Lecture Notes in Computer Science 13379

More information about this series at https://link.springer.com/bookseries/558

Osvaldo Gervasi · Beniamino Murgante ·
Sanjay Misra · Ana Maria A. C. Rocha ·
Chiara Garau (Eds.)

Computational Science and Its Applications – ICCSA 2022 Workshops

Malaga, Spain, July 4–7, 2022
Proceedings, Part III

Springer

Editors
Osvaldo Gervasi
University of Perugia
Perugia, Italy

Sanjay Misra
Østfold University College
Halden, Norway

Chiara Garau
University of Cagliari
Cagliari, Italy

Beniamino Murgante
University of Basilicata
Potenza, Potenza, Italy

Ana Maria A. C. Rocha
University of Minho
Braga, Portugal

ISSN 0302-9743 ISSN 1611-3349 (electronic)
Lecture Notes in Computer Science
ISBN 978-3-031-10544-9 ISBN 978-3-031-10545-6 (eBook)
https://doi.org/10.1007/978-3-031-10545-6

This Springer imprint is published by the registered company Springer Nature Switzerland AG
The registered company address is: Gewerbestrasse 11, 6330 Cham, Switzerland

Preface

These six volumes (LNCS 13377–13382) consist of the peer-reviewed papers from the workshops at the 22nd International Conference on Computational Science and Its Applications (ICCSA 2022), which took place during July 4–7, 2022. The peer-reviewed papers of the main conference tracks are published in a separate set consisting of two volumes (LNCS 13375–13376).

This year, we again decided to organize a hybrid conference, with some of the delegates attending in person and others taking part online. Despite the enormous benefits achieved by the intensive vaccination campaigns in many countries, at the crucial moment of organizing the event, there was no certainty about the evolution of COVID-19. Fortunately, more and more researchers were able to attend the event in person, foreshadowing a slow but gradual exit from the pandemic and the limitations that have weighed so heavily on the lives of all citizens over the past three years.

ICCSA 2022 was another successful event in the International Conference on Computational Science and Its Applications (ICCSA) series. Last year, the conference was held as a hybrid event in Cagliari, Italy, and in 2020 it was organized as virtual event, whilst earlier editions took place in Saint Petersburg, Russia (2019), Melbourne, Australia (2018), Trieste, Italy (2017), Beijing, China (2016), Banff, Canada (2015), Guimaraes, Portugal (2014), Ho Chi Minh City, Vietnam (2013), Salvador, Brazil (2012), Santander, Spain (2011), Fukuoka, Japan (2010), Suwon, South Korea (2009), Perugia, Italy (2008), Kuala Lumpur, Malaysia (2007), Glasgow, UK (2006), Singapore (2005), Assisi, Italy (2004), Montreal, Canada (2003), and (as ICCS) Amsterdam, The Netherlands (2002) and San Francisco, USA (2001).

Computational science is the main pillar of most of the present research, and industrial and commercial applications, and plays a unique role in exploiting ICT innovative technologies. The ICCSA conference series provides a venue to researchers and industry practitioners to discuss new ideas, to share complex problems and their solutions, and to shape new trends in computational science.

Apart from the 52 workshops, ICCSA 2022 also included six main tracks on topics ranging from computational science technologies and application in many fields to specific areas of computational sciences, such as software engineering, security, machine learning and artificial intelligence, and blockchain technologies. For the 52 workshops we have accepted 285 papers. For the main conference tracks we accepted 57 papers and 24 short papers out of 279 submissions (an acceptance rate of 29%). We would like to express our appreciation to the Workshops chairs and co-chairs for their hard work and dedication.

The success of the ICCSA conference series in general, and of ICCSA 2022 in particular, vitally depends on the support of many people: authors, presenters, participants, keynote speakers, workshop chairs, session chairs, organizing committee members, student volunteers, Program Committee members, advisory committee members, international liaison chairs, reviewers, and others in various roles. We take this opportunity to wholehartedly thank them all.

We also wish to thank our publisher, Springer, for their acceptance to publish the proceedings, for sponsoring some of the best papers awards, and for their kind assistance and cooperation during the editing process.

We cordially invite you to visit the ICCSA website https://iccsa.org where you can find all the relevant information about this interesting and exciting event.

July 2022

Osvaldo Gervasi
Beniamino Murgante
Sanjay Misra

Welcome Message from Organizers

The ICCSA 2021 conference in the Mediterranean city of Cagliari provided us with inspiration to offer the ICCSA 2022 conference in the Mediterranean city of Málaga, Spain. The additional considerations due to the COVID-19 pandemic, which necessitated a hybrid conference, also stimulated the idea to use the School of Informatics of the University of Málaga. It has an open structure where we could take lunch and coffee outdoors and the lecture halls have open windows on two sides providing optimal conditions for meeting more safely.

The school is connected to the center of the old town via a metro system, for which we offered cards to the participants. This provided the opportunity to stay in lodgings in the old town close to the beach because, at the end of the day, that is the place to be to exchange ideas with your fellow scientists. The social program allowed us to enjoy the history of Malaga from its founding by the Phoenicians...

In order to provoke as much scientific interaction as possible we organized online sessions that could easily be followed by all participants from their own devices. We tried to ensure that participants from Asia could participate in morning sessions and those from the Americas in evening sessions. On-site sessions could be followed and debated on-site and discussed online using a chat system. To realize this, we relied on the developed technological infrastructure based on open source software, with the addition of streaming channels on YouTube. The implementation of the software infrastructure and the technical coordination of the volunteers were carried out by Damiano Perri and Marco Simonetti. Nine student volunteers from the universities of Málaga, Minho, Almeria, and Helsinki provided technical support and ensured smooth interaction during the conference.

A big thank you goes to all of the participants willing to exchange their ideas during their daytime. Participants of ICCSA 2022 came from 58 countries scattered over many time zones of the globe. Very interesting keynote talks were provided by well-known international scientists who provided us with more ideas to reflect upon, and we are grateful for their insights.

Eligius M. T. Hendrix

Organization

ICCSA 2022 was organized by the University of Malaga (Spain), the University of Perugia (Italy), the University of Cagliari (Italy), the University of Basilicata (Italy), Monash University (Australia), Kyushu Sangyo University (Japan), and the University of Minho, (Portugal).

Honorary General Chairs

Norio Shiratori	Chuo University, Japan
Kenneth C. J. Tan	Sardina Systems, UK

General Chairs

Osvaldo Gervasi	University of Perugia, Italy
Eligius Hendrix	University of Malaga, Italy
Bernady O. Apduhan	Kyushu Sangyo University, Japan

Program Committee Chairs

Beniamino Murgante	University of Basilicata, Italy
Inmaculada Garcia Fernandez	University of Malaga, Spain
Ana Maria A. C. Rocha	University of Minho, Portugal
David Taniar	Monash University, Australia

International Advisory Committee

Jemal Abawajy	Deakin University, Australia
Dharma P. Agarwal	University of Cincinnati, USA
Rajkumar Buyya	Melbourne University, Australia
Claudia Bauzer Medeiros	University of Campinas, Brazil
Manfred M. Fisher	Vienna University of Economics and Business, Austria
Marina L. Gavrilova	University of Calgary, Canada
Sumi Helal	University of Florida, USA, and University of Lancaster, UK
Yee Leung	Chinese University of Hong Kong, China

International Liaison Chairs

Ivan Blečić	University of Cagliari, Italy
Giuseppe Borruso	University of Trieste, Italy

Elise De Donker	Western Michigan University, USA
Maria Irene Falcão	University of Minho, Portugal
Robert C. H. Hsu	Chung Hua University, Taiwan
Tai-Hoon Kim	Beijing Jiaotong University, China
Vladimir Korkhov	St Petersburg University, Russia
Sanjay Misra	Østfold University College, Norway
Takashi Naka	Kyushu Sangyo University, Japan
Rafael D. C. Santos	National Institute for Space Research, Brazil
Maribel Yasmina Santos	University of Minho, Portugal
Elena Stankova	St Petersburg University, Russia

Workshop and Session Organizing Chairs

Beniamino Murgante	University of Basilicata, Italy
Chiara Garau	University of Cagliari, Italy
Sanjay Misra	Ostfold University College, Norway

Award Chair

Wenny Rahayu	La Trobe University, Australia

Publicity Committee Chairs

Elmer Dadios	De La Salle University, Philippines
Nataliia Kulabukhova	St Petersburg University, Russia
Daisuke Takahashi	Tsukuba University, Japan
Shangwang Wang	Beijing University of Posts and Telecommunications, China

Local Arrangement Chairs

Eligius Hendrix	University of Malaga, Spain
Inmaculada Garcia Fernandez	University of Malaga, Spain
Salvador Merino Cordoba	University of Malaga, Spain
Pablo Guerrero-García	University of Malaga, Spain

Technology Chairs

Damiano Perri	University of Florence, Italy
Marco Simonetti	University of Florence, Italy

Program Committee

Vera Afreixo	University of Aveiro, Portugal
Filipe Alvelos	University of Minho, Portugal

Hartmut Asche	Hasso-Plattner-Institut für Digital Engineering gGmbH, Germany
Ginevra Balletto	University of Cagliari, Italy
Michela Bertolotto	University College Dublin, Ireland
Sandro Bimonte	TSCF, INRAE, France
Rod Blais	University of Calgary, Canada
Ivan Blečić	University of Sassari, Italy
Giuseppe Borruso	University of Trieste, Italy
Ana Cristina Braga	University of Minho, Portugal
Massimo Cafaro	University of Salento, Italy
Yves Caniou	ENS Lyon, France
Ermanno Cardelli	University of Perugia, Italy
José A. Cardoso e Cunha	Universidade Nova de Lisboa, Portugal
Rui Cardoso	University of Beira Interior, Portugal
Leocadio G. Casado	University of Almeria, Spain
Carlo Cattani	University of Salerno, Italy
Mete Celik	Erciyes University, Turkey
Maria Cerreta	University of Naples Federico II, Italy
Hyunseung Choo	Sungkyunkwan University, South Korea
Rachel Chieng-Sing Lee	Sunway University, Malaysia
Min Young Chung	Sungkyunkwan University, South Korea
Florbela Maria da Cruz Domingues Correia	Polytechnic Institute of Viana do Castelo, Portugal
Gilberto Corso Pereira	Federal University of Bahia, Brazil
Alessandro Costantini	INFN, Italy
Carla Dal Sasso Freitas	Universidade Federal do Rio Grande do Sul, Brazil
Pradesh Debba	Council for Scientific and Industrial Research (CSIR), South Africa
Hendrik Decker	Instituto Tecnológico de Informática, Spain
Robertas Damaševičius	Kaunas University of Technology, Lithuania
Frank Devai	London South Bank University, UK
Rodolphe Devillers	Memorial University of Newfoundland, Canada
Joana Matos Dias	University of Coimbra, Portugal
Paolino Di Felice	University of L'Aquila, Italy
Prabu Dorairaj	NetApp, India/USA
M. Noelia Faginas Lago	University of Perugia, Italy
M. Irene Falcao	University of Minho, Portugal
Florbela P. Fernandes	Polytechnic Institute of Bragança, Portugal
Jose-Jesus Fernandez	National Centre for Biotechnology, Spain
Paula Odete Fernandes	Polytechnic Institute of Bragança, Portugal
Adelaide de Fátima Baptista Valente Freitas	University of Aveiro, Portugal
Manuel Carlos Figueiredo	University of Minho, Portugal
Maria Celia Furtado Rocha	Federal University of Bahia, Brazil
Chiara Garau	University of Cagliari, Italy
Paulino Jose Garcia Nieto	University of Oviedo, Spain

Raffaele Garrisi	Polizia di Stato, Italy
Jerome Gensel	LSR-IMAG, France
Maria Giaoutzi	National Technical University of Athens, Greece
Arminda Manuela Andrade Pereira Gonçalves	University of Minho, Portugal
Andrzej M. Goscinski	Deakin University, Australia
Sevin Gümgüm	Izmir University of Economics, Turkey
Alex Hagen-Zanker	University of Cambridge, UK
Shanmugasundaram Hariharan	B.S. Abdur Rahman Crescent Institute of Science and Technology, India
Eligius M. T. Hendrix	University of Malaga, Spain and Wageningen University, The Netherlands
Hisamoto Hiyoshi	Gunma University, Japan
Mustafa Inceoglu	Ege University, Turkey
Peter Jimack	University of Leeds, UK
Qun Jin	Waseda University, Japan
Yeliz Karaca	UMass Chan Medical School, USA
Farid Karimipour	Vienna University of Technology, Austria
Baris Kazar	Oracle Corp., USA
Maulana Adhinugraha Kiki	Telkom University, Indonesia
DongSeong Kim	University of Canterbury, New Zealand
Taihoon Kim	Hannam University, South Korea
Ivana Kolingerova	University of West Bohemia, Czech Republic
Nataliia Kulabukhova	St. Petersburg University, Russia
Vladimir Korkhov	St. Petersburg University, Russia
Rosa Lasaponara	National Research Council, Italy
Maurizio Lazzari	National Research Council, Italy
Cheng Siong Lee	Monash University, Australia
Sangyoun Lee	Yonsei University, South Korea
Jongchan Lee	Kunsan National University, South Korea
Chendong Li	University of Connecticut, USA
Gang Li	Deakin University, Australia
Fang (Cherry) Liu	Ames Laboratory, USA
Xin Liu	University of Calgary, Canada
Andrea Lombardi	University of Perugia, Italy
Savino Longo	University of Bari, Italy
Tinghuai Ma	Nanjing University of Information Science and Technology, China
Ernesto Marcheggiani	Katholieke Universiteit Leuven, Belgium
Antonino Marvuglia	Public Research Centre Henri Tudor, Luxembourg
Nicola Masini	National Research Council, Italy
Ilaria Matteucci	National Research Council, Italy
Nirvana Meratnia	University of Twente, The Netherlands
Fernando Miranda	University of Minho, Portugal
Giuseppe Modica	University of Reggio Calabria, Italy
Josè Luis Montaña	University of Cantabria, Spain

Zequn Wang	Intelligent Automation Inc, USA
Robert Weibel	University of Zurich, Switzerland
Frank Westad	Norwegian University of Science and Technology, Norway
Roland Wismüller	Universität Siegen, Germany
Mudasser Wyne	National University, USA
Chung-Huang Yang	National Kaohsiung Normal University, Taiwan
Xin-She Yang	National Physical Laboratory, UK
Salim Zabir	France Telecom Japan Co., Japan
Haifeng Zhao	University of California, Davis, USA
Fabiana Zollo	Ca' Foscari University of Venice, Italy
Albert Y. Zomaya	University of Sydney, Australia

Workshop Organizers

International Workshop on Advances in Artificial Intelligence Learning Technologies: Blended Learning, STEM, Computational Thinking and Coding (AAILT 2022)

Alfredo Milani	University of Perugia, Italy
Valentina Franzoni	University of Perugia, Italy
Osvaldo Gervasi	University of Perugia, Italy

International Workshop on Advancements in Applied Machine-Learning and Data Analytics (AAMDA 2022)

Alessandro Costantini	INFN, Italy
Davide Salomoni	INFN, Italy
Doina Cristina Duma	INFN, Italy
Daniele Cesini	INFN, Italy

International Workshop on Advances in Information Systems and Technologies for Emergency Management, Risk Assessment and Mitigation Based on the Resilience (ASTER 2022)

Maurizio Pollino	ENEA, Italy
Marco Vona	University of Basilicata, Italy
Sonia Giovinazzi	ENEA, Italy
Benedetto Manganelli	University of Basilicata, Italy
Beniamino Murgante	University of Basilicata, Italy

International Workshop on Advances in Web Based Learning (AWBL 2022)

Birol Ciloglugil	Ege University, Turkey
Mustafa Inceoglu	Ege University, Turkey

International Workshop on Blockchain and Distributed Ledgers: Technologies and Applications (BDLTA 2022)

Vladimir Korkhov	St Petersburg State University, Russia
Elena Stankova	St Petersburg State University, Russia
Nataliia Kulabukhova	St Petersburg State University, Russia

International Workshop on Bio and Neuro Inspired Computing and Applications (BIONCA 2022)

Nadia Nedjah	State University of Rio De Janeiro, Brazil
Luiza De Macedo Mourelle	State University of Rio De Janeiro, Brazil

International Workshop on Configurational Analysis For Cities (CA CITIES 2022)

Claudia Yamu	Oslo Metropolitan University, Norway
Valerio Cutini	Università di Pisa, Italy
Beniamino Murgante	University of Basilicata, Italy
Chiara Garau	Dicaar, University of Cagliari, Italy

International Workshop on Computational and Applied Mathematics (CAM 2022)

Maria Irene Falcão	University of Minho, Portugal
Fernando Miranda	University of Minho, Portugal

International Workshop on Computational and Applied Statistics (CAS 2022)

Ana Cristina Braga	University of Minho, Portugal

International Workshop on Computational Mathematics, Statistics and Information Management (CMSIM 2022)

Maria Filomena Teodoro	University of Lisbon and Portuguese Naval Academy, Portugal

International Workshop on Computational Optimization and Applications (COA 2022)

Ana Maria A. C. Rocha	University of Minho, Portugal
Humberto Rocha	University of Coimbra, Portugal

International Workshop on Computational Astrochemistry (CompAstro 2022)

Marzio Rosi	University of Perugia, Italy
Nadia Balucani	University of Perugia, Italy
Cecilia Ceccarelli	Université Grenoble Alpes, France
Stefano Falcinelli	University of Perugia, Italy

International Workshop on Computational Methods for Porous Geomaterials (CompPor 2022)

Vadim Lisitsa	Sobolev Institute of Mathematics, Russia
Evgeniy Romenski	Sobolev Institute of Mathematics, Russia

International Workshop on Computational Approaches for Smart, Conscious Cities (CASCC 2022)

Andreas Fricke	University of Potsdam, Germany
Juergen Doellner	University of Potsdam, Germany
Salvador Merino	University of Malaga, Spain
Jürgen Bund	Graphics Vision AI Association, Germany/Portugal
Markus Jobst	Federal Office of Metrology and Surveying, Austria
Francisco Guzman	University of Malaga, Spain

International Workshop on Computational Science and HPC (CSHPC 2022)

Elise De Doncker	Western Michigan University, USA
Fukuko Yuasa	High Energy Accelerator Research Organization (KEK), Japan
Hideo Matsufuru	High Energy Accelerator Research Organization (KEK), Japan

International Workshop on Cities, Technologies and Planning (CTP 2022)

Giuseppe Borruso	University of Trieste, Italy
Malgorzata Hanzl	Lodz University of Technology, Poland
Beniamino Murgante	University of Basilicata, Italy

Anastasia Stratigea	National Technical University of Athens, Grece
Ginevra Balletto	University of Cagliari, Italy
Ljiljana Zivkovic	Republic Geodetic Authority, Serbia

International Workshop on Digital Sustainability and Circular Economy (DiSCE 2022)

Giuseppe Borruso	University of Trieste, Italy
Stefano Epifani	Digital Sustainability Institute, Italy
Ginevra Balletto	University of Cagliari, Italy
Luigi Mundula	University of Cagliari, Italy
Alessandra Milesi	University of Cagliari, Italy
Mara Ladu	University of Cagliari, Italy
Stefano De Nicolai	University of Pavia, Italy
Tu Anh Trinh	University of Economics Ho Chi Minh City, Vietnam

International Workshop on Econometrics and Multidimensional Evaluation in Urban Environment (EMEUE 2022)

Carmelo Maria Torre	Polytechnic University of Bari, Italy
Maria Cerreta	University of Naples Federico II, Italy
Pierluigi Morano	Polytechnic University of Bari, Italy
Giuliano Poli	University of Naples Federico II, Italy
Marco Locurcio	Polytechnic University of Bari, Italy
Francesco Tajani	Sapienza University of Rome, Italy

International Workshop on Ethical AI Applications for a Human-Centered Cyber Society (EthicAI 2022)

Valentina Franzoni	University of Perugia, Italy
Alfredo Milani	University of Perugia, Italy

International Workshop on Future Computing System Technologies and Applications (FiSTA 2022)

Bernady Apduhan	Kyushu Sangyo University, Japan
Rafael Santos	INPE, Brazil

International Workshop on Geodesign in Decision Making: Meta Planning and Collaborative Design for Sustainable and Inclusive Development (GDM 2022)

Francesco Scorza	University of Basilicata, Italy
Michele Campagna	University of Cagliari, Italy
Ana Clara Mourão Moura	Federal University of Minas Gerais, Brazil

International Workshop on Geomatics in Agriculture and Forestry: New Advances and Perspectives (GeoForAgr 2022)

Maurizio Pollino	ENEA, Italy
Giuseppe Modica	University of Reggio Calabria, Italy
Marco Vizzari	University of Perugia, Italy

International Workshop on Geographical Analysis, Urban Modeling, Spatial Statistics (Geog-An-Mod 2022)

Giuseppe Borruso	University of Trieste, Italy
Beniamino Murgante	University of Basilicata, Italy
Harmut Asche	Hasso-Plattner-Institut für Digital Engineering gGmbH, Germany

International Workshop on Geomatics for Resource Monitoring and Management (GRMM 2022)

Alessandra Capolupo	Polytechnic of Bari, Italy
Eufemia Tarantino	Polytechnic of Bari, Italy
Enrico Borgogno Mondino	University of Turin, Italy

International Workshop on Information and Knowledge in the Internet of Things (IKIT 2022)

Teresa Guarda	State University of Santa Elena Peninsula, Ecuador
Filipe Portela	University of Minho, Portugal
Maria Fernanda Augusto	Bitrum Research Center, Spain

13th International Symposium on Software Quality (ISSQ 2022)

Sanjay Misra	Østfold University College, Norway

International Workshop on Machine Learning for Space and Earth Observation Data (MALSEOD 2022)

Rafael Santos	INPE, Brazil
Karine Reis Ferreira Gomes	INPE, Brazil

International Workshop on Building Multi-dimensional Models for Assessing Complex Environmental Systems (MES 2022)

Vanessa Assumma	Politecnico di Torino, Italy
Caterina Caprioli	Politecnico di Torino, Italy
Giulia Datola	Politecnico di Torino, Italy

Federico Dell'Anna	Politecnico di Torino, Italy
Marta Dell'Ovo	Politecnico di Milano, Italy

International Workshop on Models and Indicators for Assessing and Measuring the Urban Settlement Development in the View of ZERO Net Land Take by 2050 (MOVEto0 2022)

Lucia Saganeiti	University of L'Aquila, Italy
Lorena Fiorini	University of L'aquila, Italy
Angela Pilogallo	University of Basilicata, Italy
Alessandro Marucci	University of L'Aquila, Italy
Francesco Zullo	University of L'Aquila, Italy

International Workshop on Modelling Post-Covid Cities (MPCC 2022)

Beniamino Murgante	University of Basilicata, Italy
Ginevra Balletto	University of Cagliari, Italy
Giuseppe Borruso	University of Trieste, Italy
Marco Dettori	Università degli Studi di Sassari, Italy
Lucia Saganeiti	University of L'Aquila, Italy

International Workshop on Ecosystem Services: Nature's Contribution to People in Practice. Assessment Frameworks, Models, Mapping, and Implications (NC2P 2022)

Francesco Scorza	University of Basilicata, Italy
Sabrina Lai	University of Cagliari, Italy
Silvia Ronchi	University of Cagliari, Italy
Dani Broitman	Israel Institute of Technology, Israel
Ana Clara Mourão Moura	Federal University of Minas Gerais, Brazil
Corrado Zoppi	University of Cagliari, Italy

International Workshop on New Mobility Choices for Sustainable and Alternative Scenarios (NEWMOB 2022)

Tiziana Campisi	University of Enna Kore, Italy
Socrates Basbas	Aristotle University of Thessaloniki, Greece
Aleksandra Deluka T.	University of Rijeka, Croatia
Alexandros Nikitas	University of Huddersfield, UK
Ioannis Politis	Aristotle University of Thessaloniki, Greece
Georgios Georgiadis	Aristotle University of Thessaloniki, Greece
Irena Ištoka Otković	University of Osijek, Croatia
Sanja Surdonja	University of Rijeka, Croatia

International Workshop on Privacy in the Cloud/Edge/IoT World (PCEIoT 2022)

Michele Mastroianni	University of Campania Luigi Vanvitelli, Italy
Lelio Campanile	University of Campania Luigi Vanvitelli, Italy
Mauro Iacono	University of Campania Luigi Vanvitelli, Italy

International Workshop on Psycho-Social Analysis of Sustainable Mobility in the Pre- and Post-Pandemic Phase (PSYCHE 2022)

Tiziana Campisi	University of Enna Kore, Italy
Socrates Basbas	Aristotle University of Thessaloniki, Greece
Dilum Dissanayake	Newcastle University, UK
Nurten Akgün Tanbay	Bursa Technical University, Turkey
Elena Cocuzza	University of Catania, Italy
Nazam Ali	University of Management and Technology, Pakistan
Vincenza Torrisi	University of Catania, Italy

International Workshop on Processes, Methods and Tools Towards Resilient Cities and Cultural Heritage Prone to SOD and ROD Disasters (RES 2022)

Elena Cantatore	Polytechnic University of Bari, Italy
Alberico Sonnessa	Polytechnic University of Bari, Italy
Dario Esposito	Polytechnic University of Bari, Italy

International Workshop on Scientific Computing Infrastructure (SCI 2022)

Elena Stankova	St Petersburg University, Russia
Vladimir Korkhov	St Petersburg University, Russia

International Workshop on Socio-Economic and Environmental Models for Land Use Management (SEMLUM 2022)

Debora Anelli	Polytechnic University of Bari, Italy
Pierluigi Morano	Polytechnic University of Bari, Italy
Francesco Tajani	Sapienza University of Rome, Italy
Marco Locurcio	Polytechnic University of Bari, Italy
Paola Amoruso	LUM University, Italy

14th International Symposium on Software Engineering Processes and Applications (SEPA 2022)

Sanjay Misra	Østfold University College, Norway

International Workshop on Ports of the Future – Smartness and Sustainability (SmartPorts 2022)

Giuseppe Borruso	University of Trieste, Italy
Gianfranco Fancello	University of Cagliari, Italy
Ginevra Balletto	University of Cagliari, Italy
Patrizia Serra	University of Cagliari, Italy
Maria del Mar Munoz Leonisio	University of Cadiz, Spain
Marco Mazzarino	University of Venice, Italy
Marcello Tadini	Università del Piemonte Orientale, Italy

International Workshop on Smart Tourism (SmartTourism 2022)

Giuseppe Borruso	University of Trieste, Italy
Silvia Battino	University of Sassari, Italy
Ainhoa Amaro Garcia	Universidad de Alcalà and Universidad de Las Palmas, Spain
Maria del Mar Munoz Leonisio	University of Cadiz, Spain
Carlo Donato	University of Sassari, Italy
Francesca Krasna	University of Trieste, Italy
Ginevra Balletto	University of Cagliari, Italy

International Workshop on Sustainability Performance Assessment: Models, Approaches and Applications Toward Interdisciplinary and Integrated Solutions (SPA 2022)

Francesco Scorza	University of Basilicata, Italy
Sabrina Lai	University of Cagliari, Italy
Jolanta Dvarioniene	Kaunas University of Technology, Lithuania
Iole Cerminara	University of Basilicata, Italy
Georgia Pozoukidou	Aristotle University of Thessaloniki, Greece
Valentin Grecu	Lucian Blaga University of Sibiu, Romania
Corrado Zoppi	University of Cagliari, Italy

International Workshop on Specifics of Smart Cities Development in Europe (SPEED 2022)

Chiara Garau	University of Cagliari, Italy
Katarína Vitálišová	Matej Bel University, Slovakia
Paolo Nesi	University of Florence, Italy
Anna Vanova	Matej Bel University, Slovakia
Kamila Borsekova	Matej Bel University, Slovakia
Paola Zamperlin	University of Pisa, Italy

Federico Cugurullo	Trinity College Dublin, Ireland
Gerardo Carpentieri	University of Naples Federico II, Italy

International Workshop on Smart and Sustainable Island Communities (SSIC 2022)

Chiara Garau	University of Cagliari, Italy
Anastasia Stratigea	National Technical University of Athens, Greece
Paola Zamperlin	University of Pisa, Italy
Francesco Scorza	University of Basilicata, Italy

International Workshop on Theoretical and Computational Chemistry and Its Applications (TCCMA 2022)

Noelia Faginas-Lago	University of Perugia, Italy
Andrea Lombardi	University of Perugia, Italy

International Workshop on Transport Infrastructures for Smart Cities (TISC 2022)

Francesca Maltinti	University of Cagliari, Italy
Mauro Coni	University of Cagliari, Italy
Francesco Pinna	University of Cagliari, Italy
Chiara Garau	University of Cagliari, Italy
Nicoletta Rassu	Univesity of Cagliari, Italy
James Rombi	University of Cagliari, Italy
Benedetto Barabino	University of Brescia, Italy

14th International Workshop on Tools and Techniques in Software Development Process (TTSDP 2022)

Sanjay Misra	Østfold University College, Norway

International Workshop on Urban Form Studies (UForm 2022)

Malgorzata Hanzl	Lodz University of Technology, Poland
Beniamino Murgante	University of Basilicata, Italy
Alessandro Camiz	Özyeğin University, Turkey
Tomasz Bradecki	Silesian University of Technology, Poland

International Workshop on Urban Regeneration: Innovative Tools and Evaluation Model (URITEM 2022)

Fabrizio Battisti	University of Florence, Italy
Laura Ricci	Sapienza University of Rome, Italy
Orazio Campo	Sapienza University of Rome, Italy

International Workshop on Urban Space Accessibility and Mobilities (USAM 2022)

Chiara Garau	University of Cagliari, Italy
Matteo Ignaccolo	University of Catania, Italy
Enrica Papa	University of Westminster, UK
Francesco Pinna	University of Cagliari, Italy
Silvia Rossetti	University of Parma, Italy
Wendy Tan	Wageningen University and Research, The Netherlands
Michela Tiboni	University of Brescia, Italy
Vincenza Torrisi	University of Catania, Italy

International Workshop on Virtual Reality and Augmented Reality and Applications (VRA 2022)

Osvaldo Gervasi	University of Perugia, Italy
Damiano Perri	University of Florence, Italy
Marco Simonetti	University of Florence, Italy
Sergio Tasso	University of Perugia, Italy

International Workshop on Advanced and Computational Methods for Earth Science Applications (WACM4ES 2022)

Luca Piroddi	University of Cagliari, Italy
Sebastiano Damico	University of Malta, Malta

International Workshop on Advanced Mathematics and Computing Methods in Complex Computational Systems (WAMCM 2022)

Yeliz Karaca	UMass Chan Medical School, USA
Dumitru Baleanu	Cankaya University, Turkey
Osvaldo Gervasi	University of Perugia, Italy
Yudong Zhang	University of Leicester, UK
Majaz Moonis	UMass Chan Medical School, USA

Additional Reviewers

Akshat Agrawal	Amity University, Haryana, India
Waseem Ahmad	National Institute of Technology Karnataka, India
Vladimir Alarcon	Universidad Diego Portales, Chile
Oylum Alatlı	Ege University, Turkey
Raffaele Albano	University of Basilicata, Italy
Abraham Alfa	FUT Minna, Nigeria
Diego Altafini	Università di Pisa, Italy
Filipe Alvelos	Universidade do Minho, Portugal

Marina Alexandra Pedro Andrade	ISCTE-IUL, Portugal
Debora Anelli	Polytechnic University of Bari, Italy
Gennaro Angiello	AlmavivA de Belgique, Belgium
Alfonso Annunziata	Università di Cagliari, Italy
Bernady Apduhan	Kyushu Sangyo University, Japan
Daniela Ascenzi	Università degli Studi di Trento, Italy
Burak Galip Aslan	Izmir Insitute of Technology, Turkey
Vanessa Assumma	Politecnico di Torino, Italy
Daniel Atzberger	Hasso-Plattner-Institute für Digital Engineering gGmbH, Germany
Dominique Aury	École Polytechnique Fédérale de Lausanne, Switzerland
Joseph Awotumde	University of Alcala, Spain
Birim Balci	Celal Bayar University, Turkey
Juliana Balera	INPE, Brazil
Ginevra Balletto	University of Cagliari, Italy
Benedetto Barabino	University of Brescia, Italy
Kaushik Barik	University of Alcala, Spain
Carlo Barletta	Politecnico di Bari, Italy
Socrates Basbas	Aristotle University of Thessaloniki, Greece
Rosaria Battarra	ISMed-CNR, Italy
Silvia Battino	University of Sassari, Italy
Chiara Bedan	University of Trieste, Italy
Ranjan Kumar Behera	National Institute of Technology Rourkela, India
Gulmira Bekmanova	L.N. Gumilyov Eurasian National University, Kazakhstan
Mario Bentivenga	University of Basilicata, Italy
Asrat Mulatu Beyene	Addis Ababa Science and Technology University, Ethiopia
Tiziana Binda	Politecnico di Torino, Italy
Giulio Biondi	University of Firenze, Italy
Alexander Bogdanov	St Petersburg University, Russia
Costanza Borghesi	University of Perugia, Italy
Giuseppe Borruso	University of Trieste, Italy
Marilisa Botte	University of Naples Federico II, Italy
Tomasz Bradecki	Silesian University of Technology, Poland
Ana Cristina Braga	University of Minho, Portugal
Luca Braidotti	University of Trieste, Italy
Bazon Brock	University of Wuppertal, Germany
Dani Broitman	Israel Institute of Technology, Israel
Maria Antonia Brovelli	Politecnico di Milano, Italy
Jorge Buele	Universidad Tecnológica Indoamérica, Ecuador
Isabel Cacao	University of Aveiro, Portugal
Federica Cadamuro Morgante	Politecnico di Milano, Italy

Rogerio Calazan	IEAPM, Brazil
Michele Campagna	University of Cagliari, Italy
Lelio Campanile	Università degli Studi della Campania Luigi Vanvitelli, Italy
Tiziana Campisi	University of Enna Kore, Italy
Antonino Canale	University of Enna Kore, Italy
Elena Cantatore	Polytechnic University of Bari, Italy
Patrizia Capizzi	Univerity of Palermo, Italy
Alessandra Capolupo	Polytechnic University of Bari, Italy
Giacomo Caporusso	Politecnico di Bari, Italy
Caterina Caprioli	Politecnico di Torino, Italy
Gerardo Carpentieri	University of Naples Federico II, Italy
Martina Carra	University of Brescia, Italy
Pedro Carrasqueira	INESC Coimbra, Portugal
Barbara Caselli	Università degli Studi di Parma, Italy
Cecilia Castro	University of Minho, Portugal
Giulio Cavana	Politecnico di Torino, Italy
Iole Cerminara	University of Basilicata, Italy
Maria Cerreta	University of Naples Federico II, Italy
Daniele Cesini	INFN, Italy
Jabed Chowdhury	La Trobe University, Australia
Birol Ciloglugil	Ege University, Turkey
Elena Cocuzza	Univesity of Catania, Italy
Emanuele Colica	University of Malta, Malta
Mauro Coni	University of Cagliari, Italy
Elisete Correia	Universidade de Trás-os-Montes e Alto Douro, Portugal
Florbela Correia	Polytechnic Institute of Viana do Castelo, Portugal
Paulo Cortez	University of Minho, Portugal
Lino Costa	Universidade do Minho, Portugal
Alessandro Costantini	INFN, Italy
Marilena Cozzolino	Università del Molise, Italy
Alfredo Cuzzocrea	University of Calabria, Italy
Sebastiano D'amico	University of Malta, Malta
Gianni D'Angelo	University of Salerno, Italy
Tijana Dabovic	University of Belgrade, Serbia
Hiroshi Daisaka	Hitotsubashi University, Japan
Giulia Datola	Politecnico di Torino, Italy
Regina De Almeida	University of Trás-os-Montes and Alto Douro, Portugal
Maria Stella De Biase	Università della Campania Luigi Vanvitelli, Italy
Elise De Doncker	Western Michigan University, USA
Itamir De Morais Barroca Filho	Federal University of Rio Grande do Norte, Brazil
Samuele De Petris	University of Turin, Italy
Alan De Sá	Marinha do Brasil, Brazil
Alexander Degtyarev	St Petersburg University, Russia

Federico Dell'Anna	Politecnico di Torino, Italy
Marta Dell'Ovo	Politecnico di Milano, Italy
Ahu Dereli Dursun	Istanbul Commerce University, Turkey
Giulia Desogus	University of Cagliari, Italy
Piero Di Bonito	Università degli Studi della Campania, Italia
Paolino Di Felice	University of L'Aquila, Italy
Felicia Di Liddo	Polytechnic University of Bari, Italy
Isabel Dimas	University of Coimbra, Portugal
Doina Cristina Duma	INFN, Italy
Aziz Dursun	Virginia Tech University, USA
Jaroslav Dvořak	Klaipėda University, Lithuania
Dario Esposito	Polytechnic University of Bari, Italy
M. Noelia Faginas-Lago	University of Perugia, Italy
Stefano Falcinelli	University of Perugia, Italy
Falcone Giacomo	University of Reggio Calabria, Italy
Maria Irene Falcão	University of Minho, Portugal
Stefano Federico	CNR-ISAC, Italy
Marcin Feltynowski	University of Lodz, Poland
António Fernandes	Instituto Politécnico de Bragança, Portugal
Florbela Fernandes	Instituto Politecnico de Braganca, Portugal
Paula Odete Fernandes	Instituto Politécnico de Bragança, Portugal
Luis Fernandez-Sanz	University of Alcala, Spain
Luís Ferrás	University of Minho, Portugal
Ângela Ferreira	Instituto Politécnico de Bragança, Portugal
Lorena Fiorini	University of L'Aquila, Italy
Hector Florez	Universidad Distrital Francisco Jose de Caldas, Colombia
Stefano Franco	LUISS Guido Carli, Italy
Valentina Franzoni	Perugia University, Italy
Adelaide Freitas	University of Aveiro, Portugal
Andreas Fricke	Hasso Plattner Institute, Germany
Junpei Fujimoto	KEK, Japan
Federica Gaglione	Università del Sannio, Italy
Andrea Gallo	Università degli Studi di Trieste, Italy
Luciano Galone	University of Malta, Malta
Adam Galuszka	Silesian University of Technology, Poland
Chiara Garau	University of Cagliari, Italy
Ernesto Garcia Para	Universidad del País Vasco, Spain
Aniket A. Gaurav	Østfold University College, Norway
Marina Gavrilova	University of Calgary, Canada
Osvaldo Gervasi	University of Perugia, Italy
Andrea Ghirardi	Università di Brescia, Italy
Andrea Gioia	Politecnico di Bari, Italy
Giacomo Giorgi	Università degli Studi di Perugia, Italy
Stanislav Glubokovskikh	Lawrence Berkeley National Laboratory, USA
A. Manuela Gonçalves	University of Minho, Portugal

Leocadio González Casado	University of Almería, Spain
Angela Gorgoglione	Universidad de la República Uruguay, Uruguay
Yusuke Gotoh	Okayama University, Japan
Daniele Granata	Università degli Studi della Campania, Italy
Christian Grévisse	University of Luxembourg, Luxembourg
Silvana Grillo	University of Cagliari, Italy
Teresa Guarda	State University of Santa Elena Peninsula, Ecuador
Carmen Guida	Università degli Studi di Napoli Federico II, Italy
Kemal Güven Gülen	Namık Kemal University, Turkey
Ipek Guler	Leuven Biostatistics and Statistical Bioinformatics Centre, Belgium
Sevin Gumgum	Izmir University of Economics, Turkey
Martina Halásková	VSB Technical University in Ostrava, Czech Republic
Peter Hegedus	University of Szeged, Hungary
Eligius M. T. Hendrix	Universidad de Málaga, Spain
Mauro Iacono	Università degli Studi della Campania, Italy
Oleg Iakushkin	St Petersburg University, Russia
Matteo Ignaccolo	University of Catania, Italy
Mustafa Inceoglu	Ege University, Turkey
Markus Jobst	Federal Office of Metrology and Surveying, Austria
Issaku Kanamori	RIKEN Center for Computational Science, Japan
Yeliz Karaca	UMass Chan Medical School, USA
Aarti Karande	Sardar Patel Institute of Technology, India
András Kicsi	University of Szeged, Hungary
Vladimir Korkhov	St Petersburg University, Russia
Nataliia Kulabukhova	St Petersburg University, Russia
Claudio Ladisa	Politecnico di Bari, Italy
Mara Ladu	University of Cagliari, Italy
Sabrina Lai	University of Cagliari, Italy
Mark Lajko	University of Szeged, Hungary
Giuseppe Francesco Cesare Lama	University of Napoli Federico II, Italy
Vincenzo Laporta	CNR, Italy
Margherita Lasorella	Politecnico di Bari, Italy
Francesca Leccis	Università di Cagliari, Italy
Federica Leone	University of Cagliari, Italy
Chien-sing Lee	Sunway University, Malaysia
Marco Locurcio	Polytechnic University of Bari, Italy
Francesco Loddo	Henge S.r.l., Italy
Andrea Lombardi	Università di Perugia, Italy
Isabel Lopes	Instituto Politécnico de Bragança, Portugal
Fernando Lopez Gayarre	University of Oviedo, Spain
Vanda Lourenço	Universidade Nova de Lisboa, Portugal
Jing Ma	Luleå University of Technology, Sweden
Helmuth Malonek	University of Aveiro, Portugal
Francesca Maltinti	University of Cagliari, Italy

Benedetto Manganelli	Università degli Studi della Basilicata, Italy
Krassimir Markov	Institute of Electric Engineering and Informatics, Bulgaria
Alessandro Marucci	University of L'Aquila, Italy
Alessandra Mascitelli	Italian Civil Protection Department and ISAC-CNR, Italy
Michele Mastroianni	University of Campania Luigi Vanvitelli, Italy
Hideo Matsufuru	High Energy Accelerator Research Organization (KEK), Japan
Chiara Mazzarella	University of Naples Federico II, Italy
Marco Mazzarino	University of Venice, Italy
Paolo Mengoni	University of Florence, Italy
Alfredo Milani	University of Perugia, Italy
Fernando Miranda	Universidade do Minho, Portugal
Augusto Montisci	Università degli Studi di Cagliari, Italy
Ricardo Moura	New University of Lisbon, Portugal
Ana Clara Mourao Moura	Federal University of Minas Gerais, Brazil
Maria Mourao	Polytechnic Institute of Viana do Castelo, Portugal
Eugenio Muccio	University of Naples Federico II, Italy
Beniamino Murgante	University of Basilicata, Italy
Giuseppe Musolino	University of Reggio Calabria, Italy
Stefano Naitza	Università di Cagliari, Italy
Naohito Nakasato	University of Aizu, Japan
Roberto Nardone	University of Reggio Calabria, Italy
Nadia Nedjah	State University of Rio de Janeiro, Brazil
Juraj Nemec	Masaryk University in Brno, Czech Republic
Keigo Nitadori	RIKEN R-CCS, Japan
Roseline Ogundokun	Kaunas University of Technology, Lithuania
Francisco Henrique De Oliveira	Santa Catarina State University, Brazil
Irene Oliveira	Univesidade Trás-os-Montes e Alto Douro, Portugal
Samson Oruma	Østfold University College, Norway
Antonio Pala	University of Cagliari, Italy
Simona Panaro	University of Porstmouth, UK
Dimos Pantazis	University of West Attica, Greece
Giovanni Paragliola	ICAR-CNR, Italy
Eric Pardede	La Trobe University, Australia
Marco Parriani	University of Perugia, Italy
Paola Perchinunno	Uniersity of Bari, Italy
Ana Pereira	Polytechnic Institute of Bragança, Portugal
Damiano Perri	University of Perugia, Italy
Marco Petrelli	Roma Tre University, Italy
Camilla Pezzica	University of Pisa, Italy
Angela Pilogallo	University of Basilicata, Italy
Francesco Pinna	University of Cagliari, Italy
Telmo Pinto	University of Coimbra, Portugal

Fernando Pirani	University of Perugia, Italy
Luca Piroddi	University of Cagliari, Italy
Bojana Pjanović	University of Belgrade, Serbia
Giuliano Poli	University of Naples Federico II, Italy
Maurizio Pollino	ENEA, Italy
Salvatore Praticò	University of Reggio Calabria, Italy
Zbigniew Przygodzki	University of Lodz, Poland
Carlotta Quagliolo	Politecnico di Torino, Italy
Raffaele Garrisi	Polizia Postale e delle Comunicazioni, Italy
Mariapia Raimondo	Università della Campania Luigi Vanvitelli, Italy
Deep Raj	IIIT Naya Raipur, India
Buna Ramos	Universidade Lusíada Norte, Portugal
Nicoletta Rassu	Univesity of Cagliari, Italy
Michela Ravanelli	Sapienza Università di Roma, Italy
Roberta Ravanelli	Sapienza Università di Roma, Italy
Pier Francesco Recchi	University of Naples Federico II, Italy
Stefania Regalbuto	University of Naples Federico II, Italy
Marco Reis	University of Coimbra, Portugal
Maria Reitano	University of Naples Federico II, Italy
Anatoly Resnyansky	Defence Science and Technology Group, Australia
Jerzy Respondek	Silesian University of Technology, Poland
Isabel Ribeiro	Instituto Politécnico Bragança, Portugal
Albert Rimola	Universitat Autònoma de Barcelona, Spain
Corrado Rindone	University of Reggio Calabria, Italy
Ana Maria A. C. Rocha	University of Minho, Portugal
Humberto Rocha	University of Coimbra, Portugal
Maria Clara Rocha	Instituto Politécnico de Coimbra, Portugal
James Rombi	University of Cagliari, Italy
Elisabetta Ronchieri	INFN, Italy
Marzio Rosi	University of Perugia, Italy
Silvia Rossetti	Università degli Studi di Parma, Italy
Marco Rossitti	Politecnico di Milano, Italy
Mária Rostašová	Universtiy of Žilina, Slovakia
Lucia Saganeiti	University of L'Aquila, Italy
Giovanni Salzillo	Università degli Studi della Campania, Italy
Valentina Santarsiero	University of Basilicata, Italy
Luigi Santopietro	University of Basilicata, Italy
Stefania Santoro	Politecnico di Bari, Italy
Rafael Santos	INPE, Brazil
Valentino Santucci	Università per Stranieri di Perugia, Italy
Mirko Saponaro	Polytechnic University of Bari, Italy
Filippo Sarvia	University of Turin, Italy
Andrea Scianna	ICAR-CNR, Italy
Francesco Scorza	University of Basilicata, Italy
Ester Scotto Di Perta	University of Naples Federico II, Italy
Ricardo Severino	University of Minho, Portugal

Jie Shen	University of Michigan, USA
Luneque Silva Junior	Universidade Federal do ABC, Brazil
Carina Silva	Instituto Politécnico de Lisboa, Portugal
Joao Carlos Silva	Polytechnic Institute of Cavado and Ave, Portugal
Ilya Silvestrov	Saudi Aramco, Saudi Arabia
Marco Simonetti	University of Florence, Italy
Maria Joana Soares	University of Minho, Portugal
Michel Soares	Federal University of Sergipe, Brazil
Alberico Sonnessa	Politecnico di Bari, Italy
Lisete Sousa	University of Lisbon, Portugal
Elena Stankova	St Petersburg University, Russia
Jan Stejskal	University of Pardubice, Czech Republic
Silvia Stranieri	University of Naples Federico II, Italy
Anastasia Stratigea	National Technical University of Athens, Greece
Yue Sun	European XFEL GmbH, Germany
Anthony Suppa	Politecnico di Torino, Italy
Kirill Sviatov	Ulyanovsk State Technical University, Russia
David Taniar	Monash University, Australia
Rodrigo Tapia-McClung	Centro de Investigación en Ciencias de Información Geoespacial, Mexico
Eufemia Tarantino	Politecnico di Bari, Italy
Sergio Tasso	University of Perugia, Italy
Vladimir Tcheverda	Institute of Petroleum Geology and Geophysics, SB RAS, Russia
Ana Paula Teixeira	Universidade de Trás-os-Montes e Alto Douro, Portugal
Tengku Adil Tengku Izhar	Universiti Teknologi MARA, Malaysia
Maria Filomena Teodoro	University of Lisbon and Portuguese Naval Academy, Portugal
Yiota Theodora	National Technical University of Athens, Greece
Graça Tomaz	Instituto Politécnico da Guarda, Portugal
Gokchan Tonbul	Atilim University, Turkey
Rosa Claudia Torcasio	CNR-ISAC, Italy
Carmelo Maria Torre	Polytechnic University of Bari, Italy
Vincenza Torrisi	University of Catania, Italy
Vincenzo Totaro	Politecnico di Bari, Italy
Pham Trung	HCMUT, Vietnam
Po-yu Tsai	National Chung Hsing University, Taiwan
Dimitrios Tsoukalas	Centre of Research and Technology Hellas, Greece
Toshihiro Uchibayashi	Kyushu University, Japan
Takahiro Ueda	Seikei University, Japan
Piero Ugliengo	Università degli Studi di Torino, Italy
Gianmarco Vanuzzo	University of Perugia, Italy
Clara Vaz	Instituto Politécnico de Bragança, Portugal
Laura Verde	University of Campania Luigi Vanvitelli, Italy
Katarína Vitálišová	Matej Bel University, Slovakia

Daniel Mark Vitiello	University of Cagliari, Italy
Marco Vizzari	University of Perugia, Italy
Alexander Vodyaho	St. Petersburg State Electrotechnical University "LETI", Russia
Agustinus Borgy Waluyo	Monash University, Australia
Chao Wang	USTC, China
Marcin Wozniak	Silesian University of Technology, Poland
Jitao Yang	Beijing Language and Culture University, China
Fenghui Yao	Tennessee State University, USA
Fukuko Yuasa	KEK, Japan
Paola Zamperlin	University of Pisa, Italy
Michal Žemlička	Charles University, Czech Republic
Nataly Zhukova	ITMO University, Russia
Alcinia Zita Sampaio	University of Lisbon, Portugal
Ljiljana Zivkovic	Republic Geodetic Authority, Serbia
Floriana Zucaro	University of Naples Federico II, Italy
Marco Zucca	Politecnico di Milano, Italy
Camila Zyngier	Ibmec, Belo Horizonte, Brazil

Sponsoring Organizations

ICCSA 2022 would not have been possible without tremendous support of many organizations and institutions, for which all organizers and participants of ICCSA 2022 express their sincere gratitude:

Springer International Publishing AG, Germany (https://www.springer.com)

Computers Open Access Journal (https://www.mdpi.com/journal/computers)

Computation Open Access Journal (https://www.mdpi.com/journal/computation)

University of Malaga, Spain (https://www.uma.es/)

University of Perugia, Italy
(https://www.unipg.it)

University of Basilicata, Italy
(http://www.unibas.it)

Monash University, Australia
(https://www.monash.edu/)

Kyushu Sangyo University, Japan
(https://www.kyusan-u.ac.jp/)

University of Minho, Portugal
(https://www.uminho.pt/)

Universidade do Minho
Escola de Engenharia

Contents – Part III

International Workshop on Geodesign in Decision Making: Meta Planning and Collaborative Design for Sustainable and Inclusive Development (GDM 2022)

International Workshop on Smart and Sustainable Island Communities (SSIC 2022)

International Workshop on Ethical AI Applications for a Human-Centered Cyber Society (Ethic AI 2022)

Linguistic Foundations of Low-Resource Languages for Speech Synthesis on the Example of the Kazakh Language

Gulmira Bekmanova, Banu Yergesh, Altynbek Sharipbay, Assel Omarbekova(✉), and Alma Zakirova

L.N. Gumilyov Eurasian National University, Nur-Sultan, Kazakhstan
omarbekova_as@enu.kz

Abstract. The article considers the linguistic foundations of the Kazakh language for the Kazakh speech synthesis system. A formalization of phonological rules is presented for the implementation of an automatic transcription of words into transcriptional notation, which can be applied to speech synthesis and recognition systems.

Keywords: Speech synthesis · Transcriptor · Phonological rules

1 Introduction

This work is carried out within the framework of the project BR11765535 "Development of Scientific and Linguistic Foundations and IT Resources to Expand the Functions and Improve the Culture of the Kazakh Language". The aim of the project is to develop scientific and linguistic foundations and IT resources to expand the functions and improve the culture of the Kazakh language as a language of interethnic communication in digital format, which is an urgent and important problem in the strategic direction of development of our state. The solution of this problem will be carried out on the basis of: an analysis of the scientific, methodological and normative foundations of the grammar of the Kazakh language and computational linguistics; research of models and methods of speech synthesis; building a formal description of the grammar of the Kazakh language, artificial intelligence technology for the development of an intelligent synonymizer, an electronic reference book, a mobile application "Fascinating Onomastics", an electronic dictionary of terminology of school textbooks, a Kazakh speech synthesizer and an intellectual system "Akhmettanu". The main approaches to conducting research are the construction of a formal description of the grammar of the Kazakh language, the creation of a database of synonymous words, proper names, and terms for the relevant subject areas (socio-political and public life, grammar of the Kazakh language and school textbooks), taking into account their history, use and possible interpretations, the formation of an audio and text corpus for the synthesis of Kazakh speech, as well as the creation of a knowledge base on Akhmet Baitursynuly's scientific heritage and on all structural tiers of the language in the light of his teachings. The solution to this problem is possible only

O. Gervasi et al. (Eds.): ICCSA 2022 Workshops, LNCS 13379, pp. 3–14, 2022.
https://doi.org/10.1007/978-3-031-10545-6_1

with the use of intelligent technologies for computer processing (analysis and synthesis) of oral and written texts (data) in the Kazakh language. This article will consider the linguistic foundations of the synthesis of Kazakh speech based on Akhmet Baitursynuly's works, as well as some ethical aspects of the perception of his scientific and cultural heritage.

2 Related Works

The development of low-resource languages is accompanied by a number of difficulties, which are different in countries depending on their historical and cultural heritage.

There are works [1–4] on natural language processing, where various ethical issues related to the processing of natural languages are solved.

Similar research and development of low-resource languages is carried out to prevent its disappearance and its development, to study the knowledge contained in the original works in these languages in [5–7]. The ethical aspects of the development of low-resource languages are also often touched upon, since often low-resource languages are infringed for various reasons in their development. When it comes to Akhmet Baitursynov, an outstanding Kazakh scientist (1872–1937), philologist, publicist [8], etc., a multifaceted scientist whose life was tragically cut short due to his patriotic and political activities, it is difficult to choose the type of his activity that made the greatest contribution to scientific and social-political life of Kazakhstan [9–12]. However, this work will use the fundamental foundations laid by A. Baitursynov in the linguistics and phonetics of the Kazakh language, which became the basis for developing a transcriptor for the Kazakh speech synthesis system. Particularly surprising is the fact that all his studies were carried out about 100 years ago [13–20], however, they most accurately reflect the modern sound and phonetic structure of the Kazakh language and allow building the highest quality speech synthesizer. Speaking about the ethical aspect of the attitude towards A. Baitursynov's works, it should be noted that the attitude towards his works changed over the years and they were completely unpopular in the Soviet era of the development of the Kazakh language, in view of the unpopularity of the views of the author, who was recognized as an enemy of the then existing government and only newfound independence made possible a fresh look at his writings. The development of artificial intelligence and the creation of systems for recognizing and synthesizing Kazakh speech only emphasized the fundamental nature and scientific validity and value of his scientific heritage.

3 Kazakh Speech Synthesis System

The Kazakh speech synthesis system is not fundamentally different from any other speech synthesis system. The peculiarity of the language has an influence mainly on the transcriptor, which feeds the transcription of the text to the input of the model that directly synthesizes the sound. Of course, phonological features of the language may influence the choice of a model. However, a number of previous works of the authors have shown that the synthesis of Kazakh speech is implemented quite effectively on existing models, whether they are probabilistic models on Hidden Markov models, models on neural networks, diphonic, phonemic and other models [21–24].

4 Transcriptor

A transcriptor of words into a transcription record is present in all natural language processing systems, such as translators, recognition systems, or speech synthesis. However, depending on the intended purpose of the system, we select one or another transcriptor model. So, for example, a simplified transcription can be used for speech recognition systems, while for speech synthesis systems it is necessary to use the most detailed transcription containing the acoustic characteristics of sounds.

The segmental phonetic transcription of the text, the construction of which completes the work of the linguistic block, is carried out by an automatic transcriptor. To do this, first of all, the standard reading rules that operate in the language are used, that is, equivalents of the type "letter ® phoneme ® sound". The degree of phonetic detail (the number of distinguishable sounds), which is selected in specific synthesis or recognition systems when constructing transcription, can be different. Often the choice is dictated by tradition, followed by phonetic descriptions of the synthesized language and the most representative and commonly used dictionaries.

In a number of languages (for example, English), the relationship between spelling and pronunciation is very complex – many words do not follow standard reading rules. Words whose pronunciation "falls out" of the standard rules have to be processed separately, either by creating narrower, specific rules for them, or by writing the phonetic transcription of the word directly into its dictionary characteristic, i.e., memorizing, and not deriving from reading rules.

Representatives of the linguistic approach emphasize the need for a wider use of phonetic and physiological knowledge in automatic speech recognition and synthesis systems.

According to the American researcher V. Zu [25], one of the most active supporters of this approach, the failures of acoustic phonetic recognition in various systems are due to two reasons:

1) the use of too simplified ideas about the relationship between the speech signal and its phonemic (allophonic) reflection in the language;
2) the use of such methods of primary acoustic processing of the speech signal, which are too far from how it is carried out in the human auditory system.

The phonetic alphabet is the basis for the operation of the speech recognition/synthesis block. The symbols of the phonetic alphabet should unequivocally correspond to those sounds, the distinction of which is essential in the process of recognition. Therefore, minimizing the size of the phonetic alphabet without compromising the quality of recognition should be carried out by identifying in the alphabet only those sounds that are closest in sound from the point of view of a person [26].

Therefore, for the correct construction of the transcriptor and the use of the phonetic alphabet, we first need to translate the record of the word into an intermediate alphabet of 31 letters, which are characteristic of the Kazakh language. At the second stage, this record of the word is translated according to the formalized linguistic (phonological) rules of the Kazakh language [27]. At the third stage, the received words are translated into a transcription record in symbols of international transcription.

It should be noted that the current Cyrillic alphabet of the Kazakh language instead of 31 letters contains 42 letters [28]. Of these, 11 letters were erroneously introduced in 1940 only to ensure that the writing and reading of Russian words in the Kazakh text were carried out in accordance with the norms of the Russian language. These include: Yo, I, Ch, Sch, Ts, һ, E, Yu, Ya, hard sign, soft sign.

Therefore, for the correct construction of the transcriptor and the use of the phonetic alphabet, we first need to translate the record of the word into an intermediate alphabet of 31 letters. Equivalence of characters is presented in Table 1.

Table 1. Symbols of the current alphabet and the intermediate alphabet

Current alphabet	Intermediate alphabet	Transcription	Current alphabet	Intermediate alphabet	Transcription
А	А	[ɑ]	Б	Б	[b]
Ә	Ә	[æ]	В	В	[v]
Е	Е	[e]	Г	Г	[g]
О	О	[ɔ]	Ғ	Ғ	[ɣ]
Ө	Ө	[ɵ]	Д	Д	[d]
Ұ	Ұ	[ʊ, u]	Ж	Ж	[ʒ]
Ү	Ү	[ʏ]	З	З	[z]
Ы	Ы	[ɯ]	Й	Й	[y]
І	І	[ɪ, i]	К	К	[k]
Э	Е	[jɪ]	Қ	Қ	[q]
Я	ЙА	[yɑ]	Л	Л	[l]
Ю	ЙУ	[yw]	М	М	[m]
Ё	ЙО	[yɔ]	Н	Н	[n]
И	ІЙ	[iy]	Ң	Ң	[ŋ]
И	ЫЙ	[ɯj]	П	П	[p]
Ч	Ш	[tʃ]	Р	Р	[r]
Щ	Ш	[ʃ]	С	С	[s]
Ц	С	[tc]	Т	Т	[t]
һ	Х	[h]	У	У	[w]
Ъ	-		Ш	Ш	[ʃ]
Ь	-		Ф	Ф	[f]
			Х	Х	[h]

5 Methods for Analyzing Natural Language Sounds

To study the sounds of natural language, phonetic methods and phonological methods of analysis will be used.

Phonetic methods of analysis are:

- articulation analysis;
- acoustic analysis;
- Perceptual analysis.

Articulatory analysis determines the organs of speech and their movements involved in the formation of the sounds of the language. The articulatory analysis of the tongue establishes the following articulatory features:

- participation of voice and noise in the formation of sounds;
- the place of formation of sounds (both active and passive organs of speech must be indicated);
- the way sounds are produced.

According to the involvement of the voice, the sounds of the language can be divided into vowels and consonants. When pronouncing the vowels of the language, the vocal cords vibrate completely, and there is no contact between the organs of speech and an obstruction in the oral cavity. When pronouncing consonants, there is an incomplete oscillation of the vocal cords (sonorous consonants and noisy consonants) or it is absent (deaf consonants), and in the oral cavity there is contact between the organs of speech and a barrier.

According to the place of formation, the vowel sounds of the language can be divided into: front-lingual (alveolar); pre-lingual; back-lingual (uvular); labial; non-labial.

According to the place of formation, consonant sounds of the language can be divided into: front-lingual dental; front-lingual front-palatal; pre-lingual pre-palatal; back-lingual pre-palatal; back-lingual post-palatal; bilabial; labial-dental. In the first place is the active organ of speech, in the second – the passive organ of speech.

According to the method of formation, the sounds of the language can be subdivided into occlusive and fricative. When pronouncing occlusive consonants in the oral cavity, a complete closure of the organs of speech occurs and the air stream, noisily overcoming the closure, finds a way out. When pronouncing fricative consonants in the oral cavity, a gap is formed between the organs of speech and the air stream seeps noisily through the gaps.

For occlusive consonant sounds, exposure turns on the moment of complete cessation of the flow of the air stream through the oral cavity. Fricative consonants can be subdivided into: explosive; confluent; nasal; flicking; explosive-lateral; vibrant.

The acoustic analysis of the language determines the presence of phonetic patterns in the formation of syllables and words from vowels and consonants. In the Turkic languages, including the Kazakh language, such phonetic regularity is vowel harmony.

Vowel harmony requires that all vowels and consonants in a syllable or a word be pronounced with a single timbre.

Vowel harmony is formed from a combination of four timbres: solid non-labial; soft non-labial; hard labial; soft labial.

Speech recognition uses acoustic analysis based on the physical characteristics of a sound.

Based on the physical nature of sounds, sounds can be classified into nine groups of features:

- vocality – non-vocality

  1. vocal sounds: Ә, А, І, Ү, Ұ, Ө, Е, Ы, О, Ң, Н, М, Р, Л, Й, У
  2. non-vocal sounds: П, Б, Т, Д, К (Қ), Г (Ғ), С, З, Щ, Ж, Ф, В, Х (Һ)

- consonance – non-consonance

  1. consonant: П, Б, Т, Д, К (Қ), Г (Ғ), С, З, Щ, Ж, Ф, В, Х(Һ), У, Р
  2. non-consonant: Ә, А, І, Ү, Ұ, Ө, Е, Ы, О

- high pitch – low pitch

  1. high pitch
  2. low pitch

- diffuseness – compactness

  1. diffuse
  2. compact

- flatness – non-flatness

  1. flat: О, Ө, Ү, Ұ, П°, Б°, М°, У, Т°, Д°, Н°, Қ°, Ғ°, Ң°, Й°, С°, З°, Р°, Ш°, Ж°, Л°, П′°, Б′°, М′°, У′, Т′°, Д′°, Н′°, Қ′°, Ғ′°, Ң′°, Й′°, С′°, З′°, Р′°, Ш′°, Ж′°, Л′°
  2. non-flat: Ә, А, І, Ы, П, Б, М, У, П′, Б′, М′, У, Т, Д, Н, Т′, Д′, Н′, Қ, Ғ, Ң, Й, К′, Г′ Ң′, Й′, С, З, Р, С′, З′, Р′, Щ, Ж, Л, Ш′, Ж′, Л′, К, Г Ң, Й

- sharpness – non-sharpness

  1. sharp: Ә, І, Ү, Ө, П′, Б′, М′, Т′, Д′, Н′, К′, Г′ Ң′, Й′, С′, З′, Р′, Ш′, Ж′, Л′
  2. non-sharp: А, Ұ, Ы, О, П, Б, М, Т, Д, Н, Қ, Г Ң, Й, С, З, Р, Щ, Ж, Л, П°, Б°, М°, У, Т°, Д°,Н°, Қ°, Ғ°, Ң°,Й° ,С°,З°, Р°, Ш°,Ж°, Л°, П′°,Б′°,М′°,У′, Т′°,Д′°,Н′°, Қ′°, Ғ′°, Ң′°,Й′° ,С′°,З′°, Р′°, Ш′°,Ж′°, Л′°

- discontinuity (pausedness) – incessancy

  1. non-continuous: П, Б, Т, Д, К (Қ), Г (Ғ)
  2. continuous: Ә, А, І, Ү, Ұ, Ө, Е, Ы, О, М, Н, Ң, С, З, Р, Щ, Ж, Л, Й, У

- sharpness – non-sharpness

1. sharp: Р,
2. non-sharp: Ә, А, І, Ү, Ұ, Ө, Е, Ы, О, П, Б, Т, Д, К (Қ), Г (Ғ), С, З, Щ, Ж, Ф, В, Х (h), У

- sonority – voicelessness

1. voiced sounds: Ә, А, І, Ү, Ұ, Ө, Е, Ы, О, Ң, Н, М, Р, Л, Й, У, Б, Г (Ғ), З, Ж, В
2. unvoiced sounds: П, Т, Д, К (Қ), С, Ш, Ф, Х(h)

Phonological methods are:

- synharmonic-articulatory analysis;
- synharmonic-acoustic analysis;
- synharmonic-perceptive analysis.

6 Formalization of Phonological Rules of Sound Combinations in the Kazakh Language

The Kazakh language has 9 vowels and 22 consonants.

Let introduce the following notation for vowels: G is the set of Kazakh vowels, G_1 is the set of hard vowels, G_2 is the set of soft vowels, G_3 is the set of non-labial vowels, G_4 is the set of labial vowels, G_5 is the set of back-lingual vowels, G_6 is a set of front-lingual vowels, G_7 is a set of open vowels, G_8 is a set of closed vowels, G_9 is a median vowel in pairwise distinguishable features of sounds in each group, i.e.

$$
\begin{aligned}
G &= \{\text{А}, \text{Ә}, \text{О}, \text{Ө}, \text{Ұ}, \text{Ү}, \text{Ы}, \text{І}, \text{Е}\};\\
G_1 &= \{\text{А}, \text{О}, \text{Ұ}, \text{Ы}\} \subseteq G;\\
G_2 &= \{\text{Ә}, \text{Ө}, \text{Ү}, \text{І}\} \subseteq G;\\
G_3 &= \{\text{А}, \text{Ә}, \text{Ы}, \text{І}\} \subseteq G;\\
G_4 &= \{\text{О}, \text{Ө}, \text{Ұ}, \text{Ү}\} \subseteq G;\\
G_5 &= \{\text{А}, \text{О}, \text{Ұ}, \text{Ы}\} \subseteq G;\\
G_6 &= \{\text{Ә}, \text{Ө}, \text{Ү}, \text{І}\} \subseteq G;\\
G_7 &= \{\text{А}, \text{Ә}, \text{О}, \text{Ө}\} \subseteq G;\\
G_8 &= \{\text{Ұ}, \text{Ү}, \text{Ы}, \text{І}\} \subseteq G;\\
G_9 &= \{E\} \subseteq G.
\end{aligned}
$$

We also introduce the notation for consonants: S – consonants of the Kazakh language, S_1 – unvoiced consonants, S_2 – voiced consonants, S_3 – sonorous consonants, S_4 – labial consonants, S_5 – anterior lingual consonants, S_6 – midlingual consonants,

S_7 – posterior lingual consonants, S_8 – stop consonants, S_9 – round-slit consonants, S_{10} – flat-slit consonants, S_{11} – tremulous consonants, S_{12} – lateral consonants, that is

$$S_1 = \{К, Қ, П, Ф, С, Т, Х, Ш\} \subseteq S;$$
$$S_2 = \{Б, В, Г, Ғ, Д, Ж, З\} \subseteq S;$$
$$S_3 = \{Й, Л, М, Н, Ң, Р, У\} \subseteq S;$$
$$S_4 = \{Б, М, П, У\} \subseteq S;$$
$$S_5 = \{Д, Ж, З, Л, Н, Р, С, Т, Ш\} \subseteq S;$$
$$S_6 = \{В, Г, К, Ф\} \subseteq S;$$
$$S_7 = \{Ғ, Й, Қ, Х\} \subseteq S;$$
$$S_8 = \{Б, Г, Ғ, Д, К, Қ, М, Н, Ң, П, Т\} \subseteq S;$$
$$S_9 = \{З, С, У\} \subseteq S;$$
$$S_{10} = \{Ж, Й, Ш\} \subseteq S;$$
$$S_{11} = \{Р\} \subseteq S;$$
$$S_{12} = \{Л\} \subseteq S;$$

Let A be the alphabet of the Kazakh language, i.e. A = G ∪ S, then the set of all chains (words) of finite length in the alphabet A is denoted as:

$$A^* = A^0 \cup A^1 \cup A^2 \cup A^3 \cup \ldots, \tag{1}$$

where $A^0 = \{\varepsilon\}$ is a set of words of 0 length, $A^1 = A$ is a set of words of 1 length, $A^2 = A \times A$ is a set of words of 2 length, $A^3 = A \times A \times A$ is a set of words of 3length, x is the sign of operations of the direct (Cartesian) product of a set.

The elements of the set A* will be denoted by lowercase (small) Greek letters: α, β, γ,…. In this case, a word of 0 length (the empty word) will always be denoted by ε.

The set of all words of non-zero length in the alphabet A are denoted by $A+$, which is formed by excluding the set of empty words from A^*, i.e.

$$A^+ = A^* \backslash \{\varepsilon\} \tag{2}$$

It is clear that any phonological unit of the Kazakh language is an element of the set A^+ [29–31].

Now we will start the formalization of phonologic rules of the Kazakh language:

1. Connection of two unvoiced consonants. On a connection of two unvoiced consonants in one word or in a case when one word ends to a unvoiced consonant, and another word begins with a unvoiced consonant, both consonants remain unvoiced:

$$\frac{\alpha \subseteq \gamma, \alpha = \alpha_1 x, \alpha_1 \neq \varepsilon, x \in S_{15}, \beta \subseteq \gamma, \beta = y\beta_1, y \in S_3, z \in S_2}{\gamma = (\alpha_1 x)(z\beta_1)} \tag{3}$$

Example: The junction of two unvoiced consonants is possible at the root of the word “akpan”, “akpar”, at the junction of the root and the affix (suffix or ending) “atakpen”, “bakpen”, at the junction of two words “ak sandyk”, “ak sausak”. In all these cases, the transformation of unvoiced consonants does not occur [28].

2. Connection of two consonants unvoiced and sonorous.

2.1. During the connection of two consonants, unvoiced and sonorous, in one word or in one case when one word ends with a unvoiced front tongue consonant (с, т, ш), and another begins with a sonorous consonant, the unvoiced consonant remains unvoiced, and soa norous consonant remains sonorous:

$$\frac{\alpha \subseteq \gamma, \alpha = \alpha_1 x, \alpha_1 \neq \varepsilon, x \in S_1 \cap S_5, \beta \subseteq \gamma, \beta = y\beta_1, y \in S_3}{\gamma = (\alpha_1 x)(y\beta_1)} \tag{4}$$

where $S_1 \cap S_5 = \{С, Т, Ш\}$.

Example: The junction of two unvoiced and sonorous consonants is possible at the root of the word "asmar", at the junction of the root and the postfix (suffix or ending) "betmonshak", at the connection of two words "zhas mal". In all these cases, the transformation of consonants does not occur [28].

2.2. During the connection of two consonants, unvoiced and sonorous, in one word or in one case when one word ends with an unvoiced non-front tongue consonant (к, қ, п, ф,), and another begins with a sonorous consonant sound, the unvoiced consonant is replaced with its matching sonorous consonant:

$$\frac{\alpha \subseteq \gamma, \alpha = \alpha_1 x, \alpha_1 \neq \varepsilon, x \in S_{15}, \beta \subseteq \gamma, \beta = y\beta_1, y \in S_3, z \in S_2}{\gamma = (\alpha_1 x)(z\beta_1)} \tag{5}$$

where $S_{15} = S_1 - (S_1 \cap S_5)$

Example: The connection of two unvoiced and sonorous consonants is possible at the junction of two roots Bekmagambet (pronounced Begmagambet), Aknur (pronounced Agnur) in compound words and at the junction of two words ak mandai (pronounced agмandai), kok nayza (pronounced kognayza). In all these cases, there is a transformation of consonants [28, 31].

3. During the connection of two consonants, voiced and unvoiced, in one word or at the connection of two words, the voiced consonant remains voiced, and the unvoiced consonant is replaced with its matching voiced consonant

or

voiced consonant is replaced with its matching unvoiced consonant and unvoiced consonant remains unvoiced

$$\frac{\alpha \subseteq \gamma, \alpha = \alpha_1 x, \alpha_1 \neq \varepsilon, x \in S_2, \beta \subseteq \gamma, \beta = y\beta_1, y \in S_1, z \in S_2}{\gamma = (\alpha_1 x)(z\beta_1)} \tag{6}$$

$$\frac{\alpha \subseteq \gamma, \alpha = \alpha_1 x, \alpha_1 \neq \varepsilon, x \in S_2, z \in S_1, \beta \subseteq \gamma, \beta = y\beta_1, y \in S_1}{\gamma = (\alpha_1 z)(y\beta_1)} \tag{7}$$

Example: The junction of two voiced and unvoiced consonants is possible at the junction of a root and a postfix and at the junction of two roots sozsiz (pronounced sozsiz), kymyzkor (pronounced kymyzkor) and at the junction of two words tez pisti (pronounced tes pisti), zhuz pyshak (pronounced zhus pyshak). However, it is possible to pronounce it as follows: kymyz kor – kymyz gor, tez pisti – tez bisti, zhuz pyshaq - zhuz byshak [28, 31].

4. During the connection of two consonants, unvoiced and voiced, in one word or at the connection of two words, the unvoiced consonants is replaced with its matching voiced consonant, and the voiced consonant remains voiced

   or

   unvoiced consonant remains unvoiced, and voiced consonant is replaced with its matching unvoiced consonant.

$$\frac{\alpha \subseteq \gamma, \alpha = \alpha_1 x, \alpha_1 \neq \varepsilon, x \in S_1, z \in S_2, \beta \subseteq \gamma, \beta = y\beta_1, y \in S_2}{\gamma = (\alpha_1 z)(y\beta_1)} \tag{8}$$

$$\frac{\alpha \subseteq \gamma, \alpha = \alpha_1 x, \alpha_1 \neq \varepsilon, x \in S_1, \beta \subseteq \gamma, \beta = y\beta_1, y \in S_2,\ z \in S_1}{\gamma = (\alpha_1 x)(z\beta_1)} \tag{9}$$

   Example: The connection of two unvoiced and voiced consonants is possible at the root of the word akbar (pronounced akpar), does not occur at the junction of the root and the postfix, at the junction of two words ak gul (pronounced akkul). In all these cases, the voiced consonant turns into an unvoiced consonant. However, you can pronounce these words in a different way: akbar (pronounced agbar), ak gul (pronounced aggul [28, 31, 32].

The formal phonological rules of the Kazakh language obtained in this way will make it possible to build a transcriptor that automatically builds a transcription of a word, which is an important element in the development of a Kazakh speech synthesis system.

7 Conclusion

This paper presents the results of the formalization of phonological rules and their application in the implementation of a transcriptor for a speech synthesis system. The transcriptor was based on the works of the Kazakh scientist, reformer of national writing, the founder of Kazakh linguistics A. Baitursynov. Formalization, digital processing of the works of A. Baitursynov contributes to the improvement of the culture of the Kazakh language, as a language of interethnic communication in digital format, will allow obtaining new scientific results in terms of the scientific and linguistic foundations of the Kazakh language for various intelligent information systems that process natural languages, will allow transferring knowledge to the future generation in implemented applications, and will also have a direct impact on the development of the ICT industry in Kazakhstan and the quality of digital services in the Kazakh language.

8 Further Work

This work is carried out within the framework of the project BR11765535 "Development of Scientific and Linguistic Foundations and IT Resources to Expand the Functions and Improve the Culture of the Kazakh Language". In total, 7 big tasks are planned in the project, 2 of which are devoted to the synthesis of the Kazakh speech, and 1 – to the creation of an intellectual knowledge system on A. Baitursynov's heritage. After the creation of the transcriptor, it is planned to create a speech synthesis system based on the integrated End-to-End model. At the same time, it is also symbolic that the modern phonetics of the Kazakh language, used as a theoretical basis for the synthesis of the Kazakh speech, is based on the works of this outstanding scientist.

Funding. This research is funded by the Science Committee of the Ministry of Education and Science of the Republic of Kazakhstan (grant no. BR11765535).

References

1. Baia, A.E., Biondi, G., Franzoni, V., Milani, A., Poggioni, V.: Lie to me: shield your emotions from prying software. Sensors **22**(3), 967 (2022). https://doi.org/10.3390/s22030967
2. Milani, A., Franzoni, V., Biondi, G.: Parsing tools for Italian phraseological units. In: Gervasi, O., et al. (eds.) ICCSA 2021. LNCS, vol. 12955, pp. 427–435. Springer, Cham (2021). https://doi.org/10.1007/978-3-030-87007-2_30
3. Atif, M., Franzoni, V., Milani, A.: Emojis pictogram classification for semantic recognition of emotional context. In: Mahmud, M., Kaiser, M.S., Vassanelli, S., Dai, Q., Zhong, N. (eds.) BI 2021. LNCS (LNAI), vol. 12960, pp. 146–156. Springer, Cham (2021). https://doi.org/10.1007/978-3-030-86993-9_14
4. Franzoni, V., Milani, A., Mengoni, P., Piccinato, F.: Artificial intelligence visual metaphors in e-learning interfaces for learning analytics. Appl. Sci. **10**(20), 7195 (2020). https://doi.org/10.3390/app10207195
5. Magueresse, A., Carles, V., Heetderks, E.: Low-resource languages. a review of past work and future challenges. ArXiv, abs/2006.07264 (2020)
6. Sebastian, R.: The 4 biggest open problems in NLP (2019)
7. Emily, B.: High Resource Languages vs Low Resource Languages. The Gradient (2019)
8. Dossanova, N., Abdimanuly, O., Kapagan, E.: The influence of Akhmet Baitursynov's literary publicistic heritage on the spiritual development of Kazakh people at the beginning of The XXth century. J. Hist. Cult. Art Res. **9**, 286 (2020). https://doi.org/10.7596/taksad.v9i4.2669
9. Allworth, Ed.: Central Asia: A Century of Russian Rule. 1st Edn. University Presses of California, Columbia and Princeton (1967)
10. Abdimanuly, O.: Akhmet Baytursynuly: zertteu-essay. Arda, Almaty, 293 b. (2007)
11. Dakenov, M.: Baitursynov's role in the development of the sociology of culture and education in Kazakhstan. Bulletin Abay Kazakh National Pedagogical University (2012)
12. Aibarshyn, A.: The Man Who Led His Nation to Enlightenment: Kazakhstan Marks 150th Anniversary of Prominent Scholar Akhmet Baitursynov. The Astana times (2022)
13. Baytursinov, A.: New primer with drawings (8–17 thousand). Qizilorda (1926). (in Kazakh)
14. Baytursinov, A.: Problems of Kazakh linguistics. Abzal-Ai, Almaty (2013). (in Kazakh)
15. Baytursinov, A.: Til – qural. Sardar, Almaty (2009). (in Kazakh)
16. Baytursinov, A.: Til tagilimi. Pavlodar (2008). (in Kazakh)
17. Baytursinov, A.: Forty examples: poems. Zhazuschy, Almaty (2001). (in Kazakh)
18. Baytursinov, A.: Alphabet: new manual. Rauan, Almaty (1998). (in Kazakh)
19. Baytursinov, A.: New rules. Zhety zhargy, Almaty (1996). (in Kazakh)
20. Baytursinov, A.: A five-volume collection of works. Volume 1: Poems, literary and scientific research. Alash, Almaty (2003). (in Kazakh)
21. Yessenbayev, Z., Karabalayeva, M., Sharipbayev, A.: Formant analysis and mathematical model of Kazakh vowels. In: Proceedings - 2012 14th International Conference on Modelling and Simulation, UKSim 2012, article№ 6205485, pp. 427–431 (2012). https://doi.org/10.1109/UKSim.2012.66

22. Yessenbayev, Zh., Saparkhojayev, N., Tibeyev, T.: Implementation of the intelligent voice system for Kazakh. J. Phys.: Conf. Ser **495**(1), статья № 012043 (2014). https://doi.org/10.1088/1742-6596/495/1/012043
23. Sharipbayev, A.A., Bekmanova, G.T., Shelepov, V.U.: Formalization of Phonologic Rules of the Kazakh Language for System Automatic Speech Recognition. http://dspace.enu.kz/handle/data/1013. Accessed 12 May 2022
24. Bekmanova, G., Yergesh, B., Sharipbay, A., Mukanova, A.: Emotional speech recognition method based on word transcription. Sensors (Basel, Switzerland) **22**(5), 1937 (2022). https://doi.org/10.3390/s22051937
25. Zu, V.V.: Linguistic approach to automatic recognition of speech signals. In: Proceedings of the Institute of Electrical and Radio Electronics Engineers (TIIER). Speech Communication with Machines, no. 73, pp. 51–54 (1985)
26. Sharipbayev, A., Torekhanov, S.: Qazaq tili dauisti dibistarinin matematikalik modeli. L.N.Gumilyov atindagi Euraziya ulttik universiteti. «Khabarshi» № 3–4, 2002. 14. Qazaq grammatikasi, Astana (2002)
27. Bekmanova, G., Nicenko, A., Sharipbayev, A., Shelepov, V.: O nekotoryh voprosah svyazannyh s raspoznavaniem kazakhskoy rechi. Bulletin ENU, Astana (2009)
28. Kazakh Grammar. Phonetics, Word Formation, Morphology, Syntax; Astana-Poligraphy: Astana, Kazakhstan (2002). (in Kazakh)
29. Babin, D., Mazurenko, I., Holodenko, A.: On the Prospects of Creating a System of Automatic Recognition of Fused Russian-Speech. Mir, Moscow (1999)
30. Bekmanova, G.: Transcript of Kazakh words for speech recognition. Bulletin NAN RK, Almaty (2009)
31. Sharipbayev, A., Bekmanova, G.: Mathematical methods of recognizing combinations of sounds of the Kazakh language. In: Proceedings of the International Scientific-Practical Conference "Innovative Technologies: Integration of Science, Education and Business" KazNTU. K. Satpayeva. Almaty (2008)
32. Bekmanova, G., Nicenko, A., Sharipbayev, A., Shelepov, V.: Algorithms for recognizing Kazakh words as a whole. Structural classification of words of the Kazakh language. Bulletin ENU, Astana (2010)

Hate Speech and Stereotypes with Artificial Neural Networks

Giulio Biondi[1], Valentina Franzoni[1,2(✉)], Alessio Mancinelli[1], Alfredo Milani[1], and Rajdeep Niyogi[3]

[1] Department of Mathematics and Computer Science, University of Perugia, Perugia, Italy
{giulio.biondi,alfredo.milani}@unipg.it, valentina.franzoni@dmi.unipg.it, alessio.mancinelli@studenti.unipg.it

[2] Department of Computer Science, Hong Kong Baptist University, Kowloon, Hong Kong, China

[3] IIT Indian Institute of Technology at Roorkee, Roorkee, India
rajdeep.niyogi@cs.iitr.ac.in

Abstract. Information technology is ubiquitously integrated into all areas of human and social life. It becomes progressively critical to build trust in systems while exposing their limitations along with utility and values. The harmonic integration of applications into society will promote the ability of the individuals to positively adapt to change (resilience and response) only if, instead of imposing an AI-centric world on humans, the central goal is to rearrange AI to environments around all aspects of human life. Current AI architectures and applications are increasingly designed taking into account ethical issues, to support the educative role of advanced research tools in improving the interaction between individuals and ultimately in the betterment of society. This work aims at detecting hate speech and stereotypes in textual communication using Artificial Neural Networks and Natural Language Processing. Starting from data from the Evalita 2020 competition, we analyse 6851 tweets which include stereotypes and hate speech, including text and emoticons. Training our neural network with the Adam optimizer, we obtain very promising results, of accuracy for the hate speech task and the stereotype prediction task.

Keywords: NLP · Affective computing · Ethical computing

1 Introduction

The debate over free speech, stereotypes and hate speech, and legislation with international protocols to be applied to digital social networks is a topic of broad interest and still without consensus on a solution [11]. In social media and in all communication channels that involve relatively short texts, including the headlines of newspaper articles, the diffusion of extremist ideas is favoured by the

This work has been supported by MIUR PRIN PHRAME Project, and EmoRe.

O. Gervasi et al. (Eds.): ICCSA 2022 Workshops, LNCS 13379, pp. 15–32, 2022.
https://doi.org/10.1007/978-3-031-10545-6_2

rapid mode of communication that does not promote depth and argumentation [9,17,18]. Extremist ideas are often exploited by politicians and journalists with click-bait marketing models. Hate speech is usually referred to lack of politically correct attitude or animated conduct where an individual or a community, often characterized by wide cultural differences, is denigrated on the basis of one of its characteristics, such as the not universally accepted concept of the human race, or skin colour, national or geographical origin, sex or gender identity, disability or health status, religious faith or beliefs, ideological orientations. While countries and companies decide what to consider a shared undesirable outcome, AI research is developing techniques to enhance the detection of hate speech and stereotypes.

Techniques based on Natural Language Processing (NLP) and Artificial Neural Networks (ANN) are among the most promising methods for stereotypes and hate speech detection [1,3,5,15]. This work considers and tests ANN and NLP on the data of the Evalita 2020 competition [6,12] for supervised classification including 6851 tweets labelled for stereotypes and hate speech. The added value of the Evalita data sets is to provide text in Italian [14], while most of the data sets for research on hate speech and stereotypes are in English only [4,8,10]. Non-English languages are being taken into consideration recently for the same classification tasks [7,13,16] because of the relevance and criticality of the issue. After a preprocessing phase, we proceed to split data into training and test sets and the proposed novel ANN prototype is tested obtaining very promising results for hate speech and good results for stereotype detection in the Italian language.

2 Architecture of the Proposed Solution

The solution we propose and discuss has been developed in different stages, see workflow in Fig. 1, where rectangles represent data, and oval shapes represent activities:

- Data Collection, data acquisition and preliminary transformation (e.g., emoticons to text)
- Data Preprocessing: cleaning, filtering, features, word embedding computation
- Data set creation & split: training set and test set split
- Training: ANNs model setup, training and generation of trained model
- Testing: application of trained model to test set
- Results analysis

2.1 Data Set Source and Preprocessing

The original data set is from the Evalita 2020 competition [6] proposing different NLP and speech challenging tasks in the Italian language. The Evalita 2020 data set consists of Twitter messages targeting specific social groups prone to stereotypes, e.g., foreigners, people of minority religions in Italy, and nomads, collected using specific keywords. Such minorities are often at the heart of the

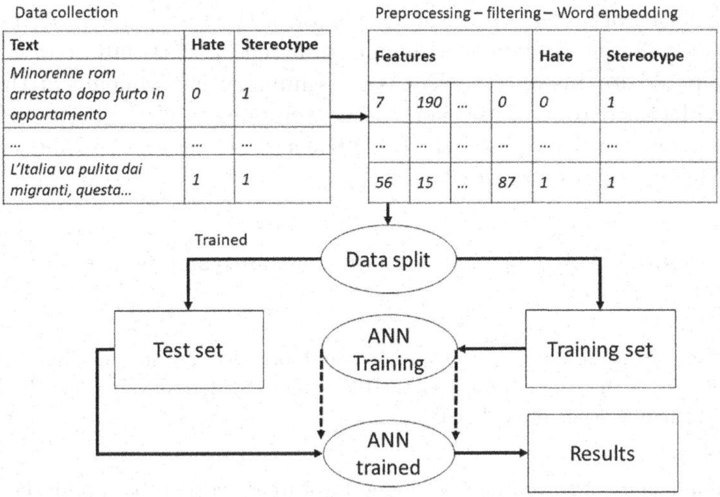

Fig. 1. Architectural flow of the solution

public social and political debate, and target of hate speech. The data set is available in a tab-separated format and contains 6851 tweets, with the following hate speech/stereotypes distribution:

- 4074 with no feelings of hate
- 2777 with feelings of hate
- 3804 with no stereotypes
- 3047 with stereotypes.

We decided to avoid balancing classes because in our case the loss due to eliminating terms is greater than the advantage of balancing them. In the data set, we consider the tweet text and the tags about *hate speech (hs)* and *stereotype*. Before transforming text into a format suitable for training the model, we exploit a preprocessing phase filtering put noisy non-meaningful words. We, therefore, eliminate some specific strings within the text, e.g. URLs or *@user* tags, and stop-words in the Italian language (i.e. prepositions, articles, possessive, demonstrative and interrogative adjectives, conjunctions). Usually, in NLP tasks, proper names and location names are also not taken into consideration. However, in our case, they can prove meaningful, e.g. Rome as the Italian seat of the government, or names/surnames of politicians involved in the public debate; therefore, we decided not to filter them out. Moreover, Particular attention has been paid to emoticons (i.e., the symbolic representation of emojis) [2], which could bring useful information that the model can learn to recognise. For their transformation, we used the emoji library that maps the analysed emoji with its respective text-symbolic representation. For the removal of stop-words, we used the nltk library that filters out articles, lexical particles and words without meaning in Italian by using a predefined list of strings. Another common technique in Natural Language Processing tasks is *stemming*, i.e., reducing inflected or derived forms of a word to the stem or root of the word to identify the same meaning in different contexts. Although Italian is a very inflected language, when compared for instance to English preliminary experiments in this work did not evidentiate any improvement using stemming, and therefore no preprocessing was done in this sense. In Table 1 sample tweets before and after the cleaning/filtering phase are shown.

Table 1. Examples of text before and after preprocessing

Original:
@user Rom ? Non illudiamoci. Loro non si cambieranno mai, non vogliono lavorare e sono disposti a tutto per rubare soldi. Il loro dio e' il denaro e non ascoltano altrove. Mi dispiace per il clochard.
Preprocessed:
rom illudiamoci cambieranno mai vogliono lavorare disposti rubare soldi dio denaro ascoltano altrove dispiace clochard
Original:
Leggendo questa notizia, mi vengono in mente la Fornero e Monti! Hanno varato una Legge per mandare in pensione gli ITALIANI a due passi dalla miglior vita, per dare i NOSTRI soldi agli IMMIGRATI? Ma chi li appoggia ancora, non si VERGOGNA? URL
Preprocessed:
leggendo notizia vengono mente fornero monti varato legge mandare pensione italiani due passi miglior vita dare soldi immigrati appoggia ancora vergogna
Original:
Zuccaro il magistrato leghista massone escluso dai suoi colleghi dalle indagini mafiose e costretto per farsi notare ad attaccare le ONG e i poveri immigrati
Preprocessed:
zuccaro magistrato leghista massone escluso colleghi indagini mafiose costretto farsi notare attaccare ong poveri immigrati thinking_face thinking_face
Original:
Penso che chi non vuole vedere che gli attentati terroristici sono motivati da volontá di sottomettersi tutti (islam) sia in malafede
Preprocessed:
penso vuole vedere attentati terroristici motivati volontá sottomettersi islam malafede
Original:
@user @user Va deindustrializzata la tratta degli africani e resa compatibile con lo stato di diritto.
Preprocessed:
va deindustrializzata tratta africani resa compatibile stato diritto

2.2 Word Frequency Features and Hate/Stereotype Classes

In this section we discuss some elements characterizing word frequency which can be used to characterize hate speech and/or stereotype. In the following we provide and analyze one Italian sentence for each of the three different classes (i.e., hate speech and stereotypes, hate speech only, stereotypes only); to make the criteria more understandable a translation in English of the sentences and the single words are shown, moreover a general statistic view of the word usage in the data set is provided:

Sentence labelled both hate speech and stereotypes: *#londonattack ask the good ol' boy what the hell they want to do with the Islamic because if I ask, all I get is insults on my mouth.*

Sentence labelled neither stereotypes nor hate speech: *@user @user in facts since they have gained with the #rom fields everything was ok with #Alemanno #Hypocrites*

Sentence labelled no hate speech but stereotypes: *Of course in #Tunisia it must not be easy to investigate extremism in #Tunisia Islamic. They are all extremists.*

Sentence labelled hate speech but no stereotypes: *#SicilyChannel has broken my balls all over the world: politicians, smugglers and immigrants. Close borders and stop.*

A the statistics of the 20 most used words is shown in Fig. 2 the corresponding English words are in order: *not, is, Roms, migrants, are, immigrants, Italy, everybody, Rome, has, Italians, immigration, foreigners, have, more, only/alone, home, camp, terrorists, away.* On the horizontal axis frequency of use is shown, while the term is shown on the vertical axis. Figure 3–Fig. 4 show a class-based analysis:

- Figure 3a shows the 20 Italian words most-used by hate speakers, in order: *not, is, are, everybody, immigrants, migrants, Italy, Roms, Italians, has, have, home, foreigners, terrorists, Islamic, Muslims, more, illegal immigrants, only/alone, Islam*
- Figure 3b shows the 20 words most-used by non-hate speakers: *Roms, non, is, migrants, are, Rome, Italy, immigrants, everybody, has, immigration, camp, nomad, foreigners, have, Italians, more, away, only/alone, Salvini*
- Figure 4a shows 20 words most-used by writers using stereotypes: *non, is, Roms, are, immigrants, everybody, migrants, Italy, has, Italians, have, Rome, foreigners, home, more, illegal immigrants, only/alone, Islamic, Muslim, terrorists*
- Figure 4b shows 20 words most-used by writers not using stereotypes: *non, Roms, is, migrants, are, Italy, immigrants, everybody, Rome, immigration, has, camp, foreigners, Italians, more, away, Salvini (italian politician), have, only/alone, nomads*

It is interesting that while the set of words is almost the same, except for some meaningful words, the frequency of use distribution is the most relevant feature to distinguish the user groups. The most used word throughout the data set is *Roms* (nomads from Romania), with 1479 occurrences. Users writing texts containing hate speech (i.e., hate speakers) use more frequently words such as *tutti* (*All*) (i.e., conveying absolute and ultimate concepts), *immigranti* (*immigrants*) and *migranti* (*migrants*), compared to non-hate speakers, using more words like *Roma* (*Rome*) and *Italia* (*Italy*), showing more conceptual focus on facts than on characteristics. The most used words by people using stereotypes are also *tutti* (*All*), *Roms* and *immigranti* (*immigrants*), while in the rest of the classes we always have the words Roma (*Rome*) and *migranti* (*migrants*). As we can see, the word *Roma* (*Rome*) is very often used by both of them since is the seat of the Italian government then is a central place often mentioned on decisions about how to manage immigration issues. The word *only* in this paper correspond to the English for the Italian word *solo*. In Italian "solo" can mean "only" or "alone", and the meaning may change in context of different tweets, but it seems apparent that the meaning *only* is the best translation, being a term used to separate classes. Figure 5 and Fig. 6 show the intersection of words present in the text both including and not including hate speech, and the intersection of words present both in the text including and not including stereotypes, which are somehow shared between different groups of users.

Regarding the intersection between the twenty most frequent words used by those who write texts containing hate speech, more than half of the words are used by both classes (i.e., from left to right correspond in English to *Roms, not, is, migrants, are, Italy, immigrates, all, has, foreigners, have, Italians, more, alone/only*) but with different frequency. The same observation applies to the intersection between the most frequent words of those who write texts containing stereotypes and not (i.e., from left to right they correspond in English to, *not, Roms, is, migrants, are, Italians, immigrants, all, Rome, has, foreigners, Italians, more, have, only/alone*).

Analysing the emoji frequency within the texts, we have circa only 282 over 7000 tweets containing emojis. The emoji angry is the most used both by those who write texts containing feelings of hate and stereotypes, while emoji face with tears of joy (i.e., laugh) is used very frequently from all classes (see Fig. 7a–Fig. 8b). Despite the trivially lower frequency of emoticons than words, the significance of emojis for the meaning understatement is apparent. It has to be noted that the problem of hate speech in the social network is particularly diffused because text messages, especially short ones and written without a cognitive filtering step taking time to re-read and correct the message, are particularly guided by emotions, and do not convey the intention of the writer. Therefore, such immediate text replays to posts can be easily misunderstood, while emoticons, despite being still supported for the emotional side and not explaining intentions, can clarify the meaning of the text.

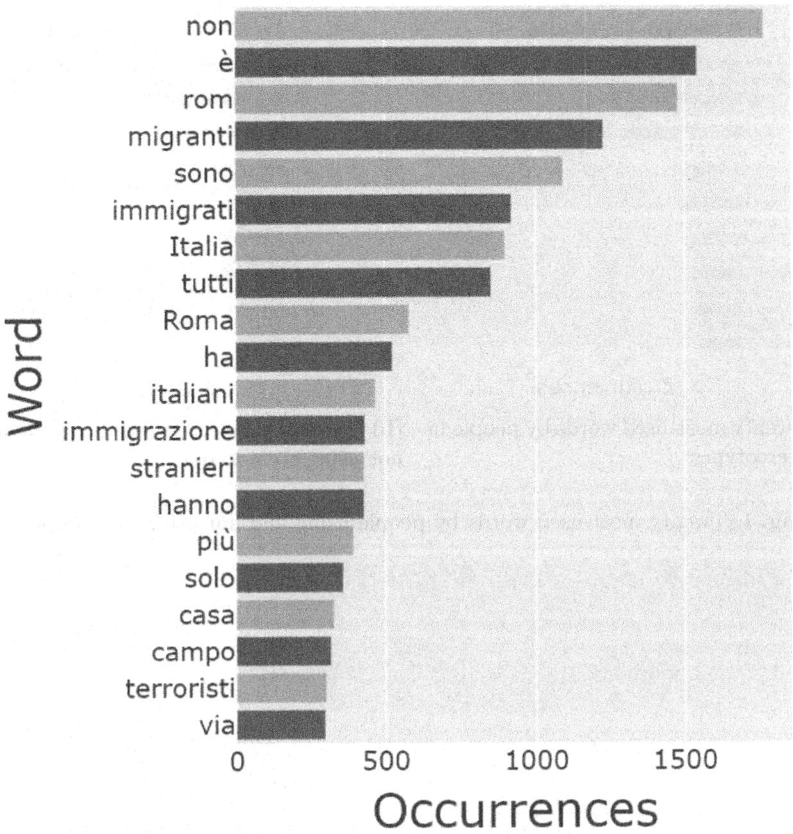

Fig. 2. Twenty most-used words in the whole data set

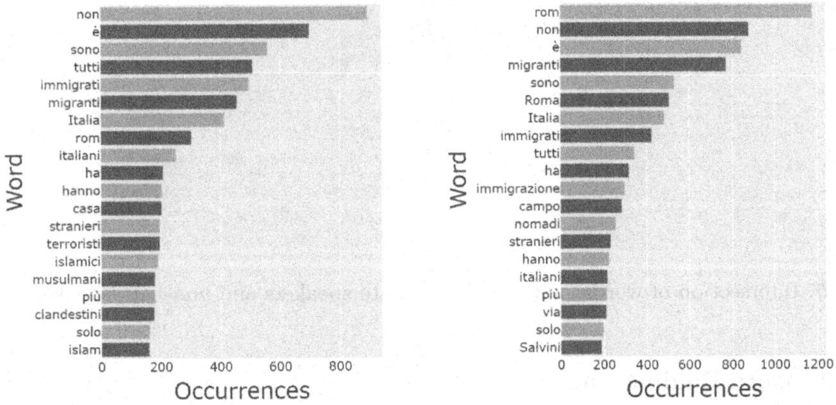

(a) Twenty most-used words by hate speakers

(b) Twenty most-used words by non-hate speakers

Fig. 3. Twenty most-used words by hate and non-hate speakers

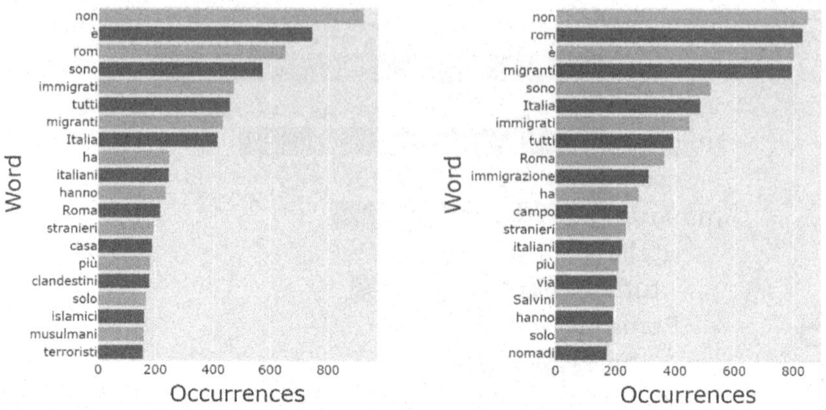

(a) Twenty most-used words by people using stereotypes

(b) Twenty most-used words by people not using stereotypes

Fig. 4. Twenty most-used words by people using and not using stereotypes

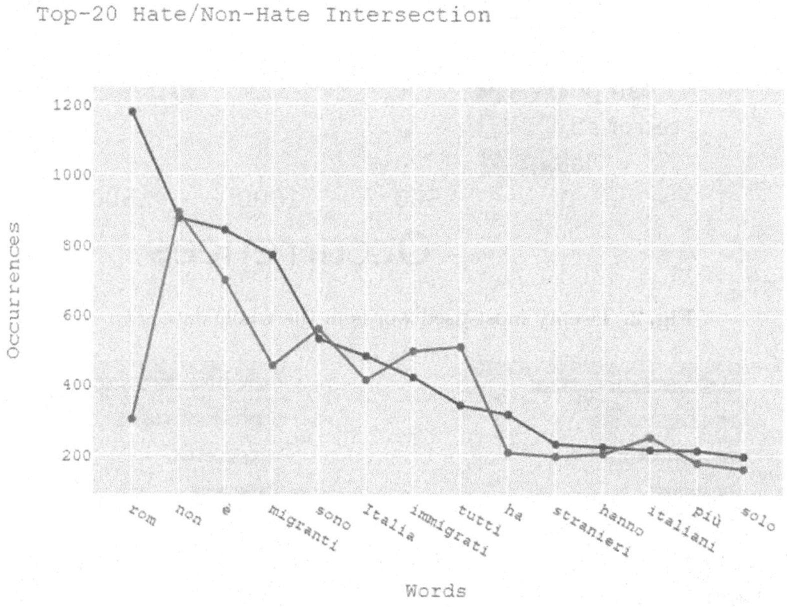

Fig. 5. Intersection of words shared between hate speakers and non-hate speakers

2.3 Feature Engineering

For the feature engineering phase, a preliminary analysis on the length of tweets was carried out, to investigate the possible correlations between text length and Hate/Stereotypes speech. The findings are reported in Table 2; on average content flagged as containing Hate Speech or Stereotypical is longer in terms of

Table 2. Average sentence length, # of characters

Class	Average # characters
Non-hate	136.40
Hate	165.73
Non-Stereotype	137.95
Stereotype	161.19

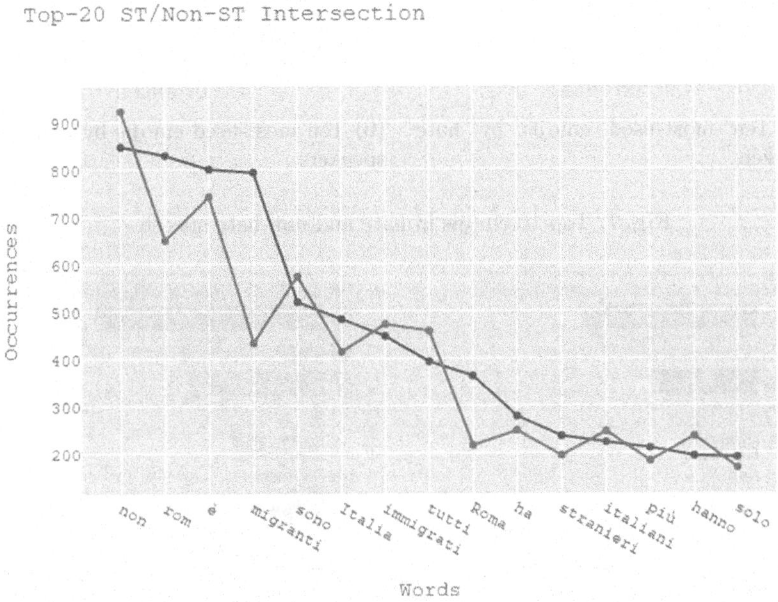

Fig. 6. Intersection of words shared between users using and not using stereotypes

characters. The previous statement is supported also by the figures in Table 3, showing the average length of tweets in terms of words; again, Hate-Speech or Stereotype tweets present a higher number of words. The following features have been computed for each tweet, on the basis of the previous figures and the data in Subsect. 2.2:

- # of words (including stop-words)
- # of characters
- Average Words Length in the sentence (including stop-words)
- Number of stop-words
- Number of words among the top 20 most used words in the whole data set
- Number of words among the top 10 most used words in hate speech tweets
- Number of words among the top 10 most used words in stereotype tweets
- Number of words among the top 10 most used words in non-hate speech tweets

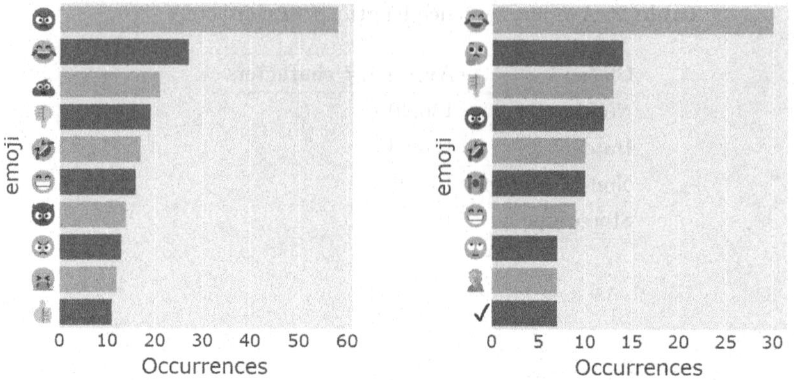

(a) Ten most-used emojis by hate speakers

(b) Ten most-used emojis by non-hate speakers

Fig. 7. Top-10 emojis in hate and non-hate speech

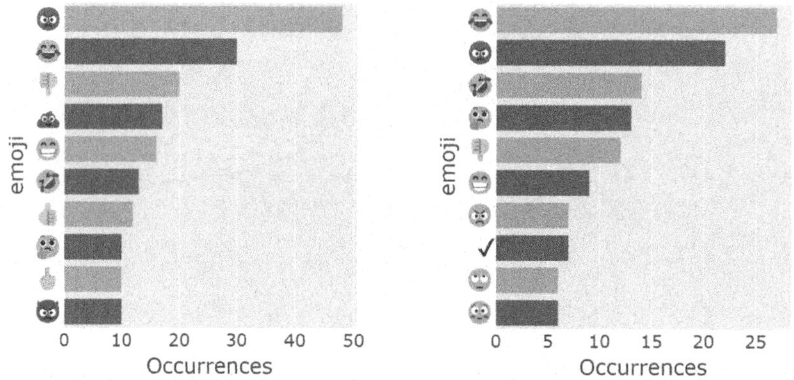

(a) Ten most-used emojis by people using stereotypes

(b) Ten most-used emojis by people not using stereotypes

Fig. 8. Top-10 emojis in stereotype and non-stereotype speech

- Number of words among the top 10 most used words in non-stereotype tweets
- # Punctuation signs
- # Exclamation marks
- # Question Marks
- # Fully capitalized words
- # Words starting with a capital letter
- # mentions (@user)
- # of Hashtag signs (#)
- # emojis in the tweet
- # of emojis among the top 5 most used words in hate speech tweets
- # of emojis among the top 5 most used words in non-hate speech tweets

Table 3. Average sentence length, # of words

Class	Average # words
Non-hate	26.34
Hate	31.44
Non-Stereotype	26.59
Stereotype	30.67

- # of emojis among the top 5 most used words in stereotype tweets
- # of emojis among the top 5 most used words in non-stereotype tweets

In the experiments, word embeddings were also calculated and employed as features. Word embedding layers create a higher-dimensional vectorial dense representation of words in a corpus. Words which frequently appear close to each other are mapped to closer vectors; embeddings are frequently employed in NLP machine learning tasks.

3 Artificial Neural Networks for Stereotypes and Hate Speech Detection

The purpose of the network described in the following is to solve two binary classification tasks. The first task classifies tweets as Hateful/Non-Hateful, and the second as containing/not containing stereotypes.

Fully connected neural networks have been employed, with several network preliminary designs tested to choose the best performing ones for the final experiments, for training the network and finally conducting the experimental test. In experiments, the data set training and test sets have been split with an 80%–20% rate.

For the HS detection task, the network has been designed as follows:

- An Embedding layer was prepended to learn the Word Embeddings, with a vocabulary size of 17986, i.e. the number of unique words in the data set after preprocessing, and output size and input length of 42, i.e. the maximum length of a sentence in the data set.
- A Flatten layer, to transform the 2D, [42*42] output of the Embedding layer, to a 1D vector of length 1764.
- A Concatenate layer, to concatenate the word embeddings to the 21 numeric features previously described in Sect. 2.3, with a final vector of 1785 features.
- Three Dense (i.e. Fully Connected) layers, respectively having 64, 32 and 2 neurons; the activation function was Softmax for the last layer, and ReLU for the others.

The structure of the network is shown in Fig. 9. The network was trained using the Adam Optimizer for 4 epochs, with a batch size of 128; the Loss function was Categorical Crossentropy. Additional experiments were performed, feeding the network either with text features only or word embeddings only. All the settings, including the network structure, were kept fixed, except for the number of training epochs, raised to 20 when only the text features were considered and lowered to 3 for the training on embeddings only. For the Stereotypes task, experiments were performed using the same network structure and combinations of features tested for the HS task. The network was trained for 4, 3 and 20 epochs for, respectively, the Text Features+Embeddings input, the Embeddings only input, and the Text Features only input. Other settings are the same as in the HSD experiment.

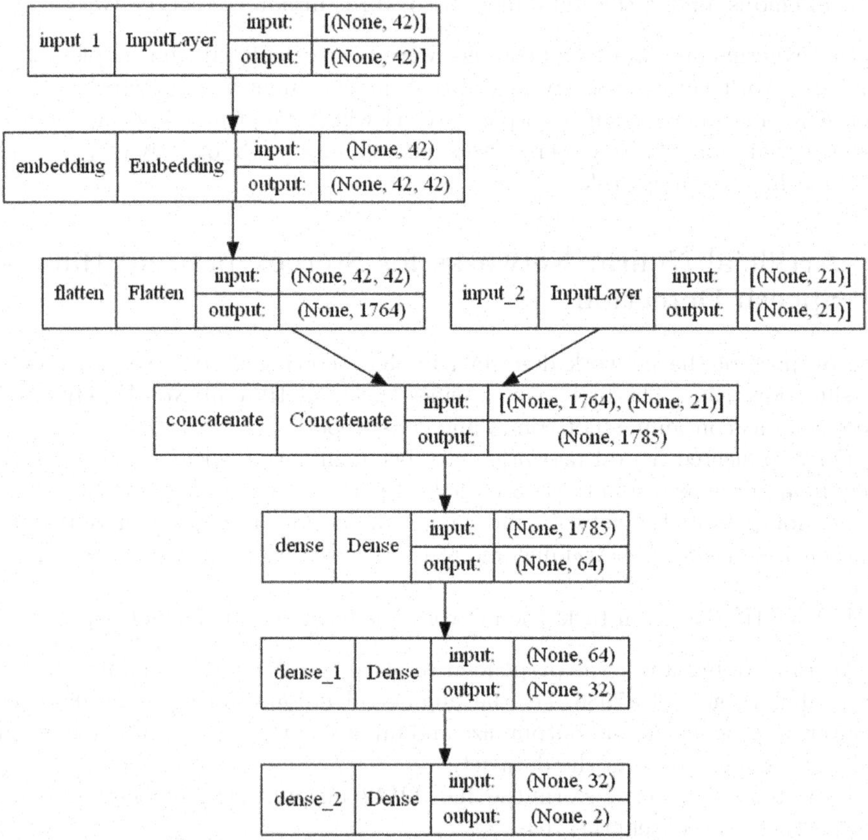

Fig. 9. Neural network structure, HS task

4 Results and Discussion

In this section the results of the experiments for the HSD and ST tasks are reported and discussed.

4.1 Evaluation Metrics

The evaluation metrics include global Accuracy and Macro-Average F1-Score and per-class Precision, Recall, and F1-Score. Let define:

- TP_{Hate} = True Positives i.e., the number of correctly classified items belonging to class Hate
- FN_{Hate} = False Negatives i.e., the number of misclassified items belonging to class Hate
- FP_{Hate} = False Positives i.e., the number of Non-Hate items erroneously classified as Hate
- TN_{Hate} = True Negative i.e., the number of correctly classified Non-Hate items

The same definitions apply to the (resp. Stereotype, Non-Hate or Non-Stereotype) All the per-class metrics are defined in terms of TP, TN, FP, FN. Precision, measuring the rate of relevant instances among the retrieved instanced:

$$precision_i = \frac{TP_i}{TP_i + FP_i}$$

Recall, measuring the rate of relevant instances that have been recalled:

$$recall_i = \frac{TP_i}{TP_i + FN_i}$$

F1, evenly weighting precision and recall, for each class i:

$$F1_i = \frac{2 * precision_i * recall_i}{precision_i + recall_i}$$

Macro-Average F1, calculated as the average of the per-class F1-Scores:

$$Macro - AverageF1 = \sum_{i=1}^{k} \frac{F1_i}{|i|}$$

Accuracy, in binary classification tasks, is defined as the ratio between the number of correctly classified items and the total number of items in the data set:

$$accuracy = \frac{TP + TN}{TP + TN + FP + FN}$$

The final results are evaluated with Accuracy and Macro-F1.

4.2 Hate Speech Detection Task

In Table 4(a) the per-class results are reported for the model exploiting both text features and word embeddings; the corresponding confusion matrix is reported in Table 5(a). The accuracy and Macro Average F1-Score values are, respectively, 75.47% and 73.5%, making this model the best performing for the HSD task.

Table 4. Per-class metrics, HSD task

(a) Word embeddings + Text features					
Class	Precision	Recall	F-Score	Accuracy	Support
0 (Non-hate)	78%	83%	80%	75.47%	833
1 (Hate)	71%	64%	67%		537
(b) Word embeddings only					
Class	Precision	Recall	F-Score	Accuracy	Support
0 (Non-hate)	78%	77%	78%	72.84%	833
1 (Hate)	65%	66%	66%		537
(c) Text features only					
Class	Precision	Recall	F-Score	Accuracy	Support
0 (Non-hate)	67%	85%	75%	65.98%	833
1 (Hate)	61%	36%	45%		537

Table 5. Confusion matrices, HSD task

(a) Word embeddings + Text features		
Class	Predicted non-hate	Predicted Hate
0 (Non-hate)	689	144
1 (Hate)	192	345
(b) Word embeddings only		
Class	Predicted non-hate	Predicted Hate
0 (Non-hate)	643	190
1 (Hate)	182	355
(c) Text features only		
Class	Predicted non-hate	Predicted Hate
0 (Non-hate)	710	123
1 (Hate)	343	194

In Fig. 10 the Accuracy and Loss values during the training process are shown. A higher number of epochs led to overfitting; therefore, the training process was stopped after four epochs. The additional experiments, exploiting either word embeddings only or text features only, delivered lower results. Complete figures are reported in Table 4(b), Table 5(b), Table 4(c) and Table 5(c).

The accuracy values for the Text Features only and Word Embeddings only experiments are, respectively, 65.98% and 72.84%, and the Macro-Average F1-Score 60% and 72%. It is apparent, from the results, that the most significant contribution to the task is given by the Word Embeddings, while the text features increase the performance only marginally.

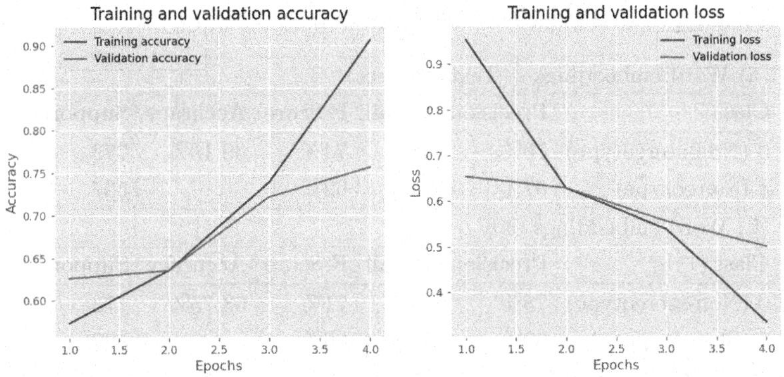

Fig. 10. Accuracy and Loss during training

4.3 Stereotypes Detection Task

Stereotypes detection proved to be a more difficult task for an automated system. For all the experimental settings, the figures are lower than the corresponding experiments for HSD. The best results, reported in detail in Table 6(a) and Table 7(a) were again obtained after training the network with the Word Embeddings and Text Features, which delivered an Accuracy of 69.19% and a Macro-Average F1-Score of 68%.

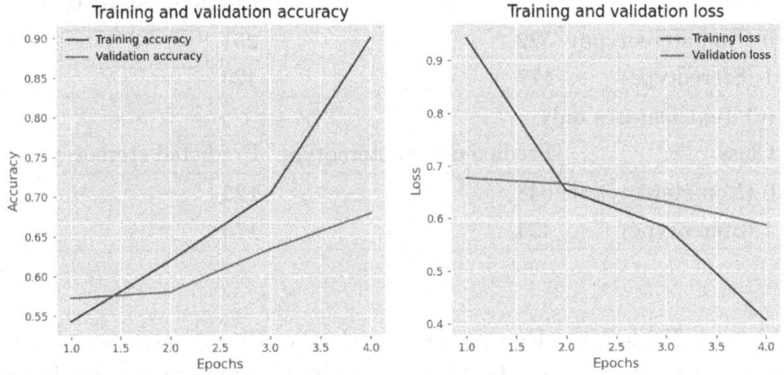

Fig. 11. Accuracy and Loss during training

In Fig. 11 the Accuracy and Loss values during the training process are shown. A higher number of epochs led to overfitting; therefore, the training process was stopped after four epochs. Feeding the network with the Word Embeddings only led to a slight loss in performance, lowering the Accuracy and Macro-Average F1-score to, respectively, 68.75% and 68.5%, showing a prominent role for the Embeddings in the ST task; complete figures are available in

Table 6. Per class metrics, ST task

(a) Word embeddings + Text features					
Class	Precision	Recall	F-Score	Accuracy	Support
0 (Non-stereotype)	70%	78%	74%	69.19%	773
1 (Stereotype)	67%	57%	62%		597
(b) Word embeddings only					
Class	Precision	Recall	F-Score	Accuracy	Support
0 (Non-stereotype)	75%	68%	71%	68.75%	773
1 (Stereotype)	63%	70%	66%		597
(c) Text features only					
Class	Precision	Recall	F-Score	Accuracy	Support
0 (Non-stereotype)	60%	84%	70%	59.92%	773
1 (Stereotype)	58%	29%	39%		597

Table 7. Confusion matrices, ST task

(a) Word embeddings + Text features		
Class	Predicted Non-stereotype	Predicted stereotype
0 (Non-stereotype)	605	168
1 (Stereotype)	254	343
(b) Word embeddings only		
Class	Predicted Non-stereotype	Predicted stereotype
0 (Non-stereotype)	522	251
1 (Stereotype)	177	420
(c) Text features only		
Class	Predicted Non-stereotype	Predicted stereotype
0 (Non-stereotype)	648	125
1 (Stereotype)	424	173

Table 6(b) and Table 7(b). Experiments with the Text Features only did not deliver any appreciable result; the system is only marginally capable of recognizing stereotypes, classifying most of the tweets in the data set as stereotypes-free. The accuracy score, in this case, is 59.92%, and the Macro-Average F1-Score is 54.5%, determined by the low F1-Score for the Stereotype class; results are reported in Table 6(c) and Table 7(c).

5 Conclusions

In this work we present a system for detecting hate speech and stereotypes usage in text communication in Italian language using Artificial Neural Networks and

Natural Language Processing; such systems prove useful in online communication contexts to promote non-aggressive and respectful dialogue between users of social networks, taking into account language-specific aspects. The system has been trained and tested on a data set used for the Evalita 2020 competition; it achieves very promising results on Hate Speech Detection, with an accuracy of 75.47% and F1-Score of 73.5%, and good results on the Stereotype Detection task, with an accuracy of 69.19% and F1-Score of 68.0%. Future experiments aim at improving the performance by experimenting additional textual features and verifying the proposed architecture for hate speech/stereotypes detection on longer texts.

References

1. Pedregosa, F., et al.: Scikit-learn: machine learning in python. J. Mach. Learn. Res. **12**, 2825–2830 (2011). http://dl.acm.org/citation.cfm?id=1953048.2078195
2. Atif, M., Franzoni, V.: Tell me more: automating emojis classification for better accessibility and emotional context recognition. Fut. Internet **14**(5) (2022). https://doi.org/10.3390/fi14050142, https://www.mdpi.com/1999-5903/14/5/142
3. Badjatiya, P., Gupta, S., Gupta, M., Varma, V.: Deep learning for hate speech detection in tweets. In: Proceedings of the 26th International Conference on World Wide Web Companion - WWW 2017 Companion, pp. 759–760. ACM Press, New York (2017). https://doi.org/10.1145/3041021.3054223, http://dl.acm.org/citation.cfm?doid=3041021.3054223
4. Benítez-Andrade, J.e.a.: José alberto. PeerJ Comput. Sci., e906 (2022). https://doi.org/10.7717/peerj-cs.906
5. Bird, S., Klein, E., Loper, E.: Natural Language Processing with Python, 1st edn. O'Reilly Media Inc, Newton (2009)
6. Bosco, C., Dell'Orletta, F., Poletto, F., Sanguinetti, M., Tesconi, M.: Overview of the Evalita 2018 Hate Speech Detection Task. In: Caselli, T., Novielli, N., Patti, V., Rosso, P. (eds.) Proceedings of the 6th Evaluation Campaign of Natural Language Processing and Speech Tools for Italian (EVALITA 2018). CEUR.org, Turin (2018)
7. Daury Cesar Fabriz, G.H.D.M.: O papel das plataformas de redes sociais diante do dever de combater o discurso de Ódio no brasil. Revista da Facultade de Direito (2022)
8. Davidson, T., Warmsley, D., Macy, M., Weber, I.: Automated hate speech detection and the problem of offensive language (2017). http://arxiv.org/abs/1703.04009
9. Del Vigna, F., Cimino, A., Dell'Orletta, F., Petrocchi, M., Tesconi, M.: Hate me, hate me not: hate speech detection on Facebook. In: CEUR Workshop Proceedings (2017)
10. Gitari, N.D., Zuping, Z., Damien, H., Long, J.: A lexicon-based approach for hate speech detection. Int. J. Multimedia Ubiq. Eng. (2015). https://doi.org/10.14257/ijmue.2015.10.4.21
11. Howard, J.W.: Free speech and hate speech. Ann. Rev. Polit. Sci. **22**(1), 93–109 (2019)
12. Manuela, S., et al.: Haspeede 2@evalita2020: overview of the evalita 2020 hate speech detection task, vol. 2765 (2020)

13. Marreddy, M., Oota, S.R., Vakada, L.S., Chinni, V.C., Mamidi, R.: Am i a resource-poor language? data sets, embeddings, models and analysis for four different nlp tasks in telugu language. ACM Trans. Asian Low-Resour. Lang. Inf. Process. (2022). https://doi.org/10.1145/3531535
14. Santucci, V., Spina, S., Milani, A., Biondi, G., Bari, G.D.: Detecting hate speech for italian language in social media. In: Caselli, T., Novielli, N., Patti, V., Rosso, P. (eds.) Proceedings of the Sixth Evaluation Campaign of Natural Language Processing and Speech Tools for Italian. Final Workshop (EVALITA 2018) Co-located with the Fifth Italian Conference on Computational Linguistics (CLiC-it 2018), Turin, Italy, 12–13 December 2018, CEUR Workshop Proceedings, vol. 2263. CEUR-WS.org (2018). http://ceur-ws.org/Vol-2263/paper041.pdf
15. Schmidt, A., Wiegand, M.: A survey on hate speech detection using natural language processing. In: Proceedings of the Fifth International Workshop on Natural Language Processing for Social Media (2017). https://doi.org/10.18653/v1/W17-1101
16. Susumu Annaka, G.K.: Can a constitutional monarch influence democratic preferences? Japanese emperor and the regulation of public expression. Social Sci. Q. (2022). https://doi.org/10.1111/ssqu.13152
17. Waseem, Z., Hovy, D.: Hateful symbols or hateful people? predictive features for hate speech detection on twitter. In: Proceedings of the NAACL Student Research Workshop (2016). https://doi.org/10.18653/v1/N16-2013
18. Zhang, Z., Luo, L.: Hate speech detection: a solved problem? the challenging case of long tail on twitter (2018). http://arxiv.org/abs/1803.03662

Student Behaviour Models for a University LMS

Giulio Biondi[1], Valentina Franzoni[1,2](✉), Alessio Mancinelli[1], and Alfredo Milani[1]

[1] Department of Mathematics and Computer Science, University of Perugia, Perugia, Italy
{giulio.biondi,alfredo.milani}@unipg.it,
valentina.franzoni@dmi.unipg.it, alessio.mancinelli@studenti.unipg.it
[2] Department of Computer Science, Hong Kong Baptist University, Kowloon, Hong Kong, China

Abstract. Learning Management Systems (LMSs) enable teachers and educational institutions to manage the organization of the courses offered and deliver courses in blended form, with LMSs offering support to in-person teaching, or fully online. LMSs, despite having been used for a long time, saw a dramatic increase in usage due to the Covid-19 pandemic; the purpose of this study is the analysis of student behaviour within the Moodle platform, by exploiting the user interaction logs as recorded by the platform itself. Two models are proposed to predict the final outcome of students' exams based on their behaviour within the platform. The first model consists of a support vector machine, while the second model consists of an artificial neural network; both models were tested on two real-world data sets, delivering outstanding results in terms of accuracy, above 90% for some of the tested configurations.

Keywords: e-learning · Behavioural models · Academic learning

1 Introduction

The term *user profiling* indicates the process of collecting personal user data aimed at creating an abstract image, which represents the cognitive and intellectual abilities, preferences and interactions that the user has with the system, which can be used to predict the user behaviour and support, facilitate or guide its activity in the interaction with the system itself. All this information will then be stored and processed dynamically, as user behaviour can still vary over time; this structured knowledge and the protocols to infer from and interact with it represent the *user model*.

This work has been supported by MIUR PRIN PHRAME Project, and EmoRe.

O. Gervasi et al. (Eds.): ICCSA 2022 Workshops, LNCS 13379, pp. 33–43, 2022.
https://doi.org/10.1007/978-3-031-10545-6_3

1.1 User Behaviour Data Sources

Information about users can be obtained in two main ways: the first one is to explicitly request from users information about themselves before they start interacting with the system. This can be achieved by an interview conducted during the registration phase, where specific data can be collected and allowed to be modified later by the user. While in principle this is a straightforward way to collect data quickly, on the other hand building a user model based on this information, exposes it to the risk of quickly becoming obsolete and most of all of not being fully objective and trustworthy. Reliability would depend entirely on the collaborative attitude of the users to provide sincere information about themselves, their attitudes, their interests, and its continuous update. It is very unlikely that further updates would happen once the initial registration process is over and, obviously, the user bias about her/himself cannot be eliminated. One advantage of this approach, however, is that it allows the user to have full control over the data that the system has access to. Another more objective approach is to allow the system itself to collect observations of user behaviour; in this case, the system monitors, as an example, the sequence of actions that the user performs to solve a given task, and therefore the information, unlike the first method, is not user provided, and it is objective. A problem in this case is that, to guarantee a high accuracy of the model without having initial data, the system has to collect a certain amount of information before being adequately performant. Therefore, it will not be able, initially, to make any prediction by facing the so called 'Cold start' [1] issue. However, when the amount of information becomes sufficient, the models will start to provide useful information and can then be adjusted automatically, allowing the model to adapt to user behaviour evolution [14].

1.2 Adaptable and Adaptive Systems

Adaptation refers to the ability of the system to react differently to each user by creating a single model of each of them, and adapting its response over the time when user behaviour evolves.

Systems with adaptation can be divided into two types based on how they use the user model: *adaptable systems* and *adaptive systems*. In the first class of systems, it is the user himself that can modify the aspect and the functionality of the system going to actively select the possible options. In the second case instead, the adaptation is executed autonomously by the system in a dynamic way, using the currently created user model [3,12,16]. Adaptability can be achieved, for instance, by manipulating the order in which content is shown to a user, thus modifying the navigation itself. One approach based on adaptive system is collaborative filtering, where information about a user is compared with that of others interaction with the same system. That is, if the characteristics of the current user match those of another, the system can make assumptions about the current user assuming that he or she has similar characteristics in areas where its model lacks enough data, by making changes based on them. Each user has his or her own characteristics and interests, as well as varying levels of familiarity with the subject under consideration; a system that knows nothing about its users would behave in exactly the same way for each of them. It is correct to consider, for instance, even the limitations of the users, such as disability, to allow the system to assist them. Considering the context of adaptive E-learning systems [17], a user model can be defined as an abstract image of the user within the system [6]. This image must contain information inherent to its domain of knowledge, such as progress in study, goals, and interests. Based on this model, the system will then be able to adapt its behaviours, providing, as an example, more detailed material for users with higher proficiency in a given subject. These elements are well summarized by the definition of an adaptive e-learning system according to Stoyanov and Kirschner:

"An adaptive e-learning system is an interactive system that personalizes and adapts e-learning content, pedagogical models, and interactions between participants in the environment to meet the individual needs and preferences of users if and when they arise."

1.3 Learning Management Systems and Moodle

A Learning Management System is typically a web based application platform that simplifies the management, distribution and analysis of an organization's online training program. These platforms allow users, typically students and instructors, to enrol, access and hold online educational activities corresponding to their role, by giving them the ability to access them at any time. Given these features, for instance, LMSs are used as verification tools for a group of company employees to assess their competence level and productivity, or for a class of university students for conducting ongoing evaluation tests to assess their knowledge level. It is particularly important the role of high-level users like administrators, whose task is to create courses and training plans, track the progress of those who use the LMS and upload contents within the platform, and instructors, which can monitor at any time the progress made by specific learners in a specific course [9]. Depending on the LMS used, different information is stored for each user, such as the total time they spend in a single course, the number of times they access the platform or performance automatically obtained in a given test (e.g. a multiple answer quiz), or assessed by the instructor for a given assignment. To promote the 'social learning' modality, an LMS can include features that support collaboration, such as forums and wikis where it is possible to create discussion groups or develop specific content on a specific topic collaboratively. In order to increase user engagement, gamification tools can also be used, through the installation of plugins, which will eventually reward the user through a system of rewards based on the score obtained. Corporate training is not the only application of LMS as they are also used within educational institutions, finding applications in schools and universities. Moodle, for instance, is an LMS distributed free of charge under an open source license, giving organizations the possibility to access the source code, thus enabling them to create numerous additional plugins aimed at adding functionality to improve the user experience of students as well as instructors. The learning style that Moodle follows is based on the interaction that the user has both with the learning material [5] and, most importantly, with other learners of the same by various forms of collaboration [11,13]. This system offers enormous advantages to teachers, since, after creating the course, it allows them to publish the material of the lessons from time to time, and also insert specific quizzes to check the student's learning progress. The platform allows the instructor, for instance, to keep track of which student has been most/least active throughout the course [2], since the system stores the logs (i.e. all the events that a user performs) in a relational database [8,15], the instructor can therefore plan learner specific activity/actions such as deepening a certain topic or repeating difficult topics. Moodle LMS stores information about user activities on more than 145 interrelated tables [4]; in this paper, we focus on the data of table mdl_logstore_standard_log: it collects all the registration of user activities and information about the events taking place in a given course, also including activities carried out within forums or wikis.

In this paper we will describe the architecture of a system using machine learning techniques to make predictions on *final exams outcomes* of university students; the system uses logs from a Moodle platform for building a meaningful user model. In Sect. 2 the data preprocessing, filtering and feature selection phases to build the data set used in the experiments are described. In Sect. 3 the machine learning architecture, the experiments held and the obtained results are presented and discussed. Conclusions are finally drawn in Sect. 4.

2 Data Preprocessing, Features Selection and Datasets

The data we considered describe the history of a university course supported by a Moodle e-learning platform in mixed modality, i.e. lessons held in physical classes, but supported by material distributed online and tests, quizzes, and assignments submitted online. The events took place over a time span of 24 months, or 101 weeks, from the actual course creation date in the LMS to the effective course ending date; a few weeks were excluded because no user events were recorded. Figure 1 and Fig. 2 show the distribution of the events, respectively, per month and per week across the selected time span.

The mdl_logstore_standard_log Moodle records for each event 21 different attributes; for the purpose of this work, four were considered:

- *userid*
- *eventname*
- *timecreated*
- *objectid*

During the first weeks, the system recorded only a few events; it is apparent that from March, i.e. the course starting month onwards, they become much more frequent with peaks in the June/July 2018 and January/February 2019 periods. The scarcity of events in the beginning weeks is due to the date of Moodle course creation not necessarily corresponding to the actual start date of

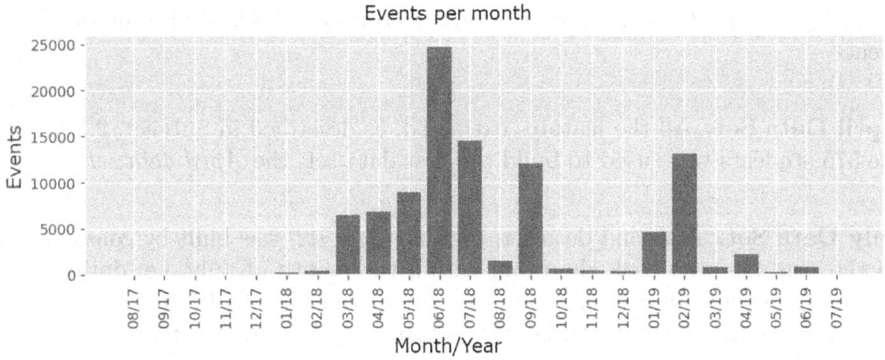

Fig. 1. Events per month

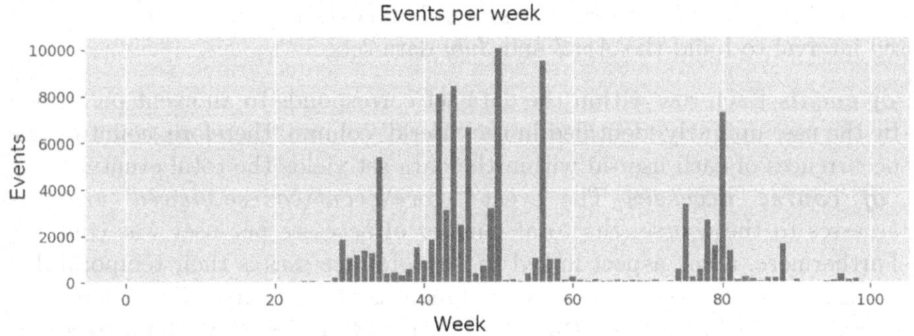

Fig. 2. Events per week

the course. The events in the first months, which constituted a tiny fraction of the total in the data set, mainly represented course enrollment events and were thus deemed not significant for the work. Therefore, 2018-01-01 was chosen as the course start date; the course ending date was set instead to April 16th 2019, the last exam session of which results were available. All of the events within the original data set were generated by 620 single users, including administrators and system applications; filtering the users to consider students only lowered the figure to 605 and applying the date-time filtering described above, the users finally fell to 575. Of these, 368 took the exam, while 207 did not attempt any session within the analysed period. The initial total number of events by the 620 users was 99011, reduced to 93024 after applying the filter on students, and finally to 91564 by considering only those events within the course period. Considering the users who passed the exam, all the events following the successful attempt were filtered out since they were deemed not meaningful to train the models. The rest of the data set consists of students who have never passed the exam or attempted it. For such students, the date of the first event recorded since the beginning of the course was also taken into account but, as the final date, April 16th, 2019, i.e. the last considered date, thus not filtering out any event.

April Data Set. All the features extracted, as described in Subsect. 2.1, from the 575 students were used to build the first data set, the *April data set.*

July Data Set. A second data set, the *July data set*, was built by considering all the students who took the exam within the month of July, i.e. during the first exam session; it contains data of events from 2018-01-01, i.e. the course beginning date, to 2018-07-24, i.e. the last July exam session date.

2.1 Feature Selection

The following per-user features were selected and extracted from data on a time-based interval to build the *April* and *July* data sets:

# of events Each row within the data set corresponds to an event performed by the user uniquely identified in the 'userid' column; therefore, counting the occurrences of each user-id within the data set yields the total events.

# of course accesses The event '\core\event\course_viewed' logs the accesses to the course; the total number of accesses per user was counted. Furthermore, a key aspect linked to the total accesses is their temporal distribution over the different weeks and months of the course. The assumption is that users who accessed the course from the earliest days, on a recurrent basis, will have better exams outcome on average and should thus be assigned more credit than those who waited for the exam sessions.

# of viewed discussions The event '\mod_forum\event\discussion_viewed' records discussions' views by users on the course forum, which is typically used to communicate course information to students, and stores the reference to the discussion in the *objectId* attribute. The number of different discussions viewed by each user is counted.

# of viewed resources similarly to obtaining the number of discussions; in this case the event considered is: '\mod_resource\event\course_module_viewed'

final exam outcome Indicates the final outcome of each user's exam, i.e. the variable that the models will predict.

3 Experiments Design and Results

In this section, the machine learning architecture, the experiments held and the obtained results are presented and discussed.

3.1 Experiments Design and Architecture

In this work two ML classifiers have been employed, i.e. Artificial Neural Networks (ANNs) [10] and Support Vector Machines (SVM) [7].

K-fold Validation. After preliminary experiments which showed a tendency to overfit with both ANN and SVM, a K-fold cross validation technique was employed to divide the data set into $k = 5$ partitions of equal size. In cross-validation, a system is trained on $k-1$ partitions and tested on the kth remaining partition; the process is repeated until each partition has been used as a test set. Considering the *April data set*, for each partition 460 of 575 users, i.e. 80% of the original data set were used as the training set and 115, i.e. the remaining 20 as the testing set. For the *July data set*, the total number of students was 340, with 272 used as training set and 68 as test set.

SVM. Two SVM kernels were tested, i.e. linear and RBF; various parameter values were tested for each kernel to find the best performing combinations. The parameter values were selected following a *grid search* approach, exhaustively testing, in selected ranges, combinations of the parameters subject to optimization, and evaluating the performance of the classifier for each parameters combination. This approach generally guarantees good results at the price of the high computational capacity required to train from the beginning a classifier for each of the combinations tested. The ranges of values used for the choice of parameters are reported in Table 1, while the final values chosen for the experiments are reported in Table 2.

Table 1. SVM grid search ranges

Parameter	Values					
C	0.001	0.01	0.1	1	10	100
γ	0.0001	0.001	0.01	0.1	1	10

Table 2. SVM parameters

Kernel	C	γ
Linear	0.1	Not applicable
RBF	100	0.0001

ANNs. A Fully Connected Neural Network has been designed, with the following architecture: the input layer has 88 neurons (resp. 41), i.e. the number of features in the *April* data set (resp. *July*). The two hidden layers are composed respectively of 32 and 16 nodes with *relu* activation function, while the final output layer consists of a single neuron with *sigmoid* activation function. The *Adam* optimizer was used in the training process; binary cross-entropy was chosen as loss function and Accuracy as performance metric.

Evaluation Metrics. The main evaluation metric chosen for the experiments is *accuracy.*

Let define:

- TP_{Passed} = True Positives i.e., the number of correctly classified items belonging to class *Passed Exam*
- FN_{Passed} = False Negatives i.e., the number of misclassified items belonging to class *Passed Exam*
- FP_{Passed} = False Positives i.e., the number of *Failed Exam* items erroneously classified as *Passed Exam*
- TN_{Passed} =True Negative i.e., the number of correctly classified *Failed Exam* items

Accuracy is defined, for binary classification tasks, as the ratio of the correctly classified records to the total number of records:

$$accuracy = \frac{TP + TN}{TP + TN + FP + FN}$$

Other computed metrics include per-class *Precision*, *Recall*, and *F1-Score.*

3.2 Experiments Result

In this section the results of the experiments on the July and April data sets are reported; all the figures in the tables are averaged over 5 folds.

July Data Set. In Table 3(a), Table 3(b) and Table 3(c) the results for, respectively, the SVM models with Linear (SVM/L) and RBF (SVM/RBF) kernels and the ANN model are reported.

The best results are achieved by the SVM/L model, with an Accuracy of 85% in predicting the exam outcome; the other models show slightly lower performance, while still equal or above 80%.

Table 3. Average results on the July data set

Class	Precision	Recall	F-score	Accuracy	Support
(a) SVM/L model, C = 0.1					
0	82%	82%	82%	85%	28
1	87%	87%	87%		40
(b) SVM/RBF model, C = 100, γ= 0.0001					
0	78%	76%	76%	81%	28
1	83%	84%	83%		40
(c) ANN model					
0	80%	71%	74%	80%	28
1	81%	87%	84%		40

Table 4. Average results on the April data set

	Precision	Recall	F-score	Accuracy	Support
(a) SVM/L model, C = 0.1					
0	95%	97%	96%	96%	52
1	98%	96%	97%		63
(b) SVM/RBF model, C = 100, γ= 0.0001					
0	91%	88%	89%	90%	52
1	90%	92%	91%		63
(c) ANN model					
0	86%	83%	84%	89%	52
1	86%	89%	87%		63

April Data Set. In Table 4(a), Table 4(b) and Table 4(c) the results for, respectively, the SVM/L, SVM/RBF and ANN models are reported.

The figures on the April data set are higher for all the models when compared to the July data set; such results can be traced to the higher number of samples and the wider set of features, covering a longer timeframe. The lowest Accuracy score, as in the case of the July data set, is obtained by the ANN model; furthermore, similarly to the other data set, the ANN and SVM/RBF models offer comparable performance, albeit with a higher ≈90% Accuracy. The SVM/L model shows the highest figure, with a remarkable 96% Accuracy on 115 samples and comparable Precision, Recall and F-score values across the two classes. All models offer better performance on the April dataset; ANN turned out to be, in both datasets, the model that offers worse accuracy, although very high. We can see that the performance of ANN and the SVM model with RBF kernel are similar, but the latter offers better performance in both datasets. In general, however, we can conclude that all the proposed models offer a good solution to the problem, guaranteeing high accuracy in assigning an exam outcome given the behaviour of a student within the platform. The model that offers better performance for the posed problem is the SVM having linear Kernel and a value of 0.1 for the C parameter.

4 Conclusions

This research work shows and analyzes how students approach the Moodle platform, how different their behaviours can be, and how such behaviours can lead to predictable consequences in terms of passing an exam. All of the proposed models showed good performance in solving the problem at hand; in particular, the SVM model achieved very high accuracy, almost always correctly predicting the outcome of the exam of the analyzed students.

References

1. Abbakumov, D.: The solution of the "cold start problem" in e-learning. Procedia - Social Behav. Sci. **112**, 1225–1231 (2014). https://doi.org/10.1016/j.sbspro.2014.01.1287
2. Bañeres, D., Rodríguez-Gonzalez, M.E., Serra, M.: An early feedback prediction system for learners at-risk within a first-year higher education course. IEEE Trans. Learn. Technol. **12**, 249–263 (2019)
3. Beck, J.E., Woolf, B.P.: High-level student modeling with machine learning. In: Gauthier, G., Frasson, C., VanLehn, K. (eds.) ITS 2000. LNCS, vol. 1839, pp. 584–593. Springer, Heidelberg (2000). https://doi.org/10.1007/3-540-45108-0_62
4. Bognár, L., Fauszt, T.: Different learning predictors and their effects for moodle machine learning models. In: 2020 11th IEEE International Conference on Cognitive Infocommunications (CogInfoCom), pp. 000405–000410 (2020). https://doi.org/10.1109/CogInfoCom50765.2020.9237894
5. Bovo, A., Sanchez, S., Héguy, O., Duthen, Y.: Clustering moodle data as a tool for profiling students. In: 2013 Second International Conference on E-Learning and E-Technologies in Education (ICEEE), pp. 121–126 (2013). https://doi.org/10.1109/ICeLeTE.2013.6644359
6. Ciloglugil, B., Inceoglu, M.M.: User modeling for adaptive e-learning systems. In: Murgante, B., et al. (eds.) ICCSA 2012. LNCS, vol. 7335, pp. 550–561. Springer, Heidelberg (2012). https://doi.org/10.1007/978-3-642-31137-6_42
7. Cortes, C., Vapnik, V.: Support-vector networks. Mach. Learn. **20**(3), 273–297 (1995). https://doi.org/10.1007/BF00994018
8. Dutt, A., Ismail, M.A., Herawan, T.: A systematic review on educational data mining. IEEE Access **5**, 15991–16005 (2017). https://doi.org/10.1109/ACCESS.2017.2654247
9. Franzoni, V., Milani, A., Mengoni, P., Piccinato, F.: Artificial intelligence visual metaphors in e-learning interfaces for learning analytics. Appl. Sci. **10**(20) (2020). https://doi.org/10.3390/app10207195, https://www.mdpi.com/2076-3417/10/20/7195
10. Haykin, S.: Neural Networks: A Comprehensive Foundation. Prentice Hall PTR, Upper Saddle River (1994)
11. Iglesias-Pradas, S., Ruiz-de Azcárate, C., Agudo-Peregrina, Á.F.: Assessing the suitability of student interactions from Moodle data logs as predictors of cross-curricular competencies. Comput. Human Behav. **47**, 81–89 (2015).https://doi.org/10.1016/j.chb.2014.09.065, http://www.sciencedirect.com/science/article/pii/S0747563214005238
12. Li, N., Cohen, W., Koedinger, K., Matsuda, N.: A machine learning approach for automatic student model discovery. In: EDM 2011 - Proceedings of the 4th International Conference on Educational Data Mining, pp. 31–40 (2011)
13. Mengoni, P., Milani, A., Li, Y.: Impact of time granularity on histories binary correlation analysis. In: Misra, S., et al. (eds.) ICCSA 2019. LNCS, vol. 11620, pp. 323–335. Springer, Cham (2019). https://doi.org/10.1007/978-3-030-24296-1_27
14. Montaner, M., López, B., de la Rosa, J.L.: A taxonomy of recommender agents on the internet. Artif. Intell. Rev. **19**(4), 285–330 (2003). https://doi.org/10.1023/A:1022850703159
15. Peña-Ayala, A.: Educational data mining: a survey and a data mining-based analysis of recent works. Expert Syst. Appl. **41**(4, Part 1), 1432–1462 (2014). https://doi.org/10.1016/j.eswa.2013.08.042, http://www.sciencedirect.com/science/article/pii/S0957417413006635

16. Sison, R., Shimura, M.: Student modeling and machine learning. Int. J. Artif. Intell. Educ. (IJAIED) **9**, 128–158 (1998). https://telearn.archives-ouvertes.fr/hal-00257111
17. Wang, Y.h., Liao, H.C.: Data mining for adaptive learning in a TESL-based e-learning system. Expert Syst. Appl. **38**(6), 6480–6485 (2011). https://doi.org/10.1016/j.eswa.2010.11.098

International Workshop on Future Computing System Technologies and Applications (FiSTA 2022)

Implementation and Proof Experiment of Communication Network for Disaster Prevention Using LPWA

Kazuaki Tanaka[1(✉)], Hiroyuki Maeda[1], Keisuke Yamashita[2], Yan Liu[3], and Hemanta Hazarika[3]

[1] Kyushu Institute of Technology, Kitakyushu, Japan
kazuaki@ics.kyutech.ac.jp
[2] CMN Co., Ltd., Tokyo, Japan
[3] Kyushu University, Fukuoka, Japan

Abstract. One of the negative influence of climate change is the occurrence of large-scale disasters. All over the world, climate change-related disasters such as torrential rains, heavy snowfalls, floods, and landslides are occurring. For example, the number of torrential rains has increased 1.4 times in the last ten years and is increasing dramatically.

In the case of a large-scale disaster, communication and power supply are not available; Typhoon No. 15 in 2019 caused a 20-day power outage in Chiba prefecture, Japan. The power outage also causes the carrier communication network inoperable, leading to a secondary disaster that prevented smooth evacuation instructions.

A system that can stably collect weather data and provide evacuation instructions at public facilities in the case of a disaster would greatly contribute to disaster prevention. The authors developed a general-purpose communication module for LPWA-based communication and designed a protocol to build an autonomous mesh communication network. This paper describes the implementation of this developed system for a ground monitoring system using soil sensors and reports on the proof experiment.

Keywords: LPWA network · Disaster prevention · Ground monitoring system

1 Introduction

Around the world, climate change-related disasters such as torrential rains, heavy snowfalls, floods, and landslides are occurring. In Japan, a power outage that lasted for hours of storage resulted in a secondary disaster in which communications systems dependent on carrier communications networks were lost and smooth evacuation instructions could not be given.

Since communication and power supply cannot be secured in the event of a large-scale disaster, a communication system that does not depend on power supply and carrier communications is desired.

O. Gervasi et al. (Eds.): ICCSA 2022 Workshops, LNCS 13379, pp. 47–56, 2022.
https://doi.org/10.1007/978-3-031-10545-6_4

A system that can stably collect weather data and also provide evacuation instructions at public facilities during a disaster will contribute to disaster prevention. The authors have developed a general-purpose communication module for LPWA-based communication and designed a protocol to build an autonomous mesh communication network. The authors implemented an LPWA communication protocol and an application that collects data from a weather meter using this protocol. This paper describes the implementation of a monitoring system using the developed system and the results of a demonstration experiment.

2 Sensing for Disaster Prevention

2.1 Requirements

This paper shows the design and implementation of a communication system for disaster prevention and disaster reduction. The proposed system will contribute to the prevention of many recent disasters.

This system includes the following elements; remote sensing with reliability, and a notification function to provide evacuation instructions at public facilities. These features are useful for disaster prevention and disaster reduction.

This communication system covers a wide area and does not depend on the networks of telecommunication providers. Furthermore, this communication mechanism has security features to prevent unauthorized communication by unauthorized parties. In addition, to make the resilient communication infrastructure to disasters, it will have redundancy and have a mechanism for reconstructing communication routes.

This communication module has an interface to attach the required sensors to detect the occurrence of disasters. Ensure those sensors, which will vary depending on the geographical situation, can be changed flexibly.

2.2 LPWA Communication

Low-power Wide-area communications, commonly referred to as LPWA, is a promising communication for IoT devices in recent years, and a variety of standards have been proposed [1]. LPWA has several standards, shown in Table 1.

For this study, the LoRa standard, one of the LPWA communication methods, was adopted to configure a flexible network and to use a proprietary protocol.

The LoRa method includes the LoRa (which stands for Long Range) modulation standard and the LoRaWAN standard. LoRa has a spread spectrum modulation scheme as a specification, and also the communication physical layer is specified. LoRa uses a license-free radio band that can be used for long-distance transmission with low power consumption. LoRaWAN, on the other hand, specifies a software communication protocol and system architecture. As the name implies, it uses LoRa modulation and specifies a bi-directional communication upper layer. LoRaWAN uses cloud-based MAC (Media Access Control) and a communication gateway managed by the Laura Alliance.

Table 1. LPWA standards

LoRa	Promoted by the LoRa Alliance and freely available for private use Only the modulation method is specified
LoRaWAN	Communication network based on the LoRa system, which requires the use of LoRa Alliance-certified equipment
NB-IoT	Using the the mobile carrier band Available only in the carrier's service area
Sigfox	Services provided by SIGFOX, Inc Commercial service and worldwide available through international roaming
LTE-M	LTE for machine-type-communication Same area as LTE service. Relatively high speed communication

In this study, we chose LoRa because this is the most cost-effective way to achieve a proprietary communications infrastructure suitable for disaster prevention and disaster reduction. The communication system will design and implement a protocol and communication control system using the LoRa modulation scheme to provide effective communication during disasters.

2.3 Security Features

Communications that use radio waves must have security measures since anyone can receive radio waves. The proposed system must not only ensure security but must also be power efficient because it must operate resiliently against disasters.

Security enhancements require computational power for their enhancement. If a system has strong cryptography capabilities, it requires a lot of computing power and consumes power. Assume that the communications required during a disaster are issuing alerts for evacuation, sending out urgent SOS, and so on. These disaster messages need not be secret. On the other hand, unauthorized messages by malicious parties should be rejected. In other words, the ability to detect unauthorized communications is an essential requirement.

Based on the above requirements, the system has a mechanism to verify that the received message was sent by the sender. This function can be regarded as a type of electronic signature. Design a lightweight verification mechanism that satisfies the requirement of power-saving.

2.4 Sensors for Disaster Prevention

While there are different types of disasters, this study will focus on heavy rainfall and the landslides caused by rain. Sensors to measure rainfall (called accumulative rain meters) and soil pressure sensors for landslides detection will be installed in the experimental field. The data acquired by those sensors will be transmitted to a central station (which will be called the head quarter; HQ) using LPWA communication.

If the values received by the HQ from the rainfall and soil pressure sensors exceed the threshold values, the HQ sends out an alert message via LPWA communication. All indicators which the LPWA communication module is connected receive alert message. Finally residents receive the alert messages.

3 Implementation

3.1 LPWA Communication Module

We have implemented communication middleware for secure LPWA communication, which uses the LoRa modulation scheme so that it can be used in disaster situations. The communication middleware has the following functions;

- Variable length messages are sent using LoRa modulation.
- The received message is verified with a pre-shared key. If the verification fails, this module discards the invalid message.

In addition, to make it simple to prototype the system and to facilitate demonstration experiments, this LPWA module also provides the following functions;

- Connect to a PC via USB cable and treat LPWA communication transparently as serial communication
- Shared keys can be updated by serial communication commands (known as AT commands)

In the LoRa system, there are legal restrictions on how often radio waves can be transmitted. After one message is transmitted, the next message is transmitted after a certain amount of time has elapsed. In the case of Japan, the legal requirement is to wait 10 times the length of time it took to transmit (Fig. 1) .

Therefore, the measurement of the time length taken to send a message and the subsequent suppression of transmission is an essential function of the LPWA module. The time length required to transmit can be calculated using the LPWA modulation rate. This time length can determine the time for next transmitting.

The LPWA module developed in this study has three FIFOs: LPWA transmit, LPWA receive, and USB serial receive. The LPWA module provides enqueue and dequeue APIs of these FIFOs, so that user applications can only make permitted FIFO accesses. The LPWA module's timer interrupt mechanism takes control of the FIFOs and sends messages using the LPWA at the appropriate time (Table 2).

Figure 2 shows the relationship between the LPWA module middleware and the user application. The FIFOs are strictly managed by the LPWA module middleware, which performs processing on each FIFO at the appropriate time through interrupts and scheduling. This middleware allows user applications to

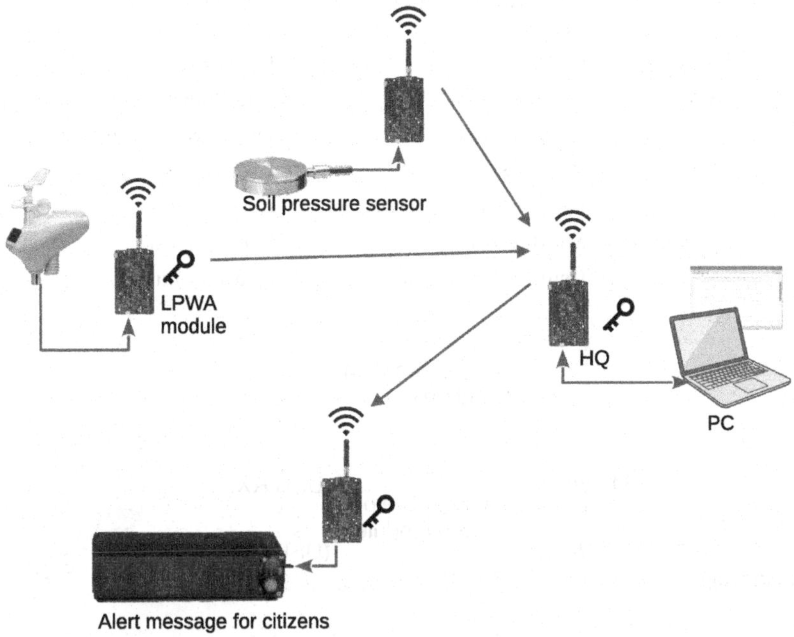

Fig. 1. LPWA communication system for disaster prevention

send and receive messages without concern about the timing (or legal restrictions) of LPWA communications.

As for the FIFO for output from the LPWA module to the PC via USB (USB TX), the PC side has a sufficient buffer that is controlled by hardware. Therefore, the LPWA module does not have a FIFO (USB TX).

With this feature, the user application developer need only implement a program such as the one shown in Listing 1.1 for the simplest bidirectional chatting.

3.2 Reconstructing Routes

LPWA modules can communicate over long distances. In previous experiments, they have successfully communicated over 10 km in open areas. However, if there are obstacles between the modules, they cannot communicate each other; the sub-giga-band radio waves used in LPWA are difficult to diffract. Therefore, relaying repeater for LPWA communications is necessary.

The communication realized in this research can be regarded as a tree structure with HQ as the root. Each node of the tree is an LPWA module, and the leaves of the tree are sensors and indicators. Just as a tree structure in programming has a pointer to the parent node of the tree, the LPWA module also keeps the parent node link information of the node on the HQ side.

Table 2. FIFO access APIs

FIFO	Enqueue	Dequeue
LPWA TX	User request Send message	Middle-wear On scheduled timing
LPWA RX	Middleware By hardware interruption	User request Receive message
USB serial RX	Middleware Using hardware flow-control	User request Console output

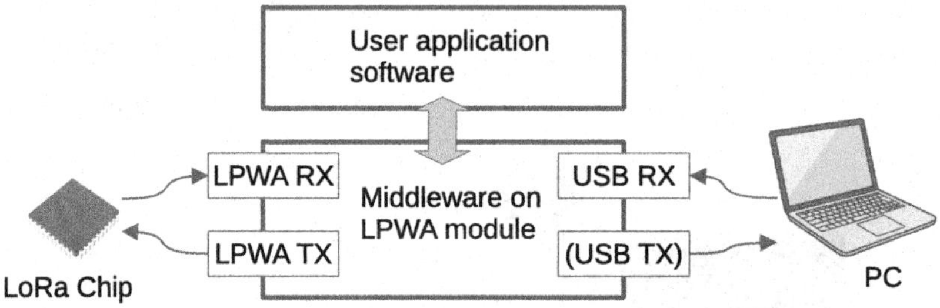

Fig. 2. FIFOs in LPWA module

A mechanism that allows flexible updating of the parent-child relationship of the nodes will result in a resilient network. Physical loss of the LPWA module due to a landslide would cause a disconnection of the communication network. This disconnection should be avoided for a disaster communication network.

Communication in the LPWA consists of (1) the transmission of a message (alert) from the HQ to the indicator and (2) the transmission of a message (sensor value) from the sensor to the HQ. This message is denoted as $Message$.

To distinguish the message in (1) from messages sent in the past, a sequence number Seq is added when HQ creates the message. Seq is a natural number that is incremented. In addition, messages in (1) and (2) have $SenderID$ as the ID of the module that sent the message. The module that created the message is the $SenderID$.

Thus, the message in (1) is

$$\{Message, Seq, SenderID\} \tag{1}$$

and the message in (2) is

$$\{Message, SenderID\} \tag{2}$$

Every module keeps $MyID$ as its ID, the parent node on the HQ side as $UplinkID$, and the $PreviousSeq$ is Seq of the last received message. The module in HQ has $UplinkID = MyID$.

Listing 1.1. example: Chat Application Program

```
void lpwa_chat_demo(void) {
        uint8_t buf[MAX_MESSAGE_SIZE+1];

    // PC(serial input) -> LPWA TX
        if (QueueSize(&fifo_serial) > 0) {
                uint8_t size = DeQueue(&fifo_serial, buf);
                EnQueue(&fifo_tx, buf, size);
        }

    // LPWA RX -> PC(console output)
        if( QueueSize(&fifo_rx) > 0 ){
                uint8_t size = DeQueue(&fifo_rx, buf);
                buf[size] = 0;
                printf("%s ", buf);  // without FIFO
        }
}
```

Now consider the message transmission in (1). When HQ sends a message $\{Message, Seq, SenderID\}$, all modules that receive this radio wave receive the message.

The receiver compares the Seq in the message with its $PreviousSeq$, and only if $Seq > PreviousSeq$, it knows that a new message has been received. At this time, the $SenderID$ is assigned to the $UplinkID$ and the parent node's information is updated. Next, change the $SenderID$ to $MyID$ and send the message again. This resending of the message is the relay function.

Next, consider the message transmission in (2). The module that wants to send a sensor value sends the message $\{Message, UplinkID, MyID\}$. The module receiving this message compares the $UplinkID$ in the message with its ID ($MyID$). If $UplinkID = MyID$, the module determines that it relays this message and sends the message $\{Message, UplinkID, MyID\}$ again. Note that HQ knows that the message has reached HQ because of $UplinkID = MyID$.

4 Experimentation and Results

We designed, developed, and implemented a communication control program for the LPWA communication module. Experiments were done in an experimental field in Soeda-Cho, Fukuoka, Japan. In Soeda-Cho, a landslide caused by heavy rainfall occurred in 2021, and the railroad track was damaged by soil and sand. The experimental field is located near the site where this landslide occurred (Fig. 4).

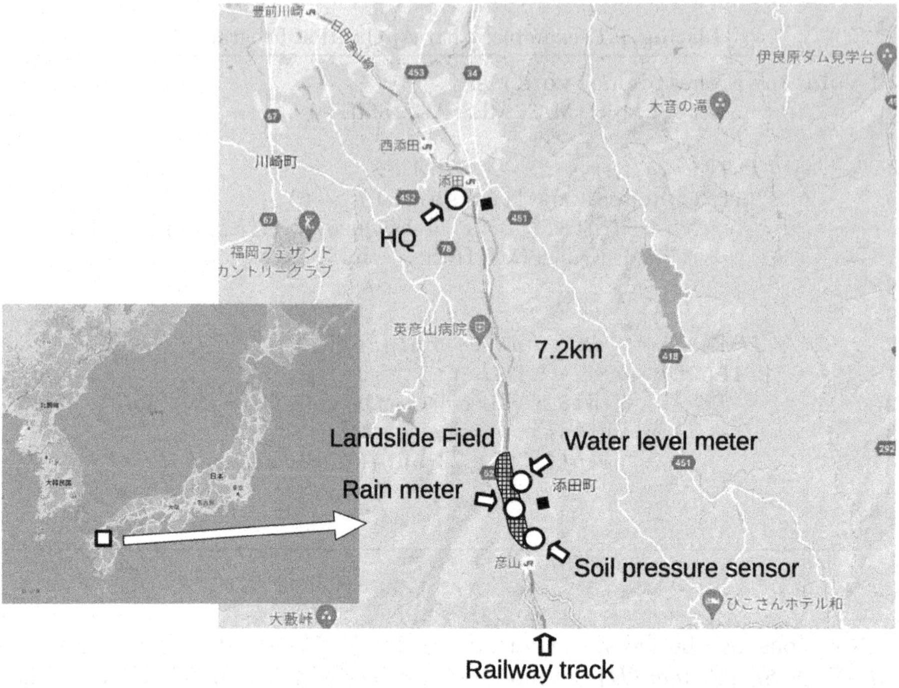

Fig. 3. Field map of experimental field

Fig. 4. Landslide field in Soeda-Cho, Japan

We deployed three sensors with an LPWA communication module; a rain meter, soil pressure sensor, and water level meter in the experimental field, where the landslide has occurred. And one HQ LPWA module in the town hall building. The distance between the experimental filed and the town hall is about 7.2 km (Fig. 3).

4.1 LPWA Modules

I developed an LPWA module using the B-L072Z-LRWAN1 from STMicroelectronics. We implemented the firmware on this microcontroller board and used it in our experiments.

The microcontroller board, solar panels, and batteries were combined and installed in the experimental field (Fig. 5).

An experiment was conducted in which one message was sent intermittently from the sensor to the HQ every 4 min, and The module was operated on battery power for 200 h. In actual operation, the module has a mechanism to continuously recharge the battery by generating electricity with the solar panel, so it can survive disasters.

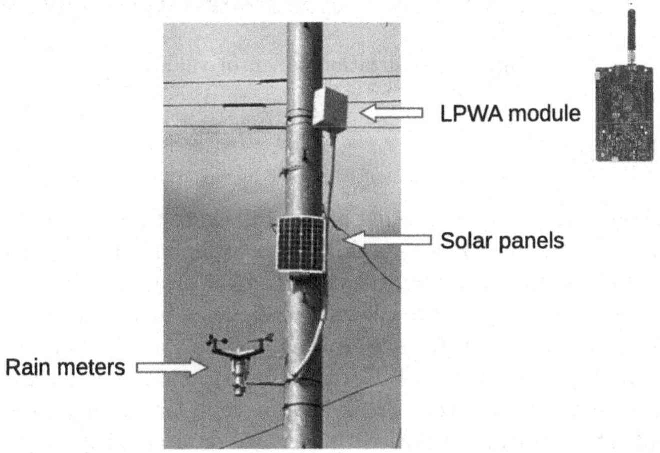

Fig. 5. Installed LPWA module

4.2 Sensor Values

The system will visualize data from weather sensors placed along with the LPWA module.

The weather sensors send messages every 4 min with data on rainfall, temperature, humidity, wind speed, and wind direction. Three weather sensors were placed in the experimental field. HQ receives the messages from these three weather sensors and stores them in a time series database.

We have implemented an application to access and visualize the time series database. The system correctly collected the sensor data (Fig. 6).

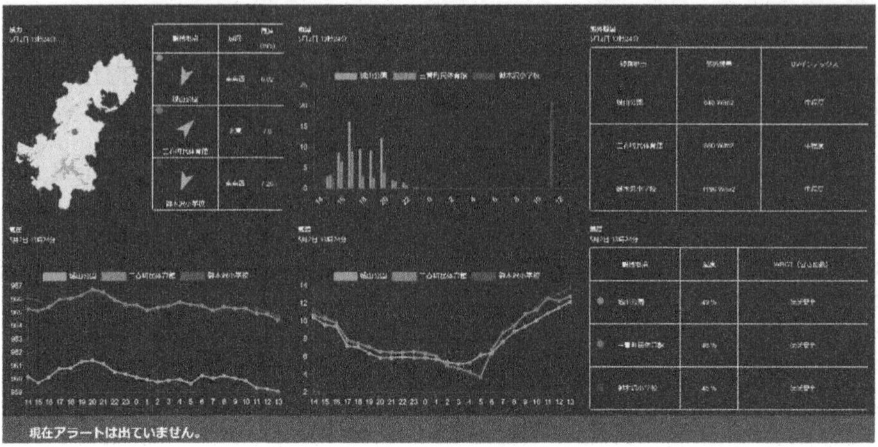

Fig. 6. Visualization of sensor values

5 Conclusion

This study showed a system consisting of a middleware that provides a platform for communication of the LPWA module, a weather meter application on the middleware, and a data collection and visualization program.

The weather meter and LPWA module were placed in an outdoor experimental field. The experiment ran for six months and had an up-time of 96%. The downtime of the experiment (4% of the experiment period) was for maintenance, and there was no communication breakdown except for the maintenance time. The results of this experiment showed that stable data acquisition was possible.

In the future, sensing with an additional soil pressure sensor and soil moisture meter will be added to the experiment to predict landslides [3].

References

1. Saari, M., Bin Baharudin, A.M., Sillberg, P., Hyrynsalmi, S., Yan, W.: LoRa - a survey of recent research trends. In: 2018 41st International Convention on Information and Communication Technology, Electronics and Microelectronics (MIPRO), pp. 0872–0877 (2018). https://doi.org/10.23919/MIPRO.2018.8400161
2. Noreen, U., Bounceur, A., Clavier, L.: A study of LoRa low power and wide area network technology. In: International Conference on Advanced Technologies for Signal and Image Processing (ATSIP) 2017, pp. 1–6 (2017). https://doi.org/10.1109/ATSIP.2017.8075570
3. Liu, Y., Hazarika, H., Takiguchi, O., Kanaya, H.: Developing a sustainable system for early warning against landslides during rainfall. In: Hazarika, H., Madabhushi, G.S.P., Yasuhara, K., Bergado, D.T. (eds.) Advances in Sustainable Construction and Resource Management. LNCE, vol. 144, pp. 917–926. Springer, Singapore (2021). https://doi.org/10.1007/978-981-16-0077-7_75

Misinformation Detection in Social Networks: A Systematic Literature Review

Zafer Duzen[1](✉), Mirela Riveni[2], and Mehmet S. Aktas[1]

[1] Department of Computer Engineering, Yildiz Technical University, Istanbul, Turkey
zafer.duzen@std.yildiz.edu.tr, aktas@yildiz.edu.tr

[2] Information System Group, University of Groningen, Groningen, The Netherlands
m.riveni@rug.nl

Abstract. Information quality is becoming an increasingly important issue as social networks have become the primary source for misinformation dissemination. Because of their ease of use, spreading behavior, and low cost, social network platforms are leveraging news consumption. Because of its negative impact on society, this term became more popular and dangerous following the 2016 U.S. presidential election. Many studies have been developed on methods to improve rumor classification, particularly on misinformation detection on social media, with promising results in recent years. Despite the growth of this type of research, it is difficult for a researcher to identify the most up-to-date literature on misinformation detection. To address this challenge, this paper presents a systematic review of the literature that provides an overview of this research area and analyzes high-quality research papers on fake news detection. According to our search protocol, more than 670 articles were discovered during this systematic literature review. Then, we put these studies through a series of scanning stages to ensure that they were of high quality. We chose 76 high-quality studies based on our selection process flow diagram, which is described in this paper. This review describes 10 years of research on social media misinformation and presents the main methods and data sets used in the literature.

Keywords: Misinformation detection · Fact check · Disinformation · Social media

1 Introduction

When compared to more traditional communication methods, such as the printed newspaper, social networks have increased news consumption due to their ease of access, broad audience reach and low cost. They have become the ideal platform for disseminating misinformation. This can have a significant impact on society's

O. Gervasi et al. (Eds.): ICCSA 2022 Workshops, LNCS 13379, pp. 57–74, 2022.
https://doi.org/10.1007/978-3-031-10545-6_5

day-to-day operations, create economic harm, and even affect a nation's political decisions directly or indirectly [90].

On the other hand, detecting fake news on social media, is a difficult undertaking since even people have been known to overlook misinformation. A fake news site also makes an effort to include sensational and very unfavorable phrases in its content. In this regard, the most recent studies in this field reveal that text mining approaches paired with Deep Learning (DL) or Machine Learning (ML) algorithms produce considerable results in terms of detecting disinformation [14,15,58]. Based on the existing work, in the near future, modern society could be able to detect misinformation automatically via information system techniques, allowing for a certain level of information transparency on social networks [50].

As a result, it is critical that users, developers and specialists in Information Systems (IS) are aware of the existing solutions to problems they may encounter throughout the usage or building of the systems. Hence, this systematic review of the literature was created to help with these and other more particular topics, such as analysing the primary sources of information, the primary data-sets used as use cases, and the primary ML and AI algorithms for each scenario. The most relevant publications retrieved in this systematic review process provide answers to these issues.

2 Systematic Review Process

A systematic literature review (SLR) is a study that tries to discover and evaluate a research issue by decreasing superficial information, and analysing and providing the gaps and greatest contributions in a research area [29]. An SLR, according to Kitchenham and Charters [40], is a three-phase process that includes planning, execution, and evaluation. In this study, we conducted a systematic mapping investigation of existing research on misinformation detection and spread in social networks.

This work is structured as follows. Section 3, Sect. 4, and Sect. 5 explain the methodology utilized in this study, including the three phases of the systematic review and the instruments employed in each. Finally, Sect. 6 and Sect. 7 reviews the findings and suggest areas for future investigation.

3 Planning the Review

3.1 Research Questions

The primary purpose of this research is to conduct an SLR on misinformation detection for social networks. The major goal of this research is to answer the following key research issues on this research topic.

- RQ1: How was the distribution of papers on misinformation detection distributed over the years?

- RQ2: What types of publications have been developed in the area of detecting misinformation?
- RQ3: Which social networks are mostly used as a case study?
- RQ4: What are the domains in which the publications are being used?
- RQ5: What type of misinformation exists on social networks?
- RQ6: What kind of approaches are proposed for misinformation detection and spread in social networks?

3.2 Data Sources and Search Criteria

A systematic search strategy is required to identify the whole population of scientific articles that could be related to the selected study topics. We were able to conduct a repeatable and transparent evaluation of external assessments. The first step in the search strategy was to define the search space. The research for this study was performed in six electronic databases.

- ACM Digital Library (https://dl.acm.org)
- IEEE Explore (https://ieeexplore.ieee.org)
- Scopus (https://www.scopus.com)
- Springer (https://www.springer.com)
- Web of Science (https://mjl.clarivate.com)
- Wiley (https://onlinelibrary.wiley.com)

After defining the search space, we specified the search phrases that would be used in electronic database search inquiry forms. The search was based on the study questions' keywords, synonyms, and alternate words. The following search string is used:

('misinformation detection' or 'misinformation spread' OR 'misinformation sharing' OR 'disinformation') AND ('social media' OR 'social network') AND ('fact check' OR 'fake news')

3.3 Inclusion and Exclusion Strategy

The inclusion and exclusion criteria have been established in order to accurately assess the quality of the available literature. The authors evaluated and discussed the papers before making an inclusion or exclusion decision. For a paper to be considered for a primary study, it must meet the following criteria:

- Research field: Computer Science
- Language: English
- Publication date 2012 to 2022
- Type of work: Scientific studies
- Availability: Full Text

3.4 Selection Process and Quality Evaluation

We assessed the scientific quality requirements of the chosen studies to determine the relevance of the review results in order to assist the analysis of the results in the included literature and to show the value of conclusions. The results of the included papers' quality rating can identify potential limitations of the current search and lead to further research on the subject. The following criteria were created to compare chosen research for an analysis or corresponding relevance to the topic.

- Are the research goals well-defined?
- What is the research article's year of publication?
- Was the proposed solution explained detailly and clearly?
- What is the distribution of detection techniques across these categories?
- Did the researcher identify which dataset to use?
- What is the size of the validation dataset?
- Do the datasets contain detailed information?
- Are the findings of the study presented in a clear and concise manner?
- Are the results consistent with the objectives?
- What are the study's limitations and recommendations for future research?

The proposed quality assessment process comprises three main measures for quantitative purposes. A 'yes' answer receives a score of 1, a partial answer receives a 0.5 score, and a 'no' answer receives a score of 0, and some questions do not apply to some articles [41]. The aggregated sum of these scores can be used to assess the relevance of the retrieved research articles.

4 Conducting the Review

The second step of our literature review includes the following: (1) searching for primary studies; (2) choosing primary articles by applying inclusion and exclusion criteria; (3) assessing the applicability and relevance; and (4) retrieving information.

The automatic search tools in the digital libraries indicated in the search strategy were used to look for primary research. We utilized a form to categorize and record the information from each document after searching the digital libraries using the stated research string pattern. The results of the search were also saved in an Excel spreadsheet and the Mendeley application.

After extracting the population of scientific publications related to the study topics, the query returned 672 unique results. The articles related to the review purpose were then chosen using the set of criteria specified in Sect. 3.3. The title, abstract, and results of the 672 findings were assessed in the first round. We examined the whole text of each article in a second round and applied quality criteria, resulting in the retrieval of 76 papers. Totally 596 studies were turned down. As a consequence, 76 studies were chosen and placed into the spreadsheet.

Each paper's inclusion and exclusion status is documented for future discussion and reassessment. The systematic review of the literature generated 76 primary studies. We have also included additional works at the time of the final editing of this report to make this study more comprehensive. Quantitative statistics for primary studies are shown in Table 1.

Table 1. Search results after phases

Database	First round	Second round	Third round
ACM Digital Library	217	32	11
IEEE Explore	128	84	33
Scopus	87	58	7
Springer	159	54	18
Web of Science	28	16	4
Wiley	53	12	3

5 Review Results

76 relevant scientific papers were found as a result of the systematic review. These are the key studies that were utilized to address the six research questions defined in Sect. 3.1. Following that, we present the results of each of these questions. All the main results obtained as the output of the SLR are detailed in Table 2 in the Appendix section.

5.1 RQ1: How Was the Distribution of Papers on Misinformation Detection Distributed over the Years?

Figure 1 reflects the intensity of publications that propose to solve the problem of spreading misinformation on social networks. It is seen that the number of papers written on this subject has increased in 2016. It is predicted that one of the biggest reasons for this is the election results in America [14,90]. It has been seen how effective misinformation is in people's political decisions, and as a result, the number of studies has increased. Since the first three months of 2022 were taken into account while conducting the study, the reason for the decrease in the graph is due to the absence of data for the rest of the year.

Considering the distribution of articles by years and digital libraries from Fig. 2, it is seen that there are more articles in IEEE and Springer. In addition, it is clear that the number of all results coming from each digital library has increased after 2016.

5.2 RQ2: What Types of Publications Have Been Developed in the Area of Detecting Misinformation in Social Networks?

Figure 3 represents an overview of which types of primary studies are most published. Conferences and journals are the primary targets of scientific effort, as seen in the diagram. The fact that conferences have a more rigid structure of publication and a smaller scope than journals can explain the larger number of papers published at conferences [41]. Furthermore, at the conferences, technical conversations between researchers take place in technical sessions, significantly enhancing knowledge regarding the conference's issues.

Another factor to consider is that detecting misinformation on social media is a very recent topic. As a result, their works are less likely to be subjected to the more time-consuming process of journal and book review and acceptance.

5.3 RQ3: Which Social Networks Are Mostly Used as a Case Study?

Figure 4 reveals that most of the selected primary studies use Twitter, Weibo, and Facebook as an environment for experimenting with social networks [63,76]. Besides that most used data set is FakeNewsNet [70] for fake news detection [62, 83]. Both of these results are expected because these are the most used social networks with widespread news reading and sharing tools [13,36,45,88].

5.4 RQ4: What Are the Domains in Which the Publications Are Being Used?

Misinformation spreads in a variety of ways, and some studies are attempting to identify domain-specific characteristics [6]. The number of publications by domain is shown in Fig. 5. There are four primary domains that have been discovered.

Papers in this general category provide methods for detecting disinformation in social media posts using common variables such as the number of followers and particular linguistic patterns, etc. This type of method may be used in a variety of domains and is unaffected by domain-specific characteristics [55,68].

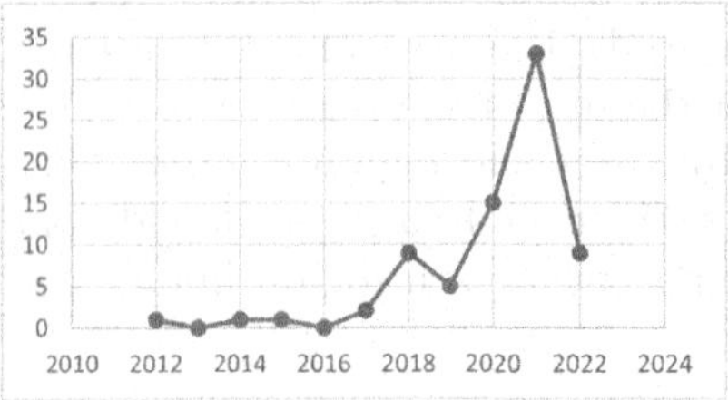

Fig. 1. Papers by year.

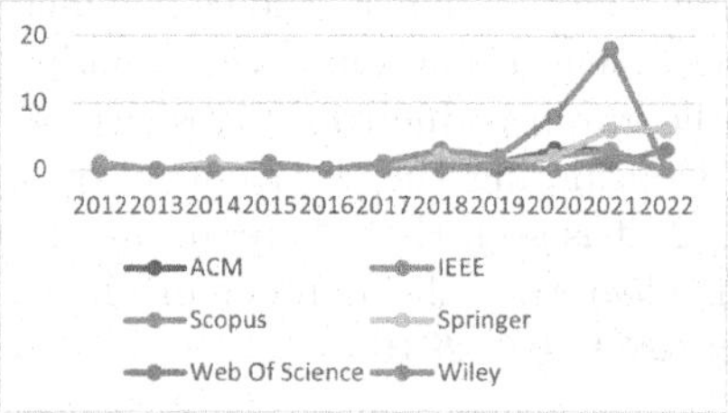

Fig. 2. Papers by year and by source.

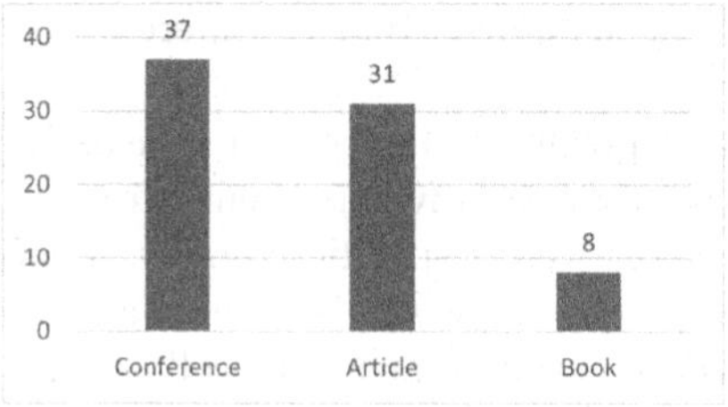

Fig. 3. Papers by publication type.

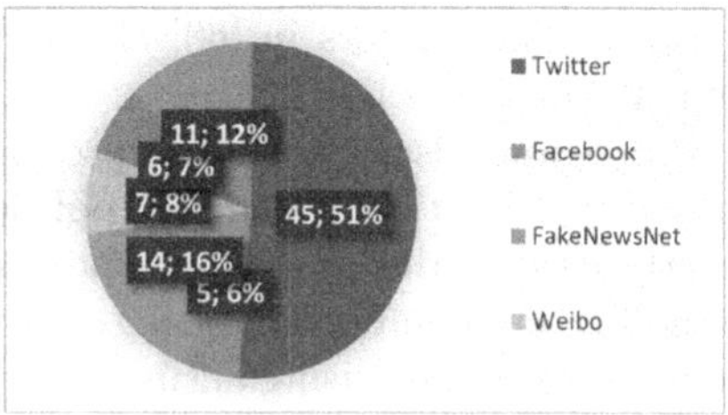

Fig. 4. Papers by dataset.

The techniques in the News category are developed particularly to deal with journalistic news. The majority of fact-checking techniques fall into this category since they aim to uncover false news by extracting and confirming the facts included in the news [12,36].

The health category contains methods for disseminating health-related disinformation. Because of the Covid 19 pandemic, this kind is currently the most prevalent [52,59]. The usage of external knowledge databases is a significant aspect of categorization in both of these efforts, and both employ information from medical databases as ground truth [61,66,81].

The Politics category contains publications which are related to rumor spreading and conspiracy theories. This kind of misinformation can identify people's political decisions and cause polarization in society [14,82].

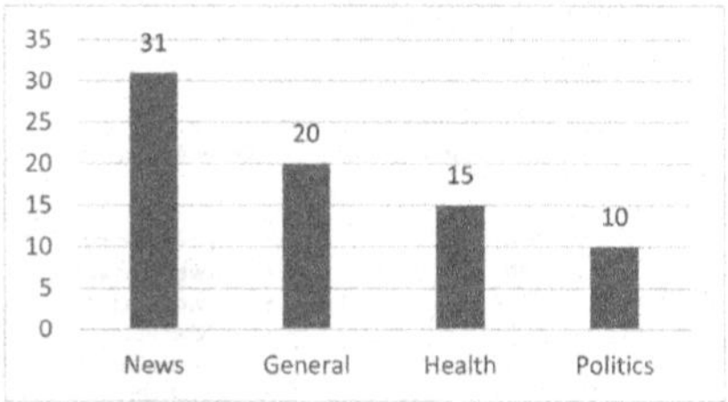

Fig. 5. Papers by domain.

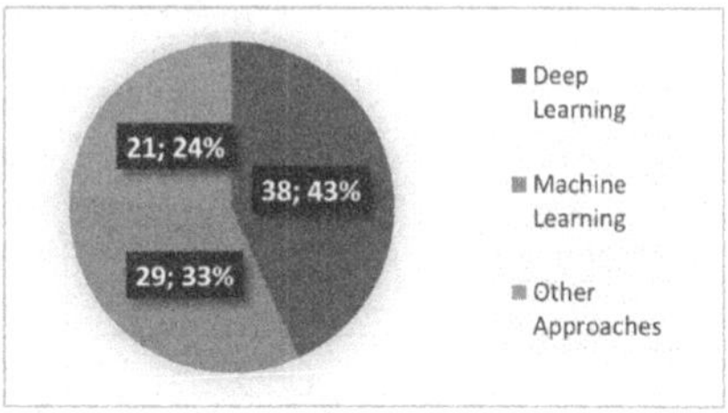

Fig. 6. Papers by solution distribution.

5.5 RQ5: What Type of Misinformation Exists on Social Networks?

Misinformation is merely incorrect information. It can be propagated inadvertently. However, sometimes the source may or may not be aware of the accuracy of the information he or she is sharing [5]. To make the distinction from false information that is shared on purpose, we use the term *disinformation*, and with it we define false information that is generated to deceive the reader on purpose. Disinformation is misleading information spread with the explicit goal of deception. While some authors have listed disinformation as another subcategory of misinformation, such as in [37], we work with an alternative taxonomy presented in Fig. 7. The authors in [60] also use the term disinformation to differentiate the malicious false news.

Propaganda is news that is produced for a specific audience and is usually utilized in a political setting. In political circumstances, advertisements are frequently used to disparage an opposition party or even a specific country. This method is often employed during political campaigns to persuade voters against the other candidate using entirely fake or partially genuine news, as well as language modifications that confuse people who consume content [82]. Propaganda is often used to polarize societies, and today we also see a rise of fabricated content and the use of deepfakes in media for this purpose.

Stories that seek to explain a situation or incident by evoking a conspiracy without providing evidence are mainly stories concerning acts committed by governments or influential persons. These ideas frequently present information with no known sources or untrusted sources as truths and reject an evidence-based approach [8]. Consideration of authenticity issues as the basic misinformation related analysis is presented in [23].

Rumors consist of news whose veracity is ambiguous or never confirmed. This type of false information is widely spread on social media. Therefore, several studies have analyzed this type of news [46].

Spams are unsolicited communications that are delivered on a mass and repeated basis with the intent of advertising, amusement, or pranking. This is a sort of diffusion circulation in which the message is reiterated so many times at a rapid pace that it begins to mix with the current and relevant data [25].

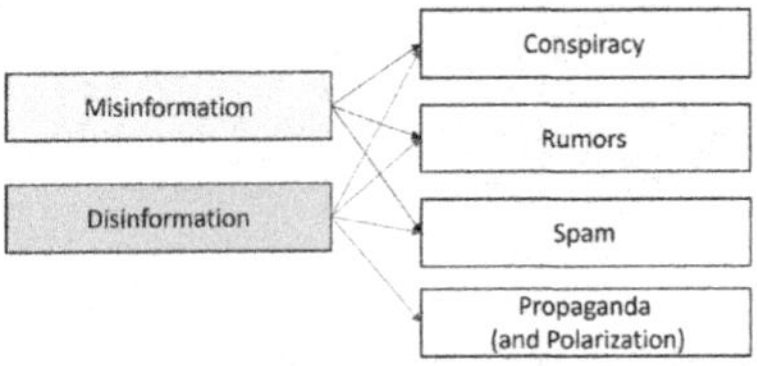

Fig. 7. Misinformation types.

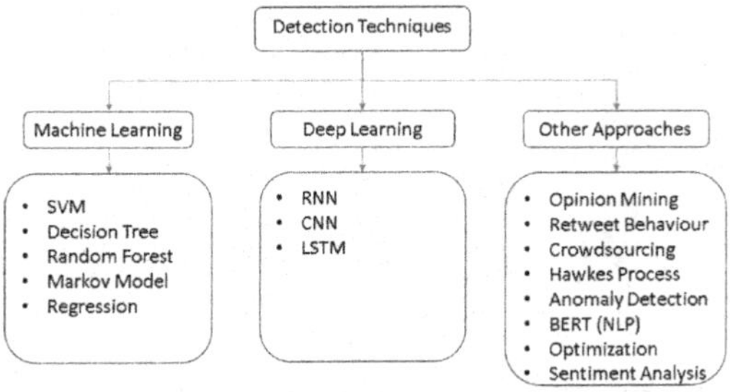

Fig. 8. Misinformation detection approaches.

5.6 RQ6: What Kind of Approaches Are Proposed for Misinformation Detection in the Literature?

Techniques. The numerous methodologies that we have investigated for our research are summarized in Fig. 8. Recently, DL and AI algorithms have been used more heavily. Also, hybrid methods were applied in some articles and better results were obtained in terms of performance. Most of the techniques for detecting misinformation presented in the literature approach the topic as a classification problem, aiming to correlate labels such as misinformation or not.

Researchers have used ML and DL methodologies in the majority of situations, with encouraging outcomes [27,67] (Fig. 6). Other researchers have used alternative techniques, such as Bidirectional Encoder Representations from Transformers (BERT), based on natural language processing techniques, to forecast the class of documents or events, or to assess their validity [38].

Parameters. We also want to point on the parameters used for misinformation detection. Of course, the *type of account* is at the front of studies. For example, an interesting work that states that misinformation is spread more widely and deeply than truthful information and it is more likely to be spread by humans than bots is presented in [80]. Thus, while doing studies on misinformation detection running the experiments with considering bots and without them will give, needless to say, also important information on misinformation detection but also spreading. Work on the type of users that spread misinformation is also presented in [30]. Another differentiating parameter that studies should consider is also the validated or non-validated types of accounts, e.g. for studies on Twitter. *Evidentiality* is another parameter that comes at the forefront of studies in both misinformation detection and misinformation spreading, such as presented in [91]. *Network indices*, such as centrality indices, are used as parameters when studying influential nodes in misinformation detection and spreading studies as well, e.g., in [60]. Homophily is also considered as a parameter in detection of misinformation and spreading patterns, e.g., [73].

6 Threats to Validity of Research

As with any systematic review process, the results of this study may contain flaws arising from the execution and analysis process and analytical imperfections. It is about quality and relevance criteria that may not be satisfactory to conceptualize a study as relevant because of the subjective criteria that each researcher develops based on his/her profile.

One of the inclusion/exclusion criteria in our work is considering works written in English only. In a way, this limits the contribution of authors who may have written in another language. Another one is the research area limited to computer sciences. This may have caused some articles that may be relevant to be excluded from the review process.

7 Conclusion and Future Work

The benefit of using a comprehensive systematic review process is that out of context publications that made it through the screening step may be deleted in the subsequent phases before the quality evaluation. This emphasizes the need of doing a thorough and systematic literature review.

The major goal of this SLR is to provide a list of the most important and relevant works on misinformation as well as their specific topics and categorizations. The responses to our study questions revealed that Twitter, Weibo,

Youtube, and Facebook are the most popular social media sites for misinformation detection studies. In addition, we can conclude that DL and AI algorithms have been widely used in the detection process in recent years, which adds value to the literature and practical applications. Finally, it was determined that using various forms of data, such as social, temporal, or emotional resources, together with, or in addition to text analysis, can increase the correctness of the offered solutions.

Finally, the findings of this systematic review revealed potential areas for future research. There are few publications focused on presenting studies for non-English language misinformation. This is unsurprising given the large group of people working on natural language processing technologies for English. As a result, future studies with this goal will be regarded as notable by the scientific community for their unique qualities, even if their detection findings do not differ significantly from those reported in this SLR. As another result of the research, fake news and video detection, spammer, and bot detection issues stand out as problems that need to be solved. Also, there hasn't been much progress in developing real-time detection systems. Last but not the least, network dynamics based on time analysis is also of crucial importance so that data about how long does misinformation survive within the network and what are the related parameters of influence can better inform our societies of the misinformation spreading dynamics and issues.

A Appendix A

Table 2. Systematic literature review results.

Ref	Year	Source	Type	Dataset	Method	Domain
[54]	2012	Scopus	Conference	Twitter	DL	News
[43]	2014	Springer	Conference	Twitter	ML	Health
[25]	2015	IEEE	Book	Twitter	DL	News
[19]	2017	IEEE	Book	Twitter	DL	General
[14]	2017	ACM	Conference	FakeNewsNet	NLP + DL	Politics
[74]	2018	Scopus	Book	Twitter	DL	General
[11]	2018	Springer	Artice	LIAR	NLP	General
[83]	2018	ACM	Conference	FakeNewsNet	ML	News
[15]	2018	IEEE	Book	Twitter	ML + NLP	News
[76]	2018	ACM	Conference	Weibo, Twitter	DL	Politics
[35]	2018	IEEE	Book	Twitter	DL	News
[2]	2018	IEEE	Book	Twitter	NLP	News

(*continued*)

Table 2. (*continued*)

Ref	Year	Source	Type	Dataset	Method	Domain
[79]	2018	ACM	Conference	Twitter	ML	Politics
[63]	2018	Springer	Article	Weibo	NLP	General
[77]	2019	IEEE	Book	Reddit	Hawkes	General
[7]	2019	Wiley	Conference	Twitter	ML	General
[64]	2019	ACM	Conference	Facebook	ML	News
[10]	2019	IEEE	Conference	LIAR	ML	News
[82]	2019	Springer	Article	Twitter	DL	General
[88]	2020	ACM	Conference	Weibo, Twitter	DL	News
[60]	2020	Springer	Article	FakeNewsNet	DL	News
[20]	2020	IEEE	Conference	Twitter	DL	Health
[49]	2020	Scopus	Article	Twitter	ML	General
[46]	2020	Scopus	Conference	Twitter	DL	Health
[78]	2020	IEEE	Conference	Twitter	ML	News
[68]	2020	Springer	Article	Twitter	ML	General
[85]	2020	ACM	Conference	Twitter	DL	News
[55]	2020	ACM	Conference	FN-COV	DL	News
[3]	2020	IEEE	Article	LIAR	DL	Health
[75]	2020	IEEE	Book	Koirala, FNSD	ML, NLP	News
[90]	2020	IEEE	Conference	Twitter	ML	Politics
[27]	2020	IEEE	Conference	Twitter	ML, DL	Politics
[23]	2020	IEEE	Conference	Twitter	NLP	News
[8]	2020	IEEE	Article	Twitter	DL	General
[13]	2021	IEEE	Conference	FakeNewsNet	ML	News
[62]	2021	IEEE	Conference	FakeNewsNet	DL	General
[4]	2021	Wiley	Article	Twitter	ML	General
[48]	2021	Springer	Article	Twitter	PageRank	News
[44]	2021	Scopus	Article	Instagram	DL	Politics
[28]	2021	IEEE	Conference	FakeNewsNet	ML	News
[87]	2021	IEEE	Conference	FakeNewsNet	ML, NLP, DL	Health
[17]	2021	ACM	Conference	Twitter	ML + DL	News
[1]	2021	IEEE	Article	philstar.com	ML	General
[89]	2021	IEEE	Conference	Twitter	ML	Health
[31]	2021	IEEE	Conference	Facebook	ML	News
[72]	2021	IEEE	Conference	Twitter	ML	News
[56]	2021	Springer	Article	Twitter	ML	Health
[18]	2021	IEEE	Conference	FakeNewsNet	DL	General
[86]	2021	Scopus	Article	Facebook	Optimize	General
[24]	2021	WebOfScience	Article	Twitter	DL	General
[22]	2021	IEEE	Conference	Twitter	ML, NLP	Health

(*continued*)

Table 2. (*continued*)

Ref	Year	Source	Type	Dataset	Method	Domain
[26]	2021	IEEE	Conference	Liar, Fakenews	Sentiment	Health
[21]	2021	IEEE	Conference	FakeNewsNet	DL	Politics
[71]	2021	IEEE	Conference	Liar	DL	Politics
[33]	2021	IEEE	Conference	FakeNewsNet	DL	News
[9]	2021	Springer	Article	Twitter	DL	Health
[12]	2021	Springer	Article	FakeNewsNet	DL	News
[47]	2021	Springer	Article	Twitter	DL	News
[36]	2021	ACM	Conference	Weibo, Twitter	DL	News
[16]	2021	Wiley	Article	Twitter	DL	General
[84]	2021	ACM	Conference	Twitter	Text Mine	General
[38]	2021	IEEE	Conference	Fake News AMT	NLP	Health
[67]	2021	IEEE	Article	Weibo	NLP	News
[42]	2021	Springer	Article	Twitter	DL	General
[66]	2021	Scopus	Article	Youtube	ML	Health
[34]	2021	IEEE	Conference	Twitter	ML + NLP	Health
[61]	2021	IEEE	Conference	Twitter	NLP	Health
[58]	2022	Springer	Article	LIAR	NLP + DL	News
[32]	2022	Springer	Article	Twitter	ML	General
[57]	2022	Springer	Article	Twitter	DL	News
[39]	2022	WebOfScience	Article	Twitter	ML	Politics
[45]	2022	WebOfScience	Article	Twitter, Weibo	DL	General
[51]	2022	Springer	Article	Twitter	DL	News
[65]	2022	Springer	Article	FakeNewsNet	ML	Politics
[69]	2022	Springer	Article	Twitter	DL	Health
[53]	2022	WebOfScience	Article	Weibo	Regression	News

References

1. Abdelminaam, D.S., Ismail, F.H., Taha, M., Taha, A., Houssein, E.H., Nabil, A.: CoAID-DEEP: an optimized intelligent framework for automated detecting COVID-19 misleading information on Twitter. IEEE Access **9**, 27840–27867 (2021). https://doi.org/10.1109/ACCESS.2021.3058066
2. Acula, D.D., Oblan, L.A.C., Pedroso, T.B., Riosa, K.J.V., Tolibas, M.A.R.: Implementing fact-checking in journalistic articles shared on social media in the Philippines using knowledge graphs. In: 2018 3rd International Conference on Computer and Communication Systems (ICCCS), pp. 462–466. IEEE (2018)
3. Al-Rakhami, M.S., Al-Amri, A.M.: Lies kill, facts save: detecting COVID-19 misinformation in Twitter. IEEE Access **8**, 155961–155970 (2020). https://doi.org/10.1109/ACCESS.2020.3019600
4. Albahar, M.: A hybrid model for fake news detection: leveraging news content and user comments in fake news. IET Inf. Secur. **15**, 169–177 (2021). https://doi.org/10.1049/ise2.12021

5. Baeth, M.J., Aktas, M.: On the detection of information pollution and violation of copyrights in the social web. In: 2015 IEEE 8th International Conference on Service-Oriented Computing and Applications (SOCA), pp. 252–254 (2015). https://doi.org/10.1109/SOCA.2015.27
6. Baeth, M.J., Aktas, M.S.: Detecting misinformation in social networks using provenance data. In: 2017 13th International Conference on Semantics, Knowledge and Grids (SKG), pp. 85–89 (2017). https://doi.org/10.1109/SKG.2017.00022
7. Baeth, M.J., Aktas, M.S.: Detecting misinformation in social networks using provenance data. Concurr. Comput. Pract. Exp. **31**(3), e4793 (2019)
8. Bahja, M., Safdar, G.A.: Unlink the link between COVID-19 and 5G networks: an NLP and SNA based approach. IEEE Access (2020). https://doi.org/10.1109/ACCESS.2020.3039168
9. Balasubramaniam, T., Nayak, R., Luong, K., Bashar, M.A.: Identifying Covid-19 misinformation tweets and learning their spatio-temporal topic dynamics using Nonnegative Coupled Matrix Tensor Factorization. Soc. Netw. Anal. Min. **11**(1), 1–19 (2021). https://doi.org/10.1007/s13278-021-00767-7
10. Benamira, A., Devillers, B., Lesot, E., Ray, A.K., Saadi, M., Malliaros, F.D.: Semi-supervised learning and graph neural networks for fake news detection. In: 2019 IEEE/ACM International Conference on Advances in Social Networks Analysis and Mining (ASONAM), pp. 568–569. IEEE (2019)
11. Boididou, C., Papadopoulos, S., Zampoglou, M., Apostolidis, L., Papadopoulou, O., Kompatsiaris, Y.: Detection and visualization of misleading content on Twitter. Int. J. Multimedia Inf. Retrieval **7**(1), 71–86 (2017). https://doi.org/10.1007/s13735-017-0143-x
12. Braşoveanu, A.M.P., Andonie, R.: Integrating machine learning techniques in semantic fake news detection. Neural Process. Lett. **53**(5), 3055–3072 (2020). https://doi.org/10.1007/s11063-020-10365-x
13. Cao, H., Deng, J., Dong, G., Yuan, D.: A discriminative graph neural network for fake news detection. In: 2021 2nd International Conference on Big Data & Artificial Intelligence & Software Engineering (ICBASE), pp. 224–228. IEEE (2021)
14. Chatfield, A.T., Reddick, C.G., Choi, K.: Online media use of false news to frame the 2016 trump presidential campaign. In: Proceedings of the 18th Annual International Conference on Digital Government Research, pp. 213–222 (2017)
15. Chen, W., et al.: Exploiting behavioral differences to detect fake news. In: 2018 9th IEEE Annual Ubiquitous Computing, Electronics & Mobile Communication Conference (UEMCON), pp. 879–884. IEEE (2018)
16. Chen, X., Zhou, F., Zhang, F., Bonsangue, M.: Modeling microscopic and macroscopic information diffusion for rumor detection. Int. J. Intell. Syst. **36**, 5449–5471 (2021). https://doi.org/10.1002/int.22518
17. Cheng, L., Guo, R., Shu, K., Liu, H.: Causal understanding of fake news dissemination on social media. In: Proceedings of the 27th ACM SIGKDD Conference on Knowledge Discovery & Data Mining, pp. 148–157 (2021)
18. Chughtai, M.A., Hou, J., Long, H., Li, Q., Ismail, M.: Design of a predictor for Covid-19 misinformation prediction. In: 2021 International Conference on Innovative Computing (ICIC), pp. 1–7. IEEE (2021)
19. Conti, M., Lain, D., Lazzeretti, R., Lovisotto, G., Quattrociocchi, W.: It's always april fools' day!: on the difficulty of social network misinformation classification via propagation features. In: 2017 IEEE Workshop on Information Forensics and Security (WIFS), pp. 1–6 (2017). https://doi.org/10.1109/WIFS.2017.8267653

20. Dhiman, A., Toshniwal, D.: An unsupervised misinformation detection framework to analyze the users using COVID-19 Twitter data. In: 2020 IEEE International Conference on Big Data (Big Data), pp. 679–688. IEEE (2020)
21. Ganesh, P., Priya, L., Nandakumar, R.: Fake news detection-a comparative study of advanced ensemble approaches. In: 2021 5th International Conference on Trends in Electronics and Informatics (ICOEI), pp. 1003–1008. IEEE (2021)
22. Garg, R., Jeevaraj, S.: Effective fake news classifier and its applications to COVID-19. In: 2021 IEEE Bombay Section Signature Conference (IBSSC), pp. 1–6. IEEE (2021)
23. Gautam, A., Jerripothula, K.R.: SGG: Spinbot, Grammarly and GloVe based fake news detection. In: 2020 IEEE Sixth International Conference on Multimedia Big Data (BigMM), pp. 174–182. IEEE (2020)
24. Giachanou, A., Ghanem, B., Rosso, P.: Detection of conspiracy propagators using psycho-linguistic characteristics. J. Inf. Sci. (2021). https://doi.org/10.1177/0165551520985486
25. Gupta, A., Kaushal, R.: Improving spam detection in online social networks. In: 2015 International Conference on Cognitive Computing and Information Processing (CCIP), pp. 1–6 (2015). https://doi.org/10.1109/CCIP.2015.7100738
26. Hande, A., Puranik, K., Priyadharshini, R., Thavareesan, S., Chakravarthi, B.R.: Evaluating pretrained transformer-based models for COVID-19 fake news detection. In: 2021 5th International Conference on Computing Methodologies and Communication (ICCMC), pp. 766–772. IEEE (2021)
27. Hassan, F.M., Lee, M.: Political fake statement detection via multistage feature-assisted neural modeling. In: 2020 IEEE International Conference on Intelligence and Security Informatics (ISI), pp. 1–6. IEEE (2020)
28. Heidari, M., et al.: BERT model for fake news detection based on social bot activities in the COVID-19 pandemic. In: 2021 IEEE 12th Annual Ubiquitous Computing, Electronics & Mobile Communication Conference (UEMCON), pp. 0103–0109. IEEE (2021)
29. Hinderks, A., José, F., Mayo, D., Thomaschewski, J., Escalona, M.J.: An SLR-tool: search process in practice: a tool to conduct and manage systematic literature review (SLR). In: 2020 IEEE/ACM 42nd International Conference on Software Engineering: Companion Proceedings (ICSE-Companion), pp. 81–84 (2020)
30. Huang, B., Carley, K.M.: Disinformation and misinformation on twitter during the novel coronavirus outbreak. arXiv preprint arXiv:2006.04278 (2020)
31. Hussna, A.U., Trisha, I.I., Karim, M.S., Alam, M.G.R.: COVID-19 fake news prediction on social media data. In: 2021 IEEE Region 10 Symposium (TENSYMP), pp. 1–5. IEEE (2021)
32. Jain, D.K., Kumar, A., Shrivastava, A.: *CanarDeep*: a hybrid deep neural model with mixed fusion for rumour detection in social data streams. Neural Comput. Appl. 1–12 (2021). https://doi.org/10.1007/s00521-021-06743-8
33. Janakieva, D., Mirceva, G., Gievska, S.: Fake news detection by using Doc2Vec representation model and various classification algorithms. In: 2021 44th International Convention on Information, Communication and Electronic Technology (MIPRO), pp. 223–228. IEEE (2021)
34. Jing, Q., et al.: TRANSFAKE: multi-task transformer for multimodal enhanced fake news detection. In: 2021 International Joint Conference on Neural Networks (IJCNN), pp. 1–8. IEEE (2021)
35. Kaliyar, R.K.: Fake news detection using a deep neural network. In: 2018 4th International Conference on Computing Communication and Automation (ICCCA), pp. 1–7. IEEE (2018)

36. Kaliyar, R.K., Goswami, A., Narang, P.: MCNNet: generalizing fake news detection with a multichannel convolutional neural network using a novel COVID-19 dataset. In: 8th ACM IKDD CODS and 26th COMAD, pp. 437–437. Association for Computing Machinery (2021)
37. Kaliyar, R.K., Singh, N.: Misinformation detection on online social media-a survey. In: 2019 10th International Conference on Computing, Communication and Networking Technologies (ICCCNT), pp. 1–6 (2019). https://doi.org/10.1109/ICCCNT45670.2019.8944587
38. Kar, D., Bhardwaj, M., Samanta, S., Azad, A.P.: No rumours please! A multi-indic-lingual approach for COVID fake-tweet detection. In: 2021 Grace Hopper Celebration India (GHCI), pp. 1–5. IEEE (2020)
39. King, K.K., Wang, B., Escobari, D., Oraby, T.: Dynamic effects of falsehoods and corrections on social media: a theoretical modeling and empirical evidence. J. Manag. Inf. Syst. **38**, 989–1010 (2021). https://doi.org/10.1080/07421222.2021.1990611
40. Kitchenham, B.: Procedures for performing systematic reviews. Keele UK Keele Univ. **33**(2004), 1–26 (2004)
41. Kitchenham, B.A., Budgen, D., Brereton, P.: Evidence-Based Software Engineering and Systematic Reviews, vol. 4. CRC Press, Boca Raton (2015)
42. Kumar, A., Bhatia, M.P.S., Sangwan, S.R.: Rumour detection using deep learning and filter-wrapper feature selection in benchmark Twitter dataset. Multimedia Tools Appl. 1–18 (2021). https://doi.org/10.1007/s11042-021-11340-x
43. Kumar, K.P.K., Geethakumari, G.: Detecting misinformation in online social networks using cognitive psychology. HCIS **4**(1), 1–22 (2014). https://doi.org/10.1186/s13673-014-0014-x
44. Kumar, A., Bhatia, M.P.S., Sangwan, S.R.: Rumour detection using deep learning and filter-wrapper feature selection in benchmark Twitter dataset. Multimedia Tools Appl. 1–18 (2021). https://doi.org/10.1007/s11042-021-11340-x
45. Luo, Y., Ma, J., Yeo, C.K.: Exploiting user network topology and comment semantic for accurate rumour stance recognition on social media. J. Inf. Sci. (2020). https://doi.org/10.1177/0165551520977443
46. Malhotra, B., Vishwakarma, D.K.: Classification of propagation path and tweets for rumor detection using graphical convolutional networks and transformer based encodings. In: 2020 IEEE Sixth International Conference on Multimedia Big Data (BigMM), pp. 183–190. IEEE, Institute of Electrical and Electronics Engineers Inc. (2020)
47. Mattei, M., Caldarelli, G., Squartini, T., Saracco, F.: Italian Twitter semantic network during the Covid-19 epidemic. EPJ Data Sci. **10**(1), 1–27 (2021). https://doi.org/10.1140/epjds/s13688-021-00301-x
48. Mehta, D., Dwivedi, A., Patra, A., Anand Kumar, M.: A transformer-based architecture for fake news classification. Soc. Netw. Anal. Min. **11**(1), 1–12 (2021). https://doi.org/10.1007/s13278-021-00738-y
49. Memon, S.A., Carley, K.M.: Characterizing COVID-19 misinformation communities using a novel twitter dataset. arXiv preprint arXiv:2008.00791 (2020)
50. Menczer, F.: The spread of misinformation in social media. In: Proceedings of the 25th International Conference Companion on World Wide Web (2016)
51. Mohapatra, A., Thota, N., Prakasam, P.: Fake news detection and classification using hybrid BiLSTM and self-attention model. Multimedia Tools Appl. (2022). https://doi.org/10.1007/s11042-022-12764-9. https://link.springer.com/10.1007/s11042-022-12764-9

52. Murić, G., Wu, Y., Ferrara, E.: COVID-19 vaccine hesitancy on social media: building a public Twitter data set of antivaccine content, vaccine misinformation, and conspiracies. JMIR Public Health Surveillance **7**, e30642 (2021)
53. Ng, K.C., Tang, J., Lee, D.: The effect of platform intervention policies on fake news dissemination and survival: an empirical examination. J. Manag. Inf. Syst. **38**, 898–930 (2021). https://doi.org/10.1080/07421222.2021.1990612
54. Nguyen, D.T., Nguyen, N.P., Thai, M.T.: Sources of misinformation in online social networks: who to suspect? In: MILCOM 2012–2012 IEEE Military Communications Conference, pp. 1–6. IEEE (2013)
55. Nguyen, V.H., Sugiyama, K., Nakov, P., Kan, M.Y.: Fang: Leveraging social context for fake news detection using graph representation. In: Proceedings of the 29th ACM International Conference on Information & Knowledge Management, pp. 1165–1174 (2020)
56. de Oliveira, D.V.B., Albuquerque, U.P.: Cultural evolution and digital media: diffusion of fake news about COVID-19 on Twitter. SN Comput. Sci. **2**(6), 1–12 (2021). https://doi.org/10.1007/s42979-021-00836-w
57. Palani, B., Elango, S., Viswanathan K.V.: CB-Fake: a multimodal deep learning framework for automatic fake news detection using capsule neural network and BERT. Multimedia Tools Appl. 1–34 (2021). https://doi.org/10.1007/s11042-021-11782-3
58. Peng, X., Xintong, B.: An effective strategy for multi-modal fake news detection. Multimedia Tools Appl. **81**, 13799–13822 (2022). https://doi.org/10.1007/s11042-022-12290-8. https://link.springer.com/10.1007/s11042-022-12290-8
59. Pennycook, G., McPhetres, J., Zhang, Y., Lu, J.G., Rand, D.G.: Fighting COVID-19 misinformation on social media: experimental evidence for a scalable accuracy nudge intervention. Psychol. Sci. **31**, 770–780 (2020)
60. Pierri, F., Piccardi, C., Ceri, S.: A multi-layer approach to disinformation detection in US and Italian news spreading on Twitter. EPJ Data Sci. **9**(1), 1–17 (2020). https://doi.org/10.1140/epjds/s13688-020-00253-8
61. Raju, R., Bhandari, S., Mohamud, S.A., Ceesay, E.N.: Transfer learning model for disrupting misinformation during a COVID-19 pandemic. In: 2021 IEEE 11th Annual Computing and Communication Workshop and Conference (CCWC), pp. 0245–0250. IEEE (2021)
62. Rani, N., Das, P., Bhardwaj, A.K.: A hybrid deep learning model based on CNN-BiLSTM for rumor detection. In: 2021 6th International Conference on Communication and Electronics Systems (ICCES), pp. 1423–1427. IEEE (2021)
63. Rath, B., Gao, W., Ma, J., Srivastava, J.: Utilizing computational trust to identify rumor spreaders on Twitter. Soc. Netw. Anal. Min. **8**(1), 1–16 (2018). https://doi.org/10.1007/s13278-018-0540-z
64. Rath, B., Gao, W., Srivastava, J.: Evaluating vulnerability to fake news in social networks: a community health assessment model. In: 2019 IEEE/ACM International Conference on Advances in Social Networks Analysis and Mining (ASONAM), pp. 432–435. IEEE (2019)
65. Raza, S., Ding, C.: Fake news detection based on news content and social contexts: a transformer-based approach. Int. J. Data Sci. Anal. 1–28 (2021). https://doi.org/10.1007/s41060-021-00302-z
66. Röchert, D., Shahi, G.K., Neubaum, G., Ross, B., Stieglitz, S.: The networked context of COVID-19 misinformation: informational homogeneity on Youtube at the beginning of the pandemic. Online Soc. Netw. Media **26**, 100164 (2021). https://doi.org/10.1016/j.osnem.2021.100164

67. Saleh, H., Alharbi, A., Alsamhi, S.H.: OPCNN-FAKE: optimized convolutional neural network for fake news detection. IEEE Access **9**, 129471–129489 (2021). https://doi.org/10.1109/ACCESS.2021.3112806
68. Santhoshkumar, S., Dhinesh Babu, L.D.: Earlier detection of rumors in online social networks using certainty-factor-based convolutional neural networks. Soc. Netw. Anal. Min. **10**(1), 1–17 (2020). https://doi.org/10.1007/s13278-020-00634-x
69. Shelke, S., Attar, V.: Rumor detection in social network based on user, content and lexical features. Multimedia Tools Appl. **81**, 17347–17368 (2022). https://doi.org/10.1007/s11042-022-12761-y. https://link.springer.com/10.1007/s11042-022-12761-y
70. Shu, K., Mahudeswaran, D., Wang, S., Lee, D., Liu, H.: FakeNewsNet: a data repository with news content, social context, and spatiotemporal information for studying fake news on social media. Big Data **8**, 171–188 (2020). https://doi.org/10.1089/big.2020.0062
71. Sridhar, S., Sanagavarapu, S.: Fake news detection and analysis using multitask learning with BiLSTM CapsNet model. In: 2021 11th International Conference on Cloud Computing, Data Science & Engineering (Confluence), pp. 905–911. IEEE, Institute of Electrical and Electronics Engineers Inc. (2021)
72. Surendran, P., Navyasree, B., Kambham, H., Kumar, M.A.: Covid-19 fake news detector using hybrid convolutional and Bi-LSTM model. In: 2021 12th International Conference on Computing Communication and Networking Technologies (ICCCNT), pp. 01–06. IEEE, Institute of Electrical and Electronics Engineers (IEEE) (2021)
73. Tambuscio, M., Oliveira, D.F.M., Ciampaglia, G.L., Ruffo, G.: Network segregation in a model of misinformation and fact checking. CoRR abs/1610.04170 (2016). http://arxiv.org/abs/1610.04170
74. Tarnpradab, S., Hua, K.A.: Attention based neural architecture for rumor detection with author context awareness. In: 2018 Thirteenth International Conference on Digital Information Management (ICDIM), pp. 82–87. IEEE (2018)
75. Thakur, A., Shinde, S., Patil, T., Gaud, B., Babanne, V.: MYTHYA: fake news detector, real time news extractor and classifier. In: 2020 4th International Conference on Trends in Electronics and Informatics (ICOEI)(48184), pp. 982–987. IEEE (2020)
76. Tschiatschek, S., Singla, A., Gomez Rodriguez, M., Merchant, A., Krause, A.: Fake news detection in social networks via crowd signals. In: Companion Proceedings of the Web Conference 2018, pp. 517–524 (2018)
77. Tyagi, S., Pai, A., Pegado, J., Kamath, A.: A proposed model for preventing the spread of misinformation on online social media using machine learning. In: 2019 Amity International Conference on Artificial Intelligence (AICAI), pp. 678–683 (2019). https://doi.org/10.1109/AICAI.2019.8701408
78. Vogel, I., Meghana, M.: Detecting fake news spreaders on Twitter from a multilingual perspective. In: 2020 IEEE 7th International Conference on Data Science and Advanced Analytics (DSAA), pp. 599–606. IEEE (2020)
79. Volkova, S., Jang, J.Y.: Misleading or falsification: inferring deceptive strategies and types in online news and social media. In: Companion Proceedings of the Web Conference 2018, pp. 575–583 (2018)
80. Vosoughi, S., Roy, D., Aral, S.: The spread of true and false news online. Science **359**(6380), 1146–1151 (2018). https://doi.org/10.1126/science.aap9559. https://www.science.org/doi/abs/10.1126/science.aap9559
81. Vraga, E.K., Bode, L.: Using expert sources to correct health misinformation in social media. Sci. Commun. **39**, 621–645 (2017)

82. Wang, L., Wang, Y., de Melo, G., Weikum, G.: Understanding archetypes of fake news via fine-grained classification. Soc. Netw. Anal. Min. **9**(1), 1–17 (2019). https://doi.org/10.1007/s13278-019-0580-z
83. Wang, Y., et al.: EANN: event adversarial neural networks for multi-modal fake news detection. In: Proceedings of the 24th ACM SIGKDD International Conference on Knowledge Discovery & Data Mining, pp. 849–857. Association for Computing Machinery (2018)
84. Wang, Y., Ma, F., Wang, H., Jha, K., Gao, J.: Multimodal emergent fake news detection via meta neural process networks. In: Proceedings of the 27th ACM SIGKDD Conference on Knowledge Discovery & Data Mining, pp. 3708–3716. Association for Computing Machinery (2021)
85. Wang, Y., Qian, S., Hu, J., Fang, Q., Xu, C.: Fake news detection via knowledge-driven multimodal graph convolutional networks. In: Proceedings of the 2020 International Conference on Multimedia Retrieval, pp. 540–547 (2020)
86. Wang, Z., Yin, Z., Argyris, Y.A.: Detecting medical misinformation on social media using multimodal deep learning. IEEE J. Biomed. Health Inform. **25**, 2193–2203 (2021). https://doi.org/10.1109/JBHI.2020.3037027
87. Watine, P., Bodaghi, A., Schmitt, K.A.: Can the Hawkes process be used to evaluate the spread of online information? In: 2021 IEEE International Symposium on Technology and Society (ISTAS), pp. 1–6. IEEE, Institute of Electrical and Electronics Engineers Inc. (2021)
88. Xie, Y., Huang, X., Xie, X., Jiang, S.: A fake news detection framework using social user graph. In: Proceedings of the 2020 2nd International Conference on Big Data Engineering, pp. 55–61. Association for Computing Machinery (2020)
89. Yang, Y.: COVID-19 fake news detection via graph neural networks in social media. In: 2021 IEEE International Conference on Bioinformatics and Biomedicine (BIBM), pp. 3178–3180. IEEE, Institute of Electrical and Electronics Engineers (IEEE) (2021)
90. Zaeem, R.N., Li, C., Barber, K.S.: On sentiment of online fake news. In: 2020 IEEE/ACM International Conference on Advances in Social Networks Analysis and Mining (ASONAM), pp. 760–767. IEEE (2020)
91. Zubiaga, A., Liakata, M., Procter, R., Hoi, G.W.S., Tolmie, P.: Analysing how people orient to and spread rumours in social media by looking at conversational threads. PloS One **11**(3), e0150989 (2016)

Mobile Prefetching and Web Prefetching: A Systematic Literature Review

Tolga Buyuktanir[1,2](✉) and Mehmet S. Aktas[1]

[1] Computer Engineering Department, Yildiz Technical University, Istanbul, Turkey
tolga.buyuktanir@loodos.com
[2] Loodos Tech., Istanbul, Turkey
aktas@yildiz.edu.tr

Abstract. Today, we see that prefetching systems are widely used to decrease the network traffic, data access latency, energy consumption, and computing performance inefficiency of data-intensive operations. However, prefetching is a concept used in different computing and IT fields such as microprocessor design, micro-controller design, hard disk design, database, network, web application, mobile application, etc. The fact that the concept of prefetching is used in different fields causes difficulties in literature review and research. Therefore, these studies need to be organized systematically for each field. This study presents a systematic literature review of prefetching related mobile and web applications to identify research gaps, define new study subject opportunities, and present future directions. We think that this study will make it easier for other researchers to work in this field with the research gaps and opportunities indicated.

Keywords: Web prefetching · Mobile prefetching · Systematic literature review · Intelligent techniques · Prefetching strategies

1 Introduction

With the development of technology, the internet has an important place in people's lives, easier to access. Companies have started to serve many users and their demands in this way. However, the users are impatient to access the services. The increased demands require improved service [20,37]. Google reported that when searches were answered 100 to 400 ms. late, the number of daily searches per user decreased by 0.2% to 0.6 % [7]. Similarly, it has been shown in various studies that delay problems are directly effective in user satisfaction and revenue growth [5,27].

Bandwidth limitations, distributed design, long query processing, etc., increase the access latency. Better hardware and technologies or intelligent techniques such as caching and prefetching can be implemented to satisfy users suffering from it [29,36,37].

Supported by Loodos Tech.

O. Gervasi et al. (Eds.): ICCSA 2022 Workshops, LNCS 13379, pp. 75–89, 2022.
https://doi.org/10.1007/978-3-031-10545-6_6

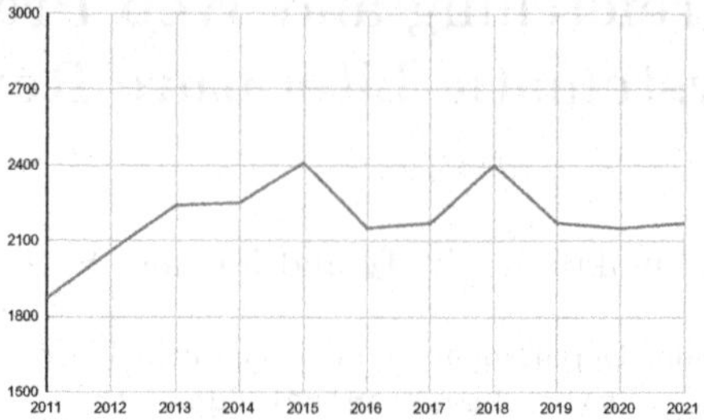

Fig. 1. Search results of "web or mobile prefetching" words on Google Scholar by years

The previously accessed data may be required near future. Because of that, it is stored for reuse in memory [11]. This approach called caching meets client needs in an instant while reducing server-side stress [17,35]. The basic approach to caching includes responding from data stores for the user's request for the first time and storing it in the cache to not occupy the server if the same request is made again. For example, thanks to Facebook's photo caching mechanism, 90.1% of the incoming requests come through the cache, while the rest is taken from the storage space [15].

User's requests in the near future can be predicted from previously accessed data, and responses to the requests can be fetched into the cache [11,29,30, 40]. This approach is called prefetching, another research area to reduce access latency. It aims to minimize user access latency using optimum memory and bandwidth [26,29].

Web prefetching and mobile prefetching is hot topic that has been studying over and over again with novel prediction approaches for near future since past. Search results of "web or mobile prefetching" words on Google Scholar by years support it. This results is shown in Fig. 1 in order to present publication counts year by year. When we scan the literature, we found a systematic literature review for web caching strategies including proxy-side and client-side prefetching [41]. There has not been a systematic literature review or mapping study on mobile and web prefetching that would identify publication trends, research gaps, and future directions.

In this paper, we share our systematic literature review steps and findings on mobile prefetching and web prefetching to identify research gaps, define new study subject opportunities, and present future directions. We share carefully selected publications on prefetching published in the last ten years and some statistics and information we have obtained from these publications. We think that this study will make it easier for other researchers to work in this field with the research gaps and opportunities indicated.

The rest of the paper is organized as follows: Sect. 2 provides information about our systematic literature review process. We answer the research question and discuss outputs obtained from the data extraction process in Sect. 3. The threats to the validity of the systematic literature review study are presented in Sect. 4, and in the last section, Sect. 5, we describe a conclusion and future work.

2 Systematic Literature Review Process

SLR or SMS aims to review all the primary studies to identify, classify and compare the research area and answer the research questions. SLR provides a clear perspective to literature for future direction through methodological steps. We follow the methodology presented by Petersen et al. [34], which includes planning, conducting, and documenting. We have applied systematic literature review method to our secondary study research on topic of "Web or Mobile Prefetching: A Systematic Literature Review".

2.1 Planing the Review

We define the research questions to obtain literature knowledge and to give a form to the review process. In the Table 1, research questions and main motivations of them are displayed.

Table 1. Research questions

Research questions	Main motivation
RQ1: What are the main practical motivations behind using prefetch?	The aim is to get ideas about the main reason for organizing the software architectures with prefetching modules
RQ2: How many studies are published on the web or mobile prefetching?	The aim is to provide a trend analysis graph
RQ3: What are the most frequently used prediction methods for prefetching?	The aim is to provide information on the most frequently used techniques
RQ4: What are the existing research issues, and what should be the future research agenda?	The aim is to understand and reveal the research gaps and identify future research directions
RQ5: Which journals include studies on the web or mobile prefetching?	Identify the journals for authors to submit their studies

2.2 Search String to Find Primary Studies

In order to find primary studies, we have defined a search string including mobile, web, and prefetching keywords. The search string we have defined is "(Mobile OR Web) **AND** Prefetching."

Using the search string, we collect results from 4 digital libraries between 2011 and march 2022. The name of libraries and how many papers are downloaded from the library are presented in Table 2. It isn't easy to download, organize, and manage the papers manually. Therefore, Zotero [3] references management tool was used. The search results were automatically imported to Zotero, the papers were organized, duplicated papers were removed, and filters and exclusion criteria were applied.

Table 2. Search results in digital libraries

No	Name	Result
1	IEEE	378
2	Science Direct	703
3	ACM	1606
4	Springer Link	1402
	Total	**4089**

Table 3. Applied filters to search results

Filter	Description
Filter-1	We excluded publications in unrelated journals and conferences and remove duplicate studies
Filter-2	We read the title and abstract of studies and eliminated irrelevants
Filter-3	We read the abstract deeply to apply the our criteria deciding inclusion or exclusion of studies

We applied three filters described in Table 3 to find out the primary studies. The number of obtained papers after the filters are shown in Fig. 2. The Filter-1 described in Table 3 is applied to search results obtained from 4 digital libraries IEEE, Science Direct, ACM, and Springer Link. At the last moment of the filtering process, we get 102 primary studies.

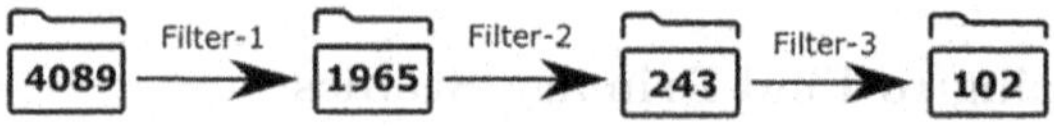

Fig. 2. This figure shows the number of studies left after applying the filters defined in Table 3.

2.3 Inclusion and Exclusion Criteria

In this systematic literature review study, we collect search results and eliminate the results according to our first two filter descriptions shown in Table 2. However, we need to select the appropriate papers objectively and answer the research question with the selected papers. For this reason, we determined inclusion and exclusion criteria, presented in Table 4, at the beginning of our study [22,31,34].

Inclusion Criteria. From the remaining paper after Filter-1 and Filter-2, We included studies whose abstract or keywords contain "prefetch" term. We also include studies that contribute to mobile prefetching and web prefetching, such as a theory, a demonstration, an approach, etc.

Exclusion Criteria. We excluded studies that do not openly associate with SLR topics. We did our searches from digital libraries, but we decided from the beginning to exclude possible blog and presentation files that we might encounter. The prefetching studies on the CPU, memory, microprocessor, flash storage devices and networks are excluded because of domain differences and SLR limitations.

Table 4. Inclusion and exclusion criteria

In/Excl	Criteria
Inclusion	Abstract/keywords include the term "prefetch"
	It is clear from abstract that it is contributes to mobile or web prefetching
Exclusion	Blogs and presentations are excluded
	Hardware-based prefetching studies, for example, prefetching studies on CPU, memory, microprocessor, flash storage devices, etc., are excluded
	The prefetching studies on networks are excluded

2.4 Classification Schema

We categorized 102 studies left after the filtering process according to places of prefetching [4,8] and prediction methods [29,41]. We created a column for each study called "objective," including the study's objective, and tried to extract some things from research fields. We also labeled the research issues and obtained a data extraction form based on this. Eventually, we classified 102 studies according to classification schema presented Table 6.

Table 5. Classification schema

Category	Subcategory	Definition
Prefetching places	Server-side	Even at the origin server, the data can be stored in a server-side for reducing the need for redundant computations or database retrievals [4]
	Client-side	It is located in the client machine [8]
	Proxy-side	It is located between client machines and origin server [4]
Prediction method for prefetching		The future access data can be predicted by a method such as lstm, k-mean, c-mean, etc., for prefetching. This the category defines the prediction method to help the prefetching decision [41]
Research issues	Long resource loading time	One of the aims of prefetching is the reducing latency and satisfying the impatient users [10,23,24,28,41]
	Energy consumption	The prefetching system, especially on mobile and IoT devices must concern with energy consumption [14,23,29]
	Computation intensive operation	The prefetching cache mechanism can improve all system performance. Computational intensive operations demanded in the near future can be calculated by a prefetching mechanism in advance [23,24,28,41]
	Network traffic	The prefetching system, especially on mobile and IoT devices, must also be concerned with network traffic issues to overcome data transfer, energy consumption, connections cost, etc. [4,9,13,33]
	Security and privacy	In the prefetching mechanism, it is necessary to use personal data securely and to protect its privacy [38,39]

2.5 Data Extraction and Mapping of the Literature

To analyze in a planned way, we extracted data from selected primary research studies. We prepared a form to extract data shown in Table 6 and used it to extract data. Research issues, prefetching places, and prediction methods fields were not filled during data extraction unless clearly defined to avoid assumptions.

At the beginning of the data extraction process for 102 studies, we selected a few studies randomly. Then, authors extracted data from the same studies set according to Table 6. We did cross-check, but we couldn't detect any conflict. After realizing that everything was fine, we started to data extraction process for 102 studies to obtain results.

Table 6. Form for data extraction

No	Data extraction column
1	Study ID (ex: S2)
2	Title: Paper's title (ex: Big data stream analysis: a systematic literature review)
3	Author: Author's name
4	Year: Publication year (ex: 2020)
5	Item Type: (ex: Book Chapter)
6	Book Title/Conference Name/Journal Name: Any book, conference or journal name
7	Objective: The propose of the study (ex: Predicting data to be accessed in the near future with association rule mining to prefetch)
8	Prediction Method: Used prediction method in the study (ex: k-means)
9	Research Issue: computation intensive operation, network traffic, latency, energy consumption, privacy or/and security
10	Dataset: Used dataset/datasets to evaluate study (ex: National Lab of Applied Network Research logs)
11	Prefetching Places: client-side, server-side, proxy-side

3 Results

In this section, we discuss outputs obtained from the data extraction process described in the previous section. Each research question presented in Table 1 is answered objectively and evaluated separately using the information in Table 5 and data extracted according to Table 6.

3.1 RQ1: What are the Main Practical Motivations Behind Using Prefetch?

The main motivation of prefetching is to satisfy users and service providers [4, 9, 11, 29]. In order to better define the motivations, it is necessary to look at the needs from the perspective of the user, provider, and system. The users surfing on the applications can be impatient. Therefore, the motivation is to satisfy the users by reducing latency [2, 11, 12]. Energy consumption and network usage are essential metrics for the things running on the edge. From this perspective, the motivation for prefetching is reducing consumption [21, 25] and network usage [18, 33]. The motivation for prefetching of the system provider can be increasing performance, optimizing system resources, and spreading the load to time [1, 6, 19]. We explained the motivation from different sides for better understanding. However, all these pointed out are the reasons behind using prefetch.

3.2 RQ2: How Many Studies are Published on the Web or Mobile Prefetching?

Within the scope of the study, the studies in the literature in the last ten years on mobile and web prefetching topics were filtered, and 102 primary studies were obtained. The frequency of primary studies by year is shown in Fig. 3. According to Fig. 3, the number of publications has decreased in the last five years. This result seems to be incompatible with search results of "web or mobile prefetching" words on Google Scholar by year shown in Fig. 1.

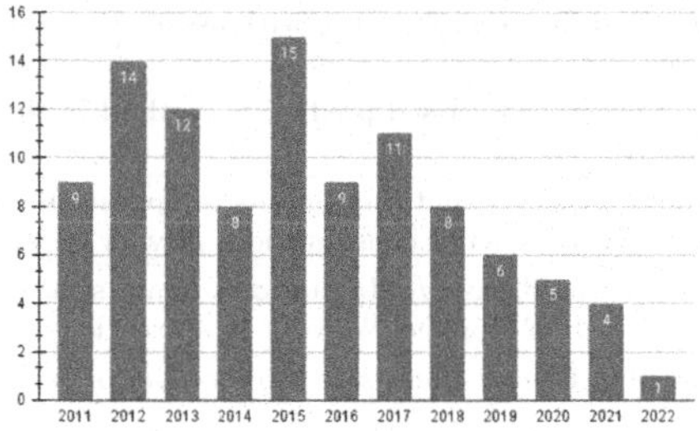

Fig. 3. Selected primary studies frequencies per year

3.3 RQ3: What are the Most Frequently Used Prediction Methods for Prefetching?

Mobile or web prefetching is the approach to predict accessed data in the near future [26,38,39]. We tried to extract prediction approaches for prefetching from obtained primary studies to answer this research question. We read studies profoundly and found out prediction approaches in the prefetching module. However, we realized that while some of the studies to be shared the algorithm's name, the concept and technique were shared in others. Therefore, we extracted terms associated with the predictions for prefetching used in the studies, wrote them down, and calculated frequencies for each term. The key terms are presented in Table 7. According to Table 7, we can group prediction approaches for prefetching as clustering-based, association rule-based, statistical-based, classification-based, and custom approaches.

The prefetching can be implemented in client-side, proxy-side and server-side [16,28,32]. While we were extracting the key terms, we tried to find the proposed prefetching place. In the studies, when we couldn't find that the prefetching place was written explicitly, we tried to understand the prefetching place from the proposed architecture. We left this field blank when we could not find it in the text and from the architecture. Also, we found in some studies that prefetching can be in more than one place. After reading all the primary studies, the frequency information we obtained about the prefetching place is shared in Fig. 4.

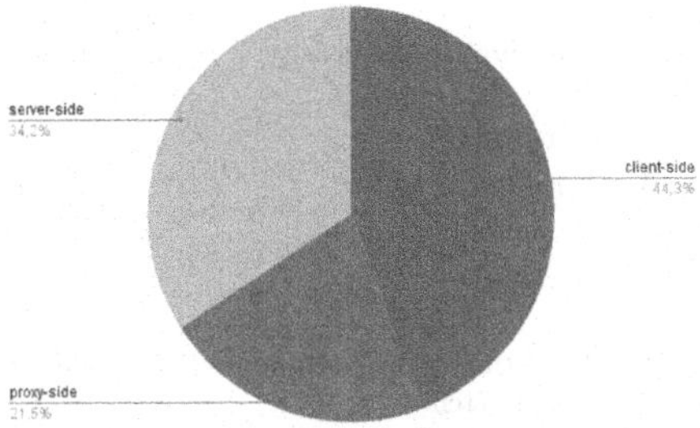

Fig. 4. Prefetching places of some primary studies

3.4 RQ4: What are the Existing Research Issues and What Should be the Future Research Agenda?

In Subsect. 3.1, we have described research motivation on prefetching from different perspectives. We have also described key terms associated with prediction approaches for prefetching in Subsect. 3.3. The answer to these questions gives an opinion about the existing research issues and solution approaches. However, we classified the research issues on prefetching as follows: computation intensive operation [10,23,24], network traffic [9,13,33], long resource loading time [10,23,24,38], energy consumption [23,29], security and privacy [38].

Figure 5 has been created according to the research issues used in our 102 primary studies. Some studies contain more than one research issue. Network traffic, long resource loading time, and energy consumption issues are hot and innovative. With the new prediction methods, novel prefetching approaches can be implemented. According to Fig. 5, prefetching for computation-intensive operation and security and privacy for prefetching are less studied issues, so these may present opportunities for identifying future research directions.

The need for prefetching on edge servers or on the client-side is increasing, especially on mobile phones and IoT devices. Even if prefetching is used, its efficiency needs to be increased. Also, there are things to be done to protect privacy and security while prefetching. Prediction for prefetching without any private data on the proxy-side and server-side are issues that need to be studied.

Table 7. Key terms associated with prediction methods for prefetching extracted from primary studies and their frequencies

Prediction method	cnt	Prediction method	cnt	Prediction method	cnt
amp	1	intentionally-related long short term model	1	prefetch state of bookmarked segments	1
appriori	1	jaccard similarity coefficients	1	prefixspan(pattern-growth dfs)	1
art1 neural network	3	joint probability density function	1	probability graph	1
association rule mining	3	k-means	3		1
bayesian network	3	k-nearest neighbor	2	quickmine	1
bi-lstm	1	k-order markov model	1	rank-based selection	2
breadth-first search latest potentialy pages for users	1	linear svm	1	rate adaption algorithm	1
c-miner	1	Long-time-to-live data types are prefetched	1	referrer graph	1
clasp (closed)	1	lstm	1	rough-set clustering	1
cluster-based	1	lstm-attention	1	semantic-based prediction	1
cluster-based latent bias model	1	markov chain	6	sequential pattern mining	1
compare-by-hash	1	markov decision process	1	skslru	1
competitive agglomeration	1	markov random fields	1	slob	1
context-aware prefetching	1	maxsp	1	social-aware prefetching	1
crowdsourcing	1	mithril	1	socially-driven learning based prefetching	1
dead-reckoning based prediction	1	most popular prefetching	2	spade	1
decision-tree induction	1	most promising pages	1	spam (apriori all bfsdfs)	1
deepevent	1	multi-class svm	1	statistical methods	1
dependency graph	3	navigation trajectory extrapolation	1	stochastic gradient boosting	1
directed graph	1	neural networks	2	stochastic gradient descent	1
directhit	1	newman clustering	1	stochastic optimization	1
double dependency graph	1	omnibox prediction	1	stochastic sequential model	1
epf-dash	1	on/off strategy	2	support vector machine	2
eschedule	1	pagerank	1	tag-based prediction	1
fp-growth	1	palpatine	1	task-level prediction	1
frequently-based prediction	1	partial maching	2	top-n prediction	2
fuzzy c-means	1	path-based next n-trace	1	transparent informed prefetching	1
gradient boosted regression tree	1	pattern-based prediction	1	user access pattern-based prediction	1
greentube	1	petri nets	1	user-aware dynamic markov chain	1
gsp	1	plwap	1	vgen (generator)	1
history-based prediction	3	popularity-based prediction	8	video content analysis	1
hits-based algorithm	2	partial match prediction	2	video slicing mechanism	1
hits-based algorithm	1	history based prediction	1	vmsp (maximal)	1
improved support vector machine	1	preference-based popularity prediction	2	weighted rule mining concept	1

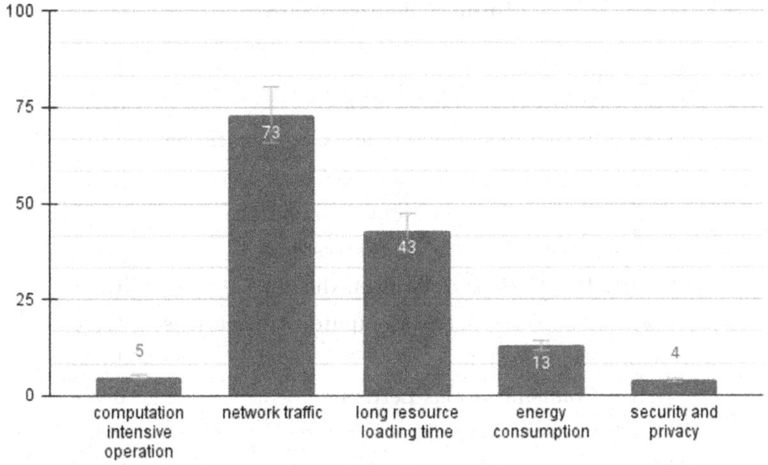

Fig. 5. Research issues on prefetching

3.5 RQ5: Which Journals Include Studies on the Web or Mobile Prefetching?

The journals which accept papers on mobile or web prefetching topics are listed in Table 8 with their scimago journal ranks.

4 Threats to Validity of Research

We discuss the thread of the validity for the mapping study steps to wrong decision makings to identify primary studies, research questions, publication selection, and data extraction.

Publication Selection: Determining the scope of the study was a challenge because prefetching is a concept used in different computing and IT fields such as microprocessor design, micro-controller design, hard disk design, database, network, web, etc. These fields use the prefetching concept in different ways and for different goals. To avoid bias, we searched prefetching terms with mobile and web words separately on digital libraries and collected results with snowballing. But, we can not guarantee that we have accessed all related studies to apply our criteria.

Research Questions: This study is a systematic literature review that logically covers the mobile or web prefetching literature with research questions. But, it may not cover in detail.

Table 8. Journal names

No	Journal name	SJR
1	IEEE Wireless Communications	3,216
2	IEEE Transactions on Wireless Communications	2,010
3	IEEE Transactions on Wireless Communications	2,010
4	IEEE Transactions on Mobile Computing	1,276
5	Future Generation Computer Systems	1,262
6	IEEE Transactions on Multimedia	1,218
7	Journal of Network and Computer Applications	1,145
8	World Wide Web	1,033
9	IEEE Communications Letters	0,929
10	IEEE Systems Journal	0,864
11	Journal of Systems and Software	0,642
12	IEEE Access	0,587
13	ACM Trans. Multimed. Comput. Commun. Appl.	0,558
14	Journal of Intelligent Information Systems	0,424
15	ACM SIGPLAN Notices	0,310
16	ACM Transactions on Storage	0,309
17	ACM SIGARCH Computer Architecture News	–

Data Extraction: The data extraction was done manually by the authors. Therefore, it may contain incorrect decisions. However, we cross-checked during the extraction process, talked together about the conflicts, and decided together.

5 Conclusion and Future Work

In this study, we aimed to investigate literature on the web or mobile prefetching topics systematically and define research gaps and future directions. The main contribution is to present the state of the literature on mobile or web prefetching. By analyzing the trends on this studies topic shown in Fig. 1, an almost equal number of studies are added to the literature each year. According to obtained key terms presented in Table 7, prediction approaches for the prefetching have been grouped as clustering-based, association rule-based, statistical-based, classification-based, and custom approaches. These key terms and groups help to find new research areas. We also defined future directions and research issues in Subsect. 3.3. Based on all this, we conclude that the mobile or web prefetching topic is open to new contributions. Significantly, research on security and privacy for prefetching and prefetching for computation-intensive operations may give good opportunities because of the lack of studies. We will focus on prefetching for computation-intensive operations and security and privacy problems for prefetching in future work.

References

1. Agustin, J.L.H., Del Barco, P.C.: A model-driven approach to develop high performance web applications. J. Syst. Softw. **86**(12), 3013–3023 (2013)
2. Ahmad, N., Malik, O., Ul Hassan, M., Qureshi, M.S., Munir, A.: Reducing user latency in web prefetching using integrated techniques. In: International Conference on Computer Networks and Information Technology, pp. 175–178. IEEE (2011)
3. Ahmed, K.M., Al Dhubaib, B.: Zotero: a bibliographic assistant to researcher. J. Pharmacol. Pharmacother. **2**(4), 303 (2011)
4. Ali, W., Shamsuddin, S.M.: Intelligent client-side web caching scheme based on least recently used algorithm and neuro-fuzzy system. In: Yu, W., He, H., Zhang, N. (eds.) ISNN 2009. LNCS, vol. 5552, pp. 70–79. Springer, Heidelberg (2009). https://doi.org/10.1007/978-3-642-01510-6_9
5. Arapakis, I., Bai, X., Cambazoglu, B.B.: Impact of response latency on user behavior in web search. In: Proceedings of the 37th International ACM SIGIR Conference on Research Development in Information Retrieval, SIGIR 2014, pp. 103–112. Association for Computing Machinery, New York (2014). https://doi.org/10.1145/2600428.2609627
6. Bellante, W., Vilardi, R., Rossi, D.: On Netflix catalog dynamics and caching performance. In: 2013 IEEE 18th International Workshop on Computer Aided Modeling and Design of Communication Links and Networks (CAMAD), pp. 89–93. IEEE (2013)
7. Brutlag, J.: Speed matters for google web search (2009). https://venturebeat.com/wp-content/uploads/2009/11/delayexp.pdf
8. Byna, S., Chen, Y., Sun, X.H.: A taxonomy of data prefetching mechanisms. In: 2008 International Symposium on Parallel Architectures, Algorithms, and Networks (i-span 2008), pp. 19–24. IEEE (2008)
9. Deng, Y., Manoharan, S.: Predicting web accesses using personal history. In: 2017 IEEE Conference on Open Systems (ICOS), pp. 7–12. IEEE (2017)
10. Esteves, S., Silva, J.N., Veiga, L.: Palpatine: mining frequent sequences for data prefetching in NoSQL distributed key-value stores. In: 2020 IEEE 19th International Symposium on Network Computing and Applications (NCA), pp. 1–10. IEEE (2020)
11. Fomin, F.V., Giroire, F., Jean-Marie, A., Mazauric, D., Nisse, N.: To satisfy impatient web surfers is hard. Theoret. Comput. Sci. **526**, 1–17 (2014)
12. Ghosh, S.S., Patra, M., Jain, A.: Reduction of web latency: an integrated proxy prefetch-cache system framework. In: Abraham, A., Dutta, P., Mandal, J., Bhattacharya, A., Dutta, S. (eds.) Emerging Technologies in Data Mining and Information Security. AISC, vol. 814, pp. 621–633. Springer, Singapore (2019). https://doi.org/10.1007/978-981-13-1501-5_55
13. Han, J., Li, X.Y., Jung, T., Zhao, J., Zhao, Z.: Network agile preference-based prefetching for mobile devices. In: 2014 IEEE 33rd International Performance Computing and Communications Conference (IPCCC), pp. 1–8. IEEE (2014)
14. Higgins, B.D., Flinn, J., Giuli, T.J., Noble, B., Peplin, C., Watson, D.: Informed mobile prefetching. In: Proceedings of the 10th International Conference on Mobile Systems, Applications, and Services, pp. 155–168 (2012)
15. Huang, Q., Birman, K., van Renesse, R., Lloyd, W., Kumar, S., Li, H.C.: An analysis of Facebook photo caching. In: Proceedings of the Twenty-Fourth ACM Symposium on Operating Systems Principles, SOSP 2013, pp. 167–181. Association for Computing Machinery, New York (2013)

16. Huang, Y.F., Hsu, J.M.: Mining web logs to improve hit ratios of prefetching and caching. Knowl.-Based Syst. **21**(1), 62–69 (2008)
17. Hurley, R.T., Li, B.Y.: A performance investigation of web caching architectures. In: Proceedings of the 2008 C3S2E Conference, C3S2E 2008, pp. 205–213. Association for Computing Machinery, New York (2008). https://doi.org/10.1145/1370256.1370291
18. Jaffrès-Runser, K., Jakllari, G.: PCach: the case for pre-caching your mobile data. In: 2018 IEEE 43rd Conference on Local Computer Networks (LCN), pp. 465–468. IEEE (2018)
19. Ji, C., et al.: Inspection and characterization of app file usage in mobile devices. ACM Trans. Storage (TOS) **16**(4), 1–25 (2020)
20. Joo, M., An, Y., Roh, H., Lee, W.: Predictive prefetching based on user interaction for web applications. IEEE Commun. Lett. **25**(3), 821–824 (2020)
21. Kim, S., Oh, H., Kim, C.: ePF-DASH: energy-efficient prefetching based dynamic adaptive streaming over HTTP. In: 2015 International Conference on Big Data and Smart Computing (BigComp), pp. 124–129. IEEE (2015)
22. Kitchenham, B., Brereton, O.P., Budgen, D., Turner, M., Bailey, J., Linkman, S.: Systematic literature reviews in software engineering-a systematic literature review. Inf. Softw. Technol. **51**(1), 7–15 (2009)
23. Ko, S.W., Huang, K., Kim, S.L., Chae, H.: Energy efficient mobile computation offloading via online prefetching. In: 2017 IEEE International Conference on Communications (ICC), pp. 1–6. IEEE (2017)
24. Ko, S.W., Huang, K., Kim, S.L., Chae, H.: Live prefetching for mobile computation offloading. IEEE Trans. Wireless Commun. **16**(5), 3057–3071 (2017)
25. Kulkarni, P., Jaini, P.: Android phone performance enhancement by energy efficient web browser. In: 2015 Global Conference on Communication Technologies (GCCT), pp. 217–222. IEEE (2015)
26. Kumar, P., Kadambari, S., Rawat, S.: Prefetching web pages for improving user access latency using integrated web usage mining. In: 2015 Communication, Control and Intelligent Systems (CCIS), pp. 401–405. IEEE (2015)
27. Linden, G.: Marissa Mayer at web 2.0. geeking with greg (2006). http://glinden.blogspot.com/2006/11/marissa-mayer-at-web-20.html
28. Liu, Q.: Web latency reduction with prefetching. Ph.D. thesis, Faculty of Graduate Studies, University of Western Ontario (2009)
29. Lotfi-Kamran, P., Sarbazi-Azad, H.: Introduction to data prefetching (2022)
30. Mohammed, H.: Continuous prefetch for interactive data applications. In: Proceedings of the 2020 ACM SIGMOD International Conference on Management of Data, pp. 2841–2843 (2020)
31. Novais, R.L., Torres, A., Mendes, T.S., Mendonça, M., Zazworka, N.: Software evolution visualization: a systematic mapping study. Inf. Softw. Technol. **55**(11), 1860–1883 (2013)
32. Pallis, G., Vakali, A., Pokorny, J.: A clustering-based prefetching scheme on a web cache environment. Comput. Electr. Eng. **34**(4), 309–323 (2008)
33. Pamboris, A., Pietzuch, P.: Edge reduce: eliminating mobile network traffic using application-specific edge proxies. In: 2015 2nd ACM International Conference on Mobile Software Engineering and Systems, pp. 72–82. IEEE (2015)
34. Petersen, K., Feldt, R., Mujtaba, S., Mattsson, M.: Systematic mapping studies in software engineering. In: 12th International Conference on Evaluation and Assessment in Software Engineering (EASE), vol. 12, pp. 1–10 (2008)
35. Rabinovich, M., Spatscheck, O.: Web Caching and Replication, vol. 67. Addison-Wesley, Boston (2002)

36. Satkar, S., Gupta, P.: Caching and prefetching web usage through improved support vector machine. In: 2019 5th International Conference On Computing, Communication, Control And Automation (ICCUBEA), pp. 1–5. IEEE (2019)
37. Song, H., Min, C., Kim, J., Eom, Y.I.: Usage pattern-based prefetching: quick application launch on mobile devices. In: Murgante, B., et al. (eds.) ICCSA 2012. LNCS, vol. 7335, pp. 227–237. Springer, Heidelberg (2012). https://doi.org/10.1007/978-3-642-31137-6_17
38. Wang, H., Kong, J., Guo, Y., Chen, X.: Mobile web browser optimizations in the cloud era: a survey. In: 2013 IEEE Seventh International Symposium on Service-Oriented System Engineering, pp. 527–536. IEEE (2013)
39. Zhao, G.F., Li, B., Hong, T.: Pre-fetching webpages on mobile social network: user-aware dynamic Markov chain. In: 2012 8th International Conference on Mobile Ad-hoc and Sensor Networks (MSN), pp. 203–210. IEEE (2012)
40. Zou, W., Won, J., Ahn, J., Kang, K.: Intentionality-related deep learning method in web prefetching. In: 2019 IEEE 27th International Conference on Network Protocols (ICNP), pp. 1–2. IEEE (2019)
41. Zulfa, M.I., Hartanto, R., Permanasari, A.E.: Caching strategy for web application-a systematic literature review. Int. J. Web Inf. Syst. **16**(5), 545–569 (2020)

Toward a Container Migration Data-Auditing Mechanism for Edge Computing Environment

Toshihiro Uchibayashi[1(✉)], Bernady Apduhan[2], Takuo Suganuma[3], and Masahiro Hiji[3]

[1] Kyushu University, Fukuoka, Japan
uchibayashi.toshihiro.143@m.kyushu-u.ac.jp
[2] Kyushu Sangyo University, Fukuoka, Japan
bob@is.kyusan-u.ac.jp
[3] Tohoku University, Sendai, Japan
{suganuma,hiji}@tohoku.ac.jp

Abstract. With the widespread use of IoT sensors and devices, it has become common to store data in the cloud. The huge and various types of data with different purposes and forms are not directly stored in the cloud but are sent to the cloud via edge computing devices. Applications are running in containers and VMs to collect data from edge computing devices and sent to the cloud. However, the current deployment and migration mechanisms for containers and VMs does not consider the conventions and regulations of the applications and data they contain. The problem is that it is easy to deploy or migrate a container and VM even if the edge computing device to which it is deployed or migrated violates the licensing terms of the application it contains, the terms of the organization, or the laws and regulations of the country in which it is located. We previously proposed a data-auditing migration control mechanism for VMs. The same problem was expected with containers as the number of edges increased. Therefore, this paper proposed a data-auditing mechanism for container migration. Implementation and evaluation of the proposed system in an edge computing environment showed that adding the proposed mechanism has minimal impact on migration time and is sufficiently practical.

Keywords: Container · Edge computing · Migration · Policy · Data audit

1 Introduction

In recent years, sensors and devices have become increasingly popular. A wide range of types of sensors and devices suitable for various applications is available in the market, including sensors for measuring environmental conditions as well as wearable devices for measuring personal health conditions. The internet of

O. Gervasi et al. (Eds.): ICCSA 2022 Workshops, LNCS 13379, pp. 90–102, 2022.
https://doi.org/10.1007/978-3-031-10545-6_7

things (IoT), where the data collected by these sensors and devices are stored in the cloud via the edge computing devices, has become common. Web services using these data are required to handle the huge volumes of data as well as data containing personal information.

Therefore, pre-processing at the edge computing device is performed before storing the data in the cloud. The aim is to reduce the volume of data or to convert information associated with individuals into data that are not associated with the individuals through secondary processing. The edge computing device is expected to be indispensable for pre-processing huge volumes of data at high speeds in the future. Pre-processing applications running at the edge computing device need to be deployed on edge computing devices in parallel, which handle huge amounts of data. For this purpose, containers and virtual machines (VMs) need to be employed. These containers and VMs can be deployed on many edge computing devices by managing them as images. It is also easy to extract an image from an active edge computing device and deploy and migrate it to other edge computing devices. Significant research work has been conducted on these migration technologies for optimizing the network connectivity by dynamically and automatically relocating edge computing devices, and likewise considering the sensors and devices density as well as the geographic location. Some of these migration technologies have already been put into service [1–3].

However, current mechanisms for deploying and migrating VMs and containers do not consider the conventions and regulations related to the applications and data they contain. VMs or containers can be easily deployed or migrated, however the edge computing device on which they are deployed or migrated may violate the licensing terms related to the application it contains, the terms of an organization, or the laws and regulations of a particular country (Fig. 1). When VMs or containers are deployed or migrated, they must be in locations that conform to the applicable license terms and conditions or the organization's policies. The restrictions are even stricter, where national laws and regulations are applied. The administrator of an edge computing device is not necessarily the administrator of a particular application. As a result, in some cases, the terms related to this application can be violated. There is a high possibility of violating national laws and regulations such as the general data protection regulation (GDPR) [4], which is a very problematic situation.

To overcome this problem, we have proposed a live migration-control mechanism for VMs. In recent years, containers, which constitute a more lightweight and flexible environment than VM, have been attracting increasing attention. Web applications previously realized in VM are being migrated to containers, one after another. Furthermore, as edge computing becomes more pervasive, the demand for containers increases and the container migration attracts more attention. Containers are often used on edge computing devices, which are very inefficient compared to the cloud. However, the inability to handle multiple containers simultaneously limits the number of containers to be used simultaneously. In this case, the container processes must be migrated to a neighboring edge computing device. The same problem with VM is expected to occur in container, as the number of edge computing devices increases. In this paper, we proposed a data-auditing mechanism for the migration of containers.

In Sect. 2, the related work along with our previous work is introduced. In Sect. 3, the current status of container migration is described. In Sect. 4, a data-auditing mechanism is proposed. In Sect. 5, the proposed mechanism is implemented and evaluated. Finally, Sect. 6 describe our conclusion and the future work.

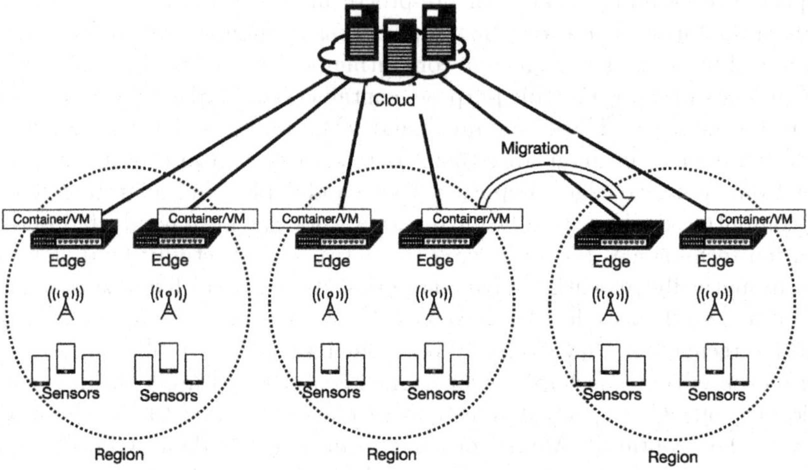

Fig. 1. Mobile sensors in edge and cloud computing environment.

2 Related Works

Shubha et al. [5] proposed a method to significantly increase the aggregation rate of data center environments by effectively managing the container state. In cloud application services, the challenge is to design efficient mechanisms, which can quickly reactivate idle containers and prevent degradation of the application's quality of service. In this paper, the proposed system is implemented on Amazon EC2, and it was confirmed that the proposed algorithm was capable of managing the container state and improving the container aggregation rate.

Omogbai [6] clarified the concept of container placement and movement on edge computing servers as well as the scheduling model and algorithm developed for this purpose. As a result, the container placement problem can be solved using a multi-objective optimization model or a graph network model and the proposed scheduling algorithm. This algorithm includes heuristic-based algorithms, which can quickly produce suboptimal solutions. It was also found that a few container-scheduling models consider distributed edge computing tasks.

Shunmugapriya et al. [7] proposed a framework, which enables a containerized evolved packet core (EPC) virtual-component migration using an open-source migration solution. This framework also provides a comprehensive experimental analysis of a live migration for two virtualization technologies (VMs and containers) and further scrutinizes container migration approaches. In their experiments, they compared several system parameters and configurations, including the arbor (image) size, the network characteristics, the processor's hardware architecture model, and the CPU load on backhaul network components. The results showed that the proposed framework successfully reduces the live migration completion time on container platforms and the end-user service interruption time for virtualized EPC components by approximately 70%.

These studies propose solutions for the quality of service and scheduling of containers in edge computing. In other words, these algorithms can automatically control a large number of containers, making it difficult for a human to determine whether a container can be movement and placement in a specific location. In this paper's method can be used to solve this problem, allowing an automated decision to be made as to whether or not to movement and placement of containers.

3 Data-Auditing for VM Migration

VM migration in the cloud is the physical transfer of a VM running in the cloud to another host machine. There are two types of migration: "live migration" and "cold migration (offline migration)". In live migration, VMs can be migrated while processes are still running without stopping. In this way, the services in the VM can be migrated while they are still alive. The memory image of the VM running on a physical host machine is entirely transferred to a VM on a different physical host machine. The operation continues on the destination physical host machine, without stopping or disconnecting the running operating system, the application software, or network connections. Although there is strictly a millisecond-long pause during switchover, but the network session is not disconnected, and the VM user is unaware that the switchover has taken place. During the cold migration, the VM is shut down, and then it is migrated to another host machine. The VM running on the physical host machine is temporarily stopped. Its memory image is moved to another physical host machine via storage, etc., and resumes operation on the destination computer. Migration has become an indispensable technology for cloud computing operations. However, the problem is that the migration process has been simplified and can be easily performed as long as the user satisfies the cloud's permissions. In this process, only the cloud's authority and the possibility of physical migration are determined, without considering any VM internal data. This could lead to violations of the internal company rules and national laws (Fig. 2). Suppose that a VM is running on the cloud of an IaaS Cloud Provider offering global IaaS services. And, the VM that contains personal data cannot cross the country borders, and that according to internal regulations, this personal data can be stored only in Region A and Region B. There is no problem if the VM manager, who controls which region the VM is launched in, migrates the VM from Region A to Region

B. However, if the VM is migrated to Region C by the VM manager's mistake ([MISTAKE] in Fig. 2), it will be a violation of the company policy. Also, if a malicious person (VM Manager (Fake) in Fig. 2) maliciously migrates the VM to Region D in Country Y ([ATTACK] in Fig. 2), it may violate the laws of the Country X. This is a very problematic situation and requires a control mechanism capable of determining whether or not a migration is allowed, considering the permissions and physical availability of the cloud and the data contained in the VM.

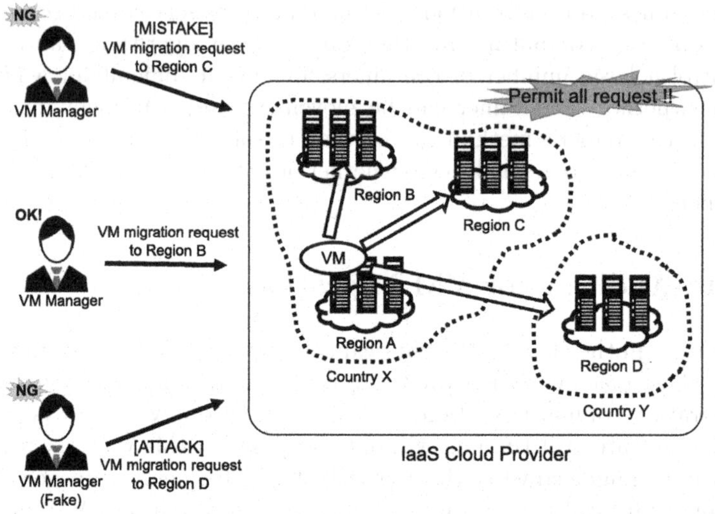

Fig. 2. VM migration problem.

To overcome the problem of an inappropriate live migration regarding data contained in VMs, we proposed a policy-based control mechanism. [8–10] The operation of the control mechanism is shown in Fig. 3. In the REGULATION, the VM administrator describes a list of identifiers of countries and organizations to which the VM data can be moved, according to the regulations attached to the data. The CountryCode indicates the countries where data movement is permitted (according to the regulations), and the OrganizationCode represents the organization that instantiates and uses the VM. When the migration is executed, the REGULATION of the VM to be moved is compared with the COUNTRY and REGULATION of the destination host machine. First, it is checked whether the CountryCode of the REGULATION is included in the CountryCode of the destination host machine.

Similarly, it is checked whether the OrganizationCode of REGULATION is included in the OrganizationCode of the destination host machine. If both checks pass, the data acquired by the VM to be moved can be moved to the country or organization where the destination host machine exists. In this way, the migration is executed. This migration process is the same as the traditional migration process. If both checks fail, the migration is not performed because the VM cannot be moved to the country where the destination host machine is located. Using these mechanisms, unintentional data breaches (caused by data migration) of the terms and conditions, which are granted by different owners of various data, national laws and regulations, and organizational rules, are avoided. In addition, by managing the policies in blockchain, and if the REGULATION, COUNTRY, or ORGANIZATION is tampered with by a malicious administrator on a host machine running various VMs, an involuntary migration can be triggered, and an inappropriate movement may occur. Therefore, to prevent malicious data tampering, a method for preventing tampering using blockchain technology was proposed. This method features a robust data protection mechanism.

The proposed mechanism was implemented in a cloud environment by registering the policies regarding VMs and host machines in the blockchain, and the decision of allowing or disallowing a VM live migration in compliance with the policies was evaluated. The execution time of the live migration using the proposed mechanism was also measured, and no overhead cost was observed.

This paper extends our proposed mechanism targeting to container in the edge. In the next section, we introduce the state of the art containers and container migration.

4 Containers and Container Migration

There are several container platforms that implement container migration.

Docker [11] is the de facto standard for containers platform. In 2016, Docker's announcement of the live migration of containers sparked much attention. Since the live migration allows containers to be migrated while processing continues, it has become an essential technology in IoT environments, where edge computing will be the de facto standard in the future. However, Docker still does not offer a pure live migration. It supported migration by Checkpoint/Restore In Userspace (CRIU).

Linux Container (LXC) [12] is a system container, which has replaced KVM and Xen. Different for LXC from Docker, which is intended to run lightweight virtual machines, the image it boots is a full OS image, complete with init and systemd. It supported migration by CRIU and live migration is implemented natively in LXD.

OpenVZ [13] runs on a single kernel, which is shared by multiple VMs on the same machine, and it has the ability to run on multiple Linux systems such as Fedora Core, CentOS, SUSE Linux, and Debian GNU/Linux. Migration functionality is available for kernels 2.6.9 or higher. It supported migration and live migration.

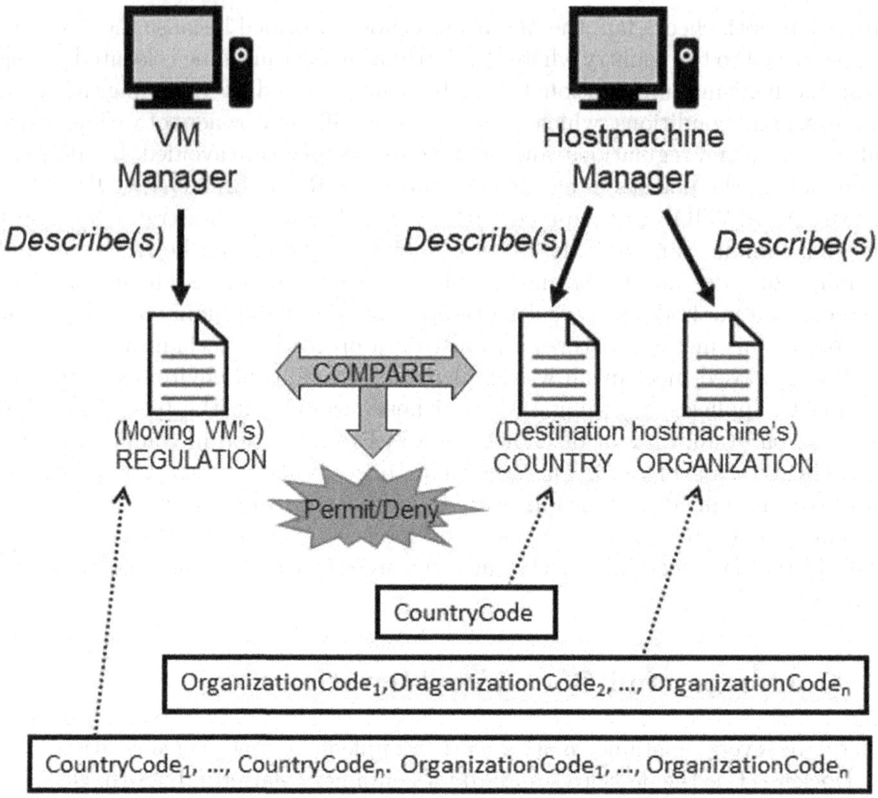

Fig. 3. The data-auditing mechanism for the live migration of VMs

5 Proposed Data-Auditing Policy Mechanism

We considered that improper movement of data is a concern in container migration like VM migration. Therefore, we propose a data-auditing mechanism and its policy during migration targeting containers by extending the policy of the data auditing mechanism for VM. In difference to the VM's host machine, the edge computing device does not have huge resources, and hardware requirements are needed in addition to information such as organization and country. Therefore, our proposed mechanism adds hardware requirements in addition to data audit requirements such as organization and country. A data-auditing operation checks whether it is acceptable to migrate data in the software. A hardware-requirement operation checks whether it is acceptable to migrate data in the hardware. These policies are stored within the container at the edge computing device. The container administrator writes and stores the container, according to the container's application and data conventions within the container. At the edge computing device, the edge computing device administrator describes and stores information similar to that of the edge computing device (Fig. 4). Usually, these written policies are assumed to be unchanged. During container migration, the container policy in the container to be migrated is compared with the policy of the destination edge computing device to determine whether migration is permitted or not. If the destination edge computing device satisfies the requirements of the policy in the container, the migration will be executed.

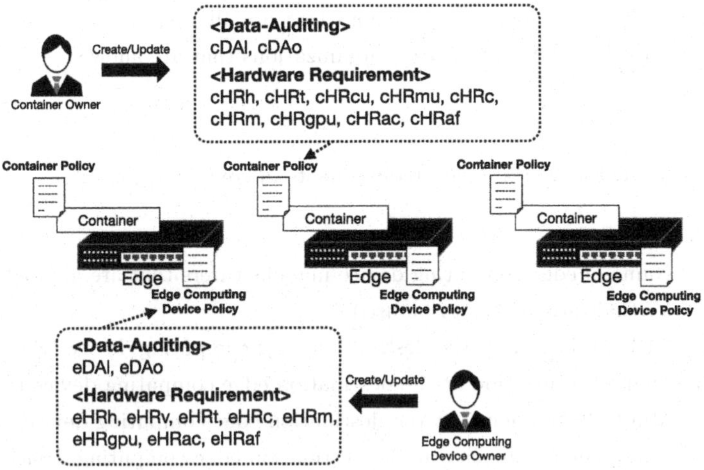

Fig. 4. Container and edge computing device policy allocation.

5.1 Container Policy

This policy establishes rules for determining whether the container created/updated by container owner can be migrated or not. Table 1 shows the elements and description of Data-Auditing in container policy. It has two Data-Auditing policies and nine Hardware Requirement policies. cDAl describes the countries or regions where containers can be placed. cDAo describes the platforms allowed to deploy containers, according to the conventions of the organization managing the containers. Table 2 shows the elements and description of Hardware Requirements in container policy. cHRh describes the allowed edge computing devices; cHRt describes the virtualization tool used by the container; cHRcu describes the CPU utilization threshold of the destination edge computing device; cHRmu describes the memory utilization threshold of the destination edge computing device; cHRc describes the minimum CPU frequency threshold of the destination edge computing device; cHRm describes the minimum memory capacity threshold of the destination edge computing device; cHRgpu describes whether the destination edge computing device must support AI processing; cHRac describes the AI accessor required at the destination edge computing device; cHRb describes the minimum memory capacity threshold of the destination edge computing device; cHRc describes the minimum memory capacity threshold of the destination edge computing device; cHRaf describes the AI framework required at the destination edge computing device.

Table 1. Data-auditing in container policy.

Element	Description
cDAl	Countries or regions that are allowed
cDAo	Administrative organizations that are allowed

Table 2. Hardware requirements in container policy.

Element	Description
cHRh	Name of edge computing device manufacturers that are allowed
cHRt	Virtualization tools to be used
cHRcu	CPU utilization at the destination edge computing device (%)
cHRmu	Memory utilization at the destination edge computing device (%)
cHRc	Min CPU frequency at the destination edge computing device (GHz)
cHRm	Min memory capacity at the destination edge computing device (GB)
cHRgpu	AI support availability the destination edge computing device
cHRac	AI accessor required the destination edge computing device
cHRaf	AI framework required the destination edge computing

5.2 Edge Computing Device Policy

This policy establishes the rules for determining whether the edge computing device which was created/updated by edge computing device owner can be migrated or not. Table 3 shows the elements and description of Data-Auditing in edge computing device policy. It has two Data-Auditing policies and eight Hardware Requirement policies. eDAl describes the country or region where the container is located; eDAo describes the organization managing the container; Table 4 shows the elements and description of Hardware Requirements in edge computing device policy. eHRh describes the manufacturer of the edge computing device; eHRv describes the available edge computing environment (VM or container); eHRt describes the name of the virtualization tool that can be used; eHRc describes the minimum CPU frequency; eHRm describes the edge computing device memory capacity threshold; eHRgpu describes whether AI processing is supported; eHRac describes the available AI accessors; eHRaf describes the available AI frameworks.

Table 3. Data-auditing in edge computing device policy.

Element	Description
eDAl	Country of placement
eDAo	Managing organization

Table 4. Hardware requirements in edge computing device policy.

Element	Description
eHRh	Edge computing device manufacturer name
eHRv	Available environment
eHRt	Available virtualization tools
eHRc	CPU frequency (GHz)
eHRm	Memory capacity (GB)
eHRgpu	AI support
eHRac	Available AI accessors
eHRaf	Available AI frameworks

6 Implementation

In this Section, an edge computing environment consisting of multiple edge computing devices, which are virtually divided into multiple regions, is implemented. All edge computing devices are assumed to run LXC and container-generated applications. In addition, since CRIU is deployed at all edge computing devices, the containers can be migrated among the edge computing devices. Furthermore, the components required to realize the proposed mechanism are assumed to be applied at all edge computing devices. The implementation configuration is shown in Fig. 5.

The implemented edge computing environment consists of eight edge computing devices and four regions. Edge 1 has a container running an application. These edge computing devices are running in an ESXi-6.5.0, which is a high-performance server. The server consists of 20 CPUs (Intel(R) Xeon(R) CPU E5-2660 v3 @ 2.60 GHz, 128 GB memory) and 3.45 TB HDD storage. All edge computing devices are configured with 2 vCPUs, 8 GB memory, 80 GB storage and Ubuntu 20.04 LTS OS. LXC and CRIU are installed and ready to run containers. The container policy for App1 which is running on edge 1 is shown in Table 5. The edge computing device policies are shown in Table 6. These policies are stored on the edge computing device for each row. App1 allows containers to be placed in JP and US. Additionally, it allows containers to be deployed on edge computing devices managed by org1, org3, and org4. This means that Application1 cannot be migrated to Edge 3, Edge 4, Edge 7 and Edge 8.

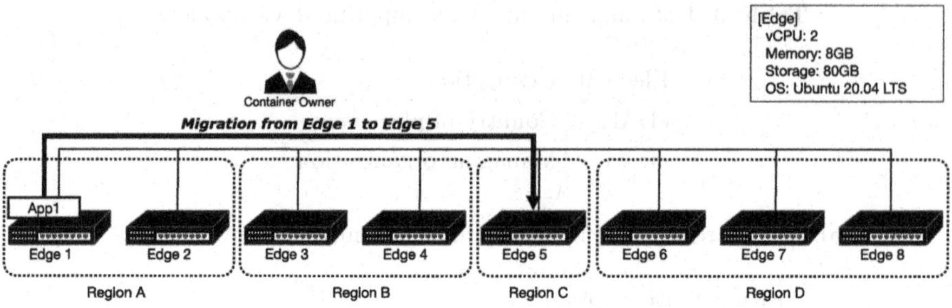

Fig. 5. Edge computing environment implementation configuration.

The execution time is measured when the container is migrated from Edge 1 to Edge 5. The average execution time is the result from ten runs for same migration condition. The difference in execution time with and without the proposed data-auditing mechanism is clearly observed. The case with the data-auditing mechanism is 220 ms. The case without the data-auditing mechanism is 217 ms. The case with the policy mechanism is slower than the case without the policy mechanism. Since the effect of the policy mechanism on the migration time is very minimal. We can say that the proposed data-auditing mechanism is sufficiently practical.

Table 5. Container attributes running on edge 1.

cDAl	cDAo	cHRh	cHRt	cHRcu	cHRmu	cHRc	cHRm	cHRgpu	cHRac	cHRaf
jp us	org1 org3 org4	app1	lcx	40	40	1.6	4	na	na	na

Table 6. Edge device attributes.

	eDAl	eDAo	eHRh	eHRv	eHRt	eHRc	eHRm	eHRgpu	eHRac	eHRaf
Edge 1	jp	org1	edge1	ctr	lxc	2.6	8	na	na	na
Edge 2	jp	org1	edge2	ctr	lxc	2.6	8	na	na	na
Edge 3	de	org2	edge3	ctr	lxc	2.6	8	na	na	na
Edge 4	de	org2	edge4	ctr	lxc	2.6	8	na	na	na
Edge 5	jp	org3	edge5	ctr	lxc	2.6	8	na	na	na
Edge 6	us	org4	edge6	ctr	lxc	2.6	8	na	na	na
Edge 7	us	org5	edge7	ctr	lxc	2.6	8	na	na	na
Edge 8	us	org5	edge8	ctr	lxc	2.6	8	na	na	na

7 Conclusion

In this paper, we focused on containers and container migration in edge computing environments, which have been in a rapidly growing demand in recent years. We proposed a data-auditing mechanism for container migration. Extended policies for VM and created policies for container in the edge. The evaluation of the proposed system in an implemented edge computing environment showed that the addition of the proposed policy mechanism has minimal impact on the migration time. We believe that using the proposed mechanism will reduce incorrect container movement and placement of containers. Therefore, the proposed policy mechanism is sufficiently practical. In the future, we aim to extend our investigation from the very compact and short-range environment examined to a real network extending over a wide area.

Acknowledgement. This work was supported by JSPS KAKENHI Grant Number JP20K19778.

References

1. Puliafito, C., Vallati, C., Mingozzi, E., Merlino, G., Longo, F., Puliafito, A.: Container migration in the fog: a performance evaluation. Sensors **19**(7), 1488 (2019)
2. Deshpande, L., Liu, K.: Edge computing embedded platform with container migration. In: 2017 IEEE SmartWorld, Ubiquitous Intelligence & Computing, Advanced & Trusted Computed, Scalable Computing & Communications, Cloud & Big Data Computing, Internet of People and Smart City Innovation (SmartWorld/SCALCOM/UIC/ATC/CBDCom/IOP/SCI), pp.1–6 (2017)
3. Karhula, P., Janak, J., Schulzrinne, H.: Checkpointing and migration of IoT edge functions. In: Proceedings of the 2nd International Workshop on Edge Systems, Analytics and Networking (EdgeSys 2019), pp. 60–65 (2019)
4. General Data Protection Regulation, GDPR. Accessed April 2022. https://eur-lex.europa.eu/eli/reg/2016/679/oj
5. Nath, S.B., Addya, S.K., Chakraborty, S., Ghosh, S.K.: Container-based service state management in cloud computing. In: 2021 IFIP/IEEE International Symposium on Integrated Network Management (IM), pp. 487–493 (2021)
6. Oleghe, O.: Container placement and migration in edge computing: concept and scheduling models. IEEE Access **9**, 68028–68043 (2021)
7. Ramanathan, S., Kondepu, K., Razo, M., Tacca, M., Valcarenghi, L., Fumagalli, A.: Live migration of virtual machine and container based mobile core network components: a comprehensive study. IEEE Access **9**, 105082–105100 (2021)
8. Uchibayashi, T., et al.: A control mechanism for live migration with data regulations preservation. In: Gervasi, O., et al. (eds.) ICCSA 2017. LNCS, vol. 10404, pp. 509–522. Springer, Cham (2017). https://doi.org/10.1007/978-3-319-62392-4_37
9. Uchibayashi, T., Apduhan, B.O., Shiratori, N., Suganuma, T., Hiji, M.: Policy management technique using blockchain for cloud VM migration. In: IEEE International Conference on Dependable, Autonomic and Secure Computing, International Conference on Pervasive Intelligence and Computing, International Conference on Cloud and Big Data Computing, International Conference on Cyber Science and Technology Congress (DASC/PiCom/CBDCom/CyberSciTech), pp. 360–362 (2019)

10. Uchibayashi, T., Apduhan, B., Suganuma, T., Hiji, M.: A cloud VM migration control mechanism using blockchain. In: Gervasi, O., et al. (eds.) ICCSA 2020. LNCS, vol. 12252, pp. 221–235. Springer, Cham (2020). https://doi.org/10.1007/978-3-030-58811-3_16
11. Home - Docker. Accessed April 2022. https://www.docker.com/
12. Middelkamp, A.: Online. Praktische Huisartsgeneeskunde **3**(4), 3–3 (2017). https://doi.org/10.1007/s41045-017-0040-y
13. Open source container-based virtualization for Linux. Accessed April 2022. https://openvz.org/

A Framework of an RL-Based Task Offloading Mechanism for Multi-users in Edge Computing

Shintaro Ide and Bernady O. Apduhan(✉)

Graduate School of Information Science, Kyushu Sangyo University, Fukuoka, Japan
bob@is.kyusan-u.ac.jp

Abstract. In recent years, the Internet of Things (IoT) has been growing rapidly, and new applications using the IoT includes autonomous driving systems, mobile health, smart homes, VR/AR technologies, and many more. While IoT applications plays important roles in enriching our lives, the size of each generated task is increasing compared to tasks generated by traditional mobile devices, which can cause high latency when deployed in traditional cloud computing. Edge computing has emerged as a method to mitigate this problem. Edge computing can provide services with lower latency than conventional cloud computing methods because the tasks are processed in the vicinity of the user's device. However, when the tasks are concentrated in one of the distributed servers, the low processing power of these servers becomes a bottleneck and high latency may occur.

In this paper, we proposed a deep reinforcement learning based offloading mechanism in an edge computing environment which can dynamically offload a task based on the performance and availability of nearby edge servers. Preliminary experiment results are promising and offered insights on related issues.

Keywords: Edge computing · Deep reinforcement learning · Task offloading

1 Introduction

Over the past decade, mobile communication systems have evolved from the 3rd and 4th generation (3G and 4G) to today's 5th generation (5G). 5G networks are characterized by extremely high speed, high capacity, low latency, and multiple simultaneous connections compared to previous generations of mobile communication systems. It is said that 5G networks will become a social infrastructure to further develop and promote the spread of existing IoT devices and applications. Examples of IoT devices or applications that are expected to develop in the future include VR/AR devices, mobile health, autonomous driving systems, and a wide range of other fields [1]. However, these intelligent devices and applications can only be realized by processing huge amounts of data in real time, which poses a great challenge for servers and network bandwidth.

In conventional cloud computing systems, data generated from edge devices such as IoT devices are processed by high-performance servers in a cloud data center. However, when the physical distance between the data source and the server is far, high latency is likely to occur [2]. Edge computing systems have emerged as a new technology to meet

O. Gervasi et al. (Eds.): ICCSA 2022 Workshops, LNCS 13379, pp. 103–114, 2022.
https://doi.org/10.1007/978-3-031-10545-6_8

the needs of real-time and low latency requirements. By distributing edge servers with a certain amount of computational power near the edge devices, edge computing can significantly reduce the response time for requested tasks and also reduce the load on cloud data centers. Edge computing is attracting attention as the next-generation computing paradigm. However, to operate it efficiently, it is necessary to consider task allocation and offloading. Task offloading here refers to uploading computationally intensive applications that cannot be processed by the local edge server and have the other server take over the processing. In general, the following cases can be considered as types of task offloading.

1. Local Execution
   It completes all tasks generated by the edge devices using only its own computational power.
2. Full Offloading
   All the generated tasks are offloaded to other edge servers, and the processing is completed by the computational power of these edge servers.
3. Partial Offloading
   Part of the task is processed locally, and the rest is offloaded to another edge server. This can be done only when the tasks can be divided.

In this paper, we study a dynamic task offloading mechanism for efficient edge computing system operation. To achieve dynamic task distribution, this paper employs reinforcement learning, which is one of the machine learning methods. Each edge device is modeled as a Markov Decision Process, and a task offloading algorithm based on multitasking and load balancing is proposed.

2 Related Work

For efficient task offloading, it is necessary to consider when, where, and to what extent tasks should be offloaded. Several studies have already been done on the optimal task offloading strategy for different scenarios.

Gao et al. developed a cooperative computing system consisting of mobile devices, edge cloud and central cloud and designed a Q-Learning based task offloading policy for optimal resource allocation and offloading based on it [3].

Mochizuki et al. focused on mobile data offloading, which is an effort by telecommunication carriers to meet the increasing demand for mobile data communications. They propose a mobile data offloading method based on distributed deep reinforcement learning [4], in contrast to the temporal offloading of existing methods (Mobile Data Offloading Protocol) to maximize bandwidth utilization efficiency.

Shino et al. proposed an autonomous distributed task offloading method in which applications autonomously determine the optimal execution node and offload tasks to provide distributed processing that can cope with the increasing number of moving applications and topology changes among nodes in edge computing environments [5].

These studies are like our work in that they adapt reinforcement learning-based algorithms for optimal task assignment and task offloading for user devices in edge computing environments. On the other hand, they only make discrete behavioral decisions for task offloading and do not support handling continuous variables that allow detailed parameter decisions. In this study, we propose a method to solve not only the discrete problem of deciding which server to offload to and determining task allocation, but also the continuous problem of making detailed decisions on migration bandwidth and other parameters during offloading.

3 System Model

In this paper, the tasks are generated from multiple user devices e = {1, 2, 3…}. Here, we assume a general edge computing scenario where tasks are generated by multiple user devices e = {1, 2, 3…, n} and processed by multiple edge servers E = {1, 2, 3…, N} as shown in Fig. 1. Each user device ranges from common computing devices such as desktop and laptop computers to web cameras and wearable devices used for mobile health monitoring. Each of these devices generates a different size of demanding tasks.

In addition, the computing power of user devices themselves varies. If a user device chooses to offload a task to an edge server, each user device thinks only of its own benefit and tries to offload the task to the edge server with the highest computational power. However, even a high-performance edge server cannot process all these tasks in real time due to its limited computing power. It may not be able to allocate the necessary resources in time, which may cause a large delay.

Therefore, task offloading in edge computing environments is important to balance the distribution of tasks and to increase the utilization rate of each edge server to a certain value.

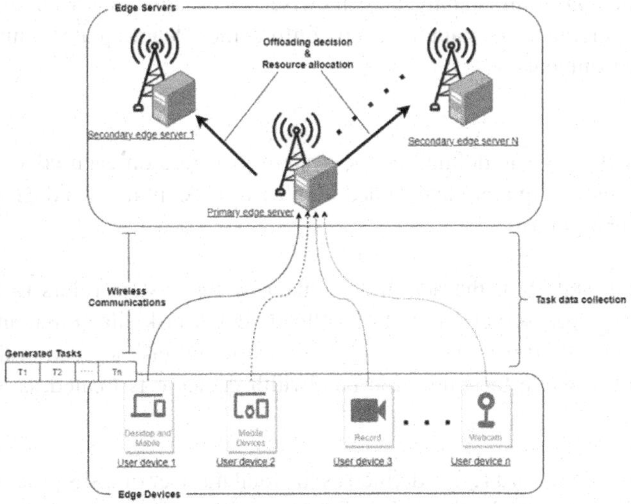

Fig. 1. An RL-based task offloading mechanism in edge computing

The Proposed Method

Deep Q-Network (DQN), a deep reinforcement learning algorithm, is one of the most effective methods for task offloading in edge computing environments. DQN is a useful method for complex resource allocation problems and high-dimensional state spaces, but it does not address the problem of continuous action spaces, and action decisions must always be made using discrete values.

In this paper, we proposed a task offloading mechanism that makes continuous action decisions in a single-agent scenario with a primary edge server as an agent. Deep Deterministic Policy Gradient (DDPG), a deep reinforcement learning algorithm based on the Actor-Critic model, is employed to realize complex decision making by the agent.

4 Reinforcement Learning – A Recap

Reinforcement learning [6, 7] is a machine learning method. It is characterized by the fact that the system itself achieves optimal system control through trial and error. It differs from supervised learning in that it does not require artificial labeling of the teacher data (correct answer data). In reinforcement learning, the computer learns behaviors to maximize the reward set as the objective in a certain environment. After a certain number of trials, it is possible to learn a policy that maximizes the long-term reward for the current environment. Furthermore, by combining this method with deep learning, it is possible to adapt to high-dimensional states and behaviors, which greatly improves the learning efficiency.

In this paper, we use deep reinforcement learning for efficient resource allocation for optimal task offloading in edge computing environments. In reinforcement learning, the dynamics of the environment are typically modeled by a Markov Decision Process (MDP), and the algorithm is analyzed. Likewise, we establish the MDP and define the following three elements to adapt the deep reinforcement learning algorithm to the edge computing environment.

- **State**
  The current state S_t is defined as the system load rate on each edge server. Each edge server queues up a predetermined number of tasks in its own data structure and processes them in turn.
- **Action**
  In the current state S_t, the action A_t taken by the system refers to the decision of the primary edge server on the task offload vector, task allocation, and migration bandwidth during offload. The task offload vector and task allocation decisions are discrete values, while the migration bandwidth decision is treated as a continuous value.
- **Reward**
  The system-wide reward R_t is defined as the total number of tasks processed by each edge server for each trial episode in reinforcement learning.

4.1 Markov Decision Process (MDP)

MDP is a stochastic model of a dynamic system in which state transitions occur stochastically, and in which state transitions satisfy Markovianity. Markovianity means that the transition to the next state depends only on the current state and action but is independent of earlier states and actions. By modeling the representation of time-series state transitions in reinforcement learning with MDPs, we can maximize the cumulative reward by simply finding the value function applied by the MDP [8].

4.2 Value Function

In reinforcement learning, the reward is a measure of the immediate goodness or badness of an action chosen from the current state, but the decision to act must consider the reward that will come later. In reinforcement learning, the cumulative reward obtained over a period is called the revenue. There are several types of revenue, but the most used revenue is the discounted cumulative reward which is expressed by discounting the value of the reward to be obtained later, as shown in Eq. (1).

$$G_t = \sum_{\tau=0}^{\infty} \gamma^{\tau} R_{t+1+\tau} 0 < \gamma < 1 \tag{1}$$

The sum of the discounted rewards is the sum of the rewards for a given interval, and the content of the interaction is determined stochastically depending on the state at the start of the interval. As a result, the revenue also becomes a value that varies stochastically. Therefore, the expected value of the revenue is obtained conditionally on the state, and the expected value is called the state value, which is used as an index for defining a good strategy.

The state value is the sum of the rewards for continuing to take actions according to the strategy π, starting from the state S_t, and can be expressed as in Eq. (2).

$$V^{\pi}(s) = \mathbb{E}_{\pi}\left[G_{t+1} | S_t = s\right] \tag{2}$$

The best strategy is called the optimal strategy π^* and is given by Eq. (3).

$$V^{*}(s) = V^{\pi^*}(s) = maxV^{\pi}(s) \tag{3}$$

Here, V^* (s) is called the optimal state value function. To improve convenience when making action decisions, we use a function called the action value function, which adds actions to the conditions in Eq. (3) above. The action value function represents the value of each action A_t in each state S_t, as shown in Eq. (4).

$$Q^{\pi}(s, a) = \mathbb{E}_{\pi}\left[G_{t+1} | S_t = s, A_t = a\right] \tag{4}$$

4.3 Deterministic Policy Gradient (DPG)

Deterministic policy gradient is a reinforcement learning algorithm presented by Silver et al. in 2014 [9]. The DPG algorithm is a policy gradient-based algorithm, which models the policy with parameter θ and performs direct optimization. The DPG algorithm uses a reinforcement learning approach called Actor-Critic, which is described later.

4.4 Actor-Critic

The DPG algorithm is a reinforcement learning algorithm based on the Actor-Critic model, which has a separate structure for representing policies, independent of the value function, as shown in Fig. 2. The structure that represents the policy is called an Actor, because it is used to select actions, and is expressed as Eq. (5), because it is a function of deterministic measures whose actions are deterministic for a given state.

$$\mu(s|\theta^{\mu}) \tag{5}$$

Here, θ^{μ} is a parameter of the measure function μ.

The part that predicts the value function is called Critic because it critiques the actions chosen by the Actor [10]. Critic is synonymous with the action value function and is therefore expressed as in Eq. (6).

$$Q(s, a|\theta^{Q}) \tag{6}$$

where θ^{Q} is a parameter of the action value function Q.

Since the strategy μ only needs to learn to maximize the current value, we can optimize θ^{μ} using the gradient shown in Eq. (7).

$$\begin{aligned}\nabla_{\theta^{\mu}} J &\approx \mathbb{E}\left[\nabla_{\theta^{\mu}} Q(s, a|\theta^{Q})|_{s=s_t, a=\mu(s|\theta^{\mu})}\right] \\ &= \mathbb{E}\left[\nabla_{\theta^{\mu}} Q(s, a|\theta^{Q})|_{s=s_t, a=\mu(s_t)} \nabla_{\theta^{\mu}} \mu(s|\theta^{\mu})|_{s=s_t}\right]\end{aligned} \tag{7}$$

In addition, the action value function Q can be defined as the error function in Eq. (8) from the Bellman equation [11], which holds for action values.

$$\begin{aligned} L(\theta^{Q}) &= \mathbb{E}\left[(Q(s, a|\theta^{Q}) - y_t)^2\right] \\ \textit{where } y_t &= r(s_t, a_t) + \gamma Q(s_{t+1}, \mu(s_{t+1})|\theta^{Q})\end{aligned} \tag{8}$$

The behavioral value function Q can be optimized by learning to minimize the error function calculated in Eq. (4) above.

As described above, in the DPG algorithm, the optimal strategy function μ^* can be obtained by simultaneously optimizing the parameter θ^{μ} of the strategy function μ and the parameter θ^{Q} of the action value function Q during the learning process.

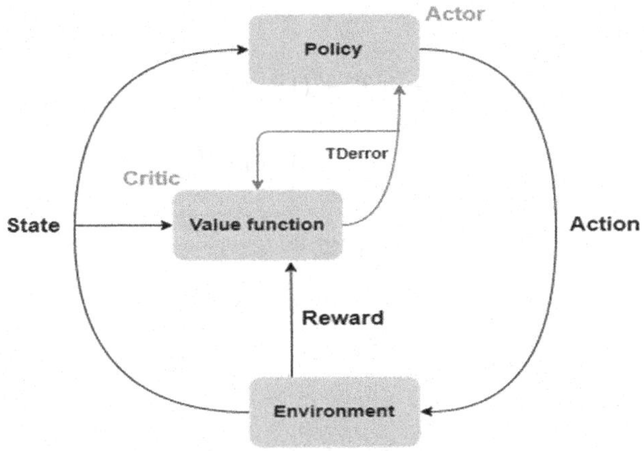

Fig. 2. Overview of actor-critic

5 Deep Reinforcement Learning

Deep reinforcement learning refers to the use of neural networks for function approximation of the value function and the policy function in reinforcement learning. In conventional reinforcement learning, linear functions are used to approximate the functions of value and policy functions. In addition, the design of the features requires human intervention. In deep reinforcement learning, however, the neural network designs the features, eliminating the need for human intervention. In addition, it was confirmed that deep reinforcement learning can significantly outperform conventional reinforcement learning simply by providing the environment directly as input [12, 13].

5.1 Deep Deterministic Policy Gradient (DDPG)

The first innovation is a method called Experience Replay [15], proposed by L. Lin in 1992. Experience Replay is a method of learning by memorizing the past actions of an agent and randomly selecting multiple memorized actions at regular intervals. This method is called Experience Replay. The number of randomly selected actions is called the batch size. By learning randomly in this way, it is possible to control the bias of the samples and to learn the same training data repeatedly, thus improving the efficiency of sample usage.

The second innovation is the fixed target Q-network. In a strategy-gradient type reinforcement learning algorithm such as DDPG, the parameters of each function are updated in the direction of optimizing the strategy function and the action value function. The fixed target Q-network can stabilize the learning by updating some parameters instead of the whole parameters. The fixed target Q-network can stabilize the learning by updating some parameters instead of the whole parameters.

The fixed target Q-network can stabilize learning by updating some of the parameters instead of updating the entire parameters. Let θ^{μ} and θ^{Q} be the parameters of the strategy function and action value function before the update, respectively, and $\theta^{\mu'}$ and $\theta^{Q'}$ after the update (Fig. 3).

$$\theta^{\mu'} \leftarrow \tau\theta^{\mu} + (1-\tau)\theta^{\mu'}$$

$$\theta^{Q'} \leftarrow \tau\theta^{Q} + (1-\tau)\theta^{Q'}$$

$$\tau \ll 1 \tag{9}$$

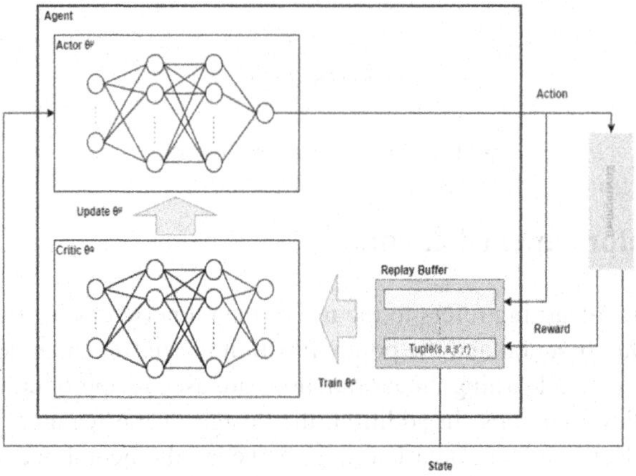

Fig. 3. The DDPG architecture

6 Experiments

In this paper, we conduct experiments to evaluate whether the task offloading mechanism learns according to the DDPG algorithm and allocates tasks to the optimal edge servers.

6.1 Experiment Methods

The simulation experiment was conducted on a virtual edge computing environment. The open-source CRAWDAD mobility dataset was used as the training dataset. This dataset shows mobility devices such as smartphones and wearable devices generating tasks at regular intervals, as shown in Fig. 4. In this experiment, we evaluate the proposed model by observing the offloading of data from this mobility dataset to multiple edge servers and measuring the rewards obtained from the environment. First, the simulations were performed with parameters such as the number of edge servers and the number of user terminals. Next, we simulate the task offloading process using a task offloading mechanism based on the DDPG algorithm. Three patterns were assumed here, i.e., 30, 50, and 80 edge devices, to evaluate the generality of the model. The parameters for each simulation are shown in Table 1. The number of training trials varies dynamically depending on the training status of the model. The specification is that if the reward obtained from the environment does not increase by the specified number of episodes, learning terminates at that point. In addition, in one episode, the movement of mobility data is divided into 3000 steps and executed. The reward defined in Sect. 5 was used as the evaluation index.

Table 1. Simulation parameters

Parameter	Value
Number of user devices (e)	50
Number of edge servers (E)	10
Maximum number of server processes (f)	5
Generation task size (r)	0–50 MB
Migration bandwidth (b)	0–1 Gbps
Number of training episodes (ep)	130
Number of steps in each episode (st)	3000
Experience replay buffer size (mem_cap)	10000
Learning rate for critic network (lr_c)	1.0×10^{-3}
Learning rate for actor network (lr_a)	2.0×10^{-3}
Bach size (batch)	32
Soft update rate for target network (tau)	1.0×10^{-2}

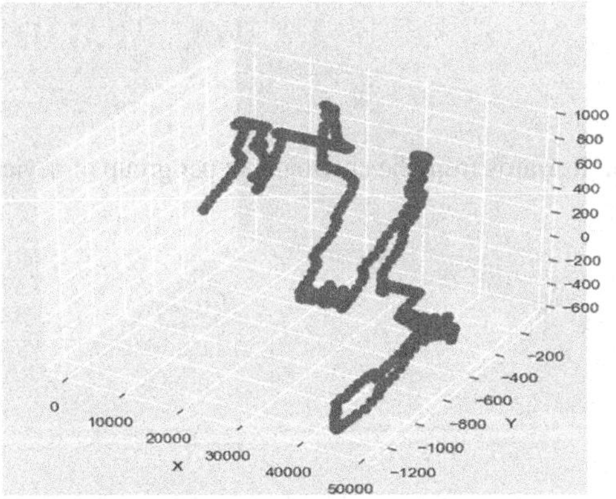

Fig. 4. The CRAWDAD mobility dataset

6.2 Experiment Results

Using the set parameters, we conducted a task offloading experiment and observed the changes in the reward obtained from the environment. The results are shown in Figs. 5 and 6.

Number of user devices	Results
30	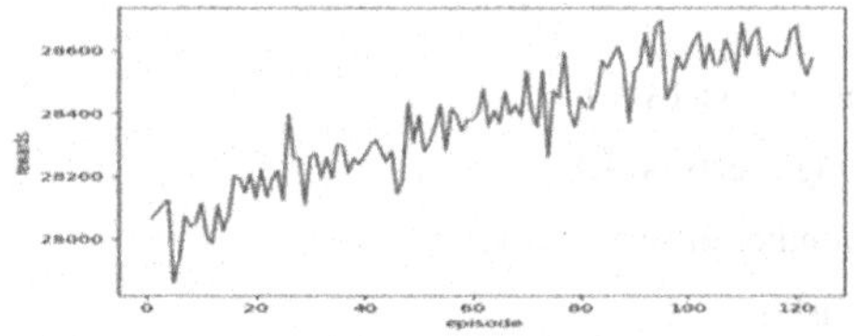
50	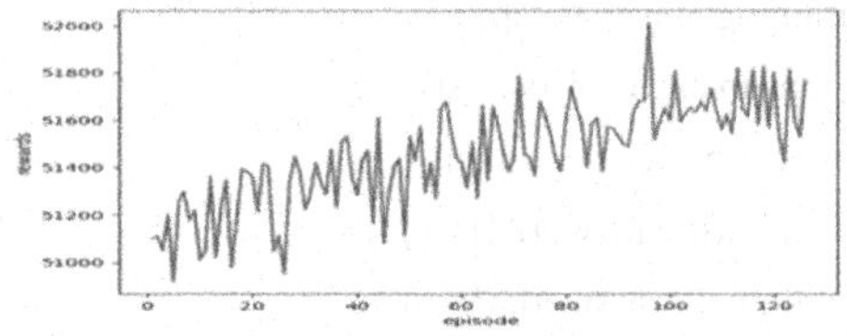
80	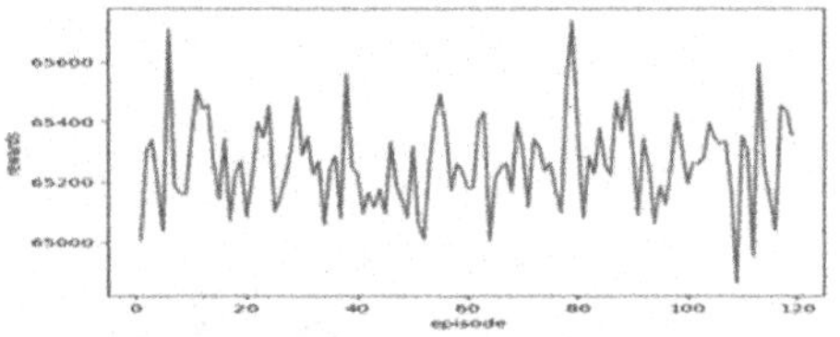

Fig. 5. Rewards from the environment per group of devices.

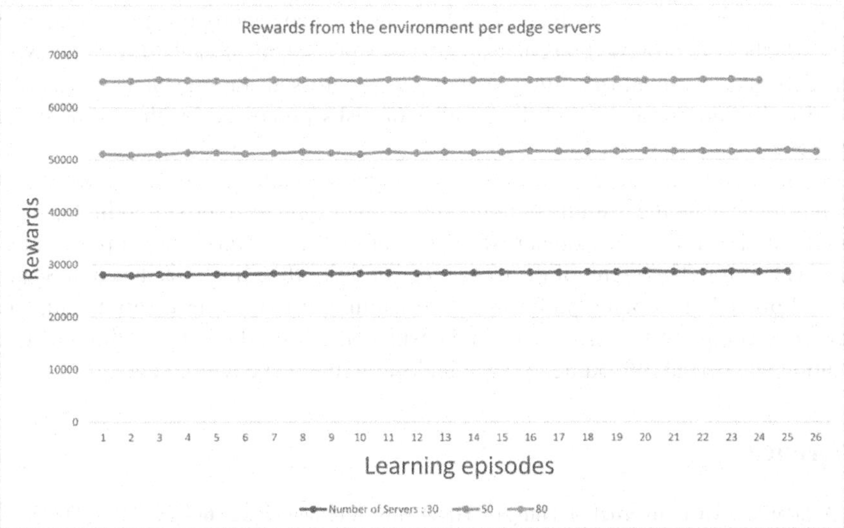

Fig. 6. Rewards from the environment per group of devices (another view)

6.3 Discussion of Results

From Fig. 5 of the experimental results, the number of system-wide task processes set as rewards varied with the learning episodes. We will look at the patterns in order of the number of user devices, starting with the lowest number. In an environment with 30 user devices, the reward tends to increase continuously, which indicates that the proposed mechanism in the environment can offload tasks to the edge server appropriately for the user devices. The same is true for the case of 50 user devices, but we can observe that the range of rewards is lower than in the case of 30 user devices. This may indicate that some episodes may have dropped out because they could not offload the task appropriately. Finally, in the case of the 80 user devices, some episodes may have high rewards, but the overall rewards are highly variable, and it is difficult to say that the rewards are on an increasing trend. This may be due to too many user devices offloading tasks relative to the number of edge servers in the experimental environment. Since all edge servers in this environment have the same performance and the number of tasks that can be processed is fixed, it is practically impossible to efficiently process too many tasks. This issue needs to be addressed in future experiments and find a solution.

7 Concluding Remarks

In this paper, we described an optimal offloading mechanism for multi-users in edge computing. Specifically, using the DDPG algorithm, which is a method of deep reinforcement learning. We define multiple user devices in the edge computing environment as agents and proposed a mechanism to offload the generated task data to the optimal edge server according to the DDPG algorithm.

In our experiments, we built and simulated a virtual edge computing environment to verify whether the proposed mechanism allocates tasks appropriately. From the experimental results, we confirmed that as learning progressed, the mechanism started to offload tasks appropriately, and the number of tasks processed by the entire system increased.

As future work, it is necessary to conduct comparison experiments with other existing methods to evaluate the usefulness of the offloading mechanism proposed in this paper. In addition, the current environment does not consider the computational power of the user device itself. Therefore, of the three types of task offloading introduced in Sect. 1, only full offloading is being performed. In the future, it will be necessary to construct a new edge computing environment that considers the two offloading methods of local execution and partial offloading to make it closer to the real environment.

References

1. Ashton, K.: That "Internet of Things." Thing Adv. Internet Things **6**(4), 97–101 (2009)
2. Buyya, R., Yeo, C.S., Venugopal, S., Broberg, J., Brandic, I.: Cloud computing and emerging IT platforms: vision, hype, and reality for delivering computing as the 5th utility. Future Gener. Comput. Syst. **25**(6), 599–616 (2009)
3. Gao, Z., Hao, W., Han, Z., Yang, S.: Q-learning-based task offloading and resources optimization for a collaborative computing system. IEEE Access **8**, 149011–149024 (2020)
4. Mochizuki, D., Abiko, Y., Mineno, H., Saito, T., Ikeda, D., Katagiri, M.: Deep reinforcement learning-based method of mobile data offloading. In: 2018 Eleventh International Conference on Mobile Computing and Ubiquitous Network (ICMU), No. 18493208, Auckland, New Zealand, 5–8 October (2018)
5. Shino, Y., Sasai, K., Kitagata, G., Kinoshita, T.: Edge computing using autonomous decentralized task offload. IPSJ Res. Rep. **2017-MBL-85**(26), 1–7 (2017)
6. Sutton, R.S., Barto, A.G.: Reinforcement Learning: An Introduction. The MIT Press, Cambridge (2014, 2015)
7. Makino, T., et al.: Future Strengthening Learning. Morikita Publishing (October 2016)
8. Kimura, G.: Basics of Reinforcement Learning. J-STAGE **52**(1), 72–77 (2013)
9. Silver, D., Lever, G., Heess, N., Degris, T., Wierstra, D., Riedmiller, M.: Deterministic policy gradient algorithms. In: 31st International Conference on Machine Learning, vol. 32, pp. 387–395 (June 2014)
10. Geron, A. (Author), Shimoda, R. (Translation), Nagao, T. (Translation): Practical Machine Learning with Scikit-Learn, Keras, TensorFlow. O'Reilly, Japan (October 2020). (Translated in Japanese)
11. Szepesvari, C. (Author), Oyamada, S. (Editor), Maeda, S., Koyama, M. (Translation): Algorithms for Reinforcement Learning Rapid Learning-Basic Theory and Algorithms, pp. 8–12, Kyoritsu Shuppan, Tokyo (July 2017)
12. Volodymvr, M., et al.: Playing Atari with Deep Reinforcement Learning. arXiv: 1312.5602 (2013)
13. Volodymvr, M., et al.: Human-level control through deep reinforcement learning. Nature **518**, 529–533 (2015)
14. Lillicrap, T.P., et al.: Continuous control with Deep Reinforcement Learning. arXiv: 1509.02971 (July 2019). (latest version)
15. Long-Ji, L.: Reinforcement Learning for Robots Using Neural Networks. No. CMU-CS-93–103, Carnegie-Mellon University PA School of Computer Science (1993)

International Workshop on Geodesign in Decision Making: Meta Planning and Collaborative Design for Sustainable and Inclusive Development (GDM 2022)

Geodesign Experience in Florianópolis Metropolitan Region: Practical Planning with Different Professional Backgrounds

Francisco Henrique de Oliveira[1(✉)], Julia Cararo Lazaro[1], Ana Clara Mourão Moura[2], Maria Carolina Soares[1], and Guilherme Braghirolli[3]

[1] Universidade do Estado de Santa Catarina (UDESC), Av. Me. Benvenuta, 2007, Florianópolis, Brazil
francisco.oliveira@udesc.br

[2] Universidade Federal de Minas Gerais (UFMG), Rua Paraíba 697, Belo Horizonte, Brazil
anaclara@ufmg.br

[3] Instituto Federal de Educação, Ciência e Tecnologia de Santa Catarina (IFSC), Av. Mauro Ramos, 950, Florianópolis, Brazil

Abstract. The work shows an application of Geodesign for metropolitan region of Florianópolis, at Santa Catarina state, Brazil, with focus on reducing carbon emissions considering the future scenarios of 2035 and 2050. The research took place with students from the discipline of Multipurpose Land Registry and Territorial Planning related to doctoral course of the Post-Graduate Program in Territorial Planning and Social-environmental Development (*Programa de Pós-Graduação em Planejamento Territorial e Desenvolvimento Socioambiental – PPGPLAN*) from the State University of Santa Catarina - UDESC in the year 2021. The students had different training and performances, but all to a greater or lesser degree had experience in urban planning, with 25% knowing the methods and concepts of Geodesign. Due to the conditions of social distancing imposed by the COVID-19 pandemic, the lessons activities took place remotely. Four official weekly meetings and also daily communication were established to carry on the activities, which were performed by WhatsApp, email or even by extra on-line meeting. To assist decision-making on the GISColab Platform, a spreadsheet was created using Excel software that ensured the organization and systematization of proposals, as well as supporting the spatialization of policies and projects. Due to the students' professional experience, the biggest challenge was shown in the proposition of ideas that corroborated with the initial goal, that was especially focused on territorial planning integrated in multifactorial parameters. In this sense, remote meetings fulfilled the role of initiating remote participatory discussion, sharing ideas and decisions for proposals adopted and approved in groups, but revealed the lack of specialized critical thinking, difficulties in developing territorial planning and defending ideas based on action and reaction that GISColab platform provides.

Keywords: Geodesign · Geoprocessing · Territorial planning · Co-creation

O. Gervasi et al. (Eds.): ICCSA 2022 Workshops, LNCS 13379, pp. 117–131, 2022.
https://doi.org/10.1007/978-3-031-10545-6_9

1 Introduction

The article shows the application process of the Geodesign Workshop based on the study area of the Metropolitan Region of Florianópolis, located at Santa Catarina State, in the south of Brazil (which in the study will be called MRSC). The study was part of a national proposal in which 13 researches groups were invited to analyze different metropolitan regions - in which they are partner, using the Geodesign method. The proposal, among others, had the challenge of inciting actions that would help in the maintenance of areas with vegetation, thus collaborating for the creation of carbon credits.

The main objective for this study was to plan the green future area to Florianópolis Region until 2050 - in this case three scenarios was planned. The first one was Scenario A: "Early Adopter" – in which initial innovations were considered, resulting in changes in 2035 and 2050; for Scenario B: "Late Adopter" – in which it was considered wait until 2035, to then adopt innovations that can lead to changes in 2025; and Scenario C: "Non Adopter" – in which no innovation was adopted, allowing for unplanned changes for 2050. Therefore, for this experiment three scenario changes were planned focusing on increasing the Carbon Credit to at least 30% more until 2050 – but clearly it was an obligation to increase the green area surface for the Florianópolis Region. Thus, the basic tool for planning the three future scenarios, as well as discussing, proposing new green áreas and also considering the United Nations Sustainable Development Goals was the Geodesign platform environment.

1.1 Study Area

For the study of MRSC the workshop was applied with the group of students of PhD course related to Postgraduate Program in Territorial Planning and Socioenvironmental Development - PPGPLAN, from the State University of Santa Catarina - UDESC.

The MRSC is one of the main centers of the technological industry (game software) in Brazil, mainly Florianópolis, where tourism, civil construction, commerce and the service sector also stand out. In the neighboring cities, mainly São José, Palhoça and Biguaçu, there is a diversified and growing industrial pole, in addition to important areas of services and business. Beyond that, most municipalities in the expansion area present themselves as important areas for agriculture. As for the relief, the region has a predominant area on coastal plain, which includes the coastal part and the mountainous region, with vegetation from the Atlantic Forest biome and still restinga (sandbank) and mangrove vegetation.

There is a strong contrast between the coastal area totally dense by buildings and real estate exploration, in contrast to the continental area, which has a predominantly rugged relief and has a predominance of tree cover with vegetation exuberance. The studied area is composed of 22 municipalities, but the actual Metropolitan Region of Florianópolis comprises 9 municipalities with a population of 1,050,000 inhabitants living in an area of 2,700 km^2, with the other 13 municipalities belonging to the Metropolitan Expansion Area (Table 1 and Fig. 1).

Notoriously, this is one of the regions with the best life quality level in the country, the Metropolitan Region of Florianópolis has the highest HDI (Human Development Index) of 0.840, among all metropolitan regions in Brazil [2].

Table 1. Municipalities from RMSC [1].

Municipalities of the Metropolitan Region of Greater Florianópolis	Águas Mornas, Antônio Carlos, Biguaçu, Florianópolis, Governador Celso Ramos, Palhoça, Santo Amaro da Imperatriz, São José, São Pedro de Alcântara
Municipalities in the Greater Florianópolis Metropolitan Expansion Area	Alfredo Wagner, Angelina, Anitápolis, Canelinha, Garopaba, Leoberto Leal, Major Gercino, Nova Trento, Paulo Lopes, Rancho Queimado, São Bonifácio, São João Batista, Tijucas

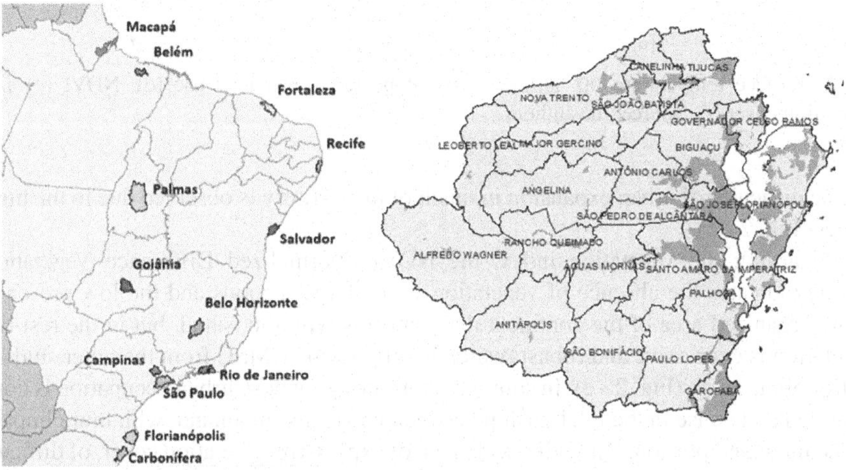

Fig. 1. The Metropolitan Region of Florianópolis (RMSC) in Brazil and other case studies in Brazil, and the municipalities of MRSC. Source: the authors.

When analyzing the set of maps on the study area, it is initially necessary to observe that the area is composed of a large island (54 km of length and 18 km width), in the municipality of Florianópolis, capital of the state of Santa Catarina, and by a significant urbanized area on the continent, corresponding to the connection with the island (Fig. 2 - d). However, in the rest of the region there is low occupation and significant vegetation cover, composed of Atlantic Forest (Fig. 2 - f).

The surface temperature has a greater impact in the central area of the island and in urban area of the continent in connection with the island, being mild in the regions of higher altitude (east–west axis to the south of the continent) and in unoccupied valleys (Fig. 2 - a). The topography is composed of the low altimetry on the island and the portion of the continent close to the island, with an east–west mountain range in the south of the continent (Fig. 2 – b). The slopes are low and favorable to use, but with the challenges of containing the risks of flooding on the edge of the island's mainland,

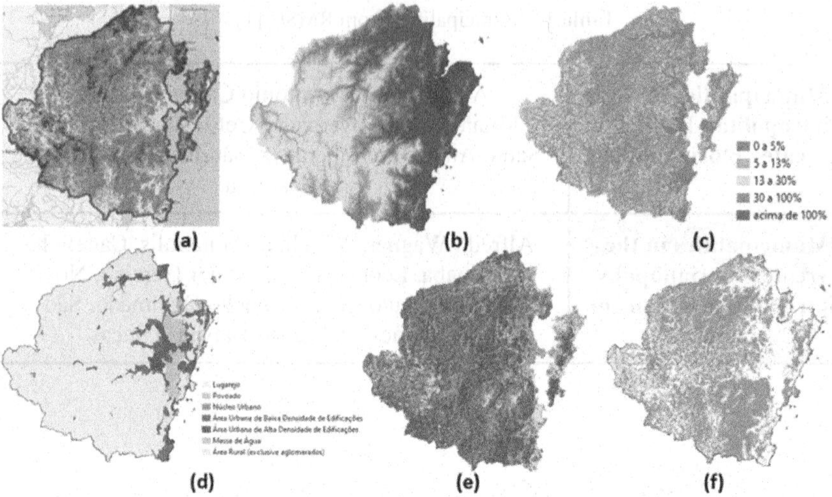

Fig. 2. Surface temperature (a), altimetry (b), slope (c), urban land use (d), NDVI (e) and vegetation cover (f). Source: the authors.

but the difficulty of urban expansion in much of the territory is observed due to the high slopes (Fig. 2 - c).

Regarding the vegetation index, the NDVI (Normalized Difference Vegetation Cover) indicates the absence of vegetation in the large lagoons and the low presence in the urbanized area of the continent that connects with the island, but in the rest the vegetation is expressive and robust, which highlights the RMSC from the other studied metropolitan areas (Fig. 2 - e). In summary, it is an area whose urban occupation is concentrated and dense in the relationship between island and mainland, with more impact on the mainland portion, but with a wide area of expressive vegetation cover, of difficult urban occupation due to slope barriers.

The distribution of commerce and service activities (Fig. 3 - a) demonstrate the importance of the mainland area connected to the island (Biguaçu, Palhoça and São José), and the same can be seen in the health services map (Fig. 3 - b), accessibility and capillarity (Fig. 3 - c). It is observed that the density of roads, in the accessibility and capillarity map, is even more expressive in this portion of the continent than on the island (Fig. 3 - c). As observed in the previous cartographic collection, the remainder is a large void, except for the axis that connects Canelinha to São João Batista and Nova Trento (north portion) and the Palhoça axis to Santo Amaro da Imperatriz (central portion). In this sense, the planning needs to consider the densification in the areas of the island's connection with the mainland and in these incipient axes of growth.

It is worth mentioning the fragility in the supply of sanitation, with the presence of water network only in the mentioned areas (Fig. 3 - d) and many limitations in the sewage network (Fig. 3 - e). It is worth noting the importance of the island area in terms of the presence of cultural and archaeological heritage, as well as the presence of indigenous land in the mainland area. (Fig. 3 - f).

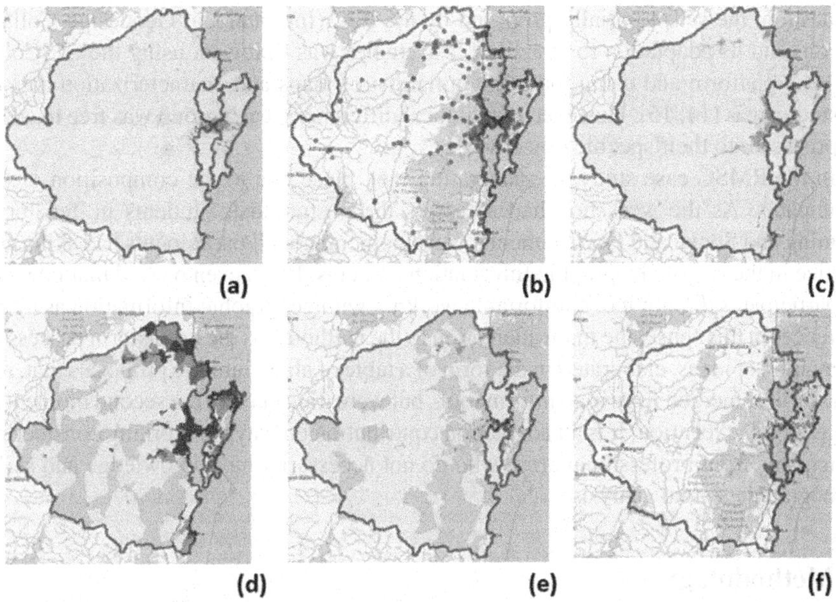

Fig. 3. Commerce and services (a), health services (b), accessibility and capillarity (c), water services (d), sanitation (e) and cultural and archeological heritage (f). Source: the authors.

The development of the study had two purposes: a) to enable the participating students to carry out a geodesign study, while expanding their knowledge about the territory of the RMSC; b) collaborate with studies on a national scale on 13 metropolitan regions in Brazil, by verifying the reproducibility of the geodesign methodological process.

1.2 Geodesign

The Project that planned the study of Brazilian metropolitan regions, was entitled: "Geodesign Brazil, Trees for Metropolitan Regions". The idea was to use the Geodesign method in a standard, simultaneous format that would allow the application in different scenarios but with a standard in the type of data used as well as in the applied methodology.

Geodesign is a methodological process that explores the potential of geospatial technologies, Geographic Information Systems and their web-based resources, for co-creation processes in shared planning. Its structure is a work framework that starts with the consumption of data, which are translated into information and generate knowledge about the area of study. As it has a geographical base, it explores geovisualization resources and access to different actors in society, so that participatory planning actually takes place [3–8].

The basis of Geodesign is the proposition of a work framework, in which steps and objectives to be accomplished, actors and teams of participants, decision support, goals to be met, negotiation and results evaluation methods are specified. In the case study in question, the script initially proposed by the IGC (International Geodesign Collaboration) and its adaptation to Brazilian case studies was followed, using the GISColab (UFMG) platform and using the same initial list of maps and characterization data of the study areas [14, 15]. However, due to local differences, each group was free to adapt the processes to their specific objectives.

In the RMSC case study, the adaptation took place due to the composition of the participants. As the workshop had as actors the postgraduate students in Territorial Planning and Social and Environmental Development, not all participants had skills and practice in the use of Geographic Information Systems. It can even be said that many of the participants did not feel comfortable working with geographic information as a first reference. In this sense, the main adaptation to the method was the brainstorm process of co-creation of ideas, elaborated in the form of a table of alphanumeric proposals that, not necessarily, emerged from map information, but were translated in the second moment to the geographic location. It is an adaptation contribution on ways of working considering participants from professional areas who do not necessarily have knowledge and skills of geographic spatial analysis.

2 Methodology

Brazil is a country of continental dimensions and of big differences in spatial, social and economic conditions. Carrying out urban planning in such complexity requires adaptability and scalability conditions, as the regions will have different conditions of participation and resources. Starting with digital inclusion and access to technological resources, there are great disparities. It was the intention of the group of Brazilian universities linked to the IGC (International Geodesign Collaboration - https://www.igc-geodesign.org/) to carry out a study together, but at the same time with freedom for the necessary adaptations due to local specificities. The 13 studies carried out presented variation in the form of development (asynchronous and synchronous), of the actors involved (undergraduate, graduate students, planning professionals of university researchers), access to additional tools (application development and specific and additional methodological procedures), in the time available for the experiment (in more concentrated processes or with more time between stages). Even with the local differences, it was possible to follow a common script and, at the same time, record and measure the adaptability condition to contemplate each local need [9–21].

All followed the schedule proposed by the IGC to consider the scenarios for the year 2021, 2035 and 2050, in view of the global climate agreements and the Sustainable Development Goals [13]. And to act according to different planning patterns, related to traditional processes, which do not adopt innovations at first and then accept them, or those that are innovative from the beginning. With this temporal scale of behavior variation, proposed by the IGC, the expectation would be to expand the capacity for innovation and, mainly, the measurement of gains in meeting the goals of sustainable development (SDG) (Fig. 4).

Also as proposed by the IGC, participants had access to a list of assumptions, a set of best practices on the different planning systems, as a way of encouraging the use of innovations. The systems proposed for all participants were: water, energy, vegetation,

Fig. 4. Sustainable development goals [10].

institutions, agriculture, transport, housing and mixed use, commerce and industry. In the opinion of the organizers, two other systems could be added, and the Brazilian group chose to include tourism and culture and to include a specific system to propose and measure contributions to the Carbon Credit (Fig. 5).

Water	**Energy**	**Institutional**
Agriculture	**Transport**	**Residential**
Green	**Industry / Commerce**	**Tourism / culture**
Carbon credit		

Fig. 5. Workshop themes. Source: authors (2021).

All Brazilian projects received the same collection of representation maps and processes (data and information on the spatialization of occurrences and their areas of influence) and the use of the Brazilian Geodesign platform, GISColab [11, 12, 19]. The EA-UFMG Geoprocessing Laboratory was responsible for assembling a collection of around 40 maps for each of the metropolitan regions involved. With this, it was possible to measure the scalability of the process of setting up a workshop, in terms of time and access to a minimum set of information. Free access data, made available on a spatial data infrastructure platform or satellite imagery, were used. The time spent on producing the maps was measured and it was observed that in order to set up a case study on a regional scale, in Brazil, a week of work would be necessary, even for regions with fewer resources [9].

It would be possible to assemble a much more robust data collection for the island of Florianópolis, but not exactly for the entire metropolitan region. In order to apply the same conditions for the entire country, the quality and resolution cut to a regional scale was carried out, as a first approach, without prejudice to the development of future studies in greater detail.

For visualization of geospatial data layers and spatialization of proposals, the GISColab platform was adopted [16]. GISColab is based on the SDI (Spatial Data Information) and OGC standards for data consumption via WMS or WFS, allowing both cases to increase performance by WPS (Web Processing Service). For training in the software navigation, the groups had videos recorded by Professor Ana Clara Mourão Moura and assistance from the monitors: Beatriz Fernandes and Thiago Lima. In use, adaptations were made to the process, demonstrating the flexibility of both the method and platform.

For standardization in the analysis proposed in the workshops, all groups had as main objectives:

- Increase the area of robust vegetation by 30% by 2050, as a contribution to carbon credits;
- Contemplate the 10 pre-determined systems (or themes) for carrying out the actions, prioritizing projects that were associated with carbon credit;
- For all possible actions, consider the 17 Sustainable Development Goals (SDGs) of the Global Compact, a UN initiative.

For the MRSC, the following specific objectives were listed:

- Informing places of conflicts of environmental interest and real estate exploitation;
- Implementing Conservation Units in areas of dense vegetation;
- Improve mobility;
- Consider sustainable technologies for civil construction;
- Deploy renewable energy sources - mainly solar energy;
- Implement a sewage treatment system;
- Improve tourism activities with a focus on ecological tourism;
- Implement policies to protect areas of the marine coastline;
- Extend the protection of springs and hill tops.

The main goals and framework developed is presented in Fig. 6. The area was divided in two: the coastal area and the continental area, according to the conditions of poor vegetation and robust vegetation. The goals were to consider the SDGs and the increasement of carbon sequestration. The consensus about the proposals were constructed using alphanumeric tables, presenting the list of ideas, the description of each of them, their relation with the main systems, the year of reference, and the place indicated for them. The column of place initially was a generic description that, with the development of the workshop, was transformed into polygons (Fig. 6).

The chronology of the activities followed the general indications of the project but with adaptations to the profile of the workshop participants. The meetings took place for 4 weeks, once a week, in the online format and the contact between the participants was carried out daily with an instant messaging application. A total of 9 students from the discipline of Multipurpose Land Registry and Territorial Planning from PPGPLAN/UDESC participated. In summary, the actions taken were as follows:

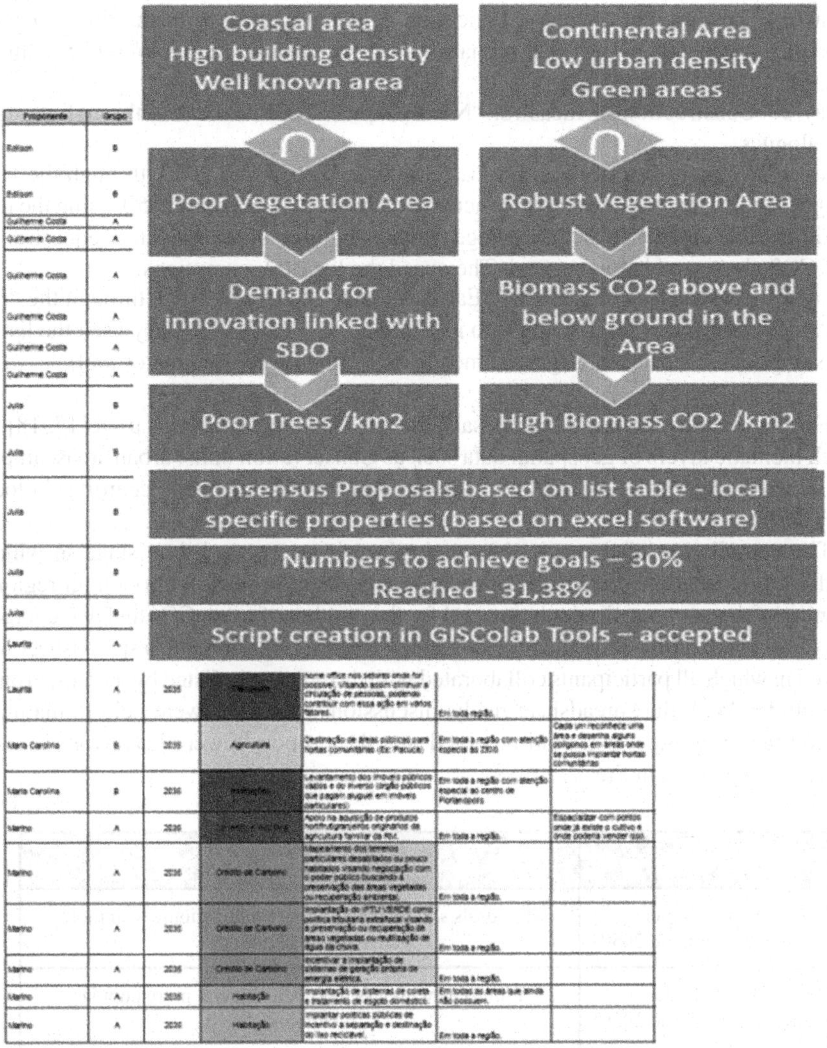

Fig. 6. Decision making process. The background figure (excel table) is a simple illustration to demonstrate that the process started with the decision of ideas by theme, followed by the negotiation on spatialization. Source: the authors (2021).

- Day 1 - Reading enrichment - Indication of potentialities, vulnerabilities, characteristics and needs in the 2020 scenario, by Annotations, using a Web-GIS with 40 maps.
- Day 2 - Construction of Ideas for "Non-Adopter" 2035 and 2050, through the tool Dialogues.
- Day 3 - Construction of ideas for "Late-Adopter" 2035 and 2050, through the Dialogues tool. They had the target to increase of 30% of CCO2 until 2050, using the tool Widgets that calculates the percentage reached, number of trees and the sequestration of CO2 above and below ground. They used the list of Assumptions.
- Day 4 - Construction of ideas for "Early-Adopter" 2035 and 2050, through the "Dialogues" tool. They used Widgets to increase of 30% of CCO2. They used the list of assumptions. Debates through comments and voting on the Dialogues tool.

For the spatialization of the proposals, the GISColab platform was used [17, 18], in which thematic layers of geospatial data such as Conservation units, urban areas, among others, were previously inserted, so that the analysis could deepen according to local characteristics.

The compilation of thematic data took place in a pre-workshop stage in which, in addition to the data collected, basemaps were created for all metropolitan regions, planning of the automated calculation tool for the number of trees, CO^2 and percentages. For better organization, after the first moment of Reading Enrichment, a spreadsheet was created in which all participants collaborated with the proposals, listed by themes, groups and authors. With the spreadsheet ready, discussions and votes were held to maintain or withdraw proposals. It should be noted that the proposals were listed for different scenarios, explained in Fig. 7.

cenario	Description
Early adopter (years of 2035 and 2050)	Proposals should contain more innovations, with more advanced technologies
Late adopter (years of 2035 and 2050)	Proposals with less innovations, with more popular technologies
Non-adopter (year of 2050)	Proposals with little innovation, standard technology

Fig. 7. Workshop scenarios. Source: the authors (2021).

After each discussion, the students spatialized the actions on the maps, through the GISColab platform. Each theme has a standard color, so in all scenarios, regardless of who was editing, it was possible to maintain visual harmony. The proposals were spatialized in pins and vegetation areas to increase carbon credits (polygons in light green) (Fig. 8).

After the elaboration of proposals for the different scenarios, voting, spatialization and confirmation of the achievement of the goal of adding carbon credit, the data from

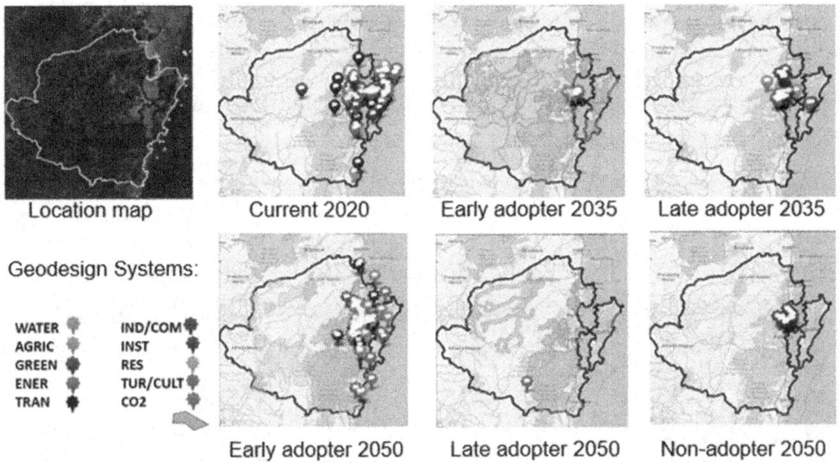

Fig. 8. Maps with proposals on the GISColab platform. Source: GISColab platform. Elaboration: authors (2021).

the GISColab platform were tabulated in two ways: 1. verifying the conformity of the proposals with the Sustainable Development objectives of UN, 2. verification of planned vegetation increase. The data for these steps will be seen in the next item of the study.

3 Discussion of Results

In general, the proposals presented a bias of more traditional technologies although with important bases in the social and environmental questions. The goal in relation to the carbon credit increase was successfully achieved, however there was a low diversity of actions related to the United Nations Sustainable Development Goals (SDG) items. In relation to the SDG, a degree of score ranging from -3 to 3 was listed, being negative when it was a bad proposal for that theme and positive when adding to the theme (Fig. 9). The following information on Fig. 9 is a summary of the actions and the results for each scenario, considering the direct or indirect correlation between each element on the first column (17 SDG) and the first line of the matrix, which describe each one of the 10 themes listed on Fig. 5.

The Fig. 10 illustrates the adherence of the 10 themes developed in the Geodesign dynamics workshop that took place in the discipline, considering the 17 goals of the SDG. The numbering highlighted within the matrix (with shades of purple and orange) refers to the intensity of adhesion (from highest to the lowest level).

Early Adopter: For this scenario, the current situation in 2020 (14) showed flaws in many items of the SDGs, being favorable only in some conditions of Agriculture and Institutions, and with weaknesses related to the other themes. When acting as an Early-Adopter, the score increased a little for 2035 (26) and a lot for 2050 (113), demonstrating that innovations can make a difference in complying with the SDG. Perhaps the group

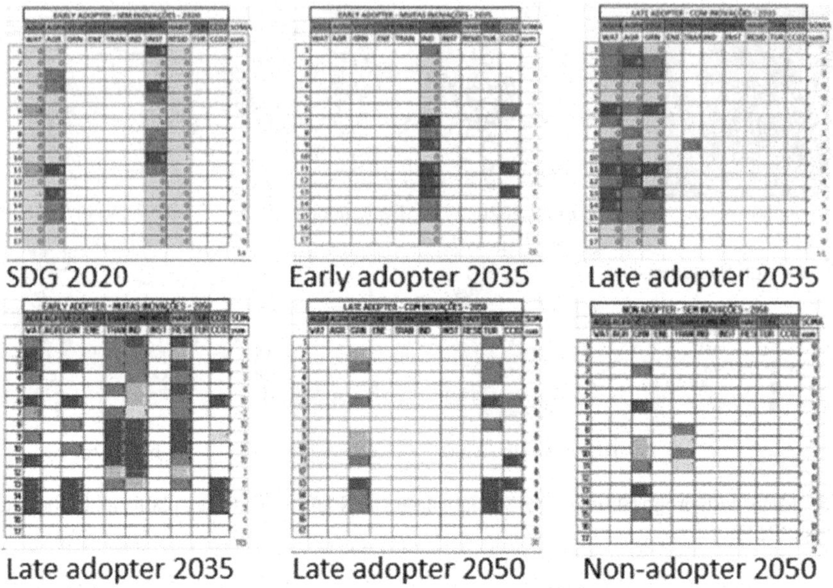

Fig. 9. Tabulation of SDG/ONU proposals in relation to the proposed themes Source: authors (2021).

Most benefit	3	#7030A0
Benefit	1	#CC66FF
Neutral	0	#BFBFBF
Detriment	-1	#FFFF00
Most Detriment	-3	#FF9933

Fig. 10. Scale of correlation SDG/ONU with workshop themes related.

was not prepared to plot all projects and policies on the GISColab platform, sharing their views.

Late Adopter: The Late-Adopter 2035 (51) had a performance far superior to the Non-Adopter 2050 (9), in values. In fact, the group had a little resistance to putting their ideas on GISColab - compiling a large part of the policies and projects in the spreadsheet that should be used as support. In this case, the graphic representation was minimal but the discussions and the main objective were achieved: to increase carbon credit. Regarding the themes, there are improvements in water, agriculture and green.

Non Adopter: It is observed that the Non-Adopter arrives in 2050 with the score (9) slightly below the current scenario (14), because the proposals, although without major innovations, did not consider the future scenario as possibilities for development. It may have been difficult to plan the future with policies and projects - given that part of the group was not used to this type of exercise.

Analyzing the data in relation to the main objective of the workshop, to increase the percentage of green area for carbon credit, it was found that the goal was achieved smoothly by the natural characteristic of the MRSC and also by the profile of the workshop participants, who put environmental actions as a priority.

4 Participants' Report and Conclusion

Throughout the process of applying Geodesign, different profiles of professional background were identified within the participating student's class, so the questionnaire was conducted at the end of the experiment to record individual and group impressions.

Considering that the whole project process took place remotely due to the COVID-19 pandemic and its implications, it was questioned whether they believed that there would be a difference in the result of applying the method if the process were in person, and for almost 70% of the group believed that yes, it would be different. Thus, was majoritary the feeling that being together and discuss face to face is better to convince or expuse the point of view related to any decision.

Regarding the degree of difficulty in carrying out collective decision -making actions, there was a balance in relation to the number of responses from those who found it easy and those who found it difficult, even so, in general the group understood that there was no conflict for decisions since the proposals were created together. But, considering the GeoDesign methodological procedure it is necessary to underline the process of definition and implementation of each proposal in order to get iteration and redefine the common focus.

About the Geodesign methodology, about 60% considered that they fully understood the method and 40% partially - besides, we must consider that for many of the participants was the first contact with the Geodesign methodology and GISColab Platform. Considering that only 3 people in the group had knowledge about Geodesign, it was a very positive margin of result.

Regarding the use of the GISColab platform in general, the group was relatively easy to use, having some ideas for improvements such as the possibility of more than one collaborator editing the map simultaneously, the creation of several polygons within the same proposal, among others. But, for the group to get skills in the GISColab platform it took a bit of time and some hours of training, as well as many messages, recommendations, orientations shared by the group.

Regarding the process as a whole, it can be said that the experiences of applying Geodesign, as well as any collective decision process, will always encompass a very unique character. In addition to what has already been mentioned, another very evident issue is that the more the individual had a connection with the place, the easier the actions could be proposed. Thus, it was noted that the proposals were largely linked to the participants' living and/or leisure places, showing the importance of people getting to know their cities and regions for effective participation in cooperation processes.

Acknowledgements. The authors thank CNPq support through the project 401066/2016-9 and FAPEMIG PPM-00368-18.

Key software used GISColab - Geoprocessing Laboratory at EA-UFMG & Christian Freitas. Accessed in April and May 2021.

Special thanks to FAPESC by support the event associated with TO nº 2019TR954.

Finally thank you to Santa Catarina State University (UDESC) for support the project, specially to Dean of Research and Graduate Studies (PROPPG). Therefore, this research received financial support from the Coordination of Superior Level Staff Improvement - CAPES - Brazil (PROAP/AUXPE).

References

1. Association of Municipalities of the Greater Florianópolis Region - GRANFPOLIS (2020). https://granfpolis.org.br/index/municipios-regiao/codMapaItem/140189. Accessed 2 May 2021
2. Brazilian Institute of Geography and Statistics (IBGE). Brazil Santa Catarina, Florianópolis (2020). https://cidades.ibge.gov.br/brasil/sc/florianopolis/panorama. Accessed 2 May 2021
3. Dangermond, J.: GIS: Designing our Future. ArcNews, Summer (2009)
4. Ervin, S.: A system for Geodesign. Keynote. Abstract, pp. 158–167 (2011)
5. Flaxman, M.: Geodesign: fundamental principles and routes forward. Talk at GeoDesign Summit (2010). https://www.esri.com/videos/watch?videoid=elk067YU2s8. Accessed 17 Jan 2019
6. Miller, W.R.: Introducing Geodesign: the concept. Esri Press, Redlands, 35 p. (2012). https://www.esri.com/library/whitepapers/pdfs/introducing-geodesign.pdf. Accessed 05 Feb 2022
7. Steinitz, C.: A Framework for Geodesign: Changing Geography by Design. ESRI Press, Redlands (2012)
8. Li, N., Ervin, S., Flaxman, M., Goodchild, M.: Design and application of an ontology for geodesign. Revue Internationale de Géomatique **22**(2), 145–168 (2012)
9. Moura, A.C.M., Freitas, C.R.: Scalability in the application of geodesign in Brazil: expanding the use of the Brazilian geodesign platform to metropolitan regions in transformative-learning planning. Sustainability **13**(12), 6508 (2021). https://doi.org/10.3390/su13126508
10. United Nations (UN): Global Compact Brazil Network. Sustainable Development Goals (SDGs) (2018). https://www.pactoglobal.org.br/ods. Accessed 2 May 2021
11. Moura, A.C.M., Freitas, C.R.: Brazilian geodesign platform: WebGis & SDI & geodesign as co-creation and geo-collaboration. In: Computational Science and Its Applications. ICCSA 2020. Lecture Notes in Computer Science(), vol. 12252. Springer, Cham (2020). https://doi.org/10.1007/978-3-030-58811-3_24
12. Marino, T.B., Rocha, C.A.B., Rosa, A.A., Mello, T.A.G.: Geodesign applied to propositional scenarios of medium and long-term sustainable projects for Rio de Janeiro Metropolitan Region, Brazil. In: Gervasi, O., et al. (eds.) Computational Science and Its Applications. ICCSA 2021. Lecture Notes in Computer Science, vol. 12954, pp 437–447. Springer, Cham (2021). https://doi.org/10.1007/978-3-030-86979-3_31
13. Pancher, A.M., de Sá, A.I., Costa, M., Aguiar, T.O.: The potential of geodesign for the optimization of land use in the perspective of sustainability: case study of the metropolitan region of Campinas. In: Gervasi, O., et al. (eds.) Computational Science and Its Applications – ICCSA 2021. ICCSA 2021. Lecture Notes in Computer Science, vol. 12954. pp. 476–490. Springer, Cham (2021). https://doi.org/10.1007/978-3-030-86979-3_34
14. Moura, A.C.M., Freitas, C.R., de Freitas, V.T., de Sa, A.I.A.: Geodesign using GISColab platform: SDI consumed by WMS and WFS & WPS protocols in transformative-learning actions in planning. In: Gervasi, O., et al. (eds.) Computational Science and Its Applications – ICCSA 2021. ICCSA 2021. Lecture Notes in Computer Science, vol. 12954. pp. 448–462. Springer, Cham (2021). https://doi.org/10.1007/978-3-030-86979-3_32

15. Moura, A.C.M., Vieira, F.C.D.V., Morais, C.F.D.: Geodesign as a support for proposing actions to fulfil the sustainable development goals. In: Proceedings of the International Cartographic Association, vol. 4, p. 75 (2021). https://doi.org/10.5194/ica-proc-4-75-2021
16. Sandre, A.A., et al.: Geodesign Brazil: trees for the metropolitan area of São Paulo. In: Gervasi, O., et al. (eds.) Computational Science and Its Applications – ICCSA 2021. ICCSA 2021. Lecture Notes in Computer Science, vol. 12954, pp 463–475. Springer, Cham (2021). https://doi.org/10.1007/978-3-030-86979-3_33
17. Moura, A.C.M., Freitas, C.R.: Co-creation of ideas in geodesign process to support opinion and decision making: case study of a slum in Minas Gerais, Brazil. In: La Rosa, D., Privitera, R. (eds.) Innovation in Urban and Regional Planning. INPUT 2021. Lecture Notes in Civil Engineering, vol. 146. Springer, Cham (2021). https://doi.org/10.1007/978-3-030-68824-0_28
18. Conti, A., Moura, A.C.M., Martinez, G.A.T., Tondelli, S., Patata, S.: Applying geodesign in the City of Bologna (Italy): the case study of the Navile Region. In: La Rosa, D., Privitera, R. (eds.) Innovation in Urban and Regional Planning. INPUT 2021. Lecture Notes in Civil Engineering, vol 146. Springer, Cham (2021). https://doi.org/10.1007/978-3-030-68824-0_29
19. Moura, A.C.M., Fonseca, B.M.: ESDA (exploratory spatial data analysis) of vegetation cover in urban areas—recognition of vulnerabilities for the management of resources in urban green infrastructure. Sustainability **12**(5), 1–22 (2020). https://doi.org/10.3390/su12051933
20. Martínez, G.A.T., de Vargas Vieira, F.C., Rocha, C.C., Palheta, A.C.M., Neri, S.H.A.: Using geodesign to plan the future of Macapa Metropolitan Region, State of Amapa, Brazil: a support to expanding collaborative technical performance. In: Gervasi, O., et al. (eds.) Computational Science and Its Applications – ICCSA 2021. ICCSA 2021. Lecture Notes in Computer Science, vol. 12954, pp 491–506. Springer, Cham (2021). https://doi.org/10.1007/978-3-030-86979-3_35
21. Moura, A.C.M.: O Geodesign como processo de cocriação de acordos coletivos para a paisagem territorial e urbana. In: Ladwig, N.I., Campos, J.B. (org.) Planejamento e gestão territorial: o papel e os instrumentos do Planejamento Territorial na Interface entre o Urbano e o Rural. Criciúma - SC: UNESC (2019). http://repositorio.unesc.net/handle/1/7018

Geodesign in Salvador Metropolitan Region: Regional Planning Based on Reproducible and Defensible Criteria

Ana Clara Mourão Moura[1](✉), Christian Rezende Freitas[1], and Susana Silva Cavalcanti[2]

[1] Escola de Arquitetura, Laboratório de Geoprocessamento, Universidade Federal de Minas Gerais (UFMG), Rua Paraíba 697, Belo Horizonte, Brazil
anaclara@ufmg.br, christianrezende@alomeioambiente.com.br

[2] Instituto de Geociências, Universidade Federal da Bahia (UFBA), Campus Universitário de Ondina, Ondina, Brazil
scavalcanti@ufba.br

Abstract. As a contribution to the meeting IGC – International Geodesign Collaboration, a group of 14 Brazilian universities developed a case study about Trees for Metropolitan Regions. One of them, and the last one developed, was about the Salvador Metropolitan Region. Being the last one, it was an opportunity to apply the observations collected during the previous experiments, in order to arrive to a framework based on reproducible and defensible criteria. The main improvements were new scripts to support decision making about the fulfillment of SDGs (Sustainable Development Goals) developed as WPS (Web Processing Service), and the composition of the groups (people from the area and not from the area). The results were analyzed according to the thematic, priority and locational assertiveness. From the collection of ideas, 67.9% were considered quite good and 23.2% were considered good. The indexes of the thematic and priority assertiveness were very high (96.4% and 89.2%), while the locational assertiveness was 73.2%. In face to these numbers, it was possible to affirm that the results were very good. It was an academic experiment, but the process of geodesign can be considered by the public administration in the regional plan that is under development.

Keywords: Participatory planning · Web Processing Services · GISColab

1 Introduction

Geodesign is a group of procedures to allow spatial planning, from the scales of landscape to local and territorial planning, considering the sense of participation, based on co-creation. It can be considered the application of contemporary values in planning, as it proposes to work with different actions, to structure different steps as a support to opinion and decision making. Moreover, it applies new digital technologies, mainly the web-based on, to give access to data, to allow the consumption of information and the creation of ideas to the area [1–6].

O. Gervasi et al. (Eds.): ICCSA 2022 Workshops, LNCS 13379, pp. 132–147, 2022.
https://doi.org/10.1007/978-3-031-10545-6_10

To have the opportunity to discuss the possibilities of the Geodesign application, a collaboration group was created, the IGC – International Geodesign Collaboration. This group is getting together annually to test and discuss frameworks, procedures to reach the defined objectives, to exchange experiences about local specificities and knowledge. There are proposals about how to achieve the SDG – Sustainable Development Goals in planning, how to face the schedules of time to correspond to global agreements (UN Agenda 2030, Paris Agreement 2050). There is also the discussion about assessments to be considered to bring innovation to new projects and policies in planning.

As part of the annual meeting of the IGC 2021, a group of 14 universities in Brazil got together to develop 13 case studies, about some of the metropolitan regions in the country. To be able to compare results with the IGC participants, all the groups had to think about scenarios for 2021, 2030 and 2050; and to divide the designs in non-adopter, late-adopter or early-adopter behavior. These conditions were to make participants understand the results of working in a traditional way (non-adopter) and to measure the results of including innovations (from late-adopter to early-adopter values). There was a list of ideas, presented as assumptions, which could be used while proposing the ideas. And, finally, the results of the workshops had to be analyzed according to the fulfillment of the goals of the 2030 agenda [7].

Specifically for the Brazilian studies the groups had to follow the same basic framework, use the same collection of around 40 initial thematic maps, but they were free to add steps, to use additional methods or technologies, to compose the groups of participants according to their reality. The name of the Brazilian project was "Trees for metropolitan regions in Brazil", with the goal to test scalability and flexibility in the use of the Brazilian Geodesign platform.

We wanted to prove scalability because we were developing 13 case studies, but there are 74 metropolitan regions in Brazil, and the same process could also be applied in other scales and areas. We wanted to prove that we were using defensible and reproducible criteria, which are the base for comparisons. And we had as keyword the sense of adaptability, as we live in a continental country that requires flexibility to consider the many differences in geography, social vulnerabilities, economic resources, access to information, and the possibilities to be part of.

While presenting a common base, as also incentivizing local adaptations, we had the best from all groups. Because all of them followed a proposed structure, received the same support of the map collection and training to use GISColab (the Brazilian Geodesign Platform), but all of them added specific adaptations to the process [8]. The results from the 13 workshops were presented in the IGC 2021 [9].

The case study presented here was the last one developed. It was held on May 2021. The Brazilian workshops started in February and ended in May, all of them planned to be developed in 4-day meetings, synchronous or asynchronous, depending on the decision of the local coordinator. In the Salvador Metropolitan Region, the studies were developed in 4 days, with synchronous meetings to propose and explain the steps, followed by the additional possibility of completing the task in asynchronous participation. It was part of post-graduation course in the Geoscience Institute, Federal University of Minas Gerais, developed in 45 h, called "*Geodesign no planejamento territorial de regiões metropolitanas*" (Geodesign in territorial planning of metropolitan regions). In addition to 20 h of the Geodesign workshop there were also lectures about the state of the art in landscape and regional planning, the role of Geodesign in contemporary planning, and to discuss the results from the workshop.

There was a group of students from Minas Gerais, UFMG, and a group of students and professionals from Bahia, from universities of the metropolitan region of Salvador, mainly the Federal University of Bahia (UFBA). The group started with 24 interested people, but ended with 13. This number is higher than the media of participants from other metropolitan regions (In Brazil, Belo Horizonte had 27, Recife had 5, the media was 11.6 and the mode was 12). From these 13, 8 were from Minas Gerais and 5 from Bahia. We believe that we had a smaller number from Bahia because they were volunteers, while from Minas Gerais they had to conclude the activities to receive the credits for the course. But the discussions and analysis were good enough to make us feel confident about the results.

As each group, from each metropolitan region had the possibility of adapting the workshop according to their expertise in knowledge and tools, as a result we had a mosaic of different possibilities about how to conduct a workshop. In Belo Horizonte they experimented the voting and agreements process in all the steps. In São Paulo they acted as projective professionals, designing the ideas. In Florianópolis they stated planning the ideas in tables and associating them with the systems and the SDGs, followed by the decision about the area, where to locate them. In Rio de Janeiro they used web-based technologies to create ideas in a VGI platform (Volunteered Geographic Information). In Fortaleza they divided the area in zones of landscape units and each participant was responsible for one of them. In Campinas they created groups of participants and tasks to be done according to the triad of sustainability: economy, social and environmental axis. In Belém they were very interested in maps and geoprocessing modeling. In Goiânia they took the opportunity to teach about the geography of the area. In Recife they tested the possibilities of developing asynchronous workshops. In Macapá they experimented geodesign developed by a group of technicians from public administration. In Palmas they were interested in understanding the area, as the metropolitan region is very new and it is not characterized as a metropolitan area. In Carbonífera metropolitan region they faced the difficulties in accepting innovations, as they are very traditional, and to discuss concepts and cultural references. Finally, in Salvador, as it was the last workshop, it was an opportunity to review the processes and to apply adjustments. The experiments were very interesting, because we prefer to analyze differences rather than similarities, because we learn with them.

1.1 The Case Study: Salvador Metropolitan Region

The RMS is composed of 13 municipalities where in 2021 almost 4 million inhabitants live in an area of 4,375 km^2, with 3,998,754 inhabitants resulting in a density of 900 inhabitants/km^2, and a GDP of 140,442 million [10]. The RMS was established by federal supplementary law number 14, of June 8, 1973. It currently comprises of the municipalities of Camaçari, Candeias, Dias D'Ávila, Itaparica, Lauro de Freitas, Madre de Deus, Mata de São João, Pojuca, Salvador, São Francisco do Conde, São Sebastião do Passé, Simões Filho and Vera Cruz. It is characterized by an extensive Atlantic coastline, in an area with strong touristic potential, composed of islets and a large island, the Island of Itaparica, in addition to the Bay of Todos dos Santos (Fig. 1).

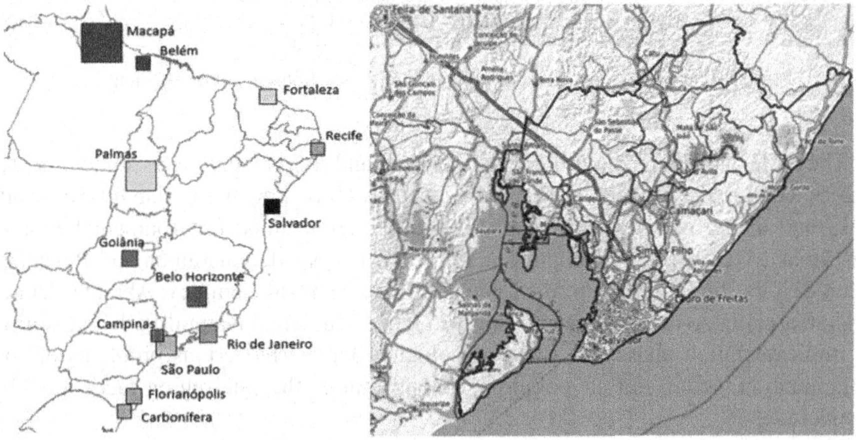

Fig. 1. Case study in Brazil and the Metropolitan Region of Salvador. Source: the authors.

It is important to emphasize that most of the municipalities that make up the RMS have the headquarters, districts and villages, in addition to rural areas. They are composed of industrial cities (Industrial Pole of Camaçari and Superintendence of Industrial and Commercial Development – SUDIC), cities developed due to oil extraction and refining activities, dormitory cities and touristic cities, for the most part. It comprises of areas of survival agriculture, extractives' activities and livestock and others not favorable to cultivation due to the regional climate (sudden variations in temperature, insolation, floods and heavy rains) and/or soil constitution.

Its main element of landscape is the tropical coastal strip, ranging from the dense urban occupation of the cities of Salvador and Lauro de Freitas to the borders destined for hotel hubs. The city of Salvador dates to 1549 and has always been an important commercial port. The capital is known for its Portuguese colonial architecture, Afro-Brazilian culture. The RMS is a composition of contrasts from very developed and qualified areas, together with areas of socially fragile occupations, where the population lives in slums and with poor sanitation conditions and services. The contrast is also observed in the economic conditions since the RMS is home to important industries at the Camaçari Petrochemical Complex and the Aratu Industrial Center. The economic base is petrochemical production, but due to its geographical position, the area has great potential for the development of alternative energy resources. The vegetation is characterized by the Atlantic Forest, but the areas delimited as conservation units are not significant, and are concentrated on the coast, in care of preservation of the shore. It is also necessary to better explore the great touristic potential for activities that are more committed to contemporary values of sustainability (Fig. 2).

Fig. 2. The complexity in landscape and land use. Source: Pinterest images.

The RMS has a large environmental heritage and tourist attraction - mineral water sources, coral reefs, beaches, dunes, remnants of Atlantic Forest, riparian forests, sandbanks and mangroves - and houses some conservation units: Environmental Protection Areas (APA) Joanes/Ipitanga, Rio Capivara, Lagoas de Guarajuba and Pinaúnas; Green Belt for the Protection of the Camaçari Petrochemical Complex; Abrantes Dunes Parks; Garcia D'Ávila; Restinga de Praia do Forte Municipal Natural Park and, still in the implementation phase, the Baiacu Ecological Park. The serious problems of soil contamination, water and air pollution, among others, that the region faces must be considered.

The region's development plan, which is still in process, will provide a Geographic Information System (http://www.emrms.ba.gov.br). In this plan, the PDUI – RMS (Integrated Urban Development Plan, Metropolitan Region of Salvador), the priority is the activities or services that one of the municipalities cannot perform alone or that impact its neighbors called Public Functions of Common Interest. The prioritized thematic areas are: Socioeconomic Development; Mobility; Planning, Land Use and Housing; and, Environment and Sanitation. During the construction of the institutional plan, the local government seeks to establish an urban sustainability agenda that encompasses the models of eco-energy rationality, metabolic balance, purity, citizenship, heritage, efficiency and equity [10].

The aforementioned plan aims to guide public proposals and actions in the RMS, especially in the area of urban mobility. It will cover the West Road System project, which includes the Salvador-Itaparica Island Bridge and actions of the Intermunicipal Urban Plan for the Island of Itaparica, the transversal corridors (Blue Line and Red Line), the Subway System and the Metro tram. The case study was an academic experiment to teach the geodesign method, and not a contribution to the institutional plan that is under development, as it. But the lessons learned can be a possibility for the future.

2 Methodology

The methodology had three levels of development: a) as a participant from the IGC meeting, it had to follow a framework proposed by them; b) as a participant from Brazilian case studies, it had to follow the framework that adapted the IGC proposal to local case studies; c) as a case study from the Salvador Metropolitan Region it had to consider the specifications of the experiment, mainly due to the participations of actors from different parts of Brazil (Minas Gerais and Bahia).

2.1 The IGC Proposal

The IGC 2021 meeting proposed a framework to be followed by all participants, while the workshops were expected to create scenarios or designs to 2021, 2030 and 2050, considering different behaviors by the actors of the society that were supposed to be "not-adopter" (traditional), "late-adopter" (initially traditional, but available to consider innovations) and "early-adopter" (available for innovations). The workshop had to consider 8 systems, and the coordinators could include 2 more. While thinking about ideas, it was important to considerer the Sustainable Development Goals. And, about the ideas of projects or policies, the organization provided a list of assumptions divided by the systems, which the participants could apply in their proposals [7].

2.2 The Brazilian Proposal

The group of 14 Brazilian universities developed 13 case studies about trees for metropolitan areas, with the goal to take part in the IGC meeting, but also to face challenges of planning in a continental country and to use some facilities developed here. The challenges are to work in areas with lack of data, lack of technological assessments, to include people that sometimes can have difficulties in using technologies, and so one. But the facilities were the use of a Brazilian Web-based Geodesign platform, called GISColab, and to have the support of the Geoprocessing Laboratory, from the Federal University of Minas Gerais.

Before the workshop itself, the mentioned Laboratory prepared all the data for all the case studies. It was a task that could be distributed or shared, but the researchers wanted to test the scalability of the process, arriving to a definition of a minimum collection of maps that could characterize the areas in the regional scale, and to measure the time required to prepare them [9]. Data from the SDIs (Spatial Data Infrastructure) were analyzed to select the best ones and the geoprocessing modelling was applied to arrive to thematic maps (i.g. Accessibility and Capillarity, Socioeconomic distribution of resources, Infrastructure, Land Use and Land Cover, Geomorphological conditions as Slope, Vegetation fragments and their metrics, and so one).

With the collection of 40 maps ready to be used, the files were uploaded in a Geographic Database in the web, they were prepared to be used as WMS or WFS (web map service or web feature service) in a Geoserver, metadata could be prepared, and finally were available to be used in a WebGis, where the "core" of Geodesign happens. The system is based on the OGC – Open Geospatial Consortium, which means it can dialogue with many other applications, as it uses common consensus standards. It was initially developed by GE21 Geotechnologies, and was optimized by scripts and programming to be used as "GISColab", the Geodesign platform [8].

The workshop starts, with all the maps organized in the WebGis as layers and distributed according to the main systems proposed by the IGC 2021 meeting. The framework proposed to the Brazilian group was planned to happen in 4 days. In the first day, the participants did the "Reading Enrichment" that is the analysis of maps collection and the register of pins called "Annotations". It is called reading enrichment because people learn about the area but also contribute with comments, alerts, additional information that are not in the presented data. These contributions are color-coded pins as annotations, colored according to the systems.

On days 2, 3 and 4 they construct scenarios, that are designs for the years and values proposed by the IGC 2021. They use the "Dialogues" resources in which they can draw points, lines or polygons with ideas of policies or projects. In these Dialogues they present the georeferenced idea, with its name and description. There is a step that all the participants read each idea to add comments, criticizing, suggesting changes or giving support with additional elements. And there is also the step of "Voting" in which the participants register if they like or dislike, approve or not the proposal (Fig. 3).

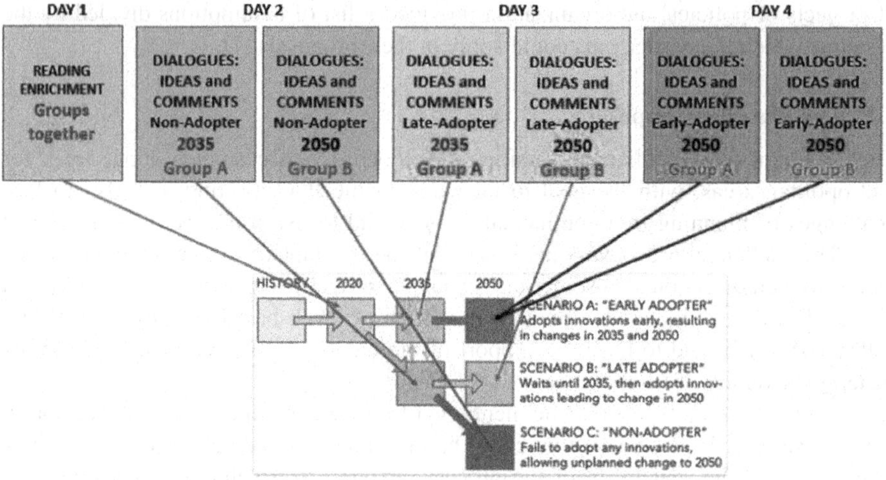

Fig. 3. Main steps proposed by the Brazilian framework. Source: the authors.

2.3 The Salvador Metropolitan Region Proposal

As the Salvador case study was the last one in the collection of 13 workshops, all the others had already been finished, we had some evaluation from participants and their coordinators, and decided to improve the framework.

The first improvement was in the use of the WPS resources (Web Processing Services) to produce dynamic information during the workshop, as support to opinion and decision making. It means that scripts were programmed to present the performances of the participants and their ideas, so that they could control whether they were achieving some workshop goals, whether they were considering the SDGs in the proposals, whether they were reaching the minimum increase of 30% in an area of qualified vegetation, and the calculation of possible carbon sequestration above and below ground resulted from the proposed ideas.

Another difference in the workshop, that happened due to the composition of the actors, the groups of participants, was to understand the role of people of the area and visitors of the area. A part of the actors were people that live in the Salvador Metropolitan Region and really knew about necessities, vulnerabilities and potentialities, from their daily life experience. But there was also a group that lives in Minas Gerais and knows the area as visitors, as tourists, and don't know all the territory of region. In that sense, it was interesting to measure the possible contribution of the two groups of actors.

The proposed framework was based on 3 steps. It started with the Reading Enrichment in which people from Salvador were more active in inserting pins with additional information about the area, highlighting the main characteristics, but also data that were not in the systems. In that step, people not from Salvador used their time to analyze the map collection in details, to construct knowledge about the area. As a result, considering the sum of all the annotations, we arrived to a mosaic of interpretations about vulnerabilities and potentialities of the area.

In the second step the participants created ideas. We observed that people from Salvador were more interested in proposing projects and policies to attend to everyday needs, and in that sense one can say they were more traditional, comparable to non-adopter and late-adopter participants. On the other hand, people that are not from Salvador were less traditional, presenting an unthinkable innovation. As a result, we arrived to o mosaic of proposals that could fit both the needs and the possibilities of the area. After registering the idea, the opportunity to write comments on all of them was there, completing the Dialogs. Finally, in the voting process, that was step 3, the participants had already analyzed the proposed ideas, had already read the collection of comments about each of them, and were able to vote and to decide about "what", "where", "when" and "why". The final decision as the selection of ideas according to thematic, locational, and priorities assertiveness (Fig. 4).

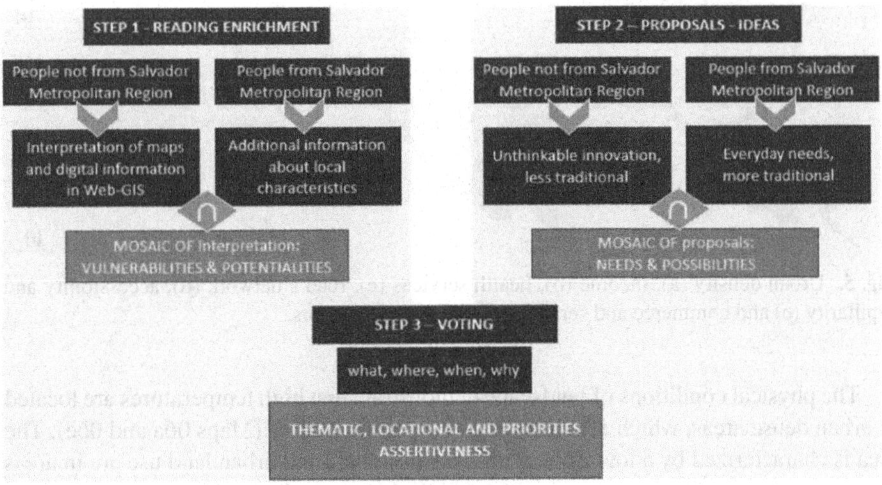

Fig. 4. Main steps proposed by the Salvador case study framework. Source: the authors.

3 The Development of the Case Study

A collection of 40 thematic maps was produced based on data present in platforms of spatial data infrastructure. From these maps it is possible to understand that urban land use in the Metropolitan Region of Salvador is mainly concentrated in a conurbated area of Salvador, Lauro de Freitas e Simões Filho, along the bay, and there is an axis of growth along the coast, in the northeast direction. In the interior the reference is Camaçari, followed by Dias Dávila, Pojuca, São Sebastião do Passé e Candeias. But it is possible to summarize that the area is dominated by the concentration along the bay, by one attractor pole in the interior and there is a narrow axis growing along the coast. Map 8a presents the densified urban area, map 8b the distribution of income demonstrating the lack of distribution, map 8c presents the distribution of health services and it´s possible to understand they are concentrated in the capital. Map 8d presents the road network that, together with map 8e, which deals with accessibility and capillarity, proves the connection in the area of Salvador and Camaçari, the line along the coast, but also the empty space in the center part of the area. Map 8f presents the concentration of commerce and services, proving the spatial dependence to Salvador and Camaçari (Fig. 5).

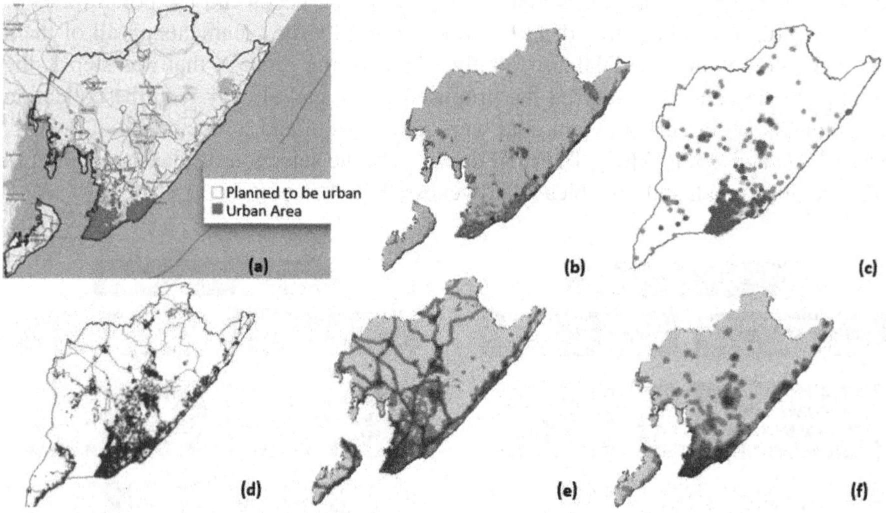

Fig. 5. Urban density (a), income (b), health services (c), road's network (d), accessibility and capillarity (e) and commerce and services (f). Source: the authors.

The physical conditions of landscape demonstrate that high temperatures are located in urban dense areas, which also have poor vegetation quality (Maps 06a and 06e). The area is characterized by a low slope with risks of floods, and urban land use are in areas of low altimetry, while the concentration of high altimetry is in the very north part, empty areas (Maps 6b and 6d). Analyzing the aspect, defined by the slope orientation, the flat areas that receive sun during all day are predominate (Map 6c). (Fig. 6).

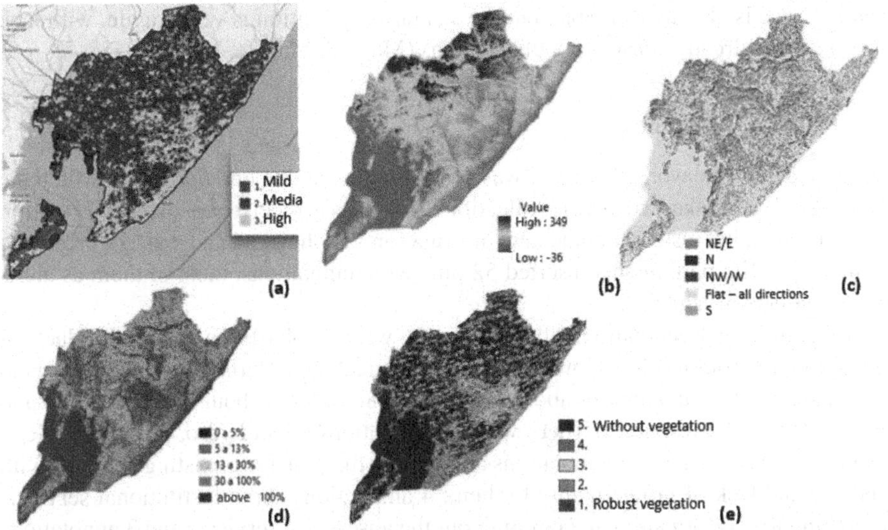

Fig. 6. Surface temperature (a), altimetry (b), aspect (c), slopes (d), NDVI – normalized difference vegetation index (e). Source: the authors.

The presence of forests with dense vegetation is not well distributed. The NDVI had demonstrated the presence of vegetation, but it is mainly composed by agriculture (Map 7a, Map 7b). The conservation units are more focused on sea areas, and are very poor in the continental area (Map 7b). There are plans to increase dense urban areas, where the

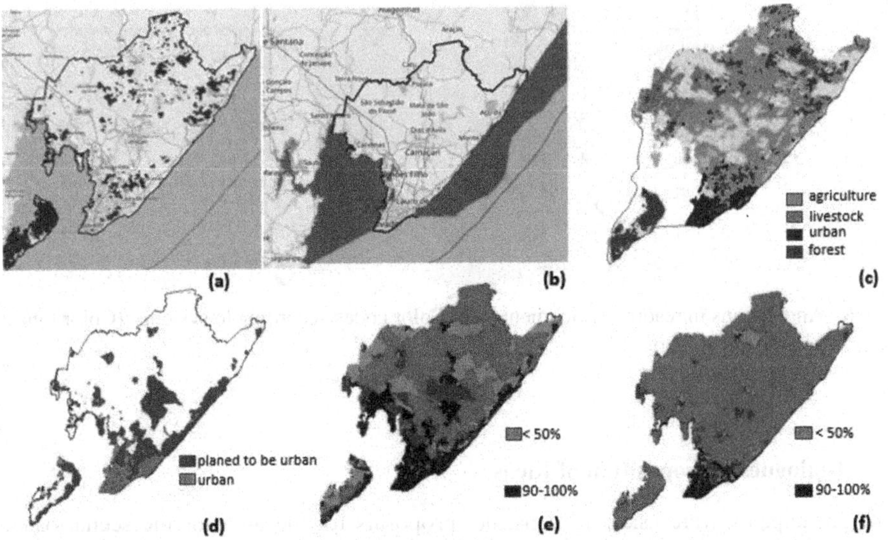

Fig. 7. Forests (a), conservation units (b), land use land cover (c), urban areas (d), water infrastructure (e), sewage infrastructure (f). Source: the authors.

water service is already available, but the sanitation condition is very fragile, with lack of services in already densely populated areas (Map 7d, Map 7e, Map 7f) (Fig. 7).

3.1 Reading Enrichment

The first step of the workshop itself was based on the reading enrichment, in which the participants were asked to read the collection of 40 maps to receive organized information about the area, but also to include new information that they had and was not presented in the maps. The participants inserted 52 pins with annotations, most of them as alerts about conflicts of land use.

There were 18 annotations about housing, with emphasis on registering lack of infrastructure, conflicts with environmental resources and alerts about incorrect land use. There were 17 annotations about green areas, all of them about conflicts of use and risks of losing the resources. There were 6 annotations about hydro, presenting alerts about risks of flood areas; 5 annotations about tourism, indicating existing conflicts with land use and lack of infrastructure to them; 4 annotations about institutional services, presenting new information and pointing out the absence of services; and 3 annotations about transport, indicating lack of services or even the inadequacy of the existing service (Fig. 8).

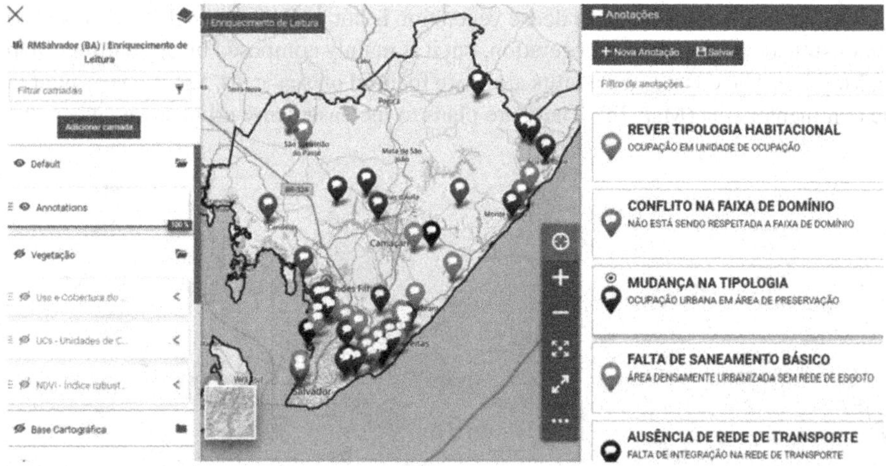

Fig. 8. Annotations in reading enrichment step. Color codes according to systems. (Color figure online) Source: the authors.

3.2 Dialogues – Proposition of Ideas

The participants were asked to construct proposals for the area for the scenarios of 2035 and 2050, considering non-adopter, late-adopter and early-adopter behavior. We understood that the scenario of 2021 was the reading enrichment, because in it they pointed out the main vulnerabilities and potentialities of the area. As the workshop was developed in the GISColab platform [8], the construction of designs to each scenario is done in boxes of contexts, that open a digital working area with all the maps and all the tools (Fig. 9).

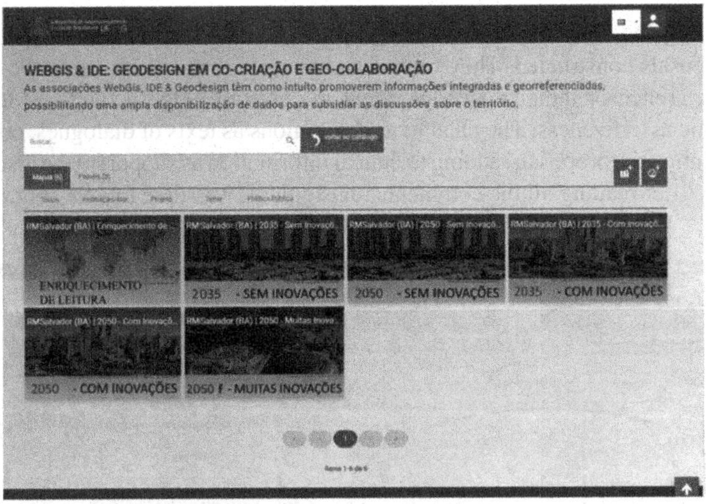

Fig. 9. The scenarios of the designs: 2035 non-adopter, 2050 non-adopter, 2035 late-adopter, 2050 late-adopter, 2050 – early-adopter. Source: the authors.

To each context, they were asked to design proposals of ideas. They could consult the list of assumptions provided by the IGC, in which there is a collection of ideas of innovations. They could use lines, points or polygons, but we asked them to use points when they were not secure about the drawing of an area but wanted to register an idea. In this sense, the idea could be developed by an expert based on the existing location, title and the description of it. It was important to use a colored spatial element, according to

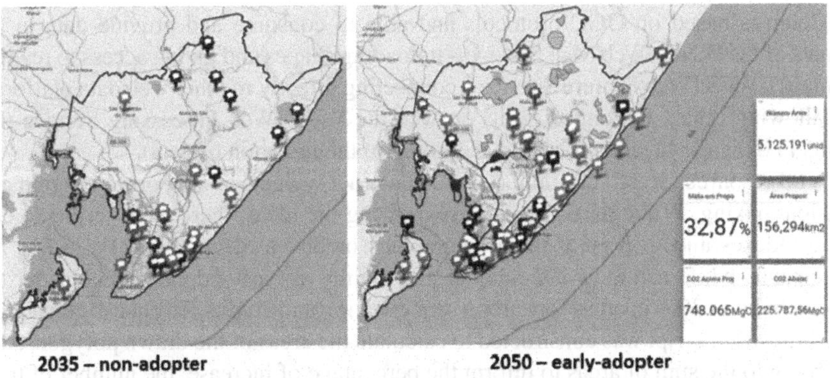

Fig. 10. Proposition of ideas to each scenario. Source: the authors.

the color code related to the systems, to add a title and a text with the description of the idea (Fig. 10).

3.3 Dialogues – Discussion of Ideas and Voting

After drawing the ideas, there was a step in which we asked the participants to read all the proposals constructed. They were asked to analyze the ideas, using the thematic maps as reference or their knowledge about the area to judge if they had locational and thematic assertiveness. They had to write opinions as texts of dialogues, criticizing, complementing the proposals, adding technical information as support to the discussions, and so on. After reading all the comments registered, it was time to vote (Fig. 11).

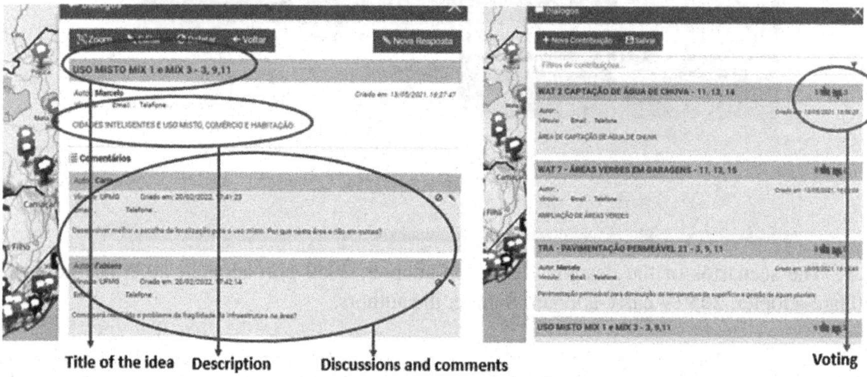

Fig. 11. Dialogues based on the title, the description, and the comments. Decision registered by voting. Source: the authors.

4 Results and Discussion

GISColab is based on OGC protocols and able to consume and provide data in the formats of the WMS (Web Map Service – uploading shapes and giving access to reading the maps), WFS (Web Feature Service – connecting directly to other web data platforms and allowing others to connect to it) or even the WPS (Web Processing Service that results in dynamic layers, processed according to the insertion of data).

WPS resources were very important to construct widgets as support to opinion and decision making. While participants were drawing the ideas, there were scripts to calculate indexes and to present them in graphics or boxes of numbers. We asked the participants, while acting as late-adopter and mainly as early-adopter, to consider the increasement of 30% in areas for carbon sequestration and credits. To check if this target was achieved, a script was constructed to calculate the areas of the drawn polygons, and according to the sum of areas to inform the percentage of increase, the number of trees that could be planted in the area, the quantity of carbon that could be sequestrated above ground and below ground. The results were presents in boxes as widgets (Fig. 12).

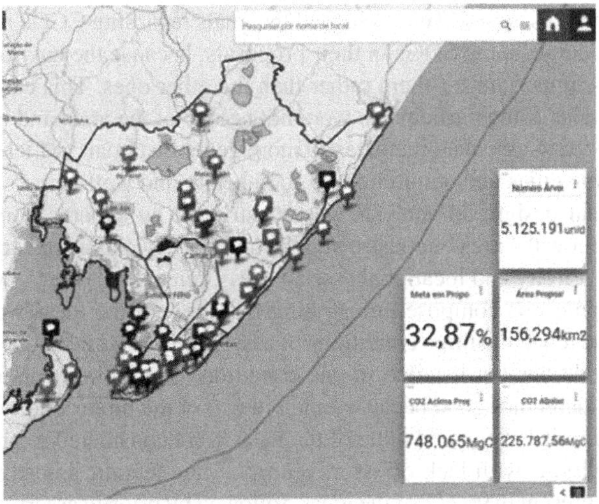

Fig. 12. Widgets based on the WPS to calculate the targets on CCO2. Source: the authors.

Also based on WPS, a script to count the number of times that an SDG was mentioned in the design was constructed. While proposing the ideas, the participant was asked to list which SDG it was contributing to, and a widget with a histogram presented the dynamic performance of the composed design (Fig. 13). Subsequently, for other case studies and workshops, the possibility to associate the negative impacts and the positive impacts to SDGs was also developed. In that case, two histograms.

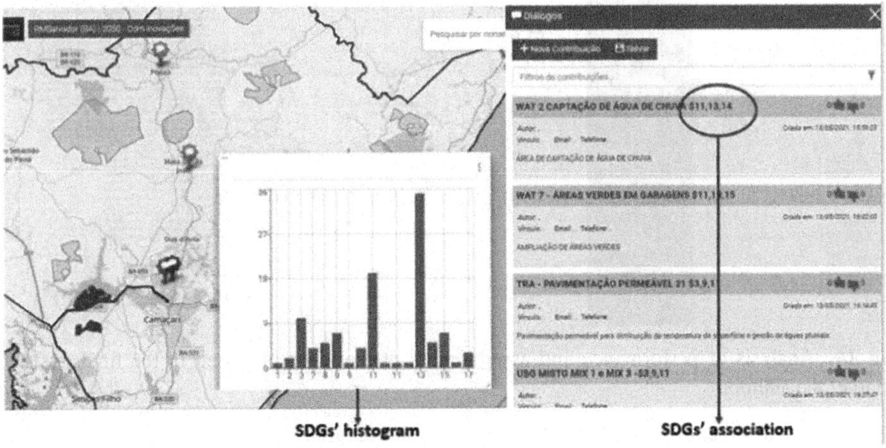

Fig. 13. Widgets based on the WPS to calculate the impacts to the SDGs. Source: the authors.

When analyzing the composition of the designs to each scenario and the participants' proposals according to non-adopter, late-adopter or early-adopter, it is very clear that they improved the design and learned with the experience. The last design was more complete, well described and discussed. They achieved the goals regarding CCO2 and understood they could considerate some SDGs in their proposals, because the environmental goals were much more important for them rather than the other ones. This can be associated to the fact that most of the participants were not people of the area, and in that sense, it is easier to think or to associate the ideas to more generalist goals, which were: climate action, sustainable cities and communities, good health and well-being.

From the final design, an analysis was constructed by experts, composed by the organizers that know the area or constructed the maps. They classified each idea according to thematic, priority and locational assertiveness, related to "what", "why/how" and "where". A graphic was composed illustrating that most of the ideas were quite good (67.9%), because it had the three conditions of assertiveness; while 23.2% of them were good in two conditions but it failed in one condition (mainly in locational one); only 8.9% were considered not good because failed in two of the three conditions (mainly in locational and priority ones); and none of the ideas were considered totally not suitable (with three conditions with lack of assertiveness). The thematic assertiveness was the most important, present in 96.4% of the ideas, followed by priority assertiveness that was observed in 89.2% of the ideas, while locational assertiveness was the most problematic, that is present in 73.2% of the ideas (Fig. 14).

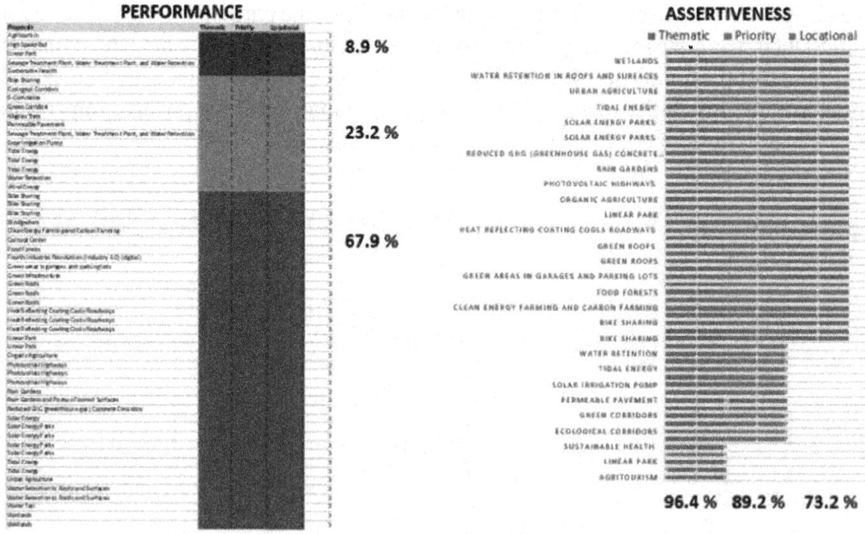

Fig. 14. Analysis of performance and assertiveness of the ideas proposed in the final design. Source: the authors.

5 Conclusions

All the indexes of performance and assertiveness were quite good, which means that the workshop arrived to a result with defensible criteria. It also means that processes have reproductible criteria and can be applied to other case studies. The main challenge is the locational assertiveness, but in a future iteration the participants can change the position of some ideas and improve their proposals.

The PDUI (Integrated Urban Development Plan, Metropolitan Region of Salvador) that is under development by the local government, should provide common guidelines to metropolitan municipalities for integrated urban development in the areas of urban transport, housing, basic sanitation and territorial planning and management. In this sense, it´s interesting to observe that the guiding principles used in the project carried out in cooperation (Geodesign RMS) include these proposals. During the workshop the participants created ideas related to actions/activities in tune with the institutional agenda, although it was an academic experiment. But it's important to highlight that the appropriate suggestions presented in the Dialogues stage can be used by the PDUI-RMS team.

Acknowledgements. The authors thank CNPq support through the project 401066/2016-9 and FAPEMIG PPM-00368-18.

References

1. Dangermond, J.: GIS: designing our future. ArcNews, Summer (2009). http://dx.doi.org/10.11606/gtp.v14i1.148381
2. Flaxman, M.: Geodesign: Fundamental Principles and Routes Forward. Talk at GeoDesign Summit (2010). https://www.esri.com/videos/watch?videoid=elk067YU2s8. Accessed 17 Jan 2019
3. Ervin, S.: A system for Geodesign. Keynote: 27 May 2011. Abstract, pp. 158–167 (2011). http://www.kolleg.loel.hs-anhalt.de/landschaftsinformatik/fileadmin/user_upload/_temp_/2012/Proceedings/Buhmann_2012_19_Ervin_Keynote_2011.pdf. Accessed 27 Jan 2018
4. Li, N., Ervin, S., Flaxman, M., Goodchild, M.: Design and application of an ontology for geodesign. Revue Internationale de Géomatique **22**(2), 145–168 (2012)
5. Miller, W.R.: Introducing Geodesign: The Concept. Esri Press, Redlands, 35 p. (2012). https://www.esri.com/library/whitepapers/pdfs/introducing-geodesign.pdf. Accessed 27 Nov 2018
6. Steinitz, C.: A Framework for Geodesign: Changing Geography by Design. ESRI Press, Redlands (2012)
7. Fisher, T., Orland, B., Steinitz, C.: The International Geodesign Collaboration: Changing Geography by Design. Esri Press, Redland (2020)
8. Moura, A.C.M., Freitas, C.R.: Brazilian geodesign platform: WebGis & SDI & geodesign as co-creation and geo-collaboration. In: Computational Science and Its Applications. ICCSA 2020. Lecture Notes in Computer Science(), vol. 12252. Springer, Cham (2020). https://doi.org/10.1007/978-3-030-58811-3_24
9. Moura, A.C.M., Freitas, C.R.: Scalability in the application of geodesign in Brazil: expanding the use of the Brazilian geodesign platform to metropolitan regions in transformative-learning planning. Sustainability **13**(12), 6508 (2021). https://doi.org/10.3390/su13126508
10. Governo do Estado da Bahia: Plano de Desenvolvimento Urbano Integrado da Região Metropolitana de Salvador (2021). https://pduirms.com.br/. Accessed 02 Feb 2022

Geodesign in Regional Green Infrastructure Planning

Maria do Carmo de Lima Bezerra[1], Rubens do Amaral[1], and Camila Marques Zyngier[2](✉)

[1] Graduate Program in Architecture and Urbanism, College of Architecture and Urbanism, University of Brasília-UnB, Campus Darcy Ribeiro Address Asa Norte, Brasília-DF, Brazil
macarmo@unb.br

[2] Graduate Program in Architecture and Urbanism and Post-graduation Course in Landscape Architecture, IBMEC-BH and IEC-PUC MG, Rio Grande do Norte Street, 300, Belo Horizonte, Brazil
camila.zyngier@gmail.com

Abstract. The patterns of consumption of natural resources and land follow the development process and mark the shapes of occupation of the territories. This process has led not only to the exhaustion of the resilience of the ecosystems but also has demanded assertive interventions in urban land management able to prevent environmental impacts and guarantee essential ecosystem services for human activities. This paper, with the aid of producing data on the support ecological processes and landscape metrics for the study area, presents some solutions anchored in the geodesign methodology for action in the Federal District of Brasília, Brazil. Aiming to improve the assertiveness in facing the depletion of environmental services in urban areas, we present the work carried out on a WebMap/WebGIS platform where strategies were proposed for four subsystems: leisure and culture, provision, green and blue infrastructure to address pressures exerted on the Cerrado ecosystem and to promote urban resilience.

Keywords: Green infrastructure · Geodesign · Landscape planning · Participatory planning

1 Introduction

The consumption patterns of natural resources and land, accompany the development process and mark the occupation forms of the territories. The contemporary framework is understood as the continuation or evolution of practices before humanity's awareness of the finitude of natural resources. This has led to the exhaustion of the self-regeneration capacity of the ecosystems. The most visible expression of this process on human survival itself can be seen in the form of various impacts such as floods, landslides, droughts, food shortages, and diseases [1–4].

This context has demanded research for the structuring of territorial planning and project actions that can simultaneously prevent environmental impacts, resulting from

O. Gervasi et al. (Eds.): ICCSA 2022 Workshops, LNCS 13379, pp. 148–164, 2022.
https://doi.org/10.1007/978-3-031-10545-6_11

territorial occupations and guarantee the provision of essential ecosystem services for human activities and the maintenance of the ecosystems [5, 9–11].

The present work is based on the research developed by the Urban Environmental Management Group of the PPGFAU/ UnB and supported by the UFMG Geoprocessing (GEOPROEA). This articulates their knowledge to develop solutions anchored by design tools to act assertively in the territory in the face of the problems of depletion of environmental services in urban areas.

The conceptual support is anchored in landscape ecology, green infrastructure, remote sensing, and geodesign, leading to the identification of ecological support processes and the construction of landscape metrics, which could support territorial design proposals to protect or promote ecosystem services and resilience.

This approach was only possible by adopting the methodology of geodesign, which can be summarized as a process that allows the co-creation of alternative futures to an area with different interests, creating a compromise through negotiation facilitated by visualization of geographic information [6]. Essentially, it is about planning and designing (future) from a geographical approach (past and present). It also strongly requires the perspective of different social actors through a dynamic construction conducted by a mediator [7, 8]. According to Steinitz [7] this process demands a methodological framework that consists of 3 iterations and 6 models, defined as the representation model, process model, evaluation model, change model, impact model, and decision model. The 3 iterations are to answer the goal "why" we are studying the area, "how" can we develop the case study, and "what, where and when" can we propose projects and policies (Fig. 1).

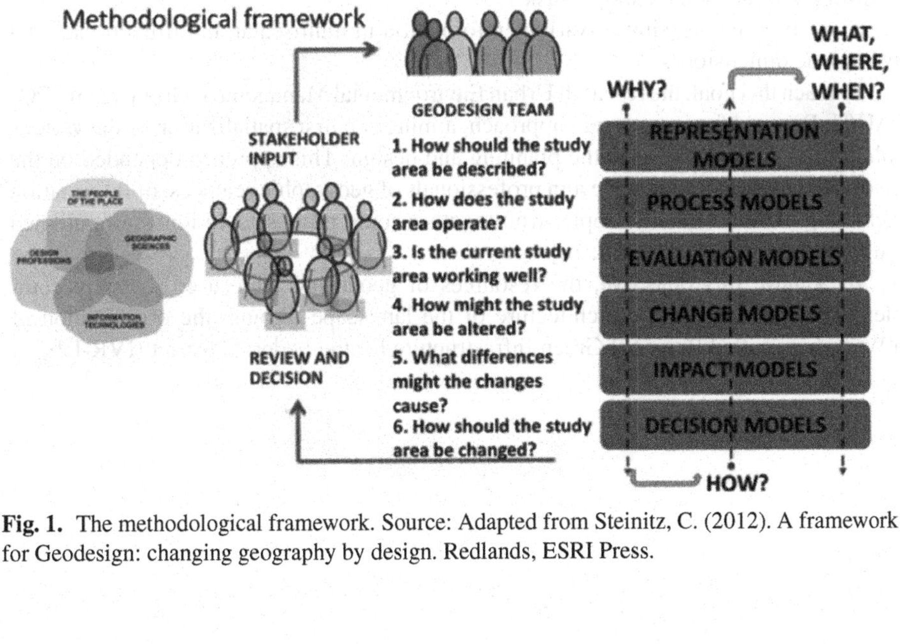

Fig. 1. The methodological framework. Source: Adapted from Steinitz, C. (2012). A framework for Geodesign: changing geography by design. Redlands, ESRI Press.

In turn, the designing process using geodesign allows for more assertive interventions in green infrastructure, at the territorial scale, focusing on both maintenance and promotion of ecosystem services.

Thus, green infrastructure as an intervention approach in the landscape can be seen not only for the conservation and for restoration of biophysical systems, but also as an agent of landscape transformation. This approach creates a system different from the previous one, more resilient, especially when ecological, economic, and social benefits become insufficient for human well-being. In this way, the greatest possible gradient of ecosystem services can be structured, whether it already exists or is under planning [17].

The research was carried out in the Federal District (DF), a federative unit of Brazil, which houses its capital, Brasília, in the Center-West region of the country [18], which, with just over 50 years of occupation, presents serious ecological risks arising from urban and agricultural uses. Among these risks, the suppression of the native Cerrado vegetation (a kind of savannah) and the loss of ability to recharge aquifers may be mentioned, causing a situation of water stress [13].

The result of the studies of the DF territory reached different conclusions regarding the performance of the vegetation. Among these conclusions are those concerning the ecological processes of support on the regional scale using the multispectral index CO_2flux. *This is* linked to the carbon flux to identify the photosynthetic efficiency of the vegetation and the Topographic Wetness Index [14, 15] that were added to the bases of the Economic Ecological Zoning of the DF (ZEE-DF). These parameters could compose a framework that allows the decision-making on the strategies of adaptability and transformability of the urban landscape of the DF.

However, the search for solutions in networked green infrastructure along the territorial mosaic is not a simple task.

It involves the crossing of various information in multiscalar, multifunctional, and synergistic dimensions.

To reach this goal, the research Urban Environmental Management Group from PPG-FAU/UnB, opted for a geodesign approach, aiming at a first spatialization of the various solutions to be considered in the planning and design. This approach depended on the involvement of environment design professionals of geographic sciences, of information technologies, and of local people, who together could propose solutions more aligned with Landscape Ecology [7, 8, 16].

To achieve this objective, the resources of geodesign were used to study complex aspects related to the architecture of the landscape through the organization of a Workshop, called Regional Green Infrastructure for the Federal District (IVR-DF).

This Workshop was carried out with the support of the Brazilian geodesign platform Giscolab, together with researchers and technicians from the Federal District Government concerned with the topic.

This experience will be reported here to demonstrate that when a consistent database is associated with adequate project tools, that is, solutions are supported by the intelligent use of technologies. This way it is possible to quickly advance in the understanding and modeling of the environment. Understanding the past and the present may be achieved, making it possible to reinterpret the landscape, in different perspectives of development consolidated in a co-design process [7, 12] built with assertive actions in the territory intending to increase resilience.

2 Methodology

One of the main reasons for choosing the Giscolab platform to support the geodesign workshop for IVR-DF was the possibility of this tool going beyond a territorial visualization platform.

Giscolab is based on a Spatial Data Infrastructure (SDI), whose ease of information circulation allows the manipulation of data and interpretation of information before planning. This software enables in-depth diagnoses of the territory, employing overlapping and combination of a supplied map system (layers).

This approach is provided by grouping four structuring components:

(i) A geographic base composed of information produced and stored in vectorial formats, raster, or BDG format.
(ii) A Geoserver map server for converting this geographic information into web services (Web Image Services-WMS; Web Feature Service-WFS or Web Processing Service-WPS).
(iii) A metadata catalog for documentation and distribution of contextualized data, used by other Spatial Data Infrastructures (IDE), standardization of documentation, as well as the search and rescue of information.
(iv) A WebMap/WebGIS platform to support visualization, shared opinion and decision-making [7].

The first step in preparing the layer systems (Fig. 2) sought to aggregate a set of information that, together, could offer different perspectives on the design of a regional green infrastructure for the DF.

These layers should together support the interpretation of essential characteristics for the definition of the required programs and projects for the proposition of the IVR-DF. This could be made through the process of a cooperative dialogue between the participants of the workshop. The layer system could neither be so simple as to lack information to support decision making nor so complex as to contain unnecessary or repetitive information.

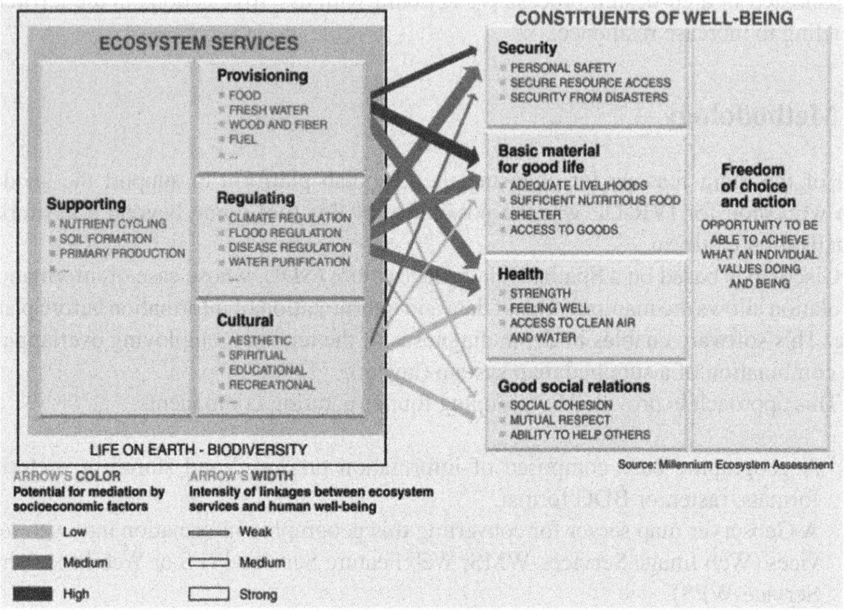

Fig. 2. Linkages between Ecosystem Services and Human Well-being. Source: Millennium Ecosystem Assessment (2005). Ecosystems and Human Well-Being: Wetlands and Water Synthesis. World Resources Institute, Washington, DC.

The system was composed of 39 layers, grouped into 6 categories as follows:

(i) Landscape ecology: shape factor, core areas, connectivity, shape factor improvement potential, core area (hotspots) improvement potential, and connectivity improvement potential;
(ii) Supporting ecological processes (SPE): CO2 flux, Topographic Wetness Index (TWI), and Ecological Restoration Potential (ERP);

(iii) Landscape support: geomorphology, geomorphological compartments, geology, pedology, agricultural suitability, hydrography, hydrographic units, fractured hydrogeology, aquifers flow in the DF, lakes and ponds, risk of loss of aquifer recharge, hypsometry;
(iv) Landscape cover: number of trees, carbon in tree biomass (above and below ground), land use and soil cover, daytime surface temperatures, nighttime surface temperatures, heat islands, highways, implanted blocks;
(v) Territorial: Ecological-Economic Zoning (ZEE-DF), Zoning of the Federal District Territorial Planning Master Plan (PDOT-DF), Integral Protection Conservation Units, Sustainable Use Conservation Units, Water Sources Protection Areas (APM), Permanent Protection Areas (APP), Legal Reserves;
(vi) Socioeconomic: Social Vulnerability Index, Housing Deficit and Purchasing Power.

Among the main models elaborated above, we can highlight those produced for the workshop, which supports the provision of ecosystem services. These models are related to the support of the ecosystem services project, essential for planning the green infrastructure supporting ecological processes and landscape ecology.

The layers of the system address: (i) carbon sequestration in vegetation, through the spectral index CO2flux; (ii) the presence of soil moisture, expressed by the spectral index TWI and the (iii) ERP, resulting from the crossing of the CO2flux with the areas with the highest topographical humidity in the TWI, as shown in Fig. 3. The three layers, when associated with the others in the system, can indicate both the strategic areas for conservation, expansion, or creation of vegetated areas.

In turn, the Landscape Ecology system presents landscape metrics (connectivity, core area, and form factor) applied in two perspectives: (i) one referring to the contemporary structure of vegetation distribution along the Federal District and (ii) a potential one, referring to a scenario of conservation and expansion of patches and ecological corridors in the areas indicated by the layer. This layer system is essential for understanding the presence and flow of biodiversity in the cerrado, in proposing a regional green infrastructure network. Figure 4, as an example, presents the connectivity layer and the potential connectivity layer.

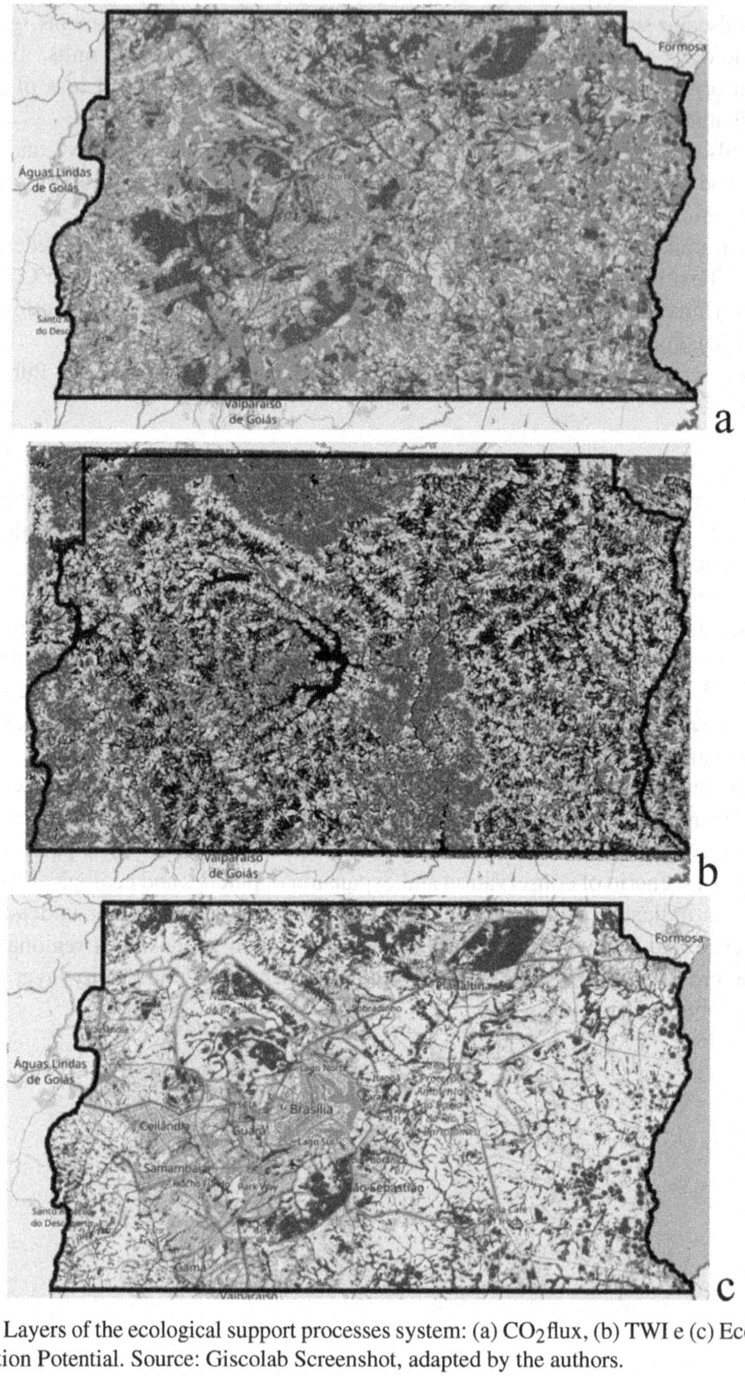

Fig. 3. Layers of the ecological support processes system: (a) CO_2flux, (b) TWI e (c) Ecological Restoration Potential. Source: Giscolab Screenshot, adapted by the authors.

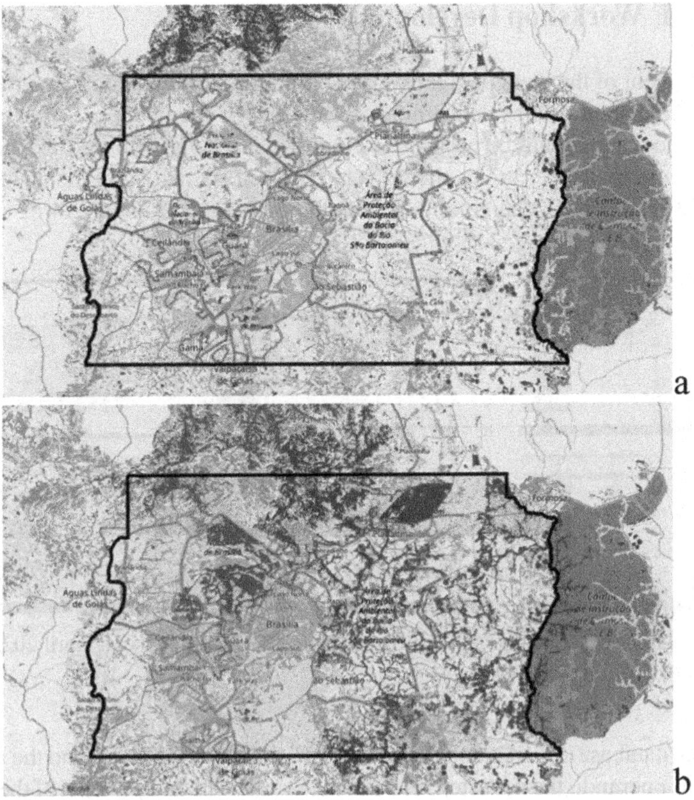

Fig. 4. Example of the landscape ecology system layers: (a) connectivity, (b) connectivity potential. Source: Giscolab Screenshot, adapted by the authors.

Aiming a conceptual alignment among the participants, a metadata spreadsheet (Fig. 5) was also provided with the description of the organizing concept of each layer and the respective source, grouped by category.

MAIN SYSTEM			
System	Data name in GeoGiscolab	Description of the layer organizer concept	Data Sources: Bibliography and or database
Socioeconomic	Social Vulnerability Index	The Social Vulnerability Index (SVI) is an indicator that allows for a breakdown of the living conditions of all socioeconomic strata of the country, identifying those who are in vulnerability and social risk. It is calculated from 3 dimensions of indicators: Urban Infrastructure; Human Capital; and Income and Work.	Codeplan and the Federal District Urban Development Department
	Housing Deficit	The Housing Deficit indicates the deficiency in housing in each region. It is usually a numerical indicator, which represents the number of deficient housing units. For its calculation, families living in conditions of cohabitation, excessive density, housing precariousness and/or excessive rent burden are considered.	https://www.geoportal.seduh.df.gov.br/geoportal/
	Purchasing power	Average monthly income per capita	Poder Aquisitivo (ssdia.df.gov.br)

Fig. 5. Example of a part of metadata presentation. Source: The authors.

3 IVR-DF Workshop Development

The development of the workshop took place online (Fig. 6), with only one recommendation for the distant groups concerning the number of members per working group. For a dynamic where it will be possible to comply with the principles of geodesign, the number of participants per group should vary between six and eight members plus the moderator who will be in charge of the operation of the geodesign platform.

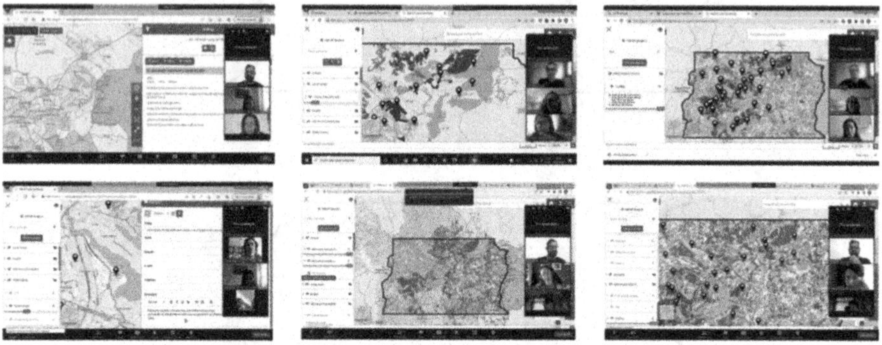

Fig. 6. Screenshots of the online participation dynamic held in March and April 2022. Source: The authors. (Color figure online)

After the database organization phase (information layers system) and the definition of the modus operandi, the next step refers to the profile and composition of the working groups to propose solutions for the regional green infrastructure.

In the case of the IVR-DF, eight participants were selected, covering three categories of participants, aiming at different perspectives on the landscape of the DF:

(i) A group of specialists in landscape architecture from outside the DF;
(ii) A group of researchers from the research project that generated the data on ecological processes (Urban Environmental Management Group from PPGFAU/UnB);
(iii) A group of technicians from the Federal District Government is already acquainted with land management planning in the environmental and urban areas.

The three sections of the Workshop were developed over 3 weeks, interspersed with days that were dedicated to individual work based on geodesign.

The works included predefined tasks of comments and complementation of ideas launched in the joint sections.

It is important to highlight that the first section was about leveling the bases of methodological information as well for the members to get to know each other. Subsequently, the participants were divided evenly into three groups (A, B, and C) (Fig. 7) that worked in two sections to develop design proposals for the DF on a regional scale.

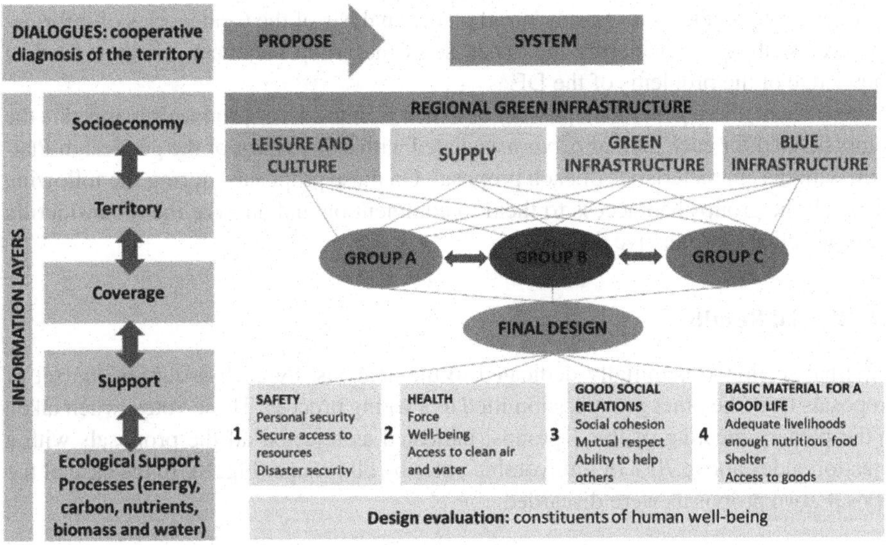

Fig. 7. Workshop framework. Source: The authors. (Color figure online)

From a methodological point of view, the geodesign proposals follow four main axes:

(i) Leisure and culture;
(ii) Provision;
(iii) Green infrastructure;
(iv) Blue infrastructure (Fig. 7).

Such axes aim to organize the discussion and not necessarily define the scope of the proposals that must adhere to the reality of each territory studied. They are axes of action in landscape architecture that helps to detect the needs of public policies for the study area, to protect, adapt and transform the landscape, aiming for its resilience.

Thus, the proposals could be composed either of programs or projects. Proposals should be divided into four subsystems: leisure and culture (gray), provision (yellow), green infrastructure (green) and blue infrastructure (blue) (Fig. 7). In addition, participants should confirm, through widgets, whether the launched proposals would affect, positively or negatively, the following well-being constituents:

(i) Safety;
(ii) Health;
(iii) Good social relations;
(iv) The basic material for a good life, which, according to the Millennium Ecosystem Assessment, configure the necessary dimensions for human beings' freedom of choice and action [5].

Each group made its proposals based on the analysis of the 6 categories of information layers, always considering the expertise of the group members and their level of knowledge of the problems of the DF.

As a result, three general maps were obtained with the set of proposals mapped in the colors defined for each thematic axis associated with a descriptor of the geodesign Platform with the characteristics of each proposal. On these proposals, during the following week, all the groups had access to them to comment on and analyze them considering the last section of collective design.

3.1 Partial Results

The final section was initially dedicated to the analysis, by each group, of the set of proposals from the other groups, submitted to a voting process. These votes, when taken to the plenary meeting of the 3 groups, indicated as rejected all the proposals with a rejection index above 70% of unfavorable votes by all groups (Fig. 8). In the case of the IRV-DF, two proposals were discarded.

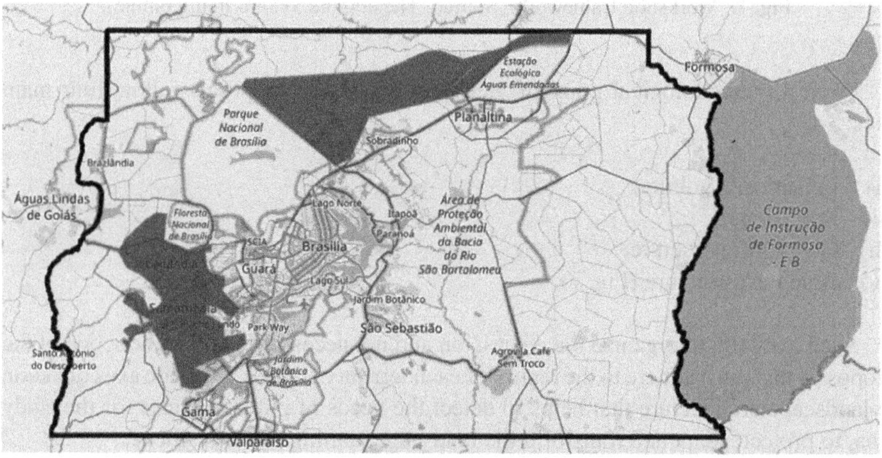

Fig. 8. Discarded proposals (red designs). Source: Giscolab Screenshot, adapted by the authors. (Color figure online)

However, when the votes reached a 60–40% or 50–50% ratio, the proposals were presented to the plenary, where a representative of each group defended their proposal, followed by the vote, which resulted in 4 approved proposals that followed the required subsystems. The following text analyzes each of these four proposals.

3.1.1 Green Infrastructure Subsystem: Approved Design

The green infrastructure subsystem denotes a common concern among most technicians and researchers. Such concern is indicated with the tracing of connections between the cores of the Cerrado Biosphere Reserve, which resulted in the design of biodiversity corridors with potential for regional connectivity. These corridors are located between Águas Emendadas, the National Park and the Jardim Botânico region, and, in another quadrant of the DF, with the need to connect and protect the vegetated areas between the cities of Taguatinga (ARIE JK), Samambaia, Ceilândia and Recanto das Emas.

This implied the necessity of a connection between ARIE JK and Santo Antônio do Descoberto in the Southwest direction (Fig. 9).

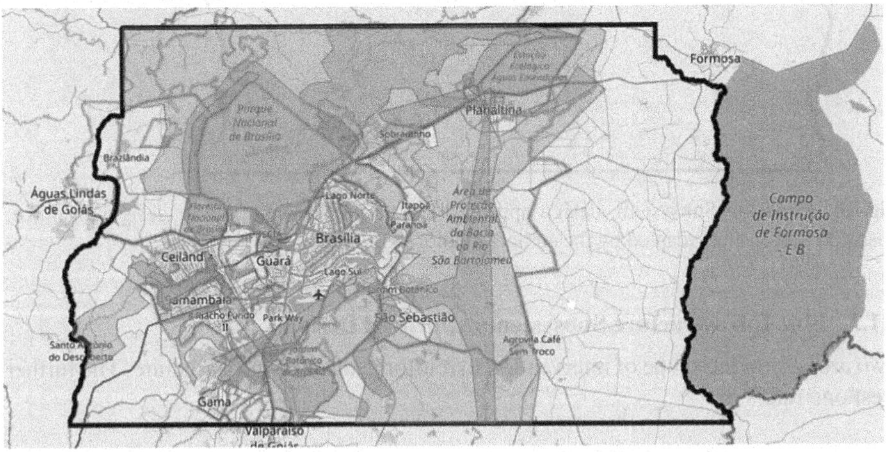

Fig. 9. Green Infrastructure Subsystem: design approved by the participants (light green designs). Source: Giscolab Screenshot, adapted by the authors. (Color figure online)

3.1.2 Provision Subsystem: Approved Design

In the provisioning subsystem, solutions were presented for the densification of the occupations along with the areas of influence of the Cerrado Biosphere Reserves through rural and/or urban occupations. These areas should be subject to Payments for Environmental Services with the promotion of agroforestry, permaculture and organic production, on the properties bordering these areas. For the essentially agricultural watershed of the basin of the Preto River in the DF, an incentive program was proposed to overcome the pattern of large monocultures based on pesticides and intensive use of water aiming carbon farming with water resilience, expanding the ecosystem functions of the region. The proposed program also aims to expand the ecological infrastructure beyond legal reserves and the introduction of other rural uses, not only monocultures but also productive farms for fruit and vegetables and rural tourism (Fig. 10).

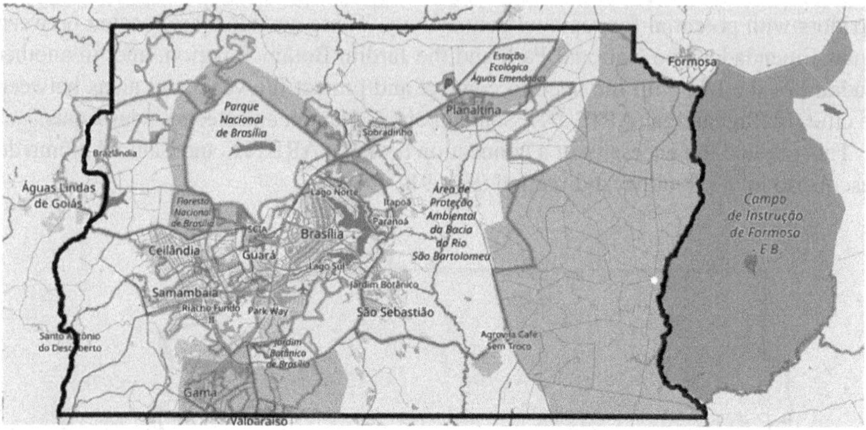

Fig. 10. Provision Subsystem: design approved by the participants (yellow designs). Source: Giscolab Screenshot, adapted by the authors. (Color figure online)

3.1.3 Blue Infrastructure Subsystem: Approved Design

Two areas form the scope of intervention to reinforce the blue infrastructure. The further west one refers to:

(i) The demand for requalification of the urban patterns of the cities located in priority aquifer recharge areas, to develop water resilience through the structuring of a system of urban green areas with the introduction of water into the landscape;
(ii) Review of permeability patterns of land and public spaces; (iii) incentives for public orchards and vegetable gardens and restoration of APP areas with native vegetation, all supported by environmental education actions (Fig. 11).

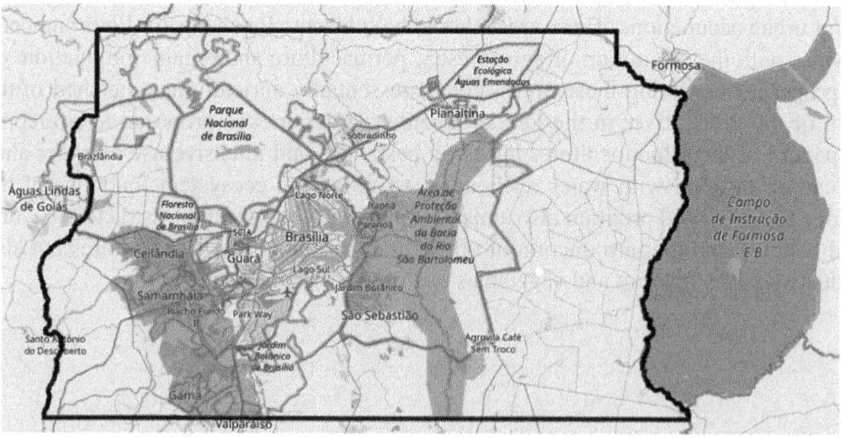

Fig. 11. Blue infrastructure subsystem: design approved by the participants (light blue designs). Source: Giscolab Screenshot, adapted by the authors. (Color figure online)

3.1.4 Leisure and Culture Subsystem: Approved Design

The final proposal was the result of a collective construction as there was only one design. The focus of this proposal was centered on rural and ecological tourism, where various potentials of the area were explored.

Among the verified potentials were the presence of waterfalls, eco-tourism, cultural tourism, sports and environmental education potentials, including the possibilities for recreation for the territory involving different income groups (Fig. 12).

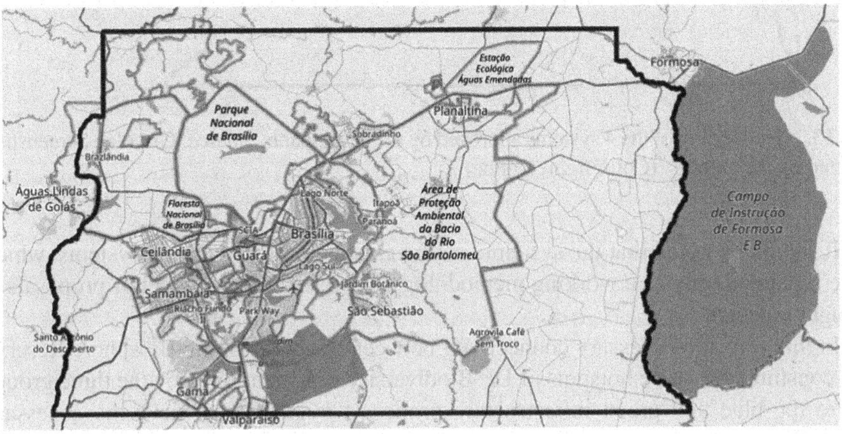

Fig. 12. Leisure and culture subsystem: design approved by the participants (gray design) Source: Giscolab Screenshot, adapted by the authors. (Color figure online)

3.2 Overlapping of Approved Design Subsystems

A proposed summary for the general understanding of the designs of the 4 overlapping subsystems in the DF territory is presented below (Fig. 13). The overlapping shows that, in general, there was a need for connection between nuclei of the Cerrado reserve and concerns about blue infrastructure in areas at risk of aquifer loss.

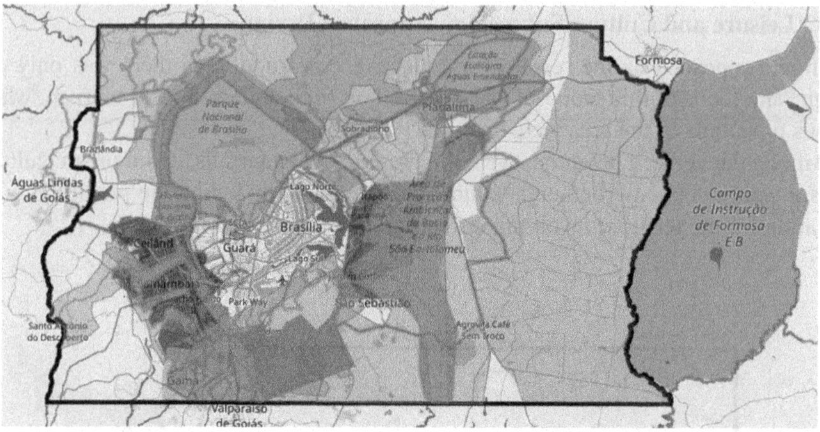

Fig. 13. Overlapping of the 4 systems approved by the participants. Source: Giscolab Screenshot, adapted by the authors. (Color figure online)

It should be noted that the systemic nature existing between the subsystems, which were separated only as a working methodology, is present when the set of proposals is brought together.

In this way, the necessary connectivity between the cores of the Biosphere Reserve that constitute the three hotspots of DF Biodiversity was mentioned by the three groups where the blue and green infrastructure proposals overlap to achieve the necessary connectivity.

Likewise, parts of the corridors formed between the three hotspots were highlighted as areas where ecotourism and leisure activities have the potential to occur, contributing to a green economy for the DF.

Another highlight regards a topic of extreme relevance to the DF, which is the water supply where the areas at risk of compromising the recharge of aquifers are occupied by settlements with high impermeability.

In this aspect, there are proposals in the southwest quadrant of the DF that outline strategies for retrofitting urban areas with the introduction of green infrastructure elements, providing soil permeability.

Also in this area, considering the existence of ARIE JK among the three largest cities in the DF, it was proposed to establish it as a biodiversity nucleus, functioning as a radiator of green wedges for the cities that surround it.

4 Results and Discussion

The use of the geodesign methodology in the planning and design process of a regional green infrastructure network, enabled through the synthesis of the adopted layers of information, the construction of a collective perception about the potential and territorial conflicts regarding its implementation. Geodesign also helped to bring out the relevance of layers related to supporting ecological processes and landscape ecology in design.

In this workshop it was possible to bring together in a co-design process, different perspectives of experts with different backgrounds, overcoming the false notion that the environment and urban development configure opposite fields.

The consensus worked out during the discussions throughout the workshop, made it possible to take a first step towards sketching, which would be a regional design for the territory studied. It also indicated the priorities for designing the project, both in terms of the project and in terms of processes and programs.

The results of the Workshop, although partial, point to some structuring bases of a more resilient occupation for the DF and can contribute to the revision of the PDOT-DF that is now under discussion. Among these, the need to create green area systems that advance from a traditional view of vegetation only for leisure and social interaction and progress towards the necessary function that a system of this nature has for the promotion of ecosystem services, has emerged as a great contribution.

A development already agreed upon between the Workshop members and the research groups involved from Universidade de Brasília (UnB), Pontificia Universidade Católica (PUC-MG) and Universidade Federal de Minas Gerais (UFMG) refers to the continuity of the geodesign process in a second iteration to consolidate the results achieved so far.

The use of geodesign tools, according to the case study presented here, provides a change in the planning and territorial design paradigm in which the design anticipates the proposition of plans, programs, and projects. This inversion indicates an important and much faster path than the "usual" for the planning, implementation and monitoring of policies without which a complex proposal such as the IVR-DF would not be able to be implemented at the time of the pressures and demands on the territorial occupation of the DF region.

Acknowledgments. FAP-DF support through the Project *Re-planejando o território: mensuração de serviços ecossistêmicos para assertivas intervenções no ordenamento do solo urbano* Edital 04/2021. The use of the GISColab platform and the guidelines about geodesign were possible due to the projects CNPq 401066/2016–9 and Fapemig PPM-00368–18.

References

1. Marsh, G.P.: Man and nature. Scribner, Armstrong & CO, New York (1864)
2. Vogt, W.: Road to survival. New York: Sloane (1942)
3. Osborn, H.F.: Our Plundered Planet. Lillte, Brown and Company, New York (1948)
4. Da Veiga, J.E.: Desenvolvimento sustentável: o desafio do século XXI. Editora Garamond (2005)
5. Millennium Ecosystem Assessment Board – MEA: Ecosystems and Human Well-being: A Framework for Assessment. Island Press, London (2005)
6. de Oliveira Monteiro, L., Moura, A.C.M., Zyngier, C.M., Sena, Í.S., de Paula, P.L.: Geodesign facing the urgency of reducing poverty: the cases of Belo Horizonte. DisegnareCon **11**(20), 6–1 (2018)
7. Steinitz, C.: A Framework for Geodesign: Changing Geography by Design. ESRI Press, Redlands (2012)

8. Moura, A.C.M., Freitas, C.R.: Scalability in the application of geodesign in Brazil: expanding the use of the Brazilian geodesign platform to metropolitan regions in transformative-learning planning. Sustainability **13**(12), 6508 (2021). https://doi.org/10.3390/su13126508
9. Carpenter, S.R., et al.: Science for managing ecosystem services: beyond the millennium ecosystem assessment. Proc. Natl. Acad. Sci. **106**(5), 1305–1312 (2009)
10. Potschin, M., Haines-Young, R.: From nature to society. In: Burkhard, B., Maes, J. (eds.) 2017, pp. 39–41. Mapping ecosystem services, Pensoft Publishers, Sofia (2017)
11. Haines-Young, R., Potschin-Young, M.: Revision of the common international classification for ecosystem services (CICES V5. 1): a policy brief. One Ecosystem, 3, n. e27108, p. 1–6 (2018)
12. Hallett, L.M., et al.: Towards a conceptual framework for novel ecosystems. In: Hoobs, R.J., Higgs, E.S., Hall, C.M. (eds.) (Orgs.). Novel ecosystems: intervening in the new ecological world order, pp. 16–28 (2013)
13. Distrito Federal. Lei nº 6.269, de 29 de Janeiro de 2019. Institui o Zoneamento Ecológico-Econômico do Distrito Federal (ZEE-DF) em cumprimento ao art. 279 e ao art. 26 do Ato das Disposições Transitórias da Lei Orgânica do Distrito Federal e dá outras providências. Diário Oficial do Distrito Federal: Suplemento B, Brasília, DF, n. 21, janeiro de (2019)
14. Amaral, R., Bezerra, M.C.L., Baptista, G.M.M.: Bases para o planejamento territorial urbano. Uso de imagens hiperespectrais para a identificação de áreas geradoras de funções ecológicas de suporte. Cidades. Comunidades e Territórios **41**, 71–89 (2020)
15. Raduła, M.W., Szymura, T.H., Szymura, M.: Topographic wetness index explains soil moisture better than bioindication with Ellenberg's indicator values. Ecol. Ind. **85**, 172–179 (2018)
16. Baptista, G.M.M.: Mapeamento do sequestro de carbono e de domos urbanos de CO_2 em ambientes tropicais, por meio de sensoriamento remoto hiperespectral. Geografia **29**(2), 189–202 (2005)
17. Hobbs, R.J., et al.: Movers and stayers: novel assemblages in changing environments. Trends Ecol. Evol. **33**(2), 116–128 (2018)
18. Instituto Brasileiro de Geografia e Estatística (IBGE): "Distrito Federal: História & Fotos". São Paulo: IBGE- Cidades (2019)

Sifting Through Historical Maps. Methodology for the Implementation of Cartographic Content in Urban Planning: Case Study of Desio

Dina Jovanović(✉) and Daniela Oreni

Department of Architecture, Built Environment and Construction Engineering, Politecnico di Milano, 20133 Milan, Italy
dina.jovanovic@polimi.it

Abstract. Numerous conventions and recommendations for the protection of cultural heritage state the importance of implementing an integrated conservation approach, taking care of built and natural elements in their settings. For small, widespread historical centres in Lombardy, historical stratigraphy is complex and often there is a lack of historical material to understand the towns' evolution. With neglected and forgotten heritage values, historical centres are suffering degradation and abandonment. The study will examine the content which can be extracted from historical maps in the form of implicit and non-implicit characteristics and focus on the means and tools for their use in urban planning. The research suggests the essential implementation of historical cartography and accompanying documents in the creation of the Municipal Urban Plan, by building the database in the Geographic Information System. The developed methodology offers adaptable approaches for analysing maps regardless of their scale or aim. Decomposition of elements, systematisation of the features presented on the historical map and application of modern urban theories, will allow researchers to compare spatial and textual elements on different maps and link them with the contemporary survey. The research criticizes the potential errors that can occur in urban plans if the historical background is not thoroughly investigated and there is no comparison between past and present data. Study will assist spatial thinking though contextualised historical data as tool for participatory planning to support GeoDesign concepts and methods.

Keywords: Historical cartography · Urban planning methods · Municipal Urban Plan of Desio (PGT) · Map deconstruction approach

1 Introduction

The practice of cartography goes beyond mere physical representation - it is a record of human history that reflects the attitudes, knowledge, and expectations of the society in which it was created [1]. Historical maps are the primary medium for transmitting ideas and knowledge about space. Additionally, they offer political, economic, religious, and social context of the towns they represent, which evoke complex meanings and responses;

O. Gervasi et al. (Eds.): ICCSA 2022 Workshops, LNCS 13379, pp. 165–180, 2022.
https://doi.org/10.1007/978-3-031-10545-6_12

thus, they record more than just space [2, 3]. Multidisciplinary cartographic practices are reflected through the difficulty of defining and studying them [4]. The available research in the field of cartography grew in number over the past decades. This renewed interest occurred through the switch in perspective on the definition of cartography through time. It was described firstly as *science* [5], then it was positioned between *art, science, and technology* [6], followed by the definition of being a *discipline* [7]. Researchers are still discussing appropriate explanations of what are *cartography* and *maps* [8]. The main reason why defining cartography is not an easy task lies in generalization which does not include the crucial variables: period, aim, production process and visual representation of maps. Moreover, technologies are changing rapidly and they are influencing mapping practices. The differences between traditional and digital maps are creating a gap, and often researchers are unable to create connections between historical and contemporary cartography [9].

A map represents, describes, and relates to other cultural heritage depicted on it. As such, historical maps can be treated as heritage that should be preserved and digitized to be protected and used. To achieve this aim, it is necessary to use modern methods and digital technologies that form the backbone of non-invasive cultural preservation and investigation of its tangible and intangible values. The level of dissemination, availability and use of historical cartography and other historical documents has changed significantly with the introduction of recommendations for their digital preservation. The European Commission has recognized the importance of digitalization of archival documents, paying special attention to historical cartography [10]. It developed projects such as'Europeana', which works with the GLAM[1] sources, and created the educational platform 'European Digital Service Infrastructure' (DSI) [11] to distribute and actively use historical material across the world. The Steering Committee of the Italian Digital Library (ital. *Comitato Guida della Biblioteca Digitale Italiana*) developed guidelines for the digitization of cartographic material and the management of its sources [4]. This was a ground-breaking step in reconstructing the public and private archives for a better propagation and protection of cartographic material. Once cartographic material is accessible, it can be used from education to preservation and participatory planning projects [12]. Nevertheless, the practice and results show that these applications of GeoDesign were not easy to attain on behalf of public administration, scholars, and individual practitioners in the studied context.

There is an increasing need to rethink the planning approaches, especially of the small, widespread historical centres. They are unique traces of the past in cities today, and it is important to consider their spatial and cultural-historical values often hidden or destroyed while creating an urbanistic plan. Numerous studies show the good and bad practices of past urban planning, damaged on the one hand by industrialization and the widening of streets to meet the needs of the car, and on the other, good practices that restored cultural values of the city and remained functional for the needs of contemporary society [13]. Historical maps are gradually being incorporated by public administrations into territorial government plans. However, they are not used constructively to provide the historical stratigraphy, which is so important for urban planning, preservation, and revitalization of cultural heritage. Usually, they are presented only in the introduction

[1] GLAM – abbreviation for Galleries, Libraries, Archives and Museums.

to the plans and their true spatial values are completely neglected [14]. This research aims to provide planners and architects with methods and tools to actively use the content extracted from historical maps and accompanying documents in the framework of digital and urban planning recommendations for contextualizing planning projects. Through techniques of geovisualisation, the study will initiate participatory planning and accelerate spatial thinking for protection and maintenance of landscape and built cultural heritage.

2 Urban Planning Declarations

Planning practices changed in the mid-20th century, bringing more attention to the preservation and management of historical centres as an undividable part of built environments. Many recommendations appeared in this period regarding the heritage protection. The Venice Charter published in 1964 decreed that architectural heritage is inseparable from its urban or rural setting [15]. This was furthermore elaborated in 1975, in the Declaration of Amsterdam, which expressed the importance of considering cultural heritage and its surroundings as a unity and implementing conservation strategies as an integral part of regional and urban planning. This was a pioneering approach to the protection of cultural heritage and a crucial step in the development of more sustainable urban plans [16]. Moreover, the European Charter of the Architectural Heritage adopted a resolution in 1976, setting out policies and regulatory requirements for integrated urban conservation, including guidelines for the protection of historic centres and landscapes as a vital part of urban planning objectives. The focus shifted from the single monument to the historic centres and landscapes, which gave a wider context to the issues of preservation included in the urban planning process. Additionally, committees called upon local authorities and citizens to participate together in the preservation of their common goods, which aligns with the research goal and concepts of GeoDesign.

In 2017, as part of the UN strategic plan, UN-Habitat adopted the'New Urban Agenda' which emphasised the importance of strengthening communities and decentralizing territories by empowering towns locally [17]. The ICOMOS's Resolution on the Conservation of Smaller Historic Towns (1975) listed threats and dangers for small historical centres: lack of economic activity, an outflow of population, and overall decay and abandonment of structures. The resolution recommends vital actions to be implemented to maintain the cultural heritage values and provides authorities with the strategies for planning and protecting indigenous spatial and cultural qualities. It stresses the importance of coordination in all planning stages [18]. The process of conservation of historical centres was significantly improved since the introduction of digitalized material which accelerated the multidisciplinary approach and engagement of various stakeholders. Digitization allowed online dissemination of accessible historical material and the creation of interconnected databases for future planning activities.

3 Location: Importance and Reasoning

The region of Lombardy was selected as a territory for the selection of the case study for numerous reasons. Firstly, the cartographic material coming from the Statal Archive of Milan (ital. *Archivio di Stato di Milano* (ASMi)) describes and presents the territory, which has remained relatively homogenous. Hence, the cartography was made for "internal purposes" by various administrations or entities [19], which also provided a good amount of diverse cartography. From the 13th century began an era of the lordship of influential families which changed the conceptualisation of public and private property [20]. In the 15th century, the progress of medieval settlements was interrupted by the turbulent period. In 1714, the Duchy of Milan passed from the hands of rulers of the Habsburgs of Spain to those of the Habsburgs of Austria. The territory was finally united in 1796, under the aegis of Napoleon Bonaparte, into the new Cisalpine Republic of which Milan was the capital [21].

This was also the period where the historical cartography available now started flourishing for tax and estimation purposes, census of population and tracking property ownership (i.e., *Catasto Teresiano*) [22]. After the defeat of Napoleon, the Duchy of Milan became a part of the Lombardo-Venetian Kingdom in 1815 (i.e., *Catasto Lombardo-Veneto*) until the unity of Italian states in 1861 (i.e., *Nuovo Catasto Terreni*) [23]. In the 19th and 20th centuries, there was increased activity in fashioning, remaking, and producing land cadastral maps with improved surveying techniques and technologies. Cities were undergoing constant rebuild and destruction phases, affected by human and natural hazards, and often heritage suffered greatly. The occurrence of various regimes produced different cadastres and thematic maps, which created the complex but fertile starting point for further research.

3.1 Case Study of Desio: Historical Background

The small historical centre of Desio, a town north of Milan, was chosen for the case study. Its strategic position since ancient times and the continuous demolition and reconstruction phases over the centuries have largely erased the cultural heritage values, and most of those remaining has been forgotten [24]. Desio emerged when Celtic Gallic tribes arrived. They were replaced by the Romans who established a military *castrum* with the main axis *Cardo* and *Decumano*, which are still traceable today. They fortified the city to control the important road that led from Milan to Como [25]. Due to the proximity of the military protection, rural houses and huts were being constructed outside of the walls of the *borgo*. With the coming of the *Longobardi*, Desio stayed an important chief town, which shape and history influenced the development of the modern town [26]. From 17th century, noble villas were emerging and the town served as a destination for leisure. Desio experienced rapid expansion during the industrial age and its heritage was slowly losing its form and authenticity. The advantage of the case study is the town's multi-layered history as a centre of a long-term establishment of administrative and religious power (see Fig. 1).

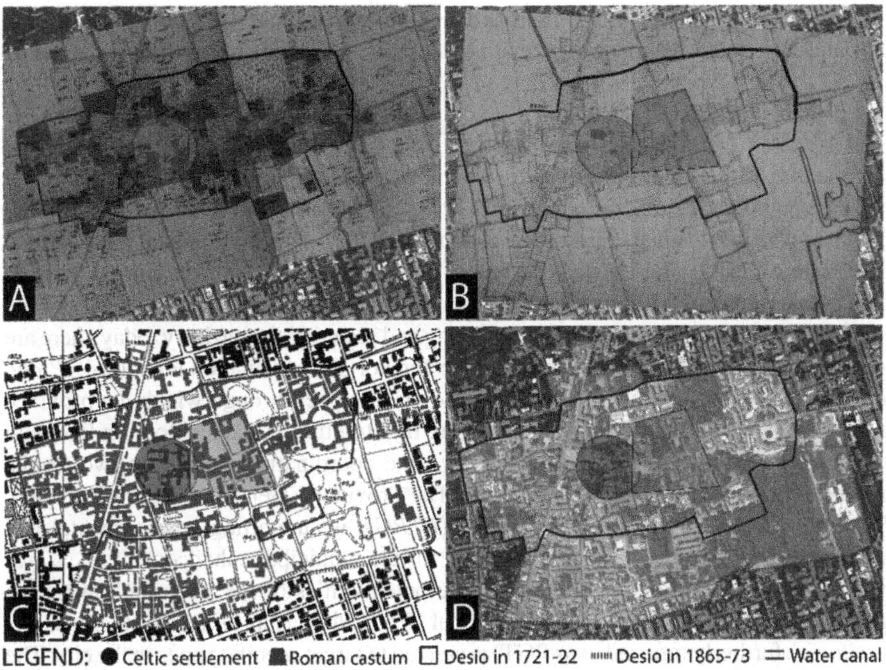

Fig. 1. Georeferenced maps of A: *Catasto Teresiano* (1721–22) (Source: ASMi); B: Georeferenced map *Catasto Lombardo-Veneto* (1865–73) (Source: ASMi); C: CTR (1980) (Source: Geoportale Lombardia); D: Orthophoto of Desio (2015) (Source: Geoportale Lombardia)[2]. The main physical characteristics of the town's transformations are schematically marked on all maps (Source: Authors).

The administrative body of the Lombardian Cultural Heritage (ital. *Beni Culturali Lombardia*) listed forty-one buildings in Desio as cultural heritage. More than half of them belong to the residential and tertiary sector architecture (51.2%). Religious and sacral architecture (22%) and rural architecture (17.1%) are especially interesting for Desio for their past agricultural activities and sacral importance. Buildings in the industrial and production sector (9.8%) are the least listed as patrimony. Desio has relatively poor architecture, mostly in the form of traditional Lombardian architecture of rural farmhouses or *cascine*. There are a few examples of *villas*, and they are distinguished with their precious artistic, architectural, and historical values from the rest of the urban area (e.g., Villa Traversi, Villa Klinkman, Villa Greppi, etc.). The villas and their gardens are unique examples of noble architecture from the 17th to 19th century. Other residential architecture, mostly houses with distinct types of courtyards, are characteristic of

[2] Archivio di Stato di Milano (ASMi), Fondo: Ufficio tecnico erariale. Milano. Catasti. Mappe sezione – Mappe piane I serie. A: - "Catasto teresiano. Mappe di attivazione (1721–1722)"; B: "Catasto lombardo veneto. Nuovo Censo. Mappe attivazione, Prima copia (1865–1873)"; C: "Carta Tenica Regionale (CTR) (1980)", sheets: B5B4, B5C4, Geoportale Regione Lombardia; D: Ortofoto Agea (2015), Geoportale Regione Lombardia.

Lombardy, too. Conversely, the Lombardian Cultural Heritage web portal did not list and categorize the natural heritage, open spaces, or water elements in the same manner.

3.2 Case Study of Desio: Municipal Urban Plan

Historical research is an undividable element of designing cities today and historical maps are an integral part of urban studies [27]. The maps on the scales from 1:1000 to 1:5000 are the most valuable for the investigation of the urban environment and physical relationships [28]. Historical cadastral maps and contemporary urban plans were made in this scale range, providing detailed explanations about the forms and functions of the buildings and land. In Lombardy, for managing and planning the territory today, there are two main plans used in the local context. 'The Territorial Coordination Plan' (ital. *'Piano Territoriale di Coordinamento' (PTC)*) is the planning act through which the province provides policies and indicators for designing the structure of the territory, in line with the territorial policies of the regional body. The coordination occurs on two levels: provincial and municipal urban planning. 'The Provincial General Planning' act (ital. *'Piano Territoriale Provinciale Generale' (PTPG)*) is supporting environmental and sustainable development. It gives indicators for the municipal enhancement, measures the municipal urban tools, and evaluates the potentialities of the areas. Following the provincial recommendations, 'The Municipal Urban Plan' (ital. *'Piano di Governo del Territorio'*, furtherly referred to as PGT) is created to target specific zones in the city. The plan has the purpose to define the structure of the entire municipal area and it consists of three distinct acts (see Fig. 2).

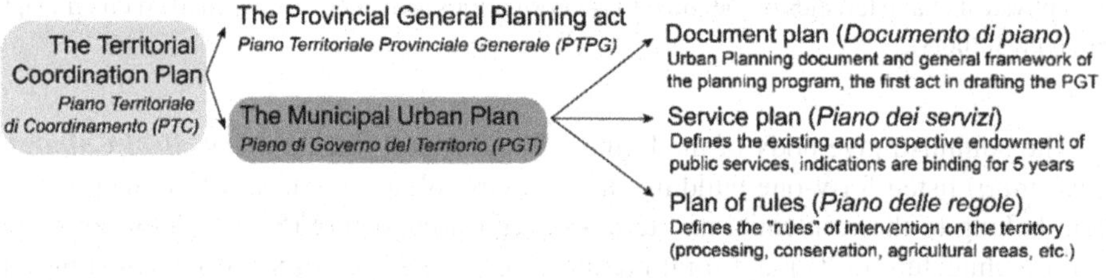

Fig. 2. The urban planning acts and plans in Lombardy and their content. Source: Authors.

Historical maps are appearing in the introduction of the PGT, in the chapter about the history of Desio, where they are mentioned as an important and initial source of information about the urban changes. Later, in the chapter'Census of Historical Heritage', the text refers to the tables in the form of the catalogue of cultural heritage, where historical maps are presented again, but not analysed [29]. The PGT made by the Municipality of Desio on the scale of 1:2000 will be the main critical point on which the developed methodology will be applied to produce better administrative plans concerning complex and not well-defined historical centres. The first problem noticed in the PGT is that in the theoretical part of the document, the administration is aware of the importance of consulting historical maps, although in practice that is not applied efficiently. Historical maps throughout the document are used as an illustration, without georeferencing and comparing maps from different periods, which does not allow professionals or planners to understand the evolution of the town. Moreover, other historical documents, such as land registers, illustrations and descriptions are not used for the census or assessment of cultural heritage.

In conclusion, the study aims to uncover implicit and non-implicit features on the historical maps, to be used for the creation of official municipal urban plans. The analyses of the spatial relationships through the different maps and documents, the use of modern urban theories and the Geographic Information System (GIS) software, can develop an elaborated study through deductive and critical analyses. This will significantly increase efficiency, nurture the communication and multi-disciplinarity between engaged parties, and allow faster and less expensive dissemination.

4 Methodology: Implementing Content from Historical Maps

Cartographic content is neglected in city designing, although it can provide insights into past functions, developments of urban areas, and changes in land use. It is essential to rethink historical documentation as a source of scientific data to build a spatial-temporal stratigraphy. The research provides a set of guidelines for using the contents of historical cadastral maps at the scale of 1:2000, produced from the 18th century onwards. Those maps are comparable with the actual PGT, geometrically measurable, and they have a vast variety of accompanying data (e.g., land registers, patterns, past planning actions, etc.). The changes in the built environment are inevitable, but the frameworks developed for GeoDesign in the past can support protection of cultural heritage, as well as design of contemporary cities with the respect to its values, above all taking care of the type of geography, scale, and size [30].

The application of the methodology starts with the systematization of the collected historical documentation and their deconstruction of primary features. To comprehend historical cartography, a combination of various skills and knowledge in different fields is required, therefore often it is not possible to study cartographic content *en bloc*. Dismantling the map on the features will focus on each element individually and on its relationship with the surrounding. The link between the flat presentation on the map and the information that the selected investigated element is providing should be broken to be rebuilt with other contemporary information. "Deconstructing maps" derived as a concept from J. B. Harley's work [31], but his research did not include the question of the purpose and scale in which extracted content would be used. This study is adding both additional criteria, specifically targeting the applications in urban plans of small widespread historical centres. Since a map is already a complex project made in the past, the elements on historical maps need to be "deconstructed" into three categories: natural elements, man-made and natural elements which are artificially shaped by man. The division of the first two categories is based on the UNESCO convention [32] and urbanist theories [33]. The study proposes adding the third category which consists of natural elements artificially made (e.g., parks, water canals or hedges) (See Fig. 3).

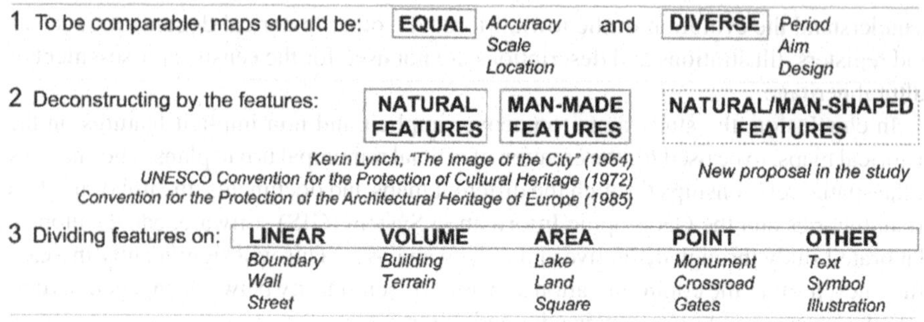

Fig. 3. Process of the selection, systematization, and deconstruction of historical maps on simplified elements for further analysis. Source: Authors.

The methodology uses theories of urban planning and design and examines physical features and cultural elements on historical maps that can be reused in planning by categorizing them in a generalized scheme. Generalized elements are divided into linear, volume, area, point and other features. This facilitates the implementation of modern concepts by selecting the features to be analysed and adapting specific methodology and techniques for in-depth study. Since all historical maps are individual scientific and artistic creations, flexible and adaptable methods are required but within well-defined and reproducible guidelines. After examining historical features and their relationship to one other and conducting a contemporary survey to create a spatial timeline, the pieces of data are reassembled using digital tools [34]. The inserted contemporary information will include administrative urban plans, photographic survey, experiences of citizens, and an assessment of the current state of cultural heritage.

The methodology provides the steps within the GIS to perform map regression analysis, allowing the user to access the metadata and link other historical material to their attributes. Georeferencing of historical maps inside the common coordinate system allows map regression for tracking the changes in the urban environment [35]. Three sets of historical cadastral maps that are held in the Statal Archive of Milan have been used for the study: *Catasto Teresiano* (1721–22), *Catasto Lombardo-Veneto* (1865–73 and 1875–1898) and *Nuovo Catasto Terreni* (1897–1902) all on the scale of 1:2000. The tool'Georeferencer' was used in the software QGIS for georeferencing maps. Deconstructed features, based on their origin and divided into simplified recognition elements, are identified and vectorized inside QGIS. Contemporary vector shapefiles are downloaded from the Lombardian geoportal (ital. *Geoportale Lombardia*), and other information about cultural heritage is imported from the SIRBeC[3] catalogue which describes patrimony. The two approaches, the decomposition of historical maps and contemporary analysis, are interdependent as good urban planning requires historical analysis and tracking transformations, both at the urban and city scale. The research criticizes the potential errors that can occur in urban plans if the historical background is not thoroughly investigated and past and present data are not compared (see Fig. 4).

[3] SIRBeC - Sistema Informativo Beni Culturali (regione.lombardia.it), accessed on 7.4.2022.

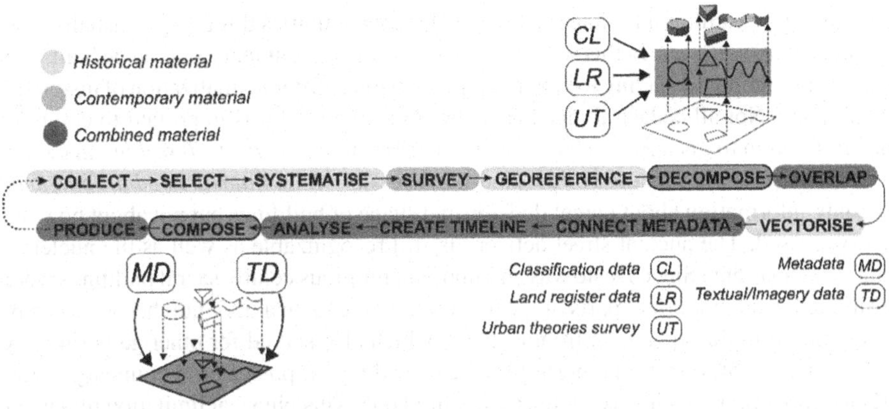

Fig. 4. Schematic preview of the developed methodology, used materials, and additional data linked to the historical and contemporary studies of the built environment. Source: Authors.

5 Results: Extracted Content and Its Evaluation

The applied methodological approach is adaptable to other sets of historical maps. Depending on the scale of the representation and typology of a map, researchers will be able to target their specific study of the urban environment of small centres. Decomposing and categorizing elements presented on the map allows the observation of single elements, and then their comparison to the related surrounding. Features on the map can be read as implicit and non-implicit. The former recognizes that what is represented should be taken as a fact: number and position of buildings, distribution of the streets, land use and surface, etc. However, the data that historical maps carry, and that is important for architects and urban planners, is often non-implicit. Those values can be read through the additional cross-referenced knowledge extracted from contemporary studies, urban theories and with the help of GIS technologies.

Non-implicit values can be translated from the map in terms of architectural style and evolution of buildings. Using land registers, it is possible to track the changes in ownership and function. The same approach can be employed for the investigation of land use, analysing why particular cultivation was in a specific area and what were the economic, social, and natural causes for those choices in the past. The use of open space, gardens, and piazzas had a significant role in the life of the community, and they are still the core of the town. Different arrangements and accessibility to those spaces can indicate the citizens' behaviour and political and economic influences. Street networks in historical centres have significantly changed, but historical alleys and ancient route can still be identified. The names of streets often suggest their previous use or that of nearby buildings, natural elements, or point to historical figures.

5.1 Urban Analysis and Thematic Maps

The study illustrates a developed methodology for investigating the cadastral historical maps on a scale of 1:2000 to be compared to Desio's actual PGT. The main aim is to find ways to improve cultural heritage studies in planning activities through geovisualisation within the GIS software. In this way, a database for other documentation can be built, and data can be compared leading to better comprehension and contextualization of historical stratigraphy. Not all cadastral maps have the same aim, and it is important to combine the information to get a full image of the built environment. *Catasto Teresiano* made for taxation purposes was focused on the land-use diversity, while *Catasto Lombardo-Veneto* had only information about parcel division and shape of buildings but not about how the land was used. The ancient street network is still recognizable as well as the nuclei of antique formations. Since Desio was an important religious centre, sacral buildings were positioned in the important parts of the town next to the main axis. Churches were easily accessible from the squares in front of them, which also served for other gatherings. A water canal running from the north to the east and south, presented a boundary in the urban development but it accelerated agricultural one. This physical limitation remained until the canal was substituted with streets like in many other towns (see Fig. 5). The GIS software helps in the creation of thematic maps for faster and clearer visualization of the aimed group of features.

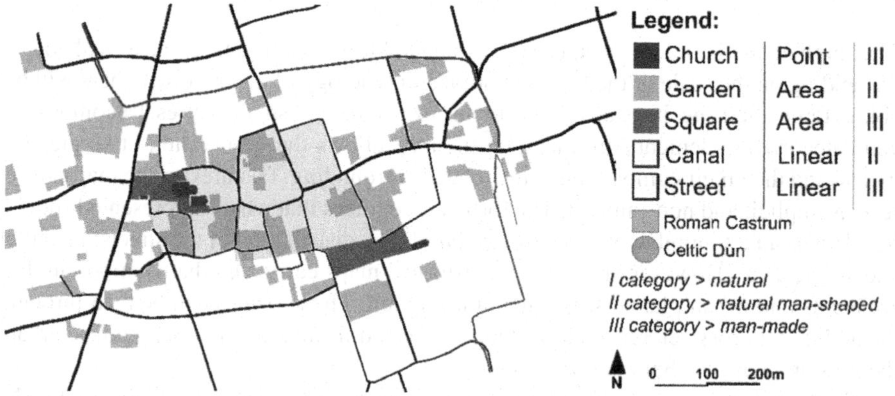

Fig. 5. Based on the *Catasto Teresiano* (1721–22) (source: ASMi, see Fig. 1 for details). Deconstructed on simplified and categorized features that were vectorised in QGIS. Source: Authors.

A newly produced thematic map can present the typology of noble villas (ital. *Ville gentilizie nell'Alto Milanese*) in Desio and building trends through time. The buildings in the city centre were built mostly in the typology house in a row and courtyard houses with several types of open and closed courtyards. In the oldest part of town, facades were facing the street, protecting the courtyards behind houses. Later on, houses were built further away, giving on to the street through open courtyards (see Fig. 6). Some future planning activities in the form of notes and sketches were directly drawn on the map (e.g., new openings, parcel divisions, paths, etc.).

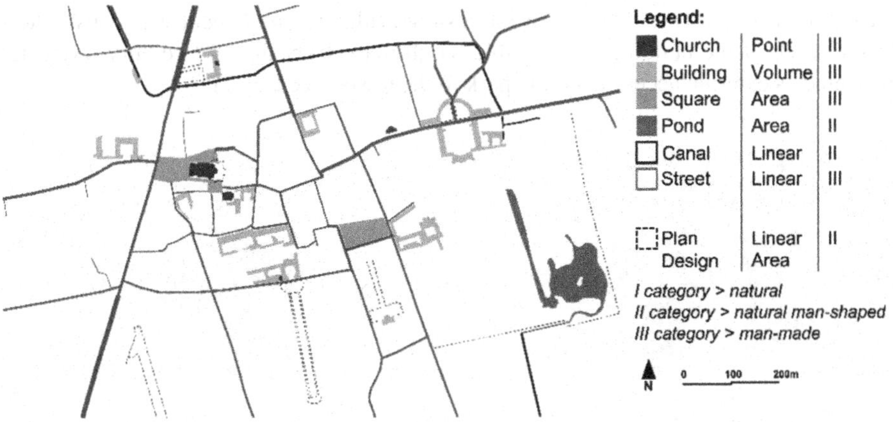

Fig. 6. Based on the *Catasto Lombardo-Veneto* (1865–73) (source: ASMi, see Fig. 1 for details). Deconstructed features vectorised in QGIS for pattern recognition. Yellow colour represents important built residential cultural heritage. Source: Authors.

5.2 Analysis of Buildings and Cross-referencing Historical Documents

Ex-convent complex and oratory of San Francesco in Desio was used to test methodology on a single cultural heritage building. The monastery was built in the first half of the 13th century and went through many changes over time, both in architectural and functional terms, which can be traced on historical maps due to the lack of other documentation. The friars of San Francesco built their convent with the scattered stones of demolished ancient structures found on the ground [25]. Around 1410, the lords of Milan, who no longer used the ancient castle residence of Bernabò Visconti, donated the surface of the castle and its adjacent areas to the convent. The donation included the site of the ancient building, the moat and part of the forest [26]. The cloister was divided into three arches and two columns on each side, which can be seen on the original cadastral map of the first survey for *Catasto Teresiano* (1720–23). At that time, the surface belonging to the convent consisted of arable land, a garden next to the cloister, and a small *piazza* in front of the oratory with mulberry trees.

On the subsequent cadastral map *Catasto Lombardo-Veneto* (1865–73) the oratory and convent lost their functions, as immediately recognised by the absence of cross symbols. The convent was transformed into a farmhouse with a part being used as a greenhouse, serving the property of Villa Tittoni Traversi. The small *piazza* that was in front of the church lost its public function and became the internal courtyard of the complex. The shift of the functions initiated a change in the structure, now more closely imitating the organization of a Lombardian *cascina* (i.e., farmhouse). The building, by this new organization, also lost the spatial relationship with the public square (i.e., *'Piazza Castello'*, today *'Piazza Martiri di Fossoli'*) signifying the private property and enclosed space. The name *'Piazza Castello'* written on the map indicates the previously mentioned structure that was in the area, the castle of Bernabò Visconti on which land convent was built. The building volume changed once more on the north side of the oratory on the map *Nuovo Catasto Terreni* (1897–1902). Arable land, which was presented on the first map, became part of the Tittoni park. An interesting bridge-ramp element was constructed on the south of the building. It is visible on all maps from the 19th century onwards, presented as external access from the park to the tower (see Fig. 7).

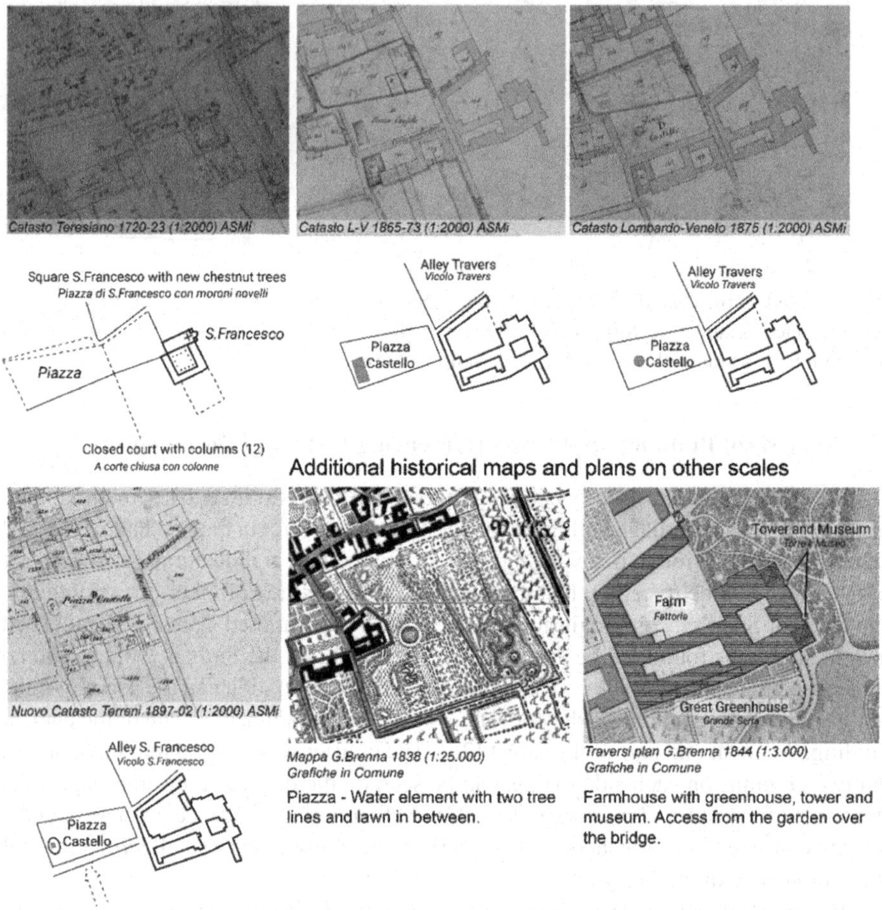

Fig. 7. Georeferenced cadastral historical maps in QGIS presenting the historical evolution of the ex-convent. oratory of San Francesco and piazza. The last two maps are not on the same scale, but they are presented as illustrations of the land use and functions of the buildings around 1840. (Map sources: indicated on the images, Analysis: Authors).

The old Cusani villa was substituted by Villa Tittoni Traversi. The architect Pelagio Palagi supervised all the works. He also built a tower, and in doing so changed the complex of the ex-convent. Torre Palagio was built in gothic style and was decorated with numerous sculptures and bas-reliefs. There is an inconsistency in examining available data deriving from the public administrations because there is no cross-referencing of the information from historical maps, land registers and other illustrative material. The catalogue of ICCD, which is a general catalogue of Lombardian Cultural Heritage (ital.

Beni Culturali Lombardia) filled by the Superintendence of Archaeology, Fine Arts and Landscape for the metropolitan city of Milan (ital. *Soprintendenza Archeologia, belle Arti e Paesaggio per la Citta' Metropolitana di Milano*), the date of construction is noted to be 1846. On the other hand, the SIRBeC documentation filled by *Beni Culturali* and Politecnico di Milano dates it between 1840 and 1844. Further investigation of historical maps and other documents suggests the tower was built a few years earlier, and other decorative elements were added through the years (see Fig. 8).

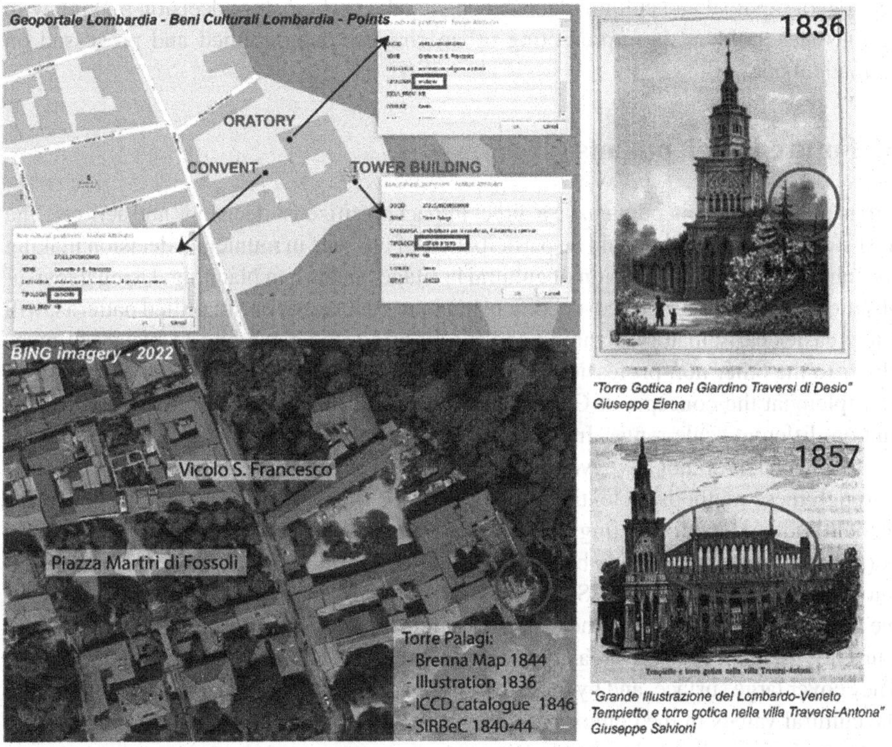

Fig. 8. Data downloaded from Geoportal of Lombardy and orthophoto are showing the current state of the building and the inconsistency of the date of construction of Torre Palagio. Illustrations are indicating that it was built at least a few years before the date indicated on administrative documents. (See changes on the illustrations from 1836 and 1857. Illustration source: Grafiche in Comune).

In the 2015 Desio PGT, under the section dedicated to the 'Census of Historical Heritage', Torre Palagio is listed as planned for restoration. It is noted that the tower is under a set of protection rules and constraints for its historical, artistic, and architectural values. Environmental qualities, in the context of the tower, are stated as"remarkable". The table was made in such a way that divides and describes single buildings but does not treat them as part of the complex or in the comparison to the surroundings and their historical timeline. In the section of the PGT, 'Plan of rules' (ital. *'Piano delle Regole'*), the map presents the investigated area restricted by two categories: 'historic-artistic valuable area' and as a 'zone of *villa urbana*'. Next to the area of interest is the cycling route, which has the potential to foster tourism and revitalize cultural values. There is a need for the creation of a database for all the collected and systematized historical and contemporary data to overcome the demonstrated inconsistencies between them.

The PGT can be improved with the georeferentiation of historical maps and linkage of historical documents and illustrations. Future administrations should revise investigation and planning activities for single buildings, built complexes and their surroundings. The core of the methodology contains geovisualisation techniques, to understand the complex set of geographical and cultural data and engage the participatory decision making with various stakeholders, by representing urban changes as simplified and processed on thematic maps.

6 Future Developments

Urban planning and mapping have a direct impact on citizens' decisions and actions. The next step in the research would be participation of citizens in municipal decision making for enhancement and protection of cultural heritage, and urban planning. Using geovisualisation techniques described, decomposing maps' elements on simplified patterns, will allow easier participatory planning and it will bring understanding of historical maps closer to the other non-professional stakeholders. Following participatory engagement, to implement the concepts of GeoDesign, would be valuable adding other set of maps and on different scale range. In this way, the natural and man-made characteristics of the towns which do not have well-defined and used urban tissue, will come to the fore. Through these methods, potential scenarios can be run, for using and designing towns, in their built and natural settings. At last, the research can be enriched with the contemporary environmental studies based on spatial-temporal data collected and assembled into one database project in GIS. The GIS can be useful in running the spatial analysis of the most endangered areas in the historical centre and target the level of their protection. Currently, selection of the areas under protection indicated in the PGT is generalised. They cover large surface, and by that block future projects on a legal level. Reconsidering the cultural values in the context, can be of the vital importance in making sustainable and participatory oriented town planning.

7 Conclusions

Urban planning and mapping have a direct impact on citizens' decisions and actions. Historical maps do not reflect the *status quo* of the place, but through comparative analysis researchers can draw conclusions, reconstruct, and eventually even predict the behavioural patterns of residents. The study will aid researchers, public administrations, and other stakeholders in conducting studies on historical maps and gaining valuable data to intersect with contemporary ones. Historical maps can provide insights into the implicit, but more importantly, the non-implicit values of past spaces. Systematization and generalization based on the recommendations and urban theories give the methodology immense potential. The methodology allows the shift of scale and focus, so that it can be replicated for other goals in research. In future, the PGT can be enriched with the creation of a database, integrating necessary georeferenced historical maps. Other historical documents can be linked through the attribute tables. The research will potentially accelerate economic, educational, social, and touristic development. The methodology will preferably provide guidelines for cartographers and creators of municipal urban plans for historical centres. The use of a GIS can increase efficiency and improve internal and external communication and data exchange. In education, knowledge can be shared among citizens and interested parties. Potentially, the public can be involved in the decision-making processes, and this collaboration can promote a sense of identity and culture. Recalling the values of the past will boost tourism and strengthen the perception of the place in the historical context.

References

1. Harley, J.B.: The New Nature of Maps: Essays in the History of Cartography. JHU Press, Baltimore (2002)
2. Pickles, J.: A History of Spaces: Cartographic Reason, Mapping, and the Geo-coded World. Routledge, Abingdon (2012)
3. Wood, D.: Rethinking the Power of Maps. Guilford Press, New York (2010)
4. Group of Authors: Linee guida per la digitalizzazione del materiale cartografico. Roma, Italia: Istituto centrale per il catalogo unico delle biblioteche italiane e per le informazioni bibliografiche ICCU (2006)
5. United Nations. Department of Social Affairs. Modern Cartography: Base Maps for World Needs. UN (1949)
6. Commission Definition International Cartographic Association: Multilingual dictionary of technical terms in cartography. Steiner (1973)
7. Krygier, J.B.: Cartography as an art and a science? Cartogr. J. **32**, 3–10 (1995)
8. Lapaine, M., Midtbø, T., Gartner, G., et al.: Definition of the map. Adv. Cartogr. GISci. ICA **3**, 9 (2021)
9. Goodchild, M.F.: Cartographic futures on a digital earth. Cartogr. Perspect. 3–11 (2000)
10. European Commission: Cultural heritage: digitalisation, online accessibility, and digital preservation. Consolidated Progress Report on the implementation of Commission Recommendation (2011/711/EU) 2015–2017. Directorate-General for Communication Networks, Content and Technology, Luxembourg (2018). www.digitalmeetsculture.net/wp-content/uploads/2019/06/ReportonCulturalHeritageDigitisationOnlineAccessibilityandDigitalPreservation.pdf. Accessed 17 June 2021
11. Europeana: Recommendations for Developing a Common Strategic Approach for Member States to Support the Digital Transformation of Europe's Cultural Heritage Sector (2019). https://pro.europeana.eu/files/Europeana_Professional/Publications/Final-Recommendations-for-a-Common-Strategic-Approach.pdf. Accessed 17 June 2021
12. Jovanovic, D., Oreni, D., Della Torre, S., et al.: Analysis of historical cartography and data presentation for an educational purpose: the case of the historical centre of Vimercate. In: Proceedings of the International Cartographic Association. Copernicus Publications, Florence, pp. 1–8 (2021)
13. Slater, T.R.: Preservation, conservation and planning in historic towns. Geogr. J. **150**, 322–334 (1984)
14. Syms, P.: Land, Development, and Design. Wiley, Hoboken (2010)
15. ICOMOS: International charter for the conservation and restoration of monuments and sites (The Venice Charter 1964). In: IInd International Congress Architecture and Technical History (1964)

16. Council of Europe: The Declaration of Amsterdam. Congress on the European Architectural Heritage Amsterdam (1975)
17. UN Habitat: New Urban Agenda. The United Nations Conference on Housing and Sustainable Urban Development Habitat III (2017)
18. ICOMOS: The Resolutions of the International Symposium on the Conservation of Smaller Historic Towns (1975)
19. Archivio di Stato di Milano: L'Immagine interessata: Territorio e Cartografia in Lombardia tra '500 e '800. Milano: Catalogo della Mostra documentaria (1984)
20. Pini, A.I.: Città, comuni e corporazioni nel medioevo italiano. Clueb (1986)
21. Desmond, G.: Napoleon's Italy. Madison Lond, pp. 75–77 (2001)
22. Monti, C.: La cartografia dall'antichità fino al XVIII secolo. Maggioli editore (2011)
23. Israel, U., Ortalli, G.: Il duello fra medioevo ed età moderna: prospettive storico-culturali. Viella (2011)
24. Malberti, P., Barzaghi, A.: Storia di Desio: Dalle origini al 1600. Amministrazione comunale di Desio (1961)
25. Cappellini, A.: Desio e la sua pieve. Edizioni del Comune (1972)
26. Brioschi, M., Conte, P., Tosi, L.: Le delizie della villeggiatura: Villa e giardino Cusani Traversi Antona Tittoni di Desio: da Bernabò Visconti a proprietà pubblica. Desio: [s.n.] (2017)
27. Cederin, K., Carlson, M.: Digital Historical Maps in Physical Planning, Beijing (2001)
28. Gomis, J., Turón, C.: The 'base map' for urban planning: cartographic representation as a fundamental tool for the representation of the town plan. Geogr. Tech. **13**, 52–61 (2018)
29. Group of Authors: Piano di governo del territorio Città di Desio. Comune di Desio (2015)
30. Steinitz, C.: A Framework for Geodesign: Changing Geography by Design. ESRI Press, Redlands (2012)
31. Harley, J.B.: Deconstructing the map. Cartogr. Int. J. Geogr. Inf. Geovisual. **26**, 1–20 (1989)
32. International Legal Materials: UNESCO Convention for the Protection of the World Cultural and Natural Heritage, vol. 11, no. 6, Cambridge University Press (1972)
33. Lynch, K.: The Image of the City. MIT Press, Cambridge (1964)
34. Jovanović, D., Oreni, D.: The methodology to systematise, present and use historical cartography: potentials and limits to analyse and enhance widespread historical centres in Northern Italy. In: The International Archives of the Photogrammetry, Remote Sensing and Spatial Information Sciences, pp. 339–346. Copernicus Publications, Beijing (2021)
35. Oreni, D., Brumana, R., Scaioni, M., et al.: Navigating on the past, as a bird flight, in the territorial scale of historical topographic maps. In: WMS on the 'Corografie delle Province del Regno Lombardo-Veneto', for accessing cadastral map catalogue. E-Perimetron, vol. 5, pp. 194–211 (2010)

Geodesign Iterations: Relevance for Planning Research, Education, and Practice

Michele Campagna(✉)

University of Cagliari, Via Marengo 2, 09123 Cagliari, Italy
campagna@unica.it

Abstract. The geodesign methodology (Steinitz 2012) proposes iterations as a way to develop a study from early scoping stages aimed at understanding how the study should be framed, to metaplanning, aiming at defining how the study should be implemented, to the final real-world implementation.

Iterations may be part of the same study, or alternatively, it is argued here, they may be implemented in different study instances on the same study area. The latter approach may indeed have benefits with relevance for planning research, education, and practice.

With reference with the Metropolitan City of Cagliari (Italy) study area, the author reports on several geodesign study instances on the same area, arguing each instance may indeed be considered as an iteration at the macro level, describing how between 2016 and 2021 several study instances helped first to scope which issues, opportunities, and challenges needed to be addressed in the study area, then to serve as a case study in academic planning courses, and eventually in setting the ground for a real-world strategic planning process involving local authorities.

Keywords: Geodesign · Metaplanning · Strategic planning · Co-design

1 Introduction

In the last two decades geodesign research and practice has attracted growing international interest in the community of scholars and practitioners in spatial planning and design, and related disciplines. Indeed the geodesign methodology approach has deep roots in the tradition of landscape planning and may offer a substantial contribution to current sustainability challenges.

Looking at one of the most recent definition of geodesign found in literature, it can be defined as a planning and design method that unites science and design in a process to make planning decisions in collaboration among design professionals, experts in geographic sciences and in geographic information technology, and the people of the place (Debnath et al. 2022 after Steinitz 2012). Geodesign applies system thinking to understand the territorial systems study area, and uses negotiation to support consensus building in collaborative decisions (Carlsson 2017).

O. Gervasi et al. (Eds.): ICCSA 2022 Workshops, LNCS 13379, pp. 181–193, 2022.
https://doi.org/10.1007/978-3-031-10545-6_13

The current interest for geodesign is documented by a growing body of literature (i.e. journal special issues, papers, books) most notably in the last decade. At the time of writing (i.e. April 2022), a simple query using "geodesign" as a single keyword on Scopus return 262 documents: excluding the first three oldest references in the query results, which referred to geodesign with a different meaning than the one intended here, since 2010 publications on geodesign flourished. As a benchmark of the growth in academic popularity on geodesign, the same query in Scopus back in 2018 and 2021 returned 91 and 197 papers respectively. Likewise, the same query in Google Scholar, which mines by a larger corpus of documents than the collection of papers in indexed journals in Scopus, returned 2,220 documents in 2018, 3,640 in 2021, and eventually 4,230 at the time of writing (i.e. April 2022).

In the geodesign body of literature, the book *A framework for geodesign: changing geography by design* by Carl Steinitz (2012) can be considered a milestone as the richest methodology references for developing geodesign studies. The International Geodesign Collaboration (IGC) a worldwide network of more than 470 members, in more than 240 organizations, in 61 countries (https://www.igc-geodesign.org/) since 2018 has extensively tested the application of the Steinitz's framework and common geodesign standards demonstrating its relevance and potential in addressing current most urgent sustainability challenges (Fisher et al. 2020).

With reference to the above context, the next session reports in synthesis the core elements of the Steinitz' framework, focusing on the role of iterations. While the geodesign framework focuses on iterations within individual studies, the concept of macro-iterations involving multiple instances of studies in the same study area is the focus here. Hence, in the remainder of this paper, several instances of the Metropolitan City of Cagliari case study are documented in synthesis as a base for analyzing the potential benefits of macro-iterations with relevance to spatial planning research, education, and practice.

2 The Steinitz's Framework: Six Models, Three Iterations

This section provides a summary description based on the authors experience of the application of the Steinitz's framework aiming at highlighting its core elements, the six models and, in particular, the importance of the study iterations.

The Representation Model (RM) describes the territorial dynamics in the study area, from the past until the present (i.e. the time of the study). The RM consists of data. From an application perspective, it should be noted that the data format from the past to current time has evolved from the analogue to the digital formats. Time frequency of data surveys has changed accordingly: while with regards to the past it is expectable to find analogue maps referring to sporadic time references, current digital geographic data detected trough remote-sensing and in-situ sensors enable to monitor territorial dynamics close to real-time, providing spatial big data. It should be noted though, that in developing a geodesign study, one should aim at gathering not the most but the least data necessary to answer the study relevant questions. If this is true, understanding how to describe the study area is not a straightforward single step, but it requires several iterations through the six models in order to find what is the least set of data needed to solve the complex design problem at hand.

The Process Model (PM) uses input from the representation model to foresee how the territorial system might evolve in the future under the hypothesis of no design/changes (i.e. *do-nothing* alternative in planning). While the representation model consists of spatial data at given times, the process model is more dynamic, in the sense simulation and forecasting are indeed dynamic in essence: thus, the space-time dimension of data become more relevant in foreseeing the evolution of territorial dynamics, so creating meaningful information.

The Evaluation Model (EM) assigns values to the expected territorial system evolution. It answers to such questions as "do we like expected future"? If answer is yes, no design change is needed; otherwise designing possible changes is required. The EM links knowledge building to design and decision-making: as such is a fundamental step in the workflow. It informs what and where changes are needed, possibly making decision more transparent and evidence-based. In this sense it may give an important contribution in informing and shaping the design. In the EM, beside the temporal dimension, values are attached to spatial data proving context for decisions (i.e. knowledge).

The Change Model (CM) consists of design proposals for the future: possible changes are collected and assembled in complex syntheses. Changes are described by spatial data presenting projects and policies.

The Impact Model (IM) aims at understanding the consequences of proposed changes assembled in alternative syntheses in the territorial systems. As in the case of the PM the time dimension becomes relevant. The consequences of possible changes, which are represented by spatial data (e.g. project or policies in space) are considered in their geographic context and described in terms of territorial dynamics, that is in their evolution along time. This is also a foresight endeavor based on forecasting and simulation, where time again becomes very relevant.

The Decision Model (DM) involve choosing, based on the information provided by the IM, and by providing values of entitled decision-makers, the preferable set of changes, or synthesis. Selecting who is entitled to make final decisions is part of the process, and it depends on the local context as well as on the purpose and scale of the study, and influences the format of the output of the other models.

According to Steinitz (2012) in addition, a geodesign study should involve three iterations across the six models. In the first iteration, the study's *scoping*, models are developed from the first to the sixth in order to understand what the main questions to be answered actually are. First data are collected, territorial dynamics of main relevance are detected, possible changes are devised and assessed, possible outcomes are framed and their impacts investigated, before it is possible to define the context for decision-making. Once it is clear who should be the actors involved at each stage, the second iteration starts. This time the models are revised in reverse order, from the sixth to the first one. In fact, in the second iteration, it is the decision-making context which provides requirements to each model: e.g. the IM should provide meaningful information to the decision-makers, so its content and format should be suitable to the purpose, and it descends from the DM. In turn, depending on what information the IM will need as input, the CM data should be shaped accordingly, and so on, until the RM is refined to be suitable as initial input of the process for the following iteration, which is eventually the *implementation* of the process. It should be noted that it is along the second iteration that actors, tasks, workflow, data, formats, supporting technologies are defined, according to a *meta-planning* approach (Campagna 2016).

While the three iterations (i.e. scoping, meta-planning, and implementation) may be formalized individually in the methodology framework, in reality they are not strictly linear, and along a study unlimited number of cycles and back-loop can be followed until the objective of the study is reached, that is, a future scenario is defined, on which consensus among involved parties is reached. In this sense, what defines the boundaries of a study are then its purpose and objectives.

A study can be indeed developed in different contexts such as research, education, or practice. If several studies are conducted on the same study area with different purposes (i.e. research, education, or practice) each with its specific objectives, each instance on the study should learn from the previous one and at the same time evolve from it, as the new study develop new additional knowledge and possibly generate new perspectives. In academia, it is not uncommon to use case studies from the real-world within planning and design studio classes, for generating knowledge and ideas informing subsequent real-world planning plan-making. In this sense each study instance can be considered as a *macro-iteration* with the final aim of building knowledge for eventually making-decisions which will be implemented in the real world. Each macro-iteration is therefore expected to enrich the understanding of current complex challenges. This assumption was tested along several macro-iterations in the Metropolitan City of Cagliari case study between 2016 and 2021. Eventually, while the results of each macro-iteration were different in terms of design, it is argued each macro-iteration provided new knowledge useful both to improve the process and in its results, or, in other words, to improve geodesign as a verb and as a noun.

It should be also noted that geodesign studies are usually fast, but at the same time very complex, with respect to both the process and its results. Thus, considering several study instances, or macro-iteration, on the same study area may indeed substantially contribute to better learn the geodesign methodology and its application technicalities, and it is therefore recommended to those who are approaching geodesign for the first time.

In the following section, several iterations of the Metropolitan City of Cagliari case study are described, each with its specific purposes, context, settings, and results, before a critical comparison on the overall experience is given in the remainder of the paper.

3 Case Studies

The case studies presented in this section contribute several macro-iterations of the geodesign study of the Metropolitan City of Cagliari (Italy). The main macro-iterations taken into consideration for this critical review are three, and were developed in 2016, 2018, and 2021 respectively. The scope of each macro-iteration was different in the three cases: research, education, and practice respectively. The structure of each macro-iteration was however substantially similar. Each case study included a knowledge building phase in which the representation, process and evaluation models were built producing the input for a subsequent intensive geodesign workshop implemented with the support of the web-based Planning Support System (PSS) Geodesignhub (http://www.geodesignhub.com). While the first two workshops were developed in presence, the last one was developed fully online with the support of the Zoom (http://zoom.us/) online meeting platform, due to COVID19 pandemic social interaction restrictions which was ongoing at the time of implementation. While the knowledge building phase usually last for a few months, the intensive workshop phase usually last between 16 (as in 2016) and 12 (as in 2021) hours, distributed either in two subsequent days (as in 2016) or in shorter three-hour section within two weeks (as in 2021). Implications of different scheduling are discussed in the next section, where the case studies are compared.

The main characteristics of each workshop are documented in the next paragraphs before a comparative critical review of similarities and differences among the cases is given.

In each case, the knowledge construction phase was fully digitally supported relaying on digital spatial data and on desktop Geographic Information System (GIS) technology, and included the following main steps:

- Data acquisition: in all the cases data from the Italian national census (ISTAT) and from the geoportal of the Regional Government of Sardinia were used, whereas in the 2021 case study additional Volunteered Geographic Information (Capineri et al. *eds* 2016; Zook and Breen 2017) data sources such as Openstreetmap.org and Flickr.com were also used to include spatial data themes otherwise not available in the regional geoportal.
- Selection of the ten systems of interest: in 2016 the ten systems were chosen looking at the study area by local researchers; in 2018 the IGC standard system were adopted; while in 2021 the system were derived with reference to an existing strategic development agenda (Table 1);
- Development of the representation, process, and evaluation models, culminating in the production of an evaluation map for each system;
- Definition of change targets for each system (i.e. total area required for changes in the system);
- Definition of a cross-systems impact model;
- Selection of the workshop participants, arrangement of the design teams, and workflow scheduling.

3.1 Case Study 1 (2016)

The first geodesign study on the future scenarios of the Metropolitan City of Cagliari was held at the University of Cagliari in 2016. This was the first ever case study on the recently established (2016) Metropolitan City of Cagliari in its current boundaries, which include seventeen municipalities. As such, there were not previous planning and design studies for the future development of the study area, and the workshop represented the first chance to reflect on its future scenarios for sustainable development. The study area is a complex territorial system including settlements, hosting a population of 431,538 inhabitants in July 2017, mountains (to the East and to the West) with natural or semi-natural landscapes, industrial areas, wetlands, and agricultural land-uses. The area is rich in natural and cultural landscape resources and in the last decades attracted a growing tourism demand.

Table 1. Selected systems in the case studies (recurrent systems in bold).

	2016	2018 (IGC standard)	2021
1	**Ecology**	**Green infrastructures**	**Green infrastructures**
2	Hazard	Water infrastructures	Water infrastructures
3	**Agriculture**	**Agriculture**	**Agriculture**
4	**Transport**	**Transport**	**Transport**
5	**Commerce/industry**	**Commerce/industry**	**Commerce/industry**
6	High density **housing**	Mixed **housing**	Energy
7	Low density **housing**	Low density **housing**	**Housing**
8	Tourism	Institutional	Tourism
9	**Cultural heritage**	**Cultural heritage**	**Cultural heritage**
10	Smart services	Energy	Smart hub

Given the size, and the territorial systems complexity, the first study was aimed at earning first insights about possible future sustainable development scenarios. Hence, the first study was exploratory in nature and it was developed from a research perspective. A total of thirty-two participants were selected by the study coordinator to form a multi-disciplinary team, including local experts, PhD and graduate students, and local stakeholders from the public and the private sectors. After the knowledge building phase was carried-on along three months by the coordination team, an intensive workshop lasting a total of 16 h within two days was held in early May 2016. Six design teams with different roles and with different objectives initially individually developed their own design syntheses, which were than compared and negotiated among teams coalitions until consensus was reached on a final future development scenario.

The relevance of this first geodesign study on the Metropolitan City of Cagliari area is that it was the first comprehensive planning and design study at its scale in the area. In fact, the traditional planning system in Sardinia includes regional landscape planning and local land-use planning, as well as a number of sector plans undertaken at the regional or at the local scale. The metropolitan planning scale was therefore a novelty which required a change in perspective. Given the research perspective of the study, moreover, a neutral scientific approach was adopted which enabled understanding the functioning and possible planning of the territorial system without having a substantial political bias. As such, this first case study represented a solid base to further studying the area for the following years for the educational and eventually real practice experiences described in the next paragraph. In addition, the final negotiated design (Fig. 1) was exported in a desktop PSS (i.e. CommunityViz) for testing interoperability and more a complex impact model. Further details on this study can be found in (Campagna et al. 2016).

3.2 Case Study 2 (2018)/IGC

In 2018, the International Geodesign Collaboration was first established. Since then, the members of the IGC, which were mainly scholars as well as educators, defined common standards to develop comparable geodesign studies around the world, this way fostering geodesign research and education. IGC standards, which were agreed as first step in the collaboration, included common formats for spatial extent, systems and colors, global assumptions and system technology innovations, as well as development scenarios and time stages (https://www.igc-geodesign.org/global-systems-research).

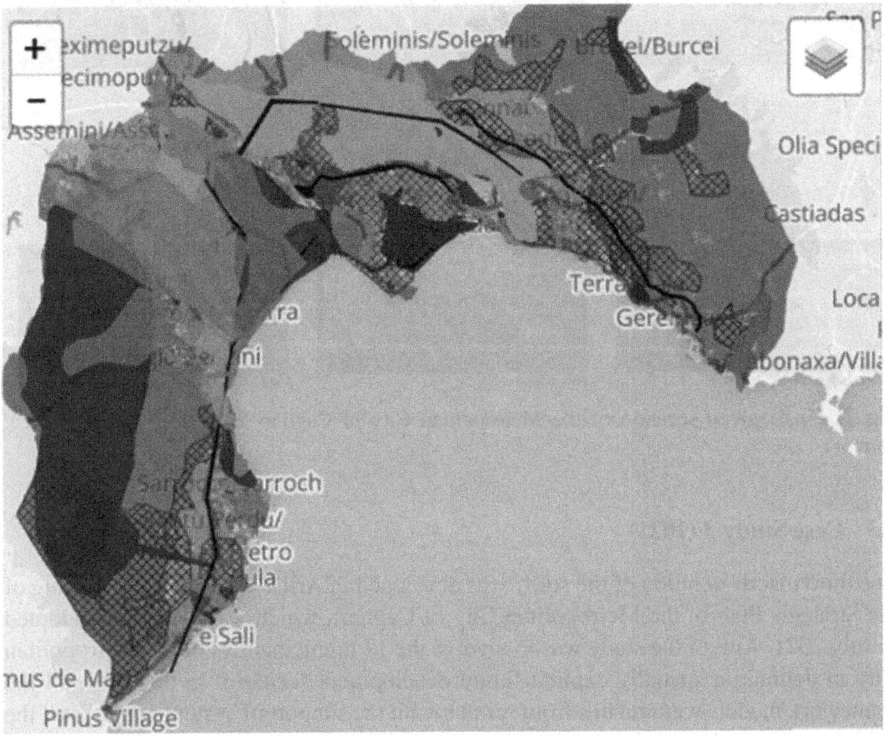

Fig. 1. Final negotiated scenario for the Metropolitan City of Cagliari 2016 study in Geodesignhub (Source: Author).

The IGC standards were adopted in the second study on the Metropolitan City of Cagliari which was developed within two studio classes at the Faculty of Engineering and Architecture of the University of Cagliari. The first class, including 56 civil engineering graduate students worked on the whole study area (i.e. a 80 × 80 km square) while the second class, including 76 undergraduate students in architecture, worked on a nested frame 20 × 20 km at a larger scale. The smaller scale study started in advance and informed the larger scale study aiming at exploring multiscale design coordination. The design teams working to build the IGC development scenarios, unlike the previous case study where design teams play different stakeholders roles, were framed using two future time horizons (i.e. 2035 and 2050) and a different approach regarding technology innovation adoption (i.e. early adopters, late-adopters – after 2035- and non-adopters). The final negotiated scenarios are shown in Fig. 2.

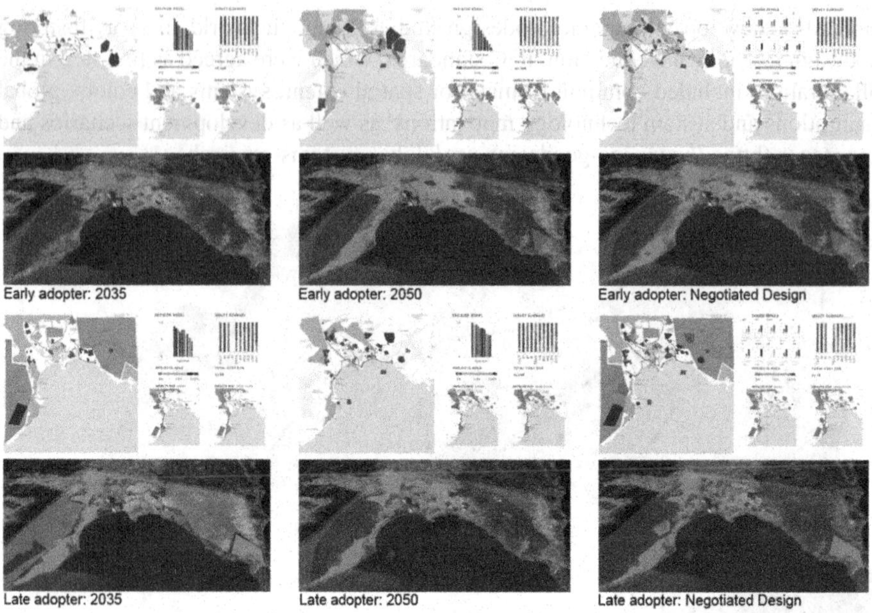

Fig. 2. Final agreed scenario of the Metropolitan City of Cagliari 2018 IGC study (Source: Author).

3.3 Case Study 3 (2021)

The third macro-iteration of the study was developed in Aril 2021 within the making of the Strategic Plan of the Metropolitan City of Cagliari, which was eventually adopted in July 2021. Aim of the study was to involve the 17 municipalities of the Metropolitan City in defining a spatially explicit future development scenario. In this case, all the framework models were rebuilt from scratch with the support of system expert; still the experience earned in of the previous iteration for framing the representation, process, and evaluation models was fundamental.

The workshop was implemented fully online in 4 three-hour sessions along two weeks, with the possibility for the participant to work remotely on the workflow tasks out of the plenary sessions, with or without the support of the coordination team which offered office-hour online slots. The final negotiated scenario was agreed in 12 plenary hours and priorities were agreed for projects and policies (Fig. 3) and the content was included in the final Strategic Plan of the Metropolitan City of Cagliari documents adopted a few months later. This workshop offered the Municipalities a substantial opportunity to have their voice heard by the higher level of government, i.e. the Metropolitan Council, which eventually adopted the plan. In addition, the collaborative design format of the geodesign workshop offered the participants an unprecedented learning experience while evolving from a local to a metropolitan wide planning and design perspective.

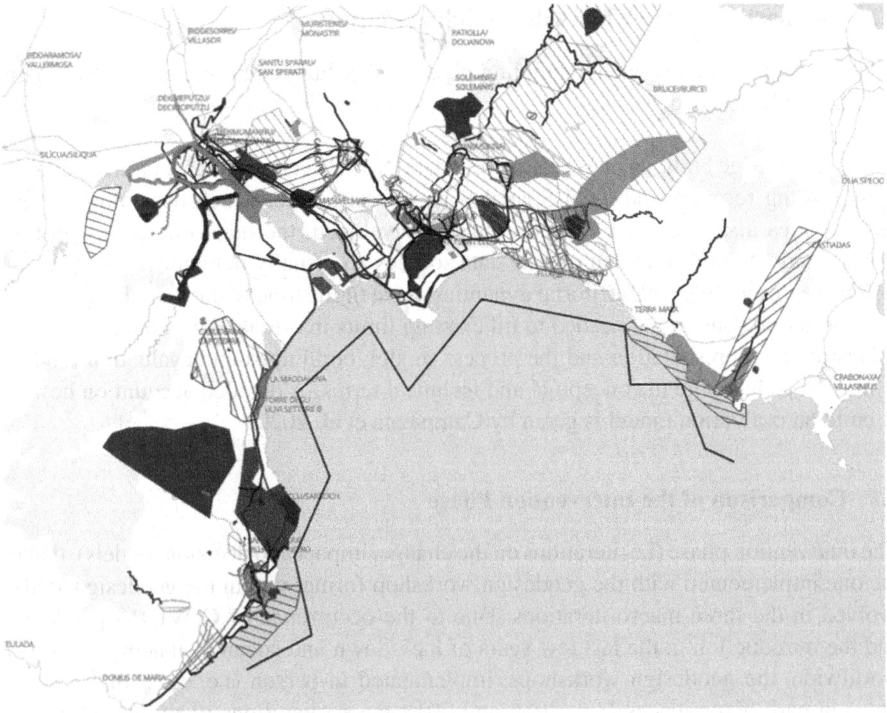

Fig. 3. Final agreed scenario of the Metropolitan City of Cagliari 2021 study (Source: Author).

3.4 Other Case Studies (2017–2022)

In addition to the three main case studies presented in the previous paragraphs, the Metropolitan City of Cagliari studies were used several times each for one-day intensive workshop tutorials aimed at teaching interested educators on geodesign methods, workflows and tools. Notably, since 2020 the in-presence workshop format was adapted to online only settings due to ongoing pandemic social interactions restrictions and occasional lock-down periods. In a few years, thanks to these initiatives hundreds educators and practitioners got familiar with the geodesign methodology, techniques and tools, and many of them successfully developed their own case studies afterwards.

4 Comparative Analysis of the Case-Studies

Geodesign is a robust methodology which proved to be effective in addressing current complex challenges of sustainable development. The critical review of several macro-iterations of a geodesign study on the same study area may offer a great deal of experience which we believe is worth sharing, with the aim of helping interest scholars and practitioner to approach this complex methodology especially at early stages. In this section, critical reflections on the different stages of a geodesign study are given.

4.1 Comparison of the Knowledge Building Phase

Looking back at the knowledge building phase in the three macro-iterations, two main lessons can be learned:

- The knowledge building phase starts from data. No matter how much data are available in existing regional and local Spatial Data Infrastructure, which depending on the study area and scale may be more or less developed, the macro-iterations on this case study demonstrate that official data sources are usually not enough to represent fully represent relevant territorial dynamics: most of the time, volunteered geographic information sources are needed to fill existing limits in official data sources.
- Beside the representation and the process model, building sound evaluation models may be a challenge in conceptual and technical terms. A detailed account on how to build an evaluation model is given by Campagna et al. 2020.

4.2 Comparison of the Intervention Phase

The intervention phase (i.e. iterations on the change, impact and decision models), that is the one implemented with the geodesign workshop format within the geodesign study, evolved in the three macro-iterations. Due to the occurrence of COVID19 pandemic and the introduction in the last few years of lock-down and social distancing measures worldwide, the geodesign workshops, implemented in-person (i.e. same place, same time) in early experiences (e.g. 2016 and 2018 macro-iterations of the Metropolitan City of Cagliari) moved online. Both in-presence and on-line formats proved to work equally well in providing robust results in term of design as well as learning experience for the participants. Nevertheless, the in-person workshop format may better support critical discussion among the participants, at the cost, though, of higher organization and logistic efforts. The latter may be sometimes relevant in eventually choosing which format to apply.

The 2016 macro-iteration was carried on in single intensive workshops during 16 h along two days. In the 2018 workshop, in order to comply with ordinary teaching schedules, a combination of five 3-h sessions totaling 15 h were arranged. Breaking the intensive workshop into shorter session proven effective as it gave participants more time to reflect on the evolution of their work. Based on this experience, and also considering time availability of public authorities decision-makers and technical staff a multi-sessions format was chosen also for the 2021 workshop. The choice was successful for it allowed representatives from municipalities more time to develop their design proposal in between sessions. Eventually in the 2021 workshop the final design with priorities was completed in four main plenary sessions, 3-h each, plus a final session for the review of the results.

4.3 Comparison of the Final Design

The main advantages in the geodesign approach are substantially two: i) developing spatially explicit and transparent alternative design syntheses informed by the geographic context; and ii) reaching consensus among the participants. These are two substantial benefits which may help to comply with the principles introduced in planning by Strategic Environmental Assessment, and eventually by sustainability of development principles such as democratic, evidence-based, transparent, responsible decision-making in spatial planning aiming at preserving natural resources, while improving the socio-economic system dynamics. Geodesign studies including intensive collaborative workshops such as those described in this research proved to be particularly effective and successful in strategic planning, where reaching in a very short time consensus of future development scenarios is of bigger importance than design precision. Indeed, when there is agreement on a future development scenario among all the actors of the affected community, a road map is given for the framing of consequent physical planning, for which broad collaboration in the implementation is somehow ensured. In Europe, this approach may be particularly useful for public authorities as it provide a solid base in applying for development funds such as the recent European Green Deal.

4.4 Comparison of the Outcomes of the Macro-iterations

The three main macro-iterations of the Metropolitan City of Cagliari geodesign study provided tangible benefits for geodesign research, education, and real-world planning practice. Each macro-iteration actually provided useful insight for research with regards to geodesign as a *verb* (i.e. the process) and geodesign as a *noun* (i.e. the design outcomes. Each macro-iterations in fact contributes new knowledge on the complex territorial system in the study area, as well as new alternatives for future development, enriching each time the understanding of the participants, including the coordination team, and inspiring new design perspective and new understanding of complex territorial sustainable development challenges.

With regards to education, in broad sense and for the reasons above, a geodesign study macro-iteration is always a rich learning experience. In this sense, it contributes to educating a community to handle its future. When it comes to university education, the 2018 IGC macro-iteration had several tangle benefits as well: considering the participating students in civil engineering and architecture had little or no previous experience in planning, they learned in a short time and with a fast learning curve how to apply system-thinking in land-use and infrastructure (e.g. green, blue, transport, energy, etc.) planning. They also learned to work with fully digital techniques and tools with ease.

When it comes from real world planning and design practice, participants from the public authorities, from the private sector and from NGOs learned to collaborate with each other with a new media, breaking consolidated power relationships which in traditional planning process often hinder the possibility of win-win situation and often end up in a zero sum game, when someone win and the other loose.

Post-workshop questionnaire surveys as well as informal feed-back from participants to the macro-iteration of the Metropolitan City of Cagliari case study, the detailed description of which is out of the scope of this paper, as well from other geodesign studies, substantially confirm these assumptions.

Last, but not least, archiving a repository of fully-digital geodesign workshops along several macro-iteration open the way to the application of geodesign process analytics techniques, as proposed by Cocco et al. (2019).

5 Conclusions

This paper aims at proposing critical insights on the role of iterations in the geodesign framework. Beside the iterations proposed by Steinitz in its framework (2012), this paper analyses macro-iterations (i.e. several studies instances on the same study areas) developed by the author in research, education, and real-world planning practice in half-decade.

It is argued macro-iterations are useful one after the other to enrich knowledge on the sustainability challenges in the study area with two major benefits: i) grasping the complexity of the territorial system so improving the final design; ii) earning experience on how to conduct the process. It is also argued that conducting preliminary studies within research and education settings may be necessary before conducting real-world planning processes, where stakes are high in deliberation.

Critically reflecting in terms of iterations, besides learning on how to build the six framework's models, may help to systematically analyses how complex planning and design processes may be improved in term of process itself and of their results. Planning several macro-iterations may be particularly useful as a strategy for those researcher and practitioners who wish to apply the geodesign framework for the first time to grasp the complexity of its application, and eventually develop the necessary experience to apply geodesign in the real-world practice.

Acknowledgements. The author is immensely grateful to Carl Steinitz, Emeritus Professor at Graduate School of Design at Harvard University, from whom he mostly learned the geodesign methodology, and with whom he coordinated the 2016 Metropolitan City of Cagliari workshop, as well as many other geodesign workshops for educators on the same study area within the International Geodesign Collaboration.

The author wish also to thank very much the anonymous reviewers for their useful comments to the early version of the paper, and to acknowledge the funding to his research on geodesign by the Fondazione di Sardegna [project: "Investigating the relationships between knowledge-building and design and decision-making in spatial planning with geodesign"], and by the Autonomous Region of Sardinia, Regional Law n. 7/2007, Fund for Development and Cohesion [project: "Rural landscapes of Sardinia: planning green and blue infrastructures and spatial complex networks"].

References

Campagna, M., Steinitz, C., Di Cesare, E., Cocco, C., Ballal, H., Canfield, T.: Collaboration in planning: the Geodesign approach. Rozwój Regionalny i Polityka Regionalna **35**, 27–43 (2016)

Campagna, M.: Metaplanning: about designing the Geodesign process. Landsc. Urban Plan. **156**, 118–128 (2016)

Campagna, M., Di Cesare, E.A., Cocco, C.: Integrating green-infrastructures design in strategic spatial planning with geodesign. Sustainability **12**(5), 1820 (2020)

Capineri, C., et al. (eds.): European Handbook of Crowdsourced Geographic Information. Ubiquity Press, United Kingdom (2016)

Carlsson, M.: Environmental design, systems thinking, and human agency: McHarg's ecological method and Steinitz and Rogers's interdisciplinary education experiment. Landsc. J. **36**(2), 37–52 (2017)

Debnath, R., Pettit, C., Leao, S.: Geodesign approaches to city resilience planning: a systematic review. Sustainability **14**(2), 938 (2022)

Fisher, T., Orland, B., Steinitz, C.: The International Geodesign Collaboration: Changing Geography by Design. ESRI press, Redlands (2020)

Steinitz, C.A.: A Framework for Geodesign. ESRI Press, Redlands (2012)

Zook, M., Breen, J.: Volunteered geographic information. In: Shekhar, S., Xiong, H., Zhou, X. (eds.) Encyclopedia of GIS. Springer, Cham. (2017). https://doi.org/10.1007/978-3-319-17885-1_1656

Geodesign Teaching Experience and Alternative Urban Parameters: Using Completeness Indicators on GISColab Platform

Ashiley Adelaide Rosa[1](✉), Ana Clara Mourão Moura[2], and Beatriz Maria Fernandes Araújo[2]

[1] Programa de Pós-Graduação em Geografia, Instituto de Geociências da UFMG, Universidade Federal de Minas Gerais (UFMG), Av. Antônio Carlos, 6627 Belo Horizonte, Brazil
ashileyrosa@ufmg.br

[2] Escola de Arquitetura, Laboratório de Geoprocessamento, Universidade Federal de Minas Gerais (UFMG), Rua Paraíba 697, Belo Horizonte, Brazil
anaclara@ufmg.br

Abstract. This paper aims to introduce a teaching experience using geodesign as a method that favors the co-creation process and the use of alternative urban parameters, in an academic graduate course about urban planning at a local scale, in Architecture and Urbanism School. In the current scenario, cities growth is oriented by the perspective of cars, by land speculation and urban sprawl. As a result, it is observed the progressive loss of the human dimension in the urban space. The students were stimulated to think about the street functions and on the possibility of measuring urban quality with alternative parameters: the Completeness Indicators. Thus, aiming to develop solutions more adapted to the reality of the area and according to the collaborative contemporary practices urban planning the methodological approach was divided into two steps. In the first step, urban parameters and urban designs were elaborated, without using Completeness Indicators, and for the second step the participants used the indicators to support and describe the ideas. Both steps were conducted in a workshop format using the web-based Brazilian geodesign platform, the GISColab. The need for changes in the urban planning paradigm highlights the need for citizen participation and the role of the urban planner as a decoder of the collective goals. Finally, the results showed that there was a maturation of the students' critical thinking about the proposals made, as well as the impacts of the proposals considering the human dimension and the quality of urban space.

Keywords: Urban spaces · Landscape quality · Environmental assessment · Co-creation process · Geovisualization · Complete streets

1 Introduction

The logic of city growth, supported by modernist and highway precepts, led Brazilian cities to growth based on the need for automobiles and the sprawl of the urban fabric. This logic is about an individual solution to the detriment of supplying collective needs.

O. Gervasi et al. (Eds.): ICCSA 2022 Workshops, LNCS 13379, pp. 194–209, 2022.
https://doi.org/10.1007/978-3-031-10545-6_14

Thus, progressively, city planning ignored the human dimension [1, 2]. Although the majority of the population needs to intensively use public urban space, such as streets, for many daily activities, as Gehl [3] classifies as "necessary, optional and social", cities are not thought of from this point of view - to people. Consequently, as car traffic, parking and congestion increase, the competition for urban space intensifies, and thus conditions for urban life and pedestrians become increasingly worse. The streets lose their function as a living space and are reduced to the displacement, directly affecting the quality and urban vitality. Such disregard for the street as a public space for people to socialize, leads to the latent need for teaching approaches in the field of architecture and urbanism that discuss issues about the quality, scale and demands of these spaces.

The predominant use in the planning of Brazilian cities of traditional urban parameters, mainly morphometric aspects (e.g., floor area ratio, volumetric coefficient, setbacks), has generated a scenario that reproduces more of the same massive constructive pattern of the urban landscape - with constant loss of environmental and cultural quality, uninviting people – and not evaluating performance or encouraging a change of mind and scenery. These parameters reproduce the interests of the real estate market, but do not manage the quality of the place based on environmental, social or cultural values.

In response to this traditional planning model, Complete Streets are an emerging concept in urban and transport planning discourse that arises to expand the focus of street design from the automobile to the safe accommodation of all modes of travel and users [4]. When approaching this concept, it proposes the democratization of the street space through a new design and a paradigm shift. Thus, arrangements are established between spaces intended for permanence, circulation, afforestation, active facades, among other aspects, which can make cities more vivid, comfortable and sustainable. There is no single Complete Street solution, that is, this approach is not replicable. Thus, better urban design alternatives can be incorporated as long as they respond to the local context of the area where they are located, reflect the street identity and the priorities of that community [5].

Therefore, the values applied to urban planning are constantly changing and are moving towards safe, living, sustainable and healthy cities [1]. This process highlights the role of the urban planner as a decoder of the collective demand, who provides the technical support and expertise for this transposition the necessarily in a collaborative way, and the need for citizen participation in urban planning process [6, 7].

The Completeness Index for Complete Streets appears as a possible solution to change the models practiced in city planning, in the design process and also in urban parameters [8]. The index consists of a set of indicators that help to assess the quality of free and public spaces in the city - especially on the streets, based on their planning functions: environment, place and movement. The "environment function" consists of the one destined to mitigate anthropic actions in the urban space, and can be measured from indicators such as efficient drainage, street afforestation and landscape quality. Meanwhile, the "place function" is one that encourages people to stay and carry out their daily activities; it is related to identity and social interaction, and can be measured through indicators of mixed use, permanent spaces, urban furniture and the flow of people. Finally, the "movement function" is linked to the street's ability to allow the movement of people, vehicles and products, and can be measured by indicators of road capacity, multimodality, and access to public transport.

The geodesign proposal presented by Steinitz [7] and Miller [9] meets the need to overcome the modern form of planning. Geodesign has a methodology designed to support opinion and the creation of ideas with the help of geographic information, in a systematic and shared way. For this reason, Dangermond [10] points out that the possibility of geovisualization enables and favors the involvement of different actors in the geodesign process, while supported by the geographical conditions of the territory, the actions simulate better and more compatible possibilities.

In general, the design of plans and projects involves a very complex technical and legislative language that does not dialogue with citizens. Geodesign can act as a connecting element of participation to actually promote broad debate among users or experts. Thus, geodesign promotes a more collaborative and equitable scenario of participatory planning. In this context, Geodesign proves to be a creative and projective process with the potential to transform consensus, as stated by Forester [11], not necessarily as a support for decision, but primarily as a support for opinion. In other words, as a support for the construction of knowledge and citizen awareness about a place.

Geoinformation technologies are undergoing a significant paradigm shift related to the use and production of georeferenced data and information - largely based on geovisualization and access through the world wide web - with as main objective supporting the construction of opinions and decision-making. In this sense, the geodesign process, when incorporated into the fundamentals of SDI (Spatial Data Infrastructure) and Web-GIS (Web-based Geographic Information System), can be a robust supporting structure for the creation of opinions and decision-making through participatory planning, taking advantage of geoinformation technology [12].

Additionally, Wilson [13] points that the join of geodesign and web create opportunities for using these platforms of geoinformation technologies, with the potentiality to transcend scales, involving more people in the discussion, to encourage spatial thinking and the use in collaborative decision making. The author also highlights the importance of geodesign education on graduation degrees, preparing future professionals to work with real problems and possible solutions around the world.

In this scenario, the architect and urban planner play a very important role. As one of the professionals trained to carry out the reading of the space, he must perform as the decoder of the collective desire, considering the social and cultural aspects of each location. Such an attitude allows exploring a truly collaborative experience, where participants visualize the impacts generated by their proposals and actions. This is a relevant factor defended by Arnstein [14] in the stages of evolution of the participatory process and the performance of the technical staff. According to the author, the emphasis is often on unilateral information, from the technicians to the citizens, without there being a communication channel that allows the return, and even less, with negotiation power for the citizens.

From this point of view, this article aims to present a didactic and methodological experience using geodesign as a process. It also presents the web-based platform as an instrument that facilitates the construction of citizen awareness. Moreover, it presents the use of alternative urban parameters, the Completeness Indicators, in a course on urban planning at the local scale, of the Architecture and Urbanism graduation course. Students learn the process of collective construction of ideas while being informed about values that favor the condition of completeness of the collective urban space. The article is structured as follows: (i) detailing of the methodological steps used in the course; (ii) presentation and description of the case study area; (iii) report on the development of activities and experiences with the virtual geodesign platform, GISColab; (iv) results and analysis of the experience, and finally (v) considerations about the experience, processes, methods, and tools explored.

2 Methods, Tools and Methodological Steps

This paper reports a methodological and teaching experience, with alternative or non-traditional urban parameters, in the course "Urban Planning: Local Scale Problems", that was held on the Architecture and Urbanism graduation, Federal University of Minas Gerais. The course was taught from October 2021 to February 2022, applying the Geodesign process as a methodology and the Brazilian web-based platform, the GISColab.

The GISColab platform, as an SDI service, was initially developed by GE21 Geotechnologies. Using this first structure, it was adapted to be used as Brazilian geodesign and co-creation platform, developed by Moura and Freitas [12]. The platform presents a map collection (layers) and tools to assist in the geovisualization, analysis, and proposition of ideas for a given place. All maps are georeferenced and are placed on the platform with pre-established legends, or can be uploaded using the connection with other SDIs.

It is up to the user to control the overlap, transparency and visualization of the layers to better qualify the relationship between the phenomena observed in the territory under study. The content of the layers can encompass phenomena of different aspects such as hydrography, vegetation, slope, distribution of roads, protected areas, slums, among others, which interfere in the perception of space. They are used as reference layers to the proposition of ideas and in the voting of a proposal. The set of maps can be customized by the workshop organizer according to the demands of each territorial context and the participants.

The tools present in the GISColab platform support the stages of the geodesign workshop. The "Annotation" tool supports the initial stages, where aspects of the territory are being identified and has points for demarcating these characteristics. This first step is called "Reading Enrichment". The "Dialogues" tool involves the propositional stage and is used to build ideas through more resources such as points, lines and polygons. This tool also has a comment feature, where participants can leave their impressions about the proposals. It is still possible in the "dialogues" tool to use the "likes and dislikes" mechanism, counting votes and recording the opinion about the ideas. Dialogues are used to the steps "Creation of Ideas", "Discussion of Ideas" and "Voting of Ideas".

Before the beginning of the workshop activities, the students attend to classes about the "traditional" and "non-traditional" urban parameters. In Brazil, the traditional ones, presented in all Master Plans, are the morphometric parameters, and the non-traditional are presented as assumptions related to cultural values, environmental studies and land use. The idea of Completeness Index for Complete Streets by Rosa [8] and about the functions of the street. They are presented to the students at this moment as non-traditional urban parameters that increase the quality of the urban space.

In the first step, the students developed their ideas in a collaborative and broader way, that is, in the form of plans of ideas for the territory, and with the aid of the digital platform GISColab. The didactic-pedagogical dynamics was established through the following sub-steps (which took place both in asynchronous and synchronous ways): (i) an introduction to geodesign, with emphasis on the Steinitz framework [7] (since this design process was unknown to most students); (ii) reading enrichment about Pampulha individually; (iii) division of students into three groups (environment, movement and place) and preparation of the first design suggesting. In the next, more detailed step, the sub-steps were: (iv) assumptions about the twelve indicators of completeness of the streets; (v) a design review including the completeness indicators, negotiation and voting of the final design, resulting in a single and collective proposal (Fig. 1). The groups worked in a "circle" logic, in which each group worked first on its own context, and then, the groups changed the contexts adding ideas in the proposal.

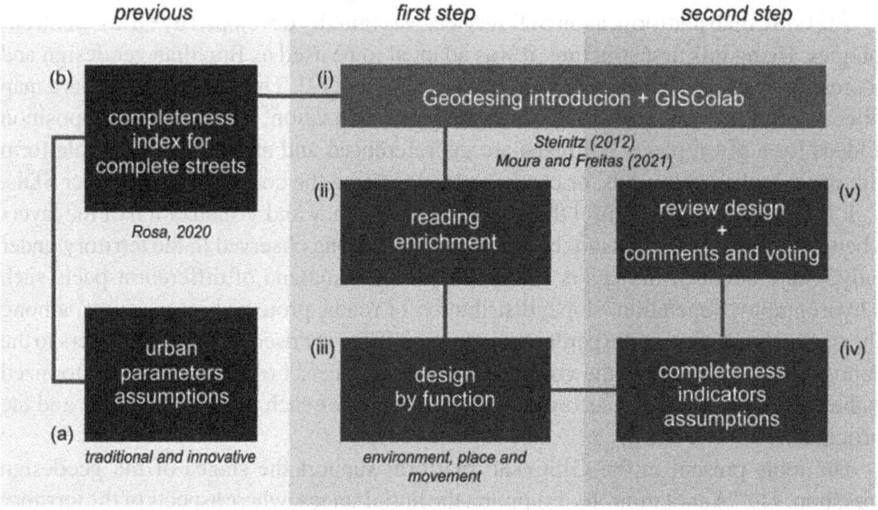

Fig. 1. Workshop activity flow. Source: the authors.

In the second step, the students were encouraged to consider twelve Completeness Indicators of the streets (e.g., street afforestation, efficient drainage, flexibility of uses, active mobility and modal connectivity) and to propose urban designs for the studied area. The idea of using these indicators is related to stimulating the use of innovative urban parameters and, consequently, resulting in more attractive urban spaces and landscape. In addition, the use of the indicators aims to facilitate the construction of ideas in line with the place, and also facilitates the gradual understanding of new concepts, such as the vocation, completeness, and planning functions of the street. This logic supported the dynamics of geodesign and was supported by it. From the description of the proposals, the use of the completeness indicators was computed, and dynamically presented in widgets on the platform, demonstrating which indicators were the most or least impacted positively/negatively, thus allowing the development of more assertive and qualified proposals.

2.1 The Study Area

The Pampulha District is located in the northern vector of the municipality of Belo Horizonte, capital of the state of Minas Gerais (Brazil) (Fig. 2). This administrative region has as its main landmark a dammed river of the same name, which originated the Pampulha Reservoir. The dam is part of the local landscape along with other landmarks such as the Governador Magalhães Pinto Stadium (Mineirão), the Mineirinho Gym, the Pampulha Airport, the São Francisco de Assis Church, the Ecological Park, the Zoo and the Botanical Garden, among others.

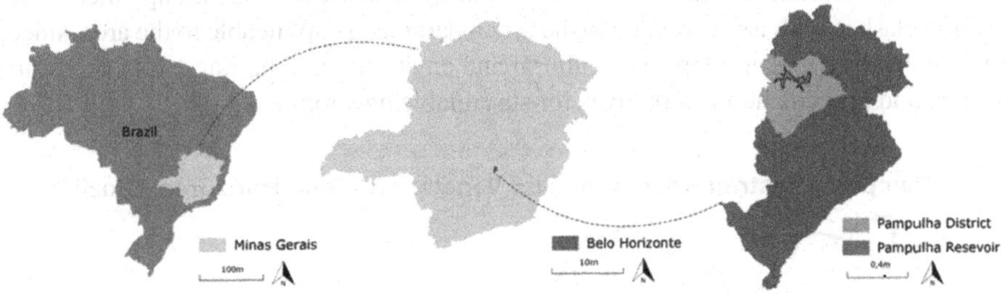

Fig. 2. Location map of the Pampulha District. Data source: PBH. Organization: the authors.

Due to the difficulty of accessing the center of the capital, the Pampulha District, which was once part of the rural area formed mainly by farms, had its urbanization process later than that of the capital, starting in the 40s. With the development of highways and of urban transport in the city, the region became accessible mainly by automobiles, in a context of modernization of the then mayor Juscelino Kubitschek, through Fernão Dias Highway and Presidente Antônio Carlos Avenue.

The Pampulha Ensemble represents a milestone in modern architecture, receiving in 2016 the title of Cultural Heritage of Humanity by the United Nations Educational, Scientific and Cultural Organization (UNESCO). The ensemble turned exceptional by the innovative way in which the formal and technological resources of its repertoire were used. Thus, the experience of Pampulha expresses the following fundamentals: innovations in form, especially in curves; the technological innovations provided by the use of the plastic potential of concrete; and innovations in landscaping, represented by early ecological interest, appreciation of native flora and botanical compositions of strong plastic expression [15].

Pampulha is an area that houses, in addition to leisure facilities and parks, regions with a lot of residential use. It is a place where the real estate pressures of densification and verticalization collide with the specific care established by the heritage protection policies for the landscape and environmental values. Thus, a conflict of interest is established in the area over the fate of the cultural and environmental landscape of Pampulha, resulting in a challenge for the dialogue between the different actors and the possible alternatives for the future of the region. This stage makes the discussion and learning about the region enriching, as it favors different analyzes and still requires new approaches and instruments to deal with these impasses. These impasses can be analyzed under the scope of the functions of movement, environment and place of the region.

Thus, the "movement function" deals with the street's ability to accommodate displacement, enable access and active mobility, and minimize travel time. In the region of Pampulha, there is an articulating character, connecting the center to the north vector by means of rapid transit intended mainly for the car. It can also observe long routes with cycle lanes and little availability of public transport, resulting in a challenge for modal connectivity, active mobility and road safety in the region.

The "environment function" also brings great discussions when observed in Pampulha, according to (Fig. 3). There it has great arboreal expressiveness that contributes to the allocation of spaces for recreation, sport, leisure and tourism and also to the maintenance of the climate, air quality, landscape quality, water drainage, among others. This function clashes with issues related to the urban parameters applicable to the area, since, in understanding its landscape as a cultural and environmental heritage, it is necessary to adapt and propose new alternatives for sustainable development.

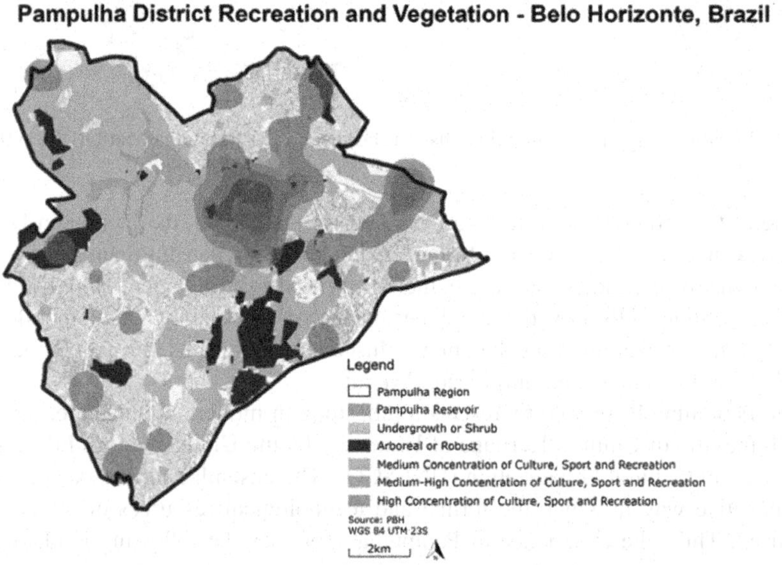

Fig. 3. Vegetation and Recreation activities map of the Pampulha District. Data source: PBH. organization: the authors.

And finally, the "place function" is evidenced in the region through the options for living there. The public space in Pampulha is attractive to the most varied people and leads to different recreational activities. However, currently, it is quite restricted to equipment present in the vicinity of the lake The concentration of commerce in Regional

Pampulha has been established outside the architectural and environmental heritage in the region (Fig. 4).

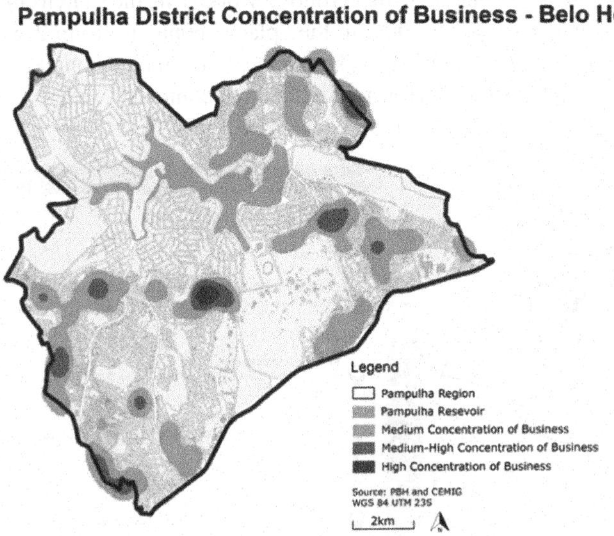

Fig. 4. Trading concentration map of the Pampulha District. Data source: PBH/CEMIG. organization: the authors.

3 The Development of the Case Study

Assuming that the students performed the previous activities: classes on traditional parameters and on alternative parameters and about completeness index and street functions (movement, environment, place), the workshop was held from January 20, 2022 to February 8, 2022, totaling six (6) meetings (synchronous/asynchronous).

For the first meeting, the students were instructed to previously watch the recorded classes about geodesign concept and about the Brazilian geodesign platform, GISColab. Thus, on January 20, 2022, they performed the reading enrichment individually, exploring the maps available on the platform and adding the observations through the "Annotation" tool (Fig. 5).

On January 25, 2022, students were separated into three groups (environment, movement and place) and the elaboration of ideas began through urban parameters (preferably represented by polygons) and urban drawings (preferably represented by points or lines), each in its own context (working windows) at GISColab.

As mentioned, the students were divided into three groups with 4 students each: environment (group 1), movement (group 2) and place (group 3). The idea was for each group to make proposals for their own context. For example, Group 1 thought about ideas of urban parameters and urban designs for the "environment function", based on what was explained in the conceptual class on the Completeness Index for Complete Streets. To make their contributions, the students used the "Dialogs" box (Fig. 6), with the author's information and description of the proposal. On January 27, 2022, students worked in the other two contexts. In the first round, group 1 worked in the "movement" context, group 2 worked in the "place" context, while group 3 worked in the "environment" context. In the second round, group 1 worked in the "place" context, group 2 worked in the "environment" context, while group 3 worked in the "movement" context. At the end of the circle, the three groups had performed in the three contexts.

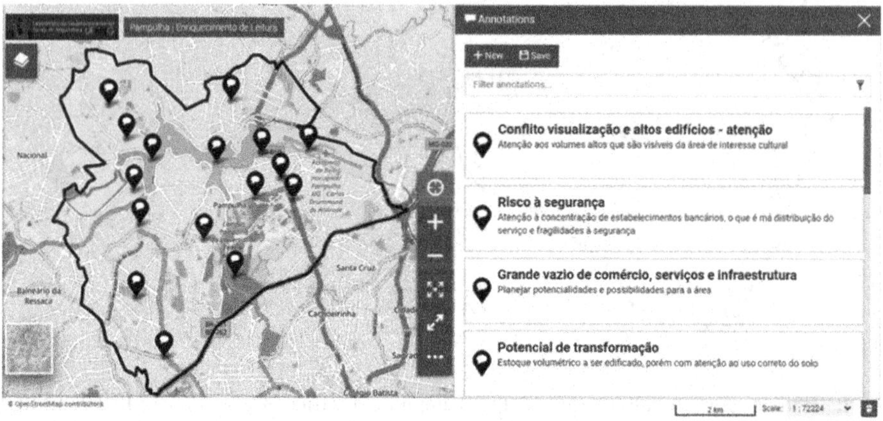

Fig. 5. GISColab interface showing the "Annotations" box (right) with the name of the idea and an explanatory text about the contribution or observation. Source: the authors.

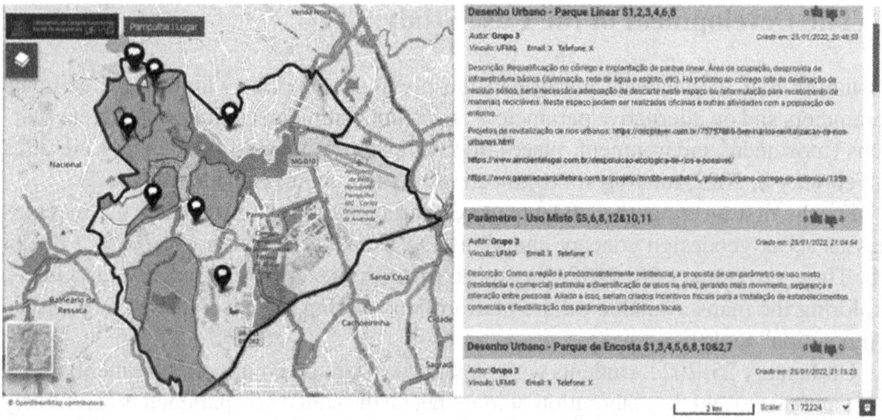

Fig. 6. GISColab interface showing the "Dialogs" box (right) with the name of the proposal, an explanatory text about the proposal, the identification of the group and the description of the completeness indicators. Source: the authors.

In addition, on February 2nd, students watched a video about the twelve indicators before class, which describes each one and exemplifies how they can be applied. The purpose of the day was to edit the proposals taking into account the Completeness Indicators. Each group in its context of origin edited the initial proposals, analyzing one by one and informing in their description to which indicators the idea could contribute positively or could cause negative impacts. For this description, the students followed the logic: Proposal Name $(comma-separated numbers from positive indicators) & (comma-separated numbers from negative indicators), for example: Permeable Sidewalks $2, 7, 9 & 3, 10, in which 2, 7 and 9 are positive contributions to the mentioned indicators, while 3 and 10 are the negatively affected indicators ones (Figs. 7, 8 and 9).

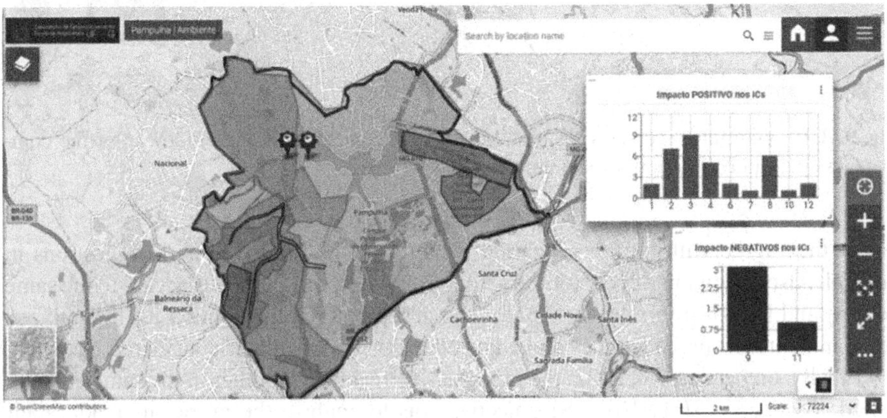

Fig. 7. GISColab interface showing the "Environment" context working window after the completeness indicators description. Source: the authors.

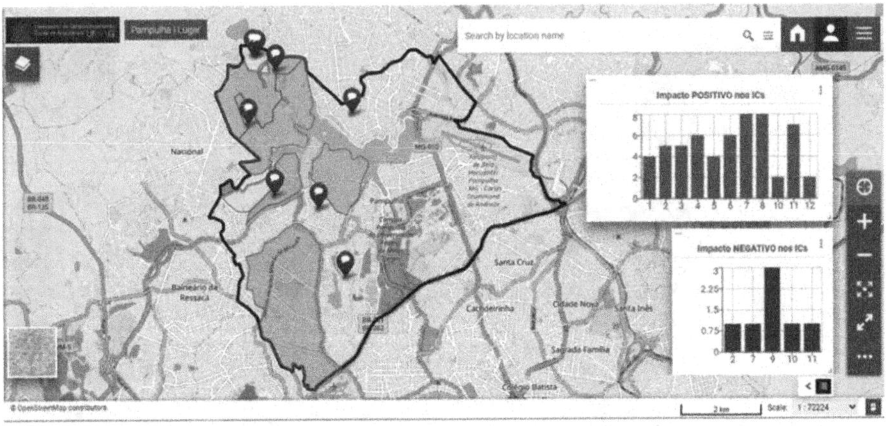

Fig. 8. GISColab interface showing the "Place" context working window after the completeness indicators description. Source: the authors.

On February 3, through video and script guidelines, students used the "Dialogues" tool to write comments for each proposal, as a discussion or debate. For example: whether

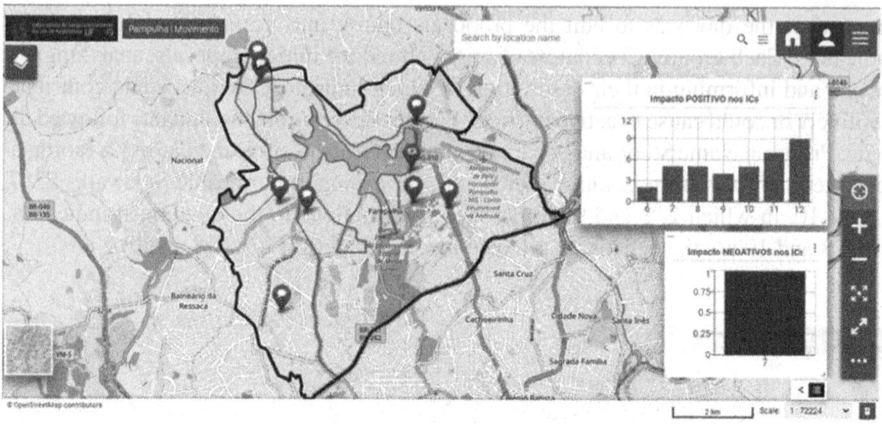

Fig. 9. GISColab interface showing the "Movement" context working window after the completeness indicators description. Source: the authors.

or not they agree with the idea/location, what could be improved and suggestions in general. Also following a cycle for the activity, avoiding simultaneous access to the same context and loss of information. Finally, the group entered the context itself, analyzed the comments left by colleagues and adjusted the proposals that it considered pertinent.

Finally, on February 8, 2022, the proposals were added together in the same context, called "Synthesis" (Fig. 10). The objective was to analyze the proposals made, their comments, keeping in mind the votes (individual opinion) that was carried out immediately afterwards in a synchronous way conducted by the workshop coordinator. The result was a unique and collectively constructed design.

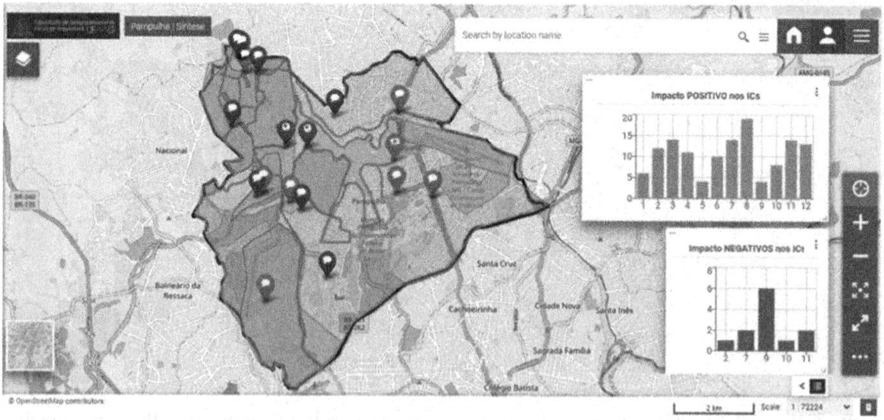

Fig. 10. GISColab interface showing the "Synthesis" context working window. Source: the authors.

4 Results and Discussion

The results were organized in an impact matrix (Fig. 11). The goal was to understand which indicators were more contemplated or not so well considered in the selected ideas. It was also a way to elucidate possibilities of representation of the results and diagnoses for the students. As can be seen, the indicator "permanence spaces" was the most contemplated, that is, with positive impacts. On the other hand, the "road capacity" indicator was identified as a negative impact at the end of the experiment. This panorama showed it was easier to the students to understand and create proposals about "place", to the detriment of proposals on "environment" and "movement".

	environment	movement	place	sum
1. street afforestation	2	0	4	6
2. efficient drainage	7	0	4	11
3. environmental comfort	9	0	5	14
4. landscape quality	5	0	6	11
5. active facades	0	0	4	4
6. flexibility of uses	2	2	6	10
7. universal accessibility	1	4	7	12
8. permanence spaces	6	5	8	19
9. road capacity	-3	4	-3	-2
10. road safety	1	5	1	7
11. mode connectivity	-1	7	6	12
12. active mobility	2	9	2	13
sum	31	36	50	117

5 Most benefit
1 Benefit
0 Neutral
-1 Detriment
-3 Most Detriment

Fig. 11. Impact matrix of completeness indicators. Source: the authors.

After the end of the workshop, the performance of the proposals was evaluated, considering thematic, locational and priority assertiveness (Fig. 12). Thematic assertiveness is related to the theme of the proposal, if it is good and appropriate to the context, in short, if it is "a good idea". Priority assertiveness is related to the workshop's objective of incorporating new concepts and alternative urban parameters, the indicators of completeness. Thus, a proposal with priority assertiveness has correctly incorporated the indicators in its description. On the other hand, locational assertiveness is related to the appropriate location of the proposal, based on the observation of the map collection offered and prior knowledge of the place.

From this analysis, it was possible to observe that most proposals achieved all the three criteria (58.40%), followed by proposals that achieved at least two criteria (34.88%). There were no proposals without some level of assertiveness. Although there is still room for further analysis on the factors that led to this situation, the first impressions show that the dynamics and methodological process incorporated in the workshop fulfilled its teaching and consensus building objectives.

Priority assertiveness was the least recurrent (69.76%), followed by locational assertiveness (88.37%), while thematic assertiveness was the predominant one (92.03%) (Fig. 13). Such a picture shows that the use of geovisualization tools and geotechnologies may have contributed positively to the understanding of the place, that is, to the locational assertiveness of the proposals. When analyzing the result of the priority assertiveness of the proposals, it became evident that the non-assertiveness was due to errors in understanding the indicators and new concepts for the students. Therefore, priority assertiveness can be improved with a previous and more in-depth approach to the indicators, adding more technical and conceptual details to the assumptions.

	proposals	thematic	priority	locational
moviment	bicycle path	1	1	1
	bus stop: bandeirantes II	1	0	1
	bus stop: vila paquetá	1	0	1
	road capacity increase	0	0	1
	road and pedestrian safety increase	0	0	1
	increase in the number of buses	1	1	1
	road improvement	1	0	1
	medium and high capacity mobility corridor	1	1	1
	medium capacity mobility corridor	1	1	0
	pampulha cultural tram	1	1	1
	tram central station and Info center	1	1	1
	bicycle racks	1	1	1
	crosswalk	1	1	1
	crosswalk	1	1	1
	interventions in unsafe stretches	1	1	0
environment	free grant benefit to increase permeability	1	1	1
	flood park	1	1	0
	shaded bus stop	1	1	1
	tax incentive to decrease surface temperature	1	1	1
	basic sanitation program	1	1	1
	green connection	1	1	0
	shaded bus stop	1	1	1
	sanitary sewage treatment and urban stream recovery	1	1	1
	water support and preservation center	1	1	1
	brazilian spotted fever monitoring center	1	1	1
	permeability parameter review	1	1	1
place	mixed use	0	0	1
	zone of sustainable urban density	1	1	1
	incentive to active facades and trading	1	1	1
	zone of restricted sustainable urban density	1	1	1
	zone of sustainable urban density	1	1	1
	slope park	1	1	1
	streets closed on weekends	1	1	1
	bus stops that encourage staying	1	1	0
	linear park	1	1	1
	bus stop	1	0	1
	bus stop	1	0	1
	bus stop	1	0	1
	bus stop	1	0	1
	bus stop	1	0	1
	bus stop	1	0	1
	bus stop	1	0	1
	basic urban infrastructure	1	1	1

number of criteria achieved
3 (58,14%)
2 (34,88%)
1 (6,98%)
0 (0%)

Fig. 12. Performance of the proposals analyzed by thematic, locational and priority: green (3), yellow (2), orange (1) and red (0). Source: the authors. (Color figure online)

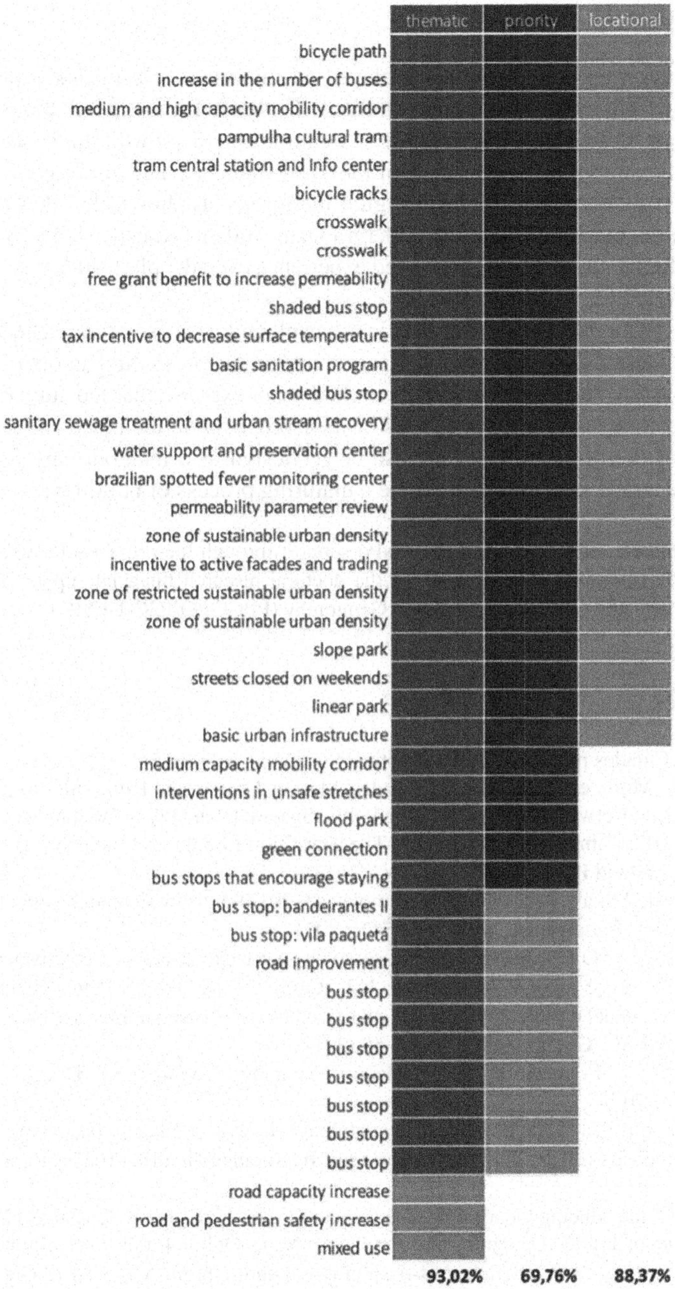

Fig. 13. Assertiveness of the proposals by thematic, locational and priority. Source: the authors.

5 Conclusions

Geovisualization and geoinformation played an important role in this experience, as it was carried out entirely remotely (online). It allowed knowledge about the place to be aggregated and built collectively. In addition, the use of digital tools facilitates communication and the consolidation of the main concepts. The use of geoinformation technologies, such as the GISColab digital platform, has shown that they have great potential on the teaching, since the undergraduate students (mostly, with 20 years old) are mostly digital natives. In this reported experience even the platform's unproven tools were explored.

The use of Completeness Indicators in urban planning course encouraged students to research innovations and other projects for reference, that is, to think about professional practice beyond what is posted. It also worked as an exercise that led students to think about the positive and negative impacts of their proposal on the place and considering the people of the place. Finally, the use of geodesign as a methodology for teaching Architecture and Urbanism proved to be a maturing process of building consensus.

Acknowledgments. The authors thank CNPq support through the project 401066/2016–9 and FAPEMIG PPM-00368–18. And, also, for the doctoral research financial support from CNPq (141092/2021–1) and Graduate Program in Geography (PPGGEO/IGC-UFMG).

References

1. Gehl, J.: Cidades para pessoas, Perspectiva, São Paulo, SP (2015)
2. Jacobs, J.: Morte e vida de grandes cidades. Martins Fontes, São Paulo, SP (2011)
3. Gehl, J.: Life Between Buildings: Using Public Spaces. Island Press, Washington, DC (2011)
4. McCann, B.: Completing Our Streets: The Transition to Safe and Inclusive Transportation Networks. Island Press, Washington, DC (2013)
5. WRI Brasil, Afinal, o que são Ruas Completas? (2017). http://wricidades.org/noticia/afinal-o-que-sao-ruas-completas. Accessed 15 Oct 2021
6. Moura, A.C.M.: O Geodesign como processo de co-criação de acordos coletivos para a paisagem territorial e urbana. In: Ladwig, N.I., Campos, J.B., (eds.), Planejamento e gestão territorial: o papel e os instrumentos do planejamento territorial na interface entre o urbano e o rural, UNESC, Criciúma, SC, pp. 16–59 (2019)
7. Steinitz, C.: A Framework for Geodesign: Changing Geography by Design. Esri Press, Redlands (2012)
8. Rosa, A.: A utilização de um índice de completude na avaliação de impacto para projetos de Ruas Completas (2020). http://repositorio.ufjf.br/jspui/handle/ufjf/11637. Accessed 15 Oct 2021
9. Miller, W.: Introducing Geodesign: The Concept, p. 36. ESRI Press, Redlands (2012)
10. Dangermond, J.:GIS: Designing our future, ArcNews Online (2009). http://www.esri.com/news/arcnews/summer09articles/gis-designing-our-future.html. Accessed 15 Oct 2021
11. Forester, J.: The Deliberative Practitioner: Encouraging Participatory Planning Processes. MIT Press, Cambridge, MA (1999)
12. Moura, A.C.M., Freitas, C.R.: Co-creation of ideas in geodesign process to support opinion and decision making: case study of a slum in Minas Gerais, Brazil. In: La Rosa, D., Privitera, R. (eds.) INPUT 2021. LNCE, vol. 146, pp. 255–264. Springer, Cham (2021). https://doi.org/10.1007/978-3-030-68824-0_28

13. Wilson, J.P.: Towards geodesign: building new education programs and audiences. In: Lee, D.J., Dias, E., Scholten, H.J. (eds.) Geodesign by Integrating Design and Geospatial Sciences. GL, vol. 111, pp. 357–369. Springer, Cham (2014). https://doi.org/10.1007/978-3-319-08299-8_23
14. Arnstein, S.R.: A ladder of citizen participation. J. Am. Plann. Assoc. **35**(4), 216–224 (1969)
15. Carsalade, F.L., Pedro, M.: O Conjunto Moderno da Pampulha como Patrimônio Cultural da Humanidade. Arquiteturas do mar, da terra e do ar? Arquitetura e Urbanismo na Geografia e na Cultura, v. 1, Lisboa: Academia de Escolas de Arquitetura de Língua Portuguesa, pp. 368–84 (2014)

Collaborative and Sustainable Strategies Through Geodesign: The Case Study of Bacoli

Maria Somma[1](✉), Michele Campagna[2], Tess Canfield[3], Maria Cerreta[1], Giuliano Poli[1], and Carl Steinitz[4]

[1] Department of Architecture, University of Naples Federico II, via Toledo 402, Naples, Italy
{maria.somma,maria.cerreta,giuliano.poli}@unina.it

[2] Department of Civil, Environmental Engineering and Architecture, University of Cagliari, Via Marengo, 2, Cagliari, Italy
campagna@unica.it

[3] CMLI, London, United Kingdom
tesscanfield@yahoo.com

[4] Graduate School of Design, Harvard University, Cambridge, MA, United States
csteinitz@gsd.harvard.edu

Abstract. The geodesign framework has supported stakeholder engagement in policy-making and planning with its innovative, practical, operational, fast, and participatory tools for a long time. Although geodesign has provided practitioners with systematic and technologically sound solutions for sustainability problems within the International Geodesign Collaboration (IGC) network, a new concept of connectivity among neighbouring cities and the regeneration of landscapes should be more stressed by the participatory workshops. The paper proposes using geodesign system thinking to spark cooperation between Academia and Public Authorities to foster integrated, spatially explicit, and strategic planning. The experimentation presented in this paper aims at providing recommendations for sustainable design with a particular focus on local problems linked to accessibility and reclamation. The peninsula of the city of Bacoli (Italy) has been selected as a best-fit case study for investigating these dynamics by involving a working group of professors, researchers, PhD candidates, and students from the Second Level Master in *Sustainable Planning and Design of Port Areas* of the University of Naples Federico II, along with professionals, citizens, and policy-makers belonging to the Municipality. The workshop experience has demonstrated how collaborative processes between people with different backgrounds and interests can elicit preferences and identify relationships among the recovery of systems connected to landscape regeneration and accessibility infrastructures.

Keywords: Geodesign · Decision-making process · Spatial planning · Collaborative design · Port areas

1 Introduction

In the last decades, a new approach to planning, integrating multi-dimensional issues and divergent points of view with technological tools, has emerged to resolve wicked

O. Gervasi et al. (Eds.): ICCSA 2022 Workshops, LNCS 13379, pp. 210–224, 2022.
https://doi.org/10.1007/978-3-031-10545-6_15

and complex decision-making [1]. From an urban and sociological point of view, this is unprecedented [2]. Conventional planning approaches are no longer suited to cope with such multi-dimensionality since they frequently fail to consider the issues endorsed by different stakeholders interested in the planning process [3]. As cities become increasingly complex, planning methods that encourage collaboration among stakeholders are needed to reach a consensus [4–7] in order to pursue the goals of the Agenda 2030 to make cities more liveable through a shared vision of integral sustainability [8].

Although geodesign has provided practitioners with systematic and technologically sound solutions to sustainability problems, new concepts of connectivity among neighbouring cities and the reclamation of landscapes [4, 9, 10] should be more stressed in specific geographical areas. The concept of sustainability is the crucial theme of territorial development policies with a specific reference to the integration of natural landscape systems with artificial urban systems, balancing public and private stakeholders' cultural backgrounds and visions oriented to priority development strategies [11]. Shared knowledge makes the planning process more effective with today's tools and methods, where teamwork is essential.In addition, geodesign methods can support decision-makers facing new and complex problems like emergency response and public participation [12, 13].

The Steinitz geodesign framework implemented into the Geodesignhub.com platform (GDH) offers suitable methods and tools for resolving complex urban problems. Through a systemic and inclusive vision, not only the expert knowledge guides a decision-making process, but all local actors contribute to building knowledge. Two fundamental components of the geodesign methodology are relevant for improving the decision-making process: digital information technology and the active participation of local communities in the planning process [14, 15]. While conventional public involvement has proven problematic in many cases [16], geodesign methods have effectively involved local community members in the design phase through virtual collaboration. As a result, the geodesign approach to spatial planning has attracted interest from academics, corporate businesses, and institutional settings [15, 17–21].

Based on these premises, the research aims to show and discuss the results of a geodesign workshop referring to the Municipality of Bacoli, in the South of Italy, nearby the City of Naples. In the following paragraphs, development strategies are described for the study area, which were pursued through a two day, iterative, online and in-person workshop that has involved different stakeholders. The geodesign workshop was supported by the online GIS-based platform Geodesignhub.com, allowing for geo-referenced analysis and design, and facilitating communication and negotiation among the stakeholders involved in the decision-making process.

The article is organized as follows: Sect. 2 shows the selected study area through a short description of its geographical, morphological, social, and cultural features; Sect. 3 describes the preparatory steps of the workshop and the involved stakeholders; Sect. 4 discusses the results obtained from the negotiation phase, while the conclusions and open questions are presented in Sect. 5.

2 The Case Study of Bacoli (Italy)

The Municipality of Bacoli (Fig. 1) near Napoli is located in a complex landscape system with a high intrinsic environmental value. It originated from an eruptive phase of a volcanic formation during the "Third Phlegraean Period", approximately 8.000 years ago. It stands on an alignment of seven volcanoes (dating back to two different historical periods), arranged on a single axis, and comprising the volcanoes of Capo Miseno, Miseno harbour. The relief characterises the entire ancient centre of Bacoli, from Punta del Poggio and Piscina Mirabile to Centocamerelle. The craters of Baia stand at the Aragonese Castle of Baia and goes up the provincial road that leads from Pozzuoli to Bacoli; the Gulf of Baia has almost wholly dismantled the remains of the volcano recognisable in Punta Epitaffio, and in the yellow tuff ridge that looks towards Lucrino. These are in the northern area outside the inhabited centre.

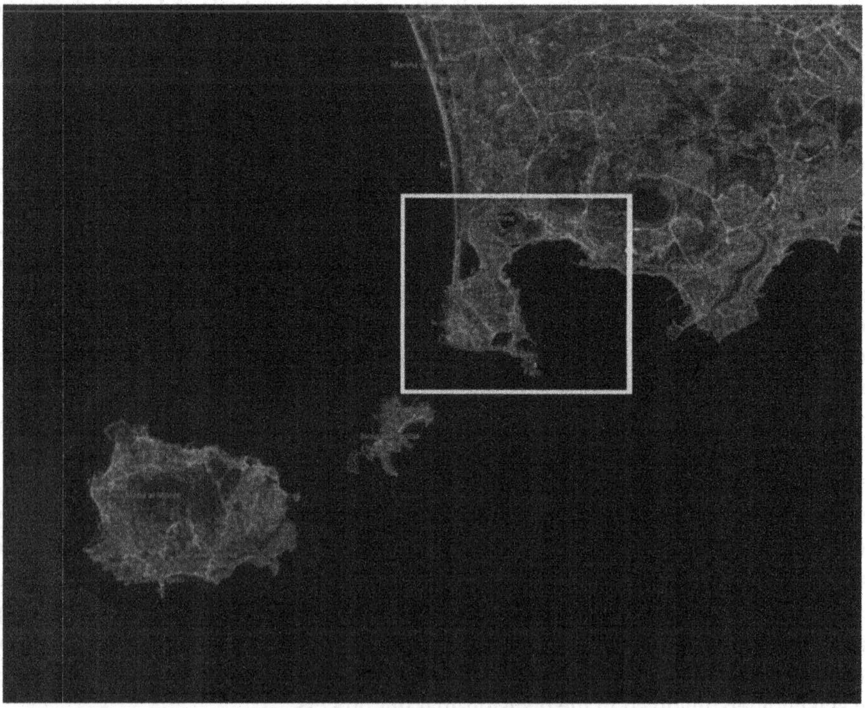

Fig. 1. The Bacoli case study (Source: the authors). (Color figure online)

The Campi Flegrei area shapes an environmental system of exceptional value, consisting of an inseparable interweaving of natural and anthropic structures, historical formation, and agricultural land uses. Over time, these four systems have created a complex ecosystem that is constantly evolving but whose fragility appears even more exposed today after the ongoing transformations between the 1960s and 1990s. At the beginning of the twentieth century, large industrial plants and specialised infrastructure boosted mono-functional urbanisation. Consequently, the Phlegraean territory has gradually lost its peculiar character because urban growth has taken place without planning and control of land use, upsetting and destructuring the traditional character of many Phlegraean towns. In Bacoli and neighbouring municipalities (Monte di Procida, Quarto and Pozzuoli), the natural boundaries - characterised by particular geomorphological-structural features - have been overtaken and partly eroded by an exponential increase in new buildings, some of which are linked to a structured planning design. This has led to the uncontrolled development of infrastructures linking land and sea, resulting in the gradual loss of Mediterranean scrub and terrace cultivation, compromising the landscape and generating degraded and disfigured places. Nowadays these places are characteristic elements of the urban system of Bacoli and need recovery, regeneration, and reclamation. Given their importance, they have been identified as one of the systems of interest to be analysed and assessed in the study. Urban sprawl has modified first the morphology of the Pozzuoli area and then Bacoli, chosen as the site for the development of some industrial plants, such as the Selenia plant at Lake Fusaro and the Baia shipyards, determining a discontinuity in the development of the coastal area and making the territory even more problematic and critical.

3 The Workflow of the Geodesign Workshop

The geodesign workshop for Bacoli was organised in November 2021 by the Second Level Master in "Sustainable Planning and Design of Port Areas" of the University of Naples Federico II. The workshop began with an introduction to the study area, the goals of development scenarios, and the presentation of ten evaluation maps developed by the coordination teams as a digital collective knowledge base from which to begin the design. Geodesign is a process that relies on the use of geographical knowledge to solve planning challenges from an interdisciplinary perspective and to produce informed and evidence-based designs and choices. The organising team devised a workshop program that condensed complicated design tasks into a time-constrained and intensive workflow agenda. As a result, the geodesign workshop is most beneficial when used at the start of research of significant complexity [20, 22]. Given the breadth and complexity of the Bacoli area and the number of people engaged, the conductors underlined that rapid, strategic thinking and decision-making is essential rather than precision.

Next, Sect. 3.1 explains the evaluation and impact geodesign models performed in the preparatory phase of the workshop, while Sect. 3.2 introduces the design, the negotiation, and preliminary results.

3.1 The Workshop Preparatory Phases

The workshop's preparatory phases started in May 2021, creating local knowledge of the context with a specific focus on citizens' needs. Local stakeholders, students, researchers, and professors of the Second Level Master in "Sustainable Planning and Design of Port Areas" at the University of Naples Federico II took part in a Living Lab workshop to learn the criticalities and potentials of the study area by exploring peculiar geographical locations. Several sources of geo-referenced information have expanded the local knowledge, including official databases of the Campania Region, of the Basin Authority, and the Copernicus Urban Atlas provided by the European Environment Agency. In addition, further spatial-explicit information was collected from the database provided by the Regional Park Authority of Campi Flegrei and the Municipality of Bacoli. These knowledge streams have highlighted landscape-environmental, historical-cultural, and economic systems. Data collection and analysis represented the base for the construction of the geodesign evaluation model [23], and ten evaluation maps were placed in Geodesignhub software. In the first phase, three main objectives have been targeted in a time horizon to 2030:

1. Port development;
2. Connectivity with neighbouring landscapes;
3. Recovery, regeneration, and reclamation of degraded and abandoned landscape linked to the infrastructure network.

Ten evaluation maps have supported the choice of change scenarios according to five degrees of suitability, as follows:

1. Dark green represents the highest feasibility for change, as there are prerequisites for new projects.
2. Green represents suitability for a transformation, as the area is already equipped with technologies to support the design.
3. Light green identifies where it is appropriate to envisage changes as far as the means to support interventions are provided.
4. Yellow identifies where changes are inappropriate.
5. Red represents areas where the system is working well, and therefore should not be changed.

The evaluation maps represent the landscape systems' spatial representation related to vegetation, hydrology, cultural and historical landscape resources, accessibility and transportation, commerce, tourist services, urban mix, and reclamation.

The ten evaluation maps (Fig. 2) have helped evaluate the study area's main characteristics. They have referred to as Water (WAT), Agriculture (AGR), Green Infrastructure (GRN), Energy (ENE), Transport (TRAN), Tourism (INDTUR), Mixed-use (MIX), Cultural heritage (CULT), Reclaim (RCLM), and Commercial (COM).

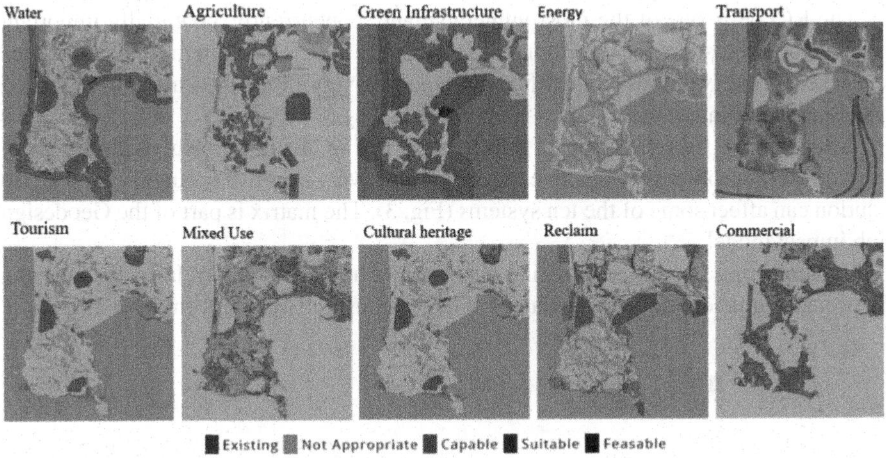

Fig. 2. Evaluation maps for the ten systems (Source: the authors).

An explanation of the meanings of the ten systems follows. The WAT system envisages actions linked to the restoration and improvement of existing water systems or the creation of blue infrastructure.

The AGR system relates to improving and developing the local agri-food sector. The system's actions envisage the creation of new enterprises, brands, circuits and structures dedicated to a market that is not only local but also able to attract tourists towards the knowledge of the local production chain.

The GRN system concerns solutions for protecting and enhancing the natural heritage, both in landscape-environmental-coastal and economic-productive aspects. Such a system encourages the creation of green infrastructures on a metropolitan scale, connecting areas of high naturalistic value and guaranteeing sustainable use of the territory and its resources [24].

The ENE system involves policy and strategies for sustainable energy efficiency, one of the most challenging targets to mitigate climate change impacts and reduce household costs.

The TRAN system is crucial for the efficiency of the study area. Therefore, it is necessary to envisage direct interventions to create and improve road infrastructures, nodes and mobility routes to support people and goods by land and water and make the territory accessible by decongesting traffic. On the one hand, in the case of transportation systems, technical issues should solve the entanglements and congestion problems. However, on the other hand, the impacts on the surrounding environment and travellers' needs have to be incorporated [25–27].

The INDTUR system relates to tourism services and assets. Therefore, it envisages interventions to protect and develop an integrated supply of cultural and environmental assets, touristic attractions, and services to boost the host capacity and accommodation facilities. These actions aim to support the enhancement of the CULT system and the economic sustainability of the MIX and COM systems.

The RCLM is one of the most vulnerable and, concurrently, potentially important systems for the sustainable development of the study area. This system needs to foresee regeneration interventions, requalification, and recovery of all the currently degraded spaces and buildings.

Afterwards, a five-class impact matrix was filled in Geodesign Hub with the likely consequences - from highly positive (dark purple) to very negative (orange) - for which a solution can affect some of the ten systems (Fig. 3). The matrix is part of the Geodesign Hub impact model.

Implementing this impact matrix, which shows how many interrelated systems are, the project's impacts can be calculated on the Geodesign Hub platform in real-time.

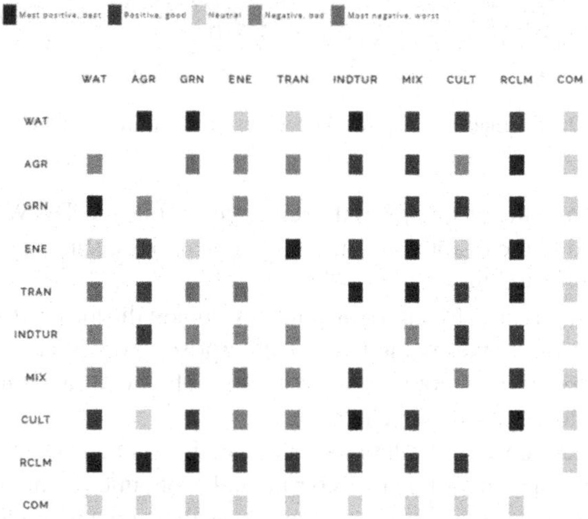

Fig. 3. The impact matrix (Source: the Authors). (Color figure online)

3.2 The Geodesign Workshop

Thirty-five participants took part in the workshop, including professors and researchers with different affiliations such as TUDelft, University of Genoa, Vanvitelli University and Federico II University, technical staff from the Public Administration of Bacoli, and stakeholders from the private sector.

The participants, most of whom had previous personal knowledge of the local context of Bacoli and the Campi Flegrei area, had various backgrounds ranging from engineering, architecture and urban planning to Geographic Information System/Information Science and Technology creating a good mix of skills for a geodesign studio.

The workshop was in a hybrid format with streaming sessions available for those participating remotely. It began with an introduction to the study area, the goals of development scenarios, and an overview of the geodesign process and the tools which would be used. (Fig. 4).

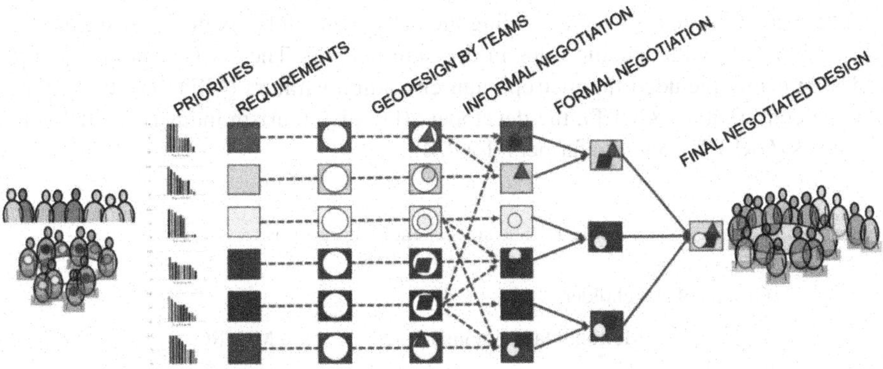

Fig. 4. Collaborative negotiation to a final design (Source: Carl Steinitz).

There then was a presentation of ten evaluation maps developed by the coordination teams as a digital collective knowledge base from which to begin the design. Then, each participant was assigned a system among the ten identified, to draw project or policy diagrams, including IGC System Innovations (https://www.igc-geodesign.org/global-systems-research). Policies are hatched, Projects are solid, and all are color coded by system. All had attributes such as public or private, timing and cost. As a result, about 250 diagrams were collected and shared among the participants by the platform into a matrix arranged by systems, representing specific policies or projects for each of the ten systems (Fig. 5).

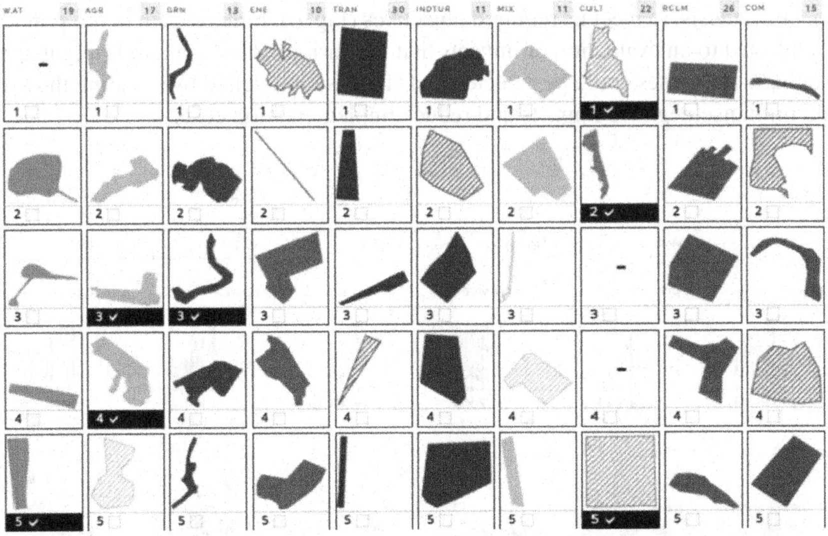

Fig. 5. Examples of policy and project diagrams (Source: the authors). (Color figure online)

The second phase started by dividing the participants into six different stakeholder groups (Table 1) with specific roles in decision-making. The six stakeholder groups, or design teams included the metropolitan city administrators (METRO), the cultural heritage conservators (CULT), the developers (DEVE), tourism industry (TOUR), the ecologists (GREEN), and the farmers (FARM).

Table 1. The six stakeholders' groups

Groups of stakeholders		
1	Metropolitan administrators	METRO
2	Cultural heritage conservation	CULT
3	Developers	DEVE
4	Tourism	TOUR
5	Green	GREEN
6	Farmers	FARM

According to their objectives, each group defined its priorities by assigning each system a value from 1 (low priority) to 10 (high priority). Then, the groups were allowed to review the incorrect diagrams, modify them, or draw new ones (Fig. 4). The GDH interface allows to view the diagrams proposed by one's group and those proposed by members of other groups.

Afterwards, each group selected diagrams of interest to compose an integrated scenario, or synthesis, to meet its required objectives (Fig. 6). Finally, each of the syntheses was subjected to an evaluation of impacts that the various transformations might generate so that weaknesses could be detected and choices remodelled by selecting those that would minimise negative impacts and reduce implementation costs.

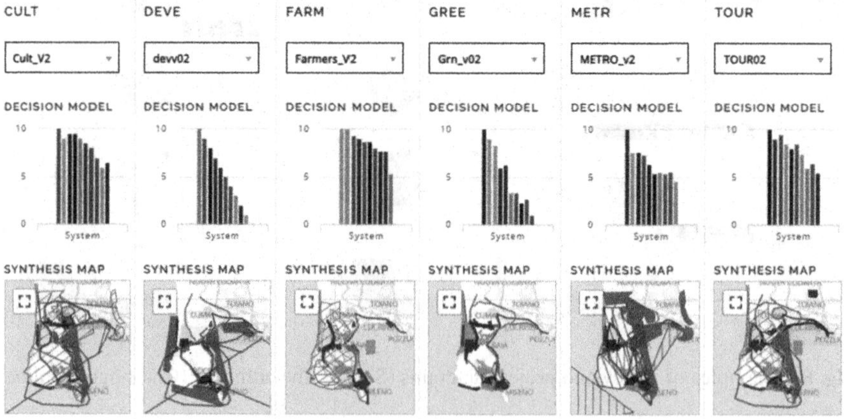

Fig. 6. The comparison design of scenarios 2 (Source: the authors).

The last phase of the workshop involved the shared construction of a project proposal by all the stakeholders involved through negotiation. Through a sociogram (Fig. 7), the affinities between the various project proposals of the six stakeholder groups were defined. Within the sociogram, each stakeholder group expressed a judgement of compatibility with the scenarios proposed by the other groups, expressing in the matrix a judgement ranging from very negative (xx) to very positive (+ +). Hence, on the base of the likelihood to collaborate, the groups were united into two coalitions, composed as follows:

- Tourism, Culture, Metropolitan teams (TCM);
- Green, Developers, Farmers team (GDH).

Fig. 7. The sociogram for negotiation agreement (original photographs by the authors).

A first negotiation phase was then launched. The two coalitions through dialogue and negotiation, constructed their two shared design syntheses (Fig. 8) which they then presented to the others.

After presenting the two designs that emerged from the respective coalitions, there was a final phase in which, through dialogue and negotiation between the two coalitions, compatible policies and projects flowed into one final shared scenario.

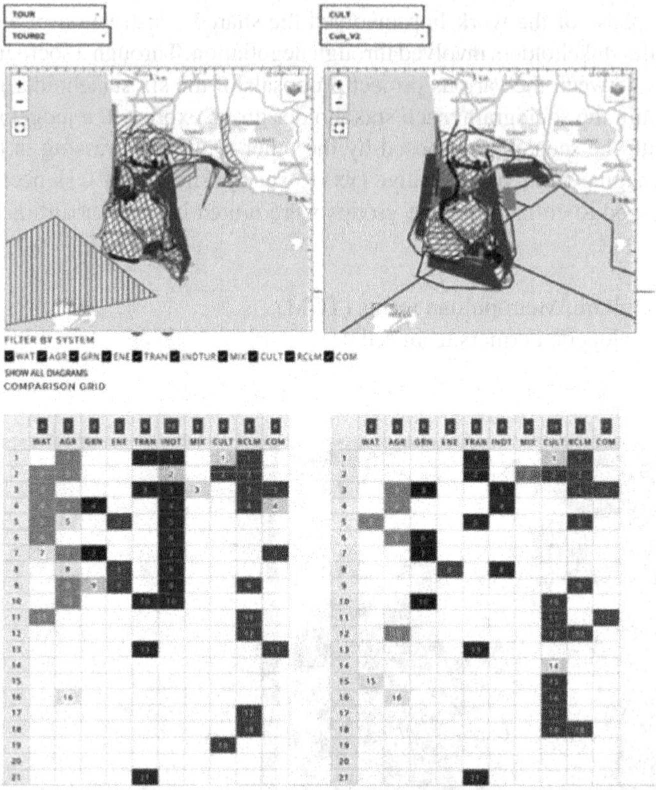

Fig. 8. The comparison of the two initially negotiated designs: TCM and GDH (Source: the authors

4 Outcomes

The proposed scenario for the city of Bacoli to 2030 fully reflects the three targets established in the preparatory phases. The diagram frequency (Fig. 9) has facilitated the comparison of the scenarios proposed by the two merged teams of stakeholders (TCM and GDF). It allowed the similarities in design and policy to emerge with a straightforward negotiation process.

In particular, the scenario proposed by the TCM team identified many more solutions aiming to solve the problem of connectivity - both by land and by the sea - and the recovery of abandoned areas, giving less importance to the design and policy interventions planned for the WAT, AGR, GRN, ENE, INDTUR, MIX and COM systems. Instead, the scenario approved by the GDF team, having selected a more significant number of project interventions for the WAT, AGR, GRN, INDTOUR, COM, and CULT systems, gave less importance to change actions in the MIX, ENE and TRAN systems. The two scenarios, therefore, turned out to be almost entirely different. However, the negotiation facilitated the construction of a scenario shared by all the stakeholders. Projects and policies linked to the final scenario (Fig. 9) were oriented to developing the network of connections. Moreover, several interventions were selected with the ambition to develop the port areas, with the related interventions for the recovery, reclamation and redevelopment of the coastal zones.

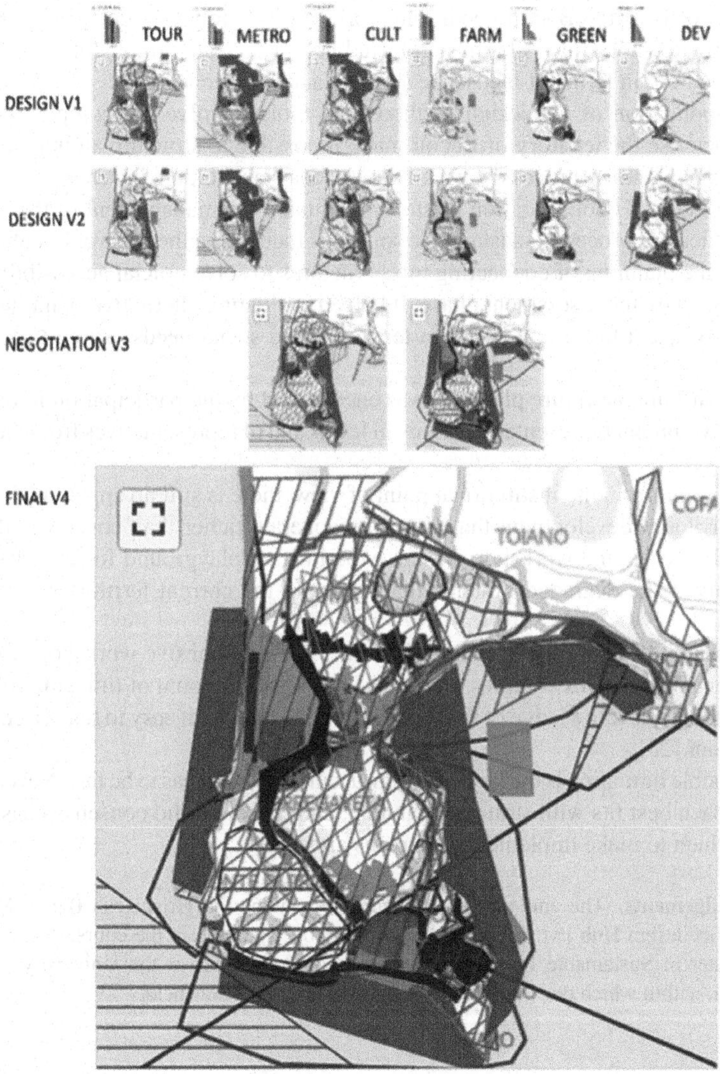

Fig. 9. Evolution of the final design syntheses by negotiation (Source: the authors).

The workshop was a great success, both for the participants and the organisers. The geodesign framework provided excellent support for the workshop, simplifying participants' activities and fostering a collaborative working environment. In less than two days, it was possible to build several alternative scenarios for the development of

Bacoli and the surrounding areas and to reach consensus through negotiation, reducing the number of potential alternative future projects to those acceptable for all.

5 Conclusions

The main focus of the Bacoli geodesign workshop was to trace scenarios of transformations in a territory that is highly protected but, at the same time, compromised and fragmented both in terms of landscape and the land-sea connections.

The application of geodesign methods and tools to solve the complex problems that characterise the territory of Bacoli made it possible to structure an interactive and collaborative planning process between the various stakeholders involved.

Using the GDH collaboration platform facilitated the management of the selection and identification process of sustainable solutions focused on the recovery of abandoned areas and the planning of connecting infrastructures to solve crucial accessibility problems detected by the assessment phase. It helped evaluating alternatives simultaneously and quickly select those that best met territorial and social needs, trying to overcome trade-offs.

More sustainable future planning was encouraged by the participation in the workshop of government representatives from all levels and of representatives from the private sector.

In addition, from the institutional point of view, there is still no apparent inclination toward territorial development that aims to regenerate rather than consume additional land. In this sense, the workshop was an experimental playground for introducing the assessment of the degraded systems that make up the current territories in planning processes.

The benefit of using the Steinitz's framework in an intensive workshop with GDH is that it enable to solves complex problems in a concise amount of time, improving the understanding and knowledge of the participants and making it easy to reach a consensus among them [28].

A possible limitation is the lack of design accuracy, which has to be fast. Nevertheless, this approach best fits with strategic planning, and it lays a solid consensus base on the base of which to make implementation plans afterwards.

Acknowledgements. The author wish to thanks very much Dr. Hrishikesh Ballal, Managing Director, Geodesign Hub Pvt. Ltd., for the use of Geodesign Hub in the courses of the Second Level Master in Sustainable Planning and Design of Port Areas of the University of Naples Federico II, within which the workshop presented in this paper was held.

References

1. Rittel, H.W.J., Webber, M.M.: Dilemmas in a general theory of planning. Policy Sci. **42**(4), 155–169 (1973). https://doi.org/10.1007/BF01405730
2. Dall'Omo, C.F., Limongi, G., Privitera, E., Somma, M., Vingelli, F.: Diary extract of five research experiences in the XXXIV Italian doctoral cycle. sharing common research questions on environment-oriented planning. Plurimondi, (19) 123–160 (2020)

3. Nyerges, T., et al.: Geodesign dynamics for sustainable urban watershed development. Sustain. Cities Soc. **25**, 13–24 (2016). https://doi.org/10.1016/J.SCS.2016.04.016
4. Cerreta, M., Mazzarella, C., Somma, M.: Opportunities and challenges of a geodesign based platform for waste management in the circular economy perspective. In: Gervasi, O., et al. (eds.) ICCSA 2020. LNCS, vol. 12252, pp. 317–331. Springer, Cham (2020). https://doi.org/10.1007/978-3-030-58811-3_23
5. Cerreta, M., Panaro, S., Cannatella, D.: Multidimensional spatial decision-making process: local shared values in action. In: Murgante, B., et al. (eds.) ICCSA 2012. LNCS, vol. 7334, pp. 54–70. Springer, Heidelberg (2012). https://doi.org/10.1007/978-3-642-31075-1_5
6. Cerreta, M., Panaro, S.: From perceived values to shared values: a multi-stakeholder spatial decision analysis (M-SSDA) for resilient landscapes. Sustainability **9**, 1113 (2017). https://doi.org/10.3390/su9071113
7. Cerreta, M., Panaro, S., Poli, G.: A knowledge-based approach for the implementation of a SDSS in the partenio regional park (Italy). In.: et al. Computational Science and Its Applications – ICCSA 2016. ICCSA 2016. Lecture Notes in Computer Science, vol. 9789, pp. 111–124. Springer, Cham (2016).https://doi.org/10.1007/978-3-319-42089-9_8
8. Scorza, F.: Training decision-makers: geodesign workshop paving the way for new urban agenda. In: Gervasi, O., et al. (eds.) ICCSA 2020. LNCS, vol. 12252, pp. 310–316. Springer, Cham (2020). https://doi.org/10.1007/978-3-030-58811-3_22
9. Cerreta, M., De, P.: Integrated spatial assessment (ISA): a multi-methodological approach for planning choices. Adv. Spat. Plan. (2012). https://doi.org/10.5772/35417
10. Attardi, R., Bonifazi, A., Torre, C.M.: Evaluating sustainability and democracy in the development of industrial port cities: some Italian cases. Sustain. **4**, 3042–3065 (2012). https://doi.org/10.3390/SU4113042
11. Di Cesare, E.A., Cocco, C., Campagna, M.: Il Geodesign come metodologia per la progettazione collaborativa di scenari di sviluppo per l'Area Metropolitana di Cagliari. ASITA 2016 Proc, pp. 333–340 (2016)
12. Keenan, P.B., Jankowski, P.: Spatial decision support systems: three decades on. Decis. Support Syst. **116**, 64–76 (2019). https://doi.org/10.1016/j.dss.2018.10.010
13. Cerreta, M., La Rocca, L.: Urban regeneration processes and social impact: a literature review to explore the role of evaluation. In: Gervasi, O., et al. (eds.) ICCSA 2021. LNCS, vol. 12954, pp. 167–182. Springer, Cham (2021). https://doi.org/10.1007/978-3-030-86979-3_13
14. Loures, L., Panagopoulos, T., Burley, J.B.: Assessing user preferences on post-industrial redevelopment. Environ. Plann. Plann. Des. **43**, 871–892. https://doi.org/10.1177/0265813515599981
15. Albert, C., von Haaren, C., Vargas-Moreno, J.C., Steinitz, C.: Teaching scenario-based planning for sustainable landscape development: an evaluation of learning effects in the cagliari studio workshop. Sustainability **7**, 6872–6892. https://doi.org/10.3390/SU7066872
16. Fisher, T.: An education in geodesign. Landsc. Urban Plan. **156**, 20–22 (2016). https://doi.org/10.1016/j.landurbplan.2016.09.016
17. Wheeler, C.: Geodesign takes root. Arc User **22**, 64–65 (2019)
18. Patata, S., Paula P.L., Moura, A.C.M.: The application of geodesign in a Brazilian illegal settlement. participatory planning in dandara occupation case study. In: Leone, C., Gargiulo, A., (eds.) Environmental and Territorial Modelling for Planning and Design, FedOAPress: Naples, pp. 673–685 (2018)
19. Pettit, C.J., et al.: Breaking down the silos through geodesign – envisioning Sydney's urban future. Environ. Plann. Urban Analy. City Sci. 46, 1387–1404 (2019). https://doi.org/10.1177/2399808318812887
20. Campagna, M., Steinitz, C., Di Cesare, E.A., Cocco, C., Ballal, H., Canfield, T.: Collaboration in planning: the geodesign approach. Rozw. Reg. i Polityka Reg. **35**, 55–72 (2016)

21. Campagna, M., Moura, A.C.M., Borges, J.: Cocco C future scenarios for the pampulha region: a geodesign workshop. J. Digit. Landsc. Archit. **1**, 292–301 (2016). https://doi.org/10.14627/537612033
22. Fischer, J.-G., Gneiting, P.: Collaborative planning processes. In: Parry, G., Graves, A., (eds.) Build to Order: the Road to the 5-Day Car, pp. 181–207 (2008). Springer London. ISBN 978–1–84800–225–8
23. Steinitz, C.: A Framework for Geodesign: Changing Geography by Design; ESRI Press, R.C. (2012)
24. Cerreta, M., Poli, G.: Landscape services assessment: a hybrid multi-criteria spatial decision support system (MC-SDSS). Sustain. **9**, 1311 (2017). https://doi.org/10.3390/SU9081311
25. Botte, M., Di Salvo, C., Caropreso, C., Montella, B., D'Acierno, L.: Defining economic and environmental feasibility thresholds in the case of rail signalling systems based on satellite technology. In: 2016 IEEE 16th International Conference on Environment and Electrical Engineering (EEEIC). https://doi.org/10.1109/EEEIC.2016.7555878
26. D'Acierno, L., Botte, M., Pignatiello, G.: A simulation-based approach for estimating railway capacity. Int. J. Transp. Dev. Integr. **3**, 232–244 (2019). https://doi.org/10.2495/TDI-V3-N3-232-244
27. Cerreta, M., di Girasole, E.G., Poli, G., Regalbuto, S.: Operationalizing the circular city model for naples' city-port: a hybrid development strategy. Sustainability **12**, 2927 (2020). https://doi.org/10.3390/SU12072927
28. Campagna, M., Di Cesare, E.A., Cocco, C.: Integrating green-infrastructures design in strategic spatial planning with geodesign. Sustainability **12**(5), 1820 (2020). https://doi.org/10.3390/su12051820

Using Geodesign Studio to Explore Alternative Local Spatial Development Scenarios in Serbia

Tijana Dabović(✉), Bojana Pjanović, Bojana Ivanović, and Dejan Djordjević

Faculty of Geography, Department of Spatial Planning, University of Belgrade, Studentski trg 3/III, 11000 Belgrade, Serbia
tijana.dabovic@gef.bg.ac.rs

Abstract. Sustainable Developments Goals (SDGs) in Serbia are reduced to the pursuit of economic growth and spatial planning in local areas is reduced to a governance mechanism for attracting investment. Similarly, if existing, digital technologies in local spatial planning are mostly used as a source of digital spatial data and not as planning support systems. Planning reforms conducted in the last two decades produce secluded, largely digitized administrative activities and technical documentation elaboration driven by the narrow, mostly national government interests. These sidestep the localization of SDGs and enhance profit-oriented interventions of powerful actors in local areas. The aim of the geodesign teaching studio conducted at the University of Belgrade in 2021 was to engage students in the elaboration of the International Geodesign Collaboration (IGC) project for the Municipality of Ivanjica and use relevant digital technologies as alternative planning themes, methods and support systems. Complying to the IGC conventions, the selection of locally relevant assumptions and innovations for the future sustainable spatial development for 10 systems was made. The Steinitz's Geodesign framework and Geodesignhub were used to design six scenarios, iteratively and collaboratively. Five scenarios differed in the starting year and intensity of implemented innovations, while the sixth reflected the "planning as usual" scenario. Consequently, the scenarios had different performance against the 17 SDGs achievement matrix. By collaboratively exploring Ivanjica's alternative spatial development scenarios and their anticipated SDGs performance, students better understood the process of localizing SDGs and learned how local stakeholders can be empowered to advocate, plan and act towards a more sustainable future.

Keywords: Geodesign education · International geodesign collaboration · Localizing sustainable developments goals

1 Introduction

Aiming at sustainable development implies a social understanding and agreement on what it is, why it is needed and how sustainable development can be localized through policies, decisions and interventions in different sub-national spatio-temporal contexts. In particular, localizing Sustainable Development Goals (SDGs) implies raising awareness, advocating, implementing and monitoring the realization of the 2030 Agenda in

O. Gervasi et al. (Eds.): ICCSA 2022 Workshops, LNCS 13379, pp. 225–241, 2022.
https://doi.org/10.1007/978-3-031-10545-6_16

sub-national communities [1]. The awareness about the importance of SDGs needs to be accompanied with the awareness of the social, political, academic and governance fragmentation and poor coordination. In such a context, local stakeholders should understand, explore, plan and implement locally specific challenges and opportunities that cross boundaries of tiers, territories, sectors, disciplines and time frames [1–4]. Localization can then relate "both to how SDGs can provide a framework for a local development policy and to how local and regional governments can support the achievement of the SDGs through action from the bottom up" [5].

In the European context, mainly since the 1990s, spatial planning has been perceived as an integrative discipline and a governance mechanism able to frame and incite different spatially relevant strategies for sustainable development in a way that is sensitive to the present and future needs of local communities and spatial conditions [6–11]. Moreover, the Charter of European Planning [6] promotes the planning profession and planners as leaders of change, scientists, designers and visionaries, political advisors and mediators, and as managers of territories. Recently, digital technologies have also been identified as crucial in enabling more transparent, inclusive, research-based decision making towards achieving SDGs [12]. With this regard, an integrated digitally enabled approach to spatial planning has been promoted by [13]. It is conceived as a people-centric process enabled by digital technologies which will generate better coordination and "engagement in the plan-making process, enhance efficiency and optimize the value of data, and it will allow stakeholders, planners, designers, and policymakers to think intelligently through an evidence-based decision-making process" [13, p. 4].

These normative standpoints indicate that the actual role of spatial planning, of planners and of digital technologies in framing the localization of SDGs varies across countries and regions in the world. Serbia belongs to the group of countries which experienced communicative self-management socialism with a decentralized and integrated approach to spatial planning (1950s – 1990s) [14] while its recent post-socialist period (2000s – 2020s) reduces the use of spatial planning and digital technologies in local areas to the investments accelerating instruments [15]. In general, planned interventions are not systematically, collaboratively or publicly considered. Investments are mostly promoted as activities of national interest and allocated to the resource extraction, infrastructure, low-tech and labour-intensive industry, tourism development, luxury housing and commerce. In turn, this kind of planning practices are beginning to experience opposition from the public demanding more transparent, locally inclusive and sensitive sustainable planning solutions. Planners in such turmoil can choose to continue doing business-as-usual or offer an alternative integrated digitally enabled approach to spatial planning.

From our perspective, the emancipation of the planning profession towards the mentioned normative roles obliges planning educators to teach planning not only as it is, but as it alternatively should and could be. We consider Geodesign within the International Geodesign Collaboration (IGC) conventions to be an appropriate pedagogical tool for such a teaching exercise. According to [16], geodesign is an interdisciplinary field with a focus on spatial thinking, geospatial technologies, the future, design as a force for good in the world, and multi-disciplinary collaboration. It has proven to be a promising pedagogical tool for exploring alternative future spatial development scenarios in the past

[17–20]. In addition, the IGC conventions aim at exploring the performance of different spatial development scenarios against the SDGs by changing not only the time-horizons of innovation adoption, but also attitudes towards current/business-as-usual planning practices. Consequently, we included the geodesign teaching studio and course in the new spatial planning curriculum as a pedagogical tool that enabled acquiring more innovative and integrative knowledge, skills and attitudes than the conventional methods used by spatial planners in the current planning practice in Serbia. The aim of this paper is to showcase this pedagogical experience and contribute to the wider consideration of Geodesign and the IGC conventions as tools for exploring the normative roles of an integrated digitally enabled approach to spatial planning [13, 21], as well as the roles of spatial planners in the process of defining the localization of SDGs.

2 The 2021 International Geodesign Collaboration Project Conventions

Geodesign is an emerging discipline usually associated with integrated land use planning, where science, system thinking and value-based spatio-temporal contexts can be interrelated. It performs as a collaborative platform for integrated spatial guidance and expression of policy areas in the study area (e. g. agriculture, infrastructure, industry, commerce and residence) crucial in meeting community's goals. Commonly, Geodesign implies that different scientific and professional place-related disciplines, IT professionals and people of the place (Fig. 1) will share their competencies in different assessment and simulated intervention processes [3, 22].

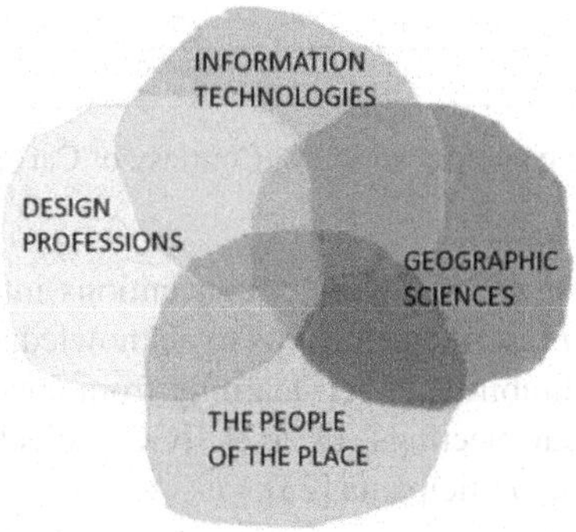

Fig. 1. The four necessary components of Geodesign. Courtesy of Carl Steinitz.

Processes are interrelated through three iterations and aim at answering six key questions: 1. How should the study area be described? 2. How does the study area function? 3. Is the current study area working well? 4. How might the study area be altered? 5. What difference might the changes cause? 6. How should the study area be changed? They enable collaborative making and exploration of alternative spatial development scenarios and understanding of their impacts before the decision on the preferable scenario is made [2, 22].

Placing geodesign in its core, in 2018 IGC was established. It is an international academic network seeking to understand how geodesign can better address design challenges in settings that are widely dispersed, differ widely in scale and in the extent of resources available to find geodesign solutions [23]. With this regard, the IGC project conventions offer a unified language and methodology for well-structured collaborative, research-based spatial development scenarios making structured in a geodesign workflow, based on [22] (Fig. 2) and supported by digital technologies and software such as Geodesignhub, GISColab and ArcGIS. As stated on the IGC website, the central aspect of effective collaboration and eventual action in the IGC project elaboration is public understanding of complex issues, which can be done without professional jargon, artistic obscurity, and scientific myopia [23].

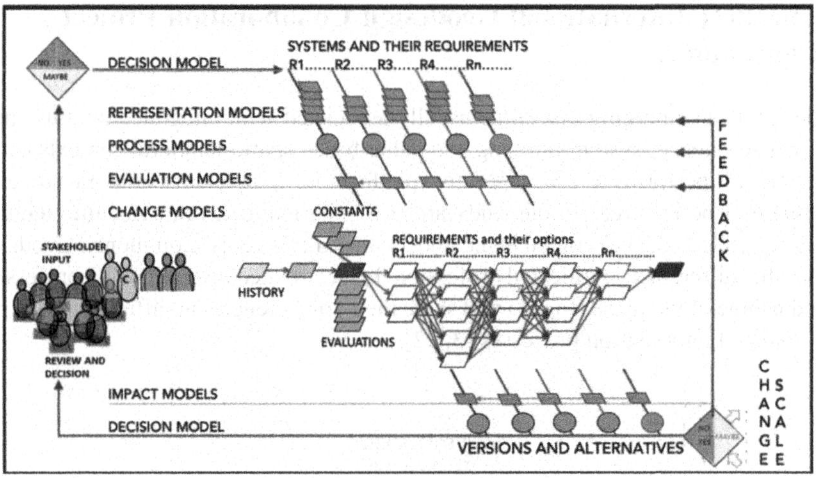

Fig. 2. Geodesign workflow. Courtesy of Carl Steinitz.

Under these conditions, the IGC project conventions intend to strike a good balance between flexible and prescribed elements to acknowledge international contextual diversity and enable comparability and co-learning from conducted projects which are presented at the IGC annual meetings. In 2021, IGC project conventions implied the following instructions to the participants [23]:

- There are eight key geodesign spatial systems plus two optional (with related color palettes). Eight land systems were pre-defined under consideration in each local study based on an examination of past Geodesign studies: 1. Water infrastructure (WAT), 2. Agriculture (AGR), 3. Green infrastructure (GRN), 4. Energy infrastructure (ENE), 5. Transport infrastructure (TRAN), 6. Industry and Commerce (INST), 7. Residential and Mixed-use Development (RES) and 8. Institutional Uses (INST). Two optional systems participants choose with the regard to the specificities of their case study.

- Global assumptions and design changes are proposed within the mentioned systems. The global assumptions and the associated specific concerns reflect current projections, forecasts, and predictions (Fig. 3). The global assumptions and system innovations were written with the awareness that individual nations and municipalities do have such goals and describe ideas that may be relevant to particular projects. Still, they will not be suitable for all projects.

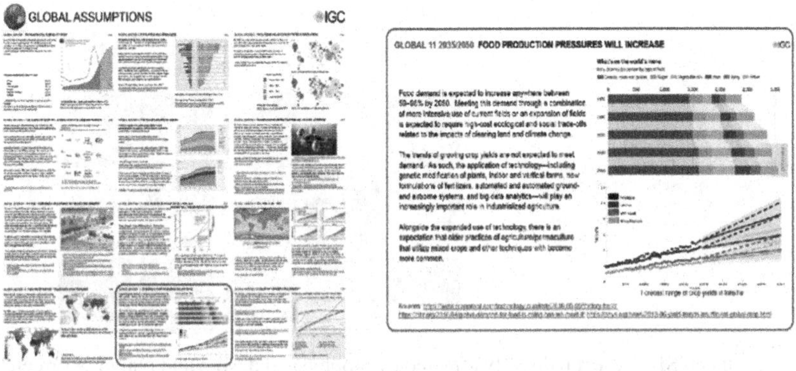

Fig. 3. Global assumptions. Source: IGC, 2021.

- All project contexts are to be defined as square spatial data "clips". With the aim to enable the direct comparison of evaluation and impact model outputs common spatial formats were established. Participants choose nested project sites at scales adhering to a square format: 0.5, 1, 2, 5, 10, 20, 40, 80, and 160 km on a side. Project goals and outcomes remain locally determined but participants are encouraged to undertake bigger-sized and nested-scales projects.
- Three design scenarios with three common time stages should be made with two future planning horizons - 2035 and 2050, and paths to achieve scenarios for those. "Early Adopters" initiate design interventions in 2020. "Late Adopters" in 2035 and "Non-adopters" continue with business-as-usual (Fig. 4).

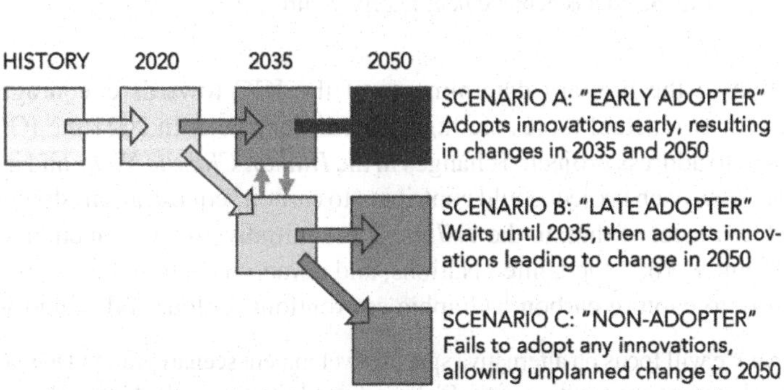

Fig. 4. IGC scenarios and time horizons. Source: IGC, 2021.

– A common impact evaluation framework based on the UN SDGs (Fig. 5), should be presented in a common format, i.e. SDGs achievement matrix (Fig. 6). IGC projects should indicate how well their design scenario outcomes would address the SDGs as a step toward addressing global sustainability truly. The assessments of performance against any SDG can be achieved by the expert judgments of the project team, or by model-based assessments [23].

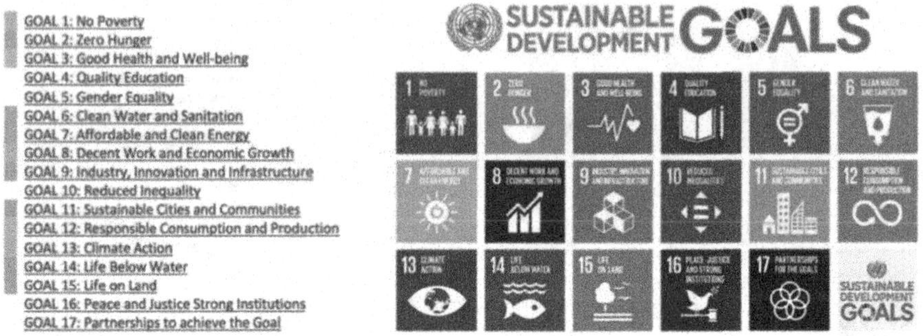

Fig. 5. Seventeen SDGs, seven directly affected by biophysical design and planning (green tabs), and five indirectly affected (orange tabs). Source: IGC, 2021 based on UN SDG, 2022. (Color figure online)

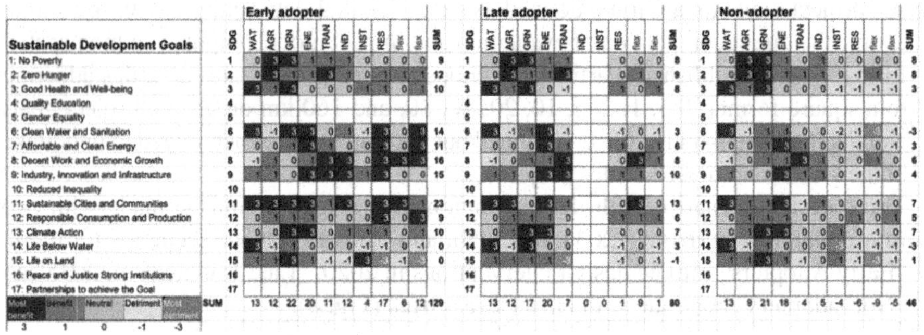

Early adopter

Sustainable Development Goals	SDG	WAT	AGR	GRN	ENE	TRAN	IND	INST	RES	flex	flex	SUM
1: No Poverty	1	0	3	3	1	1	1	0	0	0	0	9
2: Zero Hunger	2	0	3	1	1	3	1	0	1	1	1	12
3: Good Health and Well-being	3	3	1	3	0	0	0	1	1	0	1	10
4: Quality Education	4											
5: Gender Equality	5											
6: Clean Water and Sanitation	6	3	-1	3	3	0	1	-1	3	0	3	14
7: Affordable and Clean Energy	7	0	0	1	3	1	0	0	3	0	3	11
8: Decent Work and Economic Growth	8	-1	1	0	1	3	3	0	3	3	3	16
9: Industry, Innovation and Infrastructure	9	1	1	0	3	3	3	1	3	0	0	15
10: Reduced Inequality	10											
11: Sustainable Cities and Communities	11	3	3	3	3	1	3	0	3	3	1	23
12: Responsible Consumption and Production	12	0	1	1	1	0	0	0	3	0	3	9
13: Climate Action	13	0	0	3	3	0	1	1	1	0	1	10
14: Life Below Water	14	3	-1	1	0	0	0	-1	-1	0	-1	0
15: Life on Land	15	1	1	3	1	-1	-1	3	-3	-1	-3	0
16: Peace and Justice Strong Institutions	16											
17: Partnerships to achieve the Goal	17											
SUM		13	12	22	20	11	12	4	17	6	12	129

Late adopter

SDG	WAT	AGR	GRN	ENE	TRAN	IND	INST	RES	flex	flex	SUM
1	0	3	3	1	1			0	0	0	8
2	0	3	1	1	3			0	1	0	9
3	3	1	3	0	-1			1	0	1	8
4											
5											
6	3	-1	1	3	-1			-1	0	-1	3
7	0	0	0	3	1			1	0	1	6
8	-1	0	1	1	3			0	3	1	8
9	1	1	0	3	3			1	1	0	10
10											
11	3	3	0	3	1			0	3	0	13
12	0	1	1	1	0			1	1	1	6
13	0	1	3	3	0			0	0	0	7
14	3	-1	3	0	0			-1	0	-1	3
15	1	1	1	1	-3			-1	0	-1	-1
16											
17											
SUM	13	12	17	20	7	0	0	1	9	1	80

Non-adopter

SDG	WAT	AGR	GRN	ENE	TRAN	IND	INST	RES	flex	flex	SUM
1	0	3	3	1	0	1	0	0	0	0	8
2	0	3	3	1	1	1	0	-1	1	-1	8
3	3	1	3	0	0	0	-1	-1	-1	-1	3
4											
5											
6	3	-1	1	1	0	0	-2	-1	-3	-1	-3
7	0	0	1	3	1	0	0	-1	0	-1	3
8	-1	0	1	1	3	1	0	0	1	0	6
9	1	0	0	3	1	1	0	-1	-1	0	4
10											
11	3	1	1	3	-1	1	0	0	-1	0	7
12	0	1	1	1	0	0	0	1	0	1	5
13	0	1	3	3	0	0	1	0	-1	0	7
14	3	-1	1	0	0	0	-3	-1	-1	-1	-3
15	1	1	3	1	-1	0	1	-1	-3	-1	1
16											
17											
SUM	13	9	21	18	4	5	-4	-6	-9	-5	46

Most benefit	Benefit	Neutral	Detriment	Most detriment
3	1	0	-1	-3

Fig. 6. SDGs achievement matrix. Source: IGC, 2021 [23].

In addition to the primary determinants of the IGC towards encouraging global thinking, one or two actual topics are highlighted every year. In 2021 the IGC projects were supposed to address projected changes in the *Human Climate Niche* and included an assessment of how each project could contribute to carbon sequestration, slowing climate change, and as a facet of that, to the *Trillion Trees* initiative – a vision embraced by the World Economic Forum, the United Nations, and numerous national governments as an important way to capture carbon.[1] Graphic conventions, colour codes, and web-based

[1] In this paper we will focus on alternative spatial development scenarios and SDGs achievement matrix and showcase contribution to the Trillion Trees Initiative in the Municipality of Ivanjica in another publication.

communication, were founded to enable coordination and collaboration. Substantial contributed technical support from Esri and Geodesignhub was secured as these are two principal digital technologies (platforms) for Geodesign to create common datasets, data protocols, and geodesign workflow [23].

3 The 2021 Geodesign Teaching Studio of the University of Belgrade, Faculty of Geography

After a significant period of teaching the core courses[2] at undergraduate, graduate and PhD studies of the Spatial Planning programme at the Faculty of Geography in Belgrade and being introduced to Geodesign workshop in 2019 it was evident that the 2020/2021 national accreditation cycle of higher education institutions should be used to introduce a more innovative and integrative pedagogies into the new programme. Since the new programme was not accredited[3] and the onsite teaching was prohibited due to the COVID – 19 pandemics, all participants of the 2021 spring semester voluntarily participated in the 70 h online Geodesign teaching studio. In total there were 22 participants - 14 students from different stages of the undergraduate and graduate studies of Spatial Planning and graduate studies of GIS, and 1 PhD student in Geosciences with three planning educators which are co-authors of this paper. The main software used were Esri ArcGIS Pro, Geodesignhub and Microsoft Teams. In the following sections, the selection process of the case study and the IGC project elaboration for the Municipality of Ivanjica will be presented.

3.1 The Municipality of Ivanjica – An Exemplary Case of Impeded Localization of the SDGs

Even after the three decades long EU integration process and transition towards the democratic capitalism, social understanding and legitimization of sustainable development goals (SDGs) and of local spatial planning as an integrative tool for SDGs localization in Serbia is still poor. Most of the system reforms are conducted as needed governance fix for accelerating long-awaited investments aimed at economic growth. Similarly, if existing, digital technologies in local spatial planning are mainly used as sources of digital spatial data and not as planning support systems.

The Municipality of Ivanjica was chosen as the case study because of three reasons. Firstly, as a large, mostly depopulated municipality with a small municipal centre and scattered rural settlements and with a significant potential for afforestation it presents an exemplary case for most of the municipalities/local tier in the Central Serbia region.

Secondly, infrastructure development is a paradigmatic form of spatial interventions in the country. This is mostly enforced by the national interest and promoted and as an overall-beneficial development and space-activation instrument. Spatial planning for

[2] Courses of: Foundations of Spatial Planning, Planning History, Planning Theory, Process of Spatial Planning, Spatial Planning of Special Purpose Areas and Land Use Planning.

[3] Both Geodesign course and studio were officially accredited by the National Accreditation Body in 2022.

special purpose areas is the government instrument which enables faster land acquisition for infrastructure development as well as other interventions of "public interest". It has been the most used type of spatial plans in the last decade in Serbia [7]. There are three types of infrastructure development planned for the territory of the Municipality of Ivanjica: a highway (north-south transversal), ski resort infrastructure development on the Golija Mountain and construction of 57 small Hydro-Power Plants (SHPPs) scattered mostly in the rural hinterland. Even though, Strategic Environmental Assessment (SEA) is an obligatory instrument of all planning documents, the assessment of infrastructure development's negative impacts are usually poorly elaborated and/or reduced to one-two particular impacts. For the three indicated types of infrastructure development in Ivanjica we found the SEA contents to follow that rule. There is the poorly elaborated noise increase and pollutant assessment by the highway and other road transport infrastructure on the Golija Mountain; while there is no obligation for conducting SEA before the SHPPs construction. In the case of ski resort infrastructure development in the Golija Mountain, conducted environment impact assessment gives only general information and recommends investors to follow the guidelines from the relevant legislation and planning documentation.

Thirdly, almost two-thirds of the municipal territory consists of the natural areas under a different protection levels designated by the national institutions. This practically means limited possibilities of the local population in deciding about the future land use and spatial development. Also, the current approach to the natural protection land regime in Serbia has been questioned by experts and public as too strict for the local population activities and very loose for the construction by investors. It also ignores the necessity of natural areas/ecosystem connectivity which is needed for building the capacity of ecosystem services. In the case of Ivanjica, mentioned ski resort infrastructure and tourism development is planned on the Golija Mountain. The planned areas for ski resort are located in the areas of the second level protection, surrounding the areas of the first level protection. This will make especially first level protection areas mutually disconnected and fragmented.

Against this background, the Municipality of Ivanjica was chosen as the case study for the IGC project.

3.2 IGC Project Elaboration: *Ivanjica - Nursery Garden of Trees and Alternatives*

The Municipality of Ivanjica (1090 km^2, 30 800 inhabitants in 2020) is a mountainous, poorly accessible and interconnected municipality located (NW point: 43° 53′ 47" latitude 19 ° 47′ 56" longitude) in the Central Serbia region and surrounded by more developed municipalities. The region covers the surface area of 55 968 km^2 - 63% of the entire surface area, and with 4 909 000 inhabitants in 2020 - 71% of total in the Republic of Serbia without Kosovo and Metohia.[4] Before entering the IGC project elaboration of the Municipality of Ivanjica in the spring semester, students had the opportunity to

[4] By the Constitution of Serbia, Kosovo and Metohia is the integral part of the national territory. Multilateral negotiations about its future status are a stop-and-go processes lasting for more than 20 years. More of the general information can be found https://en.wikipedia.org/wiki/Political_status_of_Kosovo.

reflect and consider wider context, challenges and opportunities of the Central Serbia region during three days in the autumn semester and using the Geodesignhub as a digital technology. This enhanced the understanding of the Municipality of Ivanjica's nested context and served as an input for identifying relevant assumptions and innovations. It also placed the special focus on mitigating negative effects of the planned infrastructure development in the Municipality of Ivanjica within larger 2021 IGC themes related to the Trillion Trees Initiative, CO_2 sequestration and SDGs. Also, having in mind the spatial specificities and the planning context in the Municipality of Ivanjica students identified residential rural and tourism as additional two systems to be considered in the project elaboration.

In the next step, students were offered to use the list of global assumptions, *Human Climate Niche* and *Trillion Trees Initiative* sources from the IGC website, but also existing local and national planning documents[5] and studies relevant for the Municipality of Ivanjica to identify its main challenges and opportunities [23, 25–27]. After the reading, and consulting the data from the Statistical Office of the Republic of Serbia and the Corine Land Cover Data Set the following assumptions were selected: the population will grow older and will be concentrated in urban areas, transportation will become more automated, the built environment will be more networked and smarter, global temperature will rise, climate variability will increase, freshwater scarcity will become more prevalent, food production pressures will increase and pollution concerns intensify. In addition, national tendencies relevant for the local spatial processes were identified: rural exodus, deforestation, agricultural intensification, especially in the surroundings of the local transport infrastructure, expansion of the built-up areas as urban sprawl, but also within protected natural areas, afforestation within the protected natural areas, energy instability, more frequent and intense heavy precipitation events which together with more frequent heat waves and changing terrestrial ecosystems.

For these purposes and following the Geodesign framework tables for ten systems were prepared with three main questions: How the system can be defined? How does it function? How it should be changed?

Within a given context, students identified main requirements for the future sustainable spatial development:

- Improve population's capacity for reforestation processes, SDGs, circular economy and cross-section of activities, use of digital technology, dealing with urgencies and future needs;
- Enable decentralization of institutional and infrastructure services;
- Improve water management (floods, SHPPs and waste);
- Improve ecosystem services of natural areas;
- Apply sustainable technology for energy, transport and housing;
- Orient industrial production towards the use of local resources (herbs, berries, super-food) and recycled material (e.g. use of recycled wooden artifacts instead of clear cut trees);

[5] Those were: Spatial Plan of the Municipality of Ivanjica; Strategy of sustainable development of the Municipality of Ivanjica; Spatial Plan of the Special Purpose Area Golija Natural Park; Spatial Plan of the Special Purpose Area of the Belgrade-South Adriatic highway.

- Make agriculture and tourism more eco-friendly and resilient.

Subsequently, an integrated approach to the literature and IGC sources review resulted in identified innovations:

- INST Transdisciplinary innovation centres (circular economy, reforestation etc.); Education for urgencies and future needs; Multifunctional community centre & Coalition for Sustainable Development
- WAT Water retention & Decentralized waste management
- GRN Connectivity for resilience & Rewilding Europe Initiative
- ENE Renewable energy sources
- TRAN Electric public mini buses & Transportation with energy production
- RUR Adaptable modular housing & Natural construction and materials
- RES Urban green renewal & Communication-mediated society
- IND Wood waste recycling industry; Super food & Health cosmetics
- AGR Food forest & Shared & digital urban/rural agriculture
- TOUR Eco friendly, safe and seamless tourism & All seasons digital & green mountain

While some of these had an implicit spatial expression, as in the case of *All seasons digital & green mountain* located on the Golija Mountain and *Urban green renewal* in the municipal centre, other innovations needed to be allocated having in mind municipal spatial conditions, requirements and assumptions. For these purposes, evaluation maps needed to be prepared. With this aim, mentioned tables for ten systems were revized to resemble the one presented by [11, p. 10]. As a result, each system was assigned with the evaluation table (Table 1). Tables were then used to digitalize evaluation maps using Esri data processing software.

Table 1. Evaluation tables structure for each system

How the system can be described? Description	How does it function? assumptions		How it should be changed? requirements & innovations		
Levels of intervention	Existing	Not appropriate	Capable	Suitable	Feasible
Classification					
Description					
Data					
Operators					

Apart from following the instructed IGC workflow, participants made several independent steps before entering the scenario making workshop in Geodesignhub. Firstly, participants submitted an objection against the publicly displayed plan for the SHPP construction to the Municipality of Ivanjica's local authorities. Secondly, they defined the metaphor for its sustainable spatial development. Namely, by associating the purpose of the project elaboration with *Ivanjica* - the toponym, meaning *nursery garden of Iva*, a riverside willow, the project was entitled *Ivanjica – nursery garden of trees and alternatives*. This metaphor could inspire the change of the current reductionists' perceptions of forest benefits which result in deforestation and become a "showroom" of alternatives to current planning practices and local spatial development in the region. Also, the process of documentation review and map elaboration and interpretation enabled general spatial diversity recognition in the Municipality: agricultural area in the northeast, green northwest - southeast axes, tourism development in the northwest and southeast (Golija Mountain), industrial and institutional areas in the northern central part of the Municipality along the main transport corridor. These were important steps before entering the workshop for collaborative scenarios making.

From a more technical aspect, students needed to be trained to use Geodesignhub software. During the scenario making workshop, Green and Developers teams created their decision models, land change and innovation diagrams for each system having in mind the basic mindsets of six scenarios. Mindset behind the Early Adopter scenario(s) was: prevention i.e. there is a sense of urgency, but also political and economic uncertainty for implementing spatial innovation which will mitigate negative effects of the national spatial planning practices. Late Adopter scenario was made as a curing, more viable scenario of implementing needed spatial innovation after the implementation of the national spatial interventions i.e. when their negative and positive impacts became obvious. Non-adopter scenario reflected the mindset of the current planning approach which militated against the local sustainable spatial development. Required scenarios were made by using "pre-" scenarios instead of updating the evaluation maps. The process and its anticipated duration are presented in the Fig. 7.

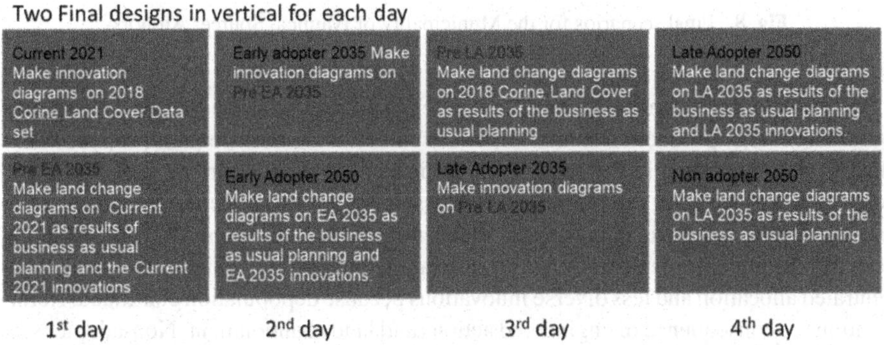

Fig. 7. Workflow and time frames for scenarios making. Source: Authors.

Once first versions of scenarios were negotiated and made, several revisions with new innovations (projects and policies) and different anticipations of resulting land use changes were drawn. For the Rural (RUR) system 33 diagrams were drawn; for Green infrastructure 51; for Water infrastructure (WAT) 33; for Energy infrastructure (ENE) 24; for Transport infrastructure (TRAN) 23; for Industry and Commerce (IND) 31, for Residential and Mixed-use Development (RES) 29; for Institutional Uses (INST) 37; for Agriculture (AGR) 38; for Tourism (TOUR) 46 diagrams were drawn. The most interesting part of the negotiation process was the role play between Green and Developer teams. Students at some point were encouraged to take these roles to the extreme and had confidence to propose and draw diagrams which they imagined could become real interventions if the current planning practice continues to deteriorate and opposition continues to grow, e.g. skyscrapers in the municipal centre vs. hobbit-like houses in the rural areas. These diagrams however, as well as some others (e.g. erroneous or redundant), were not selected in the final scenarios (Fig. 8). Final scenarios will be described in the following section.

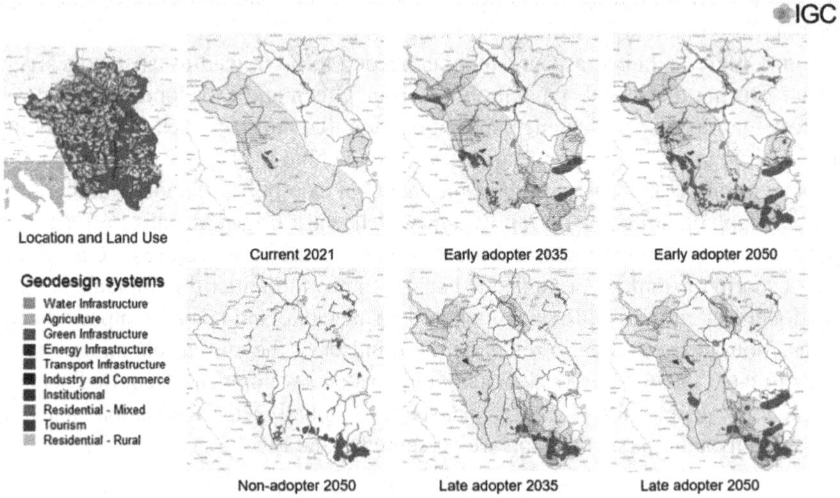

Fig. 8. Final scenarios for the Municipality of Ivanjica. Source: Authors.

Early Adopter scenarios implied complete abandonment of the SHPPs construction by adding energy production from alternative sources. Diagrams students proposed were diverse and distributed in the wider area. Policies focused on tourism, agriculture and forestry were located at the periphery. Reforestation process is a consequence of engineered actions, not natural processes which follow land abandonment. Late Adopter scenarios implied implementation of usual planning until 2035 which forces more concentrated allocation and less diverse innovations because depopulation continued. Reforestation is a consequence of engineered actions and land abandonment. Non-adopter scenario implied continued misuse of nature and local activities which intensified the depopulation. Mountain tourism center on the Golija Mountain becomes a brown-field. Most of the remaining activities are concentrated around the urban centre and the highway intersections. Reforestation is almost entirely a consequence of the land abandonment.

After making final scenarios, participants identified *All Seasons Digital Mountain Tourism*, *Shared Urban/Rural Digital Agriculture* and *Rewilding Europe* as the most significant innovations for the future local sustainable spatial development. *All Seasons Digital Mountain Tourism* implies the use of digital technology which enables tourism during a longer period of the year in accordance with the ecosystem capacities.

It enables "seamless" tourism for the calculated maximum number of the responsible visitors. *Shared Urban/Rural Digital Agriculture* implies that urban and rural actors make alliances/partnerships to share resources, benefits and risks in agricultural production. *Rewilding Europe* is the pan-European initiative with a progressive approach to conservation. The goal of this initiative is to develop and support coexistence, where wildlife comeback is beneficial for local people and socio-economic development. Therefore, it not only contributes to the implementation of the Trillion Trees initiative, but it also contributes to the sustainability of these efforts. In the next step, scenarios were evaluated in the SDGs achievement matrix (Fig. 9).

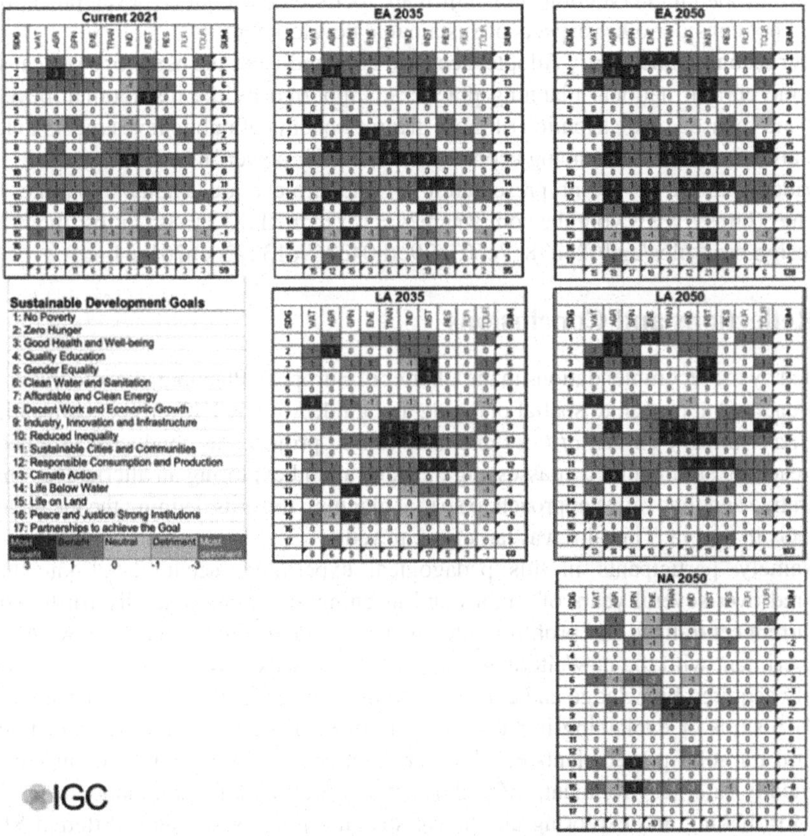

Fig. 9. SDGs achievement matrix for the Municipality of Ivanjica scenarios. Source: Authors.

The results show that Early Adopter scenarios have the best design outcomes in the context of achieving SDGs. Also, adopted innovations are often beneficial for the system to which they directly belong, but also to other systems, which contributes to the progress of all systems within the case study. Best results are achieved in goals 8 (15), 9 (18), 11 (20) and 13 (15). Worst results are in goal 15 (1). The largest contribution have AGR (19), GRN (17), ENE (18) and INST (21).

Late Adopter scenarios have a weaker performance, which is also expected, since interventions against the existing negative trends and planning practices (devastation of rivers by the SHPPs, tourism overexploitation on the Golija mountain) are undertaken after 2035. In this case, goals 9 (16),11 (16) and 8 (15) have best results. Worst results are again in goal 15 (0). The most contributing systems to SDGs are WAT (13), AGR (14), GRN (14) and INST (19).

Non-adopter scenario has the poorest SDGs performance, since innovations were not implemented. Trends continue as usual and they result with 0, which means this scenario does not contribute to SDGs implementation at all. Many goals have negative results, especially goal 15 (–8), while the best result has goal 8 (10). This showed us that the current spatial interventions in Ivanjica are focused on economic development only, and do not consider other aspects of sustainable development.

Our recommended Early Adopter scenario 2050 indicates the need for a radical shift from the current national planning practices, supported by the institutional development and focused on distribution of more diverse benefits of public investments to local population instead of enhancing economic benefits for powerful actors.

Video and Power point presentation of the project are available on the IGC website (https://www.youtube.com/watch?v=ewYmdnXktiQ&t=8s; https://www.igc-geodesign.org/_files/ugd/f24d78_7c607b79cfb04c269c13872dcb701ae4.pdf).

4 Reflections and Conclusions

Framed by the recommendations in the Charter of European Planning, the integrated digitally enabled approach to spatial planning and guided by the IGC project conventions, *Ivanjica – nursery garden of trees and alternatives* project was conducted as a geodesign teaching studio aimed at assessing the current and exploring an alternative – more integrative and innovative approach to spatial planning towards defining the localization of SDGs in Serbia. This aim was largely achieved.

Namely, participants in this pedagogical experiment accumulated knowledge acquired over several years of studies and teaching and were generally frustrated by the current centralized and profit-oriented planning practice in Serbia. They were eager to experiment with the new/alternative approach and seek ways to explore and embed already acquired knowledge and contribute to the joint endeavour using relevant skills, e.g. GIS skills or explaining impacts of ski tourism on ecosystem services or finding location for solar power plants etc. Furthermore, the studio, although conducted in a "politically safe" environment, offered a new research-based and collaborative "toolbox" for making and exploring alternative spatial scenarios and their different SDGs performances.

From the educators' perspective, the IGC conventions enabled a more intensive exposure of students to global challenges, mainly to the SDGs. By understanding how SDGs can provide a framework for a local development policy and how local governments can support the achievement of the SDGs through their actions, students can understand the importance of local spatial planning in the localization of the SDGs. It was also beneficial to engage students in a digital exploration of the ways to cross boundaries between tiers, territories, sectors, disciplines and time frames while remaining responsive to the present and future needs of local communities and local spatial conditions.

In their feedback, students emphasized the importance of collaboration and knowledge sharing, a constructive dialogue for better problem understanding and solving, clear distinction between passive and proactive approaches and a possibility to reflect on the designed scenarios (re-analyze and re-evaluate).

The main constraints identified were technical in nature and were encountered during diagram drawing and/or due to a weak online communication. They were overcome through longer and more numerous revisions and iterations during scenario making than previously anticipated. This indicates that more time should be assigned to training or adequate support to diagram drawing, as well as that proper internet connections should be secured in case digital technologies are used. From the educators' perspective, more revisions and iterations in the digital environment of Geodesignhub improved the understanding of how different local spatial innovations could be synergized and their implementation sequence more logical, so this should also be taken into account when allocating time to different stages of the process.

Finally, these reflections and conclusions will serve as an important input for the formal Geodesign teaching studio at our Department. In addition, they are already used as an important feedback for planning the Geodesign workshop aimed at enhancing the local resilience, which will be conducted in June 2022 with local stakeholders from the Municipality of Ivanjica. During the workshop we will explore the role of Geodesign in enhancing the mentioned normative approaches to spatial planning and opportunities for framing SDGs localization in the Municipality in a collaborative manner. We will also try to identify the professional and academic gaps and bottlenecks which impede these processes.

Acknowledgments. This work was funded by the Ministry of Education, Science and Technological Development of the Republic of Serbia under Grant 451–03-9/2021–14/ 200091 awarded to the University of Belgrade - Faculty of Geography. Important training in Geodesignhub software and support during the workshop sessions were provided by Hrishikesh Ballal and Chiara Cocco. Carl Steinitz, Brian Orland and Michele Campagna gave important advises on the IGC conventions. For the decision making process on the possible areas for the afforestation we used the assessment map of the Forest and Climate Project https://sumeiklima.org/sr/gde-po%C5%A1umiti offered by Tijana Ležaić. Special gratitude goes to all the students who were curious and willing to participate in this endeavour: Marina Stanić, Petar Jovanović, Jelena Tomić, Vukasin Kotrlja, Tijana Nikolić, Katarina Trbojević, Stanislav Mladenović, Lazar Tomović, Nikola Vračević, Marko Jović, Jovana Bojović, Hristina Nikolić, Aleksandra Krstić and Acquah Ebenezer.

References

1. Roadmap for localizing the SDGs: Implementation and Monitoring at Subnational Level (2022). https://sustainabledevelopment.un.org/content/documents/commitments/818_11195_commitment_ROADMAP%20LOCALIZING%20SDGS.pdf
2. IGC 2021 Project Workflow. https://www.igc-geodesign.org/project-workflow. Accessed 29 Apr 2022
3. Dabović, T.: Geodesign meets its institutional design in the cybernetic loop. J. Digit. Landscape Arch. **2020**(5), 486–496 (2020)

4. Dabović, T., Djordjević, D., Poledica, B., Radović, M., Jeftić, M.R.: Compliance with social requirements for integrated local land use planning in Serbia. Eur. Plan. Stud. **28**(6), 1219–1241 (2020)
5. Sustainable Development Goals Helpdesk: Localizing the SDGs: Strategies and Plans (2022). https://sdghelpdesk.unescap.org/e-library/localizing-sdgs-strategies-and-plans
6. The European Council of Spatial Planners – Le Conseil Européen des Urbanistes (ECTP-CEU): The Charter of European Planning. Barcelona (2013)
7. European Conference of Ministers responsible for Regional Planning (CEMAT): Guiding Principles for Sustainable Spatial Development of the European Conti-nent. CEMAT, Hanover (2002)
8. The European Commission: ESDP - European Spatial Development Perspective. Potsdam (1999)
9. European Ministers for Urban Development and Regional Planning: Leipzig Charter on Sustainable European Cities. Leipzig (2007)
10. European Ministers for Urban Development: The Toledo Declaration. Brussels (2010)
11. Campagna, M., Di Cesare, E.A., Cocco, C.: Integrating Green-Infrastructures Design in Strategic Spatial Planning with Geodesign. Sustainability **12**(5), 1820 (2020)
12. UN-Habitat: Cities and Pandemics: Towards a more just, green and healthy future. UN-Habitat (2021)
13. Batty, M., Yang, W.: A Digital Future for Planning (2022). https://digital4planning.com/wp-content/uploads/2022/02/A-Digital-Future-for-Planning-Full-Report-Web.pdf
14. Dabović, T., Nedović-Budić, Z., Djordjević, D.: Pursuit of integration in the former Yugoslavia's planning. Plan. Perspect. **34**(2), 215–241 (2019)
15. Đorđević, D., Dabović, T., Bijelić, B., Poledica, B.: Weakening of spatial planning system in Serbia: age of prevailing of spatial plans for special purpose areas (2010–2020). Bull. Serb. Geograph. Soc. **100**(2), 129–160 (2020)
16. Wilson, J.P.: Towards geodesign: building new education programs and audiences. In: Lee, D.J., Dias, E., Scholten, H.J. (eds.) Geodesign by Integrating Design and Geospatial Sciences. GL, vol. 111, pp. 357–369. Springer, Cham (2014). https://doi.org/10.1007/978-3-319-08299-8_23
17. Fisher, T.: An education in geodesign. Landsc. Urban Plan. **156**, 20–22 (2016)
18. Albert, C., Von Haaren, C., Vargas-Moreno, J.C., Steinitz, C.: Teaching scenario-based planning for sustainable landscape development: an evaluation of learning effects in the Cagliari studio workshop. Sustainability **7**(6), 6872–6892 (2015). https://doi.org/doi.org/10.3390/su7066872
19. Warren-Kretzschmar, B., Lincon, C., Ballal, H.: Geodesign as an educational tool: a case study in South Cache Valley. J. Digit. Landscape Arch. **1**, 222–232 (2016)
20. Haddad, M.A., Mourão Moura, A.C., Cook, V.M., Lima e Lima, T.: The social dimensions of the iron quadrangle region: an educational experience in geodesign. Prof. Geograph. **73**(3), 504–520 (2021)
21. Campagna, M.: Chapter 5: Spatial planning and geodesign. In: Geertman, S., Stillwell, J. (eds.) Handbook of Planning Support Science, pp. 73–86. Edward Elgar Publishing, Cheltenham, UK (2020)
22. Steinitz, C.: A Framework for Geodesign: Changing Geography by Design. Esri Press, Redlands (2012)
23. IGC 2022 Homepage. https://www.igc-geodesign.org/. Accessed 28 Apr 2022
24. UN SDG (United Nations - Department of Economic and Social Affairs Sustainable Development). https://sdgs.un.org/goals. Accessed 22 May 2022

25. Center for Urban Development: The Spatial Plan of the Municipality of Ivanjica. Belgrade (2012)
26. The Municipality of Ivanjica: Strategy of sustainable development of the Municipality of Ivanjica 2009–2014. Ivanjica (2009)
27. Dabović, T., Pjanović, B., Tošković, O., Djordjević, D., Lukić, B.: Experts' perception of the key drivers of land-use/land-cover changes in Serbia from 1990 to 2012. Sustainability **13**(14), 7771 (2021)

Training for Territorial Sustainable Development Design in Basilicata Remote Areas: GEODESIGN Workshop

Francesco Scorza(✉), Luigi Santopietro, Simone Corrado, Priscilla Sofia Dastoli, Valentina Santarsiero, Rachele Gatto, and Beniamino Murgante

School of Engineering, Laboratory of Urban and Regional Systems Engineering (LISUT), University of Basilicata, Viale dell'Ateneo Lucano 10, 85100 Potenza, Italy
{francesco.scorza,luigi.santopietro,priscillasofia.dastoli, valentina.santarsiero,beniamino.murgante}@unibas.it, simone.corrado@studenti.unibas.it, rachelegatto@outlook.it

Abstract. GEODESIGN represents an effective framework promoting collaborative planning and decision-making as an incremental process based on robust methodological guidance. In this paper, GEODESIGN has been adopted as supporting tool for preliminary activities oriented to the integrate risks mitigation and sustainable development in a wider research project MITIGO. Within this project, have been selected as case study area four Municipalities from inland areas of Basilicata Region, characterized by several risks (i.e. depopulation, hydro-geological risks, abandonment of traditional land uses…). A knowledge framework process of future scenario building was produced through GEODESIGN Workshop, based on technical information concerning environmental and anthropic risks and combined with more traditional context analysis.

A preliminary experiment of the workshop involving young engineers (in a master degree studio at the University of Basilicata) has been simulated: an useful test to refine details of the analytical framework and to calibrate workshop agenda for real case development avoiding inefficiencies. The results highlithed a comprehensive approach in terms of participation capacity of decision makers without any background in planning disciplines and unveiled the weaknesses of traditional approach mainly based on "building agreements" without any measurements of spatial evidences or scenarios comparisons.

Keywords: GEODESIGN · Participatory planning · Decision support system · Strategis design

1 Introduction

GEODESIGN represents a suitable framework in order to develop "urban vision" in urban planning practices [1]. Moreover, it demonstrates as a comprehensive methodology a horizontal applicability in any decision process concerning territorial transformation issues. This paper refers to preliminary activities in order to adopt GEODESIGN

O. Gervasi et al. (Eds.): ICCSA 2022 Workshops, LNCS 13379, pp. 242–252, 2022.
https://doi.org/10.1007/978-3-031-10545-6_17

as a main tool to support strategic design integrating risks mitigation and sustainable development in sample areas targeted by the wider research project MITIGO[1]. In facts, within a multidisciplinary research framework, emerged the need to cover with robust methodology the participatory process in structuring interaction among relevant stakeholders in specific sample contexts. In particular we selected four municipalities in Basilicata Region covering a peculiar territory in Apennine fringe where a high landscape values generates relevant tourism flows based on open-air tourism attractor (The Volo dell'Angelo[2]) but continuous depopulation process and a progressive abandonment of traditional land uses and manufacts generates additional risks condition combined with a critical hydrogeological fragility of the territory [2–8].

GEODESIGN represents relevant research focus for LISUT laboratory and several experiences had been conducted in recent years on selected case studies [9–11]. Mainly we included GEODESIGN among those technical tolls necessary to support planning processes at different scales [12] especially promoting the methodological integration of GEODESIGN with Logical Framework Approach (among others [13]).

According to C. Steinitz [2] GEODESIGN represents an inclusive approach (it involves not only technicians but all actors involved in decision making processes) supporting *"informed negotiation"*.

The specific application of GEODESIGN is not only oriented to consensus building on effective design or strategy, but mainly to generate an extensive learning process addressed to local administrators and citizens. In particular technical information concerning environmental and anthropic risks, combined with more traditional context analysis represents the technical information that through GEODESIGN has to be shared with local people. Based on the awareness of such knowledge framework a process of future scenario building has to be produced through GEODESIGN Workshop. The research actually realized a preliminary experiment of the workshop involving young engineers (in a master degree studio at the University of Basilicata) in order to have a simulated implementation useful to refine details of the analytical framework and to calibrate workshop agenda avoiding inefficiencies. Concerning negotiation, we address this concept in a positive procedural vision of building agreements: GEODESIGN it is not a way to aggregate some strong individual interests against other weakest groups of participants, but mainly a way in which the spatial evidences of decisions (namely "designs" in GEODESIGN taxonomy) becomes a way to make more and more explicit the evidences of individual proposals contributing to the strategic decision-making process.

We place this work in the stream of adopting GEODESIGN for training people, citizens, technicians and politicians in participatory planning as a component for up to date applied research project namely MITIGO.

This paper reports general consideration concerning the advantages in adopting GEODESIGN, discusses details about GEODESIGN workshop organization and conduction. Finally, the discussions and conclusions section report main evidences of the learning by doing process realized and perspectives for the "real case" implementation.

[1] https://www.mitigoinbasilicata.it/

[2] https://www.volodellangelo.com/

2 Case Study Area

The four Municipalities selected as case study in Basilicata Region (Southern Italy) are: Albano, Campomaggiore, Castelmezzano and Pietrapertosa (see Fig. 1).

These municipalities have distinguished in two groups (Castelmezzano and Pietrapertosa blue ones and Albano and Campomaggiore green ones in Fig. 1), based on their opposite placement related to Basento river valley.

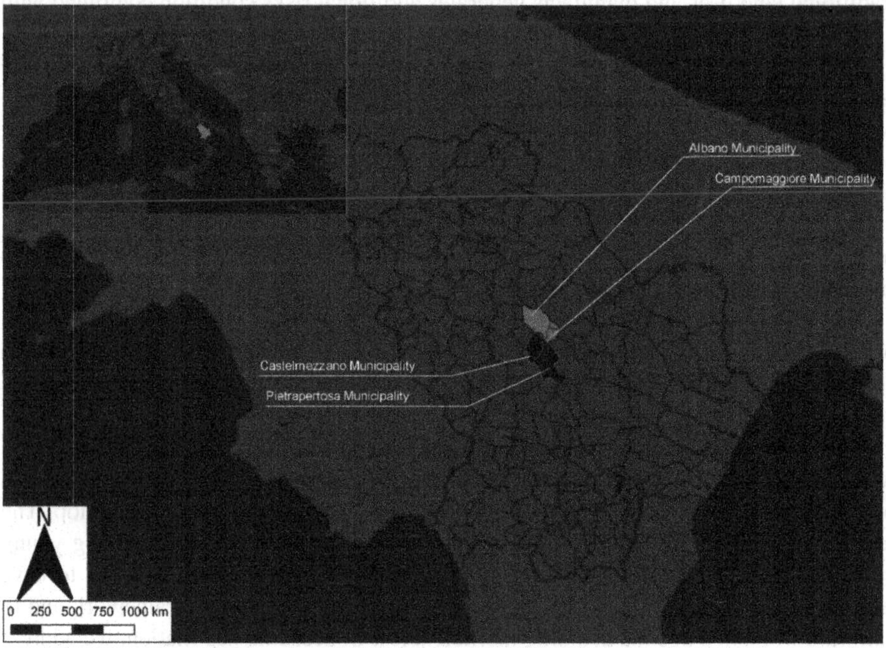

Fig. 1. Case study area

Furthermore, Castelmezzano and Pietrapertosa municipalities have a specific tourism specialization based on the "Volo dell'Angelo" tourist attractor that links the two municipalities paced in a unique mountain landscape where dolomite formations arise from the Apennine. The area is part of the "Gallipoli Cognato and Piccole Dolomiti" Regional Park (see Fig. 2).

Fig. 2. Landscape of "Piccole Dolomiti" regional park

The ex-ante context analysis of the study area is synthetized in strengths and weaknesses.

- Strengths
  - High naturalness of land: high percentage of forested area on total area per municipality (70–90% of the total municipal territory).
  - "Gallipoli Cognato and Piccole Dolomiti" Regional park: recognized at the European level as protected area
  - The "Volo dell'Angelo" tourist attraction, linking the municipalities of Castelmezzano and Pietrapertosa)
  - Areas with a high landscape value: a part of Pietrapertosa and Castelmezzano municipal territory are classified as landscape assets according to the Italian legislative decree no. 42/2004
  - Specialization of territories in the supply of receptive services: 30% of services and facilities in the study area are receptive services
  - Castelmezzano and Pietrapertosa municipalities belong to the national network of the most beautiful villages in Italy
  - Wide presence in the study area of manufacts of historic-monumental interest, protected by the Italian laws
  - In all of four municipalities there is an elementary school
  - In Albano and Pietrapertosa there are police stations

- Weaknesses
  - Depopulation: the entire study area shows a marked trend of depopulation, with a population loss from 1971to 2020 of 50% and from 2001 to 2020 of 22%. Pietrapertosa has a population decline from 2001 to 2020 of 28%

- Poor accessibility to strategic service nodes: the average travel time by own vehicle from the study area to hospitals and emergency rooms is about 40 min; to university is about 40 min; to airports is about 120 min. Pietrapertosa shows a more disadvantageous condition than the entire study area (50 min to the Potenza hospital)
- Inefficient local public transportation: high travel time to main urban center (50–60 min to Potenza). Supply is linked to the needs of the school population
- Residential building equipment is inhabited: the average value of inhabitants per residential building of 1.59 for the entire study area, with slight difference between the municipalities of Castelmezzano(1.31) and Pietrapertosa (1.22) compared to Campomaggiore (2.06) and Albano (2.08)
- Weakness of the productive system: there is a low presence of buildings for industrial use (the most lacking is Pietrapertosa with the lowest percentage of agricultural areas related to the total)
- Widespread conditions of natural and anthropogenic risks: high/extremely high fire risk, landslide risk, hydraulic risk and seismic risk for all of the four municipalities, with greater areas affected in Albano and Campomaggiore municipal territories

A criticality highlighted for all the four municipalities is related to the depopulation phenomenon: the trend in the study area overcome the average rate for all Potenza Province equal to 12% for the period 1971–2020 (see Fig. 3). Indeed, Pietrapertosa municipality has the main population reduction (41%), followed by Castelmezzano (37%), Campomaggiore (33%) and Albano (21%).

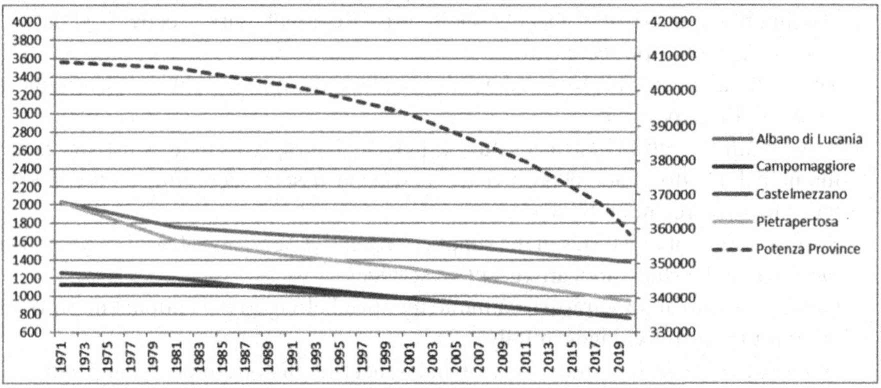

Fig. 3. Demographic trend

This represents a structural weakness for the area and therefore a central issue for approaching strategic development design through GEODESIGN Workshop.

Foreign resident population slightly increased over time (see Fig. 4) and it is possible to measure for the period 2003–2021 an increase of about 6%.(15% higher that the average data for all Province of Potenza.

These two population trends identify the issue of social integration of temporary foreign residents combined with the tourism accommodation structure.

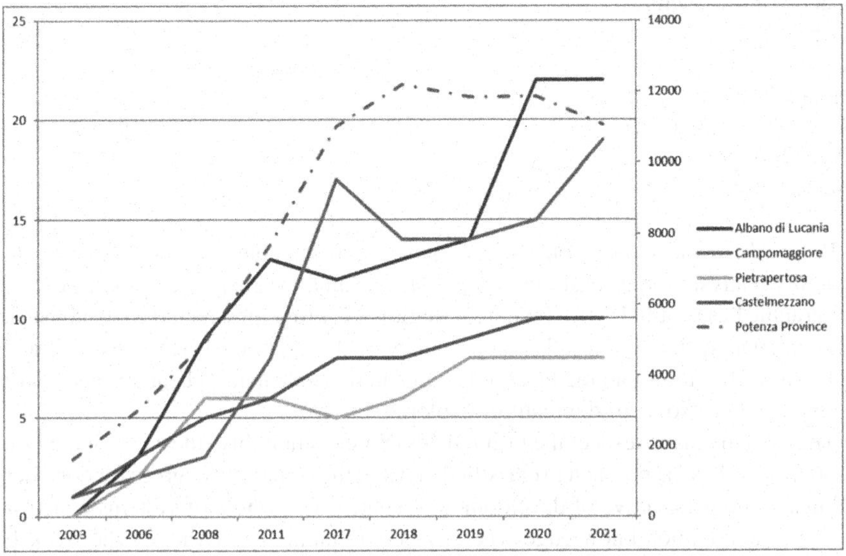

Fig. 4. Foreign population trend for the period 2003–2021

The focus on building stock and accessibility infrastructures systems, combined with environmental risks, allowed to point out a second main topic concerning degradations, abandonment, potential isolation for residents' communities. Those relevant topics integrated with the evidences of context analysis represents the input for GEODESIGN workshop.

3 The Geodesign Workshop

According with the general methodology, the GEODESIGN workshop is performed by a multi-disciplinary team consisting of planners, field engineers, decision-makers, natural and social scientists and local stakeholders. In this case the experiment was conducted with a specific group of young engineers who assumed different roles to emulate specific competing stakeholders. We place this experience in the group of simulated GEODESIGN workshop oriented mainly to tech through a learning by doing approach the methodology, generating a critical appraisal by participants on the relevant steps of the process and on the benefits of managing interactions in decision making through the "negotiation" approach.

Specifically, the workshop was attended by 8 participants emulating the following stakeholders: tour operator, environmentalist, building contractor, local promoter, mayor of the north area, mayor of the south area, agricultural entrepreneur, student and elderly citizen. These figures cover point of views and competing interests deemed to have a key-role in local development.

The "systems" selected for the analysis and design phase are:

- Green infrastructures
- Energy infrastructures
- Urban settlement
- Cultural heritage
- Hospitality
- Mobility infrastructure
- Agro-food service
- Service supply

Before the workshop session, each working group was contributed to realize the land suitability analysis for at least one system. The evaluation maps was produced on the cartographic bases of the 2013 Technical Regional Cartography including land use data and municipal scale statistics. The consistency of the existing services, as well as the level of infrastructures and the level of hazards in the area, natural beauties and tourism amenities are just some of the features explored.

The systems maps respect the GEODESIGN land suitability rules: i.e. an analytical hierarchy GIS-based approach to classified in detail the suitability degrees for considered land use in the perspective of development scenario. The whole of systems constitutes the base line common knowledge whereby begin planning activities of the workshop (see Fig. 5).

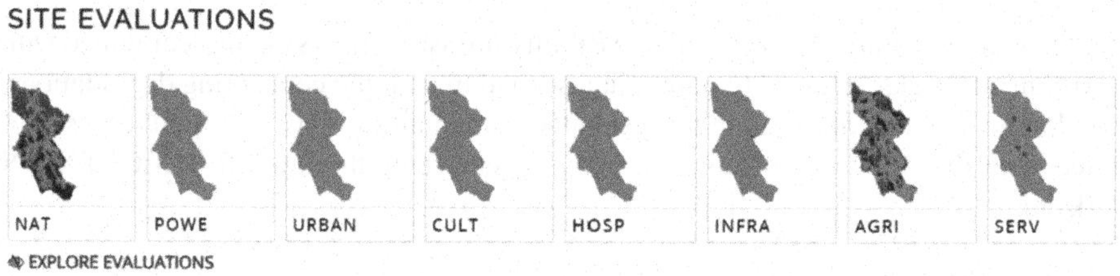

Fig. 5. Site evaluations

After the site evaluations, the workshop was conducted with the support of the GeodesignHub web-platform [14] which is useful for both the co-design and negotiation phases. The shared workspace was populated with 103 diagrams divided into 89 project proposals and 14 sectorial policies.

Therefore, the participants were divided into two groups. The first one (Team A) included the student, the environmentalist, the agricultural entrepreneur and the tour operator. The second one (Team B) contains the two mayors, the local promoter, the building contractor and the elderly citizen. Each group defined priorities and made a synthesis of the diagrams (see Fig. 6).

This selection enabled us to proceed with the negotiation phase and the development of a final shared strategy. The resulted vision of territorial development (see Fig. 7) that emerged was more comprehensive than the individual summaries. It can be understood as representing the organization of the territory through an inter-systemic proposal, thus

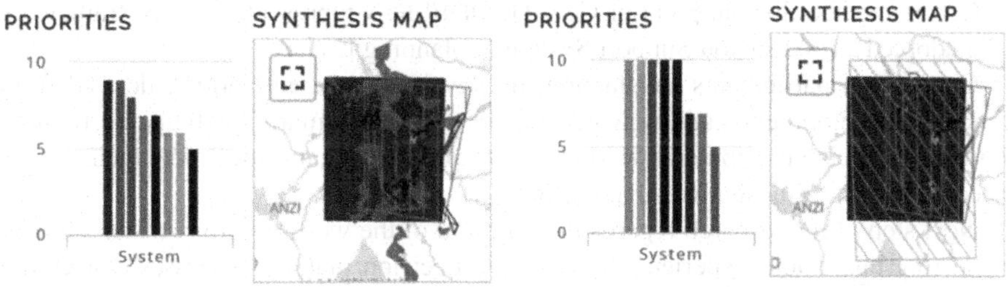

(a) Team A (b) Team B

Fig. 6. Team priorities and synthesis maps

developing synthesis that bring together ideas from every stakeholder and a deep analysis of the spatial characteristics.

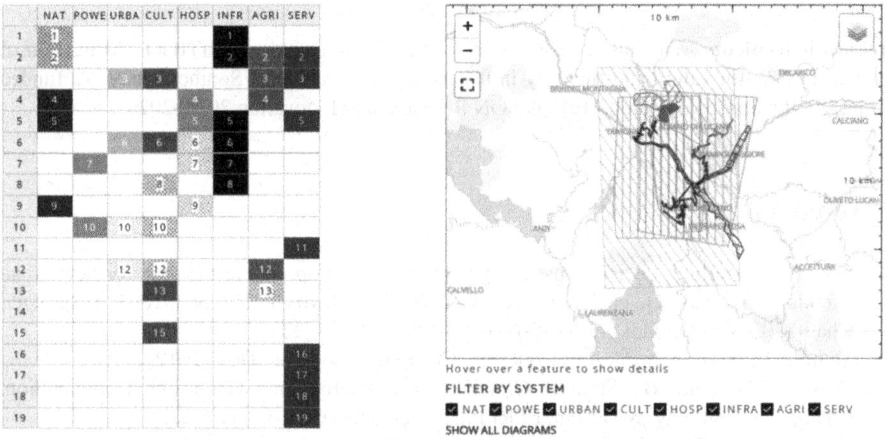

Fig. 7. Negotiated design

4 Discussions and Conclusions

The preparatory phase of GEODESIGN workshop previously described allowed the research group to point out critical issues in the strategic design: consistency of service stock in the area [15–17], alternative specialization for each municipality collective services providers, maintenance and restoration of cultural patrimony for tourism development purposes [18], the security of intermunicipal mobility infrastructure [19–21] as a precondition of local development. It is remarkable how the debate during the workshop did not consider the natural territorial components as a domain of priority interventions. Thus, probably depends on the general awareness that the naturality degree was not under pressure and it represents an available territorial value to exploit according with sustainable principles [22–26].

On the methodological point of view, GEODESIGN represents a robust framework to be adopted as a Decision Support System in planning [27].

Concerning participants satisfaction, the level of personal-learning derived from workshop development gathers a generalizes positive remark: participants (mainly politicians) declared appreciation toward the process organization and their exante expectations was almost covered at the end.

Next step of the research regards the proposal of the workshop to real stake-holder connecting this studio experience to real-case decision making processes concerning urban transformations, risks mitigation [28] and green transition [29, 30].

This application is close to the general assessment of the learning experience reported by Albert and Ott [31] for the IGC 2019. Participants learned a lot both concerning the understanding of the case study features and of the methodological background.

Additionally it was once again evident that, during the workshop, the enough time has to be spent to share the problem analysis in order to drive the participation towards relevant criticalities of the place, avoiding the so called "wicked" problems [32] risk in decision making.

Acknowledgements. This research was realized in the framework of MITIGO - Mitigation of natural hazards for safety and mobility in the mountainous areas of Southern Italy – a funded project by the European Union - ERDF, PON Research and Innovation 2014–2020.

References

1. Scorza, F.: Training decision-makers: geodesign workshop paving the way for new urban agenda. In: Gervasi, O., et al. (eds.) ICCSA 2020. LNCS, vol. 12252, pp. 310–316. Springer, Cham (2020). https://doi.org/10.1007/978-3-030-58811-3_22
2. Steinitz, C.: A frame work for Geodesign. Changing Geograph. Des. (2012)
3. Fisher, T., Orland, B., Steinitz, C. (eds.): The International Geodesign Collaboration. Changing Geography by Design. ESRI Press, Redlands, California (2020)
4. Campagna, M.: Metaplanning: about designing the geodesign process. Landsc. Urban Plan. **156**, 118–128 (2016). https://doi.org/10.1016/J.LANDURBPLAN.2015.08.019
5. Nyerges, T., et al.: Geodesign dynamics for sustainable urban watershed development. Sustain. Cities Soc. **25**, 13–24 (2016). https://doi.org/10.1016/j.scs.2016.04.016
6. Cocco, C., Rezende Freitas, C., Mourão Moura, A.C., Campagna, M.: Geodesign process analytics: focus on design as a process and its outcomes. Sustainability **12**, 119 (2019). https://doi.org/10.3390/su12010119
7. Campagna, M., Di Cesare, E.A., Cocco, C.: Integrating green-infrastructures design in strategic spatial planning with geodesign. Sustainability **12**, 1820 (2020). https://doi.org/10.3390/su12051820
8. Cocco, C., Jankowski, P., Campagna, M.: An analytic approach to understanding process dynamics in geodesign studies. Sustainability **11**, 4999 (2019). https://doi.org/10.3390/su11184999
9. Padula, A., Fiore, P., Pilogallo, A., Scorza, F.: Collaborative approach in strategic development planning for small municipalities. applying geodesign methodology and tools for a new municipal strategy in Scanzano Jonico. In: Leone, A., Gargiulo, C. (eds.) Environmental and Territorial Modelling for Planning and Design, pp. 665–672. FedOApress (2018). https://doi.org/10.6093/978-88-6887-048-5

10. Fiore, P., Padula, A., Angela Pilogallo, F.S.: Facing urban regeneration issues through geodesign approach. the case of Gravina in Puglia. In: Leone, A., Gargiulo, C. (eds.) Environmental and territorial modelling for planning and design. FedOAPress (2018). https://doi.org/10.6093/978-88-6887-048-5
11. Scorza, F.: Sustainable urban regeneration in Gravina in Puglia, Italy. In: Fisher, T., Orland, B., Steinitz, C. (eds.) The International Geodesign Collaboration. Changing Geography by Design, pp. 112–113. ESRI Press, Redlands, California (2020)
12. Casas, G.L., Scorza, F.: Sustainable planning: a methodological toolkit. In: Gervasi, O., et al. (eds.) ICCSA 2016. LNCS, vol. 9786, pp. 627–635. Springer, Cham (2016). https://doi.org/10.1007/978-3-319-42085-1_53
13. Vagnby, B.H.: Logical framework approach. **64** (2000)
14. Ballal, H., Steinitz, C.: A Workshop in digital geodesign synthesis. In: Proceedings of Digital Landscape Architecture, pp. 400–407 (2015)
15. Curatella, L., Scorza, F.: Polycentrism and insularity metrics for in-land areas. In: Gervasi, O., et al. (eds.) ICCSA 2020. LNCS, vol. 12255, pp. 253–261. Springer, Cham (2020). https://doi.org/10.1007/978-3-030-58820-5_20
16. Curatella, L., Scorza, F.: Una Valutazione Della Struttura Policentrica Dell'insediamento Nella Regione Basilicata. LaborEst. 37–42 (2020). https://doi.org/10.19254/LaborEst.20.06
17. Corrado, S., Scorza, F.: Machine learning based approach to assess territorial marginality. In: Lecture Notes in Computer Science. Springer (2022)
18. Pilogallo, A., Saganeiti, L., Scorza, F., Las Casas, G.: Tourism attractiveness: main components for a spacial appraisal of major destinations according with ecosystem services approach. In: Gervasi, O., et al. (eds.) ICCSA 2018. LNCS, vol. 10964, pp. 712–724. Springer, Cham (2018). https://doi.org/10.1007/978-3-319-95174-4_54
19. Scorza, F., Fortunato, G.: Active mobility oriented urban development: a morpho-syntactic scenario for mid-sized town. Eur. Plan. Stud. (2022). https://doi.org/10.1080/09654313.2022.2077094
20. Fortunato, G., Scorza, F., Murgante, B.: Cyclable city: a territorial assessment procedure for disruptive policy-making on urban mobility. In: Misra, S., et al. (eds.) ICCSA 2019. LNCS, vol. 11624, pp. 291–307. Springer, Cham (2019). https://doi.org/10.1007/978-3-030-24311-1_21
21. Scorza, F., Fortunato, G.: Cyclable cities: building feasible scenario through urban space morphology assessment. J. Urban Plan. Dev. **147**, 05021039 (2021). https://doi.org/10.1061/(asce)up.1943-5444.0000713
22. Scorza, F., Saganeiti, L., Pilogallo, A., Murgante, B.: GHOST PLANNING: the inefficiency of energy sector policies in a low population density region. Arch. DI Stud. URBANI E Reg. (2020)
23. Dvarioniene, J., Grecu, V., Lai, S., Scorza, F.: Four perspectives of applied sustainability: research implications and possible integrations. In: Gervasi, O., et al. (eds.) ICCSA 2017. LNCS, vol. 10409, pp. 554–563. Springer, Cham (2017). https://doi.org/10.1007/978-3-319-62407-5_39
24. Scorza, F., Santopietro, L.: A systemic perspective for the sustainable energy and climate action plan (SECAP). Eur. Plan. Stud. 1–21 (2021). https://doi.org/10.1080/09654313.2021.1954603
25. Scorza, F., Santopietro, L., Giuzio, B., Amato, F., Murgante, B., Casas, G.L.: Conflicts between environmental protection and energy regeneration of the historic heritage in the case of the city of matera: tools for assessing and dimensioning of sustainable energy action plans (SEAP). In: Gervasi, O., et al. (eds.) ICCSA 2017. LNCS, vol. 10409, pp. 527–539. Springer, Cham (2017). https://doi.org/10.1007/978-3-319-62407-5_37

26. Cerminara, I., et al.: Green chemistry, circular economy and sustainable development: an operational perspective to scale research results in SMEs practices. In: Gervasi, O., et al. (eds.) ICCSA 2020. LNCS, vol. 12255, pp. 206–213. Springer, Cham (2020). https://doi.org/10.1007/978-3-030-58820-5_16
27. Campagna, M., Ervin, S., Sheppard, S.: How geodesign processes shaped outcomes. In: Fisher, T., Orland, B., Steinitz, C. (eds.) The International Geodesign Collaboration. Changing Geography by Design, pp. 145–148. ESRI Press, Redlands, California (2020)
28. Corrado, S., Giannini, B., Santopietro, L., Oliveto, G., Scorza, F.: Water management and municipal climate adaptation plans: a preliminary assessment for flood risks management at urban scale. In: Gervasi, O., et al. (eds.) ICCSA 2020. LNCS, vol. 12255, pp. 184–192. Springer, Cham (2020). https://doi.org/10.1007/978-3-030-58820-5_14
29. Santopietro, L., Scorza, F.: The Italian experience of the covenant of mayors: a territorial evaluation. Sustainability **13**, 1–23 (2021). https://doi.org/10.3390/su13031289
30. Scorza, F.: Towards self energy-management and sustainable citizens' engagement in local energy efficiency agenda. Int. J. Agric. Environ. Inf. Syst. **7**, 44–53 (2016). https://doi.org/10.4018/IJAEIS.2016010103
31. Albert, C.: IGC 2019: What we learned. In: Fisher, T., Orland, B., Steinitz, C. (eds.) The International Geodesign Collaboration. Changing Geography by Design, pp. 139–144, Redlands, California (2020)
32. Rittel, H.W.J., Webber, M.M.: Dilemmas in a general theory of planning. Policy Sci. **4**, 155–169 (1973). https://doi.org/10.1007/BF01405730

Applying Geodesign Towards an Integrated Local Development Strategy: The Val d'Agri Case (Italy)

Priscilla Sofia Dastoli[1(✉)], Piergiuseppe Pontrandolfi[2], Francesco Scorza[1], Simone Corrado[1], and Antonello Azzato[1]

[1] School of Engineering, Laboratory of Urban and Regional Systems Engineering, University of Basilicata, 10, Viale Dell'Ateneo Lucano, 85100 Potenza, Italy
{priscillasofia.dastoli,francesco.scorza}@unibas.it, simone.corrado@studenti.unibas.it, azzato.antonello@tiscali.it

[2] University of Basilicata, DiCEM, CdS Architecture, Via Lanera, 20, 75100 Matera, Italy
piergiuseppe.pontrandolfi@unibas.it

Abstract. Geodesign is an effective collaborative methodology oriented towards designing spatial strategies with a multidisciplinary approach, involving not only the local community but also professionals from design, spatial sciences and information systems. This synergy acts as a driver for a general knowledge framework, which allows these established professional fields to develop further and collaborate effectively. This paper proposes the Geodesign workshop outcomes within the RI.P.R.O.VA.RE research project, oriented towards the definition of an integrated local development strategy in the Val d'Agri area, in the inland Basilicata region. The results, therefore, represent a component within a much broader project framework; however, the participatory design approach used in the Geodesign experience made it possible to evaluate the different project proposals, moderate the negotiation between two different focus groups and achieve a single and shared participatory design. A key role was played by the research team that moderated the organisation, localisation and expression phase of the different project proposals, having sufficient spatial and temporal knowledge to integrate the Geodesign outcomes and elaborate a future-oriented strategy.

The paper is structured in four parts. In the introduction it is specified how the use of the Geodesign tool was brought into the case study. The second part briefly outlines the study area context: the Val d'agri. The third part focuses on the Geodesign Workshop description and, finally, the outcomes are illustrated, from which the research team defined the integrated local development strategy.

Keywords: Geodesign · Inland areas · Local development strategy

1 Introduction

Geodesign is a methodology approach to decision-making which integrates spatial information science tools to support physical spatial development planning, and can help

O. Gervasi et al. (Eds.): ICCSA 2022 Workshops, LNCS 13379, pp. 253–262, 2022.
https://doi.org/10.1007/978-3-031-10545-6_18

address many of the current problems faced in urban and regional planning practices [1]. In 2012 Carl Steinitz formalised a methodological framework, called Geodesign Framework [2, 3], aimed at identifying the potential future transformations of a territory as a function of current dynamics. This framework proposes six questions and six models, which may be common to all Geodesign projects, but does not suggest a single linear process, but one characterised by several iterative cycles and possibilities for backaction.

While the relevance and interest in Geodesign research is already producing promising results and successful case studies [4–6], there is not yet a wide diffusion of its application in planning, mainly in Italy [7, 8].

Li and Milburn [9] underlined the importance of combining geodesign with increasingly advanced information and communication tools. Indeed, while geodesign continues to be used to achieve more complex goals due to its analytical skill, tools for collecting increasingly detailed data continue to evolve, including online interfaces and portable GIS tools. Idea-based graphics technologies have also been rapidly advancing. Interactive drawing devices allow designers to generate instant digital graphic products by freehand drawing on screen.

An important network for the interchange of research applied to Geodesign is the International Geodesign Collaboration linked to the GeoDesign Summit [10], where the most up-to-date applications, technologies, teaching tools and theories of GeoDesign are discussed between academia and practice.

The following sections discuss the application of the Geodesign approach to a case study, as part of the activities promoted and developed within the project "Rehabilitating Countries. Operational Strategies for the Valorisation and Resilience of Inland Areas" (RI.P.R.O.VA.RE) [11]. This project is structured around three research objectives: redrawing the Inland Areas geography [12, 13], understanding the Inland Areas resilience and defining sustainable and resilient development strategies [14]. It has as its field of experimentation the Campania and Basilicata regions.

The paper aims to illustrate the activities and results achieved with Geodesign in the Medio Agri Living Lab, an area composed of six municipalities along the Agri river basin.

The idea of starting a Living Lab in the study area is aimed at involving local stakeholders in decision-making processes and, more specifically, in co-designing area strategies, able to act on the resilience features of the systems. Therefore, actions linked to risk reduction and actions aimed at regenerating and enhancing the potential [15, 16], in terms of natural and cultural resources and productive abilities of these territories, are combined, in order to enhance the inland areas productive landscapes, recovering and strengthening local manufacturing skills.

In operative terms, the Living Lab was organised in six phases, each with a specific objective, and followed the Logical Framework Approach methodology (a rational framework to identify and organise spatial problems in a cause-effect relationship at the basis of a planning activity) [17]. The intention was to integrate Geodesign with the Logical Framework Approach methodology because the combination of these approaches is considered successful and has the potential for extensive application as a key component of planning tools. Within the Living Lab two days were spent on Geodesign, in the San Martino d'Agri and Roccanova municipalities.

2 Val d'agri Area Context

The Middle Agri area covers the central sector of the Agri river basin, one of the five rivers that cross Basilicata and flow into the Ionian Sea. The area is predominantly mountainous in its western part, with the Monte Raparo Site of Community Interest (SCI); most of the remaining area is hilly, with sandy and conglomeratic hills, which characterise it for its high hydrogeological risk. Moreover, the Val d'Agri's largest territorial unit is specialised in oil extraction activities due to the presence of Europe's largest onshore oil field [18, 19]. This generates major conflicts between oil resource industrial exploitation and environmental protection issues.

According to the SNAI classification, the six municipalities that are part of the survey group (Gallicchio, Missanello, Roccanova, San Chirico Raparo, San Martino d'Agri and Sant'Arcangelo) fall within class F - ultra-peripheral, i.e. those municipalities in the inland areas that are more than 75 min away from a pole that simultaneously has a complete upper secondary school offer, at least one hospital with a level I d.e.a. (Emergency and Acceptance Department) and at least one silver railway station. An evident migration phenomenon in the sample area leads to progressive depopulation. In the last decade, almost a thousand people have left the area; approximately 8% of the population currently stands at 10,634.

Mainly to overcome the lack of services, which compounds the marginal character of the area, the Union of Municipalities [20] of Medio Agri (Missanello, Roccanova, San Chirico Raparo, and Sant'Arcangelo) was established in 2017, recently expanded with the inclusion of the municipalities of Gallicchio and Armento. This Union aims to face up jointly to the difficulties affecting the area, starting with accessibility to essential services (education, health, transport). The setting up of the Union of Municipalities affected the choice of the area to be researched because it is believed that the smaller centers should join institutional forms of association between municipalities, both to ensure sustainable management of services and functions and to guarantee more opportunities for citizens.

The Medio Agri area has significant potential, especially in cultural and natural heritage, with a high ecological value of the ecosystems [21–24]. In particular, the area is affected by the perimeter of the Lucano Val d'Agri-Lagonegrese Apennines National Park, by a ZSC 'Murge di S. Oronzo', by a ZPS 'Lucano Apennines, Agri Valley, Monte Sirino, Monte Raparo' and by two SIC 'Lago Pertusillo' and 'Monte Raparo' [25].

3 Geodesign Workshop

Within the Medio Agri Living Lab, whose participants belonged to different professional fields, it was decided to use the Geodesign tool [3] to focus on the planning of action in the whole Medio Agri area and to concretise the ideas expressed in the description phase of eleven general objectives.

A simplified Geodesign approach was used in this case, as the activities were condensed into two days. The activities were supported by GeodesignHub (an online platform of Geodesign Hub Pvt. Ltd., Dublin, Ireland), and were set up according to the Geodesign International Collaboration (IGC) standards.

The Geodesign methodology is based on the constructive interaction of working groups, which individually develop the plan and subsequently arrive at a synthesis. There is a preliminary phase in which the research group collects a number of thematic maps representing a snapshot of the territory from different points of view (environmental, cultural heritage, economic sectors, mobility etc.). Already in this phase, it is possible to give a project outline, which, in this case, was the research group's own. This is a necessary preparatory phase in order to have qualitative and quantitative references and to identify vulnerable resources, constraints, impacts and development factors through macroscopic indicators. The reference maps (see Fig. 1) allow us to understand the actual territory condition. In the Living Lab Medio Agri case the initial reference maps proposed were:

1. ACCO – Hospitality
2. AGRI – Agriculture
3. INST – Institutional services
4. CULT – Cultural heritage
5. INFR – Infrastructure and mobility
6. NAT – Natural heritage
7. COMIND – Trade-Industry

The maps show which territorial parts, according to their own vocation, are most attractive/vulnerable for a certain land use. The seven systems maps are classified according to a precise colour coding from red (high vulnerability) to green (low vulnerability).

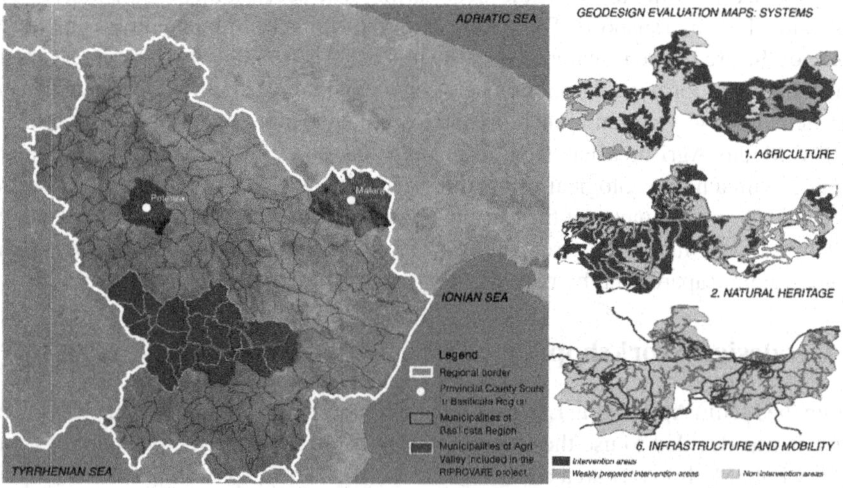

Fig. 1. Overview of the study area and assessment maps by systems to define interventions on Geodesign [25]. (Color figure online)

The maps were then loaded into the GeodesignHub main interface with simplified graphics to comply with the programme's requirements (Fig. 2).

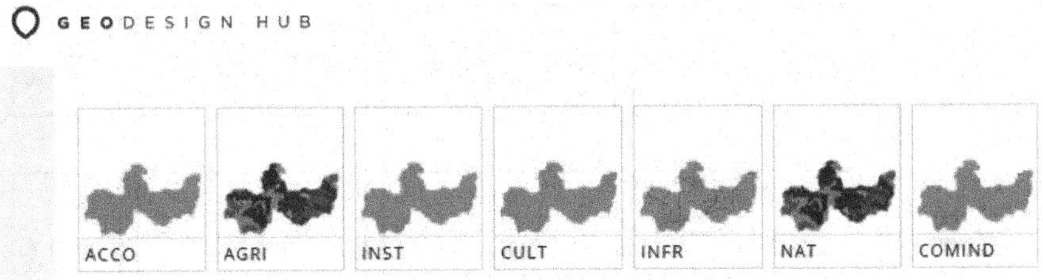

Fig. 2. System evaluation maps.

About forty participants from different profiles attended the Medio Agri Living Lab, during the days focused on Geodesign: local administrators, freelancers, researchers, university students, association and local community members. The invitation was addressed to the communities of the six municipalities belonging to the study area, which have already been on a common journey since 2017 because they established the Medio Agri Municipalities Union [25].

The participants were divided into two groups: tourism promotion and territorial protection on the one hand, local development and institutional and reception services on the other.

After a short study area and workshop objectives presentation, each participant, using a sketch-planning tool available on the platform, developed a set of geo-referenced conceptual ideas (diagrams), representing specific policies or projects for the seven systems.

A first set of proposals came up, represented and visible through an application structure supporting the groups. Each group can view and analyse the other projects by visualising and overlaying maps of the different ideas.

Eighty-six actions to be undertaken in the seven systems were located and described in this phase, divided into interventions and policies. Each diagram had to have a title, a location, a description, an estimated total amount and had to belong to one of the seven systems in which the context analysis was summarised. Updating the activities in the platform ensured that all participants could view the diagrams proposed by all group members in real time.

On the second day, the two groups' participants selected a set of project proposals in order to build a shared scenario, which was evaluated to find out the impacts generated by the transformations in the seven systems. Afterwards, the two groups were asked to negotiate the scenarios until a single strategic development scenario shared by all participants was reached (Fig. 3).

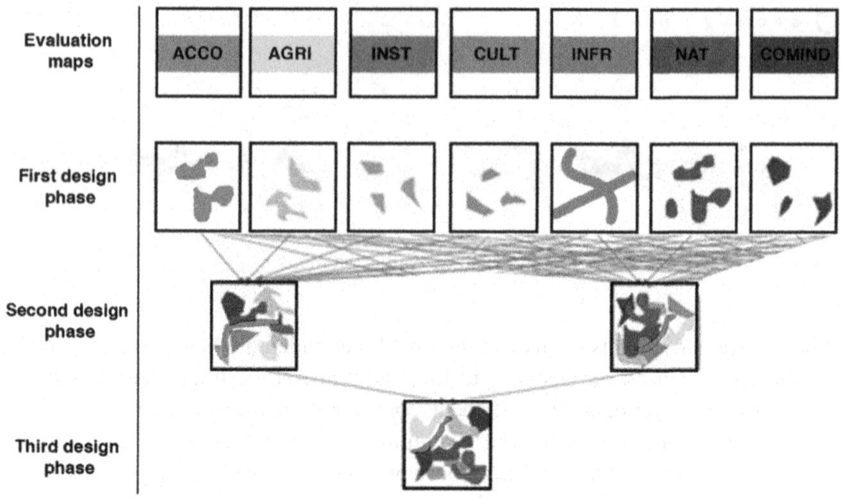

Fig. 3. The working structure of the workshop: in the first row the seven systems evaluation maps and in the second row the project and policy diagrams.

Below is a table with the interventions and policies that emerged in the Agriculture system (AGRI) and the Infrastructure and Mobility system (INFR), belonging to the final shared scenario (Table 1).

Table 1. Some actions and policies of the shared strategic development scenario.

Agricultural system	Infrastructure and mobility system
San Martino d'Agri oil mill restored and reopened	Improvement of the Roccanova-Sant Arcangelo road network
Olive plantation	Securing the SS598 crossroads
Back to the rural economy	Road public transport enforcement
Enhancing olive oil production	Public transport service adapted to the population' needs
Missanello olive oil promotion	Ecological car sharing between municipalities
Agricultural consortium	Bus service between municipalities
Service cooperative	Sports centre upgrade
Hazelnut promotion	Bus terminals
Poultry breeding	Demand responsive transport
Tax exemption for agricultural labour	Coordination between mobility services
Milk processing consortium	
Agricultural labour management consortium	

Geodesign is a valid tool to support a negotiation process among stakeholders, with the outcome of a development scenario shared by the participants. In addition, the interventions and policies are a goal at a higher level than the municipal one, where services and planning policies have a different depth, especially because the study area is composed by small municipalities.

4 Results and Conclusions

The Geodesign workshop within the Medio Agri Living Lab was aimed at co-designing and testing a place-based policy through the processing of a starting framework for the integrated local development strategy [22]. The final shared scenario is the synthesis of project alternatives and the negotiation aimed at identifying the strong elements of the project proposals.

However, this experience did not exactly follow all phases of a Geodesign workshop, but focused on the elaboration and negotiation phase. The explanation is to be found in the time that was decided to spend on Geodesign, because it was only one of the many moments in which the participants faced each other within the Living Lab. On the other hand, the participant's presence could not be extended further because the organisation of the in-person activities followed a methodology based on the Logical Framework Approach (LFA), common to the other research groups.

The very important element is the methodological approach of Geodesign which can be adapted to different situations in practice. In particular, it is argued that it can become a valuable tool in the planning techniques toolkit and contribute to its renewal. Urban and territorial planning needs a tool that keeps up with the information and communication technology development [26, 27], but has a special focus on collaboration in defining territorial strategies. One of the objectives is the creation of a stable collaboration, even after the end of the field experience promoted by experts or a research group. Finally, as in this synthetic experience, it is believed that Geodsign expresses a greater potential when combined with other techniques, such as LFA.

The Geodesign outcomes within the Living Lab were fundamental to guide the research team in the integrated strategy definition, which was defined considering the overall project framework. In particular, the preliminary knowledge phase results, the Living Lab results as a participatory moment composed by specific phases and methodologies (context analysis, SWOT analysis, problem and objective tree technique, Analytic Hierarchy Process technique to identify priority objectives) and the Geodesign experience were taken into account.

The strategy suggested for the Media Val d'Agri area cannot avoid two basic conditions:

1. The promotion of new governance forms based on the associated management of some essential functions (making stable the path started by the Local Authorities);
2. The setting up of a shared process for the area' local development in the average-long term (vision) to be pursued through policies/interventions that shall be implemented to achieve the objectives assumed.

The objective of halting the municipalities' depopulation and making the territory attractive to non-residents and/or temporary residents were considered "goals" to be achieved. The objectives priority is based on the overall integrated strategy implementation and specific strategies proposed and shared with the Living Lab participants. In general, it is expected to raise the population' awareness of a renewed approach to the sustainable development and energy transition issues.

The Geodesign tool has never been as important as now, in which the energy and natural resources decrease and the climate change crisis only require sustainable development [28–30]. Geodesign could be introduced into urban and territorial planning university courses, PhDs on the subject must be promoted (as is already being done at the UCS University of Southern California) and it must become a common working practice. People who know how to use collaborative planning tools need to be aware users of Geodesign's potential. The positive feedback received during the workshop from participants highlights the need to make people more aware of the collaborative planning benefits, especially in inland areas.

References

1. Campagna, M., Di Cesare, E.: Geodesign: lost in regulations (and in practice). In: Papa, R., Fistola, R. (eds.) Smart Energy in the Smart City. GET, pp. 307–327. Springer, Cham (2016). https://doi.org/10.1007/978-3-319-31157-9_16
2. Steinitz, C.: A Framework for Geodesign. Changing Geography by Design. Esri Press, Redlands (2012)
3. Steinitz, C., Campagna, M.: Un Framework per il Geodesign: Trasformare la Geografia con il Progetto. (2017)
4. Scorza, F.: Training decision-makers: GEODESIGN workshop paving the way for new urban agenda. In: Gervasi, O., et al. (eds.) ICCSA 2020. LNCS, vol. 12252, pp. 310–316. Springer, Cham (2020). https://doi.org/10.1007/978-3-030-58811-3_22
5. Foster, K.: Geodesign parsed: Placing it within the rubric of recognized design theories. Landsc. Urban Plan. **156**, 92–100 (2016). https://doi.org/10.1016/J.LANDURBPLAN.2016.06.017
6. Nijhuis, S., Zlatanova, S., Dias, E., van der Hoeven, F., van der SPEK, S.: Geo-design: advances in bridging geo-information technology, urban planning and landscape architecture. (2016)
7. Padula, A., Fiore, P., Pilogallo, A., Scorza, F.: Collaborative approach in strategic development planning for small municipalities. Applying geodesign methodology and tools for a new municipal strategy in Scanzano Jonico. In: Leone, A., Gargiulo, C. (eds.) Environmental and Territorial Modelling for Planning and Design, pp. 665–672. FedOApress (2018). https://doi.org/10.6093/978-88-6887-048-5
8. Fiore, P., Padula, A., Angela Pilogallo, F.S.: Facing urban regeneration issues through geodesign approach. The case of Gravina in Puglia. In: Leone, A., Gargiulo, C. (eds.) Environmental and Territorial Modelling for Planning and Design. FedOAPress (2018). https://doi.org/10.6093/978-88-6887-048-5
9. Li, W., Milburn, L.A.: The evolution of geodesign as a design and planning tool. Landsc. Urban Plan. **156**, 5–8 (2016). https://doi.org/10.1016/J.LANDURBPLAN.2016.09.009
10. Esri's 2021 Geodesign Summit, https://mediaspace.esri.com/media/t/1_7nhdnywj. Accessed 04 Apr 2022

11. Pontrandolfi, P., Dastoli, P.S.: Comparing impact evaluation evidence of EU and local development policies with New Urban Agenda themes: the Agri Valley case in Basilicata (Italy). (2021)
12. Carlucci, C., Lucatelli, S.: Aree Interne: un potenziale per la crescita economica del Paese. Agriregionieuropa. Anno 9 (2013)
13. De Rossi, A.: Riabitare l'Italia: Le aree interne tra abbandoni e riconquiste (curated by). Donzelli editore, Roma (2018)
14. Galderisi, A., Fiore, P., Pontrandolfi, P.: Strategie Operative per la valorizzazione e la resilienza delle Aree Interne: il progetto RI.P.R.O.VA.RE. BDC. Boll. Del Cent. Calza Bini. 20, 297–316 (2020). https://doi.org/10.6092/2284-4732/7557
15. Francini, M., Palermo, A., Viapiana, M.F.: Integrated territorial approaches for emergency plans. Territorio. **2019**, 85–90 (2019). https://doi.org/10.3280/TR2019-089011
16. Scorza, F., Attolico, A.: Innovations in promoting sustainable development: the local implementation plan designed by the Province of Potenza. In: Gervasi, O., et al. (eds.) ICCSA 2015. LNCS, vol. 9156, pp. 756–766. Springer, Cham (2015). https://doi.org/10.1007/978-3-319-21407-8_54
17. Dastoli, P.S., Pontrandolfi, P.: Strategic guidelines to increase the resilience of inland areas: the case of the Alta Val d'Agri (Basilicata-Italy). In: Gervasi, O., et al. (eds.) ICCSA 2021. LNCS, vol. 12958, pp. 119–130. Springer, Cham (2021). https://doi.org/10.1007/978-3-030-87016-4_9
18. Las Casas, G., Scorza, F., Murgante, B.: Conflicts and sustainable planning: peculiar instances coming from Val D'agri structural inter-municipal plan. In: Papa, R., Fistola, R., Gargiulo, C. (eds.) Smart Planning: Sustainability and Mobility in the Age of Change. GET, pp. 163–177. Springer, Cham (2018). https://doi.org/10.1007/978-3-319-77682-8_10
19. Scorza, F.: Towards Self energy-management and sustainable citizens' engagement in local energy efficiency agenda. Int. J. Agric. Environ. Inf. Syst. **7**, 44–53 (2016). https://doi.org/10.4018/ijaeis.2016010103
20. Camera dei deputati. https://www.camera.it/temiap/documentazione/temi/pdf/1105809.pdf?_1555520990223. Accessed 26 Dec 2021
21. Saganeiti, L., Pilogallo, A., Faruolo, G., Scorza, F., Murgante, B.: Territorial Fragmentation and Renewable Energy Source Plants: Which Relationship? Sustainability **12**, 1828 (2020). https://doi.org/10.3390/SU12051828
22. Las Casas, G., Murgante, B., Scorza, F.: Regional local development strategies benefiting from open data and open tools and an outlook on the renewable energy sources contribution. In: Papa, R., Fistola, R. (eds.) Smart Energy in the Smart City. GET, pp. 275–290. Springer, Cham (2016). https://doi.org/10.1007/978-3-319-31157-9_14
23. Scorza, F., Fortunato, G.: Active mobility oriented urban development: a morpho-syntactic scenario for mid-sized town. Eur. Plan. Stud. (2022). https://doi.org/10.1080/09654313.2022.2077094
24. Scorza, F., Fortunato, G.: Cyclable cities: building feasible scenario through urban space-morphology assessment. J. Urban Plan. Dev. (2021). https://doi.org/10.1061/(ASCE)UP.1943-5444.0000713
25. Dastoli, P.S., Pontrandolfi, P.: Methods and tools for a participatory local development strategy. In: New Metropolitan Perspectives (forthcoming) (2022)
26. Murgante, B., Borruso, G., Lapucci, A.: Geocomputation and urban planning. In: Murgante, B., Borruso, G., Lapucci, A. (eds.) Geocomputation and Urban Planning. SCI, vol. 176, pp. 1–17. Springer, Heidelberg (2009). https://doi.org/10.1007/978-3-540-89930-3_1
27. Scorza, F., Saganeiti, L., Pilogallo, A., Murgante, B.: Ghost planning: the inefficiency of energy sector policies in a low population density region1. Arch. DI Stud. URBANI E Reg. 34–55 (2020). https://doi.org/10.3280/ASUR2020-127-S1003

28. Pilogallo, A., Saganeiti, L., Scorza, F., Murgante, B.: Assessing the impact of land use changes on ecosystem services value. In: Gervasi, O., et al. (eds.) ICCSA 2020. LNCS, vol. 12253, pp. 606–616. Springer, Cham (2020). https://doi.org/10.1007/978-3-030-58814-4_47
29. Pilogallo, A., Scorza, F.: Mapping regulation ecosystem services (ReMES) specialization in Italy. J. Urban Plan. Dev. (2021)
30. Santopietro, L., Scorza, F.: The Italian experience of the covenant of mayors: a territorial evaluation. Sustainability. **13**, 1289 (2021). https://doi.org/10.3390/su13031289

Mission-Oriented in Geodesign Experience: Teaching About Cultural Landscape Values

Ítalo Sousa de Sena[1(✉)] and Ana Clara Mourão Moura[2]

[1] Faculty of Science, Masaryk University, 60200 Brno, Czech Republic
desena@mail.muni.cz

[2] Escola de Arquitetura, Laboratório de Geoprocessamento, Universidade Federal de Minas Gerais (UFMG), Rua Paraíba 697, Belo Horizonte, Brazil

Abstract. Citizens' inclusion in the process of urban planning brought innovative ways to produce, assess and make data available. The principle of voluntary geographic information was proposed to register people's activities and can result from motivation, as "mission-oriented". Processes emerged from the use of geospatial data by citizens, and geodesign is also presented, as a purposeful process of creating ideas, preferably in a collaborative setting. The presented workshop happened in areas of social vulnerability, whose landscape is composed of cultural values related to a historically used geodiversity. Participants had to complete tasks to design an intervention in a protected area. The objective was to motivate digital natives to think about the risks, vulnerabilities, and potentialities of the landscape. A geographic virtual environment was created from Minecraft using GIS and ETL for processing data, as a representation model. The model for dynamic interaction with the landscape was based on quests (missions) that participants had to accomplish. NPCs (Non-Playable Characters) presented contexts of restrictions and potentialities to be considered, which was the evaluation model. Once the participants had completed the step, the result considered the modification to the virtual landscape made by each pair of participants. In total, 22 design proposals met the established goals (change model). An evaluation of participants' experiences was carried out to track the increase in awareness of the subject of study. Future developments are focused on the implementation of stages for negotiation and voting for the best ideas, which can also be associated with the co-creation of proposals.

Keywords: Minecraft · Geogame · Geodiversity · VGI

1 Introduction

The possibility of people being sources of geographic data brought forth the concept of citizens as sensors [1]. It was made possible due to the many innovations in the geoinformatics field, as well as the reflection of internet popularization.

Once the possibilities of wider consumption and distribution of information were established, and the importance of citizen participation recognized, the applications turned to the VGI - Volunteered Geographic Information, which is associated with the

O. Gervasi et al. (Eds.): ICCSA 2022 Workshops, LNCS 13379, pp. 263–278, 2022.
https://doi.org/10.1007/978-3-031-10545-6_19

term user-generated content [2], associated with the potential of web 2.0 [3]. Contribution is voluntary, but it can happen passively or actively. The passive mode, according to Davis et al. [4] happens when citizens have their data and behaviors captured in sensors embedded in mobile devices (such as cell phones). The active mode, according to the same authors, happens when the citizen consciously checks in on an information capture platform or deliberately collaborates in a VGI.

The possibility of including citizens in the process has also increased interest in using platforms as a basis for planning. This begins with actions called Critical GIS, Participatory GIS, Collaborative GIS, and Community Integrated GIS [5–8]. What they have in common is the possibility of involving citizens in discussions, expanding access to analysis and criticism of the place. But they are still very much associated with the principle of collecting and making available information created collaboratively by citizens.

To further explore citizens' listening, Davis et al. [4] propose the principle of mission-oriented, whose purpose is to improve the quality of collaborations, increasing records according to broadening interests, greater spatial coverage, validation and reliability activities information, and feedback on queries. The authors relate the actions as a volunteer-task relationship (identifying the most suitable citizens to fulfill a task, depending on their profile), volunteer-region (looking for those who have specific knowledge about a spatial area), and volunteer-theme (selecting the citizens who may have more knowledge about a subject and can give more reliable answers).

At an institutional level, the availability of geospatial information gained form through Spatial Data Infrastructures (SDI). The establishment of SDIs marked a change in geospatial data available to the general public [9]. The European regulations that instituted the SDI – Spatial Data Infrastructure, INSPIRE (Directive 2007/2/EC) was a milestone, which was a reference for the Brazilian regulations, the INDE – Infraestrutura Nacional de Dados Espaciais (Decree No. 6,666 of 11/27/2008) [10, 11].

Geographic information should promote the rise of awareness of the territory by integrating the different agents of society to participate in shared planning processes. [12]. In the meantime, with the consolidation of shared geospatial data online on different styles of platforms, the concept of geodesign arose from both geospatial data analysis and public participation development. The expectation was to work as support to the collaboration of different agents of society in planning. Geodesign is preferably developed on a web-based platform, but it can also be carried out in an analogical way, as the fundamental principle is to plan "with" and "for" geography, in a shared process, by co-creation [13, 14].

Despite the many innovative ways of making geospatial data publicly available, including minorities in spatial and urban planning still remains a key issue to address. Among the underrepresented social groups are the elderly people and kids. These two groups come from completely different generations, so, they have different ways to communicate and engage with new ideas. The second generation, more specifically, falls into the group of digital natives, which are people that were born after 1995 and had to live their whole life dealing with digital technologies [15, 16]. This group of people shares the same interests and online communities, being active in online games, forums, social media, etc. Minecraft rises from this context as one of the most successful videogames in history, selling hundreds of millions of copies, holding a very active and passionate community of players, and reaching more than 50 million online players every day [17].

Considering this new generation of citizens, what should be considered when demonstrating specific values of a cultural landscape to digital natives? How to ensure that they can access information to think about designing new interventions based on these values?

One of the solutions that have been used is the game Minecraft. It can serve as a base for reproducing the framework of geodesign, by adapting its complexity to a mission-oriented experience through the virtual environment of the game.

The game design approach in implementing game mechanics for players' interaction with the represented landscape gives space for designing mission-oriented dynamics. Based on this idea, the present study aimed to involve digital natives in the process of learning about landscape values and allow them to express their views of alternative futures in a well-known environment for them. The framework of geodesign was used to lead the stages of the gameplay. A geogame was created to present how Ouro Preto's geodiversity has been used for over three centuries (Fig. 1), as well as how it still functions as part of the culture of the place (Fig. 2).

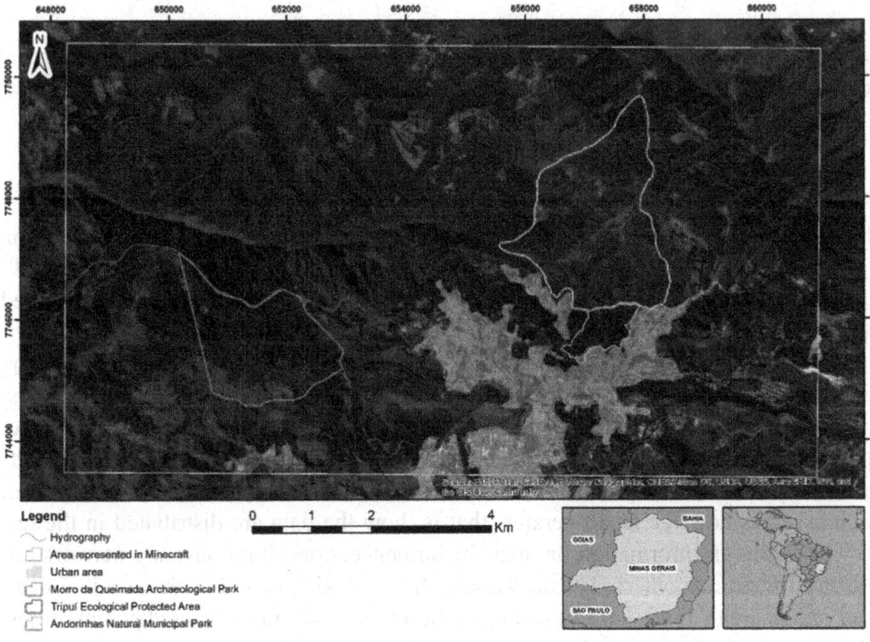

Fig. 1. Ouro Preto city and its protected areas and parks. Source: Sena, 2019 [29].

In this study, we show how Minecraft can be used as a medium for communicating the process of geodesign, by inviting kids to take part as people of the place. The proposed workshop used five out of the six models presented in the Steinitz framework. Each model is described concerning the game's virtual environment and processes that took

Fig. 2. General panorama of Ouro Preto's landscape: historical, cultural, and environmental values as part of the landscape. Perspective from the Serra de Ouro Preto area. Source: Danilo Marques Magalhães.

place based on it. The Decision Model, which consists of the process of optimizing the consensus among the participants of a workshop, was not considered in this study.

2 Geodesign and Minecraft

What stands out in geodesign is that it goes beyond the stages of analysis and evaluation of geography, and it focuses on the propositional stage, for the planning of an area [18–21]. Geodesign is based on the stages of applying group engagement methods in shared planning [13].

Among the frameworks in geodesign most used in workshops, the proposal by Steinitz [14] stands out, which establishes that a study must go through six models: three of them in the pre-workshop and three others during the workshop. The first model is the Representation one, which it is defined how the area should be described, resulting in the production of data about the case study. The second is the Process model, which assesses how the area operates, that is, how the data are distributed in the territory. It results in information on areas of influence, concentrations, and networks of relationships, among others. The third one is the evaluation model, which is a judgment based on the area's functions, drawing attention to its vulnerabilities and potentialities, and indicating where proposed changes should be placed. The fourth model, Change, is created during the workshop, as it is the design of proposals. The fifth model, Impact, is also used during the workshop as it verifies the consequences of proposed changes. Finally, the Decision Model results from the negotiation and selection of the best ideas by the participants.

All these models are adaptable considering the focal area, purpose, the public which will participate in the process, as well as the media that provide visualization options to the participants. There are several examples of digital media being used for geodesign workshops. Considering the impact of the game industry on the new generations, and how virtual environments have been developed in the past few decades, there is a visible interest in absorbing such technologies and the public by using them. One notable case of it is the use of Minecraft for urban planning processes and public participation with kids and youth.

2.1 The Participatory Process Through Minecraft

Minecraft has been used as a virtual environment for spatial and urban planning since architects, urban planners and researchers started to explore its potential for real planning processes.

There are several published experiences where Minecraft was used as a tool for public participation. In many of them, the game was used primarily to collect opinions about what should be done with a specific place [22–25]. One of the most prominent experiences using Minecraft for the participatory process was developed by the "Block by Block Foundation", with support from UN-Habitat [26]. The initiative took place in more than one hundred countries and is based on a specific methodology of three main phases (planning, Minecraft co-designing workshop, and implementation) [27]. These phases consist of activities that start from selecting a site, creating financial planning, engaging citizens to co-create and design, and reaching a point where the best design is implemented in the real world.

Nowadays statistics about Minecraft show that the game's community has a common and shared language used by the players, almost exclusively digital natives. Another major factor for choosing the game for this study is its representativeness worldwide, reaching over 112 million monthly active players [28], and its impact on a whole generation of users who, for over ten years, interacted virtually in the game's environment, creating their way of communicating ideas and strategies to deal with a 3D virtual landscape.

In this sense, as communication and geovisualization are key conditions to construct a geodesign workshop, it was employed in the use of Minecraft as the digital environment for the practice. The design thinking followed the logic of the geodesign framework, bearing in mind that the goal was to plan "with" and "for" the geography. The expectation was to make players understand their reality as local citizens and develop critical and spatially aware thinking of the following concepts: geodiversity, cultural landscape, risks, vulnerabilities, potentialities, planning, protected area, land-use change, and impacts.

3 The Workshop

The GeoMinasCraft game was created to provide a virtual environment for digital natives to learn and participate in the landscape planning process. To reproduce the framework of geodesign, the game design played a central role since most parts of the workshop were performed in the game environment by the players. The game was designed to contemplate from the representation model to the change model in one single gameplay.

The impact model is the only one that was not experienced by the players. Here, we consider the virtual environment created using geospatial data as the representation model, while the design choices of what to emphasize in the landscape representation consist of the process model. The evaluation model is the combination of the players' exploration choices and the many dialogues that they can have with the NPCs, characterizing the mission-oriented approach.

As a synthesis of the geodesign models and designed stages of the gameplay: Representation model: Landscape representation in Minecraft; Process model: Information about geodiversity and cultural landscape in Minecraft; Evaluation model: Information and contexts provided by the NPCs (Non-Playable Characters) during the exploration journey; Change model: Players' designs for visitor center of Morro da Queimada Archaeological Park; Impact model: Analysis of the possible consequences of the proposals and considering the issues presented by the NPCs.

The game was designed to be played in pairs of players in the single-player mode in the game. The purpose of putting two players to share one single computer aimed to stimulate cooperation and the rise of different strategies to deal with the virtual environment and the addressed issues.

3.1 Preparing the Representation and Process Models

The representation of the landscape was based on principal elements of the geodiversity that shaped the way human activities developed in that place over three centuries. To represent the Serra de Ouro Preto area, a set of basic geographical inputs were considered: terrain, hydrography, vegetation cover, nodal points, streets, and roads. The process of using geospatial data to create a Minecraft virtual environment was discussed by Sena et al. [27], which presents the playtesting of a prototype that, after bug corrections and new implementations, was updated and validated to be used for the present workshop. This virtual environment created in Minecraft consists of the Representation model, considering that it supports the visualization of the main features that form and give character to the landscape.

The main data input was the topography, which was represented in the game by using the satellite digital elevation model (DEM) from the PALSAR sensor (Phased Array type L-band Synthetic Aperture Radar), on ALOS (Advanced Land Observation) satellite. The used DEM has a spatial resolution of 12 m and was transformed into a 3D representation of the terrain in Minecraft. From the DEM it was also possible to extract the hydrology. ETL tools (Extract Transform and Load) were applied to create an exaggeration of the vertical axis of the DEM, to provide better geovisualization of the steepness of the Serra de Ouro Preto ridge (Fig. 3). Also using ETL tools, the hydrological features were classified according to their hierarchical level, to select those that were more representative in the landscape and to insert different widths and deepness. After preparing the topography and hydrology data, both were combined in one single in Minecraft. It was the base for several other implementations of landscape features and components.

As part of the representation model, a vegetation cover layer was created to represent the importance of the forests in context to the landscape values. The NDVI – Normalized Difference Vegetation Index was used to extract the portions of the selected area which

Fig. 3. DEM data was used as an input for recreating the city's terrain aspect, with a vertical exaggeration for the higher altitudes. Source: Sena, 2019 [29].

is covered by trees. The index is a normalized difference between the spectral responses of the red and the near-infrared bands. Sentinel-2 satellite imagery was used to calculate the index. The processing was also performed using ETL tools, in a way that it was possible to merge all the layers in one single Minecraft world file.

To create a realistic model of the area, it was also important to represent the main buildings that are landmarks on the landscape. A repository of simplified versions of common buildings was created to compose the landscape (Fig. 4). For the houses, a simple pattern of 3D buildings was produced and replicated. The main buildings were elaborate in detail, considering that those are mentioned by people of the place and recognized as landmarks when describing what they see. By having landmarks represented in their location, it would support participants in creating connections with their mental maps of the city (what they understand about the place), the reality (what the landscape is), and representation (the 3D models). This principle of connecting represented places in the game with reality was also applied to other kinds of sites and processes, like geology, land use related to mining activity, urban growth, nodal points, etc. (Fig. 4).

It was also important to represent the structure and composition of the underground, which is visible in the game when players access underground mines, as well as when they encounter a rock outcrop on steep areas. To recreate geological features a sequence of processing was performed using ETL tools that calculated the slope index from the DEM, extracting the high values of slope and transforming it into a vector layer. The vectors were used as a mask to change the terrain composition from blocks of dirt to blocks of stone, representing the rock outcrops. The underground was created using the software WorldPainter, to insert layers of blocks that represent real rocks that are found in the local banded iron formations (BIFs) (Fig. 4).

The creation of the virtual environment relied on the application of interoperability techniques between data and software, allowing the representation of landscape elements related to geodiversity aspects, such as the topography of Serra de Ouro Preto, its geology, a tailing dam, the historic gold mining sites, etc. These representations were essential to give an idea to the players of how this particular landscape works. These features, together with the NPCs dialogs, are part of the Process Model.

Considering that the purpose of the game is to explore the landscape of Serra de Ouro Preto from its aspects related to geodiversity and its uses, the choice of places of interest for geodiversity are important points for the functioning of game design. The locations were inserted considering the historical and current aspects of the formation of the cultural landscape from functions performed within the local geosystem,

Fig. 4. Examples of sites where the players interact with representations of real places and processes in the city of Ouro Preto. Source: Sena, 2019 [29].

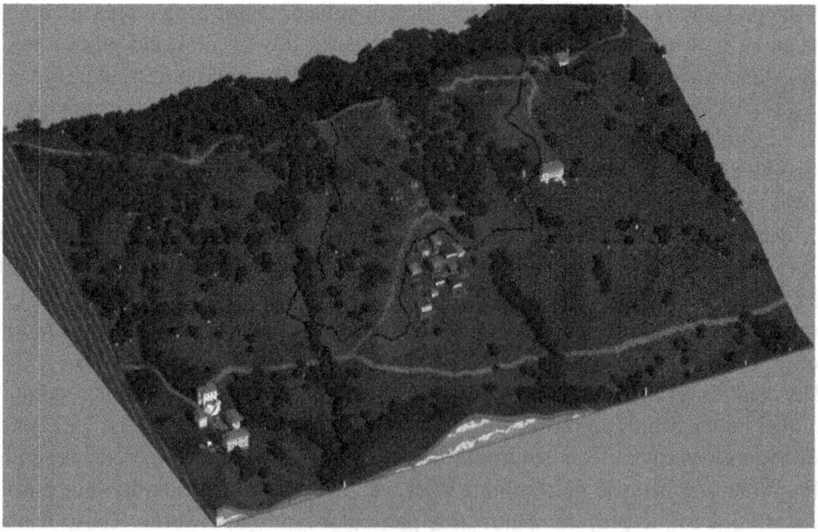

Fig. 5. Section of the virtual environment in which Morro da Queimada Archaeological Park is located. The brown line marks the park's borders. Source: Sena, 2019 [29].

in a way to evidence the connection between human activities and geodiversity. One example and focal area of the workshop is the Morro da Queimada Archaeological Park (Fig. 5). During the development of the process, fictional locations were inserted to represent phenomena related to aspects of geodiversity. For instance, a site was chosen to contextualize the occupation of steep terrain that generates a risk area due to how the geomorphological processes take place in that specific part of the area.

3.2 Evaluation Model to Be Used as a Base for a Mission-Oriented Design

During the gameplay, the participants had to accomplish a set of challenges to get permission to design and build a visiting center for Morro da Queimada Archaeological Park. On the road, they encounter NPCs that ask for help to accomplish tasks, that are designed to explain the sites they will find through their journey, as well as explain the cultural landscape's potentialities and vulnerabilities. The game intends to provide an environment for the players to learn about subjects related to the values of the landscape by visiting the places chosen to be represented in the Minecraft environment. These thematic lessons provided by the NPCs were evaluation synthesis about the place that they had to consider to go ahead (Fig. 6).

A total of 26 NPCs was in the game, each of them had a specific dialogue created to contextualize one aspect of the landscape, as well as to give players the directions to finish the quests. They were inserted in strategic positions to present information available in each specific stage of the game. There was, for example, an architect to explain about cultural landscape and the history of the place; a geologist to explain the geological structure that resulted in that landscape, a mining engineer to explain mining activities and resources; a resident to report about a sliding process after a rain period; and many others (Fig. 7).

The Change model was designed to be acquired as a result of the gameplay. A set of two quest/missions motivate the players to interact with the environment. By setting a clear objective for the players, they will collect all the resources needed to accomplish the designated task. In terms of game mechanics, the objective of the game is also the reward for finishing the landscape exploration (Fig. 8).

Fig. 6. Examples of NPCs. João, the archaeologist, Júlio, the merchant, Pedro, the geologist, Danilo, the Park Manager, Mônica, people of the place. Source: Sena, 2019 [29].

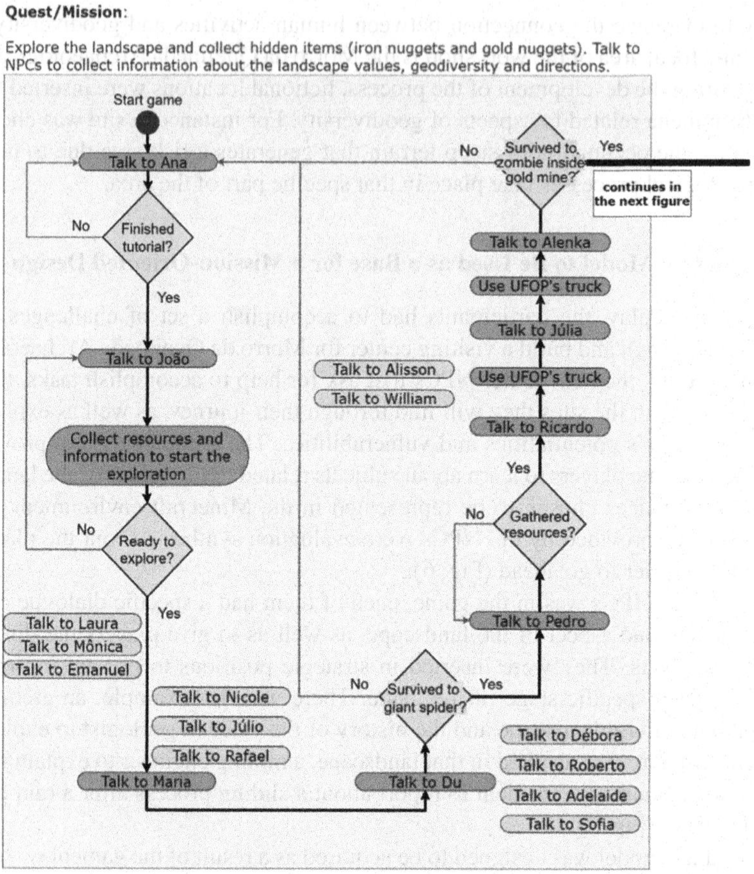

Fig. 7. Activity diagram of the first portion of the gameplay process. Green NPCs are linked to the main storyline. Light orange NPCs are secondary characters that give extra information and context. (Color figure online) Source: Created by the authors.

3.3 Post-workshop Assessment

The Impact model was created by assessing players' designs after the workshop. In this stage, the participants are not involved in the process. In combination with the proposed designs, each participant was assessed concerning their previous mental map of the landscape. This process aimed to assess the participant's perception of landscape values before and after the workshop.

One of the goals was to measure the spatial impacts generated by the players (the location of the proposed building), but also to measure the transformative learning of taking part in the experience. The locational assertiveness was analyzed by comparing the position of the buildings to the evaluation model of the area, verifying if the proposals were the within the suggested spots and if they considered the information provided by the NPCs about materials, the interventions on the field of view from the park, the risk areas and so on. The transformative learning was measured by applying questionnaires before

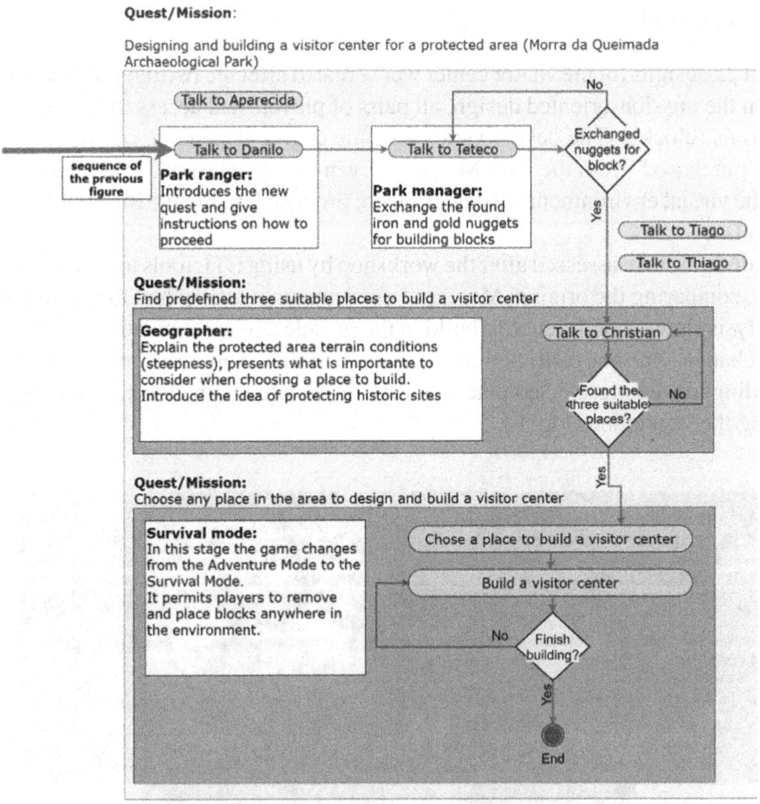

Fig. 8. Active diagram of the second portion of the gameplay process. It represents the stage when the change model is created. Source: Created by the authors.

and after the workshop, to know how much they care about the values of geodiversity before and after the experience. Together with the questionnaires, they were asked to draw the Serra de Ouro Preto area and its cultural landscape, also before and after the workshop. In the same drawing, they could add additional elements using different colors so that the organizers could evaluate the increment in information, spatial references, the score of elements represented, emphases on themes, and so on.

4 Results

The workshop took place over two days (the 6th and 7th of July), each day with one session of gameplay for kids from two neighborhoods of Ouro Preto. The invitation to play the game was made through the official program of Ouro Preto's Winter Festival of 2019. A total of 39 kids participated in the process, which was divided into two workshop sessions.

4.1 Change Model

A total of 22 designs for the visitor center were created after the two days of the workshop. Based on the mission-oriented design, all pairs of players had access to the same variety of materials (blocks). The design varies to some degree depending on which materials players 'purchased' from the Park Manager. Even though players could interfere in any part of the virtual environment, all designs were proposed within the Morro da Queimada Park limits.

The designs were assessed after the workshop by using ETL tools to perform a change analysis, comparing the original Minecraft environment with each of the modified ones. The analysis shows a preference to build in the preselected areas mentioned by the NPC, but the changes are not restricted to these spots only. There are some changes in the surroundings of the preselected places, mainly associated with changes in the terrain or removing the vegetation (Fig. 9).

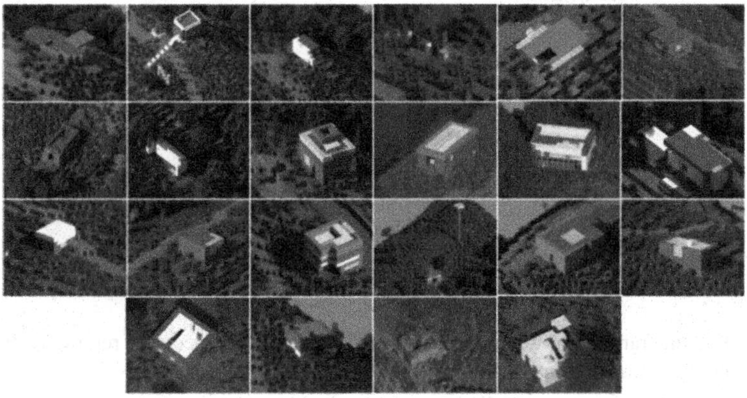

Fig. 9. Change model. Visitor center designs proposed by the players. Source: Created by the authors.

4.2 Impact Model

The impact model was created by extracting data from the game environment and comparing it to the original environment. The main principle used in this approach was to subtract the original Minecraft world from the modified one. Two types of analysis were performed from the retrieved data, one concerning the location of the design proposal and one concerning its size and components.

For the first analysis, all the designs were transformed from a Minecraft world file to a CSV file with columns for each block location and its properties (type of block). From this data, we performed a density analysis, which shows that all the designs were located within the limits of Morro da Queimada Archaeological Park (Fig. 10).

The second analysis focused on the type of material and the size of the design. The total of blocks used for each design proposal was counted to calculate the average size of the designs, which was 214 m^3. The most common blocks used by the players to design their visitor center were blocks of bricks (1089 in total), blocks of glass (465), wood plank blocks (450), and stone slabs (398). Blocks of bricks were put in the game as a product from the tailings dam, which is one of the visited places during the exploration. Glass blocks were used in almost all projects as windows or for detailing viewing spots or balconies, which shows some relationship between landscape visibility in the proposals. More than 5 billion blocks were analyzed to extract those metrics, considering all the Minecraft worlds generated after the workshop.

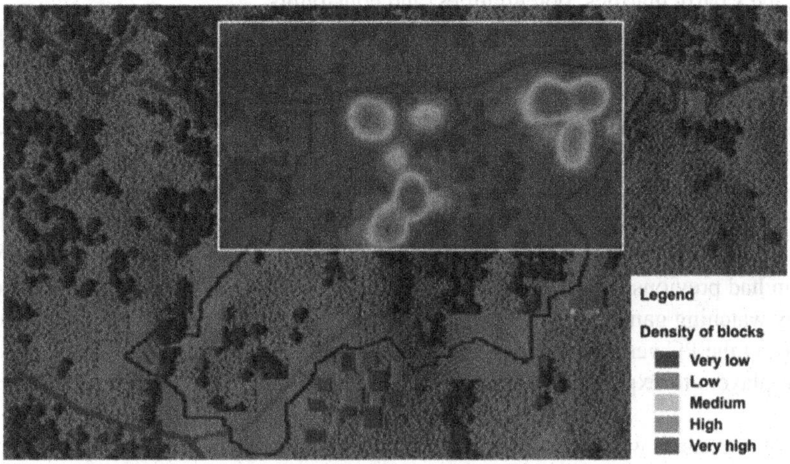

Fig. 10. Impact model. Analysis of the location of all designs. Source: Created by the authors.

5 Discussions

The case study was an example of the possibility of applying the geodesign framework to different digital media and different audiences. As the goal was to work with young people of the place, digital natives, it was selected a digital platform that is already used by them, to apply a shared language. The experiment took advantage of the immersive technologies and innovative ways to present spatial data to the general public. The goal was to support a transformative learning process, in which the participants could receive additional and organized information about their place, and were asked to use this information to design changes with and for the geography.

The participants in the GeoMinasCraft workshops are residents of Serra de Ouro Preto, with the image of Pico do Itacolomi in their daily field of vision. The mountain range is a traveled territory and not a contemplated landscape. Thus, the landscape of Serra de Ouro Preto, for some, is represented from the field of view that one has from the mountain, and not the visualization of the mountain itself, evidencing that for certain players the construction of the image is linked to landmarks. perceptible geographic features from the field of view favored by the lived space [30] (Fig. 9).

Through the designed gameplay and the stages that the participants had to complete, the Minecraft environment and its mechanics were employed to support the mission-oriented approach of the workshop. It enabled the creation of a target or main objective by the end of the process.

Limitations observed in the experiment are mostly related to representing specific aspects of the landscape and enabling design decisions (level of detail). The presented workshop shows that digital natives can perceive and communicate their thoughts through the game. On the other hand, the seriousness of the process stays on the second level of importance, since the aim was to support the learning about the cultural landscape's particularities, potentialities, and constraints.

The language used for the construction of the dialogues was adapted to favor the interpretation. The written text and the selection of key elements of the landscape presented to them were composed in capital letters, to draw the player's attention to specific textual elements. However, younger players with reading skills still in development faced some difficulties in performing the tasks given by the game, which made the monitors perform the reading of the dialogues and help them to interpret what the game asked for. Some other participants struggled to interact with the environment the fact of experiencing the game for the very first time using a keyboard and mouse as a user interface. Most of them had previous experience with Minecraft by playing the mobile edition or even only by watching gameplay videos on YouTube. These constraints can be overcome by converting the PC version of the game to the mobile version. It would make it possible for the players to experience the game outside, while they can walk through the real space.

Future research will focus on implementing the next stages of the geodesign framework, as well as improving the activity of designing and negotiation. For the presented workshop the participants were not able to visualize the Impact Model (done after the meeting by the coordinator), nor proceed with a voting/ranking stage about the best proposals. The results were composed of several ideas created in pairs or groups of participants, but they were constructed in parallel and not in a co-creation process. It is possible to use Minecraft to have a co-creation activity, by structuring an online server in which players can log in together and collectively visualize and decide about the Change Model, and negotiate towards a Decision Model. These are the future goals to be developed.

Acknowledgments. The authors thank CNPq support through the project 401066/2016-9, as well as FAPEMIG project PPM-00368-18, and CAPES support through the Overseas Sandwich Doctoral Program, under the grant process 88881.189217/2018-1.

References

1. Goodchild, M.F.: Citizens as sensors: the world of volunteered geography. GeoJournal **69**, 211–221 (2007). https://doi.org/10.1007/s10708-007-9111-y
2. Carrol, A.: Volunteered national geographic information? In: Workshop on Volunteered National Geographic Information, Santa Barbara, California, USA (2007)
3. Maguire, D.J.: GeoWeb 2.0 and volunteered GI. In: Workshop on Volunteered National Geographic Information, Santa Barbara, California, USA (2007)

4. Davis Jr., C.A., Moro, M.M., Matevelli, G.V., Machado, N.G.: ContribuiçõesVoluntárias: Impactos Potenciais dos Cidadãos Online e seus Dispositivos Móveis. In: Moura, A.C.M. (Org.). Tecnologias de Geoinformação para Representar e Planejar o Território Urbano. 1 edn, pp. 23–34. Editora Interciência, Rio de Janeiro (RJ) (2016)
5. Elwood, S.A.: Beyond cooptation or resistance: urban spatial politics, community organizations, and GIS-based spatial narratives. Ann. Assoc. Am. Geogr. **96**(2), 323–341 (2006)
6. Sieber, R.: Public participation geographic information systems: a literature review and framework. Ann. Assoc. Am. Geogr. **96**(3), 491–507 (2006)
7. Balram, S.; Dragicevic, S.: Collaborative Geographic Information Systems: Origins, Boundaries, and Structure. Idea Group Publishing, Hershey (2006)
8. Elmes, G., et al.: Local knowledge doesn't grow on trees. In: Fisher, P.F. (ed.) Advances in Spatial Data Handling, pp. 29–40. Springer, Heidelberg (2004). https://doi.org/10.1007/3-540-26772-7_3
9. Groot, R.: Spatial data infrastructure (SDI) for sustainable land management. ITC J. (3/4), 287–294 (1997)
10. Council and the European Parliament: Directive 2007/2/EC
11. Brasil, Presidência da República, Casa Civil, Subchefia para Assuntos Jurídicos. Decreto Nº 6.666 de 27/11/2008
12. Zhou, M., Nemes, L., Reidsema, C., Ahmed, A., Kayis, B.: Tolls and methods for risk management in multi-site engineering projects. In.: Arai, E., Kimura, F.; Goossenaerts, J.; Shirase, K. (eds.) DIISM 2002. IFIP, vol. 168, pp. 217–224. Springer, Boston (2002). https://doi.org/10.1007/0-387-23852-2_25
13. Li, N., Ervin, S., Flaxman, M., Goodchild, M.: Design and application of an ontology for geodesign. Revue Internationale de Géomatique **22**(2), 145–168 (2012)
14. Steinitz, C.: A Framework for Geodesign: Changing Geography by Design. ESRI Press, Redlands (2012)
15. Prensky, M.: Digital natives, digital immigrants, Part I. Horizon **9**, 1–6 (2001). https://doi.org/10.1108/10748120110424816
16. Prensky, M.: Digital natives, digital immigrants, part II: do they really think differently? Horizon **9**, 1–9 (2001)
17. Warren, T.: Minecraft still incredibly popular as sales top 200 million and 126 million play monthly. https://www.theverge.com/2020/5/18/21262045/minecraft-sales-monthly-players-statistics-youtube. Accessed 29 June 2020
18. Dangermond, J.: GIS: Designing our Future. ArcNews, Summer (2009)
19. Ervin, S.: A System for Geodesign. Keynote, pp. 158–167 (2011). Abstract
20. Miller, W.R.: Introducing Geodesign: The Concept. Esri Press, Redlands (2012)
21. Flaxman, M.: Fundamentals of Geodesign. Peer-Reviewed Proceedings of Digital Landscape Architecture 2010 at Anhalt University of Applied Sciences (2010)
22. Scholten, H., et al.: Geocraftas a means to support the development of smart cities, getting the people of the place involved - youth included. Qual. Innov. Prosper. **21**, 119 (2017). https://doi.org/10.12776/qip.v21i1.784
23. de Andrade, B.A., Poplin, A., de Sena, Í.S.: Minecraft as a tool for engaging children in urban planning: a case study in Tirol Town, Brazil. ISPRS Int. J. Geo-Inf. **9**, 170 (2020). https://doi.org/10.3390/ijgi9030170
24. Elmerghany, A.H., Paulus, G.: Using minecraft as a geodesign tool for encouraging public participation in urban planning. GI_Forum **1**, 300–314 (2017). https://doi.org/10.1553/giscience2017_01_s300

25. Opmeer, M., Dias, E., de Vogel, B., Tangerman, L., Scholten, H.J.: Minecraft in support of teaching sustainable spatial planning in secondary education - lessons learned from the Marker Wadden-project. In: Proceedings of the 10th International Conference on Computer Supported Education, pp. 316–321. SCITEPRESS - Science and Technology Publications (2018). https://doi.org/10.5220/0006764403160321
26. UN-Habitat: The Block by Block Playbook: Using Minecraft as a Participatory Design Tool in Urban Design and Governance (2021)
27. de Sena, Í.S., Poplin, A., de Andrade, B.: GeoMinasCraft: a serious geogame for geographical visualization and exploration. In: Geertman, S.C.M., Pettit, C., Goodspeed, R., Staffans, A. (eds.) Urban Informatics and Future Cities. TUBS, pp. 613–632. Springer, Cham (2021). https://doi.org/10.1007/978-3-030-76059-5_30
28. Gilbert, B.: Insider Newsletters, 14 September 2019. https://www.businessinsider.com/minecraft-monthly-player-number-microsoft-2019-9
29. Sena, I.S.: Visualização e valorização da paisagem a partir de geogame. Ph.D. thesis. Supervisor: Moura, Ana Clara M. Federal University of Minas Gerais, Geoscience Institute, Brazil (2019)
30. Lynch, K.: The Image of the City. MIT Press, Cambridge (1960)

International Workshop on Geomatics in Agriculture and Forestry: New Advances and Perspectives (GeoForAgr 2022)

A Web-Based Dashboard for Estimating the Economic and Ecological Impacts of Land Use Class Changes for Key Land Patches

Alper Bayram[1,2(✉)] and Antonino Marvuglia[1]

[1] Luxembourg Institute of Science and Technology (LIST), Esch-sur-Alzette, Luxembourg
alper.bayram@list.lu

[2] Computational Sciences, Faculty of Science, Technology and Medicine, University of Luxembourg, Esch-sur-Alzette, Luxembourg

Abstract. The increasing pressure on land coming from the raising needs of a fast-growing population puts public and private landowners and decision makers in front of difficult choices concerning the best use of limited land resources. On one hand, agricultural land and grassland need to be used to support human food requirements. On the other hand, these land uses create trade-offs with other ecosystem functions, assets and services, such as ecological connectivity, biodiversity and natural habitat maintenance. In this paper a prototype web-based dashboard is presented, that aims at allowing a fully-fledged calculation of the economic and environmental trade-offs between different land uses of any land patch (excluding urban areas and infrastructures) and in the Grand Duchy of Luxembourg. An agent-based model (ABM) coupled with life-cycle assessment (LCA) runs on the background of the dashboard. The coupled model allows the simulation of the farm business and the calculation of the revenues made by farmers in every land patch under different farm management scenarios. Crossing the information coming from the model with other tools would also allow to integrate local environmental trade-offs, such as degradation of local habitats or ecological connectivity, and not only global ones defined in a non-spatialized way. The dashboard has a potentially high value to inform policy, strategies, or specific actions (e.g., environmental stewardship programs that integrate economic convenience as a condition) and has the necessary flexibility to integrate new aspects related to territorial analyses as they become available.

Keywords: Visualization tools · Farmland · Agent-based modelling · Life cycle assessment · Decision-making · Natural capital

1 Introduction

Land is a limited resource and as such its use generates trade-off choices for landowners and public authorities who have the responsibility to incentivize and support certain land use choices over others. In this framework, simulation and visualization tools can help stakeholders to understand the possible outcomes of different strategies and select suitable alternatives.

O. Gervasi et al. (Eds.): ICCSA 2022 Workshops, LNCS 13379, pp. 281–293, 2022.
https://doi.org/10.1007/978-3-031-10545-6_20

Although intense research has been carried out and major developments have been achieved in the assessment of the impact of production systems on the environment, the complexity of the models calls for a growing need for software with user-friendly interfaces and visualization capabilities to present the results of the simulations [1]. The final impact of a project relies heavily on the easiness of communication and the accessibility and usability of its results by the target audience and relevant stakeholders.

In the case of complex systems, evaluation of different scenarios is naturally a difficult task due to existence of large amount of simulation outputs. A pre-defined set of performance metrics and a dashboard that summarizes and visualizes them can help users to draw meaningful conclusions and comparisons between scenarios. However, as it is the case for most complex systems, the analysis and visualization of simulation outcomes require a combination of data analysis methods. From the experience of the authors, building a single tool to analyze large amounts of data that includes geospatial information, network analysis, sustainability assessment indicators and financial performance, is a nonnegligible effort, but can significantly help the recipients of a final research product, whether they are researchers or not. With such a tool can be possible to achieve the important task of clarifying the model goals and parameters for people who are not involved in the modeling process task. Furthermore, comparison of different scenarios and effect of changing parameters can aid users in the decision-making process.

As suggested in modern sustainability research, when dealing with human-environment interaction a trans-disciplinary approach is required [2]. To study coupled human-natural systems, agent-based modelling has been gradually accepted as a useful modelling technique [3]. Agents are defined as autonomous entities that react to the stimuli coming from the environment and interact with one another under certain rules that are imposed by the modeler and normally defined after consultation with domain experts and stakeholders. Each of them has an objective that can be defined as optimizing the societal or individual benefit. They are capable of learning, adapting, and changing their behaviors, which end up steering their actions.

In this paper we present the first prototype of a web-based dashboard that estimates the revenue and environmental impacts that a farmer can expect applying a certain management scenario on his/her farm. The environmental impacts are calculated making use of life cycle assessment (LCA) and represent lifecycle-based (not just local) global impacts generated by the farm. Both can then be apportioned to each land patch using a given weighting procedure. Once the revenues and non-local environmental impacts are estimated and mapped, they can be overlaid onto other maps representing outputs of local analysis (e.g., habitat value, ecological connectivity, risk of soil erosion). These latter inform on the local environmental value of the land, complementing the lifecycle-based environmental assessment. The dashboard, together with local environmental analysis, would support a better-informed management of any land plot, based on the positive and negative environmental and economic outcomes of different land uses.

The calculation of the revenues and the environmental impacts is carried out using an agent-based model (ABM) of the farming system (which includes mixed farms, dealing with crops, meat and milk at the same time) coupled with an LCA calculation run on the background of the dashboard which is then used to display pre-calculated results. Future developments incorporating local environmental analysis (e.g., ecological connectivity analysis) will inform about local environmental values of the land patches using indicators and tools such as landscape metrics, connectivity indices, circuit-theory models. The maps thus generated can be easily loaded into the dashboard as it can handle georeferenced files.

In the paper, visualization techniques and technologies behind the prototype are first discussed. The prototype that shows the results from our selected case study is then presented and planned future development are outlined.

2 The Dashboard

The dashboard is created using Django web-framework and its structure is depicted in Fig. 1. It allows to run computations in the backend using other Python libraries that are already integrated into our simulation pipeline. Based on the feedback from project partners and reviewed literature, the dashboard was designed using the components depicted in Fig. 1. The data is stored using PostGIS which has the ability to manage Geographical Information System (GIS) and numerical data in one database. The PostGIS application is available in a docker container to make it compatible for different operating systems. Thanks to Django, we access the database and manipulate the tables with Python's powerful libraries. In the front-end, JavaScript allows to use interactive visualization tools to better investigate the simulation results, as well as the static properties of the farms. The dashboard can currently be used on the most common web browsers (Chrome, Firefox, Safari etc.). All the code is stored in Git and can be accessed by other contributors within the project team which allows further collaboration. The dashboard aims to provide user-friendly insights for farmers, advisors, agencies, and public administrations in terms of agricultural and financial sustainability. Although the development has been made mainly on a web-based portal, a mobile-based application

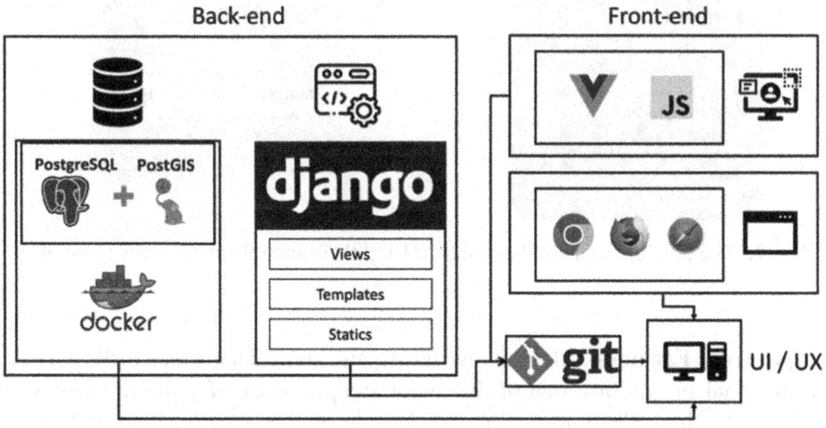

Fig. 1. The back-end/front-end structure of the dashboard.

would be necessary for farmers to make the interaction effortless. It may also be possible to allow other researchers to access the dashboard via application programming interfaces (APIs) when they want to conduct their own research.

The Two-Way Communication Between Farmers and Organizations. In our platform the farmer is the main entity and the agencies will be able to access the farmer's data as long as it is allowed by the farmer. Depending on the nature of their relationship, the agency for example can give recommendations (in case of a consultant) or send reminders (in case of a public agency). The agency will have another version of the dashboard that is suitable for its purposes. Figure 2 shows the different levels of possible users of the dashboard and their motivations to use it.

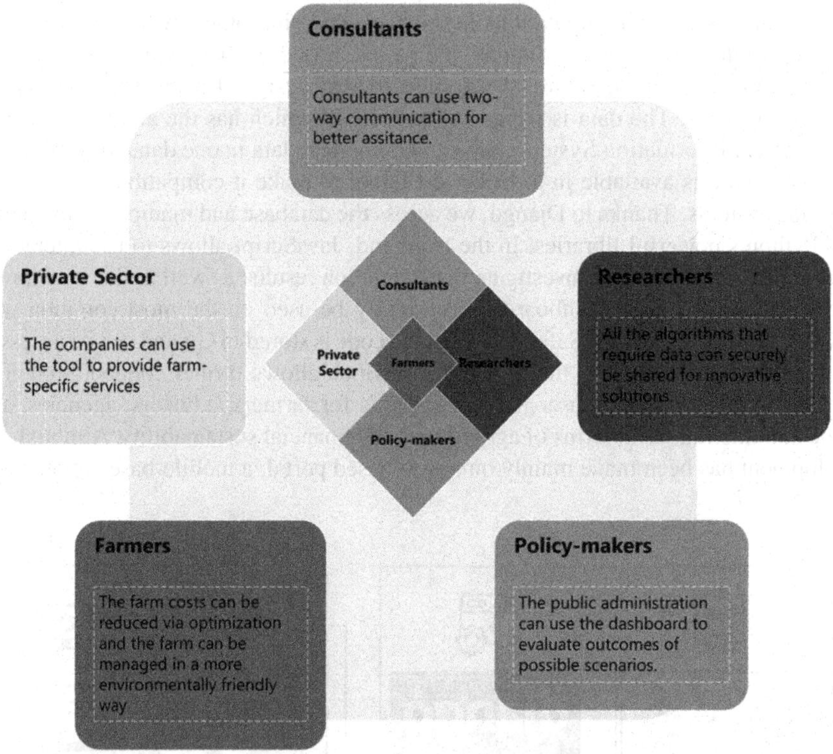

Fig. 2. The possible users of the dashboard and their possible motivations to use it.

The Input from Farmers. Although we mostly use static data, which is the data available in national inventories, one of the major steppingstones for future-work for our research can be the collection of data on a farm level. The classification of crop plantations from Sentinel imagery is possible thanks to computer vision algorithms [4], however the farmers still need to report the crop plantations to the agencies in Luxembourg. They are also required to fill out additional forms, such as grazing calendars, which would allow them to get subsidies. Our tool may allow seamless data-entry for the farmers. Apart from already required and usual data requests from agencies, farmers can choose to enter the real cost and production data to visualize and assess the business from the financial point-of-view. This can even be achieved utilizing the machinery or sensors around the farm, such as milking or feeding robots, wherever and whenever available. All these elements would result in a simplification of farmers' tasks and a fast reusability of up-to-date data.

The Fertilizer Usage and Nitrate Vulnerability. Most farmers are already aware of the nitrogen limits within and along the surroundings of their farms, however with the dashboard it is possible to show the nitrogen constraints on a map based on water body proximity. This information can help them stay below the imposed limits, thus qualifying to get subsidies. There are several subsidy programs in Luxembourg that are based on nitrogen constraints and the imposed thresholds change according to the proximity to ecological protection zones. Based on the provided algorithm for nitrogen excretion from livestock and fertilizer usage for crops, the farmers can see the already released and projected fertilizer input to the soil for a given period. It will also be possible to recommend optimum organic and inorganic fertilizer levels for each type of crop once the soil properties map is incorporated into the model.

The Weather and Climate Forecasts. This information is important for extensive farms, where the farmers let their animals graze outside, depending on the weather conditions. These forecasts can be combined with several other pieces of information such as current levels of soil moisture, grass height, barn temperature and air-quality. Some of these can be made available on the dashboard for the farms where required sensors are available. Figure 3 (left) shows the visualization of the weather forecast in the dashboard for a random commune.

Since the calculation of the revenues and the environmental impacts is based on an ABM, the mutual interactions of the agents are taken into account, as explained in [5].

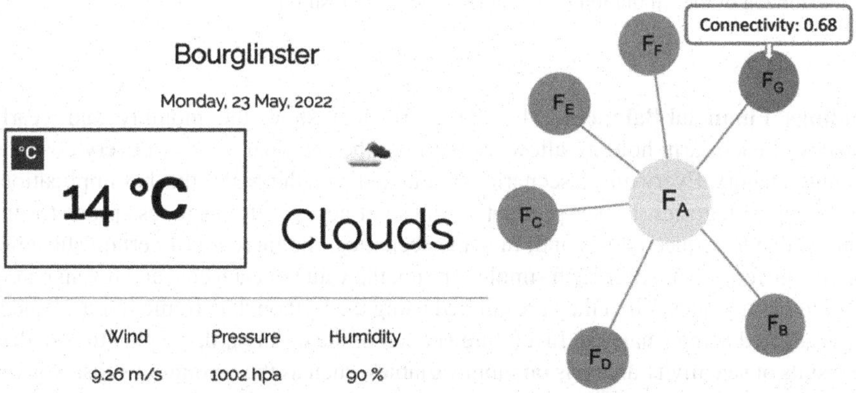

Fig. 3. (Left) The weather information for the farm's location. (Right) The connections of Farmer A (F_A).

Figure 3 (right) shows the visualization of the connection of a given farmer to the other agents in the network.

The Overview of Simulation Environment. The farmer agents act on the same fields throughout the simulations. This means that the farm and field boundaries do not change. The geospatial data that includes those boundaries is stored in a PostGIS database. It is read by GeoAlchemy2, Python object relational mapping (ORM) library for spatial databases, and then visualized with Folium, another Python library to create interactive maps. The users can interact with the map to see the crops planted and harvested in a given field throughout the simulation. Figure 4 shows a screenshot of the dashboard window where a selected farm and the life cycle impact assessment (LCIA) scores related to it can be visualized. Currently we are using the ReCiPe LCIA method [18] to calculate the impact scores, but any other existing method can be easily used in future updates of the tool. On the left-hand side of the figure one can see that each single field belonging to the farm (i.e., each polygon for which information is known at the cadaster level) is visualized.

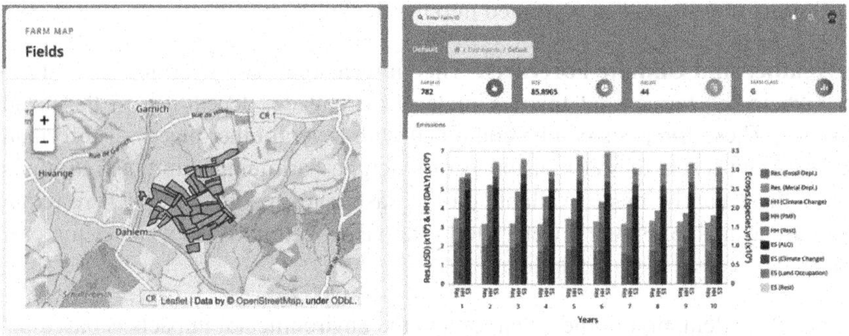

Fig. 4. (Left) The fields that belong to one farm. The user can interact with the map to visualize the field attributes. (Right) Life-cycle impact scores for a given farm in the span of 10 years (chosen as time horizon of the simulation to obtain pre-calculated results).

Holdings' Financial Balances. The 2D charts that show the monthly and yearly finances of each farm holding allow users to see the seasonal trends in every cost and revenue category. Every time a scenario is simulated with the ABM, this has implications on different categories. Lower production does not necessarily mean less profit for the farmers, due to reduced costs and, in some scenarios, the increase of certain subsidies from the government. After each simulation run, the value of each cost and revenue item is stored in CSV files. Then they are curated using the Python data frame library Pandas and visualized using Charts.js. In a future version of the dashboard, we plan to visualize the results of sensitivity analysis on input variables, such as the amount of subsidy given for a particular activity.

Life-Cycle Impact Assessment (LCIA) of Each Holding. The agricultural activities generate impacts that have short- and long-term effects on the environment that must be monitored carefully by every stakeholder in the sector if an emission reduction strategy is put in place. LCIA allows to quantify these impacts and take necessary actions to mitigate the emissions that are the reasons behind them. In our model, the Brightway2[1] LCA library is used. It was created to enable modelling functionalities that can go beyond traditional LCA software. In particular, using Brightway2 it is possible to seamlessly connect LCA calculations with other simulation engines (in this case the ABM). With Brigthway2 the so-called life cycle inventory (LCI) background data that reside in a LCI database can be recalled automatically and used (together with the foreground data that contains the crop and animal outputs) to calculate the LCIA scores during the simulations. Brightway2 is integrated in the dashboard, in a way that the users can select the impact assessment method they want to adopt for impacts calculations and the impact categories they want to monitor.

The Network of Agents. One of the crucial mechanisms in agent-based modelling is the interaction and information exchange between the agents. In our model, classes of agents were first created according to their risk aversion orientation and their geographical position, as described in [5]. The farmer agents that belong to the same risk aversion class or the ones who are geographical neighbors of one another are considered as connected in a network analysis sense. Each farmer and its connections are shown in a way that their attributes evolve over time (for instance age) and due to information exchange (e.g., environmental awareness).

Assessment of Finances and LCIs at Country-Level. Since each farmer agent acts upon the land belonging to its single farmland, this latter is the reference spatial unit we can assess in terms of economic value and environmental impact generated. However,

Fig. 5. The graph showing the trend of the net revenue of the farm over ten simulated years.

[1] https://brightway.dev/.

the policymakers have the interest to make assessments at regional level. Therefore, the dashboard allows to show the aggregated result scores as a drill-down weighted treemap with three levels, i.e., farm, commune and canton. The users can choose to visualize the farm outputs, revenues, costs or impact scores. Figure 5 shows a screenshot of the window used to visualize the net revenue of the farm over ten years as resulting from a pre-simulated scenario.

3 Case study: Farmland Revenue Generation and Impact Assessment

The dashboard prototype was used to visualize the results of a scenario which has the objective of reducing stocking rates (i.e., the density of animals per ha) throughout Luxembourgish farms. The scenario was simulated for a time span of 10 years with time steps of one month. The simulations are repeated 50 times and the results are averaged to consider the intrinsic variability induced by the random choice of certain parameters (such as behavioral attributes of a farmer, the allocation of fields of a farm, seeding and harvesting months of crops, etc.). The objective in this case study was to observe the change in the herd structure of the farms over time, and its simultaneous impact not just on the farm finances, but also on the environment. Reducing the stocking rates can help the agricultural sector to mitigate its greenhouse gas emissions. A reduction on stocking rate would be certainly pushed by a reduction of meat and dairy products' consumption coming from consumers due to change of their dietary habits. Less animals would mean less direct costs (like feed imports), as well as an improved soil quality. Within this context, certain subsidies are set for different levels of nitrogen input reduction in Luxembourg. At every year *n* of a simulation, an agent checks the nitrogen emissions into the soil caused by the herd at year *n-1*. If the objective level that was set based on the livestock unit area is exceed, then the agent chooses to get rid of the less efficient animals from the herd. Once this decision has been taken, the production of current year *n* is calculated and the corresponding revenue generation, as well as the emissions, are recorded. Afterwards, the selected animals are sent away from the herd (sold or slaughtered).

The emissions tab on the sidebar allows to see the evolution of the emissions throughout the simulation. If a farmer is logged in, the historical and simulated emissions are shown on the emissions tab; when the user is connected using administrative credentials, the country or regional level emissions are made available. In addition to monitoring the levels for whole country, we also use weighted treemaps [6], along with real maps of subregions, to see the impacts in more detail. In Fig. 6 (Right), impacts on human health (expressed in the unity DALY, which stands for *disability adjusted life years* [7]) generated by emissions due to crop and cattle farming are given per each canton of the country. The same representation is provided also as a treemap (Fig. 6 Left). The weighted treemap algorithm allows to represent the original polygons as rectangles, while respecting their boundary and topological relationships. As expected, the agricultural practices cause more emissions in northern Luxembourg than in the southern part of the country, since most farms are located in that region. The dashboard also includes the *drill-down* version of the weighted treemap, where the users can look at the treemap that is built based on a selected variable (i.e., size, production, number of livestock, impact score, revenue) in cantons' view at the highest level. By clicking on any canton, one can visualize the communes in that canton in a similar fashion. Finally, the farms in a selected commune can be visualized in the lowest level of the drill-down treemap. Figure 7 shows an example of drill-down treemap, that is built using the size of each region (canton, commune or farm). In this example, the user clicks on the canton of Esch-sur-Alzette canton and then on the commune of Pétange, to display the farms present in that area.

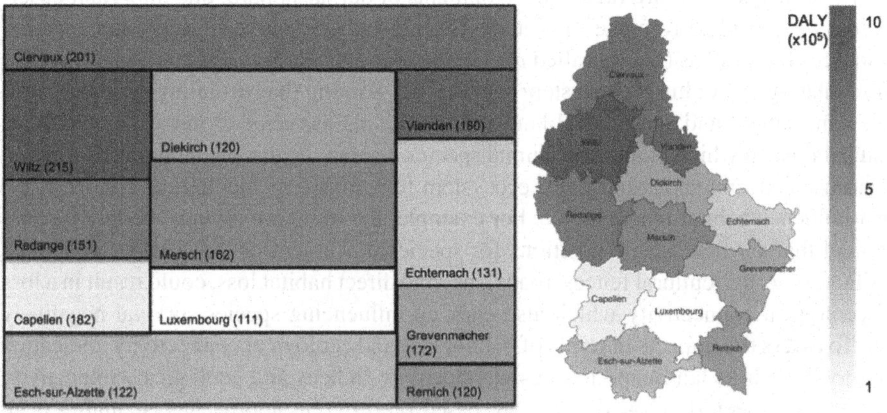

Fig. 6. Left: the weighted treemap that shows the average human health impact over 10 years of simulation and 50 different iterations. Right: the same information visualized as a traditional geographical map.

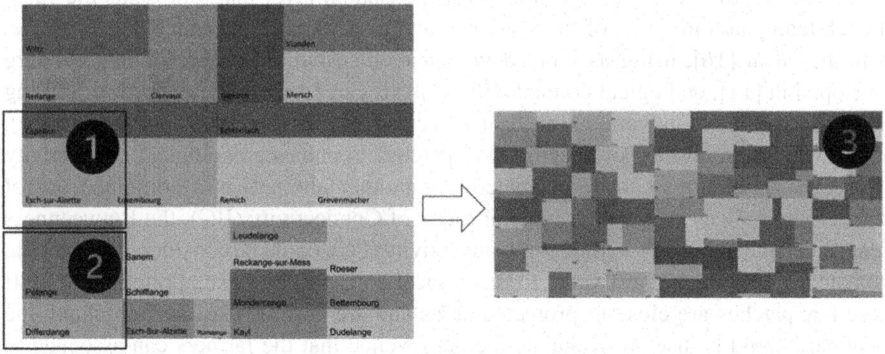

Fig. 7. The drill-down treemap implementation of geographical boundaries of Luxembourg.

4 Discussion and Conclusion

The paper presents the first prototype of a web-based dashboard that can be used to assess the economic and ecological impacts of land transformation. The direct economic value of the land patches used as cropland or pasture (i.e., the net revenue for the farmer, without considering the cost of environmental externalities) is pre-calculated using a hybrid ABM-LCA model that mimics the evolution of the Luxembourgish farming system under management scenarios that can be designed upstream. The hybrid model is also used to calculate the environmental impacts of each management scenario (which are then allocated to the single patches) using LCIA indicators [18].

Looking also at future further developments of our dashboard, one important observation we can already make is that land is not only a source of food and material resources for humans (the so-called *provisioning ecosystem services*); it is also a source of regulating and cultural ecosystem services [8]. Among the regulating services, natural, semi-natural and agricultural land support the maintenance of nursery populations and habitats on which plants and animal species depend. Anthropic land transformation (land use conversions) could harm ecosystem functions (e.g., ecological connectivity) that influence habitat maintenance. For example, the transformation of certain patches of land that are in strategic positions for species movement or the creation of human artifacts (e.g., agricultural fences, roads), beyond direct habitat loss, could result in a loss of ecological connectivity which also ends up influencing species survival negatively [9]. To assess the impacts in terms of habitat loss and ecological connectivity, indicators and tools such as landscape metrics, connectivity indices and ecological connectivity models have been developed. They are based on different approaches, spanning from least-cost path analysis [10], to circuit theory [11], matrix theory [12], agent-based or individual-based modelling [13], network analysis [14] and other techniques. A wider overview on ecological connectivity approaches and models can be found in [15].

Given the importance of these ecological functions of land, the next step we plan for the dashboard is the addition of a further geospatial layer that represents the value of each land patch in terms of their contribution to habitat maintenance. For example, as proposed in [16], using as input data species distribution models of Luxembourg developed in [17], ecological connectivity analysis can be easily developed, informing on referred routes of movement of certain species (e.g., endangered or protected ones). In this way the relevance of specific land patches to enhance ecological connectivity of species populations can be evaluated. As another alternative, a combined use of connectivity indices such as the Integral Index of Connectivity (IIC), the Betweenness Centrality (BC) and the Probability of Connectivity (PC), could be considered to estimate the patches with the highest value for ecological connectivity (also applied in [16]). If these key patches are close to protected areas and are currently used as cropland, the dashboard could be used to calculate the net revenue that the farmers can associate to those patches and therefore determine a value of a fair compensation that they should be granted if they are requested to hand over the ownership of those patches to the public administration that can then convert them into protected areas. We will therefore integrate the calculation of the value of each land patch from the habitat connectivity point of view, using landscape metrics and connectivity indices (for examples using tools such as Conefor [19] or Fragstats [20]). This will allow the identification of the most important patches that can then be selected as priority (key patches) to inform ecological planning or the definition of biodiversity action plans. When these key patches fall within existing farms (where they are used either as cropland or as pasture) the dashboard will then allow also to determine the expected monetary compensation that the farmers who own these patches should receive for the production capacity loss they would incur to reduce the pressure on the land (i.e., have a less intensive cultivation), if these patches become part of an environmental stewardship program to protect biodiversity and are therefore converted into protected areas.

Apart from technical perspectives and objectives of this tool, it is worth noting that the development procedure should be integrated with users' feedback along all the stages. That means working with agencies and farmers who understand the necessities of digitalization in agriculture and provide valuable feedback. Understanding the needs of farmers from different ages and whose farms differ in size helps building a helpful tool that reflects the characteristics of the farm system of the given territory. Moreover, the agencies that would be using this tool may decide on what to emphasize or communicate strongly to the farmers via this tool during the development phase which would possibly increase their motivation.

Acknowledgements. This research was funded by Luxembourg National Research Fund (FNR) under the project SIMBA—Simulating economic and environmental impacts of dairy cattle management using Agent Based Models (Grant INTER-FNRS/18/12987586). The authors wish to thank Javier Babi Almenar for the fruitful and very inspiring discussion on the future developments of the dashboard.

References

1. Cardinot, M., O'Riordan, C., Griffith, J., Perc, M.: Evoplex: a platform for agent-based modeling on networks. SoftwareX **9**, 199–204 (2019). https://doi.org/10.1016/j.softx.2019.02.009
2. Popa, F., Guillermin, M., Dedeurwaerdere, T.: A pragmatist approach to transdisciplinarity in sustainability research: from complex systems theory to reflexive science. Futures **65**, 45–56 (2015). https://doi.org/10.1016/j.futures.2014.02.002
3. Rounsevell, M.D.A., Robinson, D.T., Murray-Rust, D.: From actors to agents in socio-ecological systems models. Philos. Trans. Roy. Soc. B: Biol. Sci. **367**(1586), 259–269 (2012). https://doi.org/10.1098/rstb.2011.0187
4. Immitzer, M., Vuolo, F., Atzberger, C.: First experience with Sentinel-2 data for crop and tree species classifications in central Europe. Remote Sens. **8**(3), Art. no. 3, Mar. (2016). https://doi.org/10.3390/rs8030166
5. Marvuglia, A., Bayram, A., Baustert, P., Gutiérrez, T.N., Igos, E.: Agent-based modelling to simulate farmers' sustainable decisions: farmers' interaction and resulting green consciousness evolution. J. Clean. Prod. **332**, 129847 (2022). https://doi.org/10.1016/j.jclepro.2021.129847
6. Ghoniem, M., Cornil, M., Broeksema, B., Stefas, M., Otjacques, B.: Weighted maps: treemap visualization of geolocated quantitative data. In: Visualization and Data Analysis 2015, vol. 9397, pp. 163–177 (2015)

7. Kobayashi, Y., Peters, G.M., Ashbolt, N.J., Shiels, S., Khan, S.J.: Assessing burden of disease as disability adjusted life years in life cycle assessment. Sci. Total Environ. **530–531**, 120–128 (2015). https://doi.org/10.1016/j.scitotenv.2015.05.017
8. Haines-Young, R., Potschin, M.B.: Common International Classification of Ecosystem Services (CICES) V5.1 and Guidance on the Application of the Revised Structure (2018). www.cices.eu
9. Edelsparre, A.H., Shahid, A., Fitzpatrick, M.J.: Habitat connectivity is determined by the scale of habitat loss and dispersal strategy. Ecol. Evol. **8**(11), 5508–5514 (2018). https://doi.org/10.1002/ece3.4072
10. Douglas, D.H.: Least-cost path in GIS using an accumulated cost surface and slopelines. Cartographica: Int. J. Geographic Inf. Geovisualization, **31**(3), 37–51 (1994)
11. McRae, B.H., Dickson, B.G., Keitt, T.H., Shah, V.B.: Using circuit theory to model connectivity in ecology, evolution, and conservation. Ecology **89**(10), 2712–2724 (2008). https://doi.org/10.1890/07-1861.1
12. Caswell, H.: Matrix Population Models: Construction, Analysis, and Interpretation. Sinauer Associates, Sunderland, Masssachusetts (2001)
13. Allen, C.H., Parrott, L., Kyle, C.: An individual-based modelling approach to estimate landscape connectivity for bighorn sheep (Ovis canadensis). PeerJ **4**, e2001 (2016). https://doi.org/10.7717/peerj.2001
14. Pereira, J., Saura, S., Jordán, F.: Single-node vs. multi-node centrality in landscape graph analysis: key habitat patches and their protection for 20 bird species in NE Spain. Methods Ecol. Evol. **8**(11), 1458–1467 (2017). https://doi.org/10.1111/2041-210X.12783
15. Kool, J.T., Moilanen, A., Treml, E.A.: Population connectivity: recent advances and new perspectives. Landscape Ecol. **28**(2), 165–185 (2013). https://doi.org/10.1007/s10980-012-9819-z
16. Almenar, J.B., Bolowich, A., Elliot, T., Geneletti, D., Sonnemann, G., Rugani, B.: Assessing habitat loss, fragmentation and ecological connectivity in Luxembourg to support spatial planning. Landsc. Urban Plan. **189**, 335–351 (2019). https://doi.org/10.1016/j.landurbplan.2019.05.004
17. Titeux, N., Mestdagh, X., Cantú-Salazar, L.: Reporting under Article 17 of the Habitats Directive in Luxembourg (2007–2012): conservation status of species listed in Annexes II, IV and V of the European Council Directive on the Conservation of Habitats, Flora and Fauna (92/43/EEC). Centre de Recherche Public – Gabriel Lippman (2013)
18. Huijbregts, M.A.J., et al.: ReCiPe 2016. A harmonized life cycle impact assessment method at midpoint and endpoint level. Report I: Characterization. RIVM, Bilthoven, The Netherlands, Report 2016–0104 (2016)
19. Saura, S., Torné, J.: Conefor Sensinode 2.2: a software package for quantifying the importance of habitat patches for landscape connectivity. Environ. Model. Softw. **24**(1), 135–139 (2009). https://doi.org/10.1016/j.envsoft.2008.05.005
20. McGarigal, K., Marks, B.: FRAGSTATS: spatial pattern analysis program for quantifying landscape structure. U.S. Department of Agriculture, Forest Service, Pacific Northwest Research Station, Portland, OR, Generation Technical report PNW-GTR-351 (1995)

An Analysis of the Use of Hyperspectral Data for Roundwood Tracking

Georg Wimmer[1(✉)], Rudolf Schraml[1], Heinz Hofbauer[1], Alexander Petutschnigg[2], and Andreas Uhl[1]

[1] University of Salzburg, Jakob-Haringer-Strasse 2, 5020 Salzburg, Austria
{gwimmer,hofbauer,uhl}@cs.sbg.ac.at, rudolf.schraml@sbg.ac.at
[2] University of Applied Sciences Salzburg, Markt 136a, 5431 Kuchl, Austria
alexander.petutschnigg@fh-salzburg.ac.at

Abstract. Traceability of round wood from the forest to the industry is a crucial issue to secure sustainable material usage as well as to optimize and control processes over the whole supply chain. There are previous works on individual wood log tracing but there is no systematic and complete technology to track individual logs from the forest to the industry. In this work we analyze if it is beneficial to employ hyperspectral image data from log ends instead of image data from standard RGB cameras.

First, we compare the hyperspectral log image data across the spectral range using various well known image descriptors. In that way we analyze differences in the image data across the spectral range and find out which spectral ranges are best suited for log tracking. In a further step we present a novel approach to combine information across different spectra in order to gain valuable additional information on the annual ring pattern, the most important feature for log tracking.

We will show that there are clear differences of the log images at different spectra and that our proposed approach to combine the information of log images at different spectra provides a clearly better visibility of the annual ring pattern than single spectral images and also common RGB images.

Keywords: Roundwood tracking · Hyperspectral imaging

1 Introduction

Traceability of roundwood from the forest to further processing companies is a recent topic of research, as customers are getting more interested in the origin of their products. This led to certificates like the one of the Forest Stewardship Council [9] or the program for the Endorsement of Forest Certification [14] that are documenting the sustainable production of wood. Even more legal actions and agreements like the European timber regulation EUTR No. 995 2010 [7]

This project was partly funded by the Austrian Science Fund (FWF) under Project Number I 3653.

O. Gervasi et al. (Eds.): ICCSA 2022 Workshops, LNCS 13379, pp. 294–307, 2022.
https://doi.org/10.1007/978-3-031-10545-6_21

were developed. This was done to claim disclosure of the provenance of timber and timber products that are placed on the European market in order to stop illegal deforestation and trading of timber.

This topic is in the view of recent research all over the world and even scientific hackathons are organized (e.g. the Evergreen innovation camp 2019 in Vienna [8]) to solve the question of traceability of wood from the forest to the related industry. Common methods for log tracing are the application of barcodes and the usage of radio frequency identification (RFID) transponders (e.g. [22] or [1]). However, these tracking systems are only used for relatively high priced lumber up to now since they require physical markings of each tree which is expensive. An alternative to physical marking is to use biometric characteristics from log images to recognize each individual log as shown in [17,19–21,23,24]. The usage of log image characteristics for tracking logs is not a new idea. E.g. in [5] and [6], surface properties of wood logs were used for identification.

Hyperspectral images contain not only the visible spectra, but depending on the technology also parts of the ultraviolet (UV)-spectra and near infrared (NIR) spectra. Hence, this imaging technology has good chances to improve wood log tracking compared to common RGB images. The usage of hyperspectral imaging technologies ranges from large scale imaging down to lab scale sensors used in food safety, pharmaceutical applications forensic etc. (examples are shown in [2] or [15]) and therefore is very common in use. Hyperspectral images have already been employed to determine the transition between juvenile and mature wood [16] and to predict the moisture content of wood [4]. In [18], hyperspectral log images were analyzed for the use of log tracking. Using an approach developed for fingerprint tracking based on Gabor filters, hyperspectral images of logs at different spectra were compared in order to find out which spectra contain the same or different information than other spectra. This knowledge can be used to reduce the technical efforts and expenses for the collection of log image data and to improve image acquisition.

So, in [18] one concrete method was employed to compare the images at different spectra. In this work we employ several well known methods, all analyzing different image properties, to compare log images at different spectra. In that way we aim to find out what are the specific differences of images at different spectra.

The annual ring pattern is arguably the most important feature for log tracking using log end images, since it provides information about the shape of the tree cross section over the entire lifespan of the tree (the annual rings) and also the growth of the tree per year (annual ring thickness). Other features like wood coloration, knots and the saw cut pattern that are visible in the log cross section may totally change if a log is capped. Therefore, we run experiments to compare the visibility of the annual ring pattern between spectral log images and common RGB log images to find out if hyperspectral images are really better suited for log tracking than common RGB images.

So far no attempt has been made to combine information on log images across different spectra. In this work, we propose an approach to construct a new log

(a) Scanning system (b) Wood disc storage (c) Hyperspectral cube cropping

Fig. 1. The sensor system shows the line scanner which was mounted on a metal frame and the slice is moved perpendicular to the scanned line manually. The stored samples were closed airtight to avoid surface changes. Each hyperspectral cube was cropped to reduce the massive amount of data.

image by combining the information on the annual ring pattern from images of the same log at different spectra.

2 Materials

2.1 Wood Samples

Initially, 100 different Norway (*Picea Abies*) spruce logs (4.5 m length) were collected. For the experiments in this paper, a wood disc was cut from the lower end of each log. The outside of each disc was sanded to reduce the influence of manual chainsaw cuts at scanning. To avoid surface cracks due to wood shrinkage and discoloration due to oxidation processes, the slices were packed individually in plastic bags during transport and intermediate storage.

2.2 Scanning System

The samples were scanned using a FX17 multispectral line scanner, which provides scans between 990 nm to 1665 nm with a bandwidth of approx. 3 nm. The Specim FX17 uses mainly parts of the NIR spectra. For the scanning setup a resolution of 640×640 pixel was chosen. The scanning system is shown in Fig. 1. Halogen light was used for lighting. Each disc was pushed through the system by hand and the speed was synchronized with a trigger. The hyperspectral data, i.e. the translation from line scanning data to a hyperspectral cube, was performed by the acquisition software Perception Studio. For each hyperspectral cube the grayscale images (PNG) for each band were extracted and show the cross section (CS) of the disc. This results in 196 images per wood disc. This conversion enables to apply standard image processing algorithms. From 13 discs, image data was lost during acquisition and so hyperspectral data is only available from 87 discs. Unfortunately, the obtained spectral images from the FX17 scanner are a bit squeezed in height. This can be observed by comparing the spectral

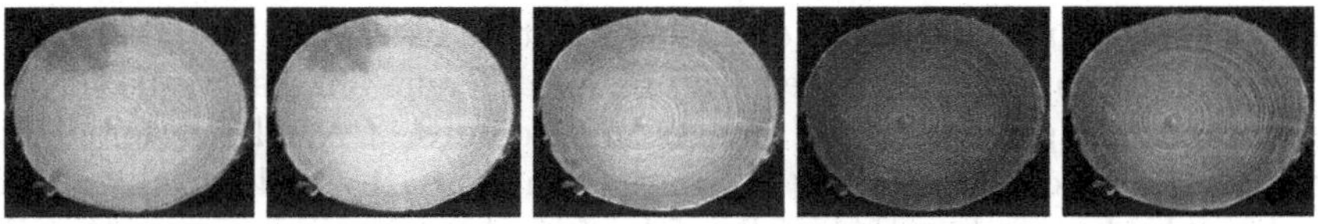

(a) 995nm (b) 1111nm (c) 1300nm (d) 1450nm (e) 1665nm

Fig. 2. Images of the same disc at different spectra.

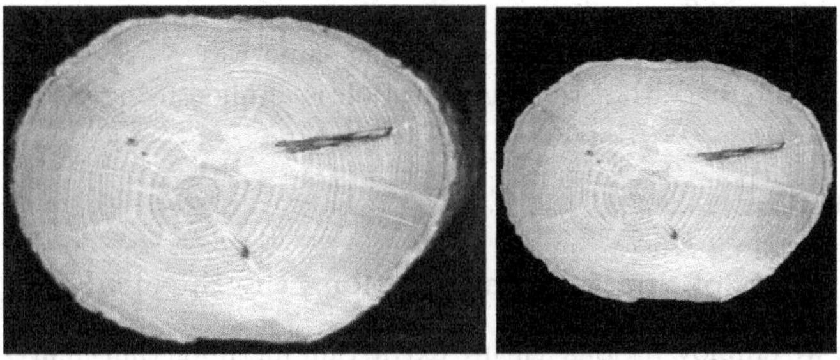

(a) Original image (b) Preprocessed Image

Fig. 3. An example of an original image and its segmented, quadratic output after preprocessing the image.

images with the RGB image of the same log in Fig. 6. We assume that this is caused by the acquisition software and an inaccurate trigger synchronization.

Exemplar images of one log at 5 different spectra are shown in Fig. 2. As we can observe, the images at different spectra have clearly different brightness distributions and also the contrast is different. The spectral image at 1111 nm is clearly the brightest and the image at 1450 nm is clearly the darkest one, so there is no constant change in one direction regarding the brightness of the images along the spectral range.

Additionally, RGB images were taken from all 100 discs using a Canon 70D camera. The camera has been fixed so that the images were all taken under the same viewpoint and the same scale. In our experiments to compare RGB and spectral image data, we employ one RGB image from each of the 87 discs for which hyperspectral data is available. An example of an RGB image together with examples of spectral images from the same disc can be observed in Fig. 6.

2.3 Image Segmentation

The spectral images are rather easy to segment since they have a nearly black background outside of the CS. Like in a previous publication on log tracing [24], we apply the active contour method [3] for the segmentation of the log images. The image is reduced to the smallest possible box shaped size so that the log is still fully included in the image and those parts of the image that have been found to be part of the background are set to black. To be able to extract information from the images using a variety of different feature extraction methods and to be able to compare the extracted features of different images, we decided to turn the box shaped segmented images into squares of equal size for all log images. This is done by making the images quadratic by padding the images with black background on the smaller side of the box shaped image so that the log is centered in the now quadratic image. Then a five pixel thick black border is added on each side of the image and the images are resized to the size of 352×352. In Fig. 3 we can see an example of an original image and its quadratic segmented output. All experiments are applied to these preprocessed images.

The 87 RGB images are processed in the same way as the spectral images with the only difference that the segmentation is applied using CNNs (see [23]).

3 Methods

3.1 Differences of Spectral Images Along the Spectral Range

In this work we employ various feature extraction methods that analyze different features of the spectral images along the spectral range. We employ image histograms that analyze the brightness distribution of the images, features extracted by CNNs, an LBP method that basically compares the brightness between pixels and their neighbored pixels, and the Gabor wavelet transform, that analyzes the frequency distribution of images along different directions. For all these methods, feature vectors are computed for each image of a log end along the spectral range. Distances between feature vectors of a log at different spectra are computed using the Euclidean distance.

Additionally to the feature extraction methods we compute the average pixel difference between images at different spectra. We further denote this method as 'Image Difference' or 'ImDiff'. Furthermore, we apply the edge metric LEG that analyzes changes in the edge information between images.

Image Histogram: Histograms of the images are build where the number of pixels for each pixels brightness value between 0 and 255 is counted. So the resulting histogram of an image has 256 bins.

CNN Transfer Learning: For CNN feature extraction, we use a DenseNet161 [11] convolutional neural network (CNN) that has been trained on the ImageNet database. As features we extract the CNN activations of an intermediate layer by simply removing the final layer of the CNN. The log images are normalized and resized to the size of 224×224 and then fed to the CNN resulting in 2208 dimensional feature vectors.

LBP: Based on a grayscale image, the LBP operator generates a binary sequence for each pixel by thresholding the neighbors of the pixel by the center pixel value. The binary sequences are then treated as numbers (i.e. the LBP numbers). Once all LBP numbers for an image are computed, a histogram based on these numbers is generated and used as feature vector. We employ the multiscale block binary patterns (MB-LBP) operator [13] with three different block sizes (3,9,15). The uniform LBP histograms of the 3 scales (block sizes) are concatenated resulting in a feature vector with $3 \times 59 = 177$ features per image.

Gabor Wavelets: The Gabor Wavelets transform (GWT) [12] is a multi-scale and multi-orientation wavelet transform that decomposes an image in subbands that contain information at different frequency bands (scales) and orientations of an image. The GWT is applied using 3 decomposition levels and 6 orientations. The feature vector of an image consists of the statistical features mean and standard deviation of the absolute values of the subband coefficients from each of the 18 (3×6) subbands.

Local Edge Gradients (LEG) The LEG [10] analyses changes in the edge information between two images. LEG combines the edge change, based on the local binary pattern concept, and the edge gradient change. The edge change is calculated in the low frequency band and the gradient change in the high frequency band of a wavelet decomposition of the images. The LEG is a quality metric, a high metric score reflects a high similarity between two images, with a normalized score in $[0, 1]$.

3.2 Combination of Spectral Images

The most important feature to trace logs is the annual ring pattern. In [24], a filtering approach was proposed for log end images that highlights the annual ring pattern and widely ignores all other features of the image. Using this filtering approach as preprocessing for a CNN-based log recognition clearly improved the results for the difficult scenario of log tracing from the forest to the sawmill using image data acquired from totally different sources (see [24]). The images were first recorded using a Canon 70D camera (the RGB data that is also used in this work) and later at the sawmill using a CT scanner.

The advantage of the filtering approach is that the filter response images offer a very good visibility of the annual ring pattern but mostly ignore features that are problematic for wood log tracing like knots that either completely change or even disappear or reappear in the log cross section after the log is capped, which is regularly done at sawmills before processing the log.

The filtering approach [24] is applied using directional Gaussian 2D filters at 8 different directions ($0°, 22.5°, 45°, \ldots 157.5°$). The filters are shown in Fig. 4 on the left side. To specifically highlight the annual ring pattern, the direction of the filters has to be similar to the direction of the annual year rings at each position of the log. This is ensured by subdividing the log into 16 different sectors, where each sector covers the part of the log within a range of 22.5° using the pith as center point. Then each sector is filtered separately with the filter that has the same direction as the annual year rings in the respective sector (see Fig. 4, right side). To ensure that mainly filter responses of the annual ring pattern remain, all filter response values that are smaller than zero are set to zero. For a better visibility of the annual ring pattern, the brightness values are normalized so that the maximum brightness value of a filter response image is 255 and the minimum

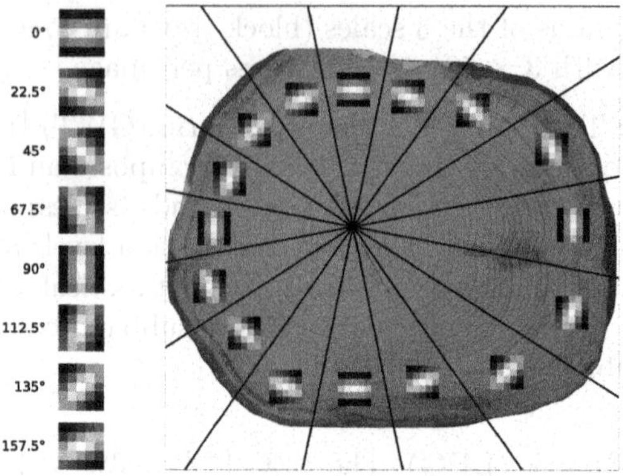

Fig. 4. Division of the log in 16 sectors and the associated filters for each sector.

is 0, followed by the application of adaptive histogram equalization. For more details on the filtering process see [24]. In Fig. 6 (a–c), we can observe spectral images (top row) and their corresponding filter responses (middle row).

A further advantage of the filter response images compared to the original spectral images is that the information on the annual ring pattern of a log across different spectra can be combined in a simple way. Our proposed approach constructs an image from the filter response images of the 196 spectral images of a log by taking the maximum pixel brightness value across the 196 filter responses at each pixel position.

This is possible because the log cross section is always positioned exactly the same for the 196 spectral images of one log. We denote this approach as Maximum Filter approach (MF). Some of the annual rings are only clearly visible under certain spectra and by taking the maximum filter response of all images along the spectral range for each pixel position separately, we aim to gain the best possible visibility of the annual ring pattern for the MF image among the spectral images at each position of the log. In Fig. 6 (d) in the middle row we show an example of an MF image along with three of the 196 spectral images (Fig. 6 (a–c)) from which it was constructed.

Now we need a way to be able to quantify the visibility of the annual ring pattern and to compare it between the spectral images, MF images and RGB images. For this, we first binarize the filter response images and the MF image using adaptive thresholding by calculating locally adaptive image thresholds which are chosen using local first-order image statistics around each pixel (using the Matlab function "imbinarize (I, 'adaptive')"). Then, skeletonization is applied to the binarized filter response images. To remove noise and components that are too small to properly indicate the annual rings, all connected components that have less than 20 pixels are removed from the skeletonized images. Examples of skeletonized filter response images can be seen in Fig. 6 in the bottom row. Now by counting the white pixels in the skeletonized images (which indicate annual rings), we get an estimation of the visibility of the annual ring pattern in the filter response images and the original images itself. The higher the number of white pixels, the better the visibility of the annual ring pattern.

4 Experimental Setup

Since we are mainly interested in the general differences between log images at different spectra and not in the differences for specific logs, we average the outcomes of the employed methods from Sect. 3.1, that are applied to each log separately, over all 87 logs.

In case of the methods extracting feature vectors (Image Histogram, CNN, LBP and Gabor Wavelets) we compute the Euclidean distances between the feature vectors of all 196 spectral images from each log separately. For LEG, we compute distances d by inverting the metric scores s between the 196 images per log ($d = |1 - s|$). Hence, for each of the methods we get a distance matrix of 196×196 for each of the 87 logs. Then each of the 87 distance matrices is normalized separately by dividing all its entries by the highest occurring distance in the matrix so that the values in each matrix are exactly between 0 and 1. Finally, the 87 normalized distance matrices are averaged by taking the average value over the 87 different distance values for each position in the matrices, so that we gain the average distances between the images at different spectra over the 87 logs in the form of a 196×196 distance matrix for each of the methods.

For the method Image Difference we proceed similar, but here we are more interested in the absolute values of the differences between images and hence we do not normalize the differences for each log. Also here we get a 196×196 matrix that shows the differences between the images per log that is averaged over the 87 logs.

The two methods 'Image Difference' and 'Image histogram' are not only applied to the original spectral images but also to images that are normalized with regard to the average pixel brightness and the image contrast. Once again, the normalization is applied separately for the images of different logs, First, the mean and the standard deviation are computed for each spectral image of a log, then the average over the 196 means (M) and standard deviations (SD) is computed per log. Finally, each spectral image I of a log is normalized by setting the standard deviation of the image to SD ($I = I \times SD/std(I)$) followed by setting the mean value to M ($I = I + M - mean(I)$). In that way, the normalized spectral images of one log all have the same mean brightness and at least similar contrast. So, by additionally applying the two methods to the normaized images, we can analyze the differences of log images at different spectra apart from the two factors average image brightness and contrast.

5 Results

In Fig. 5 (a, b) we present the results of the method Image Difference, where the mean pixel difference between images at different spectra is averaged over the 87 logs. We can observe that the differences between the normalized spectral

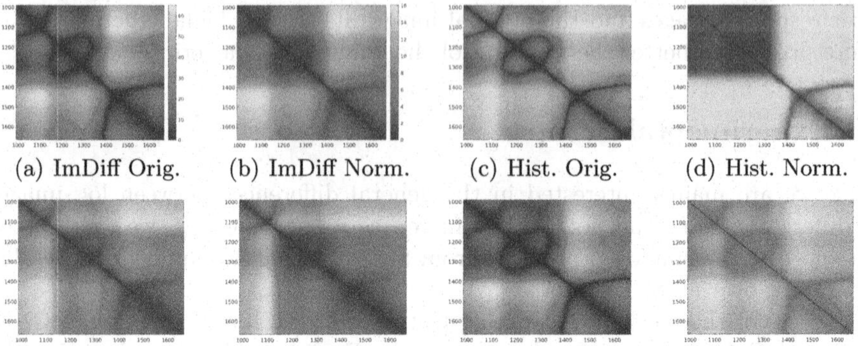

(a) ImDiff Orig. (b) ImDiff Norm. (c) Hist. Orig. (d) Hist. Norm.

(e) CNN (f) LBP (g) Gabor (h) LEG

Fig. 5. Heatmaps showing the differences (a–b) and distances (c–h) between spectral images in the range of 990–1665, averaged over the 87 logs. The Image Difference method (a, b) and the Image Histogram method (c, d) show the differences respectively distances for original and normalized images. (e), (f), (g) and (h) show the distances for the methods CNN, LBP, Gabor Wavelets respectively LEG.

images are about 4 times lower than the differences of the original image for all comparisons between images at different spectra. So, alone the normalization of the images eliminates about 3 quarters of the differences between images at different spectra. Generally, the differences between images at spectra between 990 nm and about 1350 nm are rather small and the same applies for images at spectra between about 1400 and 1665 nm. The highest differences are between images in the spectral range of 990–1150 nm and images in the spectral range of about 1400–1600 nm.

In Fig. 5 (c–h) we compare the distances between images at different spectra using 5 different methods. We can observe that for the Image Histogram method (Fig. 5 (c) and (d)), which shows the distribution of the brightness values in an image, the distances between images are quite different for original and normalized images. In case of the original images, the distances between different spectra behave similar as for the Image Difference method, but with bigger differences between images in the spectral range of 990–1150 nm and images in the spectral range of 1150–1350 nm. The distances between the normalized images at different spectra are totally different. Here, the distances are quite low between images in the spectral range of 990–1350 nm. For nearly all other comparisons of images at different spectra, the distances are high, even for rather small differences in the spectrum (>30–50 nm difference).

For the LBP method, which basically compares the brightness between pixels and their neighbored pixels, the distances are different than for the results of the previously analyzed methods. Here, the distances between images at the wide spectrum from about 1150–1665 nm are rather low. The highest difference occur between images in the spectrum of 990–1130 and images at spectra higher than 1400 nm. The distances between the CNN features are similar to those of the

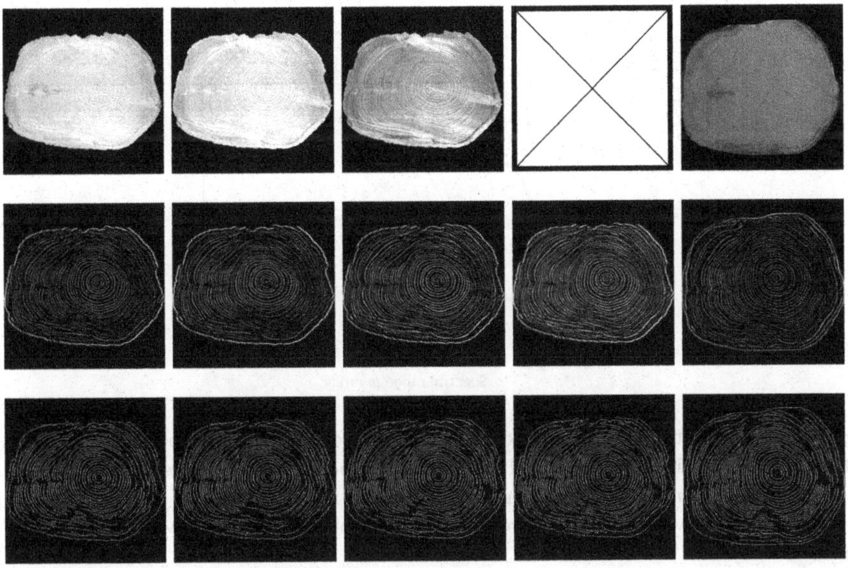

(a) 995nm (b) 1300nm (c) 1665nm (d) MF (e) RGB

Fig. 6. Original images (top row), filter response images (middle row) and skeletonized filter responses (bottom row) of images from the same log. The three columns on the left side (a–c) show spectral images at different spectra and their filter responses and skeletonization. The fourth column (d) shows the output of the Maximum Filter approach and its skeletonization. The right column (e) shows an RGB image and its filter response and skeletonization.

LBP approach and the Image Histogram method using the original images, kind of a mixture between the distances of the two methods.

The distances between images using Gabor Wavelets, which analyzes the frequency distribution of images along different directions, are quite similar in behaviour as for the Image Difference method.

The distances between images using LEG, which compares the edge information between images, are kind of similar to the results of the methods Image Histogram with the original images and CNN. Also the results in [18] on the differences between spectral log images from the FX17 scanner were similar to the outcomes of these three methods.

Summed up, the different methods produce different results regarding the difference of log images at different spectra, but the results of the methods are kind of similar with the exception of the method Image Histogram using normalized images. For all methods there are low distances between spectral images in the spectrum of 990–1150 nm and for all methods except the Image Histogram using normalized images, the same applies to images in the spectrum of about 1150–1370 nm and images in the spektrum of about 1380–1655.

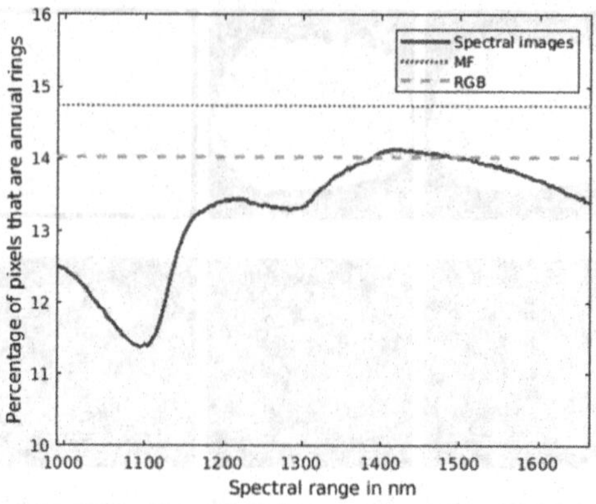

Fig. 7. The percentage of white pixels in the skeletonized filter responses in the cross section (CS) area averaged over all 87 logs. This performance measure indicates the visibility of the annual ring pattern and is shown for the spectral images along the spectral range as well as for the combination of spectral images (MF) and for RGB images.

In Fig. 6 we show five different images from the same log (three examples of spectral images at different spectra, the combined filter response MF and an RGB image) together with their filter response images and their skeletonization of the filter responses. When comparing the filter response images (middle row in Fig. 6) with each other, we can observe that the combined filter response image (MF) offers a better visibility of the annual ring pattern than the filter responses of images from only a single spectral image. The same can be observed for the images showing the skeletonization of the filter responses (bottom row in Fig. 6). For the shown skeletonized images, the number of white pixels indicating an annual ring is 9932 for the spectral image at 995 nm, 9921 for the spectral image at 1300 nm, 10528 for the spectral image at 1665 nm and 11052 for MF. However, the skeletonization of the RGB image even outperforms MF with 12048 pixels. However, as can be clearly observed in Fig. 6, the cross section area of the log in the RGB image is clearly bigger than the cross section area of the spectral images. This is because the spectral images were squeezed in height during the image acquisition process (see Sect. 2.2) and hence their cross section areas are smaller in the square images. So that comparison is clearly not fair. A much fairer approach is to compare the percentage of white pixels in the cross section area of the log (dividing the number of white pixels by the total number of pixels in the log cross section multiplied by 100). Using this fair comparison, 15.13% of the cross section area are white pixels indicating annual ring pattern for the MF image compared to 13.78% for the RGB image, whose cross section area is about 1.197 times bigger than the cross section area of the spectral images shown in Fig. 6. So, the visibility of the annual ring pattern is actually better for the MF image than for the RGB image for the exemplar images of one log shown in Fig. 6.

In Fig. 7 we present the percentage of white pixels from the skeletonized filter responses in the cross section area. This percentage is computed for each log seperately and then the outcomes are averaged over the 87 logs. This performance measure indicates the visibility of the annual ring pattern of the log images and is presented for each of the 196 spectral images along the spectral range as well as for the MF and RGB images. Here we can clearly observe that MF offers a better visibility of the annual ring pattern than single spectral images. When we compare the spectral images with the RGB images, we can see that the spectral images only show a better visibility of the annual ring pattern in the range of about 1390 nm–1490 nm. MF images offer a clearly better visibility of the annual ring pattern than the filtered RGB images.

6 Conclusion

In this work we analyzed hyperspectral log images with respect to their application on wood log tracking. First we applied experiments to find the differences between the images at different spectra (990–1665 nm). We showed that for most or even all methods there are only small differences between spectral images in the spectral ranges of 990–1150 nm, 1150–1370 nm and 1380–1655 nm. The highest differences occurred between images in the spectral range of 990–1150 nm and images in the spectral range of 1400–1600 nm. Second, we combined the images across the spectral range in order to maximize the image information. This was done using the proposed method MF, which combines filter response images that highlight the annual ring patter. We showed that MF offers a clearly better visibility of the annual ring pattern than single spectral images. Third, we compared the visibility of the annual ring pattern, the most important feature for log tracking, between spectral images and RGB images. We showed that only spectral images in the spectral range of about 1390 nm–1490 nm offer a better visibility of the annual ring pattern than RGB images of the same logs. The clearly best visibility of the annual ring pattern was achieved using MF.

References

1. Björk, A., et al.: Monitoring environmental performance of the forestry supply chain using RFID. Comput. Ind. **62**(8–9), 830–841 (2011). https://doi.org/10.1016/j.compind.2011.08.001
2. Camps-Valls, G., Tuia, D., Gómez-Chova, L., Jiménez, S., Malo, J.: Remote Sensing Image Processing. Morgan and Claypool, San Rafael (2011)
3. Chan, T., Vese, L.: Active contours without edges. IEEE Trans. Image Process. **10**(2), 266–277 (2001)
4. Chen, J., Li, G.: Prediction of moisture content of wood using modified random frog and VIS-NIR hyperspectral imaging. Infrared Phys. Technol. **105**, 103225 (2020)
5. Chiorescu, S., Grönlund, A.: The fingerprint approach: using data generated by a 2-axis log scanner to accomplish traceability in the sawmill's log yard. Forest Prod. J. **53**, 78–86 (2003)

6. Chiorescu, S., Grönlund, A.: The fingerprint method: using over-bark and under-bark log measurement data generated by three-dimensional log scanners in combination with radiofrequency identification tags to achieve traceability in the log yard at the sawmill. Scand. J. For. Res. **19**(4), 374–383 (2004)
7. EuropeanParliament: Regulation (eu) no 995/2010 of the European parliament and of the council of 20th October 2010 laying down the obligations of operators who place timber and timber products on the market
8. Evergreen: Homepage of the evergreen innovation camp 2019 in Vienna. www.evergreen-innovationcamp.io
9. FSC: Homepage of the forest stewardship council. www.fsc.org
10. Hofbauer, H., Uhl, A.: An effective and efficient visual quality index based on local edge gradients. In: IEEE 3rd European Workshop on Visual Information Processing, 6p. Paris, France, July 2011
11. Huang, G., Liu, Z., Van Der Maaten, L., Weinberger, K.Q.: Densely connected convolutional networks. In: 2017 IEEE Conference on Computer Vision and Pattern Recognition (CVPR), pp. 2261–2269 (2017). https://doi.org/10.1109/CVPR.2017.243
12. Lee, T.: Image representation using 2D Gabor wavelets. IEEE Trans. Pattern Anal. Mach. Intell. **18**(10), 959–971 (1996)
13. Liao, S., Zhu, X., Lei, Z., Zhang, L., Li, S.Z.: Learning multi-scale block local binary patterns for face recognition. In: Lee, S.-W., Li, S.Z. (eds.) ICB 2007. LNCS, vol. 4642, pp. 828–837. Springer, Heidelberg (2007). https://doi.org/10.1007/978-3-540-74549-5_87
14. PEFC: Homepage of the programme for the endorsement of forest certification. www.pefc.at
15. Richards, J.A., Jia, X.: Remote Sensing Digital Image Analysis: An Introduction. Springer, New York (2006). https://doi.org/10.1007/978-3-642-30062-2
16. Ruano, A., Zitek, A., Hinterstoisser, B., Hermoso, E.: NIR hyperspectral imaging (NIR-HI) and XRD for determination of the transition between juvenile and mature wood of pinus sylvestris l. Holzforschung **73**(7) (2019)
17. Schraml, R., Charwat-Pessler, J., Petutschnigg, A., Uhl, A.: Towards the applicability of biometric wood log traceability using digital log end images. Comput. Electron. Agric. **119**, 112–122 (2015). https://doi.org/10.1016/j.compag.2015.10.003
18. Schraml, R., Entacher, K., Petutschnigg, A., Young, T., Uhl, A.: Matching score models for hyperspectral range analysis to improve wood log traceability by fingerprint methods. Mathematics **8**(7), 10 (2020)
19. Schraml, R., Hofbauer, H., Petutschnigg, A., Uhl, A.: Tree log identification based on digital cross-section images of log ends using fingerprint and iris recognition methods. In: Azzopardi, G., Petkov, N. (eds.) CAIP 2015. LNCS, vol. 9256, pp. 752–765. Springer, Cham (2015). https://doi.org/10.1007/978-3-319-23192-1_63
20. Schraml, R., Hofbauer, H., Petutschnigg, A., Uhl, A.: On rotational pre-alignment for tree log identification using methods inspired by fingerprint and iris recognition. Mach. Vis. Appl. **27**(8), 1289–1298 (2016). https://doi.org/10.1007/s00138-016-0814-2
21. Schraml, R., Petutschnigg, A., Uhl, A.: Validation and reliability of the discriminative power of geometric wood log end features. In: Proceedings of the IEEE International Conference on Image Processing (ICIP 2015) (2015). https://doi.org/10.1109/ICIP.2015.7351488

22. Tzoulis, I., Andreopoulou, Z.: Emerging traceability technologies as a tool for quality wood trade. Procedia Technol. **8**, 606–611 (2013). 6th International Conference on Information and Communication Technologies in Agriculture, Food and Environment (HAICTA 2013). https://doi.org/10.1016/j.protcy.2013.11.087, https://www.sciencedirect.com/science/article/pii/S2212017313001497
23. Wimmer, G., Schraml, R., Hofbauer, H., Petutschnigg, A., Uhl, A.: Two-stage CNN-based wood log recognition. In: Gervasi, O., et al. (eds.) ICCSA 2021. LNCS, vol. 12955, pp. 115–125. Springer, Cham (2021). https://doi.org/10.1007/978-3-030-87007-2_9
24. Wimmer, G., Schraml, R., Lamminger, L., Petutschnigg, A., Uhl, A.: Cross-modality wood log tracing. In: 2021 IEEE International Symposium on Multimedia (ISM), pp. 191–195 (2021). https://doi.org/10.1109/ISM52913.2021.00038

International Workshop on Geomatics for Resource Monitoring and Management (GRMM 2022)

LULC Classification Performance of Supervised and Unsupervised Algorithms on UAV-Orthomosaics

Mirko Saponaro[1,2] and Eufemia Tarantino[1(✉)]

[1] Polytechnic University of Bari, Via Orabona 4, 70125 Bari, Italy
eufemia.tarantino@poliba.it
[2] Agenzia Regionale Strategica Per Lo Sviluppo Ecosostenibile del Territorio (ASSET) - Regione Puglia, Via Gentile, 52 - 70126 Bari, Italy

Abstract. Classification algorithms involve automatically categorising the response functions recorded in any image, i.e., the light reflected and recorded in the pixels by the sensors, as "virtual" representations of real-world objects in classes. These algorithms are finding increasing use in Remote Sensing (RS) applications and the scientific community is deeply engaged in investigating their performance. The substantial increase in spatial resolution that has been introduced through the onset of Unmanned Aerial Vehicle (UAV) platforms, even if equipped with low-cost sensors, has made classes recognition perform well for even the smallest scenario properties. Despite these advantages, it is emerged the need to address their limitations and to analyse their impacts in the data post-processing stages. It is necessary to validate the processing procedure so as to fully define their comparability and, in some cases, their interchangeability with other RS platforms. The aim of this research is to create a validated pixel-based classification procedure that will subsequently result in an automated method that is simple to apply, especially for end-users with limited knowledge of spatial data processing. Supervised and unsupervised approaches to testing performance were deemed more effective by adopting photogrammetric products based on UAV-acquisitions. This has mainly been accomplished by using statistical classifiers for Land Use/Land Cover (LULC) recognition based on several reflectance values across wavebands that compose an image and vegetation indexes in the visible bands. For these tests, the processing chains concerning classifications with supervised Random Forest (RF) and unsupervised K-Means Clustering algorithms were adopted.

Keywords: UAV · Vegetation extraction · Random forest · K-means · SNAP

1 Introduction

Several key developments achieved in the last decade show enormous potential in generating characterising information, in a radically new way, based merely on images and their pixels [1]. Machine learning from these images essentially translates into automatically categorising pixels based on their values and transforming them into a form of final

O. Gervasi et al. (Eds.): ICCSA 2022 Workshops, LNCS 13379, pp. 311–326, 2022.
https://doi.org/10.1007/978-3-031-10545-6_22

component or group of objects in the raster [2]. In other words, classification involves categorising the response functions recorded in the images, i.e., the light reflected from the Earth's surface and recorded in the pixels by the sensors, as "virtual" representations of real-world objects. Basic machine learning proposes a essentially different methodology by relying on programmed algorithms to classify input image data into an output map based on the statistical reflectance properties of their composite pixels. In the enhanced conceptual viewpoint of machine learning, the data and the requested output are delivered to a learning algorithm, called learner, which then generates the algorithm that converts one into the other. In a more complex and developed stage, Deep Neural Networks (DNNs) are composed of several layers between the input and output layers that collectively characterize the correct mathematical manipulation that generates the output from the input through a series of convolutions [3, 4].

These algorithms are finding increasing use in Remote Sensing (RS) applications and the scientific community is deeply engaged in investigating their performance. Even today, the variability and abundance of natural features represented as raster images and the quite coarse resolution of satellite images yield a challenge to pattern recognition algorithms. However, the significant increase in spatial resolution that has been led through the operation of Unmanned Aerial Vehicle (UAV) platforms at much lower altitudes, reducing the size of ground pixel projections by three orders of magnitude, has made machine learning perform well for even the smallest scenario properties. Even in the case of dynamic environments, i.e., subject to natural or anthropogenic change, machine learning techniques have enhanced the identification of features of interest and also tracked how they evolve over time [5].

In the case of feature detection from RS images, one of the key challenges is to agree on the most appropriate approach to reliably recognise real-world objects from a large number of pixels. So far, this has mainly been accomplished by using statistical classifiers that distinguish features or Land Use/Land Cover (LULC) based on several reflectance values across different wavebands that compose an image or by employing predefined rule sets to classify logically segmented objects from an image [6–9]. A first distinction is therefore made between pixel-based and object-based approaches to image analysis [10]. In a further distinction, a supervised approach is found within which, given an input image and a predefined training set of categories, a detection algorithm can identify all instances of pixels and/or objects that fall into these categories in an image. Secondly, quantitative classification methods applied to digital images include unsupervised pixel-based clustering [11]. In general, unsupervised clustering is a useful first step in digital image examination to reveal patterns and possible distinguishing features for purpose in more structured classification methods. Supervised classification delivers higher overall classification accuracies, commonly never less than 55%. Obviously, variations in flight altitude, illumination, shadows, partial constrictions, low sun angles and weather variability will decrease image quality and thus both visual interpretation and digital classifier performance [11].

The aim of this research is to test the performance of classification procedures that could subsequently be translated into an automated and easy-to-apply method, especially for end users with limited knowledge of spatial data processing and that is low cost in terms of the tools required.

Given the considerations discussed above, a pixel-based approach to testing performance was deemed more effective by adopting photogrammetric products based on UAV acquisitions.

In most cases, UAVs are supplied with cheap cameras able of acquiring only the visible RGB bands. These consumer cameras often come up with the problem of not being radiometrically calibrated [12, 13]. In order to offer RS data with a quantitative value, it is crucial to calibrate them both geometrically and radiometrically [14].

Despite the advantages of using UAVs and low-cost cameras, it is also necessary to address their limitations and to analyse their impacts in the data post-processing stages [15]. It is necessary to validate the processing procedure so as to fully define their comparability and, in some cases, their interchangeability with other RS platforms [16].

With a view to the democratisation of processes, accessible to end-users with a high degree of comparability, interchangeability and repeatability, the results of pixel-based classifications were tested and analysed. UAV-based orthomosaics in the radiometrically calibrated visible bands and vegetation maps in the Triangular Greenness Index (TGI) and Red–Green Ratio Index (IRG) were exported from QGIS software and uploaded to the open-source Sentinel Application Platform (SNAP) developed by Brockmann Consult, Skywatch, Sensar and CS and provided free of charge by ESA/ESRIN. In this way, Saponaro et al. [17] examined the statistical comebacks regarding the performance of vegetation indices in terms of separability between vegetated and non-vegetated areas. The impact of the most significant indices in the application of pixel-based classification algorithms was presented but a robust analysis between supervised and unsupervised classification was not assessed by the authors. Starting from the results achieved in [17], in this work the processing chains concerning classifications with supervised Random Forest (RF) [18] and unsupervised K-Means Clustering [19] algorithms were implemented.

At the end of each classification procedure, sets of test samples must be considered to verify the accuracy and precision of the classification. Confusion matrices were extracted from which the robustness and accuracy of the process can be deduced.

2 Methods

2.1 Focus Areas and Dataset Acquisition

Two study areas with different context were selected in order to demonstrate the versatility and non-specificity of the processing chain and the results that can be obtained. The areas were surveyed using different UAV sensors/cameras, using a different georeferencing strategy and at different Above Ground Level (AGL) altitudes, thus different Ground Samples Distance (GSD) values. A preview of these areas is presented in Fig. 1. In detail, in case study (a) an extra-urban environment of Grottole in the province of Matera (Italy) was selected (Fig. 1a). In this scenario, high vegetation, bare ground and, above all, a viaduct are visible. In the second case study, on the other hand, an abandoned archaeological area, called Punta Penna because of the promontory over the sea on which it stands, in the city of Bari (Italy), was considered (Fig. 1b). Unlike the first case, the presence of water is assessed in this scenario.

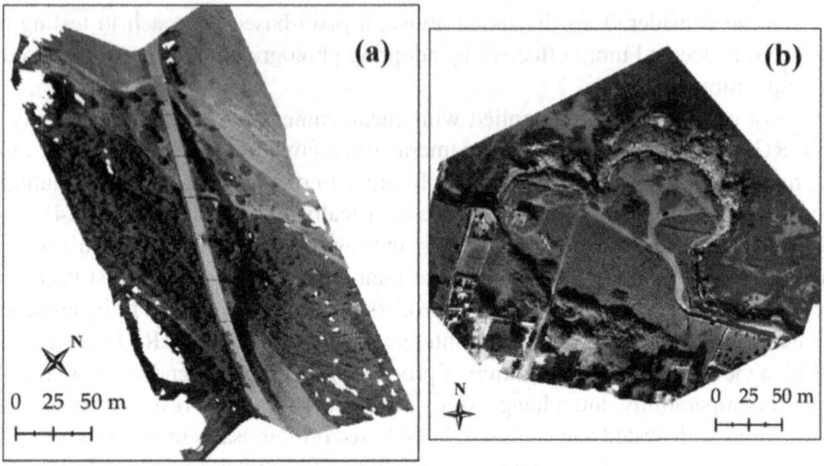

Fig. 1. Case study: (a) an out-of-town viaduct in Grottole (MT), Italy, (b) an abandoned archaeological area in Bari (BA), Italy. The icon to the left of the reader identifies the north orientation of the areas.

Table 1 highlights the assets and technologies used for each dataset.

For the first dataset, a Global Navigation Satellite System (GNSS) survey campaign of 11 Ground Control Points (GCPs) was carried out, acquired in network Real-Time Kinematic (nRTK) mode with an average accuracy of 2 cm along the three axes, in order to accomplish an Indirect Georeferencing (IG) of the photogrammetric products. For the second case study, a Direct Georeferencing (DG) was chosen, using image geo-tags determined with a low-performance GNSS receiver (average accuracy of 3 m).

Table 1. Overview of surveyed scenarios adopted technologies and acquired datasets.

	Case study (a)	Case study (b)
Location	Grottole (MT), Italy	Bari (BA), Italy
Equipment	DJI Mavic 2 Zoom RGB f-4.386, Model FC2204	DJI Inspire 1 v.2 ZenMuse X3 RGB f-3.61, Model FC350
Images	287 images (4000 × 3000 pix)	87 images (4000 × 3000 pix)
AGL/GSD	30 [m]/1.3 [cm/pix]	90 [m]/3.9 [cm/pix]
Georeferencing strategy	IG with 11 GCPs in nRTK	DG with low-cost GNSS receiver

The processing of the collected datasets was based on the workflow proposed in [20–22]. The different parameterisations for each dataset were detailed in Saponaro et al. [17]. Agisoft Metashape software (v.1.4.1, Agisoft LLC -St. Petersburg, Russia) was used during the work on Intel(R) Core (TM) i7-3970X CPU 3.50 GHz hardware, with 16 GB of RAM and an NVIDIA GeForce GTX 650 graphics card to return the photogrammetric products.

Four orthomosaics were exported for each scenario examined: beginning from the highest resolution and then doubling, tripling, and quadrupling the former. Additional down-sampling would not rationalize the use of UAV technology [23]. Specifically, the Agisoft Metashape software made it possible to export the orthomosaics at the selected resolution, resampling each time by bilinear interpolation (Table 2).

Table 2. Summary of spatial resolution down sampling in terms of GSD values performed at the orthomosaics of the two scenarios under study

	Case study (b)	Case study (c)
Orthomosaic spatial resolution *{1} min.res* *{2} min.res.x2* *{3} min.res x3* *{4} min.res.x4*	{1} 0,017 [m/pix] {2} 0,035 [m/pix] {3} 0,052 [m/pix] {4} 0,070 [m/pix]	{1} 0,036 [m/pix] {2} 0,071 [m/pix] {3} 0,107 [m/pix] {4} 0,142 [m/pix]

The orthomosaics were imported into the open-source software QGIS (3.16.5 'Hannover') [24]. Following the procedures adopted in [25], an Empirical Line Method (ELM) was applied in order to produce a radiometric calibration of the orthomosaics. Several vegetative indices in the visible bands were evaluated and their performance was analysed in terms of their ability to distinguish between vegetative and non-vegetative classes. As described in [17], the most effective vegetative indices in terms of performance were Triangular Greenness Index (TGI) (Eq. 1) and Red–Green Ratio Index (IRG) (Eq. 2), calculated as follows:

$$\mathrm{TGI} = 0.5 * [(\lambda_R - \lambda_B)(\rho_R - \rho_G) - (\lambda_R - \lambda_G)(\rho_R - \rho_B)] \quad (1)$$

$$\mathrm{IRG} = \rho_R - \rho_G \quad (2)$$

2.2 Pixel-Based Classification

The scientific literature presents a multitude of classification methodologies and the choice, in this research work, fell on pixel-based image analysis algorithms. Pixel-based image classifications are based on the simple hypothesis that the spectral response patterns of individual pixels and the textures linked with the classes of interest can be statistically categorized into a suitable set of informative classes. In object-based image analysis, in fact, the analyst is faced with an unavoidable challenge: the determination of the segmentation parameters, in particular the segmentation scale, is often very complex and, if not supported by certain expertise, is bypassed by a default parameterization or passed in overparameterization [26, 27].

In view of the classification procedures' automation, these algorithms can potentially be improved by adding data from any NIR and/or Red-Edge bands to the simple RGB bands. In other cases, one could combine data from the digital orthomosaic with height data from a DEM. In this research, however, information obtained from the calculation of visible-band vegetation indices were tested. UAV-based orthomosaics in the radiometrically calibrated visible bands and vegetation maps in the TGI and IRG indices were exported from QGIS software and uploaded to the open-source Sentinel Application Platform (SNAP) developed by Brockmann Consult, Skywatch, Sensar and CS and provided free of charge by ESA/ESRIN. SNAP provides several supervised and unsupervised raster image classification algorithms. For this tests, the processing chains concerning classifications with supervised Random Forest (RF) [18] and unsupervised K-Means Clustering [19] algorithms were adopted.

Supervised Classification. A rapid and objective tool for feature selection is a decision tree, as it is a non-parametric statistical method that is not impacted by outliers and correlations, can uncover interactions between variables and is also an outstanding data reduction tool. In a decision tree, a set of data is consecutively subdivided into increasingly homogeneous subsets until terminal nodes are established. However, a single decision tree is not performance-adequate to undertake highly complex feature classification and multi-class dimension prediction.

The Random Forest, on the other hand, is a tree-based machine learning algorithm that utilizes the power of multiple decision trees to get predictions.

This decision trees classifier is really a pixel-based classification method that then performs multi-stage classifications using a series of binary decisions to separate pixels into different classes. Each decision divides the pixels of an image into two classes on the basis of an expression. This large number of relatively unrelated decision trees essentially acts as a committee to overcome the individual constituent models. Each individual tree in the random forest makes a class prediction and so the class with the most votes joins the model prediction. In all that, the low correlation among the models is the key to the proficiency of the whole. In this sense, the trees safeguard each other from their individual errors, assuming they are not all consistently in the same direction. To ensure that RF works, the predictions and thereby the errors committed by individual trees must have low correlations with each other.

In order to do so, however, the algorithm requires training areas to be plotted so that there are real signals of the features being sought and so that models generated using these features perform better than random hypotheses screened at some nodes. In addition, the algorithm makes use of the Bootstrap aggregation method. In practice, Decision trees are very responsive to the data they are trained on: small changes to the training set can yield significantly different tree compositions. However, the random forest capitalises on this advantage by allowing each individual tree to be randomly sampled from the dataset with replacements, producing different trees. This process is commonly known as bagging. This forces even greater variation between trees in the model and eventually leads to less correlation between trees and greater diversity.

De Castro et al. [28] recommended that the Random Forest (RF) machine learning algorithm remained the best for classification automation, as it involves far fewer classification parameters than similar machine learning techniques.

In general, these classification methods are entitled supervised because they employ conventional polygons designed by an expert on the basis of ground truth identification.

Precisely, the signature area or training area is created using an area of interest (AOI) through which class signatures are collected and then applied as seeds for the extraction of the signature used in the classification. It tends to be the case that more than one training area will have to be considered for each class and then merged to overcome inhomogeneities between the AOIs selected as sample data for the respective class. This thus establishes the statistical basis for the software to recognise existing classes in a raster file. The time invested in performing this step is then spent on training the algorithm, i.e., calibrating it to work automatically in recognising the various features.

The automatic but supervised pixel-based classification method has a specific disadvantage regarding the time efficiency of the algorithm, as the time required for its completion is strongly influenced by the separate polygons created and the spectral thresholds of the bands and/or indices used, which in turn often depend on the noise level in the UAV images.

Once all of the above QGIS products from the two scenarios and in the four spatial resolutions have been imported into the SNAP software, the AOI collection was organised in such a way as to consider it balanced by classes, following the recommendations of [29] and [30]. Four types of classes were identified, labelled as asphalt, bare soil, vegetation, and water. As a consequence of the low flight height, UAV images capture a relatively small footprint on the ground, but the number of pixels in the image is comparatively high due to the high resolution. Therefore, the analysis of UAV images is even more powerful than that of conventional aerial and satellite images. Therefore, 10 AOIs per class were plotted, attempting to collect within them the spectral variability and texture of each class. The methodology used to create a training dataset for the automatic methods guarantees that the training data always covers the same percentage of area for each class, which assures the usability and robustness of the algorithm.

Unsupervised Classification. It is considered an iterative procedure with no need for prior information [30]. In general, these methods are considered as clustering algorithms, which calculate distance functions and group similar pixel values into a spectral class. In the final step, the generated categories are recognised and labelled according to the colour composition of the image and expert observations. finally, these categories can be divided into the desired classes. However, the output classes possibly do not correspond to any of the classes of interest, as they account for ambiguous spectral classes. Effectively, clustering involves dividing a large dataset into a multiplicity of data clusters, which reveal certain characteristics of each subset. This is done by estimating similarity or closeness on the basis of the distance measurement method in order to find a structure in an unnamed collection of data. Thus, a cluster is an assortment of objects that are similar to each other and are "dissimilar" to objects belonging to other clusters.

One of the most characteristic and commonly used clustering algorithms for performing unsupervised classifications of satellite-based rasters is the so-called K-means Algorithm. Tang et al. [31] positively combined a K-means method with a machine learning algorithm for weed detection. Vrindts et al. [32] applied revised K-means clustering to establish management zone gradation using soil and crop data. Indeed, from the cluster analysis the properties of the dataset and the target variable can be determined, and these come in handy when determining how to measure the similarity distance.

As described in [19], the algorithm requires as input the number of k centroids for each cluster and a database containing n data items, representing the set of all instances analysed by the algorithm. The centroids are imaginary or real points at the centre of a cluster from which the Euclidean distances to other data will be evaluated. The algorithm iteratively evaluates the distances of these data from the centroids and each is reassigned to the cluster to which the object is most similar according to the average value of the objects in the cluster. As the average value is updated, iteratively re-assignments occur until no more changes occur, i.e., a point of convergence is reached where no more cluster changes occur.

The k-means algorithm has the advantage of being quite fast, as few calculations and consequently, little computer processing time is required to calculate the distances between the data and the centroids at each iteration. On the other hand, k-means has a couple of disadvantages. Firstly, it is necessary to select how many k groups to show. This is not always trivial as it is not always possible to do this, especially for problems of higher complexity. In addition, K-means also starts with a random choice of centroids and therefore may produce different clustering results on different sequences of the algorithm. Consequently, the outcomes may not be repeatable and lack consistency. In the SNAP software, the unsupervised K-Means algorithm classifications were started. A value of the parameter K, i.e., the number of clusters, was set to 5 and the default number of iterations to 30. At the end of each processing, the clusters generated were manually labelled according to the class to which they could be identified.

2.3 Confusion Matrix

In order to verify and validate the classification results, 30 pins for each prediction class were distributed in each investigated scenario to perform the bootstrapping method. These pins represent ground truths digitally identified by the orthomosaics themselves and assigned to a certain class. Once the classification processes are complete, the predictions of the classes in the pins can be compared with the previously assigned classes and confusion matrices can be constructed.

After the algorithms have been efficiently applied, the classification results are assessed against the accuracy of the actual data. The bootstrapping method was adopted to allow a formal statistical comparison of the accuracy of the classification approaches adopted.

Adopting the guidance given in [33], the following metrics are computed to quantify the accuracy of the extracted features:

- Error Rate (ERR) is calculated as the number of all incorrect predictions divided by the total number of the dataset. The best error rate is 0 and the worst is 1.

$$ERR = \frac{FP + FN}{TN + FP + FN + TP} \tag{3}$$

- Accuracy indicates the accuracy of the model as the name implies. Therefore, the best accuracy is 1, while the worst is 0.

$$Accuracy = \frac{TP + TN}{TN + FP + FN + TP} \tag{4}$$

- F-Score: is a weighted harmonic average of the Precision and Recall metrics such that the best score is 1 and the worst is 0.

$$F - Score = \frac{2 * Recall * Precision}{Recall + Precision} \tag{5}$$

where Precision is the ability of a classifier not to label a positive instance that is negative. For each class, it is defined as the ratio of true positives to the sum of true and false positives.

$$Precision = \frac{TP}{TP + FP} \tag{6}$$

Recall, also called sensitivity, is the ability of a classifier to find all positive instances. For each class, it is defined as the ratio between true positives and the sum of true positives and false negatives:

$$Recall = \frac{TP}{TP + FN} \tag{7}$$

For this purpose, True Positives (TP), True Negatives (TN), False Positives (FP) and False Negatives (FN) are estimated for the vegetation, asphalt and bare soil classes based on ground truth data. TP signifies the correctly classified objects for the given class among all obtained objects, FP is the falsely classified objects among the extracted objects, and FN stands the missed or not extracted objects. Finally, TN denotes the objects correctly classified among all extracted objects but not within the class in question.

Confusion matrices are thus constructed for each spatial resolution of each scenario for three cases of classification, both supervised and unsupervised: using only the visible (RGB) bands, adding to these the vegetation map of the TGI index and, finally, adding to the RGB bands the information of the IRG index.

3 Results and Discussion

Figures 2 and 3 present the results of the classifications for each scenario and at each spatial resolution, obtained with the RF and K-Means algorithms, respectively. In particular, at each resolution the responses of the classification algorithms are presented when assisted by the vegetation indices in the visible bands, i.e., the TGI and IRG.

A qualitative inspection comparing the corresponding classifications reveals the difficulties of correct clustering by K-Means algorithms compared to RF. In scenario (a), if on the one hand the identification of vegetation and bare ground are quite reliable, in the unsupervised classification the difficulty in distinguishing asphalt from other classes and vice versa stands out. The same algorithm exhibits the same problems in the second study area. In this scenario, in fact, the most critical issues are found in the clustering of water, which is often included in other classes.

After performing and qualitative inspecting the supervised and unsupervised classification procedures using the RF and K-Means algorithms, respectively, the validation

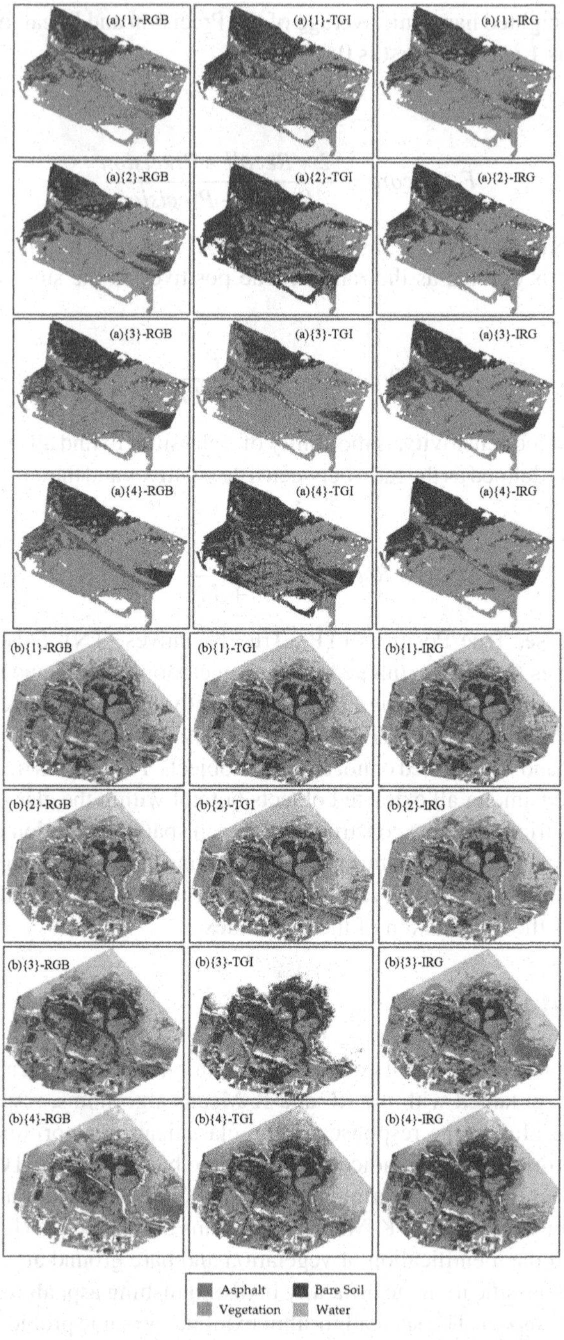

Fig. 2. RF maps for the cases analysed. In the first column, in descending order by spatial resolution, the classifications obtained using only the RGB bands. In the second by adding the TGI map, in the third by adding the IRG map.

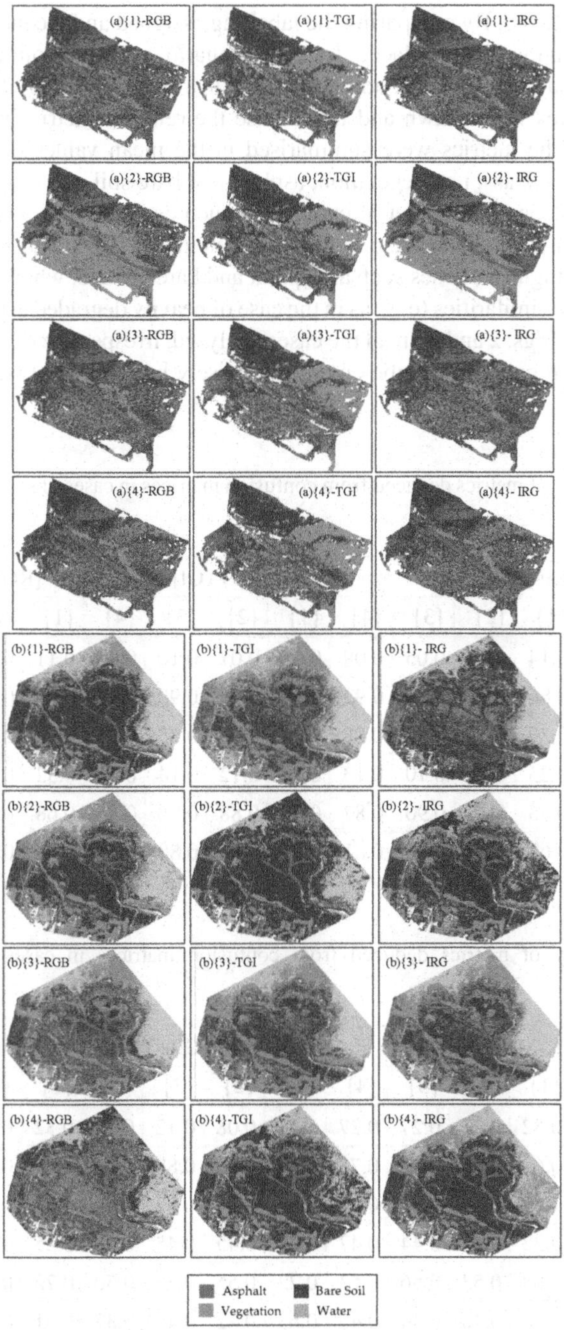

Fig. 3. K-Means algorithm maps for the cases analysed. In the first column, in descending order by spatial resolution, the classifications obtained using only the RGB bands. In the second by adding the TGI map, in the third by adding the IRG map.

metrics were extracted. By comparing the labelling assigned and the labelling predicted by the software in the 90 pins placed, for each scenario, at each resolution and for each classification mode (RGB bands, addition of the TGI band, addition of the IRG band), confusion matrices were drawn and from these the relevant metrics were derived. In Tables 3 and 4, the metrics were summarised in the mean values of the parameters calculated for each class, i.e., vegetation, asphalt and bare soil.

In general, a coarse radiometric calibration such as ELM does not permit a clear distinction to be made between and in the image elements. This results in a diminished capability to distinguish classes such as asphalt and bare ground, which in several cases may have spectral similarities (e.g., as in the case of heavily degraded asphalt). In fact, as can be seen from Figs. 2 and 3, in all the cases analysed, irrespective of the classification methods used, the greatest diatribe emerges precisely between the two classes asphalt and bare ground.

Table 3. Summary of metrics deduced from confusion matrices in cases of supervised classification

		RF [RGB]				RF [RGB+TGI]				RF [RGB+IRG]			
		{1}	{2}	{3}	{4}	{1}	{2}	{3}	{4}	{1}	{2}	{3}	{4}
(a)	Error rate	0.14	0.17	0.05	0.08	0.08	0.07	0.10	0.03	0.11	0.13	0.09	0.02
	Accuracy	0.86	0.83	0.95	0.92	0.92	0.93	0.90	0.97	0.89	0.87	0.91	0.98
	F-score	0.80	0.75	0.92	0.88	0.89	0.88	0.85	0.95	0.83	0.81	0.85	0.97
(b)	Error rate	0.25	0.13	0.10	0.13	0.22	0.12	0.14	0.16	0.32	0.17	0.15	0.11
	Accuracy	0.75	0.87	0.90	0.87	0.78	0.88	0.86	0.84	0.68	0.83	0.85	0.89
	F-score	0.62	0.82	0.86	0.81	0.67	0.83	0.80	0.78	0.58	0.76	0.75	0.84

Table 4. Summary of metrics deduced from confusion matrices in cases of unsupervised classification

		K-Means [RGB]				K-Means [RGB+TGI]				K-Means [RGB+IRG]			
		{1}	{2}	{3}	{4}	{1}	{2}	{3}	{4}	{1}	{2}	{3}	{4}
(a)	Error Rate	0.32	0.25	0.27	0.27	0.11	0.08	0.12	0.08	0.32	0.25	0.27	0.25
	Accuracy	0.68	0.75	0.73	0.73	0.89	0.92	0.88	0.92	0.68	0.75	0.73	0.75
	F-score	0.57	0.66	0.63	0.65	0.82	0.87	0.82	0.88	0.57	0.66	0.63	0.66
(b)	Error Rate	0.32	0.47	0.44	0.47	0.28	0.45	0.45	0.50	0.25	0.32	0.37	0.55
	Accuracy	0.68	0.53	0.56	0.53	0.72	0.55	0.55	0.50	0.75	0.68	0.63	0.45
	F-score	0.58	0.40	0.44	0.40	0.63	0.42	0.44	0.37	0.61	0.57	0.53	0.32

Regarding the classification with the RF algorithms, the metrics obtained from the analysis of the results are presented in Table 3. Considering the Error Rate values obtained in the two scenarios, it immediately emerges how in the second context the presence of water generates ambiguity and therefore higher values of this metric. In fact, Saponaro et al. [17] had already guessed that the algorithms are often affected in the resolution {1} due to the presence of noise and distortions in the pixels. However, the values obtained can be considered acceptable in all RF classification modes, as also ascertained by the Accuracy values averaging over 0.8. Among the classification modes, those in which the TGI vegetation index is adopted for resolutions {1} and {2} and the simple mode with the RGB bands in the other two resolution solutions prove to be effective. Looking at the F-score values, these are functional in every solution in scenario (a), in particular in the [RGB+IRG] case in resolution {4} where a value of 0.97 is even reached. This combination in fact presents the best metrics. In the second scenario instead, as already discussed, a lowering of the F-score values was recorded in the resolution {1}. In the remaining part of the cases the values can be considered acceptable. In general, from the analysed values it emerges how an efficiency of the classifications occurs at resolutions reduced with respect to the original, within which the presence of noise generates ambiguity.

On the other hand, looking at the F-score values in the cases of unsupervised classification in Table 4, one finds a drastic reduction of the general values of about 30% with respect to those obtained by supervised classification. This is also confirmed by the remaining part of the calculated metrics Accuracy and Precision. Among the analysed values, with the exception of case (a) [RGB+TGI] where the values are very functional, both scenarios where the classification used IRG maps had a slight improvement. This shows how the presence of vegetative indices improves the ability to separate classes, so using unsupervised modes requires more incisive radiometric information such as that retrievable from the NIR bands. Even in this type of classification, comparing the trends of the F-score values with respect to the spatial resolutions at which they are calculated, it is not possible to extrapolate a certain regularity.

In summary, from Figs. 2, 3 and Tables 3, 4, the best-fitting results in the case of supervised classifications result for the scenarios: (a), spatial resolution {4}, classification mode with vegetative index IRG; (b), spatial resolution {3}, basic classification mode with RGB bands.

In the unsupervised modes, however, they result for the scenarios: (a) spatial resolution {4}, classification mode with vegetative index TGI; (b), spatial resolution {1}, classification mode with vegetative index TGI. This again shows how the various datasets react unevenly to the algorithms used.

4 Conclusion

Classification algorithms involve the automatic categorisation of response functions recorded in pixels by sensors in order to identify real-world objects into predefined classes. Higher spatial resolutions, versatility of use and lower survey costs that have emerged from the use of UAVs have made class recognition perform well for even the smallest of scenery properties. Despite these advantages, the need has emerged to address their limitations and to analyse their impact in the data post-processing phases. A need has arisen to validate processing procedures in order to fully define the comparability of the products and, in some cases, their interchangeability with others obtainable from different RS techniques. The objective of this research was therefore to analyse the performance of two pixel-based classification procedures that could subsequently be translated into an automated and easy-to-apply method, especially for end users with limited knowledge of spatial data processing. A supervised classification approach using Random Forest algorithms and an unsupervised one using K-Means algorithms were tested. These are defined as statistical classifiers useful for Land Use/Land Cover (LULC) recognition and classifications were based on different reflectance values across the radiometrically calibrated wavebands that make up the UAV-based orthomosaics and vegetation indices in the visible bands.

The following observations emerged from the analysis of the results:

- As hypothesised, the supervised RF classifications returned very comfortable metrics compared to the unsupervised modes. In general, a 30% reduction in the values of the analysed metrics was found in the latter classifications.
- Especially for the unsupervised classifications, the presence of vegetative indices noticeably improves their algorithm separation capabilities. In these cases, it would be preferable to use bands in the NIR for a better automatic extraction of the vegetation.
- There is no regularity between the separation capabilities of the classification algorithms and the spatial resolution of the orthomosaics. The efficiency is very much influenced by the context and any similarities between the reflectances of the various classes, e.g. vegetation and water or bare ground and asphalt. It turns out, however, that reduced resolutions compared to the original one optimise the classification capabilities as there is a reduction of noise in the images.

In this work it is demonstrated how the orthomosaics produced by UAV acquisitions equipped with non-metric and low-cost RGB sensors can generate very valuable information for vegetation extraction. Further investigations will have to be undertaken in order to assess how additional ancillary data, such as a digital elevation model (DEM) also based on UAV acquisitions, can improve the chain of processes discussed in this work.

References

1. Hamylton, S.M., et al.: Evaluating techniques for mapping island vegetation from unmanned aerial vehicle (UAV) images: pixel classification, visual interpretation and machine learning approaches. Int. J. Appl. Earth Obs. Geoinf. **89**, 102085 (2020)
2. Alif, A.A., Shukanya, I.F., Afee, T.N.: Crop prediction based on geographical and climatic data using machine learning and deep learning. BRAC University (2018)
3. LeCun, Y., Bengio, Y., Hinton, G.: Deep learning. Nature **521**, 436–444 (2015)
4. Novelli, A., Tarantino, E., Caradonna, G., Apollonio, C., Balacco, G., Piccinni, F.: Improving the ANN classification accuracy of Landsat data through spectral indices and linear transformations (PCA and TCT) aimed at LU/LC monitoring of a river basin. In: Gervasi, O., et al. (eds.) ICCSA 2016. LNCS, vol. 9787, pp. 420–432. Springer, Cham (2016). https://doi.org/10.1007/978-3-319-42108-7_32

5. Capolupo, A., Saponaro, M., Fratino, U., Tarantino, E.: Detection of spatio-temporal changes of vegetation in coastal areas subjected to soil erosion issue. Aquatic Ecosyst. Health Manage. 1–8 (2020)
6. Xie, Y., Sha, Z., Yu, M.: Remote sensing imagery in vegetation mapping: a review. J. Plant Ecol. **1**, 9–23 (2008)
7. Capolupo, A., Monterisi, C., Saponaro, M., Tarantino, E.: Multi-temporal analysis of land cover changes using Landsat data through Google Earth Engine platform. In: SPIE (ed.) Eighth International Conference on Remote Sensing and Geoinformation of the Environment (RSCy2020), vol. 11524 pp. 447–458, August 2020
8. Tarantino, E., Novelli, A., Aquilino, M., Figorito, B., Fratino, U.: Comparing the MLC and JavaNNS approaches in classifying multi-temporal LANDSAT satellite imagery over an ephemeral river area. Int. J. Agricult. Environ. Inf. Syst. (IJAEIS) **6**, 83–102 (2015)
9. Capolupo, A., Monterisi, C., Caporusso, G., Tarantino, E.: Extracting land cover data using GEE: a review of the classification indices. In: Gervasi, O., et al. (eds.) ICCSA 2020. LNCS, vol. 12252, pp. 782–796. Springer, Cham (2020). https://doi.org/10.1007/978-3-030-58811-3_56
10. Sarzana, T., Maltese, A., Capolupo, A., Tarantino, E.: Post-processing of pixel and object-based land cover classifications of very high spatial resolution images. In: Gervasi, O., et al. (eds.) ICCSA 2020. LNCS, vol. 12252, pp. 797–812. Springer, Cham (2020). https://doi.org/10.1007/978-3-030-58811-3_57
11. Keyport, R.N., Oommen, T., Martha, T.R., Sajinkumar, K., Gierke, J.S.: A comparative analysis of pixel-and object-based detection of landslides from very high-resolution images. Int. J. Appl. Earth Obs. Geoinf. **64**, 1–11 (2018)
12. Haghighattalab, A., et al.: Application of unmanned aerial systems for high throughput phenotyping of large wheat breeding nurseries. Plant Methods **12**, 35 (2016)
13. Wang, C., Myint, S.W.: A simplified empirical line method of radiometric calibration for small unmanned aircraft systems-based remote sensing. IEEE J. Sel. Top. Appl. Earth Obser. Remote Sens. **8**, 1876–1885 (2015)
14. Pompilio, L., et al.: Application of the empirical line method (ELM) to calibrate the airborne Daedalus-CZCS scanner. Eur. J. Remote Sens. **51**, 33–46 (2018)
15. Saponaro, M., Capolupo, A., Caporusso, G., Tarantino, E.: Influence of co-alignment procedures on the co-registration accuracy of multi-epoch SFM points clouds. Int. Arch. Photogrammetry, Remote Sens. Spat. Inf. Sci. **43**, 231–238 (2021)
16. Saponaro, M., Capolupo, A., Caporusso, G., Borgogno Mondino, E., Tarantino, E.: Predicting the Accuracy of Photogrammetric 3D Reconstruction from Camera Calibration Parameters Through a Multivariate Statistical Approach. ISPRS - International Archives of the Photogrammetry, Remote Sensing and Spatial Information Sciences XLIII-B2–2020, pp. 479–486 (2020)
17. Saponaro, M., Agapiou, A., Hadjimitsis, D.G., Tarantino, E.: Influence of spatial resolution for vegetation indices' extraction using visible bands from unmanned aerial vehicles' orthomosaics datasets. Remote Sens. **13**, 3238 (2021)
18. Breiman, L.: Random forests. Mach. Learn. **45**, 5–32 (2001)
19. Jung, Y.G., Kang, M.S., Heo, J.: Clustering performance comparison using K-means and expectation maximization algorithms. Biotechnol. Biotechnol. Equip. **28**, S44–S48 (2014)
20. Capolupo, A., Saponaro, M., Borgogno Mondino, E., Tarantino, E.: Combining interior orientation variables to predict the accuracy of RPAS-SFM 3D models. Remote Sens. **12**, 2674 (2020)
21. James, M.R., et al.: Guidelines on the use of structure-from-motion photogrammetry in geomorphic research. Earth Surf. Proc. Land. **44**, 2081–2084 (2019)

22. Saponaro, M., Turso, A., Tarantino, E.: Parallel development of comparable photogrammetric workflows based on UAV data inside SW platforms. In: Gervasi, O., et al. (eds.) ICCSA 2020. LNCS, vol. 12252, pp. 693–708. Springer, Cham (2020). https://doi.org/10.1007/978-3-030-58811-3_50
23. Smith, M.W., Carrivick, J., Quincey, D.: Structure from motion photogrammetry in physical geography. Prog. Phys. Geogr. **40**, 247–275 (2016)
24. https://www.qgis.org/
25. Agapiou, A.: Vegetation extraction using visible-bands from openly licensed unmanned aerial vehicle imagery. Drones **4**, 27 (2020)
26. Safonova, A., Guirado, E., Maglinets, Y., Alcaraz-Segura, D., Tabik, S.: Olive tree biovolume from UAV multi-resolution image segmentation with mask R-CNN. Sensors **21**, 1617 (2021)
27. Shukla, A., Jain, K.: Automatic extraction of urban land information from unmanned aerial vehicle (UAV) data. Earth Sci. Inf. **13**(4), 1225–1236 (2020). https://doi.org/10.1007/s12145-020-00498-x
28. De Castro, A.I., Torres-Sánchez, J., Peña, J.M., Jiménez-Brenes, F.M., Csillik, O., López-Granados, F.: An automatic random forest-OBIA algorithm for early weed mapping between and within crop rows using UAV imagery. Remote Sens. **10**, 285 (2018)
29. Belgiu, M., Stein, A.: Spatiotemporal image fusion in remote sensing. Remote Sens. **11**, 818 (2019)
30. Gašparović, M., Zrinjski, M., Barković, Đ, Radočaj, D.: An automatic method for weed mapping in oat fields based on UAV imagery. Comput. Electron. Agric. **173**, 105385 (2020)
31. Tang, J., Wang, D., Zhang, Z., He, L., Xin, J., Xu, Y.: Weed identification based on K-means feature learning combined with convolutional neural network. Comput. Electron. Agric. **135**, 63–70 (2017)
32. Vrindts, E., et al.: Management zones based on correlation between soil compaction, yield and crop data. Biosys. Eng. **92**, 419–428 (2005)
33. Hossin, M., Sulaiman, M.N.: A review on evaluation metrics for data classification evaluations. Int. J. Data Min. Knowl. Manage. Process **5**, 1 (2015)

Exploring Stability of Crops in Agricultural Landscape Through GIS Tools and Open Data

F. Ghilardi, S. De Petris, A. Farbo, F. Sarvia, and E. Borgogno-Mondino(✉)

University of Turin, Department of Agricultural, Forest and Food Sciences (DISAFA), L.go Braccini 2, 10095 (TO) Grugliasco, Italy
{federica.ghilardi,samuele.depetris,alessandro.farbo, filippo.sarvia,enrico.borgogno}@unito.it

Abstract. Climate change is a well-known issue in both the scientific community and public opinion that, in the long term, could increase frequency and intensity of extreme weather events. Several models have been developed to estimate damages caused to crops by flooding, but most of them assume that crops are stable and unchanged over time.

Conversely, yearly crop rotation is known to be common in agricultural areas making potential flooded areas highly varying along years. In a flood damage estimation context, a proper mapping of actual crops in flooded areas is crucial to make deductions reliable. Open data from institutional players, yearly updated, can be proficiently used for this purpose, providing useful information for a more robust estimate of damages. In this work, with reference to a paradigmatic area located in the western part of the Piemonte Region (NW-Italy), stability and spatial pattern of variability of crops was investigated by coupling spatial information from cadastral maps and crop type information obtained for free from the Regional Geoportal and Agriculture Register service, respectively. Investigation considered the period 2015–2020 and was achieved by comparing crop type maps (generated at parcel level) along time. The proposed methodology is expected to be useful for assessing land use intensity. Results showed a great rate of crop variation in the area, suggesting that, to obtain a robust damage estimation in case of flood, crop type maps have to be yearly updated.

Keywords: Crop rotation · Open data · Flood damage · GIS

1 Introduction

Climate change is a well-known issue in both the scientific community and public opinion. Long term changes have important consequences although the most acute effects could be found in the increased frequency and intensity of extreme weather events (EE) [1–4].

O. Gervasi et al. (Eds.): ICCSA 2022 Workshops, LNCS 13379, pp. 327–339, 2022.
https://doi.org/10.1007/978-3-031-10545-6_23

Extreme floods events are causing important damages all over the world more and more frequently [5–8]. Agricultural areas can be subject to serious damages from flood events [9, 10], therefore an accurate damage assessment is essential for floodplain restoration and prevention actions.

Many economic models have been developed to estimate flood damages caused to cultivated areas [11, 12]. The most of them consider local crops as stable in type and position over the years [9], completely neglecting ordinary agronomic practices related to crop rotation. Consequently, some doubts arise about robustness of estimates of potential EE damage to cultivated areas. It is worth to remind that, crop rotation is an agronomic practice that goes back to antiquity and consist in planting a sequence of different crops on the same field [13, 14]. It is one of the oldest agronomic practices that permits to control environmental stresses and crop performances through the regulation of nutrient, water balances, the control of diseases, insect and weeds infestations [15–18].

Crops have increasingly moved to short rotations and monocultures due to economic market trends, technical advancements, government incentives and customer needs [19]. Intense agriculture is expected to increase in future; unfortunately, evidences indicate that short rotations or monoculture are often related to lower yield with respect to the one obtainable through longer rotations or in first time planting [20, 21].

Tracking crop rotation (CR) is a complex activity [22, 23] that, unfortunately, it is rarely recorded into the farmers' logbook, even though it is a routine activity [13, 24].

In a context where climate change leads to an intensification of EE [1], the analysis and study of the crops present on the area is crucial for an estimation of the potential damage when an event occurs [25, 26]. Consequently, crop stability is a central element in this context, since conditioning reliability of long-term predictions about potential flood damage.

In this work, with reference to the study area, authors give an answer to the above mentioned issues: can the local agricultural landscape be assumed invariant along time? If not, what is the frequency and size of changes? The answer to these questions is expected to provide operational indications to generate proper damage estimates in case of flood. The study was based on a change detection approach based on free data ordinarily obtainable by the Piemonte Region databases, namely (i) farmers' declarations about yearly crop type and (ii) cadastral maps. In particular, with reference to a study area located in the Piemonte Region (NW-Italy), the following analyses were achieved: (i) one concerning yearly crop spatial distribution; (ii) one aiming at mapping and quantifying crop changes along time (2015–2020). Future developments will allow to expand the study area considering the whole Piedmont Region and analyze further aspects related to the CRs and the crops involved in them. All acronyms used in this manuscript were reported in appendix.

2 Material and Methods

2.1 Study Area

An agricultural area located in the Piemonte Region (NW-Italy), sizing about 16079 ha, was selected as area of interest (AOI), including the municipalities of Motta de' Conti, Balzola, Casale Monferrato, Frassineto Po and Villanova Monferrato. This area, majorly devoted to agriculture that represents one on the most important economic resources, is representative of the local agronomic landscape. It is characterized by the presence of the Po River, the biggest Italian one, that is known to be potentially floodable, therefore determining a high risk for the surrounding crops (Fig. 1).

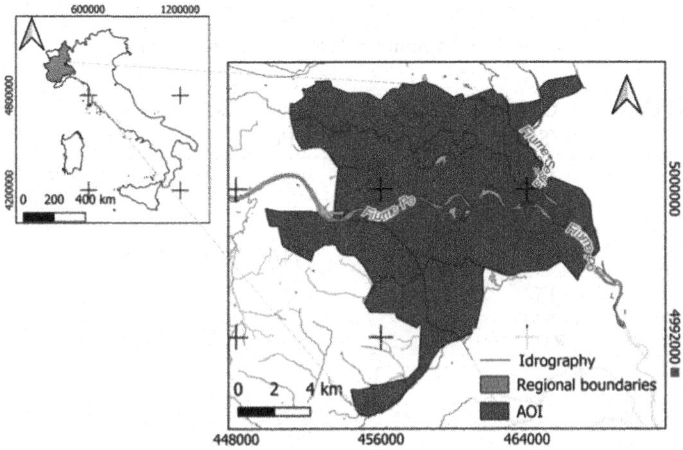

Fig. 1. Study area location – AOI (NW Italy) (Reference frame: WGS84 UTM32N).

2.2 Available Data

Cadastral maps (CM) are made available for free within the BDTRE (Territorial Reference Database for the Regional Institutions of the Piemonte Region). This can be accessed through the Piemonte Region geoportal [27].

For this work, CM was obtained as polygon vector layer (shapefile) covering AOI and including 20416 parcels. CM nominal scale is 1:2000 and was obtained by vectorization and re-projection into the WGS84 UTM32N reference frame of the native hardcopy maps of the Italian National Cadastral Office. CM is updated at 2020 and provide information about parcels geometry with no indication about associated land use.

Consequently, to qualify parcels in terms of crop type, the SIAP (Piemonte Agricultural Information System) database was accessed to obtain crop type information through the so called "Agricultural Register" (AR) service [28].

AR is an open-access system providing agricultural information (concerning crop type, livestock and farm features) at cadastral parcel level in table format (.csv).

AR data is yearly updated (on 11th November) based on declarations that farmers have to yearly provide to the Regional Administration. Typically, this data only report the main crop present in the parcel in the considered year, with no further specification about possible intra-annual rotations [13, 24]. Conversely, AR data can contain, for the same parcel, more than one record if the same parcel was split and cultivated with different crop type in the same year. AR are available for downloading since 2015. In this work, all the available years (2015–2020, hereinafter called reference period, RP) were considered.

Both cadastral map attribute table and the external one from AR contain separated codes about municipality (MC), cadastral sheet (CS) and parcel (PC). Additionally, AR table contain a further field reporting the area size devoted to the declared crop (see Table 1). These common fields made possible to operate related AR with CM, thus providing a map of yearly crop type at parcel level.

Table 1. Common fields to both reference data

Municipality Code (MC)	Cadastral Sheet Code (SC)	Cadastral Parcel Code (PC)	...	...
2082	11	18	...	...
2082	11	19	...	...
2082	15	116	...	...
2082	15	157	...	...
...	...	...	...	...

2.3 Data Processing

Geomatics offers new operative challenges to map and assess crop intensity detecting multiple crop cycles by analyzing multi-temporal spatial data [29, 30]. In this context, AR data represent a new tool, poorly explored in literature [31–33], to assess crop intensity based on farmer declaration data.

In this work, the joint use of CM and AR data were adopted to map and assess crop variability and somehow giving an estimate of crop intensity over AOI. All spatial analyses and related statistics were performed within QGIS vs 3.16.6 [34].

Crop Type Mapping. In order to assign crop type information to the correspondent parcel, a unique identification code (ID) was generated through GIS table field computation, involving strings and numbers. The code was computed for both the external table (foreign key) from AR and the attribute one linked to CM (primary key) using cadastral reference codes (Eq. 1).

$$ID = concat(MC + SC + PC) \tag{1}$$

where MC, CS and PC are respectively municipality code, cadastral sheet code and cadastral parcel code.

Data from AR were preventively filtered to ensure a one-to-one relationship between the CM attribute table and the external one. Filtering was achieved by considering the crop type associated, for the same parcel, to the biggest area as declared by farmer and recorded as additive field in AR.

An ordinary GIS join procedure was therefore applied to transfer AR information concerning crop type into the CM attribute table, thus permitting of generating 6 different yearly crop type maps.

In this work, authors focused on 8 crop types that were coded according to Table 2.

Table 2. Selected reference crops.

Reference classes	Main crop type
0	Other (vegetables, horticulture, greenhouses, minor crops)
1	Rise
2	Soya
3	Corn
4	Meadow
5	Wheet
6	Barley
7	Arboriculture (ochards, vineyards, poplar)

Temporal Crop Variability in AOI. To assess the temporal crop variability in AOI, the following conditions were tested at parcel level two years in two years: (i) parcels maintaining the same crop type for two consecutive years were coded as "unchanged" (UC); (ii) parcels where crop type changed between two consecutive years were coded as "changed" (CC) (Table 3). The areal size of CC and UC was therefore computed making possible to get an estimate of yearly changes affecting the considered crop types, namely the ones 2015–2016, 2016–2017, 2017–2018, 2018–2019 and 2019–2020. Additionally, CC was used to compute the total area that moved from one class to another assuming G = gained for increasing values and L = lost for decreasing values.

Table 3. Temporal crop variability.

ID	...	Area	2015 - 2016	2016–2017	2017–2018	2018–2019	2019–2020
20821118	...	0.37	UC	UC	UC	UC	CC
20821119	...	0.31	CC	CC	CC	CC	CC
208215116	...	0.62	CC	UC	UC	CC	CC
2082115157	...	0.07	UC	UC	UC	CC	CC
...	...	...	...	...	...	...	...

Mapping Spatial Crop Variability in AOI. Once parcels were characterized in terms of crop variation through the above mentioned UC/CC coding, CC occurrences were counted at parcel level making possible to summarize the local degree of variability (Eq. 2).

$$CV = \sum_{i=2016}^{2020} CC_i \tag{2}$$

Resulting values (CV) were recorded as a new attribute in the CM table. This permitted to map crop variability assuming CV as driver for graduation. The resulting map, hereinafter called crop variability map (CVM) was generated and the correspondent cumulative frequency distribution (CFD) explored.

3 Results and Discussions

3.1 Temporal Crop Variability in AOI

To analyze the temporal variability of crops in AOI, the total area for each crop for each year of RP was calculated (Fig. 2). Rice and corn resulted to be the most cultivated crops in AOI during RP (more than 4500 ha and 2000 ha respectively) while soya and barley the least ones (less than 500 ha). Crops extension presented very different trends in RP: arboriculture, meadows and barley showed a constant increasing trend, wheat a decreasing one, soya and rice fluctuated, corn and other crops remained slightly stable.

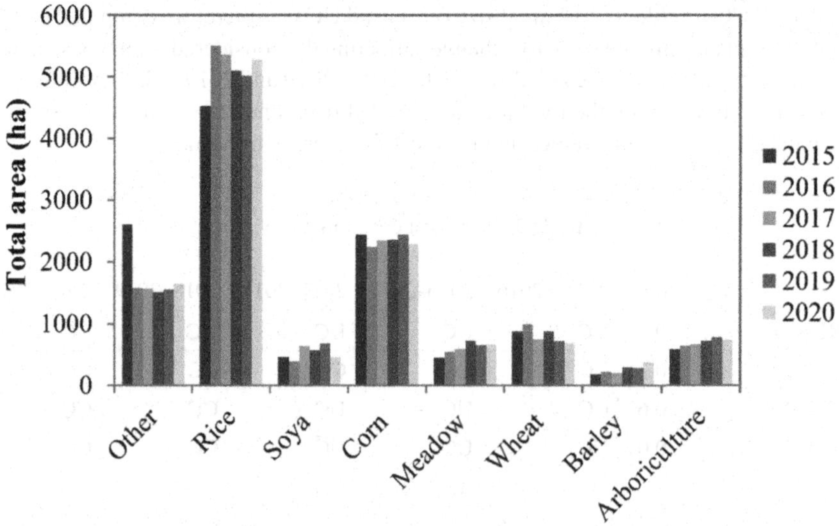

Fig. 2. Total area (ha) of crops in AOI

Yearly UC area was computed for all crops (Fig. 3). Results show that rice and corn, other crops, arboriculture and meadows were the most stable over time. For example, rice capitalized more than 4000 unchanged hectares in RP, followed by corn (>1300 ha), other crops (>1100 ha), arboriculture and meadows (~500 ha). Conversely, soybean, barley and wheat resulted the most varying one, showing a UC area of about 100 ha/y. These results are coherent to the local agricultural context. It is well known that rice tends to be cultivated on the same field for many years [35, 36]. A similarly behavior affects arboriculture class, where new plantations (e.g. orchards, vineyard and poplar stands) are expected to be maintained for 10–20 years. Barley, wheat and soya show low UC areas. In fact, they are the main rotating crops in the Piemonte region, since the firsts two (winter cereals) are frequently alternated with soya, a major soil-enriching crop [37–39].

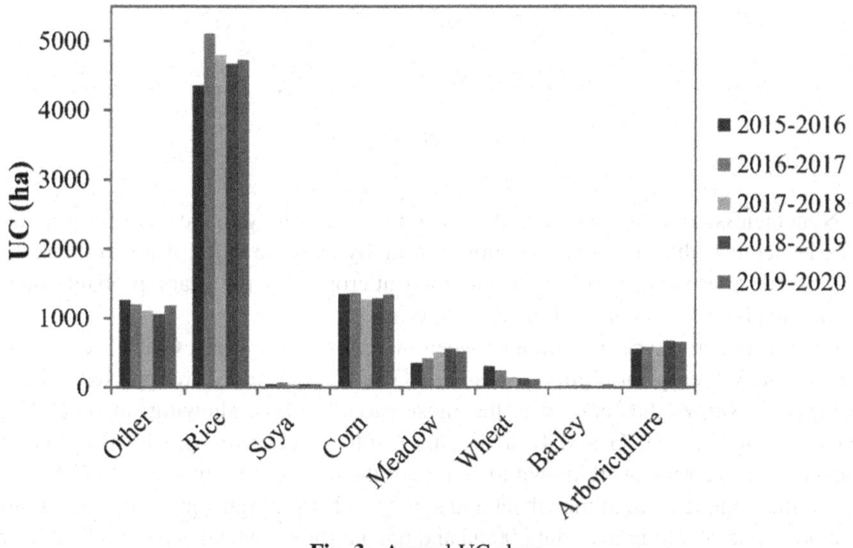

Fig. 3. Annual UC class.

Yearly CC values are reported in Fig. 4.

According to Fig. 4, CC proved to be averagely about 260 ha. The notable increase in rice in 2016 is symmetrical to the decrease in "other". Authors hypothesize that this outcome is due to the early transitional phase of the AR system. The first year of AR data availability is 2015 and is reasonable to consider that, in the first year, many rice CMs were not correctly coded in the system and consequently excluded from computation. In fact, from the following year, an increase in information and data is evident, consequently determining a migration of parcels from the "other" class to a specific crop.

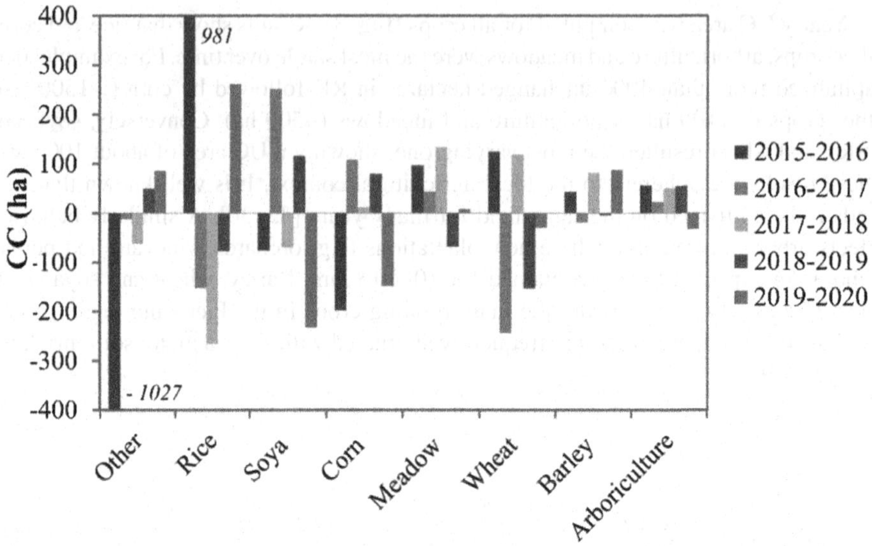

Fig. 4. Annual CC class.

Nonetheless, all crops showed alternate counts over the years, except for grassland and arboriculture that appeared to almost constantly increase in RP. Another interesting aspect is the alternating trend of soya and wheat crops over the years, probably due to the fact that both are often used in crop rotation.

Concerning crop type transition between two consecutive years, G and L can further improve the AOI crop variability assessment. G and L area values are reported in Fig. 5.

Figure 5 shows that corn was the most variable class, showing about 1000 ha exchanged in terms of G and L area. This result is coherent with local agronomic management as corn is well known to be one of the main crops subjected to CR.

For the same reason, in the wheat and soybean classes, high values of G and L area were observed, resulting in about 600 ha and 650 ha for the wheat class and 520 ha and 490 ha for the soya one respectively.

Conversely, meadows and arboriculture classes showed the smallest transition in RP, resulting in a G value of about 160 ha and 95 ha respectively, and in a L value of about 120 ha and 65 ha respectively. Additionally, it should be noted that the values of L area tend to be lower than the ones of G in RP, suggesting an increasing in terms of area for these two classes over time (Fig. 4). This result is coherent with the growing area trend previously observed in Fig. 2. Since these two classes are ordinary stable crops they are expected to remaining unchanged for many years as supported by Fig. 3 and therefore characterized by low variability and a potential increase in terms of area (Fig. 5).

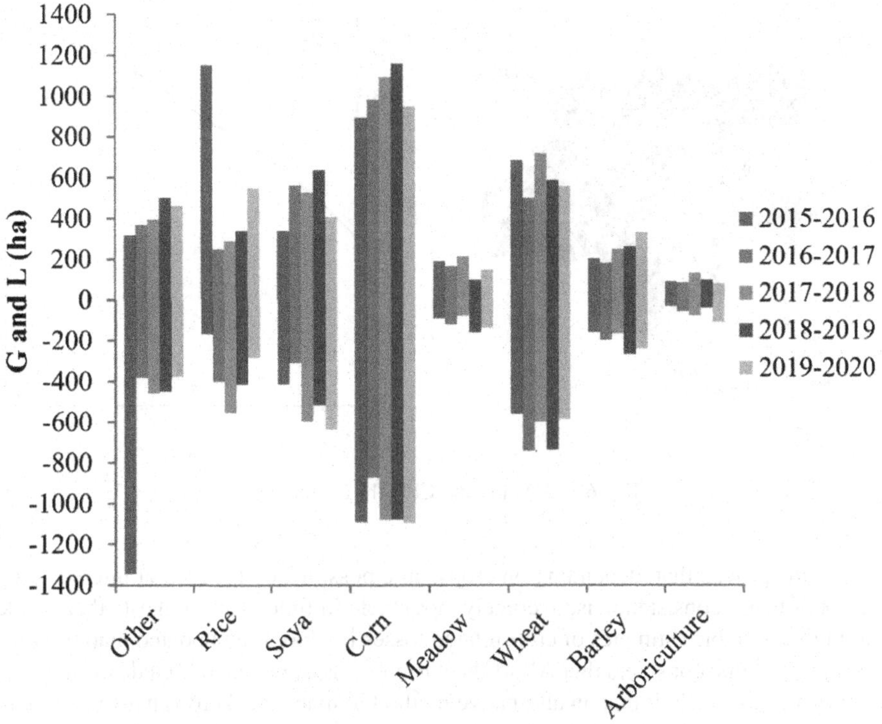

Fig. 5. G and L variability.

Regarding the rice class, both G and L values resulted to be about 350 ha. Among these results it is worth to note the high value of G (1100 ha) occurred between 2015 and 2016 (Fig. 4). However, rice remains a permanent crop with low variability in terms of G and L area. Moreover, it is worth to remind that CM size can differ considerably depending on crop. Rice extension was found to be significantly larger than other crops. Therefore, a variation of G and L of 350 ha in rice class can certainly be considered as a poorly significant.

3.2 Crop Variability Map

Crop type variability (CV) along the considered period was finally mapped in CVM (Fig. 6a). To quantitatively summarize CVM content the correspondent CFD was computed (Fig. 6b).

CFD (Fig. 6b) highlights that about 45% of the parcels did not change in RP. These areas are mainly located in the northern part of AOI where rice is the dominant crop (Fig. 6a). In fact, rice cultivation requires many irrigation infrastructures and a yearly terrain leveling to guarantee plant submersion [40]. Conversely, only less than 10% of CMs continuously changed yearly (CV = 5).

Moreover, they showed a clustered pattern suggesting that highly variable crops (e.g. wheat and soya) are rotating to each other persisting always over the same area.

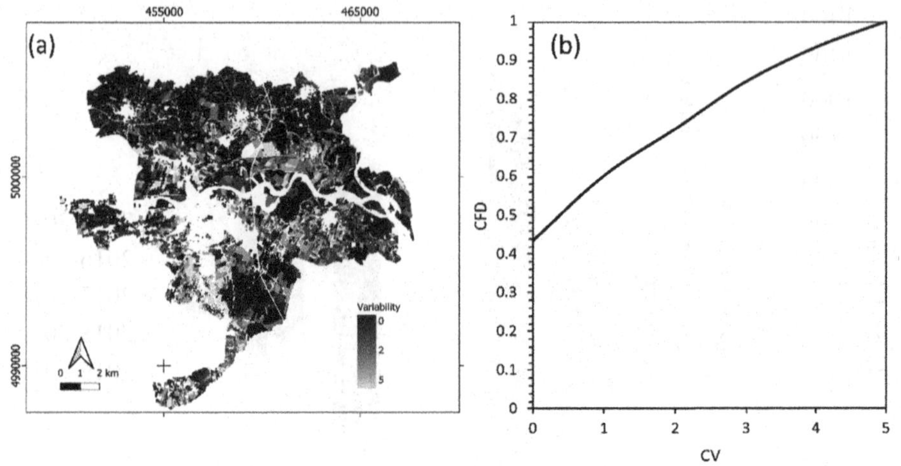

Fig. 6. CVM (a) and CFD (b) computing.

Results proved that, depending on crops, and, possibly, on the area of interest, crop distribution and consistency is, averagely, not stable in time. This suggests that, while longing for reliable estimates of crop-related losses by floods, an updated map of crops is required. If one considers that AR of the current year is, in general, made available in autumn, he has to admit that an alternative method to map actual crops has to be found. In this context, satellite-based classification can probably play an important role that has to be fostered in the next years.

4 Conclusions

In this work, crop variability in a representative agricultural area in Piemonte (NW-Italy) was explored based on free data and GIS tools.

Using AR and CM data, AOI agricultural dynamics (6 years) concerning crop type rotation was analyzed to determine if, a sort of time horizon could be eventually defined for programming crop type mapping depending on stability of crops.

To achieve this task, with reference to the main local crops and working at cadastral parcel level, authors operated a change detection analysis involving 6 years (2015–2020). Maps of transition were generated and some statistics computed. In AOI rice and arboriculture plants proved to be the most stable crops in RP. Nevertheless, in general, a high degree of variability was found; specifically soybean and wheat showed an alternating trend over the years, confirming their primary role in in crop rotation. They also showed an increasing trend in RP, demonstrated by analyzing the correspondent G and L values.

To summarize and mapping crop variability, a counter, namely CV, was mapped at parcel level. Resulting map (CVM) is expected to be used to assess land use intensity by farmers and to address the estimation process of flooded crops, suggesting, if no updated map is available, where estimates can be retained majorly reliable (Table 4.).

5 Appendix

Table 4. Acronyms used in the paper

Acronyms	Extended acronyms
EE	Extreme Events
CR	Crop Rotation
AOI	Area Of Interest
CM	Cadastral Maps
BDTRE	Territorial Reference Database for the Regional Institutions of the Piemonte Region
SIAP	Piemonte Agricultural Information System
AR	Agricultural Register
RP	Reference Period
MC	Municipality Code
CS	Cadastral Sheet Code
PC	Cadastral Parcel Code
ID	Identification Code
UC	Unchanged Crop
CC	Changed Crop
G	Gained area
L	Lost area
CV	Crop Variability
CVM	Crop Variability Map
CFD	Cumulative Frequency Distribution

References

1. Sánchez, E., Gallardo, C., Gaertner, M.A., Arribas, A., Castro, M.: Future climate extreme events in the Mediterranean simulated by a regional climate model: a first approach. Glob. Planet. Change **44**, 163–180 (2004)
2. Zwiers, F.W., Kharin, V.V.: Changes in the extremes of the climate simulated by CCC GCM2 under CO 2 doubling. J. Clim. **11**, 2200–2222 (1998)
3. Lynch, J., Cain, M., Frame, D., Pierrehumbert, R.: Agriculture's contribution to climate change and role in mitigation is distinct from predominantly fossil CO2-emitting sectors. Front. Sustain. Food Syst. **300** (2021)
4. Siwar, C., Alam, M., Murad, M.W., Al-Amin, A.Q.: A review of the linkages between climate change, agricultural sustainability and poverty in Malaysia. Int. Rev. Bus. Res. Papers (ISSN 1832–9543). **5**, 309–321 (2009)

5. Bronstert, A.: Floods and climate change: interactions and impacts. Risk Anal.: Int. J. **23**, 545–557 (2003)
6. Guhathakurta, P., Sreejith, O.P., Menon, P.A.: Impact of climate change on extreme rainfall events and flood risk in India. J. Earth Syst. Sci. **120**, 359–373 (2011)
7. Hlavčová, K., Lapin, M., Valent, P., Szolgay, J., Kohnová, S., Rončák, P.: Estimation of the impact of climate change-induced extreme precipitation events on floods. Contributions to geophysics and geodesy. **45**, 173–192 (2015)
8. Adams, R.M., Hurd, B.H., Lenhart, S., Leary, N.: Effects of global climate change on agriculture: an interpretative review. Climate Res. **11**, 19–30 (1998)
9. Brémond, P., Grelot, F., Agenais, A.-L.: Flood damage assessment on agricultural areas: review and analysis of existing methods. (2013)
10. Nelson, G.C., et al.: Climate change effects on agriculture: economic responses to biophysical shocks. Proc. Natl. Acad. Sci. **111**, 3274–3279 (2014)
11. Bremond, P., Grelot, F., Agenais, A.-L.: Economic evaluation of flood damage to agriculture–review and analysis of existing methods. Nat. Hazard. **13**, 2493–2512 (2013)
12. Molinari, D., Scorzini, A.R., Gallazzi, A., Ballio, F.: AGRIDE-c, a conceptual model for the estimation of flood damage to crops: development and implementation. Nat. Hazard. **19**, 2565–2582 (2019)
13. Bullock, D.G.: Crop rotation. Crit. Rev. Plant Sci. **11**, 309–326 (1992)
14. Yates, F.: The analysis of experiments containing different crop rotations. Biometrics. 324–346 (1954)
15. Barbieri, P., Pellerin, S., Nesme, T.: Comparing crop rotations between organic and conventional farming. Sci Rep. **7**, 13761 (2017). https://doi.org/10.1038/s41598-017-14271-6
16. Bennett, A.J., Bending, G.D., Chandler, D., Hilton, S., Mills, P.: Meeting the demand for crop production: the challenge of yield decline in crops grown in short rotations. Biol. Rev. **87**, 52–71 (2012)
17. Curl, E.A.: Control of plant diseases by crop rotation. Bot. Rev. **29**, 413–479 (1963)
18. Verhulst, N., et al.: The effect of tillage, crop rotation and residue management on maize and wheat growth and development evaluated with an optical sensor. Field Crop Res. **120**, 58–67 (2011)
19. Selim, M.: A review of advantages, disadvantages and challenges of crop rotations. Egypt. J. Agron. **41**, 1–10 (2019)
20. Huang, H.C., Chou, C.H., Erickson, R.S.: Soil sickness and its control. Allelopath. J. **18**, 1–21 (2006)
21. Sarvia, F., De Petris, S., Ghilardi, F., Xausa, E., Cantamessa, G., Borgogno-Mondino, E.: The Importance of agronomic knowledge for crop detection by Sentinel-2 in the CAP controls framework: a possible rule-based classification approach. Agronomy. **12**, 1228 (2022)
22. Stein, S., Steinmann, H.H.: Identifying crop rotation practice by the typification of crop sequence patterns for arable farming systems–A case study from Central Europe. Eur. J. Agron. **92**, 30–40 (2018)
23. Wright, R.J.: Evaluation of crop rotation for control of Colorado potato beetles (Coleoptera: Chrysomelidae) in commercial potato fields on Long Island. J. Econ. Entomol. **77**, 1254–1259 (1984)
24. Dury, J., Schaller, N., Garcia, F., Reynaud, A., Bergez, J.E.: Models to support cropping plan and crop rotation decisions. A review. Agron. Sustain. Develop. **32**, 567–580 (2012)
25. Borgogno-Mondino, E., Sarvia, F., Gomarasca, M.A.: Supporting insurance strategies in agriculture by remote sensing: a possible approach at regional level. In: International conference on computational science and its applications, Springer, pp. 186–199 (2019)

26. Sarvia, F., Petris, S.D., Borgogno-Mondino, E.: A methodological proposal to support estimation of damages from hailstorms based on copernicus sentinel 2 data times series. In: International Conference on Computational Science and Its Applications, Springer, pp. 737–751 (2020)
27. Regione Piemonte: Geoportale Piemonte. https://www.geoportale.piemonte.it/cms/
28. Sistema Piemonte - Regione Piemonte: Anagrafe agricola del Piemonte. https://servizi.regione.piemonte.it/catalogo/anagrafe-agricola-piemonte
29. Boryan, C.G., Yang, Z., Willis, P., Di, L.: Developing crop specific area frame stratifications based on geospatial crop frequency and cultivation data layers. J. Integr. Agric. **16**, 312–323 (2017)
30. Hao, P., Tang, H., Chen, Z., Le, Y.U., Wu, M.: High resolution crop intensity mapping using harmonized Landsat-8 and Sentinel-2 data. J. Integr. Agric. **18**, 2883–2897 (2019)
31. Sarvia, F., De Petris, S., Borgogno-Mondino, E.: Mapping ecological focus areas within the EU CAP controls framework by Copernicus Sentinel-2 Data. Agronomy. **12**, 406 (2022)
32. Copăcenaru, O., et al.: Copernicus data and CAP subsidies control. In: Södergård, C., Mildorf, T., Habyarimana, E., Berre, A.J., Fernandes, J.A., Zinke-Wehlmann, C. (eds.) Big Data in bioeconomy, pp. 265–290. Springer, Cham (2021). https://doi.org/10.1007/978-3-030-71069-9_20
33. Sarvia, F., Xausa, E., Petris, S.D., Cantamessa, G., Borgogno-Mondino, E.: A possible role of copernicus sentinel-2 data to support common agricultural policy controls in agriculture. Agronomy. **11**, 110 (2021)
34. QGIS. https://www.qgis.org/it/site/
35. Laborte, A.G., et al.: RiceAtlas, a spatial database of global rice calendars and production. Sci. data. **4**, 1–10 (2017)
36. Varvel, G.E.: Monoculture and rotation system effects on precipitation use efficiency of corn. Agron. J. **86**, 204–208 (1994)
37. Hammel, J.E.: Long-term tillage and crop rotation effects on winter wheat production in northern Idaho. Agron. J. **87**, 16–22 (1995)
38. Guy, S.O., Gareau, R.M.: Crop rotation, residue durability, and nitrogen fertilizer effects on winter wheat production. J. Prod. Agric. **11**, 457–461 (1998)
39. Edwards, J.H., Thurlow, D.L., Eason, J.T.: Influence of tillage and crop rotation on yields of corn, soybean, and wheat. Agron. J. **80**, 76–80 (1988)
40. Ferrero, A., Tinarelli, A.: Rice cultivation in the EU ecological conditions and agronomical practices. In: Pesticide risk assessment in rice paddies, Elsevier, pp. 1–24 (2008)

A WebGIS Prototype for Visualizing and Monitoring the Spatio-temporal Changes in Seawater Quality

Alessandra Capolupo(✉), Cristina Monterisi, Danilo Spasiano, Alberto Ferraro, Matilda Mali, Umberto Fratino, and Eufemia Tarantino

Department of Civil, Environmental, Land, Construction and Chemistry (DICATECh), Politecnico di Bari, via Orabona 4, 70125 Bari, Italy
{alessandra.capolupo,cristina.monterisi,danilo.spasiano, alerto.ferraro,matilda.mali,umberto.fratino, eufemia.tarantino}@poliba.it

Abstract. Anthropogenic pressure on the coastal areas triggers a shoreline deep evolution, impacting the marine-coastal ecosystem. A specific fact-finding tool should be developed to detect the potential damages suffered by such an environment both qualitatively and quantitatively. Web Geographical Information Systems (WebGIS), developed to store, and handle geospatial big data, as well as disseminate information generated by processing raw data, appears as an optimal solution to address those needs. Indeed, they allow integrating own data with those ones provided by external sources into a single web application, easily accessible through an interactive and straightforward interface. This may interest several types of target audiences, such as local/national authorities and scientific communities. Therefore, this research is aimed at introducing a WebGIS prototype, developed to analyze and visualize seawater quality data in the Puglia region (Southern Italy). System features and capability was designed considering potential consumers' requirements, and, in accordance with Open Geospatial Consortium and European directive INSPIRE, its infrastructure was developed using Free and Open-Source Software for Geographic information systems. Thus, after defining the end-users and capturing their needs, the platform was built using the three-tier configuration. The levels were devoted to presenting, analyzing, and storing the data, respectively. Additionally, a user-friendly interface, allowing two-dimensional data visualization, was also programmed to help the not-skilled consumers in consulting the stored data. The developed WebGIS allows both multi-temporal and multi-scale analysis to evaluate and monitor seawater quality permitting local authorities to plan the adequate remedial actions.

Keywords: Web mapping; IoT · Water pollution · Geospatial data · FOSS4G

1 Introduction

The natural phenomenon concerning the nutrients accumulation in seawater is generally called eutrophication. It, mainly linked to human pressure in the coastal areas, has been

O. Gervasi et al. (Eds.): ICCSA 2022 Workshops, LNCS 13379, pp. 340–353, 2022.
https://doi.org/10.1007/978-3-031-10545-6_24

getting worse quickly over the last few years because of population growth of about 45% in those zones [1–6]. This has caused a strong deterioration of the coastal-marine ecosystem balance, implying its goods and services degradation [7]. Indeed, as reported by Wurtsbaugh et al., [8] in 2019, an annual loss equal to $1 billion was estimated in Europe. Therefore, various European Directives, such as the Urban Wastewater Directive (UWWD-91/271/EEC), the Water Framework Directive (WFD-2000/60/EC), the Marine Strategy Framework Directive (MSFD-2008/56/EC) [9] were issued to tackle such an environmental question and to improve seawater quality. All those documents suggested the development of specific fact-finding tools aimed at evaluating and monitoring seawater quality. Therefore, the scientific community is totally dedicated on economic and effective approaches detection to meet such a purpose and to support local/national authorities in adopting the optimal management strategies.

Geographical Information System (GIS) appears as the best alternative to handle the large amount of data needed to assess and monitor the seawater quality. Moreover, thanks to the technology advancement and internet coming, GIS can be adopted to disseminate information/data too [10–12]. In fact, the Web Geographic Information System (WebGIS) permits consumers to access data directly, to visualize them both in a two and three-dimension (2D and 3D) and manage them by exploiting cloud potentialities [13].

A client-server structure, based on three-tiers configuration, is commonly selected to implement an intuitive and efficient web platform suitable for handling geospatial big data. Each layer is generally developed as an independent module in order to maximize its performance [13]. Specifically, it consists of i) an attractive easy-to-use interface with the aim of supporting skilled and not-skilled users in getting the desired information [14], ii) a geodatabase, able to store all data types [13–15], and lastly, iii) an application stage, aimed at managing and handling the data [16]. The components of each single tier can be programmed by using both proprietary and open-source software. Those last ones are usually preferred due to their versatility and competitive performance albeit they can be programmed by expert technicians [17, 18]. In addition, Free Open-Source Soft-ware (FOSS) allows also to respect the INfrastructure for Spatial InfoRmation in the European Community (INSPIRE) Directive and Open Geospatial Consortium (OCG) expectations [19].

This work is aimed at presenting the Web application prototype developed to support potential consumers in detecting the optimal eco-compatible management strategies to preserve the coastal-marine ecosystems of Puglia Region (Southern Italy). Thus, after collecting end-users' feedbacks, the external open data sources were analyzed to identify available datasets and to program the field data campaigns needed to fill the lack of information. Such a WebGIS presumes to integrate all required data to assess and monitor the coastal-marine environment. Therefore, its single component was designed properly using FOSS4G software in compliance with OCG and EU Directive INSPIRE.

Three main sections can be detected in this paper: i) "Material and methods" (Sect. 2), ii) "Results and discussion" (Sect. 3) and, lastly, iii) "Conclusion" (Sect. 4). The aim of Sect. 2 is to describe the background and the methodology, as well as the data, needed to implement an efficient, effective, and user-friendly web environment aimed at storing and handling all the available maps and information concerning the coastal-marine ecosystem. On the contrary, Sect. 3 is essentially linked to research outcomes representation and discussion in order to enhance the potentialities and the performance of the implemented Web application prototype. Its results were also compared with the main outcomes obtained by previous works. The last Section, instead, is mainly focused on describing platform strengths and weaknesses as well as outlining future work directions.

2 Material and Methods

The WebGIS application design was based on the workflow suggested by Huxhold and Levinsohm in 1995 [20] which consists of seven essential steps to comply with (Fig. 1). Thus, after detecting potential consumers of such a framework, its main characteristics, and the indispensable data, as well as the optimal architecture to adopt, were defined. That knowledge was the foundation of WebGIS platform design, later converted into a prototype whose effectiveness and efficiency were subsequently assessed. Thus, the implementation phase started by involving three key stages: i) data collection and database construction; ii) interface building and, lastly, iii) data implementation. The final performance of all the above-mentioned phases is iterative and interactive, and they are detailed in the next paragraphs.

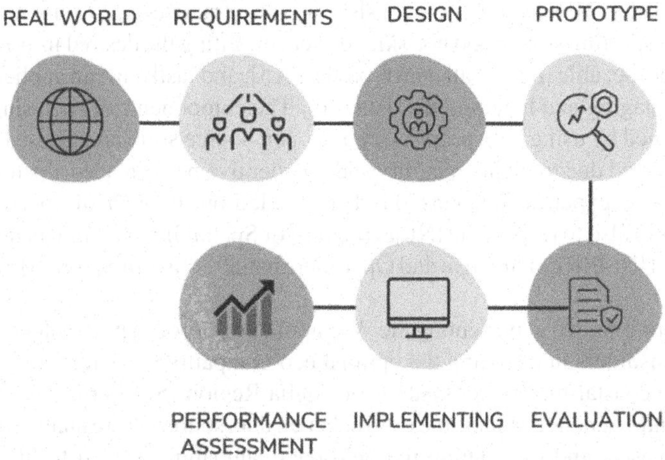

Fig. 1. Operative pipeline applied to develop and implement WebGIS application

2.1 WebGIS Framework Design

Three relevant aspects were considered to design an attractive WebGIS application. Firstly, once potential users were detected, their expectations and requirements were explored and gathered. That information was, thus, used as a substratum to define:

i) the area of interest, ii) the required data and the existing sources to consult or the best practices to acquire the unavailable data, and, lastly, iii) the optimal software and hardware needed to optimize its configuration.

Several target groups, such as the national/regional/local authorities aimed at evaluating and monitoring water quality, as well as the scientific community interested in having a unique database including all the data, may be considered as potential consumers. Individual citizens could benefit from the information provided by the platform too. Indeed, they can access the data directly and, consequently, know the actual water pollution level of the ecosystems where they live. This allows defining which features should be had by the platform and which data should be integrated and handled.

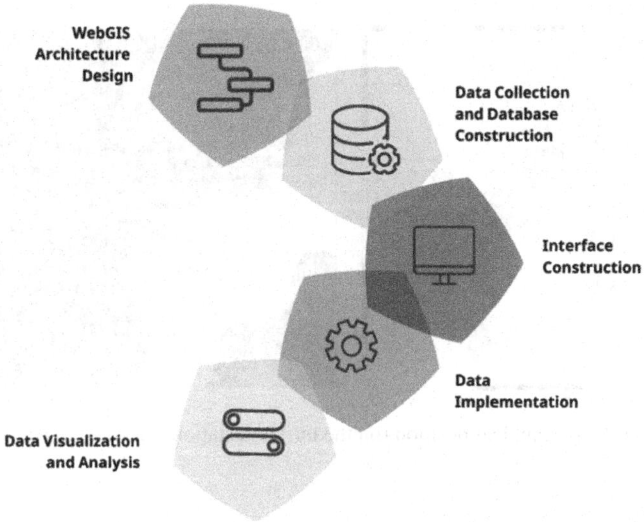

Fig. 2. Architecture operative workflow.

Therefore, the design phase was started on the basis of the operative workflow introduced by Caradonna et al., in 2016 [21]. It consists of five main stages, reported in Fig. 2. Initially, the WebGIS capability and, consequently, its structure was defined and constructed ("WebGIS architecture design" phase). Then, the most suitable data, provided by external open sources or collected during proper field data campaigns, were picked up. Due to their heterogeneous formats, the optimal strategies for their treatment and implementation in the platform were outlined too ("Data collection and database construction" step). A 2D user-friendly interface was then built for helping skilled and not-skilled users in consulting the application and getting the desired information ("Interface construction" step). Thus, the collected data were implemented in the specific drop-down menus ("Data implementation" stage) and visualized in the 2D viewer ("Data visualization and analysis" phase).

2.2 Study Area

Puglia, in Southern Italy, was chosen as a pilot site since it is the third region in terms of coastline length at the national level (Fig. 3) [22]. Indeed, as reported by the Regional Coastal Plan of 2011, its shoreline broadens to about 1000 km and it is characterized by a complex morphology, varying from sandy beaches up to river mouths including rocky cliffs too. Marine-coastal ecosystem diversity is mainly due to the influence of anthropogenic activities, such as urban sprawl and increment of population density and infrastructures. To meet the research purpose, five Apulian ports were selected as particular case studies to analyze. Specifically, the harbors of Bari, Mola di Bari, Monopoli, Brindisi, and Otranto were picked up.

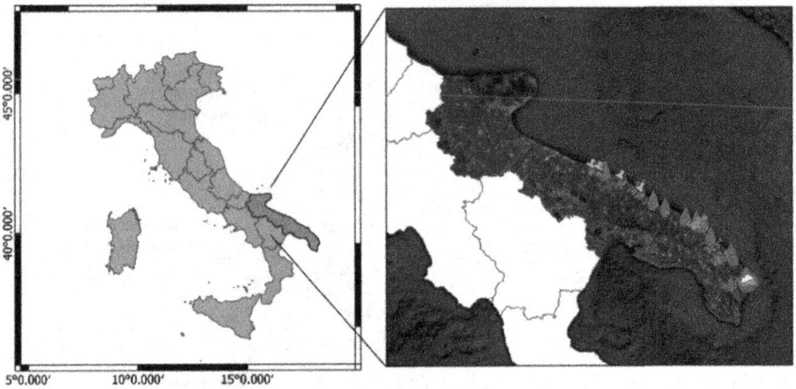

Fig. 3. Study area geographical position (on the left) and stations, devoted to data collection (on the right).

Thanks to its geographical location, the New Port of Bari is considered one of the most relevant multifunctional ports in the Southern Italy as well as the gateway to the countries of Eastern and Middle East Europe. This allows its continuous and dynamic evolution in terms of passengers and freight traffic albeit travelers movement, based on ferry and cruise, is its driving force.

The small port of Mola di Bari is characterized by an internal zone reserved for fishing boats parking and floating docks suitable for hosting recreational boats.

The structure of the Port of Monopoli is protected by two main piers: i) that one of Margherita di Savoia and ii) the Tramontana Dam. The latter, however, is not accessible because of its elbow shape and the presence of an escarpment rocky. Nevertheless, the port is still subjected to some dangers, like the shoal in Punta del Trave, especially in conditions of low tide.

The port of Brindisi is naturally characterized by an internal, medium, and external basin, which corresponds to the tourist, commercial, and industrial port, respectively. The first is delimited by two deep inlets that enclose the historic center of Brindisi. The second comprises the stretch of sea, located close to the Pigonati canal. On the north, the basin forms the "Bocche di Puglia". Lastly, the third one is delimited by the mainland on the south, the Pedagne islands on the east, Sant'Andrea island and the Costa Morena pier on the west, and the Punta Riso dam on the north.

The development of the port of Otranto is mainly linked to its touristic relevance, indeed, this small gulf is a significant point for welcoming visitors' boats. It can accommodate up to 390 berths with a maximum length of 20 m.

2.3 Data Collection and Geodatabase Building

Preserving the marine-coastal ecosystem and guaranteeing the implementation of eco-friendly actions may be ensured by a timely monitoring program aimed at assessing and controlling both natural and anthropogenic pressure factors. Therefore, in compliance with the Government Decree n. 152/2006, the most suitable parameters for meeting research purposes were identified and collected by consulting open and own data sources.

The National Geoportal [23] and Territorial Information System of Apulian Region (SIT Puglia [24]) provided the basic cartography. Conversely, the Regional Agency for Environmental Prevention and Protection (ARPA Puglia) [25], and the Italian Institute for Environmental Protection and Research (ISPRA) [26] supplied water and air quality data while the free website VesselFinder [27] gave details about the real-time maritime traffic. Additionally, to extend the information concerning the quality of seawater, sediment, and air, the dataset gathered within the AI SMART project [28], was uploaded too.

After importing those data into PostGreSQL using PostGIS extension and storing them together with style and Uniform Resource Locator (URL), their reference systems were transformed into WGS84 UTM 33N (EPSG: 32633). Each data was uploaded in the most adequate menu.

2.4 WebGIS Structure Implementation and Interface Construction

The WebGIS was structured by adopting the three tiers configuration, as depicted in Fig. 4. Thus, a specific independent module was developed for each of them, and, specifically, for i) the presentation tier (interface), aimed at visualizing the data, ii) the application layer, devoted to handling the data and producing information, and iii) the database level, dedicated to storing the data.

As outlined in Fig. 4, web browsers, session pools, static files, and rendered maps were the main tools combined to build the first level. Conversely, web servers, additional libraries, and model generation tools were adopted to construct the second tier and, lastly, an open DataBase Management System (DBMS) was, instead, applied to define the structure of the third layer.

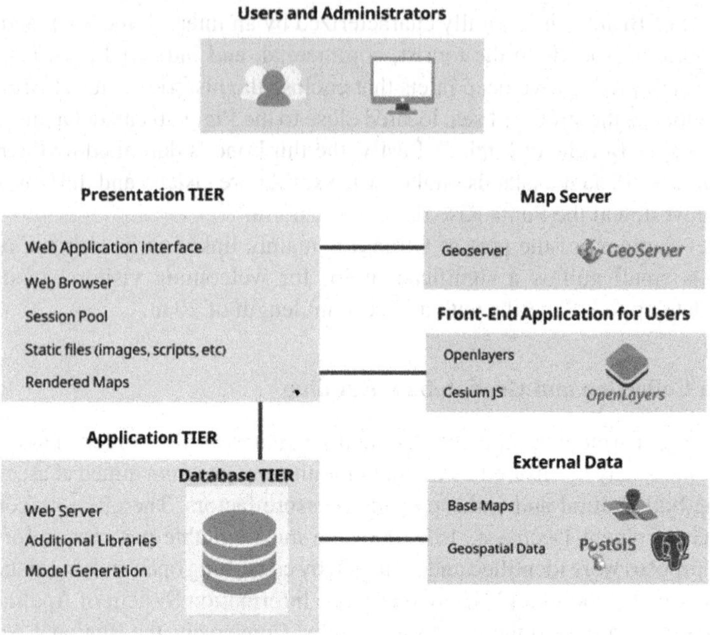

Fig. 4. Three-tiers configuration of the develop WebGIS application

Web browsers had the role of client front-end allowing web page access and consumers' queries transferee to the webserver and map server. The former, aimed at running the web scripts and forwarding the query to the implemented geodatabase, was constructed using version 9.0.39 of the open-source HTTP Apache Tomcat Server [29], realized by the Apache Software Foundation (Forest Hill, MD, USA) [14, 30]. On the contrary, the latter was mainly devoted to data treatment in the 2D viewer as well as the integration of web services available from external sources, provided in the following formats: Web Map Service (WMS), Web Feature Service (WFS); Web Coverage Service (WCS); Web Processing Service (WPS); Web Map Tile Service (WMTS) [14, 30]. Version 2.15.1 of the open-source Java-script Map server Geoserver (Boundless Spatial, GeoSolutions, Refractions Research, St. Louis, MO, USA [31]) was adopted to set the Map server. The DBMS, instead, was designed by applying version 12.0 of the PostGre Structured Query Language (PostGreSQL) database system (PostgreSQL Global Development Group [32]). Lastly, additional libraries, like, for instance, version 6.4.3 of OSGEO of OpenLayers (Boundless Spatial, GeoSolutions, Refractions Research, St. Louis, MO, USA [33]), were introduced to improve data analysis and presentation.

As above-mentioned, in compliance with the Open Geospatial Consortium (OGC) and EU directive INSPIRE, free and Open-Source Software for Geospatial Applications (FOSS4G) were adopted for every single module [34–38].

Moreover, the interface was made more attractive thanks to the adoption of version 4.5.0 and 4.7.0 of the Bootstrap [39] and version 4 of W3 [40] libraries. Additionally, a CSS style file, programmed using the HTML and JS languages, was integrated with the previously mentioned libraries, into a unique script [41]. This combination allows setting adequate menus where the data were collocated properly.

3 Results and Discussion

A web application was developed to geo-visualize and monitor air/seawater quality and sediment in the most relevant ports of the Puglia region. To meet such a purpose, the working plan comprised three basic phases: i) potential end-users needs exploration, and, thus, definition of case studies and data to collect, ii) web application design, iii) data collection and web tool implementation.

To carry out each phase, the operative workflow proposed by Huxhold and Levinsohm in 1995 [20] (Fig. 1) was adopted. Thus, potential stakeholders and users were detected, and their feedbacks were gathered. WebGIS platform was designed and calibrated on the basis of their needs through the operative workflow described in Fig. 2. After completing such a stage, the required data were collected from available external sources and AI-SMART project, and then, stored in the geo-database developed using an open-source DBMS, PostGreSQL (version 12.0) [32]. Simultaneously, the other two tiers were implemented to complete the WebGIS configuration: an attractive interface, aimed at helping users in consulting the platform, and the application layer, devoted to handling the data. All tiers were developed independently through FOSS4G in accordance with OCG and EU directive INSPIRE.

The interface, depicted in Fig. 5, is characterized by three main factors: Table of Content (ToC) and printer panel on the left, and the 2D viewer on the right. ToC groups together all the data into the most adequate menu, such as base layers (Fig. 5A), water quality monitoring, air quality monitoring, seawater surface temperature, humidity parameter, wind condition, hydrometric level, real-time maritime traffic (Fig. 5B e Fig. 5C). Each drop-down menu includes layers bringing similar information. The printer panel is located on the bottom of the ToC and it allows downloading the data by selecting the most suitable format (Fig. 5D). On the contrary, the 2D window is located on the right. Beyond the visualization of the active maps, it includes other tools too. Specifically, the navigation toolbar, comprising zoom in, zoom out, slide zoom, zoom to layer extension and full screen, is arranged on the top-left (Fig. 5E), the overview map (Fig. 5F) and the scale bar (Fig. 5G) are at the bottom-left while, lastly, the coordinates of the mouse pointer are displayed on the top-right (Fig. 5I) and the information tool is on the bottom-right (Fig. 5L).

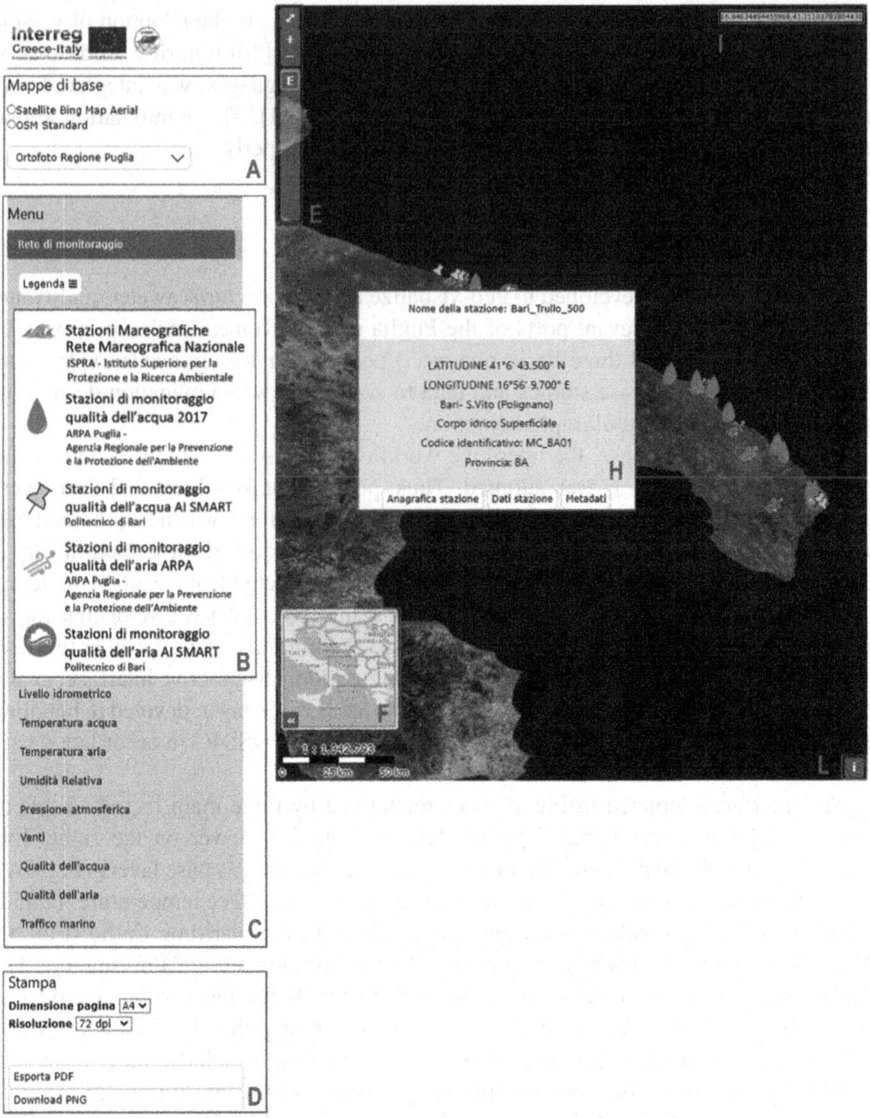

Fig. 5. 2D viewer interface: A) baseline maps; B) Sampling points; C) Table of Content (ToC); D) export tools; E) zoom in/zoom out widgets; F) frame visualization; G) scale and H) metadata panel; I) Pointer coordinates; L) information.

When active, the layer overlaps the base map and, just clinking on the corresponding panel, the users can select the information to display. Indeed, he/she can choose among the station registry panel, displayed in Fig. 5H, the data window, depicted in Figs. 6, 7, and the metadata panel.

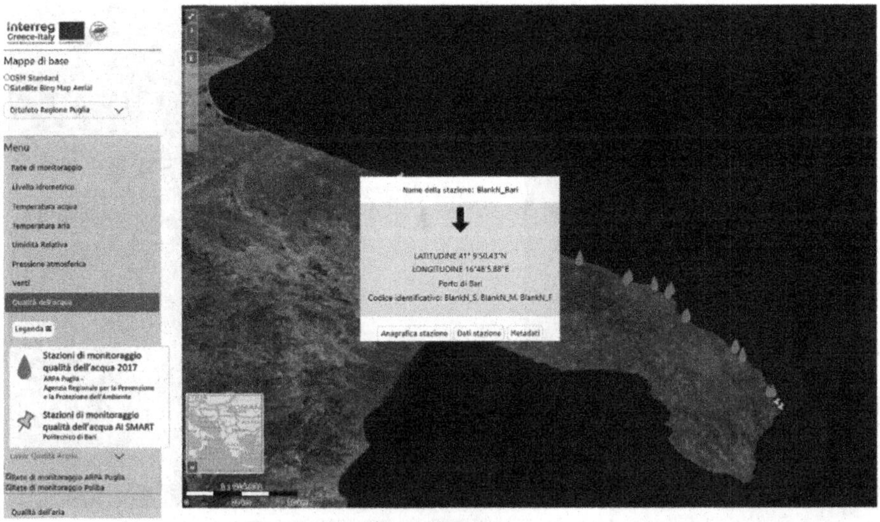

		PORTO DI BARI				DM 173/2016	
Nome stazione		Bianco			Bianco	Livelli chimici di riferimento nazionali	
Sigla		BlankN_S	BlankN_F		BlankN		
Data campionamento		Giugno 2021	Giugno 2021		Giugno 2021		
Fase		Ante operam	Ante operam		Ante operam	L1	L2
PARAMETRI CHIMICO-FISICI	U.M.			U.M.			
pH	u. pH	8,10	8,23	u. pH	8,78	-	-
Pot. Redox				mV	-83,9	-	-
Umidità a 105 °C				%	21,61	-	-
Frazione < 2mm				% s.s.	100,0	-	-
METALLI							
Arsenico	mg/l	< 0.01	< 0.01	mg/kg s.s.	6,51	12	20
Berillio	mg/l	< 0.01	< 0.01	mg/kg s.s.	0,03	-	-
Cadmio	mg/l	< 0.01	< 0.01	mg/kg s.s.	0,07	0,3	0,8
Cobalto	mg/l	< 0.01	< 0.01	mg/kg s.s.	1,75	-	-
Cromo totale	mg/l	< 0.01	< 0.01	mg/kg s.s.	9,52	50	150
Mercurio	mg/l	< 0.01	< 0.01	mg/kg s.s.	< 0.01	0,3	0,8
Nichel	mg/l	< 0.01	< 0.01	mg/kg s.s.	3,05	30	75
Piombo	mg/l	< 0.01	< 0.01	mg/kg s.s.	46,17	30	70
Rame	mg/l	< 0.01	< 0.01	mg/kg s.s.	7,92	40	52
Selenio	mg/l	< 0.01	< 0.01	mg/kg s.s.	< 0.01	-	-
Tallio	mg/l	< 0.01	< 0.01	mg/kg s.s.	< 0.01	-	-
Vanadio	mg/l	< 0.01	< 0.01	mg/kg s.s.	15,62	-	-
Zinco	mg/l	< 0.01	< 0.01	mg/kg s.s.	13,01	100	150
IDROCARBURI POLICICLICI AROMATICI (IPA)							
Naftalene	μg/l	< 5	< 5	μg/kg s.s.	< 20	35	391
Fluorantene	μg/l	< 5	< 5	μg/kg s.s.	< 20	110	1494
Antracene	μg/l	< 5	< 5	μg/kg s.s.	< 20	24	245
Acenaftene	μg/l	< 5	< 5	μg/kg s.s.	< 20	-	-
Acenaftilene	μg/l	< 5	< 5	μg/kg s.s.	< 20	-	-
Fluorene	μg/l	< 5	< 5	μg/kg s.s.	< 20	21	144
Fenantrene	μg/l	< 5	< 5	μg/kg s.s.	< 20	87	544
Pirene	μg/l	< 5	< 5	μg/kg s.s.	< 21	153	1398
Crisene	μg/l	< 5	< 5	μg/kg s.s.	< 20	108	846
Benzo[a]antracene	μg/l	< 5	< 5	μg/kg s.s.	< 20	75	500
Benzo[a]pirene	μg/l	< 5	< 5	μg/kg s.s.	< 20	30	100
Benzo[k,j]fluorantene	μg/l	< 5	< 5	μg/kg s.s.	< 20	20	500
Benzo[b]fluorantene	μg/l	< 5	< 5	μg/kg s.s.	< 20	40	500
Benzo[g,h,i]perilene	μg/l	< 5	< 5	μg/kg s.s.	< 20	55	100
Dibenzo[a,h]antracene	μg/l	< 5	< 5	μg/kg s.s.	< 20	-	-
Indeno[1,2,3-a,b]pirene	μg/l	< 5	< 5	μg/kg s.s.	< 20	-	-
$\sum$ IPA	μg/l	< 5	< 5	μg/kg s.s.	< 21	900	4000

Fig. 6. Visualization of chemical-physical features measured by the station located in Mola di Bari Port

WebGIS platform efficiency and effectiveness were assessed too. All software, selected to implement each element of the three tiers, showed a performance in line with the literature. Indeed, as already registered by [42–45], up to 10 s and 2.4 s are required by PostGreSQL and PostgreSQL/PostGIS and Geoserver to run 12 million

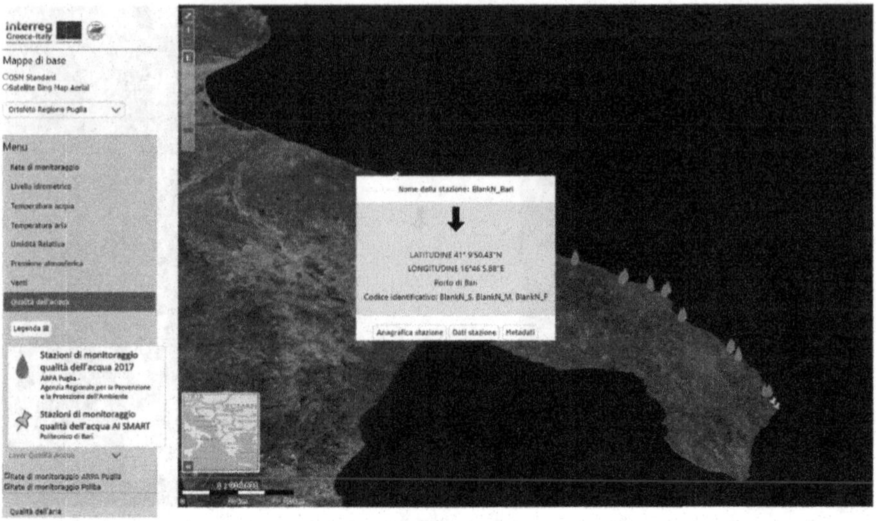

		PORTO DI BARI				DM 173/2016	
Nome stazione		Bianco			Bianco	Livelli chimici di riferimento nazionali	
Sigla		BlankN_S	BlankN_F		BlankN		
Data campionamento		Giugno 2021	Giugno 2021		Giugno 2021		
Fase		Ante operam	Ante operam		Ante operam	L1	L2
PARAMETRI CHIMICO-FISICI	**U.M.**			**U.M.**			
pH	u. pH	8,10	8,23	u. pH	8,78	-	-
Pot. Redox				mV	-83,9	-	-
Umidità a 105 °C				%	21,61	-	-
Frazione < 2mm				% s.s.	100,0	-	-
METALLI							
Arsenico	mg/l	< 0.01	< 0.01	mg/kg s.s.	6,51	12	20
Berillio	mg/l	< 0.01	< 0.01	mg/kg s.s.	0,03	-	-
Cadmio	mg/l	< 0.01	< 0.01	mg/kg s.s.	0,07	0,3	0,8
Cobalto	mg/l	< 0.01	< 0.01	mg/kg s.s.	1,75	-	-
Cromo totale	mg/l	< 0.01	< 0.01	mg/kg s.s.	9,52	50	150
Mercurio	mg/l	< 0.01	< 0.01	mg/kg s.s.	< 0.01	0,3	0,8
Nichel	mg/l	< 0.01	< 0.01	mg/kg s.s.	3,05	30	75
Piombo	mg/l	< 0.01	< 0.01	mg/kg s.s.	46,17	30	70
Rame	mg/l	< 0.01	< 0.01	mg/kg s.s.	7,92	40	52
Selenio	mg/l	< 0.01	< 0.01	mg/kg s.s.	< 0.01	-	-
Tallio	mg/l	< 0.01	< 0.01	mg/kg s.s.	< 0.01	-	-
Vanadio	mg/l	< 0.01	< 0.01	mg/kg s.s.	15,62	-	-
Zinco	mg/l	< 0.01	< 0.01	mg/kg s.s.	13,01	100	150

Fig. 7. Visualization of hydrocarbon measured by the station located in Mola di Bari Port

records and to answer a query, respectively. Lastly, to increase the application performance, the main page was divided into various JS files. This allows speeding up the procedure as well as reducing programming errors.

4 Conclusion

The developed application provides a strategic instrument for the evaluation and dissemination of seawater quality data maps concerning the Puglia region in Southern Italy. Such data may be interesting for two types of target audiences particularly: local/regional/national authorities and scientific communities. The former, indeed, can exploit platform information to make the best decision to preserve the marine-coastal ecosystem while the latter can benefit from the fact that all data are concentrated in a unique database. Additionally, the scientific community can download both raw and processed data to apply for their own research purposes. Therefore, the WebGIS provides an easy-to-use environment for the geo-visualization of free open data available on external sources as well as data and maps produced within the AI-SMART project. Both skilled and not-skilled users can access the data and visualize or download those they are interested in.

As shown in Figs. 5, 6, the application comprises several independent modules to facilitate its consultation, such as panels concerning metadata, acquisition instrument, and data acquisition point, and, lastly, ToC. Then, the consumers can select the water/air quality parameters maps or data from the ToC and overlaid them on the base maps, such as, for instance, satellite images or historical orthophotos. Moreover, they can explore maps proprieties from the metadata panel as well as the applied techniques and instruments from the stations and tools registers, respectively.

Most of the implemented data are time series, and, consequently, they allow monitoring the seawater and air quality as well as sediment both spatially and temporally. This helps the consumers to understand the actual situation and its evolution so as to predict its future development.

To achieve the research aim and to produce an easy, efficient and effective platform, a big effort was made in selecting the optimal hardware and software tool. In compliance with the OGC and EU directive INSPIRE, FOSS4G was picked up to implement every single module, guaranteeing that all browsers may access them. Nevertheless, the application still shows some limitations, such as, e.g., i) the number of contact points that can simultaneously access the database, ii) the opportunity to customize the data treatment, and, lastly, iii) the possibility to upload consumers' maps. Therefore, in the next future, the web application will be modified to face such issues.

References

1. Kay, R., Alder, J.: Coastal planning and management. CRC Press, USA (2005)
2. Boccia, L., Capolupo, A., Rigillo, M., Russo, V.: Terrace abandonment hazards in a mediterranean cultural landscape. J Hazard. Toxic Radioactive Waste **24**(1), 04019034 (2020)
3. Lama, G.F.C., Sadeghifar, T., Azad, M.T., Sihag, P., Kisi, O.: On the indirect estimation of wind wave heights over the Southern Coasts of Caspian sea: a comparative analysis. Water **14**, 843 (2022). https://doi.org/10.3390/w14060843
4. Sadeghifar, T., Lama, G.F.C., Sihag, P., Bayram, A., Kisi, O.: Wave height predictions in complex sea flows through soft computing models: Case study of Persian gulf. Ocean Eng. **245**, 110467 (2022). https://doi.org/10.1016/j.oceaneng.2021.110467
5. Peng, W., Yuan, Z., Wang, J.: Attention-enhanced neural network models for turbulence simulation. Phys. Fluids **34**, 025111 (2022). https://doi.org/10.1063/5.0079302
6. Palladino, M., Nasta, P., Capolupo, A., Romano, N.: Monitoring and modelling the role of phytoremediation to mitigate non-point source cadmium pollution and groundwater contamination at field scale. Ital. J. Agron. **13**(s1), 59–68 (2018)
7. Capolupo, A., Boccia, L.: Innovative method for linking anthropisation process to vulnerability. World Rev. Sci. Technol. Sustain. Develop. **17**(1), 4–22 (2021)
8. Wurtsbaugh, W.A., Paerl, H.W., Dodds, W.K.: Nutrients, eutrophication and harmful algal blooms along the freshwater to marine continuum. WIREs Water. **6**, 1–27 (2019)
9. Capolupo, A., Kooistra, L., Boccia, L.: A novel approach for detecting agricultural terraced landscapes from historical and contemporaneous photogrammetric aerial photos. Int. J. Appl. Earth Obs. Geoinf. **73**, 800–810 (2018)
10. Capolupo, A., et al.: An interactive WebGIS framework for coastal erosion risk management. J. Mar. Sci. Eng. **9**(6), 567 (2021)

11. Lama, G.F.C., Crimaldi, M.: Remote sensing of ecohydrological, ecohydraulic, and ecohydrodynamic phenomena in vegetated waterways: the role of Leaf Area Index (LAI). Biol. Life Sci. Forum **3**, 54 (2021). https://doi.org/10.3390/IECAG2021-09728)
12. Esposito, M., Crimaldi, M., Cirillo, V., Sarghini, F., Maggio, A.: Drone and sensor technology for sustainable weed management: a review. Chem. Biol. Technol. Agric. **8**(1), 1–11 (2021). https://doi.org/10.1186/s40538-021-00217-8
13. Alesheikh, A.A., Helali, H., Behroz, H.A.: Web GIS: technologies and its applications. In: Symposium on geospatial theory, processing and applications; ISPRS: Ottawa, Canada, (2002)
14. Kuria, E., Kimani, S., Mindila, A.: A framework for web GIS development: a review. Int. J. Comput. Appl. **178**, 0975–8887 (2019)
15. Soto-Garcia, M., Del-Amor-Saavedra, P., Martin-Gorriz, B., Martínez-Alvarez, V.: The role of information and communication technologies in the modernisation of water user associations' management. Comput. Electron. Agric. **98**, 121–130 (2013)
16. Caradonna, G., Novelli, A., Tarantino, E., Cefalo, R., Fratino, U.: A WebGIS framework for disseminating processed remotely sensed on land cover transformations. Rep. Geod. Geoinf. **100**, 27–38 (2016)
17. Caradonna, G, Tarantino, E., Novelli, A., Figorito, B., Fratino, U.: Un WebGIS per la divulgazione delle analisi dei processi di desertificazione del territorio della Puglia. In: Proceedings of the Atti Conferenza Nazionale Asita, Lecco, Italy, 29 September–1 October, pp. 217–223 (2015)
18. Kitsiou, D., Patera, A., Tsegas, G., Nitis, T.: A webGIS application to assess seawater quality: a case study in a coastal area in the Northern Aegean sea. J. Mar. Sci. Eng. **9**, 33 (2021)
19. Wheeler, D.A.: Why Open Source Software/Free Software (OSS/FS). 2007. http://www.dwheeler.com/oss_fs_why.html. Accessed 18 Jan 2020
20. Huxhold, W.E., Levinsohn, A.G.: Managing geographic information system projects. Cartographica **32**, 63 (1995)
21. Caradonna, G., Figorito, B., Tarantino, E.: Sharing environmental geospatial data through an open source WebGIS. In: International Conference on Computational Science and Its Applications (pp. 556–565). Springer, Cham (2015, June)
22. Capolupo, A., Saponaro, M., Fratino, U., Tarantino, E.: Detection of spatio-temporal changes of vegetation in coastal areas subjected to soil erosion issue. Aquat. Ecosyst. Health Manag. **23**(4), 491–499 (2020)
23. Geoportale Nazionale. http://www.pcn.minambiente.it/mattm/. Accessed 3 Jan 2020
24. SIT Puglia. http://www.sit.puglia.it/. Accessed 16 Dec 2019
25. ARPA Puglia. https://www.arpa.puglia.it/. Accessed 16 Dec 2021
26. ISPRA. https://www.mareografico.it/?session=0S307671967290K66706988JB&syslng=ing&sysmen=-1&sysind=-1&syssub=-1&sysfnt=0. Accessed 4 Jan 2022
27. VesselFinder. https://www.vesselfinder.com/it. Accessed 15 Jan 2022
28. AI SMART project. https://pugliacon.regione.puglia.it/web/sit-puglia-dipartimento/ai-smart#mains. Accessed 25 Feb 2022
29. Apache Tomcat. http://tomcat.apache.org/. Accessed 10 Mar 2020
30. Carter, B.: HTML Architecture, a Novel Development System (HANDS). An approach for web development. In: Proceedings of the 2014 Annual Global Online Conference on Information and Computer Technology, Louisville, KY, USA, 3–5 December (2014)
31. Geoserver. http://geoserver.org/. Accessed 3 Mar 2020
32. PostgreSQL: The world's most advanced open source relational database. https://www.postgresql.org/. Accessed 22 Apr 2020
33. Cesium JS. https://cesium.com. Accessed 4 Mar 2020

34. Agrawal, S., Dev Gupta, R.: Development and comparison of open source based web gis frameworks on Wamp and Apache Tomcat web servers. In: Proceedings of the International Archives of the Photogrammetry, Remote Sensing and Spatial Information Sciences,
35. Suzhou, China, 14–16 May 2014; Volume XL-4
36. Fustes, D., Cantorna, D., Dafonte, C., Arcay, B., Iglesias, A., Manteiga, M.: A cloud-integrated web platform for marine monitoring using GIS and remote sensing. Application to oil spill detection through SAR images. Future Gener. Comput. Syst. **34**, 155–160 (2013)
37. Huang, Z., Xu, Z.: A method of using geoServer to publish economy geographical information. In: Proceedings of the 2011 International Conference on Control, Automation and Systems Engineering (CASE), Singapore, 30–31 July 2011; IEEE: Piscataway, NJ, USA, pp. 1–4 (2011)
38. Brovelli, M.A., Boccardo, P., Bordogna, G., Pepe, A., Crespi, M., Munafò, M., Pirotti, F.: Urban geo Big Data. In: Proceedings of the International Archives of the Photogrammetry, Remote Sensing and Spatial Information Sciences, Bucharest, Romania, 26–30 August; Volume XLII-4/W14 (2019)
39. Getbootstrap. https://getbootstrap.com/. Accessed 21 Oct 2019
40. W3.CSS. https://www.w3schools.com/w3css/. Accessed 20 Oct 2019
41. Kommana, K. Implementation of a geoserver application for GIS data distribution and manipulation. Master's Thesis, Physical Geography and Quaternary Geology, Department of Physical Geography and Quaternary Geology, Stockholm University, Stockholm, Sweden (2013)
42. Caradonna, G., Frigorito, B., Novelli, A., Tarantino, E., Fratino, U.: Geomatic techniques for disseminating processed remotely sensed open data in an interactive WebGIS. Plurimondi (2017). http://193.204.49.18/index.php/Plurimondi/article/view/47. Accessed 19 May 2021
43. Haynes, D., Ray, S., Manson, S.M., Soni, A.: High performance analysis of big spatial data. In: Proceedings of the 2015 IEEE International Conference on Big Data, Santa Clara, CA, USA, 29 October–1 November (2015)
44. Ružicka, J.: Comparing speed of Web Map Service with GeoServer on ESRI Shapefile and PostGIS. Geoinformatics **15**, 3–9 (2016)
45. Geoext3. http://geoext.github.io/geoext3/. Accessed 16 May 2020

Dynamic Monitoring of a Railway Steel Bridge with MEMS Accelerometers: First Results on the Case Study of Portella

Alberico Sonnessa[1(✉)] and Mariano Macellari[2]

[1] Department of Civil, Environmental, Land, Construction and Chemistry (DICATECh), Politecnico di Bari, Via Orabona 4, 70125 Bari, Italy
alberico.sonnessa@poliba.it

[2] Trenitalia S.p.A. Transport Data Management, Piazza delle Croce Rossa, 1, 00161 Roma, Italy
m.macellari@trenitalia.it

Abstract. The continuous growth of demand on railway networks requires an efficient management strategy to guarantee proper levels of safety and service. Bridges are a fundamental asset for a railway infrastructure and their integrity must be ensured implementing feasible approaches aimed at avoiding critical occurrences (e.g. collapses) by quantifying infrastructure responses to standard and critical loads, in terms of vibration features and long-term displacements. The work proposes a geomatic monitoring configuration for a new steel railway bridge -the Portella bridge- located along the Roma–Napoli railway, showing the results obtained analyzing three weeks of continuous monitoring in different seasons. The system, based on triaxial MEMS accelerometers and envisaging additional sensors (GNSS receivers) in its developments, was installed at the end of the bridge construction as a lifetime tool, and is designed to highlight the effects of the train passage. Data analysis permitted to retrieve structure accelerations and vibration normal modes (natural frequencies). The findings of the investigations will be used to improve the Finite Element model of the bridge used in the design phase.

Keywords: Critical infrastructures · Railway bridges · Lifetime geomatic monitoring · MEMS accelerometers · Vibration normal modes analyses

1 Introduction

The increasing demand for mobility has significantly boosted the evolution of fast transport routes, as evidenced by the growth in the length of high-speed railways in Europe from 2.500 km to about 10.000 km in the period 2000–2022. The expansion of the Trans-European Transport Network (TEN-T), the planned network of roads, railways and airports infrastructure that is currently under development among the European Union countries [1], will make available further connections aimed at facilitating the mobility of goods and people.

O. Gervasi et al. (Eds.): ICCSA 2022 Workshops, LNCS 13379, pp. 354–368, 2022.
https://doi.org/10.1007/978-3-031-10545-6_25

Along with this rapid evolution, the need of an effective management strategy arises, which is essential for ensuring a safe use of the infrastructures and avoiding critical events (i.e. large deformations, collapses), such as those that interested the transport networks during the last decades (e.g. the collapses of the road bridge in Albiano Magra - April 2020 and the Morandi bridge in August 2018 [2] and the I-35W Bridge in Minneapolis, USA in 2007 [3]). These occurrences evidenced how bridges are often the element of a transport infrastructure most likely to be affected by instability problems, caused by design flaws, aging or subsidence of the foundation soil. Among the transport networks, the railway infrastructure has constantly increased its importance, as a direct result of the growing demand for a faster and greener handling of passengers and goods. Rail bridges often work close to their operating limit in terms of axle load, maximum transfer speed, train frequency and length [4, 5]. This can speed up deterioration processes and decrease the safety level. The need to assess their health conditions (Structural Health Monitoring-SHM) requires overcoming the traditional approach based on testing in the pre-operating phase and monitoring if damages and/or risk conditions occur. A radical change of perspective must consider a monitoring system as the standard equipment of a structure over the entire life cycle. The importance of field measurement outcomes for quantifying vibration stresses in steel bridges is clearly evidenced in [6]. The structural health of these assets must be guaranteed implementing integrated real-time monitoring approaches, fulfilling both technological and budget constraints. Integrated survey and monitoring techniques [7–9] can play a key role in their safeguard, allowing a more accurate control of their behaviour and providing timely information to the infrastructure manager.

All these things considered, an effective monitoring configuration for rail bridges, based on the use of Micro Electro-Mechanical Systems (MEMS) accelerometers is hereafter presented, and preliminary results of the analyses on the data provided by MEMS sensors is discussed. This configuration has been designed to provide high-frequency measurements (acceleration and vibration frequencies) from accelerometers. MEMS accelerometers have proven to constitute an efficient and low-cost solution for SHM in civil engineering applications concerning the bridge control [10, 11], in multi-sensor systems aimed at monitoring the dynamic response of structures and gathering information such as natural vibrating frequencies [12], and as a tool for early warning in case of critical events (e.g. earthquakes) that may affect civil infrastructures [13]. A number of experiences on the use of MEMS aimed at analysing the effects of wind, earthquake and external loads, and evaluating their performances for damage detection purposes have been presented in [14–16]. This research shows the first results of the analysis conducted on the dataset acquired by a monitoring system based on triaxial accelerometers, installed on a steel bridge located along the high-speed Roma-Formia-Napoli railway (Italy). The monitoring system was installed to track its structural behaviour since the very beginning of the structure life, enabling to collect a bulk of information useful to timely detect possible anomalies. The test phase was aimed at highlighting the effects of the rail traffic on the infrastructure in terms of acceleration peaks and, mainly, vibration modes (natural frequencies) derived through Fourier analysis of accelerations. Section 2 presents the case study and the currently installed monitoring system; Sects. 3 and 4 illustrate the data analysis results, with respect to accelerations and vibration normal modes (natural frequencies); Sect. 5 discusses the obtained results. Conclusions and planned evolution of the monitoring system are discussed in the last sections.

2 Case Study – The Portella Bridge and Its Monitoring System

The Portella steel bridge is located at km 102 + 092 of the Roma-Formia-Napoli railway, between the Priverno-Fossanova and Monte S. Biagio stations. The bridge, with a span of 28 m, consists of two reticular beams placed longitudinally at a distance of 10,30 m, with a height ranging from 4 m to 5,50 m (Fig. 1). The deck is formed by a series of transverse steel beams, an overlying steel sheet extended to the entire perimeter, and a concrete slab supporting the ballast and the two tracks. The steel bridge rests on reinforced concrete shoulders by mean of reverse-shell teflon-steel supports [17].

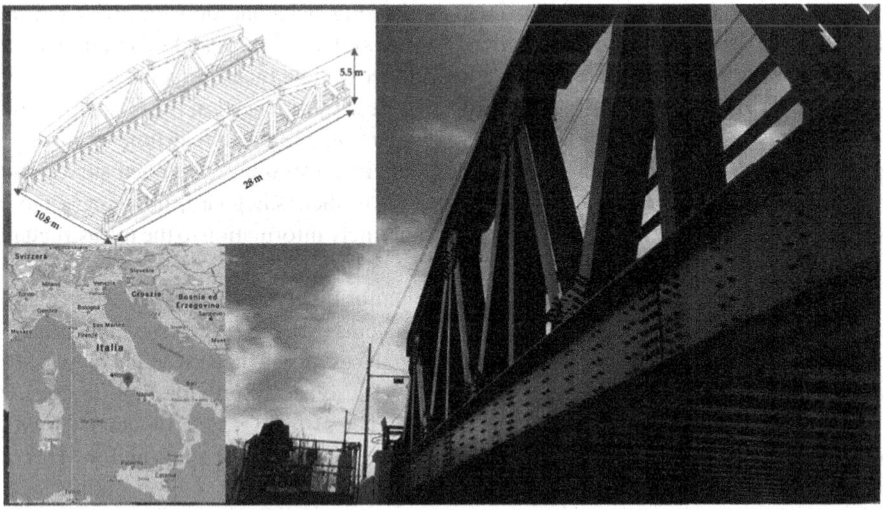

Fig. 1. The Portella bridge

The bridge crosses the Portella canal. Current line speed is 180 km/h, but the bridge is designed for allowing a maximum operative speed of 200 km/h.

The scheme of the implemented monitoring system encompasses the joint use of ten Kistler Type 8396A/2D0 high-sensitivity/low noise accelerometer (Fig. 2) simultaneously measuring acceleration on the X, Y and Z axes (A1D to A5D along the north-south track, A1P to A5P the south-north track) have been installed according to the layout in Fig. 3.

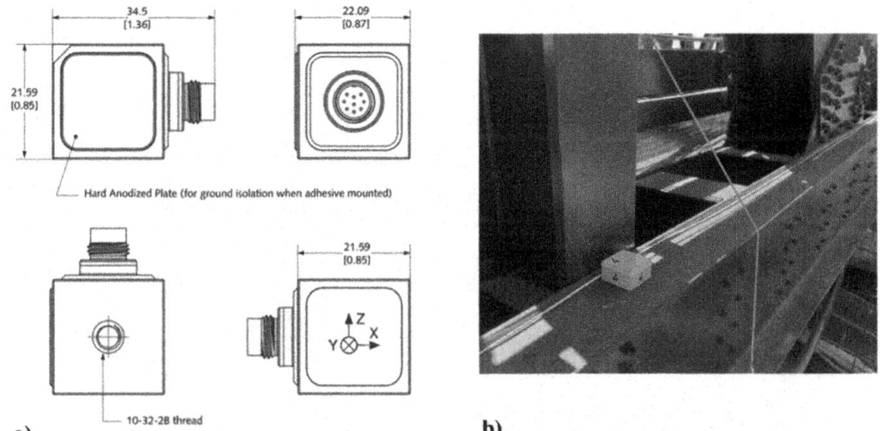

a) b)

Fig. 2. (a) Kistler accelerometer. (b) One of the sensors located on the metal structure

X axis is oriented along the tracks direction, Z axis along the gravity direction and Y (across the tracks direction) completes the cartesian reference system. A1P/D and A5P/D lie on the concrete shoulders of the structure, whereas A2, 3, 4 P/D are placed on the metal bridge. The sensors are nominally characterized by a ±2g range measurement and a frequency response ranging from 0 to 1150 Hz. The capability of better detecting the natural vibration frequencies has been the main criterion for identifying the proper sensors to be used in the system. Each accelerometer records data at a sample rate of 2000 Hz and stores the information in a proprietary format containing the acceleration value and the corresponding time epoch. Two photoelectric triggers (TRG-P and TRG-D), located approximately near A1-D and A5-P accelerometers, automatically detect the train approaching, and give the start to the beginning of the recordings. The dataset has been investigated using a code developed on purpose.

3 Data Analysis – Accelerations

A first statistical analysis has been developed on acceleration signals, directly linked to the stresses suffered by the structure, with the aim of evaluating their weekly peaks and average maximum. The acceleration values have been examined for each accelerometer to evaluate the actual stress impacting the bridge, to be compared with the design values. Data were recorded in three weeks, in different weather conditions have been considered.

- week 1 (W1), 28th April - 4th May
- week 2 (W2), 28th July - 3rd August
- week 3 (W3), 27th October - 2rd November

3.1 Analysis of Peak Accelerations

For each accelerometer, a cumulative analysis has been performed by estimating the peak accelerations on the X, Y and Z axes over the whole period W1-W3 (Table 1, Fig. 4. For

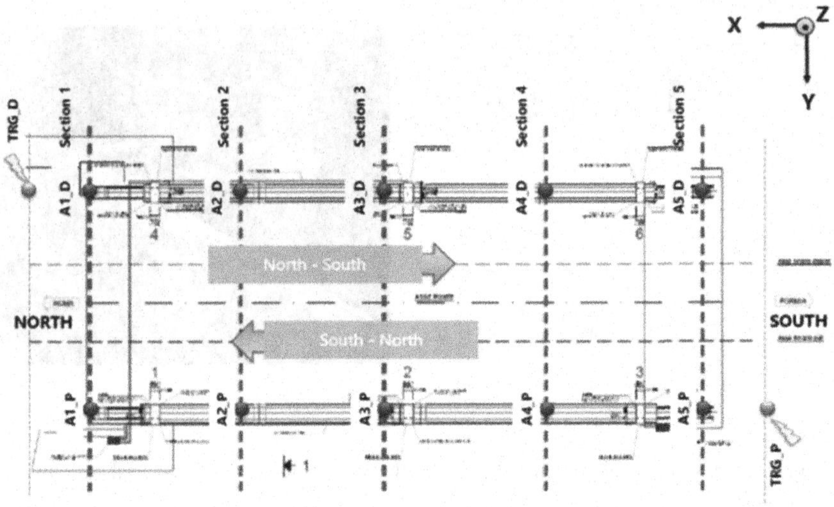

Fig. 3. Monitoring layout

each axis, the average values of the peaks are reported with relative standard deviation, and the six values (X min/max, Y min/max, Z min/max) representing the maximum accelerations affecting the structure along the three directions, are highlighted (Fig. 4).

The peak accelerations analysis evidenced that the Y and Z peaks measured by the accelerometers located on the bridge span (A2, A3, A4 D/P) are likely not fully indicative of the true peaks suffered by the structure, due to the limitations in the sensors measuring range. The example accelerogram of Fig. 5a highlights how the maximum values measured along the Y axis and the positive part of the Z axis correspond to the full scale of the instrumentation (indicated in the boxes) (Table 2).

The red squares show the reaching of the saturation of the measures for a high number of epochs in the Y (positive and negative component) and Z (positive component) directions, and for a limited number of epochs relative to the negative component in the Z direction (green square).

Therefore, the actual peak accelerations probably reach (at least) the value measured on the negative part of the Z axis, which, after being referred to the median values, is equal, in absolute value, to 33.5 m/s^2 (Fig. 5b). Since the main goal of the project was the detection of vibration normal modes, at this stage the replacement of bridge span accelerometers is not scheduled.

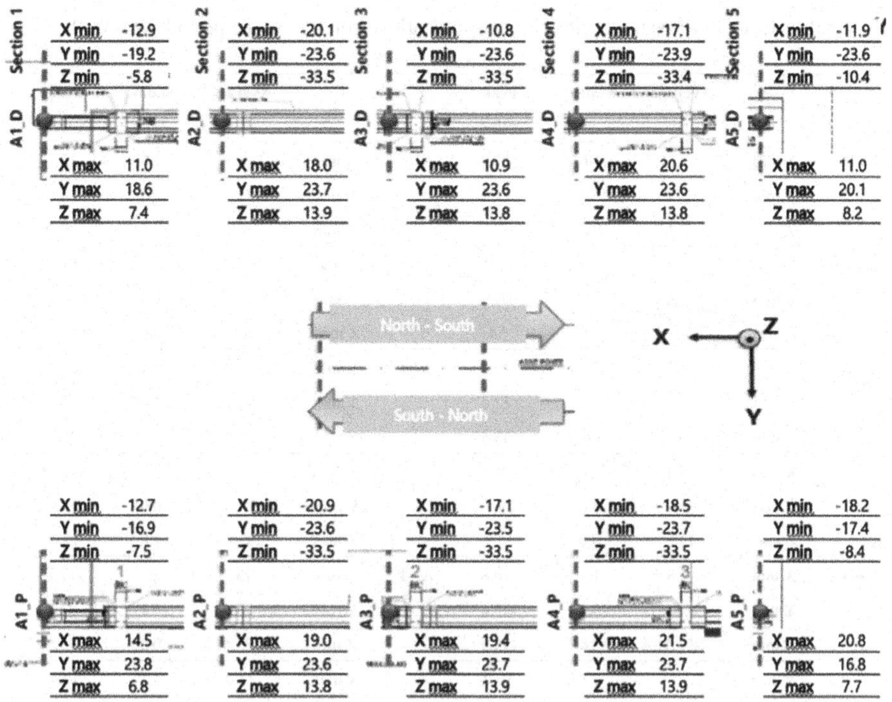

Fig. 4. Synoptic view of the peak acceleration statistics (m/s^2)

3.2 Analysis of Weekly Average Accelerations

In order to characterize the average maximum (in absolute value) stress, min/max acceleration suffered by the structure for each train passage were recorded and averaged on the whole period W1-W3. It appears that, in the average, highest absolute values (up to approximately 13 m/s^2) are related to the Y component, transversal to tracks, followed by those related to Z component. Statistics in (Table 4 in Table 2, and Fig. 7 in Fig. 6) summarize the analysis of min/max accelerations performed on the dataset over the W1-W3 period. This has been developed to characterize the accelerometer belonging to the monitoring system using 60 values (2 for each accelerometer, for each direction), namely mean and standard deviation of min and max values for all components. The six values (X min/max, Y min/max, Z min/max) which represent the maximum average accelerations to which the structure is subjected to, along the three directions are also highlighted.

Table 1. Overall peak acceleration (m/s^2) statistics on the whole period (W1-W3).

		Average	St.dev.	Peak value			Average	St.dev.	Peak value
A1-D	**X min**	-7.3	1.6	-12.9	**A1-P**	**X min**	-9.6	1.5	-12.7
	Y min	-11.0	2.3	-19.2		**Y min**	-11.3	2.6	-16.9
	Z min	-3.3	0.9	-5.8		**Z min**	-4.8	1.1	-7.5
	X max	7.0	1.3	11.0		**X max**	8.7	2.2	14.5
	Y max	11.6	2.3	18.6		**Y max**	16.6	3.4	23.8
	Z max	4.1	1.1	7.4		**Z max**	4.4	0.9	6.8
A2-D	**X min**	-15.0	2.5	-20.1	**A2-P**	**X min**	-16.1	2.5	**-20.9**
	Y min	-23.6	0.0	-23.6		**Y min**	-23.6	0.0	-23.6
	Z min	-33.5	0.1	**-33.5**		**Z min**	-33.5	0.0	-33.5
	X max	13.1	2.4	18.0		**X max**	14.6	2.2	19.0
	Y max	23.7	0.0	23.7		**Y max**	23.6	0.0	23.6
	Z max	13.8	0.0	13.9		**Z max**	13.8	0.0	13.8
A3-D	**X min**	-7.8	1.7	-10.8	**A3-P**	**X min**	-13.3	2.1	-17.1
	Y min	-23.6	0.1	-23.6		**Y min**	-23.5	0.0	-23.5
	Z min	-31.1	2.4	-33.5		**Z min**	-33.5	0.0	-33.5
	X max	7.7	1.8	10.9		**X max**	13.0	2.3	19.4
	Y max	23.6	0.0	23.6		**Y max**	23.7	0.0	**23.7**
	Z max	13.8	0.0	13.8		**Z max**	13.9	0.0	13.9
A4-D	**X min**	-13.1	2.1	-17.1	**A4-P**	**X min**	-13.5	2.3	-18.5
	Y min	-23.7	0.1	**-23.9**		**Y min**	-23.6	0.0	-23.7
	Z min	-33.0	0.7	-33.4		**Z min**	-30.9	2.0	-33.5
	X max	14.9	2.6	20.6		**X max**	16.2	2.6	**21.5**
	Y max	23.5	0.0	23.6		**Y max**	23.7	0.0	23.7
	Z max	13.8	0.0	13.8		**Z max**	13.9	0.0	**13.9**
A5-D	**X min**	-8.5	1.5	-11.9	**A5-P**	**X min**	-10.6	2.9	-18.2
	Y min	-18.4	3.4	-23.6		**Y min**	-11.7	2.6	-17.4
	Z min	-4.9	1.5	-10.4		**Z min**	-4.4	1.5	-8.4
	X max	7.2	1.4	11.0		**X max**	10.9	3.3	20.8
	Y max	12.8	2.6	20.1		**Y max**	11.9	2.3	16.8
	Z max	5.4	1.2	8.2		**Z max**	4.4	1.1	7.7

Table 2. Average values of the minimum and maximum accelerations (m/s^2) - period W1-W3.

	W1-W3									
	A1-D	**A2-D**	**A3-D**	**A4-D**	**A5-D**	**A1-P**	**A2-P**	**A3-P**	**A4-P**	**A5-P**
Min	-1.8	-3.4	-1.9	-3.1	-2.3	-2.6	**-3.5**	-2.9	-3.0	-2.3
(Average)	-2.6	**-12.8**	-8.6	-11.0	-3.8	-2.5	-11.6	-12.1	-8.9	-2.6
X,Y,Z	-0.7	-11.2	-8.3	-9.9	-1.1	-1.1	-10.9	**-11.2**	-8.9	-0.9
Min	1.3	2.7	1.5	2.5	1.6	1.8	2.9	2.4	2.5	2.0
(St.dev.)	2.2	7.8	6.9	7.8	3.6	2.2	7.5	7.8	6.7	2.2
X,Y,Z	0.6	8.4	6.7	7.9	0.9	0.9	8.3	8.7	6.5	0.8
Max	1.5	3.2	1.8	3.2	1.7	1.9	3.3	2.9	**3.3**	2.4
(Average)	2.7	**12.8**	9.5	11.4	2.9	3.6	11.1	11.8	8.7	2.7
X,Y,Z	0.8	8.5	7.0	7.8	1.2	1.0	8.5	**8.6**	7.7	0.9
Max	1.3	2.5	1.5	2.8	1.5	1.7	2.6	2.4	3.0	2.0
(St.dev.)	2.2	7.9	7.2	7.7	2.6	3.2	7.7	7.9	6.5	2.3
X,Y,Z	0.8	4.4	4.3	4.4	1.0	0.9	4.4	4.6	4.3	0.8

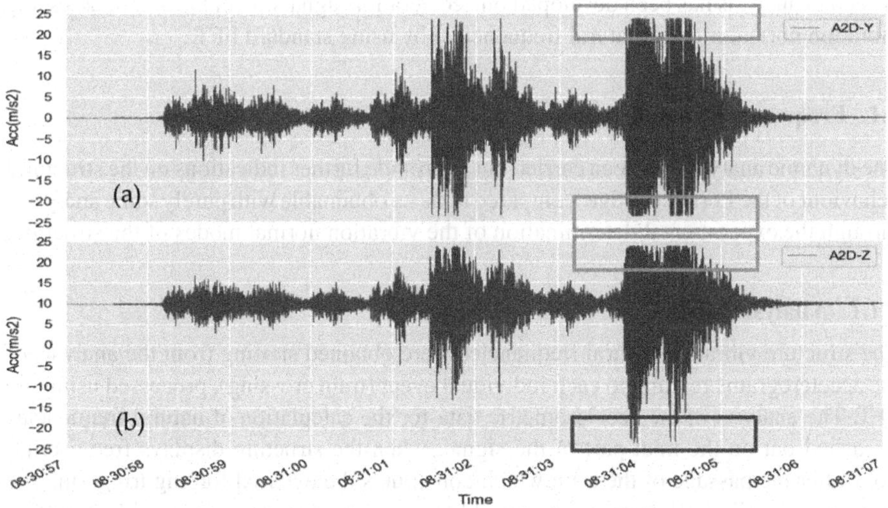

Fig. 5. Example of accelerograms related to the Y (a) and Z (b) axes. (Color figure online)

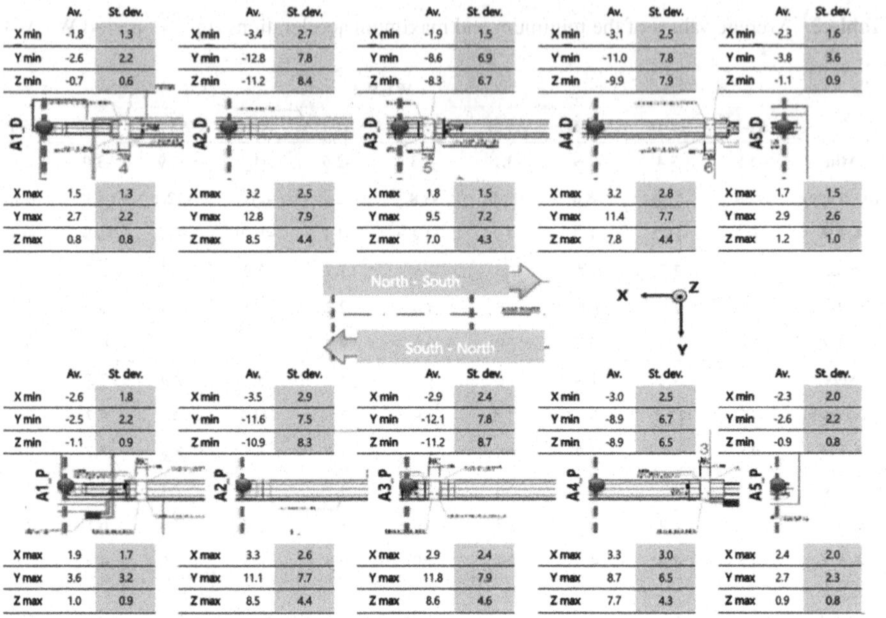

Fig. 6. Average values of the min. and max. accelerations (m/s^2) and relative standard deviations associated with each accelerometer

4 Data Analysis – Vibration Normal Modes

A second analysis has been developed on acceleration signals, with the aim of assessing vibration normal modes (natural frequencies) by using standard FFT.

4.1 Frequency Dynamic Analysis

The dynamic analysis has been carried out to provide further indications on the structural behaviour of the Portella bridge, compared to those obtainable with purely static analyses, through the experimental determination of the vibration normal modes of the structure.

4.1.1 Analysis Mode

The structure vibration natural frequencies were obtained starting from the analysis of the accelerograms relating to each individual event (train crossing), processed using the FFT. The analysis of the accelerometric data for the calculation of natural frequencies is carried out on the final part of the signal, when the structure displays free oscillations after the passage of the train which constitutes the external forcing triggering the structure vibrations. Therefore, it is possible to identify the range of natural frequencies by processing the accelerogram tail. The workflow implemented (Fig. 7) therefore provides the acquisition of accelerations values, the analysis of the signal tail, highlighted in yellow, and the extraction of the relevant frequency data.

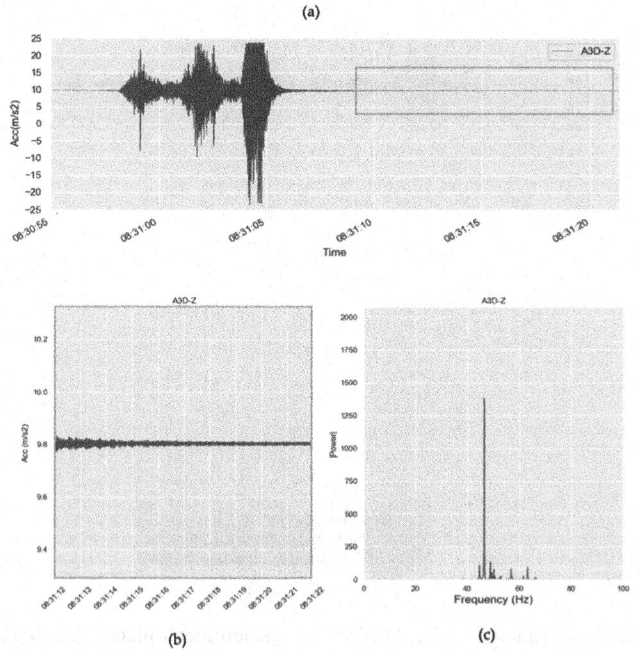

Fig. 7. Extraction of vibration frequencies, applied to the A3D-Z accelerogram

4.1.2 Frequency Calculation

Frequency analyses have been conducted on reference events, characterized by peak values in accelerations, and the peak frequency values related to each train passage investigated have been processed over the weeks W1-W3 (excluding the days 01.05.2019 and 31.07.2019, not available at the time of processing). Tables 3, 4 and 5 summarize, for the accelerometers located on the bridge span, the mean, median and standard deviation values of frequency obtained, coupled according to the transversal direction. In the cumulative analysis, the pairs of accelerometers A1D/P and A5D/P, placed on the shoulders of the bridge, were not considered as characterized, on average, by low accelerations and frequencies with not significant powers, as shown in the example in Fig. 8. The results highlight that:

- frequency distributions are almost equal for the corresponding transversal accelerometer pairs (A2D-A2P, A3D-A3P, A4D-A4P), so that the bridge behaviour appears homogeneous in transversal direction
- frequency distributions are very similar for corresponding (with respect to the bridge centerline) longitudinal accelerometer pairs (A2D-A4D, A2P-A4P), so that the bridge behaviour appears homogeneous in longitudinal direction
- frequency medians are higher for X and Z components (slightly less than 50 Hz, higher for A2D-P and A4D-P accelerometers) that for Y component (about 35 Hz for A2D-A2P and A4D-A4P accelerometers, and about 45 Hz for A3D-A3P and A4D-P)
- frequency standard deviations are within 15–20 Hz in all cases

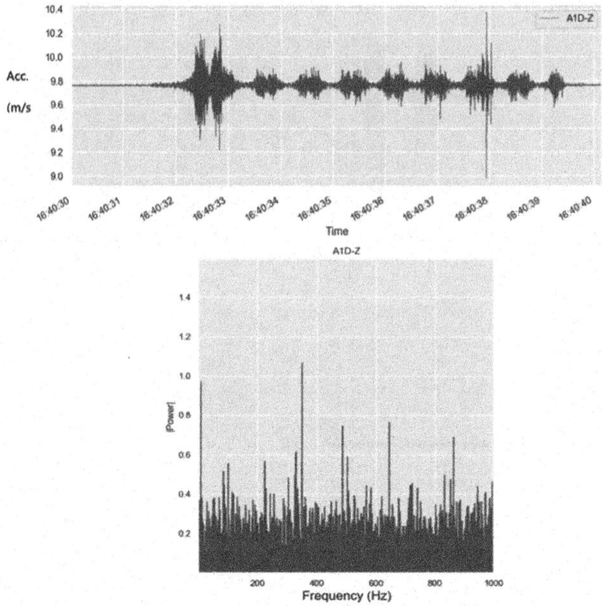

Fig. 8. Example of frequencies calculated for an accelerometer placed on a bridge shoulder

Table 3. Mean, median, and standard deviation of the natural frequency, computed on the X, Y and Z directions, related to the A2D and A2P accelerometers W3

	A2D-X	A2P-X	A2D-Y	A2P-Y	A2D-Z	A2P-Z
	Frequency (Hz)					
Mean	51,5	55,4	39,7	35,8	48,7	49,5
Median	48,5	49,2	35,0	35,0	48,7	48,9
St.dev	17,1	14,6	18,5	15,6	18,2	19,4

Table 4. Mean, median, and standard deviation of the natural frequency, computed on the X, Y and Z directions, related to the A3D and A3P accelerometers W3

	A3D-X	A3P-X	A3D-Y	A3P-Y	A3D-Z	A3P-Z
	Frequency (Hz)					
Mean	41,4	50,2	45,4	44,5	45,3	45,6
Median	49,5	49,8	45,1	43,3	46,3	46,2
St.dev	24,0	19,7	17,7	18,0	19,1	18,0

Table 5. Mean, median, and standard deviation of the natural frequency, computed on the X, Y and Z directions, related to the A4D and A4P accelerometers W3

	A4D-X	A4P-X	A4D-Y	A4P-Y	A4D-Z	A4P-Z
	Frequency (Hz)					
Mean	52,7	54,4	37,0	39,4	48,7	48,6
Median	50,0	53,4	35,0	35,0	49,7	48,9
St.dev	16,6	16,7	17,0	20,4	17,5	20,9

5 Discussion

The work describes the preliminary results obtained from the analysis of the measurements acquired by the monitoring system installed at the Portella metal railway bridge.

A comprehensive study has been performed on the data acquired by MEMS sensors, aimed at identifying the stress ranges, in terms of accelerations along the X, Y and Z axes, affecting the structure following the passage of the trains. The data analysis, conducted in three periods W1, W2 and W3, characterized by different environmental parameters, did not highlight any type of variations in the behaviour of the structure; the results obtained can therefore be considered indicative under conditions like those encountered during the events considered. It is stressed again that the events analysed are characterized by the highest acceleration values. However, as already highlighted in 3.1, the span peak values can only be inferred indirectly from the accelerometric data acquired along the Z axis, due to the limited measurement range of the instrumentation.

The accelerometric sensors also made it possible to derive the (supposed) natural frequencies, ranging in the interval 35–50 + 20 Hz for all components. The natural frequencies analysis highlighted a homogeneous transversal and longitudinal symmetric (with respect to the transversal centerline) behaviour of the bridge. Results have been compared with the outputs obtained from the Finite Element (FE) modelling of the bridge used in the design phase. The model issued natural frequencies ranging from 5 to about 10 Hz, namely one order of magnitude smaller than the experimental frequency. The reasons of these discrepancies are currently under examinations; a first hypothesis indicates the underestimation of the action of some structural constraints as a possible cause. However, a malfunctioning of the shield against electric power cannot be completely excluded. Following the findings of the investigation, an updated FE model will be developed in order to better match the results of the FE analyses and the measurement of the real behaviour of the structure. As evidenced in [18], acquired experimental dataset deliver comprehensive information regarding the behaviour of the bridge, useful for improving the initial FE model characteristics and better defining its boundary conditions.

The acquired data will allow to constantly monitor the structural integrity of the bridge and to promptly intervene if the parameters measured in real time should deviate from the typical parameters obtained from the analyses carried out, addressing the bridge maintenance process, which has a large impact on the whole life cycle cost.

6 Expected Developments

The monitoring system has provided data useful for the dynamic characterization of the investigated structure, or in the worst case, highlighted a bug in the insulation of the equipment from electric currents. Nevertheless, the system has been designed for harnessing the integration of different type of sensors and acquiring a huge amount of data.

In light of this, expected developments will encompass the full exploitation of the measurements acquired by MEMS accelerometers, by systematically processing the whole available database, in this way increasing the statistical base of analysed data and allowing a more accurate description of the structure, both in terms of vibrating natural frequencies and accelerations. The replacement (or the coupling) of the span accelerometers with different sensor units characterized by a wider measuring range could be necessary to directly measure the peak accelerations in the Y and Z directions, along which, as expected, the structure shows the greatest accelerations. Modal analyses from peak frequencies are being implemented, also taking into account the results obtained in [19], where the accuracy of MEMS accelerometers for these purposes has been experimentally assessed providing evidence of maximum expected frequency errors up to 5%. A comparison with the results obtained from an analogous monitoring system installed on concrete steel bridge is also planned.

Further improvements in the definition of the Portella bridge behaviour are expected from the evaluation of short and long-term displacements (or possible deformations) of the structure, with the availability of the monitoring system module based on GNSS sensors, as widely discussed in [20, 21]. The direct monitoring of displacements will provide the opportunity of using the original acceleration signal to retrieve velocity and displacements, starting from the experience conducted in [22], and the original approaches described in [23].

Finally, many monitoring systems have been installed on structures all over the world. Since is not easy to find detailed reports containing the achieved results, authors duty will be the reporting back on the operation, use, and success (or failure) of installed systems in future years, as intended in [24]. The already acquired acceleration big data will allow to establish a data driven model of the Portella bridge behaviour in standard conditions, both regarding maximum accelerations and natural frequencies. This model will enable to highlight eventual changes in the response to the stresses induced by railway traffic, therefore evidencing possible changes in the structural state and damages occurred.

Acknowledgments. Part of the research reported in this publication has been conducted in the frame of the collaboration between Kuaternion s.r.l., Spin-Off of the University of Rome, and ETS Ingegneria, that has in charge the design and maintenance of some rail-way structures on behalf of RFI (Rete Ferroviaria Italiana, the manager of the Italian railway network). The authors want to thank everyone at ETS for the support.

References

1. Bàlazs, P., et al.: On the first year of implementation of the core network corridors. The Trans-European Transport Network (2015)

2. Morgese, M., Ansari, F., Domaneschi, M., Cimellaro, G.P.: Post-collapse analysis of Morandi's Polcevera viaduct in Genoa Italy. J. Civ. Struct. Heal. Monit. **10**(1), 69–85 (2019). https://doi.org/10.1007/s13349-019-00370-7
3. Salem, H.M., Helmy, H.M.: Numerical investigation of collapse of the Minnesota I-35W bridge. Eng. Struct. **59** (2014). https://doi.org/10.1016/j.engstruct.2013.11.022
4. Cruz, P., León, A.D. De, Wisniewski, D., Valente, I.: Sustainable Bridges Assessment for Future Traffic Demands and Longer Lives (2007)
5. Pipinato, A.: Innovative bridge design handbook: Construction, rehabilitation and maintenance (2015)
6. Moses, F., Schilling, C.G., Raju, K.S.: Fatigue evaluation procedures for steel bridges (1987)
7. Crespi, M., Giannone, F., Marsella, M., Sonnessa, A.: Automated geomatic system for monitoring historical buildings during tunneling in Roma, Italy. In: Life-Cycle and Sustainability of Civil Infrastructure Systems - Proceedings of the 3rd International Symposium on Life-Cycle Civil Engineering, IALCCE 2012 (2012)
8. Baiocchi, V., et al.: First geomatic restitution of the sinkhole known as 'Pozzo del Merro' (Italy), with the integration and comparison of 'classic' and innovative geomatic techniques. Environ. Earth Sci. **77**(3), 1–14 (2018). https://doi.org/10.1007/s12665-018-7244-6
9. Yu, J., Fang, Z., Meng, X., Xie, Y., Fan, Q.: Measurement of quasi-static and dynamic displacements of footbridges using the composite instrument of a smartstation and an accelerometer: case studies. Remote Sens. **12** (2020). https://doi.org/10.3390/RS12162635
10. Bedon, C., Bergamo, E., Izzi, M., Noè, S.: Prototyping and validation of MEMS accelerometers for structural health monitoring—the case study of the Pietratagliata cable-stayed bridge. J. Sens. Actuator Networks. **7** (2018). https://doi.org/10.3390/jsan7030030
11. Grimmelsman, K.A., Zolghadri, N.: Experimental evaluation of low-cost accelerometers for dynamic characterization of bridges. In: Pakzad, S. (ed.) Dynamics of Civil Structures, Volume 2. CPSEMS, pp. 145–152. Springer, Cham (2020). https://doi.org/10.1007/978-3-030-12115-0_19
12. Baraccani, S., Palermo, M., Azzara, R.M., Gasparini, G., Silvestri, S., Trombetti, T.: Structural interpretation of data from static and dynamic structural health monitoring of monumental buildings. In: Key Engineering Materials (2017). https://doi.org/10.4028/www.scientific.net/KEM.747.431
13. Zheng, H., Shi, G., Zeng, T., Li, B.: Wireless earthquake alarm design based on MEMS accelerometer. In: 2011 International Conference on Consumer Electronics, Communications and Networks, CECNet 2011 - Proceedings (2011). https://doi.org/10.1109/CECNET.2011.5768502
14. Domaneschi, M., Limongelli, M.P., Martinelli, L.: Interpolation damage detection method on a suspension bridge model: Influence of sensors disturbances. Key Eng. Mater. 569–570 (2013). https://doi.org/10.4028/www.scientific.net/KEM.569-570.734
15. Ali, A., Sandhu, T., Usman, M.: Ambient Vibration Testing of a Pedestrian Bridge Using Low-Cost Accelerometers for SHM Applications. Smart Cities. **2** (2019). https://doi.org/10.3390/smartcities2010002
16. Picozzi, M., et al.: Wireless technologies for the monitoring of strategic civil infrastructures: An ambient vibration test on the Fatih Sultan Mehmet Suspension Bridge in Istanbul, Turkey. Bull. Earthq. Eng. **8** (2010). https://doi.org/10.1007/s10518-009-9132-7
17. Rete Ferroviaria Italiana S.p.A.: Ponte Portella km 102+092 - rev. C. (2018)
18. Vagnoli, M., Remenyte-Prescott, R., Andrews, J.: Railway bridge structural health monitoring and fault detection: State-of-the-art methods and future challenges (2018). https://doi.org/10.1177/1475921717721137
19. Kok, R., Furlong, C., Pryputniewicz, R.J.: Development of a wireless MEMS inertial system for health monitoring of structures. In: Materials Research Society Symposium - Proceedings (2003). https://doi.org/10.1557/proc-785-d11.5

20. Yu, J., Meng, X., Yan, B., Xu, B., Fan, Q., Xie, Y.: Global Navigation Satellite System-based positioning technology for structural health monitoring: a review (2020). https://doi.org/10.1002/stc.2467
21. Im, S.B., Hurlebaus, S., Kang, Y.J.: Summary review of GPS technology for structural health monitoring. J. Struct. Eng. **139** (2013). https://doi.org/10.1061/(asce)st.1943-541x.0000475
22. Faulkner, K., Brownjohn, J.M.W., Wang, Y., Huseynov, F.: Tracking bridge tilt behaviour using sensor fusion techniques. J. Civ. Struct. Heal. Monit. **10**(4), 543–555 (2020). https://doi.org/10.1007/s13349-020-00400-9
23. Colosimo, G., Crespi, M., Mazzoni, A.: Real-time GPS seismology with a stand-alone receiver: a preliminary feasibility demonstration. J. Geophys. Res. Solid Earth. **116** (2011). https://doi.org/10.1029/2010JB007941
24. Webb, G.T., Vardanega, P.J., Middleton, C.R.: Categories of SHM deployments: Technologies and capabilities. J. Bridg. Eng. **20** (2015). https://doi.org/10.1061/(ASCE)BE.1943-5592.0000735

Use of the Sentinel-1 Satellite Data in the SNAP Platform and the WebGNOME Simulation Model for Change Detection Analyses on the Persian Gulf Oil Spill

Giacomo Caporusso(✉), Marino Dell'Olio, and Eufemia Tarantino

Department of Civil, Environmental, Land, Construction and Chemistry (DICATECh), Politecnico di Bari, Via Orabona 4, 70125 Bari, Italy
giacomo.caporusso@poliba.it

Abstract. Oil spills in the marine environment increasingly represent a significant problem for the ecosystem. The intensification of the operations of extraction, transport and storage of hydrocarbons has in fact caused a greater frequency of the occurrence of accidents, with consequent dispersion of the material in an uncontrolled manner. Remote sensing plays a fundamental role in identifying and monitoring these phenomena. In particular, using satellite images obtained with Synthetic Aperture Radar (SAR) technology, spill recognition methodologies have been developed through automatic and semi-automatic approaches. This paper analyses the accident that occurred in March 2017 in the Persian Gulf, through the Sentinel-1 Single Look Complex (SLC) and Ground Range Detected (GRD) SAR image Change Detection technique, to evaluate the dispersion of hydrocarbons. The use of the SentiNel Application Platform (SNAP) software of the European Space Agency (ESA) made it possible to determine the amount of oil involved in the spill. Furthermore, through the Web-based application General NOAA Oil Modeling Environment (WebGNOME) the dynamic propagation model of the spilled hydrocarbons was produced based on the morphology and meteorological conditions of the site examined which further confirmed the validity of the Change Detection operations Sentinel-1 images. Finally, the results were compared with those obtained using automatic methodologies developed by ESA, confirming the greater accuracy of the procedures used in this study.

Keywords: Oil spill · Marine pollution · SAR · Sentinel-1 · SNAP · WebGNOME · Persian gulf

1 Introduction

Since 1990 there have been over 170 large-scale accidents involving tankers, bulk carriers, Floating Production Storage and Offloading (FPSO) and barges which, accidentally, caused the spill of hydrocarbons. In 2021 alone, losses totalling over 10,000 tons of hydrocarbons were recorded [1, 2]. The introduction of remote sensing techniques has

O. Gervasi et al. (Eds.): ICCSA 2022 Workshops, LNCS 13379, pp. 369–386, 2022.
https://doi.org/10.1007/978-3-031-10545-6_26

favoured a rapid and incontrovertible development in the study and monitoring of hydrocarbon spills, especially those that occur daily in the marine environment, in terms of quality and quantity of data deductible from analysis of satellite images [3]. The most widely used method for data acquisition involves the use of Aerial Photogrammetry, Unmanned Aerial Vehicle (UAV) [4–6] or satellites, especially those equipped with SAR sensors [7]. The diffusion of petroleum materials on an aqueous surface constitutes a large floating film, obviously different in terms of the chemical nature and roughness of the surrounding water surface. These characteristics determine a different ability to reflect the radar beam, determining a reduction in the backscatter detected by the instrument. Moreover, the SAR image is, thanks to the radar-type sensor, more efficient in the context of Oil Spill detection than that of a multi-spectral nature, as it is independent of lighting, cloudiness and other weather conditions that often negatively affect the quality of other types of satellite images [7]. For these reasons it was considered appropriate to analyse the oil spill that occurred off the coast of Dubai in March 2017 through Sentinel-1 images concomitant with the event. The work carried out has the following objectives ì) to compare the volume of floating hydrocarbons derived from the analysis of a single image with that derived from the Change Detection between the image acquired previously and that in conjunction with the SNAP event; ii) evaluate the effectiveness of a statistical approach in defining the backscatter value that allows you to distinguish water from oil; ììì) evaluate the behaviour of the Coherence interferometric parameter. Finally, the analysis performed was compared with the outputs produced by the Web General NOAA oil modeling environment (WebGNOME), a web application developed by NOAA [8]. This tool, starting from the data relating to the surrounding conditions of the environment and the event, allowed both to reconstruct the dynamics of the spill and to trace the quantities of hydrocarbons released into the environment.

2 Materials and Methods

2.1 Study Area

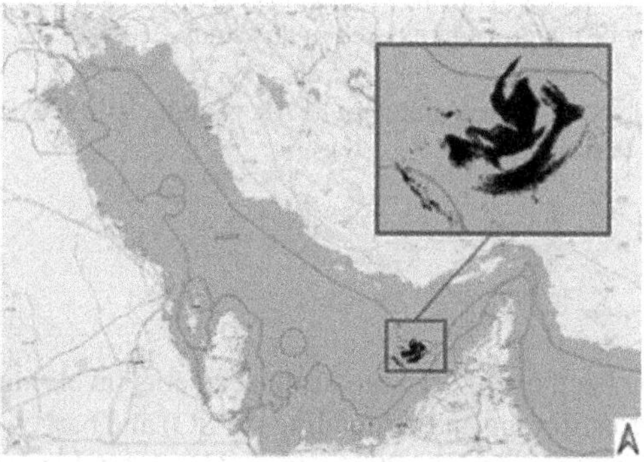

Fig. 1. Area affected by the spill. General Scale 1:10.000.000. Detail Scale 1:2.000.0000.

The region of the Persian Gulf is often subject to accidents that cause oil spills at sea, due to the richness of hydrocarbon deposits and the consequent maritime traffic; it is counted that in 2017 alone over 13,000 km^2 were spilled [2]. The event under consideration took place south of the island of Siri, in the Iranian sector of the Gulf (Fig. 1), in the first half of March 2017 when an emergency discharge occurred from the oil platform of the Siri-E field [2]. The non-profit environmental monitoring committee SkyTruth watchdog processed the SAR satellite images via the geospatial cloud platform GeoMixer, developed by Scanex, declaring that 300 to 620 m^3 of oil and / or petroleum products were spilled into the sea [2].

2.2 Dataset

The images used to study this event come from the Sentinel-1A satellite. The data used in this study are Single Look Complex (SLC) and Ground Range Detected (GRD) type belonging to Level-1 [9]. Just to get a complete idea of the actions performed on satellite data, it was decided to use SLC images in addition to the more usual GRDs as these undergo a different pre-processing with unknown parameters which, in some cases, can lead to conclusions not very exact [10]. The satellite images used for this study were acquired free of charge through NASA's Alaska Satellite Facility Data Search (ASF) portal. It was decided to use the image acquired on 12/02/17 for the image prior to the event. Instead, we chose to use the images acquired on 11/03/17 for the Change Detection procedures and those acquired on 08/03/17 for coherence estimation, given that the latter present a perfect overlap with the images of 02/12/17, a necessary condition to implement the interferometric process from which to obtain the coherence parameter. To operate through SNAP's Oil Spill tool, only the GRD-type post-event image acquired on 11/03/2017 was chosen.

2.3 Pre-processing

Images downloaded from the ASF portal require preprocessing actions. The SNAP software contains all Toolboxes for pre-processing and analysing all types of Sentinel data. Below is the list and description of the pre-processing procedures that were carried out on the SLC and GRD images (Fig. 2).

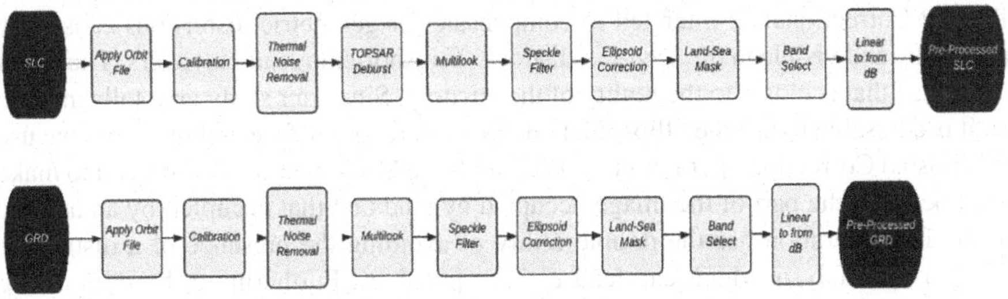

Fig. 2. SLC and GRD preprocessing workflow.

SAR products require a state orbital vector to correct spatial position accuracy. This information is present in externally hosted files, which need to be downloaded separately and are used by SNAP to update the product metadata. The Apply Orbit File process automatically downloads the OSV file and updates the metadata [12]. The objective of SAR calibration is to provide imagery in which the pixel values can be directly related to the radar backscatter of the scene. To do this, the output scaling applied by the processor must be undone and the desired scaling must be reintroduced. The radiometric scale allowed for different images by type of sensor, time and geometry of acquisition [12]. The intensity of a SAR image can be modified by the additive thermal noise. ESA provides calibrated noise vectors to subtract the power of the noise. The thermal correction of the noise can be carried out on SLC and GRD products that have not already been corrected, using a module that reduces the amount of noise from the intensity channel. The noise correction is then applied to the complex data in order to estimate the noise-free matrix [12]. TOPSAR is a progressive terrain scanning methodology performed by SAR devices; the data is acquired in bursts, then switching the antenna beam with multiple adjacent sub-bands. A product acquired with IW mode will have 3 swaths, one in EW mode will have 5. The Debursting operation merges the adjacent bursts, returning a single image by exploiting the azimuthal superposition of the individual bursts. For a GRD image, this operation has already been carried out in all the processes to obtain it starting from an SLC type image [13]. An SLC type image is acquired with a resolution ranging from 1.5 × 3.6 m to 2.3 × 14.1 m. To obtain an acquisition with a square pixel, we carry out a multilooking process of a square-sized pixel. The processing can be generated by calculating the average resolution, along the range direction or the azimuth direction, degrading the image quality but obtaining square pixels. Generally, a SAR image appears stained by the "salt and pepper noise", typical of all images of digital origin. To reduce the presence of this effect, different images are combined inconsistently, as if they correspond to different acquisitions of the same scene. Multilooking can also be used to produce an image with a reduced Speckle effect. [7]. The Speckle effect is caused by a casual constructive and destructive interference that is formed in the acquired image and which consequently forms the "salt and pepper noise". Speckle filters can be used to reduce the amount of Speckle at the cost of reduced resolution and blur. The SNAP software provides different types of Speckle filters, a Lee Sigma filter with a Windows Size 7 × 7 was used in our work [12]. Due to topographical variations of a scene and the tilt of the satellite sensor, distances can be distorted in the SAR images. Image data not directly at the sensor's Nadir location will have some distortion. Terrain Corrections and Ellipsoid Corrections are intended to compensate for geometric distortions caused by topography and visible in the scene as shadows, foreshortening, and layovers. The result is an image that is closer to the reality of the territory. Since our study area falls into the sea, it is advisable to use the ellipsoidal one as a reference surface and therefore we use the Ellipsoid Correction operator [14]. The Land-Sea Mask operator allows you to make a split between the part of the image occupied by land and that occupied by an aquatic mirror. This operation has the double utility of avoiding the presence of a disturbing action in the analysis which can lead to false positives. Furthermore, by eliminating the part of the soil that is not of interest for this study, we reduce the computational load that aggravates on the device used for the processing. This operation is carried out through the automatic download of a DEM that immediately recognizes the height of each pixel and is therefore able to deduce whether it is on the mainland or not [14]. The conversion from Digital Number to decibel transforms the backscatter intensity into a more user-friendly quantity, with a better degree of visibility and, generally, accepted as a unit of measurement for a given radar [15]. The Band Select operation is used to select the band on which we want to carry out the conversion operation (VV). At the end of the pre-processing operations we obtain, both for the SLC and GRD image, a product with the optimal characteristics for the processing required for the actual processing (Figs. 3 and 4).

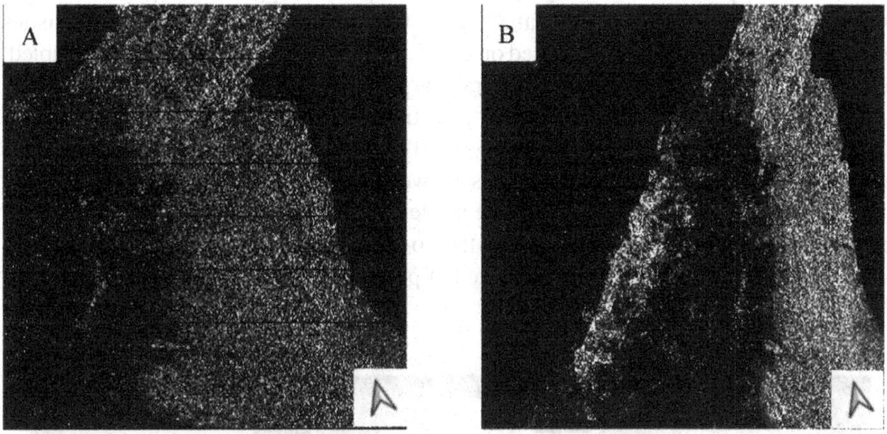

Fig. 3. SLC image before pre-processing, Scale 1:580.000 (A); GRD image before pre-processing, Scale 1:1000.000 (B).

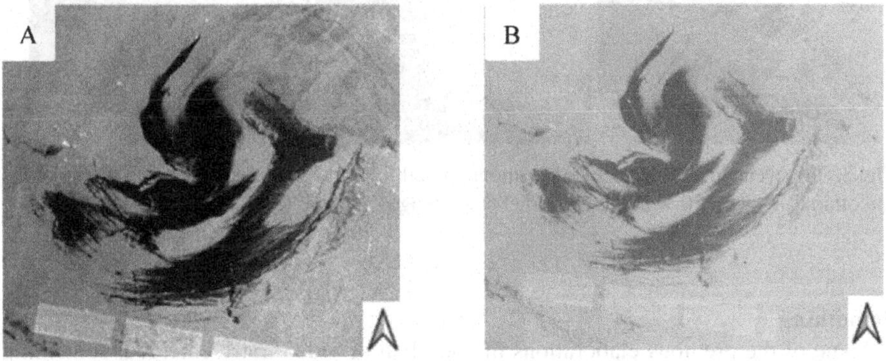

Fig. 4. SLC image after pre-processing (A); GRD image after pre-processing (B). Scale 1: 250.000.

2.4 Processing

Once the pre-processing of the images is finished, it is possible to move on to the actual processing that allowed us to achieve the originally set goals. The processing performed involves an initial phase of co-registration of the pre and post event images, the application of a smoothing filter and finally a calculation operation between the backscatter values of the two images through a mathematical expression.

Co-registration

The first step is to carry out a co-registration of the sub-pixels of the SAR images, a fundamental requirement for carrying out any comparison operation [16]. The result to be obtained through this step is to spatially align the two images so that the characteristics of a reference image are superimposed on those of the image to which the first is coupled, to be able to make a comparison as accurate as possible [17].

Co-registration is normally done by selecting an image as the reference (master) to which all other images are aligned [13]. The co-registration process requires the identification of common characteristics between the master and the slaves and the subsequent adaptation of the slaves to the master. The positions of the common features are called "Tie points" and are used by the co-registration application as a reference. Once enough binding points are generated, a polynomial function is used to align the deformed slave image to the master [17].

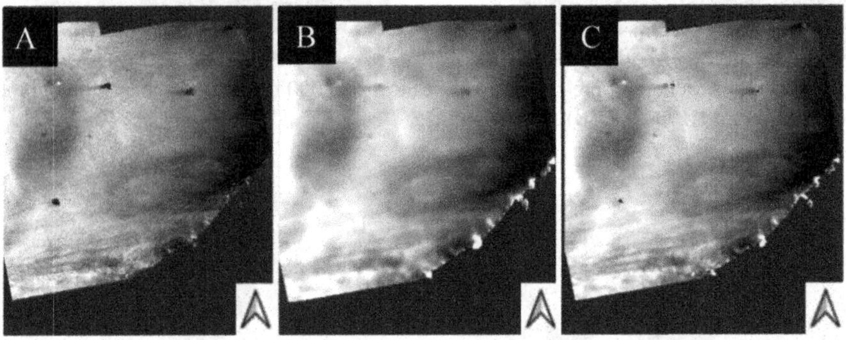

Fig. 5. Pre-event image respectively without smoothing filter (A), with 10 × 10 pixels kernel smoothing (B), with 20 × 20 pixels kernel smoothing (C). Scale 1: 800.000

Smoothing

In some of the previous elaborations the problem of video noise emerged, something common in the field of remote sensing. When it comes to detecting edges and edges, noise in images greatly affects detection accuracy; therefore, controlling the intensity of the pixel values helps the model in use to focus on general details and obtain greater precision [18]. By smoothing, we reduce the high-frequency details: the back-scatter value of each pixel is defined according to mathematical relationships with those of the backscatter of the pixels surrounding it within a kernel of a fixed size [19]. By increasing the kernel size, we increase the smoothing, thus obtaining different results; it is therefore advisable to carry out a good calibration of the values used during the procedure. Among the various mathematical filtering relationships, the choice fell on the median blurring, which averages all the pixels belonging to the same kernel and replaces the values of all the pixels with the one calculated in the kernel [20]. This filter was used exclusively on the image depicting the pre-event, to further reduce the "salt and pepper noise" caused by the irregularity of the sea surface. In our work the effects of kernels of 10 × 10 pixels and 20 × 20 pixels size were evaluated (Fig. 5).

2.5 Change Detection Analysis and Threshold Values Definition

We can define the Change Detection operation as the process that identifies the differences in the properties of an object by observing it at different instants of time [21]. The comparison is made between the image acquired prior to the event, on February 12, 2017, and that acquired in conjunction with the event, on March 11, 2017. The determination of the threshold value subsequently used as part of the Change Detection was carried out by calculating the difference of the average backscatter value of the pixels that contain the oil stain in the post-event image and the average value of the unstained ones in the pre-event image. The irregular and jagged nature of the patch did not allow to define in a precise, simple, and rapid way the average backscatter value assumed by the stained pixels and that assumed by the non-stained pixels. Not being able to use simple geometries as useful polygons to define homogeneous areas, we opted for an analysis by sections. Initially, within the image containing the oil spill, a backscatter value was determined that was able to discern the presence or less of oil by tracing Sect. 1 totally falling within the oil and Sect. 2 falling totally in the water (Fig. 6). Plotting the results, the values shown in Table 1 were obtained.

Table 1. Backscatter values in the post-event image for sections 1 and 2.

Backscatter Section 1 (oil) (dB)	
Maximum value	−28.85
Maximum value	−31.91
Average value	−30.54
Backscatter Section 2 (water) (dB)	
Maximum value	−21.11
Maximum value	−23.42
Average value	−22.26

A value of −25 dB was therefore chosen to assign or not the status of "spot-to" to the pixel in question, as the maximum value of a pixel falling within the oil spot is well below this value; conversely, an "unstained" pixel has backscatter values well above the value we have designated. Once the water-oil discriminating value had been determined,

Fig. 6. Sections 1 and 2 used to determine the oil-water discriminant backscatter value. Scale 1: 200.000.

it was possible to move on to the study of Sects. 3 to 6 which cross both floating oil and the sea without it and therefore with heterogeneous backscatter values (Fig. 7). In the post-event image, for each section, the pixels with backscatter values lower than −25 dB, in which the presence of hydrocarbons was detected, were separated from those with higher values, which were considered free from the same hydrocarbons, by calculating the average of the values of the two parts. In the pre-event image, the average backscatter value was calculated along the section uniformly made up of water. The threshold value of each section was therefore defined as the difference between the average backscatter value of the oil pixels in the post-event image and the average backscatter value of the water pixels in the pre-event image. This operation made it possible to obtain four threshold values; finally, the average of these four values allowed to obtain the threshold value which was subsequently used in the Change Detection calculations. The average threshold values of each section, both for SLC and GRD images, are shown in Table 2.

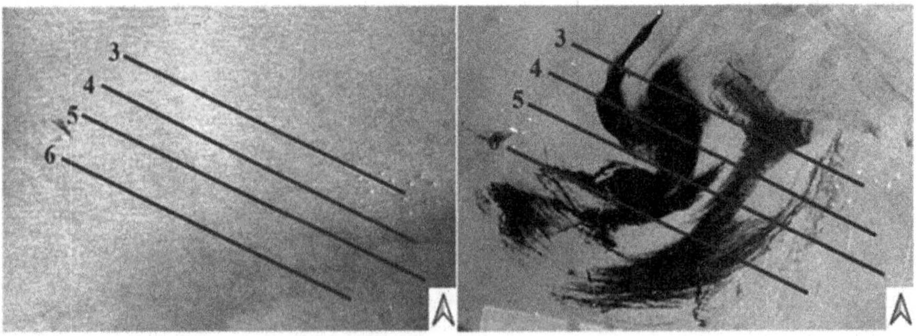

Fig. 7. Sections used to determine the Threshold value. Scale 1: 200.000.

In addition to the values determined by this procedure, it was decided to repeat the Change Detection operation also for threshold values close to the excess and defect values calculated, such as −12.5 dB, −13 dB and −14 dB. The smoothing operation was carried out exclusively for the Change Detection in which the calculated average threshold value was used. The subtraction between the backscatter values of the master image and those

Table 2. Average Threshold values calculated for SLC (left) and GRD (right).

Threshold SLC (dB)		Threshold GRD (dB)	
Section 1	13.89	Section 1	13.78
Section 2	12.96	Section 2	14.85
Section 3	13.50	Section 3	13.90
Section 4	12.67	Section 4	14.67
Average Value	13.26	Average Value	14.30

of the slave image was done through the "Band Math" operator. Subsequently, a binary mask was created composed exclusively of pixels having a threshold equal to or greater than the values we have chosen. The raster containing the mask was then exported and processed using the QGIS software. Within the latter, a vectorization operation was carried out and a Sieve Classification was subsequently carried out using the Semi-Automatic Classification Plugin tool. Sieve Classification is a procedure that allows you to replace the value of the isolated pixels with that of the surrounding pixels. This procedure is useful for removing isolated parts from the classification [22]. Finally, using the Field Calculator tool, the total area occupied by oil was calculated as the sum of the areas of the remaining polygons.

2.6 Oil Spill Detection Tool

Inside the SNAP software there is the "Oil Spill Detection" tool based on an algorithm that can be used for detecting oil spills [23]. This tool was created by training on a set of images coming from the waters of the northern European seas; generally, it performs good results, except for the presence of several false positives, caused using an adaptive algorithm for calculating the threshold based on a single image and not on a Change Detection [23]. The operator follows the following operations: a pre-processing phase, in which a calibration is performed and a Speckle filter is applied; a phase of Land-sea masking which serves to focus the detection exclusively on the area concerned; a phase of Dark Spot detection, in which dark spots are identified using the adaptive algorithm; finally a Clustering and Discrimination phase in which the identified pixels are collected in clusters or eliminated on the basis of the minimum size chosen for cluster formation [24]. The Adaptive Threshold Algorithm works by finding an average local backscatter, using a comparison kernel size chosen by the user; after which the software discriminates the spots that have a backscatter lower than the average local one as "smudged". This algorithm performs best with Radarsat and ENVISAT SAR images, for which a training activity was carried out [14]. With respect to the case in question, the image acquired on 11/03/17 was processed, to make a direct comparison with the results of the Change Detection process, for which the same data was used. The output of the process, produced after a processing time of several hours, is a raster image in which the pixels recognized as "stained" are displayed, aggregated in clusters.

2.7 Thickness Value Used to Calculate the Volumes

After having completed the processing that allowed the determination of the spilled hydrocarbon surface, it was possible to calculate the corresponding volume. To obtain this result, an estimate of the thickness that this fluid can occupy in the sea was considered. The exact determination of this parameter is very complex as it depends on various factors such as, for example, the type of hydrocarbon itself, its temperature, sea temperature, etc. [25]. Furthermore, the possibility of aggregating or not of the spilled fluid, in order to form the easily distinguishable "dark patches", depends very much on the meteorological conditions: the movement of oil is very susceptible to wind and surface currents, which can move it on the water surface and disperse it [26]. In the case of optical images, it is possible to perform a colorimetric analysis that makes a corresponding thickness correspond to a certain colour, which will therefore be spatially variable [27]. In the case of SAR images, it is not possible to carry out this type of analysis because it is not possible to appreciate the spectral characteristics that make the patch assume different colours. However, we can start from the consideration that to be detected by a SAR, a hydrocarbon must have a thickness of at least one micron [25]; starting from this assumption it was possible to make an indicative estimate of the volume of floating oil.

2.8 Coherence Estimation

The local coherence of two radar satellite images is defined as the correlation coefficient obtained by crossing two SAR images and making the ratio between the coherent and inconsistent summations calculated for each point. The value of Coherence C goes from 0 to 1; for values close to 1 we will have to deal with highly coherent pixels, typical behaviour of built structures or rocky areas, which undergo minimal change over time; for values close to 0 we will have a low coherence content, a typical behaviour of changing elements such as vegetal or aquatic ones [28]. After applying the Orbit file, a splitting operation of the SLC image was carried out. The Back Geocoding operator made it possible to co-register the two previously split SLC images. Following the co-registration of the two satellite images, the Network Enhanced Spectral Diversity (NESD) was used to estimate the azimuth shift between the radar images, to minimize the phase discontinuities between the different bursts. Then a Deburst is performed to merge the different bursts and obtain a unique Coherence image. Finally, to refine the image quality, a multilooking operation is performed, to return a square dimension to the pixel and reduce the Speckle, and an ellipsoidal correction to eliminate the deviation between the geoid and the reference ellipsoid. At the end of the processing, we moved on to the evaluation of the Coherence values: initially the Coherence values were analysed using sections that crossed the oil stain. This methodology, due to the prevailing inconsistent nature of the sea, within the scene, did not yield useful results for the purposes of our research. Given this, later, geometries were built, externally and internally to the spot displayed in the reference image, and the differences between the average values of coherence calculated inside the spot and outside were measured; the comparison was made both by means of means and by means of the ninetieth percentile.

2.9 WebGNOME

The catastrophic consequences caused by an Oil Spill event [29] have led, over the years, to the need to refine the techniques for identifying and detecting spills [30]. However, it was also necessary to develop techniques that would make it possible to reconstruct the dynamics of the accident and to predict its spread and future evolution. To meet this need, (NOAA) has developed a software, WebGNOME, equipped with a model capable of elaborating the path that the spilled hydrocarbon can follow, both from a chemical and physical point of view, based on how the latter is influenced by the atmospheric and morphological conditions of the analysed case [8].

Dataset

WebGNOME can be used by entering various data sources: the map, the wind and sea currents, the diffusion parameters, the temperature, the salinity, the type of hydrocarbon, the type and duration of Spill [8]. A spill phase duration of 3 days was set, for a total of 401,000 spilled gallons (data calibrated to obtain a quantity of floating material equal to that detected). The type of hydrocarbon chosen, in the list made available by the ADIOS Oil Database, corresponds to "DUBAI, OIL & GAS", with an API gravity equal to 31.081 and a Pour point equal to −9.0 °C. The water temperature [31] was set to 21.9 °C [32], the salinity equal to 32 psu [33] and the Sedimentation Load equal to 5 mg/l [33]. The horizontal diffusion coefficient was set to a value equal to 1e + 5 cm^2/s [34]. The wind was set for intensity and direction with a variability of six hours between one measurement and another. Finally, the currents were obtained from the GOODS website, made available by NOAA, from which it is possible to download the files necessary to correctly set the trend of the sea currents within the model [35]. The duration of the simulation was set at 6 days and 3 h, to make the end of the simulation coincide with the moment in which the post-event image used in the study was recorded.

Processing

The spilled hydrocarbon is modelled by the software through points with mass that the program calls "Lagrangian Elements" or "LE". Each LE has its location, release time, age, type of pollution and status (floating, beached or evaporated) [8]. In WebGNOME the diffusion of material is treated as a stochastic process; the effects of gravity and surface tension are ignored, because they only affect the first instants of spill. The model uses a classic diffusion equation, here expressed in Cartesian coordinates:

$$\frac{\partial C}{\partial t} = D_x * \frac{\partial^2 C}{\partial x^2} + D_y * \frac{\partial^2 C}{\partial y^2} \quad (1)$$

where C is the concentration of the material and D is the diffusion coefficient. The movement of each element is calculated moment by moment, vectorially adding the intensity transmitted by the wind and that transmitted by the current. The movement caused by the current is calculated through an algorithm called Directional Acyclic Graph (DAG) Tree, who divides the map into triangles and calculates, for each particle inside the triangle itself, on which of the adjacent triangles there is more probability that the particle moves. This procedure makes it possible to greatly lighten the complexity of the calculation with respect to the methodologies that are based on the nearest neighbour for each specific element. The Windage data entered is interpolated through a Hermite polynomial; subsequently the consequent wave motion generated is calculated from the intensity of the wind, mainly responsible for the motion of the oil particles [36]. Recent studies relating to the prediction of wave motion using neural networks could prove useful for the evolution of the oil diffusion model [39, 40]. Furthermore, for the calculation of evaporation and sedimentation, WebGNOME uses a three-phase calculation algorithm, based on the model developed by Boehm, Feist, Mackay, & Paterson [37]. Two types of solutions are obtained through the software: a "best estimate solution" and a "minimum regret solution". The "best estimate", the one chosen in this paper, considers only the Lagrangian Elements whose movement, according to the calculations made by the software, is deemed correct with excellent probability; the "mini-mum regret", on the other hand, also considers a certain uncertainty in the input data, to which a variable and uncertain output data will correspond, which contemplates within it a wider but at the same time more uncertain set of diffusion possibilities; the latter methodology is useful for determining the "worst case scenario" [8]. By using WebGNOME it was possible to validate the detection carried out via satellite image, verifying the actual matching between the spot extrapolated through the SNAP program and the one obtained from the web software calculations. Parallel to the analysis concerning the movement and diffusion of the pollutant, the WebGNOME software also performs a chemical analysis of each individual Lagrangian element. The component of the program that carries out this analysis is the Automated Data Inquiry for Oil Spills (ADIOS); this tool models oil spills to analyse physico-chemical changes [38]. Using ADIOS it was therefore possible to reconstruct, starting from the quantity of floating hydrocarbon identified by the satellite image, the sedimented quantity, that naturally dispersed and that evaporated and, consequently, also the total volume that characterized the accident in its entirety.

3 Results and Discussion

The oil surfaces obtained from the analysis carried out through Change Detection (Fig. 8) and the volumes obtained considering the thickness of one micron are collected in Table 3. The reference volume is that determined by the SkyTruth portal equal to 163876 gallons.

The Table 3 first distinguishes the results obtained for the SLC and GRD images; the threshold values used, the possible size of the Smoothing kernel, the calculated volume expressed in gallons and the percentage difference in absolute value from the comparison measure are also indicated. It is possible to notice a discrepancy between the results obtained starting from an SLC image compared to those obtained from a GRD. The result obtained using the threshold value obtained through the section method, has a percentage discrepancy with respect to the reference volume ranging from 6.7% to 6.9% as regards the SLC, of 5.5% for the GRD image. We can therefore note how the application of the Smoothing filter has a negligible contribution to the result, causing the result to vary by 0.2% in the SLC and by a value of less than 0.1% for the GRD. By carrying out the Classification Sieve process on the SLC image with a difference value equal to -13.258 with no smoothing, while obtaining a cleaner image, there is a loss of information which leads to an increase, even if minimum, of the deviation from the reference measure,

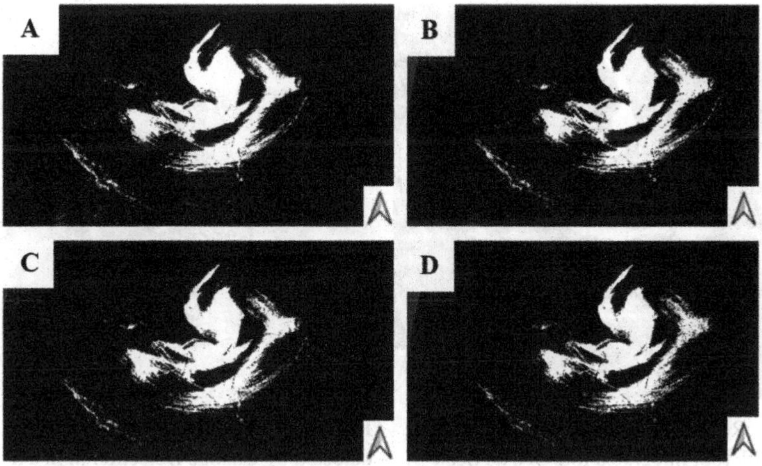

Fig. 8. Resulting images of the Change Detection process respectively with Threshold values equal to −12.5 dB (A), −13 dB (B), −13.258 dB (C), −14 dB (D). Scale 1: 55.000.

Table 3. Volume Analytics.

Declared Volume = 163876 gal				
Threshold (dB)	Smoothing filter (Pixel)	Sieve filter	Computed volume (gal)	Variation (%)
Change Detection SLC				
Difference - 12.5	NO	NO	169762.5	3.59%
Difference - 13	NO	NO	158388.0	−3.35%
Difference - 13.258	NO	NO	152911.2	−6.69%
Difference - 13.258	10	NO	152960.1	−6.66%
Difference - 13.258	20	NO	152604.0	−6.88%
Difference - 13.258	NO	YES	152624.8	−7.00%
Difference - 14	NO	NO	137349.9	−16.19%
Change Detection GRD				
Difference - 12.5	NO	NO	181226.7	10.59%
Difference - 13	NO	NO	160971.1	−1.77%
Difference - 14.301	NO	NO	154913.0	−5.47%
Difference - 14.301	10	NO	154920.6	−5.46%
Difference - 14.301	20	NO	154818.7	−5.53%
Difference -15	NO	NO	140120.0	−14.50%
SNAP Oil Spill tool				
Undefined	NO	NO	137728.4	−15.96%

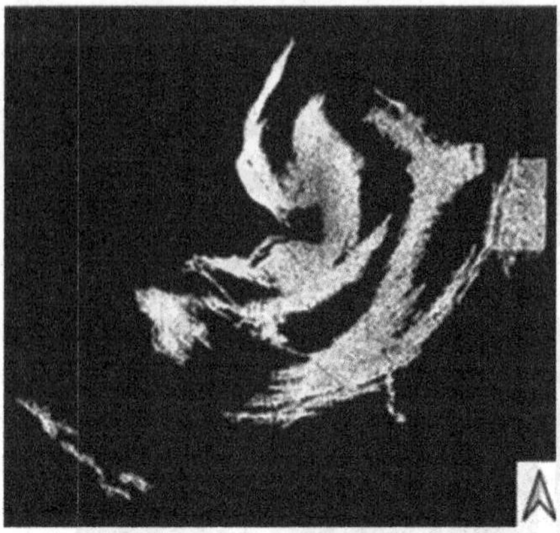

Fig. 9. Resulting image of the single image Oil Spill Tool integrated into SNAP. Scale 1: 200.000.

Fig. 10. Comparison between the spot detected by Change Detection in SNAP and Lagrangian Elements from WebGNOME. Scale 1: 200.000.

advising against its use for the purpose of a precise volumetric analysis. The best values will be obtained with a threshold value slightly lower than that calculated by us which therefore tends to undersea the actual volume value by 3–4%. The recognition obtained through the tool integrated in the single image "Oil Spill Tool" program (Fig. 9) leads to a difference of 16%, which indicates the inadequacy of the methodology in the exact recognition of the quantities spilled, moving us away by more than ten percentage points from the optimal measurements obtained from our studies. Analysing the results obtained through the Coherence Estimation procedure, it is noted that no significant and useful results emerge for the analysis: the changing nature of the aqueous medium does not lend itself, at a macroscopic level, to an interferometric analysis which allows to obtain appreciable coherence results. By examining the numerical results obtained from the coherence analysis of a geometry falling within the oil stain and comparing them with those of a geometry not falling within the stain, we obtain a deviation between the percentages of −1.5% compared to the average value and −2.2% as regards the 90th percentile. From the visual comparison between the stain detected through the SNAP procedures and that calculated through the dynamic model WebGNOME (Fig. 10) it can be seen how the two procedures, carried out in parallel, lead to a good overlap of results: the spill obtained from the satellite images it is in fact almost entirely incorporated in the cloud of points that the software developed by NOAA generates. The use of WebGNOME is therefore, from our studies, valid in predicting the behaviour of the spilled hydrocarbon, restricting the field of investigation in which cleaning operations could be carried out. In addition, this procedure allows you to reconstruct the origin and mode of diffusion of the fluid, possibly allowing you to investigate the causes; this problem is widespread in the field of detecting oil spills as it is often difficult to reconstruct the dynamics of accidents due to the unavailability of information. In this sense, the use of the ADIOS tool, which is part of the WebGNOME package, is also useful: this tool performs a chemical analysis, based on the data entered in the model, from which it obtains, moment by moment, the hydrocarbon values evaporated, naturally dispersed, settled and floating. The floating material, in the case under consideration, constitutes only 40.8% of the total volume spilled. Starting from this data it was possible to trace a quantity of spilled volume equal to 401000 gallons (Fig. 11).

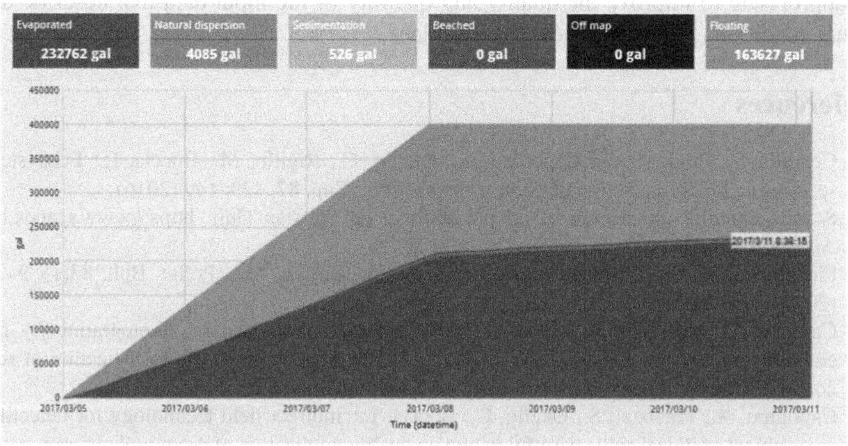

Fig. 11. Reconstruction of the event carried out using the ADIOS software.

4 Conclusions

The outputs obtained from the study confirm that more truthful results can be obtained in the identification and subsequent estimation of the mass of spilled hydrocarbons through a Change Detection process both on an SLC-type image and on an image of the GRD compared to the procedures that analyse a single image, such as the one performed by the Oil Spill Tool integrated in SNAP. The values are however affected by a degree of inaccuracy because in a SAR image it is not possible to appreciate the different densities that oil can assume in the act of floating on an aquatic surface. In this regard, it may be useful to carry out a more in-depth comparison with Change Detection procedures that have an optical type of image as the object of study, such as that obtained from Sentinel-2 satellites. The procedure used to determine the threshold value is confirmed to be suitable for recognizing an Oil Spill having given results close to those found in literature: this result could be further improved by reducing the random component that this type of measurement brings with it, by increasing the number and size of the sections used. The Coherence analysis carried out did not lead to decisive results: this is because the sea surface has a changing nature that does not lend itself well to the type of research carried out and does not give appreciable macroscopic results. This kind of procedure could therefore be more effective for the analysis of an Oil Spill phenomenon that does not occur in the marine environment but on land. The WebGNOME software was used as a validation tool for the survey carried out via satellite image; the good overlap between the results of the two models testifies to the correctness of the model and the possibility of its use for validation procedures, reconstruction of the Oil Spill event and its environmental consequences, thanks to the chemical-physical analysis performed by the ADIOS tool. For this purpose, the component of the imputed meteorological data, the type of spilled hydrocarbon and the spillage method are of particular importance for the correct functioning; to increase the reliability of the generated model, it will therefore be appropriate to improve the quality and quantity of the input data that describe the actual conditions in which the event takes place.

References

1. Cervelli, E., Pindozzi, S., Capolupo, A., Okello, C., Rigillo, M., Boccia, L.: Ecosystem services and bioremediation of polluted areas. Ecol. Eng. **87,** 139–149 (2016)
2. Scanex Satellite monitoring of oil pollution in the Persian Gulf. https://www.scanex.ru. Accessed 16 Mar 2022
3. Fingas, M., Brown, C.: Review of oil spill remote sensing. Mar. Pollut. Bull. **83**(1), 9–23 (2014)
4. Capolupo, A., Pindozzi, S., Okello, C., Fiorentino, N., Boccia, L.: Photogrammetry for environmental monitoring: the use of drones and hydrological models for detection of soil contaminated by copper. Sci. Total Environ. **514**, 298–306 (2015)
5. Capolupo, A., Pindozzi, S., Okello, C., Boccia, L.: Indirect field technology for detecting areas object of illegal spills harmful to human health: application of drones, photogrammetry and hydrological models. Geospat. Health **8**(3), S699–S707 (2014)
6. Capolupo, A., Nasta, P., Palladino, M., Cervelli, E., Boccia, L., Romano, N.: Assessing the ability of hybrid poplar for in-situ phytoextraction of cadmium by using UAV-photogrammetry and 3D flow simulator. Int. J. Remote Sens. **39**(15–16), 5175–5194 (2018)
7. Fan, J., Zhang, F., Zhao, D., Wang, J.: Oil spill monitoring based on SAR remote sensing imagery. Aquatic Procedia **3**, 112–118 (2015)
8. Beegle-Krause, J.: General NOAA oil modeling environment (GNOME): a new spill trajectory model. In: International oil Spill Conference, vol. 2001, No. 2. American Petroleum Institute (2001)
9. ESA Mission Sentinel-1. https://www.esa.int. Accessed 01 Mar 2022
10. Potin, P.: Sentinel-1 mission overview (2011)
11. Prats-Iraola, P., et sl.: Sentinel-1 assessment of the interferometric wide-swath mode. In: 2015 IEEE international geoscience and remote sensing symposium (IGARSS). IEEE (2015)
12. Filipponi, F.: Sentinel-1 GRD preprocessing workflow. Multidisciplinary digital publishing institute proceedings, vol. 18. No. 1 (2019)
13. Veci, L., Lu, J., Foumelis, M., and Engdahl, M.: ESA's Multi-mission Sentinel-1 Toolbox. In: EGU General Assembly Conference Abstracts (2017)
14. Prastyani, R., Abdul, B.: Utilisation of Sentinel-1 SAR imagery for oil spill mapping: a case study of Balikpapan Bay oil spill. J. Geospatial Inf. Sci. Eng. **1**(1) (2018)
15. Nasirzadehdizaji, R., Cakir, Z., Sanli, F.B., Abdikan, S., Pepe, A., Calò, F.: Sentinel-1 interferometric coherence and backscattering analysis for crop monitoring. Comput. Electron. Agric. **185**, 106118 (2021)
16. Mandal, D., Vaka, D.S., Bhogapurapu, N.R., Vanama, V.S.K., Kumar, V., Rao, Y.S., Bhattacharya, A.: Sentinel-1 SLC preprocessing workflow for polarimetric applications: a generic practice for generating dual-pol covariance matrix elements in SNAP S-1 toolbox (2019)
17. Usman, F., Nanda, N., Nasmirayanti, R., Sumantyo, J.T.S.: Comparative analysis on digital surface model of urban area from Sentinel-1 SAR interferometry and aerial photogrammetry for disaster mitigation plan. In E3S Web of Conferences, vol. 331, p. 04017. EDP Sciences (2021)

18. Ali, I., Cao, S., Naeimi, V., Paulik, C., Wagner, W.: Methods to remove the border noise from Sentinel-1 synthetic aperture radar data: implications and importance for time-series analysis. IEEE J. Sel. Top. Appl. Earth Observ. Remote Sensing **11**(3), 777–786 (2018)
19. Kumari, M., Murthy, C.S., Pandey, V., Bairagi, G.D.: Soybean cropland mapping using multi-temporal SENTINEL-1 data. International Archives of the Photogrammetry, Remote Sensing & Spatial Information Sciences (2019)
20. Indriasari, N., et al.: Analisa filter spekle single dan multitemporal data Sentinel 1-A. In: IOP Conference Series: Earth and Environmental Science, vol. 500. No. 1. IOP Publishing (2020)
21. Turgay, C.: Change detection in satellite images using a genetic algorithm approach. IEEE Geosci. Remote Sens. Lett. **7**(2), 386–390 (2010)
22. Al-Ahmadi, F.S., Al-Hames, A.S.: Comparison of four classification methods to extract land use and land cover from raw satellite images for some remote arid areas, Kingdom of Saudi Arabia. Earth Sci. **20**(1) (2009)
23. Misra, A., Balaji, R.: Simple approaches to oil spill detection using sentinel application platform (SNAP)-ocean application tools and texture analysis: a comparative study. J. Indian Soc. Remote Sens, **45**(6) (2017)
24. Capizzi, G., Sciuto, G.L., Woźniak, M., Damaševicius, R.: A clustering based system for automated oil spill detection by satellite remote sensing. In: International Conference on Artificial Intelligence and Soft Computing. Springer, Cham (2016)
25. Prasad, S.J., Balakrishnan Nair, T.M.: Quantification of oil lost from tanker vessel using space borne radar datasets-Case study of Haldia port oil spill. In: International Oil Spill Conference. vol. 2021. No. 1, July 2018 (2021)
26. Dąbrowska, E., Kołowrocki, K.: Hydro-meteorological change process impact on oil spill domain movement at sea. In: Zamojski, W., Mazurkiewicz, J., Sugier, J., Walkowiak, T., Kacprzyk, J. (eds) Theory and Applications of Dependable Computer Systems. DepCoS-RELCOMEX 2020. Advances in Intelligent Systems and Computing, vol. 1173. Springer, Cham. https://doi.org/10.1007/978-3-030-48256-5_17
27. Fingas, M.: The challenges of remotely measuring oil slick thickness. Remote Sens. **10**(2), 319 (2018)
28. Touzi, R., Lopes, A., Bruniquel, J., Vachon, P.W.: Coherence estimation for SAR imagery. IEEE Trans. Geosci. Remote Sens. **37**(1), 135–149 (1999)
29. Palladino, M., Nasta, P., Capolupo, A., Romano, N.: Monitoring and modelling the role of phytoremediation to mitigate non-point source cadmium pollution and groundwater contamination at field scale. Ital. J. Agron. **13**.s1 (2018)
30. D'Andrea, M. A., and G. Reddy, K.: Health consequences among subjects involved in Gulf oil spill clean-up activities. Am. J. Med. **126**(11), 966–974 (2013)
31. Tarantino, E.: Monitoring spatial and temporal distribution of Sea Surface Temperature with TIR sensor data. Italian J. Remote Sensing/Rivista Italiana di Telerilevamento **44**(1) (2012)
32. Noori, R., et al.: Recent and future trends in sea surface temperature across the Persian Gulf and Gulf of Oman. PloS one **14**(2), e0212790 (2019)
33. Dubach, H.W.: A Summary of temperature-salinity characteristics of the persian gulf. National oceanographic data center Washington D.C. (1964)
34. Al-Ghadban, A.N., Abdali, F., Massoud, M.S.: Sedimentation rate and bioturbation in the Arabian Gulf. Environ. Int. **24**, 1–2 (1998)
35. Samuels, W.B., Amstutz, D.E., Bahadur, R., Ziemniak, C.: Development of a global oil spill modeling system. Earth Sci. Res. **2**(2), 52 (2013)
36. Zelenke, B., O'Connor, C., Barker, C.H., Beegle-Krause, C.J., Eclipse, L.: General NOAA operational modeling environment (GNOME) technical documentation (2012)
37. Jung, T.H., Son, S.: Oil spill simulation by coupling three-dimensional hydrodynamic model and oil spill model. J. Ocean Eng. Technol. **32**(6), 474–484 (2018)

38. Elizaryev, A., et al.: Numerical simulation of oil spills based on the GNOME and ADIOS. Int. J. Eng. Technol. (UAE) **7**(2), 24 (2018)
39. Sadeghifar, T., Lama, G.F.C., Sihag, P., Bayram, A., Kisi, O.: Wave height predictions in complex sea flows through soft-computing models: case study of Persian Gulf. Ocean Eng. **245**, 110467 (2022)
40. Lama, G.F.C., Sadeghifar, T., Azad, M.T., Sihag, P., Kisi, O.: On the indirect estimation of wind wave heights over the Southern Coasts of Caspian Sea: a comparative analysis. Water **14**(6), 843 (2022)

Change Detection Analysis Using Sentinel-1 Satellite Data with SNAP and GEE Regarding Oil Spill in Venezuela

Giacomo Caporusso(✉), Cristian Gallo, and Eufemia Tarantino

Department of Civil, Environmental, Land, Construction and Chemistry (DICATECh), Politecnico di Bari, Via Edoardo Orabona 4, 70126 Bari (BA), Italy
giacomo.caporusso@poliba.it

Abstract. In Venezuela, according to a report by the National Aeronautics and Space Administration (NASA) dated September 2021, up to 50,000 oil spills at sea have been monitored in the 2010–2016-time frame. In the current two-year period, the situation does not seem to have changed: the state refinery of the Venezuelan oil company Petróleos de Venezuela, S.A. (PDVSA), located near El Palito (Carabobo), is estimated to have been responsible for nearly 100,000 barrels of oil spilled in just one year. The aforementioned spills, with the intensification of extraction, transport and storage operations, have given rise to a greater number of accidents resulting in uncontrolled dispersion of material, endangering local marine-coastal ecosystems. The one that took place in July 2020 stands out, reconstructed a posteriori using satellite images that have highlighted its geo-environmental impact. Remote sensing has played a fundamental role in identifying and monitoring the spread of hydrocarbons; in the present study, the same event was analysed using Sentinel-1 Synthetic Aperture Radar Image (SAR) Change Detection techniques. The use of the desktop software SeNtinel Application Platform (SNAP) of the European Space Agency (ESA) made it possible to quantify the ocean surface affected by the phenomenon under analysis; at the same time, an algorithm was formulated within the cloud platform Google Earth Engine (GEE) which confirmed the same outputs but more quickly and allowed the implementation of an algorithm that exploits the statistical concept of value of Otsu threshold. The results obtained were subsequently compared with other results extrapolated through automatic methodologies developed by ESA, which supported a better accuracy of the procedures used in this study.

Keywords: Oil spill · Marine pollution · SAR · Sentinel-1 · SNAP · Google Earth Engine · El Palito · Otsu

1 Introduction

Accidental release of hydrocarbons, caused by offshore infrastructure and oil tankers, can have a significant and far-reaching environmental, social and commercial impact [1–3]. Therefore, promptly applying protocols aimed at containing the potential damage reported by marine and coastal environments, would be decisive: among the most

O. Gervasi et al. (Eds.): ICCSA 2022 Workshops, LNCS 13379, pp. 387–404, 2022.
https://doi.org/10.1007/978-3-031-10545-6_27

common measures, the cleaning and recovery of the spill, the exact geolocation and the forecast of dispersion [4, 5]. To this end, in recent years, remote sensing technologies using radar-type satellite data have proved to be useful supports for the analysis of oil spills [6, 7]. Active remote sensing makes use of synthetic aperture radar sensors which are extremely advantageous, since the data can be acquired both day and night and in any atmospheric condition. Instead, passive remote sensing provides optical data for which an external light source (sun), cloudless and perturbation-free weather conditions are required [8, 9]. The presence of oil in the sea is manifested by a film of hydrocarbons on the water surface able to dampen the waves of the sea making it smoother [10]. Radar sensors record this condition with a lower backscatter energy intensity than natural marine conditions, causing dark streaks in the radar images depending on the quantities and types of spills and the dynamics of the ocean surface [11]. In some cases, distinguishing such spills from other contaminating factors could prove to be a particularly complicated operation, especially when dealing with rain cells, areas subject to weak wind or stains of biologic material [12, 13]. The investigated event refers to the accidental discharge of oil which took place around 26 July 2020 at the Venezuelan coast at the El Palito refinery. Sentinel-1 radar data from ESA's Copernicus program [14] was used within a Change Detection implemented both in the SNAP software and in the GEE cloud platform. The procedure consisted of a comparison between two different perfectly superimposable satellite images, one concomitant with the event and the other in the absence of hydrocarbon contamination and allowed the identification of the footprint area of the oil spill. In SNAP, the distinction between water and oil was evaluated through a backscatter threshold value deducible from the histogram statistics associated with the combination of images [15]. The speed of image processing in SNAP is strictly connected to the hardware characteristics of the device used: to get around this possible limit, it is convenient to opt for web-based and open-source cloud software, capable of managing a large amount of data and analysis directly online based on server processing in much shorter times, such as GEE [16]. Therefore, in GEE, given the need to distinguish only the two components of water and oil within the image, it was found appropriate to resort to the well-known Otsu algorithm [17], although little used for these study cases. It follows that the results obtained in both SNAP and GEE are more accurate and precise than those deriving from the automatic methodology implemented in the SNAP software, which is based exclusively on the processing of a single image concomitant to the event [18].

2 Material and Methods

2.1 The Study Area

The case study concerned the accident that occurred near the El Palito refinery, in the state of Carabobo, located near the Venezuelan coast [19] (Fig. 1). In this case, the ability to monitor, detect and manage oil spills is vital due to the persistent dangers posed to marine biodiversity, wildlife and habitats [20].

The start of the spill took place around 26 July 2020, but was silenced by the media, due to the lack of reporting by the PDVSA refinery and to the greater visibility of a simultaneous spill located off the coast of Mauritius which took place on 25 July [21].

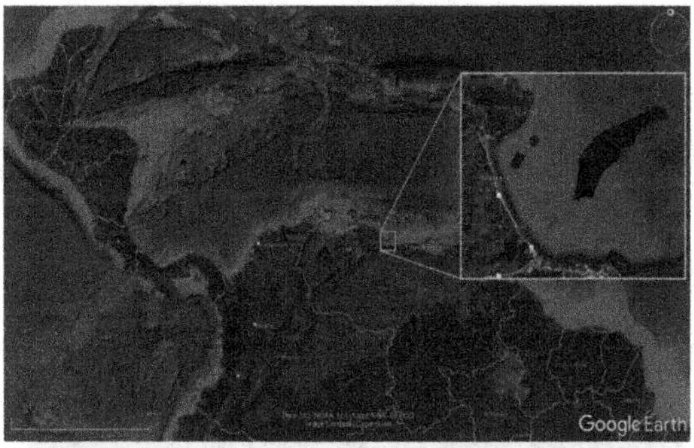

Fig. 1. Area affected by the spill on Google Earth Pro.

The lack of preparation and the inability to act in the face of similar scenarios on the part of local realities was remarked by Eduardo Klein, associate professor at the department of environmental studies at the Simón Bolívar University (USB) in Caracas. His studies on the subject allowed him to reconstruct what was happening, also using satellite research conducted by the "Remote Sensing and Geo-Spatial Analysis Laboratory", a research hub of USB [20]. The results were both instructive and alarming: based on the TerraSAR-X satellite image (Fig. 2) of 26 July, the spill remained concentrated in the immediate vicinity of the refinery (coast of Carabobo), during which time there was no measures were taken to prevent its advancement towards Morrocoy National Park and other endangered coasts. The beginning of what Klein has renamed "ecocide" has taken the form of a "language of death", so nicknamed by the same, with an extension of about 260 km^2 and a maximum length of 27 km, in front of the refining centre [20, 22].

2.2 Dataset

Despite the existence of numerous increasingly performing commercial satellites, such as the previously mentioned TerraSAR-X one, the future of Remote Sensing seems to be oriented in the use of Open Data, among which are the products of the Sentinel-1 mission [23]. The latter was built in 2014 by ESA through the Copernicus project: it consists of the two satellites Sentinel-1A and Sentinel-1B. Both satellites describe a sun-synchronous orbit and are combined in such a way as to obtain a reduced temporal resolution from 12 to 6 days. In addition, they are equipped with C-band SAR technology, operating at a central frequency of 5.405 Ghz, with an image acquisition phase independent of weather and lighting conditions [8]. The modality with which the images are obtained is divided into single polarization (VV or HH) and double polarization (VV-VH and HH-HV) [24]. In favour of users, the most used data are above all those belonging to level I, i.e., the SLC and GRD products [23]. The difference between the latter is in the type of pre-processing present. The SLC products, in fact, less processed upstream, are the result of the Instrument Processing Facility (IPF) used for raw and compressed data.

This processing consists in the application of a series of algorithms that allow to obtain SAR data of amplitude and phase focused, georeferenced and provided in slant-range geometry [25]. GRD products, on the other hand, only contain the amplitude

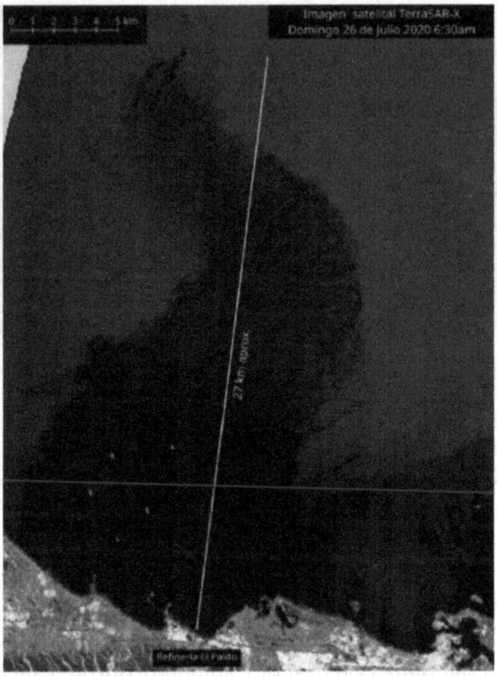

Fig. 2. TerraSAR-X radar image of 26 July 2020 processed by USB. https://newsbeezer.com

data and undergo refinement and cleaning procedures, such as a first filtering of the speckle and a Multilooking operation, which allows for square pixels [26]. The satellite images used for the case study were acquired free of charge through NASA's Alaska Satellite Facility Data Search (ASF) portal. The first data refers to a concomitant image of the event acquired on 31 July 2020. The scene shows a situation in which the spot, compared to July 26, has already moved away from the coast from which it originated and has spread to the open sea. The second image was acquired after the event, or on February 20, 2021. The choice is because it was preferred to work with both products belonging to S1A, in Descending mode, to be able to carry out interferometric operations as well. The images chosen for the study are both SLC and GRD type, with the aim of making a comparison between the surface results. Furthermore, this choice was also due to the need to ascertain the effects of the pre-processing carried out upstream on the GRD data on the final outputs [27].

2.3 SNAP Analysis

A first analysis of the event focused on the use of the Sentinel-1 toolbox of the SNAP open-source platform, software that supports the reading, visualization, processing and writing of data relating to various satellites [14]. This platform is widely used by researchers in the field of remote sensing with the intent of processing data through automatic procedures, such as the one served by ESA's toolbox for Oil Spill Detection, and semi-automatic procedures, such as the one used in the study proposed [26]. In

Fig. 3, the graph containing all the pre-processing and processing procedures for the SLC and GRD images, for the Master and Slave products, is presented.

2.4 Pre-processing

After the selection and acquisition of the satellite images, a series of semi-automatic preliminary processing was performed in order to make the data suitable for the actual processing phase. The pre-processing operations carried out on the two different inputs are reported [28].

Apply Orbit File: The orbital state vectors, contained in the metadata of SAR products, are generally not accurate. The correct orbits of the satellites are determined after several days are made available on SNAP only after the generation of the product. Through this operation it is possible to automatically download the OSV file from the ESA GNSS Hub which allows the orbital state vectors to be updated in the metadata, providing accurate information on the position and speed of the satellite [29].

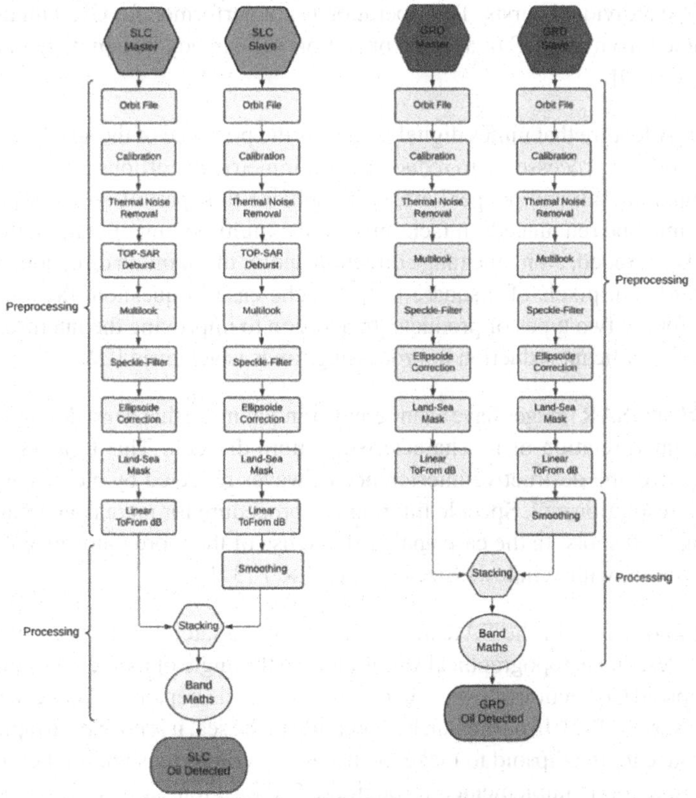

Fig. 3. SLC and GRD process workflow.

Calibration: Calibration is the procedure that converts the digital pixel values into radiometrically calibrated back-scatter values, since, in the typical first level radar data processing, a significant distortion remains. In particular, the process converts the radar reflectivity into physical units, referred to the plane perpendicular to the direction of the propagation beam. Therefore, it is necessary to apply radiometric correction to SAR products, so that the pixels numerically represent the radar backscatter value of the reflecting surface [29].

Thermal Noise Removal: Operation intended to remove the additional thermal noise of which a radar image is characterized. The removal of thermal noise reduces the distorting effects in the texture of the sub-swaths, normalizing the backscatter signal within the entire scene, favouring its reading in multi-swath acquisition mode [29].

TOP-SAR Deburst: The SAR detection devices carry out a progressive scan of the terrain through a series of images with which the data are acquired: this operation is called TOPSAR. Subsequently, the data acquired along the antenna beam are sampled in multiple adjacent sub-bands, shared by the same pixel spacing. The Debursting operation performs a merge of the adjacent bursts returning a single image by exploiting the azimuth overlap of the individual bursts. This operation is not performed for GRD images, since, being obtained from an SLC image, the operation will already be completed in the ESA pre-processes [30].

Multilook: A feature that unites digital images is the presence of the speckle; one of the objectives of these processes is to reduce any radiometric distortions present, which are shown through a "salt and pepper" effect. To achieve this, part of the initial resolution of the data must be renounced: in fact, through the multilooking operation, the original resolution is degraded, along the range direction and/or the azimuth direction, obtaining, on the other hand, pixels of a square [29]. For the case in question, the analysis was diversified for the two types of products. In addition to improving the interpretability of the image, a significant reduction in processing times is achieved [29].

Speckle-Filter: SAR images have an inherent granular noise that degrades image quality and makes interpretation of its characteristics more difficult. This trend is caused by the constructive and destructive interference of waves reflected by elementary scatters within each resolution cell. Speckle filtering is a procedure for increasing image quality by reducing such spots. In the case analysed, the use of the more innovative Lee Sigma filter was chosen, with Windows Size equal to 7×7 [31].

Ellipsoid Correction: In the SAR image there may be lateral distortions of distances and geometries, due to topographical variations and the angle of incidence of the satellite sensor. Ellipsoid Correction allows you to correct these discrepancies between the image and the real surface [32]. In particular, by operating in the sea, it is possible to approximate the real surface to an ellipsoid to make the necessary corrections within the image. The correction function is implemented through the Geolocation-Grid (GG) method which operates according to the procedures of a Range Doppler Terrain Correction [26].

Land-Sea Mask: Applies a mask that transforms all the pixels on the earth into "no data value", keeping only the pixels present on the liquid surface. The procedure consists of a quick comparison with the DEM downloaded from the software, which, by analysing the height of the pixel, will determine whether the position occupied is on the mainland or not. The operation is advantageous both in terms of processing times, significantly reduced due to the lightening of the image, and for the lack of consideration of possible false positives due to the presence of pixels that behave in a similar way to oil in terms of backscatter [32].

Linear To From dB: As the last step in the pre-processing workflow, the backscatter coefficient displayed in the Digital Number (DN) is converted to decibels (dB) through a logarithmic transformation. With this transformation, the product is made more readable by linearizing it [33]. At the end of the pre-processing workflow, clean and visibly more readable images were obtained, both for the pair of SLC products and for the GRDs, ready for subsequent processing (Fig. 4).

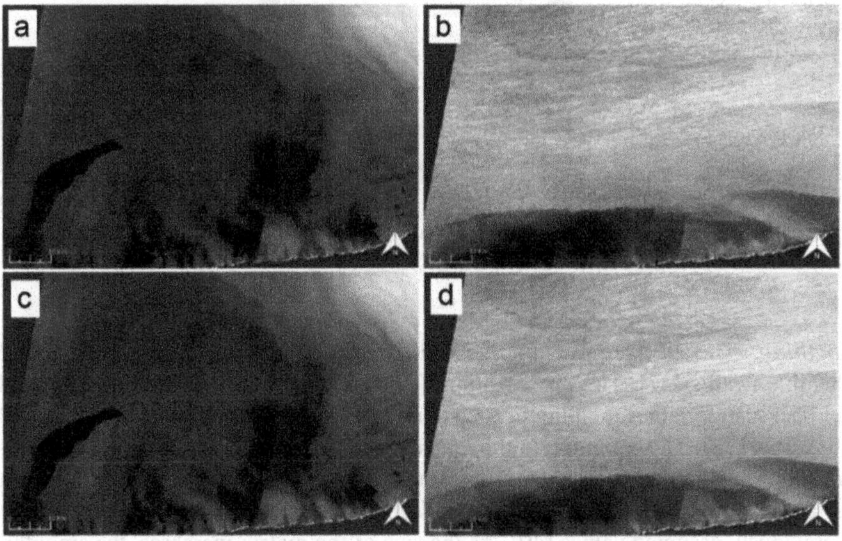

Fig. 4. Output after the SLC, Master (a) and Slave (b) image pre-processing phases, and GRD, Master (c) and Slave (d) images.

2.5 Processing

Following the SAR data pre-processing operations, products are obtained ready for processing activities through which it will be possible to recognize the spilled oil surface. Considering that oil particles have a greater influence on the amplitude of the radar signal, the analysis will be based on the latter [34].

Stacking: The toolbox interferometric modules provide for the registration of one (or more) "Slave" images with respect to a "Master" reference image [35]. This process requires, between the "Master" image and the various specificities of the "Slave" images, common characteristics called Tie Points, used as reference points for the entire operation. Following the use of a polynomial function that aligns the images, a single product ready for comparison is obtained in which the deformations of the reference image are spatially superimposed (in the geographic raster) to that of the base image. This occurs through a resampling method which, in this study, involved bilinear interpolation [36]. The co-registration procedure is completely automatic: in addition to the definition of the processing parameters, no further inputs or interventions by the user are required, as the optimization procedure is performed automatically for both images, perfecting the offsets of the operation [28]. In the proposed study, the Master data is represented by the data acquired on 07/31/2020, in which the incriminated event is present while the Slave data is represented by the image of 02/20/2021, in which there is total absence of oil.

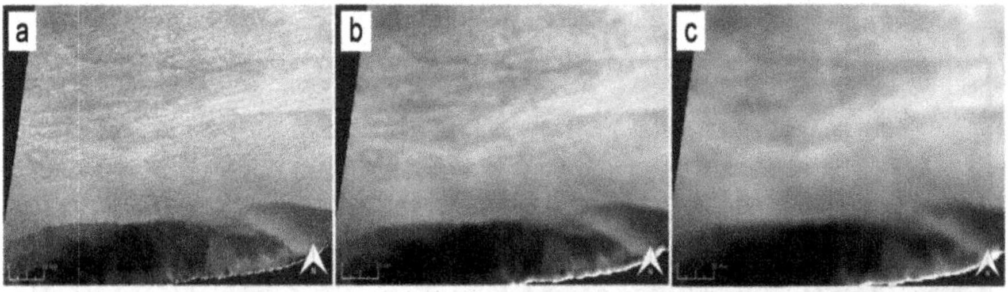

Fig. 5. Pre-processed GRD Slave image: without Smoothing filter (a), with Smoothing 10 × 10 (b) and with Smoothing 20 × 20 (c).

Smoothing: The speckle present in the SAR images compromises the precision of the deductible results [37]. The process, therefore, aims to "control" the intensity of the pixel backscatter values, helping to focus on the average of the values assumed in the same kernel [38]. The softening of the image tends to make the study area more homogeneous through a high-frequency detail filtering operation [39]. The median blurring filter assigns an average value to the pixels contained in the kernel, replacing it with the previously assumed values [40]. As the size of the matrix increases, the smoothing of the image will increase, thus obtaining different filtering effects. The operation was carried out exclusively for the Slave image, as we can say with certainty that it has pixels containing mainly water and therefore are approximately similar to each other. A series of various filtering windows was considered for the analysis, setting the kernel size of (5 × 5), (10 × 10), (15 × 15), (20 × 20) and (30 × 30) (Fig. 5). The choice of this filter was found to be the most effective for phenomena related to oil spill detection [41].

2.6 Change Detection Analysis and Threshold Values Definition

The comparison between the two pre-processed radar images is the basis of the Change Detection methodology [32]. The determination of the surface of floating hydrocarbons for the image was referred to both the SLC and GRD images using different threshold values. These values were statistically determined through a polygonal geometry within which only the petroleum pixels fall (Fig. 6). This was certainly favoured by the shape of the spot, which can be enclosed in a single geometry defined as "region of interest" (ROI), not being characterized by an irregular or fragmented shape.

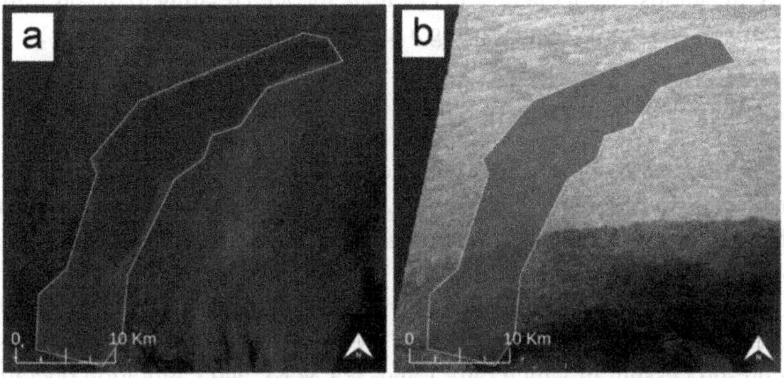

Fig. 6. ROI used to determine the threshold for the Master (a) and Slave (b) image.

Therefore, the determination of the threshold values referred to the SLC and GRD images refers to the backscatter values detected within the polygon. In particular, both the average value and the 90th percentile were considered due to the presence of some pixels characterized by anomalous backscatter values (outliers). The threshold values therefore arise from the difference between the values assumed in the ROI of the Master image and in the ROI of the Slave image.

The values for the SLC product and the GRD product are shown in Table 1.

Table 1. Threshold value.

Threshold SLC		
	Mean value (dB)	P90 value (dB)
ROI master	−27.568	24.783
ROI slave	−18.400	−16.372
Threshold	−9.168	−8.411
Threshold GRD		
	Mean value (dB)	P90 value (dB)
ROI master	−28.077	−24.978
ROI slave	−18.437	−16.341
Threshold	−9.639	−8.637

By doing so, four threshold values were obtained and subsequently used in the Change Detection. To extract the dark area that represents the release of hydrocarbons, a difference is initially made between the VV band of the Master image and the VV band of the Slave image using the Band Maths tool. The difference raster obtained is used to discriminate the "oil" pixels from the "water" pixels. This is done again through the Band Maths operator in which an inequality is set between the raster difference VV and the various thresholds. Subsequently, to calculate the area relating to the oil spill in each case, the "oil" pixels were counted using a mask.

2.7 Tool SNAP: Oil Spill Detection

The SNAP software provides the user with a collection of graphs containing preset algorithms that can be used for specific analyses. As part of the radar application, a toolbox is provided for the fully automatic mapping of oil spills, called "Oil Spill Detection". The algorithm has the substantial difference of not using Change Detection operations, going to operate exclusively on the image where the presence of the floating hydrocarbon surface is indicated. The composition of the workflow (Fig. 7) includes a first phase of image pre-processing in which only Land-Sea Mask and calibration operations are envisaged, in which a speckle filter is applied [41]. Subsequently, an image processing activity began, consisting of an operation called Oil Spill Detection, in which the "dark spots" are identified using the Adaptive Threshold Algorithm, an adaptive algorithm for calculating the Threshold based on single reference image only [42]. The survey ends with the final phase of Oil Spill Clustering, where the pixels are collected in clusters and selected with respect to the minimum size chosen by the user or performed with predefined parameters. The tool provides for the use of an average local backscatter value through the comparison Background Window Dimension freely left to the user: the software will define the pixels that will have a backscatter value lower than the one chosen [43].

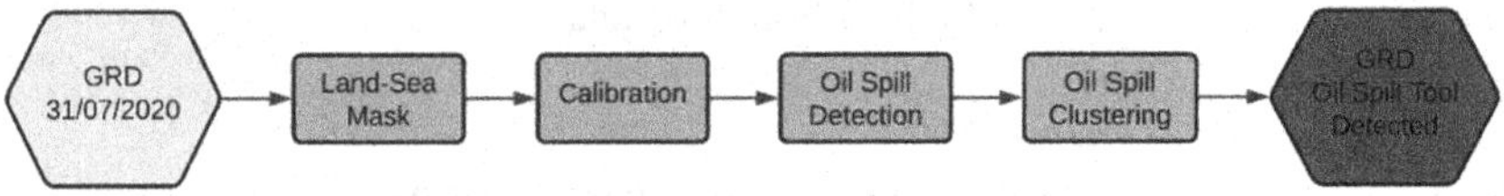

Fig. 7. SNAP oil spill detection tool workflow.

2.8 Change Detection in GEE e Threshold di OTSU

In the analysis previously carried out, the importance of lightening the processing burden was deduced in order to reduce the duration of processing times, depending on the type of hardware available to the user. The latter has often been considered a limitation of the attempt to expand the pool of users interested in the analysis of satellite images [44]. To ensure greater efficiency of these services and speed up the mechanical and repetitive phases of the process, the online platform Google Earth Engine (GEE) was created in 2011 [45]. In the study, an innovative algorithm was developed to improve and facilitate the remote sensing of floating oil surfaces in the sea. The first operation involves uploading the Sentinel-1 image collections, importing the reference data present on the Earth Engine Data Catalog, in the Work Space. From the present collection, the availability of Sentinel-1 products exclusively of the GRD type is denoted: the SLC data, in fact, are not currently supported by the GEE platform [46]. In the GEE environment, from the Copernicus/S1_GRD collection, "analysis-ready" products are imported, already pre-processed, and containing measurements of the backscattering coefficient $\sigma 0$ expressed in decibels (dB). The pre-processing steps (implemented by Sentinel-1 Toolbox) to derive the backscatter coefficient in each pixel are as follows [47]: Apply Orbit File, GRD Edge Noise Removal (has the task of removing low-intensity noise and invalid data on the edges of the scene), Thermal noise reduction, Radiometric calibration, Orthorectification and Multilook. Once the data collection has been imported, it is necessary to define the geometry of the area of interest on which to perform the calculations. A rectangle was therefore drawn, by imputing the coordinates of the four vertices, which consists of the Area of Interest (AOI) currently near El Palito and possibly translatable and modifiable in order to investigate other areas. Subsequently, the two products were selected through a series of Sentinel-1 Image Collection product filtering operations: type of VV copolarization, more effective than VH in detecting oil spills [48], IW acquisition method and Descending orbit. Once the filters have been applied, the two images referring to 07/31/2020 and 02/20/2021 are obtained, each of which has been associated with a layer of the GEE main window. The algorithm workflow also provides, before carrying out the Change Detection operations, an oil-free image smoothing operation. The "softening" of the image aims to make the study area more homogeneous through a filtering of the high-frequency pixel values [23]. The computation process, which in GEE is called convolution, performs a linear combination of the neighbouring pixels using a predefined set of weights. The results obtained are affected by the so-called "edge effect", produced by the fact that approaching the border of the image, the kernel applied to the pixel will not be totally occupied by other pixels that are part of the image [40]. To overcome this drawback, it was decided to apply this operation to a geometry with an offset of 0.02° from the margin of the previously selected one, in order to eliminate this effect. Subsequently, a comparison was made between the two radar images, the heart of the analysis based on the Change Detection methodology. The latter was processed by the Maths Operators present on GEE, which allow to obtain the Difference image, determined precisely by the subtraction, pixel by pixel, of the backscatter values of the two images purchased in the same AOI [49]. The threshold value considered was obtained using the Otsu algorithm, based on the analysis of variance between two classes of the single Difference image [50]. In satellite image analysis, there is often a need to use automated and data-driven methods to distinguish two relatively homogeneous objects, such as oil and water. For a single-band image with bimodal distribution of the pixels, it is possible to perform a two-class segmentation, finding a threshold that separates them. A bimodal image presents a plotting histogram of the backscatter values in two distinct distributions, almost separable from each other. In fact, between the two "fashions" it is possible to identify a local minimum point, in which the possibility of separating the histogram into two fronts could be considered. The binarization of Otsu, if properly performed, allows to obtain that value automatically [50]. The method, therefore, is a means that automatically searches for an optimal threshold value, based on the distribution of the pixel values. Assuming therefore that the image histogram can be interpreted with two classes, the variance value between the classes is defined by the BSS (Between-Sum-of-Squares) value which is calculated using the formula [51]. The function examines every possible partition of the input data defined by the intensity of the histogram bins; therefore, it returns the mean associated with the bin that maximizes the BSS. The algorithm works best when you strategically choose a region in which the two classes are distributed approximately in equal proportions. After implementing the code, using the standard GEE library reducers, already included in the algorithm, the Difference image histogram was obtained: this also allowed us to estimate the average of the pixel distribution. By setting as discriminant, for the Change Detection operation, both the threshold determined with the Otsu algorithm and the average backscatter value assumed by the pixels of the difference image, it was possible to determine the number of pixels with a value equal to 1 all inside of a binary mask. This last step was carried out through a counting operation of the single class of pixels, thanks to which the floating oil surface was determined [46].

3 Results and Discussion

Based on the results obtained (Table 2), compared with the reference surface of about 260 km^2, detected on 26 July 2020 by the "Remote Sensing and Geo-Spatial Analysis Laboratory" of the USB, the proposed method found with successful oil surfaces.

Table 2. Surface analysis.

SNAP						GEE		
SLC			GRD			GRD		
Thres. (dB)	Sm. filter (pixel)	Δ (%)	Thres. (dB)	Sm. filter (pixel)	Δ (%)	Thres. (dB)	Sm. filter (pixel)	Δ (%)
P90 (−8.41)	NO	1.83	SNAP Oil Spill	NO	−38.04	OTSU (−9.50)	NO	43.06
	5	−1.13	P90 (−8.64)	NO	−0.85		15	6.78
	10	−3.78		10	−4.72		30	6.67
	15	−5.13		20	−7.40	Mean (−7.19)	NO	80.37
Mean (−9.17)	NO	−21.84	Mean (-9.64)	NO	−22.08		15	76.47

Within the table, the results obtained for the different platforms used are first distinguished, namely the SNAP desktop platform and the GEE cloud platform. Below, there is a further subdivision for the type of products used SLC and GRD. Also reported are the threshold values used in the study, any smoothing filter used, indicating the size of the kernel, and the surface deviation in percentage from the comparison surface.

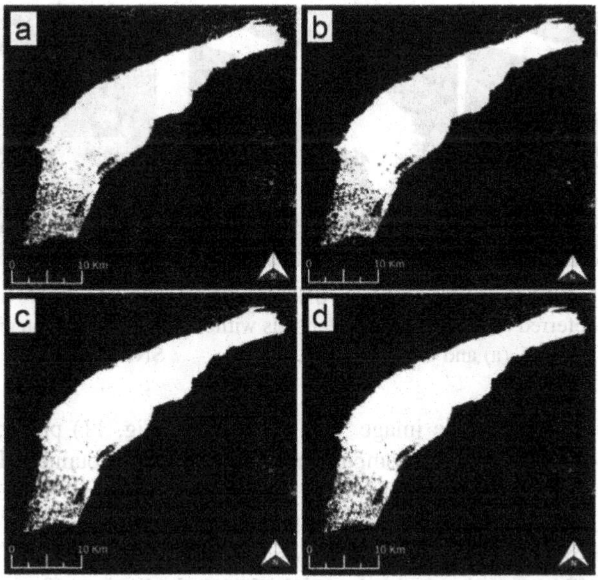

Fig. 8. Output of the Change Detection in SNAP of SLC images for threshold values P90: without Smoothing filter (a), with a Smoothing of 5 × 5 (b), with a Smoothing of 10x10 (c) and with a Smoothing of 15 × 15 (d).

Through SNAP (Fig. 8, 9, 10) compared to SLC products, using a 90th percentile threshold value from the statistical analysis of the histogram of the raster difference, with a smoothing filter with a kernel size equal to 5 × 5 on the oil-free image, a percentage difference of −1.13% with respect to the reference value. The result found with a threshold value defined by the simple average of the backscatter values within the polygon, instead, determines a percentage difference of −21.84%. For GRD products, however, a percentage deviation of −0.85% from the image with a threshold equal to the 90th percentile is reported without any smoothing filter applied. Also, for GRD products, the mean threshold value does not provide appreciably valid results considering the deviation of −22.08% from the reference value.

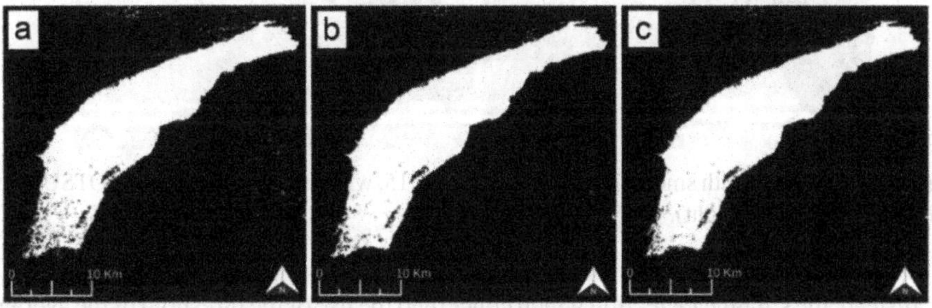

Fig. 9. SNAP Change Detection output of GRD images for P90 threshold values: without Smoothing filter (a), with a Smoothing of 10 × 10 (b) and with a Smoothing of 20 × 20 (c).

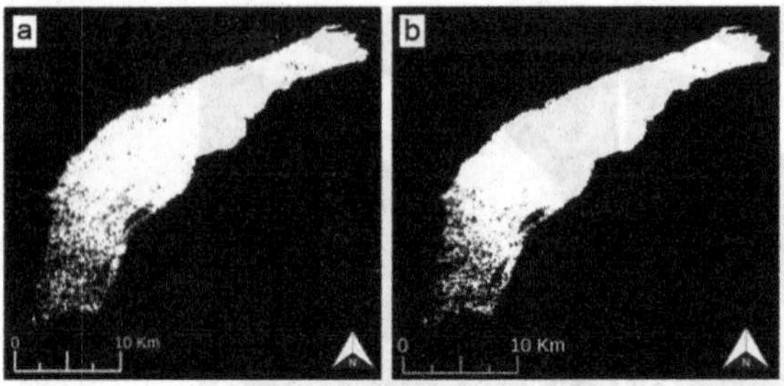

Fig. 10. Output of the Change Detection in SNAP for the threshold value referred to the average of the pixels without Smoothing filter of SLC (a) and GRD (b) images.

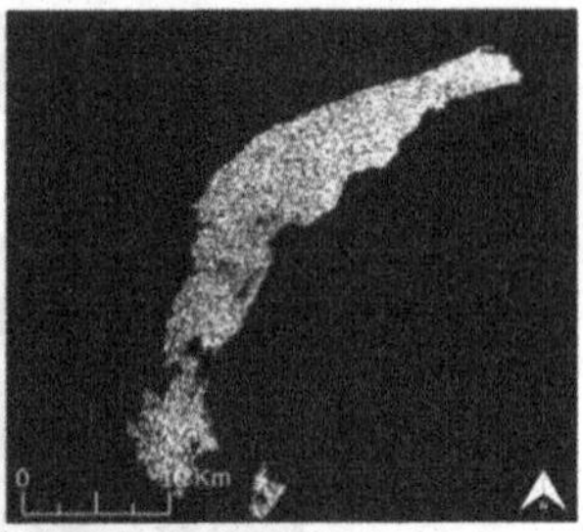

Fig. 11. Single image Oil Spill Tool output integrated into SNAP.

From the integrated single image "Oil Spill Tool" (Fig. 11) present in SNAP, a deviation equal to 38% from the comparison surface value is obtained. The cause also lies in the fact that some pixels escape the detection of the tool, as, due to the high computational capabilities required, the applied cluster is unable to "fill" the perimeter of the detected spot. It is also noted that some pixels with an oil-like behaviour are identified as oil (false positives); this is mainly due to shadowing effects, related to the presence of waves near the coast, and to the use of an adaptive algorithm for determining the threshold based on a single image [52].

Finally, the output layers from the GEE platform are reported (Fig. 12). From the analysis of the reported results, the significance of the result obtained using the algorithm devised by Otsu to determine the Threshold considered, which allows for an output that deviates by 6.67% from the reference value, is evident. To obtain a cleaner image, a Smoothing filter was applied to the event-free image which led to an important screening of false positives.

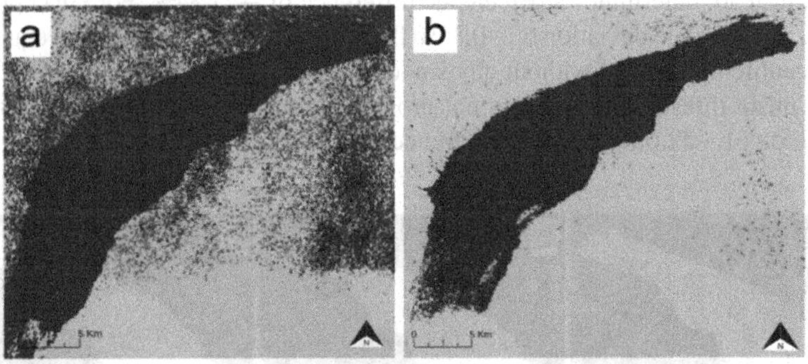

Fig. 12. GEE output with smoothing filter, Kernel size 15, with different Thresholds: OTSU value (left) and mean value (right).

Instead, the Change Detection which concerned the use of the threshold of the average pixel backscatter values, is not very effective with large areas of analysis. This result is due to a higher concentration of pixel values with a higher back-scatter value (water) which led to a higher threshold value and a deviation of more than 76% from the reference surface.

4 Conclusions

The main objective of this study was to describe and compare alternative methodologies and procedures for monitoring oil spills using open-source tools (SNAP, Google Earth Engine) and open-source radar images (Sentinel-1 SAR). The results obtained clearly show how crucial it is to carry out correct assessments on the threshold value to be taken, since, despite the work platform and the type of product used, it is the real discriminating factor for a correct and efficient Oil Spill Detection. The determination of this value requires an analysis based on statistical methods and parameters that go beyond the single average of the backscatter values assumed by the image pixels, which does not always provide fairly accurate results. The Change Detection method is more appropriate for evaluating changes in the investigated surface, allowing us to state that an automated methodology referring to a single reference data, such as the one used by the SNAP Tool, cannot offer totally satisfactory results, as, the oil detection is often influenced by the presence of double and therefore not suitable to be performed with default software parameters. The study shows that, by moving to the GEE platform, the analysis in the EO sector turns out to be more versatile and faster, from a computational point of view, compared to desktop systems, characterized by often long and redundant operations. The new algorithm presented, conceived for the case in question, has allowed to obtain a considerable automation of the process, allowing large-scale data processing in a short time. To make the process even more direct and reliable was the use of the Otsu algorithm; through this method, classification results clearly better than the threshold dictated by the average value of the pixels were obtained. Given the ever-increasing use of GEE as part of remote sensing compared to other competing platforms, thanks to the previously mentioned advantages, we are trying to intervene to eliminate the deficiencies present in the system [49].

References

1. Yu, F., Sun, W., Li, J., Zhao, Y., Zhang, Y., Chen, G.: An improved Otsu method for oil spill detection from SAR images. Oceanologia **59**(3), 311–317 (2017)
2. Naboureh, A., Ebrahimy, H., Azadbakht, M., Bian, J., Amani, M.: RUESVMs: an ensemble method to handle the class imbalance problem in land cover mapping using Google Earth Engine. Remote Sens. **12**(21), 3484 (2020)
3. Venezuela's coastal villages, fisherman suffer as oil spills rise, Reuters. https://www.reuters.com/business/environment/venezuelas-coastal-villages-fisherman-suffer-oil-spills-rise, Accessed 06 Oct 2021
4. Sánchez, J.C.: Afectacion de los ecosistemas marino-costeros por los derrames de hidrocarburos marine-coastal ecosystems pollution by hydrocarbon spills. Comisión Editorial (2020)
5. Gorelick, N., Hancher, M., Dixon, M., Ilyushchenko, S., Thau, D., Moore, R.: Google earth engine: planetary-scale geospatial analysis for everyone. Remote Sens. Environ. **202**, 18–27 (2017)

6. Cervelli, E., Pindozzi, S., Capolupo, A., Okello, C., Rigillo, M., Boccia, L.: Ecosystem services and bioremediation of polluted areas. Ecol. Eng. **87**, 139–149 (2016)
7. Palladino, M., Nasta, P., Capolupo, A., Romano, N.: Monitoring and modelling the role of phytoremediation to mitigate non-point source cadmium pollution and groundwater contamination at field scale. Ital. J. Agron **13**(s1), 59–68 (2018)
8. Klein, E.: La refinería El Palito está todo el tiempo derramando hidrocarburos. https://elestimulo.com/eduardo-klein-la-refineria-el-palito-esta-todo-el-tiempo-derramando-hidrocarburos, 21 Aug 2020
9. Kingston, P.F.: Long-term environmental impact of oil spills. Spill Sci. Technol. Bull. **7**(1–2), 53–61 (2002)
10. Al-Ruzouq, R., et al.: Sensors, features, and machine learning for oil spill detection and monitoring: a review. Remote Sens. **12**(20), 3338 (2020)
11. Solberg, A.H., Brekke, C., Husoy, P.O.: Oil spill detection in Radarsat and Envisat SAR images. IEEE Trans. Geosci. Remote Sens. **45**(3), 746–755 (2007)
12. Capolupo, A., Pindozzi, S., Okello, C., Fiorentino, N., Boccia, L.: Photogrammetry for environmental monitoring: the use of drones and hydrological models for detection of soil contaminated by copper. Sci. Total Environ. **514**, 298–306 (2015)
13. Capolupo, A., Pindozzi, S., Okello, C., Boccia, L.: Indirect field technology for detecting areas object of illegal spills harmful to human health: application of drones, photogrammetry and hydrological models. Geospat. Health **8**(3), S699–S707 (2014)
14. Moreira, A., Prats-Iraola, P., Younis, M., Krieger, G., Hajnsek, I., Papathanassiou, K.: A tutorial on synthetic aperture radar. IEEE Geosci. Remote Sens. Mag. **1**(1), 6–43 (2013)
15. Capolupo, A., Nasta, P., Palladino, M., Cervelli, E., Boccia, L., Romano, N.: Assessing the ability of hybrid poplar for in-situ phytoextraction of cadmium by using UAV-photogrammetry and 3D flow simulator. Int. J. Remote Sens. **39**(15–16), 5175–5194 (2018)
16. Brekke, C., Solberg, A.H.S.: Oil spill detection by satellite remote sensing. Remote Sens. Environ. **95**(1), 1–13 (2005)
17. Kotova, L., Espedal, H.: Oil spill detection using spaceborne SAR- A brief review. Inf. Sustainabil., 791–794 (1998)
18. Tarantino, E.: Monitoring spatial and temporal distribution of Sea Surface Tempera-ture with TIR sensor data. Ital. J. Remote Sens./Rivista Italiana di Telerile-vamento **44**(1), 97–107 (2012)
19. ESA Mission Sentinel-1. https://www.esa.int, Accessed 01 Mar 2022
20. Akkartal, A., Sunar, F.: The usage of radar images in oil spill detection. Int. Arch. Photogramm. Remote Sens. Spat. Inf. Sci. **37**(B8), 271–276 (2008)
21. Espedal, H.: Detection of oil spill and natural film in the marine environment by spaceborne SAR. In: IEEE 1999 International Geoscience and Remote Sensing Symposium. IGARSS'99 (Cat. No. 99CH36293), vol. 3. IEEE (1999)
22. Villamizar, E.: Impactos de los derrames de petroleo sobre los arrecifes coralinos y sys bienes y sercivios ecosistémicos impacts of the oil spills over the coral reefs and their ecosistémicos impacts of the oil spills over the coral reefs and their ecosystems goods and services. Comision Editorial **45** (2020)
23. Mullissa, A., et al.: Sentinel-1 sar backscatter analysis ready data preparation in google earth engine. Remote Sens. **13**(10), 1954 (2021)
24. Migliaccio, M., Gambardella, A., Tranfaglia, M.: SAR polarimetry to observe oil spills. IEEE Trans. Geosci. Remote Sens. **45**(2), 506–511 (2007)
25. Torres, R., et al.: GMES Sentinel-1 mission. Remote Sens. Environ. **120**, 9–24 (2012)
26. Gancheva, I., Peneva, E.: Verification of the SNAP ocean-tool for oil spill detection for the Bulgarian Black Sea region. In: AIP Conference Proceedings, vol. 2075, no. 1. AIP Publishing LLC (2019)

27. Potin, P.: Sentinel-1 mission overview, pp. 04–11 (2011)
28. Giancaspro, A., Candela, L., Lopint, E., Lore, V.A., Milillo, G.: SAR images co-registration parallel implementation. In: IEEE International Geoscience and Remote Sensing Symposium, vol. 3. IEEE (2002)
29. Filipponi, F.: Sentinel-1 GRD preprocessing workflow. Multidisc. Dig. Publ. Inst. Proc. **18**(1) (2019)
30. Veci, L., Lu, J., Foumelis, M., Engdahl, M.: ESA's multi-mission sentinel-1 toolbox. In: EGU General Assembly Conference Abstracts (2017)
31. Fan, J., Zhang, F., Zhao, D., Wang, J.: Oil spill monitoring based on SAR remote sensing imagery. Aquatic Procedia **3**, 112–118 (2015)
32. Prastyani, R., Basith, A.: Utilisation of sentinel-1 SAR imagery for oil spill mapping: a case study of balikpapan Bay oil spill. J. Geospat. Inf. Sci. Eng. **1**(1), 22–26 (2018)
33. Nasirzadehdizaji, R., Cakir, Z., Sanli, F. B., Abdikan, S., Pepe, A., Calo, F.: Sentinel-1 interferometric coherence and backscattering analysis for crop monitoring. Comput. Electron. Agric. 185, 106118 (2021)
34. Nunziata, F., Gambardella, A., Migliaccio, M.: On the degree of polarization for SAR sea oil slick observation. ISPRS J. Photogramm. Remote. Sens. **78**, 41–49 (2013)
35. De Zan, F., López-Dekker, P.: SAR image stacking for the exploitation of long-term coherent targets. IEEE Geosci. Remote Sens. Lett. **8**(3), 502–506 (2010)
36. Li, Z., Bethel, J.: Image coregistration in SAR interferometry. Int. Arch. Photogramm. Remote. Sens. Spat. Inf. Sci. **37**, 433–438 (2008)
37. Ali, I., Cao, S., Naeimi, V., Paulik, C., Wagner, W.: Methods to remove the border noise from Sentinel-1 synthetic aperture radar data: implications and importance for time-series analysis. IEEE J. Sel. Topics Appl. Earth Obs. Remote Sens. **11**(3), 777–786 (2018)
38. Masoomi, A., Hamzehyan, R., Shirazi, N.C.: Speckle reduction approach for SAR image in satellite communication. Int. J. Mach. Learn. Comput. **2**(1), 62 (2012)
39. Zhu, J., Wen, J., Zhang, Y.: A new algorithm for SAR image despeckling using an enhanced Lee filter and median filter. In: 2013 6th International congress on image and signal processing (CISP), vol. 1. IEEE (2013)
40. Adrian, J., Sagan, V., Maimaitijiang, M.: Sentinel SAR-optical fusion for crop type mapping using deep learning and Google Earth Engine. ISPRS J. Photogramm. Remote. Sens. **175**, 215–235 (2021)
41. Longépé, N., Mouche, A.A., Ferro-Famil, L., Husson, R.: Co-cross-polarization coherence over the sea surface from sentinel-1 SAR data: perspectives for mission calibration and wind field retrieval. IEEE Trans. Geosci. Remote Sens. **60**, 1–16 (2021)
42. Liu, D., Yu, J.: Otsu method and K-means. In: 2009 Ninth International Conference on Hybrid Intelligent Systems, vol. 1. IEEE (2009)
43. Marghany, M.: RADARSAT automatic algorithms for detecting coastal oil spill pollution. Int. J. Appl. Earth Obs. Geoinf. **3**(2), 191–196 (2001)
44. Brigham, T.J.: Taking advantage of Google's Web-based applications and services. Med. Ref. Serv. Q. **33**(2), 202–210 (2014)
45. Tamiminia, H., Salehi, B., Mahdianpari, M., Quackenbush, L., Adeli, S., Brisco, B.: Google Earth Engine for geo-big data applications: a meta-analysis and systematic review. ISPRS J. Photogramm. Remote. Sens. **164**, 152–170 (2020)
46. Mutanga, O., Kumar, L.: Google earth engine applications. Remote Sens. **11**(5), 591 (2019)
47. Vollrath, A., Mullissa, A., Reiche, J.: Angular-based radiometric slope correction for Sentinel-1 on google earth engine. Remote Sens. **12**(11), 1867 (2020)
48. Chaturvedi, S.K., Banerjee, S., Lele, S.: An assessment of oil spill detection using Sentinel 1 SAR-C images. J. Ocean Eng. Sci. **5**(2), 116–135 (2020)

49. Xing, H., Hou, D., Wang, S., Yu, M., Meng, F.: O-LCMapping: a google earth engine-based web toolkit for supporting online land cover classification. Earth Sci. Inf. **14**(1), 529–541 (2021). https://doi.org/10.1007/s12145-020-00562-6
50. Yousefi, J.: Image Binarization Using otsu Thresholding Algorithm. University of Guelph, Ontario (2011)
51. Yang, X., Shen, X., Long, J., Chen, H.: An improved median-based Otsu image thresholding algorithm. Aasri Procedia **3**, 468–473 (2012)
52. Misra, A., Balaji, R.: Simple approaches to oil spill detection using sentinel application platform (SNAP)-ocean application tools and texture analysis: a comparative study. J. Indian Soc. Remote Sens. **45**(6), 1065–1075 (2017)

Comparative Analysis of the Remotely Sensed Coastline with Geological Cartography: The Case Study of the Puglia Region

Umberto Fratino(✉), Alessandro Reina, Maria Francesca Bruno, and Mauro Palombella

Polytechnic of Bari, Bari, Italy
umberto.fratino@poliba.it

Abstract. As part of the Polytechnic of Bari's research project on the evaluation of the geological risk in the coastal environment (DICATECH), the planimetric position of the coastline of the Puglia Region was analyzed using a digitally extracted orthophoto made available from the Office of the State Property of the Puglia Region in 2017.

Remote sensing data analysis led to the geometric extraction of the shoreline from orthophoto maps through automatic extraction and visual digitization techniques. Particular attention was paid to the geological analysis of the coast, with respect to its morphological characters. A comparison study was conducted using the most recent cartographic surveys available on the official geological cartography (CARG project).

The results have allowed a more detailed and in-depth definition of some aspects of geological cartography and the various elements of geohazard as well as a clearer reconstruction of the mechanisms of interaction between the various processes involved in geohazard.

The detailed analysis of some of the most representative cases has also confirmed the complexity of the coastal issues and highlighted some crucial questions about the making of geological cartography and coastal maps of the ongoing CARG project to further investigate.

We call for a greater in-depth knowledge of the geomorphological and meteo-marine characteristics of the coastal environment to observe its evolution through accurate and continuous monitoring over time. This allows the analysis of evolutionary trends and both natural and anthropogenic factors influencing the delicate balance of the coastline.

1 Introduction

As part of the Polytechnic of Bari's research project on the evaluation of the geological risk in the coastal environment (DICATECH), the planimetric position of the coastline of the Puglia Region was analyzed using a digitally extracted orthophoto made available from the Office of the State Property of the Puglia Region in 2017.

Starting from a summary of the geomorphological and evolutionary characteristics of the Apulian coast as can be deduced from the most recent sector studies, a scientific

O. Gervasi et al. (Eds.): ICCSA 2022 Workshops, LNCS 13379, pp. 405–422, 2022.
https://doi.org/10.1007/978-3-031-10545-6_28

method was followed that is able to contribute to the updating of the thematic supporting cartography to identify and evaluate the degree of geological risk, by virtue of the geometric evolution conditions of the Apulian coastline.

A Bibliographic survey of the geological knowledge already available in the GIS environment was carried out and it was decided to take the coastline of the Hydrogeomorphological Map and the Regional Coastal Plan from the Puglia Region (2011) as a reference for this update.

Remote sensing data analysis led to the geometric extraction of the shoreline from orthophoto maps through automatic extraction and visual digitization techniques. Particular attention was paid to the geological analysis of the coast, with respect to its morphological characters. A comparison study was conducted using the most recent cartographic surveys available on the official geological cartography (CARG project). The analyzes were performed using the Free Geographic Information System and Open Source QGIS.

In some coastal stretches, coinciding with the most recent cartographic surveys available on geological sheets of official cartography (CARG project), the existing strengths and criticalities were analyzed with the aim of continuing the methodological studies aimed at the problem of the uniqueness of the data useful in the analysis of integrated territorial planning and soil defense.

The results have allowed a more detailed and in-depth definition of some aspects of geological cartography and the various elements of geohazard as well as a clearer reconstruction of the mechanisms of interaction between the various processes involved in geohazard.

The detailed analysis of some of the most representative cases has also confirmed the complexity of the coastal issues and highlighted some crucial questions about the making of geological cartography and coastal maps of the ongoing CARG project to further investigate and the consequent need to complete the updating of the official Geological and Geomorphological Cartography.

We call for a greater in-depth knowledge of the geomorphological and meteo-marine characteristics of the coastal environment to observe its evolution through accurate and continuous monitoring over time. This allows the analysis of evolutionary trends and both natural and anthropogenic factors influencing the delicate balance of the coastline.

2 Materials and Methods

The planimetric position of the coastline assumes particular importance in the space of the interface between the submerged and emerged sector and in the points where the "free surface" of the water meets the land. This interface is a line that can be considered continuous. Awareness is widespread on the variation of the position of the water surface. However, the effects of the variations due to the different configuration and position of earth over time (i.e., tectonic, volcanic phenomena, with uplift or lowering effects and sedimentary processes, both erosive and depositional) should not be overlooked.

To this study, the shoreline and coastline take the form of a sector in space, within which the real line is present with a certain level of reliability. The digitization of the coastline considers its variability due to factors related to the movements of the sea and land surfaces (vertical and horizontal variations of the coast profiles and sea level) and the uncertainties related to the procedures used. It will therefore be considered conceptually as the expression of an area of uncertainty conditioned by the scale of restitution.

The only directly detectable line has been digitized. This was obtained by measuring the position of the shoreline at a given instant, namely the instantaneous shoreline. This generalized line leads back to INSPIRE's definitions of shoreline or coastline.

The remote sensing investigations had a two-dimensional approach which can be rendered in three dimensions by making the appropriate considerations on the spatial variations of the coast and its consequent final uncertainty of positioning and representativeness.

The geometric extraction of the shoreline from orthophotos directly on the visible bands or through the automatic extraction techniques typical of remote sensing was considered a method applicable to the regional context of this study. Particular attention was paid to the standard coding of the shoreline, with clearly assigned attributes and codes.

For the instantaneous shoreline to be transformed into a shoreline (and in its case coastline), it was considered as a first approximation to a standard tide level.

In this work, the coastline was digitized on video using the 2017 orthophotos as a basis.

Contourlines were subsequently extracted from the DTM obtained from the frames of the same 2017 flight. But it was not possible to obtain contourline 0 for the entire coast. in the stretches of high coast, a good correspondence was noted between the digitized coastline on video and the coastline extracted from the 2017 DTM coinciding with the 0.5 m contourline. Also, all the stretch coinciding with UF1_2017 (beetwen Marina Di Chieuti and Vieste) was acquired observing the frames in rough sea conditions. This could have caused problems in acquiring the 0m altitude level. Therefore, due to the objective technical problems it was decided to use the extracted level lines only as a further comparison with the coastline typed on the screen and to better refine the digitization itself.

Both the physiographic units defined by the Regional Coastal Plan and the municipal, provincial, and regional ISTAT limits of 01/01/2020 have been attributed to the coastline thus obtained. The analyzes described below were carried out on the level thus organized. Information on the characteristics of the coast has been included in the GIS, such as the division of the coast into Physiographic Units and Subunits. The coast has been classified, maintaining the typological subdivision of the Hydro geomorphological Map shown in Fig. 3.

3 Geological and Cartographical Framework

Structurally, the Puglia Region is mainly included in the geological domain of "Avampaese" and subordinately in the geological domain of "Fossa" (Fig. 1).

The geological considerations developed in this study were inspired by the cognitive tool available to the Puglia Region: the "Hydrogeomorphological map", which was considered a starting point for the appropriate detailed investigations of both scientific and applicative nature (Palumbo 2009).

Despite the apparent "simplicity" and "uniformity" of the morphological and hydrological-hydraulic structures of the great morphogenetic regions that constitute it, the Apulian Region contrasts an extreme variability and complexity of numerous and often interacting dynamic phenomena taking place, some capable of directly threaten man and his activities.

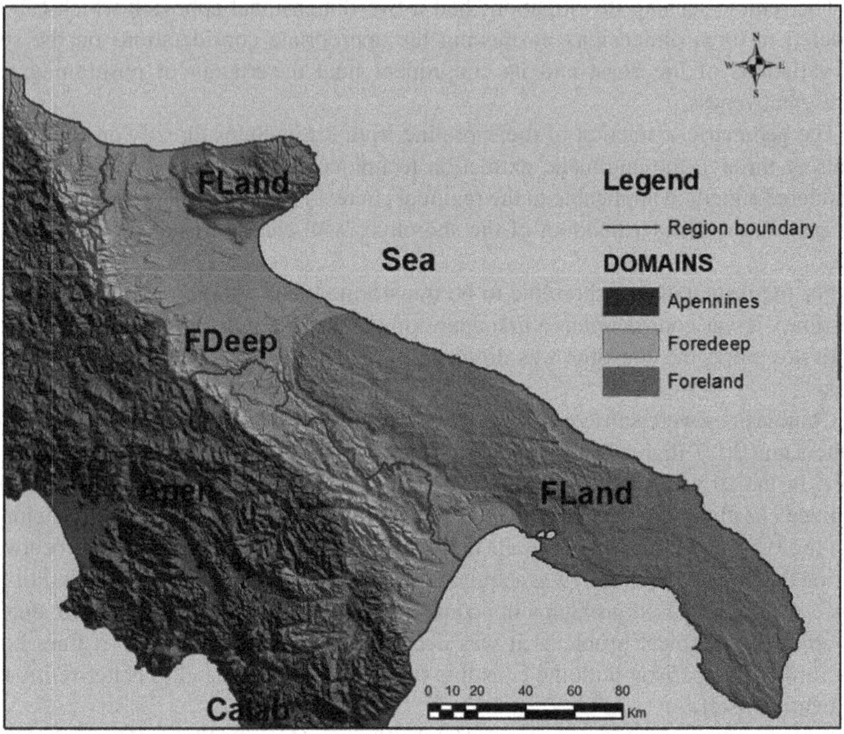

Fig. 1. Geological-structural schematic. Image by (Palombella and Gallicchio 2012) - High-resolution DTM for studying quaternary morphology and stratigraphy of plain areas (Ascoli Satriano, FG). Rend. Online Soc. Geol. It., Vol. 19 (2012), pp. 52–54, 3 figg. © Società Geologica Italiana, Roma.

The geological-structural set-up is crucial to better understand the origin of the different types of coasts present in the area. Among the rocky and/or cliff-like coasts, the coastal stretches of the eastern and southern slopes of the Gargano as well as the southernmost portion of Salento are worthy of note, characterized by steep slopes, in some cases over a hundred meters high.

The Hydrogeomorphological Map of Puglia aims to constitute a coherent and updated framework of knowledge of the various physical elements that contribute to the current configuration of the natural landscape, with reference to the morphological and hydrographic attitude. It delineates its morphographic and morphometric characteristics and interprets its origin according to geomorphic processes, natural or induced by man. The geo-lithological characters contribute significantly to the understanding of the structural elements of the coastal geomorphology.

Figure 2 shows the lithological distinctions that have been entered in the database of the hydrogeomorphological map.

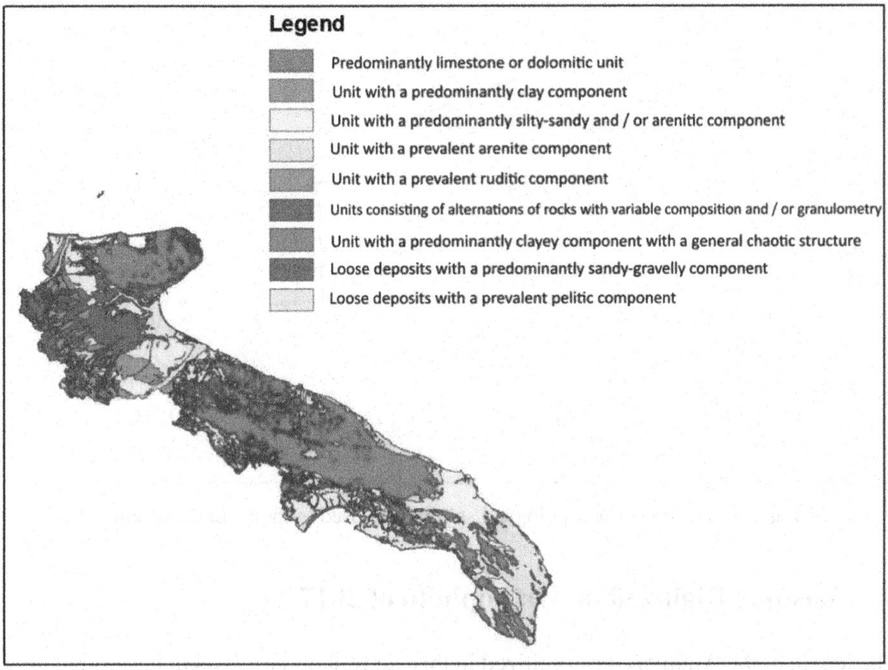

Fig. 2. Geo-lithological characters of Puglia region (by the Hydrogeomorphological Map of Puglia)

In the database, geomorphological details such as the coastline, the forms of river modeling, the slope forms, the hydrographic network "le lame" and rivers were also considered. Figure 3 shows the information level of the coastline.

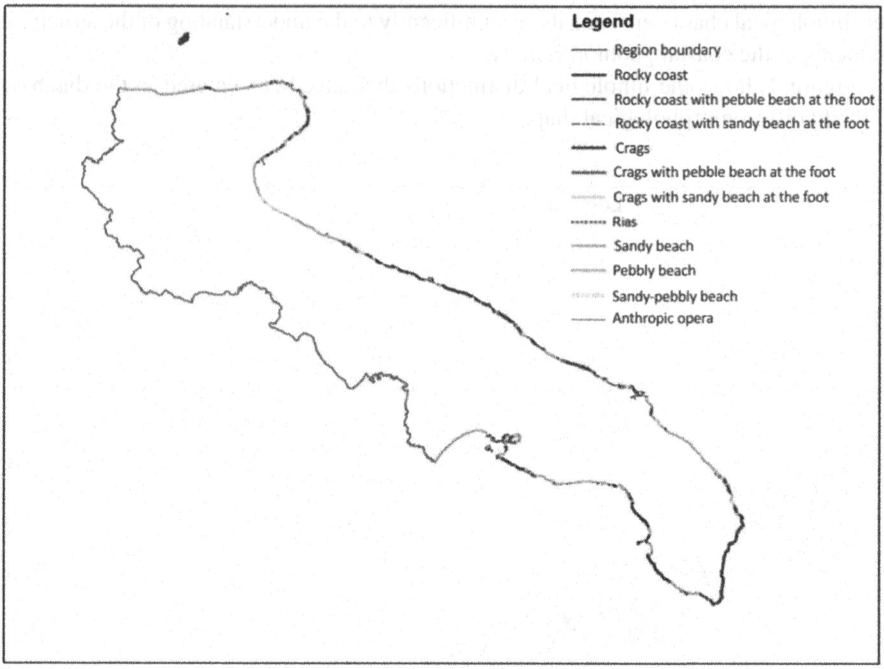

Fig. 3. Coastline. The typological subdivision used is shown in the legend.

4 Coastline Digitized on Orthophoto of 2017

The length of the Apulian coast digitized in this study shows a 1250 km development of the coast from the mouth of the Saccione Torrent in the Adriatic Sea to the outlet of the Bradano River in the Ionian Sea, including the coastal strip of the Mar Piccolo basin of Taranto.

The coastal strip is a particularly sensitive area at the interface between land and sea; its morphology is influenced by both natural and anthropic factors, which directly determine its equilibrium and evolution. Coasts can be classified on the basis of the lithoid elements that constitute them, and therefore are divided into: rocky coasts (high and low) and beaches. Then there are the coastal stretches characterized by Anthropic operas.

Table 1 shows the overall linear extension (in km) of the different types of coastal morphology, as identified in the Regional Coastal Plan (Reina 2011), updated with the new digitization performed on aerial shots in 2017, and the relative frequency in percentage terms referred to the entire Apulian coastal perimeter. The table includes to the overall length of the anthropic works resulting from the digitization.

Table 1. Types of coast updated with the new 2017 digitization.

Type of coast	Lenght (km)	% Lenght
Rocky coast	329.26	26.20
Rocky coast with pebble beach at the foot	8.99	0.72
Rocky coast with sandy beach at the foot	33.61	2.67
Crags	173.10	13.77
Crags with pebble beach at the foot	3,85	0,31
Rias	4.38	0,35
Pebbly beach	12,24	0,97
Sandy beach	298.55	23,76
Sandy-pebbly beach	1.00	0,08
Anthropic opera	370.22	29,46
Fictitious trait	0.84	0,07
TOTAL	1256.70	100

In summary, the Apulian coast, digitized on orthophotos of 2017, is mainly made up of the following coastal types: 27% of low rocky coasts plus 29% anthropic opera stretches; sandy beaches make up 24% while we have 15% of crags. The coastal development also includes the anthropic works overall length.

The results of the photo interpretation performed on the 2017 orthophotos are shown in Fig. 4.

Using the hydrogeomorphological map as a basis, the lithologies were mapped as follows:

1. Primarily calcareous or dolomitic unit.
2. Unit with a prevalent arenite component.
3. Units consisting of alternations of rocks with variable composition and/or granulometry.
4. Unit with a predominantly clayey component with a general chaotic structure.
5. Unit with a prevalent ruditic component.
6. Unit with predominantly clay component.
7. Unit with predominantly silty-sandy and/or arenitic component.
8. Loose deposits with a predominantly sandy-gravelly component.
9. Loose deposits with a prevalent pelitic component.

An analysis was carried out on the lithologies mapped along the coast, focusing on the four main typologies of the Apulian coast: sandy beach 23.76%, rocky coast 26.20%, crags 13.77 and anthropic operas works 29.46%. The four types of coasts make up over 93% of the Apulian coast.

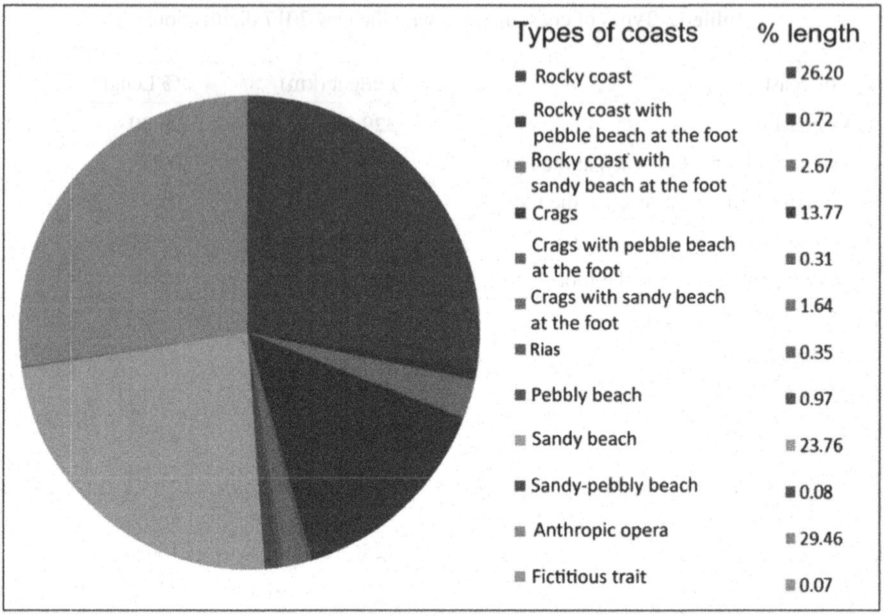

Fig. 4. Morphological classification of the Apulian coast (photo interpretation on the 2017 orthophotos)

The lithologies that have been found along the coastline for the four types of coasts are the following:

sandy beach = 1, 2, 6, 7, 8, 9
rocky coast = 1, 2, 6, 7, 8, 9
crag = 1, 2, 6, 7, 8, 9
anthropic opera = 1, 2, 6, 7, 8, 9

The prevailing lithologies, in percentages:
298.55 km of sandy beach are made up of 78% of the lithology 8.
329.26 km of rocky coast are made up of 1 31%, 2 32% and 7 31% lithologies.
173.10 km of crag are mainly made up of lithologies 1 42% and 2 35%.
The anthropic operas are made mainly out in the lithologies 7 24%, 8 25% followed respectively by the lithologies 1 e 2 19 e 18%.
The following lithologies were not found along the coastal strip: 3, 4, 5.
The dominant lithologies along the natural coastal development, grouped by provinces, are divided as follows:

	Bari	*BAT*	*Brindisi*	*Foggia*	*Lecce*	*Taranto*
Dominant lithologies	1 e 2	8	2 e 7	1 e 8	1, 2, 7 e 8	7 e 8
Percentages %	33 e 71	59	60 e 44	41 e 58	31, 20, 22 e 26	36 e 45

5 Problems Related to the Univocity of the Data: Section of Coast of the Geological Map 1: 50.000 Ugento

The Official Geological Cartography of Italy, surveyed at the scale of 1: 25,000, provides for a coverage of the entire national territory and is drawn up by the Geological Service of Italy (SGI).

Since the late 1980s, state resources have been made available such as to allow the launch of the "CARG Project" for the creation and computerization of the new official geological map of Italy. The surface of the national territory has been divided according to the framework of union IGMI at scale of 1: 50,000; scale of cartographic restitution of printed geological sheets.

The Project is characterized using national technical regulations, specially drafted by the SGI with the collaboration of experts and published in the Geological Service Notebooks series. They constitute the reference guidelines for the survey, cartographic representation, and computerization of both geological and geothematic sheets, allowing them to be homogeneous at national level.

The geological data collected are computerized and constitute the ISPRA geological database (Palombella 2010).

In the Puglia region, the CARG Project was interrupted due to a lack of funding and resumed at the end of 2020 thanks to the Budget Law no. 160/2019, with the funding of Sheet no. 493 "Taranto" of which the detection and computerization of both the emerged and the submerged area is envisaged. Four years are foreseen for the realization of the Sheet. Therefore, out of 54 Sheets needed to cover the entire Apulian territory, 39 Sheets have not yet been funded (Fig. 5).

In this study, the geometric elements of the coastline digitized on the Orthophotos of 2017 and compared with the Hydrogeomorphological map of 2011, were compared also with that of the database of the Sheet "Ugento" Geological of the CARG Project (Fig. 6).

The information level "coastline", of the geological Sheet "536 Ugento", digitized on topographic base at a scale of 1: 25,000 published in the years 1947–1948 by I.G.M.I., it was overlapping to the digitized one on Orthophoto of 2017 (Fig. 7).

The coastal stretches were examined on screen and a good coincidence appeared between them, considering the limits of digitization and the objective errors deriving from the transformations of the Reference Systems.

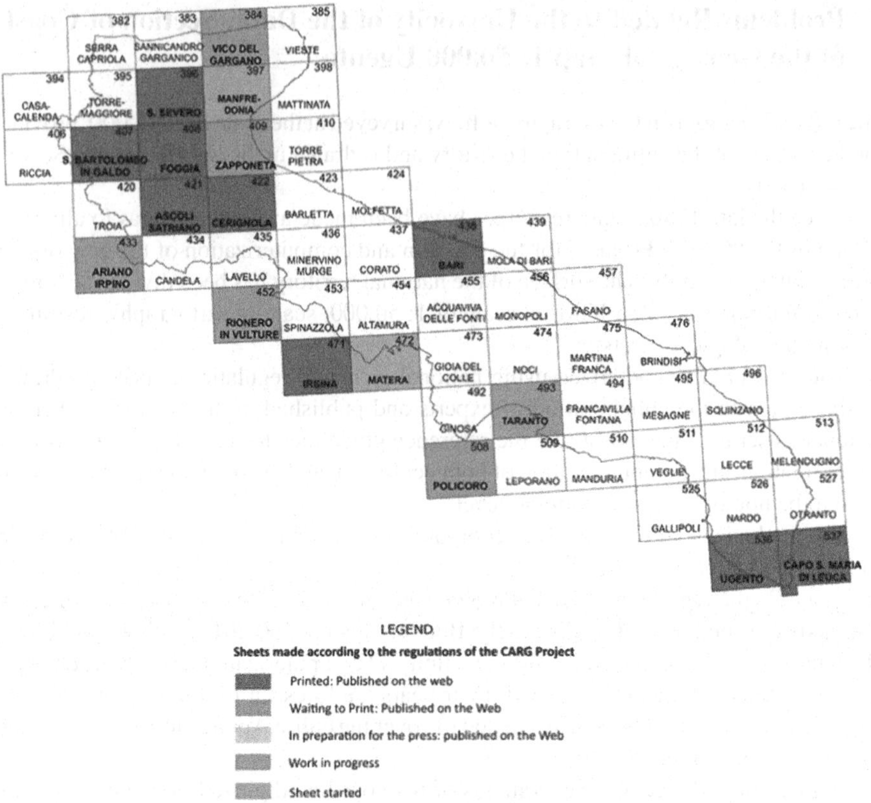

Fig. 5. Implementation status of the CARG Project in the Puglia Region (https://www.isprambiente.gov.it/Media/carg/puglia.html)

Subsequently, some numerical considerations were made. The length of the coastline included in the limit of Sheet 536 Ugento has been calculated:

- Coastline Length of the Sheet 536 Ugento: **46.724,85 mt.**
- Same stretch digitized on 2017 orthophoto: **56.196,23 mt.**

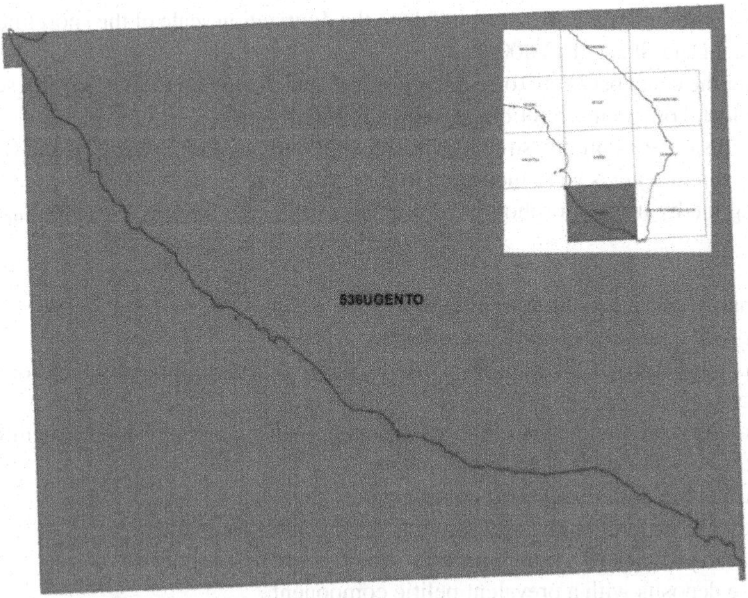

Fig. 6. Coastline extracted from the database of 536 Ugento (CARG Project).

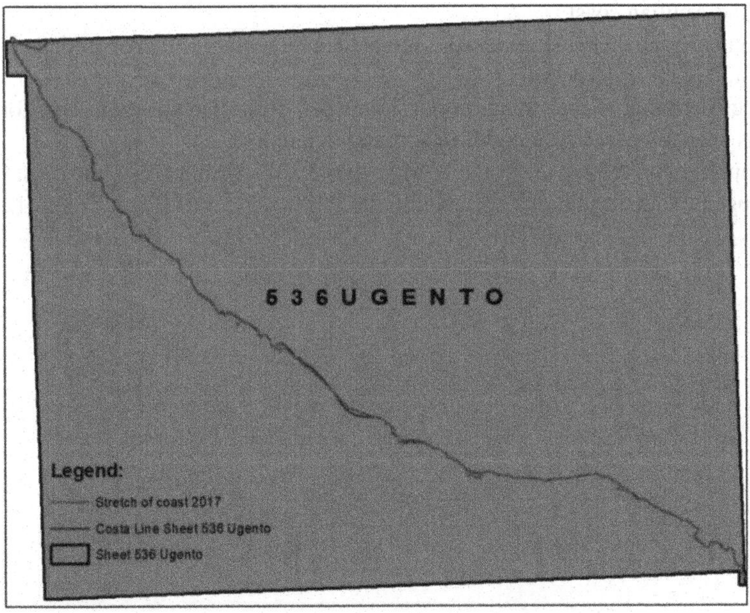

Fig. 7. Overlap of the coastal line information level extracted from the database of Geological 536 Ugento (CARG Project) on the one digitized on the 2017 orthophoto.

These differences are also attributable to the digitization scale of the shoreline of the Geological Data Sheet (1: 25,000).

Along the coast between Torre San Giovanni and Torre Pali there are some sections in erosion and others in accretion, as shown in Fig. 8.

The erosion areas in this stretch of coast were measured in 259,268.65 m^2 (Fig. 9).

The accretion areas were measured in 234,746.68 m^2.

Using the hydrogeomorphological map as a basis, the lithologies were mapped as follows:

1. Primarily calcareous or dolomitic unit.
2. Unit with a prevalent arenite component.
3. Units consisting of alternations of rocks with variable composition and/or granulometry.
4. Unit with a predominantly clayey component with a general chaotic structure.
5. Unit with a prevalent ruditic component.
6. Unit with predominantly clay component.
7. Unit with predominantly silty-sandy and/or arenitic component.
8. Loose deposits with a predominantly sandy-gravelly component.
9. Loose deposits with a prevalent pelitic component.

An analysis was carried out on the lithologies mapped along the coast, focusing on the four main typologies of the Apulian coast: sandy beach 23.76%, rocky coast 26.20%, crags 13.77 and anthropic operas works 29.46%. The four types of coasts make up over 93% of the Apulian coast.

In some points, the erosion can be calculated in more than 150 m of eroded coastline, as shown in the Fig. 10 detail.

It is evident that in the stretch of coast between Torre San Giovanni and Torre Pali there has been a real rebalancing of the coastal dynamics.

Comparing the reference stretch IGM with the 2017 Orthophotos, the most evident anthropogenic transformations occurred in the following points (Figs. 11 and 12).

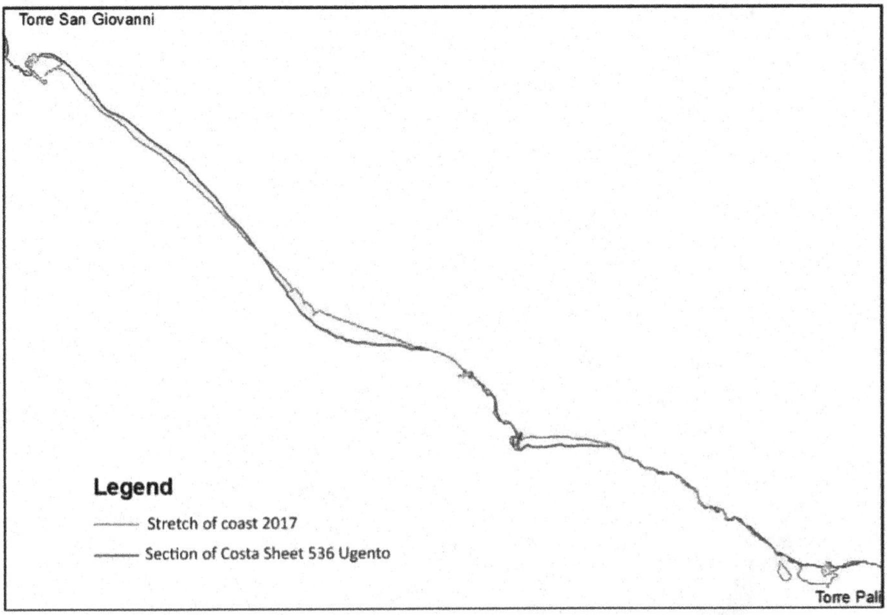

Fig. 8. Stretch of coast between Torre San Giovanni and Torre Pali

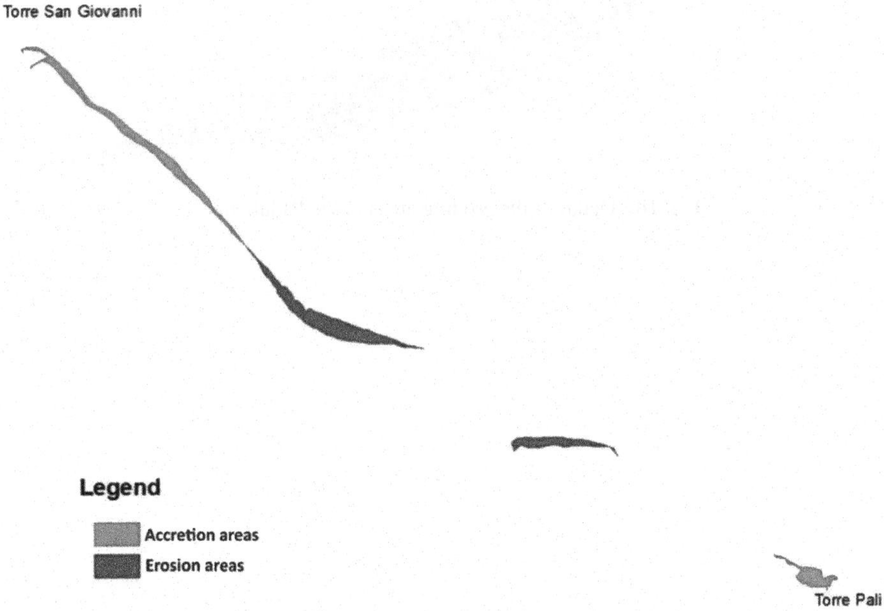

Fig. 9. Areas in erosion and growth in the stretch of coast between the localities of Torre San Giovanni and Torre Pali

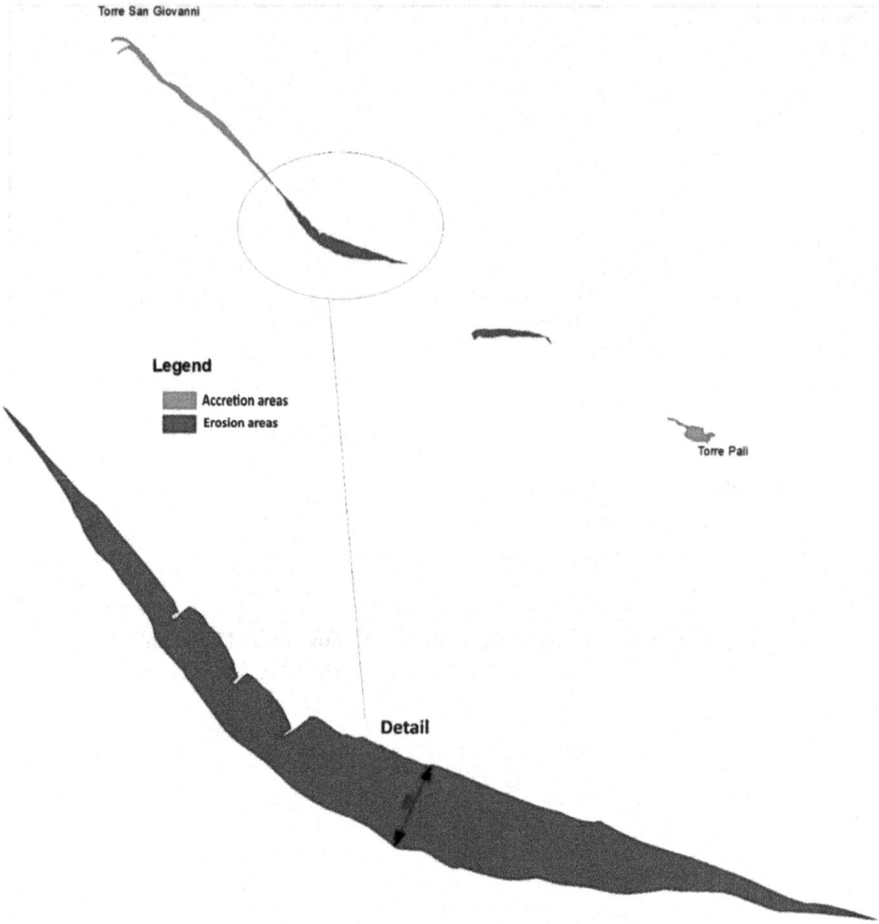

Fig. 10. Detail of the eroding areas in the Paduli area.

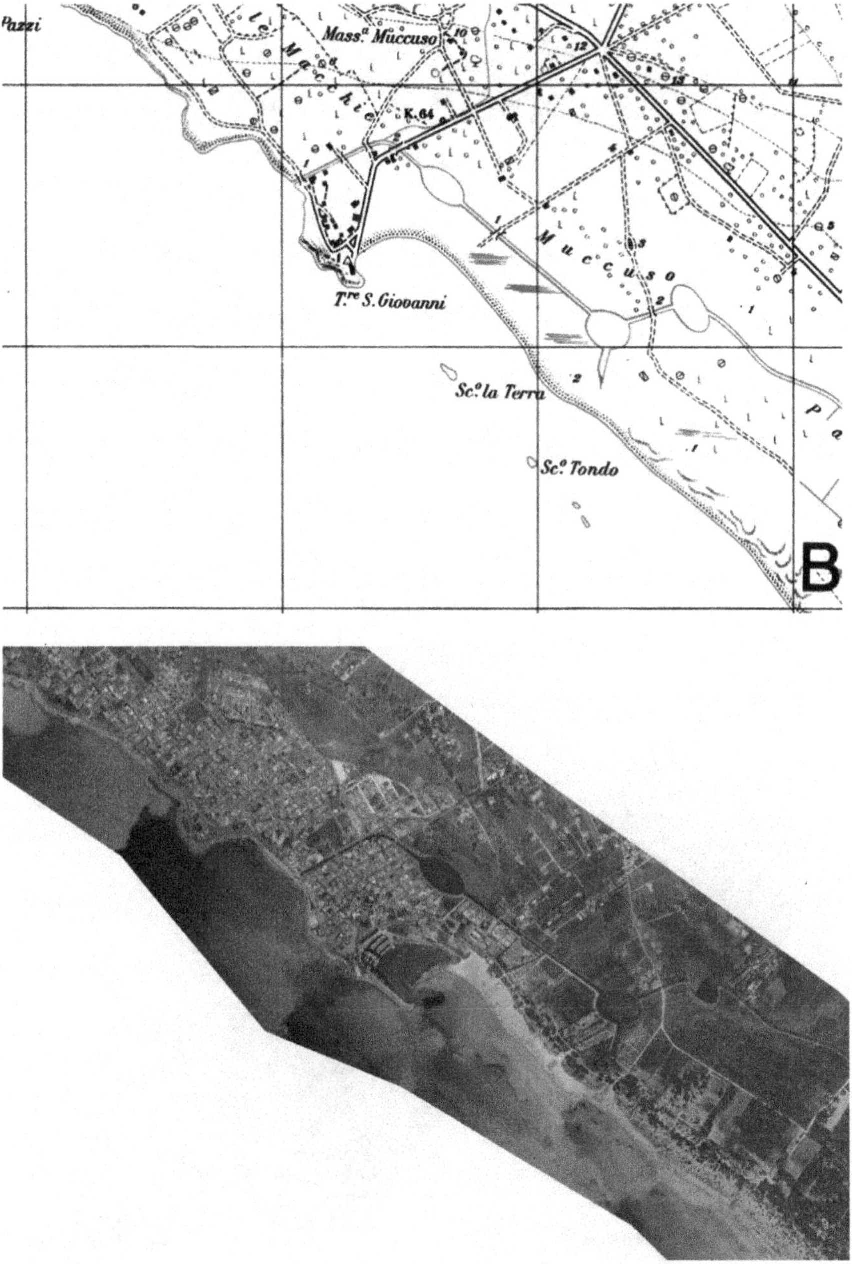

Fig. 11. Torre S. Giovanni: area comparison 1947–1948 excerpt of I.G.M.I. and orthophoto 2017.

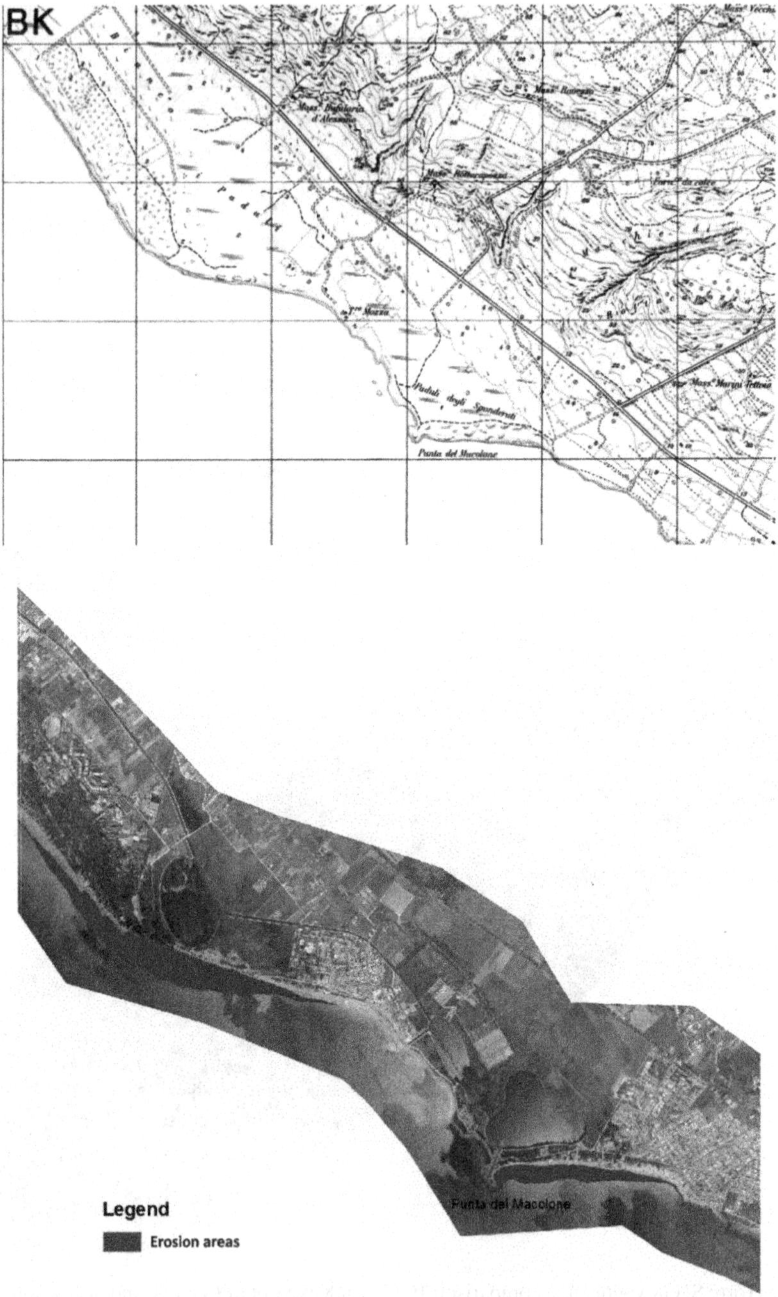

Fig. 12. The Paduli-Punta del Macalone: area comparison 1947–1948 excerpt of I.G.M.I. and Orthophoto 2017.

6 Analysis of the Results

The 2017 digitized coastline was used to carry out numerical and morphometric analyses. The analysis shows that the stretches of coast in 2017 with anthropogenic works (27%) have now equalled the type of natural coast prevalent in Puglia consisting of low rocky coasts. Sandy beaches constitute 24% of the length of the entire Apulian coast. The coastal development also includes the anthropic works on its overall length.

To continue to monitor the dynamism of the coastline, it appears necessary to continue the studies to develop automatic or semi-automatic methods for updating the coastline. This would allow to obtain better data with good spatial resolution that are comparable with the regional data available, considering the possibility of integrating information from different types of sensors and platforms (e.g., drones, aerial photos, high resolution satellite images). As a non-secondary objective, we also have returned the data on the coastline to the tolerance provided for cartographic rendering at the 1: 25,000 scale.

From the comparison of the digitized coastline on orthophotos of 2017 with the new geological cartography of the Geological Survey of Italy, we highlighted the strong coastal rebalancing taking place between Torre S. Giovanni and Torre Vado. The correlation appears clear between the anthropization of this stretch of coast and the coastal dynamics of the last seventy years. Hence, our results suggest there is a need to consider the problems associated with sedimentary inputs in the planning and management phase of coastal territories.

In Italy, the waterproofing process on coastal areas is a documented phenomenon: 19.4% of soils between 0 and 300 m from the sea are already sealed, and even 16% are sealed at between 300 and 1,000 m. However, the environmental effects of this phenomenon are poorly explored due to the extensive substitution of land use. It appears necessary to develop subsequent studies to explore the qualitative effects of the sealing process by considering changes in ecosystem services as a key factor for environmental assessment as well as to link these issues to the ongoing climate changes. The loss of biodiversity on coastal areas is one of the main problems for the sustainability of the urban development process.

Furthermore, it is necessary to ensure uniformity of data of reference maps, such as those of the CARG Project. The coastline present in the two cartographic databases analysed should be the same in order not to create confusion for the planner and the manager of the territory. They should be updated periodically and at the same time. In this way, starting from the common geometric element, the different specific databases would contain all the other peculiar informations. For example, the same geometric element "coastline" should be able to connect and dialogue with the information contained in the geomorphological cartography model approved and published by ISPRA in 2018 and the data of the Regional Coastal Plan of the Puglia Region (Reina et al. 2011).

Some strengths and criticalities existing in institutional geological cartography were analyzed. The problem of the uniqueness of the data should be analyzed in subsequent methodological studies, also with reference to other elements existing in the database of the Hydro geomorphological maps and useful in the analysis of integrated territorial planning and soil defense such as: forms of river modeling, slope forms, hydrography (the hydrographic network "le lame" and rivers).

The results obtained allowed, in sample areas, a more detailed and in-depth definition of some aspects of geological cartography and some elements of geohazard which deserve further study for a clearer reconstruction of the interaction mechanisms between the various processes responsible for their genesis and evolution.

References

Palumbo N.: Carta Idrogeomorfologica della Puglia (2009)

Istituto Idrografico della Marina: Linee guida per lo studio e la descrizione ai fini cartografici della zona costiera (2017)

ISPRA: Banca dati geologici alla scala 1:50.000. QUADERNI serie III, vol. 6 (1997)

ISPRA: Aggiornamento ed integrazioni delle line guida della carta geomorfologica d'Italia alla scala 1:50.000: QUADERNI serie III, vol. 13 – Fascicolo I - (2018)

Regione Puglia: Piano regionale delle coste (2011). www.sitpuglia.it

Reina, A., Rotondo, F., Selicato, F.: Il Piano Regionale delle Coste. Geologi e Territorio, no. 2, pp. 4–8 (2011)

Palombella, M.: La Carta Geologica d'Italia. Geologi e Territorio (2010)

Di Santo, R., Palumbo, N., Buzzanca, L.: Contenuti e indirizzi dei più recenti atti di pianificazione e programmazione territorial e settoriale ai fini della gestione della dinamica dei litorali della costa pugliese. Geologi e Territorio (2012)

Bruno, M.F., Saponieri, A., Molfetta, M.G., Damiani, L.: The DPSIR approach for coastal risk assessment under climate change at regional scale: the case of apulian coast (Italy). J. Marine Sci. Eng. **8**(7), 531 (2020)

Palombella, M., Gallicchio, S.: High-resolution DTM for studying quaternary morphology and stratigraphy of plain areas (Ascoli Satriano, FG). Rend. Online Soc. Geol. It. **19**, 52–54 (2012). 3 figg.©Società Geologica Italiana, Roma

First Flush Occurrence Prediction and Ranking of Its Influential Variables in Urban Watersheds: Evaluation of XGBoost and SHAP Techniques

Angela Gorgoglione[1](✉), Cosimo Russo[2], Andrea Gioia[3], Vito Iacobellis[3], and Alberto Castro[1]

[1] Universidad de la República, 11300 Montevideo, Uruguay
{agorgoglione,acastro}@fing.edu.uy
[2] Politecnico di Milano, 20133 Milan, Italy
cosimo.russo123@gmail.com
[3] Politecnico di Bari, 70126 Bari, Italy
{andrea.gioia,vito.iacobellis}@poliba.it

Abstract. In the last decades, the quality of the surface-water bodies has been increasingly threatened mainly due to anthropogenic activities (i.e., urbanization and the consequent increase of impervious surfaces). This leads to the generation of runoff even more rich in pollutants and difficult to adequately treat in the specific first-flush treatment plant. Consequently, accurate water-quality predictions in urban areas and related detections of events that may generate first flush are the key to enhancing urban water management and pollution control. In this study, the ability of a supervised machine-learning technique (XGBoost) to predict the occurrence of first flush was demonstrated. The model showed outstanding performance in predicting first flush for three of the most detected pollutants in urban areas (total suspended solids, total nitrogen, and total phosphorus) by using rainfall-runoff variables as input. Furthermore, by exploiting a non-model-biased method based on game theory (SHAP), such variables were quantified and ranked based on their level of importance in pollutant first-flush predictions. The findings of this work proved that the XGBoost model is a functional tool for enhancing the accuracy of first-flush predictions in urban watersheds and, thus, contributes to the development of an effective design of first-flush treatment plants.

Keywords: First flush · Urban runoff · XGBoost · Hydroinformatics

1 Introduction

Accurate prediction of water quality in urban areas plays a crucial role in minimizing stream pollution and protecting the health of aquatic ecosystems. Due to anthropogenic activities, such as agriculture, urbanization, sewage discharge, and water extraction, the quality of the surface-water bodies has been increasingly threatened by affecting the ecosystems and populations that benefit from such resources [1, 2].

O. Gervasi et al. (Eds.): ICCSA 2022 Workshops, LNCS 13379, pp. 423–434, 2022.
https://doi.org/10.1007/978-3-031-10545-6_29

The water-quality field counts of a long history of developing discharge and water-quality prediction models: for several watershed scales, based on different datasets, and evaluated with different performance criteria. However, it is still challenging to identify "the best model" under certain conditions [3].

To simulate and predict water quality in urban regions, several physically-based models have been successfully adopted, such as SWMM, STORM, FLUPOL, and InfoWorks [4, 5]. However, such models are limited by several factors: *i)* data availability since they require rainfall-runoff information along with catchment and drainage-network characteristics as input; *ii)* they are time-consuming and labor-intensive since they require a meticulous implementation in a specific geographic area and an adequate data pre-processing [6, 7].

Supervised machine-learning algorithms have been proving to be a very useful tool for predicting surface-water quality [8, 9]. Even though researchers were initially diffident about adopting machine-learning models since they are often black-box predictors, during the last years, more and more scholars have been using data-driven models to predict water quality [10, 11]. One of the most widespread algorithms in machine learning is ensemble learning. It employs the basic idea of gathering weak learners (*decision trees*) to create a powerful model with a higher prediction rate, to enhance the robustness and the generalization ability by combining multiple learners [12]. Currently, ensemble learning such as random forest (RF) and Gradient Boosting Decision Tree (GBDT) are widely adopted [13]. Extreme gradient boosting (XGBoost) is also an excellent algorithm for ensemble learning [14]. Compared with other ensemble models, XGBoost can enhance the model's robustness by introducing terms for regularization and column sampling. When each decision tree chooses the split point, a parallelization strategy is adopted to improve the model's running speed [15]. Furthermore, it can be exploited for both classification and regression, requiring less training and prediction time. However, to our knowledge, XGBoost's ability to predict the occurrence of first flush (FF) in urban watersheds was never investigated.

An important aspect to take into account in water-quality modeling is the dynamic and random nature of urban runoff quality [16]. Numerous studies demonstrated that it is influenced by a multitude of variables, such as pollutant type, physical water-quality characteristics, and spatial and temporal factors [2, 17, 18]. However, only a few works ranked such variables based on their level of importance in predicting FF.

Based on these considerations, this study aims to *i)* assess the XGBoost algorithm's ability to predict FF occurrence in urban areas; *ii)* identify and rank the input variables in terms of their importance in predicting FF.

The water-quality variables considered for this study were total suspended solids (TSS), total nitrogen (TN), and total phosphorus (TP) since they are the most detected pollutants in urban runoff [19, 20].

2 Materials and Methods

2.1 Study Site

The study area selected for this study is an urban watershed located in Sannicandro di Bari, Southern Italy. It is a catchment with the following characteristics: surface =

31.24 ha, slope = 1.56%, average elevation = 169 m a.s.l., mean annual rainfall = 586 mm, mean annual temperature = 15.0 °C, impervious area = 70% of the total area.

The sewage network is 1.96 km long. It collects water into a rectangular concrete channel (1.20 m × 1.70 m).

The watershed under study, along with its sewage network and the discharge point, is represented in Fig. 1.

Fig. 1. Study area located in Southern Italy [2].

2.2 Dataset Creation

A thorough description of the dataset creation process can be found in Gorgoglione et al. [2].

It is essential to highlight that the dataset is constituted by 141 rainfall-runoff events (data points) from three different data sources: *observations*, *simulations*, and *generations*. The *observations* are time series of discharge (Q_{obs}), precipitation (P_{obs}), and pollutant concentration (C_{obs}) observed during a monitoring campaign carried out at the study site. The *simulations* are rainfall-runoff events characterized by recorded rainfall (P_{obs}) and simulated discharge (Q_{sim}), and pollutant concentration (C_{sim}). The simulations were obtained with the Stormwater Management Model (SWMM) [21] implemented and calibrated for the study site [22]. P_{obs} along with watershed and drainage-network characteristics were used as model input. The *generations* are rainfall-runoff events constituted by synthetic precipitation (P_{gen}) obtained from the Iterated Random Pulse (IRP) model [23], used as input of SWMM, and simulated discharge (Q_{sim}) and pollutant concentration (C_{sim}). It is important to highlight that the dataset used for this study is a subset of the one described in Gorgoglione et al. [2]. A summary of the dataset creation is reported in Table 1.

Table 1. Dataset creation.

Data type	Composition	Data source
Observations	$P_{obs}, Q_{obs}, C_{obs}$	Monitoring campaign (*obs*)
Simulations	$P_{obs}, Q_{sim}, C_{sim}$	Monitoring campaign (*obs*), SWMM (*sim*)
Generations	$P_{gen}, Q_{sim}, C_{sim}$	IRP (*gen*), SWMM (*sim*)

The water-quality variables considered for this study are total suspended solids (TSS), total phosphorus (TP), and total nitrogen (TN). This is justified by the fact that TP and TN are among the primary nutrients detected in urban runoff, and their adsorption to particles is the main form by which their offsite movement takes place; therefore, TSS were also taken into account for this work.

The rainfall-runoff and water-quality variables (hereafter also called *features* or *attributes*) calculated and used as input/output of the model are the following: antecedent dry period (*ADP*), average rainfall intensity (I_{ave}), rainfall duration (*D*), total rainfall (*TR*), maximum rainfall intensity (I_{max}), runoff volume (*RV*), and TSS, TN, and TP event mean load (EML_{TSS}, EML_{TN}, EML_{TP}). It is noteworthy mentioning that prior data analysis was adequately carried out with the aim of choosing appropriate rainfall-runoff features to avoid correlated variables from overshadowing meaningful relationships between rainfall-runoff characteristics and the FF phenomenon.

2.3 First Flush Analysis: 30/80 First Flush Definition

A FF analysis was conducted to identify how many rainfall-runoff events among the 141 generate FF for the three pollutants under study. This was done on the basis of the 30/80 FF definition [24]: an event generates FF for a particular pollutant when at least 80% of such pollutant load is washed off by the first 30% of the runoff volume. In Fig. 2, we reported, as an example, the FF occurrence calculated for TN for the rainfall event of June 19, 2008 (a data point of the 141 that constitute our dataset). In this plot, the blue curve V(t) represents the cumulative runoff volume divided by the total volume; the red curve M(t) represents the cumulative pollutant mass (TN in this case) divided by the total TN mass. Since the 80% of TN load (red dotted line) "occurs" before the 30% of runoff volume (blue dotted line), this event generates TN FF.

This FF definition was applied to the entire dataset. Such results are presented in Table 2. Almost 70% of the events does not generate FF for TSS and TP (71% and 74%, respectively). In contrast, almost 70% of the events generates FF for TN (68% precisely).

This information was used as ground truth to train the XGBoost model.

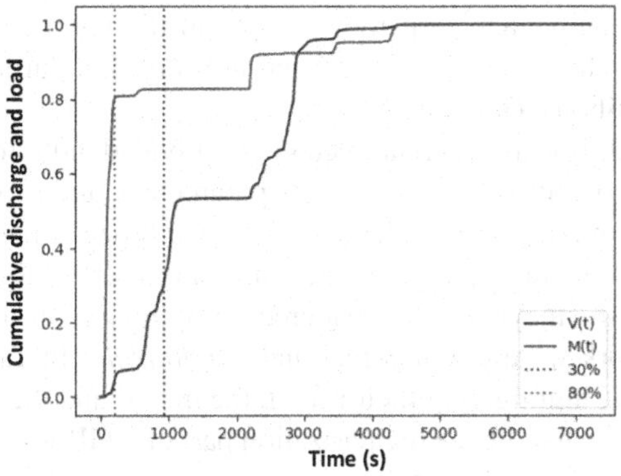

Fig. 2. TN FF occurrence for the event of June 19, 2008. (Color figure online)

Table 2. Datapoint distribution in the two classes "No FF" and "Yes FF" based on the 30/80 FF definition.

Pollutant	No FF occurrence (No FF)	FF occurrence (Yes FF)
TSS	71.0%	29.0%
TN	32.0%	68.0%
TP	74.0%	26.0%

2.4 eXtreme Gradient Boosting (XGBoost) Model

XGBoost model, proposed by Chen and Guestrin [25], belongs to decision tree-based machine-learning models. Such models have the advantages of handling missing data well and reaching fast high performance by just building the decision tree.

XGBoost is one of the most adopted supervised machine-learning models in the environmental field since it has been showing good performance [13, 26, 27]. It is able to couple several weak learners (*decision trees*) into one robust learning machine by generating and iterating multiple trees. This algorithm is characterized by the following features: *i) parallelization*: it can automatically use the CPU multithreading for parallelism while enhancing the algorithm to improve accuracy (this represents the most notable feature of XGBoost). *ii) Regularization:* it includes different regularization penalties to avoid overfitting and adequately generalize the model. *iii) Non-linearity*: it can detect and learn from non-linear data patterns. *iv)* Big amounts of data can be handled at high speed according to block technology. *v)* It is a learning algorithm based on the decision-tree model and can automatically process scarce data [27].

2.5 Model Training and Testing

A 5-fold cross-validation was adopted to calibrate and test the XGBoost algorithm. In particular, 75% of the rainfall-runoff events were used for training the model and the remaining 25% for testing it.

During cross-validation, a hyperparameter optimization process that aims at obtaining an accurate and reliable model was carried out. For this purpose, we adopted the open-source Python library *Optuna* [28].

Generally, the XGBoost hyperparameters are divided into four groups: general parameters, boosting parameters, learning task parameters, and command-line parameters. Before running an XGBoost model, the first three types of parameters must be set up. In contrast, the command-line parameters are only used in the console version of XGBoost and, therefore, they are not considered for optimization. The hyperparameters considered in this work were *n_estimators* and *reg_lambda*. In Table 3, we described such hyperparameters, highlighting their role in the model and their range of variation. *reg_lambda* was used to handle the regularization part of XGBoost since increasing this value will make the model more conservative.

Table 3. Selected hyperparameters for optimization.

Group	Hyperparameter	Description	Range of variation
Boosting parameters	*reg_lambda*	It is responsible for L2 regularization on leaf weights	0.00–1.00
Learning task parameters	*n_estimators*	It is the number of decision trees	1000–2000

After identifying the best set of hyperparameters, the final scoring was computed by using such a set on the training dataset (25% of the dataset).

2.6 Goodness-of-Fit Indicators

Model performance was evaluated by computing the *F1 score* and the *Accuracy*. The latter represents the number of correctly classified samples (i.e., true positives (*TP*) and true negatives (*TN*)) (*CORRs*) divided by the total number of samples (*TOTs*) (Eq. 1):

$$Accuracy = \frac{CORR_s}{TOT_s} \tag{1}$$

It represents the percentage of correctly classified samples related to the total amount of samples. Therefore, it ranges between 0 and 1: the closer to 1, the higher the model performance. Since the *Accuracy* is not particularly descriptive on its own in case of class imbalance and, therefore, it does not take into account false positives (*FP*) and false negatives (*FN*), it is often complemented with the *F1 score* (Eq. 2):

$$F1score = 2\frac{P * R}{P + R} \tag{2}$$

where the precision (*P*) and the recall (*R*) are respectively represented in Eqs. 3 and 4:

$$P = \frac{TP}{TP + FP} \tag{3}$$

$$R = \frac{TP}{TP + FN} \quad (4)$$

F1 score varies between 0 and 1. Also in this case, the closer to 1, the better the model performance.

2.7 Shapley Additive exPlanations (SHAP) Analysis

SHapley Addictive exPlanation (SHAP) was adopted to carry out the feature-importance analysis [29].

It is based on the Shapley Values, the cooperative game-theory solution [30]. The main objective of SHAP is to estimate the expected marginal contribution of a feature among all possible contributions. In other words, it explains the prediction of an instance by calculating the contribution of each variable to the prediction.

To run this analysis, the SHAP python package was adopted.

3 Results and Discussion

3.1 Hyperparameter Optimization

Optuna was set up to run T = 1000 trials, with a sliding window size t = 100. F1 score was used as the objective function during the training process. The search space definition and the best hyperparameters found for the XGBoost models for the three pollutants under study are provided in Table 4.

Table 4. Hyperparameters optimization.

Hyperparameter	Range of variation	Pollutant	Value chosen
reg_lambda	0.00–1.00	TSS	0.65
		TN	0.30
		TP	1.00
n_estimators	1000–2000	TSS	2000
		TN	2000
		TP	1000

3.2 Model Performance

The XGBoost model was tested using the best hyperparameter configuration found.

To summarize its performance, the three confusion matrices (one per pollutant) resulting from the model testing are reported in Fig. 3. Following Eq. 3, P is equal to 0.73, 0.90, and 0.72, respectively for TSS, TN, and TP. Following Eq. 4, R is equal to 0.86, 0.95, and 0.59, respectively for TSS, TN, and TP. In other words, this means that the probability of predicting a FF- and non-FF event as they actually are for the three pollutants is relatively high (low false positives and false negatives, respectively).

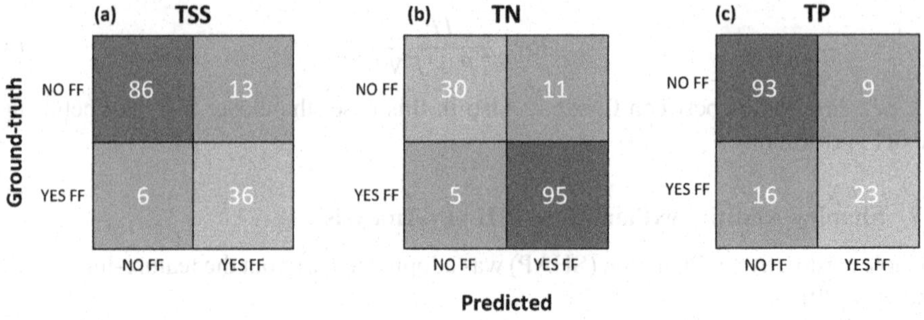

Fig. 3. Confusion matrix for (a) TSS, (b) TN, and (c) TP.

Goodness-of-fit indicator values were calculated for the three pollutants under study and are summarized in Table 5. Overall, the XGBoost model developed shows very satisfactory results. In particular, slightly lower performance was found for TP. The level of *Accuracy* reached in this study (always higher than 80%) is a good step forward, considering that the current approach for predicting pollutant FF is based on a graphical representation with 50% of *Accuracy* (FF occurrence or not). Furthermore, Perera et al. [31] in their work found an *Accuracy* of 71% for predicting TSS FF occurrence in a two-class scenario like the one under study. We were able to enhance such state-of-the-art, reaching an *Accuracy* of 87%.

Table 5. XGBoost model performance.

Goodness-of-fit indicator	Pollutant	Results
Accuracy	TSS	0.87
	TN	0.89
	TP	0.82
F1 score	TSS	0.79
	TN	0.92
	TP	0.65

3.3 Feature-Importance Analysis

Based on the best XGBoost model, the SHAP values were calculated for the input features, and the critical variables for predicting FF occurrence were ranked. The variables are ranked in terms of their degree of influence in predicting FF occurrence. The feature ranking for the three pollutants under study is reported in Fig. 4. Overall, high values of all the input variables have a positive impact on the model outcomes (red dots); while low values may not have an influence or have a negative impact on model results (blue dots). In particular, it is possible to see that I_{ave} is always among the most important

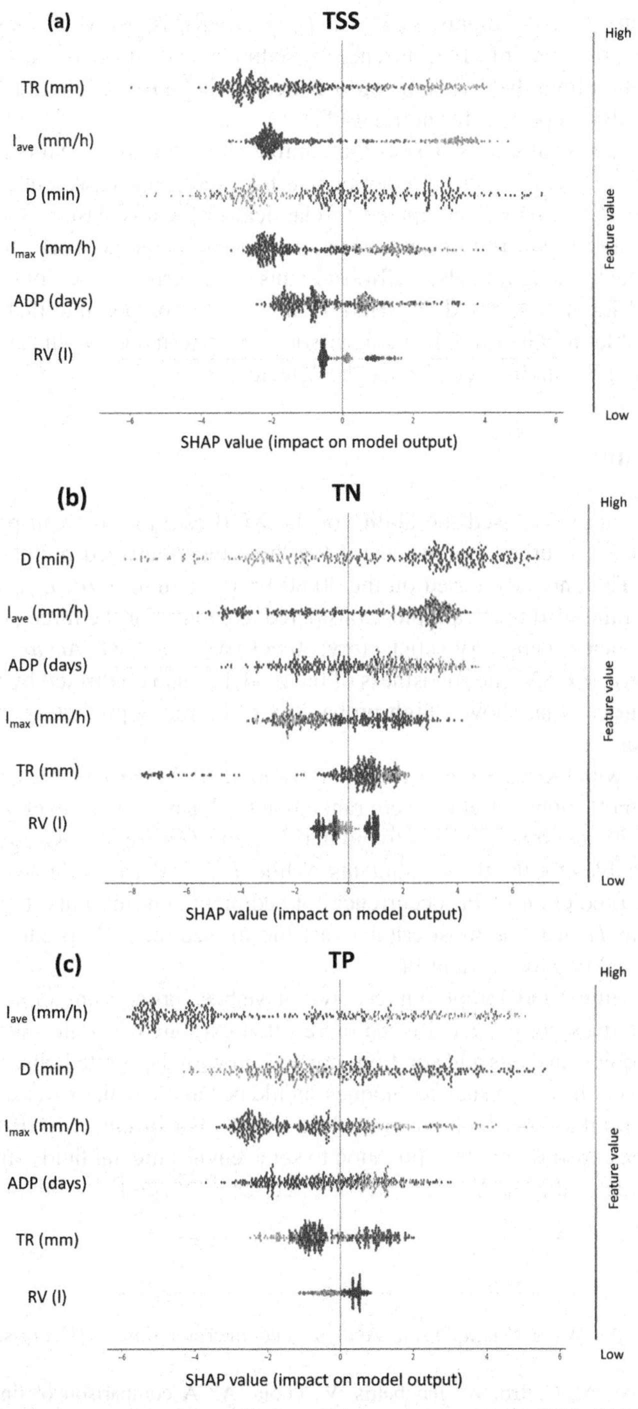

Fig. 4. SHAP values to explain the prediction of FF occurrence for (a) TSS, (b) TN, and (c) TP. (Color figure online)

variables for the three pollutants, as well as *D*. While, *RV* is always the least important variable in the prediction of FF occurrence for sediment and nutrients. Furthermore, it is interesting to highlight that *TR* is the most critical variable for sediment FF prediction; while it is not that important for nutrient FF.

Based on such results, we can state that rainfall characteristics are more critical than the runoff ones in FF occurrence prediction in urban areas. This represents an advantage of machine-learning models compared to classical physically-based models. In fact, the latter require rainfall-runoff data, watershed and drainage network characteristics. While, machine learning models, XGBoost in this case, performs well only considering rainfall-runoff input and, based on SHAP results, it may be possible that by reducing the input variables to only rainfall characteristics, its performance would continue being good even though a slight decrease may be detected.

4 Conclusions

This research study assessed the ability of the XGBoost algorithm in predicting the occurrence of FF in urban watersheds of the three most detected pollutants in urban runoff (TSS, TN, and TP), based on the 30/80 FF definition. *ADP*, I_{ave}, *D*, *TR*, I_{max}, and *RV* were rainfall-runoff variables considered as input. For the three pollutants, the model performance were very satisfactory: $Accuracy_{TSS} = 0.87$, $Accuracy_{TN} = 0.89$ and $Accuracy_{TP} = 0.82$. The robustness of the model is also confirmed by the resulting confusion matrices that show a high probability of correctly predicting true positives and false negatives.

Moreover, with the aid of a non-model biased method (SHAP) based on game theory, the rainfall-runoff input variables were ranked on the basis of their level of importance in predicting FF occurrence. It was found that I_{ave} and *D* were always among the most important variables for the three pollutants. While, *RV* was always the least significant feature in the prediction of FF occurrence for sediment and nutrients. Furthermore, it was found that *TR* was the most critical variable for sediment FF prediction; while it was not a critical one for nutrient FF.

Since algorithms and computing resources have been progressing rapidly, machine-learning techniques are expected to be more often exploited in water-quality studies, mostly when quick analysis and solutions are needed with the limited observation availability. However, the use of such techniques should be handle with extra care taking into account their limitations which could mislead results. For instance, XGBoost is sensitive to outliers, constraining its application to some environmental fields, and it tends to overfit the model if the latter is not early stopped (as it was done for this study).

References

1. Hounslow, A.: Water Quality Data: Analysis and Interpretation. CRC Press, Boca Raton (2018)
2. Gorgoglione, A., Castro, A., Iacobellis, V., Gioia, A.: A comparison of linear and non-linear machine learning techniques (PCA and SOM) for characterizing urban nutrient runoff. Sustainability **13**(4) (2021)

3. Vilaseca, F., Narbondo, S., Chreties, C., Castro, A., Gorgoglione, A.: A comparison between lumped and distributed hydrological models for daily rainfall-runoff simulation. IOP Conf. Ser. Earth Environ. Sci. **958**(1), 012016 (2022)
4. Hur, S., Nam, K., Kim, J., Kwak, C.: Development of urban runoff model c-qual for first-flush water-quality analysis in urban drainage basins. J. Environ. Manag. **205**, 73–84 (2018)
5. Gorgoglione, A., Gioia, A., Iacobellis, V., Piccinni, A.F., Ranieri, E.: A rationale for pollutograph evaluation in ungauged areas, using daily rainfall patterns: case studies of the apulian region in southern Italy. Appl. Environ. Soil Sci. **2016** (2016)
6. Rodríguez, R., et al.: Water-quality data imputation with a high percentage of missing values: a machine learning approach. Sustainability **13**(11) (2021)
7. Vilaseca, F., Castro, A., Chreties, C., Gorgoglione, A.: Daily rainfall-runoff modeling at watershed scale: a comparison between physically-based and data-driven models. In: Gervasi, O., et al. (eds.) ICCSA 2021. LNCS, vol. 12955, pp. 18–33. Springer, Cham (2021). https://doi.org/10.1007/978-3-030-87007-2_2
8. Sun, A., Scanlon, B.: How can big data and machine learning benefit environment and water management: a survey of methods, applications, and future directions. Environ. Res. Lett. **14**(7) (2019)
9. Wang, F., Wang, Y., Zhang, K., Hu, M., Weng, Q., Zhang, H.: Spatial heterogeneity modeling of water quality based on random forest regression and model interpretation. Environ. Res. **202** (2021)
10. Russo, C., Castro, A., Gioia, A., Iacobellis, V., Gorgoglione, A.: A stormwater management framework for predicting first flush intensity and quantifying its influential factors. Earth Space Sci. Open Arch. **44** (2022). https://doi.org/10.1002/essoar.10510381.1
11. Jeung, M., Baek, S.-S., Beom, J., Cho, K., Her, Y., Yoon, K.: Evaluation of random forest and regression tree methods for estimation of mass first flush ratio in urban catchments. J. Hydrol. **575**, 1099–1110 (2019)
12. Gudiyangada, T., Piralilou, S.T., Gholamnia, K., Ghorbanzadeh, O., Blaschke, T.: Flood susceptibility mapping with machine learning, multi-criteria decision analysis and ensemble using dempster shafer theory. J. Hydrol. **590**(125275) (2020)
13. Ma, M., et al.: XGBoost-based method for flash flood risk assessment. J. Hydrol. **598**(126382) (2021)
14. Hosseiny, H., Nazari, F., Smith, V., Nataraj, C.: A framework for modeling flood depth using a hybrid of hydraulics and machine learning. Sci. Rep. **10**(1) (2020)
15. Budholiya, K., Shrivastava, S.K., Sharma, V.: An optimized XGBoost based diagnostic system for effective prediction of heart disease. J. King Saud Univ. Comput. Inf. Sci. (2020)
16. Gorgoglione, A., Castro, A., Gioia, A., Iacobellis, V.: Application of the self-organizing map (SOM) to characterize nutrient urban runoff. In: Gervasi, O., et al. (eds.) ICCSA 2020. LNCS, vol. 12252, pp. 680–692. Springer, Cham (2020). https://doi.org/10.1007/978-3-030-58811-3_49
17. Gorgoglione, A., Gioia, A., Iacobellis, V.: A framework for assessing modeling performance and effects of rainfall-catchment-drainage characteristics on nutrient urban runoff in poorly gauged watersheds. Sustainability **11**, 4933 (2019)
18. Gorgoglione, A., Gregorio, J., Ríos, A., Alonso, J., Chreties, C., Fossati, M.: Influence of land use/land cover on surface-water quality of Santa Lucía river, Uruguay. Sustainability **12**(11) (2020)
19. Pitt, R.: Characterizing and controlling urban runoff through street and sewerage cleaning. Water Eng. Res. Lab. (1985)
20. Sartor, J.D., Boyd, G.B., Agardy, F.J.: Water pollution aspects of street surface contaminants. J. (Water Pollut. Control Fed.) **46**, 458–467 (1974)

21. Rossman, L.A.: Storm Water Management Model User's Manual Version 5.1, U.S. Environmental Protection Agency (EPA), National Risk Management Research Laboratory Office of Research and Development U.S. Environmental Protection Agency, Cincinnati, OH, USA (2015)
22. Di Modugno, M., et al.: Build-up/wash-off monitoring and assessment for sustainable management of first flush in an urban area. Sustainability **7**, 5050–5070 (2015)
23. Veneziano, D., Iacobellis, V.: Multiscaling pulse representation of temporal rainfall. Water Resour. Res. **38**, 131–1313 (2002)
24. Saget, A., Chebbo, G., Bertrand-Krajewski, J.L.: The first flush in sewer systems. Water Sci. Technol. **33**(9), 101–108 (1996)
25. Chen, T., Guestrin, C.: XGboost: a scalable tree boosting system. In: Proceedings of 22nd ACM SIGKDD International Conference on Knowledge Discovery and Data Mining, pp. 785–794. ACM (2016)
26. Osman, A.I.A., Ahmed, A.N., Chow, M.F., Huang, Y.F., El-Shafie, A.: Extreme gradient boosting (Xgboost) model to predict the groundwater levels in Selangor Malaysia. Ain Shams Eng. J. **12**, 1545–1556 (2021)
27. Lu, H., Ma, X.: Hybrid decision tree-based machine learning models for short-term water quality prediction. Chemosphere **249**(126169) (2020)
28. Akiba, T., Sano, S., Yanase, T., Ohta, T., Koyama, M.: Optuna: A Next-Generation Hyperparameter Optimization Framework, pp. 2623–2631. Association for Computing Machinery, New York (2019)
29. Lundberg, S.M., Lee, S.-I.: A unified approach to interpreting model predictions. In: I. Guyon, U.V., Luxburg, S., Bengio, H., Wallach, R., Fergus, S., Vishwanathan, R.G. (eds.) Advances in Neural Information Processing Systems, vol. 30, pp. 4765–4774. Curran Associates, Inc. (2017)
30. Shapley, L.S.: A value for n-person games. In: Classics in Game Theory (1997)
31. Perera, T., McGree, J., Egodawatta, P., Jinadasa, K., Goonetilleke, A.: Taxonomy of influential factors for predicting pollutant first flush in urban stormwater runoff. Water Res. **166**(115075) (2019)

Exploring the Potentialities of Landsat 8 and Sentinel-2 Satellite Data for Estimating the Land Surface Albedo in Urban Areas Using GEE Platform

Carlo Barletta, Alessandra Capolupo(✉), and Eufemia Tarantino

Department of Civil, Environmental, Land, Building Engineering and Chemistry (DICATECh), Politecnico di Bari, via Orabona 4, 70125 Bari, Italy
{carlo.barletta,alessandra.capolupo,eufemia.tarantino}@poliba.it

Abstract. Albedo quantifies the capacity of a certain surface to reflect incident solar radiation. Therefore, this parameter is relevant in environmental and climate studies as it drives both the land surface energy balance and the interaction between surfaces and atmosphere. It can be estimated and monitored at different scales using Remote Sensing technique. However, its assessment is pretty difficult as factors, such as resultant map accuracy, processing time, and complexity of the algorithm used to retrieve it, should be considered.

The goal of this paper is to develop a proper JavaScript code in Google Earth Engine cloud environment in order to estimate surface albedo using two different satellite data, Landsat 8 and Sentinel-2, over two different study areas: Bari (Southern Italy), and Berlin (Northeastern Germany). To achieve this purpose, Landsat 8 and Sentinel-2 images, acquired in close date, were processed in GEE environment by implementing an appropriate JavaScript code. After obtaining albedo maps over both investigated sites, the two algorithms' performances, the Silva for Landsat 8 data and the Bonafoni for Sentinel-2 images, were statistically analyzed and compared. Furthermore, to investigate the outcomes deeply, statistics metrics were computed for different land cover classes also. UrbanAtlas provided by Copernicus was used to classify the whole case studies. Both approaches showed satisfying results albeit Landsat 8 algorithm provided higher mean values than the other one.

Keywords: GEE · Geospatial big data · Climate change · Cloud computing · Copernicus program · UrbanAtlas

1 Introduction

Albedo, a bio-geophysical variable that quantifies the capacity of a surface to reflect solar radiation, plays a fundamental role in environmental studies and climate change investigations as it drives the land surface energy balance and the interaction between surfaces and the atmosphere [1, 2]. Therefore, the Global Climate Observing System (GCOS) considers Albedo as an Essential Climate Variable (ECV) [3].

O. Gervasi et al. (Eds.): ICCSA 2022 Workshops, LNCS 13379, pp. 435–449, 2022.
https://doi.org/10.1007/978-3-031-10545-6_30

The urbanization process, resulting in land use/land cover (LU/LC) changes and, consequently, the energy balance modification, triggers the Urban Heat Island (UHI) phenomenon [2, 4–8]. Anthropogenic surfaces, in fact, are mainly composed of non-reflective materials and, thus, absorbed incident solar radiation is released as heat [5]. Furthermore, in built-up areas, effective surface albedo values are influenced not only by the presence of land cover features such as buildings, roads and vegetation (including both parks and urban forests) but also by the topography of the so-called "urban canopy" [9].

Albedo can be estimated and monitored both at regional and global scales using Remote Sensing (RS) technique effectively. Indeed, RS is very suitable for studying environmental phenomena [10–13]. However, the albedo estimation from the Top Of the Atmosphere (TOA) corrected satellite images is not easy and the optimal strategy to evaluate it should be based on the compromise among resulting map accuracy, processing time and complexity of the implemented algorithm [14]. On the other hand, the knowledge of the atmospheric conditions and land surface characteristics, obtained from multispectral satellite data, are required for improving results accuracy [2, 15–19].

Various approaches have been proposed in literature to retrieve the surface albedo from different satellite sensors. Among them, Liang's simplified method (2000) [15] and Silva *et al.* (2016) algorithm [20] are largely applied to process Landsat data, characterized by a geometric resolution of 30 m [2]. Those methods require TOA reflectance knowledge in visible (RGB), near infrared (NIR) and shortwave infrared (SWIR) bands. In particular, the Silva *et al.* algorithm, specific for Landsat 8 data, provides accurate albedo estimations albeit a high implementation and operational time are needed. Conversely, Liang's method permits to produce albedo maps in a faster way but with a lower accuracy, compared to Silva's algorithm [2].

The launch of Sentinel-2A and Sentinel-2B satellites of the European Union (EU) Copernicus Program (https://www.copernicus.eu/) in 2015 and in 2017, respectively, brought relevant changes in the observation of land surface processes. Sentinel-2 sensors have, indeed, higher resolution (10 m) than Landsat (30 m), and, thus, it is more suitable for tackling many environmental applications, like land monitoring [21]. In addition, the Multi Spectral Instrument (MSI) on board Sentinel-2 satellites acquires thirteen bands of the Earth with a temporal resolution of five days at the equator [22].

An easy-to-use narrow-to-broadband algorithm, developed by Bonafoni *et al.* (2020) [23] allows retrieving surface albedo from Sentinel-2 Level-2A surface reflectance in RGB, NIR and SWIR spectral bands, assuming the hypothesis of Lambertian surfaces and clear sky conditions [23].

However, analyzing and processing a large volume of geospatial data require considerable time and using a traditional desktop software is not always a feasible solution [2, 24]. The advent of cloud services as Google Earth Engine (GEE) opens up new opportunities to use and integrate diverse Earth Observation (EO) datasets for mapping and monitoring Earth's surface processes [24]. GEE is a cloud-based platform developed for geospatial analysis, that allows users to process geospatial big data using Google's massive computational capabilities. GEE consists of a multi-petabyte free-to-use and continuously updated data catalog of remote sensing imagery, co-located with a high-performance computation service. This last one is accessible through an Application

Programming Interface (API) with an associated web-based Interactive Development Environment (IDE). JavaScript, Python and REST are the available API in GEE [25].

The aim of this paper is to develop a proper JavaScript code in GEE environment to: i) extract surface albedo information from two different satellite data, Landsat 8 and Sentinel-2, and, ii) evaluate and compare their performances to detect the corresponding pros and cons. To meet this purpose, two territories, Bari (Southern Italy) and Berlin (Northeastern Germany), were selected as pilot sites. Such urban areas are extremely different in terms of climatic and geo-morphological characteristics point of view. This allows testing the two approaches in various environmental contexts. Silva *et al.* algorithm (2016) [20] and Bonafoni *et al.* (2020) [23] narrow-to-broadband conversion method were applied to estimate surface albedo from Landsat 8 and Sentinel-2 images, respectively. The performances of those algorithms were statistically analyzed and compared. Lastly, they were also evaluated in accordance with the LU/LC classification provided by the Copernicus program.

2 Materials and Methods

2.1 Study Areas and Data

Bari (Fig. 1), in Southern Italy, and Berlin (Fig. 2), in Northeastern Germany, cities were picked up as pilot sites because of their great diversity in terms of morphological as well as climatic features.

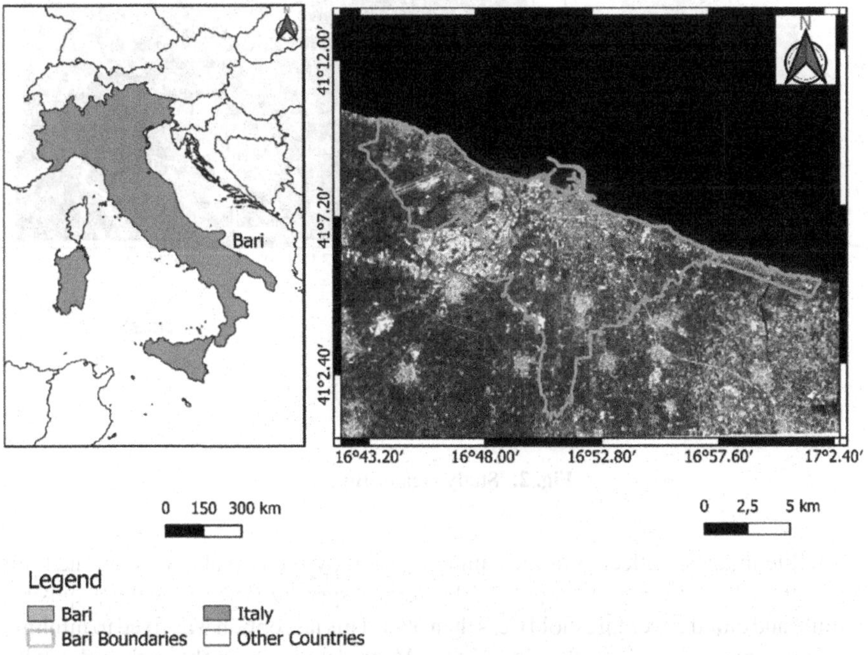

Fig. 1. Study area of Bari.

Bari is a Mediterranean coastal city with hot summers and mild winters [26]. The city has experienced an urban sprawl since the mid twentieth century which causes an expansion of its inner core, built until then, along preferential directions or nuclei. Such an area has a flat topography, and it is mainly characterized by the presence of erosive karstic grooves called "lame". Apart from these grooves, surface water bodies are absent and green urban spaces are scarce [27–29]. Moreover, UHI phenomenon is more evident in the zones close to the city center, even if it is mitigated, especially near the coast, by the sea breeze [26].

Berlin is the capital city of Germany. It has a humid warm temperate climate with cold winters and warm summers. The territory of Berlin, extended for almost 900 km^2, is essentially characterized by a flat topography and a great number of green spaces and water bodies [30, 31]. Its growth started when, in 1871, it was named the capital of Germany. Nevertheless, its sprawl continued during the twentieth century and, in 1920, the "Greater Berlin" became one of the largest and most populated cities in the world [32]. Nowadays, Berlin is characterized by about 35% of built-up areas that results in an evident UHI phenomenon, especially during summer periods [33].

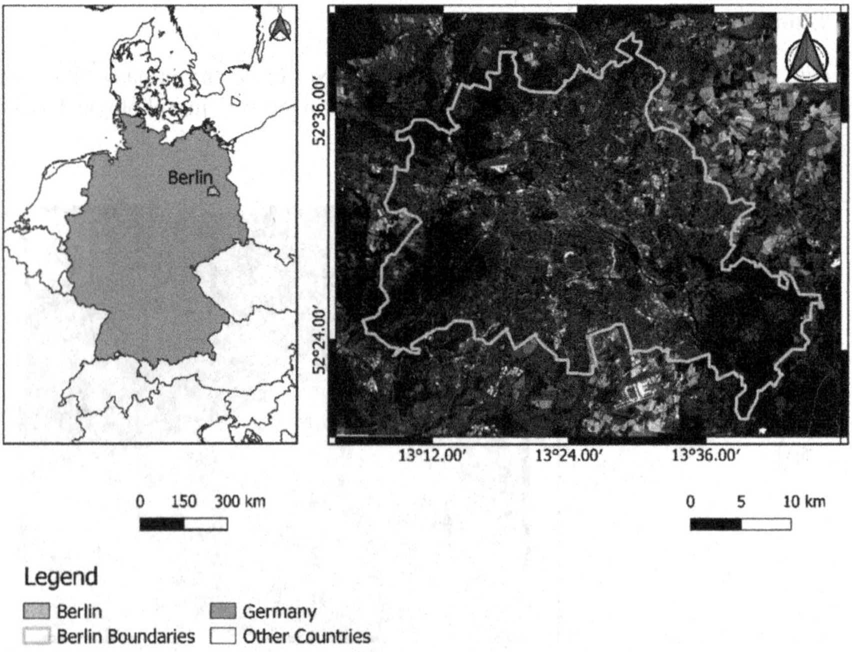

Fig. 2. Study area of Berlin.

Satellite images, collected in the summer period by the two above mentioned missions, were selected for each study area by setting specific criteria, as the acquisition date/time and cloud cover threshold (less than 3%). This last option was fixed to minimize clouds influence on the final thematic maps. More details about the gathered satellite data are reported in Table 1. Concerning the area of Berlin, various Sentinel-2 scenes, with the same acquisition time but covering different territory portions, were collected and, then, mosaicked by adopting a proper code in GEE.

Table 1. Features of the selected satellite images. OLI: Operational Land Imager; MSI: MultiSpectral Instrument.

Study area	ID	Mission	Sensor	Acquisition date (mm/dd/yyyy)	Acquisition time	Cloud cover (%)
Bari	1	Landsat 8	OLI	07/28/2021	09:34	0.51
Bari	2	Sentinel-2	MSI	07/28/2021	09:40	2.11
Berlin	3	Landsat 8	OLI	07/26/2019	10:02	0.04
Berlin	4	Sentinel-2	MSI	07/26/2019	10:20	0

2.2 GEE Cloud Platform and Workflow

Figure 3 describes the operative workflow applied in this study to estimate surface albedo. Once the collection phase was completed, the new dataset was built and processed in GEE environment by applying Silva *et al.* and Bonafoni *et al.* algorithms on Landsat 8 and Sentinel-2 scenes, respectively. After retrieving surface albedo maps, algorithms performances were statistically evaluated considering both the whole territory of the two case studies, and each LU/LC class. To meet such a purpose the information provided by Copernicus UrbanAtlas 2018 was used [34].

2.3 Surface Albedo Estimation

Two different algorithms were implemented to retrieve surface albedo: the Silva *et al.* method (2016) [20], developed for Landsat 8 satellite images, and the Bonafoni *et al.* algorithm (2020) [23] specific for Sentinel-2 images.

The Silva *et al.* algorithm is expressed as follows:

$$\alpha_{TOA} = p_2 * r_2 + p_3 * r_3 + p_4 * r_4 + p_5 * r_5 + p_6 * r_6 + p_7 * r_7 \quad (1)$$

where α_{TOA} is the TOA albedo, p_i are the weighting coefficients, which represent the ratio between the solar constant of each OLI band and the sum of all solar constant used in the calculation of albedo, and r_i are the TOA reflectances for Landsat 8 spectral bands. The surface albedo α is retrieved by:

$$\alpha = \frac{(\alpha_{TOA} - \alpha_{ATM})}{\tau_{sw}^2} \quad (2)$$

where α_{ATM} is the atmospheric albedo, which value was set equal to 0.03, and τ_{sw} is the atmospheric transmissivity for shortwave radiation, function of local atmospheric pressure, water in the atmosphere, solar zenith angle and air turbidity coefficient [20, 35].

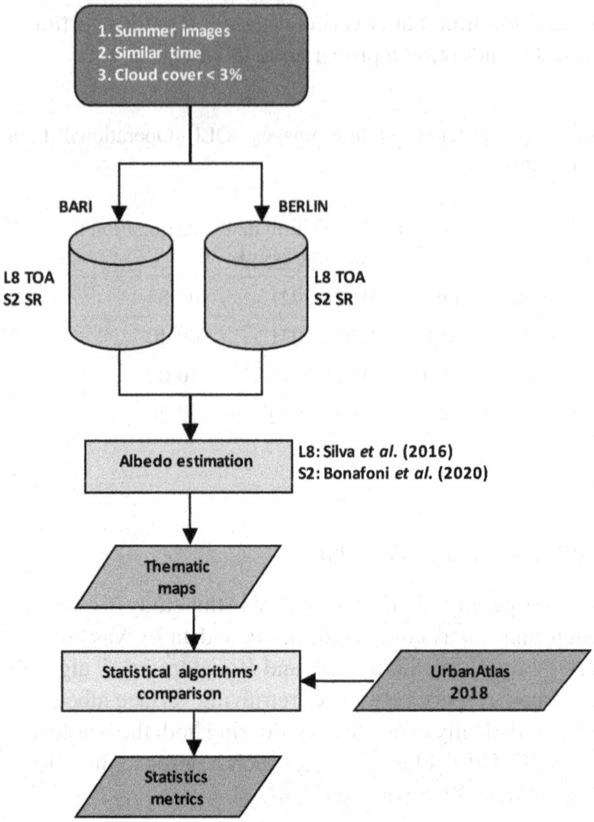

Fig. 3. Operative workflow of satellite data processing. L8: Landsat 8; S2: Sentinel-2.

The easy-to-use Bonafoni *et al.* narrow-to-broadband conversion method is represented by the following equation:

$$\alpha = \omega 2 * \rho 2 + \omega 3 * \rho 3 + \omega 4 * \rho 4 + \omega 8 * \rho 8 + \omega 11 * \rho 11 + \omega 12 * \rho 12 \quad (3)$$

where ω_i are the weighted coefficients, which represent the weight of the portion of the at-surface solar radiation encompassing the range of each MSI spectral band, ρ_i are the surface reflectance for Sentinel-2 bands [23].

A proper JavaScript code was created using GEE platform to retrieve the surface albedo from the selected images with the above-mentioned methods.

2.4 Statistical Comparison of Algorithms' Performances

After obtaining land surface albedo maps from Landsat 8 and Sentinel-2 scenes, a statistical analysis was performed to assess their accuracy and quality. In particular, scatterplots, Mean (μ), Correlation Coefficient (ρ), Standard Deviations (SD) and Root Mean Square Error (RMSE) were calculated.

Moreover, to validate the results, the above-mentioned statistics were extracted for each land cover class, taken from Copernicus Land Monitoring UrbanAtlas 2018, which is a data provided by the Copernicus Program of the European Union, that includes LU/LC categories for many European cities [34].

3 Results and Discussion

Figures 4 and 5 show the land surface albedo maps obtained through the application of the aforementioned algorithms on the selected Landsat 8 and Sentinel-2 satellite images. These maps represent the albedo variability within urban territories of the two investigated sites.

Berlin maps (Fig. 5A and 5B) are darker than those of Bari. This is partly caused by the abundant presence of water bodies in Berlin, which have albedo values close to 0, as well as by other factors such as different LU/LC, climate and latitude. Furthermore, for each study area, the Sentinel-2 map (Fig. 4B for Bari and Fig. 5B for Berlin) result darker than the Landsat 8 map (Fig. 4A for Bari and Fig. 5A for Berlin). Lastly, the albedo map of Bari obtained from Landsat 8 (Fig. 4A) has the highest values.

Figure 6 and Table 2 report the results of the statistical comparison of algorithms' performances, both for Bari and Berlin study areas. In particular, Fig. 6 shows the scatterplots between land surface albedo retrieved by applying the two algorithms, while Table 2 reports the fundamental statistical metrics. The scatterplots show a good correlation among the albedo computed on the same case study with different algorithms. This is evident in Figs. 4 and 5, where it is possible to notice a certain correspondence of albedo trend between Landsat 8 and Sentinel-2 outcomes. Nevertheless, several outliers, in particular in the site of Berlin (Fig. 6B), can be detected due to its greater heterogeneity in LU/LC.

As already highlighted in Fig. 6, a strong correlation between the albedo estimated through the application of the two different algorithms for both sites is outlined in Table 2. Nevertheless, Bari shows the higher ρ, RMSE and μ. These results are also confirmed by the visual inspection of the albedo maps in Figs. 4 and 5 (darker maps for Berlin) and from the boxplots, reported in Fig. 7. This outcome is mainly due to the different climate, that characterizes the two cities, and their diverse latitude. Boxplots highlight outliers in both study areas, probably due to the diverse size and heterogeneity of the investigated territories.

To investigate the results deeply, the main statistical metrics were explored for each LU/LC class. The outcomes of such an analysis are reported in Fig. 8. Figure 9, on the other hand, reports RMSE values, between Landsat 8 and Sentinel-2 albedo products, calculated for each LU/LC class.

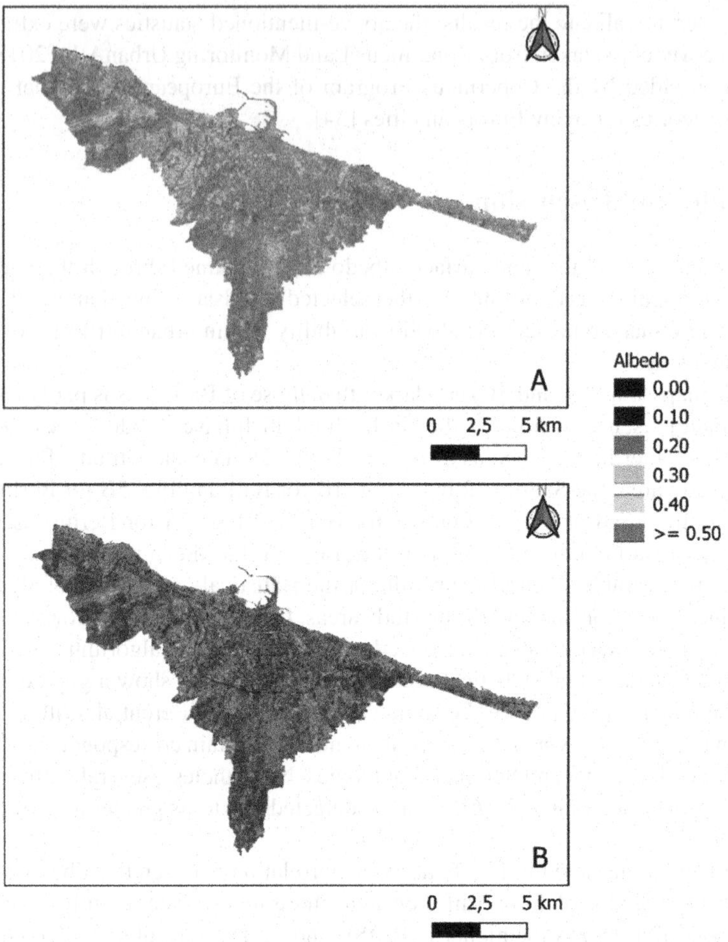

Fig. 4. Land surface albedo maps obtained from L8 Bari (A) and S2 Bari (B) satellite images. L8: Landsat 8; S2: Sentinel-2.

Figure 8 underlines that Silva *et al.* method [20] provides higher albedo values than Bonafoni *et al.* algorithm [23] and that, as expected, Bari has higher values than Berlin for most of the investigated LU/LC classes. Nevertheless, values detected by applying both algorithms are comparable with that one obtained by previous research works. For example, Taha (1997) [36] reported that albedo in urban areas is comprised between 0.10 and 0.20 (0.15 to 0.20 for many US and European cities as 0.20 in Los Angeles and 0.16 in Munich). These values, sometimes, can be exceeded as occurred in the North African cities or Adelaide, in Australia, which values are between 0.30 and 0.45 and equal to 0.27, respectively.

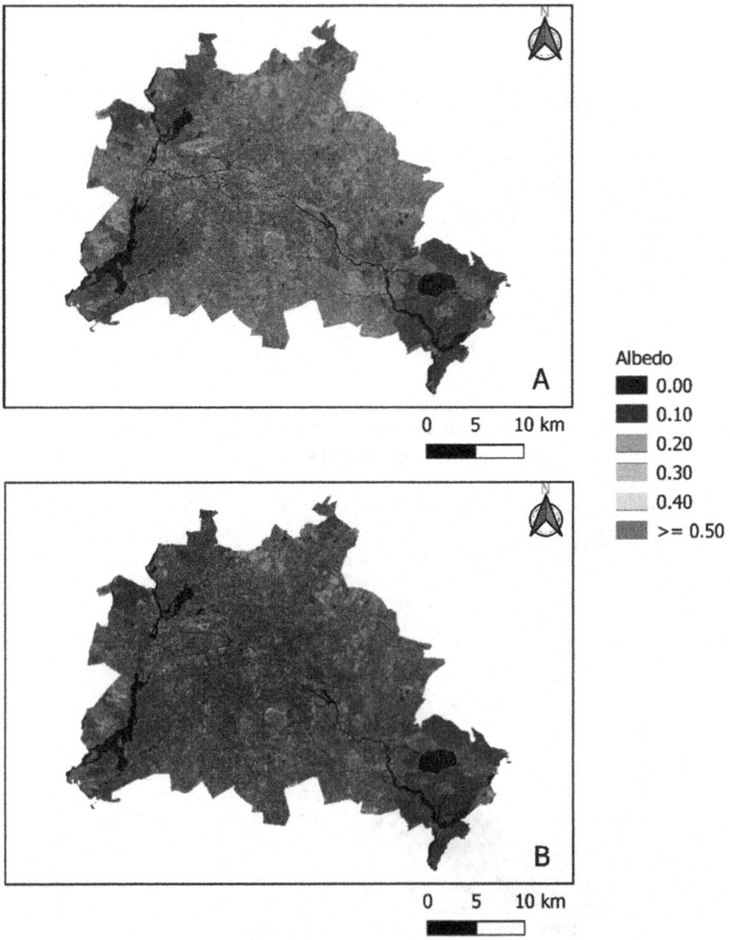

Fig. 5. Land surface albedo maps obtained from L8 Berlin (A) and S2 Berlin (B) satellite images. L8: Landsat 8; S2: Sentinel-2.

Furthermore, Waters *et al.* (2002) [37] reported typical albedo values for various natural or agricultural LU/LC classes. For example, the albedo of coniferous forests is in the range of 0.10–0.15, grass or pastures is between 0.15 and 0.25, agricultural areas, such as corn fields and rice fields, is comprised between 0.14 and 0.22, while the water between 0.025 and 0.348, respectively.

Except for some LU/LC classes, the RMSE trend of L8 and S2 surface albedo is similar for the two study areas (Fig. 9). Just a difference of about 0.02 is, indeed, assessed between Bari and Berlin.

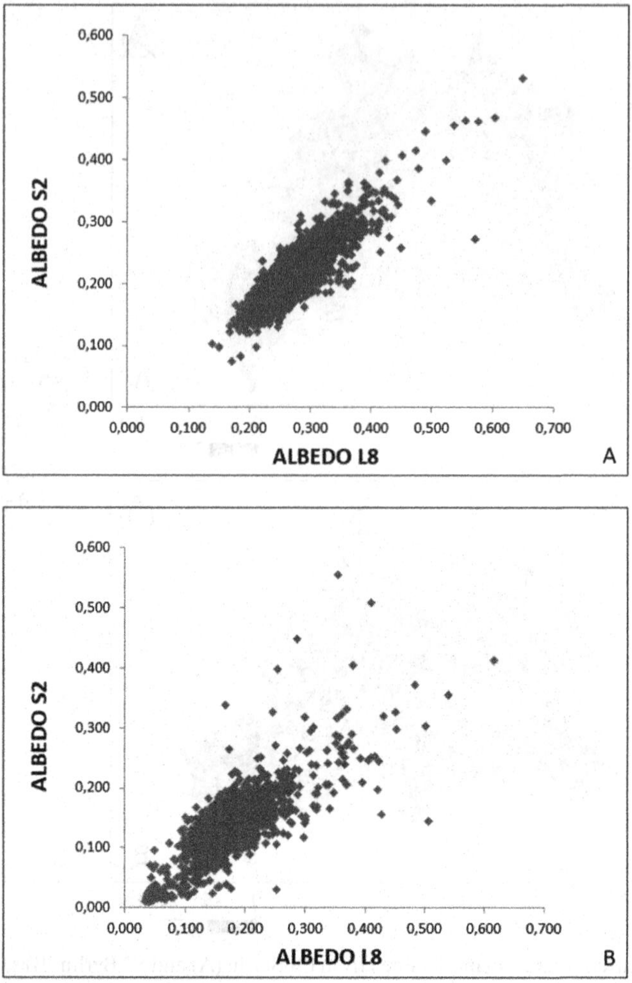

Fig. 6. Scatterplots between the surface albedo retrieved by implementing Silva *et al.* (2016) algorithm for L8 images and Bonafoni *et al.* (2020) method for S2 scenes, for Bari (A) and Berlin (B) study areas, respectively. L8: Landsat 8; S2: Sentinel-2.

Table 2. Main statistics metrics of albedo estimations. L8: Landsat 8; S2: Sentinel-2.

Study area	Images	Mean	SD	ρ	RMSE
Bari	L8	0.256	0.043	0.892	0.057
	S2	0.202	0.037		
Berlin	L8	0.155	0.045	0.805	0.039
	S2	0.127	0.039		

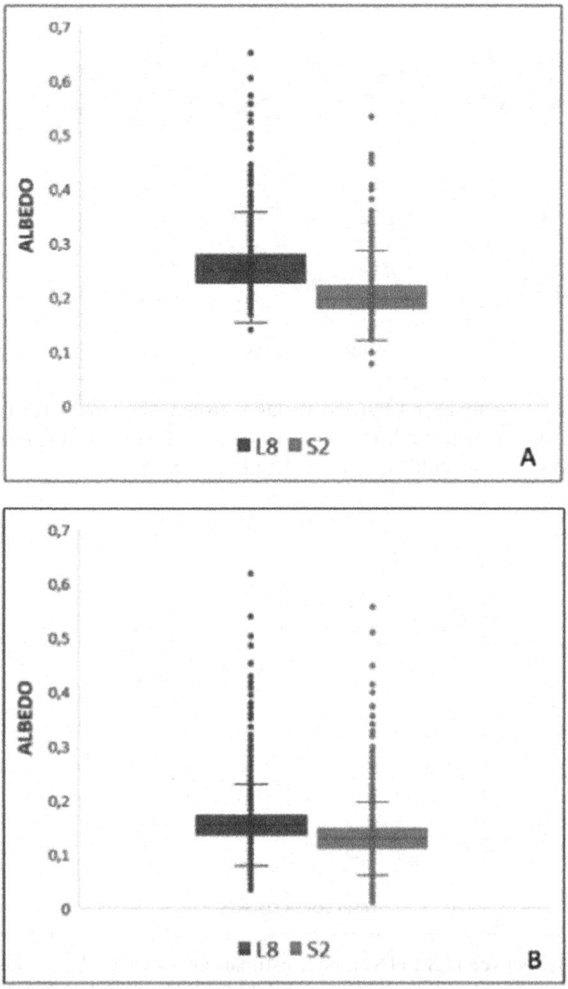

Fig. 7. Boxplots of albedo values in Bari (A) and Berlin (B), respectively. L8: Landsat 8; S2: Sentinel-2.

Conversely, "port areas" show a difference of about 0.04. This outcome is mainly due to the scattering problems of the sea and the different geometric resolution. Also, the classes "construction sites" and "forests" show a higher difference, about 0.05 and 0.04, respectively. Perhaps, this is due to the scarce presence of such LU/LC categories in Bari.

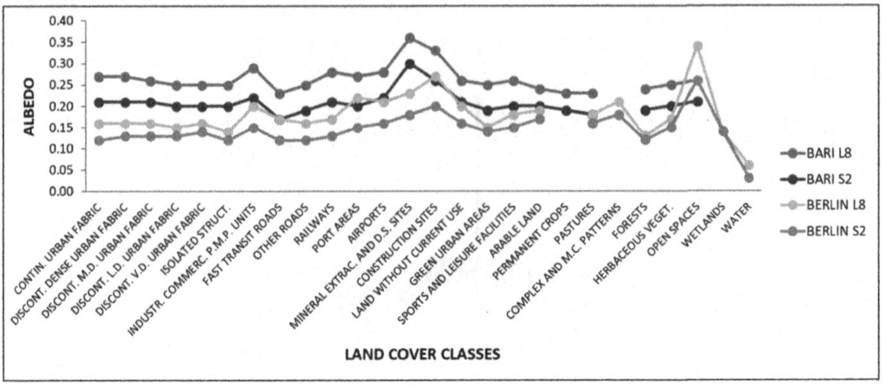

Fig. 8. Mean albedo value for each LU/LC class taken from Copernicus UrbanAtlas 2018. M.D.: medium density; L.D.: low density; V.D.: very low density; P.M.P.: public, military and private; D.S.: dump sites; M.C.: mixed cultivations. L8: Landsat 8; S2: Sentinel-2.

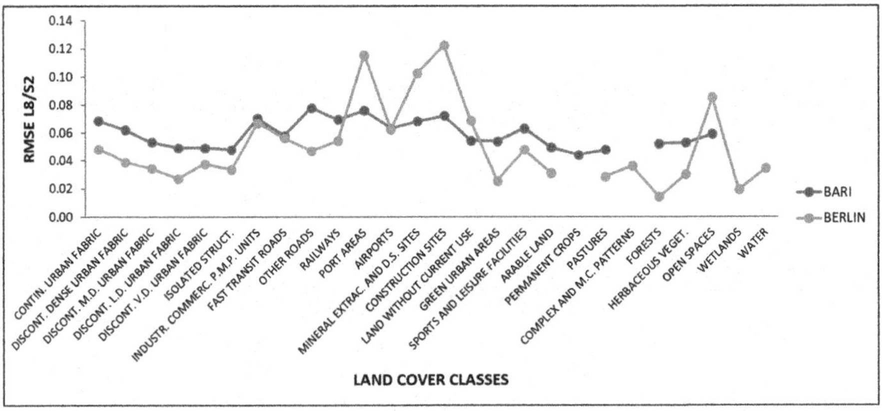

Fig. 9. RMSE values between L8 and S2 albedo estimations for each LU/LC class. M.D.: medium density; L.D.: low density; V.D.: very low density; P.M.P.: public, military and private; D.S.: dump sites; M.C.: mixed cultivations. L8: Landsat 8; S2: Sentinel-2.

4 Conclusion

The objective of this paper is to estimate land surface albedo using two different satellite datasets and to explore their potentialities over two study areas, the cities of Bari and Berlin, respectively. Such sites were selected because of their great diversity in terms of climatic and geo-morphological features. This gives the possibility to test algorithms performances in a diverse urban context. Indeed, this research contributes also to investigating LU/LC impact on albedo changes. Because of natural areas replacement with impervious material, the urbanization process influences urban climate, as well as land surface energy balance [5, 26, 38–41]. Therefore, investigating the albedo trend in urban areas may improve the knowledge of UHI phenomenon and identify the optimal strategy to face it [6, 9]. To achieve such a goal, two algorithms, the Silva *et al.* (2016) [20], specific for Landsat 8 data, and the Bonafoni *et al.* (2020) [23] for Sentinel-2 images, were implemented. Their outcomes were satisfying results in terms of correlation, SD and RMSE albeit Landsat 8 algorithm provided higher mean values, for both study sites, than Sentinel-2 algorithm.

To implement the processing procedure, a proper JavaScript code was developed in GEE environment. It was preferred to desktop software because of its many advantages in comparison to desktop software, such as the capability to i) customize codes to meet users needs, ii) implement complex algorithms, and, lastly, iii) minimize acquisition and operational times [42]. At the same time, it also has some disadvantages such as the need to export maps, which have to be imported into another software like QGIS in order to improve the visualization of the results. Nevertheless, GEE can be recognized as the optimal tool for investigating satellite geospatial big data because of the benefits above mentioned.

Lastly, this paper introduces additional innovative elements in comparison to previous studies. Indeed:

1. potentialities of Landsat 8 and Sentinel-2 data were explored and compared;
2. algorithms performance was assessed by comparing their results both visually and statistically considering the whole case study and each LU/LC class.

References

1. Liu, Q., Wen, J., Qu, Y., He, T., Zhang, X., Wang, L.: Broadband albedo. In: Liang, S., Li, X., Wang, J. (eds.) Advanced Remote Sensing: Terrestrial Information Extraction and Applications, 1st edn, pp. 173–231. Academic Press, Cambridge (2012)
2. Capolupo, A., Monterisi, C., Barletta, C., Tarantino, E.: Google earth engine for land surface albedo estimation: comparison among different algorithms. In: Proceedings of SPIE 11856, Remote Sensing for Agriculture, Ecosystems, and Hydrology XXIII, p. 118560F. International Society for Optics and Photonics (2021)
3. Essential Climate Variables. https://gcos.wmo.int/en/essential-climate-variables. Accessed 28 Nov 2021
4. Voogt, J.A., Oke, T.R.: Thermal remote sensing of urban climates. Remote Sens. Environ. **86**(3), 370–384 (2003)
5. The Urban Heat Island (UHI) Effect. https://www.urbanheatislands.com/. Accessed 13 Dec 2021
6. Sangiorgio, V., Capolupo, A., Tarantino, E., Fiorito, F., Santamouris, M.: Evaluation of absolute maximum urban heat island intensity based on a simplified remote sensing approach. Environ. Eng. Sci. **39**(3), 296–307 (2022)
7. Capolupo, A., Monterisi, C., Saponaro, M., Tarantino, E.: Multi-temporal analysis of land cover changes using Landsat data through google earth engine platform. In: Proceedings of SPIE 11524, Eighth International Conference on Remote Sensing and Geoinformation of the Environment (RSCy2020), pp. 1152419. International Society for Optics and Photonics (2020)
8. Capolupo, A., Boccia, L.: Innovative method for linking anthropisation process to vulnerability. World Rev. Sci. Technol. Sustain. Dev. **17**(1), 4–22 (2021)

9. Trlica, A., Hutyra, L.R., Schaaf, C.L., Erb, A., Wang, J.A.: Albedo, land cover, and daytime surface temperature variation across an urbanized landscape. Earth's Future **5**, 1084–1101 (2017)
10. Lama, G.F.C., Sadeghifar, T., Azad, M.T., Sihag, P., Kisi, O.: On the indirect estimation of wind wave heights over the Southern Coast of Caspian sea: a comparative analysis. Water **14**(6), 843 (2022)
11. Lama, G.F.C., Crimaldi, M.: Remote sensing of ecohydrological, ecohydraulic, and ecohydrodynamic phenomena in vegetated waterways: the role of leaf area index (LAI). Biol. Life Sci. Forum **3**(1), 54 (2021)
12. Sadeghifar, T., Lama, G.F.C., Sihag, P., Bayram, A., Kisi, O.: Wave height predictions in complex sea flows through soft-computing models: case study of Persian Gulf. Ocean Eng. **245**, 110467 (2022)
13. Esposito, M., Crimaldi, M., Cirillo, V., Sarghini, F., Maggio, A.: Drone and sensor technology for sustainable weed management: a review. Chem. Biol. Technol. Agric. **8**(1), 1–11 (2021). https://doi.org/10.1186/s40538-021-00217-8
14. Capolupo, A., Monterisi, C., Sonnessa, A., Caporusso, G., Tarantino, E.: Modeling land cover impact on albedo changes in google earth engine environment. In: Gervasi, O., et al. (eds.) ICCSA 2021. LNCS, vol. 12955, pp. 89–101. Springer, Cham (2021). https://doi.org/10.1007/978-3-030-87007-2_7
15. Liang, S.: Narrowband to broadband conversions of land surface albedo I algorithms. Remote Sens. Environ. **76**, 210–238 (2000)
16. Tarantino, E.: Monitoring spatial and temporal distribution of sea surface temperature with TIR sensor data. Italian J. Remote Sens. **44**(1), 97–107 (2012)
17. Caprioli, M., Tarantino, E.: Identification of land cover alterations in the Alta Murgia National Park (Italy) with VHR satellite imagery. Int. J. Sustain. Dev. Plan. **1**(3), 261–270 (2006)
18. Capolupo, A., Saponaro, M., Fratino, U., Tarantino, E.: Detection of spatio-temporal changes of vegetation in coastal areas subjected to soil erosion issue. Aquat. Ecosyst. Health Manag. **23**(4), 491–499 (2020)
19. Sarzana, T., Maltese, A., Capolupo, A., Tarantino, E.: Post-processing of pixel and object-based land cover classifications of very high spatial resolution images. In: Gervasi, O., et al. (eds.) ICCSA 2020. LNCS, vol. 12252, pp. 797–812. Springer, Cham (2020). https://doi.org/10.1007/978-3-030-58811-3_57
20. da Silva, B.B., Braga, A.C., Braga, C.C., de Oliveira, L.M.M., Montenegro, S.M.G.L., Barbosa, J.B.: Procedures for calculation of the Albedo with OLI-Landsat 8 images: application to the Brazilian semi-arid. Revista Brasileira de Engenharia Agrícola e Ambiental **20**, 3–8 (2016)
21. Varghese, D., Radulović, M., Stojković, S., Crnojević, V.: Reviewing the potential of Sentinel-2 in assessing the drought. Remote Sens. **13**(17), 3355 (2021)
22. Vanino, S., et al.: Capability of Sentinel-2 data for estimating maximum evapotranspiration and irrigation requirements for tomato crop in Central Italy. Remote Sens. Environ. **215**, 452–470 (2018)
23. Bonafoni, S., Sekertekin, A.: Albedo retrieval from Sentinel-2 by new narrow-to-broadband conversion coefficient. IEEE Geosci. Remote Sens. Lett. **17**(9), 1618–1622 (2020)
24. Hird, J.N., DeLancey, E.R., McDermid, G.J., Kariyeva, J.: Google earth engine, open-access satellite data, and machine learning in support of large-area probabilistic wetland mapping. Remote Sensing **9**(12), 1315 (2017)
25. Gorelick, N., Hancher, M., Dixon, M., Ilyushchenko, S., Thau, D., Moore, R.: Google earth engine: planetary-scale geospatial analysis for everyone. Remote Sens. Environ. **202**, 18–27 (2017)
26. Martinelli, A., Kolokotsa, D.-D., Fiorito, F.: Urban heat island in Mediterranean coastal cities: the case of Bari (Italy). Climate **8**(6), 79 (2020)

27. Leone, A., Gobattoni, F., Pelorosso, R., Calace, F.: Nature-based climate adaptation for compact cities: green courtyards as urban cool islands. Plurimondi **18**, 83–110 (2020)
28. Peschechera, G., Tarantino, E., Fratino, U.: Crop water requirements estimation at irrigation district scale from remote sensing: a comparison between MODIS ET product and the analytical approach. In: Proceedings of SPIE 10773, Sixth International Conference on Remote Sensing and Geoinformation of the Environment (RSCy2018), p. 1077318. International Society for Optics and Photonics (2018)
29. Tarantino, E., Novelli, A., Aquilino, M., Figorito, B., Fratino, U.: Comparing the MLC and JavaNNS approaches in classifying multi-temporal LANDSAT satellite imagery over an ephemeral river area. Int. J. Agric. Environ. Inf. Syst. (IJAEIS) **6**(4), 83–102 (2015)
30. Vulova, S., Meier, F., Fenner, D., Nouri, H., Kleinschmit, B.: Summer nights in Berlin, Germany: modeling air temperature spatially with remote sensing, crowdsourced weather data, and machine learning. IEEE J. Sel. Top. Appl. Earth Observ. Remote Sens. **13**, 5074–5087 (2020)
31. Dugord, P.-A., Lauf, S., Schuster, C., Kleinschmit, B.: Land use patterns, temperature distribution, and potential heat stress risk – the case study Berlin, Germany. Comput. Environ. Urban Syst. **48**, 86–98 (2014)
32. Kühn, M., Gailing, L.: From green belts to regional parks: history and challenges of suburban landscape planning in Berlin. In: Amati, M. (ed.) Urban Green Belts in the Twenty-first Century, Chapter 10, pp. 185–202. Ashgate (2008)
33. Li, H., et al.: A new method to quantify surface urban heat island intensity. Sci. Tot. Environ. **624**, 262–272 (2018)
34. Urban Atlas 2018. https://land.copernicus.eu/local/urban-atlas/urban-atlas-2018. Accessed 26 Feb 2022
35. Allen, R.G., Tasumi, M., Trezza, R.: Satellite-based energy balance for mapping evapotranspiration with internalized calibration (METRIC) – model. J. Irrig. Drain. Eng. **133**(4), 380–394 (2007)
36. Taha, H.: Urban climates and heat islands: albedo, evapotranspiration, and anthropogenic heat. Energy Build. **25**, 99–103 (1997)
37. Waters, R., Allen, R., Tasumi, M., Trezza, R., Bastiaanssen, W.: SEBAL (surface energy balance algorithms for land). Idaho implementation. In: Advanced Training and Users Manual. Version 1.0 (2002)
38. Lai, S., Leone, F., Zoppi, C.: Spatial distribution of surface temperature and land cover: a study concerning Sardinia, Italy. In: Gervasi, O., et al. (eds.) ICCSA 2020. LNCS, vol. 12253, pp. 405–420. Springer, Cham (2020). https://doi.org/10.1007/978-3-030-58814-4_29
39. Crocetto, N., Tarantino, E.: A class-oriented strategy for features extraction from multidate ASTER imagery. Remote Sens. **1**(4), 1171–1189 (2009)
40. Novelli, A., Tarantino, E., Caradonna, G., Apollonio, C., Balacco, G., Piccinni, F.: Improving the ANN classification accuracy of Landsat data through spectral indices and linear transformations (PCA and TCT) aimed at LU/LC monitoring of a River Basin. In: Gervasi, O., et al. (eds.) ICCSA 2016. LNCS, vol. 9787, pp. 420–432. Springer, Cham (2016). https://doi.org/10.1007/978-3-319-42108-7_32
41. Boccia, L., Capolupo, A., Rigillo, M., Russo, V.: Terrace abandonment hazards in a Mediterranean cultural landscape. J. Hazardous Toxic Radioactive Waste 24(1) (2020)
42. Capolupo, A., Monterisi, C., Caporusso, G., Tarantino, E.: Extracting land cover data using GEE: a review of the classification indices. In: Gervasi, O., et al. (eds.) ICCSA 2020. LNCS, vol. 12252, pp. 782–796. Springer, Cham (2020). https://doi.org/10.1007/978-3-030-58811-3_56

3D Surface Reconstruction and Change Detection of Miage Glacier (Italy) from Multi-date Archive Aerial Photos

Arsalan Malekian[1(✉)], Davide Fugazza[2], and Marco Scaioni[3]

[1] Politecnico di Milano, Lecco Campus, via G. Previati 1/c, 23900 Lecco, Italy
arsalan.malekian@mail.polimi.it

[2] Department of Environmental Science and Policy, Università Degli Studi di Milano, Via Celoria 2, Milan, Italy
davide.fugazza@unimi.it

[3] Department of Architecture, Built Environment and Construction Engineering, Politecnico di Milano, via Ponzio 31, 20133 Milan, Italy
marco.scaioni@polimi.it

Abstract. Historical aerial images provide valuable information for monitoring and change detection in different areas such as glaciers. Using aerial images, 3D models can be created and the geometry of the glaciers can be digitized manually to analyse their surface extent and evolution. Here, we use archive images to reconstruct 3D models of Miage glacier in the Val Veny region, Mont Blanc, Italy. First, the features of each dataset photos are inspected, and they are pre-processed to be used in the 3D reconstruction phase. This pre-processing is conducted to not only minimize the dataset's problems, including shadows covering the glaciers and insufficient image overlapping over crucial places, but also to generate the best achievable dense 3D point clouds from each dataset. Point clouds of reconstructed 3D models may be used to detect variations in the Val Veny region and determine the rate of retreat and height differences for each glacier in the area over time. This could be done by computation of distances between points in cloud pairs in consecutive years. In this phase, no manual shifting and translating of point clouds are required as they were georeferenced in the 3D reconstruction phase and automatically co-registered with Iterative Closest Point algorithm. Miage glacier in the Val Veny area was chosen to be assessed considering the quality of generated point cloud during the 3D reconstruction phase. The results of the comparisons indicate how the Miage glacier volume has varied throughout time. While volume changes of the evaluated glacier were almost negligible until the mid-1990s, investigations demonstrate a significant rise in volume decrease at the beginning of 21st century.

Keywords: 3D reconstruction · Photogrammetry · Change detection · Glacier monitoring · Archive aerial images

O. Gervasi et al. (Eds.): ICCSA 2022 Workshops, LNCS 13379, pp. 450–465, 2022.
https://doi.org/10.1007/978-3-031-10545-6_31

1 Introduction

People and economic infrastructure in mountain areas are at risk as a result of natural processes related to the melting of glacier ice. Glacier avalanches, landslides, and slope instability produced by debuttressing, as well as catastrophic outburst floods from moraine-dammed lakes and outburst floods from glacier-dammed lakes, are examples of these phenomena [17]. The threat of cryospheric hazards as a consequence of climate change necessitates the implementation of preventive techniques [25]. Remote sensing is regarded as a valuable method for generating supporting data, such as Digital Elevation Models (DEM) and multispectral images. DEMs are especially effective for detecting glacier thickness and volume changes, as well as identifying steep places that are more susceptible to geomorphodynamic changes, such as mass movements [12].

Archive aerial photos, in particular, are one of the oldest data sources for glacier monitoring. Indeed, they are extremely useful for glacier observation in terms of extension, length, volume, and mass change [9]. In general, these archives consist of historical aerial photos collected for local topographic mapping projects based on photogrammetric techniques. In glaciological studies, they may be used to create geometrically precise 3D models of glaciers by using cutting-edge digital photogrammetric methods, such as Structure-from-Motion (SfM) and Multi-View Stereo (MVS) dense matching [13].

The majority of historical photos in the archives were captured by using analogue film cameras and then transferred onto digital images by photogrammetric scanners. Only in the two last decades, Digital Airborne Cameras (DAC) started to take over analogue cameras in order to directly record digital aerial imagery. Today the almost complete production in the photogrammetric market relies on the use of DACs.

Historic aerial photos were already used in the past to calculate comprehensive elevation and volume analyses. Sixteen Antarctic glaciers were analysed by using aerial photos since 1950s [10]. Between 1959 and 1990, DEMs and orthophotos were created for a glacier in Sweden based on consistent photogrammetric processing of aerial images [20]. Also, a dataset including scans of 300 (analogue) aerial images that were obtained between August and October of 1954 by the U.S. Air Force over the province of Trento was used for 3D modelling of glaciers and change analysis. The comparison between the 3D models of 1954 and 2015 showed changes up to 70–80 m in the height of glaciers in the region [24].

This paper investigates how historical aerial photos may be used to derive 3D models of Alpine glaciers, to be compared between different times in order to detect morphological and volumetric changes. The area of Val Veny in Aosta Valley (Northern Italy) is assumed as case study (see Sect. 2). Here some important glaciers are located, with the Miage Glacier being the largest one. Section 3 presents the adopted archive aerial photos that derive from the online repository of the National Geographic and Forestry Institute of France (IGNF). Sections 4 and 5 describe the methods applied for the photogrammetric 3D reconstruction and for comparing multi-temporal point clouds of glaciers, respectively. Results are shown and discussed in Sect. 6, while Sect. 7 draws some conclusions and addresses future work.

2 Study Area

This work is mainly focused on the evaluation of glacier changes in Val Veny area (see Fig. 1), which is located the Aosta Valley, a high elevation and relatively small administrative region in the Italian Western Alps (3,262 km^2). The Aosta Valley has the largest glacier coverage of any area in Italy, based on the latest Italian Glacier Classification [28]. There are 192 glaciers in the Aosta Valley Region with a total area of 133.7 km^2, accounting for 36 percent of the Italian glacier area (data from 2005–2011). The glaciers range in altitude from roughly 1400 to 4800 m a.s.l. [29].

Val Veny is a lateral valley of the Mont Blanc massif located west of Courmayeur town. This mountain valley is split into three sections: the section that runs parallel to the Mont Blanc massif between the Seigne pass (2,512 m a.s.l.) and part of the Miage Glacier, the middle part that is called Plan Vény, and the valley's entrance (1,444 m a.s.l.), which is surrounded by Mont Blanc and the lower Brenva Glacier [29]. The existence of significant geological components and varied outcropping lithologies, which are molded by glacial activity and result in a diverse geological environment, is an important aspect of this small region [13].

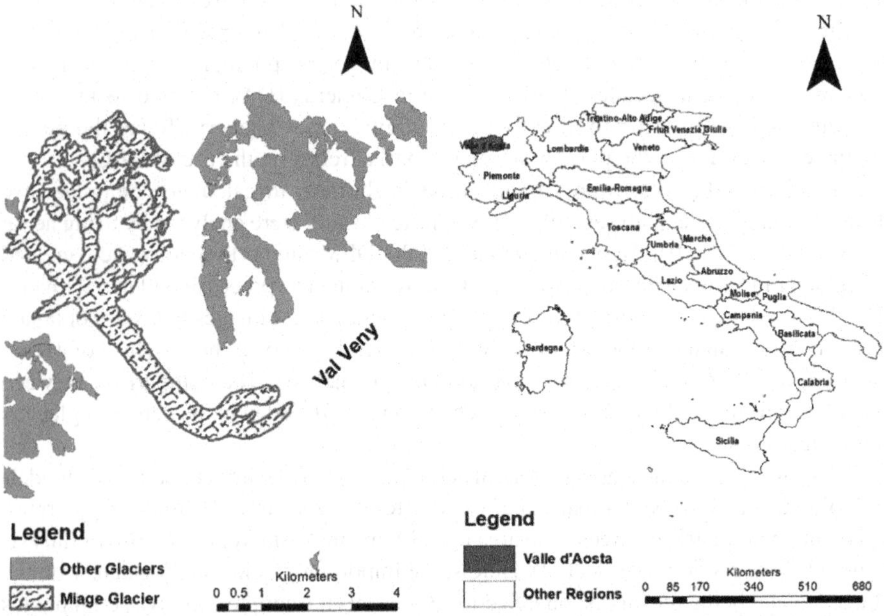

Fig. 1. Location of Aosta Valley in Italy and of Miage glacier among other glaciers of the region.

Miage Glacier are one of the primary glaciers in this area. It is the longest glacier in Italy and the largest debris-covered glacier in Europe, measuring roughly 10 km in length [7]. Debris covers approximately 5 km^2 out of its 11 km^2 total area, mostly from rockfall from neighbouring flanks and avalanching in deposition regions of its four tributaries [21]. Due to the quick thinning of the glacier tongue, debris transported along within the glacier is also being exposed at an accelerated pace. The variety of supraglacial debris sources, as well as the peculiar mica schist-dominated lithology of the rock walls surrounding the glacier, results in a diverse debris lithology. The debris cover becomes continuous below 2,400 m a.s.l. and continues intact until the terminus. Crevasses or moulins, on the other hand, may cause inconsistent areas [26]. Although the spatial distribution of thicknesses is uneven, especially on sections of the northern terminal lobe, debris thickness usually increases between a few centimetres at 2,400 m a.s.l. to over 1 m at the terminus at 1,775 m a.s.l. [27].

Because of several key features, the Miage Glacier is the best example of a 'Himalayan Glacier of the Alps,' including its accumulation zone, steep cliffs characterised by avalanches, avalanches that indirectly feed the glacier, a notable difference in altitude between the accumulation area and the terminus, and variations in ice thickness in the frontal area [25].

3 Photogrammetric Data Description

The archive aerial photos used in this research over the Val Veny were obtained from multiple aerial missions operated from1967 to 2006. Images are provided in digital form through the WEB portal of the National Geographic and Forestry Institute of France (IGNF - *Institut National de l'Information Géographique et Forestière*). All datasets include a calibration certificate containing information on the camera and lens used (see Kraus 2008). Image orientation parameters computed after aerial triangulation or recorded by onboard GNSS/INS (Global Navigation Satellite System-Aided Inertial Navigation System) sensors are not generally provided, while mission information is generally limited to the average flight height, acquisition scale, and side overlap. Most missions were flown using analogue film cameras of different types, but all equipped with standard focal lens (150 mm) and film format (23 cm × 23 cm). Analogue panchromatic or colour photos were then transformed into digital using photogrammetric scanners. The selected pixel size was around 20 μm. Data sets collected in the last two decades (such as the one in 2006) were directly captured using a *frame* digital airborne camera (Table 1).

In all datasets, the variation of flying altitude is between 4.7 and 6.35 km, with photos from the 2001 dataset featuring the lowest flying height and the ones from 1967 showing the highest flying altitude, respectively. The coverage area of the photos from 1996 to 2001 is between 300 and 345 km^2, whereas the data from 1967, 1979, and 2006 cover an area of 132 to 173 km^2. Coordinates of camera perspective centres recorded by onboard GNSS are only provided for three datasets: 1996, 2000 and 2001. All of the photographs were acquired during the warmer months, from June to September, with the exception of the 1967 photos, which were taken in October.

The image quality was evaluated by taking into consideration some factors. Firstly, the aerial photographs completely encompass the Val Veny, particularly the glaciers. In flat, hilly, and mountainous locations, the ground coverage is acceptable for aerial triangulation and orthophoto generation. Secondly, the analogue photos were transformed into digital data after scanning, which degraded the image quality even further. [1]. The presence of steep terrain that characterize the mountains around Val Veny resulted in dark shadows on the photos (Fig. 2). Shadows frequently look as uniform black surfaces due to limited dynamic range [3]. Snow may also be a concern since it may smooth out the original terrain topography and create problems for image matching algorithms used for image orientation ad 3D surface reconstruction [31].

The information impressed on the lateral borders of each photograph is useful for a variety of objectives. The date and time of each set of images helps to better understand the dynamics of the glaciers by identifying the mean temperature in that region. The GNSS camera location could be used as approximation to help automatic image orientation [6], as described in the following section.

Table 1. Properties of dataset over Val Veny area from 1967 to 2006 downloaded from IGNF online repository.

Year	Date	No. images	Camera coordinate	Camera model	Flying Altitude [km]	Coverage area [km^2]
2006	Aug 23rd to Sep 5th	78	Not available	Digital	5.54	173
2001	Aug 1st to 13th	73	Available	RMKTOP15	4.78	345
2000	Jun 23rd to Aug 1st	25	Available	RMKTOP15	5.54	310
1996	Jul 3rd to Aug 4th	35	Available	RMKTOP15	5.02	301
1988	Jul 26th	23	Not available	RC10	6.15	321
1979	Sep 5th	19	Not available	RC10	5.7	144
1967	Oct 11th & 12th	24	Not available	RC10	6.35	132

Fig. 2. Example of dark shadows on glaciers near vertical surfaces in 1996 image.

4 3D Model Reconstruction

The purpose of this work is to apply the described methodologies to reconstruct a 3D model from aerial historical photos over a 40-year period covering the Val Veny region. The photogrammetric procedure to reach this aim is presented in the following paragraphs.

4.1 Image Pre-processing

For categorization and editing, the images were loaded into Adobe Photoshop Lightroom Classic 9.4 release®. Lightroom is a professional-grade program for managing photography catalogues that is both affordable and user-friendly, in addition to having efficient processing algorithms [24]. The radiometric image balancing and adjustment was used in this investigation to mitigate differences in different photos due to different lighting conditions and presence of shadows. In all datasets the clarity and contrast are adjusted according to properties of the images. This procedure increases the capability of Structure-from-Motion and Multi-View Stereo matching techniques adopted for image orientation and dense point cloud generation [15].

4.2 Image Orientation

In this work 3D point cloud reconstruction has been performed by using a standard SfM and MVS approach, as implemented in the popular software package Agisoft Metashape® (www.agisoft.com). Agisoft Metashape® is a stand-alone software package that perform photogrammetric processing on digital photos and provides 3D spatial data for use in different applications. Here, “Professional” version 1.7.5 of the software has been used.

The *image orientation* (“Alignment” in the software jargoon) is the initial phase in the process. During this phase, Images are sought for corresponding *keypoints* that are matched across images to create manifold *tie points* [11]. The availability of approximate values for camera stations (e.g., from onboard GNSS observations) may help speed up this process and limit the number of blunders. In the case these approximations are not provided, the image orientation process is applied first on sub-sampled low-resolution images, and then iteratively transferred to the ones at full resolution.

Tie points are then fed into a *bundle block adjustment* (BBA) internal module, which at the same time computes camera calibration parameters (including Inner Orientation and Additional Parameters for lens distortion compensation), Exterior Orientation (EO) parameters, and 3D coordinates of tie points. The latest ones are used to generate the “sparse point cloud” [8], that is then used to drive the successive dense matching phase [17]. Due to multiple overlapping of images, this step additionally assessed camera calibration and EO quality thanks to the data redundancy in the BBA. Prior to the more computationally intensive generation of dense point clouds, the user can assess precision and recognize problematic tie points using the sparse point cloud. The BBA solution was referred to an arbitrary reference system, since so far no ground constraints were included (e.g., ground control points).

4.3 Georeferencing

In order the define the coordinates of the output 3D point clouds in a mapping grid, some ground control points (GCPs) were needed. Unfortunately, GCPs were not measured in the archive photos from IGNF. To overcome the problem of georeferencing, natural features have been selected to serve as GCPs in stable areas over time and across all datasets, and their coordinates determined using accessible satellite data from Google Earth®. Even though in some regions of the area of interest the location of GCPs has been difficult if not impossible, GCPs have been selected to be well distributed in each photogrammetric block, avoiding weak configurations such as GCPs concentrated around the same line [25]. Typical stable objects within time are buildings and houses, that unfortunately are available only in villages and in the bottom part of the valley. Much more challenging has been to find stable parts in the upper parts of glaciers. The spots chosen to be GCPs are the same in all datasets, and 12 GCPs are considered in each dataset based on their availability.

Once a set of GCPs has been selected, a new BBA including their observations in the images has been run. Due to the low quality of measured GCPs, corresponding ground coordinated have been properly weighted not to result in deformation in the EO and, consequently, on the output point clouds.

4.4 Assessment of Exterior Orientation and Georeferencing

The residuals of the GCPs are provided by BBA, which indicate the difference between measured coordinates and newly calculated values. Errors in the photogrammetric network of observations are indicated by relatively large residual values. Large residuals in

GCPs were modified or deleted until an optimal solution has been found. The nature of these errors may be due to two different aspects: errors in the measurement of 3D coordinates of GCPs from satellite observations, or in the measurement of their 2D coordinates in the images.

Nevertheless, removing too many GCPs might reduce the photogrammetric model validity, especially if numerous parameters were to be estimated.

4.5 Dense Cloud Generation

Agisoft Metashape® software can create a dense point cloud based on the computed EOs and the photos themselves based on dense Multi-View Stereo (MVS) matching. The first step in the MVS process is the computation of *depth maps* on the basis of image disparities in normalized image pairs. In a second step, *depth maps* are used to generate a dense point cloud [18]. Multiple pairwise *depth maps* created for every camera are integrated into a combined *depth map*, with extra information in overlapping locations used to filter out incorrect depth measurements [14]. The camera's combined *depth maps* are turned out into partial dense point clouds, which are then blended into a final dense point cloud with further noise filtering done in overlapping locations. Subsequently, the dense cloud was modified to eliminate points that were not on continuous surfaces, such as supraglacial lakes, as well as visible outliers.

All procedures were carried out in a "high-quality" setting in Metashape®, which has been retained as the best compromise between the obtainable quality and the processing time.

5 Point-Cloud Analysis

Photogrammetric point clouds obtained from the archive aerial photos are utilized to compute the variations in glacier thickness between different epochs. In this paper we focus on the evolution of the Miage Glacier in the period from 1967 to 2006.

In order to compare point clouds, the open-source software package CloudCompare (www.cloudcompare.org) has been used. Prior to analysing cloud pairs, some pre-processing steps have been applied to improve data quality in different data sets. The first step is to eliminate all outliers and noisy points from each point cloud. One approach to generate a clean point cloud with a homogenous surface density, is to extract the related components using a 3D grid which is called Label Connected Component [30]. Another technique is S.O.R Filter/Noise Filter. These methods are fairly similar between them since they both eliminate points that are over a specific distance from the plane fitting a particular number of neighbours for each point (kNN) [12]. As a result, Label Connected Component is applied to each point cloud to remove outliers that are separated from the point cloud by a substantial distance, and S.O.R or Noise filter are applied if there are more noises near the surface of the point clouds.

Because each point cloud has been independently georeferenced in the national geodetic datum (RDN 2008.0/UTM32N), but this operation resulted in some residuals due to non-homogenous errors, a refinement of the co- registration between each pair of point clouds to compare has been applied in CloudCompare. Due to the vastness of the area of interest, different approaches for co-registration have been examined. Indeed, point clouds to compare feature some unstable areas where changes occurred: these regions should not be considered to select control points for co-registration. Consequently, some stable areas have been selected and point clouds segmented to extract subsets there. The ICP (Iterative Closest Points – see Pomerleau et al. 2013 [25]) method for point cloud co-registration as implemented in CloudCompare has been applied. After a preliminary initial co-registration, that in this case was obtained from the use of GCPs in photogrammetric processing, the ICP techniques computes the rigid-body transformation which minimizes the distances between points in both point clouds to co-register. Here this process has been limited to the stable areas. Then the transformation parameters computed in this way have been applied to the remaining parts of both point clouds. Stationary regions in the model have been investigated to check out the quality of co-registration. To this purpose, the ICP distance between both clouds has been calculated in those regions.

After co-registration refinement, the M3C2 (*Multi-scale Model to Model*) technique has been applied to detect changes. M3C2 is well-suited to assessing statistically significant changes between point clouds where the geometry varies in three dimensions, and it is resistant to changes in point density and point cloud noise [20]. For example, in some studies where this method was used for estimating geomorphologic variations in channel sedimentation, M3C2 emerged as the most reliable method for highlighting erosion and deposition rates from point cloud comparisons, due to the fact that this procedure does not use interpolation, which might cause errors, particularly for complex landforms [17]. Therefore, M3C2 is considered as main method for comparison of data sets in this research.

5.1 Volume Computation

For the evaluation of volume change of glaciers between two epochs when photogrammetric point clouds were derived, CloudCompare implements a specific function to this purpose. This function derives the volume between two point clouds after selecting a reference plane, to be used for deriving 2.5D raster Digital Elevation Models (DEMs)[26]. The volume is derived from the computation of the DOD (DEM of Differences) between both DEMs to compare. Then the DOD is used to derive the volume by using the area of the grid step. The smaller the size of each elementary cell, the more accurate the computed volume. On the other hand, the grid step should be coherent with the density of the point cloud [4]. The percentage of average neighbours in each cell should be considered. It should be kept close to 8, or gaps would emerge between the cells, resulting in an incorrect volume estimation.

The percentage of cells in a DEM that have a matching cell in the second DEM shows how completely both point clouds overlap. Step size of generated grid should be optimized to make "Average neighbours per cell" as close as possible to 8. In all the comparison cases, the step value is optimized between 3 and 5 to obtain a value of 7.9 for the "Average neighbours per cell". Due to importance of height difference in these comparisons, the projection direction for the volume calculation is considered to be the Z direction and the height of each cell is considered to be the average of the points inside the cell.

6 Result and Analysis

The approach described in Sect. 5 has been applied to process all datasets. For datasets including images from multiple cameras, a pre-calibration procedure is used before applying SfM/MVS algorithms in Agisoft Metashape®. With the exception of data from 1967, all data sets downloaded from the IGNF geoportal were provided with pixel size and focal length information. In addition, for image sets containing camera position GNSS coordinates, the SfM has been computed by using these data as starting camera locations. This resulted in reducing the time for computing the EO at the full image resolution (options: "high-quality" alignment precision and exclusion of stationary tie points). After the alignment process, the error of chosen GCPs is obtained for each dataset (Table 2). GCPs are chosen in a way that they have at least two projections on the images and are spread out as much as feasible throughout the whole region, avoiding weak configurations (Fig. 3).

Table 2. The root mean square error of GCPs in X-easting, Y-northing and Z-altitude for each dataset.

Year	X error (m)	Y error (m)	Z error (m)	XY error (m)	Total (m)
2006	1.293	0.704	1.380	1.473	2.018
2001	0.570	3.156	0.331	3.208	3.225
2000	1.328	2.429	0.679	2.768	2.850
1996	1.465	3.239	2.453	3.556	4.320
1988	1.486	4.300	0.693	4.550	4.603
1979	2.480	1.789	0.197	3.058	3.064
1967	0.218	0.941	0.939	0.965	1.347

For all the datasets except 2006 and 1967 photogrammetric blocks, fiducial marks have been used in the BBA. Then in this case the alignment procedure can be done either using fiducial marks or masking them. In most cases, masking the fiducials results in better alignment and denser point cloud. In 1996, 2000, and 2001 datasets camera location coordinates are available. The dataset from 1996 contains 35 photos from two separate cameras: 27 images taken with the RMK TOP 15 camera type, which has a calibration certificate, and 8 images taken with another camera, for which a calibration certificate was not available. The 8 photographs acquired by separate cameras will not be aligned with the other 27 images if the conventional methodology is followed, i.e., by measuring fiducial marks in photos. To overcome this issue, two groups are aligned independently in two chunks, and then the camera calibration properties exported from each other. Pre-calibration parameters will indeed be based on the calibration data of both groups of images. For the dataset from 1979, the calibration certificate allows the use of fiducial marks, but the camera coordinates are missing. This is the only dataset in which utilizing fiducial marks in the alignment operation results in an increased number of aligned images and a denser 3D model. In addition, in images of the dataset from

1967, because it is the oldest dataset in this study and because there is no corresponding calibration certificate, using fiducial marks has not been feasible, and they were masked.

Fig. 3. An example of reconstructed 3D dense cloud from the 2001 dataset representing the position and distribution of GCPs.

6.1 Assessing the Evolution of Miage Glacier

To compute the volume changes of glaciers over time, 3D surface models are compared. Thanks to GCPs, different photogrammetric blocks have been georeferenced in the same coordinate system, and then co-registration has been improved by exploiting overlap between pairs of point clouds. To ensure the quality and reliability of co-registration, points within five stable windows have been segmented and used for co-registration refinement based on ICP. Residual distances in these windows after this process have been adopted for the assessment of the co-registration accuracy (Table 3).

Table 3. Residual co-registration errors in five sample windows of stable parts around Miage Glacier.

Time period	Points in sample widows	Mean of M3C2 distances [m]	Standard deviation of M3C2 distances [m]	RMSE (root mean square error) of M3C2 distances [m]
2001–06	114k	1.31	1.61	2.82
2000–01	74k	0.90	2.60	2.70
1996–2000	158k	1.61	2.94	3.20
1988–96	218k	0.67	2.26	2.27
1979–88	230k	1.95	4.67	4.95
1967–79	128k	0.67	3.27	3.53

The accuracy of the co-registration resulted in a mean difference from 0.5 to 1.5 m (Table 2) and root means square error of distances varying between 2 and 5 m.

The evaluation of changes in glacier thickness has been done over an area of approximately 5 km^2 of the glacier tongue. The maximum average height reduction occurred between 2001 and 2006 with 3.5 m of decrease, while the variation is minimum from 2000 to 2001. Similarly, the largest volume changes mostly occurred from 2001 to 2006. In contrast, the only major increase of glacier thickness occurred in from 1979 to 1988. After 1988, the glacier started losing mass. Distribution of height variation of point clouds (Fig. 4) suggest mostly mass loss condition in Miage glacier through the decades and the last 5 years showed the largest contribution. The comparison between 2001 and 2006 shows that glacial mass loss occurred largely in the lower regions of the Miage tongue, whereas in 2000–01, the losses happened in the middle part, while the lower part showed little change. From 1996 to 2000, the volume and height decreased primarily in the lower half of the glacier tongue, with some gain was observed in the top half. In contrast, in the lower section of Miage glacier mass increased from 1967 to 1988. Due to huge shadows covering the middle sections of Miage in the photos of the dataset of

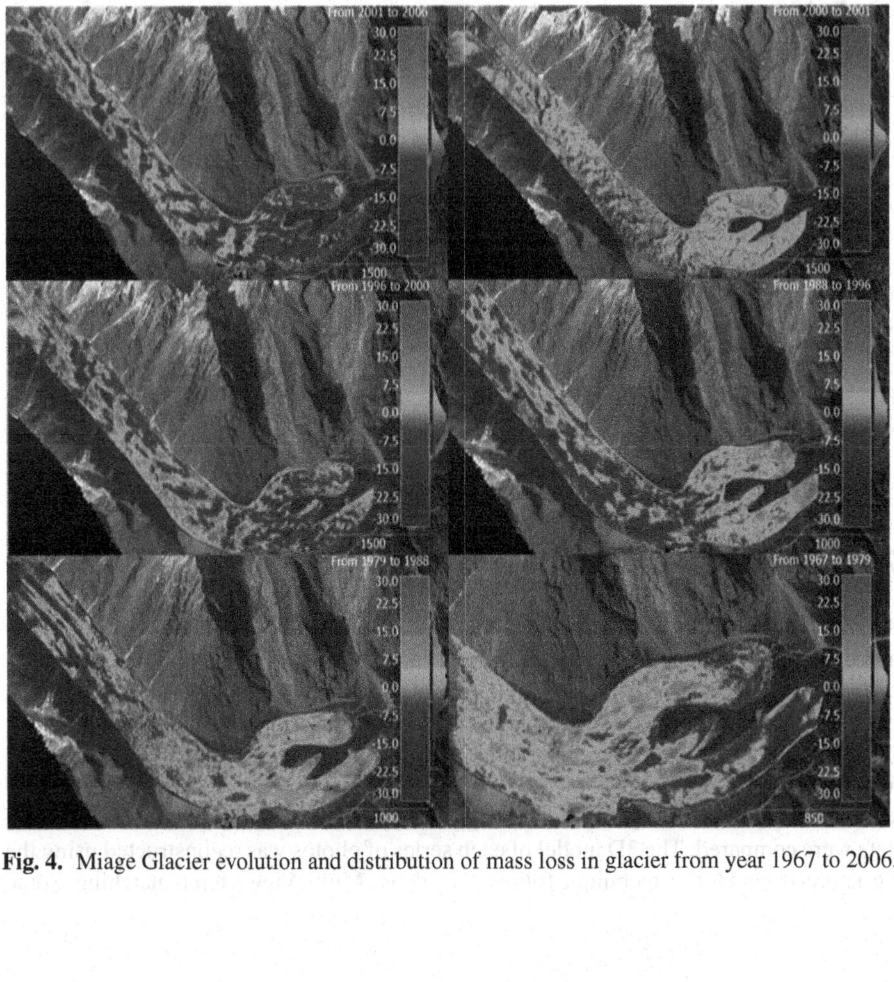

Fig. 4. Miage Glacier evolution and distribution of mass loss in glacier from year 1967 to 2006.

1967, the 3D model of this dataset has numerous outliers and noise in the middle part of Miage glacier tongue, and only the bottom half of Miage is considered for comparison in the 1967 point-cloud. Overall, the Miage glacier experienced a slight mass gain until 1988, then a gradual decrease in thickness over time, although not abrupt. In addition, the rate of mass loss tends to rise over time. Similarly, the thickness of the upper branches of Miage has remained consistent, with the exception of 2000, when a high retreat rate of -3 m per year was observed, resulting in a decrease in height.

Furthermore, the volume variation calculation throughout the years when cloud pairs are compared may be used to calculate the Miage glacier mass loss rate, by subtracting the volume of the glacier from two distinct point clouds and taking the surface area into account. This method allows us to comprehend the fluctuation of the Miage across all years until 2006, not only during the time that datasets are available (Fig. 5).

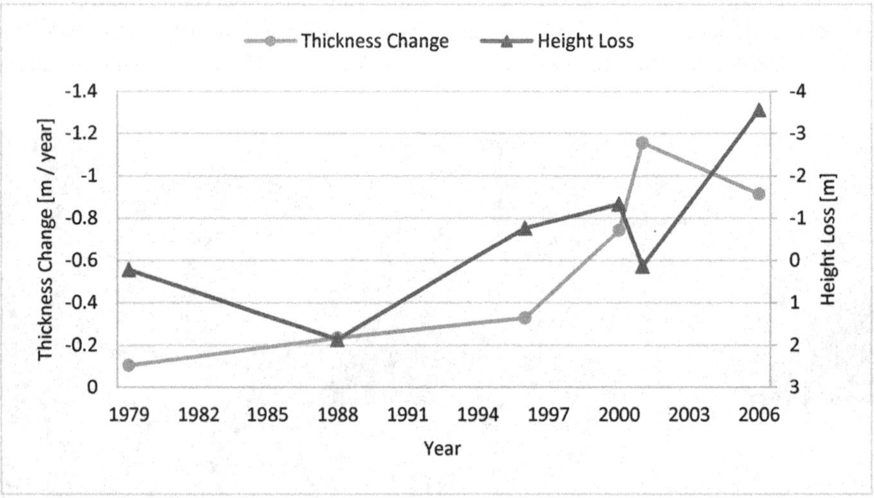

Fig. 5. Mean height and thickness change rate variation of Miage glacier in Val Veny through the years.

7 Conclusions

Archival photographs were utilized in this research to better understand the evolution and dynamics of Miage glacier in Val Veny from 1967 to 2006. Photogrammetric methods can be used to interpret morphological change captured in a sequence of aerial photographs. These data were acquired by IGNF (National Geographic and Forestry Institute of France) and covered an area ranging from 132 to 345 km^2. The data were acquired with various airborne cameras during the warmer months of the year. To understand the variation of Miage glacier through these years, 3D models obtained from these data were compared. The 3D model of each series of photos was reconstructed using the Structure-from-Motion technique followed by dense Multi-View Stereo matching. Some pre-processing was conducted before the main procedure to improve keypoint extraction from photographs. According to availability of calibration certificates for some datasets, it was possible to try the alignment procedure by using fiducial markers. However, in most of the datasets, masking the fiducial markers leads to better or equivalent results. Satellite data was used to identify stable points that were used as GCPs in all images, resulting in improved initial alignment of the 3D models during the comparison phase. The appearance of shadows on the glacier in some zones is due to the presence of high cliffs and improper photography timing, and this fact leads to missing data in some portions of the 3D model.

To use 3D models to investigate variations in Miage glacier, noise must be filtered and model alignment must be accurate enough to provide an accurate result. The distances between the stable zones may be used to measure the co-registration quality between two point clouds. The error in the co-registration procedure may be evaluated in the mean distances in stable areas after co-registration refinement based on ICP. The registration error varies depending on the quality of the 3D model in different zones of Val Veny, but it is usually between 1 and 2 m. *Multi-scale Model to Model* (M3C2) method for cloud comparison was employed to determine distances, as recommended by prior studies, especially for complex landforms.

In the Miage Glacier, height loss was determined to be 1 m/y between 2000 and 2006, after being almost negligible until the 1990s. however there is a general increasing trend in both height and volume loss from 1979 to 2006. Furthermore, the findings of this study may be integrated with more contemporary models acquired by using more advanced photogrammetry technology to assess whether the variations in Miage glacier follow the same trend as before. The methodology applied in this research may be transferred to various applications or locations if archival photographs are available. Unidentified causes of natural disasters, including landslides, floods, and droughts, can be identified by analysing archival photographs of the region and using the results for risk mitigation and planning in the long term.

References

1. Aguilar, M., Aguilar, F., Fernandez, I., Mills, J.: Accuracy assessment of commercial self-calibrating bundle adjustment routines applied to archival aerial photography. Photogram. Rec. **28**(141), 96–114 (2013)
2. Azzoni, R.S., et al.: Recent structural evolution of Forni Glacier tongue (Ortles-Cevedale Group, Central Italian Alps). J. Maps **13**(2), 870–878 (2017). https://doi.org/10.1080/17445647.2017.1394227
3. Baumann, P.: Aerial Photography: History and Georeferencing. The Geographic Information Science & Technology Body of Knowledge, 2nd Quarter edn. (Ed. by, J.P. Wilson) (2019)
4. Costa, J.E.: Physical geomorphology of debris flows. In: Costa, J.E., Fleisher, P.J. (eds.) Developments an Applications of Geomorphology, pp. 268–317. Springer, Berlin (1984). https://doi.org/10.1007/978-3-642-69759-3
5. Cox, S.C., et al.: Rock avalanche on 14 July 2014 from Hillary Ridge, Aoraki/Mount Cook, New Zealand. Landslides **12**(2), 395–402 (2015). https://doi.org/10.1007/s10346-015-0556-7
6. De Michele, C., et al.: Using a fixed-wing UAS to map snow depth distribution: an evaluation at peak accumulation. Cryosphere **10**, 511–522 (2016)

7. Deline, P.: Etude géomorphologique des interations écroulements rocheux/glaciers dans la haute montagne alpine (versantsud-est du massif du Mont Blanc). Thèse de doctorat de géographie, Université de Savoie, p. 539 (2002)
8. Eltner, A., Kaiser, A., Castillo, C., Rock, G., Neugirg, F., Abellán, A.: Image-based surface reconstruction in geomorphometry – merits, limits and developments. Earth Surf. Dyn. **4**, 359–389 (2015)
9. Fey, C., Wichmann, V., Zangerl, C.: Reconstructing the evolution of a deap seated rock-slide (Marzell) and its responseto glacial retreat based on historic and remote sensing data. Geomorphology **298**, 72–85 (2017)
10. Fox, A.J., Cziferszky, A.: Unlocking the time capsule of historic aerial photography to measure changes in Antarctic Peninsula Glaciers. Photogramm. Rec. **23**(121), 51–68 (2008)
11. Fraser, C.S.: Automatic camera calibration in close range photogrammetry. Photogramm. Eng. Remote. Sens. **79**(4), 381–388 (2013)
12. Fugazza, D., et al.: Combination of UAV and terrestrial photogrammetry to assess rapid glacier evolution and map glacier hazards. Nat. Hazards Earth Syst. Sci. **18**, 1055–1071 (2018). https://doi.org/10.5194/nhess-18-1055-2018
13. Fugazza, D., et al.: Highresolution mapping of glacier surface features. The UAV survey of the Forni Glacier (Stelvio National Park, Italy). Geografia Fisica e Dinamica del Quaternario **38**, 25–33 (2015)
14. Giordano, S., Le Bris, A., Mallet, C.: Fully automatic analysis of archival aerial images current status and challenges. In: Joint Urban Remote Sensing Event (JURSE) (2017)
15. Haala, N., Kada, M.: An update on automatic 3D building reconstruction. ISPRS J. Photogramm. Remote Sens. **65**, 570–580 (2010)
16. Huggel, C.: Recent extreme slope failures in glacial environments: effects of thermal perturbation. Quat. Sci. Rev. **28**, 1119–1130 (2009)
17. James, M.R., Robson, S., Smith, M.W.: 3-D uncertainty-based topographic change detection with structure-from-motion photogrammetry: precision maps for ground control and directly georeferenced surveys. Earth Surf. Proc. Landforms **42**(12), 1769–1788 (2017)
18. Kaufmann, V.; Ladstädter, R.: Quantitative analysis of rock glacier creep by means of digital photogrammetry using multitemporal aerial photographs: two case studies in the Austrian Alps. In: Proceedings of the 8th International Conference on Permafrost, Zurich, Switzerland, 21–25 July 2003, pp. 21–25 (2003)
19. Koblet, T., et al.: Reanalysis of multi-temporal aerial images of Storglaciären, Sweden (1959–99) – Part 1: determination of length, area, and volume changes. Cryosphere **4**, 333–343 (2010). https://doi.org/10.5194/tc-4-333-2010
20. Kraus, K.: Photogrammetry - Geometry from Images and Laser Scans. Walter de Gruyter, Berlin (2008)
21. Lague, D., Brodu, N., Leroux, J.: Accurate 3D comparison of complex topography with terrestrial laser scanner: application to the Rangitikei canyon (N-Z), ISPRS J. Photogramm. Remote Sens. (2012)
22. Micheletti, N., Chandler, J.H., Lane, S.N.: Section 2.2. Structure from Motion (SfM) photogrammetry. In: Cook, S.J., Clarke, L.E., Nield, J.M. (eds.) Geomorphological Techniques (Online Edition), pp. 2047–2371. British Society for Geomorphology, London (2015)
23. O'Connor, J.E., Costa, J.E.: Geologic and hydrologic hazards in glacierized basins in North America resulting from 19th and 20th century global warming. Nat. Hazards **8**, 121–140 (1993)
24. Poli, D., Casarotto, C., Strudl, M., Bollmann, E., Moe, K., Legat, K.: Use of historical aerial images for 3d modelling of glaciers in the Province of Trento. ISPRS Int. Arch. Photogramm. Remote Sens. Spat. Inf. Sci. **XLIII-B2**, 1151–1158 (2020)
25. Pomerleau, F., Colas, F., Siegwart, R., Magnenat, S.: Comparing ICP variants on realworld data sets. Auton. Robot. **34**, 133–148 (2013)

26. Scaioni, M., Roncella, R., Alba, M.I.: Change detection and deformation analysis in point clouds: application to rock face monitoring. Photogramm. Eng. Remote. Sens. **79**(5), 441–456 (2013)
27. Scaioni, M., et al.: Structure-from-motion photogrammetry to support the assessment of collapse risk in Alpine Glaciers. In: Altan, O., Chandra, M., Sunar, F., Tanzi, T. T. (eds.) Gi4DM 2018. LNGC, pp. 239–263. Springer, Cham (2019). https://doi.org/10.1007/978-3-030-05330-7_10
28. Scaioni, M., Corti, M., Diolaiuti, G., Fugazza, D., Cernuschi, M.: Local and general monitoring of Forni glacier (Italian alps) using multi-platform structure-from-motion photogrammetry. Int. Arch. Photogramm. Remote Sens. Spat. Inf. Sci. **42**(Part 2/W7), 1547–1554 (2017). https://doi.org/10.5194/isprs-archives-XLII-2-W7-1547-2017
29. Scaioni, M., et al.: Technical aspects related to the application of SfM photogrammetry in high mountain. Int. Arch. Photogramm. Remote Sens. Spat. Inf. Sci. **XLII**(Part 2), 1029–1036 (2018)
30. Schneider, D., Huggel, C., Cochachin, A., Guillén, S., García, J.: Mapping hazards from glacier lake outburst floods based on modelling of process cascades at Lake 513, Carhuaz, Peru. Adv. Geosci. **35**, 145–155 (2014). https://doi.org/10.5194/adgeo-35-145-2014
31. Smiraglia, C., Diolaiuti, G., D'Agata, C.: I ghiacciai delle Alpi italiane: variazioni areali e volumetriche e dinamica geomorfologia recente. Relazione contratto di ricerca n8 R1877. CESI, Milano (2001)
32. Smiraglia, C., Diolaiuti, G., Casati, D., Kirkbride, M.: Recent areal and altimetric variations of Miage Glacier (Monte Bianco Massif, Italian Alps). In: Nakawo, M., Raymond, C.F., Fountain, A. (eds.) Debris-Covered Glaciers, vol. 264, pp. 227–233. IAHS Publ. (2000)
33. Tavakoli, K., Zadehali, E., Malekian, A., Darsi, S., Longoni, L., Scaioni, M.: Landslide dam failure analysis using imaging and ranging sensors. In: Gervasi, O., et al. (eds.) ICCSA 2021. LNCS, vol. 12955, pp. 3–17. Springer, Cham (2021). https://doi.org/10.1007/978-3-030-87007-2_1
34. Walstra, J., Dixon, N., Chandler, J.H.: Historical aerial photographs for landslide assessment: two case histories. Quart. J. Eng. Geol. Hydrogeol. **40**, 315–332 (2007)
35. Westoby, M.J., Brasington, J., Glasser, N.F., Hambrey, M.J., Reynolds, J.M.: 'Structure-from-motion' photogrammetry: a low-cost, effective tool for geoscience applications. Geomorphology **179**, 300–314 (2012). https://doi.org/10.1016/j.geomorph.2012.08.021

Evaluation of eCognition Developer and Orfeo ToolBox Performances for Segmenting Agrophotovoltaic Systems from Sentinel-2 Images

Claudio Ladisa[1], Alessandra Capolupo[1(✉)], Maria Nicolina Ripa[2], and Eufemia Tarantino[1]

[1] Department of Civil, Environmental, Land, Construction and Chemistry (DICATECh), Politecnico Di Bari, via Orabona n. 4, 70125 Bari, Italy
{claudio.ladisa,alessandra.capolupo,eufemia.tarantino}@poliba.it
[2] Department of Agricultural and Forest Sciences (DAFNE), Università Degli Studi Della Tuscia, Via S. Camillo de Lellis Snc, 01100 Viterbo, Italy
nripa@unitus.it

Abstract. A deep energy transformation will be tried out across the globe in the next decades in order to detect potential green and renewable sources able to replace fossil fuels. Among the various alternatives, photovoltaic technology, recognized as sustainable, clean, and environmentally friendly essence, is considered one of the most relevant solutions. To date, the Remotely Piloted Aircraft System has been largely used to inspect solar parks albeit the treatment of very high-resolution satellite images through object-based models may be a valid option. In this work, the potentialities of two segmentation approaches (multi-resolution and mean-shift algorithms, implemented in eCognition Developer and Orfeo Toolbox software, respectively) in extracting photovoltaic panels from Sentinel-2 time series were explored and compared. Such techniques were tested in Montalto di Castro in Viterbo (Italy). Multi-resolution algorithm was applied by varying scale and shape parameters between 20 and 100 and 0.1 and 0.5, respectively. Conversely, the mean-shift approach was used by considering the default values of spatial radius and range radius. Their segmentation outcomes were compared on the base of i) minimum Euclidean Distance 2 (ED2), calculated in AssesSeg environment, ii) segmentation polygons statistics and areas value, and, lastly, iii) their performance in terms of processing time, versatility, ability of handling heavy data, and cost. ECognition Developer demonstrated a better performance in segmenting Sentinel 2-images for extracting PV systems in terms of segmentation parameters management and outcomes interpretation ability.

Keywords: Object-Based Image Analysis (OBIA) · Segmentation · Agrophotovoltaic panels · Copernicus Program · Medium-resolution satellite images

O. Gervasi et al. (Eds.): ICCSA 2022 Workshops, LNCS 13379, pp. 466–482, 2022.
https://doi.org/10.1007/978-3-031-10545-6_32

1 Introduction

The need to tackle climate change and the imminent depletion of oil, coal, and natural gas reserves is leading the World to rely on renewable sources such as solar, wind, biomass, and geothermal energy [1]. Currently, the actual green energy capacity is expected to grow of about 50% by 2024 [2]. The strong, though now stable, construction and design costs decline, mainly due to the higher energy productivity of PV modules, have promoted PV deployment albeit PV solar installation implies a consistent soil loss [3]. As shown in the statistical report edited by the Gestore Servizi Energetici (GSE) in 2019 [4], 880,090 PV systems, with a total capacity of 20.865 MW, were installed up to December 31, 2019, in Italy. 92% of them were small systems with a power less than or equal to 20 kW. and an average system size of 23.7 kW. Nevertheless, the land is considered a commodity and, thus, specific studies have been carried out to investigate PV impact on land use [5, 6]. For this reason, in recent years, agrovoltaic or agrophotovoltaic systems have been implemented to allow the simultaneous cultivation and production of renewable energy, reducing high land consumption [7]. The choice of the adequate lands where to install PV systems is affected by many factors, such as geographical position, morphological characteristics of the territory and climatic conditions. As a result, their distribution is very heterogeneous among the different regions [4]. An additional key factor to be considered concerns the defects brought out by their permanent exposition to harsh environmental conditions [8]. Therefore, a constant inspection of their health status performed with various methods, such as field-of-view diagnosis, infrared thermal imaging, and electricity-based techniques, is required [1]. All these traditional techniques have proven to be obsolete for monitoring large structures and, therefore, valid alternatives based on digital image analysis have been introduced [9]. Remotely Piloted Aircraft System (RPAS) image-based assessment systems are considered as the optimal solution to meet such a purpose because of its competitive costs and the fastness of monitoring the efficiency of systems made up of many photovoltaic modules [10]. Nevertheless, the development of many large-scale PV systems in recent years has made RPAS an ineffective technique for monitoring them [11, 12]. The recent introduction of free medium and high-resolution satellite images could go beyond those limitations. Among the several techniques developed to process them, the object-based analyses are mainly adapted to extract land use/land cover information [13–16]. Object-Based Image Analysis (OBIA) principle is to group together spectrally and geomorphologically similar pixels to form objects which will be then classify [13, 17, 18]. The step allowing object identification is commonly called "Segmentation". This step can be performed by applying various software, such eCognition Developer (Trimble, Sunnyvale, California, USA) and Orfeo Toolboxes (OTB). As demonstrated by previous works [19], eCognition Developer is suitable for segmenting satellite images or mosaics at larger scales because of its ability of producing a number of segments closer to the number of objects defined as ground truth data and its processing speed. Nevertheless, it cannot be applied in the projects with limited budgets because of its high license cost. On the other hand, OTB is a free open-source software able to generate satisfying outcomes albeit it needs a high processing time [20]. ECognition Developer and OTB were used for extracting PV systems and roofs from satellite data by Xia et al. [21] and Khan et al. [22], respectively. Both works showed satisfying results without any excessive computational costs. Nevertheless, Plakman et al. [23] demonstrated an improved of PV systems extraction outcomes using Sentinel-2 (S2) satellite images thanks to the many spectral bands provided by the sensor mounted on it. To the best of authors' knowledge, any researches based on the combination of the two above-mentioned software and S2 images have not been proposed in the literature for extracting PV systems. In this paper, the performance of eCognition Developer environment, a leading commercial software, and the open-source OTB for extracting PV solar panels from S2 time series were evaluated and compared. To achieve such an objective, two different segmentation algorithms (multi-resolution and mean-shift) were tested on the experimental site of Montalto di Castro, located in Viterbo, Italy. Such a site was selected because of the presence of the largest solar parks in Europe up to 2011. Software' outcomes quality as well as its ability and versality were evaluated by computing the modified version of Euclidean Distance (ED2) index, statistical metrics of the generated segmented polygons and processing time.

2 Study Area

The pilot site is located in Montalto di Castro, 42 km far from Viterbo city (northern part of Lazio Region, Central Italy) (Fig. 1).

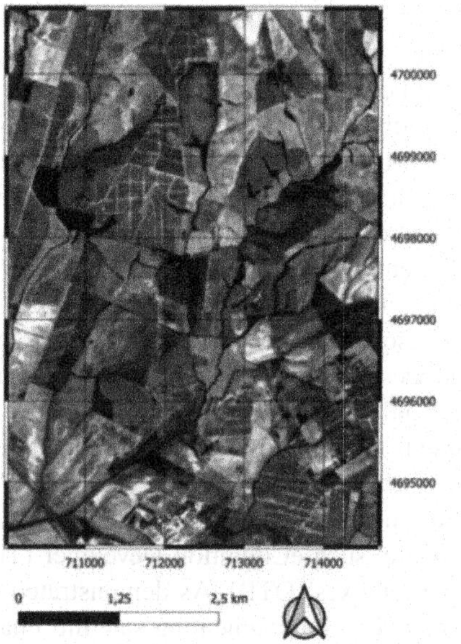

Fig. 1. Study site world geodetic system 84 Universal Transverse Mercator (UTM) zone 32N.

Such rectangular area covers a surface of about 6.2 km^2, characterized by a predominant flat morphology. It was selected as a test site due to the presence of the largest photovoltaic plant system in Europe up to 2011[24, 25], subsequently blocked-in accordance with the Italian Ministry for Cultural Heritage activities and tourism, worried about its impacts on cultural heritage landscapes, archaeological and historical areas, located close by [26].

3 Datasets

3.1 Sentinel-2 Imagery

Ten cloud-free Sentinel-2 (S2) scenes were collected over the study area from the European Space Agency (ESA) Copernicus Scientific Data Hub instrument website [27] (Table 1). Level 2A (L2A) was selected and all data were provided in World Geodetic System 84 (WGS84) Universal Transverse Mercator (UTM) zone 32N. The S2 multispectral (MS) sensor collects up to 10 bands with three different geometric resolutions ranging from 60 up to 10 m. Among them, four bands (Blue (B): 458–523 nm, Green (G): 543–578 nm, Red (R): 650–680 nm and Near Infrared (NIR8): 785–900 nm) have a resolution of 10 m, while six bands (Red Edge 1 (RE1): 694–713 nm, Red Edge 2 (RE2): 731–749 nm, Red Edge 3 (RE3): 769–797 nm, Narrow Near InfraRed (NIR8a): 848–881 nm, Shortwave Infrared-1 (SWIR1): 1565–1655 nm and Shortwave Infrared-2 (SWIR2): 100–2280 nm) have a resolution of 20 m. In this study, both 10 m and 20 m resolution bands were used because of the low reflectance of solar panels in VIS and NIR spectrum [28]. Lastly, S2 images were clipped in Quantum GIS (QGIS) environment (version 3.22) on the selected study area.

Table 1. Input Sentinel-2A and Sentinel-2B images.

Date of acquisition (D/M/Y)	Sensor	Orbit	Level
24/02/2021	S2B	R122	2A
31/03/2021	S2A	R122	2A
25/04/2021	S2A	R122	2A
28/05/2021	S2B	R022	2A
29/07/2021	S2A	R122	2A
21/08/2021	S2A	R022	2A
30/09/2021	S2A	R022	2A
30/10/2021	S2A	R022	2A
24/11/2021	S2B	R022	2A
31/12/2021	S2B	R122	2A

4 Software

4.1 eCongnition Developer 9.5

eCognition is a powerful object-based environment for image analysis [29]. It classifies and analyzes images, vectors, and point clouds using all the semantic information needed to interpret them correctly. It does not examine single pixels or points, but it investigates the mutual relationships among neighboring pixel of the same layer and across various input data [29]. Thus, similar pixels are generally grouped together in objects[29]. ECognition suite offers three different components that can be used individually or in combination to solve the most challenging image analysis tasks: i) eCognition Developer; ii) eCognition Server and, lastly, iii) eCognition Architect. ECognition Developer is a software created for object-based image analysis. It is widely used in the field of remote sensing because of the simplicity of creating rule sets suitable for performing automatic data analysis. It contains a large collection of algorithms that can be combined to facilitate rapid development of geospatial analysis applications [29]. The eCognition Server software is a processing environment for simultaneous multiple data development and transferability testing, while eCognition Architect enables non-technical professionals to perform OBIA. Users can easily customize the ruleset created a proper rule-based model in eCognition Developer [29].

4.2 Orfeo ToolBox

Orfeo ToolBox is an open-source project for satellite data investigation [30]. Based on the backs of the open-source geospatial community, it can process optical, multispectral, hyperspectral and radar resolution imageries up to the terabyte scale. Therefore, it can be applied by a wide variety of applications, including orthorectification, pansharpening, supervised and unsupervised classification, feature extraction. All the implemented algorithms are accessible from Monteverdi, QGIS [30], Python, command line, and C++. Monteverdi is a visualization tool that allows users looking at high-resolution images and accessing all toolbox commands [30]. It is available on Windows, Linux, and Mac OS X.

4.3 AssesSeg

AssesSeg is a command line tool based on the computation of the modified version of the Euclidean supervised Distance (ED2) aimed at assessing the segmentation quality by calculating the Potential Segmentation Error (PSE) and the Number-of-Segments Ratio (NSR). These two parameters measure the geometric and the arithmetic discrepancy between the manually digitized ground truth and the corresponding segments, respectively. A high ED2 value indicates a high geometric and/or arithmetic discrepancy, while a low ED2 value implies a good level of segmentation [31]. AssesSeg's goal is to evaluate segmentation quality [31]. It was produced by the cooperation between the University of Almeria (Almeria, Spain) and the Politecnico di Bari (Bari, Italy). AssesSeg outputs allow detecting the best bands combination and showing a clear positive correlation between segmentation accuracy and the amount of available reference data [31].

4.4 Quantum GIS (3.22)

QGIS is an open-source Geographic Information System (GIS). The project was born in May 2002, and it was established by SourceForge in June of the same year. Currently, it runs on the most relevant platforms, such as, for instance, Unix, Windows, and macOS. It is developed using the Qt toolkit [32] and C++ [33]. Its intuitive graphical user interface (GUI) allows users conducting advanced GIS analysis easily [33]. QGIS supports a huge number of raster and vector data formats, and many free plug-ins can be downloaded for any geomatics applications. [33].

5 Methodology

The digitalization of PV panels located in the study area allows having the Ground Truth for assessing segmentation quality. Thus, after digitalizing the solar park manually, the operative workflow reported in Fig. 2 was applied. Once S2 images were collected, they were segmented in eCognition Developer and OTB software separately. A multi-parameter approach, based on scale, shape, and compactness parameters, was applied in eCognition platform.

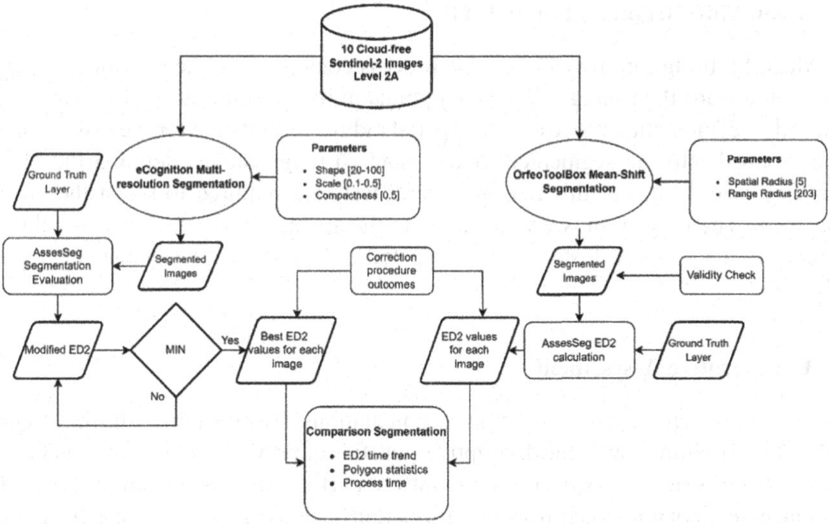

Fig. 2. Workflow of the applied methodology.

A mean-shift segmentation algorithm was, instead, used in OTB platform. Contrary to the technique adopted in eCognition, fixed values were picked up in this case. Then, for each segmented image, ED2 was calculated. The smallest ED2 value corresponds to the best segmentation parameter set for each image. ED2 outcomes were compared. Some output segmentations from the two software that showed abnormal ED2 values were subjected to correction procedures, aimed at masking all pixels characterized by an anomalous reflectance value. Lastly, software performances were also investigated in terms of processing time, versatility, and costs.

5.1 Multi-resolution Segmentation in eCognition

The Multiple Resolution Image Segmentation (MRS) algorithm, already implemented in the eCognition Developer environment, was applied to gathered S2 images. MRS performance depends on three main parameters: (i) Scale parameter (SP), responsible for defining the maximum admissible heterogeneity. The larger the value, the larger the resulting objects is [29]. SP ranged between 20 and 100 (with an increment step of 1.0); (ii) the weight of color and shape criteria (Shape), which assigns a weight to the shape and spectral color of the objects. When the shape weight is zero, only the value assigned to col-or is considered, while when it is greater than zero, the shape of the objects is taken into account along with the color [29]. It was between 0.1 and 0.5 (with an increment step of 0.1); lastly, (iii) the weight of compactness and smoothness (Compactness) criteria useful for optimizing overall compactness [29]. It was set at 0.5 for all cases. As proposed by Novelli et al. [34], the optimal combination of MRS parameters was selected by applying AssesSeg.

5.2 Mean-Shift Segmentation in OTB

The Mean-Shift algorithm is an iterative process consisting on the shift of each single data point toward the average of the data points in its proximity [35]. Two parameters control the segmentation process: i) the spatial radius, responsible for the pixels number to be grouped into the segmented images, and ii) range radius, defining the objects of interest size. [36]. For this reason, several tests are required to select the optimal parameters. The range radius was set equal to the average number of pixels within the Ground Truth segments. Instead, for the spatial radius, the default value was used in OTB.

5.3 Comparative Assessment

Three methods were used to compare the segmentations: i) evaluation of the time trend of ED2 index; ii) estimation of the descriptive statistics of polygon geometries and Ground Truth; iii) assessment of the processing times to perform the segmentation procedures. The total number of polygons provides information on the detail level that can be captured as well as the time needed to run the segmentation procedure and basic analytic analysis, such as raster conversion into vector and zonal statistics computation [19]. The area was calculated for each polygon using the 'field calculator' tool implemented in QGIS environment. A set of descriptive statistics (minimum, maximum, range, sum, mean, median and standard deviation) was also evaluated through the "basic field statistics" tool. The metrics extracted from Ground Truth and polygons were explored. Images reporting an anomalous ED2 values were subsequently corrected by masking all pixels with inconsistent reflectance values. Then, the whole procedure was applied again on the corrected maps.

6 Results

6.1 Multi-resolution Segmentation Outputs

Figure 3 reports the trends of the modified ED2 index for all the segmented images produced by applying eCognition Developer. Most of the images reach the lowest ED2 value setting the shape equal to 0.5 and the scale ranges between 36 and 55.

The best ED2 value (0.454) was shown from the image acquired in August using 53 and 0.3 for the scale and the shape, respectively. On the other hand, instead, the images belonging to October and November reported an anomalous trend and November showed the highest value of ED2 and scale. Scale and shape values useful to obtain the corresponding minimum ED2 value for each image is reported in Table 2.

6.2 Mean-Shift Segmentation Products

Table 3 describes the ED2 values computed on the images segmented using the Mean-Shift Segmentation algorithm. Even in this case, the lowest ED2 value was generated in August while November reported an anomalous trend. In this case, the ED2 value registered for October is in line with that one obtained in the other months.

6.3 ED2 Trend Comparison Outcomes

Figure 4 describes the trend of the minimum value of ED2 obtained by processing the images in eCognition Developer and OTB, respectively. A quite similar trend is detected using both software from February till September. Such a Figure enhances the anomalies already noted in November and October outcomes generated using eCognition Developer. Also OTB shows an anomaly in November albeit it is less marked. On the contrary, any anomalies are not detected in OTB for October.

6.4 Polygons Statistics Results

Tables 4 report the total amount of obtained polygons generated using eCognition Developer and OTB, respectively. Furthermore, the number of polygons intersected with Ground Truth is shown too. ECognition Developer produced more polygons than OTB except in November. Polygons intersecting Ground Truth are greater in eCognition Developer than in OTB.

Figure 5 shows the metrics calculated on the polygons intersected with the Ground Truth samples. In particular, in Fig. 5a, it can be seen that the areas of the polygons intersected with Ground Truth, produced by OTB, have a higher average value than those obtained from the Ground Truth polygons for all months under analysis, while eCognition Developer produced results with a more fluctuating trend always below the average value of Ground Truth, except in September. In Fig. 5f, the coefficient of variation (CV) values show more heterogeneity in the polygons generated by eCongnition Developer. The values of standard deviation, median, CV and minimum show more small segments for eCognition Developer in November. Table 5 describes the processing time needed in eCognition Developer and OTB, respectively. eCognition Developer time involves

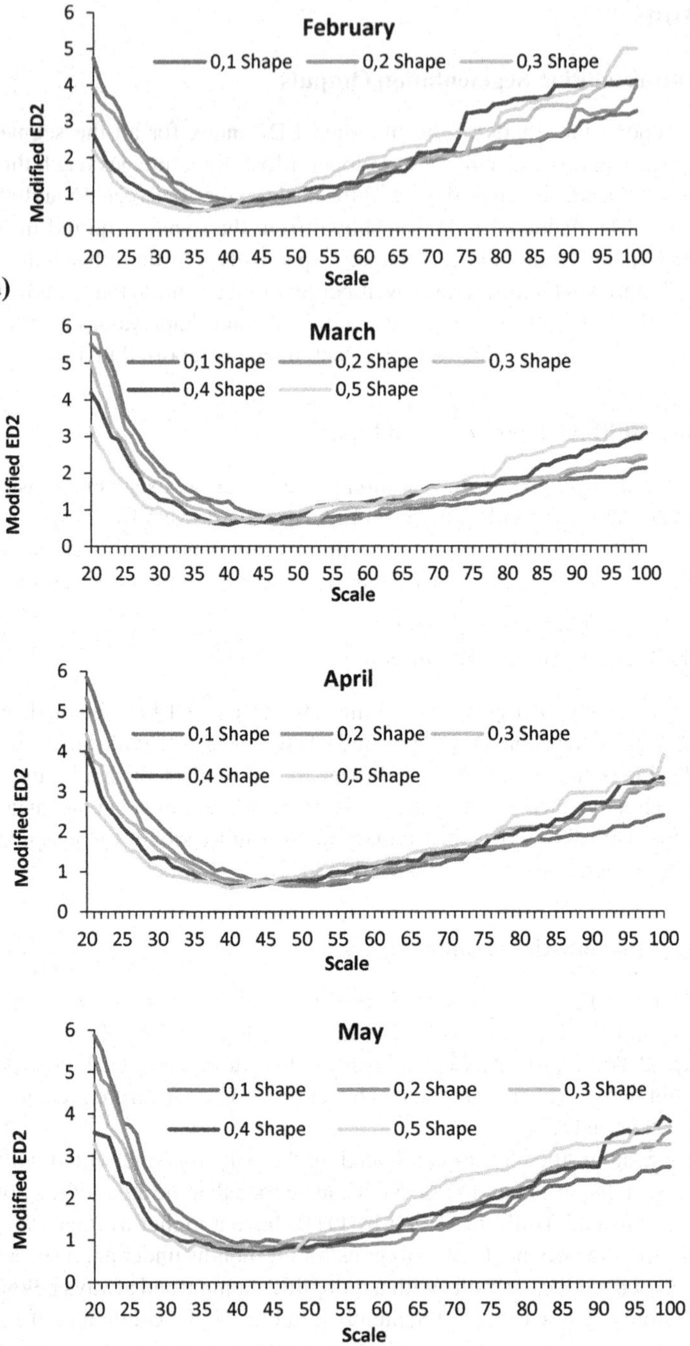

(a) (b) (c) (d)

Fig. 3. ED2 value trend computed on the images collected in: (a) February; (b) March; (c) April; (d) May; (e) July; (f) August; (g) September; (h) October; (i) November; (j) December.

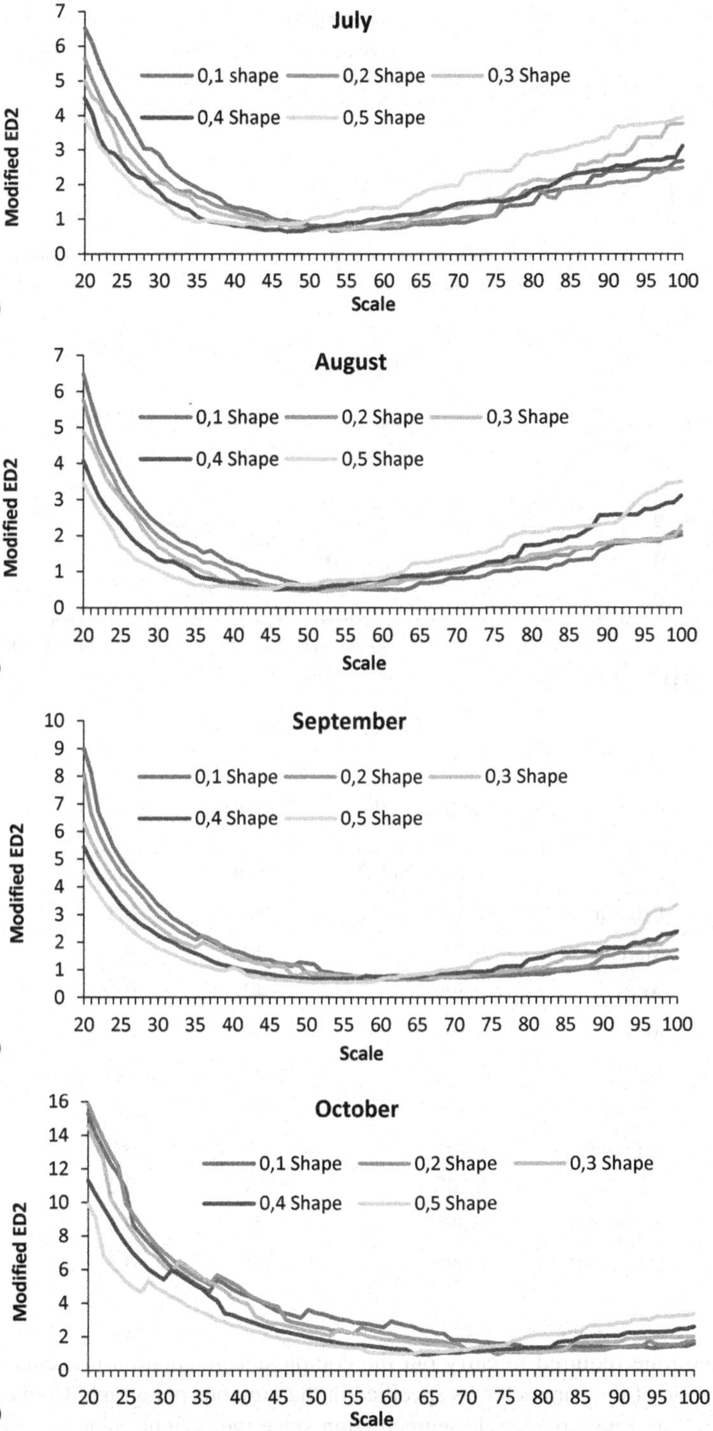

(e) (f) (g) (h)

Fig. 3. continued

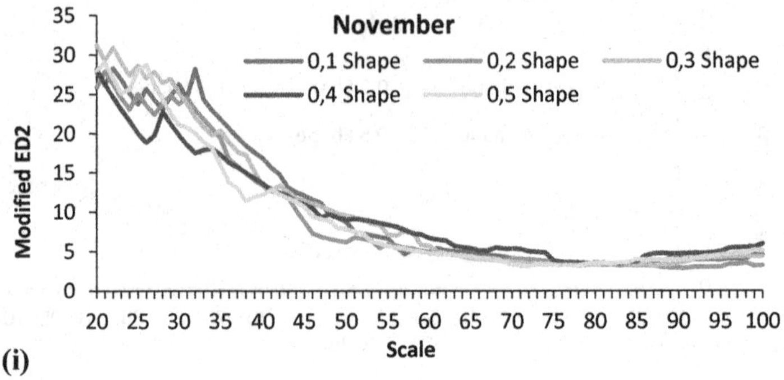

(i)

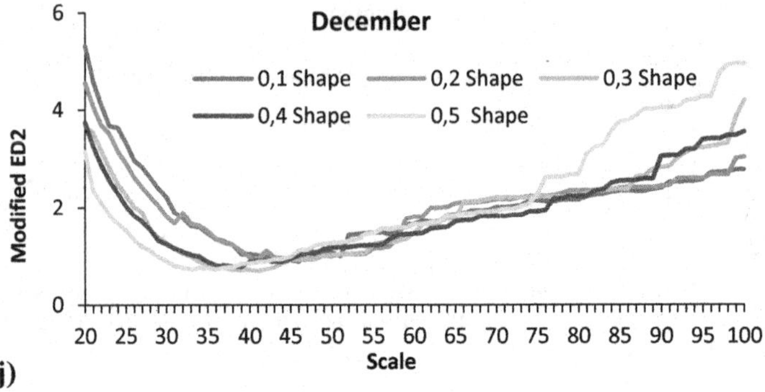

(j)

Fig. 3. continued

Table 2. Best Shape and Scale values obtained using eCognition Developer.

Month	Minimum ED2	Scale	Shape
February	0.507	36	0.5
March	0.598	40	0.4
April	0.599	40	0.5
May	0.632	40	0.5
July	0.641	47	0.4
August	0.454	53	0.3
September	0.537	55	0.5
October	0.942	74	0.2
November	2.895	91	0.2
December	0.695	41	0.3

the whole time required to carry out the complete segmentation procedure including the variation of the parameter, as specified in the previous paragraph. Conversely, OTB time is referred just to a single segmentation since the default value are used. In both

Table 3. Best shape and scale values obtained using OTB.

Month	Minimum ED2	Spatial radius	Range radius
February	0.651	5	203
March	0.573	5	203
April	0.627	5	203
May	0.660	5	203
July	0.712	5	203
August	0.559	5	203
September	0.707	5	203
October	0.716	5	203
November	1.023	5	203
December	0.743	5	203

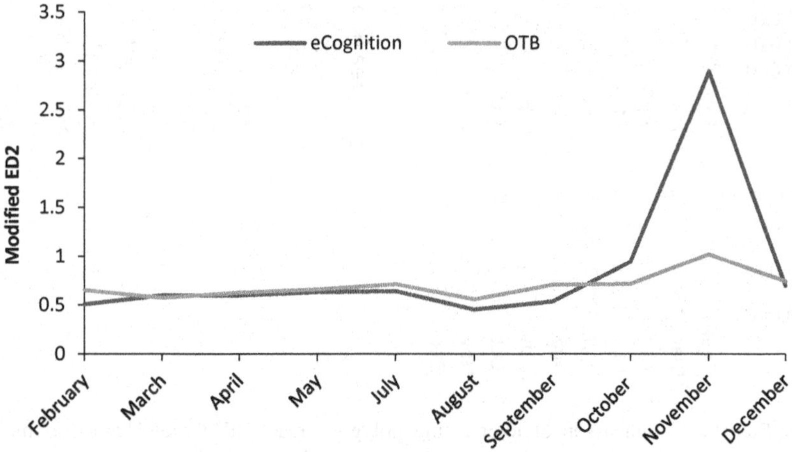

Fig. 4. Comparison of ED2 trends extracted using eCognition Developer (in blue) and OTB (in orange). (Color figure online)

Table 4. Statistics of eCognition Developer and OTB polygons. GT: Ground Truth.

		GT	Feb.	Mar.	Apr.	May	Jul.	Aug.	Sept.	Oct.	Nov.	Dec.
eCognition	Pol	152	4428	5055	4271	4210	4242	3917	2943	2623	1979	4719
	Inters. pol. & GT	\	409	477	417	416	381	369	333	425	498	474
OTB	Pol	152	2586	2332	2640	2597	2556	2577	2501	2539	2586	2545
	Inters. pol. & GT	\	326	319	332	320	329	331	306	314	322	317

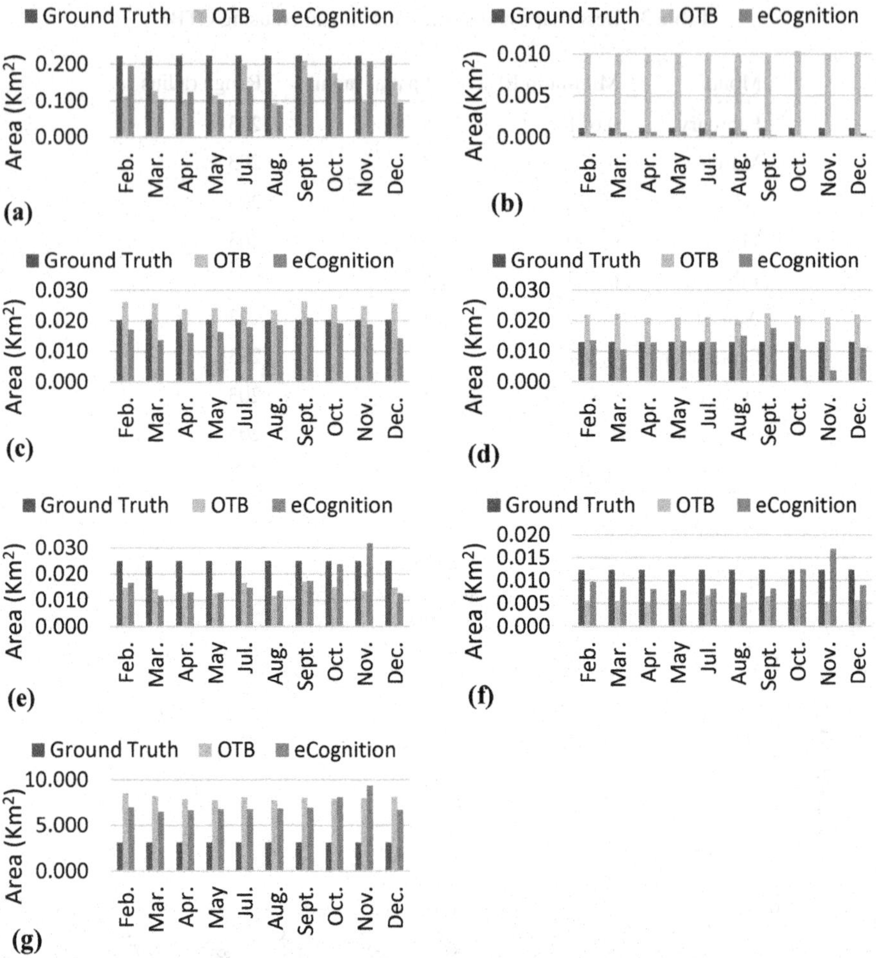

Fig. 5. Statistical comparison of intersecting polygon areas with GroundTruth: (a) max; (b) minimum; (c) mean; (d) median; (e) standard deviation; (f) CV; (g) Sum.

cases, the HP Pavillion Gaming Laptop 16-a0xxx computer with Intel(R) Core (TM) i7-10750H CPU @ 2.60 GHz and RAM was applied.

Table 5. Processing time required by eCognition Developer and OTB to segment the S2 time series.

Software	Feb. (sec)	Mar. (sec)	Apr. (sec)	May (sec)	Jul. (sec)	Aug. (sec)	Sep. (sec)	Oct. (sec)	Nov. (sec)	Dec. (sec)
eCo. Dev.	10:19.0	10:12.3	10:05.2	09:59.8	10:05.7	10:09.4	10:07.6	09:56.7	09:46.3	15:13.4
OTB	00:04.3	00:03.4	00:04.0	00:03.4	00:03.3	00:03.5	00:03.5	00:03.5	00:03.6	00:03.5

6.5 Correction Procedure Outcomes

The results in showed anomalies in October and November. For this reason, as already explained in the "Methodology" Section, the areas of the images characterized by unusual reflectance values were masked and, both segmentation algorithms were reapplied on the resultant maps. As showed in Table 6, in eCognition Developer, ED2 values were lowered compared to the original images. In OTB, on the other hand, slightly higher

Table 6. Correction procedure outcomes.

	October			
	eCogntion		OTB	
	Before	After	Before	After
ED2	0.9420	0.4270	0.7150	0.8780
Pol.	2623.0000	4860.0000	2539.0000	2243.0000
Inters. pol. & GT \	425.0000	358.0000	314.0000	238.0000
Min (km^2)	0.0001	0.0004	0.0103	0.0103
Max (km^2)	0.1481	0.2346	0.1748	0.2346
Mean (km^2)	0.0191	0.0150	0.0253	0.0274
Median (km^2)	0.0105	0.0113	0.0216	0.0221
Dev. Sta. (km^2)	0.0237	0.0182	0.0150	0.0225
CV (km^2)	0.0124	1.2165	0.0059	0.8238
Sum ($km^{2)}$	8.1153	5.3695	7.9320	6.5130
	November			
	eCogntion		OTB	
	Before	After	Before	After
ED2	2.8950	0.9420	1.0220	1.1930
Pol.	1979.0000	4703.0000	2586.0000	2250.0000
Inters. pol. & GT \	498.0000	358.0000	322.0000	240.0000
Min (km^2)	0.0001	0.0001	0.0101	0.0101
Max (km^2)	0.2063	0.2346	0.0982	0.2346
Mean (km^2)	0.0188	0.0164	0.0249	0.0276
Median (km^2)	0.0037	0.0107	0.0210	0.0211
Dev. Sta. (km^2)	0.0318	0.0215	0.0135	0.0228
CV (km^2)	0.0169	1.3100	0.0054	0.8264
Sum ($km^{2)}$	9.3807	5.8703	8.0228	6.6251

ED2 values were obtained in October and November than in the unmasked images. Regarding polygon statistics, in eCognition Developer, the total number of polygons is much bigger than that one reported in Table 4. This is due to scale value change (scale = 40 in October; scale = 47 in November) (see Table 2. for unmasked value). In OTB, the total polygons value did not change much. Polygons intersected with Ground Truth decreased both in eCognition Developer and OTB. Areas statistics show an increment of median value in eCognition Developer for November and a decrement of standard deviation value. This suggests that a lower number of small segments can be detected.

7 Discussion and Conclusion

The aim of this work was to compare the performance of the commercial software eCognition Developer with the open-source platform Orfeo ToolBox in segmenting S2 time-series covering Montalto di Castro (Viterbo, Italy). Such a zone was selected because of the presence of the largest solar park in Europe until 2011. Furthermore, to the best of the authors' knowledge, any researches have been proposed in the literature to detect PV systems from S2 images by applying OBIA. After segmented the images, the modified ED2 index was evaluated using AssesSeg software. The corresponding temporal trends of ED2 extracted using eCognition Developer and OTB were similar, except for the months of October and November where anomalies were detected and subsequently corrected. Then, polygons statistics, shown in Table 4, were computed. eCognition produced more polygons than OTB and, consequently, their intersection with Ground Truth samples was higher albeit the area sum was higher in OTB case (Table 6) This is confirmed also by the relatively high median value and relatively low standard deviation value that enhance the tendency of the mean-shift algortim to create larger polygons than Ground Truth samples. Additionally, OTB produces a narrow range of polygon sizes. Thus, polygons generated by eCognition Developer were more adapted to the selected Ground Truth samples. Although the same laptop was used to process the data, eCognition Developer showed a better performance considering that a range of parameters were tested, and non-self-intersected polygons were generated. Indeed, in the case of OTB, just single default values were evaluated and all the segmented polygons produced by OTB were characterized by self-intersected polygons, subsequently fixed. This made the process slower and complex. In addition, eCognition Developer demonstrated greater versatility and completeness in managing segmentation parameters than OTB as well as better handling heavy geospatial data. In conclusion, both software showed promising results since they generated acceptable segmentation outcomes. However, some differences have to be considered: i) eCognition Developer allowed extracting fewer large segments than those ones obtained using the other software; ii) considering the whole time needed to remove self-intersected polygons, eCognition Developer environment was faster in meeting the goal; iii) eCognition Developer amplified the anomalies detected in October and November, and, therefore, the images used in the multiresolution algorithm may be preprocessed adequately. Thus, eCognition Developer can be recognized as the optimal option for segmenting large input images. Nevertheless, its higher cost is a strong limitation in those projects characterized by a limited budget. In this case, OTB is preferable although much more time is required to produce satisfying polygons adapted for further classification purpose. In the future, other segmentation algorithms will be tested and compared to segment Sentinel-2 images to identify the optimal strategy to adopt to improve PV parks classification accuracy.

References

1. Heinberg, R., Fridley, D.: Our Renewable Future: Laying the Path for One Hundred Percent Clean Energy; Island Press/Center for Resource Economics: Washington, pp. 1–15. DC, USA (2016)
2. Souffer, I., Sghiouar, M., Sebari, I., Zefri, Y., Hajji, H., Aniba, G.: Automatic extraction of photovoltaic panels from UAV imagery with object-based image analysis and machine learning. In: Bennani, S., Lakhrissi, Y., Khaissidi, G., Mansouri, A., Khamlichi, Y. (eds.) WITS 2020. LNEE, vol. 745, pp. 699–709. Springer, Singapore (2022). https://doi.org/10.1007/978-981-33-6893-4_64
3. Feldman, D., Ramasamy, V., Fu, R., Ramdas, A., Desai, J., Margolis, R.: U.S. Solar Photovoltaic System and Energy Storage Cost Benchmark (2020)
4. Agrillo, A., Surace, V., Liberatore, P.: Direzione Studi e Monitoraggio di Sistema Funzione Statistiche e Monitoraggio. Gestore dei Servizi Energetici S.p.A, (2019)
5. Sahu, A., Yadav, N., Sudhakar, K.: Floating photovoltaic power plant: a review. Renew. Sustain. Energy Rev. **66**, 815–824 (2016)
6. Pindozzi, S., Faugno, S., Cervelli, E., Capolupo, A., Sannino, M., Boccia, L.: Consequence of land use changes into energy crops in Campania region. J. Agric. Eng. **44**(s2) (2013)
7. Katsikogiannis, O.A., Ziar, H., Isabella, O.: Integration of bifacial photovoltaics in agrivoltaic systems: a synergistic design approach. Appl. Energy **309**, 118475 (2022)
8. Ferrara, C., Philipp, D.: Why do PV modules fail? Energy Procedia **15**, 379–387 (2012)
9. Balzategui, J., et al.: Semi-automatic quality inspection of solar cell based on Convolutional Neural Networks. In: 2019 24th IEEE International Conference on Emerging Technologies and Factory Automation (ETFA), pp. 529–535. IEEE, September 2019
10. Zhang, D., et al.: Aerial image analysis based on improved adaptive clustering for photovoltaic module inspection. In: 2017 International Smart Cities Conference (ISC2), pp. 1–6. IEEE, September 2017
11. Wang, M., Cui, Q., Sun, Y., Wang, Q.: Photovoltaic panel extraction from very high-resolution aerial imagery using region–line primitive association analysis and template matching. ISPRS J. Photogramm. Remote. Sens. **141**, 100–111 (2018)
12. Novelli, A., Tarantino, E., Caradonna, G., Apollonio, C., Balacco, G., Piccinni, F.: Improving the ANN classification accuracy of landsat data through spectral indices and linear transformations (PCA and TCT) aimed at LU/LC monitoring of a river basin. In International Conference on Computational Science and Its Applications, pp. 420–432. Springer, Cham, , July 2016. https://doi.org/10.1007/978-3-319-42108-7_32
13. Blaschke, T.: Object based image analysis for remote sensing. ISPRS J. Photo-gramm. Remote Sens. **65**(1), 2–16 (2010)
14. Santoro, F., Tarantino, E., Figorito, B., Gualano, S., D'Onghia, A.M.: A tree counting algorithm for precision agriculture tasks. Int. J. Digital Earth **6**(1), 94–102 (2013)
15. Crocetto, N., Tarantino, E.: A class-oriented strategy for features extraction from multidate ASTER imagery. Remote Sens. **1**(4), 1171–1189 (2009)
16. Tarantino, E.: Features extraction from multi-date ASTER imagery using a hybrid classification method for land cover transformations. In: Sixth International Symposium on Digital Earth: Models, Algorithms, and Virtual Reality, vol. 7840, p. 78401T. International Society for Optics and Photonics (2010)

17. Sarzana, T., Maltese, A., Capolupo, A., Tarantino, E.: Post-processing of pixel and object-based land cover classifications of very high spatial resolution images. In: International Conference on Computational Science and Its Applications, pp. 797–812. Springer, Cham (2020). https://doi.org/10.1007/978-3-030-58811-3_57
18. Capolupo, A., Boccia, L.: Innovative method for linking anthropisation process to vulnerability. World Rev. Sci. Technol. Sustain. Dev. **17**(1), 4–22 (2021)
19. Sideris, K.: Review of image segmentation algorithms for analysing Sentinel-2 data over large geographical areas. JNCC (2020)
20. Grizonnet, M., Michel, J., Poughon, V., Inglada, J.: Mickaël, S., Cresson, R.: Orfeo ToolBox: Open source processing of remote sensing images. Open Geospatial Data, Software Stand. **2**(1), 15 (2017)
21. Xia, Z., et al.: Mapping the rapid development of photovoltaic power stations in northwestern China using remote sensing. Energy Rep. **8**, 4117–4127 (2022)
22. Khan, J., Arsalan, M.H.: Implementation of open source GIS tools to identify bright rooftops for solar photovoltaic applications–a case study of creek lanes, DHA, Karachi. J. Basic Appl. Sci. **12**, 14–22 (2016)
23. Plakman, V., Rosier, J., van Vliet, J.: Solar park detection from publicly available satellite imagery. GISci. Remote Sens. **59**(1), 461–480 (2022)
24. SMA Solar. https://www.sma-italia.com/. Accessed 21 Mar 2022
25. Infobuildenergia. https://www.infobuildenergia.it/. Accessed 15 Mar 2022
26. New tuscia. https://www.newtuscia.it/2020/06/14/. Accessed 10 Mar 2022
27. Scihub.copernicus. https://scihub.copernicus.eu. Accessed 15 Mar 2022
28. Czirjak, D.W.: Detecting photovoltaic solar panels using hyperspectral imagery and estimating solar power production. J. Appl. Remote Sens. **11**(2), 026007 (2017)
29. Trimble Geospatial Inc., https://geospatial.trimble.com/what-is-ecognition. Accessed 20 Mar 2022
30. Orfeo ToolBox. https://www.orfeo-toolbox.org/. Accessed 20 Mar 2022
31. Novelli, A., Aguilar, M.A., Aguilar, F.J., Nemmaoui, A., Tarantino, E.: AssesSeg—a command line tool to quantify image segmentation quality: a test carried out in southern spain from satellite imagery. Remote Sens. **9**(1), 40 (2017)
32. Qt. https://qt.io. Accessed 15 Mar 2022
33. QGIS Documentation. https://docs.qgis.org/3.10/it/docs/index.html. Accessed 20 Mar 2022
34. Novelli, A., Aguilar, M.A., Nemmaoui, A., Aguilar, F.J., Tarantino, E.: Performance evaluation of object-based greenhouse detection from Sentinel-2 MSI and Landsat 8 OLI data: a case study from Almería (Spain). Int. J. Appl. Earth Obs. Geoinf. **52**, 403–411 (2016)
35. Cheng, Y.: Mean shift, mode seeking, and clustering. IEEE Trans. Pattern Anal. Mach. Intell. **17**(8), 790–799 (1995)
36. Sarkar, P.R.: Comparison of Segmentation Algorithms and Estimation of Optimal Segmentation Parameters for Very High-Resolution Satellite Imagery. Indian Institute of Space Science and Technology (2016)

International Workshop on Geographical Analysis, Urban Modeling, Spatial Statistics (Geog-An-Mod 2022)

Using GIS for Analyzing the Effectiveness of Urban Growth Boundary in Karaj, Iran

Mohamad Molaei Qelichi[1](✉), Rahmatollah Farhoudi[2], and Beniamino Murgante[3]

[1] Faculty of Encyclopedia Research, Institute for Humanities and Cultural Studies, Tehran, Iran
m.molaei@ihcs.ac.ir

[2] Faculty of Geography, University of Tehran, Tehran, Iran

[3] School of Engineering, University of Basilicata, Potenza, Italy

Abstract. Nowadays, physical development is essential in any integrated urban development program. The rapid expansion in the physical form of cities in an unplanned and uneven growth in line with the various causes of irregular migration is considered one of the significant problems in Iran's cities, resulting in urban sprawl. With its numerous economic and environmental impacts, sprawling urban areas forced urban experts to explore strategies to deal with this phenomenon. The primary purpose of this research is to evaluate the effectiveness of urban growth boundaries in the Iranian metropolis of Karaj. This paper prepared the required data to explain the studied problem. The study was conducted using survey techniques, field operations, and GIS software to evaluate the measure of success and effectiveness of the urban growth boundary. Moreover, analyses and quantification of the spatial dimension of the urban expansion have been extracted using multi-classification techniques by Envi, ArcMap, and Snap software. On the other hand, the study collects multi-temporal and multi-sensor satellite data, Landsat ETM with L8. The quantification and mapping of urban growth enabled us to quantify and spatially characterize urban growth and create a model to make sustainable cities. As a whole, outputs from our investigations highlight that the currently available free of charge long-term satellite time series provides an excellent low-cost tool for several applications, including urban growth analysis.

Keywords: Urban growth boundary · Urban containment policies · Change detection · Karaj (Iran)

1 Introduction

The issue of urban growth, along with management policies and control as a causal issue, affects many metropolitan and regional programs and plans (Khalili et al. 2018). The physical growth and expansion of the city is a process that, despite being affected by existing structures, has directly or indirectly involved all urban systems and structures. For this reason, if this process does not follow the spatial approach, it will have many adverse effects on various parts of the city, resulting in poverty and imbalance, economic problems and unemployment, psychological problems of city dwellers, large-scale migration to cities, the main result of which is marginalization. And the creation of slums.

O. Gervasi et al. (Eds.): ICCSA 2022 Workshops, LNCS 13379, pp. 485–498, 2022.
https://doi.org/10.1007/978-3-031-10545-6_33

The change in the proportion of the urban population is the physical expansion outside the city plan and has involved cities with many problems. The dimensions and generality of this issue have further affected the cities of developing countries. However, if we think about the physical expansion of cities, we will see that cities are living organisms whose growth is an inevitable phenomenon. The city's physical development considered in this study is unplanned and scattered. In this regard, Nelson and Dawkins argue that "the uncontrolled expansion of urban growth and the dispersal of urbanization is due to many individual behaviors, especially the tendency for more space and the migration of minorities, as a result of some policies." Since invisible market groups cannot locate and allocate land use efficiently, public policies are needed to prevent the dispersal and control the rampant growth of cities. Cities are policies that inhibit urban growth, and their use by local governments is increasing (Nelson and Dawkins 2004). To this end, in the middle of the twentieth century, comprehensive plans were prepared for cities with the development of knowledge of planning and urban planning based on empirical-rational approaches. These plans proposed tools and strategies to deal with acute urban issues and problems, especially urban sprawl. One of these tools and strategies was the "boundary or urban growth boundary," whose mission was to prevent the uncontrolled physical growth of cities.

Previous studies have evaluated the effectiveness of urban growth boundaries in the studied areas (Ding 1996; Jun 2004; Bhatta 2009; Tayyebi et al. 2011; Guoen and Yuanyuan, 2012; Cho et al. 2006; Zheng et al., 2017; Chakraborti et al. 2018; Samat et al. 2021, Amer et al. 2021; Yi et al. 2022; Niu et al. 2022). Aware that developed countries imitate the majority of the planning system of developing countries, comprehensive plans were transferred to these countries within a short time interval and prepared for the cities and capitals of these countries. In comprehensive plans, policies range from the green belt to defining the physical urban growth boundaries (the urban growth boundary). Karaj was also one of the cities for which a comprehensive plan was prepared. In the comprehensive plans designed in Iran, the "urban growth boundary" policy has been used more or less from the beginning until now, and almost no such content change has occurred in them. The primary purpose of this study is to evaluate the success of the policy of urban growth control measures included in the Karaj metropolis's comprehensive plans and, in particular, the "urban growth boundary." In summary, this study tries to determine the degree of compliance of the planned urban growth boundary with actual conditions, determine the planning process and its implementation, and analyze the effectiveness and success of this policy.

2 Study Area

Karaj is the capital of Alborz Province in Iran, spanning between latitudes 35°67′–36°14′N and longitudes 50°56′– 51°42′E and covers a total area of about 141 km^2. (Iranian Statistics Center 2016). Over the last three decades, Karaj has been experiencing a significantly growing, primarily due to its socioeconomic attractions. Past developments and challenges have led to environmental, socio-cultural, political-security, economic, and spatial (Sakieh et al. 2014) (Fig. 1).

Karaj, in 1956, had a population of fifteen thousand people. However, in 2016, the population of Karaj city reached 1592492 people. The area of the city has increased from about 3900 ha in 1956 to about 17000 ha now. Karaj is a city whose main structure and texture is the product of developments in Iran from 1340 onwards and the achievement of the Renaissance in the country.

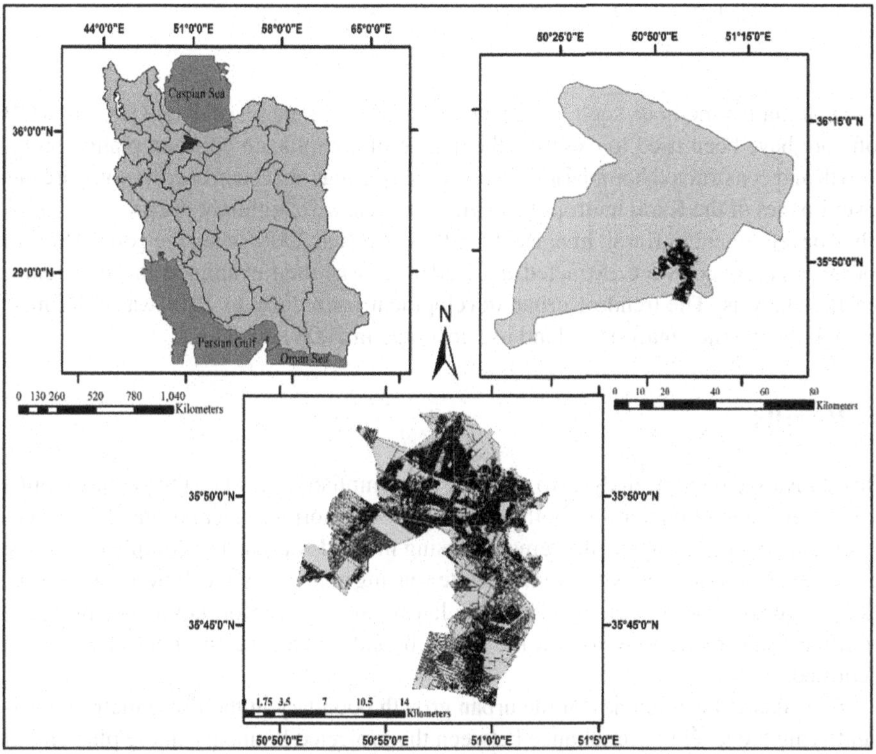

Fig. 1. The study area of Karaj City, Iran

3 Material and Methodology

Multi-temporal data sets of Landsat ETM 2008 and L8 (OLI) 2014 images were collected from the USGS and GLCF websites for the study area. Image processing was done using Arc GIS 10.8 and Envi 5.3 software tools. The analyses were addressed to detect the changes in the urban areas based on comparing the outputs obtained from the classification and geospatial analysis of the past and present data (Santarsiero et al. 2022). Table 1 summarizes the data used for remote sensing analysis and overlay analysis.

Table 1. Data collection properties of the study area of Karaj

Satellite	Sensor	Resolution (M)	Acquisition date
Landsat	ETM	30 m	Aug 2008
Landsat	L8	30 m	Jul 2014

Quantitative methods such as distance measurement analysis using GIS and ENVI software have been used to examine the degree of compliance between planned urban growth and constructed boundaries. Overlay analysis has also been used to compare land cover images of the Karaj metropolis in different years. To highlight the process of rapid urban development in Karaj, images of land use status in 2008, when the comprehensive plan was approved, were extracted until 2014. It was then examined through remote sensing analysis. The trend of urban development from 2008 to 2014 was determined through the overlay analysis of land use coverage in 2008 and 2014.

4 Results

This study used overlay analysis to examine the compliance between the planned boundary and the actual boundary in both quantitative and morphological terms. Before land cover and land use analysis, the remote sensing method was used to complete the existing Karaj land boundary extraction. Remote sensing analysis is a technique that is often used for geographic processing. Thus, the latest land cover information was processed from the Karaj metropolis so that the actual boundary built on the land of Karaj was identified.

To evaluate the efficiency of the urban growth boundary in the Karaj metropolis, by identifying the level of compliance between the projected boundary in the plan and the actual boundary, the researcher can conclude to what extent the policies have successfully controlled urban growth and dispersion. This section presents empirical evidence on the success of the 2008 plan's urban growth boundary, as evaluated by compliance. Three general parts of this part: (1) urban development in 2008–2014, (2) the level of compliance between the actual boundary built in 2014 and the urban growth boundary planned in the 2008 plan; (3) Details of developments that occurred outside the urban growth boundary (Azizi et al. 2019).

After analyzing the distance and classifying land use information, the lands constructed in the metropolis of Karaj at the time of preparation of the comprehensive plan (2008) have been estimated at 9620 ha. After six years and in 2014, the area of land built in Karaj has changed to 12033. The cultivated land has increased by about 2400 ha in 6 years, which shows a growth rate of 25.08% (Fig. 2).

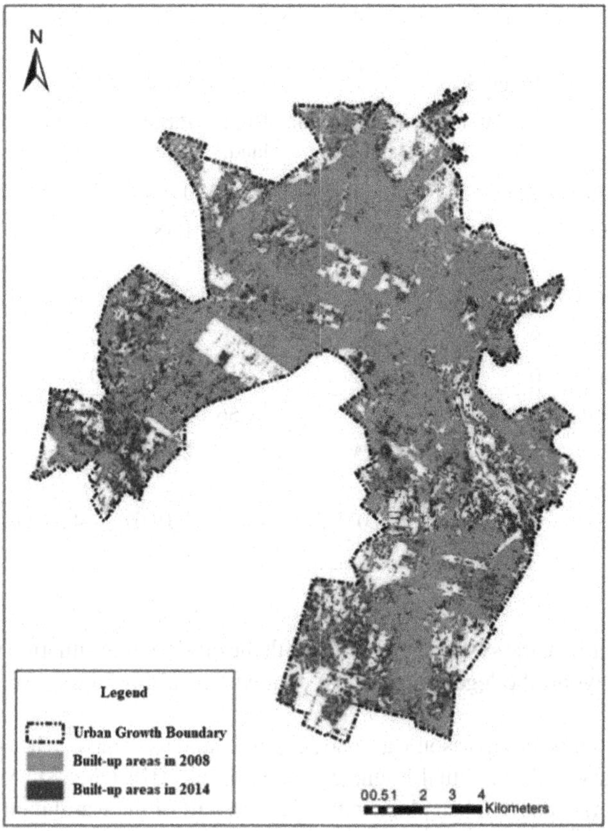

Fig. 2. Evolution of built-up areas in Karaj from 2008 to 2014

When we compare the urban morphology of 2008 with 2014, we find that most lands built-in 2014 have expanded in the vicinity of the lands built-in 2008. As can be seen in the picture, during the comprehensive plan period of 2008, most of these increases occurred in the western and southern parts of Karaj. The majority of these developments have resulted from the conversion of barren and agricultural lands into urban lands so that 24 km^2 of agricultural lands, barren lands, and orchards have undergone land use changes and gone under construction. The details of these changes and developments of the user class are detailed in Table 2.

Since the purpose of the urban growth boundary is to control urban development until all the new developments have taken place in the form of the urban growth boundary, it can be said that the result of planning and design is by the plan. Analysis of satellite images and Google Earth software shows that in 2008 when the urban growth boundary was prepared in the comprehensive plan, many changes were taking place in the physical outskirts of Karaj (especially in the west and south). Also, it seems that these added spots and settlements, although delayed, have been gradually integrated within the legal limits of the municipality, and no plan has been made to manage (or remove) them. In the lack of

Table 2. Amount and area of land use and change the share of each of them (square kilometer)

		Initial State						
		Unclassified	Agricultural land	Built land	Barren land	Green land	Row total	Class total
Final State	Unclassified	223.94	0	0	0	0	223.94	223.94
	Agricultural land	0	5.51	0.04	1.48	3.21	10.25	11.59
	Green land	0	1.71	0	0.03	3.66	5.4	5.98
	Barren land	0	0.78	3.2	29.39	0.3	33.67	42.21
	Built land	0	2.01	34.16	13.2	0.25	49.62	82.09
	Class total	223.94	19.66	39.56	52.88	10.34	0	0
	Class Changes	0	14.15	5.39	23.49	6.69	0	0
	Image Difference	0	−8.07	42.54	−10.67	−4.37	0	0

laws and regulations, the system for dealing with the city's actual situation has frequently disregarded (beyond the legal boundaries) contexts, resulting in the over-expansion of these contexts.

A morphological comparison was made through land use analysis between the urban growth boundary and the actual boundary made up to 2014 (Fig. 3). As can be seen, many developments have taken place in the western part of the Karaj metropolis outside the urban growth boundaries and connected to its physical fabric. These developments outside the urban growth boundary are 3.17 km^2, equal to 13.20% of the total increase in the area built in 2008–2014 (2400 ha). This statistic shows that the urban growth boundary has not effectively controlled the urban growth of Karaj, at least in the west. In addition, most illegal extensions in 2008 and the start of the comprehensive plan have not been eliminated, and the expansion around them has continued.

However, despite the expansion outside the urban growth boundary, there is still a large amount of land within the city and the urban growth boundary, which is included in the classification of satellite images in the form of barren lands (Fig. 4). At the end of the comprehensive plan period, the area of these lands is about 5279 ha. With an increase of approximately 2400 ha of urban land between 2008 and 2014, approximately 41 km^2 of barren land remains within the legal urban growth boundaries, demonstrating that, despite the possibility of development within the urban growth boundaries, much of the activity construction has occurred outside the urban growth boundaries.

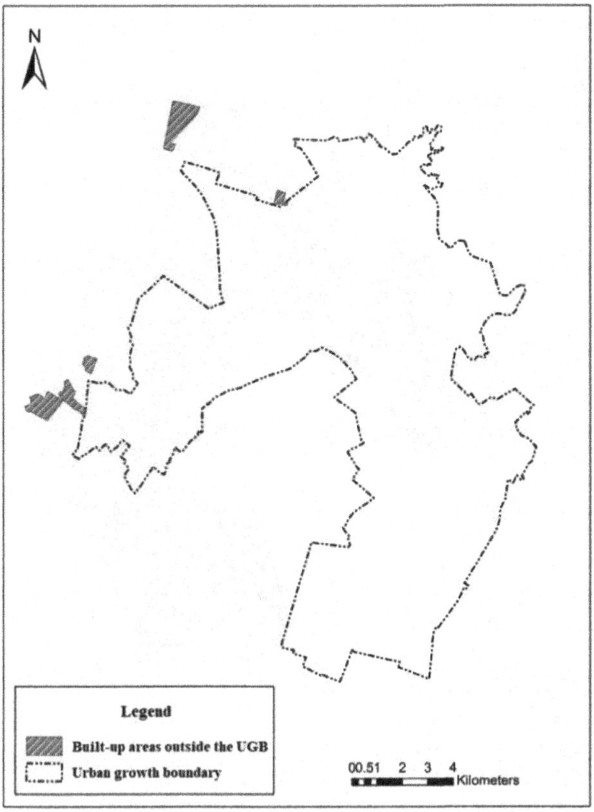

Fig. 3. Built-up areas outside the urban growth boundary

The boundary containment ratio (BCR) is one of the indicators presented by Han et al. (2009) that deals with the degree of containment in urban growth boundaries. This index is measured by calculating the ratio between areas built outside the urban growth boundary (3.17 km^2) and areas built within the urban growth boundary (52.79 km^2). The higher the ratio, the lower the degree of success and effectiveness of the urban growth boundary. The ratio of this index for the Karaj metropolis is calculated to be 0.13. In this paper, due to the lack of necessary information and resources, only the extensions outside the boundary and connected to the west of Karaj have been calculated and taken into account; naturally, the value of this index has a low number. Although this index is low at first glance and shows the success of the urban growth boundary in curbing urban development, as mentioned, because only the developments west of Karaj were considered, this index indicates the failure of the urban growth boundary in the siege of urban development in Karaj.

According to the above analysis, it can be seen that the urban growth boundary has not effectively restrained and besieged the new developments of the Karaj metropolis. So that 13.20% of the increase in land built-in 2008–2014 has spread beyond urban growth limits. However, from a quantitative point of view, the total amount of land increase made

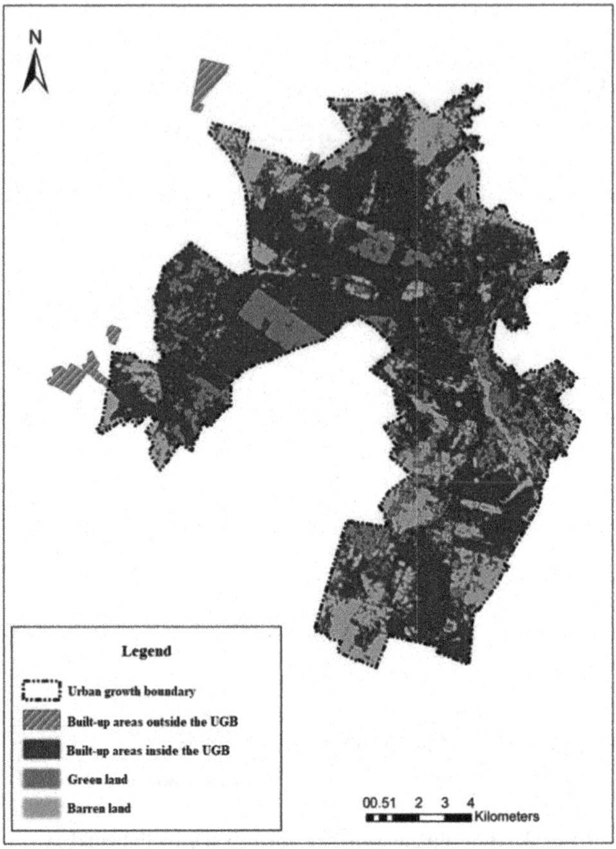

Fig. 4. Barren lands inside the urban growth boundary

in 2008–2014, both inside and outside the urban growth boundary, is 27.3 km^2 (including lands developed outside the urban growth boundary) smaller. One of the available lands for development inside the boundary is the comprehensive plan of 2008 (approximately 41.02 m^2). That indicates that until 2014, the urban growth boundary had somewhat limited urban development. In other words, there is a quantitative (numerical) adaptation in the period 2008–2014. Of course, it is necessary to mention that this adaptation is partly due to the large area of the Karaj metropolitan boundary in the comprehensive plan. Table 3 provides an overview of the above analysis (Figs. 5 and 6).

Table. 3 A summary of the UGB's effectiveness analysis

Indicators	Values
Area of increased built-up land during 2008–2014 (A1 + A2)	27.3 Km^2
Area of increased built-up areas inside the UGB during 2008–2014 (A1)	24.13 Km^2
Area of increased built-up areas the outside UGB during 2008–2014 (A2)	3.17 Km^2
Area of urban land allowed by UGB in 2008 (A3)	52.79 Km^2
Area of barren land inside the UGB in 2014 (A4)	41.02 Km^2
The boundary containment ratio (BCR) (A2/A1)	0.13

(Zheng 2014)

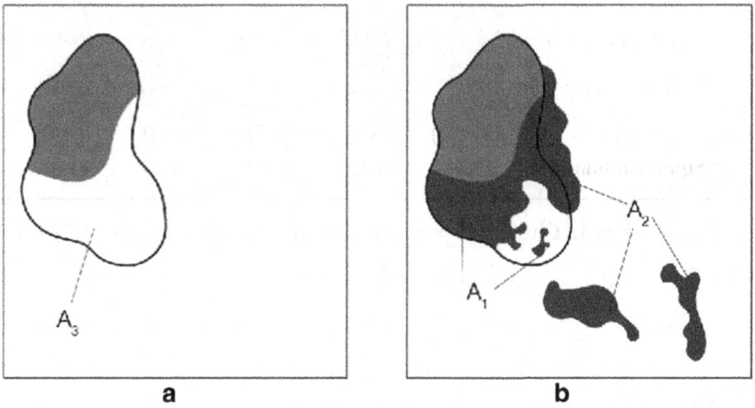

Fig. 5. Illustration of the areas and boundaries of analysis. (a) The start of the planning period; (b) The end of the planning period (Han et al. 2009; Zheng 2014).

In general, it can be inferred that until 2014, the level of morphological compliance between the urban growth boundary predicted in the comprehensive plan and the constructed boundary was low. A significant part of the new developments has occurred outside the urban growth boundary (in the western part of the Karaj metropolis), and the value of the urban growth inhibition index is 0.13. In contrast, the level of compliance is somewhat high as calculated by the size and breadth of uses.

By examining the lands built outside the urban growth boundary and the aerial images of the Karaj metropolis, it can be found that most of these lands have residential use and, in some cases, industrial use. In order to confirm the accuracy of the judgment, field research was conducted at four sites, which can be seen in Figs. 7, 8, 9 and 10.

Research has shown that site (a) is the residential town of Golha in the northwest of Karaj, and site (b) in the northwest is dedicated to the Baharestan industrial town and is located outside the legal growth zone of the city. Site (c) also has a residential use (Abrisham Town). Site (d), as shown in the picture, has a military use and is manifested outside the urban growth boundaries.

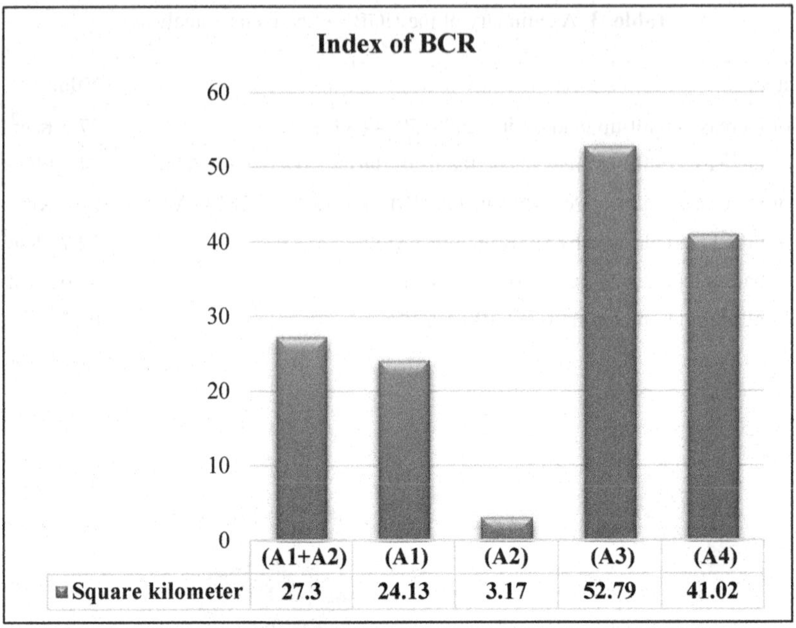

Fig. 6. Changes in boundary containment ratio (BCR)

Fig. 7. Site (a)

Fig. 8. Site (b)

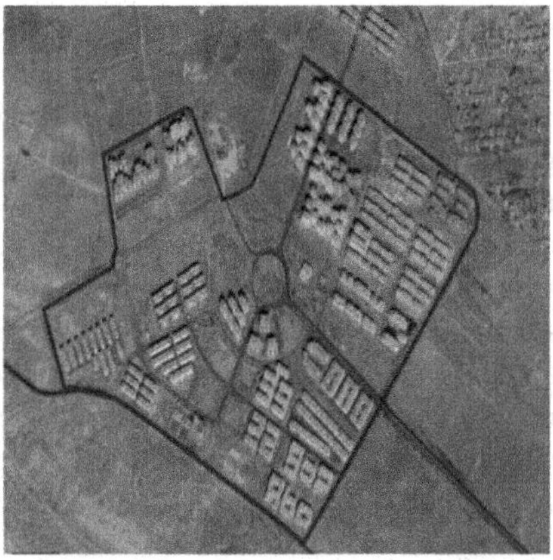

Fig. 9. Site (c) (Google earth, 2020)

Fig. 10. Site (d) (Google earth, 2020)

By imposing restrictions on the growth of the city of Karaj based on their approved physical development plans and the relative increase in land prices in them, the low-income migrant population turned to villages near the two city centers to have both shelter and the opportunity to use the facilities of these cities. And have Tehran. In this way, agricultural lands and gardens were separated and made available to the people in small plots in charters. In the 1990s, the government approved converting these rural areas into cities.

The concentration of urban centers in the east of the constituency is more than in the west due to the strong attractiveness of the labor market, Tehran services, and the comparative advantage of communication facilities in this sector. Being located in a standard communication network, daily use of services and employment and training facilities, and attracting the overflow of Tehran population are signs of functional connection with Tehran metropolis. Except for Karaj, most of these cities have become small, densely populated villages with very limited development capacity, as they are among the finest agricultural lands, and their growth has destroyed much of the region's environmental potential.

5 Conclusion

The Industrial Revolution and the subsequent developments that led to the urbanization revolution in the second half of the nineteenth century made the settlement of human beings in cities different and led to the unprecedented expansion of cities. Rapid urbanization disrupts land use patterns and poses severe threats to natural resources, so it is necessary to delineate urban growth boundaries (UGB) to encompass large-scale urban development (Ma 2020).

In the present century, scattered urban development is a common phenomenon in many metropolises and cities of Iran. Fundamental changes in social, economic, and political institutions have led to an increase in Iran's urban population of about 60% over four decades. This excessive increase in population has led to the growth and expansion of cities, which manifested that the growth of cities in Iran has also led mainly to suburban expansion. One of the cities facing the problem of horizontal irregular growth is the city of Karaj. This city had the appearance of a garden city until 1345. However, with the growth of migration, destruction of gardens and green lands on the other hand and the transfer of agricultural water to Karaj, drying of gardens and the emergence of new urban neighborhoods, unprincipled construction along roads and connecting multiple systems around the outskirts of Karaj, it has become modern Karaj. One of the main challenges of this city is its physical development, which has led to the destruction of gardens and agricultural lands and increased the cost of urban services (Bozorgmehr et al. 2013) because the city of Karaj has gone through the process of urban development and evolution much faster than the natural pace and in a short time and has experienced uneven horizontal growth.

In order to counter the urban sprawl and distribution in Iran from the middle of the present century, comprehensive urban plans that had policies at the heart of controlling and limiting urban growth were used. In the framework of these comprehensive plans, urban growth control policies include the green belt, the boundary of urban services, And the city growth boundary (the city's physical growth zone). More than four decades after preparing the first comprehensive plans for Iranian cities and the definition of growth boundaries for cities, a comprehensive and accurate assessment of the success and effectiveness of these urban growth control tools has not yet been done. This factor caused this research to do this essential and selected its study sample in the metropolis of Karaj and by examining it to evaluate the success rate and effectiveness of the urban growth boundary.

The topic selected for this study is to evaluate and evaluate the success of urban growth control policies in the comprehensive plans of the Karaj metropolis. This macro goal assessed the compliance of the "urban growth boundary" policy planned in the comprehensive plans and its actual situation. Research findings show that the urban growth boundary has not effectively controlled urban development. Among the reasons that have contributed to the failure of the urban growth boundary are the plan's low quality, poor quality of implementation, and lack of political support from governments; Cited. From 2008 to 2014, some of the new developments have been located outside the urban growth boundary. When the ability to control the urban growth boundary was measured using the "boundary containment ratio" index, it was shown that the value of this index was 0.13, which indicates the inability of the urban plan to limit urban development in the Karaj metropolis.

Developments outside the growth of the Karaj metropolis mainly include residential and military settlements and industrial projects. Of course, their construction time is different, and as mentioned, some existed before the comprehensive plan was prepared, and some are still being developed and under construction. In short, all the reasons that have led to the failure and effectiveness of comprehensive plans and consequently the urban growth boundary can ultimately be summed up by policymakers' insufficient understanding of urban growth boundary and the resulting problematic urban management. To create a deeper understanding of the failure of the urban growth boundary in the comprehensive plans of the Karaj metropolis, the weaknesses of this research must be filled. Therefore, further research on assessing the urban growth boundary of the Karaj metropolis can refine the above aspects and achieve better results.

Acknowledgments. The authors would like to thank the Iran National Science Foundation (INSF) for funding this work through grant no. 96000426.

References

Amer, M.S., Majid, M.R., Ledraa, T.A.: The riyadh urban growth boundary: an analysis of the factors affecting its efficiency on restraining sprawl. Int. J. Built Environ. Sustain. **8**(3), 17–25 (2021). https://doi.org/10.11113/ijbes.v8.n3.704

Azizi, D., Taghvaee, A., Adineloofard, M.: Evaluation of the success of the urban growth boundary comprehensive plans in the containment of the growth of metropolitan Tehran. Hoviatshahr **13**(3), 5–18 (2019)

Bhatta, B.: Modelling of urban growth boundary using geoinformatics. Int. J. Dig. Earth **2**(4), 359–381 (2009). https://doi.org/10.1080/17538940902971383

Bozorgmehr, N., Habibi, M., Barakpour, N.: Assessment of Karaj current development plan based on the smart growth. J. Archit. Urban Plan. **6**(11), 131 (2013)

Chakraborti, S., NathDas, D., Mondal, B., ShafizadehMoghadam, H., Feng, Y.: A neural network and landscape metrics to propose a flexible urban growth boundary: a case study. Ecol. Ind. **93**, 952–965 (2018)

Cho, S.-H., Chen, Z., Yen, S.T., Eastwood, D.B.: Estimating effects of an urban growth boundary on land development. J. Agric. Appl. Econ. **38**(2), 287–298 (2006). https://doi.org/10.1017/S1074070800022331

Ding, C.: Managing urban growth for efficiency in infrastructure provision: dynamic capital expansion and urban growth boundary models. Thesis (Ph.D.) -- University of Illinois at Urbana-Champaign (1996)

Guoen, W., Yuanyuan, Z.: Urban growth boundary efficacy and its influence on administrative boundary adjustment. Planners **28**(3), 21–27 (2012)

Han, H.Y., Lai, S.K., Dang, A.R., Tan, Z.B., Wu, C.F.: Effectiveness of urban construction boundaries in Beijing: an assessment. J. Zhejiang Univ., Sci., A **10**(9), 1285–1295 (2009)

Iranian Statistics Center, Karaj statistical yearbook 2016. Tehran, Iran (2016)

Jun, M.-J.: The effects of portland's urban growth boundary on urban development patterns and commuting. Urban Stud. **41**(7), 1333–1348 (2004). https://doi.org/10.1080/0042098042000214824

Khalili, A., Zebardast, E., Azizi, M.: Typology of urban growth management politics in urban based regions. Armanshahr Archit. Urban Dev. **10**(21), 291–308 (2018)

Ma, Q.: Integrating ecological correlation into cellular automata for urban growth simulation: a case study of Hangzhou China. Urban Forestry Urban Greening **51**, 126697 (2020)

Nelson, A.C., Moore, T.: Assessing growth management policy implementation: case study of the united states' leading growth management state. Land Use Policy **13**(4), 241–259 (1996). https://doi.org/10.1016/0264-8377(96)84555-8

Nelson, A.C., Dawkins, C.J.: Urban containment in the United States: History, models, and techniques for regional and metropolitan growth management. APA Plan. Advisory Serv. Rep. **520**, 1–82 (2004)

Niu, W., et al.: Understanding the corrective effect of the urban growth boundary policy on land finance dependence of local governments in China. Int. J. Environ. Res. Public Health **19**(8), 4785 (2022). https://doi.org/10.3390/ijerph19084785

Sakieh, Y., Amiri, B.J., Danekar, A., Feghhi, J., Dezhkam, S.: Simulating urban expansion and scenario prediction using a cellular automata urban growth model, SLEUTH, through a case study of Karaj City Iran. J. Hous. Built Environ. **30**(4), 591–611 (2014)

Samat, N., Mahamud, M.A., Tilaki, M.J.M., Abu Bakar, M.A., Mou, L.T., Mohd Noor, N.: Investigating urban growth boundary as mechanism to plan for sustainable urban development. Plan. Malaysia **19**(18) (2021). https://doi.org/10.21837/pm.v19i18.1050

Santarsiero, V., NolÃ, G., Lanorte, A., Tucci, B., Cillis, G., Murgante, B.: Remote sensing and spatial analysis for land-take assessment in Basilicata Region (Southern Italy). Remote Sen. **14**(7), 1692 (2022)

Tayyebi, A., Pijanowski, B.C., Tayyebi, A.H.: An urban growth boundary model using neural networks, GIS and radial parameterization: an application to Tehran Iran. Landscape Urban Plan. **100**(1), 35–44 (2011)

Yi, D., Guo, X., Han, Y., Guo, J., Ou, M., Zhao, X.: Coupling ecological security pattern establishment and construction land expansion simulation for urban growth boundary delineation: framework and application. Land **11**(3), 359 (2022). https://doi.org/10.3390/land11030359

Zheng, L.: Evaluating the Effectiveness of Urban Growth Control Boundary in Comprehensive Land Use Plan through a Conformance-Based Approach an Empirical Study of Hangzhou, China, Master's Thesis, MSc PLANET Europe European Spatial Planning, Environmental Policy and Regional Development (2014)

Zheng, Q., et al.: Delimiting urban growth boundary through combining land suitability evaluation and cellular automata. Sustainability **9**(12), 2213 (2017). MDPI AG. http://dx.doi.org/10.3390/su9122213

GLCF http://glcf.umd.edu/

USGS: http://edcsns17.cr.usgs.gov/EarthExplorer/

Building a Rule-Based Generalisation Service for Geovisualisation of Business Data

Marion Simon[1] and Hartmut Asche[2(✉)]

[1] Faculty of Science, University of Potsdam, Karl-Liebknecht-Str. 24-25, 14476 Potsdam, Germany
marion.simon@uni-potsdam.de

[2] Computer Graphics System Group, Hasso Plattner Institute, University of Potsdam, Prof.-Dr.-Helmert-Str. 2-3, 14482 Potsdam, Germany
hartmut.asche@hpi.de

Abstract. Effective geovisualisation is characterised by the fact that the application context, the output medium and the visual-cognitive abilities of the targeted audience are carefully considered when it comes to an informed (carto)graphic representation of a spatial data set. In this way, an optimal visual communication and analysis of the spatial facts is made possible. An essential key to this is the absence of graphic conflicts that tend to impede proper visual perception. At the level of (carto)graphic modelling, this is achieved by application-specific generalisation measures that are bundled in a toolbox. In the automated generation of effective map graphics, these generalisation measures are used in a rule-based manner. To avoid specific graphical conflicts, interactive components are integrated into the processing chain that support expert generalisation solutions. To date, such tools, some of which work automatically, exist for specific visualisation systems and GIS only. A professional generalisation solution that is automated and can be implemented across systems and platforms is currently missing. Against this background this paper discusses a modular, web-based concept for the rule-based generalisation service of quantitative business data.

Keywords: Geovisualisation · Cartographic modelling of spatial data · Graphical conflicts · Cartographic generalisation · Automated generalisation

1 Introduction

The aim of visualisation is the transformation of (spatial) alphanumeric data into a graphical form of representation. Every alphanumeric representation is scale-free. Every graphic representation of spatial data is subject to scaling and it causes abstraction or generalisation. Geovisualisation enables "visualisation" of semantic relationships in their spatial reference [1]. The lack of generalisation, e.g., when zooming in and out, destroys or hinders the transmission of information. That is why it is not an expert requirement, but a shere communication necessity. Experts make generalisation possible. The spatial reference of alphanumeric data is established by assigning characters to data objects (theme) in connection with their mapping onto a data-related base map. A

O. Gervasi et al. (Eds.): ICCSA 2022 Workshops, LNCS 13379, pp. 499–513, 2022.
https://doi.org/10.1007/978-3-031-10545-6_34

characteristic of the thematic map is the variety of cartographic design modalities. These are directly dependent on the data basis, and indirectly on the scale. This results in the problem of ineffective information transfer. The basic spatial method basis of object-sign referencing finds its application in applied cartography in the form of cartographic representation methods.

A generalisation of spatial visualisation without expertise leads to ineffective map graphics. Effectiveness requires intuitive interpretability from a visual representation [2]. Generalisation is thus considered a decisive influencing factor in the practical application of representation methods. Here the problem arises that generalisation is scale-dependent, but semantically based. This results in the imperative need for expertise. With regard to a largely automated generalisation service, the system should be able to mirror this expertise. Richardson and Müller [3] comment that "automated solutions to generalization should emulate the cartographer's decision making." "However, it is not clear that algorithms and procedures can suffice by themselves" Buttenfield [4] points out.

The solution must be a professional web service that constructs the necessary production steps of a high-quality graphical representation into a process as automatically as possible. One of these essential construction steps is generalisation. While the cartographic generalisation of topographic representations is confronted with graphical conflicts that arise due to the derivation of a subsequent map, i.e., the transfer of map contents of a smaller scale map, the generalisation in thematic cartography is independent of scale. Digital generalisation is defined by McMaster and Shea [5] "as the process of deriving, from a data source, a sybolically or digitally-encoded cartographic data set through the application of spatial and attribute transformations." Regnauld and McMaster [6] see in McMaster and Shea's remarks "the maintenance of graphical clarity at the target scale" as one of the goals of digital generalisation. For the technical implementation of a professional web service for semi-automated generalisation, theoretical cartographic knowledge has to be formalised. This comprises solutions for map construction including the generalisation of thematic maps as well as modalities of further conflict types. Standardised map construcxtion including the required generalisation procedures. Starting from a map image as an intermediate result after running through a map construction pipeline [7], the generalisation is run through in the further processing to create the final visualisation model (Fig. 1).

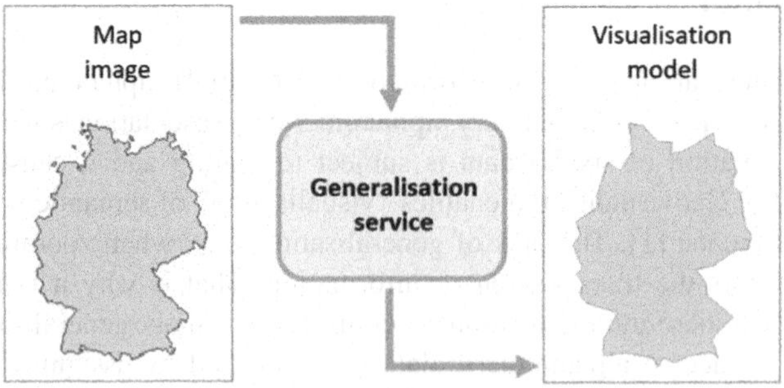

Fig. 1. Simplification of shape throught generalisation service

2 Solution Approach

The mapping of spatial business data is often done by means of choropleth or area diagram maps (Fig. 2). These represent the results of the cartographic representation methods used. The latter are characterised, among other things, by certain requirements for the data to be depicted (e.g., scaling level). The unique signatures for different map types and cartograms to convey the information content (e.g., area signatures or diagrams) also require special properties of the data to be displayed [8]. For the visualisation of statistical business data in area diagram maps and choropleth maps, mostly diagrams (circles, columns, bars) or area colours are used. Kishimoto [9] describes choropleth maps, which are also used under other names, as "undoubtedly one of the largest groups of maps for the representation of statistical data". Unfortunately, they are often used improperly. Therefore, the focus of this paper is on area diagram maps, which are an adequate professional alternative.

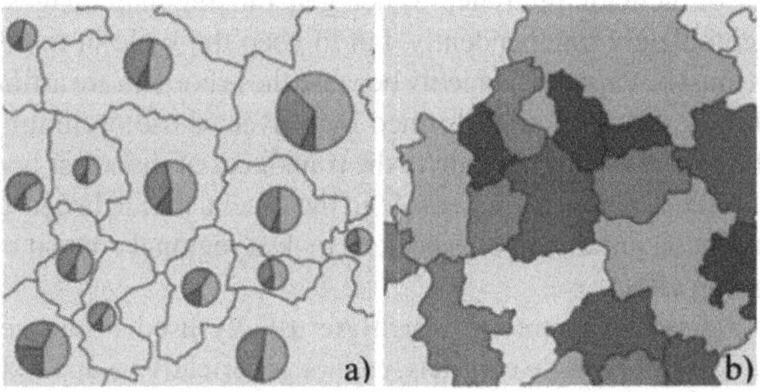

Fig. 2. Mapping principle of (a) area diagram maps and (b) choropleth maps

The above-mentioned diagrams and area fillings are embedded in the respective administrative unit, regardless of their form and colour, and represent an information layer. The administrative reference units themselves form a separate information layer. The filling of these administrative units occurs in the cartographic representation method of area cartograms and could be combined with the layer of area diagram maps if certain conditions are met. Thus, a statistical map representation entails several information layers that require generalisation measures coordinated with the layers.

A base map serves to locate the topic in order to ensure regional comparability. The content of a base map depends on the topic to be depicted. In addition to the core element for embedding the topic, representation of water bodies, depiction of administrative or other territorial units support orientation. There is disagreement on the question of relief representation and forest areas. Various sources show different opinions on the necessity of base map content.

The thematic information to be conveyed by the map will generate different generalisation needs depending on the cartographic means of expression used. In some cases, data generalisation has been done in advance for map image production. A recursion to this already completed data generalisation module may be useful in the course of the generalisation. When these circumstances occur is to be investigated in the course of processing identified conflicts within the generalisation process.

One aim of the generalisation is to harmonise the base map elements in order to achieve the map objective of an optimal graphical representation of the thematic spatial content. The need for generalisation of the base map used as the map basis for establishing the spatial reference and of the thematic representation layer can be determined at the level of model generalisation and map generalisation [11]. Furthermore, an emerging need for generalisation after the merging of both layers has to be identified. Generalisation measures to be introduced must be found to solve the problem graphically.

Automation requires a form of standardisation. This can be implemented through rules. Therefore, in addition to special map type-dependent generalisation modalities, the complexity of a map representation should be described in a rule-based manner by defining the degree of generalisation. Since the contents of the base map depend on the topic, as mentioned above, the strict scale independence of generalisation measures recedes in favour of thematic reference. When generalising map images, it is important not to proceed completely independently, but to keep the scale in mind. For example, national borders must be depicted jaggedly because these borders are artificial (not visible in the real world). A natural border, formed by a river whose oscillating centre line is real and has to be generalised according to the roundness of the water body. Objects and their regional distribution play a greater role in the special theme because they represent the theme. AI (artificial intelligence) can take a look at regional context of the topic after appropriate learning effect.

Certain generalisation operators, which are usually used in the generalisation of topographic maps to resolve rule conflicts, cannot generically be applied in the generalisation of tematic maps because they are strictly scale-bound. An example of this is the mathematically based Töpfer's root law [12], which can positively influence a reduction of quantities and thus the graphic map load. However, scale-boundness must also be kept in mind when generalising thematic map representations in connection with the desired output parameters. A screen presentation, for example, has different requirements for the presentation than a print edition.

Both forms of presentation (see Fig. 2) require a two-dimensional irregular surface representation of the reference unit. Other contents of the base map are used as needed for each application. This requires a regulation in the form of a catalogue, which can be expanded in each application depending on the map topic. Other contents besides the representation of delimited, irregular area units to which the data to be mapped directly or indirectly refer depend on further factors. The density of the map content (also map load) describes the map complexity. When assessing map load, thematic elements must be prioritised.

The need for generalisation results from the conflicts that a first map image brings with it after object-character referencing has taken place. In order to identify conflicts a catalogue of rules is necessary. For this purpose, generally valid visualisation rules are taken into account as far as possible in the application of cartographic representation methods. The aim of these rules is to ensure the readability of the representation. Occasionally they reach their limits due to subject matter and scale, and leave behind graphic conflicts. At the latest, however, when several information views interact or when localities are referred to purely semantically.

Generalisation operations must be specified in a standardised way for grouping use cases. Even if regional diversity requires individual case solutions, a rule set must first be set up to start generalisation, on which potential machine learning systems can base the use case group extension. When it comes to thematic generalisation, the user enjoys greater freedom. This implies more responsibility and consequently requires subject matter expertise. Solutions for the generalisation of visualisation models, consisting of map theme as well as base map, are first converted into process diagrams. The representation of the conceptual processes is module-based using SysML activity diagrams. The resulting process diagrams are algorithmised in a modular way and related in a rule-based way by connectors.

This generalisation service is not necessarily to be called up in its entirety. Rather, a specific process is requested for each use case, which determines the necessity of individual generalisation operators based on rules, connects to them and initiates their execution. This approach ensures maximum effectiveness in the computational effort and minimisation of the time required to perform the service. An implementation takes place within the development of the "expertly" web-based map construction service, which provides high-quality, semi-automatic map construction. A qualitative advancement through AI focuses on the regional context, which cannot be considered in the full automation due to the diversity for a generic solution. In any case the final decision on the success of a generalisation solution is left to the expert user.

The following work packages result from the explanations:

1. compilation of a generalisation rule catalogue,
2. identification of the resulting conflicts and further conflicts to justify the need for generalisation,
3. highlighting and describing solution options,
4. description of the way from map image to generalised visualisation model via process modelling for the development of the modularised generalisation service.

3 Implementation Strategy

Generalisation "is a selection of the most important, essential and its purposeful generalisation, in which it is important to depict reality on the map in its most important, typical features and characteristic peculiarities according to the purpose, the subject and the scale of the map" [13].

While going through a visualisation process [7] or after applying a system to create a map image, the user receives at one break point a map image that is aligned with the desired spatial section for the output parameters selected by the user (e.g., size for printing, or screenwidth). Such a graphic is mapped on the interface within the framework of the user-system interaction as a graphical draft of a map representation (presented as an example in Sect. 4). This map image requires generalisation.

WHY generalisation is necessary can have various reasons. Not all conflicts can be avoided by pre-selected parameter and signature decisions. If conflicts can be completely excluded, this also means a restriction of freedom in design. The process step of generalisation should not be dissolved even in such a case, because this would exclude a subsequent change of output parameters, such as the size of the map display on the screen.

In principle, generalisation should be carried out when ineffective map images are presented. In order to be able to assess the intended effectiveness, a comparison of the actual state with a defined target state is necessary. Such a comparison can be carried out semi-automatically on the basis of a rule catalogue. Generalisation is used in the case of control deviation. The need for generalisation can also arise when the user makes subsequent changes to decisions made in the map production process, for example:

- Changes to the data to be mapped,
- Extension/reduction of the room section,
- Modification of the output parameters (reproduction via beamer instead of laptop)
- Change of the design medium for the reproduction of the map theme (e.g. bar sectors instead of circle sectors for diagrams)

A representation of map objects is scale-bound, but there is also a need for generalisation that is detached from this. On the one hand, graphic conflicts are taken into account during generalisation, which are of pictorial origin on the raster level. They are considered to be the result of object sign referencing (OSR). On the other hand, within the framework of the generalisation of content-related or thematic object features, model generalisation (e.g., classification of objects) can bring about a changed graphic representation.

Generalisation measures answer the question HOW generalisation takes place. Slocum et al. [14] list ten "Fundamental Operations of Generalization":

- "Simplification: Selectively reducing the number of points required to represent an object;
- Smoothing: Reducing angularity of angles between lines,
- Aggregation: Grouping point locations and representing them as areal objects,
- Amalgamation: Grouping of individual areal features into a larger element,
- Collapse: Replacing an objekt's physical details with a symbol representing the object,
- Merging: Grouping of line features,
- Refinement: Selection specific portions of an object to represent the entire object,
- Exaggeration: To amplify a specific portion of an object,
- Enhancement: To elevate the message imparted by the object,
- Displacement: Separating objects."

These generalisation measures are used in topographic cartography. Simplification and displacement, for example, can also be used in thematic cartography. Effects on other map objects are far less significant than those produced during generalisation within topographic maps. In this work, the generalisation of thematic map representations for mapping statistical data is considered. Partial automation is aimed at and embedded in a generalisation service. "The aim, like that of all generalising, is to simplify a complex process to manageable proportions" [15]. These sub-processes must be broken down to the operator level so that they can be implemented in an algorithmised way.

3.1 Rule Base

The automation of generalisation processes first requires the definition of generic generalisation rules and editorial guidelines. The automation of individual generalisation processes requires a definition of the generalisation sequence, because the results of the individual measures have an impact on the other measures, or are the first to trigger them. This means that conflict identification must be carried out iteratively after each generalisation process. "There is no natural order for the execution of each generalisation operation." [16]. When setting up a rule catalogue, such an order must be determined.

The following rule catalogue (excerpt) (Table 1) applies to an intermediate map image that aims to be an area diagram map after completion of all process steps required for map creation:

Table 1. Excerpt of a rule catalogue for generalisation of an area diagram map (see Sect. 4)

Object	Rule
Administrative unit	Data basis: Polygons 1:3,000,000 from Eurostat simplificated by Mapshaper.org (Visvalignam Weighted Area, degree of generalisation 90%)
Administrative unit	Contour: line width 0.0706 mm, colour RGB 99, 99, 99
Administrative unit	Filling thematic polygons: RGB 230, 230, 230
Labelling	Country names: placement under diagram
Labelling	Diagram labeling: at the upper right corner of the diagram or diagram section
Diagram	Typ: rectangle, vertical, subdivided
Diagram	Filling: greater value RGB 240, 240, 240 and hatching pattern (ancle 45°, line width 0.0706 mm, hatch width 1 mm, structured: prarallel, coloured in grey tone of smaller value), smaller value RGB 99, 99, 99
Diagram	Area proportionality: none
Diagram	Width: maximum until smaller value subdivision of diagram reaches line width of 1.7 mm
Diagram	Height: minimum 3.4 mm

3.2 Conflict Identification

According to McMaster and Shea [17], the specific case in which generalisation is necessary is determined by a cartometric evaluation of Geometric Conditions, Spatial and Holistic Measures. The authors differentiate the generalisation measures according to spatial transformations (simplification, smoothing, aggregation and so on) and attribute transformations (classification and symbolisation). In this work, however, the symbolisation of attributes is considered as OSR, which must precede the generalisation service within process design of map production, since only then do graphical conflicts arise.

Generally, classification is prior to graphic generalisation. In case of graphic conflict, it may be useful to reclassify the data.

In order to identify existing conflicts and to specify solution models, a comparison with a rule base is necessary. Töpfer [12] is convinced that "the use of numerical criteria [.] ensures the correct evaluation of the details and thus the correct generalisation". Ruas and Duchene [18] take these specifications into account by terming it a "required value" of the object when establishing the principles of their "Generalisation Model". To ensure a future full automation of the generalisation procedures, we apply this approach.

3.3 Solution Options

Solutions exist for various conflicts. Some are implemented as tools, others as a mathematical approach, others again on a conceptual level. Some conflicts do not yet have generic solutions, which are solved individually by hand by experts. For example, freeing map characters (e.g., bridges or lettering) solves a graphical conflict that does not classically belong to generalisation measures. Also, not every solution is suitable for every application. Slocum et al. [14] show the problem that a line generalisation solution is not generally applicable due to semantics. Not even within an information category like borderline generalisation of administrative reference units.

For individual generalisation measures, tools exist, which were mostly designed and developed to meet the requirements of topographic maps. For thematic map display, for example, MapShaper and ColorBrewer can be used. MapShaper is a web-based solution software running in the browser to simplify the geometry of lines (e.g., administrative boundary lines and other contours). The user determines which of three available algorithms is to be used for the simplification (Douglas-Peucker, Visvalingam, modified Visvalingam-Whyatt [14], and the degree of generalisation can also be set individually. ColorBrewer is used for the selection of colour scales. Conditions such as colour blindness, printability or even colour selection using relief shading can be set.

3.4 Process Modelling

For the processing of a generalisation service, the rules relevant for the applied representation method and the map elements required with it must be specified in the rule catalogue, as exemplified in Sect. 3.1. Furthermore, generalisation measures on the algorithmic level of operators must be assigned to the conflict cases. For this purpose, a generalisation catalogue is used according to the scheme developed by Ruas and Duchene

Table 2. Generalisation catalogue principle [18]

Agent	Constraint	Conflict	Operator
A geographical object	Required value of characteristic of an object/two objects/a set of objects	Fact that one object does not satisfy a specific constraint	A generalisation action

[18] (Table 2). The values to be determined per conflict type and object element or group per use case are also entered in this. The order of the cases listed in the generalisation catalogue determines the prioritisation during processing, starting at the top.

The conflict column is variable for each process iteration, as values are currently recalculated. The generalisation service is to be regarded as a box in which, according to the SysML model concept, there are various roles that manage subordinate roles on their part (Fig. 3). Each role can contain an activity that can be executed independently as a process section. This hierarchical modularised concept should make it easier for the developer to set up and later maintain the components. Since each generalisation operator can be controlled individually as a role, they can be edited or deleted individually. Apart from the GenToolConnector, which must be adapted for each change, all other modules of the service remain untouched and unaffected. It is also possible to add further operators, which are integrated via the GenToolConnector. A new creation of solution operators is possible both comando-based and via a GUI (graphical user interface), or as an implementation in an outsourced web application. An application-specific adaptation of the generalisation tool to be used is also guaranteed. The changes are saved separately after execution for the purpose of reusability and the GenOperator resets itself to its original state if it is an on-board operator. GenOperator roles can also integrate APIs (interfaces) of external services such as Mapshaper, Colorbrewer or similar. In order to determine whether one of the mentioned roles is used at all, the generalisation service begins with the generalisation identification (GenIdentifier).

When this comes into action (act GenIdentifier), the underlying geometry data is first checked by the TopologyChecker. This looks for line intersections, non-closed polygons, voids in adjacent surfaces and other conflicts in the database. In order not to influence the determination of generalisation conflicts of quality deficiencies of the data set, this role must be upstream of all other process sections. Once any corrections have been made within the TopologyChecker action using TopoRepair, the search for generalisation conflicts in the map image (act GenCartoEvaluator) begins.

This connects each agent with the current feature class and reads out the associated constraints. An agent stands for an object or an object class in the map display and behaves in a 1:n relationship to the instance constraint. All target values of different object features are loaded. Then, for each potential conflict area, current values for occurring map elements are determined iteratively (act GenCalculator). The target-actual comparison is carried out by the action act GenController, which outputs boolean values (conflict present: yes, no) and saves the sizes of the deviations in a file. This can be queried by the user. In this way, e.g. minimal deviations can be judged as tolerable by the business user and thus removed from the generalisation catalogue. If no deviation from the target value is determined for the loaded agent, the loop is executed iteratively for the subsequent agent listed in the generalisation catalogue. However, if a need for generalisation has been determined, whether as a default decision after calculation by the service or corresponding assessment by the business user, the operators assigned to the individual conflicts in the generalisation catalogue are called one after the other. A generalisation operator stands for exactly one stored solution algorithm. For each line in the stored conflict value file, the respective generalisation operator is integrated successively via act GenToolConnector. After all generalisation cases have been processed, the

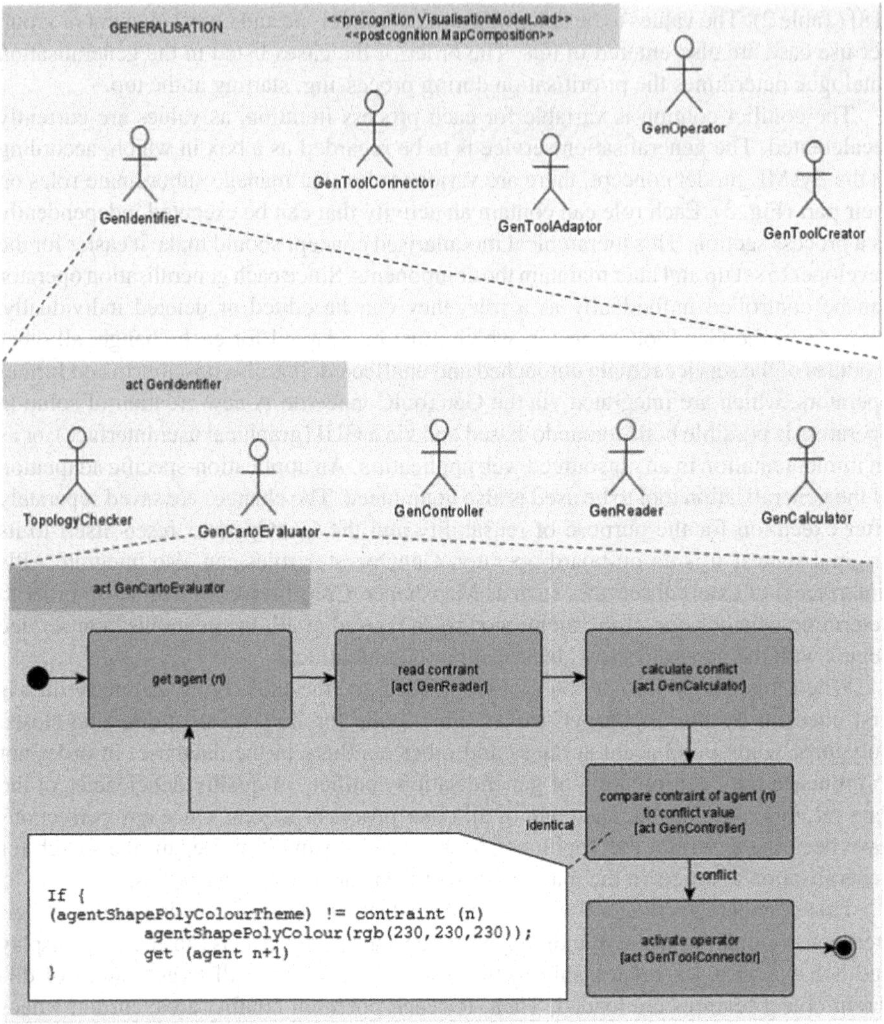

Fig. 3. Conceptual model of the generalisation service based on SysML

generalised visualisation model is mapped for evaluation and is available for any further editors that may be required or directly for further processing within the framework of map composition.

After the shape generalisation as the first measure, the action of TopologyChecker must be repeated before further processing in the generalisation catalogue. In this way, conflicts such as intersections or undercutting of minimum distances resulting from changes in the shape of the base map or its base point reduction can be eliminated.

4 Use Case

For the map image in this use case, following map purpose was defined:

Representation of a company's own exports of a product type (in tons) to Scandinavia (defined here: Denmark, Sweden, Norway, Finland). In comparison, import quantities from the entire EU are to be indicated for the same product category and year. This pursues the map objective of market analysis. The informative gain should consist of 1) highlighting one's own market position in the target region for this particular product category and furthermore making it easy to read how much market potential can be exploited in the short term, possibly without major operational investments. The interim result of the visualisation process (Fig. 4) was based on the following data:

Fictitious export quantities of a product category of a producing and exporting company were used, which has a near monopoly position in production in a certain country and knows the European competitors. Furthermore, import quantities for the product category in question were taken from Destatis for Scandinavia. Base map data (administrative units) available at Eurostat was downloaded for the selected spatial section.

Output parameters are now set for this example:

- given is a maximum image area of 12 * 19 cm, portrait format,
- black and white output, on screen, printable,
- insular map presentation,
- spatial section Scandinavian countries as described above,
- coordinate system used ETRS1989_LAEA (Lamberts Azimuthal Equal Area),
- spatial section and available mapping area define an output scale of 1:20,000,000.

This map image shows various visualisation problems. The boundary lines, especially the outer boundary lines, are displayed in a too differentiated manner. In doing so, the minimum dimensions for the representation of the islands are undershot and the minimum distances are not observed. Recesses are not always clearly recognisable as such. The map theme is implemented with a vertically positioned rectangle. However, these do not dominate, so that the map background seems to have a higher visual weight. Perceptionwise, it needs the other way around. To achieve this, colouring has to be changed, the optimal location of the diagrams needs to be checked, too. When placed within the reference area, the limiting factor is the smallest available space. The diagram for Denmark fits in exactly, but it influences the size of the other diagrams and thus limits the visual weighting. A solution to this could be: Balance out Norway and Finland as far as possible, taking up space, and place the Denmark diagram, which has now become too large for embedding in, outside the reference area and connect it with a line to the reference area. This measure is also possible if the underlying statistical data entail an enlarged diagram representation for Denmark and smaller ones for the other countries. Placing the represented values next to the diagrams increase the effectiveness of the visualisation model.

The generalisation service has traversed the presented rule catalogue for the described map target with the desired spatial section, specified data basis, taking into account the required output parameters (e.g., mapping area size, black/white representation) (Fig. 5).

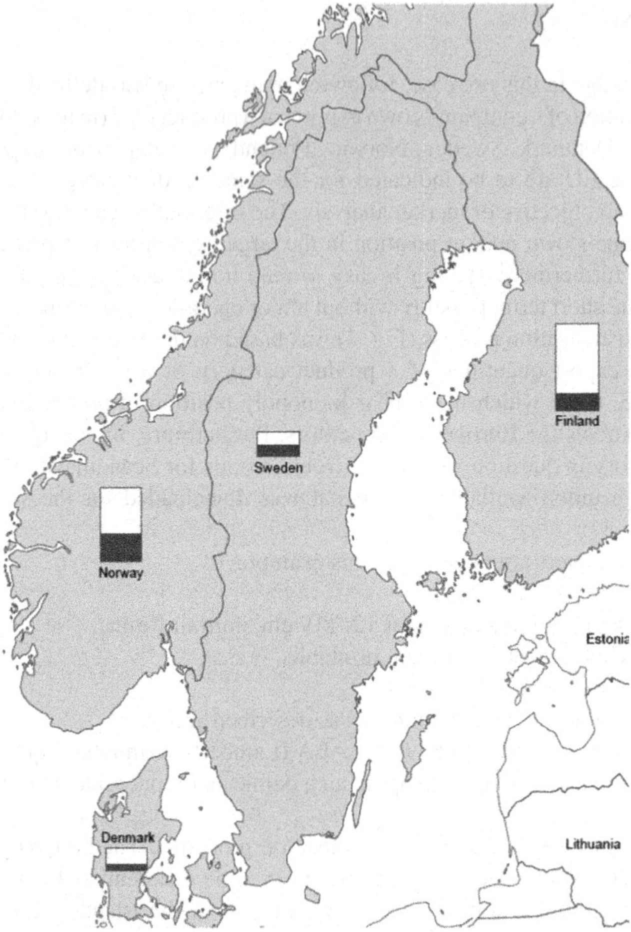

Fig. 4. Map image prior to generalisation: business export volumes in comparison to EU-import volumes to Scandinavian countries for a certain year and product category

The base map areas are no longer dominant, but rather appropriate for the purpose: the theme. The portion of imports which is not served by companie's exports are now expressed as potential volumes. Former map image ignores the potential due to whitening related diagram section. Applicated colouring based on the classification of colorbrewer2.org. Three grey tones have been used for the visualisation model with one minimally intensification in favour of an optimised figure-ground distiction.

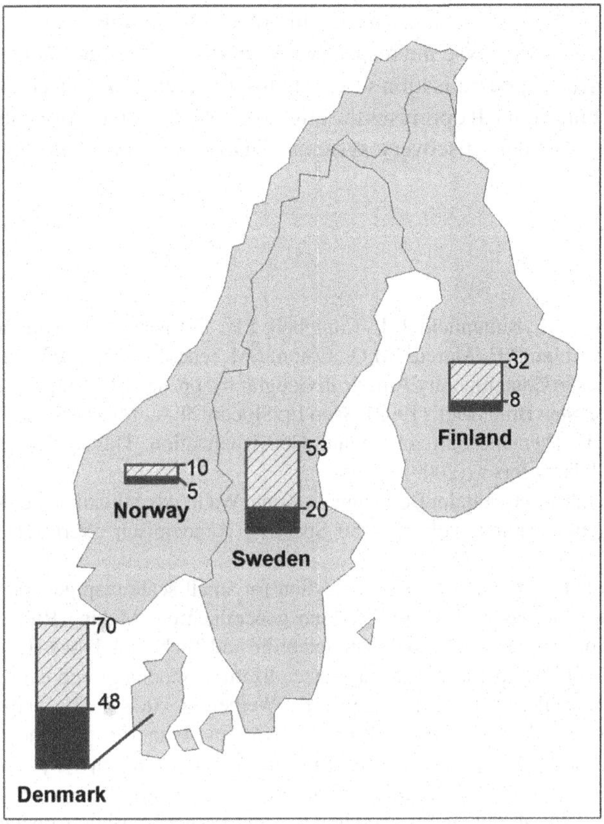

Fig. 5. Generalised visualisation model at map scale 1:20,000,000

5 Conclusion and Outlook

Graphical transformation of spatial data forces generalisation. This results in the resolution of graphical conflicts: effective information transfer via the visual channel is ensured. A rule catalogue for generalisation has been created, a comparison with the actual state of a map image carried out and solution options used. A process section has been presented and the work steps have been run through using an example. The result presentation of the generalised visualisation model is included in the previous chapter.

A use of the generalisation service with mass data enables a grouping of the use cases. These serve to develop a form of standardisation of the generalisation process. Generalisation service has interfaces for various web-based generalisation services, as well as an embedded editor, for subsequent editing by the user.

To support this, self-learning systems can be used at break points where a expert user still have to make decisions. This can, after a suitable number of training sessions, enable automatic case-specific generalisation. AI (artificial intelligence) can analyse and cluster use cases by means of machine learning, so that adapted standard solutions with a view to regional context can be developed through an increasing number of cases of resolved conflicts by the specialist user. This requires the definition of scale areas in order to be able to standardise the respective generalisation requirements.

For businesses the generalisation service helps to increase or even enable information value for represented data. It optimises the effectiveness of visualisation models produced by map functions of data discovery systems (DDS) or business intelligence software (BIS).

References

1. MacEachren, A.M., Buttenfield, B.P., Campbell, J.B., DiBiase, D.W., Monmonier, M.: Visualization. In: Abler, R.F., Marcus, M.G., Olson, J.M. (eds.): Geography's Inner Worlds: Pervasive Themes in Contemporary American Geography, pp. 88–137. Rutgers University Press, New Jersey& New Brunswick (1992). Seen In: Slocum, T.A., McMaster, R.B., Kessler, F.C., Howard, H.H.: Thematic Cartography and Geovisualization. Third Edition, p. 12. Pearson/ Prentice Hall, New Jersey (2009)
2. Schumann, H.: Effektivität. In: Bollmann, J., Koch, W.G. (eds.): Lexikon der Kartogaphie und Geomatik. In two volumes, vol. 1., p. 180. Spektrum Akademischer Verlag, Heidelberg/Berlin (2001)
3. Richardson, D.E., Müller, J.C.: Rule selection for small scale map generalization. In: Buttenfield, B.P., McMaster, R.B. (eds.): Map generalization. Making Rules for knowledge Representation, pp. 136–149. Longman Scientific and Technical, Essex (UK) (1991)
4. Buttenfield, B.P.: Object-oriented map generalization: modeling and cartographic considerations. In: Müller, J.-C., Lagrange, J.-P., Weibel, R. (eds.): Gis and Generalization. Methodology and Practice, Gisdata 1, p. 91. Taylor and Francis Ltd., London (1995)
5. McMaster, R.B., Shea, K.S.: Generalization in Digital Cartography, p. 3. Association of American Geographers, Washington D.C. (1992)
6. Regnauld, N., McMaster, R.B.: A synoptic view of generalisation operators. In: Mackaness, W.A., Ruas, A., Sarjakoski, L.T. (eds.): Generalisation of Geographic Information: Cartographic Modelling and Applications, p. 38. Elsevier Ltd., UK/The Netherlands (2007)
7. Simon, M., Asche, H.: Designing a semi-automatic map construction process for the effective visualisation of business geodata. In: Gervasi, O., et al. (eds.) ICCSA 2020. LNCS, vol. 12252, pp. 435–447. Springer, Cham (2020). https://doi.org/10.1007/978-3-030-58811-3_32
8. Simon, M., Asche, H.: Automated spatial data processing and refining. In: Leveraging Applications of Formal Methods, Verification, and Validation – 6th International Symposium, IsoLA 2012, Heraklion, Crete, Greece, 15–18 October 2012, Revised Selected Papers, CCIS, pp. 38-49. Springer, Heidelberg (2016). https://doi.org/10.1007/978-3-319-51641-7_3
9. Kishimoto, H.: Generalisierung von statistischen Karten aus der Sicht des Kartenbenutzers: Choroplethen-Darstellung mit oder ohne Klassenbildung?. In: Schweizerische Gesellschaft für Kartographie. Kartographische Publikationsreihe. N°. 10, p. 91. SGK Publikationen, Zürich (1990)
10. Tainz, P.: Choroplethenkarte und Flächendiagrammkarte. In: Bollmann, J., Koch, W.G. (eds.): Lexikon der Kartogaphie und Geomatik. In two volumes, vol. 1, p. 118, 248. Spektrum Akademischer Verlag, Heidelberg/Berlin (2001)
11. Bollmann, J.: Kartographische Generalisierung. In: Bollmann J., Koch, W. G.(eds.): Lexikon der Kartogaphie und Geomatik. In two volumes, vol. 2, p. 22. Spektrum Akademischer Verlag, Heidelberg/Berlin (2002)
12. Töpfer, F.: Kartographische Generalisierung. 2nd ed., p. 25, 238. VEB Hermann Haack, Geographisch-Kartographische Anstalt, Gotha, Leipzig (1979)

13. Salistchew, K.A.: Einführung in die Kartographie. In two volumes, vol. 1, 1st edn., p. 19. VEB Hermann Haack, Geographische-Kartographische Anstalt, Gotha/Leipzig (1967)
14. Slocum, T.A., McMaster, R.B., Kessler, F.C., Howard, H.H.: Thematic Cartography and Geovisualization. Third Edition, p.102, 106, 110. Pearson/Prentice Hall, New Jersey (2009)
15. Robinson, A.H., Morrison, J.L., Muehrcke, P.C., Kimerling, A.J., Gubtill, S.C.: Elements of Cartography. 6. ed., p. 451. John Wiley & Sons Inc., NY/Chinchester/Brisbane/Toronto/Singapore (1995)
16. Bobzien, M.: Methodische Aspekte der Generalisierung von Geodaten, p.23. doctoral thesis, Rheinische Friedrich-Wilhelms-Universität Bonn, Bonn (2006) https://hdl.handle.net/20.500.11811/2359
17. McMaster, R.B., Shea, S.: Generalization in digital cartography, p. 68. Association of American Geographers, Washington DC (1992)
18. Ruas, A., Duchene, C.: A prototype generalisation system based on the multi-agent system paradigm. In: Mackaness, W.A., Ruas, A., Sarjakoski, L.T. (eds.) Generalisation of Geographic Information: Cartographic Modelling and Applications. Elsevier. UK/Amsterdam, pp. 269–284 (2007)

A New Approach to Assess the Vulnerability of a *Road Infrastructure System* Affected by Rockfalls

Lucia Losasso(✉), Carmela Rinaldi, and Francesco Sdao

University of Basilicata, Potenza, Italy
lucialosasso1@gmail.com

Abstract. To assess the rockfall risk of a road infrastructure system, it is very important to obtain detailed information about the territory and the road.

This paper aims to create a model for analyzing the vulnerability of a road infrastructure system.

The new proposed approach consists in different phases linked to the different parameters contributing to the assessment of the final risk: the rockfall intensity, the susceptibility assessment (by using an Artificial Neural Network approach), the exposure to the risk and the value of the exposed elements (road and human life).

Definitely, this paper deals with the development of an integrated numerical model allowing to obtain the vulnerability level of a road infrastructure system due to rockfall phenomenon. This approach can be used to obtain more useful information on a territory prone to mass movements allowing planners to manage emergencies in the best possible way.

Keywords: Element at risk · Magnitude · Province of Potenza · Rockfalls · Vulnerability

1 Introduction

The most conspicuous natural processes that occur along the slopes and can involve road communication lines are the landslides and the mass movement.

This last general term indicates all the phenomena of rockfalls, toppling or sliding that may involve rocky masses, surface soils or both, due to the gravity.

This phenomenon represents one of the most frequent geological risks in the national territory, especially in mountain environments, with serious consequences on the viability of the road sections, on infrastructures, and consequent serious inconvenience to inhabited areas.

The detachment of the blocks from one side of a slope is strongly influenced by the structural conditions of the rocky mass (discontinuity families, persistence, spacing), by the geometry (position and orientation of the discontinuities with respect to the slope), by the mechanical characteristics (shear strength of the discontinuities, traction resistance

O. Gervasi et al. (Eds.): ICCSA 2022 Workshops, LNCS 13379, pp. 514–530, 2022.
https://doi.org/10.1007/978-3-031-10545-6_35

of some rock bridges) and possible external stresses (presence of pressurized water in the discontinuities, earthquakes, etc.) (Losasso et al. 2017a).

The risk on the transportation infrastructures and on roads due to such particularly dangerous phenomena, can be assessed in successive phases by estimating the hazard, the exposure and the vulnerability and then overlapping the above information (Losasso et al. 2017b). The first step for the assessing of the risk level on the road infrastructures, therefore, consists in the assessing of the hazard. It regards, in principle, the prediction of the event and its possible effects. The hazard is a measure to assess the level of expectation with respect to the occurrence of a given event and tries to establish its magnitude, as well as its spatial and temporal definition. In other words, a depth study of the hazard should be able to establish where, how and with what consequences a particular event can occur. The second step that needs to be done for the risk assessment, after the hazard analysis, is the exposure assessment. The study of exposure allows to identify areas particularly sensitive to the presence of people, artifacts, goods, etc. The distribution of these elements at risk is clearly not uniform on the territory, it is large where the density of the population is greater, or where there is a higher concentration of products (for example in the industrial areas). As it is clear, population, artefacts and goods do not have the same degree of priority, in fact the safeguarding of human life always has a greatest importance.

The analysis of the population exposure is the main step to assess the final vulnerability level but it is also the most difficult. The population can't be considered only as a static entity, but it has its own dynamism, given the possibility that it has to move in the territory (Budetta and Nappi 2013). For this reason, there will be several areas, especially in the urban ones, particularly exposed to the risk; moreover, this exposure varies in time in a cyclical way, so that the exposure will also have a temporal dimension, as well as a spatial one. In the Table 1 there some of the typologies and definitions of vulnerability proposed by several authors.

The vulnerability study of a transportation infrastructure is an important topic of growing interest in terms of road infrastructure. The concept of vulnerability does not have a univocal and commonly accepted definition, but it has been defined according to the context. There are, therefore, different definitions of the vulnerability in the literature, as there are different ways to evaluate it.

Vulnerability (V), in general, expresses the degree of loss of an element or group of elements exposed to the risk and therefore depends on both the type of element at risk and the intensity of the mass movement phenomenon. Ultimately, it is a particularly relevant parameter in the risk assessment (Leone et al. 1996) which links the intensity of the phenomenon to its possible consequences.

The vulnerability assessment can be based on statistical criteria and on particularly more subjective criteria. As regards the statistical methods, it is possible to adopt them in the case of repeatable and frequent phenomena.

For example, in the case of rockfalls, it is possible to estimate, on a statistical basis, the probability that the detachment of a boulder produces a certain damage on a structural and infrastructural element (Canuti and Casagli 1996).

However, as previously mentioned, in general the estimation of vulnerability is based on particularly subjective criteria; moreover, there are different currents of opinion: some include in the estimation of vulnerability an evaluation of the unpredictability of the phenomenon, while the other ones include simply considerations on the elements at risk. This is a fundamental step in the analysis of landslide risk along the road transportation corridors. It is expressed in a scale from 0 (no loss) to 1 (total loss) (Fell 1994; Wong 1998) and is therefore a function of the intensity of the phenomenon and the type of involved element at risk. In general, when the element at risk is represented by human life, the vulnerability may express the probability that the occurrence of a mass movement may cause death, injuries and/or homelessness.

For this reason, it can be considered directly proportional to the population density of an area exposed to the risk. On the other hand, if an infrastructure is considered as an element at risk, many authors usually express the vulnerability as a percentage of the economic value (by considering structure or homogeneous areas) that can be impaired following the occurrence of a landslide phenomenon (Canuti and Casagli 1994).

In the following table, different definitions of Vulnerability proposed by several authors are briefly described.

As presented for the general concept of vulnerability, there is not a univocal definition of vulnerability of a road network in the literature. Husdal (2004) identifies the vulnerability as the composition of three types of vulnerability of a road network, the composition of which determines the global vulnerability:

- Structural Vulnerability, referring to the construction characteristics of the road, such as the geometry of the road and the works connected to it;
- Natural Vulnerability, referring to the characteristics of the territory crossed by the road;
- Relative/generated by traffic Vulnerability; referring to the traffic flow affecting the infrastructure and its variations in particular situations (peak times, maintenance operations, special days, etc.).

The difference between vulnerability and reliability of the network is very important: the first one is linked to the malfunction and collapse of an element, while the second one is linked only to its work. Not everyone, however, considers a clear distinction between the two concepts; in fact, according to Berdica (2002), reliability is a concept that allows to assess the vulnerability of the network.

Vulnerability is defined as the susceptibility of a network to accidents, where an accident means a reduction in serviceability, ie the possibility of using a transportation network during a given period. In other words, the vulnerability does not concern the safety of a road network, but the reduction of accessibility due to the event, where accessibility means the possibility for people to take part in the activities that take place in the territory thanks to the transportation systems.

Reliability becomes a measure of vulnerability because it is linked to the probability that an event can occur (Husdal 2004). Other authors (Bleukx et al. 2005), link the concept of vulnerability to the configuration of the network, identifying the most vulnerable scheme in particular traffic conditions or network interruptions.

Table 1. Some of typologies and definitions of Vulnerability

Type of vulnerability	Definition
Sistemic Vulnerability (Sdao et al. 2013)	It measures the relationship between extreme event's magnitude and direct and indirect consequences of this event on the territory system
Direct Vulnerability (Cafiso et al. 2011, D'Andrea and Condorelli 2006)	Propensity of a single element, simple or complex, to be damaged by a natural event
Induced Vulnerability (Cafiso et al. 2011, D'Andrea and Condorelli 2006)	It refers to the effects on the organization of the territory due to the collapse of one or more elements that make it up
Deferred Vulnerability (D'Andrea and Condorelli, 2006)	It refers to all the effects that occur in the phases following the event such as the modification of the habits and behavior of the populations located in those areas
Functional Vulnerability (Cafiso et al. 2011; D'Andrea and Condorelli 2006)	It refers to the lack of functionality of some elements that could cause significant damage after the occurrence of a calamitous event
Socio-economic Vulnerability or Social Vulnerability (Cutter et al. 2003)	It refers to the social, economic, politic conditions that characterize the territory affected by an event
Structural Vulnerability (Cafiso et al. 2011; Husdal 2004)	It refers to the infrastructure and to its constructive characteristics
Natural or Biophysical Vulnerability (Cutter et al. 2003; Husdal 2004)	It refers to the characteristics of the territory and to the natural risk of the territory
Vulnerability of the traffic (Husdal 2004)	It refers to the characteristics that describe the traffic flow and the conditions deriving from the variation of the traffic flow

2 Materials and Methods: A New Approach to Assess the Road Infrastructure System Vulnerability in the Rockfall Prone Areas

In this paper a new approach to assess the vulnerability of Road Infrastructure System in areas prone to landslides and in particular characterized by intensive rockfall events has been presented.

According to the authors, the road infrastructure system is a network system that connects various spatial areas guaranteeing a multitude of essential and indispensable services for the survival of the population, not less important the possibility of providing aid in places affected by natural disasters. Because of the importance of the transportation network, ensuring its functionality is of central interest both for the system users and for the managers. For these latter, it is also essential to have the tools available to effectively manage the limited financial resources available to reduce their vulnerability as far as possible.

In the proposed methodology, the vulnerability is expressed, in general terms, as the susceptibility of an element to be damaged by a natural event of a given intensity. According to the authors, in the proposed approach the vulnerability concept considers three characteristics: the type of risk the network is vulnerable to, the most vulnerable elements and the ways in which the vulnerability occurs.

The final level of vulnerability can be assessed by following several consecutive steps as shown in the following flowchart and description (Fig. 1).

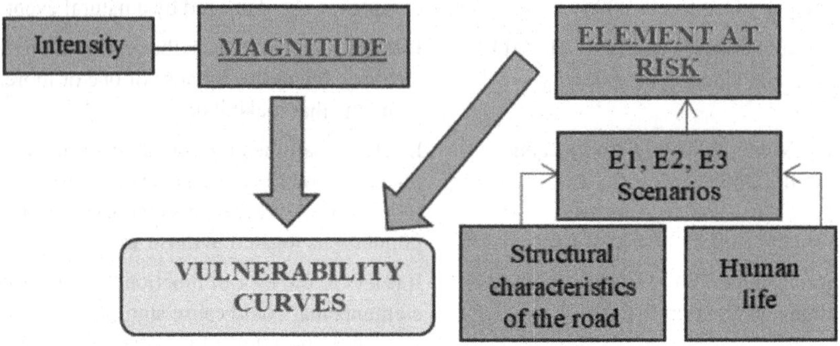

Fig. 1. Different phases to assess the vulnerability

2.1 Intensity Assessment of the Rockfall Phenomenon

Intensity assessment (or severity) of a phenomenon is a topic of the increasing interest for local technicians, administrators and local programmers.

The concepts of intensity and localization in the space generally is linked to the definition of the hazard expressed as the probability that a given phenomenon of a given intensity will occur in a given area (Varnes et al. 1978).

The first step for the assessment of the mass movement risk along the transportation corridors consists, therefore, in analyzing the geometric severity of the phenomenon by considering the parameters enumerated in the Table 2.

The intensity of the phenomenon is expressed in a relative scale describing the parameters related both to the physical characteristics of the phenomenon (volume, energy, etc.) (Canuti and Casagli 1996) and to the speed, as proposed by Hungr (1990), since it is not possible to precisely define a functional relationship between them.

In this case the definition of the intensity is linked to hypotheses on the possible consequences of the phenomenon; moreover, different speed thresholds are provided delimiting seven well-defined classes (Cruden and Varnes 1996).

Rockfalls are phenomena from rapid to extremely rapid (Cruden and Varnes 1996); in particular, the estimation of speeds in general can be obtained from the type of phenomenon and its state of activity.

The zoning of the territory in intensity classes occurs through the critical interpretation of the data collected in the inventory map, integrated with the information derived from the other basic documents.

The mass movement phenomena recorded in the inventory maps must be classified according to the area extension and the presumed speed.

The phenomena characterized by low intensity, in principle, do not compromise the structural integrity of the road infrastructure, nor the integrity of human life.

The medium intensity processes, on the other hand, can cause, depending on the circumstances, serious damages, without compromising, however, the structural stability of the infrastructure.

High intensity processes cause significant structural damages. In fact, the stability of the roads can be severely compromised and this could therefore imply large costs for repairs. Total restoration is often unavoidable (Table 3).

Another problem related to high-intensity rockfall phenomena is certainly linked to the deposit of collapsed material in the riverbed, that can compromise the normal flow of water, forming natural barriers (Landslide dams) (Dal Sasso et al. 2014) causing landslide lakes, debris flows, poor stability, overflowing of rivers and soil erosion.

The intensity mass movement scale proposed with the present assessment method, therefore, takes into account the speed of the movement and is associated with a scale of damages similar to the Mercalli scale of earthquakes (Canuti and Casagli 2004), divided into 10 classes.

The parameters to be analyzed in order to obtain the corresponding intensity class are listed in the table and described below.

The definition of the intensity is linked to hypotheses on the possible consequences of the phenomenon; moreover, different speed thresholds are provided delimiting seven well-defined classes (Cruden and Varnes 1996).

The landslides and particularly the rockfalls are phenomena from rapid to extremely rapid (Cruden and Varnes 1996); in particular the estimation of speeds in general can be obtained from the type of phenomenon and its state of activity. The zoning of the territory in intensity classes occurs through the critical interpretation of the data collected in the inventory map, integrated with the information derived from the other basic documents. The mass movement phenomena recorded in the inventory maps must be classified according to the area extension and the presumed speed.

The phenomena characterized by low intensity, in principle, do not compromise the structural integrity of the road infrastructure, nor the integrity of human life. The medium intensity processes, on the other hand, can cause, depending on the circumstances, serious damages, without compromising, however, the structural stability of the infrastructure. High intensity processes cause significant structural damages. In fact, the stability of the roads can be severely compromised and this could therefore imply large costs for repairs. Total restoration is often unavoidable.

The parameters to be analyzed in order to obtain the corresponding intensity class are listed in the Table 2.

Table 2. Rockfall intensity assessment matrix.

ROCKFALL INTENSITY ASSESSMENT				
PARAMETERS	**RATING CRITERIA BY SCORE**			
Volume of rockfall per event (m³) - y = 3^x	$Y = 3^{V/2.3}$			
Block size (cm)	$Y = 3^{Db/30}$			
Speed (m/s)- (Hungr, 1981; Cruden & Varnes, 1994)		**5*10^-4 - 5*10^-2 RAPID (for neoformed and reactivated rock slides)**	**5-10^-2 - 5 VERY RAPID (for rockfalls and neoformed rockslides)**	**>= 5 - EXTREMELY RAPID (for Rockfalls and avalanches)**
SCORE		9	27	81
Run out (Km)	**< 10^-3**	**10^-3 - 10^-2**	**10^-2 - 10^-1**	**10^-1 - 10^-0**
SCORE	3	9	27	81
Affected area (Km²)	**< 0,01**	**0,01 - 0,5**	**0,5 - 0,75**	**> 0,75**
SCORE	3	9	27	81

2.2 Block Diameter and Rockfall Volume Per Event

The rockfall intensity assessment involves, first of all, the evaluation of the dimensions of the collapsing rock. In the RHRS method (Pierson et al. 1990) and in many subsequent modifications it is not specified if the block diameter is considered before or after the detachment; this aspect is very important to proceed to the intensity assessment of the phenomenon since, during the fall, substantial changes may occur with regard to the shape, size, conditions of motion, the variation of instantaneous kinetic energy that the boulder can undergo during the course and before the impact on the carriageway (Budetta 2004). Therefore, the roads that can be traveled in this direction can be mainly 2 to obtain the level of intensity or geometric severity with which a rockfall phenomenon can occur along a road:

1) Potential intensity assessment by considering mainly outcrops that, due to their size, homogeneity in the distribution of families of discontinuity, lack of vegetation and persistence of situations of potential risk, allow to better define the characteristics of the rock mass and, subsequently, the level of the potential risk of the underlying road;
2) Evaluation of the Rockfall Intensity Assessment (RIA) that has already occurred in the past by parameterizing all the predisposing factors and by determining the phenomenon through a back-analysis identifying the reach angle (see Losasso et al. 2016) and consequently the hazard levels of the slope, the vulnerability and the value of elements at risk.

In the first case the size of the phenomenon can be assessed considering the volume of the block (V_b) possessed at the time of the estimated rockfall, evaluating the spacing data for each system of joints and the angles that they form. Once this value has been obtained, the diameter can be assessed indirectly as:

$$D_b = \sqrt[3]{V_b}$$

In the second case, to obtain the size of the phenomenon, it is possible to consider the total volume of the "swarm" of already collapsed blocks in order to parameterize the original volume of the cluster by means of a back analysis.

Table 3. Magnitude class and Intensity level for the Rockfall phenomenon.

TOTAL SCORE	15	16-58	59-101	102-144	145-187	188-230	231-273	274-316	317-359	360-405
MAGNITUDE	I	II	III	IV	V	VI	VII	VIII	IX	X
INTENSITY	VERY LOW								VERY HIGH	VERY LOW

2.3 The Hazard Assessment

The parameter linked to the intensity, in addition to the vulnerability, is the hazard (Losasso and Sdao 2018). The maps of spatial hazard can be realized by using different modeling approaches with different complexity degrees. In particular, it is possible to use qualitative or quantitative methods. Quantitative approaches can be traced back to statistical models (Ayalew and Yamagishi 2005), probabilistic (Chung and Fabbri 1999) and may also refer to Soft Computing methods such as Artificial Neuronal Networks (ANNs). The ANNs are the reference evaluation models for many approaches and are used in the implementation of the hazard map for the study area, considering as input parameters the rockfall potential source areas, the detachment niches of already collapsed rock masses, the values of kinetic energy of propagation, lithology, slope and land use (Losasso and Sdao 2018).

2.4 The Element at Risk: Two Exposure Scenarios

Table 4. Typology of element at risk: two scenarios

TIPOLOGY OF ELEMENT AT RISK: TWO SCENARIOS				
RATING CRITERIA BY SCORE				
STRUCTURAL CARACTERISTICS OF THE ROAD	**POINTS 3**	**POINTS 9**	**POINTS 27**	**POINTS 81**
Ditch Effectiveness	Good catchment: properly designed according to updates of Ritchie's ditch+passive defense works	Moderate catchment: properly designed according to updates of Ritchie's ditch design chart without passive defense works	Limited catchment: wrongly designed	No catchment
Roadway width **(Pierson, 1990)**	Y = 3 ^(21.5-Lc)/6			
	21.5	15.5	9.5	3.5
Number of lines per each direction	3	2	2	1
HUMAN LIFE	**POINTS 3**	**POINTS 9**	**POINTS 27**	**POINTS 81**
% of decision sight distance	Y = 3^(120-%Da)/20			
	100%	80%	60%	40%
Average Veihcle Risk	Y = 3 ^AVR/25			
	25%	50%	75%	100%

To assess the final risk level, it is necessary, after the hazard assessment, to evaluate the element at risk, represented by population, goods, economic activities, public service and environmental goods present in a given area exposed at risk, that is to say more prone to the danger after a calamitous event. In the presented approach, an index that takes into account two categories for the assessment of the exposure degree of a road traveled by a vehicle has been considered. The element exposed at risk is, first of all, the road; for this reason, the expected damage is strictly connected to the design characteristics of the road. That's why 2 categories have been considered: in the category 1, represented by the road, the design characteristics of the road (such as the presence of rockfalls valley, the road width, the number of lines in each direction, …) has been assessed by using a scoring method. To assess the direct exposure of a road infrastructure and, consequently, of the vehicles passing through it (Category 2), it is possible to assess the Average Vehicle

Risk, a parameter directly proportional to the Average Daily Traffic, that is a parameter capable of representing the ordinary conditions of circulation (Table 4).

The sum of the scores relating to category 1 and category 2 provides three exposure classes (Table 5) that is to say 3 scenarios to be used later in the assessment of Vulnerability.

Table 5. Exposure classes

E1	LOW EXPOSURE	15-101
E2	MEDIUM EXPOSURE	102-273
E3	HIGH EXPOSURE	274-405

2.5 The Vulnerability Assessment of the Road Infrastructure System

The curves representing the vulnerability values according to the intensity of the phenomenon have been realized by considering different approaches proposed in the literature: for example the probability of human consequences for the different types of intensity (DRM 1990), or the vulnerability evaluation (possibility of death or injury) considering the intensity of the phenomenon based on the speed of movement (for speed > 1 m/s human life can be directly vulnerable as proposed by Hungr 1981; for Cruden and Varnes (1994), on the other hand, this limit is reduced to 0.05 m/s or about 3 m/min).

In general, vulnerability curves are represented by an expression such as:

$$\mathbf{1 + e^{\alpha t}} \tag{1}$$

represented by a Gaussian curve known as the Gauss function corresponding to an exponential mathematical function.

There are numerous studies in the literature about the curves of the elements vulnerable to disasters, such as mass movement and floods (Pascale et al. 2009) considering as elements exposed at the risk constructions and communication lines (ie elements with different physical, social and economic characteristics).

For this reason, the elements at risk, to assess their vulnerability, are categorized in general into three groups with different physical, social and economic characteristics: A, B and C (Fig. 2), each of which has a different response to the stress to which it is.

The vulnerability of the elements exposed to the risk ranging from 0 to 1 (Fig. 2), therefore, it is described by the following Eq. (2010; Sdao et al. 2013, Pascale et al. 2010; Papathoma et al. 2015):

$$y = 1 - \frac{ae^{-\alpha\xi^{2.2}}}{\left(1 + e^{-\alpha\xi^{2.2}}\right)} \tag{2}$$

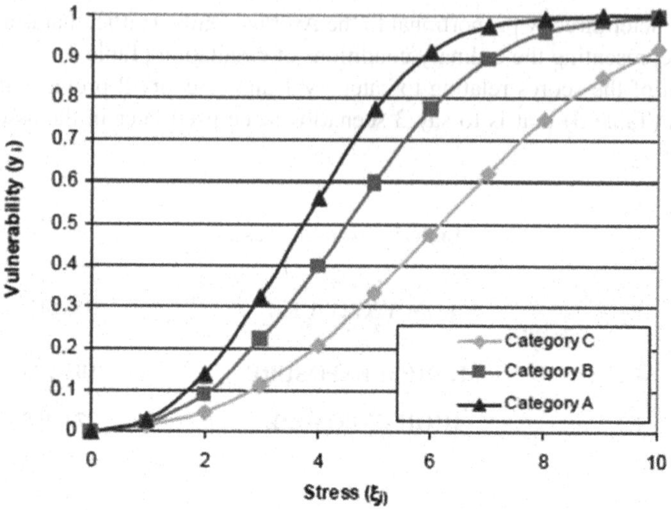

Fig. 2. Vulnerability curves for different types of risk elements

where: **y** represents the vulnerability on the occasion of the specific considered natural disaster;

ξ stands for a deterministic variable calculated from a scenario analysis (speed, dimension, energy,… of the analyzed process) that identifies the intensity of the phenomenon expressed as a scalar quantity;

a is a constant obtained by setting boundary conditions while **α** represents a variable introduced to model the curves.

The above-described approaches have therefore been further modified to be adapted to the assessment of the vulnerability of the road infrastructure system (Eq. 3) in order to obtain three curves for each scenario (for a total of 9 curves) that allow to assess the degree of vulnerability based on the importance of the artery in terms of practicability.

$$y = 1 - a\frac{e^{-\alpha\xi^{\gamma}}}{\left(1 + e^{-\alpha\xi^{\gamma}}\right)} \tag{3}$$

In Eq. 3, ξ indicates the magnitude (intensity) and is expressed by a scalar quantity (previously evaluated and divided into 10 classes according to the obtained score), the constant has been calculated by setting specific boundary conditions, that is to say by imposing y = 0 representing zero vulnerability (no loss) for ξ = o.

The parameter α is also assessed by imposing boundary conditions: for example, for the curve belonging to the E3 category when the phenomenon falls in the 6, 7, 8, 9 and 10 intensity classes, the vulnerability varies from 0.9 to 1, for intensity equal to 3, 4, 5, and 6, the vulnerability falls in the middle class in a vulnerability range of 0.3–0.9, finally low vulnerability for disastrous phenomena characterized by a stress or intensity level of 1, 2 and 3, obtaining three different values for the three different curves (Sdao et al. 2013).

In the considered approach, vulnerability is expressed as a function of the elements at risk, represented by the road (structural characteristics) and by the vehicles that can cause damage to human life.

Since the elements at risk are closely correlated (and for this reason expressed through three scenarios), the vulnerability has been considered with reference to three curves showing the three different exposure scenarios (Scenario E1, Scenario E2 and Scenario E3).

Therefore, the scenarios E1, E2, and E3 (Fig. 3) represent the elements exposed to the risk in the infrastructure system (ie vehicles and roads).

The relevance of these scenarios increases passing from class E1 (lower exposure) to class E3 (high exposure).

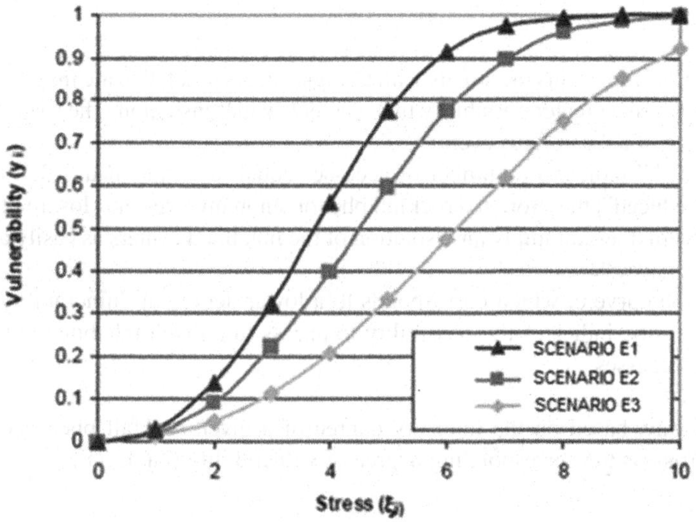

Fig. 3. Vulnerability curves for the different risk exposure scenarios

In this specific case, the values necessary for the implementation of the vulnerability curves relating to the road infrastructure system are summarized in the following table (Table 6):

In the light of the above, it is possible to represent the final graph (Fig. 4) which shows the 9 vulnerability curves with the different risk exposure scenarios representing the values of magnitudes in abscissa and the levels of relative vulnerabilities in the ordinate. The different exposure scenarios are reported with three different colors: the green curves represent the elements most exposed to landslide risk i.e. corresponding to E3 scenario, the red curves represent the E2 scenario and finally the blue curves the E1 scenario. Each curve in turn contains three different curves: a, b and c which correspond to a different degree of vulnerability and take into account the "exposure density" of the elements at risk, i.e. they represent the number of accesses to the road;

Table 6. Assessment of the parameters related to the vulnerability curves

PARAMETERS	VALUES	ASSESSMENT
γ	2.2	travel alternative>2
γ	2.4	travel alternative =2
γ	2.6	travel alternative =1
α	0.02	E1 scenario
α	0.04	E2 scenario
α	0.06	E3 scenario

- the curve "a" represents the streets with a single access point, this means greater traffic flow, therefore a greater possibility that a vehicle can transit along the road during the occurrence of a calamitous event;
- the curve "b" indicates a number of accesses equal to 2: this means that the traffic can be "reduced", therefore if a rockfall phenomenon involves the closure of the road, this problem does not imply any isolation of the inhabited centers as easily accessible from other accesses.
- Finally, the curve c, which corresponds to a lower degree of vulnerability with the same intensity, indicates the possibility to access to a given inhabited area through different accesses.

In this way, based on the intensity degree of a given rockfall phenomenon, it is possible to assess the corresponding degree of vulnerability (Table 7).

2.6 Conclusion

In this study, some existing methods for vulnerability assessment related to landslides has been reviewed. From the analysis of the different approaches, a lot of difficulties in their implementation has been detected (for example data availability).

The new proposed approach allows to assess the rockfall vulnerability of each element at risk by considering a process of a given magnitude as a function of rockfall hazard.

The proposed curves for the evaluation of the road infrastructure system vulnerability are objective and the reproduction is possible and applicable for other studies and regions. In particular, the effects of changing the vulnerability of elements at risk can be analyzed, so scenarios of potential future developments can be calculated.

The most important advantage of the new proposed methodology is its versatility and the its user friendliness.

Table 7. Values relative to the vulnerability curves of the road infrastructure system

E1	>2 γ=2.6	0.03066	0.12522	0.30874	0.545844	0.784871	0.918601	0.976585	0.994804	0.999104	0.999851
	2 γ=2.4	0.03072	0.14244	0.37625	0.667189	0.898155	0.978688	0.99717	0.999762	0.999987	0.999999
	1 γ=2.2	0.03078	0.16195	0.45467	0.7856	0.965552	0.996987	0.999877	0.999997	0.999999	0.999999
E2	>2 γ=2.6	0.02044	0.08372	0.20961	0.387024	0.607713	0.783098	0.901203	0.962842	0.988357	0.996476
	2 γ=2.4	0.02048	0.09532	0.25783	0.490794	0.750921	0.906995	0.975085	0.995176	0.999324	0.999913
	1 γ=2.2	0.02052	0.10849	0.31586	0.608512	0.873588	0..974036	0.996895	0.999787	0.9999991	0.999999
E3	>2 γ=2.6	0.01022	0.04193	0.10598	0.201358	0.338718	0.482828	0.628719	0.758105	0.8557837	0.919362
	2 γ=2.4	0.01024	0.04776	0.013113	0.262278	0.452255	0.638216	0.798053	0.906267	0.963906	0.986926
	1 γ=2.2	0.01026	0.05441	0.016208	0.339279	0.587615	0.794229	0.924129	0.979602	0.996007	0.999303
		I	**II**	**III**	**IV**	**V**	**VI**	**VII**	**VIII**	**IX**	**X**

LOW VULNERABILITY
MEDIUM VULNERABILITY
HIGH VULNERABILITY
VERY HIGH VULNERABILITY

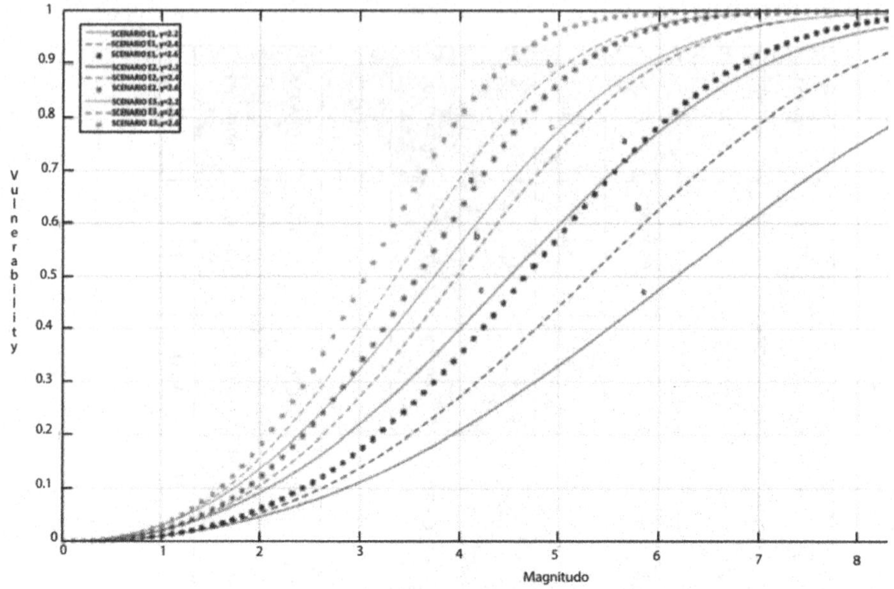

Fig. 4. Vulnerability curves of the road infrastructure system

References

Ayalew, L., Yamagishi, H.: The application of GIS-based logistic regression for landslide susceptibility mapping in the Kakuda-Yahiko Mountains. Central Japan. Geomorphol. **65**, 15–31 (2005)

Berdica, K.: An introduction to road vulnerability: What has been done, is done and should be done". Transp. Policy **9**(2), 117–127 (2002)

Bleukx, J., Stada e B. Immers: «3rd International SIIV Congress "People, Land, Environment and Transpor Infrastructures - Reliability and development (Session C1 "Network reliability) » in The effect of network layout on the reliability of travel time, Bari (2005)

Budetta, P., Nappi, M.: Comparison between qualitative rockfall risk rating system for a road affected by high traffic intensity. Nat. Hazards Earth Syst. Sci. **13**, 1643 (2013)

Budetta, P.: Assessment of rockfall risk along roads. Nat. Hazards Earth Syst. Sci. **4**, 71–81 (2004)

Cafiso, S., García, A.G., Cavarra, R., Rojas, M.A.R.: Crosswalk safety evaluation using a Pedestrian Risk Index as traffic conflict measure. In: 3rd International Conference on Road Safety and Simulation, Indianapolis, IN (2011)

Canuti, P., Casagli, N., Ermini, L., Fanti, R., Farina, P.: Landslide activity as a geoindicator in Italy: significance and new perspectives from remote sensing. Environ. Geol. **45**, 907–919 (2004)

Canuti, P., Casagli, N., Pini, G.: Zonazione del rischio di frana nelle coste alte: la ripa costiera di Talamone (Orbetello, Gr), Università di Firenze, "Studi di Geologia applicata e Geologia dell'Ambiente", 29, Firenze (1994)

Canuti, P., Casagli, N.: Considerazioni sulla valutazione del rischio di frana. CNR-GNDCI Publication 846, p. 57 (1996)

Chung, C.F., Fabbri, A.G.: Probabilistic prediction models for landslide hazard mapping. Photogramm. Eng. Remote Sens. **65**(12), 1389–1399 (1999)

Cruden, D.M., Varnes, D.J.: Landslide types and processes. In: Turner, A.K., Schuster, R.L. (eds.) Landslides Investigation and mitigation: Transportation Research Board, US National Research Council, Special Report 247, pp. 36–75. DC, Washington (1996)
Cutter, S., Boruff, B, Shirley, W.: Social vulnerability to environmental hazards. Soc. Sci. Q. **84**(2), 242–261 (2003)
D'Andrea, A., Condorelli, A.: Metodologie di valutazione del rischio sismico sulle infrastrutture viarie, Comitato Tecnico 3.2 "Gestione dei rischi legati alle strade" Associazione Nazionale della Strada, AIPCR, Comitato Nazionale Italiano, XXV Convegno Nazionale Stradale, Napoli, 4–7 ottobre 2006
Dal Sasso, S.F., Sole, A., Pascale, S., Sdao, F., Bateman Pinzòn, A., Medina, V.: Assessment methodology for the prediction of landslide dam hazard. Nat. Hazards Earth Syst. Sci. **14**, 557–567 (2014)
Fell, R.: Landslide risk assessment and acceptable risk. Can. Geotech. J. **31**, 261–272 (1994)
Hungr, O.: A mass-change model for the estimation of debris-flow runout: a discussion. J. Geol. **98**, 791 (1990)
Hungr, O.: Dynamics of rock avalanches and other types of mass movement. PhD Thesis. Univerity of aAlberta (1981)
Husdal, J.: Reliability/vulnerability versus Costs/Benefits. In: Proceedings of the 2nd International Symposium on Transportation Network Reliability,Queenstown and Christchurch, New Zealand, 20–24 August 2004, pp. 180–186 (2004)
Jenelius, E.: User inequity implications of road network vulnerability. J. Transp. Land Use, Winter 2010 **2**(3/4) (Winter 2010), pp. 57–73 Published by: J. Transport Land Use (2010)
Leone, F., Aste, J.P., Leroi, E.: Vulnerability assessment of elements exposed to mass-moving: working toward abetter risk perception. In: Landslides. Senneset K., Balkerma, Totterdam, pp. 263–269 (1996)
Losasso, L., Derron, M.-H., Horton, P., Jaboyedoff, M., Sdao, F.: Definition and mapping of potential rockfall source and propagation areas at a regional scale in Basilicata region (Southern Italy). Rendiconti Online Societå Geologica Italiana **41**, 175–178 (2016)
Losasso, L., Jaboyedoff, M., Sdao, F.: Potential rock fall source areas identification and rock fall propagation in the province of Potenza territory using an empirically distributed approach. Landslides **14**(5), 1593–1602 (2017). https://doi.org/10.1007/s10346-017-0807-x
Losasso, L., Rinaldi, C., Alberico, D., Sdao, F.: Landslide risk analysis along strategic touristic roads in basilicata (southern Italy) using the modified RHRS 2.0 method. In: Gervasi, O., et al. (eds.) ICCSA 2017. LNCS, vol. 10404, pp. 761–776. Springer, Cham (2017). https://doi.org/10.1007/978-3-319-62392-4_55
Losasso, L., Sdao, F.: The artificial neural network for the rockfall susceptibility assessment. A case study in Basilicata (Southern Italy) – Geomatics. Nat. Hazards Risk **9**, 1, 737–759 (2018)
Papathoma-Kohle, M., Zischg, A., Glade, T., Keiler, M.: Loss estimation for landslides in mountain areas – an integrated toolbox for vulnerability assessment and damage documentation. Environ. Modell. Softw. **63**, 156–169 (2015)
Pascale, S., Giosa, L., Sdao, F., Sole, A.: Assessment of systemic vulnerability in flood prone areas. In: Fourth International Conference on Sustainable Development and Planning, Cyprus, 13–15 May 2009
Pascale, S., Sdao, F., Sole, A.: A model for assessing the systemic vulnerability in landslideprone areas. Nat. Hazards Earth Syst. Sci. **10**, 1575–1590 (2010)
Pierson, L.A., Davis, S.A., Van Vikle, R.: Rockfall hazard rating system – implementation manual. Federal Highway Administration (FHWA), report FHWA-OR-EG-90–01. FHWA. U.S. Department of Transportation. Press Clark University, USA, p. 328 (1990)
Sdao, F., Lioi, S.D., Pascale, S., Caniani, D., Mancini, M.: Landslide susceptibility assessment by using a neuro-fuzzy model: a case study in the Rupestrian heritage rich area of Matera. Nat. Hazard. **13**(2), 395–407 (2013)

Varnes, D.J.: Slope movement types and processes. In: Schuster, R.L., Krizek, R.J. (eds.) Landslides, analysis and control, special report 176: Transportation research board, National Academy of Sciences, Washington, DC, pp. 11–33 (1978)
Wong, C.K.L.: The new priority classification systems for slopes and retaining walls, GEO report no. 68. Hong Kong: Geotechnical Engineering Office (1998)

Evaluating Territorial Capital of Fragile Territories: The Case of Sardinia

Ivan Blečić[1(✉)], Arnaldo Cecchini[2], Valeria Saiu[1], and Giuseppe A. Trunfio[2]

[1] University of Cagliari, Via Corte d'Appello 78, Cagliari, Italy
ivanblecic@unica.it
[2] University of Sassari, Viale San Pietro, 07100 Sassari, Italy

Abstract. We present a framework for the evaluation of "territorial capital", specifically devised as support for policy design on fragile territories, the so called "inner areas". The evaluation procedure leverages open data sources in a multi-criteria spatial evaluation procedure, yielding a dashboard with geographical distribution of indicators of territorial capital, subdivided into its eight constituent dimensions (human, social, cognitive, infrastructural, productive, relational, environmental, and settlement capital). To showcase the working, outputs, and possible uses of the evaluation framework for territorial analysis and policy design, we present the results of a case study application on the Island of Sardinia. The interest and novelty of this research is possibly threefold: the conceptualisation of the notion of "territorial capital" in terms of capabilities for development; its operationalisation in a spatial evaluation model which accounts also for potential spatial interactions; and finally, the application in the case study, illustrating possible employment and usefulness of such results for territorial analysis and policy design.

Keywords: Territorial capital · Multi-criteria spatial evaluation · Fragile territories · Internal areas · Sardinia

1 Introduction

In Europe, many non-coastal territories with historical settlements distant from, or poorly connected with major urban centres, especially in mountainous or agricultural areas, experience demographic stagnation or decline accompanied by general impoverishment. In Italy, this phenomenon is often identified as the "crisis of inner areas" (*crisi delle aree interne*).

In Sardinia, given it being an island with a peculiar morphology, the geographical traits of this phenomenon have been synthesised as a "donut with a hole" [1].

The history of human settlements has frequently seen phenomena of dislocation of populations and activities from the coast to the interior and vice versa, from high-density areas to more sparse areas and vice versa, and the disappearance of prosperous communities for climatic, economic, and social factors, or due to conflicts of various kinds [2, 3]. But perhaps we live in an epoch in which it is possible not to passively surrender

O. Gervasi et al. (Eds.): ICCSA 2022 Workshops, LNCS 13379, pp. 531–545, 2022.
https://doi.org/10.1007/978-3-031-10545-6_36

to this happening, also because the consequences of the abandonment of many such territories can trigger calamitous environmental effects as well as lead to the destruction of histories and cultures.

Yet not all inner areas are created equal. Perhaps not all can and should be "rescued": for some it may be unavoidable to accept the demographic decline and only to ensure their environmental integrity and preservation of ecosystem services; for others it could be apt to put in place suitable safeguard measures, perhaps providing for forms of temporary human uses; other inner areas can perhaps be "defended" as stable settlements, protecting their fragility, and subsidising housing and not-fully competitive economic activities; yet others, with appropriate policies and investments, may become innovative production centres in the fields of agriculture, tourism, services, and research, attracting new populations [4, 5].

But to identify which is which, it is necessary to measure, evaluate and compare the territories. Assessing different dimensions of their fragility and capabilities for development is relevant both for such strategic choices, and for designing appropriate policies.

In this paper we propose one such evaluation framework specifically devised as support for policy design on the "inner areas". The evaluation framework is based on the concept of "territorial capital" and leverages open data sources in a multi-criteria spatial evaluation procedure, yielding a dashboard with geographical distribution of indicators of territorial capital, subdivided into its eight constituent dimensions (human, social, cognitive, infrastructural, productive, relational, environmental, and settlement capital). To showcase the working, outputs, and possible uses of the evaluation framework for territorial analysis and policy design, we present the results of a case study application on the Island of Sardinia. The interest and novelty of this research is possibly threefold: the conceptualisation of the notion of "territorial capital" in terms of capabilities for development; its operationalisation in a spatial evaluation model which accounts also for potential spatial interactions; and finally, the application in the case study, illustrating possible employment and usefulness of such results for territorial analysis and policy design.

In the next section we present the background, main sources, and relevant previous research. In Sect. 3 we describe the evaluation methodology, the structure of the evaluation model, its articulation in eight dimensions of territorial capital, and the data sources used for calculating the respective indicators. Section 4 is dedicated to presenting and discussing the results of the case study we conducted on the island of Sardinia. The article ends with concluding remarks on employment and usefulness of such results for territorial analysis and policy design, indicating possible future developments of the presented framework.

2 Background and Previous Research

The National Strategy for Inner Areas adopted in Italy in 2013 points at the so called "territorial capital" among the factors for contrasting the decline of inner areas (the expression "territorial capital" is used 18 times in the text of the National Strategy): «For the construction of an economic development strategy for inner areas, this relationship starts from the unused "territorial capital" present in these territories: the natural, cultural capital and cognitive, the social energy of the local population and potential residents, production systems (agricultural, tourism, manufacturing)».

An expression used in conjunction with territorial capital is "economic development potential" (8 times in the text).

Hence, our starting point for the assessment of fragility and development potential of inner areas was to refer, with all due cautions, to the concept of territorial capital.

Following ([6], p.1387), territorial capital can be defined as «the set of localised assets – natural, human, artificial, organizational, relational and cognitive – that constitute the competitive potential of a given territory». The concept of territorial capital is dynamic and changes according to the social, political, economic, and cultural conditions of a specific time and place. Following the report by Farrell, Thirion and Soto ([7], p. 19), within the European LEADER program aimed at supporting integrated development of rural areas, the territorial capital includes «all of the elements available to the area, both tangible and intangible, which in some respects constitute assets and in others constraints» and underlies the development of a territorial project (or vision of the future) conceived as «a multi-faceted living entity (with economic, social, institutional, cultural and other facets) that evolves over time». This characteristic is also corroborated by the Organisation for Economic Co-operation and Development (OECD) ([8], p. 15) that highlight the factors that determine the region's territorial capital:

> *"[G]eographical location, size, factor of production endowment, climate, traditions, natural resources, quality of life or the agglomeration economies provided by its cities... Other factors may be 'untraded interdependencies' such as understandings, customs and informal rules that enable economic actors to work together under conditions of uncertainty, or the solidarity, mutual assistance and co-opting of ideas that often develop in small and medium-size enterprises working in the same sector (social capital). Lastly there is an intangible factor, 'something in the air', called 'the environment' and which is the outcome of a combination of institutions, rules, practices, producers, researchers and policy-makers, that make a certain creativity and innovation possible. This territorial capital generates a higher return for certain kinds of investments than for others since they are better suited to the area and use its assets and potential more effectively...".*

The concept of territorial capital has become significant in the context of the place-based approach, the guiding principle of European Union Cohesion Policy (Barca 2009). Many studies suggest a positive relationship between territorial capital and economic growth [9]. Territorial capital can significantly affect the impact of policies on regional growth [10] and of specific expenditure axes [11, 12]. In this context Barca et al. [13] pay attention on the "unused" territorial capital of inner areas, considered as a measure of the economic development potential.

More recently, this concept is taken up in the Territorial Agenda of the European Union for 2020 "Towards an Inclusive, Smart and Sustainable Europe of Diverse Regions" [14] and for 2030 "A future for all places" [15] which point out the central role of a place-based approach based on the territorial capital to long-term development and competitiveness for places.

While we are aware of the limits and risks of referring to the concept of "capital", we can interpret it by purifying the term of its many connotations and from its purely productive orientation (i.e., the set of goods intended for productive uses to obtain new production) and relate it instead to the concept of "endowments", of stock of resources in the broad sense. In this sense, we hold, the of concept of territorial capital can be fruitful as an operational framework for evaluating of the fragilities, opportunities, and development potential of inner areas as fragile territories.

3 Methodology

Based on the above premises, we have developed a spatial evaluation model assessing territorial capital on the spatial scale of municipalities. Despite the importance of this local geographical scale to calibrate and ensure effectiveness to territorial policies, municipal dimension is still little studied in economic and territorial studies on territorial capital that are usually focused on a major spatial scale (e.g. provincial) [16]. Therefore, in the proposed evaluation model, the territorial capital is expressed at this spatial scale as an aggregate measure combining eight constituent dimensions (capitals): human, social, cognitive, infrastructural, productive, relational, environmental, and settlement capital, each assessed as aggregating a set of indicators. Our choices to articulate territorial capital in these eight dimensions is in many respects provisional since the concept is not consolidated in the literature. However, we settle with this structuring to make our results somewhat comparable with a 2012 study at the national level [17], which proposes similar framework, and in accordance with several studies which have suggested conceptual and analytical frameworks to capture a range of issues encompassed by the concept of territorial capital [17–24].

Our choice of indicators was also guided by the need to have data available, and possibly updatable in a quasi-automatic way.

The proposed methodology allows to evaluate and map the capital of a given territory at municipal level, providing a platform to investigate the performance of eight different categories of capital (see Table 1). For each, we identify a set of relevant indicators – some already used in the literature and others developed by us – that highlight existing or potential assets and their accessibility that can increase the capital base of a given territorial context.

The 33 indicators included in the eight categories of the proposed territorial capital framework encompass a range of different physical (e.g. infrastructure and building structures, natural resources) and immaterial dimensions (e.g. wellbeing, knowledge, productivity, entrepreneurial dynamism and innovation) that integrate multiple perspectives and levels of analysis from different disciplines and sectors of government responsible for health and social care, education, environmental protection, transport development and other critical services. These indicators simplify the complex reality of a territory into easily communicable data and for this reason are applicable to a large spectrum of contexts, then allowing to achieve uniformity of reporting and easily compare different territories.

The definition and indicators used to assess each capital is shown in Table 1 and briefly described in the following text.

Table 1. The eight categories of capitals that compose the proposed "Territorial Capital Index" and related indicators.

Territorial sub-capitals	Indicators	Territorial sub-capitals	Indicators
HUMAN	1.1) Old-age index; 1.2) Specific employment rate; 1.3) Education index; 1.4) Migratory balance	PRODUCTIVE	5.1) Entrepreneurship index; 5.2) Tourism accomodation capacity; 5.3) Start-up companies; 5.4) Average income
SOCIAL	2.1) Voting population; 2.2) Voluntary associations; 2.3) Expenditure for social services; 2.4) Socio-educational users	RELATIONAL	6.1) Public funding; 6.2) University students; 6.3) Bank branches; 6.4) Business networks
COGNITIVE	3.1) Cultural and recreational services; 3.2) Expenditure for culture; 3.3) Broadband accessibility; 3.4) Social promotion associations	ENVIRONMENTAL	7.1) Parks and protected areas; 7.2) Utilized agricultural area; 7.3) Areas at risk; 7.4) Waste sorting; 7.5) Sustainable energy
INFRASTRUCTURAL	4.1) Health services; 4.2) Suburban public transport; 4.3) Postal offices; 4.4) Police stations	SETTLEMENT	8.1) Uninhabited housing; 8.2) Housing quality; 8.3) Average age of buildings; 8.4) Average income from buildings

1. Human Capital (HC) is considered central by many studies [25–27]. We refer to [28] that conceives the human capital as a qualitative attribute of a territory, directly related to the level of education, training and skills of its inhabitants that are positively related to their ability to perform labour and individual's productivity. Thus, investments in human resource can be viewed as strategic investments for increasing territorial wealth. We evaluate the HC through four indicators related to "Educational level", "Employment rate", but also "Population ageing" and "Migratory balance" that provide information about territorial attractiveness and the risk of population decline.

2. Social Capital (SC) emphasises the importance of shared norms, values and understandings that balances societal and individual interests and facilitate co-operation within or among groups [8] and endogenous bottom-up development processes [29–35]. In this context the social capital includes the territorial "relational capital" as the solidarity and active citizenship, associated with a higher propensity to work together toward shared goals [19, 20, 36–41]). According to this notion, we evaluate SC using four indicators that measure "Voluntary associations", "Voting population", "Socio-Educational Users" and "Expenditure for social services".

3. Cognitive Capital (CC) incorporates information about knowledge and individual's ability to learn new skills [42, 43] that are enhanced by new technologies and reinforced by cultural experiences [44–46]. Thus, the CC can be defined as «the result of the application of accumulated knowledge and intangible fundamental human intellectual activity, manifested in the generation of innovations, ideas, invention or improvement of techniques and technologies, including endo-resources technologies» ((Kirshin and Titov 2012) cit in [47]). Proposed indicators are: one the one hand, "Broadband Accessibility" and, one the other hand, "Cultural and recreational services" and "Expenditure for culture" both for heritage and cultural activities and "Social promotion associations".

4. Infrastructural Capital (IC) is the fixed capital of territories, including infrastructural assets, railways, pipelines, communications towers and lines, dams and plants [18, 48] as resources that guarantee local connections and significant interactions with non-local actors [24], attract people and investments and promote local economic growth and the competitiveness of the territory [49, 50]. Thus, the IC is a public good «characterized by long duration, technical indivisibility and a high capital-output ratio» [51], complementary to the productive capital [52]. Proposed indicators are "Suburban Public Transport", "Postal Offices", "Police Stations" and "Health services".

5. Productive Capital (PC) refers to the classical "capital" theory, and it can be distinguishing between variable and constant capital. The first adds value in production and consist in labour services, the second is the system of physical systems necessary for the production. We consider the business networks, incubators, production of sophisticated or intermediate goods which provide information about the productive potential of a given territory [8, 20]. Thus, suitable indicators are: "Entrepreneurship Index", "Start-up companies", "Tourism Accommodation Capacity" and "Average Income" of inhabitants.

6. Relational Capital (RC) is related to the category of "relational goods" introduced by researchers from different disciplines: the philosopher Martha Nussbaum [53], the sociologist Pierpaolo Donati [54], the economists Benedetto Gui [55] and Carole Uhlaner [56]. Accordingly, a relational good refers to that good that are linked with interpersonal experiences, where it is the relationship itself that matters: this kind of goods are both co-produced and co-consumed by the subjects involved [57]. Thus, the RC is the ability of a territory to activate physical and immaterial exchanges between firms, institutions and people [58]. A high level of relational capital can improve production and efficiency of public service delivery [59]. We propose as indicators for RC: "Public Funding", "University Students", "Bank Branches" and "Business Networks".

7. Environmental Capital (EC) is an essential prerequisite for human survival and economic activity, which includes goods and services provided by natural environments [60–63]. EC comprises the endowment of renewable and non-renewable stocks of natural resources that can create a competitive advantage both in terms of cost and differentiation [64]. Among these, agriculture is increasing in importance as a provider of opportunities for income generation and environmental protection. According to this concept, we propose these four indicators: "Parks and Protected Areas" and "Utilized Agricultural Area" but also those factors that have an impact on their quality, such as the potential exposure to "Environmental Risk" and the management of environmental resources to prevent pollution such as "Waste sorting" and "Sustainable Energy".

8. Settlement Capital (SC) in our study refers to the housing supply and quality which is an important part of the infrastructural capital of cities that significatively affects the people's lives [17, 22]. Human settlements, in fact, as a part of the physical infrastructure essential for development [65], must ensure the right to adequate housing for all, according to the 2030 Agenda Sustainable Development Goal (SDG) 11 "Sustainable Cities and communities" [66]. Thus, the SC measures those factors that allow identify inadequate housing such as the structural quality of the building "Housing Quality" and the "Average age of buildings" that can be directly related to energy consumption and, consequently, to the housing costs. Furthermore, we consider the "Uninhabited Housing" as a consistent risk factor of degradation and the "Average income from buildings" that in general is associated with their quality.

Aggregation Procedure. The eight categories of capital are calculated at municipal level. For each municipality, the aggregate index of each capital is calculated as a mean value of scaled min-max (in [0, 1]) sub-indicators respective to that category capital (see Table 1). This scale is constructed by considering the value of the indicator for the municipality from which the minimum regional value is subtracted; it is then divided by the difference between the maximum regional value and the minimum value. In some cases, the complement to one of the result must be considered. The calculation (in this first processing) is done by giving equal weight to each indicator in the calculation of each of the capitals and to each capital in the calculation of the territorial capital. Finally, the aggregate Territorial Capital Index (TCI) for each municipality is calculated and the average of indices of each capital.

The user frontend of the software tool, deployed through web mapping platform Mango, further allows to manipulate the evaluation structure by modifying or adding indicators, weighing them, spatially aggregate the municipalities by proximity or by administrative division, and producing historical series and customisable maps.

4 Case Study: Sardinia

We have applied the proposed methodology to evaluate the territorial capital of municipalities of Sardinian Region in Italy. The Sardinian territory is made up of 377 municipalities, that are very different from each other in population size, infrastructural and structural facilities, environment characteristics, demographic and socio-economic attributes. The scale of analysis highlighted these differences which are difficult to observe in aggregate data at the provincial or regional level.

We calculated the value of each indicator of the eight TCI categories and for each administrative boundary using a wide range of local data available from National and

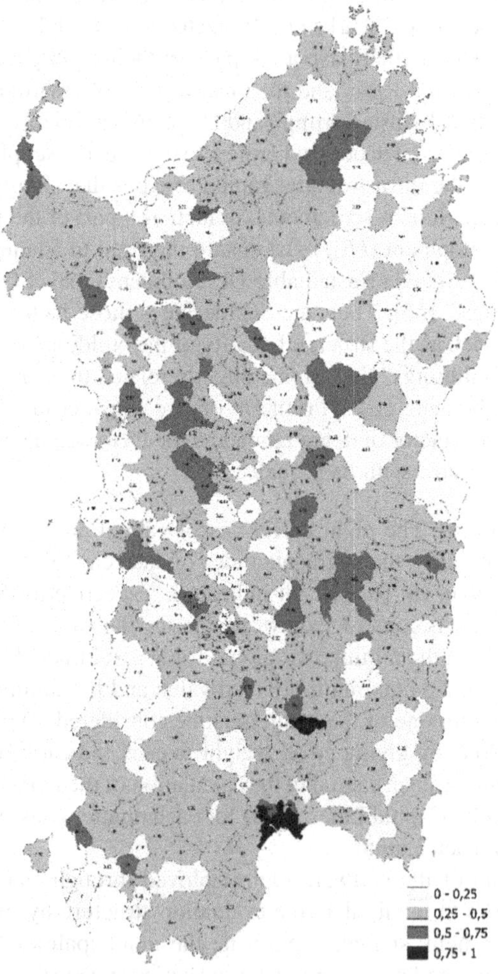

Fig. 1. The "Territorial Capital Index" (TCI) of the 377 Sardinian municipalities: values range from: 0–0.25 (low), 0.25–0.5 (middle), 0.5–0.75 (middle-high), 0.75–1 (high).

Regional authorities and statistical institutions (e.g. the Italian National Institute of Statistics - ISTAT, the Italian Ministry of the Environment, the Institute for Environmental Protection and Research – ISPRA, Regional Information System) and open data sources that include information about mobility and transport (see Table 1).

As Fig. 1 shows, only the Metropolitan City of Cagliari and Sant'Andrea Frius have a high TCI value, with the majority of municipalities having an intermediate TCI middle value.

The analysis of the eight TCI categories shows different scenarios (see Figs. 2 and 3).

Small municipalities generally have greater values of Social, Cognitive, Relational and Infrastructural capital.

Only 7 of 377 municipalities have a high level of Social Capital – Sant'Antonio di Gallura, Padria, Romana, Sarule, Turri, Vallermosa and Tratalias – all with a population of less than 2,000 inhabitants and four of these with less than 600 inhabitants.

Only five municipalities have a high level of Cognitive Capital – Semestene, Villanova Tulo, Turri, Elini – all with a population of less than 1,000 inhabitants and one of these (Semestene) with about 150 inhabitants.

The highest level of the Relational Capital is reached by seven municipalities – Ardara (784 ab.), Monteleone Rocca Doria (102 ab.), Semestene (156 ab.), Sagama (201 ab.), Fonni (3,942 ab.), Osini (790 ab.) and Sant'Andrea Frius (1,786 ab.) – one of these with about 100 inhabitants.

Surprisingly the Infrastructural Capital reaches higher values only in five little municipalities – Romana, Osidda, Sorradile and Boroneddu - all with a population of less than 600 inhabitants.

Instead, the Human and Settlement Capital are higher in larger cities: the Metropolitan City of Cagliari (MC-Cagliari), Sassari, Olbia, Nuoro and Oristano. Only Quartu Sant'Elena, the third largest cities of Sardinia, have a middle-high level of HC.

The Settlement Capital is greater in Nuoro, Arborea, Sant'Andrea Frius, the MC-Cagliari, Capoterra, Elmas, Sestu and Selargius, most of them with a population over 1,000 inhabitants.

Furthermore, the comparison between the seven largest cities of Sardinia – MC-Cagliari, Sassari, Quartu Sant'Elena, Olbia, Alghero Nuoro and Oristano – shows the differences in the global TCI values and specific TC categories.

The MC-Cagliari have a high level of Human, Productive and Settlement Capital but a very low value of Environmental and Infrastructural Capital.

Sassari have a middle value of TCI, that hides a high level of Human Capital and a very low level of Infrastructural Capital.

Quartu Sant'Elena, Olbia and Alghero have a middle value of TCI coherent with the middle-high value of the Settlement Capital and a low value of Cognitive and Infrastructural Capital.

Nuoro and Oristano have a middle-high value of TCI and a low value of Cognitive Capital.

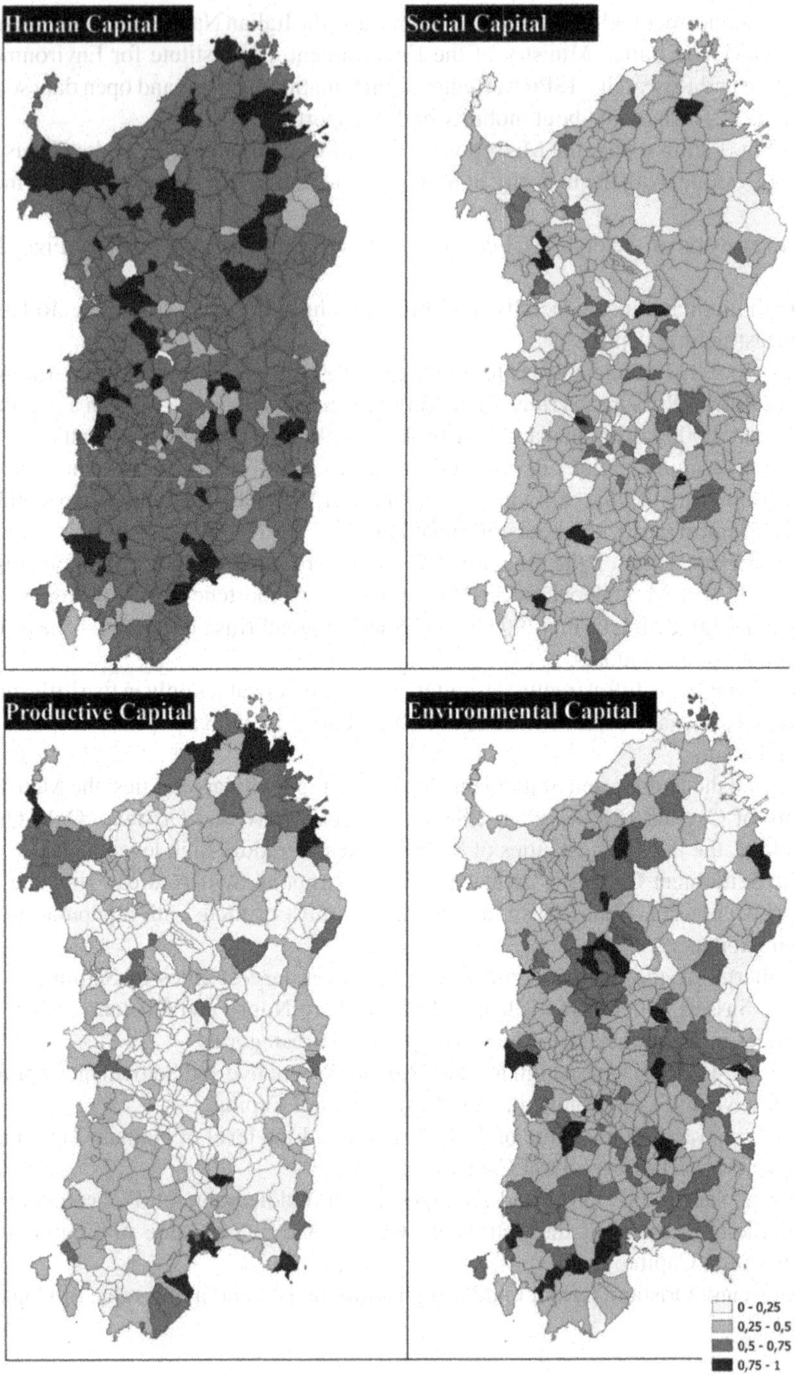

Fig. 2. Four of the eight TCI categories: human, social, productive and environmental.

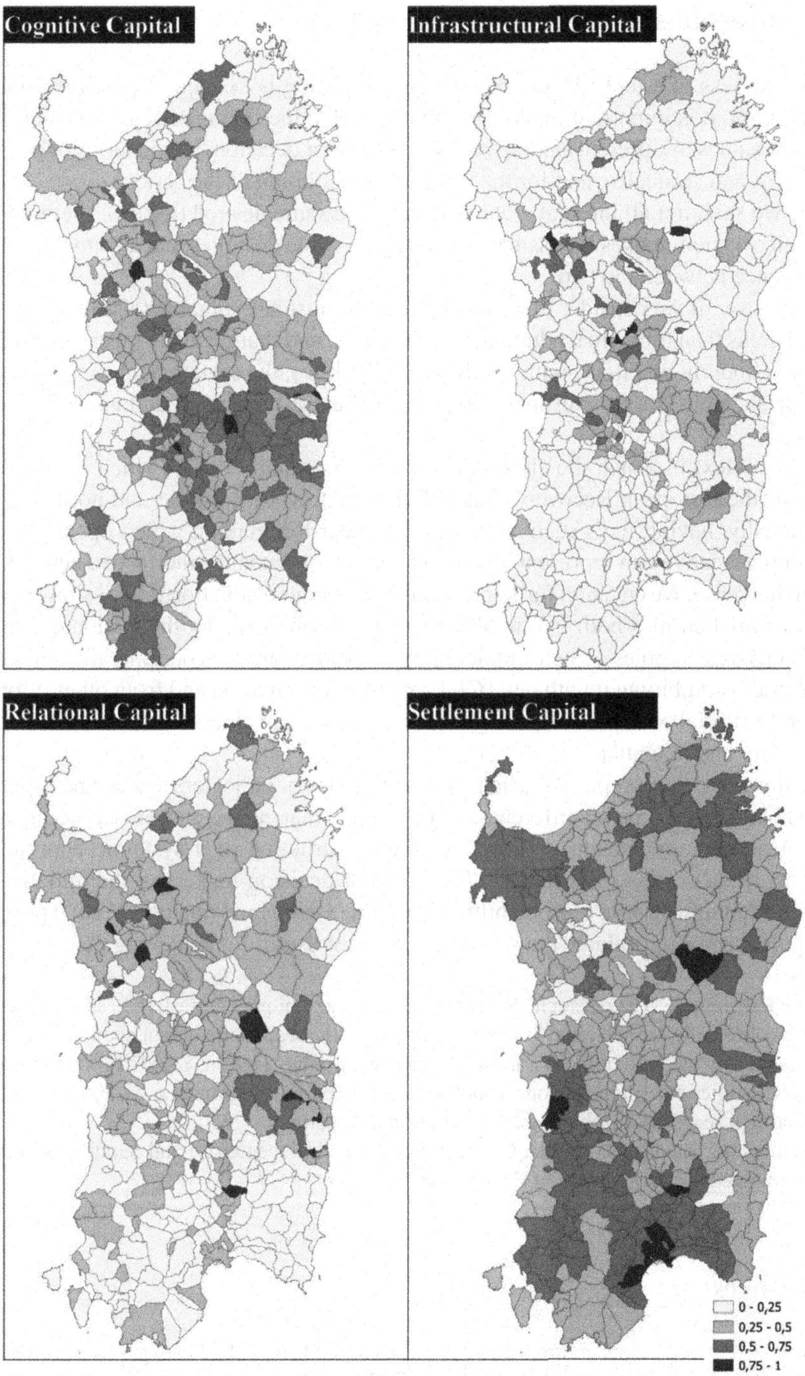

Fig. 3. Four of eight TCI categories: cognitive, infrastructural, relational and settlement.

5 Conclusions

The usefulness of a tool like the one we are proposing is to suggest possible policies. In this sense, it is important to observe similar TCI values on aggregate can result from different values of different capitals, offering clues for decision both in terms of possible objectives and strategies, and for the temporal articulation of the actions.

As we said, not all internal areas may have the same desired destiny. The proposed evaluation system makes it possible to identify possible destinies and also to "measure" the distance between the two.

Moreover, if we consider that some indicators must be evaluated (also) in wider territorial areas than municipal administrative borders, and that there are (also) phenomena with neighbourhood effects with nearby municipalities, the system helps to identify the appropriate areas for policies and to plan for diffusive impacts of actions within these areas.

In a context in which the choices related to the Italian PNNR (which is the articulation of the European Recovery Plan) often appear to be episodic and not conceived systemically, having tools such as this to help decision-making which operate from a system perspective can represent a way to avoid inconsistent or ineffective actions.

In this sense, we envision further development of our evaluation tool to allow to classify territorial entities both in one of the categories proposed by the National Strategy for Inner Areas ("poles", "belt municipality", "intermediate", "peripheral" and "ultra-peripheral") combining it with out TCI. From this combination and from other information on territorial endowments of higher rank, classes can emerge that group territories by fragility and potential.

In this sense, our proposal – which is based on a set of indicators that can be expanded and whose weights can be different, and on "units" that can be chosen according to the type of actions undertaken – allows for the construction of a systemic approach to policies. In fact, it does not replace the choice of decision-makers or the initiatives of local communities whose responsibility is to define visions and objectives, but it provides a tool that serves to evaluate the set of actions most useful for achieving them.

Acknowledgement. The research "Scenari, strategie e azioni per contrastare lo spopolamento e la marginalità delle aree interne. Un sistema di aiuto alle decisioni e alcuni spunti progettuali" was financed by the Autonomous Sardinia Region within the "L. R. n. 7/2007 Promozione della ricerca Scientifica e dell'innovazione tecnologica in Sardegna" (Regional Law 7/2007–Promotion of scientific research and technological innovation in Sardinia).

Authors are thankful to Andrea Cappai that have built the database and Serafino Scanu that have elaborated the maps shows in Figs. 1, 2 and 3.

References

1. Rete delleAssociazioni contro lo spopolamento in Sardegna: Manifesto per lo sviluppo delle Aree Interne e la Rinascita della Sardegna (2020). http://www.ninocarrus.it/new/index.php/blog/680-manifesto-della-rete-associazioni-comunita-per-lo-sviluppo.html. Accessed 10 Jan 2021

2. Graeber, D., Wengrow, D.: The Dawn of Everything: A New History of Humanity. Penguin UK (2021)
3. Harmaan, H.: Culture dimenticate (orig. Vergessene Kulturen der Weltgeschichte Bech Munchen). Bollati Boringhieri, Torino (2020)
4. Blečić, I., Cecchini, A.: Antifragile planning. Plan. Theory **19**, 172–192 (2020)
5. Blečić, I., Cecchini, A.: Verso una pianificazione antifragile: come pensare al futuro senza prevederlo. FrancoAngeli, Milano (2016)
6. Camagni, R., Capello, R.: Regional competitiveness and territorial capital: a conceptual approach and empirical evidence from the European Union. Reg. Stud. **47**, 1383–1402 (2013). https://doi.org/10.1080/00343404.2012.681640
7. Farrell, L., Thirion, S., Soto, P.: Territorial competitiveness creating a territorial development strategy in light of the LEADER experience. Rural Innovation, Dossier n. 6 – Part1 Leader European observatory, December 1999
8. OECD: OECD Territorial Outlook. OECD Publishing, Paris (2001)
9. Perucca, G.: The role of territorial capital in local economic growth: evidence from Italy. Eur. Plan. Stud. **22**, 537–562 (2014)
10. Dall'Erba, S., Llamosas-Rosas, I.: Does federal expenditure promote growth in the recipient countries? In: NARSC Conference, Atlanta, 13–16 November 2013
11. Fratesi, U., Perucca, G.: Territorial capital and the effectiveness of cohesion policies: an assessment for CEE regions. Investigaciones Regionales **29**, 165–191 (2014)
12. Fratesi, U., Perucca, G.: Territorial capital and EU cohesion policy. In: Bachtler, J., Berkowitz, P., Hardy, S., Muravska, T. (eds.) EU Cohesion Policy: Reassessing performance and direction, pp. 255–270. Taylor & Francis, Oxon (2017)
13. Barca, F., Casavola, P., Locatelli, S.: A strategy for inner areas in Italy: definition, objectives, tools and governance. In: Public Investment Evaluation Unit, Material UVAL, Series 31, Territorial Cohesion Agency (Ministry for Economic Development), Rome (2014)
14. European Commission: Territorial Agenda of the European Union 2020: Towards an Inclusive, Smart and Sustainable Europe of Diverse Regions. Agreed at the Informal Ministerial Meeting of Ministers Responsible for Spatial Planning and Territorial Development on 19th May 2011, Gödöllő, Hungary (2011). http://www.eu2011.hu/files/bveu/documents/ta2020.pdf. Accessed 6 May 2022
15. European Commission: Territorial Agenda 2030 "A future for all places". Adopted at Informal meeting of Ministers responsible for Spatial Planning and Territorial Development and/or Territorial Cohesion 1 December 2020, Germany (2020). https://territorialagenda.eu:443/ta2030/. Accessed 7 May 2022
16. Benassi, F., D'Elia, M., Petrei, F.: The "meso" dimension of territorial capital: evidence from Italy. Reg. Sci. Policy Pract. **13**, 159–175 (2021)
17. Brasili, C.: Gli indicatori per la misura del capitale territoriale. Rapporto di ricerca Regio Cycles & Trends, Bologna (2012)
18. Dematteis, G., Governa, F.: Territorialità, sviluppo locale, sostenibilità: il modello SLoT. FrancoAngeli, Milano (2005)
19. Camagni, R.: Regional competitiveness: towards a concept of territorial capital. In: Capello, R. (ed.) Seminal Studies in Regional and Urban Economics, pp. 115–131. Springer, Cham (2017). https://doi.org/10.1007/978-3-319-57807-1_6
20. Camagni, R.: Territorial capital and regional development. In: Capello, R., Nijkamp, P. (eds.) Handbook of Regional Growth and Development Theories, pp. 118–132. Edward Elgar, Cheltenham (2009)
21. Franzato, C.: Il capitale territoriale come porta d'accesso al progetto e al design del territorio. Glob. Manag. **16**, 19–30 (2009)
22. Camagni, R., Dotti, N.F.: Il sistema urbano. In: Perulli, P., Pichierri, A. (eds.) La crisi italiana nel mondo globale. Economia e società del Nord. Einaudi, Torino (2010)

23. Amodio, T., Bencardino, M., Iovino, G.: Emerging topics in Italy: the territorial capital value. Bollettino della Società Geografica Italiana **14**, 75–89 (2019)
24. De Rubertis, S., Mastromarco, C., Labianca, M.: Una proposta per la definizione e rilevazione del capitaleterritoriale in Italia (2019). https://doi.org/10.13137/2282-572X/29676
25. Woodhall, M.: Human capital concepts. In: Psacharopoulos, G. (ed.) Economics of Education, pp. 21–24. Pergamon (1987)
26. Bontis, N., Dragonetti, N.C., Jacobsen, K., Roos, G.: The knowledge toolbox: a review of the tools available to measure and manage intangible resources. Eur. Manag. J. **17**, 391–402 (1999). https://doi.org/10.1016/S0263-2373(99)00019-5
27. Goldin, C.: Human capital. In: Diebolt, C., Haupert, M. (eds.) Handbook of Cliometrics, pp. 55–86. Springer, Heidelberg (2016). https://doi.org/10.1007/978-3-642-40406-1_23
28. Becker, G.S.: Human Capital: A Theoretical and Empirical Analysis, with Special Reference to Education. The University of Chicago Press, Chicago (1964)
29. Bourdieu, P.: Le capital social. Actes de la Recherche en Sciences Sociales **31**, 2–3 (1980)
30. Bourdieu, P.: Distinction: A Social Critique of the Judgement of Taste. Harvard University Press, Cambridge (1984)
31. Coleman, J.S.: Social capital in the creation of human capital. Am. J. Sociol. **94**, 95–120 (1988)
32. Putnam, R.D.: Making Democracy Work. Princeton University Press, Princeton (1993)
33. Lin, N.: Social Capital: A Theory of Social Structure and Action. Cambridge University Press, Cambridge (2002)
34. Dini, F.: Despecializzazione, rispecializzazione, autoriconoscimento. L'evoluzione dei sistemi locali nella globalizzazione. Brigati, Genova (2007)
35. Conti, S.: I territori dell'economia. Fondamenti di geografia economica. Utet, Torino (2012)
36. Putnam, R.D.: Bowling alone: America's declining social capital. J. Democracy **6** (1995)
37. Fratesi, U., Senn, L.: Growth and Innovation of Competitive Regions: The Role of Internal and External Connections. Springer, Heidelberg (2008). https://doi.org/10.1007/978-3-540-70924-4
38. Capello, R.: Spatial and sectoral characteristics of relational capital in innovation activity. Eur. Plan. Stud. **10**, 177–200 (2002)
39. Camagni, R.: Uncertainty, social capital and community governance: the city as a Milieu. In: Contributions to Economic Analysis, pp 121–149. Elsevier, Amsterdam (2004)
40. Camagni, R., Capello, R.: Apprendimento collettivo e competitività territoriale. FrancoAngeli, Milano (2002)
41. Camagni, R.: La ville comme Milieu: de l'application de l'approche GREMI à l'évolution urbaine. Revue d'Economie Régionale et Urbaine **3**, 591–606 (1999)
42. Camerer, C.F., Hogarth, R.M.: The effects of financial incentives in experiments: a review and capital-labor-production framework. J. Risk Uncertain. **19**, 7–42 (1999). https://doi.org/10.1023/A:1007850605129
43. Ballinger, T.P., Hudson, E., Karkoviata, L., Wilcox, N.T.: Saving behavior and cognitive abilities. Exp Econ **14**, 349–374 (2011). https://doi.org/10.1007/s10683-010-9271-3
44. Costa, A.L., Garmston, R.J., Zimmerman, D.P.: Cognitive Capital: Investing in Teacher Quality. Teachers College Press (2014)
45. Caragliu, A., Nijkamp, P.: Cognitive capital and islands of innovation: the Lucas growth model from a regional perspective. Reg. Stud. **48**, 624–645 (2014). https://doi.org/10.1080/00343404.2012.672726
46. Murphy, E.R.: Collective Cognitive Capital. Social Science Research Network, Rochester (2021)
47. Rozhdestvenskaya, E.: Cognitive capital and its profitability. In: The European Proceedings of the International Scientific Symposium on Lifelong Wellbeing in the World Tomsk Polytechnic University, Tomsk, pp 383–392 (2017)

48. Baldwin, J.R., Dixon, J.: Infrastructure capital: what is it? Where is it? How much of it is there? In: Canadian Productivity Review Research Paper, vol. 16 (2008)
49. Prezioso, M.: Short-term territorial investment for Europe's long-term future. J. Transit. Stud. Rev. **23**, 61–77 (2016)
50. Crescenzi, R., Di Cataldo, M., Rodríguez-Pose, A.: Government quality and the economic returns of transport infrastructure investment in European regions (2016)
51. Torrisi, G.: Public infrastructure: definition, classification and measurement issues. Econ. Manag. Financ. Mark. **3**, 100–124 (2009)
52. Weitzman, M.L.: Aggregation and disaggregation in the pure theory of capital and growth: a new parable. Cowles Foundation for Research in Economics at Yale University Discussion Paper no. 292 (1970)
53. Nussbaum, M.C.: The Fragility of Goodness: Luck and Ethics in Greek Tragedy and Philosophy. Cambridge University Press, Cambridge (1986)
54. Donati, P.: Introduzione alla sociologia relazionale. FrancoAngeli, Milano (1986)
55. Gui, B.: Eléments pour une définition d'économie. Notes Doc. **19–20**, 32–42 (1987)
56. Uhlaner, C.J.: "Relational goods" and participation: incorporating sociability into a theory of rational action. Publ. Choice **62**, 253–285 (1989)
57. Bruni, L., Zarri, L.: La grandeillusione. False relazioni e felicità nelle economie di mercato contemporanee. In: AICONN Working Paper n.39, Facoltà di Economia, Forlì (2007)
58. Capello, R., Faggian, A.: Collective learning and relational capital in local innovation processes. Reg. Stud. **39**, 75–87 (2005)
59. Youndt, M.A., Subramaniam, M., Snell, S.A.: Intellectual capital profiles: an examination of investments and returns. J. Manag. Stud. **41**, 335–361 (2004)
60. Banchiero, F., Blečić, I., Saiu, V., Trunfio, G.A.: Neighbourhood park vitality potential: from Jane Jacobs's theory to evaluation model. Sustainability **12**, 5881 (2020). https://doi.org/10.3390/su12155881
61. Blečić, I., Saiu, V.: Assessing urban green spaces availability: a comparison between planning standards and a high-fidelity accessibility evaluation. In: La Rosa, D., Privitera, R. (eds.) INPUT 2021. LNCE, vol. 146, pp. 339–347. Springer, Cham (2021). https://doi.org/10.1007/978-3-030-68824-0_37
62. Blečić, I., Saiu, V., Trunfio, G.A.: Towards a high-fidelity assessment of urban green spaces walking accessibility. In: Gervasi, O., et al. (eds.) ICCSA 2020. LNCS, vol. 12252, pp. 535–549. Springer, Cham (2020). https://doi.org/10.1007/978-3-030-58811-3_39
63. Pinna, F., Saiu, V.: Greenways as integrated systems: a proposal for planning and design guidelines based on case studies evaluation. Sustainability **13**, 11232 (2021). https://doi.org/10.3390/su132011232
64. Morretta, V., Syrett, S., Ramirez, L.S.: Territorial capital as a source of firm competitive advantage: evidence from the North and South of Italy. Eur. Plan. Stud. **28**, 2390–2408 (2020). https://doi.org/10.1080/09654313.2020.1722067
65. Rodwin, L.: Shelter, Settlement & Development. Routledge, London (2022)
66. Saiu, V., Blečić, I.: Sustainable development goals (SDGs) evaluation for neighbourhood planning and design. In: New Metropolitan Perspectives 2022 Symposium. Springer, Reggio Calabria (2022)

A Comparative Study on Site Selection Methods for Modeling Hospital Locating in Urban Area, A Case Study in Iran

Fu Fang-yu[1], Mohamad Molaei Qelichi[2(✉)], Farrokh Namjooyan[3], and Ahmad Asadi[4]

[1] School of Architecture and Urban Planning, Huazhong University of Science and Technology, Wuhan, Hubei, China

[2] Faculty of Encyclopedia Research, Institute for Humanities and Cultural Studies, Tehran, Iran
m.molaei@ihcs.ac.ir

[3] Department of Geography and Planning, University of Toledo, Ohio, USA

[4] Faculty of Humanities, Bozorgmehr University of Qaenat, Qaen, Iran

Abstract. Urban managers are faced with complex decisions, including the decision to select a suitable location for service centers, based on several conflicting criteria noted. The purpose of this research is a comparative study on site selection methods for modeling hospital locating. According to the present article, new locations were found to manage better and complete Amol city coverage with eight specified criteria. The research area in terms of proximity to major roads, green spaces, fire stations and distance from the river, industrial land uses, education land uses, hospitals and sport land uses has been studied. As well as for weighing the criteria, the model of AHP was implemented. Then, using the TOPSIS model in ArcGIS software, the valuation of standards was analyzed, and suitable maps were created that show the best place for the hospital building. In the next step, using the Fuzzy Logic model in ArcGIS, another appropriate map is prepared, and the results of the two models have been compared together. The results revealed that the Multi-Criteria Decision Making (MCDM) system with GIS could be an effective hospital site selection tool. Anyway, there are some differences between the results of the models. Fuzzy Logic is better suited to the hospital locating. The location of hospitals away from existing spaces in the Fuzzy Logic model shows this model's ability in comparison with the TOPSIS model.

Keywords: Hospital planning · Site selection · TOPSIS · Fuzzy logic · Amol city

1 Introduction

Health is the product of a dynamic relationship between socioeconomic conditions, the natural environment, and the built environment as emerging on individual and social levels (Rydin et al. 2012; Rydin 2012; Sarkar et al. 2014). Despite the considerable advancements in today's healthcare, studies show a massive gap in healthcare access and

O. Gervasi et al. (Eds.): ICCSA 2022 Workshops, LNCS 13379, pp. 546–563, 2022.
https://doi.org/10.1007/978-3-031-10545-6_37

health outcomes. One of the essential public services is the hospital that provides the citizens' health. The selection of a hospital site is essential to hospital management (Zhou and Wu 2012). Several researchers have used geographical information systems (GIS) to help with hospital site selection. To overcome the MCDA problems of hospital site placement, Vahidnia et al. (2009) implemented the model of FAHP. Their observations demonstrate the best way to figure out how much each alternative is worth. Zhou and Wu (2012) applied the GIS-based MCA method with AHP and ROM for the weighting factor criteria. Senvar et al. (2016) used a TFHFWA operator. They claim that it is possible to propose their methodology for other multi-criteria site selection issues. Şahin et al. (2017) used the AHP method for hospital site selection. They believe that the best hospital site selection must consider both macro and micro parameters to work effectively for several years. Choosing the best hospital location would also help to improve public health in the region.

This paper focused on the choice of proper hospital sites in Amol city, Iran. Therefore, the GIS program is used to assess hospital building positions in a comparative analysis of two techniques (TOPSIS and Fuzzy Logic). To this goal, multiple factors were included in the screening process based on literature and related study experiences.

Table 1. Recent researches about hospital site selection

Researchers	Year	Applied method
Wu et al.	2007	AHP
Behzadi & Alesheikh	2013	Belief-Desire-Intention (BDI)
Chiu & Tsai	2013	AHP
Abdullahi et al.	2014	OLS technique
Kumar et al.	2016	ELECTRE

2 Study Area

Amol is in Iran's province of Mazandaran. It is situated on the southern side of the Caspian Sea, spanning between latitudes 26°25′N and longitudes 52°2′E and covers a total area of about 31 km^2. (Iranian Statistics Centre 2016). (Fig. 1).

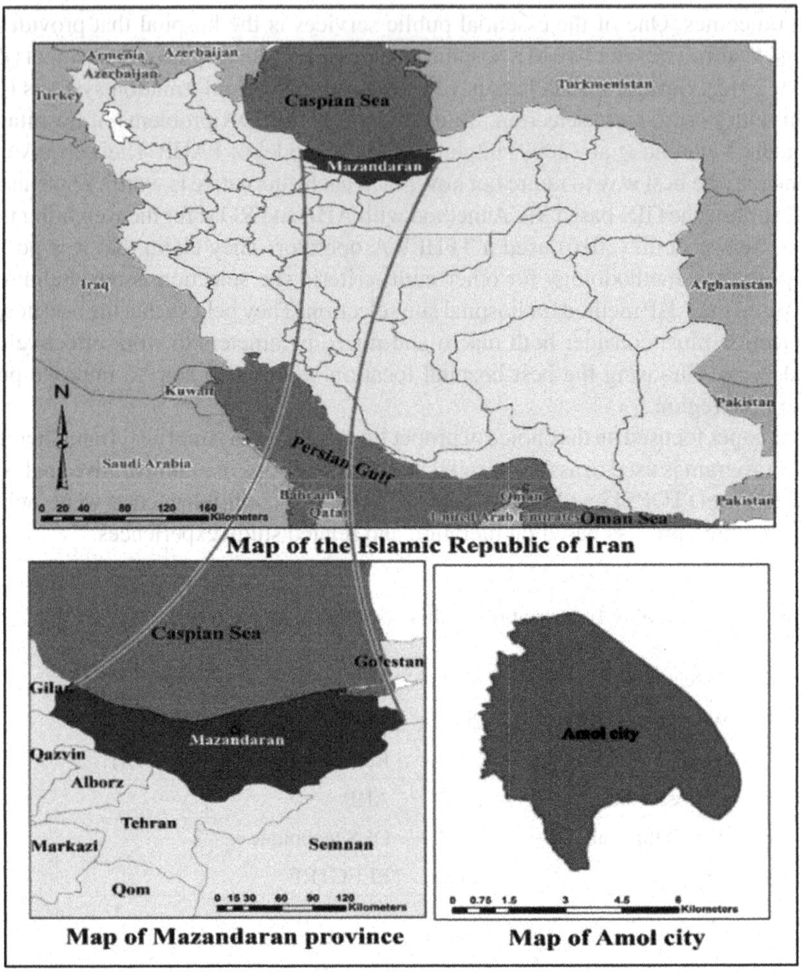

Fig. 1. Study area of Amol City, Iran

3 Methodology

Generally, scientific research needs to apply proper methods and tools while doing any investigation. Regarding the research identity, the method is analytical and descriptive. "Hospital site selection is one of the multi-criteria decision-making problems" (Şahin et al. 2019). In this research, GIS techniques were used within field data to select the hospitals sites. Furthermore, the method of TOPSIS and Fuzzy Logic were implemented. At first, in this paper, for assessing hospitals' spatial distribution patterns, the "Nearest Neighborhood" method is used. Then effective criteria in identifying appropriate locations for hospitals are listed. According to literature and the views of the experts, we determined the following criteria: distances from industrial land use, education land uses, river, hospitals, sport land uses and proximity to fire stations, areas of green space, and major roads. The use of multi-attribute decision-making methods and spatial analysis capability by the ArcGIS assess the data and the location of hospitals in Amol city (Fig. 2).

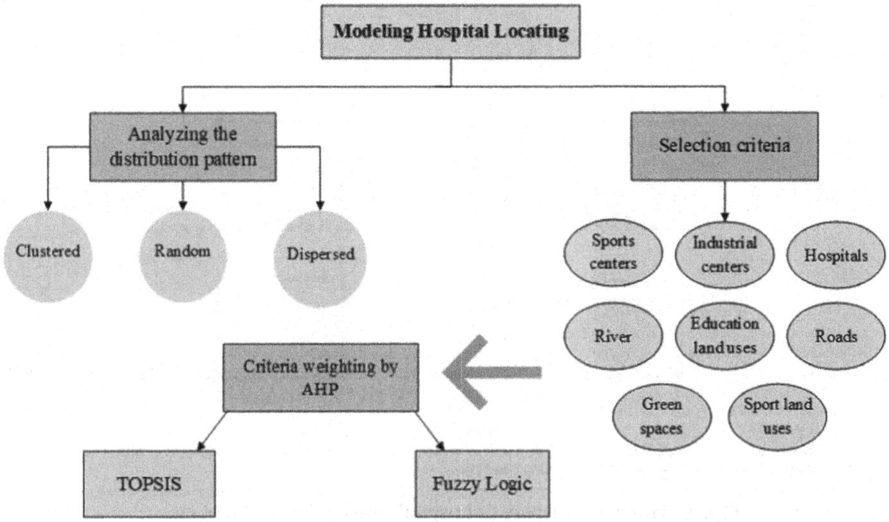

Fig. 2. Research methodology

4 Results

One of the most crucial approaches for analyzing urban land usage is the Nearest Neighborhood technique. According to this formula, when the criterion is between 0 and 0.5 the distribution form is clustered; it is random when between 0.5 and 1.5. When it is between 1.5 and 2.15 the distribution form is regular and ordered (Ali Akbari and Emadodin 2012).

According to numeric results, the observed nearest neighborhood among hospitals is 1461 m, and the expected average distance is 369 m. Thus, the nearest neighbor ratio is 3.95 that presents a dispersed distribution of hospitals in Amol. Z-Score is applied to explain the disparity in the number found with a random distribution. This value amounts to 9.80. On the basis of this quantity and the presumption that the trend of distribution was dispersed, the assumption is accepted with a significance level of 95%, and there was no significant difference between the distribution observed and the random distribution. The P-value of 0.00 demonstrates the credibility of the findings (Fig. 3).

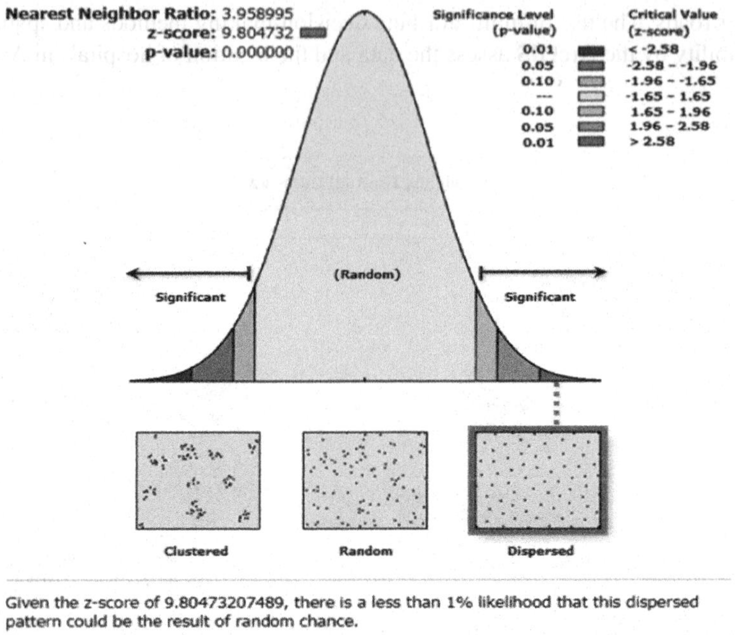

Fig. 3. Graphical display of hospital distribution in Amol city

The Nearest Neighborhood analysis results show that the hospital distribution is not acceptable and does not have a rational foundation in the case study. This issue provides rise to the notion that these hospitals must be organized. Table 2 shows the results of the ANN (Tables 1 and 3).

Table 2. The results of Nearest Neighborhood for analysis of the hospitals

The observed average distance	1461.4711 m
The expected average distance	369.1520 m
Nearest Neighbor Ratio (R)	3.958995
z-score	9.804732
p-value	0.000000

Table 3. Weights of criteria

Criteria	Proximity to major roads	Proximity to areas of green space	Proximity to fire stations	Distance from sport land uses
Weight	0.210	0.124	0.164	0.078
Criteria	Distance from hospitals	Distance from education land uses	Distance from industrial land uses	Distance from river
Weight	0.136	0.136	0.080	0.072

TOPSIS technique has been presented in Chen and Hwang (1992), concerning Hwang and Yoon (1981) that alternatives should have the shortest distance from a positive ideal solution and the most distant from a negative ideal solution (Jahanshahloo et al. 2009). After defining effective criteria in locating urban hospitals, data layers of criteria were entered in GIS. In the first step, raster layers were created based on the number of criteria used in this study using spatial analyst and the distance tool. Raster layers of used criteria are shown within the following figures (Figs. 4, 5, 6, 7, 8, 9, 10, 11).

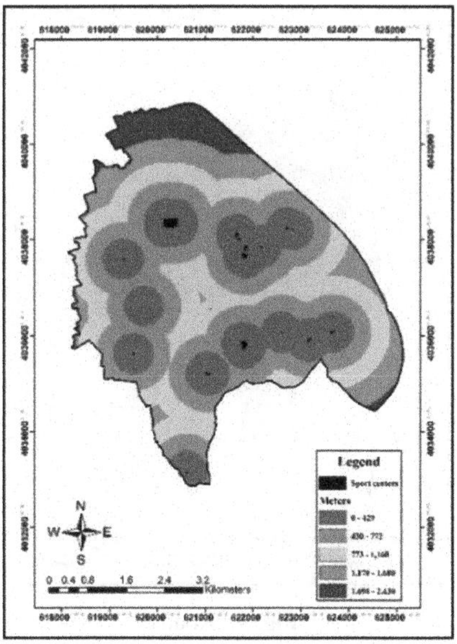

Fig. 4. Sports centers

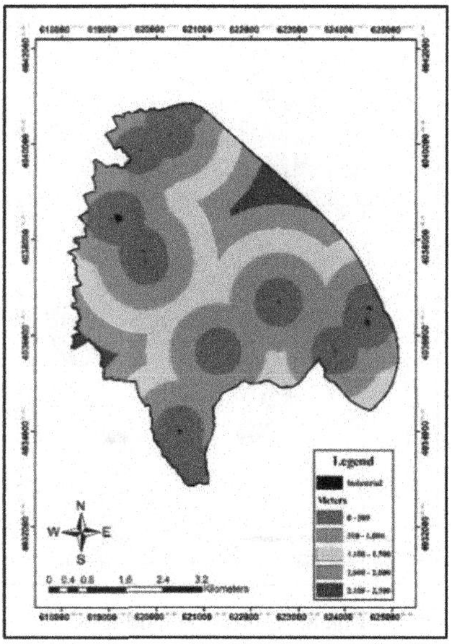

Fig. 5. Industrial centers

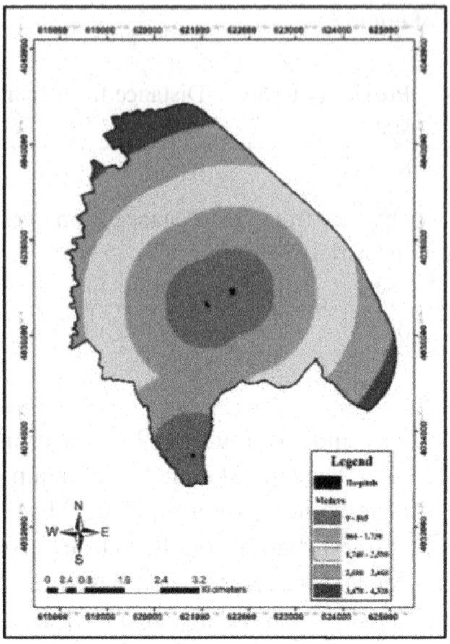

Fig. 6. Hospitals

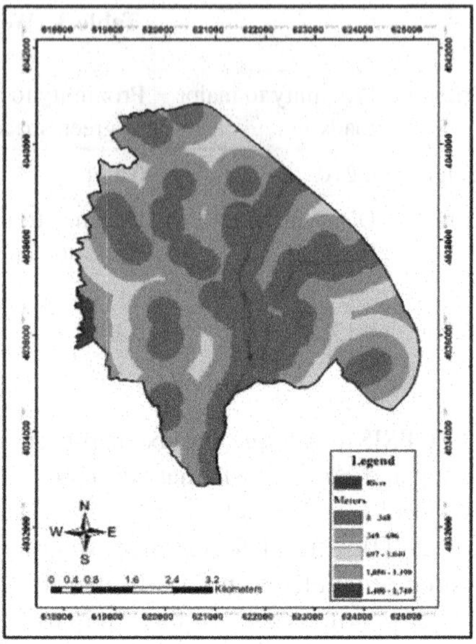

Fig. 7. River

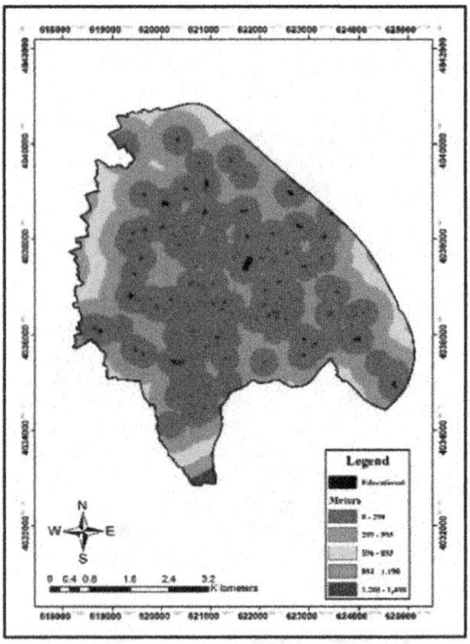

Fig. 8. Education land uses

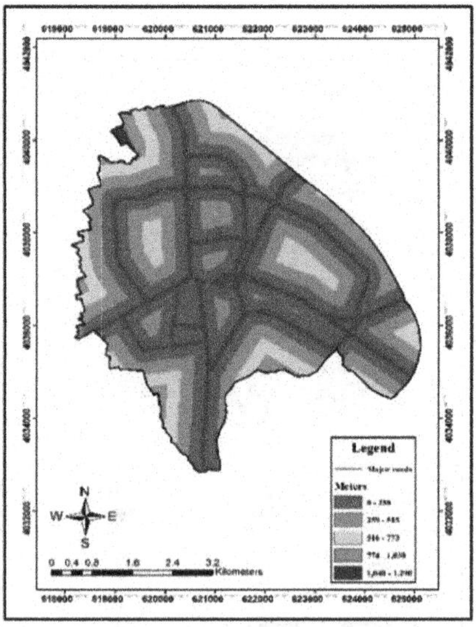

Fig. 9. Roads

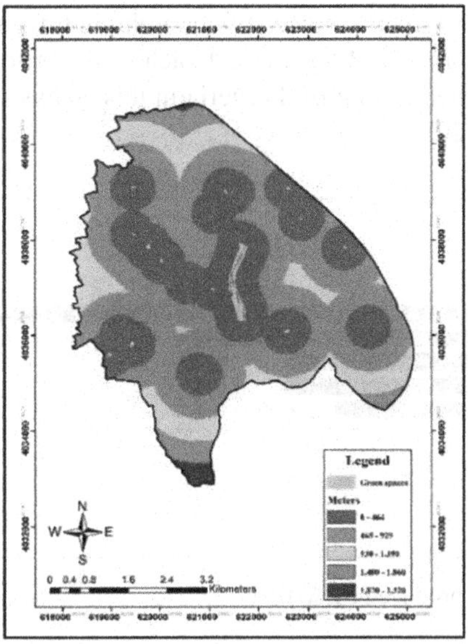

Fig. 10. Green spaces

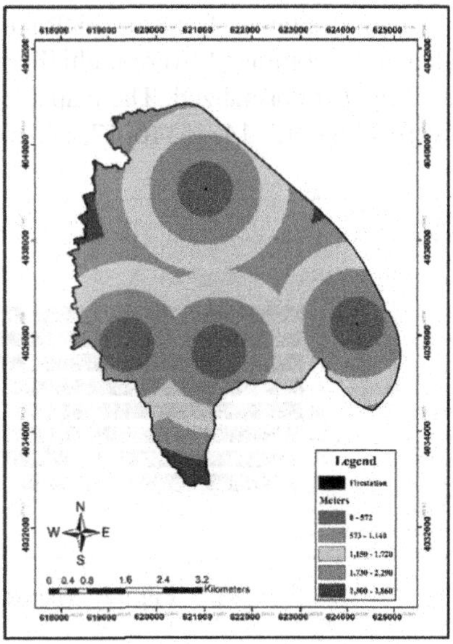

Fig. 11. Sport land uses

(Raster output of hospital locating criteria in the study area)

In hospital locating, the next step of TOPSIS is normalizing criteria that each of the criterion based on their effect (positive or negative) normalized by using the following formula, and a linear method is used for this purpose:

$$N_{ij} = \frac{r_{ij}}{Max\, r_{ij}}$$

After normalization, each layer is assigned a weight depending on its relative value in locating hospitals. For this purpose, the AHP model is used in Expert Choice software. AHP is one of the weighting methods that formulate the problem hierarchically. AHP is based on (1) hierarchy construction, (2) pairwise comparison, (3) relative-weight computation, (4) consistency ratio, and finally (5) aggregation of relative weights. In this research, we used the Expert Choice software that computes each criterion's weight according to the AHP model (Fig. 12). The consistency ratio of pairwise comparison is 0.01. That is acceptable because it is less than 0.1. In Fig. 12, see weights obtained from the AHP model.

Weights obtained from the AHP model in Expert Choice software, through Raster Calculator's command, were multiplied in normalized layers, and each of the criteria was weighted normalized. The map of weighted normalized criteria in this analysis is shown in Figs. 13, 14, 15, 16, 17, 18, 19 and 20.

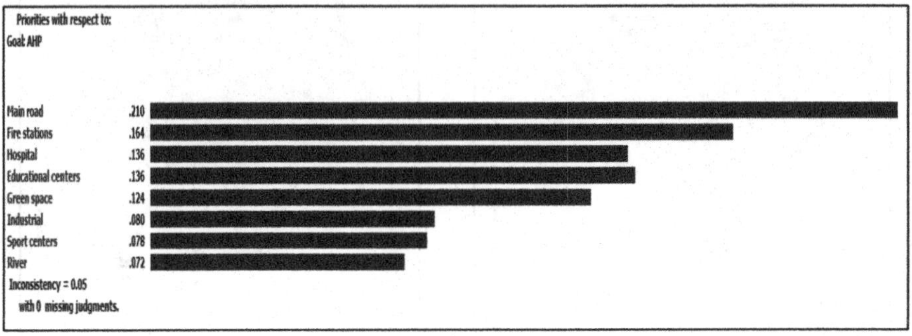

Fig. 12. The weights produced by AHP

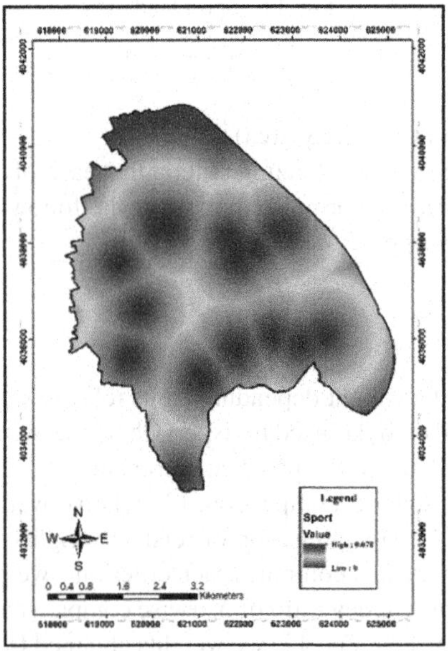

Fig. 13. Sports centers

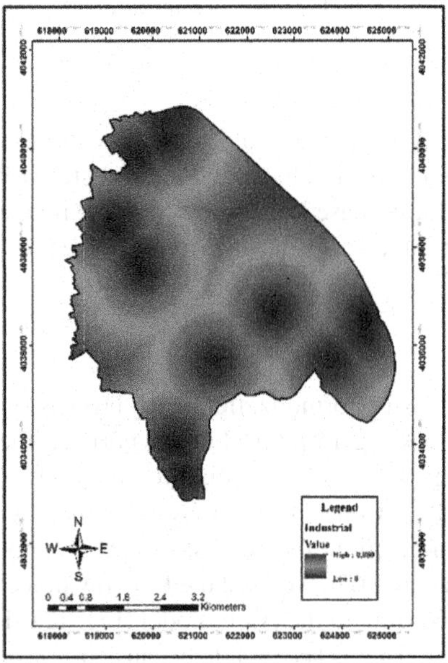

Fig. 14. Industrial centers

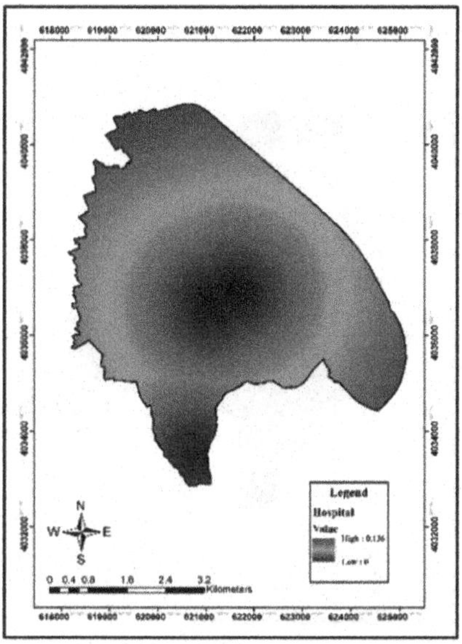

Fig. 15. Hospitals

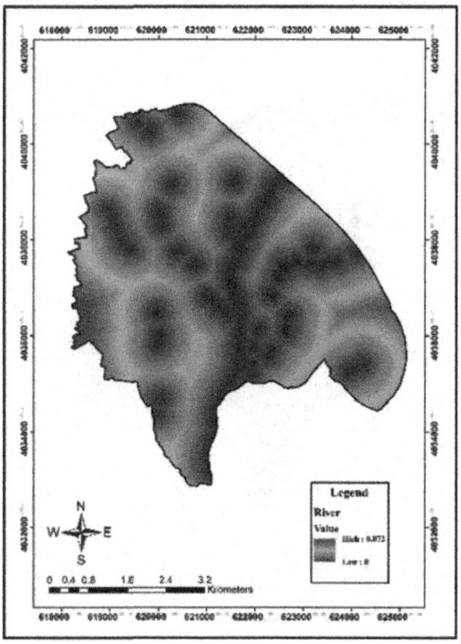

Fig. 16. River

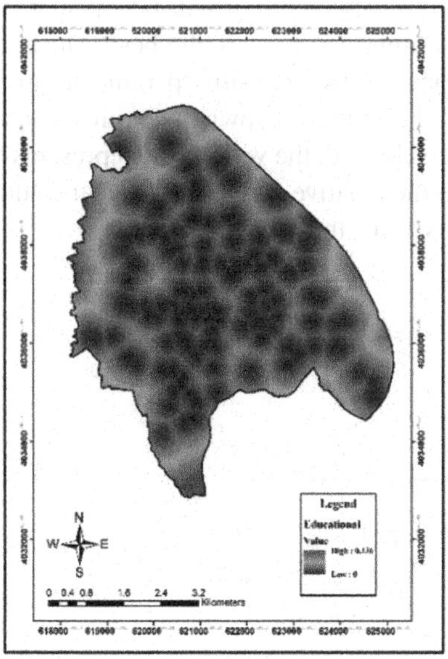

Fig. 17. Education land uses

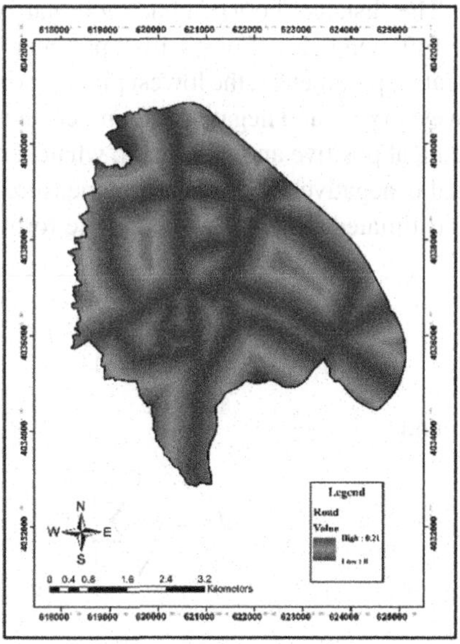

Fig. 18. Roads

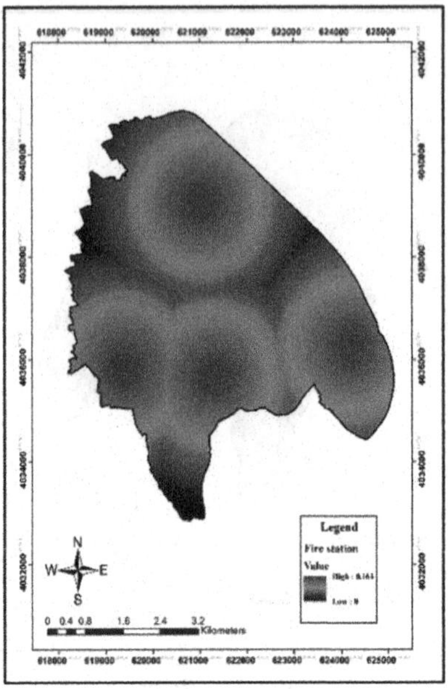

Fig. 19. Green spaces

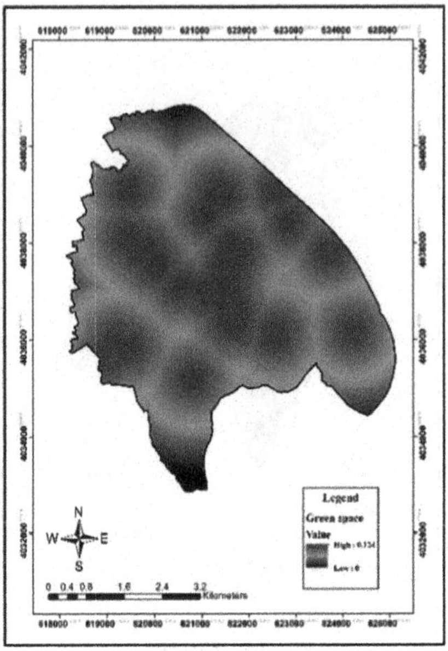

Fig. 20. Sport land uses

(The maps of weighted normalized for each option).

The distance between each alternative and the ideal solution will be calculated in the following step. For positive parameters, the highest pixels are the best values. For negative parameters, the lowest pixels and the worst values for positive parameters are the lowest pixels, and negative parameters are the highest pixels. Brown pixels are closest to the ideal positive and vice versa; whatever we are close to, the yellow hue represents the ideal is negative. The Separation measures from the positive and negative ideal solution are estimated (Figs. 21 and 22). The formulae used for this step are:

$$d_i^+ = \sqrt{\sum_{j=1}^{n} (v_{ij} - v_j^+)^2}, \quad i = 1, 2, \ldots, m,$$

and

$$d_i^- = \sqrt{\sum_{j=1}^{n} (v_{ij} - v_j^-)^2}, \quad i = 1, 2, \ldots, m.$$

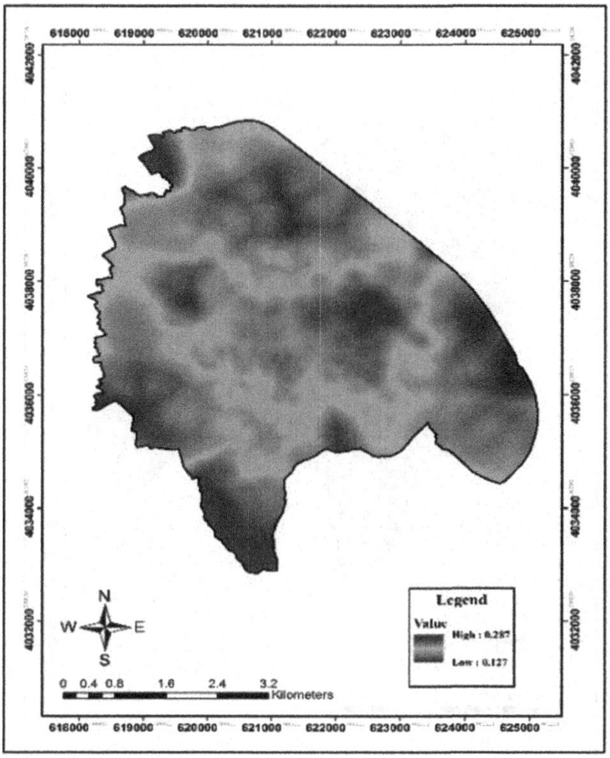

Fig. 21. Separation measure from positive ideal solution

For the positive ideal, the value of the pixels is between 0.29 and 0.13 which means that pixels closer to 0.29 have a good capability, and pixels with the value of 0.13 have the minimum ability for locating the hospitals. On the other hand, for the negative ideal layer, the location's value is also between 0.31 and 0.12, which means that pixels closer to 0.31 have the minor capability, and pixels with a value of 0.12 have a better ability for locating the hospitals.

Following the TOPSIS model for the spatial classification, for finding suitable places to locate hospitals in the case study, Ri factor is anticipated in a spectrum between 0.31 and 0.69. Ri factor is predicted by the following formula (Soufi et al. 2015):

$$R_i = \frac{d_i^-}{d_i^- + d_i^+}$$

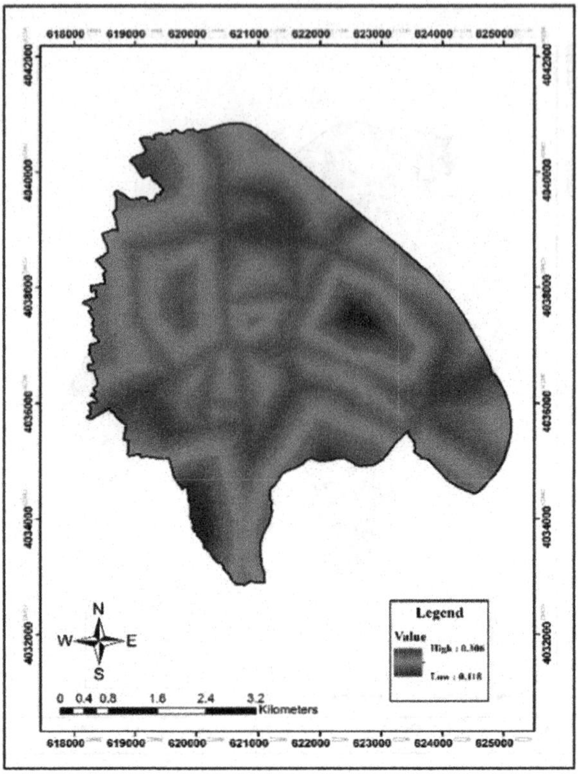

Fig. 22. Separation measure from the negative ideal solution

Spatial multifactor decision-making analysis reveals that if the location value is high, that place will be a good choice for locating a hospital. With this worth decreasing, this location loses its suitability for hospital building.

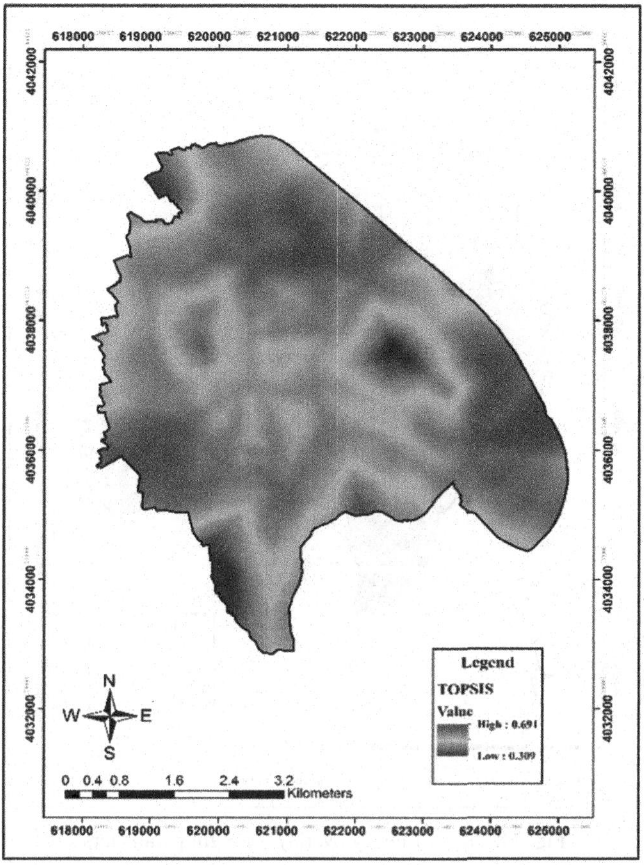

Fig. 23. Hospital site selection using TOPSIS model

The Fuzzy Logic theory was first suggested by Zadeh (1965), who believes that a descriptive variable of linguistics would more adequately represent a complex system (Cox et al. 1998); Dixon (2005). Due to the Fuzzy membership functions having more excellent compatibility with urban issues, using this system to analyze urban systems in decision making would be more effective. In Fuzzy Logic, an element's membership in a set was determined with a value ranging from 0 (non-membership) to 1 (entire membership) (Bonham-Carter 1994). It can prepare the map of a factor so that each pixel's amount includes the relative value of parameters compared with other hospital site selection parameters (Beheshtifar et al. 2010). For overlying the factors, some Fuzzy operators, like AND, OR, Product, Sum, and Gamma operator can be implemented (Kamran 2008; Esri (2011). The Overlay type for hospital locating was Gamma. Figure 24 is the final map and presents the best spaces for locating hospitals in the study area.

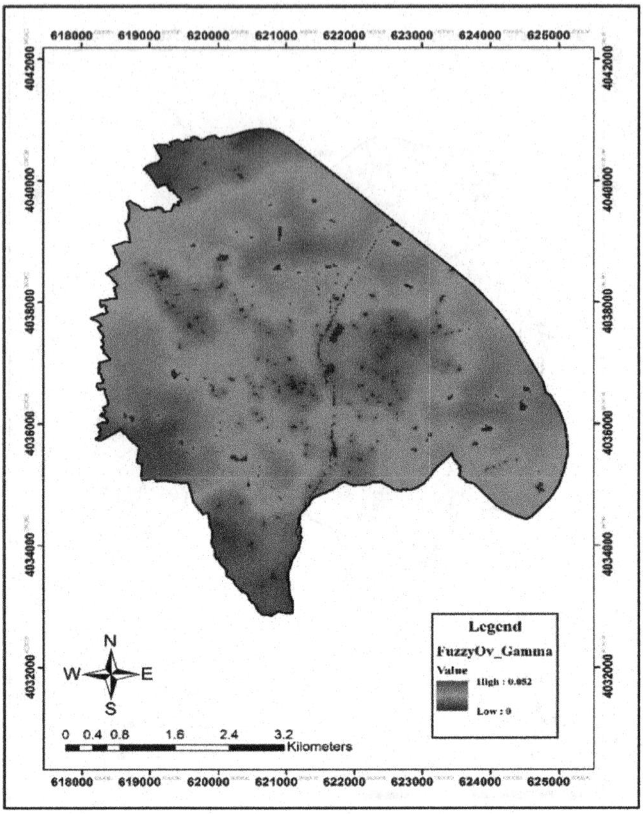

Fig. 24. Map of Fuzzy overlay for eight parameters

The TOPSIS method results show that the existing hospitals in the city are under the appropriate spaces. Still, in the Fuzzy Logic method, the existing hospitals are in concordance with the new hospitals' appropriate areas.

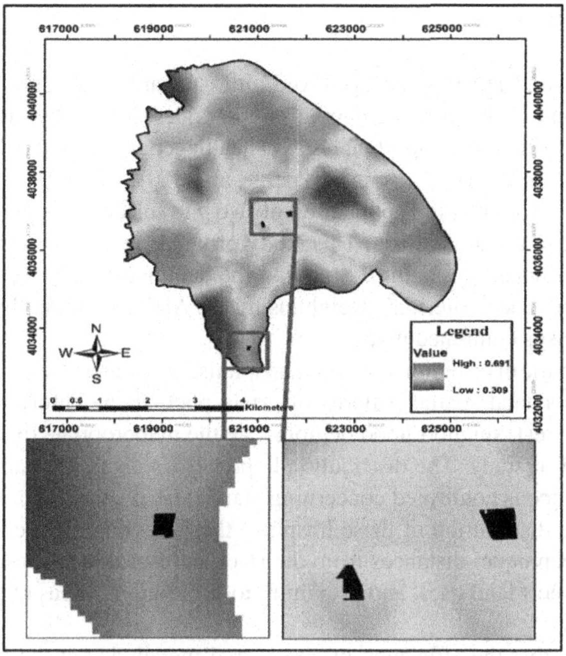

Fig. 25. Hospital locating map extracted by TOPSIS

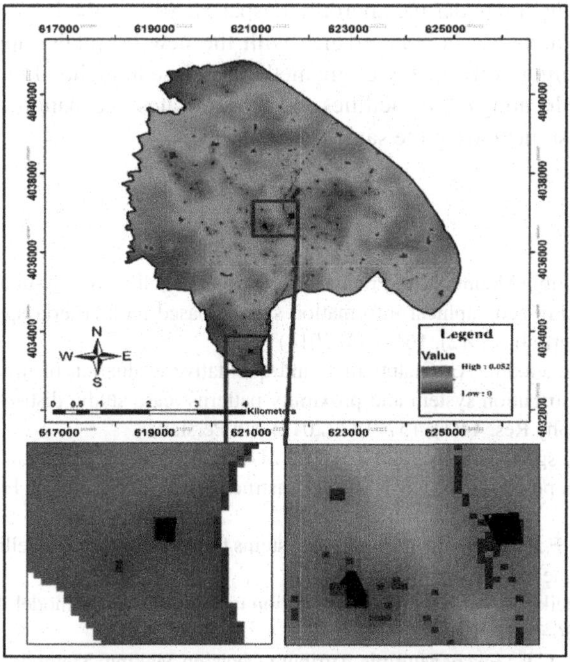

Fig. 26. Hospital locating map extracted by Fuzzy Logic

5 Conclusion

The shortage of land in urban areas moved cities toward adopting excessive density policies to respond to the growing demand for services, especially in big urban areas (Ranjbarnia et al. 2017). An important issue in health geography and health policy is the analysis of the accessibility to hospitals (Paez et al. 2010).

This research examined the application of two site selection methods for modeling hospital locating in urban land use. This study provides an application of the GIS for modeling hospital locating in cities. Studying the parameters and storing them in GIS software calculates each criterion's weight using the AHP technique (by Expert Choice software) and makes combined maps.

For analyzing the distribution pattern of hospitals, the Nearest Neighborhood method was used to understand spatial patterns of urban phenomena before assessment. The results of the Nearest Neighborhood demonstrate the inappropriate distribution of hospitals in the area of study. The distribution hypothesis's dispersed pattern with a 95% level of significance is confirmed concerning standardized scores. So, for reorganizing the inappropriate distribution of these hospitals the following eight criteria were used from the AHP technique: distances from the river, industrial land uses, education land uses, hospitals, sport land uses, and proximity to fire stations, areas of green space and major roads.

Results show that the efficiency of considered models is not the same in hospital site selection. The case study indicated the Fuzzy Logic model's desirable function in hospitals' location in Amol city. The TOPSIS method results show that the existing hospitals in the city are under the appropriate spaces. Still, in the Fuzzy Logic method, the existing hospitals are in concordance with the new hospitals' appropriate areas. Therefore, the ability of the Fuzzy Logic method is close to reality. In general, GIS is a powerful tool for locating urban facilities and demonstrates its capabilities by employing diverse and robust methods at the same time.

References

Abdullahi, S., Rodzibin Mahmud, A., Pradhan, B.: Spatial modelling of site suitability assessment for hospitals using geographical information system-based multicriteria approach at Qazvin city, Iran. Geocarto Int. **29**(2), 164–184 (2014)

Ali Akbari, A., Emadodin, A.: Quantitative and qualitative evaluation of urban land use with emphasis on distribution system and proximity patterns (case study: district 1 Gorgan City). Human Geography Res. **44**(1), 157–172 (2012). (In Persian)

Beheshtifar, S., Mesgari, M.S., Veldan Zoj, M.J.: Using fuzzy logic in gis environment for site selection of gas power plant. Civil Eng. Infrastructures J. (J. Faculty of Eng.) **44**, 583–595 (2010)

Bonham-Carter, G.F.: Geographic information systems for geoscientists: modelling with GIS, vol. 13. Access Online via Elsevier (1994)

Behzadi, S., Alesheikh, A.A.: Hospital site selection using a BDI agent model. Int. J. Geography Geology **2**(4), 36–51 (2013)

Chen, S.J., Hwang, C.L.: Fuzzy Multiple Attribute Decision Making: Methods and Applications. Springer, Berlin (1992)

Chiu, J.E., Tsai, H.H.: Applying analytic hierarchy process to select optimal expansion of hospital location: the case of a regional teaching hospital in Yunlin. In: 2013 10th International Conference on Service Systems and Service Management, ICSSSM 2013, Hong Kong (2013)

Cox, E., O'Hagan, M., Taber, R., & O'Hagen, M., (1998). The Fuzzy Systems Handbook with Cdrom: Academic Press, Inc.

Dixon, B.: Groundwater vulnerability mapping: a GIS and fuzzy rule based integrated tool. Appl. Geogr. **25**(4), 327–347 (2005)

Esri: Environmental Systems Research Institute (2011). How Fuzzy Overlay works, ArcGIS Resource Center

Hwang, C.L., Yoon, K.: Multiple Attribute Decision Making: Methods and Applications. Springer, Berlin (1981)

Iranian Statistics Centre. (2016). General census of population and housing of Amol City

Jahanshahloo, G.R., Lotfi, F.H., Davoodi, A.: Extension of topsis for decisionmaking problems with interval data: Interval efficiency. Math. Comput. Model. **49**(5), 1137–1142 (2009)

Kamran, K.V.: Comparison of boolean, overlay index and fuzzy logic methods for hazardous material disposal center site selection. Islamic Azad University-Ahar Branch Geographic Space An Approved Scientific. Res. Based J. **25**, 9–24 (2008)

Kumar, P., Kumar Singh, R., Sinha, P.: Optimal site selection for a hospital using a fuzzy extended ELECTRE approach. J. Manage. Anal. **3**(2), 115–135 (2016). https://doi.org/10.1080/23270012.2016.1152170

Paez, A., Mercado, R., Farber, S., Morency, C., Roorda, M.: Accessibility to healthcare facilities in Montreal Island: an application of relative accessibility indicators from the perspective of senior and non-senior residents. Int. J. Health Geogr. **9**(1), 52 (2010)

Ranjbar, B., Murgante, B., Molaei, M., Rustaei, S.: A comparative study employing CIA methods in knowledge-based urban development with emphasis on affordable housing in iranian cities (Case: Tabriz). In: Gervasi, O., et al. (eds.) ICCSA 2017. LNCS, vol. 10407, pp. 485–501. Springer, Cham (2017). Doi: https://doi.org/10.1007/978-3-319-62401-3_35

Robinove, C.J.: Principles of logic and the use of digital geographic information systems: Department of the Interior, US Geological Survey (1986)

Rydin, Y.: Healthy cities and planning. Town Plann. Rev. **83**, 1–6 (2012)

Rydin, Y., et al.: Shaping Cities for Health: the complexities of planning urban environments in the 21st century. Lancet **379** (Special Issue), 2079–2108 (2012)

Şahin, T., Saffet, O., Mehmet, T.: Analytic hierarchy process for hospital site selection. Health Policy Technol. **8**(1), 42–50 (2019)

Sarkar, C., Webster, C., Gallacher, J.: Urban built environment configuration and psychological distress in later life: cross-sectional results from the Caerphilly Prospective Study (CaPS). Healthy Cities. Public Health through Urban Planning, pp. 255–276 (2014)

Dehghani Soufi, M., Ghobadian, B., Najafi, G., Sabzimaleki, M.R., Yusaf, T.: TOPSIS multi-criteria decision modeling approach for biolubricant selection for two-stroke petrol engines. Energies **8**(12), 13960–13970 (2015)

Vahidnia, M.H., Alesheikh, A.A., Alimohammadi, A.: Hospital site selection using fuzzy AHP and its derivatives. J. Environ. Manag. **90**(10), 3048–3056 (2009)

Wu, C., Lin, C., Chen, H.: Optimal selection of location for Taiwanese hospitals to ensure a competitive advantage by using the analytic hierarchy process and sensitivity analysis. **42**(3), 1431–1444 (2007)

Zadeh, L.A.: Fuzzy sets. Information and control **8**(3), 338–353 (1965)

Zhou, L., Wu, J.: GIS-Based Multi-Criteria Analysis for Hospital Site Selection in Haidian District of Beijing, Master thesis in Geomatics, Hogscolan I Gavlee, China (2012)

The SDGs Indicators for the Statistical Analysis of Land and Water Resource Protection

Paola Perchinunno[1(✉)], Domenico Leogrande[1], Samuela L'Abbate[1], and Francesco Rotondo[2]

[1] Department of Economics, Management and Business Law, University of Bari "Aldo Moro", Italy, via C. Rosalba, 53, 70100 Bari, Italy
{paola.perchinunno,domenico.leogrande,samuela.labbate}@uniba.it
[2] DICEA-Dipartimento di Ingegneria Civile, Edile e Architettura, UNIVPM, Via Brecce Bianche 12, 60131 Ancona, Italy
f.rotondo@univpm.it

Abstract. The evolution of the concept of sustainability and the availability of new statistical information requires constant checks on the set of indicators so that they accurately carry out the task of representing well-being in our society. The Sustainable Development Goals refer to several domains of development related to environmental, social, economic, and institutional issues. For the environmental sustainability is particularly interesting territorial protection and the water resource issues and how statistical indicators can be helpful for urban planning and decisions support systems. The numerous data available have been analysed at regional level through multivariate statistical methodologies (Totally Fuzzy and Relative method) capable of synthesizing the multiple information to assess the current situation in the different Italian regions. The presence of multiple data updated to 2019 allows researchers to develop a holistic approach to the evaluation of the policies of government of the territory in place and to monitor the progress of subsequent policies of intervention of the Italian government.

Keywords: Water discomfort · Ecological development · Sustainable development goals

1 Introduction

At the heart of the United Nations 2030 Agenda of great importance is the theme of sustainable development in the economic, social and environmental dimensions. Among the many objectives are those concerning urgent ecological measures to combat climate change, to protect the oceans, seas and marine resources and to manage forests by combating desertification.

Clean water is an essential resource for human health, agriculture, energy production, transport and nature. Also, if it is under multiple pressures. Currently, only 40% of

The contribution is the result of joint reflections by the authors, with the following contributions attributed to Rotondo (paragraphs 4.3 and 5), to Leogrande (paragraph 1, 3.1), to Perchinunno (paragraphs 4.1, 4.2) and to L'Abbate (paragraphs 2, 3.2).

O. Gervasi et al. (Eds.): ICCSA 2022 Workshops, LNCS 13379, pp. 564–575, 2022.
https://doi.org/10.1007/978-3-031-10545-6_38

Europe's surface water bodies achieve good ecological status. In addition, even though EU countries have managed to reduce selected pressures, the status of our freshwater bodies remains unsatisfactory [1].

In Europe, in 2000, with the adoption of the Water Framework Directive, an integrated ecosystem-based approach to managing water was introduced. Public safety and health objectives were persued by the Drinking Water, Bathing Water and Floods Directives [2]. While the directives tend to be very specific, the importance of water in relation to biodiversity and marine policies is pursued through the EU biodiversity strategy to 2020 [3] and the priority objectives of the Seventh Environment Action Europe's waters are affected by pressures from pollution, overabstraction and physical changes.

Hydromorphology is considered a key parameter, because interaction between water, morphology, sediments and vegetation creates habitats that determine the river's ecological status. Hydromorphological pressures are one of the main reasons that surface water bodies fail to achieve good ecological status.

What is Italian evaluation of protection, and the water resource issues? How is it possible to evaluate it?

The Sustainable Development Goals refer to various development domains relating to environmental, social, economic and institutional issues [4]. This paper deals with analyzing the relationships between the domains of the Sustainable Development Goals (SDGs) and the statistical indicators relating to the protection of the territory and of the water resource.

The numerous data available were analyzed at regional level using multivariate statistical methodologies (Totally Fuzzy and Relative method) capable of synthesizing the various information to evaluate the current situation in the various Italian regions. The presence of multiple data updated to 2019 allows for the development of a holistic approach to the evaluation of the local government policies in place and the ability to monitor the progress of the subsequent intervention policies of the Italian government.

2 The Statistical Indicators of the Sustainable Development Goals Report (SDGs)

2.1 SDGs Project

The "Sustainable Development Goals" indicate what changes the nations and peoples of the world are committed to achieving, by virtue of a global consensus, obtained through a long, complex and difficult process of international and interdisciplinary dialogue and collaboration.

The 2030 Agenda consists of 17 objectives that refer to different development domains relating to environmental, social, economic and institutional issues, outlining a global action plan for the next 15 years. The 17 objectives are divided into 169 Targets (sub-objectives) that refer to different domains of economic, social and environmental development; the United Nations Inter Agency Expert Group on SDGs (UN-IAEG-SDGs) in 2017 proposed a system of over 230 indicators necessary for their monitoring, which constitute the reference framework worldwide [5].

It is a highly complex system of indicators that includes both consolidated indicators available for most countries, and indicators that are not currently produced or that have not yet been precisely defined at an interactional level. Starting from 2018, Istat makes available, every six months, many indicators for Italy and publishes the "SDGs Report. Statistical information for the 2030 Agenda in Italy".

We briefly describe the 17 Sustainable Development Goals (SDGs): No Poverty; Zero Hunger; Good Health and Well-Being; Quality Education; Gender Equality; Clean Water and Sanitation; Affordable and Clean Energy; Decent Work and Economic Growth; Industry, Innovation and Infrastructure; Reduce inequalities; Sustainable Cities; Responsible Consuption and Production; Climate Action; Life Below Water; Life on Land; Peace, Justice, and Strong Institution; Partnership for the Goals.

3 Statistical Indicators for the Protection of the Territory and Water Resources

3.1 SDGs Indicators

The Italian National Recovery and Resilience Plan (NRRP) is part of the Next Generation EU (NGEU) program, the 750-billion-euro package, about half of which is made up of grants, agreed by the European Union in response to the crisis pandemic. The main component of the NGEU program is the Recovery and Resilience Facility (RRF), which has a duration of six years, from 2021 to 2026, and a total size of 672.5 billion euros (312, 5 grants, the remaining 360 billion loans at subsidized rates).

The Plan is developed around three strategic axes shared at European level (digitization and innovation, ecological transition and social inclusion) and 6 missions. The subject of territorial safety also finds space in the Mission, with prevention and restoration interventions in the face of significant hydrogeological risks, the protection of green areas and biodiversity, and those relating to the elimination of water and soil pollution, and the availability of water resources.

The Sustainable Development Goals [5] refer to various development domains relating to environmental, social, economic and institutional issues. In particular, the Goals considered for the purposes of the analysis for the protection of the territory and of the water resource are shown in Table 1.

Table 1. Goals, indicators, measures and data source.

Goal	Indicators	Measures	Data source
Goal 6.1.1:	Percentage of population benefiting from safely managed drinking water services	Irregularities in water distribution	(Istat, 2020, percentage values)
Goal 6.1.1:	Percentage of population benefiting from safely managed drinking water services	Water supplied per capita	(Istat, 2018, litres per capita per day)
Goal 6.3.1:	Percentage of civil and industrial wastewater treated safely	Urban wastewater with secondary or advanced treatment	(Istat, 2018, No. of plants)
Goal 6.3.1:	Percentage of civil and industrial wastewater treated safely	Coverage of the public sewerage service	(Istat, 2018, percentage values)
Goal 6.4.1:	Change in efficiency in the use of water resources	Efficiency of drinking water distribution networks	(Istat, 2018, percentage values)
Goal 11.3.1:	Ratio of land use rate to population growth rate	Sealing and land use per capita	(Ispra, 2019, m2 per inhabitant)
Goal 11.7.1:	Average percentage of the urbanized area of cities that is used as public space, by sex, age and people with disabilities	Incidence of urban green areas on the urbanized surface of cities	(Istat, 2019, m^2 per 100 m^2 of urbanized surface)
Goal 15.3.1:	Share of degraded land out of the total land surface	Soil waterproofing by artificial cover	(ISPRA, 2019, percentage values)
Goal 15.3.1:	Share of degraded land out of the total land surface	Fragmentation of natural and agricultural land	(ISPRA, 2019, percentage values)

3.2 SDGs Index and Their Italian Distribution

Let's carry out a first analysis by territorial division for the different sets:

- **Set 1: Protection of water resources**
  - Water supplied per capita
  - Efficiency of drinking water distribution networks
  - Irregularities in the distribution of water
  - Coverage of the public sewerage service

- **Set 2: Protection of the territory**

  - Waterproofing and land use per capita
  - Soil waterproofing by artificial cover
  - Fragmentation of the natural and agricultural territory
  - Incidence of urban green areas on the urbanized surface of cities

From an initial analysis of the indicators for the protection of water resources, Italy is among the European countries in the Mediterranean area that use the most groundwater, springs, and wells; these represent the most important freshwater resource for drinking water use on the Italian territory (84.8% of the total withdrawn). The infrastructural situation remains critical in some areas of the country, mainly due to the presence of physical losses (deterioration of the systems, breakages in the pipes, defective joints, etc.) and to a minimum part of physiological and administrative losses (unauthorized connections, measurement errors of the counters).

The volume supplied per capita increases with the growth of the resident population and in the territories where there is a greater concentration of non-residential uses. In the municipal drinking water distribution networks, 215 L per inhabitant are supplied daily in 2018 (Table 2), about 5 L less than in 2015.

The efficiency of municipal drinking water distribution networks has been steadily worsening since 2008: the share of injected water reaching end users was 58.0% in 2018 (0.6 percentage points less than in 2015). Efficiency is declining for more than half of the regions. The most critical situations are concentrated above all in the regions of the Centre (51.3%) and the South (52.1%).

In 2018, 10.4% of families complained of irregularities in the water supply service in their home. In the North, the percentage of families reporting inefficiencies reaches minimum values (3%); in the Centre, almost one in ten families (10.6%) complains of irregularities, while in the South this percentage rises to 21.2%.

About nine out of ten inhabitants (87.8% of residents) in 2018 are connected to the public sewerage system, regardless of the subsequent purification treatment. There are 7.3 million residents not connected to the public sewerage system. The area with the greatest coverage of the sewerage service is the North (90%).

Table 2. Indicators for the protection of water resources by territorial division (year 2018)

Territorial distribution	Water supplied per capita	Efficiency of drinking water distribution networks	Irregularities in the distribution of water	Coverage of the public sewerage service
North	238	65.7	3.0	90.0
Centre	190	51.3	10.6	85.5
South	199	52.1	21.2	86.3
Italy	**215**	**58.0**	**10.4**	**87.8**

Fonte: our elaboration on SDGs.

The degradation of the territory, understood as the loss of ecological functionality, is monitored through the dynamics of land consumption, which Italy has committed to eliminating by 2030 with the National Strategy for Sustainable Development (2017). The "consumed" soil is that occupied by urbanization and made waterproof by artificial coverings (soil sealing). However, an excessive fragmentation of open spaces is also a degradation factor, since the barriers constituted by buildings and infrastructures interrupt the continuity of ecosystems, making even unoccupied but not large enough spaces ecologically inert and unproductive. Furthermore, in a fragile territory like the Italian one, soil consumption is also a significant factor of hydrogeological risk and deterioration of the landscape.

The per capita waterproofing and land use index in 2018 increased for the fifth consecutive year, resulting in 357 m^2 per inhabitant (Table 3). The soil sealed by artificial coverings is equal to 7.1% of the national territory (8.5% in the North, 6.5% in the Centre, 5.9% in the South). However, the goal of zero land use is not yet within reach.

According to Ispra estimates, 44.3% of the Italian natural and agricultural territory has a high or very high degree of fragmentation. A joint representation of the variations in fragmentation and soil sealing over the last two years summarizes the recent trends in soil consumption and their impact on the environment and landscape.

Another goal for 2030 is to provide universal access to safe, inclusive and accessible public green spaces, especially for women and children, the elderly and people with disabilities. In 2018, the incidence of urban green areas on the urbanized surface of cities was 8.5% in Italy with slightly higher values in the North and lower in the South.

Table 3. Indicators for the protection of the territory by territorial division (year 2018)

Territorial distribution	Waterproofing and land consumption per capita	Waterproofing of the soil from artificial cover	Fragmentation of the natural and agricultural territory	Incidence of urban green areas on the urbanized surface of cities
North	409	8.5	43.8	11
Centre	389	6.7	47.5	7.8
South	426	5.9	43.3	5.5
Italy	**357**	**7.1**	**44.3**	**8.5**

Fonte: our elaboration on SDGs.

4 A Multidimensional Approach for the Identification of the Areas

4.1 The Fuzzy Approach

The development of fuzzy theory initially stems from the work of Zadeh [6] and subsequently was conducted by Dubois and Prade [7]. The fuzzy theory develops starting from the assumption that each unit is not univocally associated with only one but simultaneously with all the categories identified on the basis of links of different intensity (degrees of association).

The first measurement based on the fuzzy set theory, named TF (Totally Fuzzy), was suggested by Cerioli and Zani [8]. This logic can be applied to both continuous and ordinal variable cases. However, in the latter case, the maximum and minimum values can be determined by assuming the value of the lowest category as minimum and the highest as maximum.

Cheli and Lemmi [9] have proposed a generalization of this approach, called *Totally Fuzzy and Relative* (TFR). This method is also called "totally relative" because the value of the membership function is entirely determined by the relative position of the individual in the distribution of the population. The fuzzy TFR approach consists in defining the measurement of an individual's *degree of belonging* to the totality fuzzy, included in the interval between 0 (with an individual who does not demonstrate a clear belonging) and 1 (with an individual who demonstrates a clear belonging). Mathematically, such a method consists of the construction of a function of membership to "the fuzzy totality of the poor" which is continuous in nature, and "able to provide a measurement of the degree of poverty present within each unit". Supposing the observation of k indicators of poverty for every family, the function of membership of i-th family to the fuzzy subset of the poor may be defined thus:

$$f(x_{i.}) = \frac{\sum_{j=1}^{k} g(x_{ij}).w_j}{\sum_{j=1}^{k} w_j} \qquad i = 1, \ldots, n \tag{1}$$

The values w_j in the function of membership are only a *weighting system*, as for the generalization of Cerioli and Zani, whose specification is given:

$$w_j = \log\left(1/\overline{g(x_j)}\right) \tag{2}$$

Theoretically when $\overline{g(x_j)} = 1$ all units demonstrate the *j*-th symptom and the corresponding weight w_j results equal to zero; when $\overline{g(x_j)} = 0$ then w_j is not defined, or rather X_j is not an appropriate indicator for that collective.

The weighting operation is fundamental for creating synthetic indexes, by the aggregation of belonging functions of each single indicator. An alternative, by Betti, Cheli and Lemmi [10] starts from the conjoint use of the coefficient of variation as the first component of the set of weights, with the correlation coefficient, as the second component. The new set of weights, that is proposed for continuous variables, considers two factors, described in the following multiplicative form:

$$w_j = w_j^{(a)} * w_j^{(b)} \tag{3}$$

where:

$$w_j^{(a)} = \frac{\sigma_j}{\mu_j} \tag{4}$$

is given from the coefficient of variation of X_j

$$w_j^{(b)} = 1 - \frac{\sum\limits_{l \neq j} \rho(X_j, X_l)}{\sum\limits_{l=1}^{k} \rho(X_j, X_l)} \quad (5)$$

is given from the complement to one of the ratio between the sum of all correlation coefficients, left out the j array, and the whole sum of correlation coefficients referring to X_j. For further analyses please refer to other works [11, 12].

The indices were grouped into several sets characterized by different situations in the different components considered (Set 1 Protection of the water resource; Set 2 Protection of the territory). The Total Fuzzy and Relative method was applied to the data of all the Italian regions, obtaining a value of the individual weights wi, which varies according to the level of importance in determining the quality of the situation.

4.2 The Results Deriving from the Application of the Totally Fuzzy and Relative Approach

Once the sets of indicators for the 2 considered components were identified, the minimum, maximum and average values were found for each indicator of the different sets (Table 4). The indicators have been transformed in such a way that high values are significant for regional situations of poor health, conversely low values are significant for favourable conditions that do not require public intervention.

Table 4. Results of the application of the TFR method in relation to the distribution function and the weights of the various indices.

Indicators	Minimum	Maximum	Mean	gmean	Weight w_j
- Water supplied per capita	152	446	235	0.4	0.8
- Efficiency of drinking water distribution networks	0.0	1.0	0.6	0.6	0.5
- Irregularities in the distribution of water	0.7	39.6	10.0	0.3	1.3
- Coverage of the public sewerage service	2.7	24.0	10.6	0.4	0.8
- Waterproofing and land use per capita	2.1	562	6.3	0.6	0.6
- Soil waterproofing by artificial cover	240	12.0	410	0.4	0.8
- Fragmentation of the natural and agricultural territory	1.2	66.7	39.2	0.5	0.6
- Incidence of urban green areas on the urbanized surface of cities	0.0	1.0	0.5	0.5	0.7

For each set of indicators, the fuzzy value and the relative values connected to it have been calculated. Of particular interest is the analysis of the weights w_j which indicate the relevance of the indicator on the set considered. As already specified, high values of this indicator denote a strongly discriminating condition in determining the result. In our case the values of the weights of the indicators relating to the irregularity in water distribution ($w_j = 1.3$), those relating to the quantity of water supplied, the coverage of the sewerage service and the waterproofing of the soil are particularly discriminating. from artificial roofing ($w_j = 0.8$). Conversely, the weights of the indicators relating to the inefficiency of the drinking water distribution networks appear less discriminating ($w_j = 0.5$).

As a result of the application, we have classified the Italian regions based on fuzzy values, obtaining the classification shown in Table 5. We recall that high values are significant for regional situations of water or territorial degradation which therefore require national interventions.

Table 5. Composition in absolute values and percentages of the provinces by belonging to the fuzzy classes

Fuzzy value	Number of regions		%	
	Water protection	Territory protection	Water protection	Territory protection
0.0–0.2	2	0	10%	0%
0.2–0.4	9	6	45%	30%
0.4–0.6	6	7	30%	35%
0.6–0.8	2	5	10%	25%
0.8–1.0	1	2	5%	10%
Total	**20**	**20**	**100**	**100**

4.3 Spatial Distribution of Fuzzy Values

In this paper, the representation of the values attributed to the individual geographic areas, corresponding to the regions, occurs through cartograms, associated with "natural" interval classes, defined within the distribution.

Applying the *Total Fuzzy and Relative* method on the data of all Italian regions, as described in the previous paragraph, three synthetic indices were obtained (Table 5) that describe the territorial distribution of the indicators that are represented in the next Fig. 1.

It thus emerges that for the set related to the indicators related to the protection of the water resource most of the regions are in an average condition while 3 regions have strong deficiencies with fuzzy values between 0.6 and 1 (Calabria, Molise, Sicilia).

Regarding the indicators linked to the protection of the territorial resource, there is instead a greater equidistribution in all classes with the presence of 7 regions in

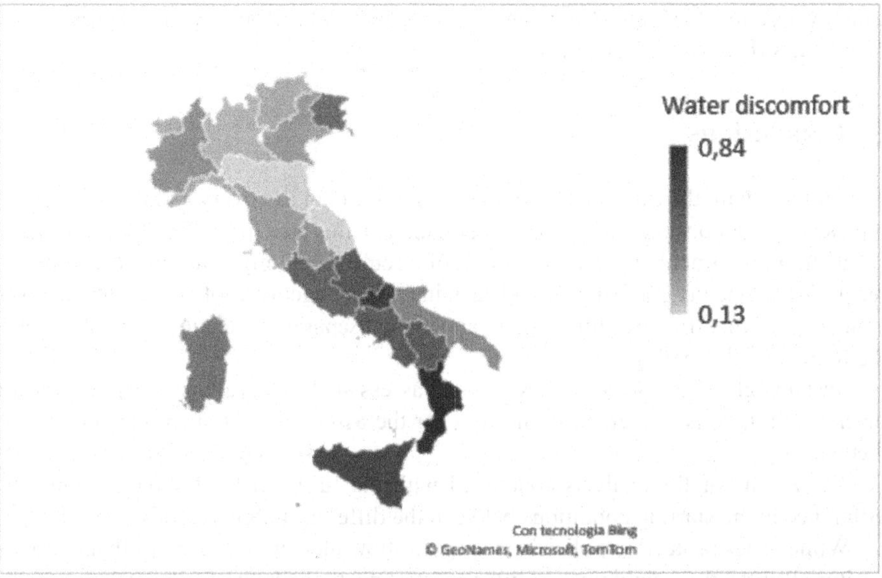

Fig. 1. Territorial distribution by region of the fuzzy values for *Water protection* assessed through indicators for the achievement of the Sustainable Development Goals Agenda 2030.

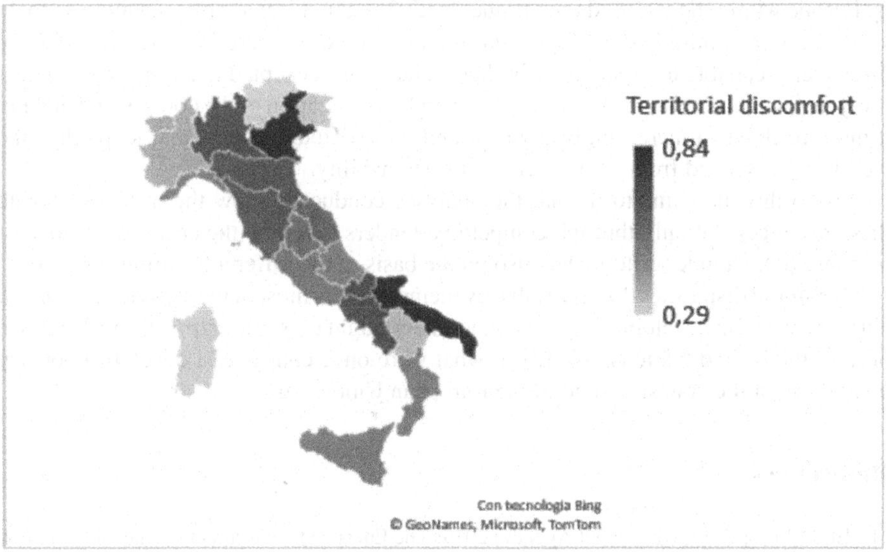

Fig. 2. Territorial distribution by region of the fuzzy values for *Territory protection* assessed through indicators for the achievement of the Sustainable Development Goals Agenda 2030.

conditions of territorial degradation (Fig. 2): Puglia, Veneto with very high degradation values (close to 1), Molise, Campania, Lombardy, Emilia-Romagna and Tuscany with high values (between 0.6 and 0.8).

5 Conclusions

In continuity with the European Green Deal, the National Recovery and Resilience Plan represents an opportunity for further development in this area, providing for reforms and substantial investments for the promotion of circular economy solutions, the improvement of the capacity for efficient and sustainable management. of waste, the strengthening of the infrastructures for waste treatment and separate collection, the reduction of the Italian North/South gap.

Sustainability indicators are key tools to assess such integration, but initiatives are diverse and there is no agreed framework for the assessment of such interactions and feedbacks.

The results of the analysis conducted with the fuzzy method show a significant difference in the starting conditions between the different Italian regions.

While water protection policies once again show the gap between North and South, territorial protection highlights a different starting point between the Italian regions which is independent of this gap and appears more linked to more articulated regional differences.

It is certainly important and necessary to spend the huge resources made available by Europe within the required time frame (by 2026), but it is perhaps even more so to do so that they can multiply their effectiveness and become not mere expenses but effective investments capable to offset the debt that Italians have accepted to assume for the next few years with a view to restructuring the overall organization of the country and making it more resilient to increasingly frequent and unpredictable events that jeopardize the well-being achieved from a perspective of sustainability.

To do this, it seems to us that the analyses conducted show the need to allocate these resources not only through competitive tenders based on the criterion of the best response to the tender criteria, but also on the basis of the different starting conditions.

Territorial disparities do not resolve by themselves, as most of the experiences carried out in the world in development policies have now taught us, starting from the well-known ones of the United Nations [13–15] in what were once called least developed country up to those of the cohesion fund of the European Union [16].

References

1. EEA (European Environment Agency) 2019: The European environment—state and outlook 2020. Knowledge for transition to a sustainable Europe. Luxembourg: Publications Office of the European Union
2. EU, 2007: Treaty of Lisbon amending the Treaty on European Union and the Treaty establishing the European Community, signed at Lisbon, 13 December 2007 (2007/C 306/01)
3. EC, 2011a: Communication from the Commission to the European Parliament, the Council, the European Economic and Social Committee and the Committee of the Regions—Energy Roadmap 2050 (COM (2011) 885 final)

4. Griggs, D., et al.: A guide to SDG interactions: from science to implementation, International Council for Science, Paris (2017). https://council.science/cms/2017/05/SDGs-Guide-to-Interactions.pdf. Accessed 8 Oct 2017
5. Istat: Rapporto SDGs 2021. Informazioni Statistiche per l'agenda 2030 in Italia. Ed. Anno 2021. Collana: Letture statistiche–Temi
6. Zadeh, L.A: Fuzzy sets, information and control **8**(3), 338–353 (1965)
7. Dubois, D., Prade, H.: Fuzzy Sets and Systems. Academic Press, Boston, New York, London (1980)
8. Cerioli, A., Zani, S.: A fuzzy approach to the measurement of poverty. In: Dagum, C., Zenga, M. (eds.) Income and Wealth Distribution, Inequality and Poverty. Studies in Contemporary Economics. Springer, Berlin, Heidelberg (1990). https://doi.org/10.1007/978-3-642-84250-4_18
9. Cheli, B., Lemmi, A.A.: Totally fuzzy and relative approach to the multidimensional analysis of poverty. Econ. Notes **24**(1), 115–134 (1995)
10. Betti G., Cheli B., Lemmi A.: Disoccupazione e condizione di vita: dinamiche e relazioni nella realtà italiana degli anni novanta. Studi Sulla povertà: Franco Angeli (2002)
11. Montrone, S., Perchinunno, P., Di Giuro, A., Rotondo, F., Torre, C.M.: Identification of hot spots of social and housing difficulty in urban areas: scan statistics for housing market and urban planning policies. In: Murgante, B., Borruso, G., Lapucci, A. (eds.) Geocomputation and Urban Planning. Studies in Computational Intelligence, vol. 176, pp. 57–78. Springer, Berlin, Heidelberg (2009). https://doi.org/10.1007/978-3-540-89930-3_4
12. Perchinunno, P., Rotondo, F., Torre, C.M.: A multivariate fuzzy analysis for the regeneration of urban poverty areas. In: Gervasi, O., Murgante, B., Laganà, A., Taniar, D., Mun, Y., Gavrilova, M.L. (eds.) Computational Science and Its Applications–ICCSA 2008. ICCSA 2008. LNCS, vol. 5072, pp. 137–152. Springer, Berlin, Heidelberg (2008). https://doi.org/10.1007/978-3-540-69839-5_11
13. UNDP–United Nations Development Programme Evaluation Office, Handbook on Monitoring and Evaluating for Results, Evaluation Office Press, New York (2002). https://www.oecd.org/derec/undp/35134974.pdf. Accessed 01 Apr 2022
14. UN–Committee for Development Policy: Handbook on the Least Developed Country Category. United Nations publication, New York (2008)
15. United Nations: System of environmental-economic accounting for water, United Nations, New York (2012)
16. Bachtler, J., Wren, C.: Evaluation of European Union cohesion policy: research questions and policy challenges. Reg. Stud. **40**(2), 143–153 (2006)

Migration Studies with a Compositional Data Approach: A Case Study of Population Structure in the Capital Region of Denmark

Javier Elío[1(✉)], Marina Georgati[1], Henning S. Hansen[1], and Carsten Keßler[1,2]

[1] Department of Planning, Aalborg University, Copenhagen, Denmark
javierdem@plan.aau.dk

[2] Department of Geodesy, Bochum University of Applied Sciences, Bochum, Germany

Abstract. Computing percentages or proportions for removing the influence of population density has recently gained popularity, as it offers a deep insight into compositional variability. However, data are constrained to a constant sum and therefore are not independent observations, a fundamental limitation for applying standard multivariate statistical tools. Compositional Data (CoDa) techniques address the issue of standard statistical tools being insufficient for the analysis of closed data (i.e., spurious correlations, predictions outside the range, and subcompositional incoherence) but they are not widely used in the field of population geography. Hence, in this article, we present a case study where we analyse at parish level the spatial distribution of Danes, Western migrants and non-Western migrants in the Capital region of Denmark. By applying CoDa techniques, we have been able to identify the spatial population segregation in the area and we have recognised patterns in the distribution of various demographic groups that can be used for interpreting housing prices variations. Our exercise is a basic example of the potentials of CoDa techniques which generate more robust and reliable results than standard statistical procedures in order to interpret the relations among various demographic groups. It can be further generalised to other population datasets with more complex structures.

Keywords: Population geography · Migration · Compositional data · Cluster analysis · House prices

1 Introduction

In population geography, it is often more interesting to analyse proportions, such as the percentage of people in a region with an income below the poverty line or the proportion of people fully vaccinated against COVID-19, than absolute

O. Gervasi et al. (Eds.): ICCSA 2022 Workshops, LNCS 13379, pp. 576–593, 2022.
https://doi.org/10.1007/978-3-031-10545-6_39

population numbers. In this sense, the variable of interest is normalised so that it does not depend on the total population of the region [9], thus allowing an intuitive analysis of spatial patterns (e.g., distribution of poverty or vaccinate rates across regions). This normalisation explicitly describes the internal structure of the explored system. However, the data are constrained to a constant sum (e.g., 1 for proportions or 100 for percentages) and, therefore, they are dependent; if the share of one subgroup increases, another one has to decrease to retain the sum [24]. This violates a fundamental assumption of most standard statistical analysis and alternative methods are thus required.

These data are known as compositional data (CoDa) and have been widely used in many kinds of interdisciplinary analysis [2]. Aitchison first described the theoretical background to handle such data based on log-ratio transformations [1]. However, this approach is still not widely used despite the associated issues that arise when analysing them with standard statistical procedures; i.e., spurious correlations, predictions outside the range, or problems with subcompositional coherence [20]. In fact, CoDa methods have been mainly applied in the geosciences but even in this field it is not a standard procedure [5]. Instances of CoDa application range from soil and geochemical surveys [34], water and groundwater studies [6], to the evaluation of the link between indoor radon and topsoil geochemistry [14]. Outside of the geosciences, the technique is gaining popularity across different studies in various fields including the evaluation of urban water distribution [10], health studies [22], nutrition research [7], and forecast of energy consumption structures [32].

Human geography is no exception regarding the limited use of CoDa techniques. Often geographers apply standard statistical and geostatistical tools to analyse compositional data (e.g. percentage of young, working age and elderly population in a region; percentage of rented/owner households; unemployment rates) even though these tools have been designed for unconstrained data and are deemed insufficient or unsuitable for such analysis. Lloyd, among others [19], warned about these problems and introduced tools for dealing with compositional data in population studies. Nonetheless, the research community has not widely adopted these tools with the exception of some recent studies. Specifically, CoDa techniques have been utilised for evaluating socio-spatial segregation [8], studying child mortality levels and trends [13], forecasting population age structure [33], or visualising three part compositions in demographic analysis [27]. To the best of our knowledge, there are no studies that use the full range of CoDa techniques to analyse migration data and only Nowok [23] has proposed the use of ternary diagrams for evaluating migration flows.

In this article, we therefore show the applicability of compositional data techniques in population geography analysing the spatial population structure of the capital region of Denmark as a case study. Our aim is to stress the need of CoDa techniques in this type of studies to get robust and reliable results about the compositional variability of the population. We used parish-level data for the year 2020 from Statistics Denmark to analyse the spatial distribution of the three main population categories as defined by the national statistics based on migration background: people of Danish origin, Western and non-Western migrants. After performing a log-ratio transformation (i.e., balances), we carried out a hierarchical cluster analysis for detecting areas where migrants settle down preferentially in the Capital region of Denmark. Furthermore, we explored the association between migration, considering also the area of origin, and housing prices.

It is well known that house prices and migration are closely related with profound implications on urban planning. There is a two-way causal relationship between migration and house prices [18]. On the one hand, a rise in house prices increases a household's housing equity and, therefore, ability to migrate, since homeowners have a higher financial flexibility for purchasing a new house. At the same time, high house prices make the house unaffordable, thus limiting the number of potential buyers. This way, price differences between regions where migrants live and regions where they intend to move affect in- and out- migration rates. Moreover, the expectation of future house prices also plays an important role in the decision to move [25]. On the other hand, migration increases housing demand and consequently prices [31]. An example of this effect has been found in Sweden where "a 1% increase in the foreign-born population results in a 0.8% increase in house prices, which increases to 1.2% if internal migration is also accounted for" [30]. However, data that contain relative information (e.g., percentage of young, working age and elderly population; share of the population with a certain education level; or percentage of migrants) were used in the models and thus the analysis would be benefited from applying CoDa techniques to avoid possible issues with non-independent observations.

2 Theoretical Background

The main idea in Aitchison's proposal for analysing compositional data was to transform them in a way that allows their analysis with standard statistical tools, designed for unconstrained data. He therefore introduced the concept of log-ratio transformations: the additive log-ratio transformation (alr) and the centred log-ratio transformation (clr). In 2003, Egozcue [11] proposed a new family of transformations called isometric log-ratio transformations (ilr) to overcome some of the limitations of the alr and clr transformations. However there is no single best transformation and all of them have their strengths and limitations [22]. In all types of transformations special attention should be put on the case of zeros, since the logarithm of 0 is undefined [20,21].

The alr transformation for a compositional vector $x = [x_1, x_2, \ldots, x_D]$, with positive components ($x_i > 0$) summing to a constant ($\sum_{i=1}^{D} = k$), is defined as [20]:

$$alr(x) = log(\frac{x_1}{x_D}, \frac{x_2}{x_D}, ..., \frac{x_{D-1}}{x_D}) \tag{1}$$

The alr transformation is useful for parametric modelling. However, it is not invariant under permutation of the components and it is not isometric between the simplex (the sample space of compositional data; $x = [x_1, ..., x_D] \in S^D$)

and the real space (R^{D-1}) [2,5]. In order to address the limitations of the alr transformation, the clr transformation was proposed:

$$clr(x) = log(\frac{x_1}{g(x)}, \frac{x_2}{g(x)}, ..., \frac{x_D}{g(x)}) \tag{2}$$

where g(x) is the geometric mean of the part of the composition. The clr transformation solves the problem of symmetry and, unlike the alr-transformed variables, ordinary distances can be computed [20]. The clr transformation is useful for generating biplots [3,20], but it cannot be used for parametric modelling [5]. Considering this constraint, Egozcue et al. [11] finally proposed the ilr transformation:

$$y = ilr(x) = (y_1, y_2, ..., y_{d-1}) \in \mathbb{R} \tag{3}$$

where:

$$y_i = \frac{1}{\sqrt{i(i-1)}} \ln \left(\frac{\prod_{j=1}^{i} x_j}{(x_{i+1})^i} \right) \; for \; i = 1, ..., D-1 \tag{4}$$

The ilr transformation allows using all the standard multivariate procedures [11] but the ilr coordinates may be difficult to interpret. The Sequential Binary Partitions method was therefore developed [12]. The result is a particular case of ilr coordinates (i.e., balances) that represent the relationship between two groups of parts allowing the interpretation of their inner connections. The difficulty is to select the correct partitions for obtaining meaningful interpretations and it should be done based on expert knowledge and/or by compositional biplots [20]. The general formula for balances is:

$$b_i = \sqrt{\frac{rs}{r+s}} \ln \left(\frac{(\prod_{+} x_j)^{\frac{1}{r}}}{(\prod_{-} x_k)^{\frac{1}{s}}} \right) \; for \; i = 1, ..., D-1 \tag{5}$$

where $\prod_{+}$ and $\prod_{-}$ are the parts coded as + or – in the partitioning scheme and r and s the number of components in the + and – partition.

3 Data and Methods

This section introduces the population data and the data on housing prices used for the study. Moreover, it describes the application of CoDa techniques on the data.

3.1 Population Data at Parish Level

Data at parish level have been obtained from Statistics Denmark [29]. The table contains information about the population at the first day of the year and divides it in five ancestry groups: persons of Danish origin, immigrants from Western countries, immigrants from non-Western countries, descendants from Western countries, and descendants from non-Western countries. The concepts of '*immigrants and descendants*' and '*western and non-western countries*' do not occur in other countries and are defined by Statistics Denmark (DST). According to DST, western countries are all 28 EU countries, Andorra, Iceland, Liechtenstein, Monaco, Norway, San Marino, Switzerland, Vatican State, Canada, USA, Australia, and New Zealand, while all other countries are non-western countries.

We selected only the data referring on the capital region of Denmark in 2020. We also assumed that immigrants and their descendants behave similarly and thus we merged them to simplify the interpretability of our case study. Finally, we closed the dataset to represent percentages over the total population in each parish. Table 1 and Fig. 1 show the summary statistics of the percentages and the spatial distribution respectively.

Table 1. Summary statistics of population data (in percentage) by parish (N = 127).

Value	Danes	Non-western	Western
Mean	77.8	14.5	7.7
Median	79.6	11.5	7.1
IQR	72.9–84.3	7.7–17.7	4.9–9.7
Range	21.2–94.6	2.7–69.9	2.7–19.9

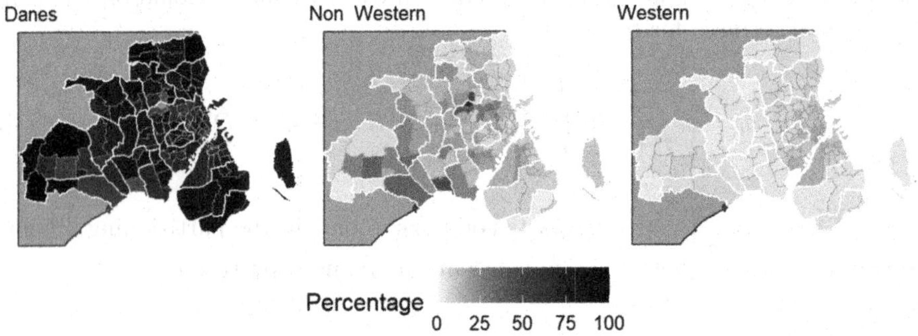

Fig. 1. Population distribution [%] in the capital region of Denmark.

3.2 House Prices

We obtained the individual house prices from the Building and Dwelling Register (BBR - https://teknik.bbr.dk/forside). We used all residences for year-round living (i.e., excluding summer houses and similar seasonal housing) and we selected from the main residential buildings only those that are on the ordinary free trade (sales between parties who are not members of the same family and sales that are not considered as a partial gift) or public sales, assuming that they also represent a market value. Furthermore, we filtered out dwellings that are not used for residential purposes, are smaller than $10\,m^2$, or have no value. Colleges and residential buildings for institutions (i.e., different kinds of dormitories) were excluded from the data analysis since they are mainly outside of the free market. We calculated the mean and the median prices in 1.000 Danish kroner per square meter ($kDKK \cdot m^{-2}$) along with the number of dwellings per parish (Table 2 and Fig. 2).

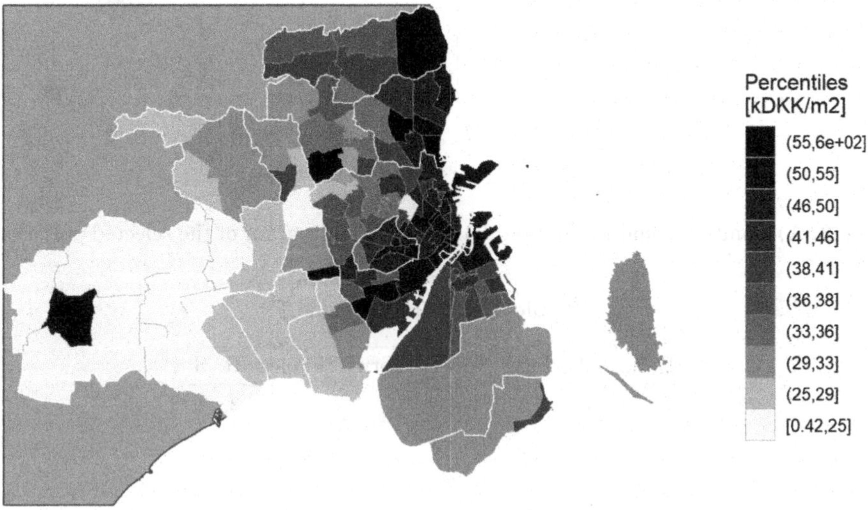

Fig. 2. Spatial distribution of parish-level median house price in 2020.

Table 2. Summary statistics at parish level (N = 125)

Value	N. House	House prices ($kDKK \cdot m^{-2}$).	
		Mean	Median
Mean	150.1	82.8	46.2
Median	127.0	42.3	38.0
IQR	85.0–182.0	33.2– 61.2	31.1–47.4
Range	7.0–637.0	22.1–1,132.9	0.4–602.6

3.3 Compositional Data

The Sequential Binary Partition for our balance calculation has been carried out based on the compositional biplot as presented in Fig. 3(A). The first component differentiates mainly non-Western migrants from other inhabitants, and

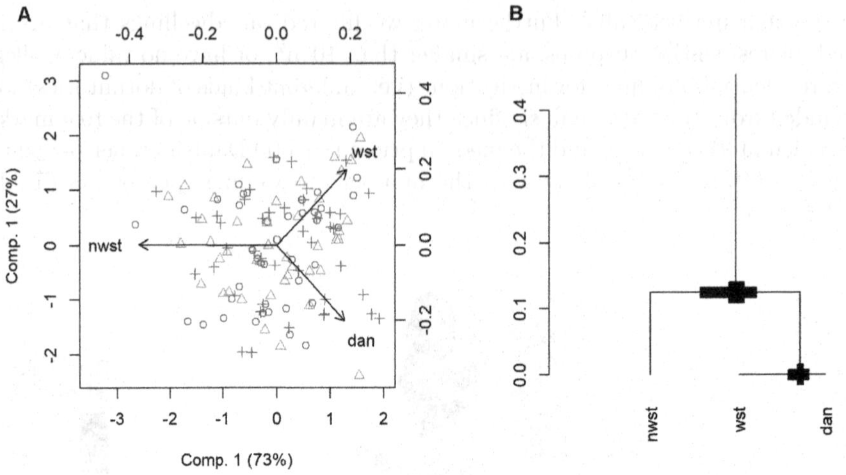

Fig. 3. A) Compositional Biplot, and B) balance-dendrogram of the selected partition.

Table 3. Partition scheme.

Danes	Western	Non-Western	Balance	R	S
1	1	−1	b_1	2	1
1	−1	0	b_2	1	1

it accounts for about 73% of the variance. The second component explains the remaining 27% and mainly separates the native population from Western migrants (Fig. 3A).

Table 3 and Fig. 3B display the selected partition for the balances.

The equations for estimating the two balances are:

$$b_1 = \sqrt{\frac{2}{3}} \ln \left(\frac{(Danes \cdot Western)^{0.5}}{NonWestern} \right) \tag{6}$$

$$b_2 = \sqrt{\frac{1}{2}} \ln \left(\frac{Danes}{Western} \right) \tag{7}$$

where Danes, Western, and Non-Western are the percentages of each population group in the parish.

Using these balances, we performed a hierarchical cluster analysis to investigate whether there are parishes with similar population distributions and whether they are spatially aggregated or not. We used an agglomerative clustering with the Ward's method, which minimises the total within-cluster variance. The analysis was carried out with the function hclust (see complementary material) of the R-software [26]. Finally, we evaluated the spatial autocorrelation of the balances.

4 Results

This section summarises the obtained findings in our case study area. Our aim is to demonstrate the applicability of CoDa techniques not only in migration studies but generally in population geography showing how log-ratio transformations can be used in spatial data analysis (e.g., cluster analysis). For this purpose, we analyse the structure of the population divided in three groups following initially a ternary-balance scheme technique and then examining the similarities among nearby observations and clusters.

4.1 Ternary Diagram of Population Structure

Population structure varies significantly across the capital region of Denmark. The use of colour composition with the rainbow-like surfaces consists an efficient way to visualise the proportions among the three investigated groups and immediately indicates the composition of the population. Figure 4 illustrates the population structure in the ternary plot centred over the compositional mean (80.1%, 7.4%, 12.5% of Danes, Western, and non-Western population respectively). Specifically, the shades of brown indicate parishes with higher proportions of Danes than the compositional mean while the shades of green and pink indicate higher proportions of Western and non-Western migrants correspondingly. As the map shows, Western populations prevail in parishes in the city centre while non-Western citizens tend to settle down in the western peripheral parishes with percentages up to 41.6%, 49.61%, and 69.85% for Husumvold, Haralds and Tingbjerg parishes respectively.

4.2 Balances

The compositional biplot (Fig. 3A) shows similar patterns as observed in the ternary diagram. Non-western migrants dominate component 1, with an opposite direction than Danes and Western migrants. Therefore, we selected a partitioning scheme (Table 3 and Fig. 3) that separates mainly non-Western migrants from Danes and Western migrants (b1), and then Western migrants and Danes (b2). High values of b1 indicate a smaller proportion of non-Western population and high values of b2 a smaller proportion of Western citizens (Fig. 5).

The balances show positive spatial autocorrelation (Table 4), suggesting some degree of spatial structure in the population by its origin. The local indicators of spatial association (LISA - [4] for both balances (Fig. 6) confirm that non-Western migrants tend to live in the peripheral western parishes (blue colours in b1) while Western migrants tend to settle down around the city centre (blue

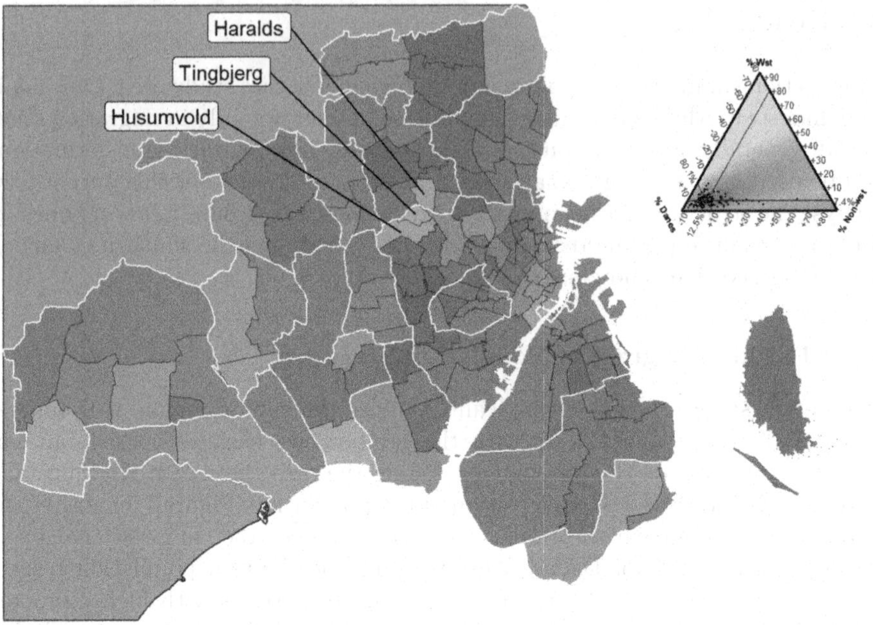

Fig. 4. Ternary diagram of the population distribution in 2020 (Danes - people of Danish origin, Wst - Western population, Non-wst - Non-Western population).

Table 4. Moran's I for each balance.

Balance	Index	Expectation	Variance	Statistic	p-value
b_1	0.470	–0.008	0.003	8.563	5.503×10^{-18}
b_2	0.542	–0.008	0.003	9.837	3.915×10^{-23}

Method: Moran I test under randomisation. Alternative: greater

colours in b2). Furthermore, the presence of non-Western migrants is reduced in the Eastern coast of the capital region (red colours in b1). On the other hand, Danes avoid the city centre and the parishes to the south, north and west tend to have high percentage of national residents (red colours in b2).

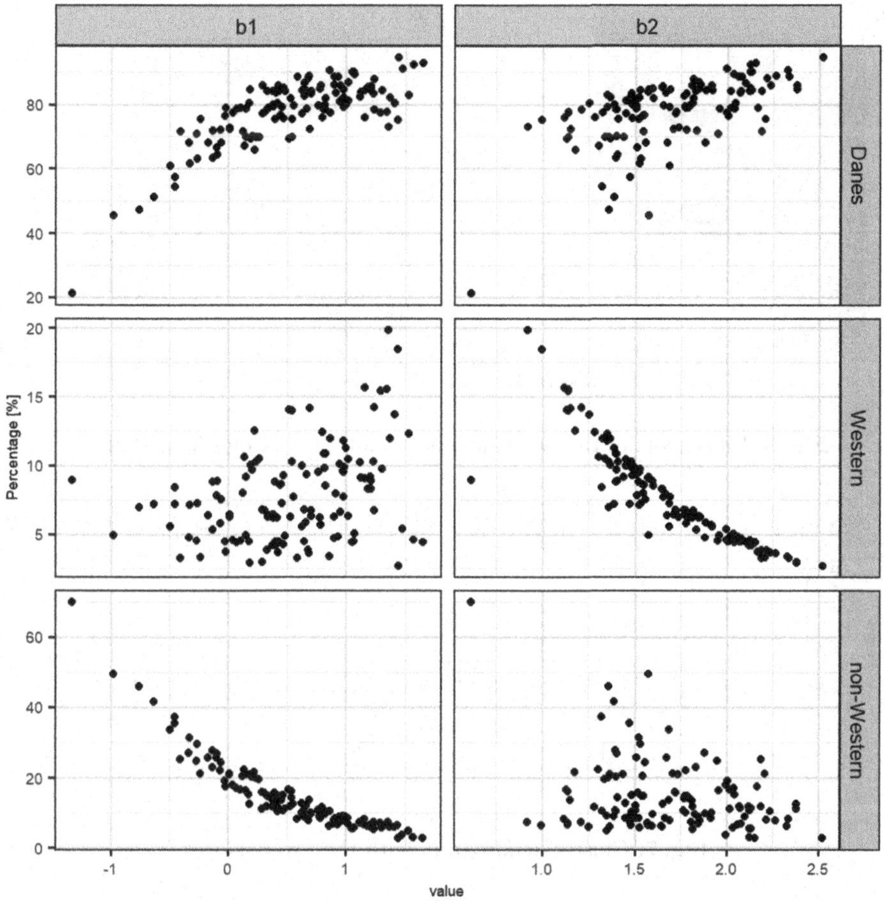

Fig. 5. Balances vs. population distribution percentages.

4.3 Hierarchical Cluster

We identify two main clusters in the data with different proportions of Western migrants and then each one of them is further divided based on the proportion of non-Western migrants. The cluster dendrogram of Fig. 7 shows the first level of division by low and high proportions of Western migrants in the blue boxes (upper) and the second level of division based on the proportions (low/high) of non-Western migrants in the orange boxes (lower). We summarise the compositional means of these four clusters in Table 5 where CL1 and CL2 concentrate a high percentage of Western migrants with a respectively low and high percentage of non-Western migrants. Correspondingly, CL3 and CL4 have low concentration of Western migrants with a respectively low and high concentration of non-Western migrants.

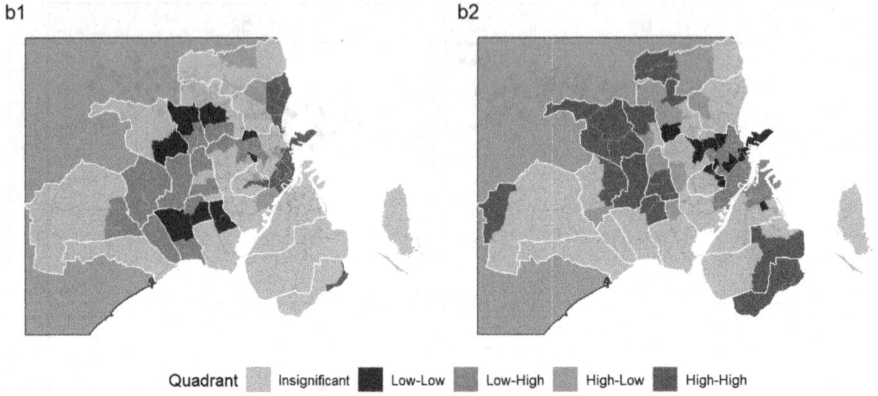

Fig. 6. LISA plots of the two balances (b1 and b2). (Color figure online)

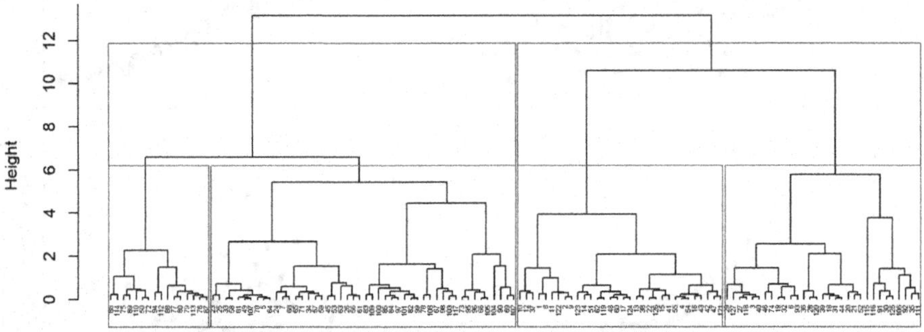

Fig. 7. Cluster dendrogram with the two balances.

Figure 8 spatially maps the distribution of these clusters by parish. Cluster CL1-2 (blue colours) has a median percentage Western migrants of around 10%, while their proportion in CL3-4 (orange colours in Fig. 8) is approximately 5%. This supports the findings of the previous subsections about the tendency of the Western migrants to live in the central parishes. These two main clusters are further divided into four clusters (CL1-2 into CL1 and CL2; and CL3-4 into CL3 and CL4) based on the proportions of the non-Western population. In this regard, CL2 has a higher proportion of non-Western population than CL1 (i.e. 24.1% and 7.8%, respectively), while CL4 has a higher proportion of non-Western than CL3 (i.e. 20.5% and 8.9%, respectively). Again, we observe the preference of non-Western population for the peripheral western parishes (CL2 - light blue; and CL4 - light orange; Fig. 8). Finally, CL3 shows the parishes with the highest proportion of national citizens with values around 85.9%.

Table 5. Compositional mean of the four clusters.

Cluster	N Parishes	Danes	Western	Non-western
1	32	81.0	11.2	7.8
2	31	66.6	9.3	24.1
3	48	85.9	5.2	8.9
4	16	74.8	4.7	20.5

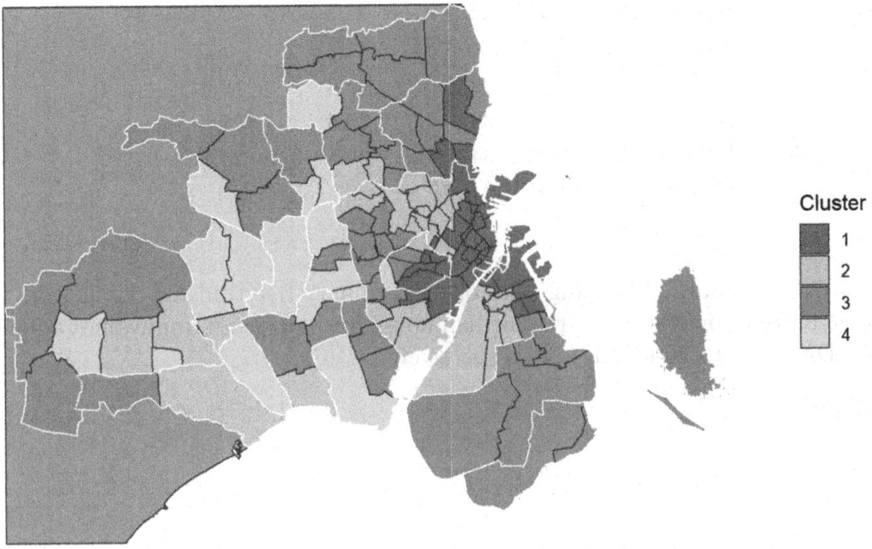

Fig. 8. Spatial distribution of the four clusters.

4.4 House Prices

Analysing the housing prices in the four clusters, there are some clear differences in the mean and median values (Table 6). In general, CL1 and CL2 have higher values (i.e. mean around 57.0 and 41.7 kDKK/m^2; and median of 50.7 and 38.6 kDKK/m^2, respectively) than CL3 and CL4 (i.e. means of 38 and 27 kDKK/m^2, and medians of 35.6 and 27.0 kDKK/m^2, respectively).

A ternary diagram with the median housing prices and the population distribution in Fig. 9 also shows the differences in the median house prices by parish and their association with the clusters. The parishes of CL1, where the proportion of Western migrants is the highest and the proportion of non-Western migrants is relatively low, have the highest median housing prices. Furthermore, house prices decrease with the proportion of non-western migrants, being CL2 the cluster where we observe it clearer. In this sense, in CL2 the proportion of non-Western migrants change remarkably from around 10% to up to approximately 45% (there are two parishes with even more proportion of non-Western migrants; i.e. Haralds and Tingbjerg with 49.61%, and 69.85% respectively, but

Table 6. House price statistics in each cluster.

Cluster	CL1 (N = 32)	CL2 (N = 29)	CL3 (N = 48)	CL4 (N = 16)
Mean values ($kDKK \cdot m^{-2}$)				
Mean	119.8	82.9	65.7	59.9
Median	57.0	41.7	38.2	27.2
IQR	50.7–98.7	37.3–60.8	31.4–49.8	24.8–33.5
Range	39.4–1,132.9	22.1–554.6	22.2–554.7	22.5–333.6
Median values ($kDKK \cdot m^{-2}$)				
Mean	67.6	37.3	35.8	50.9
Median	50.7	38.6	35.6	27.0
IQR	46.9–54.5	34.2–42.0	30.1–40.2	24.7–32.0
Range	37.1–602.6	0.4–70.8	20.5–55.6	5.1–367.3

there were no data of housing sales on the ordinary free trade or public sales in these parishes in 2020), and the median house price decrease from values around 45 kDKK/m^2 to 25 kDKK/m^2, respectively.

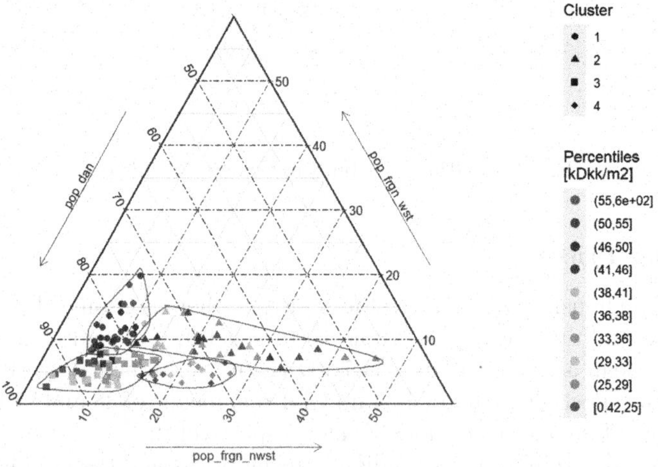

Fig. 9. Population distribution (in percentage) and housing prices (median values in $kDKK \cdot m^{-2}$).

5 Discussion

The hierarchical clusters analysis over the log-ratio transformed data has allowed us to detect four main spatial clusters which clearly characterise parishes according to their population structure (i.e., people of Danish origin, Western migrants, and non-Western migrants). As expected, Danes are the main population in the region. They tend to avoid the city centre and are more attracted by the parishes of southern Amager and the north-west capital region. Western migrants, on the other hand, prefer the central areas while the proportion of non-Western migrants increases in the western peripheral parishes. Additionally, the ternary diagram (Fig. 4) has also allowed us to graphically identify parishes with a very high percentage of non-Western migrants; i.e., Husumvold, Haralds and Tingbjerg parishes with values up to 41.6%, 49.61%, and 69.85%; respectively, and manly due to a diminution of Danes (51.20%, 45.47%, 21.24%; respectively) rather than Western migrants (7.20%, 4.91%, 8.90%; respectively). These parishes are examples of what the Danish authorities call '*parallel societies*' or '*ghettos*', which trigger political actions [17,28]. Our observations also are in agreement with previous studies [15] and confirm a degree of socio-spatial segregation in the capital region of Denmark.

It is important to note that different phenomena can lead to the same proportions in the data. Compositions only give information about the relative magnitude of its components but not the absolute values [2] and additional information would be needed in order to make inferences with the absolute values. In our study, for example, we have seen the spatial segregation of the population by its origin but we cannot interpret its causes; e.g., if it is an effect of socio-economic segregation or diaspora, where immigrants tend to settle down in areas with existing migrant networks and an ethnicity background similar to their country of origin. This is actually a limitation of any observational study, which helps to make hypothesis about the phenomena we are investigating but further studies would be needed to verify them. CoDa techniques are however more robust than ordinary statistics methods because they alleviate issues with spurious correlations and they avoid problems with sub-compositions since the results obtained by using the whole dataset do not contradict results obtained by only a subset [2].

Regarding house prices and migration, we interpret that the differences in the median house prices we observed in each cluster are probably influenced or related more by their location than the population structure. On the one hand, CL1 and CL2 parishes are central parishes close to the city centre where we can expect more amenities and, therefore, people may be willing to pay more for their house in these areas than for further away ones. On the other hand, the central area of the capital region is more densely populated than the periphery [15] so we can expect a higher demand for houses in these parishes which may lead to an increase in the housing prices. However, if we compare the values within the two main clusters (i.e., CL1 vs. CL2 and CL3 vs. CL4), the prices are lower in the parishes where the proportion of non-Western population is relatively high (around 20%, Table 5). It seems therefore that the relative numbers of non-Western and Western migrants are also associated with the median housing prices (Table 6) and thus population structure should also be taken into account when we evaluate house prices.

While our analysis is limited to a small number of socio-economic variables, our results point to two different kinds of segregation that can be observed in the Danish capital region. The clustering of native Danes and Western immigrants on the one hand and high concentrations of non-Western immigrants in a relatively small number of parishes on the other hand indicates racial segregation. Taking into account house prices, we further see that Western migrants are concentrated in the central parishes, which are characterised by higher prices, whereas the parishes with high numbers of non-Western show lower house prices. This correlation therefore also indicates socio-economic segregation.

6 Conclusions

CoDa techniques are more robust and appropriate than standard statistical and geostatistical methods when we are analysing closed data (e.g. percentages) because they avoid spurious correlations, predictions outside the range, and have no problems with sub-compositional coherence. However, they still are not widely used in population geography. In the present study, we demonstrate a showcase applying CoDa techniques in order to promote their use and adoption in a wider range of applications in population studies and spatial analysis. We specifically carried out a case study from the capital region of Copenhagen and evaluated the obtained results and the ways of interpreting them along with the applicability of the methodology in this field. In this regard, we studied the population distribution divided into people of Danish origin, Western immigrants, and non-Western immigrants and its possible relationship with house prices.

Our analysis facilitates the analysis and the interpretation of the socio-spatial segregation in the capital region of Denmark. We detected four main cluster regions with clear differences in the composition of population in terms of migration backgrounds. Furthermore, we performed an analysis to relate these variation in migration patterns to the median house prices at parish level. CoDa techniques show great potential in recognising such trends and patterns but we only shortly discussed the associations between migration and house prices. Differently put, despite a broad range of factors (e.g. property size, condition, proximity to transportation) influences house prices, they all are considered out of the scope of this study apart from the migration component. Our results, therefore, need to be taken with caution and further investigation is required to evaluate the causal relationship between migration and house prices in the capital region of Denmark.

We showed how balances can be used for alleviating the issue of data interpretation with CoDa methods. There is still some complexity in the interpretation of models based on balances and some researchers [16] have proposed the use of amalgamated logratios (i.e., sum of compositional parts) which produce more comprehensible results with minimal cost. We aim on further investigating their use in population geography in the future. Overall, our exercise is a good example of how CoDa methods could be used for exploratory spatial data analysis of various demographic groups. Although it may be a basic case study with only three components, it can be generalised to other population datasets with numerous possible applications and advantages ranging from getting a general insight into the compositional variability of population structures to the identification of clusters and the interpretation of complex socio-economic phenomena.

Acknowledgements. This work has been supported by the European Union's Horizon 2020 research and innovation programme under grant agreement No 870649, the project Future Migration Scenarios for Europe (FUME; https://futuremigration.eu); and by the Aalborg University Strategic Fund, through the project: "Global flows of migrants and their impact on north European welfare states - FLOW" (www.flow.aau.dk).

References

1. Aitchison, J.: A new approach to null correlations of proportions. J. Int. Assoc. Math. Geol. **13**(2), 175–189 (1981). https://doi.org/10.1007/BF01031393
2. Aitchison, J.: A concise guide to compositional data analysis. CDA Workshop Girona **24**, 73–81 (2002). https://doi.org/10.2307/4355794
3. Aitchison, J., Greenacre, M.: Biplots of compositional data. J. Roy. Stat. Soc. Ser. C: Appl. Stat. **51**(4), 375–392 (2002). https://doi.org/10.1111/1467-9876.00275
4. Anselin, L.: Local indicators of spatial association-LISA. Geograph. Anal. **27**(2), 93–115 (2010). https://doi.org/10.1111/j.1538-4632.1995.tb00338.x, https://onlinelibrary.wiley.com/doi/10.1111/j.1538-4632.1995.tb00338.x
5. Buccianti, A., Grunsky, E.: Compositional data analysis in geochemistry: are we sure to see what really occurs during natural processes? J. Geochem. Explor. **141**, 1–5 (2014). https://doi.org/10.1016/j.gexplo.2014.03.022
6. Buccianti, A.: Water chemistry: are new challenges possible from CoDa (compositional data analysis) point of view? In: Daya Sagar, B.S., Cheng, Q., Agterberg, F. (eds.) Handbook of Mathematical Geosciences, pp. 299–311. Springer, Cham (2018). https://doi.org/10.1007/978-3-319-78999-6_16
7. Corrêa Leite, M.L.: Compositional data analysis as an alternative paradigm for nutritional studies. Clin. Nutr. ESPEN **33**, 207–212 (2019). https://doi.org/10.1016/j.clnesp.2019.05.011, https://linkinghub.elsevier.com/retrieve/pii/S2405457718304236
8. Cruz-Sandoval, M., Roca, E., Ortego, M.I.: Compositional data analysis approach in the measurement of social-spatial segregation: towards a sustainable and inclusive city. Sustainability **12**(10), 4293 (2020). https://doi.org/10.3390/su12104293, https://www.mdpi.com/2071-1050/12/10/4293
9. Dailey, G.: Normalizing Census Data Using ArcMap. ArcUser (January-March), 52–53 (2006). www.esri.com
10. Ebrahimi, P., Albanese, S., Esposito, L., Zuzolo, D., Cicchella, D.: Coupling compositional data analysis (CoDA) with hierarchical cluster analysis (HCA) for preliminary understanding of the dynamics of a complex water distribution system: The Naples (South Italy) case study. Environ. Sci. Water Res. Technol. **7**(6), 1060–1077 (2021). https://doi.org/10.1039/d0ew01123a
11. Egozcue, J.J., Pawlowsky-Glahn, V., Mateu-Figueras, G., Barceló-Vidal, C.: Isometric logratio transformations for compositional data analysis. Math. Geol. **35**(3), 279–300 (2003). https://doi.org/10.1023/A:1023818214614

12. Egozcue, J.J., Pawlowsky-Glahn, V.: Groups of parts and their balances in compositional data analysis. Math. Geol. **37**(7), 795–828 (2005). https://doi.org/10.1007/s11004-005-7381-9
13. Ezbakhe, F., Pérez Foguet, A.: Child mortality levels and trends: a new compositional approach. Demographic Res. **43**(43), 1263–1296 (2020). https://doi.org/10.4054/DemRes.2020.43.43, https://www.demographic-research.org/volumes/vol43/43/
14. Ferreira, A., et al.: Indoor radon measurements in south west England explained by topsoil and stream sediment geochemistry, airborne gamma-ray spectroscopy and geology. J. Environ. Radioact. **181**, 152–171 (2018). https://doi.org/10.1016/j.jenvrad.2016.05.007, https://linkinghub.elsevier.com/retrieve/pii/S0265931X16301515
15. Georgati, M., Keßler, C.: Spatially explicit population projections: the case of Copenhagen, Denmark. AGILE: GIScience Ser. **2**, 1–6 (2021). https://doi.org/10.5194/agile-giss-2-28-2021, https://agile-giss.copernicus.org/articles/2/28/2021/
16. Greenacre, M., Grunsky, E., Bacon-Shone, J.: A comparison of isometric and amalgamation logratio balances in compositional data analysis. Comput. Geosci. **148**, 104621 (2021). https://doi.org/10.1016/j.cageo.2020.104621
17. Gulis, G., Safi, M., Linde, D.S.: Rapid health impact assessment of a Danish policy document: One Denmark without parallel societies: no ghettos in 2030. J. Public Health (2020). https://doi.org/10.1007/s10389-020-01375-z
18. Jeanty, P.W., Partridge, M., Irwin, E.: Estimation of a spatial simultaneous equation model of population migration and housing price dynamics. Reg. Sci. Urban Econ. **40**(5), 343–352 (2010). https://doi.org/10.1016/j.regsciurbeco.2010.01.002, https://linkinghub.elsevier.com/retrieve/pii/S0166046210000037
19. Lloyd, C.D.: Analysing population characteristics using geographically weighted principal components analysis: a case study of Northern Ireland in 2001. Comput. Environ. Urban Syst. **34**(5), 389–399 (2010). https://doi.org/10.1016/j.compenvurbsys.2010.02.005
20. Lloyd, C.D., Pawlowsky-Glahn, V., Egozcue, J.J.: Compositional data analysis in population studies. Ann. Assoc. Am. Geographers **102**(6), 1251–1266 (2012). https://doi.org/10.1080/00045608.2011.652855, http://www.tandfonline.com/doi/abs/10.1080/00045608.2011.652855
21. Martín-Fernández, J.A., Barceló-Vidal, C., Pawlowsky-Glahn, V.: Dealing with zeros and missing values in compositional data sets using nonparametric imputation. Math. Geol. **35**(3), 253–278 (2003). https://doi.org/10.1023/A:1023866030544
22. McKinley, J.M., et al.: Investigating the influence of environmental factors on the incidence of renal disease with compositional data analysis using balances. Appl. Comput. Geosci. **6**, 100024 (2020). https://doi.org/10.1016/j.acags.2020.100024
23. Nowok, B.: A visual tool to explore the composition of international migration flows in the EU countries, 1998–2015. Demographic Res. **42**, 763–776 (2020). https://doi.org/10.4054/DemRes.2020.42.27, https://www.demographic-research.org/volumes/vol42/27/
24. Pawlowsky-Glahn, V., Egozcue, J.J.: Exploring compositional data with the CoDa-dendrogram. Aust. J. Stat. **40**(1&2), 103–113 (2011). https://doi.org/10.17713/ajs.v40i1&2.202
25. Peng, C.W., Tsai, I.C.: The long- and short-run influences of housing prices on migration. Cities **93**, 253–262 (2019). https://doi.org/10.1016/j.cities.2019.05.011
26. R Core Team: R: A language and environment for statistical computing (2021). https://www.r-project.org/

27. Schöley, J.: The centered ternary balance scheme: a technique to visualize surfaces of unbalanced three-part compositions. Demographic Res. **44**, 443–458 (2021). https://doi.org/10.4054/DemRes.2021.44.19, https://www.demographic-research.org/volumes/vol44/19/
28. Seemann, A.: The Danish 'ghetto initiatives' and the changing nature of social citizenship, 2004–2018. In: Critical Social Policy, pp. 1–20 (2020). https://doi.org/10.1177/0261018320978504
29. Statistics Denmark: KMSTA001: Population 1. January by parish, ancestry and member of the National Church (2021)
30. Tyrcha, A., Abreu, M.: Migration diversity and house prices - evidence from Sweden. SSRN Electron. J., 1–36 (2019). https://doi.org/10.2139/ssrn.3394234, https://www.ssrn.com/abstract=3394234
31. Wang, X.R., Hui, E.C.M., Sun, J.X.: Population migration, urbanization and housing prices: evidence from the cities in China. Habitat Int. **66**, 49–56 (2017). https://doi.org/10.1016/j.habitatint.2017.05.010
32. Wei, Y., Wang, Z., Wang, H., Li, Y.: Compositional data techniques for forecasting dynamic change in China's energy consumption structure by 2020 and 2030. J. Clean. Prod. **284**, 124702 (2021). https://doi.org/10.1016/j.jclepro.2020.124702
33. Wei, Y., Wang, Z., Wang, H., Li, Y., Jiang, Z.: Predicting population age structures of China, India, and Vietnam by 2030 based on compositional data. PLOS ONE **14**(4), e0212772 (2019). https://doi.org/10.1371/journal.pone.0212772
34. Zheng, C., et al.: Application of compositional data analysis in geochemical exploration for concealed deposits: a case study of Ashele copper-zinc deposit, Xinjiang. China. Appl. Geochem. **130**, 104997 (2021). https://doi.org/10.1016/j.apgeochem.2021.104997

Estimation of Groundwater and Salinity for the Central Biscayne Bay Coast, Florida, USA

Vladimir J. Alarcon[1](✉), Anna C. Linhoss[2], Paul F. Mickle[3], Christopher R. Kelble[4], and Alexandra Fine[4]

[1] Civil Engineering Department, Universidad Diego Portales, 441 Ejercito Av., Santiago, Chile
vladimir.alarcon@udp.cl

[2] Department of Biosystems Engineering, Auburn University, 3101, Shelby Center, Auburn, AL 36849, USA
alinhoss@auburn.edu

[3] Northern Gulf Institute, 1021 Balch Blvd., Stennis Space Center, Starkville, MS 39529, USA
pmickle@ngi.msstate.edu

[4] NOAA Atlantic Oceanographic and Meteorological Laboratory, 4301 Rickenbacker Causeway, Miami, FL 33149, USA
{chris.kelble,alexandra.fine}@noaa.gov

Abstract. Estimating groundwater flows in karst-dominated landscapes is difficulted by the lack of observed groundwater flows and the uncertainty in hydrogeological parameters (hydraulic conductivity, specific storage and yield, porosity, anisotropy, etc.). The State of Florida (USA) landscape is dominated by the largest geographic area of geologically young carbonate and rocks with well-developed karst features in North America. In this research, a MODFLOW groundwater model for central Biscayne Bay is presented. The Bay is surrounded by karst terrain. The groundwater model is loosely linked to a hydrodynamic model to estimate salinity concentrations at the Biscayne Bay's central coast. The loose-link model framework is shown to improve salinity estimations in 50% from estimations that do not include groundwater contributions to the Bay. A statistical comparison of simulated concentrations versus observed data demonstrates that the loose-link model simulates salinity concentration values and trends within acceptable margin of errors ($0.72 < R < 0.77$; $0.52 < R^2 < 0.59$; $0.62 <$ K-G < 0.70; $d > 0.76$; 4.1% < PBIAS < 13.5%). These results have the potential to be applied to other coastal locations in Florida and the world where karst terrain is predominant.

Keywords: Biscayne Bay · Groundwater · Salinity · Southeast Florida · Karst · Aquifer · MODFLOW

1 Introduction

Karst landscapes cover 7–12% of Earth's continental area, and approximately 25% of the world's population partially or completely relies on drinking water from karst aquifers

O. Gervasi et al. (Eds.): ICCSA 2022 Workshops, LNCS 13379, pp. 594–606, 2022.
https://doi.org/10.1007/978-3-031-10545-6_40

[1]. Therefore, knowledge of the effects of surface and groundwater flow through karst terrain is paramount for optimizing regional water resources use.

The global percentage of land covered by karst soils is distributed unevenly in the world: Europe (23.54%), Middle East and Central Asia (20.97%), East and Southeast Asia (18.27%), the Russian Federation Plus (17.87%), North America (16.31%), Africa (10.49%), Australia (6.81%), and South America (4.31%) [2]. In the United States extensive carbonate karst occurs in Mississippian and Ordivican age limestones (Fig. 1). The southeastern United States has extensive carbonate karst in Florida, Alabama, and Georgia [2].

Florida landscape is dominated by the largest geographic area of geologically young carbonate and rocks with well-developed karst features in North America (Fig. 1) and it is a one of the largest karst areas in the world. [3]. Because of the abundant pore space in Florida's karst terrain, water movement occurs through fractures and other secondary openings (highly permeable conduits). This double set of open pore spaces and high permeability results in the high productivity of the aquifers.

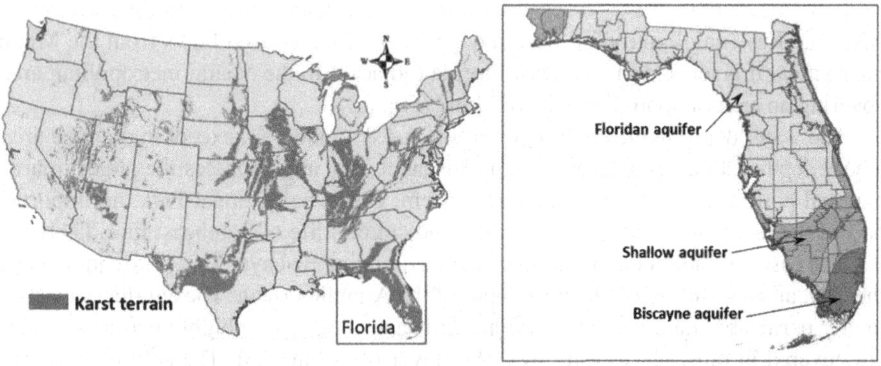

Fig. 1. Karst terrain in North America and main karst aquifers in Florida (USA) (modified from [3]).

The zone of karst-dominated landscape in Florida correlates with areas of unconfined and semi-confined conditions of the Floridan Aquifer [4]. Unconfined aquifers feed fresh water to the Northern Gulf of Mexico and the Atlantic Ocean. Coastal aquifers are an important freshwater resource for significant portions of the global population. Understanding the dynamic relationship between aquifer recharge, storage and discharge is fundamental for sustainable groundwater management [5].

In coastal locations where groundwater produces low salinity zones, estimating the salinity regime at the coast has implications for biological communities and for urban settlements [6]. A recent modeling study on the hydrodynamic regime and salinity spatial distribution in Biscayne Bay (Southeast Florida, USA) was able to replicate salinity concentration values and seasonal trends occurring within the bay [7]. In this study, salinity estimations were poorest for locations close to the coast, especially during the wet season. Unknown groundwater flow sources seem to be lowering salinity concentrations at the coast. Also, freshwater flow to the Florida Northern Gulf of Mexico is greatly enhanced by the substantial groundwater contributions from aquifer base flow [8]. Estimating groundwater flow in the Florida peninsula would not only positively impact management of water resources, but also would help characterizing salinity regime at the Florida coasts.

The United States Geological Service's Modular Three-dimensional Finite-difference Groundwater Flow Model (MODFLOW) has been applied in the past to quantify groundwater contributions to South Florida coasts. However, those estimations were not used to explore the effect of groundwater flow in salinity concentrations.

This research presents a MODFLOW groundwater model developed to estimate groundwater contributions to the central coast of Biscayne Bay, Florida, USA. The model-estimated flows are introduced into a hydrodynamic/salinity model of the bay to quantify salinity concentrations in the coastal waters at Biscayne Bay.

2 Methods

2.1 Study Area

Biscayne Bay (an oligotrophic water body) receives land-based flows from the Miami metro area. It is located in southeast Florida (adjacent to the Miami metropolitan area) covering an area of approximately 700 km^2 (Fig. 2).

The water depth in the bay ranges between 1.8 m and 4 m, except in dredged areas where depths can exceed 12 m [9]. The Biscayne Bay area includes the largest marine national park in the U.S. national park system: Biscayne National Park, an important part of the recreational, social, economic, and cultural life of Southeast Florida [10].

The Biscayne aquifer underlies the area surrounding Biscayne Bay, it extends beneath the Bay, and also underlies the near shore of the Atlantic Ocean. The aquifer consists of highly permeable interbedded limestone and sandstone. These highly permeable rocks are covered in most places only by a thin layer of porous soil. The aquifer is wedge-shaped and ranges in thickness from 0.6 m on its western edge, to more than 100 m toward the coast [11].

Most of the geologic formations comprising the aquifer are of Pleistocene age but, locally, Pliocene rocks also are included in the aquifer. Its water table is a subdued replica of the land surface, meaning that the water table is at a higher altitude under hills and at a lower altitude under valleys. The water table fluctuates rapidly in response to variations in recharge (precipitation), natural discharge, and pumping from well fields (common in southeast Florida). Natural discharge is by seepage (into streams, canals, or the ocean), and evapotranspiration [12].

The geology and lithology of the Biscayne aquifer are dominated by sand layers at the surface and carbonates and minor sandstone layers at greater depth. This is important from a hydrodynamic point of view. These types of fractured and karstic rocks facilitate the formation of far-reaching regional groundwater flow systems even at the moderate elevation differences of less than 10 m between recharge and discharge areas [13].

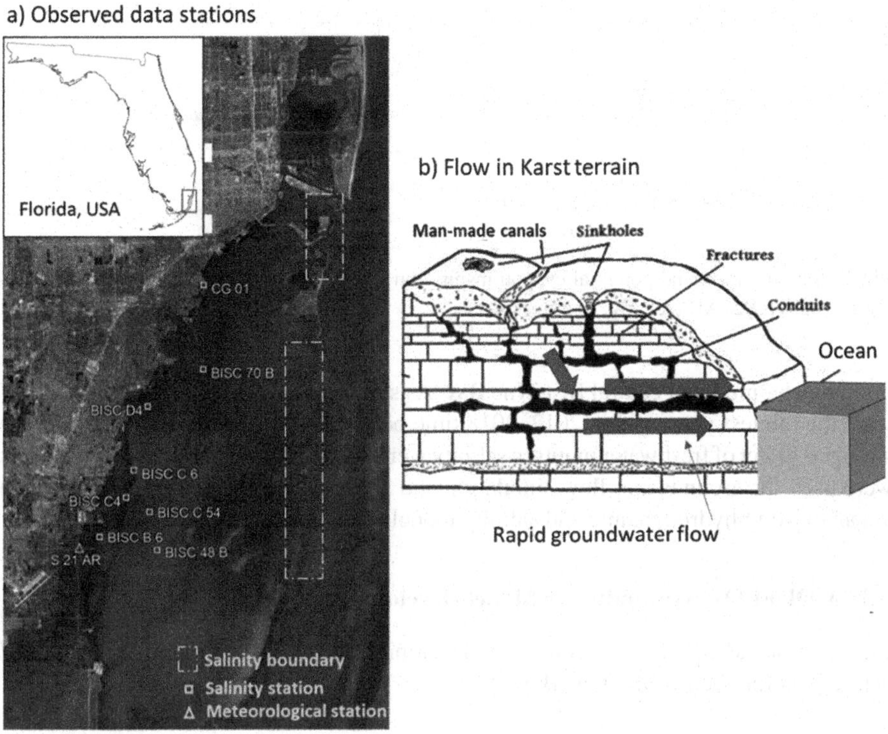

Fig. 2. Study area. a) Biscayne Bay and location of salinity stations in the Bay and salinity boundary conditions. The meteorological station (S21AR) is also shown. b) Flow in karst terrain: sinkholes, fractures, and preferential flow conduits promote rapid groundwater flow to the ocean.

Figure 2 shows the location of salinity stations in the Biscayne Bay. Three salinity stations located in the central coast (BISC C4, BISC C6, BISC D4) are chosen in this research as representative of the coastal salinity regime in the central coast. Hourly salinity concentration data collected at those stations were used in this research.

2.2 Meteorology

Salinity in estuarine systems is influenced by climate and weather. The climate in Southeast Florida is characterized by hot and humid rainy summer, and mild winters (Fig. 3). The annual average minimum, mean, and maximum temperatures in the area are 15 °C, 26 °C, and 32 °C, respectively, and the total annual precipitation average is 1507 mm. The total annual average potential evapotranspiration (ETP) loss in the area ranges from 1220 mm to 1320 mm per year. Stalker et al. [14] estimated a freshwater input ratio canal/precipitation/groundwater of 37%:53%:10% in the wet season, and 40%:55%:5% in the dry season, with an error of ±25%. Approximately 75% of the total precipitation falls in the wet season, generating substantial run-off.

Figure 3 shows precipitation and potential evapotranspiration data from Miami Airport meteorological station that were used to implement meteorological forcings to the

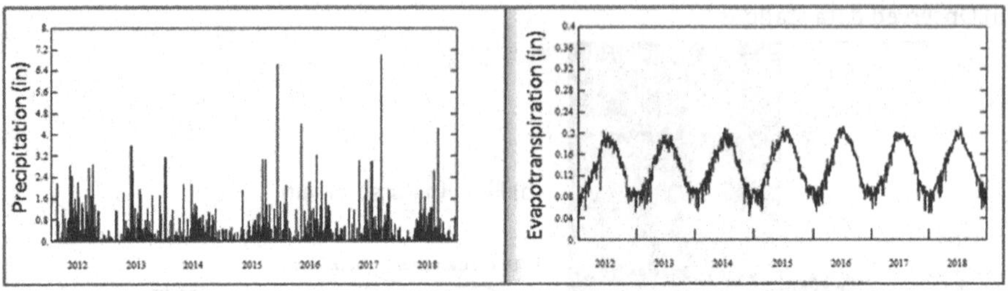

Fig. 3. Precipitation and potential evapotranspiration in Southeast Florida. Data from meteorological station S21AR (see Fig. 2) are shown.

groundwater model of central Biscayne Bay. As shown in the figure, years 2015 to 2017 were the rainiest years within 2012–2018 time period. In those years (2015–2017), the strongest effect of freshwater inputs in salinity were observed. For that reason, those years were used for groundwater flow simulation and subsequent coastal salinity simulation via an existing hydrodynamic and salinity model (detailed in [15]).

2.3 MODFLOW Groundwater Model Development

This section details the procedure for developing a groundwater flow MODFLOW application for central Biscayne Bay.

Aquifer Limits Delineation

Topographical data from the US National Elevation Dataset (NED) was used to delimit the boundaries of the Biscayne aquifer that drain into central Biscayne Bay.

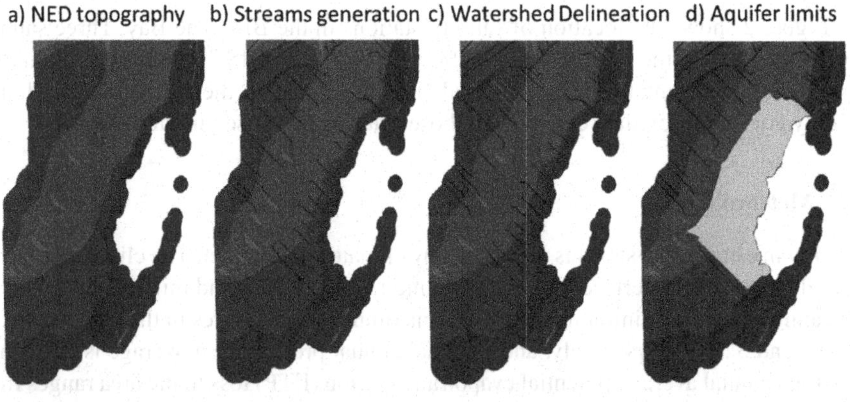

Fig. 4. Delimitation of the inland aquifer. a) NED topography used to delimit inland areas that drain into central Biscayne Bay, b) stream digitalization based on topography, c) watershed delineation to identify areas that drain to Biscayne Bay, and d) topographical mask that delimits the Biscayne aquifer in coastal Biscayne Bay. It is assumed that groundwater recharge area is similar to surface water drainage area.

Since groundwater in an unconfined aquifer is gravity driven, watershed delineation of surface waters gives a good estimate of the area of the inland aquifer that feeds groundwater to the Bay. Figure 4 illustrates the use of NED topography to delimit the inland aquifer boundaries that feed freshwater to central Biscayne Bay. Standard hydrological geoprocessing was performed to generate the geographical boundaries: stream generation, watershed delineation, and merging of all surface watershed areas that drain to central Biscayne Bay into a mask. The NED topographical layer was intersected with the mask and a topographical raster for the aquifer was produced. This raster was used to develop the corresponding MODFLOW model for groundwater flow simulation.

MODFLOW Model

The development of the groundwater model was performed using ModelMuse: a graphical user interface (GUI) for the U.S. Geological Survey MODFLOW [16]. In ModelMuse, the spatial data for the model are independent of the grid, and the temporal data are independent of the stress periods [16]. The topographical raster representing the inland aquifer was the basic data for defining recharge areas and model output locations.

The MODFLOW computational grid consists of a structured non-curvilinear mesh (Fig. 5) consisting of 3 layers, and 6500 active cells. Each active cell is of 300 m × 300 m. Horizontal isotropy was enforced and vertical hydraulic conductivity was defined as one

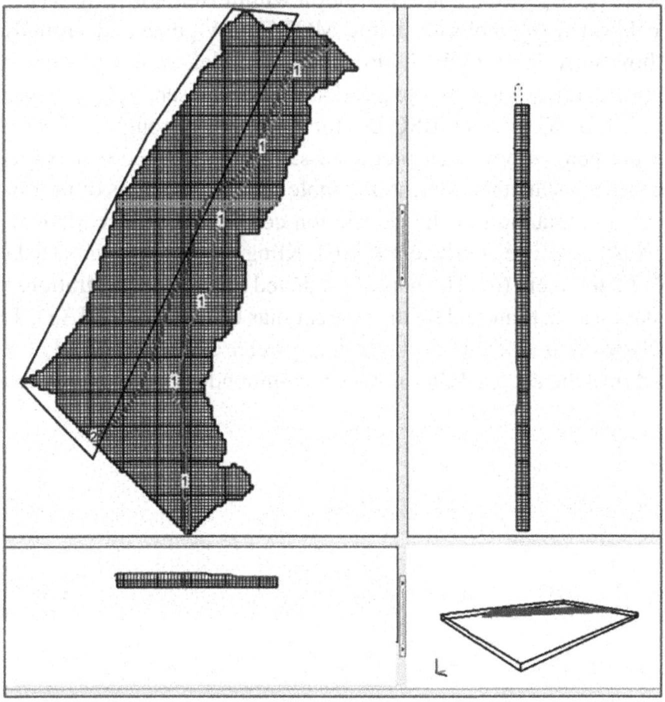

Fig. 5. MODFLOW model for the inland aquifer. View of the model through the ModelMuse interface. Topographical contour lines are also visualized.

tenth of horizontal conductivity. Hydraulic conductivity, specific storage, specific yield, and porosity were used calibrating parameters.

The MODFLOW-Newton (MODFLOW-NWT) solver was used in this research because it was considered more appropriate to model groundwater processes of an unconfined aquifer such as the Biscayne aquifer. This solver is commonly used to simulate groundwater flow involving wetting and drying under unconfined groundwater-flow conditions. MODFLOW-NWT was used with the Upstream-Weighting (UPW) Package for calculating intercell conductance.

Total simulation time was 4 years (2014–2017), being year 2014 used for model warm-up, i.e., results from the modeling process correspond to years 2015 to 2017. Stress periods of 86400 s were implemented for recharge data (input) and groundwater flow (output data). Total number of stress periods was 1463, representing 4 years. Therefore, currently the model generates daily groundwater flow data, although it can also generate hourly output. However, processing time and output visualization of hourly data was proven to be time-wise inefficient.

Indirect Calibration Based on Coastal Salinity

Since there are not observed data of groundwater at Biscayne Bay coast, the groundwater model was indirectly calibrated by inputting the MODFLOW output in an existing hydrodynamic and salinity model of Biscayne Bay (detailed in [15]). The hydrodynamic model computes hourly salinity at any location within Biscayne Bay. The MODFLOW model was calibrated by exploring if the MODFLOW-generated groundwater flows, when those flow were input to the hydrodynamic model, would produce salinity concentrations statistically similar to observed salinities. Observed hourly salinity data at stations BISC C4, BISC C6, and BISC D4, for years 2014 through 2017 were compared.

The measurement of how well predicted salinities matched observations was performed using several statistical indicators (Table 1). The goodness of fit was statistically assessed by the computation of the correlation coefficient (R), coefficient of determination (R^2), Nash Sutcliffe coefficient (NSE), Kling-Gupta efficiency (K-G), and Willmott's index of agreement (d). The bias of predicted salinity concentrations with respect to observed data was determined by the percent bias coefficient (PBIAS). These indicators are widely used to assess hydrological and water quality modeled output [17–19]. Table 3 also shows the acceptability ranges recommended by the cited literature.

Table 1. Statistical indicators of fit and acceptability ranges.

Indicators of fit	Formulae	Range
Percent bias, *PBIAS*	$\frac{\sum_{i=1}^{n}(Y_i^{Obs}-Y_i^{Sim})*100}{\sum_{i=1}^{n}(Y_i^{Obs}).}$	$< \pm 18\%$
Correlation coefficient, *R*	$\sqrt{\frac{\sum_{i=1}^{n}(Y_i^{Sim}-Y_i^{Mean}).^2}{\sum_{i=1}^{n}(Y_i^{Obs}-Y_i^{Mean}).^2}}$	> 0.71
Coefficient of determination	R^2	> 0.50
Nash–Sutcliffe efficiency, *NS*	$1-\frac{\sum_{i=1}^{n}(Y_i^{Obs}-Y_i^{Sim}).^2}{\sum_{i=1}^{n}(Y_i^{Obs}-Y_i^{Mean}).^2}$	> 0.50
Kling-Gupta efficiency, *K-G*	$1-\sqrt{\left(\frac{Y_{Sim}^{Mean}}{Y_{Obs}^{Mean}}-1\right)^2+\left(\frac{STDEV_{Sim}}{STDEV_{Obs}}-1\right)^2+(R-1)^2}$	> 0.50
Willmott's index of agreement, *d*	$1-\frac{\sum_{i=1}^{n}(Y_i^{Obs}-Y_i^{Sim}).^2}{\sum_{i=1}^{n}(\lvert Y_i^{Sim}-Y_{Obs}^{Mean}\rvert+\lvert Y_i^{Obs}-Y_{Obs}^{Mean}\rvert).^2}$	> 0.65
Y_i^{Obs} = Observed salinity Y_i^{Sim} = Simulated salinity Y_{Obs}^{Mean} = Mean of observed salinity Y_{Sim}^{Mean} = Mean of simulated salinity n = Total number of hourly salinity data		

3 Results

3.1 Calibration Phase

Table 2 Summarizes the main MODFLOW parameters resulting from the calibration phase. The parameter values shown in the table were selected from sensitivity analysis, where each parameter was varied until the model produced predictions of salinity concentrations (for the control salinity stations) that matched observed concentrations.

As shown in Table 2, a relatively high horizontal hydraulic conductivity (0.007 m/s) was implemented in the model. The adopted value is consistent with karst hydraulic conductivities published in the literature [20,21]. All other parameters were varied until salinity estimations produced by the hydrodynamic model matched observed salinity values. Adopted porosity and specific storage are consistent with values reported in the literature [22].

Figure 6 shows MODFLOW-estimated groundwater flows at the control stations (BISC C4, BISC C6, BISC D4).

Groundwater flow hydrographs at control stations are very similar (Fig. 6). Peak flows, however, vary depending on the station location. The highest groundwater flow

Table 2. Resulting MODFLOW calibration parameters

Feature	Adopted value
Number of layers	3
Layer depth	2 m
Horizontal hydraulic conductivity	0.007 m/s
Vertical hydraulic conductivity	7E−4 m/s
Specific storage	0.003
Initial head	Saturated
Porosity	0.25
Specific yield	0.2
Number of stress periods	1463
Stress period length	86400 s

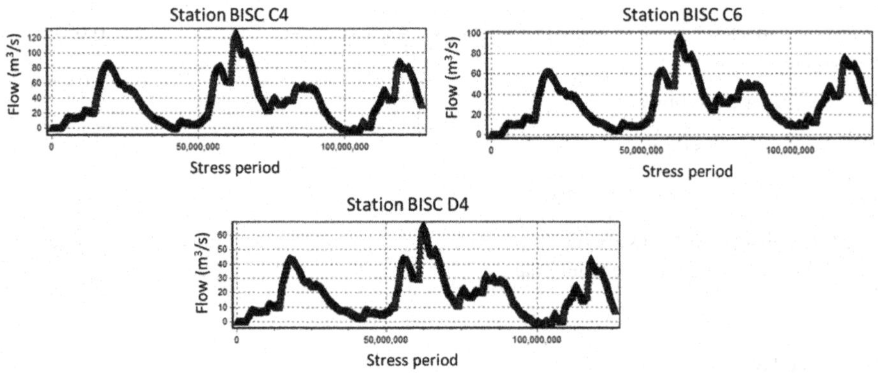

Fig. 6. Groundwater flows at control stations BISC C4, BISC C6, and BISC D4.

is estimated to occur at BISC C4 (130 m^3/s), and the lowest peak flow corresponds to BISC D4 (70 m^3/s). Since stations BISC C6 and BISC D4 are located farther east than BISC C4, i.e., farther from the recharge zone, these results were expected.

3.2 Salinity at Biscayne Bay's Central Coast

As stated in previous sections, the MODFLOW model output was input into an existing hydrodynamic and salinity model that predicts hourly salinity concentrations the control stations for years 2015 through 2017. Figure 7 shows a comparison of observed salinities at the control stations (BISC C4, BISC C6, and BISC D4), salinity estimation by the hydrodynamic model without groundwater inputs, and estimated salinities with groundwater inputs (generated by MODFLOW).

As shown in Fig. 7, when the hydrodynamic model does not account for groundwater contributions, salinity estimations (red line) fail to replicate the low observed salinities during years 2016 and 2017 (blue line). As shown, salinities in the range of 5 PSU to 20 PSU were observed during those years (blue line). When groundwater contributions (estimated by MODFLOW) are taken into account, those low salinities are captured at the control stations. Also, inputting groundwater flows allows capturing the salinity temporal dynamics better than the hydrodynamic model.

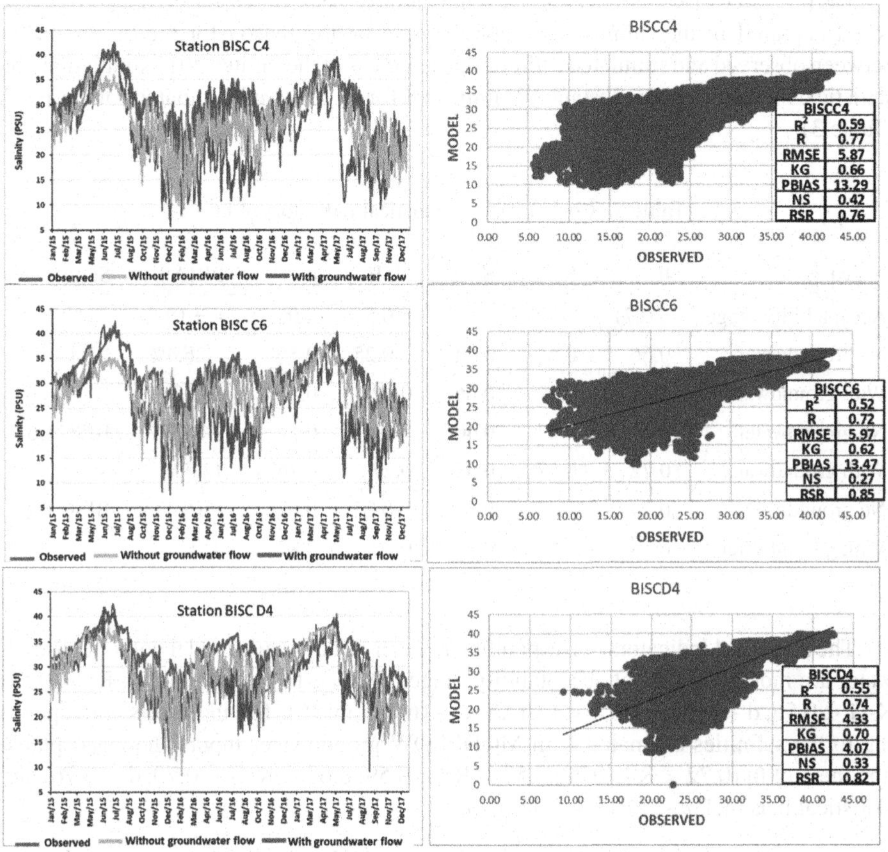

Fig. 7. Comparison of observed and simulated salinity for years 2015 to 2017. Simulated and observed hourly salinity concentrations at stations BISCC4, BISCC6, and BISCD4 are compared (Color figure online).

A statistical comparison of estimated salinities against observed salinities was performed. The goodness of fit indicators described in Table 1 (and shown in Fig. 8) were calculated to determine if the introduction of groundwater flows (calculated by the MODFLOW model) are actually beneficial to characterize the salinity regime at central Biscayne Bay.

As evidenced in Figs. 7 and 8, and Table 3, the MODFLOW groundwater model developed in this research allows simulating hourly salinity concentration values and trends (for years 2015 through 2017) well. When the hydrodynamic model does not account for groundwater inputs (Table 3), 14 statistical indicators of fit (out of 18) are outside acceptability ranges (78%). When groundwater contributions calculated by MODFLOW are introduced to the hydrodynamic model, only 5 out of 18 statistical indicators are not within acceptability ranges (28%). Half of the statistical indicators corresponding to BISC C6 (when groundwater is accounted for) are not optimal. The indicators that are out of acceptability range correspond to statistics that are very sensitive to extreme values (R^2, NSE). The extreme salinity peak observed in July 2015, that is not captured in the salinity simulations could be the reason for the disagreement between observed and simulated salinities. Regardless of the limited 2015 simulation, the statistical indicators were substantially improved for all observed/simulated comparisons (Table 3).

Table 3. Comparison of statistical indicators of fit.

Indicator	R	R^2	K-G	NSE	d	PBIAS	Station
Acceptability range	>0.71	>0.5	>0.5	>0.5	>0.65	<±18%	
No groundwater	0.66	0.44	0.42	−0.25	0.56	−26.4%	BISC C4
With groundwater	0.77	0.59	0.66	0.42	0.81	13.3%	
No groundwater	0.65	0.42	0.40	−0.41	0.51	−24.9%	BISC C6
With groundwater	0.72	0.52	0.62	0.27	0.76	13.5%	
No groundwater	0.74	0.55	0.56	−0.23	0.62	−16.4	BISC D4
With groundwater	0.74	0.55	0.70	0.33	0.83	4.1%	

The statistical indicators corresponding to the hydrodynamic model without groundwater are mostly outside of acceptability ranges: $0.65 < R < 0.74$; $0.42 < R^2 < 0.55$; K-G < 0.56; d < 0.62; −26.4 < PBIAS < −16.4 (Table 5). The indicators corresponding to the salinities estimated with MODFLOW groundwater inputs show acceptable goodness of fit ($0.72 < R < 0.77$; $0.52 < R^2 < 0.59$; 0.62 < K-G < 0.70; d > 0.76) and statistical bias (4.1% < PBIAS < 13.5%).

4 Conclusions

In this research, a MODFLOW groundwater model for central Biscayne Bay (Florida, USA) allowed successful simulation of hourly salinity concentrations for 3-years (2015 through 2017). Salinities calculated by an existing hydrodynamic/salinity model using groundwater inputs calculated by MODFLOW were statistically compared to observed salinities at three coastal salinity stations located in central Biscayne Bay: BISC C4, BISC C6, and BISC D4. Calibration of the groundwater model was performed by inputting the MODFLOW output in an existing hydrodynamic and salinity model of Biscayne Bay. The hydrodynamic model computed hourly salinity at the control stations explored in this research. The MODFLOW model was considered calibrated when model-generated groundwater flows produced salinity concentrations statistically similar to observed salinities.

Statistical indicators of goodness of fit show that the MODFLOW groundwater flows can improve the estimation of salinities at the central coast of Biscayne Bay. Loosely linking the MODFLOW outputs to a hydrodynamic model improved salinity estimations performed by the hydrodynamic model allowed a 50% improvement in the quality of statistical fit. The groundwater model could be improved in capturing salinity peaks occurring during year 2015. However, in its current form the MODFLOW-hydrodynamic model combination allows better simulation of salinity concentrations and trends, than an existing hydrodynamic model without groundwater inputs.

The methodology presented in this paper have the potential to be applied to other coastal locations in the Florida Peninsula and elsewhere in which karst terrain is predominant and groundwater contributions are unknown.

References

1. Ye, Q., Li, Z., Duan, L., Xu, X.: Decoupling the influence of vegetation and climate on intra-annual variability in runoff in karst watersheds. Sci. Total Environ. **824** (2022). https://doi.org/10.1016/j.scitotenv.2022.153874
2. Hollingsworth, E.: Karst regions of the world (KROW): populating global karst datasets and generating maps to advance the understanding of karst occurrence and protection of karst species and habitats worldwide. Thesis, University of Arkansas (2006). https://digital.lib.usf.edu/SFS0052617/00001
3. Upchurch, S., Scott, T.M., Alfieri, M., Fratesi, B., Dobecki, T.L.: The Karst Systems of Florida: Understanding Karst in a Geologically Young Terrain, pp. 1–15. Springer, Cham (2019). https://doi.org/10.1007/978-3-319-69635-5
4. Bahtijarevic, A.: Karst landforms in Florida, Geomorphological analysis. Thesis, Department of Geology, University of South Florida (1996)
5. Klammler, H., Jawitz, J.W., Annable, M.D., Yaquian, J.A., Hatfield, K., Burger, P.: Decadal scale recharge-discharge time lags from aquifer freshwater-saltwater interactions. J. Hydrology, **582** (2020). https://doi.org/10.1016/j.jhydrol.2019.124514
6. Conrads, P.A., Darby, L.S.: Development of a coastal drought index using salinity data. Bull. Am. Meteor. Soc. **98**, 753–766 (2017). https://doi.org/10.1175/BAMS-D-15-00171.1
7. Alarcon, V.J., Linhoss, A.C., Kelble, C.R., Mickle, P.F., Bishop, J., Milton, E.: Estimation of hourly salinity concentrations using an artificial neural network. In: Gervasi, O., et al. (eds.) ICCSA 2021. LNCS, vol. 12954, pp. 629–640. Springer, Cham (2021). https://doi.org/10.1007/978-3-030-86979-3_44
8. Orlando, S.P.Jr., Rozas, L.P., Ward, G.H., Klein, C.J.: Salinity Characteristics of Gulf of Mexico Estuaries. Silver Spring, MD, National Oceanic and Atmospheric Administration, Office of Ocean Resources Conservation and Assessment (1993). 209 pp.
9. Caccia, V., Boyer, J.: Spatial patterning of water quality in Biscayne Bay, Florida as a function of land use and water management. Mar. Pollut. Bull. **50**, 1416–1429 (2005). https://doi.org/10.1016/j.marpolbul.2005.08.002
10. Fernald, E.A., Purdum, E.: Water Resources Atlas of Florida. Institute of Science and Public Affairs, Florida State University (1998). https://fga.freac.fsu.edu/gaw/2001/resources/waterpdf/biscayne_aquifer.pdf
11. Miller, J.A.: Ground Water Atlas of the United States: Alabama, Florida, Georgia, South Carolina. U.S. Geological Survey, Publication HA 730-G (1990). https://www.nrc.gov/docs/ML1002/ML100290484.pdf

12. Weyer, K.U.: The case of the Biscayne Bay and aquifer near Miami, Florida: density-driven flow of seawater or gravitationally driven discharge of deep saline groundwater? Environ. Earth Sci. **77**(1), 1–16 (2017). https://doi.org/10.1007/s12665-017-7169-5
13. USGS: Changing Salinity Patterns in Biscayne Bay, Florida. Prepared in cooperation with South Florida Water Management District and Biscayne National Park (2004). https://doi.org/10.3133/fs20043108
14. Stalker, J., Price, R., Swart, P.: Determining spatial and temporal inputs of freshwater, including submarine groundwater discharge, to a subtropical estuary using geochemical tracers, Biscayne bay South Florida. Estuaries Coasts **32**, 694–708 (2009). https://doi.org/10.1007/s12237-009-9155-y
15. Alarcon, V.J., Linhoss, A.C., Kelble, C.R., et al.: Coastal inundation under concurrent mean and extreme sea-level rise in Coral Gables, Florida, USA. Nat Hazards **111**, 2933–2962 (2022). https://doi.org/10.1007/s11069-021-05163-0
16. USGS. ModelMuse: A Graphical User Interface for Groundwater Models (2022). https://www.usgs.gov/software/modelmuse-graphical-user-interface-groundwater-models
17. Moriasi, D.N., Arnold, J.G., Van Liew, M.W., Bingner, R.L., Harmel, R.D., Veith, T.L.: Model Evaluation Guidelines for Systematic Quantification of Accuracy in Watershed Simulations. Trans. ASABE, **50**, 885–900 (2007). https://doi.org/10.13031/2013.23153
18. Ang, R., Oeurng, C.: Simulating streamflow in an ungauged catchment of Tonlesap Lake Basin in Cambodia using Soil and Water Assessment Tool (SWAT) model. Water Sci. **32**, 89–101 (2018). https://doi.org/10.1016/j.wsj.2017.12.002
19. Knoben, W.J.M., Freer, J.E., Woods, R.A.: Technical note: Inherent benchmark or not? Comparing Nash-Sutcliffe and Kling-Gupta efficiency scores. Hydrol. Earth Syst. Sci. **23**, 4323–4331 (2019). https://doi.org/10.5194/hess-23-4323-2019
20. Schrader, A., Erasmus, E., Winde, F.: Determining hydraulic parameters of a karst aquifer using unique historical data from large-scale dewatering by deep level mining - a case study from South Africa (2014). Water SA. https:// doi.org/40 .555.10.4314/wsa.v40i3.20
21. Kovács, A.: Geometry and hydraulic parameters of karst aquifers: a hydrodynamic modeling approach (2003). Ph.D. dissertation, Université de Neuchâtel, Switzerland, p 1724 (2003)
22. Kuang, X., Jiao, J.J., Zheng, C., Cherry, J.A., Li, H.: A review of specific storage in aquifers. J. Hydrol. **581** (2020). https://doi.org/10.1016/j.jhydrol.2019.124383

On the Applied Efficiency of Systematic Earthquake Prediction

V. G. Gitis, A. B. Derendyaev(✉), and K. N. Petrov

The Institute for Information Transmission Problems, Moscow, Russia
gitis@iitp.ru, wintsa@gmail.com, stranger12@list.ru

Abstract. The systematic forecast of earthquakes is regularly performed with a step of Δt in a predetermined analysis zone. At each step, the training set of target earthquakes is augmented, new data about the seismic process is loaded, the data is processed, transformed into grid-based fields, and the machine learning program calculates a solution using all available data from the beginning of the training to the moment t^* of the earthquake forecast. The result is a map of the alarm zone in which the epicenter of the target earthquake is expected in the interval $(t^*, t^* + \Delta t]$. At the next step, the learning interval is increased Δt.

Usually, the quality of the forecast is estimated by the percentage of detection of target events for a given average value of the alarm zone. Here, we consider a generalization of the method of minimum area of alarm, designed to improve another characteristic of the forecast quality: the probability of occurrence of at least one target event in the expected alarm zone. The difference between the methods is that at the moment of forecasting t^* two decisions are made: forecast in time and in space. The first solution determines the possibility of an earthquake epicenter with a target magnitude in the forecast interval. If it is decided that the target event is possible, then a map with an alarm zone is calculated. A target earthquake is predicted if its epicenter falls into the calculated alarm zone.

Predictive modeling is carried out for California. The initial data are earthquake catalog and GPS time series. The results showed rather high estimates of the probability of detecting target events and very small values of estimates of the probability of predicting the appearance of the epicenter of a target event in the alarm zone. At the same time, the estimates of the probability of a systematic forecast are much higher than the similar forecast probabilities for random fields.

Keywords: Earthquake forecast · Machine learning · Method of minimum area of alarm · Forecast quality · Spatio-temporal processes

---

The paper is supported by the Russian Science Foundation, project No20-07-00445.

O. Gervasi et al. (Eds.): ICCSA 2022 Workshops, LNCS 13379, pp. 607–624, 2022.
https://doi.org/10.1007/978-3-031-10545-6_41

1 Introduction

Strong earthquakes cause great social and economic damage. Timely warning of a devastating earthquake can reduce loss of life and property damage. In this case, the damage from earthquakes is determined by the losses both from the destruction of the event missed during the forecast and from the implementation of protective measures in case of a false alarm.

The task of earthquake forecasting is usually to indicate an alarm zone limited in size, in which an earthquake epicenter with a magnitude greater than a certain threshold is expected within a certain time. Ideas about the possibility of predicting earthquakes are based on the data of physical modeling of the process of destruction of rocks and real observations, which show that an earthquake is preceded by processes that form anomalous changes in the geological environment in the area of the source of the expected earthquake [30–32]. So, for example, in the area of preparation for a strong earthquake, anomalous deviations were recorded in the frequency and strength of seismic events, in deformations of the earth's surface, in the chemical composition of fluids, in the level of groundwater, in the time of passage of seismic waves, in the magnitudes of the electric and geomagnetic fields, etc. [15,20,22,25,30,32]. This testifies in favor of the assumption that an earthquake can be predicted from local changes in the geological environment.

Earthquake forecasting works are being carried out in many directions. They include the study of rock destruction mechanisms, the study of various earthquake precursors, the development of mathematical models and forecasting methods. At the same time, there is an opinion that earthquake prediction is impossible [8,12,16]. The complexity of earthquake prediction is mainly due to two factors. Methods based on the physical features of the seismological and geodynamic regime require that the models of earthquake source preparation be determined by quantitative indicators available for instrumental measurements. Statistical forecasting methods require improvement of the network for monitoring seismic and geodynamic processes, increasing the types of instrumental observations, and increasing their accuracy.

Currently, machine learning methods are widely used for earthquake prediction [2,7,13,17,21,24,28,29]. In a number of works, artificial neural networks [1,23,27], as well as their hybrid and recurrent modifications [3,26], are used for forecasting. These methods require sufficiently large samples of target events for training. At the same time, it is known that for a number of seismically active regions, the number of strong seismic events during training intervals is small. Therefore, some simpler models may have similar or better predictive capabilities.

In this paper, we develop the approach to systematic earthquake prediction presented in [9–11]. A systematic prediction algorithm with a constant time step is regularly trained on occurred earthquakes and calculates a map of the alarm zone in which the target earthquake is expected. The alarm zone is determined by the function of the grid of spatio-temporal fields of features, calculated on the basis of the initial data. The approach is based on a machine learning method called the method of the minimum area of alarm. During training, the method uses a mathematical model that allows you to identify anomalies in the feature fields preceding the target earthquakes, compare these anomalies with each other, and then highlight similar anomalies in the attribute fields during the forecast. This model introduces constraints on the prediction rule that help to compensate to some extent for the small number of strong earthquakes used for training.

In our previous works, the main characteristic of the quality of a systematic forecast was the proportion of detected earthquake epicenters with a target magnitude for a given value of the alarm zone. Here we consider a generalization of the method designed to improve one more characteristic of the forecast quality: the probability of the target event occurring in the selected time interval and in the zone of expected alarm. The main elements of the approach are presented in Sect. 2. In Sect. 3, the generalized method of the minimum alarm zone is considered. Sections 4 and 5 present the results of approbation of the earthquake prediction method on the seismological and geodynamic data of California.

2 Main Elements of the Approach

2.1 Formulation of the Problem

The fundamentals of the technology for an automatic system for systematic earthquake prediction were developed in 2018 [11]. A demo version of the system is available at https://distcomp.ru/geo/prognosis-gps/. Earthquake forecasts are given in increments of Δt. At each step, the selection of target earthquake epicenters is replenished from remote servers and new initial data on the seismic process are loaded. The data is processed, transformed into spatio-temporal fields of the grid of predictive features, and machine learning is performed on the data from the beginning of training until the prediction moment t^*. As a result, the alarm zone is calculated, in which the epicenter of the target earthquake is expected at the interval $(t^*, t^* + \Delta t]$. At the next step, the learning interval is increased by Δt.

The approach to systematic earthquake prediction is based on the method of minimum area of alarm. In [9–11], the quality of the forecast was estimated by the probability of detecting the epicenters of the target earthquakes, which was defined as the fraction of predicted target events. In this article, we generalize our method to bring the approach closer to practical applications. In the simplest case, it is important in practice to know the estimate of the probability of at least one target event falling into the calculated alarm zone. Let the forecast be given regularly with a step Δt, the number of forecasts N, and all target events in the analysis zone are contained in M intervals. Estimation of the probability of choosing an interval with a target event $P = M/N$. This value is an upper estimate of the probability that at least one target event will fall into the alarm zone within a given interval. In a number of seismically active regions, with a long-term forecast of strong earthquakes for relatively short time intervals Δt, the estimate of the probability P of forecasting the interval containing the target event is too small for making practical decisions about declaring an alarm.

This explains the need to develop an approach to the systematic prediction of earthquakes and to generalize the machine learning method.

The difference of the generalized method of the minimum area of alarm is that at the forecast moment t^* the algorithm makes two decisions. The first solution determines the possibility of an earthquake epicenter with a target magnitude in the analysis zone at the forecast interval $(t^*, t^* + \Delta t]$. This solution does not depend on the spatial position of the expected earthquake epicenter. Let's call this decision *time forecast.* If it is decided that a target event in the analysis zone is possible, then this time interval is declared an alarm interval, and the alarm zone is calculated on it. We will call this solution *spatial forecast.* A target earthquake is predicted if its epicenter falls within the calculated alarm zone. The more successful the forecast, the greater the product $s(t^*)\Delta t$. At the same time, it is obvious that the size of this spatio-temporal area should be reasonably limited in forecasting.

2.2 Model

We assume that, within the analysis zone, the precursors of occurred earthquakes may precede similar future earthquakes.

1. *Fields of forecast features.* The processes associated with the preparation of strong earthquakes can be represented by spatial and spatio-temporal grid fields. The field values at the grid nodes correspond to the vectors of the multidimensional feature space.
2. *Abnormality of features.* Strong earthquakes are preceded by anomalous values of grid fields close to maximum or minimum.
3. *Precursor cylinder.* The field grid node corresponding to a possible earthquake precursor is located in the cylinder preceding this earthquake, with the center of the base at the epicenter.
4. *Condition of monotonicity.* Let the vector $\mathbf{f}^{(q)}$ be a precursor of an earthquake q. Let the attribute fields be known, the anomalous values of which f_i^+ are close to the maximum, and the fields, the anomalous values of which f_i^- are close to the minimum. Then any vector $\mathbf{f}$, the values of whose components are equal to $f_i^+ \geq f_i^{(q)+}$ or $f_j^- \leq f_j^{(q)-}$, can also be a precursor of a similar event.

The monotonicity condition corresponds to the ideal situation when the fields of features contain complete information about earthquake preparation processes. In a real situation, this information is not complete. Therefore, for some earthquake precursors, the monotonicity condition is not satisfied. However, the monotonicity condition allows us to introduce a measure of the anomalousness of the earthquake precursor. This measure is used by the learning algorithm to find the prediction rule.

Further, in Sect. 2, to simplify the explanation of the method of minimum area of alarm, without loss of generality, we will assume that the anomalous components of earthquake precursors take only values of the fields of predictive features that are close to the maximum.

2.3 Generalized Method of the Minimum Area of Alarm

The method of the minimum area of alarm uses fields of spatio-temporal features and earthquake epicenters with target magnitudes for training. The training begins with the fact that the algorithm of the method finds anomalous values in the grid fields, which are further considered as possible earthquake precursors. As a result, the training sample set consists of vectors of earthquake precursors $\mathbf{f}^{(q)} = (f_1^{(q)}, f_2^{(q)}, \ldots, f_I^{(q)})$ and unlabeled vectors of values of the field $\mathbf{f}^{(g)}$ in all other nodes of the coordinate grid, among which there may be earthquake precursors not represented in the training set. Based on these data, in the learning process, it is required to learn how to determine the largest number of earthquake epicenters provided that the number of selected unmarked vectors is limited. Machine learning algorithms in this setting refer to one-class classification methods [5,14,18].

Let it be known that the event q is preceded by a precursor $\mathbf{f}^{(q)}$. Associated with the precursor is a set $w^{(q)}$ of vectors in the feature space $\mathrm{I\!R}^I$ whose components are greater than or equal to $\mathbf{f}^{(q)}$, i.e., $w^{(q)} = \{\mathbf{f}^{(g)} \in \mathrm{I\!R}^I : f_i^{(g)} \geq f_i^{(q)}, i = 1, 2, \ldots, I\}$. We call this set the orthant $w^{(q)}$ with vertex at the point $\mathbf{f}^{(q)}$, and the vectors $\mathbf{f}^{(g)} \in w^{(q)}$ as the *base vectors* of the target event q.

The basis vectors of the event q, according to the monotonicity condition, are also precursors of such events. In geographic coordinates, each base vector forms an *alarm cylinder* of radius R and element T. Each base vector forms, in geographic coordinates, an alarm cylinder of radius R and element T. The alarm cylinder of the base vector $\mathbf{f}^{(g)}$ has its base centered at grid node g with coordinates $(x(g), y(g), t(g))$, the radius of the base R and the element $[(x(g), y(g), t(g)), (x(g), y(g), t(g) + T)]$, where $t^{(g)} \in [t_0, t^*]$, t_0 is learning start time, t^* is the moment of prediction. An earthquake can only be predicted if its epicenter falls into one of the alarm cylinders. The union of the alarm cylinders formed by the base vectors of the orthant $w^{(q)}$, selects the set of grid nodes $W^{(q)}$, $|W^{(q)}| = L^{(q)}$. The learning algorithm uses the alarm cylinders to calculate the space-time alarm field.

Note now that an earthquake q with epicenter coordinates $(x(q), y(q), t(q))$ can fall into the alarm cylinder and, therefore, can be predicted if and only if its precursor $\mathbf{f}^{(q)}$ corresponds to some grid node from a cylinder with base center at point $(x(q), y(q), t(q))$, radius R and element $[(x(q), y(q), t(q) - T), (x(q), y(q), t(q))$. Let's call this cylinder the *cylinder of the precursor* of the event q. The precursor of the event q is the vector $\mathbf{f}^{(q)}$, which has the minimum value $v^{(q)} = L^{(q)}/L$ among all vectors corresponding to the nodes of the predecessor cylinder of the grid, where $|W^{(q)}| = L^{(q)}$, L is the number of all grid nodes of the spatio-temporal area of analysis on the interval $[t_0, t^*]$. The value $v^{(q)}$ (the *volume of the precursor*) determines the measure of the anomaly of the precursor of the event q.

The scheme of the learning algorithm for the method of the generalized minimum area of alarm is as follows. The forecast of the target event at the moment t^* of the interval $(t^*, t^* + \Delta t]$ is carried out in two stages. At the 1st stage, the problem of choosing the time interval for the forecast is solved, at which the target event is expected within the analysis zone. If it is decided that the target event is possible at this interval, then the 2nd stage of the forecast is performed: the problem of determining the alarm zone in which the target event is expected is solved.

Stage 1: Forecast in Time. At the 1st stage, the radius of the cylinders R is chosen so that the circle centered at any grid node of the analysis area covers the entire analysis area. This leads to the fact that the earthquake precursor can refer to any grid node of the analysis area. Thus, the precursor loses its spatial localization and the alarm cylinder degenerates into an alarm time interval, and the space-time alarm field degenerates into an alarm time series Ψ.

The algorithm for calculating the time series of alarms for the time t^* is as follows.

1. Find earthquake precursors $\mathbf{f}^{(q)}$ for each target event $q = 1, 2, \ldots, Q$. Let the event q occur at the moment $t^{(q)}$. The precursor $\mathbf{f}^{(q)}$ of the event q is sought on the interval $[t^{(q)} - T, t^{(q)})$ among the vectors corresponding to the grid nodes $g = 1, 2, \ldots, G$ of the precursor cylinder. Each of these vectors $f^{(g)}$ selects the orthant $w^{(g)}$ of base vectors and selects a set of samples of the time series of signals $W^{(g)}$, $|W^{(g)}| = N^{(g)}$. The precursor of the event q is the vector $\mathbf{f}^{(q)}$ with the minimum volume of the precursor $v^{(q)} = N^{(q)}/N$ among the vectors corresponding to the grid nodes of the precursor cylinder, where $N^{(q)}$ is the number of signal intervals when choosing the orthant $w^{(q)}$ with vertex $\mathbf{f}^{(q)}$, N is the number of all intervals from the beginning of training to the moment t^*.
2. Sort all the precursors $\mathbf{f}^{(q)}$ by increasing their alarm volume: $v^{(1)} \leq v^{(2)} \leq \cdots \leq v^{(q)} \leq \cdots \leq v^{(q)}$.
3. Calculate the alarm time series Ψ.
   (a) Set the values $\psi(t) \equiv 1$.
   (b) Replace the values 1 to the value $\psi(1) = v^{(1)}$ in the set $W^{(1)}$; replace the value 1 with the value $\psi(2) = |W^{(1)} \cup W^{(2)}|/N$ in the set $W^{(2)} \setminus W^{(1)}$; replace the value 1 with the value $\psi(3) = |W^{(1)} \cup W^{(2)} \cup W^{(3)}|/N$ in the set $W^{(3)} \setminus (W^{(1)} \cup W^{(2)})$ and then sequentially replace the values 1 with the corresponding values of alarm volumes. The resulting alarm time series Ψ takes the values $\psi(1) \leq \psi(2) \leq \cdots \leq \psi(q) \leq \cdots \leq \psi(Q) \leq 1$.

Thus, at the forecast moment t^*, the values of the time series Ψ are updated. The decision to declare an alarm on the interval $(t^*, t^* + \Delta t]$ is made if $\psi(t^*) \leq \psi_0$, where ψ_0 is the value of the specified threshold. Intervals Δt of a series of alarms Ψ with sample values $\psi(t^*) \leq \psi_0$ will be called alarm intervals. The number M^* of detected alarm intervals with target events, depends on the value $\Psi = N^*/N$, where N^* is the number of alarm intervals, N is the total number of all forecast intervals. The quality of the forecast at the 1st stage is determined by the following statistics: $U^* = M^*/M$ is an estimate of the probability of successful detection of an interval in which at least one target event occurred, where M is the number of all intervals containing at least one target event, and

$P_1 = M^*/N^*$ is an estimate of the probability that at least one target event will occur in the predicted alarm interval.

Stage 2: Spatial Forecast. The spatial forecast defines alert zones where target earthquakes are expected. Alarm zones are calculated only on alarm intervals with values $\psi(t^*) \leq \psi_0$. In this case, as in the previous stage, all data available by the time of forecasting t^* are used for training: grid fields $\mathbf{F}_1, \mathbf{F}_2, \ldots, \mathbf{F}_I$ and target events $q = 1, 2, \ldots, Q$.

The learning algorithm uses the following parameters:

1. The area of analysis and the time step of the coordinate grid do not change compared to the 1st stage.
2. The grid of spatial coordinates is determined by the accuracy of the data.
3. The parameters of the signal and precursor cylinders are the same and depend on the accuracy of the data, the grid spacing, and the features of regional seismicity.

The alarm field calculation algorithm consists of three steps:

1. Calculate earthquake precursor vectors $\mathbf{f}^{(q)}$, $q = 1, \ldots, Q$ (see previous section)
2. Generate training sample $\{f^{(q)}, v^{(q)}\}$. Order cases $f^{(q)}$ by increasing volume of alarms for the target event $v^{(1)} \leq v^{(2)} \leq \cdots \leq v^{(q)} \leq \cdots \leq v^{(Q)}$.
3. Calculate the alarm field Φ.
   (a) Set the grid nodes of the alarm field to 1.
   (b) Replace the value 1 of the field Φ with $\phi(1) = v^{(1)}$ for the set $W^{(1)}$ of grid nodes corresponding to the base points of $\mathbf{f}^{(1)}$; replace the value 1 with $\phi(2) = |W^{(1)} \cup W^{(2)}|/L$ at the grid nodes, $W^{(2)} \setminus W^{(1)}$; replace value 1 with $\phi(3) = |W^{(1)} \cup W^{(2)} \cup W^{(3)}|/L$ at grid nodes $W^{(3)} \setminus (W^{(1)} \cup W^{(2)})$, and then sequentially replace the values of 1 with the corresponding alarm volume values. The resulting field Φ takes the values $\phi(1) \leq \phi(2) \leq \cdots \leq \phi(q) \leq \cdots \leq \phi(Q) \leq 1$.

Thus, at each step of the forecast Δt, new values of the spatio-temporal alarm field Φ are calculated. The time interval of the alarm field at time t^* is used for prediction. The decision on the success of the forecast of an earthquake with a target magnitude on the interval $(t^*, t^* + \Delta t]$ is made if its epicenter falls into the alarm zone $\phi(t^*) \leq \phi_0$, where ϕ_0 is the value of the specified threshold. The number of events M^{**} in the alarm zones, calculated in the alarm intervals selected at the 1st stage, depends on the value of the alarm volume $\phi_0 = L^*/L$, where L^* is the average number of grid nodes in the signal zones, L is the total number of grid nodes in the analysis zone for all intervals Δt on which the forecast decision was made. The quality of the forecast at the 2nd stage is determined by the following statistics: $U^{**} = Q^{**}/Q$ is the estimate of the probability of successful detection of the target event at alarm intervals, where M is the number of intervals with the target event in the analysis zone, M^{**} is the number of alarm intervals with target events in the alarm zone, and $P2 = M^{**}/N^*$ is an estimate of the probability that at least one target event that falls into the alarm interval will also fall into the predicted alarm zone.

3 Modeling

3.1 Initial Data

Earthquake prediction modeling was performed on data from the California region. The initial data include the earthquake catalog of the National Earthquake Information Center (NEIC) [4] for 01/01/1995–11/14/2020 with magnitude $m \geq 2.0$ and hypocenter depth $H \leq 160$ km, as well as GPS time series of daily horizontal displacements of the earth's surface in the interval 01/01/2008–11/14/2020 from the Nevada Geodetic Laboratory (NGL), http://geodesy.unr.edu/about.php [6]. The average distance between GPS receiving stations is 9.38 km, with a standard deviation of 5.74 km. The forecast is calculated for earthquake epicenters with target magnitude $m \geq 5.5$ and hypocenter depth $H \leq 60$ km. The analysis zone is defined by the intersection of two zones. The first zone is calculated from seismological data. The zone is limited by the threshold spatial density of earthquake epicenters in the interval 1995–2008, at which, for the alarm volume $\phi_0 = 0.2$, the probability of detecting earthquake epicenters with magnitude $m \geq 5.5$ in this field will not exceed 0.3–0.4. The second zone is limited to an area for which the distance to the ground receiving GPS stations does not exceed 50 km. The area of analysis is shown in Fig. 1. The circles show the epicenters of target earthquakes with magnitude $m \geq 5.5$ used for training (yellow) and forecast (red).

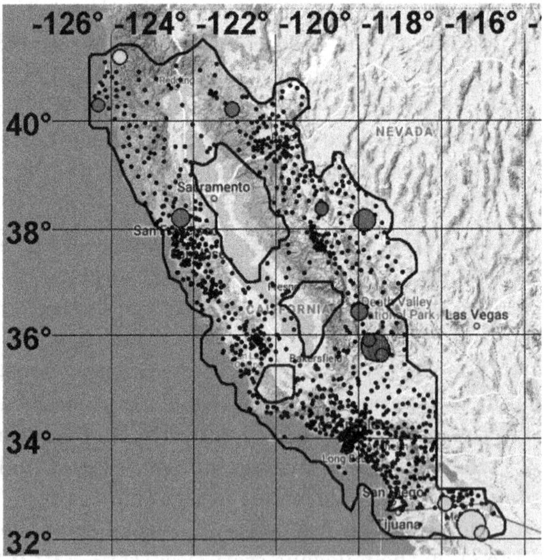

Fig. 1. Zone of analysis. Circles are epicenters of target earthquakes with magnitudes $m \geq 5.5$ used for training (yellow) and testing (red). Black dots are GPS receiving stations. (Color figure online)

3.2 Preprocessing

Seismological Data. are presented in the form of the following main spatial and spatio-temporal grid fields, similar to those used in our previous works [9–11]:

1. $\mathbf{S}_1$ is the 3D density field of earthquake epicenters.
2. $\mathbf{S}_2$ is the 3D field of medium magnitude earthquakes.
3. $\mathbf{S}_3$ is the 3D field of variations in the density of earthquake epicenters over time. The values of the field $s_{3n}(t)$ at grid node n are equal to the ratio of the difference between the average values of the density of epicenters $(\overline{s_{1n}} - \overline{s_{2n}})$ in two successive intervals T_1 and T_2 to the sample standard deviation of this difference $\sigma_n(s_1)$.
4. $\mathbf{S}_4$ is the 3D field of variations of mean magnitudes of earthquakes over time. The field values are calculated similarly to the values of the $\mathbf{S}_3$ field,
5. $\mathbf{S}_5$ is the 3D field of quantiles of the background density of earthquake epicenters in the interval from the beginning of the analysis to the start of training, the values of which correspond to the density of earthquake epicenters in the analysis interval.
6. $\mathbf{S}_6$ is the 2D density field of earthquake epicenters in the interval from the beginning of the analysis to the start of training.

When choosing the most informative fields of features, in addition to the fields indicated in the list, fields equal to their products and ratios were used.

Geodynamic Data. are presented as time series of the $x(t)$ and $y(t)$ components of the coordinates of daily horizontal displacements of GPS receiving stations in the west-east and north-south directions. The efficiency of using space geodesy data for earthquake prediction was studied in [10]. Calculation of fields from GPS time series is performed in two stages. At the first stage, a useful signal is extracted from the time series of GPS receiving stations, then the space-time fields of prognostic features are calculated.

The daily displacement velocity of the earth's surface $g_x(t)$ and $g_y(t)$ are calculated over the interval $T_0 = 30$ days: $g_x(t) = (x(t) - x(t - T_0))/T_0$ and $g_y(t) = (y(t) - y(t - T_0))/T_0$. Changes in the $x(t)$ and $y(t)$ station coordinates over a thirty-day interval are comparable to the measurement noise. For each coordinate of the time series, there are a large number of discontinuities. If after each break you start counting the speed again, then the number of missing values increases significantly. To limit the number of gaps in the time series of velocities, we linearly interpolate the values of the station coordinates at discontinuities not larger than T_0. When the breaks in the series of coordinates are more than T_0, we end the calculation of the speed at the last value before the break and again continue estimating the speeds, starting from the first value after the break.

Spatio-temporal fields are calculated in the grid $\Delta x \times \Delta y \times \Delta t = 0.1° \times 0.075° \times 1$ day. Time series values are interpolated using the well-known method of weighted inverse distances. As a result of interpolation, the gaps in the velocity time series related to the nodes of the spatial grid are filled with data from neighboring receiving stations. After field interpolation, the velocity components $\mathbf{V}_x$ and $\mathbf{V}_y$ were spatially smoothed with a sliding window of 25×25 km^2.

We assume that the precursors of strong earthquakes can be detected in spatio-temporal fields of anomalous changes in the mode of deformations of the earth's surface. Anomalies in time were calculated in three fields of strain rate invariants:

- $\mathbf{F}_1$ is the strain rate divergence field: div $V_g = \frac{\partial V_{xg}}{\partial x} + \frac{\partial V_{yg}}{\partial y}$
- $\mathbf{F}_2$ is the rotor strain rate field: rot $V_g = \frac{\partial V_{xg}}{\partial y} - \frac{\partial V_{yg}}{\partial x}$
- $\mathbf{F}_3$ is the field of shear deformations: sh $V_g = \frac{1}{2}\sqrt{(\frac{\partial V_{xg}}{\partial x} - \frac{\partial V_{yg}}{\partial y})^2 + (\frac{\partial V_{xg}}{\partial y} + \frac{\partial V_{yg}}{\partial x})^2}$
- $\mathbf{F}_4$ is the field of variations in the strain rate divergence. The values of the field $f_{4g}(t)$ at the grid node g are equal to the ratio of the difference between the average divergence values $(\overline{div_{2g}} - \overline{div_{1g}})$ in two successive intervals T_1 and T_2 to the standard deviation of this difference $\sigma_g(div)$, where $T_1 = T_2 = 361$ days and $\overline{div_{2g}}$ is calculated from the values of the field $\mathbf{F}_1$ on the interval $(t - T_2, t)$, $\overline{div_{1g}}$ is calculated on the interval $(t - T_2 - T_1, t - T_2)$.
- $\mathbf{F}_5$ is the field of variations of the rotor deformation rate. The values of the field f5(t) are calculated similarly to the values of the field $\mathbf{F}_4$, $f_{5g}(t) = (\overline{rot2g} - \overline{rot_{1g}})/\sigma_g(rot)$.
- $\mathbf{F}_6$ is the field of shear strain variations: $f_{6g}(t) = (\overline{sh2g} - \overline{sh_{1g}})/\sigma_g(sh)$.

The fields $\mathbf{F}_4$, $\mathbf{F}_5$, $\mathbf{F}_6$ were calculated in the coordinate grid $\Delta x \times \Delta y \times \Delta t = 0.1° \times 0.075° \times 30$ days.

3.3 Forecast

Detection of Target Events. The following forecast parameters were used. The training interval starts on September 23, 2009 and ends at the time of the next forecast. The forecast is performed regularly with a step of $\Delta t = 30$ days in the testing interval until 11/14/2020. During the test period, 12 epicenters of earthquakes with magnitude $m \geq 5.5$ fall into the analysis zone. The parameters of the alarm and precursor cylinders are $R = 18$ km and $T = 61$ days. To calculate the alarm field, the same 4 fields were used as in the article [10]: (1) field $\mathbf{F}_6$—maximum values of variations in time of shear deformations of the earth's surface with parameters $T_1 = T_2 = 365$ days; (2) field $\mathbf{F}_4$—the maximum values of variation in time of divergence of the earth's surface with parameters $T_1 = T_2 = 365$ days; (3) field $\mathbf{S}_{12}$ - minimum values of variations in the field $\mathbf{S}_2$ of average magnitudes of earthquakes in time with parameters $T_1 = 1095$ and $T_2 = 730$ days; (4) field $\mathbf{S}_{13} = \mathbf{S}_1/\mathbf{S}_5$—ratios of the density values of earthquake epicenters in field $\mathbf{S}_1$ and quantiles in field $\mathbf{S}_5$. For comparison, the forecast was calculated from the $\mathbf{S}_6$ fields of the spatial density of earthquake epicenters. The main results are shown in Fig. 2 and summarized in Table 1.

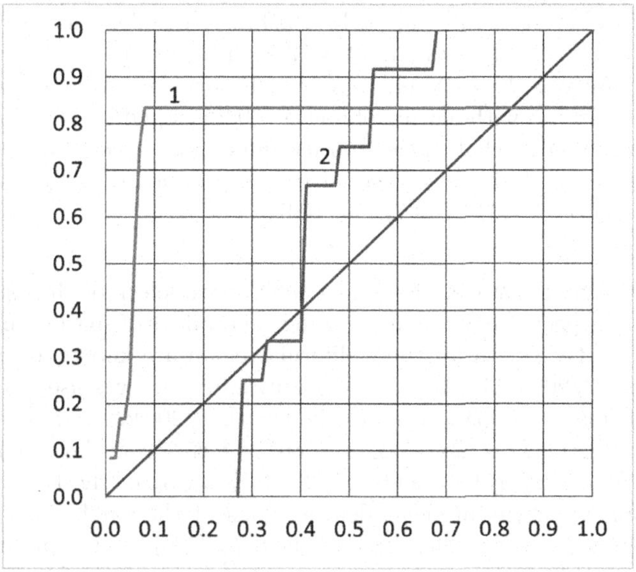

Fig. 2. Plot $U(\phi)$ of the probabilities of detecting target events U on the alarm volume ϕ: 1—forecast for the selected spatio-temporal fields, 2—forecast for the spatial density field of earthquake epicenters.

Table 1. Probability of detecting target events.

Alarm	Fields F_4, F_6, S_{12} and S_{13}		Field of 2D earthquake density S_6	
volume threshold ϕ	Number of Events Q^*	Probability $U = Q^*/Q$	Number of Events Q^*	Probability $U = Q^*/Q$
0.05	3	0.39	0	0
0.10	10	0.83	0	0
0.15	10	0.83	0	0
0.20	10	0.83	0	0
0.25	10	0.83	0	0
0.30	10	0.83	3	0.25

It can be seen from the figure and tables that the values of the probability of detecting target events when using the indicated spatio-temporal fields are much higher than when using the spatial density field of earthquake epicenters. This indicates the spatial homogeneity of target events in the selected areas of analysis.

The California testing interval 01/19/2013–11/14/2020 contains $N = 95$ forecast intervals Δt. All target events $Q = 12$ with magnitude $m \geq 5.5$ fall within the forecast intervals $M = 7$. The number of alarm intervals for which target events falls into zones with alarm volume $\phi = 0.2$ is equal to $M^{**} = 6$. The estimate of the probability that in the forecast interval Δt at least one target event will fall into the analysis zone is equal to the proportion of forecast intervals with target events $P = M/N = 7/95 = 0.07$.

Stage 1. At the 1st stage, the alarm interval is selected, during which the target event is expected in the analysis zone. The values of spatio-temporal fields calculated from GPS data for the California region are known for a very short interval of 09/23/2009–11/14/2020. This entire interval was used for testing.

Feature fields were spatially smoothed with a 200 km radius window and converted to a grid $\Delta x \times \Delta y \times \Delta t = 1.85° \times 1.85° \times 30$ days. The temporal forecast was made using two fields: (1) field $F_{6smoothed}$—the maximum values of the field of variations in shear deformations of the earth's surface in time with parameters $T_1 = T_2 = 365$ days; (2) field $F_{4smoothed}$—the minimum values of the field of variations in the divergence of the earth's surface in time with the parameters $T_1 = T_2 = 365$ days. Parameters of the minimum alarm zone algorithm: $T = 61$ days, $R = 3000$ km. The decision to assign a forecast interval as an alarm interval is made if the values of the time series Ψ do not exceed the threshold value $\psi_0 = 0.35$.

Figure 3 shows the dependence of the probability estimate $U^* = M^*/M$ of detecting test earthquakes in alarm intervals Δt on the proportion of alarm intervals $\psi = N^*/N$, where N^* is the number of alarm intervals, N is the number of all predictive intervals, M is the number of all alarm intervals with target events, M^* is the number of alarm intervals in which target events are present, P_1 is the probability that at least one target event falls into the analysis zone during the alarm interval. Figure 4 shows a plot of the alarm time series Ψ and the sequence of target earthquakes in the testing interval.

The Table 2 shows that the threshold $\psi_0 = 0.35$ corresponds to the estimate of the probability of hitting at least one target event in the analysis zone during the alarm interval $P1 = M^*/N^* = 7/41 = 0.17$. The value P_1 is the upper limit for estimating P_2 the probability that at the 2nd stage at least one target event will fall into the alarm zone of one of the N^* alarm intervals selected at the first stage.

Table 2. Testing the 1st stage of the forecast.

Alarm volume threshold ϕ	N^*	M^*	$U^* = M^*/M$	$P_2 = M^*/N^*$
0.25	30	5	0.71	0.17
0.45	41	7	1.00	0.17

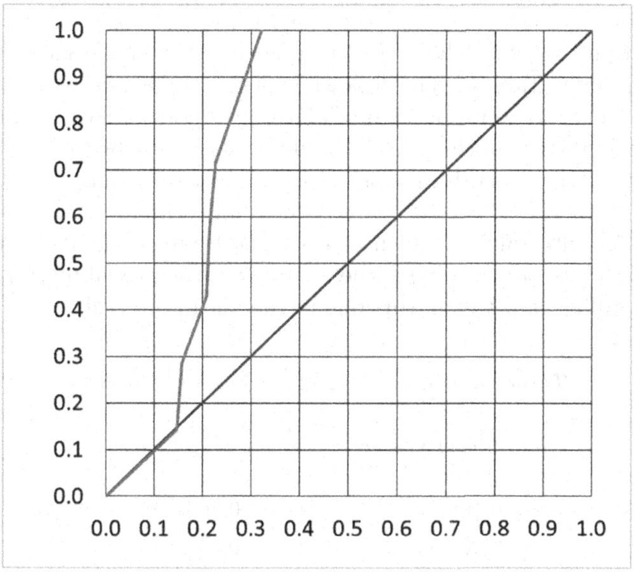

Fig. 3. Graphs of dependence $U^*(\psi)$.

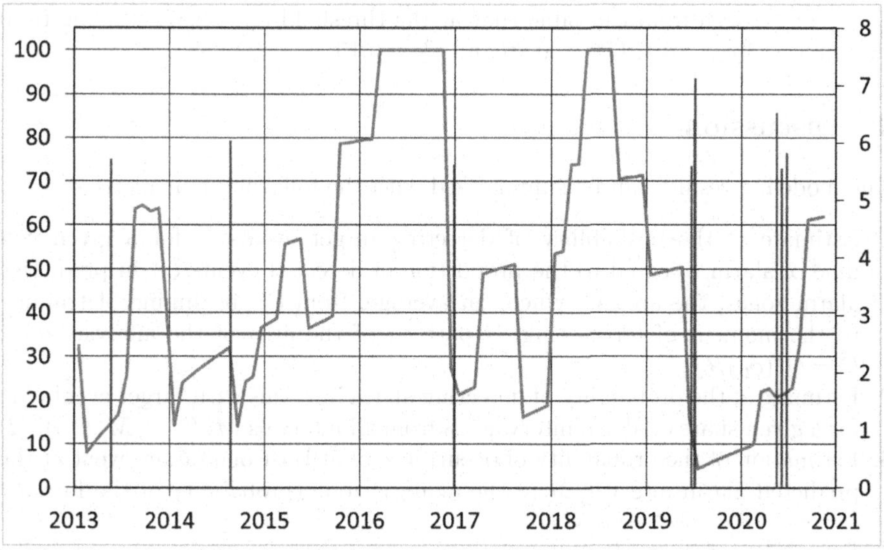

Fig. 4. Time series of alarm intervals Ψ and test sequence of target earthquakes with $m \geq 5.5$. The decision to alarm is made if the values of the time series do not exceed the value $\psi_0 = 0.35$.

Stage 2. For spatial forecasting, the same fields were used as in the "Target Event Detection" section. The results of modeling the 2nd stage of the forecast are summarized in Table 3. The following designations are used in the table: $\phi = L^*/L$ is the average proportion of alarm grid nodes relative to the analysis zone; N^* is the number of selected alarm intervals during testing; $M^{**}(\psi_0, \phi_0)$ is the number of alarm intervals in which at least one target event fell into the alarm zone during testing; $U^{**} = M^{**}(\psi_0, \phi_0)/M$ is an estimate of the probability of detecting alarm intervals for which at least one target event fell into the alarm zone; $P_2 = M^{**}(\psi_0, \phi_0)/N^*(\psi_0)$ is the estimate of the probability of at least one target event falling into the alarm zone in the alarm interval.

Table 3. Testing the 2nd stage of the forecast.

Alarm volume threshold ϕ	M^{**}	U^{**}	P_2
0.10	6	0.86	0.15
0.20	6	0.86	0.15
0.30	6	0.86	0.15

It can be seen from the table that at the threshold $\psi_0 = 0.35$, starting from the threshold $\phi_0 = 0.1$, $U^{**} = 0.86$ and $P_2 = 0.15$.

4 Discussion

The modeling results can be summarized with the following four metrics:

1. Estimate of the probability of detecting target events U for a given volume of alarm ϕ, equal to the proportion of detected events Q^* in predictive alarm zones, the area of which, on average, from the beginning of training to the moment of forecasting, is part ϕ_0 of the area of the analysis zone: $U = Q^*(\phi_0)/Q$.
2. Estimate of the probability of detecting alarm intervals with target events M* for a given share of alarm intervals ψ_0 from all intervals M: $U^* = M^*(\psi_0)/M$.
3. Estimation of the probability of occurrence of at least one target event at the predicted alarm interval Δt in the analysis zone (probability of the forecast in time): $P_1 = M^*(\psi_0)/N^*(\psi_0)$.
4. Estimation of the probability of occurrence of at least one target event at the signal interval Δt in the predicted alarm zone (spatio-temporal probability of the forecast): $P_2(\psi_0, \phi_0) = M^{**}(\psi_0, \phi_0)/N^*(\psi_0)$.

For comparison, we will use the values of the same indicators when predicting target events for random fields.

1. The probability of detecting target events when choosing an alarm zone by a random field with an alarm volume ϕ: $U_{rand}(\phi) = \phi = L^*/L$.

2. Probability of detecting alarm intervals Δt with target events when choosing N^* intervals from N random field values: $U^*_{rand}(\psi) = \psi = N^*/N$.
3. The probability that, under the condition of a uniform distribution of intervals Δt with target events, a randomly selected interval will contain at least one target event: $P_{1rand} = M/N$.
4. Probability P_{2rand} that, with a random selection of the alarm zone, at least one of the target events, provided that they are evenly distributed in the analysis zone, will appear in the randomly generated alarm zone. Let X be a random variable equal to the number of events in the alarm zone. The average value $\overline{X} = \phi Q/N$, where the alarm volume ϕ is equal to the ratio of the average value of the area of the alarm zone to the area of the analysis zone, the number of intervals N is equal to the ratio of the testing time to the value of the forecast interval Δt. Assuming that the empirical mean X is equal to the mathematical expectation $\mathrm{E}\,X$, one can estimate P_{2rand} using the Markov inequality [19]: $P_{2rand}(X \geq 1) \leq \phi Q/N$.

Table 4 compares the results of a systematic earthquake forecast and the results of a forecast based on random fields.

Table 4. Results of systematic and random forecasts.

№	Indicator	Systematic forecast	Random forecast
1	Detection of target events $U(\phi) = Q^*(\phi)/Q$	$U(0.10) = 10/12 = 0.83$ $U(0.20) = 10/12 = 0.83$ $U(0.30) = 10/12 = 0.83$	$U_{rand}(\phi) = \phi = 0.10$ $U_{rand}(\phi) = \phi = 0.20$ $U_{rand}(\phi) = \phi = 0.30$
2.	Detection of intervals with events $U^*(\psi) = M^*(\psi)/M$	$U^*(0.25) = 5/7 = 0.71$ $U(0.35) = 7/7 = 1.00$	$U_{rand}(\psi) = \psi = 0.25$ $U_{rand}(\psi) = \psi = 0.35$
3.	Interval prediction with target events $P_1(\psi) = M^*(\psi)/N^*(\psi)$	$P_1(0.25) = 5/30 = 0.17$ $P_1(0.35) = 7/41 = 0.17$	$P_{1rand} = M/N = 7/95 = 0.07$
4.	Forecast of target events $P_2(\phi,\psi) = M^{**}(\phi)/N^*(\psi)$	$P_2(0.2, 0.35) = 6/41 = 0.15$ $P_2(0.3, 0.35) = 6/41 = 0.15$	$P_{2rand} \leq \phi Q/N = 0.2 \times 12/95 = 0.03$ $P_{2rand} \leq \phi Q/N = 0.3 \times 12/95 = 0.04$

The results show that with a systematic forecast, the estimates of the probability of detecting target events $U(\phi)$ and alarm intervals with events $U^*(\psi)$ take quite high values. However, for the practical application of earthquake prediction methods, it is more important to estimate the forecast probabilities $P_1(\psi)$ and $P_2(\psi,\phi)$, the probability of at least one target event occurring in the predicted alarm intervals and the alarm zone. It can be seen that the experimental estimates of these values take small values. At the same time, these estimates of forecast probabilities are higher than similar values obtained when using random attributive fields for forecasting, and also higher than those obtained in section "Detection of target events", when using the previous version of the minimum alarm zone method: $P_1 = 0.07$ at $\psi_0 = 0.35$ and $P_2 = 0.06$ at $\phi_0 = 0.2$.

5 Conclusion

We have considered the main elements of the approach to systematic earthquake prediction. The forecast decision is made regularly for the time interval Δt. We determine the quality of the forecast using two types of estimates. We estimate: (1) the probability of detecting target events, which is equal to the share of detected events in the forecast, and (2) the probability of predicting target events, which determines the measure of the possibility of a target event occurring at the next alarm interval Δt in the analysis zone and in the predicted alarm zone. The predictive decision is made regularly for the time interval Δt. The first assessment determines the effectiveness of the initial data, methods of their processing, and the method of forecasting. The second assessment is necessary for making practical decisions related to seismic hazard prediction.

The solution to the second problem required the development of the method of minimum area of alarm. The generalized method consists of two steps. At the first stage, the possibility of an earthquake epicenter with a target magnitude in the analysis zone is predicted, and a decision is made to announce an alarm at the interval Δt. At the second stage, in the alarm interval, the spatial position of the alarm zone is calculated, in which the appearance of the epicenter of this earthquake is expected.

This method has been experimentally investigated for the California region. The forecast of earthquakes with magnitude $m \geq 5.5$ was made according to the catalog of earthquakes and time series of displacements of the earth's surface obtained using GPS. The simulation results show that for alarm zones, the area of which on average is from 10% of the area of the analysis zone, the estimates of the probability of detecting target events are more than 0.8. At the same time, the probabilities that at least one target earthquake is expected in the predicted alarm zone take on a very small order of magnitude, less than 0.15. At the same time, it can be seen that estimates of the probability of a systematic forecast are significantly higher than similar forecast probabilities based on random fields.

We believe that in order to develop an approach to systematic earthquake prediction in the direction of solving applied problems, it is advisable to conduct research on optimizing the method of systematic earthquake prediction and studying new grid fields representing the processes of preparation of sources of strong earthquakes.

Acknowledgements. This work was partially supported by RFBR grant 20-07-00445. The authors are grateful to E.N. Petrova and S.A. Pirogov for their helpful remarks.

References

1. Alves, E.I.: Earthquake forecasting using neural networks: results and future work. Nonlinear Dyn. **44**(1), 341–349 (2006)
2. Amei, A., Fu, W., Ho, C.H.: Time series analysis for predicting the occurrences of large scale earthquakes. Int. J. Appl. Sci. Technol. **2**(7) (2012)

3. Asim, K.M., Idris, A., Iqbal, T., Martínez-Álvarez, F.: Earthquake prediction model using support vector regressor and hybrid neural networks. PLoS ONE **13**(7), e0199004 (2018)
4. Barnhart, W.D., Hayes, G.P., Wald, D.J.: Global earthquake response with imaging geodesy: recent examples from the USGS NEIC. Remote Sens. **11**(11), 1357 (2019)
5. Bishop, C.M.: Machine learning and pattern recognition. In: Information Science and Statistics. Springer, Heidelberg (2006). ISBN:978-1-4939-3843-8
6. Blewitt, G., Hammond, W.C., Kreemer, C.: Harnessing the GPS data explosion for interdisciplinary science. Eos **99**(10.1029), 485 (2018)
7. Corbi, F., et al.: Machine learning can predict the timing and size of analog earthquakes. Geophys. Res. Lett. **46**(3), 1303–1311 (2019)
8. Geller, R.J., Jackson, D.D., Kagan, Y.Y., Mulargia, F.: Earthquakes cannot be predicted. Science **275**(5306), 1616 (1997)
9. Gitis, V., Derendyaev, A.: The method of the minimum area of alarm for earthquake magnitude prediction. Front. Earth Sci. **8**, 482 (2020)
10. Gitis, V., Derendyaev, A., Petrov, K.: Analyzing the performance of GPS data for earthquake prediction. Remote Sens. **13**(9), 1842 (2021)
11. Gitis, V.G., Derendyaev, A.B.: Machine learning methods for seismic hazards forecast. Geosciences **9**(7), 308 (2019)
12. Gufeld, I.L., Matveeva, M.I., Novoselov, O.N.: Why we cannot predict strong earthquakes in the earth's crust. Geodyn. Tectonophys. **2**(4), 378–415 (2015)
13. Keilis-Borok, V., Soloviev, A.A.: Nonlinear dynamics of the lithosphere and earthquake prediction. Springer Science & Business Media (2013)
14. Khan, Shehroz S.., Madden, Michael G..: A survey of recent trends in one class classification. In: Coyle, Lorcan, Freyne, Jill (eds.) AICS 2009. LNCS (LNAI), vol. 6206, pp. 188–197. Springer, Heidelberg (2010). https://doi.org/10.1007/978-3-642-17080-5_21
15. King, C.Y.: Gas geochemistry applied to earthquake prediction: an overview. J. Geophys. Res. Solid Earth **91**(B12), 12269–12281 (1986)
16. Koronovsky, N., Naimark, A.: Earthquake prediction: is it a practicable scientific perspective or a challenge to science? Mosc. Univ. Geol. Bull. **64**(1), 10–20 (2009)
17. Kossobokov, V., Shebalin, P.: Earthquake prediction. In: Nonlinear Dynamics of the Lithosphere and Earthquake Prediction, pp. 141–207. Springer (2003). https://doi.org/10.1007/978-3-662-05298-3
18. Kotsiantis, S.B., Zaharakis, I., Pintelas, P.: Supervised machine learning: a review of classification techniques. Emerg. Artif. Intell. Appl. Comput. Eng. **160**, 3–24 (2007)
19. Kremer, N.S.: Probability theory and mathematical statistics. YUNITI-DANA, M p. 573 (2004)
20. Lighthill, J.: A critical review of VAN: earthquake prediction from seismic electrical signals. World scientific (1996)
21. Marzocchi, W., Zechar, J.D.: Earthquake forecasting and earthquake prediction: different approaches for obtaining the best model. Seismol. Res. Lett. **82**(3), 442–448 (2011)
22. Matsumoto, N., Koizumi, N.: Recent hydrological and geochemical research for earthquake prediction in Japan. Nat. Hazards **69**(2), 1247–1260 (2013)
23. Mignan, A., Broccardo, M.: Neural network applications in earthquake prediction (1994–2019): meta-analytic and statistical insights on their limitations. Seismol. Res. Lett. **91**(4), 2330–2342 (2020)

24. Moustra, M., Avraamides, M., Christodoulou, C.: Artificial neural networks for earthquake prediction using time series magnitude data or seismic electric signals. Expert Syst. Appl. **38**(12), 15032–15039 (2011)
25. Murai, S.: Can we predict earthquakes with GPS data? Int. J. Digital Earth **3**(1), 83–90 (2010)
26. Panakkat, A., Adeli, H.: Neural network models for earthquake magnitude prediction using multiple seismicity indicators. Int. J. Neural Syst. **17**(01), 13–33 (2007)
27. Priambodo, B., Mahmudy, W.F., Rahman, M.A.: Earthquake magnitude and grid-based location prediction using backpropagation neural network. Knowl. Eng. Data Sci. **3**(1), 28–39 (2020)
28. Rhoades, D.A.: Mixture models for improved earthquake forecasting with short-to-medium time horizons. Bull. Seismol. Soc. Am. **103**(4), 2203–2215 (2013)
29. Shebalin, P.N., Narteau, C., Zechar, J.D., Holschneider, M.: Combining earthquake forecasts using differential probability gains. Earth, Planets and Space **66**(1), 1–14 (2014). https://doi.org/10.1186/1880-5981-66-37
30. Sobolev, G.: Principles of earthquake prediction (1993)
31. Sobolev, G., Ponomarev, A.: Earthquake physics and precursors. Publishing house Nauka, Moscow.-2003 (2003)
32. Zavyalov, A.: Intermediate term earthquake prediction. Nauka, Moscow. In: Zhang, L.Y., Mao, X.B., Lu, A.H. (eds.) (2009) Experimental Study of the Mechanical Properties of Rocks at High Temperature, Sci. China Ser. E, vol. 52(3), pp. 641–646 (2006)

International Workshop on Smart and Sustainable Island Communities (SSIC 2022)

SDGs Implementation in Italy: A Comparative Assessment of Subnational Strategies for Sustainable Development

Valeria Saiu(✉) and Ivan Blečić

University of Cagliari, 09124 Cagliari, Italy
{v.saiu,ivanblecic}@unica.it

Abstract. Currently, many countries are committed to achieving the Sustainable Development Goals (SDGs) included in the United Nations Agenda 2030. The subnational governments are playing a key role in SDGs implementation at local level. In Italy, the "National Strategy for Sustainable Development" (NSDS) for 2017–2030 defined an integrated system of objectives and actions for guiding policies and interventions towards SDGs. Italian subnational governments (Regions and Autonomous Provinces) must adapt the NSDS to their contexts through local-specific strategies, according to different territorial features and priorities. This paper provides a comparative assessment between four Italian subnational Strategies for Sustainable Development – Liguria and Marche Regions, Autonomous Region of Sardinia and Autonomous Province of Trento – in order to highlight differences and similarities in vision, approaches and implementation mechanisms for embedding SDGs across local strategies, action plans and programs. Thus, the main aim is to provide a first detailed insight of the implementation strategies for SDGs in Italy and to contribute to the growing knowledge in the field of strategic and operational planning related to sustainable development.

Keywords: 2030 agenda · Sustainability assessment · SDGs implementation · Strategy for sustainable development · Subnational policies

1 Introduction

In 2015, the 17 Sustainable Development Goals (SDGs) of the UN 2030 Agenda [1], provided a unified framework for addressing the main global challenges such as poverty, climate change, food security, economic crisis, resource scarcity, environmental degradation, and biodiversity loss.

These universal goals can be achieved by each member state through a process of SDGs localization that allows to move from global to the national and subnational levels of government [2–4]. The 2030 Agenda, in fact, recognise the central role of the local action in addressing sustainable development and, therefore, in SDGs progress. Thus, «despite the need for global outcomes, most implementation will be local» ([5], p. 1483). The importance of context-specific indicators has been highlighted by many academics

O. Gervasi et al. (Eds.): ICCSA 2022 Workshops, LNCS 13379, pp. 627–638, 2022.
https://doi.org/10.1007/978-3-031-10545-6_42

and practitioners [6–13] that have also highlighted influence that the local action can have in shaping the global [12, 14].

Italy is one of the 193 world Countries that have signed the 2030 Agenda in September 2015 and after just over two years, on the 22 December 2017, the Italian government has approved their National Strategy for Sustainable Development (NSSD) [15] as the main tool for the implementation of the SDGs within the Italian territory for the period 2017/2030 [16].

The NSSD established a set of strategic priorities and objectives, articulated into the five pillars of 2030 Agenda (People, Planet, Prosperity, Peace, and Partnership) which must be pursued by Italian subnational governments – Regions and Autonomous Provinces with law-making powers – through local adapted policy and interventions [17–19]. Through a cascade mechanism, subnational governments are accountable for developing local strategies based on specific local priorities and for the setting-up related indicators to measure and monitor their progress towards SDGs.

Since 2018 and 2019, the Italian Ministry of the Environment and Protection of the Territory and the Sea (now Ministry for Ecological Transition) has supported through specific collaboration agreements Regions and Autonomous Provinces in the development of their own local strategies and in the definition of a regulatory framework consistent with the financial framework of the European Cohesion Policy for the 2021–2027 programming period [20], one of the main economic tools for the implementation of NSSD [21–23].

Until now, among the 20 Regions and two Autonomous Provinces (Trento and Bolzano) into which the Trentino Alto-Adige Region is divided, 11 subnational Strategies are formally approved (Bolzano, Emilia-Romagna, Lazio, Liguria, Lombardia, Marche, Piemonte, Sardinia, Toscana, Trento, Veneto) and 10 are under development (Abruzzo, Basilicata, Calabria, Campania, AR Friuli Venezia Giulia, Molise, Puglia, Sicilia, Umbria, Valle D'Aosta) [24].

This study analyzes and compares four of these strategies – Liguria and Marche Regions, Autonomous Region of Sardinia and Autonomous Province of Trento – that provide a significant sample of the strategies approved so far, to evaluate similarities and differences in the SDGs implementation.

Thus, encompassing the universal nature of the 2030 Agenda, the main aim of this study is to contribute to advancing knowledge about different approaches and actions carried out by subnational governments for the adaptation of global goals to local realities and contexts.

2 Methodology

2.1 Data Collection

This study analyses and compares four selected Strategies for Sustainable Development elaborated by different Italian subnational governments (see Table 1).

Table 1. The characteristics of the four selected Italian subnational governments.

Local government	Inhabitants (2021)	Surface (km2)	Density (inh/km2)	Municipalities
Liguria Region	1.518.495	5.416,15	280,36	234
Marche Region	1.498.236	9.401,18	159,37	225
Autonomous Region of Sardinia	1.590.044	24.099,45	65,98	377
Autonomous Province of Trento	542.166	6.206,87	87,35	166

These strategies are easily comparable with one another regarding their structures, implementation mechanisms and monitoring procedures (see Fig. 1 and Table 2).

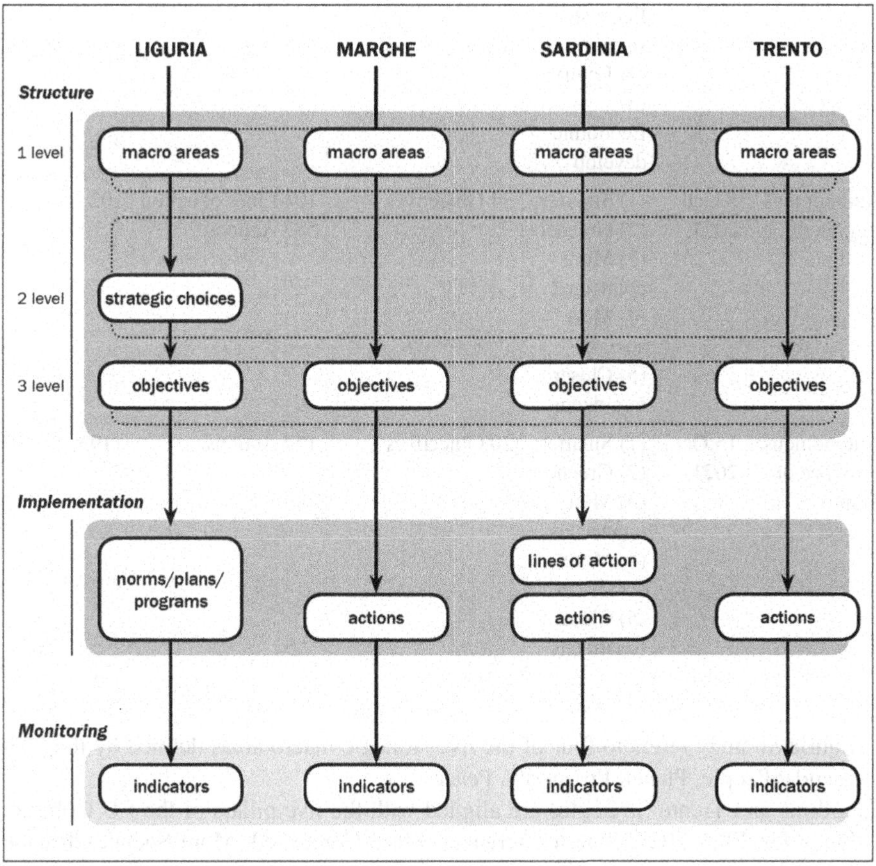

Fig. 1. A graphic representation of the structure and contents of the selected strategies.

Each of the four strategies is articulated in strategic macro-areas:

Table 2. The four selected Italian subnational Strategies for Sustainable Development: structure, implementation mechanisms and monitoring procedures (data sources: [25–29].

Subnational government	Date	Strategic macro areas	Implementation Choices/Themes/Objectives/Actions		Monitoring: Indicators
Liguria Region	29.Jen 2021	(1) People; (2) Planet; (3) Prosperity; (4) Pace	13 Choices 49 Objectives	369 Norms/ Plans/Programs	111
Marche Region	13.Dec 2021	(1) Resilience; (2) Climate change; (3) Ecosystem services; (4) Equity; (5) Economic develop	19 Objectives (+ 4 related to selected vectors of sustainability)	59 Actions (+ 31 related to selected vectors of sustainability)	98
Autonomous Region of Sardinia	8.Oct 2021	(1) Smarter; (2) Greener; (3) More connected; (4) More social; (5) Closer to citizens	34 Objectives	104 Lines of action 587 Actions	102
Autonomous Province of Trento	15.Oct 2021	(1) Smarter; (2) Greener; (3) More connected; (4) More social; (5) Closer to citizens	20 Objectives	177 Actions	119

- Liguria Strategy refers to four of the five strategic macro areas defined by the 2030 Agenda: People, Planet, Prosperity, Peace;
- Sardinia and Trento Strategies are aligned with the five pillars of the EU Cohesion Policy for 2021–2027: Smarter, Greener, More Connected, More Social, Closer to Citizens;
- Marche Strategy is structured into five region-specific macro-areas: Resilience; Climate change; Ecosystem services; Equity; Sustainable Economic development.

Each strategic macro-area (1 level) is divided in themes and/or strategic choices (2 level) and/or objectives (3 level). For each of these, implementation mechanisms (e.g., norms, plans, programs, actions) and procedures for monitoring the extent and impacts of these mechanisms (e.g., specific indicators) are provided.

These different structures and contents depend on subnational priorities derived from the data analysis provided by local "Positioning Reports" that provided a preliminary full assessment of the distance to the SDGs at regional or provincial level.

2.2 Data Analysis

This study analyses and compares a selection of Italian subnational Strategies for Sustainable Development. For each strategy it applies the following assessment criteria:

1. Systemic Vision: Are all SDGs addressed?
2. Balanced Approach: Have all SDGs the same weight?
3. Implementation: Are all SDGs associated with an adequate number of objectives?

To this end, for each selected strategy we used descriptive statistics to evaluate:

- Which SDGs are addressed by different macro-areas;
- How many SDGs was addressed in different strategic macro-areas;
- How often each SDGs was addressed by different objectives in relation to the total number of objectives defined by each strategy. This assessment was carried out on the basis of information and data provided by official documents (see "data source" column in Table 2).

3 Results and Discussion

3.1 Systemic Vision of SDGs

All 17 SDGs were addressed only by one of the five selected Italian subnational Strategies (Sardinia), while one of these (Marche) doesn't consider the SDG 16 "Peace, Justice and Strong Institutions" and other two (Liguria and Trento) don't consider the SDG 17 "Partnership for the Goals" (see Fig. 2).

However, these two SDGs are implicitly linked to all Strategies because these are developed through a multi-stakeholder consultation process that leaded to different Public Administrations, private-owned organizations and citizens working together to define a shared vision and corresponding strategies (Target 17.7), accommodating competing interests and enhancing policy coherence for sustainable development (Target 17.14). Thus, this "global partnership for sustainable development" allowed to mobilize and share knowledge, expertise, and financial resources to support the achievement of the SDGs (Target 17.16) and to develop effective, accountable, and transparent public institutions (Target 16.6). Only the Sardinia Strategy has evaluated the contribution of all strategic macro-areas in the achievement of SDG 16 and 17.

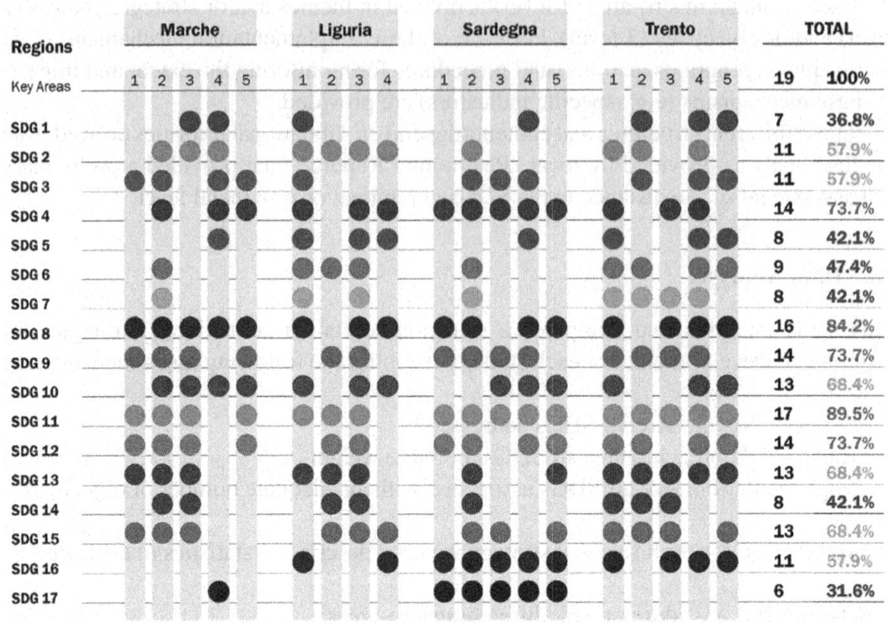

Fig. 2. Interrelations between SDGs and the subnational Strategies: a detailed overview of the different Goals which are associated to each strategic macro area of the four selected subnational strategies (graphically indicated with coloured dots) and the overall relevance of single SDGs expressed in number and in percentage. (Color figure online)

3.2 Balanced Approach to SDGs

The analysis of the four selected Strategies reveals different weights that are given to various SDGs (see Fig. 2). Overall, the SDG 11 "Sustainable Cities and Communities" (89.5%) and the SDG 8 "Decent work and economic growth" (84.2%) are the most prevailing goals. All the five macro-areas of the Marche Strategy contribute to achieve the SDG 8 and all the five macro-areas of Sardinia and Trento Strategies the SDG 11.

With 73.7% SDG 4 "Quality Education", SDG 9 "Industry Innovation and Infrastructure" and SDG 12 "Responsible production and Consumption" are in an intermediate position. All the five macro-areas of the Sardinia Strategy have an impact on the SDG 4. In addition to the SDG 17 already discussed above, the SDG 1 "No Poverty" (36.8%), the SDG 5 "Gender Equality", the SDG 7 "Clean Water and Sanitation" and the SDG 14 "Life below Water" are among the goals that are less addressed by all strategies. Compared to the others, the Trento Strategy seems to make the greater effort to achieve these SDGs.

3.3 SDGs Implementation

Overall, most objectives outlined by selected strategies, have an impact on SDG 11: about the 79% in the Marche Strategy, 35% in Trento Strategy and the 26.5% in Liguria and Sardinia strategies (see Table 3).

Table 3. Summary of metrics deduced from confusion matrices in cases of supervised classification

Strategic Macro areas	SDGs	1	2	3	4	5	6	7	8	9	10	11	12	13	14	15	16	17
LIGURIA	Objectives Tot: 49	10%	18%	10%	14%	26%	22%	6%	20%	12%	12%	26%	18%	6%	14%	22%	12%	0%
(1) People	10	5	4	5	3	7	4	1	2		3	2					1	
(2) Planet	17		2				6			1		7	2	2	3	9		
(3) Prosperity	16		3		2	2	1	2	7	5	1	4	7	1	4	1		
(4) Pace	6				2	4			1		2					1	5	
MARCHE	Objectives Tot: 19	17%	21%	42%	21%	5%	17%	5%	42%	40%	21%	79%	63%	37%	17%	42%	0%	5%
(1) Resilience	4			3					2	2		4	2	3		2		
(2) Climate	5			2			2	1		1		5	5	3	1	3		
(3) Ecosystem	4	1	3				1		2	1	1	3	3	1	2	3		
(4) Equity	3	2	1	2	2	1			2	1	2	2						1
(5) Economic	3			1	2				2	1	1	2	2					
SARDINIA	Objectives Tot: 34	3%	6%	29%	29%	15%	6%	9%	44%	35%	23.5%	26%	38%	15%	15%	29%	26%	38%
(1) Smarter	4				1				4	2		1	1				2	2
(2) Greener	13		2	3	2		2	3	2	4		1	8	4	5	8		3
(3) Connected	4			2	2				1	3	3	3				1	1	2
(4) Social	9	1		5	4	5			5	3	4	3	1				2	4
(5) Closer	4				1				3		1	1	3	1		1	4	2
TRENTO	Objectives Tot: 20	45%	30%	20%	30%	50%	25%	25%	50%	40%	20%	35%	30%	55%	20%	45%	30%	0%
(1) Smarter	5	2	1		2	2	1	1	5	1	1	2	2	2	2	3	1	
(2) Greener	4	1	1	1			2	1		1		2	1	4	1	4		
(3) Connected	2				1			2	1	1		1		2	1	1	1	
(4) Social	6	3	4	3	3	6	1	1	3	1	5	1	2	2			2	
(5) Closer	3	3		1		2	1		1		3	1	1	1		1	2	

After SDG 11, the goals accorded the most importance are SDG 8, SDG 9, SDG 12 and SDG 15 "Life on land". Besides these goals, SDG 3 "Good health and Well-being", SDG 4 and SDG 5 "Gender Equality" and SDG 13 "Climate Action". Finally, SDG 1 and SDG 16 in Trento and SDG 17 in Sardinia (see Table 3).

Furthermore, the analysis shows the integrated nature of many subnational objectives that allow to achieve different goals, according to the interrelated nature of SDGs. The number of SDGs related to a single subnational objective varies from one to nine.

In the Trento Strategy one of 20 total objectives is linked with nine SDGs, 5 to seven SDGs and 8 to five SDGs.

In the Marche Strategy five of 19 total objectives are linked with six SDGs, 4 with five SDGs and 6 with four SDGs, while only 4 objectives with three or two SDGs.

In the Sardinia Strategy 11 objectives of the 34 totals are linked with five SDGs, 13 with four SDGs; only 4 are related with two SDGs.

In Liguria only 4 objectives of the 49 totals are linked with five SDGs and 3 with 4 SDGs, most of these (respectively 17 and 15) are related with 3 or 2 SDGs and 10 with a single SDG.

4 Discussion and Conclusions

Subnational strategies for Sustainable Development can play a key role to achieve all 17 SDGs at subnational level. Nevertheless, in different regional or provincial contexts certain SDGs are addressed and prioritized more than others. As shown by the results presented in Sect. 3, the four Italian subnational strategies assign different importance to specific SDGs for delivering local needs and the major environmental, economic, social, and political concerns, as highlighted in Fig. 3.

Considering the strategic macro-areas, the most prevailing goals are the SDG 2 in Liguria, SDG 8 in Marche, SDG 11 and SDGs 13 in Trento, while in Sardinia several goals – SDGs 4, 11, 16 and 17 – have the same importance. In general Liguria and Trento strategies present an equilibrate balance between different goals while the differences are more evident in Marche and Sardinia strategies. If instead considering the objectives, differences between SDGs are low in Liguria strategy (range from 6% to 27%), greater in Sardinia (range from 6% to 44%) and Trento (range from 20% to 50%) strategies, and more pronounced in Marche strategy (range from 5% to 79%).

The study described in this paper starts with the data collection and the analysis of a representative sample of Italian subnational strategies. Although the sampling was limited to four strategies, in fact, their complex articulation and the significant number of macro-areas and objectives included in the analysis nevertheless offer a first comprehensive review on the status of SDGs implementation in Italy conducted by subnational governments. It addresses the three research questions that are aimed at creating a comprehensive understanding of different approaches, structures and actions towards SDGs by verifying if all SDGs: (1) are addressed by each strategy; (2) have the same weight in different strategic macro areas; (3) are associated with a high or low number of objectives.

The findings of this study highlight differences and similarities in the way that sub-national governments interpret and translate SDGs into operational actions towards achieving local objectives. The participatory approach adopted by regional and provincial administrations, in fact, creates an opportunity to meet local needs more effectively, and allows to increase the responsiveness of public investments to local priorities using clear objectives and measures [30–32].

Furthermore, these results could be useful to address further questions on SDGs implementation also in other subnational contexts. SDGs, in fact, are a common basis for tackling many global issues and a shared framework for sustainability reporting and accounting which can be easily adapted to different territorial realities with their own characteristics and dynamics.

The overview of the different strategies that we have presented, on one hand, constitutes a guide for evidence-based monitoring and impact assessment of subnational

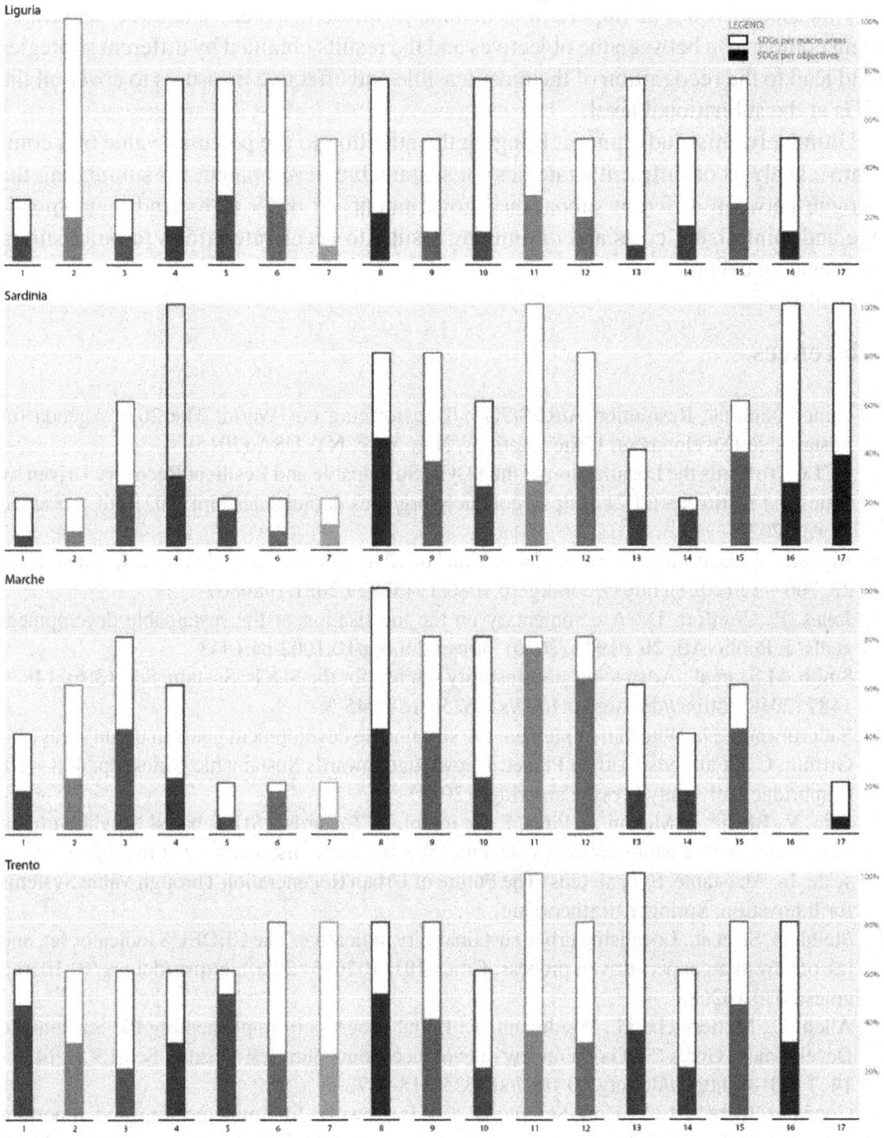

Fig. 3. Relation between SDGs and the macro areas and objectives of different strategies, the values are expressed in percentage (based on data in Fig. 2 and Table 3).

initiatives (policies, programs, plans and projects) that indicates what we are doing and what we should do for orienting the decision-making process towards SDGs. On the other hand, this articulated whole suggests a set of different "best practices" that can be revised and applied to other territorial realities to achieve specific SDGs, allowing for innovative solutions.

This aspect would be important to include in future research. The direct and transparent comparison between the objectives and the results obtained by different strategies could lead to the recognition of the most feasible and effective measures to cover all the SDGs at the subnational level.

Ultimately, this study aims at bringing the attention to the potential value of a comparative analysis of different strategies for sustainable development for stimulating the dialogue between different subnational governments in order to expand their knowledge and minimizing costs and optimizing results to accelerate efforts to build strong governance mechanisms.

References

1. United Nations: Resolution A/RES/70/1. Transforming our World: The 2030 Agenda for Sustainable Development. United Nations, New York, NY, USA (2015)
2. UCLG: Towards the Localization of the SDGs. Sustainable and Resilient Recovery Driven by Cities and Territories (2021). https://gold.uclg.org/sites/default/files/hlpf_2021.pdf. Accessed 10 Apr 2022
3. Biggeri, M.: Editorial: a "Decade for Action" on SDG localisation. J. Hum. Dev. Capabilities **22**, 706–712 (2021). https://doi.org/10.1080/19452829.2021.1986809
4. Jones, P., Comfort, D.: A commentary on the localisation of the sustainable development goals. J. Public Aff. **20**, e1943 (2020). https://doi.org/10.1002/pa.1943
5. Smith, M.S., et al.: Advancing sustainability science for the SDGs. Sustain. Sci. **13**(6), 1483–1487 (2018). https://doi.org/10.1007/s11625-018-0645-3
6. Satterthwaite, D.: Who can implement the sustainable development goals in urban areas? In: Griffith, C., et al. (eds.) Urban Planet: Knowledge towards Sustainable Cities, pp. 408–410. Cambridge University Press, Cambridge (2018)
7. Saiu, V., Blečić, I., Meloni, I., Piras, F., Scappini, B: Towards a SDGs based Neighbourhood Sustainability Evaluation Framework: a tool for assessing sustainability at the urban microscale. In: Abastante, F., et al. (eds) The Future of Urban Regeneration Through Value Systems for Innovation. Springer (forthcoming)
8. Steiniger, S., et al.: Localising urban sustainability indicators: The CEDEUS indicator set, and lessons from an expert-driven process. Cities **101**, 102683 (2020). https://doi.org/10.1016/j.cities.2020.102683
9. Allen, C., Metternicht, G., Wiedmann, T.: Initial progress in implementing the Sustainable Development Goals (SDGs): a review of evidence from countries. Sustain. Sci. **13**(5), 1453–1467 (2018). https://doi.org/10.1007/s11625-018-0572-3
10. González-Torre, P.L., Suárez-Serrano, E.: A framework for implementing and reporting United Nations sustainable development goals in Spanish higher education institutions. Int. J. Sustain. Higher Educ. (2022). ahead-of-print: https://doi.org/10.1108/IJSHE-03-2021-0118
11. United Nations: Compendium of National Institutional Arrangements for implementing the 2030 Agenda for Sustainable Development. United Nations, New York (2019)
12. Jiménez-Aceituno, A., Peterson, G.D., Norström, A.V., Wong, G.Y., Downing, A.S.: Local lens for SDG implementation: lessons from bottom-up approaches in Africa. Sustain. Sci. **15**(3), 729–743 (2019). https://doi.org/10.1007/s11625-019-00746-0
13. Croese, S., Green, C., Morgan, G.: Localizing the sustainable development goals through the lens of urban resilience: lessons and learnings from 100 resilient cities and cape town. Sustainability 12 (2020)

14. European Commission: Delivering the Sustainable Development Goals at local and regional level (2018). https://ec.europa.eu/info/sites/default/files/delivering-sdgs-local-regional-level.pdf. Accessed 21 Jul 2021
15. MATTM: Strategia Nazionale per lo Sviluppo Sostenibile (2017). https://www.mite.gov.it/sites/default/files/archivio_immagini/Galletti/Comunicati/snsvs_ottobre2017.pdf. Accessed 11 Apr 2022
16. Khussamov, R., Galiy, E., Anisimov, E., Ershova, L., Nemkov, D.: National Strategies for Sustainable Development G-7: Trends 2010–2020. In: E3S Web of Conferences. EDP Sciences, Les Ulis, France (2020)
17. Saiu, V., Blečić, I., Cocco, G., Meloni, I.: Urban Sustainability and SDGs Implementation between Regional strategy and Local Practice: Case of Sardinia. In: Filho, W.L. (ed.) SDGs in the European Region. Springer (forthcoming)
18. Saiu, V., Blečić, I., Meloni, I.: Making sustainability development goals (SDGs) operational at suburban level: potentials and limitations of neighbourhood sustainability assessment tools. Environ. Impact Assess. Rev. 96 (2022). https://doi.org/10.1016/j.eiar.2022.106845
19. Richiedei, A., Pezzagno, M.: Territorializing and monitoring of sustainable development goals in Italy: an overview. Sustainability **14**, 3056 (2022). https://doi.org/10.3390/su14053056
20. European Commission: EU cohesion policy: Priorities for 2021–2027 (2021). https://ec.europa.eu/regional_policy/en/policy/how/priorities. Accessed 19 Jan 2022
21. Cavalli, L., et al.: Sustainable development goals and the European Cohesion Policy: an application to the autonomous Region of Sardinia. J. Urban Ecol. **7** (2021). https://doi.org/10.1093/jue/juab038
22. Cavalli, L., et al.: The contribution of the European cohesion policy to the 2030 agenda: an application to the autonomous Region of Sardinia. SSRN Journal (2020). https://doi.org/10.2139/ssrn.3706003
23. Assumma, V., Datola, G., Mondini, G.: New cohesion policy 2021–2027: the role of Indicators in the assessment of the SDGs targets performance. In: Gervasi, O., et al. (eds.) ICCSA 2021. LNCS, vol. 12955, pp. 614–625. Springer, Cham (2021). https://doi.org/10.1007/978-3-030-87007-2_44
24. AsviS: I territori e gli Obiettivi di sviluppo sostenibile (2021). https://asvis.it/public/asvis2/files/Rapporto_ASviS/Rapporto_2021/Rapporto_ASviSTerritori2021.pdf. Accessed 26 Jan 2022
25. Provincia Autonoma di Trento: Strategia Provinciale per lo Sviluppo Sostenibile (2021). https://agenda2030.provincia.tn.it/content/download/8212/151863/file/SproSS%20def_15.10.2021.pdf. Accessed 4 Jan 2022
26. Regione Marche: Strategia Regionale per lo Sviluppo Sostenibile (2021)
27. Regione Autonoma della Sardegna: Sardegna2030. La Strategia della Regione Sardegna per lo Sviluppo Sostenibile (2021). https://delibere.regione.sardegna.it/protected/57127/0/def/ref/DBR57095/. Accessed 4 Oct 2021
28. Regione Autonoma della Sardegna: Sardegna2030. Report di posizionamento Obiettivi di Sviluppo Sostenibile Agenda 2030 ONU (2021). https://delibere.regione.sardegna.it/protected/57127/0/def/ref/DBR57095/
29. Regione Liguria: Strategia regionale per lo Sviluppo sostenibile (2019). https://www.regione.liguria.it/homepage/ambiente/sviluppo-sostenibile/strategia-regionale-sviluppo-sostenibile.html. Accessed 29 Mar 2022
30. Saiu, V.: The three pitfalls of sustainable city: a conceptual framework for evaluating the theory-practice gap. Sustainability **9**, 2311 (2017). https://doi.org/10.3390/su9122311

31. Saiu, V.: Evaluating outwards regeneration effects (OREs) in neighborhood-based projects: a reversal of perspective and the proposal for a new tool. Sustainability **12**, 10559 (2020). https://doi.org/10.3390/su122410559
32. Blečić, I., Saiu, V.: Il futuro della rendita (ripetere Sullo). Archivio di Studi Urbani e Regionali (2020). https://doi.org/10.3280/ASUR2020-129-S1001

Small Frontier Islands in the Clean Energy Transition Era_ Emerging Patterns and Planning Approaches

Yiota Theodora(✉) and Sotiris Piperis

Department of Urban and Regional Planning, School of Architecture, National Technical University of Athens, Athens, Greece
ptheodora@arch.ntua.gr, sotirispiperis@yahoo.gr

Abstract. In the climate crisis era, energy security or even more autonomy is critical in developmental policies of countries worldwide. This crisis, coupled with the recent geopolitical crisis in Europe and its socio-economic repercussions, calls for dedicated national strategies in support of the transition towards a carbon-free economy, largely based on domestic energy networks that utilize renewable sources (RES/MRE). Islands, in this respect, are of particular concern, as fragile natural-cultural and anthropogenic ecosystems, already under multiple pressures due to urban sprawl, over-concentration of land/maritime activities and mass tourism, all largely intensifying peak energy demand pattern. Having Aegean small frontier islands as a study reference, the article explores their energy dynamics and sketches restrictions in clean energy transition set by the scale and specificities of insular vulnerable locales. Towards this end, current conditions and trends are evaluated; and a spatial energy database is produced for serving typological classification of islands. The latter is based on a multifactorial approach for assessing small islands' energy autonomy and degree of RES/MRE utilization; identifying main factors of their energy diversification; and unveiling critical issues to be addressed in renewable energy planning. The proposed methodology aspires to step forward the discussion on sustainable energy transition of insular territories in the Mediterranean Region and beyond.

Keywords: Sustainable energy development and planning · Renewable energy sources · Green and blue infrastructures · Low-carbon energy transition policies · Insular regions and communities · Small islands

1 Setting the Stage

At a time of climate crisis and energy poverty, states across the world seek to ensure their energy autonomy and reinforce their position in strong energy networks. To this end, the policy objective is to develop sustainable national strategies for the transition to a zero carbon economy through the development of domestic energy production networks for the use of renewable energy sources [1, 2]. Nevertheless, achieving energy neutrality in practice remains an intractable issue for two main reasons. On the one hand, the

O. Gervasi et al. (Eds.): ICCSA 2022 Workshops, LNCS 13379, pp. 639–656, 2022.
https://doi.org/10.1007/978-3-031-10545-6_43

dominant countries generating and exporting polluting energy do not intend to lose the lead even if they use clean energy at national level. On the other hand, energy-dependent countries (regardless of population size and prosperity level) lack to secure their energy independence mainly due to their increased needs (e.g. intense urbanisation, transport hubs, entrepreneurship), or failure (technological, legislative, etc.) to utilise their existing domestic sources and/or discover new forms of energy. The former case includes mainly developed countries with strong administration and infrastructure centres, while the latter concerns countries with a low technological development index that are in the process of productive reconstruction and/or modernization of their national administration, development, planning and legislation systems. In Europe, specifically, which is the broader field of the pilot focus area, the former case includes mostly the developed northern countries, while the latter includes the EUMed9 countries of eastern basin. Greece, Cyprus and Malta demonstrate special research interest due to their cross-border character; abundant natural and cultural wealth; vulnerable national economies; and the new development challenges they face in the context of global competition in the shipping and tourism sectors, which intensify their energy requirements [3–6].

Against the backdrop of intense political, social and economic upheavals at global level and they geopolitical uncertainty they induce to countries at national level, increased concerted efforts to prevent the looming ecological catastrophe -most recently at the UN Climate Change Conference (COP26, Glasgow 31.10. 2021)- have brought back to the forefront of political and scientific discussions at international level the need to change the current energy model [7]. This finding is becoming more critical following the dramatic developments in Eastern Europe and the broader SE Mediterranean region, which confirm: a) the failure to use gas as a sustainable and socially just 'transition bridge' from conventional to renewable energy sources; and b) the dependence of countries' energy transition on strong global investment interests. Through the aggravation of inequalities this causes across spatial levels, there are constant disruptions to the global energy map with a variety of consequences on the development dynamics as well as territorial/socio-economic cohesion of the countries and their regions, regardless of whether they are energy-dominant or dependent. In these extremely adverse conditions, the search for new forms of clean energy and innovative methods/technologies to use them, as well as the formulation of flexible alternative transition scenarios, pose challenges for states [8–10]. In this respect, hydrogen is already promoted as the new energy key of the 21st century, due to its fuel and energy storage capacity, while the use of marine renewable energy (MRE) is seen as the solution for the energy neutrality of coastal and island countries [11–13].

In a climate of intense concern, the energy transition of island areas (i.e. states, regions, islands) poses special research interest, mainly due to their differences in scale, structure, dynamics and needs (i.e. surface, spatial fragmentation/dispersion, climatic specificities, fragility of natural- cultural- anthropogenic ecosystems and landscapes, urbanization characteristics, density and seasonality of habitation, type of activities and degree of over-concentration on land and at sea, quality of technical/ social infrastructure, tourism development, dependence on mainland areas, etc.) [14]. These diversifications, due to a number of spatio-functional and socio-economic factors, affect the energy requirements of island regions and their variations during the year (*seasonality*) [15,

16]. At the same time, the above diversifications raise the issue of energy autonomy, especially in remote island regions with adverse climatic conditions (e.g. the Azores and Iceland in the North Atlantic ocean, Mauritius and Reunion in the Indian ocean), but also in countries with many islands and a strong concentration of small remote and border islands that are inhabited (e.g. Sweden and Greece). The diversity of island regions introduces different conditions, priorities and constraints in their energy transition process. This makes it necessary to address specifically the energy planning of insular regions and islands in the framework of national development and energy policies. The specificity of island regions has been recognised at EU level [17–23]. Hence, the relevant debate on their energy transition is constantly enriched with new initiatives in the broader EU policy framework for climate and energy neutrality[1]. These initiatives refer not only to island states, but also to countries with an island part [i.e. insular regions (NUTS2), islands NUTS3)]. Small islands are highly interesting mainly due to the strong emigration trend of their inhabitants, and the various pressures they face from their urbanization/conversion into 'pockets' of tourism development and/or energy utilization [24–26]. Greece, although intensely insular with a significant number of small islands, still lacks an integrated clearly formulated policy on energy modernization.

Given the ongoing climate and energy crises, the main question is: *how should the energy transition of islands be conducted so as to ensure their energy autonomy without threatening the local identity and carrying capacity of their natural-cultural-anthropogenic ecosystems and landscapes*? The answer is sought in the selection of a sustainable energy model. Thus, the dilemma is whether the energy transition of islands should be aimed at meeting their local needs/demands, or satisfying wider scale requirements (inter-regional, national, supranational). Undoubtedly, the choice will affect the sustainability, resilience, and competitiveness of these fragile locales. Thus, the energy planning challenge is *how to prevent any environmental and socio-economic impact on the islands to be exploited for energy* (RES/MRE).

Focusing our study on the small frontier Greek Aegean islands, this article attempts to contribute to the discussion at a critical time for the country and the world. That is, in the context of the intended withdrawal from polluting forms of energy, where pressures for immediate use of RES/MRE can degrade the island environment unless there is an integrated energy policy encompassing protection, sustainability and social justice [17, 21]. In this context, the objective is to assess the energy dynamics of small border islands and to identify the favourable/constraining factors for their energy transition-autonomy [23, 25]. To this end, fifteen islands were selected with a view to recording, mapping and evaluating existing energy conditions/trends per island. The above process results in a pool of spatial and energy data that is then used for their typological classification. It is supported that research shall be implemented on the basis of a multifactorial approach in order to: a) assess the energy autonomy of the islands and the degree of

[1] EU Legislation on Energy Transition (Laws/Directives] 1997–2021: COM(1997)599; COM(2006)105; COM(2007)575; L.2008/56/EC; COM(2008) 768; Renewable Energy L.2009/28/EC; Blue Growth COM(2012)494; Blue Energy COM(2014)8; COM(2014)254; EUCO/169/14; Climate Change Policy COM (2015)80; COM(2018)773; European Climate Law (2018/1999/EU); 2018/2001/EU; European Green Deal (COM(2019)640); COM (2020)741; COM(2021)82; COM(2021)240.

RES/MRE utilization; b) identify the factors that have played a role in the evolution of their energy dynamics; c) highlight the critical issues that must be addressed in the national energy planning so as not to burden the small islands with the development of renewable sources. The proposed methodology enables various correlations among the selected criteria and can be applied applicability across spatial units; hence it can contribute to the recent debate on the sustainable energy transition of countries with an island part in the Mediterranean and beyond.

For the approach of the research object the article is organized in six sections. The first presents the research object; the second refers to the spatial field of study and the research methodology, the third describes the development and energy dynamics of Greek insular regions focusing on the small frontier islands of the Aegean; the fourth concerns the findings of the investigation, the fifth describes the proposed typological classification for islands, while the sixth expresses thoughts on a sustainable energy transition-autonomy for insular territories.

2 Methodological Steps and Sources

This research on the energy transition of the small frontier islands[2] of the Aegean is part of a wider ongoing study on the energy neutrality of the Greek island territory in a context of multifaceted crisis and evolving climate change. The Aegean small boarder islands were not selected by chance. The occasion was previous researches on the Greek island territory [14, 27], through which emerged: α) the complexity and vulnerability of insular regions and islands, as well as their specific dynamics, as a result of their particular geographical and spatial characteristics; and b) the existence ambiguities in the practices of RES/MRE utilisation and in the relevant national legislation. However, a key role was played by a study on small border islands of the Aegean and their typological classification on regional criteria, which can identify the specificities of these vulnerable areas, as well as their ability to function as both autonomous entities and hubs of broader island networks with supra-local reach [28]. This is because, this research highlighted the critical role of the characteristics and development prospects of small islands (especially those demonstrating geographical/socio-economic isolation and *seasonality*) in their integration into the international economic system, on the one hand, and in their energy transition and neutrality, on the other. The main causes are issues pertaining to scale, adequacy of resources and infrastructures, quality of natural-cultural-built environment/landscape, accessibility and networking, development orientation, inhabitation pattern, *seasonality*. Therefore, this research is used at this stage (after the necessary data updates and enrichment of the spatial sample/assessment criteria) as a 'basis' for the establishment of the wider framework conditions/trends within which the energy transition-autonomy of the small Aegean border islands will be assessed at local level. Specifically, regarding the research area, the criteria for assessing the development and energy dynamics of islands, and the process of their typological classification, the following are noted:

[2] In the absence of an official definition of small frontier island at national and European level the selection criteria were: a) an area of < 96 km^2 and a permanent population of $< 8{,}000$ inhabitants, b) islands constitute municipalities, and c) frontier islands are considered to be those bordering another country on at least one side [28].

Place of Reference: fifteen small Aegean border islands of different development - energy dynamics were selected. Islands per region (from north to south) are: North Aegean: Ag. Efstratios, Psara, Oinousses and Fournoi, South Aegean: Leros, Kasos, Symi, Tilos, Nisyros, Patmos, Halki, Lipsi, Agathonisi, Megisti, and Crete: Gavdos.

Assessment Criteria: their selection allows simultaneous understanding of the broader developmental and spatial context (qualities, vulnerability, and prospects) of islands, and more specifically their energy dynamics- autonomy. On this basis, a pool of assessment criteria established, falling into ten themes, namely: (i) geographical location [cross-border character (distance from neighbouring country], (ii) locus [i.e. surface area, density (inhabitants/km^2), geomorphology, climate], (iii) nature-culture [i.e. historic and memorial sites, natural-cultural heritage sites, protected areas], (iv) population [inhabitants and % population change (1991, 2001 and 2011)], (v) local economy - production sectors [primary, secondary, tertiary (% change by sector 2001–2011)], (vi) accessibility/networking (Multimodal Hub (MH: port and airport)], (vii) services/infrastructures of supralocal reach (administrative, technical, social), (viii) construction activity [number of buildings per island, rate of change (2001–2011)], (ix) tourism [indicators: ship/ferry passengers, overnight stay, full occupancy (2011–2020), and cruise passengers arrivals (2015–2020)], (x) energy [i.e. energy demand, energy consumption rate, production rate from conventional/renewable sources (2016–2020)]. The criteria are deliberately selected and can assess both the competitiveness and the rate of energy transition-autonomy of small border islands at the national and global level. The geographical location coupled with locus features and high quality services and infrastructures of supralocal reach bring out important specificities for islands' supralocal role. The population size indicates islands' dynamics, especially in combination with locus, local economy-production sectors, accessibility/networking and high quality services-infrastructures of supralocal reach. In addition, geographical location in combination with locus and nature-culture features can either favour or restrict islands' energy transition, as they can simultaneously meet energy demands, but also burden local identity and resilience due to the overexploitation of natural resources. Moreover, population especially coupled with local economy-production sectors, accessibility/networking, supralocal infrastructures, construction activity, and tourism may lead to increased energy demands (especially during peak seasons) with multiple effects to landscapes and biodiversity, as well as the environment. Finally, energy highly interacts with all other criteria, as it is affected by them and vice versa.

Research Process-Sources: for approaching the research object, the correlation of the criteria was done in two spatial levels (region, island) aiming at understanding: a) the broader geographical-administrative environment where the small islands interact with larger islands and continental areas, b) local peculiarities and the restrictions they set on islands' energy transition-autonomy. This was attempted by implementing two investigation procedures. The first investigation procedure pertained to the generation of six tables through the correlation of the proposed criteria [i.e. Table 1 [(i), (ii), (iii), (vii)]; Table 2 [(v), (vi)]; Table 3 [(v), (viii), (ix)]; Table 4 [(xi)]; Table 5 [(i), (vi)]; and Table 6 [(i), (ii), (iv), (x)]. The six tables provide data on administrative structure, while islands are presented by region and regional unit (from north to south), and by size, starting with the smallest in area. In the second procedure, the data of the above tables was correlated for the typological classification of the small islands according to their energy demands and the barriers they face in energy transition-autonomy. The main sources were EU texts and the current Greek institutional framework for insular/energy planning, as well as official databases of international, European and national bodies [29, 30]. The data has been processed using spatial analysis methods in a GIS environment.

Under conditions of an intense multifaceted crisis, the article aims at contributing to the relevant discussion by proposing a methodology to identify the factors that may affect energy transition and autonomy, in such a way that it can be used as a planning tool of energy policy at various territorial levels, while paving the way for subsequent re-evaluation of existing criteria for the selection/delimitation of RES/MRE areas.

3 Greek Insular Regions and Small Frontier Aegean Islands in Times of Energy Transition _ A Multifactorial Overview

In this section, the development and energy dynamics of the Greek insular regions are briefly presented focusing on the small boarder islands of the Aegean Sea based on a multifactorial approach of simultaneous monitory of the proposed criteria [(i)–(x)].

3.1 Identifying Local Characteristics and Developmental Dynamics

3.1a Greek Insular Regions

Greece is among the countries with the largest number of islands in the world. The multi-insular structure in concert with the fragmentation of its insular regions makes the Greek insular phenomenon quite unique [28]. The purely insular regions (15% of Greek territory/4 out of 13 administrative regions) constitute extremely complex spatio-functional entities of intense fragility and diverse dynamics due to the number of islands and their peculiarities. In particular, the Greek insular regions/islands of the Aegean (EU's external

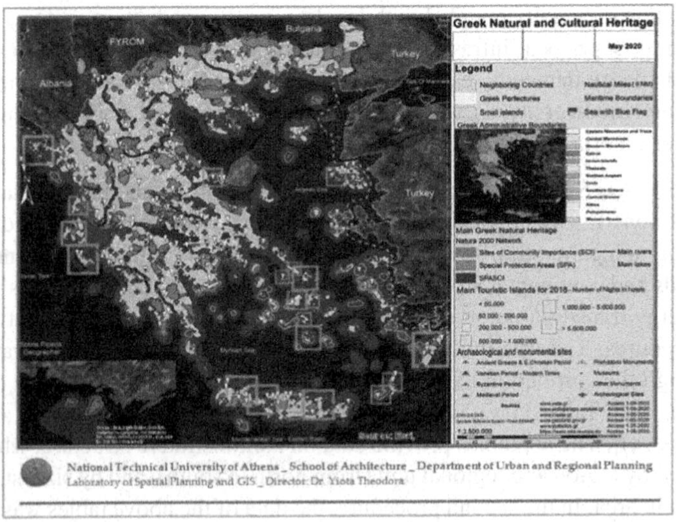

Fig. 1. Protected areas and natural - cultural heritage Sites in Greece [own elaboration]

borders) where issues of geopolitical importance, spatial discontinuity/heterogeneity - mainly in terms of expanse, identity, dynamics- coexist with incompatible activities and transnational networks (e.g. shipping, commerce, tourism, energy etc.), a concentration of natural-cultural wealth and unique landscapes/seascapes, as well as a pressure because of the strong migrant/refugee flows and the ever-increasing energy interest [14, 27] (Fig. 1).

Based on the assessment criteria, the following are briefly stated: a) South Aegean has the largest territorial fragmentation and the most significant concentration of small frontier islands; b) all insular regions are characterized by seismicity and have similar climatic conditions; especially those of the Aegean Sea which provide strong wind dynamic; c) South Aegean (5th and 1^{rst} place respectively in the national ranking), Crete (6th and 5th), North Aegean (11th and 7th) and the Ionian Islands (8th and 11th) have the most intense concentration of nature and culture protection areas (i.e. Natura, archaeological and historical sites, underwater culture heritage); d) North Aegean in total and parts of South Aegean (small frontier islands) face significant networking issues; e) low population increase (2001–2011) is noted in Crete (+4.83%) and South Aegean (+3.54%), whilst the North Aegean (−2.93%) loses its population; f) increase of tertiary sector (>24%) with simultaneous contraction of primary (−33% up to −49.79%) and secondary sector (−12% up to −15%) was detected. The primary/secondary sectors decreased mainly in North Aegean and the Ionian Islands, whilst the tertiary sector increases mainly in South Aegean (+37.91%) and the Ionian Islands (+32.55%); g) the rate of change in building stock (2001–2011) increases mainly in North Aegean and the Ionian Islands (+16.86% and +9.26% respectively); and h) indicators of overnight stays (>−52%), occupancy (>−29,5), and cruise (>−99,45%) (2011–2020) dramatically decline due to dramatic effects of the pandemic [28, 30].

3.1b Aegean Small Frontier Islands

When it comes to the small frontier islands of the Aegean, the following are noted [14, 28, 30]: a) Ag. Efstratios, Psara, Agathonisi and Lipsi are in a more unfavorable networking situation. Leros, Symi and Megisti provide ferry connections to Turkey, Oinousses and Patmos only during the summer; b) the majority of islands has an area <50 km^2, thus creating special conditions for their economy; c) the most intense wind dynamics is to be found in North Aegean, whilst the greatest depths are to be found in Patmos, Halki and Gavdos; d) all insular regions provide a rich natural and cultural heritage on land as well at sea and belong to the Natura network of protected areas. The biggest concentrations of such areas are to be found in Gavdos, Leros, Nisyros, Psara, Halki, Patmos, and Fournoi [30(f)] (Fig. 1); e) Leros is by far the island with the greatest population followed by the smaller (in area) islands of Patmos and Symi. The majority of islands (78.57%) have a population of <1500 inhabitants. The largest population increase (2001–2011) (>50%) was recorded in Gavdos (+88%), Halki (62%) and Tilos (50%), while islands that lost population were: Ag. Efstratios, Psara, Leros and Oinousses; f) the highest unemployment rates (>50%) (2001–2011) were noted in Halki, Psara, Leros, Ag. Efstratios, Kasos and Agathonisi, with the exception of Oinousses (60% reduction in unemployment). In primary sector an increase of > 50% was recorded in Megisti (250.0%) and Nisyros (53.3%), while a decrease (>50%) was recorded in Halki (−65.6%) and Fournoi (−50.0%). In the secondary sector an increase

>50% was recorded in: Gavdos (83.3%), Halki (58.3%), Oinousses (52.0%), while a decrease >30% was recorded in: Psara (−53.6%) and Ag. Efstratios (−35.0%). In the tertiary sector the increase exceeds >100% in Gavdos (311.1%), Halki (273.7%), Agathonisi (258.35%), Lipsi and Psara, while a decrease 30% was recorded in Fournoi and Patmos. Decreases in primary/secondary sectors are mainly associated with the contraction of residents and the strengthening of tourism; g) construction activity (mainly associated with tourism development) was increased in Fournoi (344.5%), Tilos (52.1%) and Agathonisi (51.1%), and a decrease >20% was recorded in Halki and Psara [30(a)].

In particular, when it comes to tourism development, regardless of the year 2020 when indicators were dramatically decreased due to the COVID-19 pandemic, islands with positive rates (>100%) of tourism growth (after 2011) were Gavdos, Megisti and Nisyros. Based on a) the rate of change of ferry passengers disembarking, the highest positive change was recorded by Gavdos, Megisti, Nisyros and Tilos, while the highest negative one by Symi (−57.30%), Halki (−26.74%), and Fournoi (−25.80%); b) the rate of change in hotels, a positive change >300% was recorded by Agathonisi and Gavdos, while a negative one by Kasos (−20.19%), Leros (−5.14%) and Patmos (−1.14%); c) the occupancy rate change, positive changes >30% were recorded by Nisyros, Megisti, Leros and Lipsi, while negative ones (>13%) by Psara, Tilos and Fournoi; and d) rate of change in cruise passenger arrivals (2015–2020): strong differentiation was found between Patmos (+574%) and Symi (−92%). The study of the indicators is of great importance as it highlights the types of tourism and consequently the pressure that islands encounter, their role in the local economy as well as the energy demands they cause [30(e)].

3.2 Monitoring Existing Energy Patterns _ Peculiarities and Perspectives

3.2a Greek Insular Regions

As regard spatial dependence of insular regions from the mainland of the country, the most interconnected regions (underwater networks) are the Ionian Islands (along with the regions of Epirus and Western Greece) and the northern Cyclades (Andros, Tinos, Mykonos, Kea, Gyaros, Syros, Paros) of South Aegean (along with the regions of Attica and Central Greece). On the other hand the regions of the Northern Aegean and Crete (in total) and northern Cyclades and Dodecanese Islands of the South Aegean belong to the non-interconnected islands due to their geographical location and spatial structure (i.e. polynesia, intense spatial dispersal, etc.). To meet the energy needs, the islands have local production stations that face several problems in their operation, especially those on the smaller and more remote islands. For this reason, there is a project aiming at the gradually interconnection of all islands by 2030 [30(d)].

Based on the official data of the Hellenic Statistical Authority (ELSTAT 2020), the dependence of insular regions on the utilization of polluting forms for energy production remains high. Greater dependence show, in descending order, the regions of Crete, S. Aegean, Ionian Islands, N. Aegean. As regard the RES utilization insular regions are at the bottom of the national ranking [Crete 10th, Ionian Islands 11th, S. Aegean 12th, N. Aegean 13th], while they do not harness MRE. An exception is Crete, where wave energy is harnessed in an experimental phase [30(a)].

As regard energy consumption and future demands, the highest annual energy consumption (2020) show, in descending order, the regions of Crete, South Aegean, Ionian Islands and North Aegean. The region ranking based on the % change in energy consumption (2016–2020) was: Crete (+5.2%), South Aegean (+4.7%), Ionian Islands (+2%) and North Aegean (+1.5%)]. Growth trends in energy consumption in regions of South Aegean, Ionian Islands and North Aegean is mainly attributed to tourism development and less to permanent resident population growth. This is also ascertained by the % changes of population [(2001–2011): South Aegean (+2.08%), North Aegean (+2.06%), Crete (+0.03%)]; construction activity [(2001–2011): South Aegean (+16.86%), Ionian Islands (+9.26%) and Crete (+0.03%)] and tourism [(2016–2020): South Aegean (+89.3%), Crete (+24.3%), North Aegean (+21.4%)] [30(a–e)].

3.2b Aegean Small Frontier Islands

The small border islands of the Aegean belong to non-interconnected islands to the national electricity network of the mainland. They have power plants, which however face significant adequacy issues and are energy dependent on neighboring larger islands, as follows: Ag. Efstratios energy dependent from Lemnos, Oinousses from Chios, Fournoi from Ikaria, Leros from Kalymnos, Kasos from Karpathos, Symi-Tilos-Halki from Rhodes, Nisyros from Kos, Patmos-Lipsi-Agathonisi from Kalymnos, Gavdos from Crete. Furthermore, during periods of increased demands (summer months) small islands are supplied by oil tankers [30 (b–d)].

In 2016–2020 period, islands with the higher electricity consumption increase were Gavdos (17%), Agathonisi (10.0%), Megisti (3.0%) and Symi (2.0%). The majority of the islands (Ag. Efstratios, Psara, Oinousses, Fournoi, Leros, Kasos, Tilos, Nisyros, Halki, and Lipsi) maintained a stable consumption, while a significant decrease is observed in Patmos (−22.0%) which is worth studying. In 2020 the rate of electricity generation from conventional forms was at 100% for 10 of the 15 islands (i.e. Ag. Efstratios, Oinousses, Fournoi, Kasos, Tilos, Nisyros, Halki, Lipsi, Agathonisi and Megisti). In the rest of islands it exceeded 80% [i.e. Gavdos (99.9%), Symi (98.3%), Psara (96.9%), Leros (96.2%), Patmos (83.7%)]. In these islands the participation rate of RES in electricity production was limited. Finally, there is no small frontier island harnessing MRE [30(b–d)] (Fig. 2).

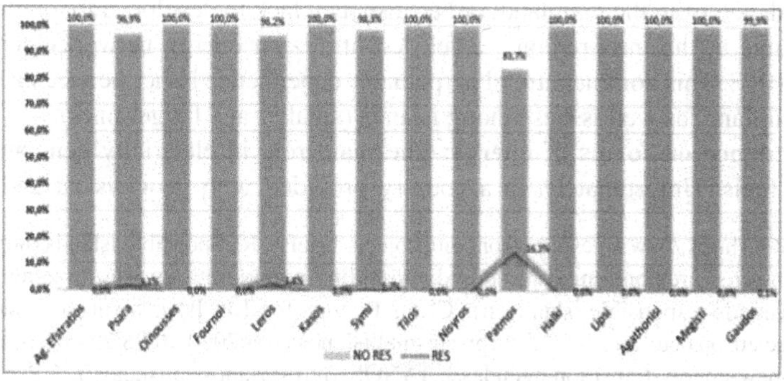

Fig. 2. Small Frontier Aegean Islands: Percentage of participation of conventional and renewable energy sources in electricity generation (2020) [30(b-d)]

Furthermore, for the assessment of the energy dynamic of small frontier islands the monitoring of energy dynamic indicators during the year is of particular interest. Through such a perspective, the multiplicity of effects of *insularity*, *seasonality* and *remoteness* on energy dynamics of islands and changing trends is ascertained. Thus, from the study of changes in the rate of energy consumption per quarter for the year 2020 it was ascertained that the highest prices were noted during 3rd and 4th quarter due to tourism. The monitoring of fluctuations among islands emerged from their rate of *seasonality*, as well as the supralocal character of tourism development.

As regard the future of energy transition, several of the under investigation small islands are found in proposals formulated at scientific/political levels. Among them, an indication reference is made to recent initiatives[3] promoted by the EU [e.g. NESOI (Nisyros, Tilos), RESponsible Islands (Tilos), Clean Energy for EU Islands (Halki, Kasos, Symi), IANOS (Nisyros)] and Greek government [GR-eco Islands (Halki)], as well as projects by private bodies in cooperation with Greek administration (central/decentralized) and research entities for the development of innovative technologies [e.g. MUSICA (Oinousses)] for the harnessing of RES/MRE in the context of smart sustainable development and the European Green Deal [2, 5, 6, 22, 23]. It is noted that Tilos is the first Greek small border island to develop an innovative model of energy autonomy through the utilization of solar-wind energy and battery energy storage awarded by the pan-European RESponsible Islands competition.

4 Conclusions Based on a Synthetic Approach of the Proposed Criteria

From the multi-criteria approach of the development and energy dynamics of insular regions and the small frontier islands of the Aegean emerged findings that highlight critical issues that must be addressed at a time of global climate-energy crisis and established absence of national insular and energy policy in Greece [14, 27, 28, 30]. In conclusion, the following are noted by thematic:

a. **Spatial dependence from the mainland and insular regions**: the rate of energy autonomy of islands is limited due to two reasons. Either because of their energy dependence from the mainland, or because they lack to develop autonomous energy structures at the intra-regional level decentralizing energy networks that harness RES/MRE. This dominant trend perpetuates dependence issues between islands and the mainland, as well issues among islands (smaller and bigger ones).
b. **Dependence on forms of energy**: The main role in electricity generation plays fossil fuels. Unfortunately, in a country provided with geophysical and climatic

[3] i.e. NESOI (https://www.nesoi.eu/content/projects-briefs), RESponsible Islands (https://ec.europa.eu/info/research-and-innovation/funding/funding-opportunities/prizes/prize-renewable-energy-islands-responsible-island_en), Clean Energy for EU Islands (https://clean-energy-islands.ec.europa.eu/ and https://europeansmallislands.com/2020/10/28/29-european-islands-publish-new-energy-transition-agendas/), IANOS (https://ianos.eu/islands/), GR-eco Islands (https://ypen.gov.gr/i-chalki-ginetai-to-proto-gr-eco-island/), MUSICA (https://musica-project.eu/).

comparative advantages the harnessing of RES is still limited, whilst that of MRE is absent.

c. **Energy consumption and new demands**: Differentiations are found both between regions and at the intra-regional level (between islands). The highest consumption and growth trends are found in regions that include islands with a significant population size, which simultaneously function as gateways, supra-local tourist destinations and enclaves of development activities in primary/secondary sector (Crete, South Aegean). Moreover, lower consumption with significant fluctuations due to *seasonality* are presented by insular regions of islands of small population size, with weaknesses in their productive structure and low tourism development (mainly in North Aegean and less in the Ionian Islands). At intra-regional level, the highest energy consumption/demands are found in developed islands, but also in less developed ones that experience tourism development (regardless of their surface area and the size of their population). To this category belong several small frontier islands of the Aegean. Examples are Gavdos, Agathonisi and Megisti, due to the significant population growth (>22%) in 2001–2011 combined with the positive percentage changes in tourism in the last 10 years (>14%) in construction activity and other sectors of production (2001–2011) [i.e. primary: Megisti (250%); secondary: >50% in Gavdos; tertiary: >100% in Gavdos and Agathonisi] [30].

Based on the above, findings of general and more specific interest which could be utilized in the development of sustainable energy policy are emerged for: a) the establishment of necessary context of planning principles and guidelines and the approached methodology (phases and assumptions), b) the selection of assessment criteria and how they are correlated, c) the prioritization of energy transition options (typological classification/hierarchy of islands based on existing energy needs as well as their changing trends). In particular, it is ascertained that:

- Energy demands of islands vary depending on the degree of *insularity* [territorial fragmentation (type/intensity), spatial/socio-economic isolation and networking, local economy], *seasonality* (permanent population, multifunctionality, etc.), and *remoteness* (geographic position, connection with the mainland/insular regions). Crucial parameters in the differences in consumption between insular regions and islands in particular are: population size (inhabitants/visitors), type and number of activities and infrastructures and level of tourism development.
- The increase in quantitative indicators associated with population, local economic activity and infrastructures of supralocal reach [i.e. (iv), (v), (vi), (vii), (viii), (ix)] variously affect the energy requirements [(x)] of insular regions and islands.
- The type and intensity of the correlation of criteria related to the local economy and supra-local infrastructures [i.e. (v), (vi), (vii), (ix)] may have simultaneously positive (i.e. enhancing competitiveness by limiting *seasonality*) and negative (i.e. increasing pressures on natural-built environment and carrying capacity) effects on islands' sustainability and resilience. This raises the issue of choosing energy patterns depending on the specifics of islands.

- Criteria related to specific characteristics, local identity and carrying capacity of the natural-cultural-anthropogenic ecosystems of the islands [(ii), (iii)], especially in combination with criteria that affect their accessibility and networking [(i), (vi)] can be favorable (e.g.geomorphology, climate) or restrictive (e.g. protection areas, landscape) in their energy transition - autonomy, mainly in smaller (surface area, population size, range of local economy) and frontier islands (spatial and socio-economic isolation).

5 The Typological Classification of Islands as a Means of a More Sustainable Energy Transition

In this section, the small boarder islands are included in energy priority categories, based on the findings for their development (i.e. local identity, economy) and energy dynamics (energy transition-autonomy, new demands), as well as their evolutionary trends (risks/prospects). Thus, the proposed criteria [(i)–(x)] are related in the context of two main assumptions. The first assumption supports the importance of taking into account the parameters that affect the energy demands of the islands, while the second focuses on those that function favorably or restrictively in their energy transition and autonomy. In the first case, emphasis is given to the quantitative dimension of the parameters, while in the second case their qualitative dimension is of high importance too. The aim of the proposed typological classification is actually to highlight groups of islands with common problems and crucial issues that need to be addressed in a sustainable energy policy at local and regional level. In this sense, the classification could be used as a 'basis' for a -in a later phase- pilot implementation of energy transition-autonomy actions at island level and/or in groups of islands (Fig. 3).

Along this line, the criteria are divided into two groups. The first group includes those that affect the energy demands of islands (first assumption) [(iv) population, (v) local economy - production sectors, (vi) accessibility/networking, (vii) services/infrastructures of supralocal reach, (viii) construction activity, (ix) tourism], while the second group focuses on criteria that highlight the uniqueness of the islands (second assumption) [(i) geographical location, (ii) locus, (iii) nature-culture]. The criteria are evaluated in two phases. The first combines criteria of the first group [(iv), (v), (viii), (ix)] with energy, aiming at including islands in energy priority categories, according to their resettlement and tourism development trends and perspectives (regardless of island area or population size) [(A) 1st priority islands; and (B) 2nd priority islands]. In the second phase, the criteria of the second group [(i), (ii), (iii)] are also taken into account in order to highlight the barriers set by the particular characteristics of the islands and which affect their energy transition and autonomy (geographical location, climate, nature-culture, landscape etc.). It is argued that the consideration of the later criteria is a precondition for the sustainable energy transition of these vulnerable sites.

More specifically, the main methodological steps followed in the first phase were:

A table with the percentage changes of the criteria of the first group [(iv)–(x)] was organized in order to monitor and evaluate their changes (2001–2020).

The islands were divided into groups/subgroups based on the percentage changes in inhabitants (2001–2011) and visitors (2011–2020). The choice was not random. It reflects the tendencies of the abandonment by the inhabitants and the strengthening of tourism in islands; parameters that can affect in various ways islands' energy demand and its variation in the year. Thus, based on population change, three groups emerge: (I) islands that are losing population (abandonment trends) [North Aegean (in total), South Aegean (Leros)]; (II) islands that are gaining population (resettlement trends) [Kasos, Tilos, Nisyros, Halki, Lipsi, Agathonisi, Megisti, Gavdos], and (III) islands that maintain a stable population [Symi, Patmos]. The biggest negative change was found in Ag. Efstratios (-12%) and the highest positive in Gavdos (+88%) and Halki (+62%). To better understand the effects of *seasonality* on the small islands' energy needs, the above groups were divided into subgroups depending on the correlations of increase and decrease of residents-visitors. Hence, groups (I), (II) were divided into: (I − −), (I − +) and (II ++), (II + −), while group (III) remains, due to a stable population and reduction of visitors in Symi (−57.3%) and Patmos (−24.14%). In particular, the distribution of islands by subgroup is as follows: a) (I− −): decrease in inhabitants and visitors [Psara, Oinousses, Fournoi, Leros], (I − +): (decrease in inhabitants/increase in visitors) [Ag. Efstratios]; and b) (II ++): increase of inhabitants and visitors [Tilos, Nisyros, Lipsi, Agathonisi, Megisti, Gavdos], (II + −): increase of inhabitants/decrease of visitors [Kasos, Halki]. Of particular interest are: Fournoi (I − −) with the smallest negative change in residents (−2%) and the largest negative in visitors (−25.8%); Ag. Efstratios (I− +) with the largest negative change in inhabitants (−12%) and the largest positive in visitors (+25.1%); Gavdos (II ++) with the largest increase in residents (+88%) and visitors (+837%); and Halki (II + −) with the largest positive change in residents (+62%) and the largest negative in visitors (−26.74%) [30].

Consideration of economic activity and energy demands by island (% changes 2001–2011). The islands with the largest positive change in the primary sector were Megisti (+250%), Nisyros (+53%) and Psara (+14%). This increase in Megisti and Nisyros was accompanied by positive changes in residents (+22% + 9% respectively) and tourism (+438.27% and 198.74% in visitors respectively, and in Nisyros + 112.4% in hotel occupancy), while in Psara from negative changes in residents and visitors (−4%, −3.68% respectively). The most dynamic islands in the secondary sector were Gavdos (+83%), Halki (+58%), Oinousses (+52%) and Megisti (+36%) mainly due to construction activity. In Gavdos, Halki and Megisti the increase in the secondary sector was accompanied by an increase of inhabitants (+88%, + 68% and + 22% respectively) while especially for Gavdos and Megisti islands an explosive increase in visitors was observed in the same period (+837%, +438.27% respectively). In Halki and Oinousses the visitors decreased (−26.74% and −23.38% respectively) adjusting the energy requirements. In the tertiary sector the biggest positive changes were found in Gavdos (+311%), Halki (+274%), Agathonisi (+258%) and Lipsi (+115%) and were accompanied by an increase in population [mainly in Gavdos and Halki (+88%, +62% respectively)] and visitors [mainly in Gavdos (+837%) and less in Agathonisi (+23%) and Lipsi (+13.98%)]. Of particular interest is the increase of the hotel potential index in Gavdos (+837%) and Lipsi (+54%), and the changes in the construction activity that are mainly connected with the tourism development. At the same time, in Halki, despite the increase in population (+62%), there is a decrease in construction activity (−30%), visitors (−26.74%) and hotel staff (−53.5%). Symi and Patmos (group III) -the only islands of the sample cruise destinations-showed a decrease in the primary sector (−28%

and −45%) and in visitors (−57.3% and −24.4%). Based on the % changes of tourism indicators, Nisyros, Agathonisi, Gavdos, Oinousses are emerging as potential 'poles' of tourism and holiday residence. Regarding the energy sector, increasing consumption trends highlighted mainly in Gavdos (+17%) and Agathonisi (+10%), while the most active islands in RES assessment were Patmos (+16.3%) and Leros, Psara and Symi with percentages <4%. The negative changes in the tourism indicators are attributed to the health crisis (COVID-19) that broke out in 2020 and are worth re-examining in relation to the 2021 updated data of ELSTAT when available [30].

Taking into account the % changes of the indicators, which are expected to affect future local need and demands, the small islands fall into the following two categories of energy intervention priority (Fig. 3):

(A) 1st priority islands due to threats/risks [(I− −): Psara, (I− +): Ag. Efstratios, (III): Symi, Patmos] and opportunities/perspectives [(II ++): Tilos, Nisyros, Agathonisi, Megisti, Gavdos, and (II + −): Halki]
(B) 2nd priority islands due to threats/risks [(I− −): Oinousses, Fournoi, Leros] and opportunities/perspectives (II ++): Lipsi, and (II + −): Kasos]

Having the above classification as a basis, in the second phase are highlighted those small frontier islands that, due to their geographical location, scale (area/population size), and intense concentration of natural-cultural resources, require special attention in their energy transition-autonomy. Based on the research, the following are noted: a) 9 out of 15 islands (60%) have an area of <45 km^2, and of those four are <20 km^2 [Oinousses, Lipsi, Agathonisi, Megisti]; b) the most remote islands (distance from Turkey <15 km) are Oinousses, Symi and Megisti (<10 km) followed by Agathonisi, Nisyros, Tilos; c) there are favorable prospects for the development of RES/MRE in all islands; d) the most intense concentrations (> six sites) of nature-history-culture-protection areas (Natura, archeological sites, historical sites, underwater heritage, etc.) are found in Gavdos, Leros, Nisyros, Halki and Psara while high concentration of supralocal infrastructures (>3 types) and good accessibility (Multimodal Hub) have Leros, Kasos, Megisti followed by Symi, Patmos and Halki. Finally, Psara, Oinousses and Kasos are islands with strong historic naval tradition [28, 30(f)].

Based on the above insights, it is estimated that special attention should be given to the energy transition-autonomy of islands that: a) simultaneously experience trends of abandonment and tourism development (Ag. Efstratios, Fournoi), especially if they are among the smallest and most remote (Psara, Oinousses) [local identity alteration]; b) experience conditions of resettlement and simultaneous rural-tourist development (Nisyros, Megisti) [balanced local development prospects]; and c) have oriented their development exclusively to tourism (i.e. Halki, Symi, Kasos, Tilos, Patmos, Leros), especially if they are among the smallest and less populated (i.e. area <30 km^2, <1,000 inhabitants) since pressures tend to be more intense on their territories (i.e. Gavdos, Agathonisi, Lipsi) [carrying capacity alteration].

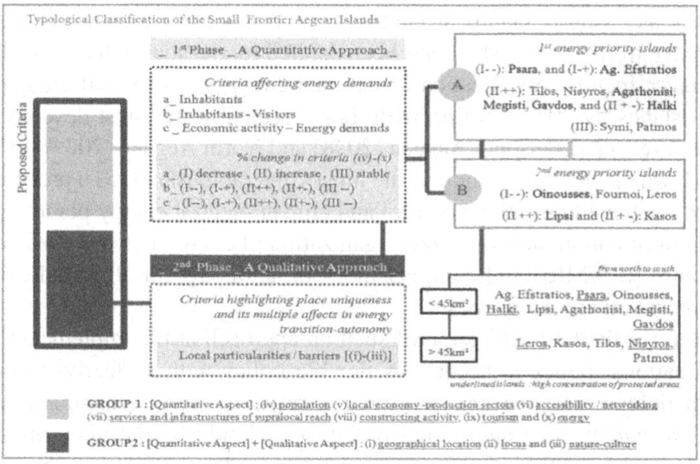

Fig. 3. Small frontier Islands: proposed energy priority categories [own elaboration]

Recognizing the importance of mitigating inequalities and preserving the climate neutrality of insular regions it is argued that priority should be given to islands (<45 km^2) with strong resettlement trends (Gavdos, Halki) and to the frontier ones that are losing inhabitants (Ag. Efstratios, Psara, Oinousses) or are being faced with the management of strong deviations in regards to the ratio of residents/visitors during the year [Lipsi, Agathonisi, Megisti (MH)]. However, of equally importance is the case of islands (>45 km^2) with increased energy demands due to population size (>3,000 and <8,000 inhabitants) and high concentration of supralocal infrastructures (i.e. transport, administration, production, social) [Leros (MH), Patmos] and those less populated (<1,000 inhabitants) with a high concentration of supralocal infrastructures and tourism [i.e. Kasos (MH), Tilos, Nisyros].

6 Paving the Way for Clean Energy Insular Regions/Islands

The need to ensure sustainable energy transition and autonomy for insular regions is not disputed. However, implementing such a goal is a real planning challenge, as it requires a balance between meeting energy demands, satisfying different investment interests, and protecting fragile natural-cultural-manmade ecosystems. Challenges and dilemmas are increasing in the case of small remote islands. There are two reasons for this phenomenon. On one hand, these islands impose their energy autonomy thanks to their strong spatial and socio-economic isolation. On the other hand, they raise special terms and restrictions in regards to their energy planning (i.e. choice of energy model, location, extent of development, etc.) due of their limited scale and high concentration of quality elements of nature-culture-landscape.

Recognizing that sustainable energy transition - autonomy in these vulnerable areas is a prerequisite for their resilience and competitiveness, it is argued that in order to achieve such an objective the answer must be sought in the typological classification of islands by simultaneous assessing the local energy demands and the barriers that each island sets (scale, natural- manmade environment, landscape/seascape). This is a different perspective from the one which has been applied for decades to the official planning level in Greece [central organization of national energy network and gradual connection of all islands by 2030, starting with those located in the most developed insular regions, i.e. Crete (2023), South Aegean (2028) and North Aegean (2029)] [30(d)]. It is an approach which chooses to support the most vulnerable islands as a precondition for a more fair (spatial and socio-economic) and climate-neutral energy planning. In other words, it aims at a more decentralized organization of energy networks oriented to the exploitation of RES/MRE with a higher index of autonomy for all islands, mainly for the smallest and most remote ones.

However, for the best utilization of such an approach at the implementation level, an overall national policy is needed. A flexible policy with a clearly defined vision and a methodological framework structured in respect to three planning assumptions, namely: a) *insularity*, *seasonality* and *remoteness* should be the main pillars of this policy framework, due to their effects on the energy demands of insular regions and islands, and the barriers/priorities they set up on a case-by-case and time basis; b) energy transition-autonomy of insular regions/islands should be sought on the basis of equal consideration of local peculiarities integrated into the national and broader international energy environment. Small frontier islands should gain an additional interest due to their vulnerable natural and manmade environment and geopolitical significance; and c) energy planning should be carried out in the context of a multifactorial approach with simultaneous evaluation of geographical, environmental, spatial and socio-economic criteria. In a difficult juncture of a multifaceted crisis, no matter how difficult could be to move toward this direction, we should reconsider the current trends and assume responsibility as active citizens, especially those of us who serve the planning process as policymakers, planners and academic teachers [31].

References

1. International Renewable Energy Agency (IRENA): Global Energy Transformation. Energy Roadmap 2050, ISBN 978-92-9260-059-4. (2018). https://www.irena.org/-/media/Files/IRENA/Agency/ Publication/2018/Apr/IRENA_Report_GET_2018.pdf
2. Gjorgievski, V., Markovska, N., Pukšec, T., Duić, N., Foley, A.: Supporting the 2030 agenda for sustainable development: Special issue dedicated to conference on sustainable development of energy, water and environment systems 2019. Renewable and Sustainable Energy Rev. **143** (2021). Accessed 6 Jan 2022
3. European Commission: European Council- Council of the European Union 2020, Climate Action-2050 Long term Strategy (2020). https://ec.europa.eu/clima/eu-action/climate-strategies-targets/2050-long-term-strategy_en. Accessed 8 Apr 2022
4. European Commission: A European Green Deal. Striving to be the first climate neutral continent (2019). https://ec.europa.eu/info/strategy/priorities-2019-2024/european-green-deal_en. Accessed 21 Apr 2021
5. European Commission: Clean Energy. The European Green Deal, Decarbonising the EU's energy system is critical to reach our climate objectives (December 2019). https://ec.europa.eu/commission/presscorner/detail/en/fs_19_6723. Accessed 10 Apr 2021
6. European Commission: Energy and the Green Deal: A Clean Energy Transition (2021). https://ec.europa.eu/info/strategy/priorities-2019-2024/european-green-deal/energy-and-green-deal_en. Accessed 10 Apr 2022

7. UN Climate Change Conference UK 2021: COP26 The Glasgow Climate Pact (2021). https://ukcop26.org/wp-content/uploads/2021/11/COP26-Presidency-Outcomes-The-Climate-Pact.pdf. Accessed 8 Apr 2022
8. Nouicer, A., Kehoe, A., Nysten, J., Fouquet, D., Meeus, L,. Hancher, L.: The EU Clean Energy Package. European University Institute (2020). https://cadmus.eui.eu/bitstream/handle/1814/68899/QM-01-20-700-EN-N.pdf?sequence=1
9. Pelleri-Carlin, P., Vinois, J., Rubio, J., Fernandes, S.: Making the energy transition a European success. Tackling the democratic, innovation, financing and social challenges of the energy union. Notre Europe Jacques Delors Institute. Studies & Reports (2017). https://institutdelors.eu/wpcontent/uploads/2018/01/makingtheenergytransitionaeuropeansuccess-study-pellerincarlinfernandesrubio-june2017-bd.pdf. Accessed 10 Apr 2022
10. Gui, E., MacGill, I.: Typology of future clean energy communities: an exploratory structure, opportunities and challenges. Energy Res. Soc. Sci. **35**, 94–107 (2018). ISSN 2214-6296. https://doi.org/10.1016/j.erss.2017.10.019
11. COM. 494Blue Growth. Opportunities for marine and maritime sustainable growth (2012). https://eur-lex.europa.eu/legal-content/EN/ALL/?uri=CELEX%3A52012DC0494
12. Ocean Energy Europe (OEE): Ocean Energy Strategic Roadmap 2016. Building ocean energy for Europe (2016). https://www.oceanenergy-europe.eu/files/ocean-energy-roadmap/
13. Khare, V. R, Dubey, R.: Blue Energy: Power from the Sea. National Conference of Green Technology (2016). https://www.researchgate.net/publication/288839358_Blue_Energy-_Power_from_the_Sea. Accessed 23 Sept 2021
14. Theodora, Y.: Aegean sea - challenges and dilemmas in management and planning for local development in Fragmented Insular Regions. Heritage **2**(3), 1762–1784 (2019). https://doi.org/10.3390/heritage2030108
15. Kuang, Y., et al.: A review of renewable energy utilization in islands. Renew. Sustain. Energy Rev. **59**, 504–513 (2016). ISSN 1364–0321. https://doi.org/10.1016/j.rser.2016.01.014. Accessed 10 Apr 2022
16. Wimmler, C., Hejazi, G., de Oliveira Fernandes, E., Moreira, C., Connors, S.: Multi-criteria decision support methods for renewable energy systems on islands. J. Clean Energy Technol. **3**(3) (2015). https://repositorio.inesctec.pt/server/api/core/bitstreams/b48ac2be-a80f-490a-9f03-8932b5bfc908/content. Accessed 10 Apr 2022
17. European Commission, Clean Energy for EU islands. Providing a long-term framework to help EU islands generate their own sustainable, low-cost energy (2022). https://energy.ec.europa.eu/topics/markets-and-consumers/clean-energy-eu-islands_en
18. European Commission: Clean Energy Vision to Clean Energy Action. Clean Energy for EU Islands Community (2022). https://clean-energy-islands.ec.europa.eu/
19. New Energy Solutions Optimised for Islands (NESOI). European Islands Facility. (2022). https://www.nesoi.eu/. Accessed 6 Jan 2022
20. Islands Commission of the CPMR: The Final Declaration adopted by its members. In: 36th Annual General Meeting, 19–20 May, Rhodes, South Aegean, Greece (2016). https://europeansmallislands.files.wordpress.com/2016/05/agenda-cpmr-rhodos.pdf
21. European Parliament: Research for REGI Committee: Islands of the European Union: State of play and future challenges. Policy Department for Structural and Cohesion Policies. Directorate-General for Internal Policies. PE 652.239 - March (2021). https://www.europarl.europa.eu/RegData/etudes/STUD/2021/652239/IPOL_STU(2021)652239_EN.pdf. Accessed 10 Apr 2022
22. Smart Islands Initiative: Smart Islands Declaration. New Pathways for European Islands (2022). https://www.smartislandsinitiative.eu/en/index.php. Accessed 8 Apr 2022

23. Groppi, D., Pfeifer, A., Garcia, D., Krajačić, G., Duić, N.: A review on energy storage and demand side management solutions in smart energy islands. Renew. Sustain. Energy Rev. **135** (2021). https://doi.org/10.1016/j.rser.2020.110183
24. Blechinger, P., Seguin, R., Cader, C., Bertheau, P., Breye, Ch.: Assessment of the global potential for renewable energy storage systems on small islands. Energy Procedia **46**, 325–331 (2014). https://doi.org/10.1016/j.egypro.2015.01.071. Accessed 2 Dec 2021
25. Andaloro, A., Salomone, R., Andaloro. L.: Alternative energy scenarios for small islands: a case study from Salina Island (Aeolian Islands, Southern Italy). Renew. Energy **47**, 135–146 (2012)
26. Ricardo Energy & Environment: Small Islands Energy System Overview. Local Carbon Energy Systems Framework. Report for Highlands and Islands Enterprise (2016). https://www.hie.co.uk/media/8139/hie-small-islands-low-carbon-energy-overview-final-report-for-publication-pdf-060420-a3410152.pdf. Accessed 8 Dec 2021
27. Theodora, Y.: Cultural heritage as a means for local development in Mediterranean historic cities-the need for an urban policy. Heritage **3**(2), 152–175 (2020). https://doi.org/10.3390/heritage3020010
28. Theodora, Y.: Tracing sustainable island complexes in response to insularity dilemmas _ methodological considerations. In: Gervasi, O., et al. (eds.) ICCSA 2020. LNCS, vol. 12255, pp. 278–293. Springer, Cham (2020). https://doi.org/10.1007/978-3-030-58820-5_22
29. International and European Databases: International Renewable Energy Agency (IRENA). https://www.irena.org; European Environment Agency (EEA). https://www.eea.europa.eu/
30. Greek Databases: (a) National Statistical Authority of Greece (ELSTAT). http://www.statistics.gr; (b) Hellenic Electricity Distribution Network Operator (HEDNO) https://deddie.gr/en/; (c) Public Power Corporation (DEI). https://www.dei.gr/en/; (d) Independent Power Transmission Operator (IPTO/ADMIE). https://www.admie.gr/en; (e) Institute of Greek Tourism Confederation-INSETE (INSETE). https://insete.gr/?lang=en; (f) Hellenic Ministry of Culture. https://www.culture.gov.gr/en/SitePages/default.aspx
31. Theodora, Y.: Landscape at Risk _ Why Planning Matters? National Symposium on the Implementation of the Council of Europe Landscape Convention in Greece. Round -Table: Landscape-based Public Policies. European Landscape Convention, Council of Europe, Trikala, Greece (2022). https://www.coe.int/en/web/landscape/trikala-march-2022

Sustainable Building Material: Recycled Jute Fiber Composite Mortar for Thermal and Structural Retrofitting

Arnas Majumder[1(✉)], Flavio Stochino[2], Andrea Frattolillo[2], Monica Valdes[2], Fernando Fraternali[1], and Enzo Martinelli[1]

[1] Department of Civil Engineering, University of Salerno, Via Giovanni Paolo II n. 132, 84084 Fisciano, SA, Italy
amajumder@unisa.it

[2] Department of Civil Environmental Engineering and Architecture, University of Cagliari, Via Marengo 2, 09123 Cagliari, CA, Italy

Abstract. The construction sector requires a major part of the produced energy (around 36% globally) and emits the highest amount of greenhouse gases (around 39% globally). Therefore, it has an important impact on global warming and climate change. For centuries the irrational use of natural resources of non-renewable raw materials in the construction and building sector have damaged the eco-system and also hindered the sustainable development.

This experimental research work contributes to the United Nations (UN) sustainable development goals by adapting the use of natural fiber (which is recyclable, bio-degradable) to create new sustainable composite building materials.

In this work recycled-jute fibers have been used to replace the plastic insulation material used to improve the thermal resistance of construction mortar. These jute fibers were collected during jute net fabrication process as production scrapes and testify to the possibility of using a natural material for an extended life cycle.

The mechanical and thermal performance of jute fiber reinforced mortar have been tested in order to evaluate the effectiveness of this material for integrated retrofitting of existing masonry buildings. About 34.11% (with respect to the mortar mass) of the plastic insulation materials (already present in the original manufactured mortar product) have been replaced with 6.33% (with respect to the mortar mass) recycled jute-net fibers.

Due to the presence of jute fibers (residual from net fabrication) in composite samples, approximately around 7.13%, improvement in the thermal insulation capacity has been obtained with respect to the non-reinforced mortar samples. Moreover, an increment in strain energy of the same composite mortar about 632.26% has been assessed.

Keywords: Sustainability · Sustainable materials · Natural fiber composite · Recycled fiber · Recycled jute fiber · Recycled jute net fiber composite · Recycled building materials

O. Gervasi et al. (Eds.): ICCSA 2022 Workshops, LNCS 13379, pp. 657–669, 2022.
https://doi.org/10.1007/978-3-031-10545-6_44

1 Introduction

Mankind has historically used the locally available natural resources (clay, fibers etc.) as construction and building materials and, in the past centuries (only from the end of the XIX° century) the man-made building materials (inorganic fibers, steel and concrete etc.) have dominated this sector. The rapid change in the global climate conditions, poses enormous challenge to the existence of the animal and its surrounding ecosystem.

Among all greenhouse gases (Methene 16%, Nitrogen 6% and F-gases 2% [1]), CO_2 is primarily (76% [1]) responsible for rising the global near-surface air temperature [2]. Notably, the Construction and Building (C&B) sector is singularly responsible for releasing 39% (globally) and 36% (in EU) of the produced CO_2 [3]. According to [4], the electricity generated by burning of fossil fuels accounts for 40% (+) of the energy related CO_2 emissions, whereas the C&B sector consumes 36% (globally) and 40% (in EU) of the total energy [3]. On the other hand, a building, in its whole life cycle generates a huge combination of recyclable and non-recyclable wastes. This value can be quantified as in [5], approximately 160 tons and plus wastes per European Union (EU) citizen are produced during total lifetime. The EU encourage all those countries come under its influence, to recycle majority of the building Construction and Demolition (C&D) (around 70%). According to the directive EU 2008/98/EC [6], limiting them to dispose hundred percentage of the demolition wastes. A major part of the C&D wastes is dumped as land filling and responsible for damaging the environment and ecosystem, conversely sometime these wastes are also very harmful to the human health [7].

Therefore, with increasing consciousness to minimize the global warming, by limiting the greenhouse gases emission and to reduce the carbon footprint (with use of green, natural, recyclable, and sustainable raw materials) have forced scientists and engineers to search for newer and innovative sustainable building materials.

On the other hand, various goals and constrains (like [8–10]) implemented by UN, EU and various governments, have also encouraged the researchers to explore the natural fiber composite materials [11–14].

Locally produced typical natural fibers are widely available [15] in all continents. These fibers are cheap, bio-degradable and recyclable [16].

Majority around 80–85% (India and Bangladesh) of the total jute production come from the Gangetic delta [17]. The jute fiber has many advantages [18, 19]) and uses [20–27]), due to its adequate availability and good mechanical and thermal properties [19].

The present paper aims at investigating the use of the recycled jute net fibers for the composite mortar preparation. The used net fibers are the residuals/wastes, and these fibers are collected during the jute net manufacturing process. These recycled fibers were utilized to cast composite mortars with the intention to study its mechanical and thermal properties and behavior.

Moreover, these fibers were used to replace original insulation materials (typically expanded perlite/polystyrene granules or plastic balls) already present in the commercial dry-mixed mortar. Therefore, contributing towards the UN's sustainable development goals [28], this experiment proposes recycling of jute net fibers as alternative to the insulating granules.

Section 2 highlights the materials and methods used for the recycled jute net fiber preparation: the sample composition and the mix design can be found in this section, together with the procedure for the samples casting. The mechanical properties and the thermal behavior of both normal and recycled jute net fiber-composite mortars are described in the Sect. 3 and Sect. 4, respectively. Finally, the conclusive remarks are stated in Sect. 5.

2 Materials and Methods

2.1 Materials

Two different compositions, normal mortar and recycled jute fiber composite mortar were fabricated by using a commercial dry-mixed "Thermal Mortar" (TM).

The TM is a lime-based mortar and it has pre-fabricated insulation materials (expanded perlite/polystyrene granules or Plastic balls (PB)), (see Fig. 1). The TM is classified according to EN ISO 13788 [29] and it is certified as R and T / CSII. The jute fibers were recycled from the jute-net fibric fabrication (see Fig. 2).

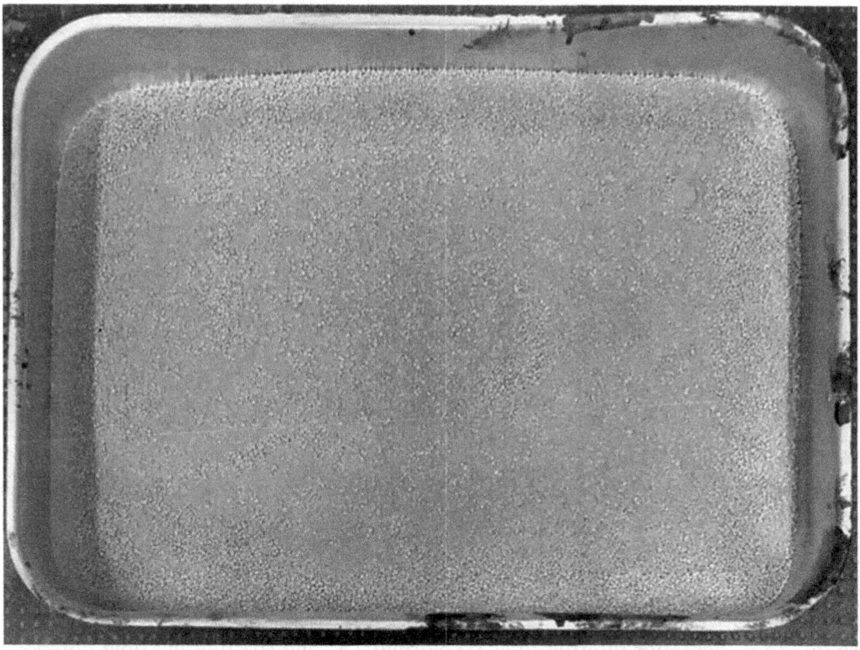

Fig. 1. Thermal mortar (TM) with plastic insulation materials (PB)

Fig. 2. Recycled jute net fibers

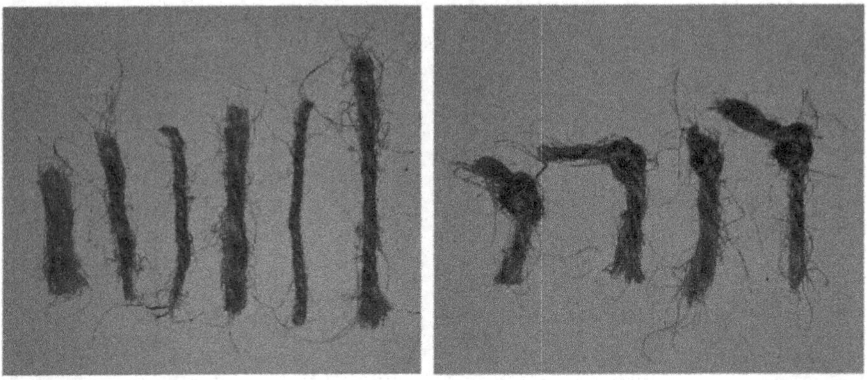

(a) (b)

Fig. 3. (a) Thread fiber pieces of various sizes; (b) Presence of knots in some of the recycled jute net fibers

2.2 Methods

Two mixtures, hereafter referred to as (i) Normal TM and (ii) Jute-net fiber composite mortar without plastic balls, were prepared according to UNI EN 1015-2: 2007 [30] (Fig. 4). The normal TM samples are nominated and grouped under M (without fiber), whereas the jute Net Fiber (NF) composite mortar without/No Plastic Balls (nPB) are nominated and grouped under M(nPB)F6.5(NF).

The inherent insulation materials (i.e. PBs) of the original mortar, take up to 1/3 of the total product/mortar mass (Table 1). Before preparing the jute net fiber composite mortar, the PBs have been removed and separated (Fig. 4c and Fig. 4d) from the original mortar (Fig. 4a) using a powder sifting machine.

The recycled jute-net fibers have been introduced to replace PBs, are the jute-net production wastes (Fig. 4b). These recycled fibers were added to perform both as insulation and binding materials. These residual fibers do not have fixed length (see, Fig. 3a), as their size ranges from 5 mm to 50 mm; in some cases, some of them also have knots (see, Fig. 3b).

Table 1 presents the mix design for normal and composite mortar mixtures. After pouring adequate amount of water (see, Table 1), the normal mortar and composite mortar mixture were stirred (Fig. 4f) approximately for 5 min. The consistency and workability of the mixture was determined by means the flow table test according to UNI EN 1015-3: 2007 [31]. For each mixture, two types of samples were cast: Mechanical Samples (MS) and Thermal Samples (TS). The empty molds sized $160 \times 40 \times 40\ mm^3$ for MS and $160 \times 140 \times 40\ mm^3$ for TS respectively, were initially half-filled initially and 25 strokes for MS and 75 strokes for TS were applied in order to remove the inside trapped air. Then, the molds were completely filled and again the same number of strokes were applied. Then the top of the molds was leveled and the extra materials were removed.

For the sample curing the UNI EN 1015-11: 2019 [32] has been followed. The curing period can be divided into two phases, the first phase is the period from casting day up to the 8th day and the second phase is the natural drying period (from 8th until 28th day).

First initial two days, the samples were left inside the molds and plastic bags, whereas during next five days samples were kept only inside plastic bags.

During the last phase, samples were placed outside the plastic bags in an environment-controlled room, with quasi-constant ambient temperature and relative humidity of 20 °C (±3) and 65% (±5), respectively.

Table 1. Composition of TM in samples without and with recycled jute-net fiber.

Sample type	Insulation materials	Percentage of insulation materials with respect to mortar mass	Water used for the mixture
M(without fiber)	Plastic balls (Already present in the manufactured product)	34.11%	30%
M(nPB)F6.5(NF)	Jute net fiber (Added externally replacing PB)	6.33%	58%

Where, nPB = No Plastic Balls; NF = Net Fiber

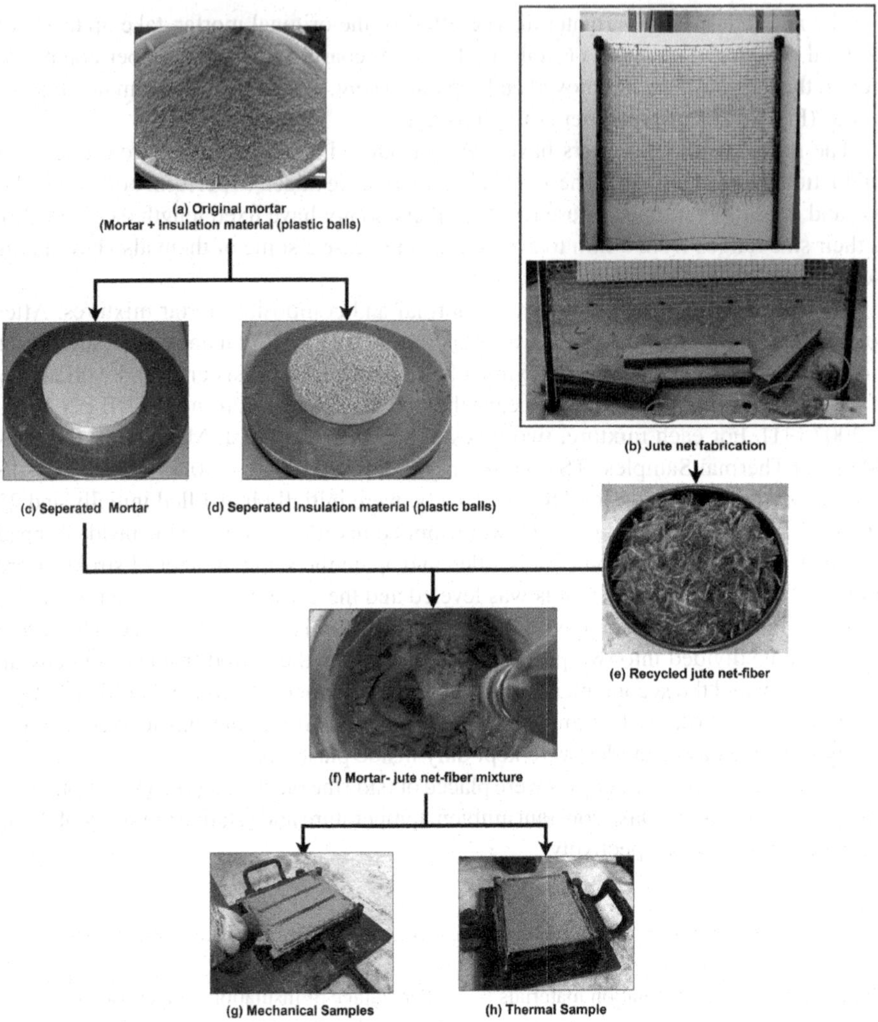

Fig. 4. The recycled jute net fiber composite mortar preparation scheme

3 Experimental Results: Mechanical Properties of the Jute-Net Fiber Composite Mortars

The mechanical behaviour of each prismatic sample ($160 \times 40 \times 40$ mm^3) was determined through flexural (Fig. 5) strength tests. The tests were conducted on the 28th day of casting, and the strain energy (U), the flexural strength (ft) and flexural strain of each sample were determined. Three samples of each category were tested.

A universal displacement-controlled machine: Metrocom-1 has been used to conduct the three point bending flexural test (UNI EN 1015-11:2019 [32]). The loading machine has maximum load capacity of 4.9 kN, with sensibility/scale division of 0.02 kN. The machine is equipped with a load cell of class 1 (measuring capacity of 5 tons and with nominal sensitivity of 2 mV/V) and a transducer (max. range 50 mm, nominal sensibility output 2 mV/V and linearity - <0.10%F.S) in order to measure the applied central load and displacement, respectively. The load was applied with displacement rate of 1.5 mm/min.

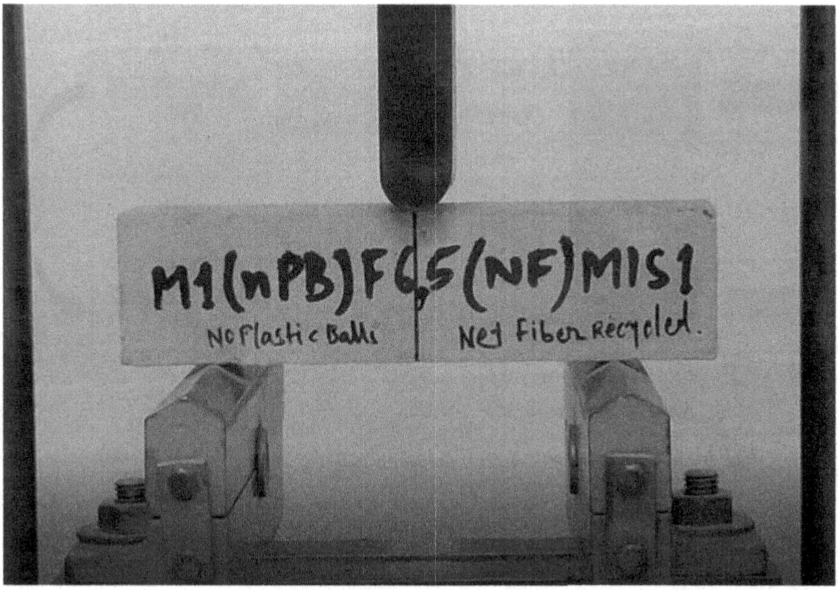

Fig. 5. Flexural strength test

With the removal of PB from original mortar and the addition of jute fibers (recycled from net fabrication), the strain energy improved more than 600% (see, Table 1), when compared with the samples without fiber and with PB. This was due to unequal and longer fibers (some with knots, see Fig. 3b) whose presence helped in binding and gripping mortar materials better than that of PBs; imbodied fibers helped in absorbing and dissipating the applied load, too. During the flexural tests the samples with fibers have shown ductile behavior.

Table 2. Change in mechanical properties with addition of jute fiber and removal of insulation materials: the sample M(nPB)F6.5(NF) Vs. M (without fiber)

Flexural properties	
Stain energy	Flexural stress/strength (σ)
kNmm	MPa
+632.26%	−50.01%
Where, nPB = No Plastic Balls; NF = Net Fiber	

4 Experimental Results: Thermal Charactristics of the Jute-Net Fiber Composite Mortars

Thermal characteristic of each sample (160 × 140 × 40 mm^3) was evaluated by measuring the Thermal Conductivity (TC) value using a heat flow meter (TAURUS TCA300).

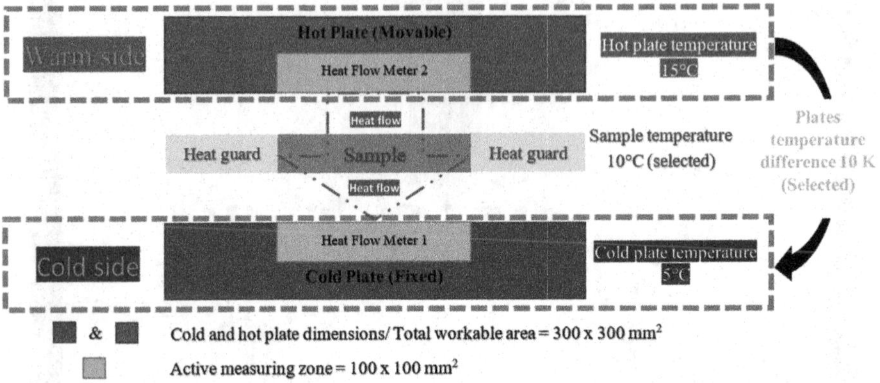

Fig. 6. Schematic diagram of the heat flow meter (TAURUS TCA300).

Normal mortar samples (M) with plastic balls and without fiber, and composite mortar samples (M(nPB)F6.5(NF)) (Fig. 7a) without plastic balls and with recycled jute net fiber were used to conduct measurements following ISO 8301 [33] and DIN EN 1946-3 [34].

After 28th day of restricted and natural drying (see, Sect. 2.2) each sample was placed in oven for forced drying and this period range from 7 to 14 days. The range of the forced oven drying period was varied, due to the presence of different amount of moisture contained in each sample. According to UNI EN 12667 [35], samples were dried in oven at 50 °C in order to reduce the moisture level, as presence of humidity influence the TC measurement. Existence of no moisture was confirmed, when two successive measurements have same (±0.1 g sample mass) value.

The TC measurements were conducted on the day, when the ambient temperature and relative humidity were found to be 22 ± 2 °C and 60 ±10%, respectively. The samples (160 × 140 × 40 mm^3) need to be placed exactly at the center of the measuring plates (300 × 300 mm^2). The instrument has one hot (moveable) and a cold (fixed) plates, as in Fig. 6 and Fig. 7b. The plates' function can be reversed as desired. The active measuring area (100 × 100 mm^2) is located at the center of each plate which is equipped with one heat flux sensor. The protective zones surround the active zones.

A woolen heat guard/insulating ring has been used (Fig. 7b) to have quasi-uniform monodirectional heat flow and also to minimize the heat losses around the edge of the measuring sample.

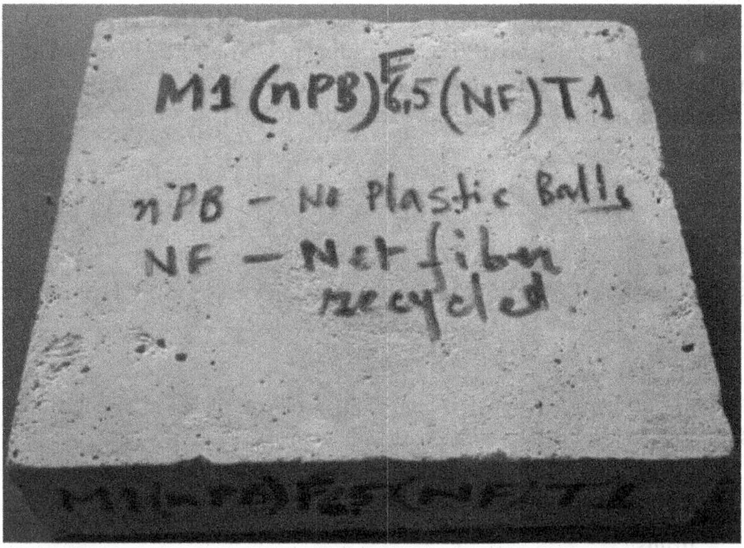

(a)

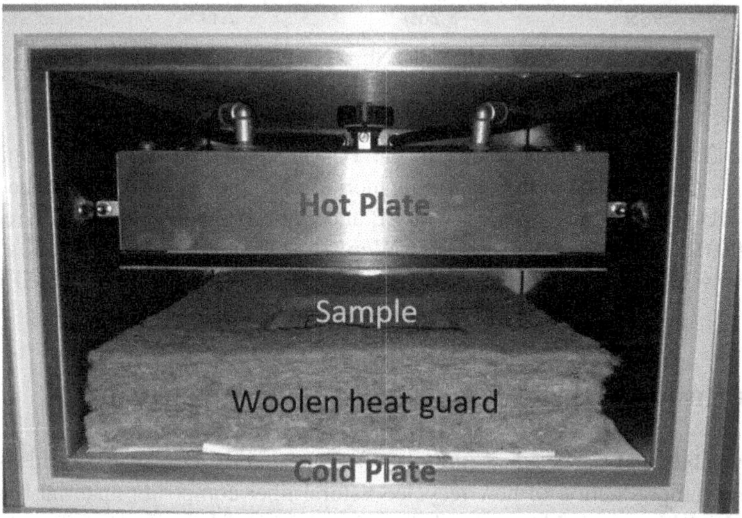

(b)

Fig. 7. (a) Recycled composite sample (160 × 140 × 40 mm^3); (b) Sample placed inside the flow meter, surround with woolen heat guard.

The instrument has the pre-set data sampling time at every 5 s. while the intermediate measuring time and total measuring time were set as 1 min and 300 min, respectively.

The plates temperature difference was chosen to be 10 K. The sample mean temperatures selected as 10 °C, 20 °C and 30 °C, according to UNI EN 12939 [36]. The heat flux $\dot{Q}$ [W/m^2] and the plates temperatures were measured and the Thermal Conductivity λ [W/mK] is calculated by TAURUS TCA according to [21]:

$$\lambda = \dot{Q}\frac{S}{(t_H - t_C)}\left[\frac{W}{mK}\right] \quad (1)$$

where:

$\dot{Q}$ is the heat flux [W/m^2]; S is the sample thickness [m]; t H is the hot plate temperature [°C]; t C is the cold plate temperature [°C].

Table 3. Change in thermal properties with addition of jute fiber and removal of insulation materials: the sample M(nPB)F6.5(NF) Vs. M(without fiber)

Thermal conductivity (λ)		
W/mK		
at 10 °C	at 20 °C	at 30 °C
−7.98%	−8.26%	−7.11%
Where, nPB = No Plastic Balls; NF = Net Fiber		

Table 3 shows the improvement in the TC values at three different temperatures (10 °C, 20 °C and 30 °C) of the composite mortars (without PB and with jute net-fibers) with respect to the normal mortars (with PB and without jute net-fibers). The reduction in TC of 0.017 W/mK at 10 °C, of 0.018 W/mK at 20 °C and of 0.016 W/mK at 30 °C, respectively have been observed when PBs were replaced with the recycled jute-net fibers.

5 Conclusions

The recyclability of the residual jute fiber from net fabrication process and its applicability in the production of new recycled natural fiber composite material have been evaluated in this paper. Moreover, the thermo-structural behaviors of the composite material and its potential use as duel-retrofitting (i.e., structural and thermal) purposes have been studied.

In this process, the insulation materials (expanded perlite/polystyrene granules or plastic balls) already present in the commercial dry-mixed mortar have been replaced with the above-mentioned recycled jute-net fibers. Interestingly, promising results have been obtained with the improvement in strain energy and thermal conductivity. Only three samples of normal mortar (without fiber and with PB) and jute net-fiber composite mortars have mechanical and thermal properties have been compared during this research work. Therefore, further studies need to be conducted to assess the feasibility of using these fibers in construction and building sector.

Different masonry-wall thermo-structural retrofitting composite systems would be developed using jute-composite mortar and jute fiber nets. It would be followed by the in-plane shear tests and thermal performance evaluations.

Future developments are also expected from the recycling of other processing scraps [37, 38] or construction and demolition waste [39] in concrete and mortar for structural retrofitting.

References

1. Change, I.C.: Mitigation of climate change. Contribution of working group III to the fifth assessment report of the intergovernmental panel on climate change. 1454, 147 (2014)
2. Gao, Y., Gao, X., Zhang, X.: The 2 C global temperature target and the evolution of the long-term goal of addressing climate change—from the United Nations framework convention on climate change to the Paris agreement. Engrg **3**(2), 272–278 (2017)
3. Benzar, B.E., Park, M., Lee, H.S., Yoon, I., Cho, J.: Determining retrofit technologies for building energy performance. J. Asian Archit. Build. Eng. **19**(4), 367–383 (2020)
4. https://www.world-nuclear.org/information-library/energy-and-the-environment/carbon-dioxide-emissions-from-electricity.aspx. Accessed 12 Mar 2022
5. European Union, EU Construction and Demolition Waste Protocol and Guidelines Homepage. https://ec.europa.eu/growth/news/eu-construction-and-demolition-waste-protocol-2018-09-18_en. Accessed 12 Mar 2022
6. European Parliament. European waste framework directive: Directive 2008/98/EC of the European Parliament and of the Council of 19 November 2008 on Waste and Repealing Certain Directives
7. Mah, C.M., Fujiwara, T., Ho, C.S.: Environmental impacts of construction and demolition waste management alternatives. Chem. Eng. Trans. **63**, 343–348 (2018)
8. United Nations Climate Change, The Paris Agreement Homepage. https://unfccc.int/process-and-meetings/the-paris-agreement/the-paris-agreement. Accessed 12 Mar 2022
9. European Commission, Climate Action Homepage. https://ec.europa.eu/clima/eu-action/climate-strategies-targets/2050-long-term-strategy_en. Accessed 12 Mar 2022
10. European Commission, Energy Homepage. https://energy.ec.europa.eu/topics/energy-efficiency/energy-efficient-buildings/nearly-zero-energy-buildings_en. Accessed 12 Mar 2022
11. Elanchezhian, C., Ramnath, B.V., Ramakrishnan, G., Rajendrakumar, M., Naveenkumar, V., Saravanakumar, M.K.: Review on mechanical properties of natural fiber composites. Materials Today. Proc. **5**(1), 1785–1790 (2018)
12. AL-Zubaidi, A.B.: Effect of natural fibers on mechanical properties of green cement mortar. In AIP Conference Proceedings, vol. 1968, no 1, p. 020003. AIP Publishing LLC. (2018)
13. Formisano, A., Dessì Jr, E., Landolfo, R.: Mechanical-physical experimental tests on lime mortars and bricks reinforced with hemp. In: AIP Conference proceedings, vol. 1906, no. 1, p. 090006. AIP Publishing LLC (2017)
14. Sassu, M., Giresini, L., Bonannini, E., Puppio, M.L.: On the use of vibro-compressed units with bio-natural aggregate. Buildings **6**(3), 40 (2016)
15. Discover Natural Fibers Initiative Homepage. https://dnfi.org/coir/natural-fibres-and-the-world-economy-july-2019_18043/. Accessed 12 Mar 2022
16. Majumder, A., Stochino, F., Fernando, F., Enzo, M.: Seismic and thermal retrofitting of masonry buildings with fiber reinforced composite systems: a state of the art review. Int. J. Struct. Glass Adv. 41–67 (2021)
17. Roy, S., Hassan, K.M.: Scenario of water pollution by retting of jute and its impact on aquatic lives. In: Proceedings of the 3rd International Conference on Civil Engineering for Sustainable Development, pp. 164–169 (2016)

18. Islam, M.S., Ahmed, S.K.: The impacts of jute on environment: an analytical review of Bangladesh. J. Environ. Earth Sci. **5**, 24–31 (2012)
19. Chand, N., Fahim, M.: Tribology of natural fiber polymer composites. Woodhead publishing (2020)
20. Ferrara, G., Caggegi, C., Martinelli, E., Gabor, A.: Shear capacity of masonry walls externally strengthened using Flax-TRM composite systems: experimental tests and comparative assessment. Constr. Build. Mater. **261**, 120490 (2020)
21. Majumder, A., Canale, L., Mastino, C.C., Pacitto, A., Frattolillo, A., Dell'Isola, M.: Thermal characterization of recycled materials for building insulation. Energies **14**(12), 3564 (2021)
22. Islam, M.S., Ahmed, S.J.: Influence of jute fiber on concrete properties. Constr. Build. Mater. **189**, 768–776 (2018)
23. Majumder, A., Stochino, F., Farina, I., Valdes, M., Fraternali, F., Martinelli, E.: Physical and mechanical characteristics of raw jute fibers, threads and diatons. Constr. Build. Mater. **326**, 126903 (2022)
24. Formisano, A., Chiumiento, G., Dessì, E. J.: Laboratory tests on hydraulic lime mortar reinforced with jute fibres. Open J. Civ. Eng. **14**(1)
25. Ferreira, J.M., Capela, C., Manaia, J., Costa, J.D.: Mechanical properties of woven mat jute/epoxy composites. Mater. Res. **19**, 702–710 (2016)
26. Saleem, M.A., Abbas, S., Haider, M.: Jute fiber reinforced compressed earth bricks (FR-CEB)–a sustainable solution. Pakistan J. Eng. Appl. Sci. (2016)
27. Rashid, K., Haq, E.U., Kamran, M.S., Munir, N., Shahid, A., Hanif, I.: Experimental and finite element analysis on thermal conductivity of burnt clay bricks reinforced with fibers. Constr. Build. Mater. **221**, 190–199 (2019)
28. https://sdgs.un.org/goals. Accessed 12 Mar 2022
29. EN ISO 13788: Hygrothermal Performance of Building Components and Building Elements Internal Surface Temperature to Avoid Critical Surface Humidity and Interstitial Condensation - Calculation Methods
30. UNI EN 1015-2:2007, Methods of test for mortar for masonry - Part 2: Bulk sampling of mortars and preparation of test mortars
31. UNI EN 1015-3:2007, Methods of test for mortar for masonry - Part 3: Determination of consistence of fresh mortar (by flow table)
32. UNI EN 1015-11:2019, Methods of test for mortar for masonry - Part 11: Determination of flexural and compressive strength of hardened mortar
33. ISO 8301:1991. International Organization for Standardization. Thermal Insulation—Determination of Steady-State Thermal Resistance and Related Properties—Heat Flow Meter Apparatus; Geneva, Switzerland (1991)
34. EN 1946-3. European Committee for Standardization. Thermal Performance of Building Products and Components—Specific Criteria for the Assessment of Laboratories Measuring Heat Transfer Properties—Part 3: Measurements by the Guarded Heat Flow Meter Method; CEN: Brussels, Belgium (1999)
35. UNI EN 12667: 2002. Italian National Unification. Thermal Performance of Building Materials and Products-Determination of Thermal Resistance by Means of Guarded Hot Plate and Heat Flow Meter Methods-Products of High and Medium Thermal ResistanceMilan, Italy (2002)
36. UNI EN 12939:2002: Italian National Unification. Thermal Performance of Building Materials and Products—Determination of Thermal Resistance by Means of the Hot Plate with Guard Ring and the Heat Flow Meter Method—Thick Products with High and Medium Thermal Resistance; Milan, Italy (2002)
37. Martínez-Barrera, G., del Coz-Díaz, J.J., Álvarez-Rabanal, F.P., López Gayarre, F., Martínez-López, M., Cruz-Olivares, J.: Waste tire rubber particles modified by gamma radiation and their use as modifiers of concrete. Case Studies in Construction Materials **12,** e00321 (2020)

38. Suárez González, J., Lopez Boadella, I., López Gayarre, F., López-Colina Pérez, C., Serrano López, M., Stochino, F.: Use of mining waste to produce ultra-high-performance fibre-reinforced concrete. Materials **13**(11), 2457 (2020)
39. Pani, L., Francesconi, L., Rombi, J., Mistretta, F., Sassu, M., Stochino, F.: Effect of parent concrete on the performance of recycled aggregate concrete. Sustainability **12**(22), 9399 (2020)

Protocols of Knowledge for the Restoration: Documents, Geomatics, Diagnostic. The Case of the Beata Vergine Assunta Basilic in Guasila (Sardinia)

Silvana Maria Grillo[2], Elisa Pilia[1], and Giuseppina Vacca[1](✉)

[1] Department of Civil and Environmental Engineering and Architecture, University of Cagliari, 09123 Cagliari, Italy
vaccag@unica.it

[2] Department of Chemical Sciences and Geology, University of Cagliari, 09042 Monserrato, Italy

Abstract. For several decades, the conservation and maintenance of the historical architectural heritage in Italy have become one of the central problems within the scientific community of architects, restorers, and engineers. In fact, historic buildings represent not only an important symbol of the country's culture but also a significant economic resource linked to tourist flows. Unfortunately, many historic buildings are in a state of neglection or in a dangerous state of conservation. It is therefore important to activate a series of actions to preserve and conserve this built heritage. In this context, a transdisciplinary approach that includes an accurate historical, dimensional, and material knowledge has fundamental importance to allow a correct design for restoration actions and the possible reuse as well as to allow this heritage to be usable and active. This article presents this integrate approach carried out for the specific case of the Basilica of the Beata Vergine Assunta in Guasila (Sardinia) with a particular focus on the results obtained from historical-documentary investigations, geomatics and petrographic surveys. These studies have been a fundamental base of knowledge for the last interventions of safety and extraordinary maintenance of the monument implemented in 2019.

Keywords: Geomatics · Diagnostics · Transdisciplinarity · Conservation · Cultural heritage

1 Introduction

In the last decades, the conservation and maintenance of the historical architectural heritage in Italy have become one of the central problems within the scientific community of architects, restorers, and engineers. In fact, historic buildings represent not only an important symbol of the country's culture but also a significant economic resource linked to tourist flows. Of this vast Italian historical built heritage only 33% is declared to be of cultural interest and therefore subject to direct constraint by the Italian Ministry of

O. Gervasi et al. (Eds.): ICCSA 2022 Workshops, LNCS 13379, pp. 670–685, 2022.
https://doi.org/10.1007/978-3-031-10545-6_45

Culture [1]. The rest, for reasons of different nature but mainly for economic issues, very often lies in a state of neglection or in a precarious state of conservation. Numerous management initiatives have been planned for this huge heritage at risk, including the establishment of the Risk Card Territorial Information System, developed by the Higher Institute for Conservation (formerly ICR) [2] and focused on the concept of vulnerability for the assessment of the conservation status of the heritage. Another example is the "red lists" of Italia Nostra [3], which collect the sites to be defended on a regional basis. These are tools still in a phase of implementation where a clear numerical data is not yet assumed. What is clear is that more than half of the existing heritage would require maintenance actions to avoid getting into the current precarious state of conservation and requiring restoration.

These aspects make important to activate actions to protect this heritage, especially against the destructive events related to climate and territorial changes such as earthquakes, floods, pollutions as well as weathering linked to the historical passage of time.

If from an economic point of view, the scarcity of facilitations for interventions does not encourage their continuous maintenance, on the other hand, it is also true that restoration projects very often follow one another, without an in-depth knowledge bases and therefore not understanding the real causes of deterioration. As it is well-known, in order to carry out all the conservation actions, the understanding of the state of conservation of buildings has paramount importance. In fact, only with this information the conservation project can be really activated, giving new life to heritage.

Therefore, the trans-disciplinary approach, which offers the study and synergic involvement of different figures such as that of architectural historians for the analysis of the documentary and photographic archives of the major protection bodies, such as Superintendencies and private parish archives, geomatics for the survey aimed at geometric and dimensional knowledge and, finally, petrographers for the material analysis and the assessment of the material state of conservation, is certainly the most effective protocol for reaching this in-depth knowledge [4–8].

This paper presents this approach declining for the specific case of the Basilica of the Beata Vergine Assunta in Guasila (Sardinia) and the results obtained, fundamental bases knowledge for the last intervention of safety and extraordinary maintenance of the monument implemented in 2019. This late nineteenth-century basilica showed signs of dangerous infiltration of rainwater both on the dome and on the plaster with alarming detachments, the walls showed dangerous cracks and signs of humidity deserving of careful investigations. The bell tower, attacked by vegetation that has settled in the cracks, threatens devastating collapses, and requires safety measures. Thanks to the results of this in-depth and integrated study it has been possible to set the bases of knowledge, the current state of conservation of the fabric and the causes of its structural problems, suggesting to architects and restorers balanced guidelines for the intervention of restoration, especially to optimize timing, money, and the usability of this monument.

2 The Transdisciplinary Protocol for the Restoration

Every restoration project needs to be based on a transdisciplinary knowledge protocol to be effective and long-term. This is intended "not only as the integration of knowledge of a specific research topic but also as the assimilation of reciprocal bodies of knowledge, overcoming the concepts of multidisciplinary and interdisciplinary works [9]. In such an approach, there are no boundaries between sectorial disciplines that are fully integrated with the aim of a deep knowledge of the monument in every aspect: from the historical-archival point of view to the geometric-architectural and material-structural features, as well as to those related to pathologies of decay and their causes, crucial information regarding the state of conservation. Then, it is possible to hypothesize the possible interventions to be performed.

This approach considers the integrated use of different techniques and different skills that, according to the current standards of good practice of conservation and preservation of the architectural heritage such as the ISO 13822:2010 "Bases for design of structures-Assessment of existing structures", should involve the use of non-destructive methodologies and tools [10, 11] designed to ensure the geometric surveys, detailed inspections, material testing and structural analyses [12–14].

In particular, the transdisciplinary protocol for the knowledge of the cultural heritage carried out, consists by the integration of three fields of research:

a) architectural history with the analyses of documents and iconographic materials, useful to reconstruct the unknow construction history of the fabric and its evolution considering its context and the previous restoration works. In this phase all information can be indirectly investigated through the consultation of all the documents regarding the monument: bibliographic, archival, cartographic, iconographic, and archaeological studies have paramount importance for reconstructing the building's history and evolution, providing important information about the building materials and techniques as well as possible previous interventions. Also, prior geometrical surveys, when available, can help in this phase of knowledge. This phase of analysis should be conducted through the consultation of National, Civil, Ecclesiastic and Council Archives, the documentary, photographic, iconographic archives of the Superintendence for Architectural, Landscape, Historic, Artistic and Ethno-Anthropologic Heritage and the Archaeological Superintendence.
b) geomatics surveys, fundamental basis for the geometric knowledge and health assessment of a building. During the last decade, the Terrestrial Laser Scanner (TLS) has been one of the main methods for the 3D survey and modelling of historical and cultural heritage, providing high data acquisition rates and high spatial data density [15–17]. Interesting reports on point clouds from TLS to 3D reconstruction can be found in Napolitano, 2019 and in Remondino, 2011 [18, 19]. Many works with the TLS have also involved the survey of paintings or frescoes to obtain orthophotos to be used for the construction of virtual paths [20]. On the other hand, there are countless works for the study of deformations or for the conservation of the architectural heritage [21, 22]. Currently another geomatics technique, widely used to produce high-density point clouds is the multi-image Close Range Photogrammetry (CRP) which is based on the Structure from Motion (SfM) algorithm [23, 24]. CRP

produces dense point clouds with high accuracy [25] that can be treated like those from TLS. The state-of-the-art of dense image-matching is discussed in Remondino, 2014 [26], where a comparison of the available software is also presented. Most of the published studies [27–29] estimate the accuracy of the point cloud using targets or through sections extracted from the point cloud and compared with the design ones or to preservation of archaeology and cultural heritage based on point cloud surveys. In Remondino, 2012 [30] a critical review of the developments in automated image processing is discussed. In architectural surveying it is common to find complex geometries with different configurations, the combination of the two TLS and CRP methods must therefore be seen as an integration that can provide a more complete 3D model than the use of individual techniques [31]. The main advantage of this technique is surely its ability to accurately acquire the colour of the surveyed object. This is a substantial difference with the TLS technique, due to the nature of the data acquisition method [32, 33] for this reason, the two techniques are often used together.

c) material analyses, investigated through a detailed diagnostic protocol with minero-petrographic analyses such as optical microscope and Xray-diffraction. Materials represent topography and the interaction between nature and builders' skills and abilities. Not only stones but also mortars, mixtures of aggregates and binder are investigated because an integral part of historical masonry with the functional role of bonding or protecting. In this light, this step of the protocol underlines the importance of the characterisation, the identification of historical mortars and the analysis of their state of conservation considering composition, shape, size, particle size of aggregates, binder type, and to the assessment of the level of degradation. This analysis allows to define the nature of the natural materials, to hypothesize the origin and the extractive sites, and to identify the different types of decay [34].

3 Results

The codified methodology has been carried out for the study of the Beata Vergine Assunta Basilic placed in Guasila (CA), a neoclassic monument designed by the local famous architect Gaetano Cima in the middle nineteenth century (Fig. 1). Since its construction, this monument has shown signs of decay and structural failure such as cracks and infiltration of rainy water mainly located on the dome, on all the smaller vaults, arches, and headers. All these problems concerning the quality of the building materials, a local sandstone historically quarried in the surroundings hills, and the poor building skills have been investigated to understand the origin of the current state of decay and to define, after several years of unsuccessful restorations works, effective guidelines for the safeguard of the monument.

In the following paragraphs results arisen from the application of the protocol are presented, with specific regard to historical, geomatics and diagnostic investigations carried out on the Basilica in wider research titled *Architectural and structural survey of the Santuario della B.V. Assunta in Guasila,* financed by the Guasila council [35].

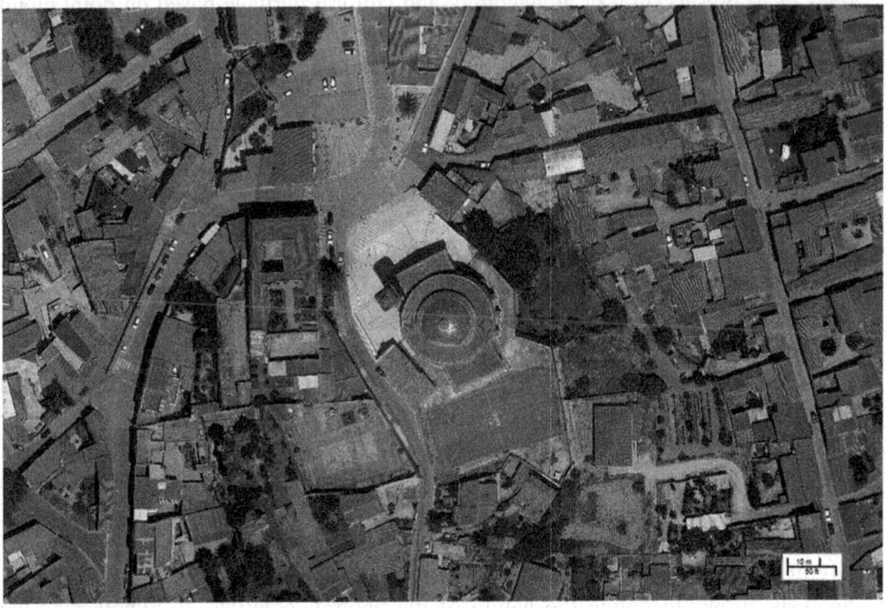

Fig. 1. Aerial view of the Basilic (Pilia E.)

3.1 From the Document to the Monument

The study of the documents has been essential to reveal the controversial construction history of the basilica, built on the ruins of a previous church and as already known, characterised by several building issues related to the poor quality of craftsmanship and materials used. Three archives concerning documents, photographs and iconographies were consulted in order to reconstruct the historical events related to monument: the first one is the Parish archive, which provided important information about the foundation phase of the church with drawings and written documents (reports of project, sketches and correspondence about the construction site) that state detailed design intentions of the architect Gaetano Cima, the ongoing planned changes, problems and outcomes of the construction site; the archive of the Superintendence of Architecture, Landscape, Historical, Artistic and Ethno-anthropological Heritage of the Provinces of Cagliari and Oristano and of the Guasila municipality which instead provided projects, drawings and photographic evidence of the restorations carried out on the monument, interventions that start as early as 1897, after only forty years since the consecration and opening to the community happened.

Thus, the data contained has been for the first time crossed with the aim of reconstructing not only the chronology and the overall stratigraphy of the monument, in some phases still unknown, but also to identify materials and construction techniques used in the construction and restorations phases, going to understand the possible causes of decay in place. All the materials have been then cross-checked with the direct analysis of the monument, finding interesting and crucial findings and differences for planning the last intervention of restoration.

The Parish Church of the Beata Vergine Assunta was built in 1839 by Gaetano Cima [36]. The construction site started in 1842 is immediately linked to controversy with the impresario Crobu who realised several variations during the execution phase of the building site. It is so clear that the main structures and the decorative apparatus are therefore different from the original project placed in the Parish archive.

It is precisely because of these faults during the construction that it is already necessary to require a first restoration in 1897, when Vivanet, Director of the Regional Office of Antiquities and Fine Arts receives the first report concerning the presence of injuries and recommends the use of concret instead of ordinary mortar, for "profiling of the lesions". From this first intervention of restoration, highly incompatible with the materials of the structure, several ineffective interventions were designed and conducted, all aimed at solving two issues that are recurring with continuity during time: the lesions on the elevation structures and the infiltrations of water from the roofs.

As reported in the archives of the Superintendence, the interventions included: the consolidation of masonries with the application of iron chains, the compensation of injuries with iron bars and grout and the mending of damaged masonry (arch. Crudeli, 1954); the construction of a new reinforced concrete retaining wall (1988), operations of "*cuci e scuci*" and armed seams with iron bars (199–1993), the waterproofing of the dome as well as the complete demolition of all the decorated plaster of the dome and its reconstruction (Arch. Rollo, Ing. Medda and Mameli, 1978), the waterproofing and the complete replacement of the roof covering and finally, interventions on the rainwater disposal system and on the fixtures of the lantern to promote the air circulation in the dome (Arch. Secci and Morand, half 80s) [37].

Despite this long series of interventions, we are still facing the same problems of decay: the presence of moisture and water infiltration from the roofs, and widespread injuries on the dome and arches.

Overall, during these restoration activities, prolonged for over a century, it has been possible to recognise the total incompatibility of materials used and the interventions, often not connected to each other creating significant further discontinuities on the masonries. The indirect study of the monument has therefore, accurately outlined the historical facts concerning the monument, providing important information to re-read the factory thanks to the support and integration of direct analysis, focused on studying with reliability the geometries and anomalies already witnessed at the design level and modified over time due to subsidence and diagnostic analysis of characterisation of materials (natural and artificial), considering the specific properties of building and restoration materials, their compatibility and their current state of conservation (Fig. 2).

Fig. 2. Drawing of the main façade of the church. Cima's project is conserved in the Archive of the church.

3.2 Geomatics Survey

The Terrestrial Laser Scanner (TLS) and Close Range Photogrammetry (CRP) techniques were used and integrated for the metric-dimensional survey and 3D modeling of the Basilica. In particular, the entire internal and external building was detected with the TLS. The CRP was used for the internal 3D survey of the dome. The need for this integration was to improve the texture of the 3D survey of the dome and its paintings, a result that could not be achieved with the TLS survey alone, both due to the distance of the TLS from the dome and due to the resolution of the digital camera associated with the laser scanner used.

3.3 Terrestrial Laser Scanner

For the TLS technique, the Faro Focus 3D Terrestrial Laser Scanner was used. It is a compact scanner characterized by an operative range that varies between 0.6 and 120 m, with a ranging error of ±2 mm for scanner–object distances between 10 and 25 m. The scans were processed using the JRC Reconstructor software v. 3.1.0 by Gexcel Ltd.

For the design of the scans, we started by thinking about the geometry of the building and the scale of restitution. The presence of architectural details and the situation of the deformations to be detected were taken into account. From these considerations, it was decided to perform the scans at a resolution of ¼, with 3x quality, which corresponds to a resolution of 7 mm/10 m. To ensure an overlap between the scans of at least 30%, 33 internal scans from the ground and 8 internal scans from the elevator basket were performed to survey some niches not directly accessible by the detector. The external scans were 15 from the ground and 8 from a crane equipped with a telescopic arm on which the TLS was mounted (Figs. 3 and 4).

Fig. 3. TLS survey of the roof

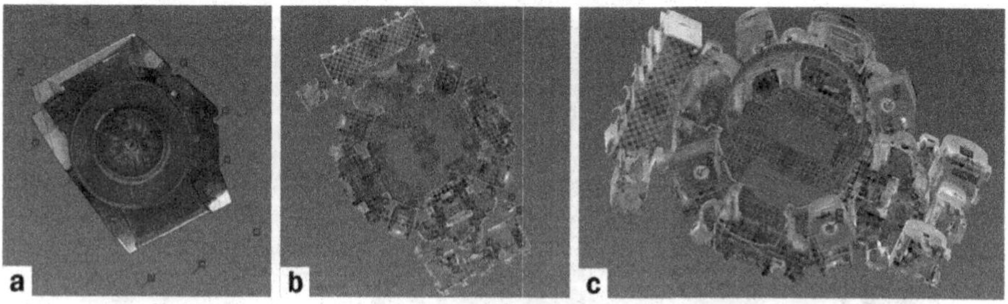

Fig. 4. a) Outdoor TLS stations; b) Indoor TLS stations, ground floor; c) Indoor TLS stations of chapels.

The survey was carried out on 12 October 2017, a non-windy day, and with the crane engine turned off to avoid harmful vibrations that could have affected the scans The 64 scans were initially pre-processed and subsequently, using only natural features, they were pre-aligned and then aligned obtaining closure errors of less than one centimetre. The complete point cloud of the Basilica was therefore geo-referenced in the ETRF2000 reference system (with geoidal heights), through the use of 20 Ground Control Points located outside the Church (Fig. 5) and surveyed with a GNSS survey in RTK mode, using the differential corrections from the SARNET network of permanent stations in Sardinia [http://www.geodesia.biz/sarnet/].

Fig. 5. GCPs position (image from Google Earth)

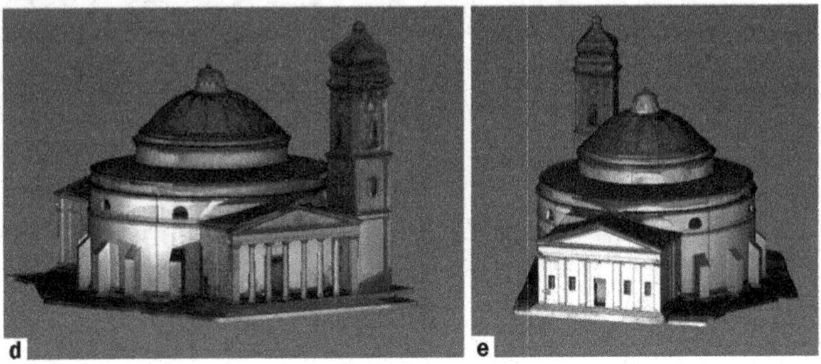

Fig. 6. Front (d) and rear (e) 3D model

After processing the 64 point clouds and obtaining a single point cloud, still using JRC 3D Reconstructor, we produced the mesh and then the 3D model. From this we extracted the following graphic elements:

- horizontal sections at different heights: ground level, ground + 3 m, ground + 6 m (Fig. 7);
- vertical sections;
- orthophotographs of the vertical and horizontal elements, both on the inside and outside, with ground sampling distance (GSD) of 2 cm.

From the sections and orthophotos, through a long editing work, all the drawings of the Basilica's plans, sections and elevations have been prepared (Fig. 6).

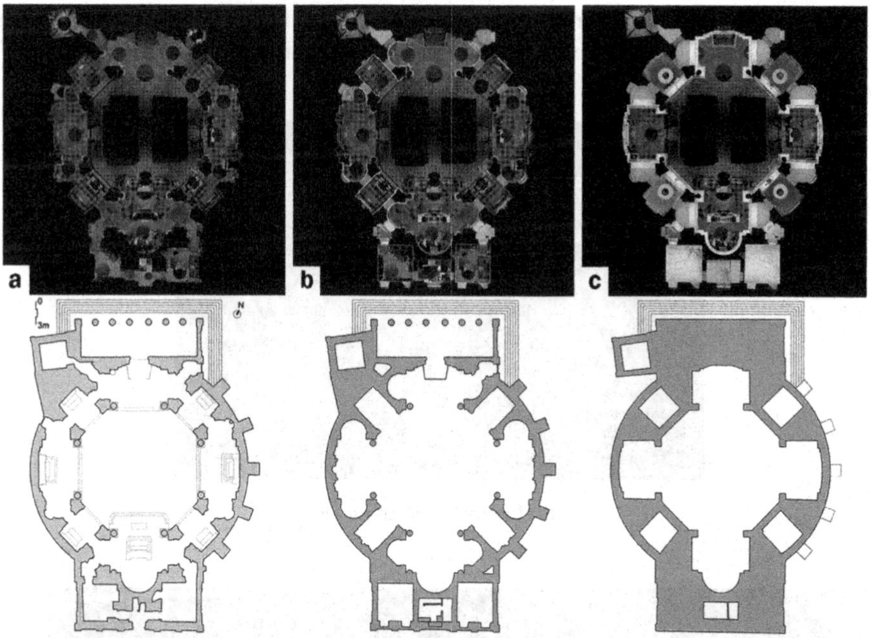

Fig. 7. Orthophotographs and horizontal sections at different heights: a) ground level, b) ground + 3 m, c) ground + 6 m (edited by Pilia, E)

3.4 CRP Survey

The CRP survey was used exclusively to survey the dome of the basilica and thus allow to obtain a high-resolution 3D relief with a high definition of the paintings shown on it (texture).

We used a digital non-metric camera (Canon EOS M3) with a CMOS 22.3 × 14.9 mm (3.7 mm pixel dimension) sensor, Field of View (FoV) 81.5 g, and 24.2 Megapixel resolution; objective EF-S 18–55 mm; the output data formats are Exif 2.3 (JPEG) and RAW (CR2 Canon original).

In order to obtain high metric and texture resolutions, the photogrammetric survey was performed using an elevated platform, with distances between the camera position and the dome varying between 3 and 8 m.

The images were processed with Metashape, a commercial software by Agisoft, using the "Structure from Motion" algorithm. 97 photos have been acquired by the EOS M3 and processed on an HP Z420 workstation with 64 GB RAM, Intel Xeon E5-16200 3.60 GHz CPU, and NVIDIA Quadro K2000 video card.

The image processing workflow follows the standard steps of SfM software with the solution of the Bundle Adjustment on sparse point cloud, external orientation of the block and generation of the dense point cloud. All images have been elaborated in Medium mode, in fact, as verified in Grillo, 2019 [38] the accuracy does not vary with respect to UltraHigh mode and processing times are reduced. The processing produced a point cloud of 11,315,919 points with a processing time of 6 h. The cloud was georeferenced using 10 GCPs extracted from the TLS point cloud. The global RMS of georeferencing is 2 cm. Figure 9 shows the textured point cloud of the dome.

Fig. 8. Internal view of the dome.

Fig. 9. Dome 3D model

3.5 Diagnostic for Materials

The analysis of the materials consisted of the systematic study of natural and artificial materials both used during the construction and the restorations. All these materials studied have allowed us to define the nature of materials, to hypothesize their origin and the quarry of extraction.

Particular attention has been given to the characterization of mortars and plasters in order to define their minero-petrographic nature: composition, shape, size, aggregates grain size, type of binder and to assess their state of conservation. Therefore, a reasoned sampling was carried out on mortars and plasters with scalpel and micro chisels for more compact materials, in accordance with the "Normal Recommendation UNI EN 16085:2012 Conservation of Cultural property - Methodology for sampling from materials of cultural property - General rules ICS: [97.195]".

The number of samples collected, sufficient to represent all the different types of materials, is the result of a preliminary analytical survey conducted in different parts of the structure with the help of a crane during the endoscopic survey campaign. So, different types of mortars, plasters and paint layers made with different techniques at different times have been sampled. These samples were characterised by investigations carried out under transmitted microscopy light. All the investigations were carried out at the laboratories of the DICAAR of LabMast (Mediterranean Laboratory for Materials and Historical-Traditional Architectures). The basilica is located in a landscape that presents a flat and hilly morphology called Trexenta, specifically characterized by silky marl, alternating with arenaceous levels from medium coarse to fine with strong vulcanoclastic component", and anthropic deposits, Eluvio-colluvial and terraced alluvial cultivars. Nine samples taken during endoscopic investigations were characterised by optical microscopy in transmitted light. From the macroscopic analysis of the Church, it was clear that all the load-bearing structures were made of local sandstone as also confirmed by the results provided by the geotechnical surveys. The building material are those extracted in the nearby historic quarries around the mining poles of Nuraminis-Samatzai, Pimentel and reused materials from the previous church and other monuments in the area, The sands, instead, as prescribed by Cima (ACCA, Carte Cima, b.2 fasc. 84) came from the cava de is Concas located in the same municipality of Guasila and now closed.

In summary, the analysis of the material samples shows that these are elements attributable to restoration work (C 02, C 04a-b, C 05, C07 I C 04, C 02). Hypothetically, historical mortars show a finer aggregate and a lower aggregate/binder ratio (C 04b, C 05, C 01). The forms of decay such as the strong decohesion, the presence of biological patinas, as in sample C03, are attributable to the strong presence of water infiltrations from the walls and roofs (Figs. 10 and 11).

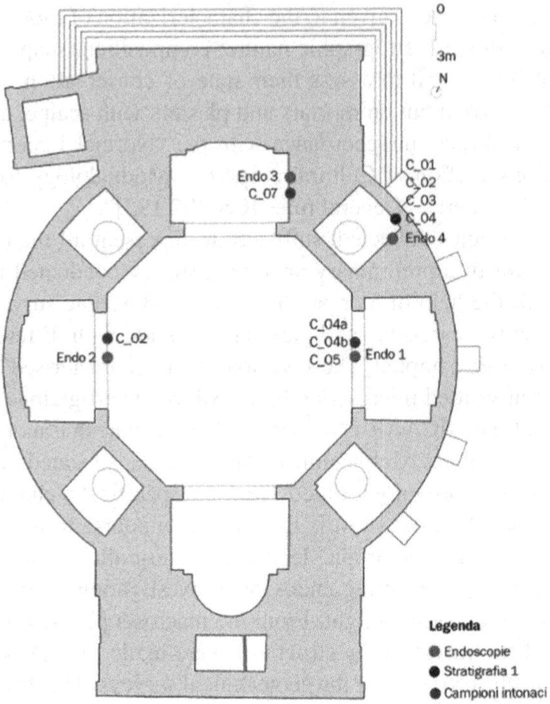

Fig. 10. Map of the samples at the level + 6 m (Pilia E.)

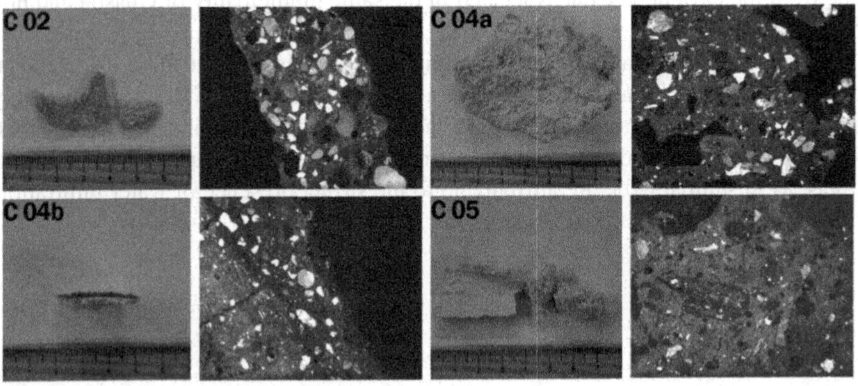

Fig. 11. Minero-petrographic analysis. From the left: macro photo and thin sections under the optical microscope in Transmitted Light (Laboratory analysis: Grillo S.M., LabMaST. Graphic elab.: Pilia E.).

4 Discussion and Conclusions

The research, conducted according to an integrated approach of the investigative field of research, has allowed to outline the history of the case study from the connexion between direct and indirect sources, to define its state of conservation with regard to geometries, techniques and materials, to provide a valid knowledge base for future insights, studies and for the preparation of a restoration project truly suited to the needs of the monument. From the sources we learn the information relating to the reconstruction of the schedule from its origins to today, which we know to be different from the one designed by Cima also from the feedback in the graphic rendering of the geometries of the asset. These geometries highlight a stable structure from a structural point of view, albeit characterized by the presence of widespread lesions present above all in correspondence of arches and vaults, attributable to the typical collapse of the platbands and their consolidation passed with cementitious binder mortars, and other superficial lesions, mainly due to the material degradation caused above all by the continuous infiltration of rainwater. As for the materials, on the other hand, a widespread use of concrete as a restoration material was found, which, being totally incompatible with the factory, has led to further problems of detachment of plaster and loss of decorative apparatus, which can be compensated by means of the constitution of a compatible mortar similar to the historical ones analysed.

Finally, no less important from this cross study is the possibility of having put up for tender the last intervention of 2019 for "safety and extraordinary maintenance of the Sanctuary of the Beata Vergine Assunta" concerning the problems that were still present in the monument such as the arrangement of the lantern, the rehabilitation of the recessed downspouts, the rehabilitation of the mezzanine walls from humidity, the reconstruction of the roof covering on the connection with the bell tower, appropriate natural and mechanical ventilation systems against condensation humidity.

Acknowledgments. The research *Architectural and structural survey of the Santuario della B.V. Assunta in Guasila* has been financed by the Guasila council, Scientific coordinators: Prof. Fausto Mistretta and Paolo *Sanjust. V;* architectural surveys (1:50) - conducted by the DICAAR, Unity of Geomatics of the DICAAR; Scientific Coordinator: Prof. G. Vacca; non-destructive and partially destructive controls - performed by the DICAAR, LabMAST - Mediterranean Laboratory for Historical materials and architectures, Scientific Coordinator: Prof. S.M. Grillo.

This paper, furthermore, was supported by Fondazione di Sardegna through grant Surveying, modelling, monitoring and rehabilitation of masonry vaults and domes i.e. Rilievo, modellazione, monitoraggio e risanamento di volte e cupole in muratura (RMMR) (CUP code: F72F20000320007).

References

1. http://vincoliinrete.beniculturali.it/VincoliInRete/vir/utente/login. Accessed 01 Apr 2022
2. http://www.icr.beniculturali.it/. Accessed 01 Apr 2022
3. https://www.italianostra.org/listarossa/#:~:text=La%20campagna%20nazionale%20di%20Italia,tutela%2C%20siti%20archeologici%20meno%20conosciuti. Accessed 01 Apr 2022
4. Pilia, E.: Urban ruins in historical centres. An integrated methodology for sustainable interventions in Cagliari, Sardinia. In: ArcHistoR architettura storia restauro - architecture history restoration, anno IV (2017) no. 8, pp. 174–217 (2017). ISSN 2384–8898

5. Fiorino, D.R., Grillo, S.M., Pilia, E.: Interdisciplinary Knowledge for conservation of Ruins: Stratigraphic Investigations of San Giovanni Battista Church (Sardinia, Italy). ATINER'S Conference Paper Series, No: ARC2015-2123, Athens (2015)
6. Moropoulou, A., Delegou, E.T., Avdelidis, N.P., Athanasiadou, A.: Integrated diagnostics using advanced in situ measuring technology. In: Proceedings of the 10th International Conference on Durability of Building Materials and Components, Lyon, France, 17–20 April 2005, pp. 1116–1123 (2005)
7. Letellier, R., Schmid, W., LeBlanc, F.: Recording, Documentation & Information Management for the Conservation of Heritage Places, Guiding Principles. J. Paul Getty Trust, Los Angeles, CA, USA (2007)
8. Delegou, E.T., Mourgi, G., Tsilimantou, E., Ioannidis, C., Moropoulou, A.: A multidisciplinary approach for historic buildings diagnosis: the case study of the Kaisariani Monastery. Heritage **2**, 1211–1232 (2019)
9. Pilia, E.: Urban Ruins. Memorial Value and Contemporary Role. DOM Publishers, Berlin (2019). ISBN 978-3-86922-708-5
10. Kioussi, A., Karoglou, M., Bakolas, A., Moropoulou, A.: Integrated documentation protocols enabling decision making in cultural heritage protection. In: Ioannides, M., Fritsch, D., Leissner, J., Davies, R., Remondino, F., Caffo, R. (eds.) EuroMed 2012. LNCS, vol. 7616, pp. 211–220. Springer, Heidelberg (2012). https://doi.org/10.1007/978-3-642-34234-9_21
11. Juanes, D., Ferrazza, L.: Computed Tomography Studies Applied to Polychromed Sculpture: The Making Process in Three Different Times. In: Ioannides, M., et al. (eds.) EuroMed 2012, LNCS, vol. 7616, pp. 884–893 (2012)
12. International Organization for Standardization. 13822 Bases for Design of Structures-Assessment of Existing Structures, CEN Brussels, Bruxelles, Belgium (2005)
13. Carpinteri, A., Invernizzi, S., Lacidogna, G.: In situ damage assessment and nonlinear modelling of a historical masonry tower. Eng. Struct. **27**, 387–395 (2005)
14. Costanzo, A., Minasi, M., Casula, G., Musacchio, M., Buongiorno, M.F.: Combined use of terrestrial laser scanning and IR thermography applied to a historical building. Sensors **15**, 194–213 (2014)
15. Costa, E., Balletti, C., Beltrame, C., Guerra, F., Vernier, P.: Digital survey techniques for the documentation of wooden shipwrecks. In: The International Archives of the Photogrammetry, Remote Sensing and Spatial Information Sciences, XLI-B5. XXIII ISPRS Congress, 12–19 July 2016, Prague, Czech Republic (2016)
16. Alshawabkeh, Y., El-Khalili, M., Almasr, E., Bala'awi, F., Al-Massarweh, A.: Heritage documentation using laser scanner and photogrammetry. The case study of Qasr Al-Abidit, Jordan. Digit. Appl. Archaeol. Cult. Heritage **16**, e00133 (2020). ISSN 2212-0548
17. Vacca, G., Quaquero, E.: BIM-3D GIS: an integrated system for the knowledge process of the buildings. J. Spat. Sci. **65**(2), 193–208 (2020). https://doi.org/10.1080/14498596.2019.1601600
18. Napolitano, R., Hess, M., Glisic, B.: Integrating non-destructive testing, laser scanning, and numerical modeling for damage assessment: the room of the elements. Heritage **2**, 151–168 (2019). https://doi.org/10.3390/heritage2010012
19. Remondino, F.: Heritage recording and 3D modeling with photogrammetry and 3D scanning. Remote Sens. **3**, 1104–1138 (2011). https://doi.org/10.3390/rs3061104
20. Balletti, C., Bertellini, B., Gottardi, C., Guerra, F.: Geomatics techniques for the enhancement and preservation of cultural heritage. Int. Arch. Photogramm. Remote Sens. Spatial Inf. Sci. **XLII-2/W11**, 133–140 (2019). https://doi.org/10.5194/isprs-archives-XLII-2-W11-133-2019
21. Mateus, L., et al.: Terrestrial laser scanning and digital photogrammetry for heritage conservation: case study of the historical walls of Lagos, Portugal, Int. Arch. Photogramm. Remote

Sens. Spatial Inf. Sci. **XLII-2/W11**, 843–847 (2019). https://doi.org/10.5194/isprs-archives-XLII-2-W11-843-2019
22. Pesci, A., Casula, G., Boschi, E.: Laser scanning the Garisenda and Asinelli towers in Bologna (Italy): detailed deformation patterns of two ancient leaning buildings. J. Cult. Herit. **12**, 117–127 (2011)
23. Luhmann, T., Robson, S., Kyle, S., Boehm, J.: Close Range Photogrammetry: 3D Imaging Techniques. Walter De Gruyter Inc., Berlin (2014)
24. Szeliski, R.: Computer vision: algorithms and applications. Springer Science & Business Media (2010)
25. Mistretta, F., Sanna, G., Stochino, F., Vacca, G.: Structure from motion point clouds for structural monitoring. Remote Sens. **2019**, 11 (1940). https://doi.org/10.3390/rs11161940
26. Remondino, F., Spera, M.G., Nocerino, E., Menna, F., Nex, F.: State of the art in high density image matching. Photogramm. Rec. **29**, 144–166 (2014). https://doi.org/10.1111/phor.12063
27. Morgan, J.A., Brogan, D.J., Nelson, P.A.: Application of structure-from-motion photogrammetry in laboratory flumes. Geomorphology **276**, 125–143 (2017)
28. Vacca, G.: Overview of open source software for close range photogrammetry. Int. Arch. Photogramm. Remote Sens. Spat. Inf. Sci. **XLII-2/W14**, 239–245 (2019). https://doi.org/10.5194/isprs-archives-XLII-4-W14-239-2019
29. Kersten, T.P., Lindstaedt, M.: Automatic 3D object reconstruction from multiple images for architectural, cultural heritage and archaeological applications using open-source software and web services. Photogramm. Fernerkund. Geoinf. (PFG) **6**, 727–740 (2012)
30. Remondino, F., Del Pizzo, S., Kersten, T.P., Troisi, S.: Low-cost and open-source solutions for automated image orientation – a critical overview. In: Ioannides, M., Fritsch, D., Leissner, J., Davies, R., Remondino, F., Caffo, R. (eds.) EuroMed 2012. LNCS, vol. 7616, pp. 40–54. Springer, Heidelberg (2012). https://doi.org/10.1007/978-3-642-34234-9_5
31. Mateus, L., et al.: The role of 3D documentation for restoration interventions. The case study of Valflores in Loures, Portugal. Int. Arch. Photogramm. Remote Sens. Spatial Inf. Sci. **XLIV-M-1-2020**, 381–388 (2020). https://doi.org/10.5194/isprs-archives-XLIV-M-1-2020-381-2020
32. Zhang, R., Schneider, D., Strauß, B.: Generation and comparison of TLS and SfM based 3D models of solid shapes in hydromechanic research. Int. Arch. Photogramm. Remote Sens. Spat. Inf. Sci. **XLI-B5**, 925–929 (2016). https://doi.org/10.5194/isprs-archives-XLI-B5-925-2016
33. Carraro, F., et al.: The 3D survey of the roman bridge of San Lorenzo in Padova (Italy): a comparison between SfM and TLS methodologies applied to the arch structure. Int. Arch. Photogramm. Remote Sens. Spat. Inf. Sci. **XLII-2/W15**, 255–262 (2019). https://doi.org/10.5194/isprs-archives-XLII-2-W15-255-2019
34. Fiorino, D.R., Grillo, S.M., Pilia, E.: Interdisciplinary Knowledge for conservation of Ruins: Stratigraphic Investigations of San Giovanni Battista Church (Sardinia, Italy). ATINER'S Conference Paper Series, No: ARC2015-2123, Athens (2015)
35. AA.VV. Il santuario della Beata Vergine Assunta in Guasila. Storia, analisi e prospettive future per la conservazione, CG Creazioni (2017)
36. Virdis, F., Puddu, T.: Gaetano Cima. Il tempio della villa di Guasila, documenti di archivio (2003)
37. Sanjust, P., Mistretta, F., Pilia, E.: The pantheon of Gaetano Cima in Guasila. Interdisciplinary studies for its structural conservation. In: TeMA, vol. 5, no. 2, pp. 158–169 (2019). ISSN 2421-4574
38. Grillo, S.M., Pilia, E., Vacca, G.: Integrated study of the Beata Vergine Assunta dome with Structure from Motion and diagnostic approaches. Int. Arch. Photogramm. Remote Sens. Spatial Inf. Sci. **XLII-2/W11**, 579–585 (2019). https://doi.org/10.5194/isprs-archives-XLII-2-W11-579-2019

Locus of Underwater Cultural Heritage (UCH) in Maritime Spatial Planning (MSP): A Data-Driven, Place-Based and Participatory Planning Perspective

Dionisia Koutsi(✉) and Anastasia Stratigea

Department of Geography and Regional Planning, School of Rural, Surveying and Geoinformatics Engineering, National Technical University of Athens, Athens, Greece
{koutsidionisia,stratige}@central.ntua.gr

Abstract. During the last decade, the rising interest in the marine world has enriched the planning discourse with issues such as the protection, preservation, sustainable and resilient exploitation of marine resources. At the European level, Maritime Spatial Planning (MSP) has come to the forefront in this respect, as part of the EU blue growth strategy and a powerful tool for facilitating the transition from traditional maritime sectoral approaches to an integrated, place-based, data-driven, participatory and multi-dimensional new maritime planning rationale. Among the maritime resources concerned, Underwater Cultural Heritage (UCH) gains ground as a valuable asset in pursuing developmental objectives of coastal/insular communities. Towards this end, MSP endeavours need to successfully incorporate UCH management and compromise UCH-related uses with other sectoral ones in the sea. Along these lines, this paper aims at highlighting the context of sustainable and resilient UCH management within the MSP realm by innovatively integrating the conceptual framework for its understanding and the key methodological steps for its implementation. The aforementioned context is parallelized to current UCH management reality in order to explore UCH handling within MSP in practice; and illuminate successful UCH management in MSP approaches in selected countries/regions at the EU level.

Keywords: Underwater Cultural Heritage · Marine Spatial Planning · Sustainable coastal and insular communities · Participatory planning · Place-based approach

1 Introduction

Megatrends of the last few decades, such as the globalization, urbanization, resource-intensive developmental pathways, digital transition, overpopulation and lifestyle, have led to more demanding resource consumption patterns, with severe impacts on resource availability and sustainability objectives [1]. The already visible strain of continental reserves has shifted interest in ocean ones, bringing to the surface the *blue economy concept*. This concept, already highlighted in the Blue Growth Strategy of the European

O. Gervasi et al. (Eds.): ICCSA 2022 Workshops, LNCS 13379, pp. 686–702, 2022.
https://doi.org/10.1007/978-3-031-10545-6_46

Commission [2], is getting flesh and bones as technological advances offer the means for gathering significant data about the marine environment at more and more greater depths, unveiling the benefits that can be reaped by the oceans and the abundance of their resources in comparison with the terrestrial ones [3]. Such an ascertainment has placed maritime resources at the epicenter of the discourse about a maritime-based sustainable future of humanity [4].

Marine world exploration, however, brings also to the forefront cultural resources of global significance that lay at the sea bottom and form the *Underwater Cultural Heritage* (UCH). UNESCO [5] defines UCH as all traces of human existence having a cultural, historical or archaeological character; and being partially or totally, periodically or continuously, under water for at least 100 years. These may concern sites, structures, buildings, artifacts and human remains; vessels, aircraft, other vehicles or any part thereof, their cargo or other contents; and objects of prehistoric character. UCH constitutes an essential element of the marine world that bears social, environmental, cultural and economic value [6, 7]; and is currently highly appreciated as the *humanity's trace* in the marine world through centuries [7–13]. Nonetheless, UCH in many cases remains largely unknown, unexplored and, most importantly, unprotected, being thus placed at significant risk of degradation and even loss [14]. Deterioration of UCH state is further stressed by the lack of available data as to the exact location, current status, historical documentation as well as conditions of the surrounding environment, in which these submerged parts of heritage are laid [15, 16].

The growing interest in the blue economy and related maritime economic activities further threatens UCH integrity in multiple ways. In fact oceans, during the last decade, have become extremely crowded places due to the development of maritime economy. Thus, the need for managing conflicting interests and regulating maritime uses, including UCH-related ones, is rising. In response to this need, the European Union (EU) has published the 2014/89/EU Directive [17], introducing *Marine Spatial Planning* (MSP) as a powerful and essential spatial tool, capable of handling conflicts among sectoral interests and reconciling marine resource conservation along with maritime economic stakes. Based on an *ecosystem and place-based approach* and taking into account the distinct levels of the sea world (seabed, water column and ocean surface), MSP attempts to effectively organize a complex, highly complicated range of activities that are interwoven in both sectoral as well as spatial and temporal terms [17, 18]. Furthermore, MSP presents a great chance for the preservation and sustainable exploitation of UCH in the blue economy realm.

Managing UCH, as a maritime asset serving multiple objectives – e.g., environmental protection; cultural heritage acquaintance, awareness and valuation; as well as authentic diving tourism experiences [19] – constitutes a challenging planning task and a distinct dimension of MSP duties. Along these lines, this paper aims at highlighting the context of sustainable and resilient UCH management within MSP, by firstly delimiting the conceptual framework for grasping UCH. Based on that, key methodological concerns for implementing UCH planning exercises in MSP studies are sketched and their practical implementation is explored. The structure of the paper has as follows: in Sect. 2, UCH management is framed by MSP's key principles that demarcate methodological adjustments/guidance of related planning processes; Sect. 3 elaborates on two MSP examples

(Finland and Estonia), in an effort to parallelize conceptual/methodological concerns with current practice; while, finally, in Sect. 4 discussion and conclusions are drawn.

2 Framing UCH Management Perspectives within MSP

MSP is a spatial tool in support of policy making as to the allocation, in a sustainable and resilient way, of competing economic activities/uses in the marine environment [20]. Its practice is challenging planners, so far accustomed to a more stable and easier to explore ground, the land. This holds even truer when comes to UCH and maritime uses, addressing UCH protection/preservation and sustainable exploitation in coastal and insular contexts. Below, conceptual and methodological issues, addressing planners' concerns for grasping UCH within MSP studies, are discussed.

2.1 Highlighting the Locus of UCH along the Key Principles of MSP

According to the United Nations (UN) [21] and UNESCO-IOC/European Commission [22], successful MSP outcomes are grounded in nine *commonly accepted principles*, featuring key concerns of the planning process and placing stakeholders and community engagement as an integral part. These are discussed below, in the effort to locate UCH within MSP.

A. Multiple spatial scale (or multi-scale) approach to MSP
This principle delineates the need for properly demarcating the spatial scale of an MSP endeavour in order to adjust for the unique attributes of each single marine environment (e.g. geographical features, existence of vulnerable areas), but also kind of maritime uses (e.g. intensity, synergies or conflicts among different uses) and diversifying legal/administrative jurisdictions in charge. According to the UN [21], the recommended spatial scales can range from the local to the regional/sub-regional or even national ones. In order for plans to be successful, actors from different spatial scales should share common visions and objectives; and display a sort of hierarchical relationship/cooperation for building consensus as to the action plans that are capable of reaching this vision. The multi-scale approach is quite essential when managing UCH that is of *glocal* (global and local) concern, since UCH is in many cases a heritage of global resonance and interest [5]. Achieving a certain balance among divergent hierarchical priorities at multiple spatial scales [23] implies *governance* and *engagement* of a range of actors and stakeholders (authorities, NGOs, businesses etc.) [24]. Thus governance and stakeholders' engagement lie at the heart of UCH management as a means for UCH location identification, exploration, excavation, documentation, conservation, valuation, sustainable and resilient exploitation according to local beliefs and experiential knowledge [13], monitoring and safeguarding; and are issues aptly pronounced in the 2001 UNESCO Convention [25].

B. Integration
The term accounts for different meanings and approaches. Thus, it may refer to the integration of:

- environmental, social, economic objectives in pursuing marine sustainability goals;
- sectors' perception for establishing synergies (e.g., UCH management and diving tourism/recreation) [26] and handling conflicts;
- vertically- (across different spatial levels) and horizontally-related (stakeholders, community, decision-making bodies, NGOs, etc. within a specific spatial level) actors' engagement for accommodating all stakes/interests in the planning process;
- land- and maritime-based planning endeavours for assuring harmonization and coherence among interacting parts of the same coastal system [27].

When it comes to UCH, integration further relates to the inseparable consideration of the:

- cultural (UCH) and natural dimension (marine environment) [13, 28]. UCH is inextricably linked with its hosting land and sea environment; it is largely interpreted by use of locational aspects of this environment; and is, in most of the cases, adjusted to or formed by such an environment, e.g., UCH as artificial reefs [29];
- tangible and intangible dimensions of UCH and their interconnection with elements of the terrestrial world, e.g., monuments, war installations, maritime museums.

In addition, the aforementioned interrelationships render synergies among a variety of stakeholders (in both vertical and horizontal terms) quite essential in order for conflicts between developmental and protection prospects to be eliminated; and a sustainable and resilient exploitation of UCH to be accomplished.

C. Land-sea interactions

Such interactions are of high importance in MSP studies, seeking to achieve the sustainable use of maritime resources. These may relate to natural processes embedding land-sea interaction (e.g. coastal erosion); land- and sea-related uses and activities (e.g. ports); outcomes of policy decisions for land and sea areas and respective planning-related land-sea interactions (e.g. areas designated for tourism or aquaculture activities). In case of UCH in particular, the neighboring coastal area largely determines the way UCH can be utilized, the pressures it receives by e.g. intense coastal activities, but also the linkages with land-based activities or even terrestrial cultural heritage sites. The relationship with the coastal land is also determined by the intangible elements attached to UCH, such as nautical stories, legends and myths that accompany the local (U)CH[1] narrative [7, 30].

D. The MSP 'four dimensions' of reference

MSP should include planning directions for all four marine dimensions, namely the: ocean surface, sea water column, seabed and time. Same holds for UCH management within MSP, where these dimensions can ensure: UCH protection and handling of conflicts with other uses, e.g., diving activities (all dimensions), surface observation/snorkeling (ocean surface), maritime transport [surface, seabed (anchoring)], material extraction (seabed), to name but a few. Time is also of high importance in the marine

[1] (U)CH: the term refers to both UCH and land-based Cultural Heritage (CH).

environment, perceived both in a short term, demarcating the changing marine conditions (e.g. season weather); and a longer one, displaying alterations of the marine state (e.g. climate change, changing water texture) and related repercussions to UCH.

F. Knowledge-based projects
MSP has to rely on high-quality spatio-temporal data, used for demonstrating the state of play of the marine environment. These data are coupled with empirical knowledge, emanating from actors' engagement and delineating expectations/priorities that need to be factored into the MSP (Fig. 1). Data and related sources, when implementing MSP, are also essential for monitoring/evaluating results and fueling relevant adjustments to both the MSP outcome and related policy paths (Fig. 1).

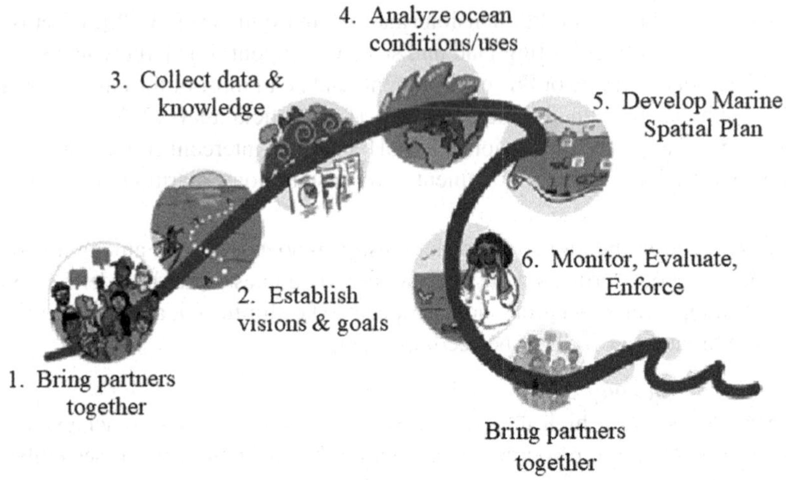

Fig. 1. The Marine Spatial Planning process, Source: Adapted from [31]

Data availability is also of utmost importance for *UCH management*. Gathering and interpreting data about UCH sites is a multi- and inter-disciplinary endeavour, shedding light on the: *tangible* attributes, e.g., current physical condition of submerged relics, state of the surrounding environment, location and depth, cargo in case of a shipwreck; and *intangible* ones, e.g., historical evidence/references, sinking conditions, human and material losses, to name a few [15]. Of course, gathering such UCH data is not an easy task; and despite the technological progress in the field of data collection, resulting crop still remains limited due to considerable time and cost constraints [32]. Considering that currently only 20% of the oceans are mapped [33], valuable data as to the location and current status of a large part of UCH is lacking, a deficit that places formidable barriers to their very protection at first and, subsequently, their sustainable management within MSP endeavours.

G. Suitability and spatial efficiency
During the last decade, attractiveness of marine resources has rendered oceans highly contested spaces. However, prioritizing uses in the sea space within MSP endeavours

is crucial for the sustainable exploitation of marine resources. Such a prioritization can be accomplished by the identification of immovable and non-renounceable resources that normally gain priority in marine space allocation [21]; and the multi-use of marine space by establishing synergies among uses. UCH, as an immovable and valuable to community heritage [34], gets high priority in marine space for in situ preservation and protection [5]. As stated also by Stancheva and Stanchev [35], UCH management allows multi-use of marine space by establishing the triptych of cultural heritage management, environmental protection and recreation/diving tourism.

H. Connectivity

This is realized in terms of networking among, e.g., sectors or activities of the same nature; areas with similar characteristics or interrelated uses or functions, such as networks of protected areas; but also connections among marine stakeholders, establishing 'bridges' for sharing knowledge and coordinating maritime activities. Connectivity is essential among UCH-related activities, e.g., cultural and natural maritime protection and recreation/diving tourism, a fact also related to the aforementioned multi-use dimension. Spatial connectivity can strengthen common developmental directions of sites that have similar characteristics or fall into the same historical narrative (e.g. WWII remains in coastal/marine areas). It can support exchange of knowledge and good practices, thus broadening the benefits reaped in societal, environmental and economic terms. Speaking of stakeholders' connectivity, a robust, well-structured and impactful UCH management perspective presupposes networking and interaction among interested stakeholders, falling into UCH-related sectors, such as marine archeology, tourism, maritime and diving communities [36].

I. Cross-border cooperation

Although MSP can be seen primarily as a state-based process, cross-border cooperation is essential to ensure coherence of MSP plans; and coordinated action across coastal zones and marine regions. Cross-border cooperation addresses also the transboundary dimension of marine problems and challenges, the resolution of which requires common regional or sub-regional approaches [37]. This holds true for UCH management as well, taking into account that submerged cultural assets do not always originate from the country these are eventually detected. Especially when it comes to e.g., war shipwrecks, jurisdiction issues arise between the wreck's origin country and the country in which the wreck is sunk, being in charge for its preservation [38]. In such a context, cooperation between both sides is critical. Cross-border cooperation can also be perceived among regional, and/or local plans within a single national territory.

G. Adaptive approach

This constitutes one of the most critical principles in MSP. It follows a process of interactive and repetitive planning cycles (Fig. 2) for continually improving maritime plans, policy outcomes and management practices. Each repetition of a planning cycle steps forward understanding, learning and knowledge gains with regard to goal achievements and inexpediencies. Steady monitoring of results of each planning cycle lies at the heart of the adaptive approach, resulting in data collection that is capable of drafting outcomes of the allocation of MSP uses and related maritime activities in the marine environment. Such data emanates from *field observation* and *experiential knowledge*, collected from stakeholders who are active in the marine environment. The latter is quite valuable for monitoring and evaluating the performance of maritime uses, as these are allocated by the MSP.

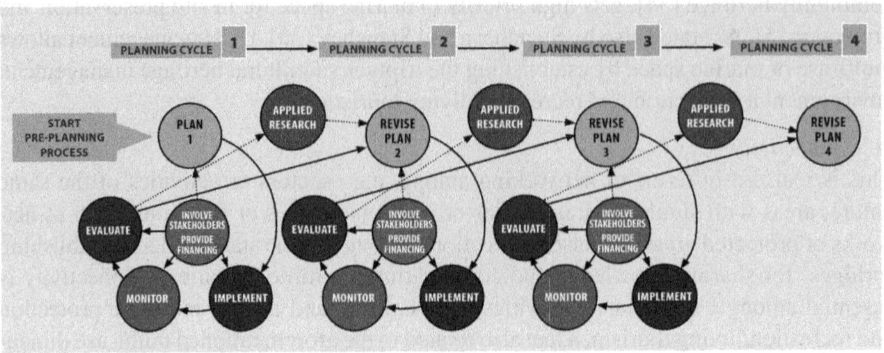

Fig. 2. The adaptive approach of MSP, Source: [21]

When it comes to UCH, the adaptive approach as a process of repetitive planning cycles (Fig. 2) can be regarded in alignment with the *Cultural Heritage Cycle* (CHC) (Fig. 3). CHC presents a participatory stepwise process that guides understanding, valuing, caring and enjoying cultural heritage, both in land and at sea; and a process that strengthens appreciation and awareness raising as to the value of UCH and desire to keep it intact [13, 39]. Furthermore, it broadens community's understanding as to the role of UCH for safeguarding local identity and pursuing sustainable development goals in coastal and insular regions; and renders local people the guardians of their UCH [30]. A better understanding and valuation of UCH can be a precious feedback in the MSP monitoring process, steadily improving results of each single planning cycle and providing a clearer, more powerful and motivating image of the true nature of UCH [30].

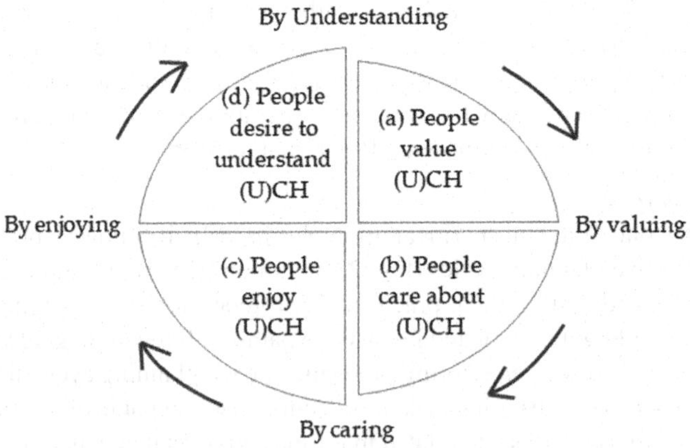

Fig. 3. The people-centered Cultural Heritage Cycle, Source: [13]

As stated by the Spanish Ministry of Culture [40], involvement of fishermen, divers and local inhabitants in the conservation of local marine sites has proved to be the most effective measure for UCH protection.

2.2 UCH Handling Within the MSP Context

Having described the way UCH can be embedded in the key MSP principles, some critical *methodological concerns* arise, when it comes to UCH management for serving local/regional sustainable development goals in coastal and insular regions, in harmony with the general directions provided by an MSP plan.

In particular, seeking to achieve sustainable and resilient exploitation of UCH in coastal and insular regions implies the need for a methodological approach that roughly consists of *three closely interrelated components* (Fig. 4), namely the: core component, representing steps of an *integrated and adaptive planning process*, accompanied by a *monitoring mechanism* for assessing and retrofitting the outcome of the planning process; and two essential for the core component pillars, being *spatial data analysis* and *public engagement* (Fig. 4, Pillar 1 and 2) [12, 13], also recognized as the bedrocks of well-documented and robust MSP decisions. These two pillars crosscut both compartments of the core component, i.e. the planning and monitoring process; provide essential information and valuable feedback for coping with the complexity and dynamic nature of the marine environment and land-sea / sea-land interactions; and guide well-informed and robust planning choices for sustainable and resilient UCH management. The way conceptual principles of MSP and CHC (Fig. 4) are instilled into the components of such a methodological framework is shortly discussed below.

More specifically, all *MSP principles* are infused into all concrete steps of the core planning component and accompanied pillars, addressing sustainable management of UCH and defining the way decision-making is taking place and policy directions are drawn. In more detail, the aforementioned principles frame choices as to the *spatial data* collection, processing and visualization for planning the sustainable exploitation of UCH within the MSP general directions. These data are used to unfold the current spatial context and the dynamics of the coastal and marine environment in which UCH is located. They strengthen knowledge as to the: natural and cultural attributes of land and marine environment; MSP uses allocated in the surrounding area and respective interactions, assessing whether these are in harmony or conflict with predicted UCH uses; and complementary uses, shaping an integrated and multi-use approach of marine space. Regarding the purely *planning steps* of UCH management, MSP principles highlight all those dimensions that need to be addressed in order for the most suitable planning decisions for allocation of UCH maritime uses and complementarity/appropriateness of their coexistence, but also potential reallocation of uses currently or potentially in conflict with UCH to be made. *Monitoring*, as an integral part of the planning discipline in general and MSP in particular is the mechanism for assessing and redefining UCH planning exercises and related policy decisions according to the dynamics of the wider marine environment. It is based on spatio-temporal data management and constitutes the means for initiating adaptive planning cycles. Finally, MSP principles frame the context of *community and stakeholders' engagement*, as a defining element of UCH management for demarcating who is going to be part at which stage of the planning process; what kind of synergies is essential to be established; and what should be the role or power given to stakeholders in the planning process, ranging from pure awareness raising or consultation to co-design or co-decision.

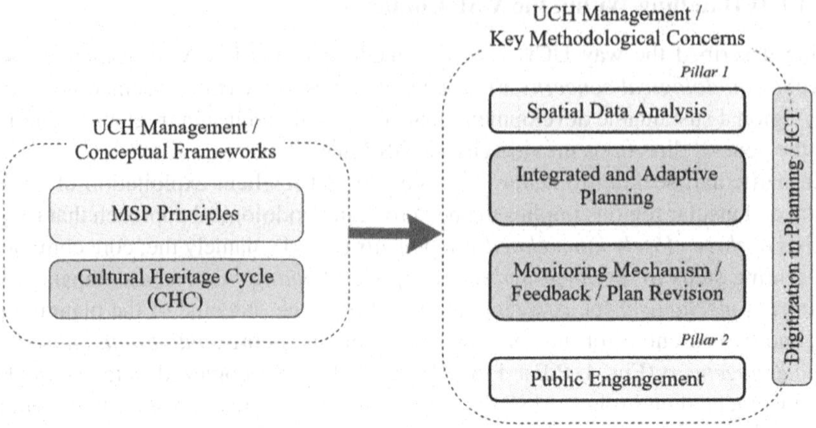

Fig. 4. Linkages between the conceptual and methodological framework for UCH management in coastal and insular communities, Source: Own elaboration

The *Cultural Heritage Cycle* is also a key asset from a methodological point of view of UCH management. It is strongly related to qualitative and quantitative *spatial data collection/analysis*, demarcating the value attached to tangible and intangible aspects of UCH as well as the prevailing attitude as to its protection/preservation. Distinct stages of CHC result in the: maturing of community with respect to the understanding, valuing, caring and enjoying cultural heritage and its surrounding environment (Fig. 3), both in land and at sea; and steadily broadening of willingness to keep it intact for the next generations, rendering thus locals the guardians of UCH. The *planning process* itself is also fueled by the deepening of knowledge on the local perception of UCH, guiding planning outcomes that fit well with the value system, historical paths and position of UCH in each single local context. Gradual awakening of the value of cultural heritage, as realized by the maturing process presented by the Cultural Heritage Cycle, goes hand-in-hand with the *monitoring process*. Indeed, assessment of the impacts of the UCH management plan, coupled with the gradually enhancement of UCH knowledge, awareness, appreciation and valuing, sharpens UCH consciousness, deepens willingness to engage in UCH planning endeavours and provides valuable feedback for further improving such planning outcomes (Fig. 2). Finally, proper integration of the Cultural Heritage Cycle in planning is strongly associated with the collaboration among planners, decision makers and local communities, broadening *public engagement* and resulting in community-driven UCH protection/preservation and sustainable exploitation plans [7, 12].

Last, but not least, comes Information and Communication Technologies (ICT) as a significant enabler of effective UCH management [41]. Speaking of *spatial data collection/analysis*, ICT offer the means for collecting, elaborating, visualizing and communicating a vast amount of planning-related content. Crowdsourcing can also be a valuable mean for enriching tangible, but notably intangible aspects of UCH, thus enabling the placement of UCH within the right historical, value, social etc., context. Such a potential creates a more fertile ground for conducting *planning exercises*, a fact that is further enhanced by the ICT potential for opening up the planning exercise in the Web – e-planning [42] – and thus strengthening planners-community interaction at the various planning stages. Web-based Geographical Information Systems (Web-GIS), social networks, participatory platforms etc., constitute complementary valuable tools for broadening communicative and interaction potential; opening also up planning data to local communities [7]. ICT's role is also exceptional when it comes to the *monitoring stage*. ICT-enabled tools can support online monitoring of UCH site, but also gather feedback from stakeholders in order for continuously adjusting the UCH management plan. Furthermore, e-engagement can facilitate or even broaden potential for more active stakeholders' commitment at this stage.

All in all, sustainable management of UCH implies a local value-driven problem and, at the same time, an integral part of a highly controversial MSP process. Furthermore, handling of UCH is carried out within a highly dynamic environment – the marine one – and, in most of the times, in adjacent to lagging behind, from a developmental point of view, neighbourhoods, such as *remote coastal or insular regions*. Thus integrated, place-based, data-driven, and highly community-engaging planning procedures seem to be the prevailing option in handling UCH to the benefit of such regional contexts, but also society as a whole. Such procedures should be embedded into the MSP process, setting priority to the protection/preservation and sustainable exploitation of, among others, this particular marine cultural resource. Towards this end, integration of the conceptual principles of MSP and CHC into the methodological approach of UCH management seems to establish a rather more powerful and community-valued decision-making process.

3 Gathering Successful European Experiences of UCH Integration into MSP

The complexity of allocating maritime uses in a harmonizing and conflicts' alleviating way; and the need to establish multi-scale and multi-stakeholders' interaction across the different spatially-defined administrative levels, render spatial data availability/analysis and their unimpeded flow as well as multiple stakeholders' consultation the *bedrocks* for well-documented and robust MSP decisions, including UCH management decisions as well. Further to that, of crucial importance is the expansion of the participatory planning process beyond the stage of plan development, i.e., in plan evaluation, implementation and revision [20]. In both MSP and UCH management, this denotes a dynamic process for constantly reconsidering, adjusting and improving policy decisions as well as alleviating potential conflicts among maritime uses, based on proper and stable monitoring and feedback mechanisms. But how are the aforementioned attributes embedded in efforts carried out at the EU level along the blue growth strategy and MSP; and in particular how UCH is integrated into MSP plans and aligns with the previously discussed conceptual and methodological ground? An effort to respond to this question follows in this section, by indulging into two examples of MSP from the European scene and the way UCH is managed within respective plans.

At present, most of the 22 member states of the EU, disposing a maritime border, have adopted MSP practices, adjusting key priorities to their own needs. According to data published in the European MSP Platform [43], 45% of these states have already adopted the final version of their national MSP plans, 36% of them are at the stage of MSP preparation and 18% have not yet embarked upon this duty. From a geographical point of view, the majority of already in place MSP plans concerns spatial units of the Baltic Sea, covering almost 78% of the Baltic countries.

Thus the MSP examples presented in the following refer to two neighboring countries of the Baltic Sea, namely Finland and Estonia. Assessment of the two case studies is conducted by use of the below presented *five criteria*, highlighting aspects of integrated, data-driven and participatory approaches in alignment with the key principles of MSP and having a specific focus on UCH. These have as follows:

- C1: Alignment with the multi-scale approach.
- C2: Integration/inseparable consideration of UCH and surrounding natural marine environment, tangible/intangible UCH dimensions as well as vertical/horizontal integration of UCH-related stakeholders.
- C3: Land-sea interaction with a focus on cultural assets.
- C4: Data-driven planning choices and maritime spatial plans.
- C5: Public and stakeholders' engagement for gathering empirical knowledge and enriching both the planning process and outcomes with local flavor.

3.1 Case Study Finland

Finland has taken the first steps in Maritime Spatial Planning in 2010, by chance of the Bothnian Sea Transboundary Pilot Project between Finland and Sweden (2010–2012). This experience has fueled work carried out in the first *Finland's MSP 2030*, in alignment with the MSP Directive [17]. This National Marine Spatial Plan is composed by three regional MSPs, following a *place-based approach* and covering both territorial waters and the Exclusive Economic Zone (EEZ) (Fig. 5a).

UCH in the Finnish National Marine Spatial Plan is designated as one of the blue growth sectors. Known UCH sites are categorized and managed by means of regional zones, integrating both terrestrial and maritime sites and delimiting *zones of cultural significance*. These are clusters of nation-wide: valuable landscape areas, significant built cultural environments, UCH landscapes, traditional coastal fishing areas, etc.; but also entities related to maritime cultural heritage, e.g., military history, seafaring, traditional biotopes, landscape as well as coastal and archipelago areas [46]. Among the strategic objectives of the plan fall the protection/preservation of (U)CH, enhancement of cultural values, accessibility of cultural areas as well as integration of cultural and natural values, both in land and at sea. Stakeholders' engagement is grasped as a powerful tool for

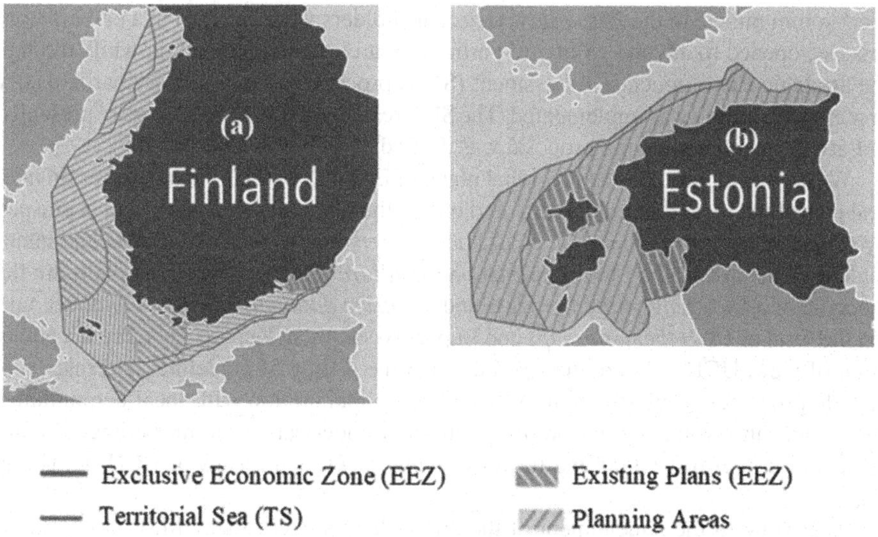

Fig. 5. National Maritime Spatial Planning of: (a) Finland [44] and (b) Estonia [45]

successful MSP and long-standing regional cooperation in Finland. Indeed, decision-making processes in the Finnish MSP have at their heart *participatory approaches*, including *consultation workshops* with local authorities and targeted stakeholders [47] as well as *public hearings* for the general public [44]. Based on these collaborative procedures, an interaction plan was prepared, providing an MSP overview and the chance for stakeholders and citizens' engagement in order for their involvement in all planning stages to be deepened [48]. Finnish MSP is also a subject of matter in the Baltic Cultural Heritage Committee [49], in which Finland is a member; and in the Working Groups on UCH and Coastal Heritage, addressing a holistic, cross-border cooperation in the Baltic Sea [50].

3.2 Case Study Estonia

Estonia is one more state of the Baltic Sea with previous experience in MSP. Since 2010, two pilot MSP plans were carried out (Fig. 5b) – one in the surrounding area of Hiiu Island and another one in the Pärnu Bay Area, around Kihnu Island – both driven by the growing interest in *offshore energy* [45]. These MSP Projects stimulated the government to establish, in 2011, legal processes resulting in MSP legislation; and have led to two legally binding *county plans* of Hiiu Island (2016) and Pärnu Bay (2017). In Hiiu MSP, designation areas for offshore wind energy were abolished by the National Court in 2018; while with regard to other topics the Hiiu MSP remains still valid.

The two aforementioned MSPs reveal differences as to the level of participation of interested stakeholders. In *Hiiu Island*, representatives approached stakeholders and invited them to take part in the leading group, engaged with the development of the MSP Plan. The planning process was thus led by a multi-scale steering board, consisting of members from different national authorities, sectoral stakeholders (energy, fisheries) and local communities. In the *Pärnu Bay Area*, stakeholders were engaged in a participatory process, opened to anyone willing to participate at each single meeting; while through the Strategic Environmental Assessment (SEA) process, a transboundary participatory process with Latvia was implemented. The SEA results and the MSP plan were presented to Latvia when the planning proposal was drafted.

Within the aforementioned regional plans of Estonia, UCH is considered as an integral part of the local cultural identity and one of the blue growth sectors; and is grasped by means of natural and cultural, coastal and underwater as well as tangible and intangible dimensions, leading to the formation of *cultural clusters*. Finalized plans are the outcome of a *knowledge-based process* and *intensive data collection and analysis*, taking the form of *UCH thematic maps* and Impact Assessment Reports [51]. From a policy point of view, UCH sites are managed through the setting of guidelines and rules; and include processes of information exchange and collaboration with local communities and organizations, having a stake in coastal and underwater cultural heritage. In situ preservation prevails, taking the form of *diving parks* as a means of UCH protection [52].

According to the Amendment of the 2015 Planning Act, today MSP in Estonia is developed at the national level. The new Planning Act makes a clear distinction between terrestrial planning and MSP. The finalization of the MSP plan is the result of several *public discussions* and also *transboundary consultations* with national authorities of the neighbouring states of Finland, Latvia and Sweden. The plans' extroversion is also evident through the participation of Estonia in the Baltic Region Heritage Committee, recognising the need for UCH governance by adopting a multi-level, multi-scale and transborder approach. Worth noticing is also the fact that in the newly established MSP, *land-sea clusters* are also drawn, integrating coastal and UCH assets and supporting, within MSP, the land-sea and sea-land interaction principle.

4 Discussion and Conclusions

Completion of national MSP strategies at the European level – ought to be delivered already by March 31, 2021 [17] – displays a certain delay. This leads to a blurred image as to the way MSP is being carried out in the European seas; and what position UCH holds in this effort. Experience gained from the two MSPs in Finland (already in force) and Estonia (at the final stage, expected to be adopted in May 2022) unveils the interest of both states in preserving *underwater cultural and natural heritage*, being perceived as a distinct objective of related MSP plans. It also reveals certain convergences but also divergences with respect to the previously defined set of criteria.

More specifically, a certain deviation is noticed as to the *criterion C1*. Finland, in this respect, follows a more regional approach that is marked by collaborative schemes embedding local municipalities. On the contrary, Estonia pursues a more centrally-driven (national government) approach, apart from the two legally binding county-based regional MSPs of Hiiu Island and Pärnu Bay. MSPs in both states conform to the *integrated approach – criterion C2* – featuring (U)CH as an interwoven complex of tangible and intangible, land and underwater, natural and cultural dimensions. This aspect is also in favor of *C3 criterion*, considering *land-sea and sea-land interactions of UCH* and land-based cultural heritage in general, fulfilled by both states. In addition, *data analysis and unimpeded information flow – criterion C4* – are considered of high importance in both Finland and Estonia's MSPs; unfolding through deep insights into the current state of areas concerned, mapping of their attributes and intense use of GIS, both at the preparation and finalization stage. Finally, certain divergences between the MSPs of the two states appear in the way *stakeholders and citizens* are engaged in the process – *criterion C5*. In Finland, co-operation among stakeholders at the regional level is top priority and occurs at both the stage of analysis and the one of visioning and scenario building steps, engaging experts and the general public. Extroversion of MSP, however, is not so obvious at the stage of preparation. Nonetheless, the country's involvement in the Baltic Region Heritage Committee provides the ground for getting also feedback at the transnational level. In Estonia, stakeholders' engagement is accomplished at the national/regional and the transboundary level, with public engagement at the national/regional level being open at each single stage of the process. Compulsory public displays and discussions are also held at different stages of the MSP process.

In general, it could be inferred that UCH has not yet gained the eminent position it deserves within the MSP process [53]. As revealed by the studied examples, prevailing sectors in MSP still remain energy, maritime industry and logistics, fishing and aquaculture as well as tourism and recreation. However, the rising importance attached to UCH resources in society as a whole, coupled with academic research works and policy guidelines that shed light on respectful UCH management for serving local development purposes, are already noticeable trends; and are pushing forward the interest in UCH, properly valuing this resource within MSP; and managing it as an equally important maritime resource and in harmony with other maritime resources and related activities. Along these lines, keeping track with the conceptual frame of UCH management within MSP as well as its counterpart in the planning arsenal, presented in this paper, seems to be critical when dealing with UCH in MSP studies. In particular, the role of integrated, data-driven and place-based approach for UCH management is stressed; while same holds for collaborative planning as a means to overcome MSP complexity/conflicts; and properly grasp the value and position UCH should gain within such a marine spatial planning exercise. At present, MSP seems to present a priceless chance for effectively protecting/managing UCH, provided that this can be adapted to the multiple considerations and understanding of UCH; and shift from a process of purely allocating maritime uses for managing conflicts and establishing synergies, to a more creative one, socially- and culturally-sensitive, aiming to keep up with peculiarities of the marine world as well as the valuable for the community land- and sea-scapes, including the cultural ones [54]. Future research ambition of authors, as soon as relative MSP studies are accomplished, is a comparative study of the locus of UCH in practical MSP exercises in two quite distinct marine spatial contexts, such as the Mediterranean and the Baltic Sea, in order for a more robust UCH management approach to be established and assessment of MSP in UCH protection, preservation and sustainable exploitation to be grasped.

References

1. ISSA: Climate change and natural resource scarcity. Security and Society Megatrends (2014). https://ww1.issa.int/sites/default/files/documents/publications/2-megatrends-climate-change-web-29854.pdf. Accessed 10 Mar 2022

2. COM(2012)494 final: Blue Growth Opportunities for Marine and Maritime Sustainable Growth, Communication from the Commission to the European Parliament, the Council, the European Economic and Social Committee and the Committee of the Regions, European Commission, Brussels, 13 September 2012
3. Zhong, H.: Exploitation and utilization of marine resources and protection of marine ecology. IOP Conf. Ser. Earth Environ. Sci. **369**(1), 012009 (2019). https://doi.org/10.1088/1755-1315/369/1/0120
4. COM(2021) 240 final: Communication on a new approach for a sustainable blue economy in the EU Transforming the EU's Blue Economy for a Sustainable Future, Commission of the European Communities, Brussels, 17 May 2021
5. UNESCO: Convention on the protection of the underwater cultural heritage. In: General Conference of UNESCO. UNESCO, Paris (2001)
6. Papageorgiou, M.: Underwater cultural heritage facing maritime spatial planning: legislative and technical issues. Ocean Coast. Manag. **165**, 195–202 (2018). https://doi.org/10.1016/j.ocecoaman.2018.08.032
7. Koutsi, D., Stratigea, A.: Unburying hidden land and maritime cultural potential of small islands in the mediterranean for tracking heritage-led local development paths. Heritage **2**(1), 938–966 (2019). https://doi.org/10.3390/heritage2010062
8. Forrest, C.J.: Defining 'underwater cultural heritage'. Int. J. Naut. Archaeol. **31**(1), 3–11 (2002). https://doi.org/10.1006/ijna.2002.1022
9. Barr, B.: Understanding and managing marine protected areas through integrated ecosystem-based management within maritime cultural landscapes: Moving from theory to practice. Ocean Coast. Manag. **84**, 184–192 (2013). https://doi.org/10.1016/j.ocecoaman.2013.08.011
10. Koutsi, D., Stratigea, A.: Integrated maritime policy and management of underwater cultural heritage. In: Defner, A., Skagianis, P., Rodakinias, P., Psatha, E. (eds.) 3rd National Conference of Urban and Regional Planning and Regional Development, pp. 565–577. University of Thessaly, Volos (2018). (in Greek)
11. Argyropoulos, V., Stratigea, A.: Sustainable management of underwater cultural heritage: the route from discovery to engagement—open issues in the Mediterranean. Heritage **2**(2), 1588–1613 (2019). https://doi.org/10.3390/heritage2020098
12. Koutsi, D., Stratigea, A.: Releasing cultural tourism potential of less-privileged Island communities in the Mediterranean: an ICT-enabled, strategic, and integrated participatory planning approach. In: Marques, R.P., Melo, A.I., Natário, M.M., Biscaia, R. (eds.) The Impact of Tourist Activities on Low-Density Territories. THEM, pp. 63–93. Springer, Cham (2021). https://doi.org/10.1007/978-3-030-65524-2_4
13. Koutsi, D., Stratigea, A.: Sustainable and resilient management of underwater cultural heritage (UCH) in remote Mediterranean Islands: a methodological framework. Heritage **4**, 3469–3496 (2021). https://doi.org/10.3390/heritage4040192
14. ICOMOS: Heritage at risk (2006). https://www.icomos.org/risk/2006/fulldocan.pdf. Accessed 12 Mar 2022
15. Koutsi, D., Stratigea, A.: Shipwrecks' underwater mysteries—identifying commonalities out of globally-distributed knowledge. Heritage **4**(4), 3949–3969 (2021). https://doi.org/10.3390/heritage4040217
16. Koutsi, D., Stratigea, A.: Indulging in the 'mediterranean maritime world' – diving tourism in insular territories. In: Gervasi, O., et al. (eds.) ICCSA 2021. LNCS, vol. 12958, pp. 59–74. Springer, Cham (2021). https://doi.org/10.1007/978-3-030-87016-4_5
17. Directive 2014/89/EU: Establishing a Framework for Maritime Spatial Planning. European Parliament and European Council. Off. J. Eur. Union **L257**, 135–145 (2014)
18. Douvere, F., Ehler, C.N.: New perspectives on sea use management: initial findings from European experience with marine spatial planning. J. Environ. Manag. **90**(1), 77–88 (2009). https://doi.org/10.1016/j.jenvman.2008.07.004

19. Stancheva, M., Stanchev, H., Zaucha, J., Ramieri, E., Roberts, T.: Supporting multi-use of the sea with maritime spatial planning. The case of a multi-use opportunity development - Bulgaria, Black Sea. Marine Policy **136**, 104927 (2022). https://doi.org/10.1016/j.marpol.2021.104927
20. COM(2008) 791 final: Roadmap for Maritime Spatial Planning: Achieving Common Principles in the EU, Commission of the European Communities, Brussels, 25 November 2008
21. UN Environment: Conceptual Framework for Marine Spatial Planning in The Mediterranean (2018). shorturl.at/loN14. Accessed 14 Mar 2022
22. UNESCO-IOC/European Commission: MSPglobal International Guide on Marine/Maritime Spatial Planning. UNESCO, Paris (2021). (IOC Manuals and Guides no 89)
23. Lagabrielle, E., Lombard, A.T., Harris, J.M., Livingstone, T.-C.: Multi-scale multi-level marine spatial planning: a novel methodological approach applied in South Africa. PLoS ONE **13**(7), e0192582 (2018). https://doi.org/10.1371/journal.pone.0192582
24. Matczak, M., Przedrzymirska, J., Zaucha, J., Schultz-Zehden, A: Handbook on Multi-level Consultations in MSP. PartSeaPate Project. http://www.partiseapate.eu/wp-content/uploads/2014/09/PartiSEApate_handbook-on-multilevel-consultations-in-MSP.pdf. Accessed 16 Mar 2022
25. Martin, J.B.: Harnessing local and transnational communities in the global protection of underwater cultural heritage. Transnatl. Environ. Law **10**(1), 85–108 (2021). https://doi.org/10.1017/S2047102520000369
26. Przedrzymirska, J., et al.: Multi-use of the sea: from research to practice. SHS Web Conf. **58**, 01025 (2018). https://doi.org/10.1051/shsconf/20185801025
27. Tissier, M.: Unravelling the relationship between ecosystem-based management, integrated coastal zone management and marine spatial planning. In: O'Higgins, T.G., Lago, M., DeWitt, T.H. (eds.) Ecosystem-Based Management, Ecosystem Services and Aquatic Biodiversity, pp. 403–413. Springer, Cham (2020). https://doi.org/10.1007/978-3-030-45843-0_20
28. Barbash-Riley, L.: Application of environmental legislation to protect underwater cultural heritage on the outer continental shelf. Presented at Society for Historical Archaeology, Quebec City, Quebec, Canada (2014). tDAR id: 437284
29. UNESCO: Underwater cultural heritage (2008). https://unesdoc.unesco.org/ark:/48223/pf0000181217. Accessed 14 Mar 2022
30. Pérez-Reverte Mañas C., Cerezo Andreo F., López Osorio, P., González Gallero, R., Mariscal Rico, L., Arévalo González, A.: Underwater cultural heritage as an engine for social, economic and cultural development. State of Research at the University of Cadiz (Andalusia, Spain). Heritage **4**(4), 2676–2690 (2021). https://doi.org/10.3390/heritage4040151
31. National Indigenous Fisheries Institute. http://indigenousoceans.ca/en/marine-spatial-planning/. Accessed 14 Mar 2022
32. Varinlioglu, G.: Digital in Underwater Cultural Heritage. Cambridge Scholars Publishing, Cambridge (2016)
33. Amos, J.: Mapping quest edges past 20% of global ocean floor. BBC News (2021). https://www.bbc.com/news/science-environment-57530394. Accessed 16 Mar 2022
34. Papageorgiou, M.: Stakes and challenges for underwater cultural heritage in the era of blue growth and the role of spatial planning: implications and prospects in Greece. Heritage **2**, 1060–1069 (2019). https://doi.org/10.3390/heritage2020069
35. Stancheva, M., Stanchev, H.: Addressing the Multi-Use Concept with Maritime Spatial Planning in the Cross-Border Region (Bulgaria). MARSPLAN-BS II Project (EASME/EMFF/2018/1.2.1.5/01/S12.806725), Deliverable: WP2, Activity 2.4 (2020)
36. Gambin, T., Sausmekat, M., Kovacevic, D.: The innovative and state of the art public access management of Malta's underwater cultural heritage. Heritage **4**(4), 3365–3381 (2021). https://doi.org/10.3390/heritage4040187

37. Hill, R., Kring, K.: European Territorial Co-Operation Maritime Cross-Border Programmes: The Maritime Dimension (2013). https://www.interact-eu.net/download/file/fid/1186. Accessed on 14 Mar 2022
38. Staniforth, M., Hunter, J., Jateff, E.: International approach to underwater cultural heritage. In: Harris, W.J. (ed.) Maritime Law Issues, Challenges and Implications, pp. 2–24. Nova Science Publishers, New York, USA (2011)
39. Thurley, S.: Into the future-our strategy for 2005–2010. Conserv. Bull. **49**, 26–27 (2005)
40. Spanish Ministry of Culture: Green Paper - Spanish National Plan for the Protection of Underwater Cultural Heritage (2009). https://www.libreria.culturaydeporte.gob.es/ebook/3640/free_download/. Accessed 14 Mar 2022
41. Virtudes, A., Sá, J.: Approach of ICT application to governance in urban planning. IOP Conf. Ser. Mater. Sci. Eng. **245**(5), 052086 (2017). https://doi.org/10.1088/1757-899X/245/5/052086
42. Panagiotopoulou, M., Stratigea, A.: Spatial data management and visualization tools and technologies for enhancing participatory e-planning in smart cities. In: Stratigea, A., Kyriakides, E., Nicolaides, C. (eds.) Smart Cities in the Mediterranean. PI, pp. 31–57. Springer, Cham (2017). https://doi.org/10.1007/978-3-319-54558-5_2
43. European MSP Platform: Overview of MSP Authorities & Plans per Country (2022). https://maritime-spatial-planning.ec.europa.eu/sites/default/files/overview_of_msp_0.png. Accessed 16 Mar 2022
44. MSP Country Information Profile Finland 2022: Finland. https://maritime-spatial-planning.ec.europa.eu/sites/default/files/download/finland_january_2022.pdf. Accessed 14 Mar 2022
45. MSP Country Information Profile Estonia 2021. https://maritime-spatial-planning.ec.europa.eu/sites/default/files/download/estonia_june_2021.pdf. Accessed 14 Mar 2022
46. Finnish MSP Official Page. https://meriskenaariot.info/merialuesuunnitelma/en/vm7-eng/. Accessed 11 Mar 2022
47. Lehtimäki, M., Tikkanen, S.: Maritime Cultural Heritage integrated in MSP/BalticRIM project (2021). https://vasab.org/wp-content/uploads/2021/06/02_WS3_Marianne_lehtimaki.pdf. Accessed 16 Mar 2022
48. Finland's Maritime spatial plan 2030: Interactive Map. https://mspfinland.maps.arcgis.com/apps/webappviewer/index.html?id=97f9d24e2771487995a7cc41fdca11c4. Accessed 16 Mar 2022
49. Baltic Region Heritage Committee. https://baltic-8326.wilhelm-osl.servebolt.cloud/working-groups/underwater-cultural-heritage/. Accessed 16 Mar 2022
50. Altvater S., et al.: Integrating Cultural Heritage into Maritime Spatial Planning in the BSR (2020). https://www.submariner-network.eu/images/BalticRIM_handbook_Dec_2020-1.pdf. Accessed 12 Mar 2022
51. Pikner, T., et al.: Sociocultural dimension of land-sea interactions in maritime spatial planning: three case studies in the Baltic sea region. Sustainability **14**(4), 2194 (2022). https://doi.org/10.3390/su14042194
52. Estonian MSP Draft Plan (2020). http://mereala.hendrikson.ee/dokumendid/Eskiis/Estonian_MSP_main-solution_ENG.pdf. Accessed 15 Mar 2022
53. European MSP Platform: Marine Cultural Heritage (MCH) and MSP. https://maritime-spatial-planning.ec.europa.eu/faq/marine-cultural-heritage-mch-and-msp. Accessed 16 Mar 2022
54. Kyvelou, S.S., Ierapetritis, D.: Discussing and analyzing "maritime cohesion" in MSP, to achieve sustainability in the marine realm. Sustainability **11**, 3444 (2019). https://doi.org/10.3390/su11123444

Author Index